The Revelations of Daniel:
YAH's Prophetic Utterances To Black America And All Mankind

COPYRIGHT

The Revelations of Daniel: YAH'S Prophetic Utterances To Black America And All Mankind

Copyright© 2019 by Yehoshaphat Israel

All material and rights are reserved exclusively to the author. Any part of book that is reproduced or transmitted in any form, whether electronically, social media, print, visual, or any form of human transmission, must be first approved by the author with written permission. Submit all requests to: Yehoshaphat Israel, P.O.Box 9673, Memphis, TN 38190 or jcn365@hotmail.com.

ISBN: 978-0-578-52348-2
Published and Exclusively Owned by the *JCN* Foundation

Dedication

I dedicate this book **THE REVELATIONS OF DANIEL:** *YAH'S Prophetic Utterances To Black America And All Mankind* **[Chapters 1—3]** exclusively to the Name of **YHWH** our Eternal Saviour and Redeemer. **The Everlasting ONE** to whom all praises, glory, and honor belongs. This book is also dedicated to all of HIS Israelite people throughout the diaspora, and to all the righteous men, women, and children of all nations, languages, and tongues who walk in HIS commandments. The goal of this book has been to provide spiritual clarity and DIVINE insight into the hereafter based on YAH's Prophetic timeline that HE revealed to our ancestor Daniel. **YAH KHAI!!!**

O **YHWH** of host(**sabaot**), Enthroned on the Cherubim, YOU alone are ELOHIM. O all the great and glorious kingdoms that exist, it is YOU O YHWH who created the heavens and the earth and the great waters of the sea. **O YHWH,** the kings of gold, silver, brass, iron, and miry clay have ruled YOUR earth from the Prophetic Time Zone of the head of gold down until this very day of the toes of iron and miry clay. These kings have annihilated various people and destroyed many movements. These rulers have invaded various lands, annihilated many nations and occupied their lands, and committed the conquered people's gods to the flames of fire. Those **kings of gold, silver, brass, iron, and miry clay** have destroyed many nations because those nations did not trust in YOU. Their beliefs and trust were in man's handiwork, even man-made religions and not YAH.

But now, O YHWH, we the descendants of Daniel, Hannaniah, Mishael, and Azariah, invoke YOUR DIVINE NAME , **O YHWH**, and humbly request that YOU, **O YHWH** our ELOHIM return to our midst and deliver us, the lost sheep of Israel in the diaspora, near and far, from the tyrannial power of **the kingdoms of gold, silver, brass, iron, and miry.** O YAH, make known that YOU alone **O YHWH are THE STONE CUT OUT WITHOUT HANDS.** YOU, **O YAH** are the only true ELOHIM possessing all DIVINE POWERS from everlasting to evertlasting. Selah.

The purpose of this book is to predict that **YHWH** shall once again become the Great KING of HIS people Yisrael and Yehudah. This book also envisions our redemption at the appointed time. When you read this book, **YHWH** will reveal, and you will discover, that Daniel's interpretation of the dream was sure. And **YHWH'S** terrifying dream to Nebuchadnezzar was certain.

Last, but not least, for many ages, arrogant religious Jewish, Christian, and Islamic scholars among the nations have regarded the prophecies of Daniel as a myth. The book, **The Revelations of Daniel: YAH'S Prophetic Utterances to Black America and All Mankind**, will shatter those lies that have been told for the past two thousands years.

Aleph

Acknowledgements

First and foremost I acknowledge and give all praise, glory, and honor to the Creator of the Universe, YAH, ELOHIM of our ancestors, the ELOHIM of Abraham, the ELOHIM of Isaac, and the ELOHIM of Yaacov our Eternal Saviour and Redeemer. I thank the ETERNAL for all DIVINE wisdom, understanding, and knowledge on this subject matter.

I also give thanks my family, my beloved wife Leah, and all of our children, 8 in all, (Israel, Samaria, Sarai, Judaea, Ophrah, Yoshua, Aijalon, and last by not least, Ariel *"Little Nathan"*) for their faithfulness and steadfast support inspite of, and throughout all the struggles we have experienced, and overcame with the help of YAH. They are truly builders of the **Walls of Jerusalem.**

I will never forget the legacy of Aaron Casey, of Chicago and Cairo, Illinois, my first Hebrew teacher whom I first met in November of 1978. YAH sent him to raise me and the Memphis community up out of the valley of dry bones. Inspite of his imperfections, the Words of YAH which he shared with us were perfect, more relevant today in 2019 than they were when he spoke them 40 years ago. His teachings served as an inspiration and foundation for the eventual development of the *Jerusalem Chronicle Newspaper* which YAH helped me to start back in March of 1990.

I acknowledge all the anointed brothers, sisters, morehs, rabbis, elders, friends, supporters, members of Yis-SAC, especially the encouragement from Elder Brother Yachanan Daveed Yisrael, and the readers of the *JCN,* and to all of the new ones coming into the Israelite community whom YAH is raising up for the future. The goal of this writing is to assist us in our journey towards DIVINE Enlightment.

Last but not least, I would like to acknowledge my beloved father **[Elbert Earl Payne Sr.]**, my beloved mother[**Me-ma, Betty Jean Payne**], my real brother[**Ba Bra, Elbert Earl Payne Jr.**]. My family will always be indebted to my brother. Back in the day in 2004, my Israelite family was on the brink of homelessness. My maternal brother told me and my family to come on over and stay with him. We lived in his beautiful palace with him for seven months. We were living so good we couldn't even tell we were homeless because we had everything we needed at his home. My family will remember him forever. He passed in April of 2018. Ba-Bra, we will never forget your practice of true Hebrew love). I also acknowledge my beloved baby sister **[Emily Payne]**. Much love.

GLOSSARY
(The meaning of certain words used throughout this book)

In this you will read certain words and Hebrew terms that may be unfamiliar to some readers or those new in the Hebrew culture. I will explain the meaning of certain ones to help you in reading the book.

YHWH: These four consonants Y-H-W-H *pronounced* (Yod-Hey-Waw-Hey) are known as the Tetragrammaton. Tetragrammaton is a Greek term that means four letters. The Sacred Name YHWH is replaced with the word LORD throughout many English translations of the Hebrew scriptures. The Sacred Name is transliterated and pronounced as the following variations: YEHOWAH, YAHAWAH, YAHOWAH, YAHWEH or the shortened poetic transliteration YAH. Throughout the book you will also read the term YHWH ELOHIM Israel, which is translated in English as the Lord God of Israel.

ELOHIM: The word ELOHIM is a Hebrew word meaning POWERS which expressed the ancient Hebrew realization that YHWH possessed all POWERS. YHWH is ELOHIM. The word ELOHIM itself is transliterated as God. The term God is actually a pagan Germanic term used to describe their pagan deities. All of them were known as God. Therefore the proper Hebrew manner to address the true CREATOR is YHWH ELOHIM instead of LORD GOD or Lord Jesus. YHWH is the true Spiritual POWER who governs Creation. YHWH is regarded as the only true Spirituality of the children of Israel.

Sabaot: The Hebrew word *sabaot* is pronounced [sa-ba-ot] which means host. The sabaot are the Angelic host that serve YHWH's interest throughout creation. Many times in the Hebrew scriptures, known as the Old Testament, you will read the term YHWH sabaot which is transliterated the LORD of host.

Shalom: The word "Shalom" means "Peace" in Hebrew. It is also regarded as an expression of greeting. Oftentimes you will hear the Shalom used as a saluation for "Hello" and "Goodbye".

While reading Chapter 2 in the section entitled the "Battle of Armageddon" you will find this following verse used repeatedly as I discuss one conflict after another. I used the book of Zechariah, 14th chapter and the thirteenth verse, which states: *"In that day, a great tumult from YHWH shall fall upon them, and everyone shall snatch at the hand of another, and everyone shall raise his hand against everyone else's hand"*. What do that term actually mean? The answer is this. The reason I chose that verse over and over again was because, as I explained, the Battle of Armageddon is an ongoing process inwhich wars will occur year after year, one after another, until ultimately, the nations are drawn into the last battle which the prophet Yoel foresaw. Therefore, Zechariah 14:13 applies to each of those separate wars as we the Countdown To The Final Conflict of the Battle of Armageddon. So, I used that verse for each Middle East conflict.

Gimel

Preface

By Leah Baht Israel

The Revelations of Daniel: YAH'S Prophetic Utterance To Black America and All Mankind is an authentic book that can be used as a reference when you are reading the Torah, or the Old Testament as some may describe it. In reading this book, it will bring YAH'S Words and prophecies back into the present for the minds of the readers. **The Revelations of Daniel** will definitely broaden your horizon. It will give you a certain intellect of history, and the worlds of other nations of people that you may have never known existed.

I know the book will have different effects on different people. Some will rejoice. Some will get angry, some will be afraid of what's been revealed, while others will be in total disbelief, and others in denial. The book will show you how this present world order was created and the status of all nations in YAH'S Creation. **The Revelations of Daniel** can, and *will be*, a wealth of information for those who want to know the **Truth** and *seeking* Everlasting Divine Spiritual Guidance, Divine Peace, Divine Protection, Divine Prosperity, and most all, the Divine Understanding of **YAH and His Host, THE STONE CUT WITHOUT HANDS**. I ask that the Divine Powers of YAH watch over you and your family. I love you YAH! Todah **YAH** for blessing my Ish to write this book. We have many brilliant Hebrew authors in the Israelite community, but this one is truly like none other. On a personal note, this book was completed in the year 2019, our 40th marriage anniversary **[January 23, 1979—January 23, 2019]**, and the 400th year of our captivity in this kingdom**[August 19, 2019]**.

Leah Israel
Wife of Yehoshaphat Israel
on behalf of the family-based *JCN* Foundation

By Yachanan Daveed Israel

In this book the author is speaking directly to the Hebrew Israelites, who **YAHOWAH our ELOHIM** gave HIS Laws, Statutes, and Judgement. **The CREATOR of the heavens and earth name is YAHOWAH our ELOHIM. HE is also the CREATOR of all Mankind on earth.**

HIS Laws were given to Moses in **Exodus chapter 20**. All the prophets from Moses to Malachi kept all the Laws. These Laws were not just for Hebrew Israelites only, they were, and continue to be, for all nations of the earth to keep forever.

This book talks about **The AGE of YHWH** upon the face of the earth. This countdown began with Nebuchadnezzar, King of ancient Babylon who ruled from **605—561 B. C. E.**, who made a statue 90-feet tall whose Head was made of pure gold which represent King Nebuchadnezzar as the first king of seven kings of Babylon on the face of the earth that would eventually lead up to the beginning of **The Age of YAH.** The ten toes of the feet, *which were part of iron and part of clay,* represented the last kings before **The AGE OF YAH** is finally ushered in upon the face of the earth. And in the days of these kings shall **YAHOWAH ELOHIM of heaven and earth** set up a kingdom, and it shall stand forever as spoken in **Daniel 2:44.** This will be the beginning of **The AGE OF YAH** of Host on earth. This is why the author of this great book, through the **Spirit** of our Heavenly Father, put this book together to uncover, and expose, the wicked kings of the nations on earth. For nearly 3,000 years these kings and their nations have always hated **YAHOWAH our ELOHIM, the CREATOR of the heaven and earth,** and all HIS Laws that HE gave to Moses at Mount Sinai. Nations have always loved the traditions of men, with their wicked idols, more than the Laws of the CREATOR. The author of this book, **The Revelations of Daniel,** with **the Spirit of our CREATOR** in him, the same **Spirit** that was in Daniel when he interpreted the dream to King Nebuchadnezzar which he had dreamed, has unearthed those esoteric historical truths. The author knew that it was time to sound the trumpet of **YAHOWAH our ELOHIM** to this evil, wicked, adulterous generation before the final destruction of mankind. Nations will rise against nations and kingdoms shall war against kingdoms until 2/3 of mankind is destroyed from off the face of the earth. Weapons of mass destruction, such as chemical and nuclear weapons, will cause the destruction upon the earth as in the days of Noah because of the refusal to obey the Laws of **YAHOWAH our ELOHIM.** Today's world is the same as it was in the days of Noah. We are headed for a great destruction and it's because mankind's hatred for the Laws of **The Most High ELOHIM.** Right after this great destruction, **YAHOWAH ELOHIM** will usher in a new kingdom that will be ruled by **the CREATOR of heaven and earth** through HIS righteous people who will obey HIS Laws forever throughout their generations forever. This will be the beginning of **The AGE of YAH** upon the face of the earth.

I give total praise to **YAH** for blessing the author of this book with such wisdom, understanding, and knowledge to do the work that he has done is this book. When it is all said and done, we must always remember what our ancestor King Solomon, the wisest man to ever live upon the face of the earth, said in **Ecclesiastes 12:13:** He said, *"Let us hear the conclusion of the whole matter. Fear YAHOWAH our ELOHIM and keep HIS commandments and live. For this is the whole duty of man, forever throughout all your generations".*

YAHOWAH our ELOHIM, I thank **YOU** again, for giving the author of this book the **Spirit** to sound the Trumpet before destruction comes upon the earth. **The AGE of YAH** is sure to come soon. *Wake Up!, Wake Up!, Wake Up* nations of the earth before it is *too* late.

Yachanan Daveed Israel
Founding Member of Yisraelite Spiritual Action Committee(Yis-SAC)

By Chanak Abisawa

Seifer Daniye'l
The Scrolls of Daniye'l
The Present is reflected in the Past; Visions in the Past foretelling the Future

The **Book of Daniye'l** *is like holding a mirror made of the past which allows one to see the present standing before them. The present will be reflected in the mirror of the past in every detail, in the same way our image is reflected in a conventional mirror.*

The history of the "**African American**" is familiar to the majority of humankind. As spoils of war and conquest the ancestors of "African Americans" were sold/kidnapped into enemy lands and were transported across great oceans of water to distant lands. They were horribly mistreated before, during, and after the transport from their homes to what would amount to hell on earth. But that was only the beginning of **the Holocaust.** While their lands were taken over, plundered, and laid waste, their ancestors were undergoing the most diabolical form of brainwashing and re-education endured by any people in the history of humankind. So all encompassing, so intense and relentless, *was,* and, *is,* this process that the efforts can be observed in the present generation, who are descended from those ancestors who "survived" that horrible initial process.

In today's perfected and refined state, we witness the best and brightest descendants of those infiltrated ancestors serve in this kingdom of darkness. If this tale of woes sounds familiar to you, it should. For it also happened nearly 3,000 years earlier, and is recorded in **the Book of Daniel** in detail. The first 7 verses in chapter one in the book describes the, *why,* and, *how,* a people being chastised by the **CREATOR of the Univers**e could fall into enemy's hands, have their names, education, clothing, diet, and purpose for living changed, not temporarily, but for a lifetime.

The Four Israelites that are highlighted and followed in **the Book of Daniel** were exceptional individuals and were exceptionally blessed. The vast multitude of Israelites/Judeans were absorbed by Babylon, killed or worse. They were the nameless, faceless Israelites that were simply overcome and assimilated into Babylonian society. As it was then, so it is now. Aside from a few exceptional and blessed few, the Israelite/Judeans were a nameless face in a crowded field of history. The Israelite royalty was assimilated into a decadent society in a new empire with a new god to serve. They had no clue as to *who* or *what* they truly were.

However, as **YHWH** would have it, prophets were raised up throughout our sojourn in the these strange lands just as they were raised up for us all throughout our history.

As Daniel's record of his life and the visions given to him were recorded, so too is this book you are holding in your hand dear reader. It is nothing short of a **YAH** ordained prophetic record of *what was, what is,* and *what is to come.* By reading **the Book of Daniel,** one can see that it has two parts. In **the first 6 chapters,** Daniel primarily speaks in the third person about things that happened to him and his compatriots as well as interpreting the dreams and visions of others. In **chapters 7 thru 12,** you have him speaking in the first person primarily about dreams and visions he himself received.

Aside from the guidance offered to all humanity through Daniel's recorded vision (covered thoroughly in this in this book) **"Black"** America in particular can gain a good deal of wisdom by carefully reading about how our Hebrew ancestors regularly faced down death (and life) behind enemy lines with their hands firmly bound by the hand of their enemy's power (and our hands are bound too).

Perhaps by imitating their examples we can learn how to respond to very similar challenges we face today. After all, Danyie'l was considered a Standard of Righteousness, **(Read Ezekiel 14:14,20),** and a Standard of Wisdom, **(Read Ezekiel 28:3),** and a Prophet worthy to be quoted by "New Testament" *prophets* such as Yahshua and Yochanan. As a matter of fact, material from every chapter in Danyie'l is either directly or indirectly quoted in the *Book of Revelations.* Only two chapters from the *Book of Revelations* are free of any background in the **Book of Danyie'l.** And of course, the highest praise anyone can receive is from **YHWH Himself.** After Danyie'l Powerful Prayer in chapter 9, **YAH** sent a Malakim (Angel) to respond to him and let him know that he was precious and highly esteemed in HIS sight.

May we strive to live lives that are respected by our peers and pleasing in the sight of YHWH as our ancestor Daniye'l, <u>Judge of God</u>, and, one who <u>pleads the cause</u> of his brethren, did.

Chanak Abisawa
Founding Member of Yisraelite Spiritual Action Committee(Yis-SAC)

By Seth Ben Israel
"Daniel"

I give all Honor, Praise, and Exaltation to the **Almighty YAH our FATHER, KING of Universe** and All that it contains. HalleluYAH!

I thank YAH for giving our brother Yehoshaphat the vision and will to put these great writings and words of wisdom together to read, learn, and prepare.

I often remember a cliche **my Abba[Moreh Kahishmiyah Ben Yisrael],** who was great teacher in the Israelite community, would quote: *"There is nothing new under the sun".* Abba would say, *"What is has been".* I also remember one of my very first scriptures my Abba taught us and committed to memory was **Psalms 83:3-5**. The Hebrew culture that **Daniel** and all Judah had once embraced no longer existed. They were forced to eat the king's meat, drink the king's wine, and participated in all of the wicked practices of the kingdom of Babylon. We have seen these same occurrences against Israel over and over again from the days of **Daniel** to the times of the Maccabees to the atrocities of slavery. *"There is nothing new under the sun"*. These are the same things that have happened, and, happening today as in the days of old. Their customs are not our customs and their ways are not our ways. *"What we see today has already been"*—We—black people in the Diaspora and many of our families on the continent—are the only people in world history that share the link to **Daniel** and his people of ancient Babylon which is stated in this awesome book. This is not a coincidence.

As I reflect on **Psalms 83:3** reads: *"They have taken crafty counsel against thy people and consulted against thy hidden ones"*. This means they have made their counsel crafty, cunning, and malignant, and may I add, they were artful. We can see that from the time of the Council of Nicaea during the reign of Emperor Constantine in 325 C.E. to the Willie Lynch Era in America, and in the Diaspora. Constantine and his henchmen canonized the Bible, forced the Israelites to stop worshipping on the Shabbat, outlawed circumcision, stopped new moon services, and created a new calendar. Israelite women were raped, creating a new look of people in the region called the Middle East. Israelite men were murdered and their leaders savagely put to death.

In the early 1700s, Willie Lynch instructed the plantation owners on ways to break the slave and his spirit which he likened to that of braking a horse. Lynch taught that the slave must fear his master even when his master isn't present, so they wouldn't poison their master, kill their livestock, or sabotage the fields. They must worship what their master say worship, their families separated, and men humiliated in front of their wives and children. Fear was put in the hidden ones—the children yet to be born. These horrific experiences are not a coincidence.

As I reflect on **Psalms 83:4**, I remember that it reads: *"Come let us cut them off them from being a nation, that the name of Israel shall be no more in remembrance"*. It is a historic fact that the people of Northeast Africa were cast off their land. It is a historical fact that these people fled to many provinces throughout Africa, including the Ivory Coast. It's also a historical fact that the enslaved Africans, which were "our ancestors", were taken to the Americas and the Caribbean by the ancestors of the Europeans. Those same Europeans were the descendants of Constantine the Roman in 325 C.E. and his predecessor Alexander the Great during the era of 333—323 B.C.E.

We, the descendants of the enslaved African Hebrews, are a people that have been cut off from their nation who no longer remember who we are. This is the only match in world history to these prophetic utterances. These biblical prophecies definitely match those historical facts. Do you think this is a coincident?

As I reflect on **Psalms 83:5**, it also says, *"They have consulted together with one consent, they are confederate"* who are joined together by an agreement or treaty in alliance" against "YAH's chosen people". After slavery ended, European nations found alternative sources to continue their wealth other than Black Gold. They found diamonds, gold, minerals, and other valuable metals, as well as a beautiful assortment of animals and ivory. Europeans in their greed for these great things began fighting one another and dying in bloody warfare. To alleviate this problem, they called for a meeting "Treaty". This agreement in Berlin was called **the 1884-1885 Berlin Conference**. They took crafty counsel on how they would colonize our people and rob Africa, making their kingdoms wealthy with growing infrastructures. England, Norway, Germany, Spain, and several others participated in this plot. They took the fight out of our ancestors; their intellect, their spirituality, their soldiers and missionaries caused them to repeat history matching the prophecy of **Psalms 83:5**. Coincidence? I repeat, my Abba always said, *"There is nothing new under the sun"* and *"What is has already been"*.

In this book **"The Revelations of Daniel"** we will see how historical matters repeat themselves over and over again with the same people, and we will see how it relates to today's times. We'll see that, yes, we are the descendants of an enslaved people, but, on the other hand, we'll also see that we were the descendants of kings and queens and a royal people. The end of the matter is that the world fears that we are the historical match with these biblical prophecies which proves beyond a doubt that the people that were colonized and the children of the Diaspora are are the true children of Israel. Not just kings and queens, but rulers of this world under YAH.

We are Israel. It's not a matter of "if". It's a matter of when. We know redemption is going to be a little rocky and it will try our faith, so let us make strives to better ourselves, stop judging others who don't believe like you believe, whether Messianic or non-Messianic, and begin to prepare. Divide and conquer has always been a method to conquer us. Let's not keep allowing this to happen. Find people you trust and build teamwork and prepare. It may be one year or it could be 10 years, even if it's not for you. It could be your descendants, your "grand, and great grandchildren". My brother, the author has done an excellent job in giving us **The Revelations of Daniel:** *YAH's Prophetic Utterances To Black America and All Mankind*. May YAH continue to be with **Yis-SAC** in our travels to Ghana as we're connecting with our Israelite families abroad. We say thank you YAH from **Me, My Congregation Or-Ami** and **Zikneh Yisrael from Atlanta, Georgia.**

Seth Ben Israel
Son of Zakain-Moreh Kahishmiyah Ben Israel
Lifetime Supporter of the Jerusalem Chronicle Newspaper<i>(JCN)</i>
Zikneh Yisrael
Or-Ami
Yis-SAC Ghana Mission

A captive of Judah
from the Trans-Atlantic
Slave Holocaust

August 11, 1847—August 4, 1908

From
Daniel, Hananiah, Mishael, Azariah,
To
William Saunders Crowdy
"Men Who Brought Back The Ancient Of Days"
"THE STONE CUT OUT WITHOUT HANDS!"

Table of Content

Chapter 1
Ancient Israel Lost Their Freedom--------------------------------Page 1
(The Fall of Jerusalem, Yehudah, Benyamin, and Levities and the beginning of slavery for the chosen people. Known today as so-called Negroes)

The Kingdom of Judah(Yehudah) and the ancient Hebrew concept of "the anointed" "HaMashiach"—"The Messiah------------------------Page 5
Kingdom of Israel and Judah---------------------------------------Page 11
The History of the House of David---------------------------------Page 11

Chapter 2
How Long, O YAH? Will You Be Angry Forever? Shall Your Jealousy burn like fire?--Page 15
YAH'S Heavenly Divine Court of Justice-------------------------Page 20
YAH'S Heavenly Verdict Against His People---------------------Page 21
Understanding The Vision---Page 25

Prophetic Time Zone
The Gold Age—The History of The Head of Gold----------------------Page 27
Historical Profile of Neo-Babylonian Chaldean Dynasty

Prophetic Time Zone
The Silver Age—Its Breast and Arms Were of Silver--------------------Page 40
Historical Profile of Persian Dynasty

Prophetic Time Zone
The Brass Age—Its Belly and Thighs of Brass-----------------------------Page 51
Historical Profile of Classical Greek Dynasty
Historical Profile of Philip the Great--Page 66
Historical Profile of Alexander the Great-----------------------------------Page 69

Prophetic Time Zone
The Brass Age—Its Belly and Thighs of Brass—Continues-------------Page 75

Hey

Divided Grecian Empire

1) The Antipatrid Dynasty (<u>Macedonia</u>)----------------------------------Page 76
Historical Profile of Macedonian Dynasty
The Antigonid Dynasty (Macedonia)
Historical Profile of Macedonian Dynasty
2) The Ptolemy Dynasty (<u>Egypt</u>)—The Beginning of The White Man's Takeover of Africa---Page 89
Historical Profile of Ptolemaic Dynasty
3) The Seleucid Dynasty (<u>Mesopotamia and Syria</u>)--------------------Page 103
Historical Profile of Seleucid Dynasty
4) The Thrace Dynasty (Southeastern Europe)<u>(Thrace)</u>-------------Page 139
Historical Profile of Thracian Dynasty

<u>Prophetic Time Zone</u>—Part 1
The Iron Age—Its Pelvis and Legs of Iron-------------------------------Page 149
The History of the Rome
The Roman Republic

<u>Prophetic Time Zone</u>—Part 2
The Iron Age—Its Pelvis and Legs of Iron-------------------------------Page 156
The Roman Empire
From 27 C.E. to 476 C.E.
The Black Emperors of Rome---Page 193

<u>Prophetic Time Zone</u>—Part 3
The Iron Age—Its Long Legs of Iron
The Divided Roman(Global) Empire
Western Iron Leg begins--Page 273
The History of The Divided Eastern Leg
Eastern Iron Leg begins---Page 321

<u>Prophetic Time Zone</u>
The Feet of Iron---Page 403

<u>Prophetic Time Zone</u>—*"The Latter-days"*
Toes of Iron and Miry Clay—The United Nations, EU, G-20--------Page 403

<u>Prophetic Time Zone</u>—*"Return of the Presence of YAH to Zion"*---Page 462
THE AGE OF YHWH—THE STONE CUT OUT WITHOUT HANDS
a) YAH Victorious through Natural Disasters and the Battle of Armageddon---Page 469
b) Universal Worship of ELOHIM of Israel
c) The Deliverance of the 12 tribes of Israel
d) Re-establishment of the Kingdom of YAH on earth with Israel and Yehudah
e) The Holiness of YAH rule the earth forever.

Chapter 3

The Great Whoredom "that ruleth the nations, languages, and tongues"
Global Falsehood--Page 516
A Prayer For Victory In Our Spiritual Struggle--------------------Page 529
(King Nebuchadnezzar)
(The Personification of the Evil & Wicked Man)------------------Page 530
A Psalms of Praise Dedicated to YAH---------------------------------Page 532
A Psalms to YAH who is my Strength---------------------------------Page 532

Chapter 1

Ancient Israel Lost Their Freedom

The fall of Jerusalem
(Yehudah, Benyamin, and Levites)
and
the beginning of slavery for
the chosen people.
(Known today as so-called Negroes)

The writings of Daniel continues to be one of the most important prophetic books of the ancient Hebrew scriptures. It reveals firsthand how and when the chosen people of God[**ELOHIM**]—who are the true Messiah the Prince—fell from power and were cruified. It also details how they would be eventually resurrected from the graveyard of the nations once again in *"the latter-days"*.

One of the greatest lessons to be learned from studying this book is that prophecy has dual aspects, meaning that prophecies applies to both the past, present, and future, and their occurrences would be repeated over and over again. What happened to Daniel in ancient times was destined to happen again in succeeding generations. The offsprings of these Israelites would also be taken into captivity to foreign lands just like their ancestors Daniel, Hananiah, Mishael, and Azariah. Another example of this book's duality is found in the fact that Daniel and his brethren were bound in chains, shackled, and carried into exile to the ancient kingdom of Babylonia. After the holy people's arrival in Babylon, Daniel was castrated, placed on an auction block, then sold as a palace slave where his name was changed to Belteshazzar. The Hebrew culture that Daniel and all Judah once embraced no longer existed. They were forced to eat the king's meat and drink his wine. Those developments occurred over and over again wherever Israel and Judah went into slavery, starting at the ancient **Head of Gold** and continuing down to the modern **Ten Toes of Iron and Miry clay**.

Black people in America should be able to relate to these horrific experiences because this is what has happened to them in these modern times. In fact, when you study history, you will see that black people's origins in America began under the same exact circumstances as Daniel and his people's in ancient Babylon, thus unmistakably proving the link between the ancient people of Judah and the so-called black people here in America today. This is no coincidence.

Historically speaking, the book of Daniel opens with the military defeat of Jerusalem by King Nebuchadnezzar of Babylon. The Temple of **YAH**(the Lord) **ELOHIM**(God) of **Israel** which had been built by King Solomon four centuries earlier was completely destroyed. The holy vessels and all remaining spiritual artifacts were carried away to the temple of Marduk. The entire city was razed. Ancient Judah, Benjamin, and Levi were exiled into captivity. The DIVINE freedom of the anointed prince, the holy people was gone. **[See Jeremiah 39:1-9]**.

However, before we can discuss this subject matter any further it should be stated that it is very important for us to understand exactly who these ancient people were. The reason being, the prophecies of ancient Daniel were, and continues to be, directed specifically towards the descendants of his people. Those prophetic utterances cannot be transferred to another nation of people, ethnicity, or be turned into a religion. For the record, the appearance of ancient people of Judah and Israel were the same as the ancient Egyptians, Ethiopians, Canaanites, or surrounding Shemites-Hamites. They were, and they continue to be, of the same appearance today, thousands of years later. This is another duality of prophecy, and the descendants of ancient Judah and Israel need to understand these historic and spiritual connections today.

The Kingdom of Judah

Yehoiakim, a son of David was one of the last kings of Judah, who ruled in Jerusalem from 607 B.C.E.

until 597 B.C.E. During Yehoiakim's reign, Nebuchadnezzar assumed the throne of his father Nabopolassar in Babylonia. Nebuchadnezzar began his military career as an administrator and builder in the Chaldean army. Nebuchadnezzar immediately launched wars against Syria, Egypt, and Judah during his first years of rulership. During his reign, the Babylonian ruler also spent most of his time and efforts rebuilding and modernizing the Babylonian infrastructure, launching massive projects that included paving the roads, rebuilding the numerous temples, and digging canals for luxurious travel throughout the royal city. His most famous construction project was known as the Hanging Gardens of Babylon which is still regarded as one of Seven Wonders of the Ancient World. Meanwhile in Jerusalem, Yehoiakim's rulership was marred with crimes against the commandments of YAH. The ancient Hebrew scribes wrote the following about this black king of Judah:

> "Yehoiakim was twenty-five years old when he began to reign, and he reigned eleven years in Jerusalem: and he did that which was evil in the sight of the LORD (**YAH**) his God (**ELOHIM**). Against him came up Nebuchadnezzar king of Babylon, and bound him fetters (shackles), to carry him to Babylon.
> Nebuchadnezzar also carried of the vessels of the house of the LORD (**YAH**) to Babylon, and put them in temple at Babylon."
>
> **II Chronicles 36: 5-7.**

Again in **II Kings 24:1-4** it is written:

> "In Yehoiakim's days Nebuchanezzar king of Babylon came up, and Yehoiakim became his servant three years; then he turned and rebelled against him.
> And the Lord (**YAH**) sent against him bands of the Chaldees, and bands of the Syrians, and bands of the Moabites, and bands of the children of Ammon, and sent them against Judah to destroy it, according to the word of the Lord (**YAH**), which he spake by his servants the prophet.
> Surely at the commandment of the Lord (**YAH**) came this upon Judah, to remove them out of HIS sight for the sins of Manesseh, according to all that he did; and also for the innocent blood that he shed: for he filled Jerusalem with innocent blood which the LORD (**YAH**) would not pardon."

Yehoiakim ruled for one year and in the following year he broke the peace treaty with Nebuchadnezzar. In the third year after the rebellion began, Nebuchadnezzar, the king of Babylon, invaded Jerusalem with his entire army, laying seige with battering rams and fury. **YAHAWAH** delivered Yehoiakim into his hand. Nebuchadnezzar completely destroyed the city of David, its walls, the Temple, the palaces, the great houses of learning, and the vessels of the CREATOR which Israel had dedicated to **YAH** during the reign of King Solomon. The wrath of the CREATOR had come upon the holy city and the holy people. After the third invasion, YAH eventually cast the kingdom of Judah out of HIS DIVINE PRESENCE because of their disobedience and rebellion.

The final blow to the kingdom of Judah came when Zedekiah, the brother of Yehoiakim reigned. Zedekiah rulership started in 597 B.C.E. after the death of his brother. You can verify this when you read **II Kings 24:11-20, II Kings 25:1-21**, and **II Chronicles 36:11-20**.

Zedekiah also rebelled against King Nebuchadnezzar and attempted to sign a defense pact with Egypt against Babylon. The ancient prophet **Isaiah** spoke of this spiritual and political error in his book in **chapters 30** and **31**. Zedekiah lost this third war with Babylon in 586 B.C.E.. He was captured, stripped naked, bound in chains, his eyes plucked out, and he was carried into Babylon where he joined the other prisoners from the previous two wars. The first Babylonian invasion came in 606 B.C.E.. The second war came in 597 B.C.E.., and this final war ended in 586 B.C.E. You can verify this history in **Jeremiah 52: 1-11**. The prophet Jeremiah made the following predictions:

> "For thus said YAH: I am going to deliver you and all your friends over to terror; they will fall by the sword of their enemies while you [Jeremiah] look on. I will deliver all Judah into the hands of the king of Babylon; he will exile them to Babylon or put them to the sword. And I will deliver all the wealth, all the riches, and all the prized possessions of this city, and I will also deliver all the treasures of the kings of Judah into the hands of their enemies: they shall seize them as plunder and carry them off to Babylon."
> **Jeremiah 20: 4-5**

Again **Jeremiah** answered them:
> "Thus shall you say to Zedekiah: Thus said YAH, ELOHIM of Israel: I am going to turn around the weapons in your hands with which you are battling outside the wall against those who are besieging you—the king of Babylon and the Chaldeans—and I will assemble them into the midst of this city, and I Myself will battle against you with an outstretched mighty arm, with anger and rage and great wrath. I will strike the inhabitants of this city, man and beast: they shall die by a terrible pestilence. And then—declares YAH —I will deliver King Zedekiah of Judah and his courtiers and the people—those in this city who survive the pestilence, the sword, and the famine—into the hands of King Nebuchaddnezzar of Babylon, into the hands of their enemies, into the hands of those who seek their lives. He will put them to the sword without pity, without compassion, without mercy."
> **chapter 21: 3-7.**

To a large degree, it was the Nation of Israel who had been acting like the Defiant and Wayward Son spoken of in the Torah in **Deuteronomy 21:18.** For example when we read this particular law, let us not forget that YAH, in HIS DIVINE words, in **Exodus 4: 22**, told us that the people of Israel were HIS son, even HIS firstborn—the anointed one (the true Messiah the Prince).

> Then you shall say to Pharoah, Thus says YAH, Israel is MY firstborn SON."
> **Exodus 4: 22**

So we must bear in mind that YAH our ELOHIM disciplines us—HIS people—in the same manner that we discipline our children. The law reads: "When a man has a wayward and defiant son who does not heed his father and mother, and does not obey them, even after they discipline him, his father and mother shall take hold of him and bring him out to the elders of his town, they shall say to the elders of his town, this son of ours is disloyal and defiant; he does not heed us. He is a drunkard and glutton. Therefore the men of his town shall stone him to death. Thus shall you sweep evil out of your midst; all Israel will hear and be afraid," in **Deuteronomy 21: 19-23**. The word *Defiant* means open, bold resistance to authority, and opposition or challenge to leadership.

The definition of the word *Wayward* is: difficult to control or predict because of unusual or perverse behavior; stubborn, contrary, headstrong (stiffnecked), disobedient, undisciplined. When you read the holy scriptures you will find that all these terms were used by the prophets of Israel to describe the people of Israel—YAH's Son. The prophets said Israel and Judah were a wayward and defiant people who would not heed the DIVINE Instructions of their **HEAVENLY FATHER—YAH.** These people did not obey the voice of their spiritual father and mother. They strayed and turned away defiantly. They opposed the commandments of YAH by choosing to practice the customs of the nations, and challenged YAH's DIVINE and MORAL authority. Therefore the Angels (host) of heaven, who served as the elders of the town, stood before **the Judge-YAH,** and brought the disloyal and defiant Son, Israel before Seat of Judgement. The prophets, who served as the father and mother, testified that "this son (people) of ours is disloyal and defiant; he does not heed the commandments (voice) of YAH. He is a glutton and drunkard. Therefore the prophet (father and mother) brought Israel before the Angels (elders of the town) and they stoned them to death (DIVINE Judgement).

> "YAH said to me, "Even if Moses and Samuel were to intercede with ME, I would not be won over to that people. Dismiss them from MY presence, and let them go forth! And if they ask you, To what shall we go forth? answer them, "Thus said YAH; Those destined for the plague, to the plague; Those destined for the sword, to the sword; Those destined for famine, to famine; Those destined for captivity, to captivity. And I (YAH) will appoint over them four kinds [of punishment]—declares YAH—the sword to slay, the dogs to drag, the birds of the sky, and the beast of the earth to devour and destroy. I will make them a horror to all the kingdoms of the earth, on account of King Mannesseh son of Hezekiah of Judah, and what he did in Jerusalem. But who will pity you, O Jerusalem, Who will console you? Who will turn aside to inquire about your welfare? You cast ME (YAH) off declares YAH. You go ever backward. So I have stretched out MY hand to destroy you; I cannot relent (stone them to death).
> **Jeremiah 15: 1-6**

Now that the disloyal, defiant, and wayward Son, the kingdom of Judah—the true Messiah the Prince—was dead, *stoned to death*, and turned into dust and ashes, there was no physical, spiritual, or political entity to represent **YAH ELOHIM of Israel** on earth The exiles were now spiritually dead existing in the graveyards of the nations, in pagan, idol-laden societies where all the commandments of YAH were disrespected and violated on a daily basis. The social pressure to embrace the prosperous, luxurious, materialistic Babylonian culture was intense. The minds and souls of Judah were highly impressed with their new environment. The Babylonian-Judaean war was over, second-class citizenship was available for all the exiles who complied with the rules and regulation of the **head of gold.** Many Judaeans became wealthy in Babylon. All they had to do was eat the king's meat and drink his wine. Of course, there was a spiritual price to pay for this material gain. Judah would have to integrate into this society where Idolatry replaced the worship of YAH. Profanity replaced Sacredness. Heathen Idolatry replaced the Hebrew concept of righteousness, and last but not least, Sin became the rule of law. Welcome to Babylon O house of Israel.

The spiritual meaning of eating the king's meat and drinking his wine was that the captives would accept Nebuchadnezzar's food for thought and join his new path of life and serve his gods, thereby forsaking YAH and HIS commandments. The Hebrews were expected to form social and political ties with their captors. Whosoever accepted the rule of law was a honorary Babylonian. The smart Hebrews were placed in institutions of higher learning to study the academics, sciences, arts, and mystery system of Babylon. These institutions certainly caused ancient Israel to go astray. The goals of the Babylonian schools were to teach dedication to the new world order, new diet, new habits, new dress, new protocol, and develop a new mindset. Once the majority of Israelites graduated from these schools, they were good for nothing in the eyes of YAH. Many became homeborn slaves to the new Babylonian order defiantly opposing the Torah more than they did before the exile. Instead of being priests and ministers of YAH, the anointed prince Israel, now served the kingdoms of the earth, using their YAH-given spiritual powers to advance Babylon. This can be verified in **Daniel 1: 18-19**.

Hebrew slaves were now highly valued in the halls of Babylonian power. Daniel, Hananiah, Mishael, and Azariah were among those sold to officials of a Babylonian college where they studied three years to gain certification. They were given government jobs upon graduation. Although a majority of Israelites forsook their ancient culture, there were remnants of Judah—anointed ones—who refused to go astray and forsake YAH. Daniel, Hananiah, Mishael, and Azariah represented this remnant in ancient times, and they continue to represent the proper way for us—the resurrected anointed ones—to conduct ourselves in captivity even today. Again, as I said earlier, this is the duality of prophecy.

Everyday Daniel faced professors who taught necromancy, astrology, humanistic philosophies, magic, and sorcery. *"But Daniel purposed in his heart that he would not defile himself,"* see **Daniel 1:8**. Daniel represented those who would remember the commandments, laws, judgements, and statutes of YAH given to Moses thousands of years earlier. Although, he was a slave and forced to attend these schools, Daniel vowed not to convert to his slavemaster's religion. Therefore he invoked the name of the true and living God **(YAH)**, and asked for DIVINE assistance in this new Prison Land. Unfortunately, all humanity would suffer due to the death of the kingdom of Judah and Israel, the true Messiah-Prince.

It is important for us, the descendants of the ancient Israelites, to understand the truth about the ancient Hebraic concept of who and what was the Messiah the Prince. The true Hebrew meaning of this term 'Messiah the Prince' has been grossly distorted by religious authorities. Contrary to Christian mythology, the term Messiah didn't apply to one individual. Instead, the term 'Messiah' applied to a historic process that included several individuals spanning several millenniums. In fact, the *Messiah*, or *anointed one*, is a term that represented "a people under the righteous DIVINE order consisting of the prophets, priests, king, and the 12 tribes of Israel who faithfully followed the Instructions of YAH according to HIS laws, commandments, judgements, and statutes delivered by HIS servant Moses. These anointed servants were, and continue to be, the Messiah the Prince. The meaning of the Messiah (HaMashiach) was, and continues to be, the "Anointed." Let's examine the Hebrew scriptures and see who this term actually applies to:

> "If it is the 'anointed' [which means Messiah] priest who has incurred guilt, so that blame falls upon the people, he shall offer for the sin of which he is guilty, a bull of the herd without blemish as a sin offering to YAH."
> **Leviticus 4: 3**

> "And the 'anointed' [Messiah] priest shall take some of the bull's blood and bring it into the Tent of Meeting."
> **Leviticus 4: 5**

> "The anointed [Messiah] priest shall bring some of the blood of the bull into the Tent of Meeting."
> **Leviticus 4: 16**

> "This is the line of Aaron and Moses at the time that YAH spoke with Moses on Mount Sinai. These were the names of Aaron's sons: Nadab, the firstborn, and Abihu, Eleazar and Ithamar; those were the names of Aaron's sons, anointed [HaMashiach-Messiah] priests who were ordained for priesthood."
> **Numbers 3: 1-3**

> "And let designate the Levites before YAH as an elevation offering from the Israelites, that they perform the service of YAH."
> **Numbers 8: 11**

> "Thereafter the Levites shall be qualified for the service of the Tent of Meeting, once you have cleansed them and designated them as an elevation offering. For they are formally assigned to ME [YAH's

Anointed Servants-Messiahs] from among the Israelites; I have taken them for Myself in place of all the first issue of the womb, of all firstborns of the Israelites. For every firstborn among man as well as beast, is Mine; I consecrated them to Myself at the time that I smote every firstborn of the Israelites; and from among the Israelites I formally assign the Levites to Aaron and his sons to perform the service for the Israelites in Tent of Meeting and to make expiation for the Israelites, so that no plague may afflict the Israelites for coming to near the sanctuary." **Numbers 8: 15-19**

As we see, only the tribe of the Levites were anointed to make atonement for Israel's sin. These spiritual truths and established decrees written in the Torah would automatically exclude the lone individual, 'man of Galilee,' from the tribe of Judah spoken of in the New Testament. The religious positions embraced by those early Christian theologians at the Council of Nicea were a total contradiction of the commandments of **YAH** decreed by Moses. Only the Levites were, and continue to be, ordained to make an atonement for the 12 tribes of Israel's sin, and not a man who was hung on a tree pole two thousand years ago. It is stated, *"your [Aaron's] sons shall be careful to perform your priestly duties in everything pertaining to the altar and what is behind the curtain. I make your priesthood a service of dedication; any outsider* [non-Levite] *who encroaches shall be put to death,"* in **Numbers 18: 7.** Read **2 Chronicles 26: 16-26** to see what happened to King Uzziah, a son of David of the tribe of Judah [an outsider], when he entered the area of the sanctuary reserved only for the Levites. Again, YAH chose only the Levites to make atonement for Israel's sin, and NOT a man from the tribe of Judah. Those non-Israelites of the 1st Century Common Era were in error when they started the global lie that a non-Levite could make expiation for Israel's sin. This contradicts the Word of **ELOHIM** written in stone by Moses centuries earlier. This global falsehood has deceived the majority of the inhabitants of the earth for over 2,000 years.

Furthermore we read in the inscribed Words of God **ELOHIM** that:

"The priest [Levites] shall make expiation for the whole Israelite community and they shall be forgiven; for it was an error, and for their error they have brought their offering, an offering by fire to YAH and their sin offering before YAH."
Numbers 15: 25

"And YAH said to Aaron: You shall, however, have no territorial share among them or own any portion in their midst; I [YAH] am your portion and your share among the Israelites. And to the Levites I [YAH] hereby give all the tithes in Israel as their share in return for the services that they perform, the services of the Tent of Meeting."
Numbers 18: 20-21

These verses prove beyond a shadow of doubt the importance of the Levites when it comes to Israel's eternal salvation in both ancient and modern times.. They were, and continue to be, YAH's Sons speaking in HIS name and proclaiming HIS laws, commandments, and judgements in the midst of the earth. Through these anointed men the nation of Israel and all the foreign nations shall be saved. They, the Levites, were first in the nation be called YAH's Messiahs [HaMashiach]..

Secondly, the prophets of Israel were also known as the anointed ones within the kingdom of Israel. In **Psalms 105: 14-15**, King David said, "YAH allowed no one to oppress them; He [YAH] reproved kings on their account, Do not touch *"My anointed* **[HaMashiach]** ones; do not harm *MY prophets."* The majority of the prophets were Levites also. This fact is documented in **Deuteronomy 18: 15** where Moses wrote:

YAH your ELOHIM will raise up [anoint] for you [Israel] a prophet from among your own people [one of the Levitical priests] like myself [Moses, a Levite. See **Exodus 4: 12-16, Exodus 7: 1-2**]; him you shall heed. This is just what you asked of YAH your ELOHIM at Horeb, on the day of the Assembly; saying, "Let me not hear the voice of YAH my ELOHIM any longer or see this wondrous fire any more, lest I die. Whereupon YAH said to me, They have done well speaking thus. I will raise up a prophet for them from among their own people, like yourself [Moses the Levite]; I will put MY words in his mouth and he will speak to them all that I command him; and if anybody fails to heed the words he speaks in MY name, I myself will call him account."

Deuteronomy 18: 15-19

"YAH replied to Moses, "See, I [YAH] place you in the role of **ELOHIM** to Pharoah; with your brother Aaron [a Levite] as your prophet. You shall repeat all I command you, and your brother Aaron shall speak to Pharoah to let the Israelites depart from his land."

Exodus 7: 1-2

The anointed prophet Jeremiah was a Levitical priest from the city of Anathoth. You can verify this in **Jeremiah 1:1**. The prophet Ezekiel was a Levite. This also can be verified in **chapter 1: 3**: *"the word of YAH came to the priest Ezekiel son of Buzi, by the Chebar River, in the land of the Chaldeans. And the hand of YAH came upon me there."* The prophet **Isaiah** was also a Levitical priest. You can read of this in chapter **6: 1-7**. Only a Levitical priest could enter into the inner court of the Holy of Holies where the prophet Isaiah saw the vision of YAHAWAH. The prophets Elijah and Elisha were also Levite priests. Zechariah, the son of Berechiah, the son of Iddo, was a Levite. This also can be confirmed in **Nehemiah 12:16**. Haggai was a Levite as well. These two anointed priest-prophets, along with Ezra the chief priest, assisted in the rebuilding of the temple of **YAH ELOHIM** of Israel during the reign of ancient Persian empire in the 6th century B.C.E. Of course, we cannot forget to mention Samuel the Levite, the priest-prophet, who started working as an attendant in Tent of Meeting as a young boy. His genealogy is recorded in **I Chronicles 6: 17-19** where the scribe wrote: *"They served at the Tabernacle of the Tent of Meeting with song until Solomon built the House of YHWH in Jerusalem; and carried out their duties as prescribed for them. Those were the appointed men; and their sons were the Kohathites; Heman the singer, son of Joel son of Samuel, son of Elkanah, son of Jeroham, son of Eliel, son of Toah, son of Zuph, son of Elkanah, son of Mahath, son of Amasai."*

This is the same genealogy in **I Samuel 1:1**:

"There was a man of Ramathaim of the Zuphites, in the hill country of Ephraim, whose name was Elkanah, son of Jeroham, son of Elihu, son of Tohu, son of Zuph, an Ephraimite."

Young Samuel was in the service of YAH under Eli. In those days the word of YAH was rare; prophecy was not widespread. One day Eli was asleep in his usual place; his eyes had begun to fail and he could barely see. The lamp of ELOHIM had not yet gone out, and Samuel was sleeping in temple of YAH where the Ark of ELOHIM was. YAH called out to Samuel, and he answered, "I'm coming." He ran to Eli and said, Here I am; you called me." But he replied, "I didn't call you; go back to sleep. So he went back and lay down. Again YAH called, "Samuel!" Samuel rose and went to Eli and said, "Here I am; you called me." But he replied, "I didn't call, my son; go back to sleep." Now Samuel had not experienced YAH; the word of YAH had not been revealed to him. YAH call Samuel again, a third time;

and he rose and went to Eli and said, "Here I am; you called me."
Then Eli understood that YAH was calling the boy. And Eli said to
Samuel, "Go lie down, if you are called again, say speak YAH for
your servant is listening." And Samuel went to his place and lay
down. YAH came, and stood there, and HE called as before
"Samuel!" "Samuel!", And Samuel answered, "Speak YAH, for
your servant is listening."

I Samuel 3: 1-10

This chapter—**I Samuel 3: 1-18**—confirms what **Deuteronomy 18: 15** was actually talking about. It was prophecy of men like Samuel, Elijah, Elisha, Isaiah, Jeremiah, Ezekiel, Zechariah, Haggai, all Levites like Moses. They were priests who transcended to the spiritual realm of Seer. They were all termed "anointed" [HaMashiach/Messiah] prophets. The point I'm making is that the term Messiah applied to several individuals within the kingdom of YAH. Furthermore, these verses also confirm that **Deut. 18: 15** had nothing to do with the coming of Jesus or Yeshua. When you read verse 1 of chapter 18, it will plainly tell you that this chapter is about the Levites, and their future mission within the kingdom of YAH.

"The Levitcal priests, the whole tribe of Levi, shall have no territorial portion with Israel. They shall live off YAH's offerings by fire as their portion. And shall have no portion among their brother tribes; YAH is their portion.

Deuteronomy 18: 1-2

The Levites were the chosen ones among the chosen people—the true Sons of ELOHIM among the 12 tribes of Israel, and according to this chapter, Israel was prohibited from consigning their children to the flames of Baal, seeking augurs, soothsayers, diviners, sorcerers, wizards, necromancers, instead YAH would elevate a Levite priest to a prophet, through visions and dreams. Israel was commanded to seek DIVINE insight from them, and not use the customs of the foreign nations who practiced using pagan sources for esoteric insight. Let us continue. Additional examples of levitical priests serving as prophets can be found in these following verses which provides more indisputable truth that **Deuteronomy 18: 15** was referring to Levites as prophets:

"But he shall present himself to Eleazar the priest, who shall on his behalf seek the decision of Urim before YHWH. By such instruction they shall go out and by such instructions they shall come in, he and all the Israelites, the whole community."

Numbers 27:21

"The priests, sons of Levi, shall come forward: for YAH your ELOHIM has chosen them to minister [prophesied] to HIM and pronounce blessing in the name of YHWH, and every lawsuit and case of assault is subject to their ruling."

Deuteronomy 21: 5

"Then the spirit of **ELOHIM** enveloped Zechariah son of Jehoiada the priest; he stood above the people and said to them, "Thus **ELOHIM** said: Why do you transgress the commandments of YAH that you cannot succeed?
Since you have forsaken YAH, HE has forsaken you."

2 Chronicles 24:20

"The priest shall make expiation for the whole Israelite community and they shall be forgiven; for it was an error, and for their error they have brought their offering, an offering by fire to YAH and their sin offering before YAH.
Numbers 15:25

The Israelites inquired of YAH (for the Ark of ELOHIM's Covenant was there in those days, and Phinehas son of Eleazar son of Aaron the priest ministered before HIM in those days), "Shall we again take the field against our kinsmen the Benjaminites, or shall we not? YAH answered, "Go up tomorrow I will deliver them into your hands."
Judges 20: 27-28

Then in the midst of the congregation the spirit of YAH came upon Jahaziel son of Zechariah son of Benaiah son of Jeiel son of Mattaniah the Levite, of the sons of Asaph, and he said, "Give heed, all Judah and the inhabitants of Jerusalem and King Jehoshaphat; thus saith YAH to you, Do not fear or be dismayed by this great multitude, for the battle is God's, not yours."
2 Chronicles 20: 14-15

Again, I know I mentioned these facts previously in this same chapter, but I must say it over and over. *(And I know I will certainly reiterate it in this chapter, and in chapters 2 and 3.)* Christian theologians have corrupted the meaning of this chapter and used it to enforce falsehood among the nations. Thus, the Christian church has attempted to rob the Levitical priesthood of their historic and prophetic mission of serving as YAH's Messiahs and spokesmen in Israel and among the nations of the earth by misinterpreting this particular chapter—**Deut. 18, verse 15**. One of their main theories used to justify the worship of Jesus/Yeshua is their misuse of that chapter. The sons of Aaron, are the anointed ones, who should be the moral force in the world today, not preachers or the Popes of Rome. The world, including the children of Israel, have been deceived. Christians are notorious when it comes to cherry-picking the Hebrew scriptures. Instead of reading the entire chapters they only read one verse then falsely believe they have the proper Hebraic understanding of the entire ancient Hebrew scriptures.

So far we have discussed the priests and prophets as the "anointed" [HaMashiach/Messiahs] "ones." The next position in Israel that became known as the "Anointed" was the kingship, first under King Saul, of tribe of Benjamin, then later under King David and his son Solomon of the tribe of Judah. The ascension of David, of Bethlehem-Judah, represented the fulfillment of Genesis[Bereshith] 49:8-12 which states: *"Judah, thou are he*[**David**] *whom thy brethren shall praise: thy hand shall be in the neck of thine enemies; thy father's children shall bow down before you."* [Read **1 Kings 1: 23-37** for the fulfillment of Jacob's prophecy. You can also read **2 Samuel 7: 1-29** or **1 Chronicles 17: 1-27** for further confirmation of the fulfillment of Jacob's ancient prophecies. It should be clearly stated that these prophecies had nothing to do with the prediction of Jesus/Yeshua the carpenter and everything to do with prophecy of future kings of Israel and Judah). *"Judah is a lion's whelp: from the prey, my son, thou art gone up: he stooped down: he crouched as a lion' and as an old lion: who shall rouse him.*[**David**]. *The sceptre shall not depart from Judah, nor a lawgiver from between his feet;* [**Prophecy of the perpetual dynasty of King David.** Please read **2 Samuel 7:8-16** and **1 Chronicles 3:1-16** again to understand that prophecy because, as I emphasized earlier it had nothing to do with the coming of the New Testament character Jesus/Yeshua who was a carpenter and not a king who sat upon the throne of **David]** *"until Shiloh*[**YHWH**] *come;*[return in the midst of HIS people as spoken of in **Joshua 18:1**]. *and unto him*[**Shiloh-YHWH**] *shall the gathering of the people be.* [This prophecy was fulfilled in **I Chronicles 28:1-21** and **I Chronicles 29:1-30**. In the book of Ezekiel the prophet envisioned a future restoration of **Shiloh** in **chapter 37: 24-28:**

"And **David/Shiloh** MY servant shall be king over them; and they all shall have one shepherd; they shall also walk in MY judgements, and observe MY statutes, and do them. And they shall dwell in the land that I have given unto Jacob MY servant, wherein your fathers have dwelt; and they shall dwell therein, even they, and their children, and their children's children for ever; and MY servant David [**Shiloh**] shall be their prince for ever. [This will be the fulfillment of Jacob's prophecy: *"thy father's children shall bow down before thee,"* and *"The sceptre shall not depart from Judah, nor a lawgiver from between his feet until Shiloh come, and unto him shall the gathering of the people be."*]

"Morever I will make a covenant of peace with them; it shall be everlasting covenant with them: and I will place them, and multiply them, and will set MY sanctuary in the midst of them forevermore. MY tabernacle[**The Tent of Meeting which was moved from the city of Shiloh to the Temple of YHWH in Jerusalem by King David**] also shall be with them; I will be their ELOHIM(God), and they shall be MY people. And the heathen shall know that I, YHWH, do sanctify Israel, when MY sanctuary [**Shiloh**] shall be in the midst of them for evermore."

As the following verses prove the term Shiloh has a doublefold meaning. Number one, it represented the future establishment of the Tabernacle of YAH in the midst of the people where all 12 tribes gathered. Number two, it also represented the prophecy of the coming of King David and his sons as the kings upon the throne of Israel over the 12 tribes of Israel. When you combine both projections, they represent a vision of David and his sons gathering the people together before the Presence of YAH to obey HIS Voice and walk in HIS ways. This DIVINE truth is also revealed in **Ezekiel 34: 23-31, Jeremiah 33: 19-26, Hosea 3: 4-5, Amos 9:11, and Haggai 2: 21-23**. Again, I reiterate these prophecies are not referring to a poor carpenter or a second coming. Those falsehoods have been prepetuated by earlier Christian theologians and their followers.

Continuing, our ancestor Jacob said in **Genesis 49:11-12:***"Binding his foal unto the vine, and ass's colt unto the choice vine*[**I Kings 1: 33**]: *he washed his garments in wine, and his clothes in the blood of grapes: His eyes shall be red with wine, and his teeth white with milk."*

The reason I explained all of those verses was to prove to you that the term "Anointed" HaMashiach was a term that applied to an entire people comprised of several individuals, the priest, the prophets, and the kingship. We as the resurrected Israelites must publicly demystify the term Messiah because the Christian teachers have distorted the concept over the past two-thousand years with the individual known as Christ.

It was the individual David whom YAH singled out by name as HIS anointed servant. In fact, YAH said *"MY servant David, who kept MY commandments, and followed ME with all his heart, to do that only which is right MINE eyes,"* in **I Kings 14:8**. King David became the spiritual father of all the successive sons of David. He was the standard which YAH used to judge all of his offsprings who would occupy his seat of power. Take time and read the following verses that verify that David was the spiritual father and the standardbearer for the throne of David forever. You will need to open your Hebrew scriptures for a moment and read these: **I Kings 11: 31-39, II Kings 18: 1-3, II Kings 14: 1-3, II Chronicles 17: 1-6, I Kings 22: 41-43, I Kings 15:24, I Kings 15: 1-5, I Kings 8: 14-18,24-26, I Kings 2:4, II Chronicles 13:5,8, II Chronicles 21:4-7, II Chronicles 26:4, II Chronicles 27:2,6, II Chronicles 28:1-2, II Chronicles 29:2, II Chronicles 33:2-4, II Chronicles 34:1-3.** Those above verses confirm the point that King David became the role model for all his successors. Oftentimes you read the statements such as *"MY servant David"* or *"he did good in the sight of YAH like unto David his father,* or *"he did evil in the eyes of YAH and did not walk in the ways of David his father"*, when in fact, David was not the actual biological father of these men. Instead, he was the spiritual father who set the standard for good leadership, as it is until this very day.

KINGDOM OF ISRAEL & JUDAH
"Judah is a lion's whelp;"

THE HISTORY OF THE HOUSE OF DAVID
David (**David I**)
Solomon(**David II**)
Rehoboam(**David III**)
Abiyah(**David IV**)
Asa(**David V**)
Yehoshaphat(**David VI**)
Yehoram(**David VII**)
Azariah(**VIII**)
Yehoash(**David IX**)
Amaziah(**David X**)
Uzziah(**David XI**)
Yotham(**David XII**)
Ahaz (**David XIII**)
Hezekiah(**David XIV**)
Manasseh(**David XV**)
Amon(**David XVI**)
Yosiah(**David XVII**)
Jehoahaz (Shallum)(**David XVIII**)
Yehoiakim(**David XIX**)
Yehoiachin(**David XX**)
Zedekiah(**David XXI**)

Zerubbabel(**Worked to restore the throne of David**)
Nehemiah(**Worked to restore the throne of David**)

Psalms 89:18-46
The Spiritual History of Throne of David

For YHWH is our defence; and **the Holy One of Israel is our KING**. Then thou spakest in vision to thy holy one, and saidst, I have laid help upon one that is mighty; I have exalted one chosen out of the people. I have found David MY servant; with MY holy oil have I[**YHWH**] anointed [**HaMashiach**] him; With whom MY hand shall be established; MINE arm also shall strengthen him. The enemy shall not exact upon him; nor the son of wickedness afflict him. And I will beat down his foes before his face, and plague them that hate him. But MY faithfulness and MY mercy shall be with him; and in MY NAME shall his horn be exalted. I will set his hand also in the sea, and his right hand in the rivers. He shall cry unto ME, thou are MY FATHER, MY ELOHIM, and the rock of my salvation. Also I will make him MY firstborn [**David and his sons**], higher than the kings of the earth. MY mercy will I keep for him for evermore, and MY covenant shall stand fast with them. His seed [**David's sons**] also will I make to endure for ever, and his throne as the days of heaven. If his children forsake MY law, and walk not in MY commandments; Then will I visit their transgression with the rod, and their iniquity with stripes. Nevertheless MY lovingkindness will I not utter take from him, nor suffer MY faithfulness to fail; MY covenant will I not break, nor alter the thing that is gone out of MY lips. Once have I sworn by MY Holiness that I will not lie unto David. His seed [sons] shall endure for ever, and his throne as the sun before ME. It shall be established for ever as the moon, and as a faithful witness in heaven. Selah. But thou hast cast off [**into slavery among the kingdoms of gold, silver, brass, iron, and miry clay**] and abhorred, thou hast been wroth with thine anointed [**HaMashiach**]. Thou hast made void the covenant of thy servant: thou hast profaned his crown by casting it to the ground. Thou has broken down all his hedges; thou has brought his strongholds to ruin. All that pass by the way spoil him: he is a reproach to his neighbours. Thou hast set up the right hand of his adversaries: thou hast made all his enemies to rejoice. Thou hast also turned the edge of his sword, and hast not made him to stand in the battle [**against Babylon-The Head of Gold**]. Thou hast made his glory to cease, and cast his throne down to the ground. The days of his youth hast thou shortened; thou has covered him with shame.[**Deuteronomy 28:15-68**]. Selah.

How Long YAH? will you hide thyself for ever? shall thy wrath burn like fire?

Now, let's look at another group of Israelites to which the term anointed "HaMashiach" also applied. It applied to the entire 12 tribes of Israel—the people. That's right, the people of Israel were known as the anointed people or "HaMashiach" people. This is why Israelite scholars totally disagree with the Greco-Roman Chrisitan perspective of one person being God's only begotten Son. That perspective is totally false. It is based on non-Hebrew unenlightened speculation and erroneous Gentile assertions. Again, as I said earlier, when you read **Exodus 4:22-23** it stated: *"And you shall say unto Pharaoh, Thus saith YAH, Israel* [**the people**] *is MY son, even MY firstborn; And I say unto thee, Let MY son go, that he may serve ME; and if you refuse to let him go, behold, I will slay your son, even your firstborn."*

So, as you see, the Torah clearly states YAH'S feelings. The people of Israel were God Almighty's son—the anointed one. Furthermore the prophets confirm the same point with the following words of YAH:

"Thou[**O YAH**] went forth for the salvation of YOUR **people,** even for the salvation of YOUR **anointed [HaMashiach] people;** thou [**O YAH**] woundest the head out of the house of the wicked, by discovering the foundation unto the neck. Selah. **Habakkuk 3:13**.

"And [**YAH**] said unto me[**Isaiah**], You are **MY servant, O Israel,** in whom I[**YAH**] will be glorified. **Isaiah 49:3**.

"Now therefore, if you will obey **MY VOICE** indeed, and keep **MY covenant,** then you shall be a **peculiar treasure unto ME above all people**: for all the earth: And you shall be unto ME[**YAH**] a **kingdom of priests,** and **an holy nation**. These are the words which you shall speak unto the **children of Israel**." **Exodus 19:5-6**.

"I have forsaken MINE house, I have left MINE heritage; I have given **the dearly beloved of MY soul** into the hand of her enemies." **Jeremiah 12:7-8**

"But now thus saith YAH that **created thee,** O Jacob, and HE that **formed thee,** O Israel, Fear not: for I have redeemed thee, I have called thee by thy name, thou art MINE." **Isaiah 43:1**

"Yet now hear, O Jacob MY servant; and Israel, whom **I have chosen**." **Isaiah 44:1** . . . ."Thus saith **YAH thy Redeemer, and HE that formed thee from the womb**, I am YAH that maketh all things; that stretcheth forth the heavens alone; that spreadeth abroad the earth by **MYSELF**." **Isaiah 44:24**.

"For Jacob MY servant's sake, and **Israel MINE elect**, I have even called thee by thy name:

I have surnamed thee, though thou hast not known ME." **Isaiah 45:4.**

Those verses which I mentioned proves YAH's feelings towards HIS people. In HIS eyes they are the dearly beloved of HIS soul, which is another way of saying MY anointed. YAH reminds the people of Israel that they were created, formed, and will be redeemed by HIM because Israel is "MINE" HE said. That too is another way of saying **Israel is MY anointed**. YAH even goes further and said "I have chosen you", **"I am your REDEEMER"**, "I formed you, Israelite people, in your mother's womb", and **"Israel MINE elect."** That too is another way of simply saying **Israel is "My anointed. "— "My Messiah."**

So the truth of the matter is this: YAH's Messiah—consisting of the throne of David, the Levitical priesthood, the Hebrew prophets, and the 12 tribes of Israel— fell from power in 586 B.C.E. when the kingdom of YAH was invaded and destroyed by King Nebuchadnezzar, the ruler of the Neo-Babylonian empire. This Messiah we're referring to is not based on a Christian interpretation of the controversial term. As I stated previously, the Gentiles have attempted to rob the ancient Israelite people of their role as the "anointed" by attempting to transfer their title of "Messiah" over to one man whom they claimed was the Christ/Messiah who founded Christianity/Messiah-worship. Those New Testament writings by the apostles focused on a mythological individual and not the true ancient Hebrew concept. That false doctrine has deceived and misled the entire world, including certain segments of the Israelite community that embrace their Gentile-inspired perverse outlook.

Once the people of Israel and Judah—the true Messiah the Prince—were scattered among the nations(**into the kingdoms of gold, silver, brass, iron, and miry clay**) as slaves, they were disrespected, persecuted, forced to convert to foreign religions, given foreign names and diets. They ceased to be known as the people of YAH or the children of Israel. From the head of gold down to the toes of iron and miry clay, the history of the ancient Israelites was erased from the minds of the inhabitants of the earth. They became the lost sheep of Israel, who were hated by all men, and reduced to the status of bondmen and bondwomen known as—The Suffering Servant described in **Isaiah chapter 53.**

YAH continuously sent HIS servant the prophets to instruct Israel and to bring them back into HIS fold. Regrettably in those days, and even in these latter-days, the people of Israel and Judah have eaten sour grapes and their children's teeth are set on edge. Therefore YAH told the prophet **Yeremiah** in **chapter 29, verses 17 and 18:** *"Thus saith YAH sa-ba-ot (of hosts): Behold, I will send upon them the sword*[**oppression**]*, the famine*[**poverty**]*, and pestilence*[**diseases**]*, and will make them like vile figs, that cannot be eaten; they are so evil. And I will persecute them with the sword*[**oppression**]*, with the famine*[**poverty**]*, and with the pestilence*[**diseases**]*, and will deliver them to be removed to all the kingdoms of the earth*[**slavery**]*, to be a curse, an astonishment, and an hissing, and a reproach, among all nations whither I have driven them."*

QUESTION: Why would YAH do this to **HIS Messiah the Prince—the people of Israel and Judah, HIS firstborn?**

Our ANSWER is found in **Jeremiah 29:19:** *"Because they have not hearkened to MY Words, saith YAH, which I sent unto them by MY servants* [**HaMashiachs**] *the prophets, rising up early and sending them: but you would not hear, saith YAH."* Israel's punishment, as foretold in **Deuteronomy 28:15-68,** would be spiritual death causing them to become a valley of dry bones, dead men and women without the Spirit of YAH. This long, continuous decline into the graveyard among nations started with the Babylonian captivity and has progressed well into the 21st century here in America.

Nevertheless, for those who remained focused on the disciplines of YAH's commandments like the four young Hebrew men, who represented the remnant, YAH would guide his chosen ones through the dark tunnel of continuous captivities. Our beloved elders Daniel, Hananiah, Mishael, and Azariah were the ones who remained steadfast to the covenant that YAH made with Israel at Mount Sinai. Now Daniel and his brethren dwelt in Babylon and they were ready scribes in the law of Moses which **YAH ELOHIM of Israel** had given to HIS people Israel. *(We must also uphold the law of the Most High in this land where we have been carried* *away into captivity.)*

Every since the days of Daniel, YAH has made it possible for the Hebrews to remain lawful according to the commandments, proving that HIS WILL was still in effect although earthly power had been transfered over to Nebuchadnezzar. We should also learn from that moment in history that those who invoke the name of YAH would be able to overcome foreign opposition, beginning with the **(head of gold)** down to **(toes of iron and miry clay)** in the latter-days . That DIVINE Truth can be verified in Daniel **1: 9-16.**

1500 B.C.E. wall relief of Arameans praying. The Arameans, also known as ancient Syrians, were kinsmen of the ancient Israelites. Both were descendants of Shem. The Arameans were the offspring of Aram and the Israelites were the descendants of Arphaxad. Both were black Shemitic people. [See Genesis 10:22].

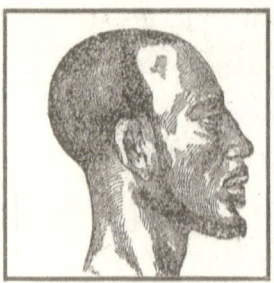

A potrait of a typical Egyptian man. The photo clearly reveal the Afro-Asiatic features of the Egyptian people. Moses was mistaken for an Egyptian man, proving that he was a black man as well.

This is another wall relief from Egypt depicting an ancient Afro-Asiatic Hebrew man. Again, these drawings clearly demonstrate that the ancient Hebrews were people of color.

Chapter 2

How Long, O YAH? Will You Be Angry Forever? Shall Your Jealousy Burn Like Fire?

> YAHAWAH saved Israel and Israel had faith in YAHAWAH and in Moses YAH's servant.
> **Exodus 14: 30-31.**

> YAHAWAH's portion is HIS people and they are the measure of HIS inheritance.
> **Deut. 32: 9.**

> Blessed be the name of YAHAWAH, ELOHIM of the entire heavens, earth, and the great seas, all therein. May YAHAWAH bless you out of Zion. Selah.

The disobedience of ancient Israel and Judah set in motion the fall of Jerusalem and the rise of the heathen kingdoms to global prominence. The writings of Daniel opened with the scribe detailing how he and his people arrived in the land of the Chaldeans. As we already discussed in Chapter one, King Nebuchadnezzar triumphed over Yehoiakim because he was disobedient to HIS God (YAH). This great forsaking of YAH in the midst of the land was a **Spiritual Crime** committed by the servants of YAHAWAH. After these abhorrent acts by the children of Israel, YAH's judgement manifested itself against them in the physical realm. Therefore the **Spiritual Judgement** spoken of by Moses and the prophets became a reality. The Israelites had been bound in chains and shackles as Moses had warned:

> "I know how defiant and stiffnecked you are: even now, while I am still alive in your midst, you have been defiant toward YAH; how much more, then, when I am dead! Gather to me all the elders of your tribes and you officers that I may speak all these words to them and that I may call heaven and earth to witness against them: For I know that, when I am dead you will act wickedly and turn away from the path that I enjoined upon you, and that in time to come misfortune will befall you for having done evil in the sight of YHWH and vexed HIM by your deeds.
> **Deut. 31: 27-29.**

> "I will scatter them, I will cause their memory to cease from men."
> **Deut. 32: 26.**

The Babylonian name Belteshazzar was given to Daniel. Hananiah's name became Shadrach, Mishael was given the name Meshach and Azariah was renamed Abednego. Judah was now exiled in ancient Babylon—a strange land full of the religions (gods) of others. These new names given to these captives honored the pantheon of gods of Babylon—Bel, Nebo, Merodach (Marduk), Anu, and Nergal, which were all graven images. The meaning of the Hebrew name Daniel was "ELOHIM(God) is Judge." The meaning of the name Hananiah was "YAHAWAH is gracious." Mishael means "Who is like God (ELOHIM)." Azariah means "YAHAWAH has helped." On a spiritual level King Nebuchadnezzar was acting as an agent of Satan (the adversary) seeking to destroy the Words, Names, and separate the people of ELOHIM from their historical and spiritual past. This is what the changing of their Hebraic names represented. It is also the same thing it represented when the European slave masters changed the Afro-Asiatic names of our African American ancestors when they arrived at Jamestown, Virginia in 1619. This is the duality of prophecy spoken of earlier. By changing their name, the king replaced the worship of YAHAWAH with the worship of the gods of Babylonia in the earth.

On a human level Nebuchadnezzar also sought to enrich himself and his royal court by enslaving and exploiting the people of Judah using them as palace servants, field hands, officers, and laborers. His hope was that the people of the kingdom of YAH would remain his slaves in this new strange land and never experience a national rebirth.

'O Israel' welcome to your new home away from home, the land of the lawbreakers—Torahbusters. A world where people did not recognize the commandments of YAH. Their personal, public, and national policies did not incorporate the Torah into their day-to-day lives. This new homeland, Babylon, was now the total focus of their attention. Jerusalem was gone. It laid desolate. All the holy dwelling places such as the temple, palaces, the walls, and gates were in total ruin, thereby erasing the physical presence and memory of YAH from among nations. This beacon of light in Zion no longer shined.

The question in the minds of Daniel, Hananiah, Mishael, and Azariah, along with the remnant of Israel and Judah was, would YAH remember His Mercies towards them and restore their kingdom once again? Would YAH's tender mercies remember the covenant with Abraham, the oath to Isaac, the confirmation with Jacob, and the eternal pact with the tribes of Israel? Of course, the people's spirits were low because of their new social status as bondmen and bondwomen. Some thought, where is the Omniscient Power of YAH? Where is His outstretched arm and mighty hand?

Little did they know that the mysteries of YAHAWAH would manifest itself through a dream to the ruler of Babylon. This dream would be an answer to these questions that the remnant had longed to know. How Long Heavenly Father? How long would they have to sigh under the yoke of Babylon. When would they regain their strength to return and re-establish the kingdom of Judah as in days of old with Jerusalem as their spiritual capital? To the physical eye, it seemed as if YAH had plowed under His chosen people, however, on a DIVINE level YAH was creating a new beginning that would take root, blossom, and bring forth fruit thousands of years later. At that moment only YAH, the all-knowing ELOHIM, understood the esoteric meaning behind Nebuchadnezzar's dream. The reason being, it was YAH who gave him the visions of the dream upon his bed in the first place.

Judgement Day

It had been a normal day for the king. He had handled the vast affairs of the empire. The evening had ended with a nightly feast before Nebuchadnezzar went to retire in the royal palace bedroom. It was during this night, YAHAWAH would reveal Himself and His eternal Sovereignty through a terrifying nightmare.

"I, YHWH, make Myself known to him; in a dream shall I speak with him."

Numbers 12: 6.

YAH in His Infinite Wisdom knew that King Nebuchadnezzar had great admiration for graven images. In fact, he had spent his civilian career as a builder of national monuments throughout the Chaldean kingdom. He envisioned these gods as superpower entities that could fly, fight wars, descend into the netherworld, ascend up to the stars, give divine instructions, and serve as a national patron. So YAH, the True and Living ELOHIM gave him a mental motion picture of a statue made of diverse metals, gold, silver, brass, iron, and miry clay. This was highly unusual because stautes are always made of one solid metal such as pure gold, pure silver, pure brass, pure iron, or all earthenware (miry clay), not an image of mingled and diverse metals. Then to make matters worse, instead of the statue being revered and honored, it was destroyed by a great stone cut out without human hands and became worthless chaff for a summer threshingfloor. This was very disturbing to a man who did nothing but design, construct, and worship graven images as God. Imagine. This dream was disturbing. To understand the severity of it, you could compare it to a U.S. president having a nightmare of the White House and the U.S.being devastated by a nuclear attack. Nebuchadnezzar woke up perplexed, in a night sweat, and to make matters even worse, he forgot what he had seen. The dream vanished from his mind.

YAH had two DIVINE purposes for this incident: One purpose was to prove that HE was the all-Knowing, all-Seeing, Eternal Power who was greater than all the gods (magicians, diviners, astrologers, sorcerers, soothsayers, and Chaldeans) of Babylon. Secondly, as I said earlier, YAH used this incident to answer the prayers of the remnant of children of Israel, which was to inform them of the duration of their captivity which would extend from the head to the base of the great image.

This awesome experience caused the king to summon all of his inner circle to the palace for an emergency meeting. Nebuchadnezzar demanded: Tell me what I dreamed. Tell me the meaning of what I just dreamed! These advisors were extremely confused by this unusual early morning request. They responded: *"Let the king tell his servants the dream and we will show you the interpretation of it. There is not a man upon the earth that can show the king's matter. Furthermore, there is no king, lord, nor ruler that has asked such things from any magician, or astrologer, or Chaldean, and it a rare thing that the king requireth, and there is none other that can show it before the king except the gods whose dwelling is not with flesh."*

When you think about it, there have been times in our own lives when we've had dreams, only to awaken and forget everything in the dream. This is what happened to King Nebuchadnezzar in 584 B.C.E.. In this particular case, YAH also revealed that true spirituality includes being able to reveal the unknown. If your beliefs or system of divination could not answer the king's question, you had to be fake: *"there is but one verdict for you. You have conspired to tell me something false and fraudulent until circumstances change; so relate the dream to me and I will then know that you can tell its meaning."* This challenge which confronted these wise men of Babylon would prove their integrity, or lack of it, one way or another. In Babylon, necromancers, astrologers, sorcerers, and members of the sercet Chaldean societies were respected as the ultimate sources of esoteric insight who could reveal the unknown. Astrologers claim to know your future based on the movement of the sun, moon, planets, and constellations from birth and throughout your life. Necromancers claim to speak to the ancestors to gain insight. Sorcerers and magicians claim to be able to produce favorable occurrences according to their personal will. Surely, they should be able to recall the dream and tell the interpretation, Nebuchadnezzar thought. These high-paid government employees were expected to be all-knowing. All they had to do was enquire of the zodiac, ask the gods, hypnotize, or cast a spell to find the answer concerning the dream.

It is written:
For ELOHIM speaks once, yea, twice, yet man perceiveth it not. In a dream, in a vision of the night, when deep sleep falleth upon men, in slumbering upon the bed; Then he opens the ears of men; and seals their instruction;   **Job 33: 14-16**

Furthermore, YAH commanded Moses to tell the children of Israel:

"When you are come into the land which YAH thy ELOHIM give you, you shall not learn to do after the abominations of these nations. There shall not be found among you any one that make his son or his daughter to pass through the fire, or that use divination, or an observer of times, or enchanter, or a witch, or a charmer, or a consulter with familiar spirits, or a wizard, or a necromancer. For all that do these things are an abomination unto YAH; and because of these abominations YAH thy ELOHIM will drive them out from before you. You shall be perfect with YAH your ELOHIM.
Deut. 18: 9-13

The truth of the matter was, and continues to be, YAH is the source of True Spirituality throughout eternity. So we can see now that when the chosen people lived in their own land and turned their backs on YAH for necromancers, astrologers, magicians, sorcerers, diviners, and secret societies, we see that they made a tragic mistake and exchanged their glory for falsehood. **See II Chronicles 33: 3-6.** The fact that these Chaldean wise men could not recall or interpret the king's dream proved the folly of Israel's earlier decision to turn their backs on YAH, and it further revealed the folly of these heathen kingdoms to trust in these esoteric pseudo-sciences instead of the Almighty God **(YAH)** who created the heavens, sun, moon, stars, constellations, the earth, the seas, and all therein.

Upon hearing the royal decree to execute all the faculty members of the Babylonian Institute of Higher Knowledge, including the Hebrew captives employed there, Daniel, Hananiah, Mishael, and Azariah, who were caught up in the purge, continued to remain faithful to their Hebrew way of life. Instead of seeking an astrological reading, or conjuring a magic potion, they humbly besought YAH to preserve them. YAH, according to His steadfast mercies, in return, answered their petition according to His Holy Words in the Torah:

It is written:

> "YAH will scatter you among the peoples, and only a scant few of you shall be left among the nations to which YAH will drive you. There you will serve man-made gods of wood and stone, that cannot see or hear or eat or smell, but <u>if you search there for YAH your ELOHIM, you will find Him, if only you seek Him with all your heart and soul—when you are in distress because all these things have befallen you and, in the end, return to YAH your ELOHIM and obey Him. For YAH your ELOHIM is a compassionate ELOHIM: He will not fail you nor will He let you perish;</u> He will not forget the covenant which He made on oath with your fathers.
>
> **Deut. 4: 27-31**

YAH did not fail Daniel, Hananiah, Mishael, and Azariah, nor did He allow them to perish at the hands of the mighty king of Babylon. He did not forget His covenant with the seed of Abraham, Isaac, and Yaacov. When they sought YAH with all their hearts and souls in the hour of their distress, YAH answered them. Although, the kingdom of Judah had fallen and the people of Judah were captives scattered among the nations. These men returned to YAH their ELOHIM and obeyed His voice. YAH, the Most Compassionate, gave them the answer. YAH gave Israel a sign by revealing what the dream was, and what was the interpretation of dream, thereby proving that He was God of gods, LORD or lords, KING of kings, the all-Knowing Eternal.

By giving Daniel, the seed of Abraham, Isaac, and Yaacov, the answer to the mystery and not giving the solution to the Chaldean mythmakers, YAH also proved that He had not forgotten the covenant with the ancient twelve tribes of Israel although evil had befallen Judah's and Israel's earthly kingdom. YAH proved that He ruled in the realms of men. Even King Solomon once said: *"Like channels of waters is the mind of the king in the hand of YAHAWAH. He directs it* [his mind] *to whatever He wishes,* in **Proverbs 21: 1**. The message was clear. It was YAH who was in control of man's destiny, not Nebuchanezzar. This message still resonates to the descendants of the twelve tribes of Israel today, YAH continues to be in control of man's destiny in the 21st century and He still rules in the realm of the children of men although they hold sway over global politics.

When Daniel and his companions received the DIVINE insight, they immediately assembled and gave thanks to YAH, the ELOHIM of their ancestors, Abraham, Isaac, and Yaacov, the Eternal Saviour and Redeemer. The historic development confirmed that YAH lives throughout eternity, in every generation from beginning to end, even during the Babylonian captivity which was represented by **The Head of Gold**.

On a Spiritual level this dream was really an act of the Divine Court of Justice. Let me explain. The prophet Micaiah once said:

YAH's Heavenly Divine Court of Justice

"I call you to hear the word of YAH! I saw YHWH seated upon His throne, with all the host of heaven standing in attendance to the right and to the left of Him."
I Kings 22: 19

"As I looked on, Thrones were set in place, And the Ancient of Days (YHWH) took His seat, His garment was like white snow, and the hair of His head was like lamb's wool. His throne was tongues of flame, his wheels were blazing fire." **Daniel 7: 9.**

For YHWH is our JUDGE, YAH is our Lawgiver, YHWH is our [Israel's] King. He will save us.
Isaiah 33:22

YAH's Heavenly Court was now in session. One of the holy angels, serving as the prosecutor (the accuser) stepped forward to testify against Israel for their offenses and crimes against the Sovereign YAH. The Spirit read the long list of indictments, or should I say, the list of Spiritual Crimes Israel had committed. The **Spiritual Indictment** read: *"They sacrificed to demons, no-gods, gods they had never known, new ones, who came but lately whom your father's feared not. You neglected the ROCK (YAH) that begat you, forgot ELOHIM who brought you forth. YAH saw and was vexed and spurned His sons and His daughters,"* Moses prophesied earlier in **Deut. 32: 17-19.**

"This happened because the Israelites sinned against YAH their ELOHIM, who had freed them from the land of Egypt, from the hand of Pharaoh king of Egypt. They worshipped other gods and followed the customs of the nations which YAH had dispossessed before the Israelites and the customs which the kings of Israel had practiced. The Israelites committed against YAH their ELOHIM acts which were not right. They built for themselves shrines in all their settlements, from watchtowers to fortified cities. They set up pillars and sacred posts for themselves on every lofty hill and under every leafy tree, and they offered sacrifices there, at all the shrines, like the nations whom YAH had said to them, "You must not do this thing..... But they did not obey; they stiffened their necks, like their fathers who did not have faith in YAH their ELOHIM; they spurned His laws and the covenant that He had made with their fathers. ...They rejected all the commandments of YAH their ELOHIM; they made molten idols for themselves—two calves—and they made a sacred post and they bowed down to all the host of heaven, and they worshipped Baal. They consigned their sons and daughters to the fire, they practiced augury and divination, and gave themselves over to what was displeasing to YAH ," the scribe wrote in **II Kings 17: 7-17**. Continuing: *"YAH said to me, a conspiracy exists among the men of Judah and the inhabitants of Jerusalem. They have returned to the iniquities of their ancestors of old, who refused to heed My words; They too, have followed other gods and served them. The House of Israel and the House of Judah have broken the covenant that I made with their ancestors, ...Even if Moses and Samuel were to intercede with Me, I would not be won over to that people. Dismiss them from My Presence, and let them go forth! And if they ask you, To what shall we go forth? Answer them, Thus saith YAH, those destined for the plague, to the plague, Those destined for the sword, to the sword. Those destined for famine, to the famine; Those*

destined for captivity, to captivity," the prophet **Jeremiah** iterated in **chapter 11: 9-10** and **15: 1-2.**

"Ah, those who call evil good and good evil; Who present darkness as light and light as darkness, who present bitter [falsehood] as sweet [truth], and sweet [truth] as bitter [falsehood]! Ah, those who are so wise in their own opinion, so clever in their own judgement," the prophet **Isaiah** added in **chapter 5: 20-21.**

After these SPIRITS of truth finished their deplorable testimony recalling Israel's crimes, YAH, the Self-Existing ONE, lifted up His hand holding the holy gavel, struck the bench, and said: "I hereby sentence you: *"I will hide My countenance from you, and see how you fare in the end. For you are a treacherous breed, children with no loyalty in you. You incensed Me with no-gods, vexed Me with your futilities. I'll incense you with a no-folk, and vex you with a nation of fools,"* in **Deut. 32: 20-21.**

YAH's Heavenly Verdict against His People

VERDICT: Thus saith YHWH: You O Israel and Judah are sentenced to captivity among the nations as bondmen and bondwomen. You have refused to be My servants. Therefore you will become slaves to strangers. Your duration of jail time will extend from the head of gold down to the ten toes of iron and miry clay. Remove them from this courtroom!!! (My Presence in the holyland). So this great image in Nebuchadnezzar's dream represented a SPIRITUAL JUDGEMENT and DIVINE SENTENCE against the children of Israel for their disobedience against YAH's commandments. Yet at the same time, the dream answered the question of remnant of Judah in exile, which was, How Long, O YAH?

For Nebuchadnezzar the great image represented another aspect of YAH's DIVINE truth. For him and succeeding rulers, the great image represented time zones of empowerment, dominion, strength, and glory for heathen and gentile empires. For ancient Israel, the golden head of this image began with the conquest of Jerusalem in 586 B.C.E.. The chosen people would experience captivity after captivity throughout the annals of time from the head to the toes of this image. No man would be able to free them. Only YAH, the Eternal, would be able to open the door to freedom for His people to return at the appointed time in the latter-days. This was YAH's verdict against His people and His plan for their eventual redemption after the reign of these heathen empires. This was the meaning of the mysterious dream and its interpretation which Nebuchadnezzar had forgotten. YAH was the Giver of this dream and He revealed the verdict to His faithful Hebrew servants there in ancient Babylon. No longer would Israel have to wonder: when will this horrific storm pass over their nation. Again, as I stated earlier, YAH answered their prayers with a spirit of knowledge to Daniel and a spirit of perplexity to the Babylonian rulership. YAH is the Ruler of all Spirits.

"They fell on their faces and said, O (God) ELOHIM, the <u>Source of the spirit for all flesh</u>!
Numbers 16:22

Nebuchadnezzar and his Chaldean mythmakers were dullards who had no knowledge of YAH's Heavenly Court of Justice. They didn't even know ELOHIM (YAH) existed. Their lawless spirits scorned the truth: Who is YAH that we need to serve Him? We have our own religion. Instead they consulted the sun, moon, stars, and charted the position of the planets. cast spells, made magic potions, or consulted with the deceased. None of those pagan mediums could reveal the mind of YAHAWAH. We all learn from this historic experience that eating from the tree of life, which is, total obedience to YAH's commandments, laws, judgements, and statutes can reveal deep, esoteric truths. The Chaldeans would have never figured out this matter because they eat from the tree of the knowledge of good and evil. Their arrogant eyes were opened to other beliefs, gods, and schools of thought which could not compare to YAH.

Once the revelation came to Daniel in a night vision, he created <u>A Psalm of Thanksgiving to YAH</u> in **chapter 2: 19-23,** which stated: *"Let the name of ELOHIM (YAH) be blessed forever and ever. For wisdom and power is His(YAH'S). He (YAH) changes times and seasons, removes kings and installs kingdoms; He gives the wise their wisdom and knowledge to those who know. He (YAH) reveals deep and hidden things, knows what is in the darkness, and light dwells with Him. I acknowledge and praise You, O God of my fathers(God of Abraham, Isaac, and Jacob), You who have given me wisdom and power, For now You have let me know what we asked of You; You have let us know what concerns the king."* This prayer served, and continues to serve, as a spiritual compass providing direction for the Israelite people throughout their various captivities around the globe. For example, the exiled remnant in this country is divided between those who have Messianic and others who maintain a Torah based school of thought. When we examine this Psalm of Thanksgiving, this compass points us in the correct direction and provides us with proper understanding. Lets go over this prayer line by line.

The first line reads: Let the name of ELOHIM (YAH) be blessed forever and ever. This means Israelites should bless the name of the God of Israel forever and ever. We should never turn away from total reverence of the God of Israel for anything or anyone else. Therefore Israelites who praise men, teachers, leaders, apostles, Christ, Messiahs, or any other deities, have violated the principles of Daniel's prayer. The prayer was based on the first commandment: *"I am YAH thy ELOHIM who brought you out of the land of Egypt, the house of bondage."* He proceeds to revere YAH by attributing Wisdom and Power to Him. He acknowledged YAH as He who created the great lights and heaven. The sun to illuminate by day and the moon, stars, and constellations to illuminate in the darkness of night. YAH was responsible for the changing of the seasons from winter, spring, summer, and autumn. He controlled the winds, the raging of the seas, providing rain, snow, warmth and coldness, in Daniel's eyes. Daniel didn't believe in Mother Nature as the source and controller of stormy winds, seasons, and floods. Daniel didn't ask for DIVINE Insight in the name of Jesus, Buddha, or Allah and neither should the descendants of the children of Israel today who are exiled here among the Gentiles in **ten toes of iron and miry clay**. Daniel should be our people's spiritual role model, and not the other man that our people love to praise and glorify as God in flesh. You know who I'm talking about.

Continuing, Daniel said: YAH reveals all deep and hidden things. Therefore, a wise person should understand that deep and hidden truths belong to God Almighty, and no one else. Just think. If our people wanted to know some deep and hidden things like who are the descendants of the ancient children of Israel, or who assassinated Dr. King, we could Ask Him, and He would reveal it to us. Instead our people reject YAH, the God of Israel and His commandments for the man-god and the gospels. This is a deviation from the path that Daniel laid out in this prayer. YAH knows what goes on in the secret places of the earth, in the darkness where no one else can see. YAH reads the minds and probes the thoughts of man. Daniel understood DIVINE light came from **ELOHIM of Israel** who revealed the esoteric meaning of Nebuchadnezzar's dream. Daniel didn't praise his slave master's gods, and neither should the children of Israel today. He acknowledged the ELOHIM of his fathers, Abraham, Isaac, Jacob as Moses had commanded him in **Exodus 3:15**. YAH gave Daniel wisdom, knowledge, and understanding concerning the king's matter. Meditate on verse 23. We, the descendants of the remnant, should not turn to the left or right. We should walk steadfastly in the name of YAH alone as Daniel, Hananiah, Mishael, Azariah did. There shouldn't be any deviation from these role models even in the 21st century and beyond.

After YAH revealed the mystery to Daniel, he immediately went to tell his overseer who was named Arioch. Arioch brought Daniel before the king claiming he had found Daniel instead of telling the truth. He told the king: *"I have found a man from the people of the captives of Judah who will make known the interpretation to the king."* That was not true. It was YAH who had found Daniel and revealed the interpretation of the dream to him. Arioch wanted to take credit because he was influence-peddling, looking for a promotion and salary increase. That's why he lied. He was a cheese-eater, attempting to make himself look good in the eyes of the king.

The king had already issued and signed an executive decree to execute all the wise men of Babylon. So when Daniel was brought before the royal throne at the last minute, Nebuchadnezzar was extremely agitated and very skeptical. His arrogance made him look down on Daniel and doubt his capability. Certainly this mystery was too deep for this captive. In his mind, Daniel couldn't know. If his own royal advisers hadn't found a last-minute resolution, so how could this slave know?: *"Are you capable of making known to me the dream that I saw and its interpretation? Daniel answered before the king, and said, the secret the king requests, no wise men, astrologers, necromancers, or demonists are able to tell the king. But there is a ELOHIM (God) in Heaven who reveals secrets, and He has informed you King Nebuchadnezzar what will be at the end of days."* Nebuchadnezzar became speechless. Daniel proceeded to explain the mystery.

> "You, O king, were watching and behold a great image (statue); This statue, which was huge and its brightness surpassing, stood before you, and its appearance was awesome. The head of that statue was of fine gold; its breast and arms were of silver; its belly and thighs, of bronze; its legs were of iron, and its feet part iron and part clay. As you looked on, a stone was hewn out, not by hands, and struck the statue on its feet of iron and clay and crushed them. All at once, the iron, clay, bronze, silver, and gold were crushed, and became like a chaff of the threshing floors of summer; a wind carried them off until no trace of them was left. But the stone that struck the statue became a great mountain and filled the whole earth."
>
> **Daniel 2: 31-35**

Upon hearing Daniel's explanation, a mental motion picture began to illuminate once again in king Nebuchadnezzar's mind. He realized what he had just heard corresponded with the forgotten vision. While attempting to maintain his kingly posture, he was elated. It was definitely what he had seen in the dream. Now he wondered, what was the meaning of the dream? *"Such was the dream, and we will now tell the king its meaning,"* the Hebrew prophet continued.

> "You, O king—king of kings, to whom ELOHIM of Heaven has given kingdom, power, might, and glory; into whose hands He has given men, wild beasts, and the fowls of heaven, wherever they may dwell, and to whom He has given dominion over them all—you are the head of gold. But another kingdom will arise after you, inferior to yours; then yet a third kingdom, of bronze, which will rule over the

whole earth. But the fourth kingdom will be strong as iron; just as iron crushes and shatters everything—and like iron smashes—so will it crush and smash all these. You saw the feet and the toes, part of potter's clay and part iron; that means it will be a divided kingdom; it will have only some of the stability of iron, inasmuch as you saw iron mixed with common clay. And the toes were part iron and part clay; that means the kingdom will be part strong and in part brittle. You saw iron mixed with common clay; that means: they shall intermingle with the offspring of men, but shall not hold together, just as iron does not mix with clay. And in the time of those kings, the ELOHIM (God) of Heaven will establish a kingdom that shall never be destroyed, a kingdom that shall not be transferred to another people. It will crush and wipe out all these kingdoms, but shall itself last forever—just as you saw how a stone was hewn from the mountain, not by hands, and crushed the iron, bronze, clay, silver, and gold. The great ELOHIM (God) has made known to the king what will happen in the future. The dream is sure and its interpretation reliable."

Daniel 2: 37-45

King Nebuchadnezzar was startled. His memory was revived and he recognized the dream. The Babylonian ruler experienced a total recall and realized the Hebrew slave was telling him the truth. YAH's outstretched arm manifested itself through Daniel by solving the mystery. It proved that the Holy Spirit (Ruach HaKodesh) was greater than all the mystic abilities of the wise men of Babylon. In a physical sense Nebuchadnezzar heard Daniel's words. However, in a spiritual sense, his ears were stopped by his long years of habitual trust in Babylonian paganism. We know that to be true because in Chapter 3, he went on to erect and commission a new Babylonian religion. In Chapter 4, he defied YAH and said: *"This is great Babylon which (I) have built by (my) vast power to be a royal residence for the glory of (my) majesty,"* as if YAH had never interpreted this dream for him. So this brings us to this question. Who was the interpretation of this dream really for? The answer is, it was for the children of Israel to inform them of their prophetic future.

According to this vision, the children of Israel would be in slavery for a long time: **How Long?:** from the head of gold down to the ten toes of iron and miry clay. These non-Israelite people of the idolatrous-empires, were seen as wicked transgressors in the eyes of YAH, nevertheless, He would grant them permission to enslave the chosen people due to their past behavior, which was "offensive in the sight of YAH." These idol-worshipping kingdoms would not seek truth, righteousness, nor justice during their reign. These empires would be brilliant, knowledgeable, technologically innovative, and highly humanistic, but, dedicated towards worshipping the works of their own hands and spreading iniquity throughout the earth. The knowledge and worship of the God of Israel (YAH) would be non-existent among these populations. They would not adhere to YAH's sacred Counsel, as it is this day.

"If his sons forsake My law and do not live by My rules, if they violate My laws, and do not observe My commands, I will punish their transgression with the rod, their iniquity with plagues . . . . .You have exalted the right hand of his adversaries, and made all his enemies rejoice . . ."

Psalms 89: 1, 43

" . . . .who eat up My people as they eat bread, and not call upon YAH."

Psalms 14: 4

The ancient Israelite visionaries foresaw YAH exalting the right hand of their adversaries. These people were ordained as the world rulers. At this point, YAH chose the heathen empires in the same manner he had once cared for ancient Israel. There was one major difference, however, and that was the fact that YAH did not anoint the "goyims" (heathens) to be teachers of the Word of ELOHIM. YAH never chose, nor would He ever choose these strange nations to be His priests, prophets, or anointed ones to replace His relationship (covenant) with the seed of Abraham, Isaac, and Jacob.

Notwithstanding, the Babylonian, Persian, Grecian, Macedonian, Ptolemaic, Seleucid, Thracian, Roman, Arabian, European, Chinese, Japanese, Indian, American, and all other pagan priests, seers, apostles, and teachers from the idol-kingdoms have taught that their wisdom, understanding, and knowledge is equal to, or even greater than the way of life practiced by the ancient Israelites. These brutish people have practiced their own religious doctrines, erected their own local or regional shrines, and bowed before them. All of the beliefs from these kingdoms continue to be considered *"other gods"* which YAH commanded Israel not serve nor bow down before. It would be a spiritual error in the 21st century for Israelites in the diaspora to follow any strangers and adopt their foreign religious doctrines. Israelites should be steadfast and not eat these kingdom's meat or drink their wine.

Again, YAH never chose any foreigners, from **the head of gold down to the ten toes of iron and miry clay**, to teach His people a new way of life. Therefore it would be safe to say that all of the religious beliefs of these pagan nations are FALSE, according to the Torah. All of these new foreign religions are the works of men's hand and wicked minds. None of those pagan philosophers are qualified to be Israelite spiritual leaders. Israelites were supposed to remember the commandment which forbid strangers from serving as their kings, priests, and prophets. Even today, Israelite spirituality should remain separate from the foreign concepts found in all world religions which violate the teachings found in **Exodus 20: 1-17**.

People of the Image-Idol-worshipping Kingdoms (Empires)

"All the gods of the peoples are idols; but YAHAWAH made the heavens; Glory and majesty are before Him; strength and splendor are in His temple."
Psalms 96: 5-6

"Their idols are silver and gold, the works of men's hands, they have mouths, but cannot speak, eyes, but cannot see; they have ears, but cannot hear, noses, but cannot smell; they have hands, but cannot touch, feet, but cannot walk; they can make no sound in their throats. Those who fashion them, all who trust in them, shall become like them."**(Spiritually Dead)**
Psalms 115: 4-8

"The idols of the nations are silver and gold, the work of men's hands. They have mouths, but cannot speak; they have eyes, but cannot see; they have ears but cannot hear, nor is there breath in their mouths. Those who fashion them, all who trust in them, shall become them. **(Spiritually Dead)**. O house of Israel, bless YAH; O house of Aaron, bless YAH.
Psalms 135: 15-19

Understanding the Vision

One thing the Torah teaches us for sure is that YAH's Holy Spirit does not dwell in the midst of graven images. It is written in the commandments: *"You shall not make for yourself a sculptured image, any likeness of what is in the heavens above, or on the earth below, or in the waters below the earth. You shall not bow down to them or serve them."* Nevertheless in this case, YAH had to reach out and touch pagan Nebuchadnezzar in a manner in which he understood: a dream highlighting a graven image. However, in reality, this statue in the dream was actually a parable of people, nations, and tongues, and the rise and fall of their idol-worshipping global empires. This was not a vision glorifying a pagan god. YAH confirmed this when he told Nebuchadnezzar: "You, O king are the head of gold." Each metal and body part represented a time zone when these idolatrous global empires would rule over the earth. Israel would remain in captivity under the yokes of these powers.

Lets look at each age of rulership for each of the ancient kingdoms whose dominion would extend into the modern age in which we live today. This is what makes this dream so relevant and important 2,600 years later.

The Gold Age—(The Head of Gold)
Babylonian Era

Land of Gold
"A river issues from Eden to water the garden, and it then divides and becomes four branches. The name of the first is Pishon, the one that winds through the whole land of Havilah (Africa), **where there is gold. The gold of that land is good;** bdellium is there, and lapis lazuli . . . ."
Genesis 2:10-12

The land of Kemet, Nubia, and Kush were always known as **the land of gold.** In fact, gold and mineral deposits are still being unearthed all across the continent today. **He who controlled the land of gold would be the Head of Gold.** In antiquity, there were times when the Kushite, Nubian, and Egyptian empires controlled the land of the Chaldees. There were also other times when the Chaldean empire reigned over Egypt, Kush, and Nubia. Both of these regions, stretching from the Nile River in the west to the Euphrates River in the east, were known as the Twin Pillars of Ancient Civilization. Similarly today, Western Europe and North America enjoy a parallel reputation as the Twin Pillars of the Industrial and Technological world. The European governments on both of these continents still rely on gold, silver, nickel, cobalt platinum, oil, and countless other mineral resources from **the land of gold** Havilah (Africa) to maintain their rulership of the world economy. Remember, he who controls the land of gold is the temporal head of gold. All global empires, beginning with the head of gold down to the ten toes of iron and miry clay, have sought to conquer and control the land of gold.

In 605 B.C.E. the armies of Babylon and Egypt engaged in the Great Battle of Carcemish which was near the modern-day border of Syrian-Turkey. Egypt was defeated and forced to retreat to the African mainland. This territory from the Euphrates to the Nile was then ceded to Nebuchadnezzar II and the Babylonian empire. Pharaoh had marched north to support the rebels who opposed Nebuchadnezzar. Nebuchadnezzar had already inherited the Assyrian empire in the north and was now moving to eliminate any opposition or Egyptian interference. This victory established the kingdom of Babylon as the ancient superpower ruling over an empire stretching from Egypt to Persia. This is why Daniel told King Nebuchadnezzar these following words:

"You O king are king of kings, to whom ELOHIM (GOD) of Heaven has given the kingdom, power, might, and glory, into whose hands HE has given men, wild beasts, and the fowl of heaven, wherever they dwell, it is you whom HE has given dominion over them all—you are the head of gold.   **Daniel 2: 37-38**

The History of the Head of Gold

The head of gold has been the brainchild for humanity to establish the mindset, intelligence, outlook, and spirit needed to build future civilizations around the globe. This head of gold dates back to the earliest human civilization consisting of ancient Hamitic (Kemitic), Kushite, Egyptian, Nile Valley, and Canaanite city-states. In this territory early man developed and flourished. Here, the principles of architecture, astrology, the written word, codified law, mathematics, measurements, the invention of wheel, commerce, religion, and concepts of nobility were introduced to the human family. These arts and sciences still provide intellectual insight to modern civilizations during this common era inwhich we live today.

In the ancient Hebrew scriptures, Moses spoke to ancient Israel about these city-states which were built by these early men. In Genesis 11th chapter, you read about this ancient world located in the region of the land of Shinar. These wise men were great builders who constructed the world's first tower-temples, monuments, ziggurats, pyramids, and walled cities. These tower-temple structures were used to study and observe the movement of the sun, moon, the constellations, and for burial grounds. These people were among the world's first astral observers and worshippers. The Kemitic (Black) people were the first rulers of ancient Babylon and surrounding cities.

> "The descendants of Khem (Ham): Kush (Ethiopia), Mizraim (Egypt), Put (Libya), and Canaan (Phoenicians). The descendants of Kush (Ethiopia): Sheba (Abyssinia), Havilah (Nubia), Sabtah (Ethiopia), Raamah (Canaanite) civilizations. The descendants of Raamah: Sheba (Kush) and Dedan (Arabia) people. And Kush begat the Nimrud people who became the first men of might on the earth. They were mighty hunters by the grace of YAH. The beginnings of their kingdoms were Babylon, Erech, Akkad, and Calneh in the land of Shinar. From that land Asshur (the Asshurites) went forth and built Nineveh, Rehoboth-ir, Kalah, and Resen between Nineveh and Kalah, that is the great city."
>
> **Genesis 10: 6-12**

> "Canaan begot Sidon, his firstborn, Heth (Hittites), and the Jebusites (black people living in ancient Jerusalem), **the Amorites, (King Hammurabi of Babylon in 1750 B.C.E.—was the Sixth and best known Babylonian ruler of the Amorite Dynasty),** Girgashites, Hivites, Arkites, Sinites, Arvadites, Zemanites, and the Hamathithes. Afterwards the kingdoms (city-states) of the Canaanites spread abroad.
>
> **Genesis 10: 15-18**

The Kushite empire was the first great civilization and center of intelligence on the earth. The empire extended from northeastern Africa to Babylonia, Erech, Akkad, and Calneh. The Akkadites—another Hamitic people—were also renown as one of the first builders of city-states. The city-state Erech was also an ancient Mesopotamian city located northwest of Ur on the Euphrates River. It was one of the greatest cities of Sumer. It was enclosed with brickwork walls, which according to legend, was built by the mythological hero Gilgamesh (the worship of Nimrod). Continuous excavations have uncovered successive cities that date from prehistoric Ubaid period (5000 B.C.E.) down to the Parthians era (126 B.C.E. to 224 C.E.).

In ancient Ur, the Ubaids, along with other Shemitic and Hamitic people, developed the skill of building a thriving city. They were among the first to make bricks from mud. They learned to use these bricks to build walls, homes, and temples dedicated to various gods. In the skyscraper-temple dedicated to the moon-god Dubial-Makh. Archaeologists have unearthed clay tablets that provided monthly accounts of all trade and business contracts inside the temple. Women developed the skill of weaving fabric from wool. Details from the clay tablets said a procession of moon-god priests once marched up and down the stairway of the house of god. Trees were planted on both sides of pavement. Inside was a jeweled sanctuary.

All the people in this region built these temple-towers known as ziggurats. These tall monuments stood in Ur, Babylon, Nimrud, Akkad, Sumer, Kish, Nippur, Erech, and Lagash in the east. Meanwhile to the west in the land of gold, Egypt, Kush, Nubia, Ethiopia, and other Nile Valley city-states also built ziggurats which were called pyramids.

Clay tablets discovered by British archaeologists during 1914-1918 described religious life at the temple-tower in approximately 1800 B.C.E.. It stated: "Men brought their tithes and offerings to the moon-god. Donkeys laden with grain sacks, jars of oil, cheese, droves of sheep and goats were traded as payments and offerings to the gods. Temple servants weighed the roped wool bales, scribes kept records, and handed out receipts on damp clay tablets. At the temple of Gig-Par-ku, patrons cooked on outdoor stoves in outdoor kitchens. The area included a large area with a water well and water tank. Men drew water that was placed on fireplaces for hot water. In the cooking center there were chopping blocks where animals were slaughtered. In the background, there was a cooking range to bake bread and meats. In the far corner, men and women would grind grains into flour. The modern kitchens still use these same basic layouts in the 21st century. The only difference is indoor plumbing, electricity, and refrigeration.

Sumer

The first people to settle in the southern portion of ancient Babylonia were the Sumerians. The city-state Sumer was located in the midst of the Tigris-Euphrates Valley. As I said earlier, the Ubaidians—a Hamitic people were the founders whom anthropologists have traced back to 4500 B.C.E. to 4000 B.C.E. They were the first civilizing force, draining the marshes to create farmland, and developing trade with surrounding city-states. The Sumerians spoke the Semitic language and by 3300 B.C.E. they became the dominant power and developed one of the world's first known city-state empires. Their skills of pottery-making, sculpture-building, brickmaking, candle-making, housing construction, utensil and tool inventions, and countless other human advancements made them **the head of gold**. These early men and women served as the brains of the human family. Their ideas and mentality still affects the thoughts and actions of the body that make up the human family today. All nations continue to use their skills and knowledge for survival even in the 21st century.

Sumer's prominence created a rivalry among the people in surrounding city-states. Neighboring city-states copied the Sumer model and created their own institutions of kingship.

Kish

The city-state Kish was founded around 2008 B.C.E. along with Erech, Ur, Nippur, and Lagash. These city-states vied for the leadership role for hundreds of years. The Shemitic people—the Elamites controlled the area from 2530-2450 B.C.E. Later, the Akkadians, who were led by King Sargon, united the city-states and ruled for fifty-five years from 2334 to 2279 B.C.E. After his reign, the confederation collapsed and each city-state became independent kingdoms.

Erech

Erech was another ancient Mesopatamian city-state located northwest of Ur. It too was situated on the banks of the Euphrates River. It became one of the greatest cities of the Sumerian civilization. It continues to be famous for brick walls. According to legend, the walls were built by the mythological hero Gilgamesh. Excavations have traced successive cities that date back to the prehistoric Ubaid period (5000 B.C.E.) up to the Parthian times, beginning in 126 B.C.E. to 224 C.E.

Ur

The Third Dynasty among these city-states came from Ur. Located on the Euphrates River near the Persian Gulf, the city became the capital of a kingdom known as Chaldea. The inhabitants were known as the Chaldeans. Eventually they conquered the entire region and also became known as the Babylonians. These Semitic people began their first reign in the 11th century B.C.E. Their second reign came during the Neo-Baylonian dynasty in 625 B.C.E. under the rulership of Nabopolasar in 625 B.C.E.

The first reign of Ur lasted for a century from 2100 to 2000 B.C.E. Ultimately, the final Sumerian kingdom declined after foreign invasions. The native Sumerians were replaced and the region became a part of the Babylonian empire beginning in 1800 B.C.E. In conclusion, the Sumerian's legacy had included a number of standard technological innovations, such as the first wheel, the potter's wheel, cuneiform writing, codes of law, and measurements.

An important invention that originated in the Tigris-Euphrates Valley was the concept of a graven image (man-god) as a deity to be honored in society. The god Gilgamesh became one of the first heroes worshipped in the Epic of Gilgamesh. The mythological character Gilgamesh was probably based on the historic king named Gilgamesh who ruled Uruk in 3000 B.C.E. In the epic, Gilgamesh is portrayed as a great warrior and builder who rejected marriage with the goddess Ishtar. Many biblical scholars associate this mythology with the worship of King Nimrod and his mother Semiramis.

> Canaan begat Sidon, his firstborn Heth (Hittites) and the Jebusites (blacks in Jerusalem for centuries), **(the Amorites)**, Girgashites, Hivites, Arkites, Sinites, Arvadites, Zemarites, and Hamathites. Afterwards the kingdoms (city-states) of the Canaanites spread out."   **Genesis 10: 15-18**

The Amorites

The Kemitic (Hamitic) people known as the Amorites were a branch of the Canaanite people. They were scattered across the ancient world in areas that make up Turkey, Syria, Iraq, and Iran today. These Canaanite people were known as Indo-European because they migrated and maintained city-states in southeastern Europe as well. They were a nomadic people who invaded cities, plundered and killed inhabitants, and assumed control of new territories. After invading ancient Babylon during 1800 B.C.E., the Amorite dynasty assumed power. The greatest and the most widely known ruler of that dynasty was Hammurabi, who was the sixth Babylonian ruler from that dynasty (1787-1750 B.C.E.). Hammurabi was known as a great thinker, war strategist, builder, restorer of temples, and writer of the Code of Hammurabi, which was a collection of 282 of his legal decisions from four decades of rulership. Some historians have compared several of his rulings with those found among the ordinances in the Law of YAH given to Moses centuries later.

The Kassites

The city-state Babylonia continued to change hands between various invaders such as Egypt, the Hittites, Mitanni, Assyria, and Elamites.. However, regardless of who ruled the city, the system of Babylon always remained intact. Each conquering ruler made only slight variations. Thai was also the case for the Kassites who ruled the city-state from 1595 B.C.E. to approximately 1158 B.C.E. Historians have stated that these people originated from the Zagros mountains in neighboring Persia and quickly assimilated into Babylonianism. During their four centuries of rule, the Kassites united lower and upper Babylonia as an independent city-state. During their reign, the Kassite kings rebuilt temples in Ur, Uruk, Nippur, and Larsa which had deteriorated under previous rulers. Their renovations were recorded on stone monuments by scribes who served in the capital city Dur-Kurigalza at their new palace. In retrospect, the Kassites are really known for their complete assimilation into Babylonian culture. Their native language remains unknown even today. The Kassite dynasty continued to rule until 1158 B.C.E. when the Elamite invaders overthrew them. Elam carried many Babylonian artifacts back to Susa.

Second Dynasty of Isin

Babylonia remained under Elamite control for nearly thirty-two years. In 1126 B.C.E., however, things began to change when a ruler named Nebuchadnezzar I rose to power. Nebuchadnezzar I liberated the kingdom from Elamite domination. Afterwards, his forces marched onto the city Susa and destroyed the Elamite capital. The victory gave him the opportunity to recover the statue of the god Marduk and return it to its temple in Babylon. He then restored the Temple Marduk along with the other Babylonian temples. His military victories are detailed in the famous Enuma Elish. The Enuma Elish is an ancient Babylonian composition which glorified Marduk accepting his leadership as the chief diety over the other gods. In Babylonian mythology Marduk was regarded as the sovereign diety in heaven who granted Babylon its earthly power. Babylon enjoyed a revival during the 21-year reign of Nebuchadnezzar 1.

Arameans

Shortly after the reign of Nebuchadnezzar I, the revived Babylon city-state began to crumble slowly. In fact, there is not much known about those who succeeded him as a part of the Second Dynasty of Isin. During this time in the 12th century B.C.E., a large population of people who had not established a homeland began to migrate across the Near East. Known as the Sea People, these people started a migratory movement that lasted for many decades. This was called the Aramean invasion. The large population of these people was felt by all the neighboring city-states, including Assyria. King Tiglathpileser I, said during his thirty-eight year reign between 1115-1077 B.C.E., that *"twenty-eight times I have crossed the Euphrates to chase the Arameans."* Tiglathpileser I was unsuccessful in his attempts to halt the Arameans. They conquered northern Syria and eventually moved on to penetrate the great walls of the royal city Nineveh to become the rulers of northern Mesopotamia before moving southwards to lay waste to city-state Babylon. According to historiographers, the Arameans continued the traditions of ancient Babylon without making any distinctions that separated them from the previous occupiers of the throne.

The Aramean ruler Nabu-apla-iddina ruled Babylon from 888 to 855 B.C.E., Marduk-zakir-shumi I succeeded him in 854 B.C.E. After Marduk-zakir-shumi's reign, the Aramean rulership of Babylon faded from the scene for one-hundred thirty-three years before the 11-year reign of Merodach-Baladan from 721 to 710 B.C.E.. The next ruler was Assur-nadin-shumi whose 5-year reign extended from 699 to 694 B.C.E. before Babylon was destroyed in 689 by the re-emerging Assyrians. Of the four Aramean rulers, Nabu-apla-iddina was accredited with reviving the cult of Babylonian gods and rebuilding great sanctuaries in the capital city, Borsippa, Sippar, and Uruk. He was also known for literary and scientific accomplishments.

Assyrians

The native Assyrians began to slowly recover in the 10th century with the ascension of King Adad-nirari in 911. His reign marked the beginning of a 300-year Assyrian conquest of the entire Near East, sacking Gozan, Haran, Rezeph, Hamath, Arpad, Lair, Sepharvaim, Hena, Ivvah, Babylon, Syria, Zidon, Samaria, Memphis, Egypt, Thebes, Susa, and even threatening Jerusalem during the reign of King Hezekiah in 701. The chronology of Assyrian kings included Adad-nirari II (911-891), Tukuti-Ninurta II (890-884), Assurnasirpal II (883-859), Shalmaneser III (858-823), Shamshi-Adad V (823-811), Adad-nirari III (810-783), Tiglath-pileser III (744-727), Shalmaneser V (726-722), Sargon II, *(named after the earlier King Sargon I, who was known as the Great, ruler of ancient Mesopotamia from the royal city of Akkad from 2334-2279 B.C.E.)*, Sennacherib (704-681), Esarhaddon (680-669), and Assurbanipal (669-627). This Assyrian dominion should be divided into three periods which includes: Assyrian Reconquest, Civil War, and the Neo-Assyrian Empire.

ASSYRIAN RECONQUEST: Assurbanipal ascended to the Assyrian throne in 853. He was famous for his military prowess, engaging in brutality unheard of, such as skinning their captives alive, piercing their eyes causing blindness, and beheadings. The fame of Assyrian brutality caused many kingdoms to surrender instead of facing Nineveh on the battlefield. The Assyrian empire extended its control from the Mediterranean to Egypt. After conquering these city-states, Assurnasirpal introduced a strategy of pillaging and deporting native populations back to Assyria. **(See 2 Kings 17: 24-33).** These captives were used as a part of a forced labor workforce which built a new capital in Calah, which is modern Nimrud, south of the northern Iraqi city Mosul. The new royal city consisted of massive walls, lavish palaces, several temples for the pantheon of Assryo-Babylonian deities. Many of his extravagant projects were not completed during his twenty-four year reign. His son, Shalmaneser III, succeeded him, and continued to turn the capital into a great metropolis. By 850 B.C.E., he went on to conquer Babylon after receiving a request for help from Marduk-zakir-shumi I to put down a rebellion by Marduk's own brother. After helping Marduk, Shalmaneser worshipped in the famed Babylonian temples in the cities of Kutha, Babylon, and Borsippa.

Several years later in 798 B.C.E., Queen Semiramis, the mother of Adad-nirari III, spent massive amounts of the empire's riches to build a temple to her god **(graven image)**.

ASSYRO-BABYLON CIVIL WAR: By 823 B.C.E., the powerful clans of the Chaldeans in the south and the Assyrians in the north were locked into a contentious situation. In the north, a family feud broke out in the House of Shalmaneser. One of his sons conspired against him in an attempted coup. The infighting raged on for seven years until his successor Shamshi-Adad V came into power. On top of that in southern Mesopotamia, the Chaldeans of Babylonia mounted a serious rebellion against Assyrian rule. Under the rulership of his successor, Adad-nirari III, the kingdom of Assyria began a steady decline.

In 781, Shamshi-ilu broke away from the throne in Calah and undertook a military campaign against the western portion of the Assyrian empire. After gaining control, he made peace between the Neo-Hittite empire and the Aramean kingdoms in an area known today as southern Turkey and northern Syria. Shamshi-ilu's actions did not strengthen Assyria. Chaos, rebellions, and other internal conflicts, both in Babylon, Assyria, and in Syria, raged on. Finally, major epidemics began to affect the Assyrian throne from 765 to 759 killing large numbers and spreading more instability. These negative actions took an unbearable toll on the land of Asshur.

THE NEO-ASSYRIAN EMPIRE: In this last era, the kingdom of Assyria became a global power with territorial control stretching from Thebes, Egypt to Susa, Persia. All kingdoms in Assyria's path were turned into provinces of the empire. The rulers of this Dynasty started with King Tiglath-pileser III (744-727). Tiglath-pileser III is recorded in the Hebrew scriptures in **2 Kings 16:7-10),** Shalmaneser V (726-722). (Shalmaneser V is recorded in the Hebrew scriptures in **2 Kings 17: 3, 2 Kings 18: 9-12**), Sargon II (721-705)(Sargon II was a worshipper of the god Assur), his son was Sennacherib (704-681) (Sennacherib is recorded in the Hebrew scriptures in **2 Kings 18: 13-37, 2 Kings 19: 20**), Esarhaddon (680-669) (Esarhaddon is recorded in Hebrew scriptures in **2 Kings 19: 37.** Esarhaddon also conquered Thebes and Memphis and ruled Egypt from 679-673 B.C.E. There were several Assyrian military campaigns into **the land of gold**), and last but no least, it was campaign of Assurbanipal whose reign lasted from 669 to 627. Assyria was a strong military power with a large calvary and chariotry. Their military campaigns in this era included the invasion of Taurus in Asia Minor, Scythia, and the land of the Medes. This made the Assyrians, which were an ancient black people, instrumental and among one of the first people to help civilize the uncultured Indo-European Japhethic Medes and Scythians. In the country that we now called Lebanon, the Phoenicians (northern Canaanites of the Mediterranean Sea), did the same thing for the Greeks, Romans, and Turks in terms of lifting them up out of the *Dark Ages* and bringing culture into southeastern Europe. This intermingling represented the first stages of the transfer of global power from black Shemitic and Hamitic people to non-black rulership.

By 612 B.C.E., continuous infighting among heirs of throne caused major instability in the palace at Nineveh. As Sennacherib's reign came to an end, his eldest son, Arad-mullissu was suppose to succeed him on the throne. Instead, Sennacherib decided to relinquish his crown to his younger son Esarhaddon. This decision caused a family feud in the royal palace. The infighting caused Esarhaddon to flee the palace. Sennacherib was then assassinated by his son Arad-mullissu. After this, a civil war raged on for nearly two months. This contention was recorded in the Hebrew Scriptures in **2 Kings 19: 36-37**.

> "So King Sennacherib of Assyria broke camp and retreated, and stayed in Nineveh. While he was worshipping in the temple of his god Nisroch, his son Adrammelech and Sarezer struck him down with the sword. They fled to the land of Ararat, and his son Esarhaddon succeeded him as king."
>
> **2 Kings 19: 36-37**

Esarhaddon eventually returned to Nineveh after the insurgency and the murder of his father Sennacherib. His enemies then fled the capital and headed towards the country we call Turkey today—the land of Ararat. Esarhaddon reigned twelve years in Nineveh serving the idol gods of his fathers, seeking advice from astrologers, exorcists, wizards, and specialists who stood before him. His rule was marred with reports of bad health and a wild lifestyle. Numerous clay tablets have been unearthed which recount how Esarhaddon sought health advice and other counsel from familiar spirits on how to avoid bad fortune. For Babylon, the intervention of the Assyrians was a good thing. The Assyrians loved the culture of Babylonia and they spent plenty of their kingdom's treasure on its revival and restoration. Although the southern kingdom of Babylon was a vassal to its northern superpower, Babylonian nobility experienced new levels of fortune and prosperity.

Another threat to Assyria was the encroaching Indo-European Scythians from the north. Meanwhile inside the palace of Nineveh, Esarhaddon made arrangements to secure a peaceful transition for his succession. He made all the crown princes swear to support Assurbanipal as the next king. Esarhaddon died in Harran, Syria in the midst of another invasion of Egypt. So in 669 B.C.E., Assurbanipal assumed the throne of Nineveh and continued the conquest of foreign lands. Five years later, he invaded Egypt again in 664 B.C.E. He also won a hard-fought victory over Elam. In the west, however, the Assyrians could not maintain their grip and lost control of Egypt after Psamtik I and his army regained rulership in 653. Assyria was unable to keep the yoke around Egypt's neck and decided to write off the land of Kemet. Instead he concentrated his energies on maintaining dominion over Persia in the east. During 652 to 648, Babylon rebelled against Assyrian rule again. Assyria squashed the uprising and regained control, exacting vengeance on all the supporters of the uprising including the Elamites, Arabs, and Chaldeans. Many of the Babylonian artifacts were taken from the temples and libraries of Babylon and carried off to the temples and libraries in the Assyrian capital of Nineveh.

Assurbanipal's reign over Assyria lasted for 42 years from 669 to 627. In fact, he was the longest reigning monarch of the Neo-Assyrian Dynasty. In 627 his reign finally came to an end. During the following fifteen years, Assyria began to gradually fall apart—both internally and externally. Inside the palace in Nineveh, continuous infighting prevented the rulers from preparing or paying attention to foreign threats. By 612 Cyaxares, ruler of the Medes and Persians to the east, and Nabopolassar, ruler of the Babylonians in the south, united to jointly rise up against Assyria. Assyria was already weakened from more than a decade of steady decline, so this attack was the final blow. In Babylon, General Nabopolassar, the Chaldean, had risen to prominence. His influence now provided independence for all the territory of ancient Babylonia in the south. Once he was crowned as the new king, Nabopolassar, became emperor of the Neo-Babylonian Dynasty which extended from 625 to 539 B.C.E..

Neo-Babylonian Chaldean Dynasty

As I stated earlier, the head of gold was the one who ruled **the land of gold.** This same head of gold represented all the ancient various dynasties that ruled the ancient Babylonian and Egyptian (Nile Valley) civilizations. The land of gold was and continues to be, the continent of Africa where the ancient civilizations of Kush, Nubia, Ethiopia, and Egypt flourished for thousands of years. It also includes the various city-state empires of the Tigris-Euphrates Valley. Together, these two ancient powerhouses were the brainchildren and twin pillars of ancient civilization extending from the Nile to the Euphrates. During the lifetime of Daniel, the Chaldean Dynasty of Babylon, which included Nabopolassar and his successors, were rulers of all of this region with a **golden** fist. Thus, the Neo-Babylonian Empire became the **HEAD OF GOLD.** The Neo-Babylonian Chaldean Dynasty included Nabopolassar (625-605 B.C.E.), Nebuchadnezzar II (604-562), Evil Merodach (561-560), Neriglissar (559-556), Labashi-Marduk (556), Nabonidus (555-539), and ended with Belshazzar (549-539 B.C.E.).

NABOPOLASSAR
(625 B.C.E.—605 B.C.E.)

Nabopolassar, [Nabu-apla-usur which means *"O Nabu watch over my heir"*] was considered the first king of Neo-Babylonian Dynasty. He was an Aramean (Asiatic black) who came from the Kaldu tribes living in the extreme southern coastal area near the Persian Gulf residing in Chaldea. He began his career as the administrative assistant for the Neo-Assyrian empire. When the Assyrian empire began to crumble in 612, he became the general of the rebel Chaldean forces and declared independence from the superpower Assyria in the north. This rebellion gave birth to the Neo-Babylonian dynasty and the rise of the Chaldean empire. During his reign which began in 625 B.C.E., he defeated Assyria and established peace with Elam (Persia) in the northeast. Nabopolassar then commissioned several renovation projects that included restoring temples, erecting new monuments, and expanding trade. His 20-year rulership brought a new level of wealth and commerce to the royal city. He restored the Sippar Temple and groomed his son to become his successor. He named him [Nabu-kudurri-usur II, translated, **Nebuchadnezzar II**], in honor of a prior great Babylonian king [Nabu-kudurri-usur I] who had ruled from 1124—1103 B.C.E., five centuries earlier. The name means *'Nabu, guard my border.'* His 43-year reign lasted from 605 to 562 B.C.E.

NEBUCHADNEZZAR II "The Great"
(605 B.C.E.—562 B.C.E.)

Nebuchadnezzar II [Nabu-kudurri-usur II] was embroiled in a war with Egypt near Syria and Asia Minor when news of his father's death reached him on the battlefield. He hastily returned to the royal residence. The various kingdoms in Syria and Israel used this opportunity to rebel, along with the kingdom of Egypt. The Babylonian Chronicle also states that the king of Babylon returned a second time and defeated the Egyptian armies in a major battle at Carchemish. Pharaoh Necho had attempted to regain control over Syria and Israel after the collapse of the Neo-Assyrians, but Nebuchadnezzar had plans of restoring Babylon to its former glory as a world power **(head of gold)**. During the next two years Nebuchadnezzar placed this territory, including King Yehoiakim and Judah, under heavy tribute.

The Babylonian Chronicle also reported, "all the kings of Hatti-land came before him and he received heavy tribute." In 601-600, Nebuchadnezzar launched another attack on Egypt. This encounter between the two ancient black global superpowers ended with Babylon as the clear victor. Afterwards, the new Chaldean leader mustered his entire army to invade the land of Judah during December 598 B.C.E. According to the Babylonian Chronicle: "Nebuchadnezzar encamped against the city of Jerusalem on the second day of the month Adar which was March 16, 597 B.C.E., and seized the city of Jerusalem and captured the King Yehoiachin. He then appointed a king of his own choice who was named Zedekiah. Nebuchadnezzar imposed heavy tribute upon the remaining people and carried Yehoiachin captive to Babylon.

Meanwhile at home Nebuchadnezzar lavishly restored old religious monuments, including the ancient temples of Marduk, Esogil, Ezida, the Ishtar Gate, the Hanging Gardens. He restored a network of dilapidated canals, a stone bridge, and other spectacular architectural projects throughout the cities of Babylonia. These actions gained him support among the Chaldean augurs. At the same time the Babylonian king fought wars against the Elamites in the east and internally he suppressed an Akkadian revolt. To his west, in Syria and Israel, those kingdoms rebelled again.

While he was detained away in Chaldea, Egypt promised king Zedekiah support against the Mesopotamian strongman if Judah agreed to form an alliance with them. This proved to be a fatal mistake for the Israelite kingdom of Judah. Another Babylonian siege came during this summer of 586. This time Nebuchadnezzar breached the fortified walls and captured the city of David. The **Temple of YAH** was totally destroyed and burned to the ground. The survivors were carried away into slavery. King Zedekiah's eyes were plucked out. His sons and officers were executed. The defeated city became a vassal province of the Babylonian Empire. This new phenomenon would prove to be a precedent for Jerusalem for the next 2,600 years. Read **2 Kings 25:6-17** to witness for yourself.

Nebuchadnezzar continued his global conquest, attacking the kingdoms of Damascus, Tyre,

Phoenica, Sidon, northern Arabia, and parts of Asia Minor. His war against Tyre lasted for 13 years, ending in a stalemate with Tyre withstanding the fierce Chaldean assault. The Chaldean conqueror was unable to capture the island kingdom. He also turned his attention towards the continent of Africa and invaded the Egyptian mainland, becoming the first Babylonian king to rule the land of the Pharaohs. This was the beginning of a downward spiral for Egypt, a civilization that had been flourishing for nearly 4,000 years.

Again, Nebuchadnezzar was domestically regarded as a genius administrator who revived the royal city and built a palace large enough to be used for national affairs, religious, ceremonial purposes, and serve as a royal residence. According to historians, the city of Babylon itself covered three miles surrounded by moats and a double circuit of walls. The Euphrates River flowed through the center of the city. A huge stone bridge spanned across the city. In the city's center was a giant ziggurat called Etemenanki located next to the Temple of Marduk. Etemenanki means *"the house of the frontier between heaven and earth."* During his reign, Babylon was the center of extraordinary luxury with the world latest technology of that era.

Although Nebuchadnezzar viewed himself as a god, his personal life was another story and less than divine. Like all the pagan emperors before and after him, he reportedly participated in many unclean sexual fetishes. It had been reported by the rabbis of ancient Babylon and other foreign sources that Nebuchadnezzar forced many of the conquered kings to engage in homosexual relations. It was reported that he practiced pederasty, meaning he had anal and oral sex with young palace boys on a regular basis. Nevertheless, the Neo-Chaldean ruler was a married man. When his father, Nabopolassar, formed an alliance with Media to fight against the Assyrian empire, he sealed the confederation with a political marriage between his son Nebuchadnezzar and the Indo-European (mulatto) princess. In hindsight, this interracial marriage between a black man and fair-skinned woman was actually an ancient omen that the world was in gradual transition from thousands of years of total black hegemony to what we have today—mulatto and Indo-European dominion over world affairs.

Babylon was indeed the dominant power in the Near East. Its famous walls strongly fortified the seat of power. It grew into a cultural center, a religious center, and a scientific center whose influence reached as far as the shores of Europe and even America. This makes both Europe and North America the modern-day *"daughters of Babylon."* Ancient Babylon was renowned for large sculptures of gods, statues of rulers, arts, literature recorded on cuneiform, architectural marvels, literary canons, and world influence. Babylon represented one of the oldest, highly civilized areas of the ancient world—**head of gold**. It was also the place where the worship of materialism began.

This is what Strabo Geography Book XVI, Chapter 1 stated: *"Babylon, too, lies in a plain and the circuit of its wall is three hundred and eighty-five stadia. The thickness of its wall is thirty-two feet, the height thereof between the towers is 50 cubits, 9 of that of the towers is sixty cubits and passage on top of the wall is such that a 4-horse chariots can easily pass one another, and it is on this account that this and Hanging Gardens are called one of Seven Wonders of the World."* Continuing, he wrote: *"There were in it also several artificial rocks that had the resemblance of mountains; with nurseries of all sorts of plants, and a kind of hanging garden suspended in the air by the most admirable contrivance. This was to gratify his wife, who being brought up in Media, among the hills, and in the fresh air found relief from such projects."* The Hanging Gardens stood on terraces supported by brick arches. The capital city was surrounded with double walls 10-miles long with an elaborate entry called the Ishtar Gate.

The historian Herodotus wrote: *"These walls are the city's outer amour, within them there is another encircling wall nearly as strong as the other, but narrower."* He also said: *"On the top along the edges of the wall, they built houses of a single room, facing each other with space enough between to drive a 4-horse chariot. There are a hundred gates in the circuit of the wall, all of bronze, with posts and lintels of the same."*

Like all mortals, in 562 B.C.E. the forty-three year reign of Nebuchadnezzar the Great came to an end. The Psalmist, King David once said:

"I saw a wicked man, powerful, well-rooted like a robust native tree. Suddenly he vanished and was gone; I sought him, but he was not found." **Psalms 37: 35-36.**

Again in **Psalms 103:15-18** it is written: *"Man, his days are those of grass; he blooms like a flower of the field; a wind passes by and it is no more; its own place no longer knows it. But YAH's steadfast love is for all eternity towards those who fear Him; and His beneficence is for children's children, towards those who keep His covenant."*

"He brings potentates to naught, makes rulers of the earth as nothing, Hardly are they planted, Hardly are they sown, Hardly has their stem taken root in earth, When He blows upon them and they dry up, And the storm bears them off like straw."

Isaiah 40: 23-24

After Nebuchadnezzar's death, his son Evil Merodach assumed the throne of Babylon as the successor on the throne of Babylon.

Evil Merodach
(562 B.C.E.—560 B.C.E.)

Evil-Merodach, whose name is a Akkadian translation of Amel-Marduk, means *"man of Marduk"* came to the throne during a time of treachery among the officials in the royal court. Various cliches of power vied to give their choice the mantle of power. Some of the Babylonian priests supported him while others viewed him as weak and inexperienced. This internal strife led to a plot to remove him from office. During his brief two-year reign, however, the Babylonian monarch acted favorably towards the children of Israel and announced plans to allow the Hebrew exiles return to Jerusalem. This presidential pardon was recorded in the book of Jeremiah:

"In the thirty-seventh year of the exile of King Jehoiachin of Judah, on the twenty-fifth day of the twelfth month, King Evil Merodach of Babylon, in the year he became king, took note of King Jehoiachin of Judah and released him from prison. He spoke kindly to him and gave him a throne above the other kings who were with him in Babylon. He removed his prison garments and Jehoiachin ate regularly in his presence the rest of his life. A regular allotment of food was given him by order of the king of Babylon, an allotment for each day to the day of his death—all the days of his life."

Jeremiah 52: 31-34

Jehoiachin was an 8-year-old when he first arrived in Babylon as a child-slave. He had turned into a 45-year-old middle-aged man when the king issued the royal decree to pardon him. Evil-Merodach, who was a mulatto, attempted to become a reformer who sought to change his father's policies. I'm quite sure his new liberal policy toward the captives of Judah didn't set well with all the Babylonian aristocracy. The older loyalists opposed his new direction. It can be safely assumed that this was one of the reasons why he was later assassinated in a palace coup by his brother-in-law Neriglissar, a military leader who was married to his princess-sister, who was one of the daughters of the late Nebuchadnezzar.

Neriglissar
(559 B.C.E.—556 B.C.E.)

Neriglissar [*pronounced* Nergal-shar-usur means *"Nergal protect the king"*] was the son-in-law of the late great emperor Nebuchadnezzar. According to the Hebrew Bible and Babylonian Chronicles, he was a mighty warrior. His military exploits enabled him to marry into the royal family where Nebuchadnezzar's daughter became his wife. Neriglissar was one of the commanding generals during the siege and destruction of Jerusalem in 587 B.C.E.

"In the ninth year of King Zedekiah of Judah, in the tenth month, King Nebuchadnnezar of Babylon moved against Jerusalem with his whole army, and they laid siege to it. And in the eleventh year of Zedekiah, on the ninth day of the fourth month, the walls of the city were breached. All the officers of the king of Babylon entered and took up quarters at the middle gate— Nergal-sarezer, Samgar-nebo, Sarsechim the Rab-sais, Nergal-sarezer the Rabmag, all the rest of the officers of the king of Babylon."

Jeremiah 39: 1-3

Viewed as a strong leader who would maintain the course of Nebuchadnezzar, Neriglissar sought to foster close ties with the powerful Babylonian priesthood by restoring and renovating the temples. He also sought to upgrade all the cities of the empire during his brief four year reign. He was also a traditionalist who served the gods of Nebuchadnezzar. The classic Babylonian pantheon of deities consisted of the statue Ea, which was regarded as the son of Anu. Ea was also regarded as the ruler of all other gods after Apsu, another classic Babylonian statue-god. The statue Anu was regarded as the husband-god of the female statue called Damkina. The sculptured image Anu was also believed to be the father of Marduk. The statue Marduk became the national patron deity of the Neo-Babylonian Empire. This graven image was believed to be god (power) of wisdom, arts, and crafts.

For some strange reason, Neriglissar reign came to an end after only four years.

Labashi-Marduk
(556 B.C.E.)

Labashi-Marduk was the son of Neriglissar. Historical sources stated that he was a young man who was considered to still be a boy by the ruling cliche in the Babylonian priesthood. He was murdered in a conspiracy only 9 months after his inauguration. The palace coup removed him, but the coup itself revealed a deepening crisis for the Babylonian empire: ineffective and poor leadership. A poor system of electing a successor without a democratic process. After the death of Nebuchadnezzar six years earlier in 562, none of his successors experienced lengthy and stable rulerships. The situation presented internal and external dangers for the long-term well-being of the greatest kingdom on earth. Whoever amassed the most political influence would muscle themselves into power. This was the case for Labashi-Marduk, and this was one of the main weakness of their system. Bitter losers always plotted coups for revenge.

Nabonidus
(555 B.C.E.—539 B.C.E.)

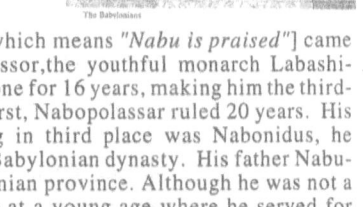

Nabonidus [The Akkadian translation is *Nabu-na'id* which means *"Nabu is praised"*] came to power in 556 B.C.E. after overthrowing his successor, the youthful monarch Labashi-Marduk. After assuming power, he remained on the throne for 16 years, making him the third-longest reigning king of the Neo-Chaldean Dynasty. First, Nabopolassar ruled 20 years. His successor Nebuchadnezzar reigned 43 years. Coming in third place was Nabonidus, he reigned 16-years and was also the last king of the Neo-Babylonian dynasty. His father Nabu-balatsu-iqbi was the chief governor of Haran, a Babylonian province. Although he was not a native Chaldean, Nabonidus was inducted in the army at a young age where he served for nearly 40 years. Eventually he became a military commander before rising to the position of king of Babylon. He continued the policy of temple renovation throughout the royal city. The kingmakers of the Babylonian priesthood preferred him because he was a courageous middle-aged soldier with experience as a military commander helping the kingdom fend off its enemies and maintain Babylonian hegemony.

Archaeologists and historians have unearthed a cuneiform that detail his rulership. This cuneiform, known as the Nabonidus Chronicle, is a basalt stela. this document details his rise to power and his efforts to rebuild the religious sancutaries within the royal city and throughout the empire. He restored the famous zigguarat of ancient Ur, which was known as the temple of Esagila, the great temple of national deity Marduk, the temple of Uruk, and the temple of the moon-god Sin in the city of Haran.

Militarily, Nabonidus sought to regain control of his native city Haran which had fallen under the control of the Medes. The Medes had controlled the city since 610 B.C.E. when they joined in the confederation with Babylon to overthrow the Assyrian empire. Changing a sixty-year-old policy, Nabonidus chose to form a new alliance with a new Persian emperor named Cyrus. Cyrus agreed to the new arrangement and his armies moved to defeat the Medes in northern Mesopotamia, Syria, and Asia Minor. The Persian leader also captured Astyages [Ast-ya-ges], the king of the Medes and united the two kingdoms of Media and Persia into one. Ironically, Astyages was the grandfather of Cyrus. Although Nabonidus gained control of the city of Haran, the unexpected consequence of this arrangement gave birth to the united Medo-Persian global empire less than two decades later.

Nabonidus also fought wars in Syria and Arabia. He also conquered the city of Hamath in Asia Minor. In Arabia, he conquered the cities of Adumma and Tema. Nabonidus went on to build Tema into a royal residence where he lived for several years. Some historians believe infighting and treachery in the royal city Babylon is what caused Nabonidus to make this decision to build Tema as a second royal residence. He did not want to be assassinated in a palace coup like his predecessors. So, he appointed his son as crown prince to handle day-to-day affairs in his absence. For some reason Nabonidus was infatuated with the worship of the moon-god Sin and revived the worship of that ancient Mesopotamian religion. The god Sin dated back to the times of Sargon I of Akkad which involved the veneration of the crescent moon. He elevated his daughter to the High Priestess in the city of Ur, further aggravating the priesthood. This crescent-moon symbol is still used today on most Islamic flags world-wide.

His mother Adda-Guppa lived to become a very eldery queen-mother. As a native of Haran, she was also closely connected with the local temple of the Akkadian moon-god Sin. Some historical sources maintain that inspite of his military prowess,Nabonidus was a poor politician who should have known that the magicians, sorcerers, exorcists, astrologers, and priesthood of the national-god Marduk would feel betrayed and plot to remove him.

As I said earlier, In 549 B.C.E., which was six years into his 16-year reign, Nabonidus totally transferred power to his son Belshazzar and spent the last ten years in a self-imposed exile in the city of Tema, located in northern Arabia. After the year 555 B.C.E., he also served as co-regent for his father.

Belshazzar
(555 B.C.E.—539 B.C.E.)

Belshazzar [The Akkadian translation is Bel-sar-usur *which means* "O Bel, guard the king"] reign was marked by ceremonial celebrations, feasting, and self-indulgence. This was done to keep internal politics off the minds of high officials and the priesthood. The truth of the matter is that Babylon had already been penetrated by Persian intelligence agents who had secret contacts with Babylonian officials. In the royal court, corrupt palace officials had already sold out the country to the enemy for the love of money. Belshazzar was actually a weakened monarch, second-in-command to his father who was detached from daily affairs. Belshazzar policy of appeasement and partying did not alleviate the threats of an internal coup. Yet, Belshazzar continued to live lavishly. The kingdom's treasury was in a deficit. The spoils from military excursions were limited by internal factors and the ascension of Persia.

In the final days of the Neo-Babylonian dynasty, Belshazzar commissioned a royal banquet for his high officials. He called the feast to commemorate the fact that 70 years had passed since the exile of the Israelite tribes of Judah, Benjamin, and Levi and redemption had not occurred as predicted by the Hebrew prophets. In the minds of the Babylonian aristocracy this reality proved that the gods of Babylon were superior to **YHWH**. The kingdom of Judah was still enslaved by the golden grip of the kingdom of Babylon. Null and void was the counsel of YAH, therefore it was time for a high national celebration to exalt the powers of the gods of Babylon over the God **(ELOHIM)** of Israel. He commissioned his palace courtiers to bring out the Israelite artifacts taken by King Nebuchadnezzar from the **Temple of YAH** which were then held in the temple of Marduk. These golden and silver drinking cups were brought into the royal banquet hall. The evening included music, songs of praise to the gods of Babylon, dance, food, revelry, and other fetishes. The theme of the evening was the God of Israel was dead. Long live the deities of great Babylon. The palace waiters and waitresses served the wine. It was time to toast to the gods of Babylon—Marduk, Nebo, Nergal, Anu, Sin, and all the other powers of Babylon.

The Babylonians were a very proud people, self-indulgent, and extremely materialistic. Nabonidus, Belshazzar, or none of the high officials had respect for **the Words of YAH ELOHIM Israel**. Little did the participants realize, Babylon was in its final days. Nabonidus and Belshazzar would be the last two monarchs of the empire. The downfall of Babylon which had been predicted by the Levite prophets, Jeremiah, Ezekiel, and Isaiah, was finally coming to pass. *"Babylon the great, the glory of all kingdoms, the proud splendor of the Chaldeans,—* **the head of gold** *was falling!"*

"King Belshazzar gave a great banquet for his thousand nobles, and in the presence of the thousand he drank wine: Under the influence of the wine Belshazzar ordered the gold and silver vessels that his father Nebuchadnezzar had taken out of the temple at Jerusalem to be brought so that the king and his nobles, his consorts, and his concubines could drink from them. The golden vessels that had been taken out of the sanctuary of the House of ELOHIM **(YHWH)** in Jerusalem were then brought and the king, his nobles, his consorts, and his concubines drank from them. They drank wine and praised the gods of gold, silver, bronze, iron, wood, and stone." **Daniel 5: 5**

As I mentioned before, the Babylonian priesthood approved of the invasion because the Marduk priesthood hated Nabonidus because of his decision to advance the cult of Sin at the expense of Marduk, the patron Babylonian deity. In the midst of the Persian siege, certain segments of the population unsuccessfully rose up against Nabonidus. He massacred all the inhabitants of Opis. This didn't prevent his general Sippar from surrendering to Cyrus. Nabonidus fled the city. The next day, the priests of Marduk who hated him opened the gates of Babylon to the Persian emperor and his forces. These dissatisfied officials had given Cyrus a blueprint to the royal city, providing him with the knowledge he needed to redirect the canal waters entering the city. Cyrus made a victorious entrance into the royal city. The population cheered him and spread twigs on the ground symbolizing their acceptance of the new head of the ancient world—**The Breast and Arms of Silver.** Babylonians greeted him as *"the mighty king of Sumer and Akkad, king of the four quarters of the world."* In return, Cyrus declared a state of peace with Babylon. Nabonidus was captured and placed under house arrest in the central Iranian city of Carmania. Babylon became a colony of Achaemenid Persia. Cyrus portrayed himself as the saviour chosen by Marduk to restore order and justice.

In conclusion, Babylon was the ancient head of gold. It was the dominant power of the Near East beginning in the days of Nimrod(people of Nimrud) and finally collapsing with the Neo-Babylonian dynasty several millenniums later. Its fertile lands were considered the breadbasket of the ancient Near East. The famous fortified walls of this great city with its outer and inner circuits could not prevent **the Words of YAH** from coming to pass. The region of Babylonia, along with the Nile Valley, was one of the oldest, highly civilized areas in the world. It was also the place where the worship of money, materialism, humanism, and the construction of monuments began—**The Head of Gold**.

Babylon was also a place of massive immigration where large populations from poorer areas came to be a part of the vibrant urban centers. These centers became the main routes of ancient world trade. Babylon became more than a state, it became a cultural center of the entire Near East whose pagan spiritual influences reached the shores of Europe and North America thousands of years later. In the 21st century, Europe and North America are now the Twin Pillars of Modern Civilization, even the *"the daughters of Babylon"*.

The Silver Age—(Its Breast and Arms were of Silver)
Media-Persia Era
"But another kingdom will arise after you, inferior to yours"
"Its breast and arms were of silver;"
Daniel 2: 32, 39

"YAH changes times and seasons, HE removes kings (kingdoms) and install kings (kingdoms), He gives the wise their wisdom and knowledge to those who know" **Daniel 2: 21**

Persis means the land of the Persians. It was formerly the eastern portion of the Elamite dominion. The Persian Empire was an ancient empire in Southwest Asia whose modern name is Iran. This kingdom consisted of a mixture (intermingling) of people. This included the dark-brown skinned Elamites of the lineage of Shem(Shemitic people), **See Genesis 10:22**, and the Indo-European people of Scythia (the Medes of the lineage of Japheth) **See Genesis 10:2**. These Indo-European nomads migrated down into northern Persia, beginning in 1000 B.C.E. Centuries of intermarriage produced a mulatto people whose physical features ranged from dark brown, light brown, to pale-skin. This mulatto empire reached its peak in 500 B.C.E. extending from the Indus River in the far east to the western borders of Asia Minor, down into Egypt on the continent of Africa. Persepolis was its capital which was near the modern city of Shiraz. Persia is credited with giving Europe some of its favorite fruits and vegetables, such as peaches, oranges, limes, pistachio nuts, date-palms, and most importantly, spinach. Many of the plants cultivated by Persia originated in the Far East countries such as India and China. Persia was famous for long camel caravans loaded with carpets, spices, and other expensive merchandise traveling from Sidon and Tyre all the way to India. In eastern Turkey, which was also a portion of the ancient Persian empire, the Persians were owners of fine horses. Most homes had expensive carpets. Silver mining and large mineral deposits were found in the northern borders of Media-Persia, near Barburt, Armenia. They traded rare gems, elephant teeth, and silks.

Near the Caspian Sea, the Persians and Scythians (Medes) traded silk fabrics, grew cotton, and manufactured textiles. The Persians were the first in southwest Asia to maintain trade and diplomatic relations with the Mongols. The Mongols went on to build a bridge between Europe and Asia centuries later.

The Persian Empire built paved roads throughout its kingdom. Their travelers used mariner's compasses, and introduced other ancient Eastern innovations to southwestern Asia and southern Europe. Persians were also accredited as the fathers of fiction writing. They used boxwood for construction of homes and other buildings. The average home contained a garden with delicious fruits. The vineyards were also renown for producing high-quality wines. Their farms produced milk, honey, and were known for clean drinking water. Persian women were considered some of the most beautiful women of the ancient world, and known for their sexual charm.

The **kingdom of Persia (silver)** replaced **Babylon (gold)** as the center for architectural wonders, fortresses, and magnificent palaces. The empire was founded by Cyrus, who was known as *"Cyrus the Great"*, during the 6th century B.C.E. The Pesian empire comprised a succession of 13 monarchs extending from 538 B.C.E. until 331 when it fell to Indo-Aryan conqueror, Alexander the Great of Greece in 330 B.C.E.**(brass)**.

The Persian Achaemenid dynasty—**The Breast and Arms of Silver**—prophetic time zone started with the ascension of Cyrus II in (538-530 B.C.E.), Cambyses (529-522 B.C.E.), Bardia (522 B.C.E.), Darius I (521-486 B.C.E.), Xerxes I (485-465 B.C.E.), Artaxerxes I (464-424 B.C.E.), Xerxes II (424), Sogdianus (424), Darius II (423-405 B.C.E.), Artaxerxes II (404-359 B.C.E.), Artaxerxes III (358-336 B.C.E.), Ares (337-336 B.C.E.), and ended with Darius III (335-331 B.C.E.).

Cyrus II
(538 B.C.E.—530 B.C.E.)

Cyrus II [which is *translated* Kurush in the Persian language] was also known as "the Great." His father Cambyses I married the daughter of Median crown-prince Astyages, who later became the Medes king. Cyrus II was born out of that union. He rose to power as a conqueror. He was regarded as the founder of Persian culture, the Achaemenian dynasty, and the "father of the people." Cyrus, the grandson of Astyages, king of the Medes, usurped his grandfather's throne and united it with mainland Persia. Once empowered, he established a massive bureauarcy to govern an empire that extended from Ecbatana, Sogdiana, Khorasan (modern Khurasan), all the people of the steppes, Media, Ionia, Lydia, Mesopotamia, Syria, Israel, Phoenicia, northern Arabia, the western coast of Grecia, on down to the doorsteps of Egypt. The territorial range of the empire far surpassed the size of all the previous Near Eastern empires. Some of the kingdoms were conquered through diplomacy as well as with the sword. His influence and empire continued to expand for the next two centuries long after his death. He was then worshipped by the Persian people as a god. In the year 1971, the Iranian government of Shah Pahlavi commemorated the 2,500 anniversary of the founding of Persian civilization.

In the Hebrew scriptures, Cyrus is viewed as *"YAH'S Liberator"* of the captive kingdom of Judah. After conquering the royal-city of Babylon, Cyrus issued a decree to allow the Israelite to return to rebuild the city of Jerusalem, restore the walls, and resurrect the temple of YAH. This announcement was seen by ancient Israelites as the fulfillment of the prophecies of Isaiah, Jeremiah, and Daniel. Below are several of the prophecies spoken by these men concerning this future event:

Achaemenid dynasty ruled the Persian royal court from 536 B.C.E. to 331 B.C.E.

1) "I confirm the word of MY servant, and fulfill the prediction of MY messengers. It is I who say Jerusalem, "It shall be inhabited," and of the towns of Judah, "They shall be rebuilt; And I will restore their ruined places." I who said to the deep, "Be dry; I will dry up your floods, I am the same who said of Cyrus, "He is MY shepherd," He shall fulfill all MY purposes! He shall say of Jerusalem, "She shall be rebuilt, and to the temple You shall be founded again."   **Isaiah 44: 26-28**

Through the Spirit of YAH's prophecy, Isaiah foretold the rebuilding of Jerusalem. The above scriptures proves this point. Another reference to the restoration of Jerusalem after its destruction in 586 B.C.E., is found in **Isaiah 45:1-2** which states:

2) "Thus said YAH to Cyrus, His anointed one—whose right hand, HE (YAH) has grasped, treading down nations before him, ungirding the loins of kings, opening doors before him and letting no gate stay shut. I (YAH) will go before you (Cyrus) and make the crooked places straight; I will break in pieces the gates of brass, and cut in sunder the bars of iron."

YAH in HIS Infinite wisdom revealed to the prophet Isaiah that ancient Babylon would fall and the captives of Judah would be set free. "YAH said this about the waters flowing into the royal city of Babylon:

3) "I (YAH) say to the deep, "Be dry," and I will dry up your rivers." **Isaiah 44: 27.**

As I said earlier, in 539 B.C.E. dissatisfied Chaldean officials had given Cyrus a blueprint to the royal city, allowing him knowledge needed to redirect the canal waters entering the city. Cyrus made a victorious entrance into the royal city. The population cheered him and spread twigs on the ground symbolizing their acceptance of the new head of the ancient world—**The Chest and Arms of Silver,** thus confirming the words of HIS servant Isaiah.

4) "And this whole land shall be a desolation, and an astonishment; and these nations shall serve the king of Babylon (Neo-Chaldean dynasty) seventy years."   **Jeremiah 25:11**

Jeremiah prophesied in the above verse that the Neo-Chaldean dynasty of Babylon would collapse after 70 years of global power. It had extended from approximately 609 to 539 B.C.E. Isaiah also foresaw YAH using Cyrus to render HIS DIVINE judgement upon ancient Babylon to fulfill Jeremiah's and Daniel's visions:

5) "Know therefore and understand, that from the going forth of the commandment *(by Cyrus II)* to restore and to build Jerusalem unto the anointed prince—*(Zerubbabel, Sheshbazzar, Yeshua, Ezra, Zachariah, Haggai, Malachi, Nehemiah, and the entire remnant: Judah, Levi, and Benyamin)*—shall be seven weeks: the street shall be built again, and the wall, even in troublous times:"   **Daniel 9: 25.**

This remnant, Judah, Levi, and Benyamin, would remain in the holyland for the next five centuries until 70 C.E. when Titus, the general of the Roman Empire, came and destroyed the city of Jerusalem to cut off the anointed prince once again.

As we can see, each and every move made by great rulers and kings of the earth is ultimately controlled by YAH, the Creator of the heavens, earth, and seas. As King Solomon once said in **Proverbs 21: 1**: *"The king's heart* **(core of mind)** *is in the hand of YAH, as rivers of water: HE (YAH) turns it wherever HE will."* Cyrus the Great, like Nebuchadnezzar II before him, was actually YAH's servants of DIVINE judgement for, and against, HIS people.

As fate would have it, in 530 B.C.E. Cyrus II and his entire army were destroyed while fighting Massagetae nomads deep inside the interior of Central Asia. This area is known as Kazakhstan today. These diverse groups of Japhetic(Aryan) and mulatto (mingled Aryans and Shemites) nomads lived in territory which extended from the eastern borders of the Persian empire in Central Asia all the way towards the borders of what we call modern India, Mongolia, and China. The Far East city-states also maintained a much lower living standard than those in ancient Kemet, Kush, Canaan, and Mesopatamia. This is why YAH told Daniel in **chapter 2 verse 39**: "But another kingdom (civilization) will arise after you (Kemetic-Neo-Babylon), inferior to yours (the ancient Afro-Asiatic world)."

Cambyses II
(529 B.C.E.—522 B.C.E.)

Cambyses II [which is *translated* Kambuziya in Persian language] was the son of Cyrus the Great. He was named after his grandfather Cambyses I. His father appointed him the ruler of the city of Babylon and overseer of the entire western portion of the empire. One of his first major assignments was to invade Africa and conquer the kingdoms of Egypt, Ethiopia, and Libya. Once the news of his father's death reached him in Africa, Cambyses withdrew his seige of those kingdoms. As he journeyed home towards Persia, he became ill and died in route. In absence of their father's presence, a man who claimed to be his brother Bardiya seized the throne in Pasargadae as the heir of the Achaemenids. Pasargadae was the imperial city in central Persia that contained several palaces, parks, a fortified treasure-house, and a sanctuary to praise the gods of Media-Persia. But, Cambyses, in a deathbed confession, told his commanders that the supposedly new monarch was an imposter because he had already murdered his own brother Bardiya before he departed for his invasion of the land of Kemet.

Bardiya
(522 B.C.E.)

Whoever this Bardiya was, his mysterious reign did not endure for one complete year. According to Cambyses, this so-called Bardiya was actually Gaumata, a Median magi. Nevertheless, it seems that Bardiya resented the Persian aristocracy and spent his mere twelve months attempting to rein in the nobility by taking away their benefits such as paid entourages, family property grants, and government positions. This new policy was popular with the commoners, but it caused resentment among the wealthy. Commanders who had been leaders in Cambyses II's Republican Guard conspired with the displaced nobility to murder Bardiya. This assassination occurred in 522 B.C.E.. This confusion concerning what was the true identity of the Bardiya caused a leadership crisis in the Persian empire. The next leader had to be, without a doubt, a true heir of the Achaemenid dynasty.

Through military conquest, the Achaemenid Persian Empire expanded all the way to southeast Europe in the West to India in the far East.

Darius I
(522 B.C.E.—486 B.C.E.)

Darius I [which is *translated* Da-ra-ya-wah-ush in Persian language means *"he who possesses goodness, truth, and light"*] was also known as Darius the Great. He began as a military commander. When he heard that Bardiya had usurped the throne after the death of Cambyses II, he moved with force to kill Bardiya and his allies and proclaimed himself king of Persia. Darius claimed to be a descendant of the Ariarannes dynasty. He inscribed himself the son of Hystapes, a satrap of Parthia.

The majority of the citizens in the empire did not support Darius claim to the throne, therefore he had to militarily suppress his own population one province at a time in order to bring stability. Darius then enacted social reforms that transferred large tracts of land from supporters of old order to supporters of the new administration. In terms of foreign policy, he divided the empire into a system of satraps [provinces]. Darius also initiated massive renovation projects that included the building of a new magnificent imperial city named Persepolis—"the city of the Persians." The former royal city, Susa, then became the imperial winter residence of the Persian court. Susa consisted of three royal courtyards built with glazed decorated bricks. Darius was also well known for the sculptured monument he constructed on the peaks of the mountains near Kirmanshah. Although Susa was demoted to a winter residence, he still had four gigantic Egyptian-style statues erected in the former capital.

Darius, militarily, continued the conquest of his predecessors, subduing Thrace, Macedonia, and some of the Aegean islands. The series of wars between the Indo-Aryan Greek states and the mulatto Persian empire persisted. However, Darius failed in his war efforts against the Scythians in 513 B.C.E. Fourteen years later in 499 B.C.E., he succeeded in his campaign to put down the Ionian revolt. Yet, he could not conquer the Grecian mainland although he attempted two invasions. Grecian resistance angered the Persian monarch and he purposed in his heart to invade the entire country. Yet in 492 his fleet was destroyed by a terrible storm (**Act of YAH**). Two years later in 490, he assembled his huge army on a plain near Athens. Nevertheless, misfortune continued when he experienced another devastating reversal when the forces of Athens defeated his army at the Battle of Marathon. He died before he could launch a third expedition. Still, Darius was viewed as a an administrative genius and great builder.

Xerxes I
(485 B.C.E.—465 B.C.E.)

Xerxes I [which was *translated* Khsharyasha in the Persian language meaning *"hero among kings"* was the son of Darius I. He ascended to the throne in 485 B.C.E. as the King of Persia. He was a member of the Achaemenid dynasty. Like many of his predecessors, he sharpened his political teeth as a governor of the city of Babylon and the western section of the empire. In 484 he fiercely quashed an Egyptian revolt, and again in 482, he extinguished the

Babylonian desire for independence. In fact, he cast away the title of "king of Babylon" and launched a war against those whom he described as the *"den of the false gods."* He no longer pursued a policy of peace with the priesthood of the former royal city. In fact, he went on to pillage all the gods of Babylonia. Historical records report that the punishment Xerxes inflicted on the *"Kings of the Lies"* was savage.

Xerxes had one major aim when he came to power: Avenge the lost of his father Darius who had been defeated at the Battle of Marathon in 490 B.C.E. For three years he launched a massive army rebuilding program. During this time a storm also destroyed the bridges he had built to cross Hellespont, nevertheless, he rebuilt the bridges in an amazing seven days. He then officially reviewed the crossing of his 360,000-man army, which was probably the largest military force in the Near East, marching off to the war zone supported by over 1000 ships. This could be considered an ancient World War which would eventually shift the balance of power from the ancient Near East and Africa to the continent of what we called Europe today.

When the conflict actually broke out, the Persians broke through the Grecian forces at Thermopylae and destroyed the city of Athens. On the other hand, Xerxes naval forces, suffered a setback against the Greek navy in the Battle of Salamis in 480 B.C.E.. This time all Greeks united to war against the Persians. Sparta controlled the army while Athens was in charge of the navy. After a series of battles, Xeres decided to return to Persia leaving his army behind to continue the fight. Xeres then formed an alliance with Carthage to attack Greek garrisons in Sicily. Nevertheless, he formally withdrew all forces after another defeat at the Battle of Plateau the following year. These Greek-Persian wars continued for another 30 years. At home in Persepolis, he continued the extensive building projects of prior rulers. His losses abroad, however, brought challenges to his personal authority. There was palace infighting and conspiracies to assassinate him. Xerxes killed his brother's family at the request of his queen-wife. Those actions did not thwart his enemies. He was later murdered by members of his own court. In terms of Persian foreign policy, historians regard his repeated setbacks in Greece as the beginning of the gradual decline of the Achaemenid empire. **Xeres I is identified as Ahasuerus in the Book of Daniel** in the Hebrew scriptures. It was during his reign that Ezra the priest returned to Jerusalem in 458 B.C.E. You can read about his experiences in the Book of Ezra beginning with chapter one.

Domestically, Xerxes I was renown for his grand beautification of Persepolis. There he added opulent splendor to the fortified citadel that included giant sculptures and magnificent palace complexes all constructed on massive limestone platforms.

Artaxerxes I
(464 B.C.E.—424 B.C.E.)

Artaxerxes I [surnamed Makrocheir *which meant* "long-arm" by the Greeks] was the throne name for the second son of Xerxes I. His birth name was Ar-de-shir and his reign began in 464 after the murder of his father. The commander of the palace guards Artabanus was the chief conspirator behind the murderous plots against his father Xerxes I and his oldest brother Darius. After securing power, Artaxerxes turned on Artabanus and slew him. During his 40-year rulership, Artaxerxes stamped out a rebellion in the land of the Pharaohs (Egypt). He announced a peace pact with Athens ending the war with the Aryans and the other Grecian cities in Asia Minor. Artaxerxes also announced peace to the children of Israel when he anointed Nehemiah as the governor of Judah and sanctioned the return of the Jerusalem captives in 445 B.C.E. He also ordered the walls of Jerusalem to be rebuilt and later commissioned Nehemiah and Ezra to complete the work. You can read about this in chapter one of **the Book of Nehemiah.** Artaxerxes died in 424 and his wife Damaspia was said to have also died on the exact same day. Although Artaxerxes was a womanizer who fathered several children by other women besides the queen, their son Xerxes II assumed the throne as his successor. It should also be noted that Artaxerxes was regarded as the great father of the Persian religion Zoroastrianism which became the official belief system throughout the vast empire. Many historians compare him to Rome's Constantine who made Christianity the official state religion of the ancient Roman empire. Zoroastrianism was founded by 30-year-old Zarathustra, a 6th century B.C.E. Persian cult leader, who believed in a man-made philsopy along with, an idol-god named Ahura Mazda who was regarded as the creator of all that was good. The graven symbol for the deity consisted of a sun-disc with a human upper body situated on top of the sun with two wings. This image was called Faravahar [farohar]. Inside the Iranian temples, there were altars of fire with giant flames burning like the eternal flame monument in Washington, D.C. today. The Persian priests were known as 'The Magi.' The Zoroastrian sacred text was known as the Avesta (The Book of Law) which included spells against demons, hymns praising Zarathustra, and instructions on how to observe of Persian festivals.

Xerxes II
(424 B.C.E.)

Xerxes II, which is *translated* Khsharyasha in the Persian language meaning *"hero among kings"*, was the second Persian ruler to possess that name. He had the shortest reign of all the rulers of the Achaemenid dynasty. After seizing the throne, he attempted to maintain the peace and stability of his father Artaxerxes I. Palace infighting and sibling rivalry, nevertheless, would not allow that to come to pass. Xerxes announced a great feast for his inauguration and invited all his family members, even his half-brothers whose mothers were Babylonian concubines. One half-brother named Sogdianos was a covetous and power-hungry soul. Now Sogdianos wrought an evil scheme to seize the Persian throne for himself. On the forty-fifth day of Xerxes II rulership, the king had been partying, drinking heavy, and went to lay in his bed. Sogdianos sneaked into the palace bedroom and murdered Xerxes II. This treacherous act alienated Sogdianos's future relationship with the palace guards who were responsible for the king' security.

Sogdianos
(424 B.C.E.)

Sogdianos, *translated* as Sugdyana in Persian language, was one of the illegitimate sons of Artaxerxes I. Ancient documents reveal that he was the son of a Babylonian concubine. Sogdianos was also known as Smerdis and Diodorus. He slew his half-brother Xerex II in a personal feud to seize power. Ochus, a military officer, secretly assembled an army and was joined by other commanders of the household cavalry and the satrap of Egypt, moved against Sogdianos. He was forced to surrender, and immediately put to death. Sogdianos's fate wasn't too much better than Xerxes II. His reign lasted merely 6 1/2 months. General Ochus was chosen to be king and assumed the title of King Darius II.

Darius II
(423 B.C.E.—405 B.C.E.)

Darius II, *translated* Da-ra-ya-wah-ush in Persian language *means*" **he who possesses goodness, truth, and light**", named himself after his predecessor Darius I, who was regarded as a true heir of the Achaemenid dynasty. As I stated earlier, his original name was General Ochus, the satrap of Egypt, who took up arms against his half-brother Sogdianus. After a short battle Sogdianus was slain, and his army scattered. Another skirmish broke out with his maternal brother Arsites. General Ochus, an experienced commander, also quashed that rebellion.

His arch-enemies, the Greeks, termed him *"Nothos"* which meant *"Bastard."* Most of Darius reign was regarded as peaceful and uneventful. During this quiet time he started a monument building campaign adding more splendor and beautifying the homeland of the Persian empire. In 409 B.C.E., however, a conflict arose close to home when he was forced to suppress an insurgency in Media.

Ancient Persian documents reveal that his wife Parysatis was one of his main advisors. For most of his reign, Darius refrained from intervening in Greek affairs as long as Athens remained stable and a non-threat to Persian interest. But in 413 B.C.E. a ruling faction within the Greek hierarchy double-crossed King Darius and supported the rebel forces of a Persian usurper named Amorges who lived in the city of Caria in southwest Asia Minor. Amorges rebelled against Perseopolis and launched attacks against Persian allied forces in his region. Meanwhile, Grecian armies from the city of Syracuse warred against Athens. Although Syracuse was not an ally of Persia, this instability caused King Darius to order his satraps and armies stationed in Asia Minor to squash the mutiny and invade the Greek mainland. Those troops then marched to Athens, sacking it, and all other towns which supported the rebellion.

Five years later in 408, Darius II entered a new alliance with the Grecian city-state of Sparta. He then dispatched his son Cyrus to Asia Minor to redouble efforts to secure the western flank of the Persian empire. Shortly after this in the year 405, Darius II died in the ninteenth year of his reign before he could complete his goals.

Artaxerxes II
(404 B.C.E.—358 B.C.E.)

Artaxerxes II, also known as Arsakes, began his 46 year reign, in 404 B.C.E. and continued until 358 during the height of the Achaemenid glory. Artaxerxes, who was surnamed "Mnemon" which *meant "Mindful and he whose reign is through truth"* was known as the **Great king (Shah)** of Persia. He was the son of Darius II. His mother's name was Queen Parysatis. During his reign, Athens was temporarily crushed and subdued as the ongoing Peloponnesian wars waned. At home in Persepolis, his younger brother Cyrus plotted against him with a mixture of Greek mercenaries and Persian turncoats. Nevertheless, Artaxerxes slew him in 401 and his forces surrendered. Cyrus had masterminded a plot to support the Grecian city-state Sparta against his own country. Sparta readily joined in the rebellion hoping to expel Persian forces from the mainland. Sparta hated the Persian monarch because he had already forced them to abandon several coastal Greek cities and islands. This short war became known as the Corinthian war which ended with the signing of the Treaty of Antalcidas. This treaty restored Persia's control over the Grecian cities of Ionia and Aeolis. Artaxerxes proposed a peace pact with Athens promising to assist with rebuilding efforts in hopes of using them as proxies against Sparta. Athens temporarily gained from Persian support, but Artaxerxes double-crossed Athens and secured a new peace agreement with his former foe Sparta. During Artaxerxes reign, the Grecian city-states were deeply divided. This provided Persia the opportunity to pursue a divide and conquer strategy against Aryan Greece. Towards the end of his forty-six year reign, Persian satraps in several provinces rebelled against the crown weakening the empire. Even Egypt revolted against Artaxerxes II. He was forced to dispatch forces in an attempt to reconquer **the land of gold**. By 373 B.C.E., Persia was forced to withdraw from the land of Kemet to confront new threats involving a joint Egyptian-Sparta alliance to claim Phoenicia (modern Lebanon). This new development forced him to withdraw and caused his campaign in Egypt to fail.

Artaxerxes II marriage with Stateira was ended when his mother, Queen Parysatis, poisoned her in 400 B.C.E. He was reported to have 115 sons from 350 wives. Much of the kingdom's wealth was spent on several building projects, including restoring the palace of Darius I at Susa, renovating the cities of Ecbatana and Persepolis. In its glory the boundaries of the

Persian empire consisted of India towards the Far East, down into Lower Egypt on the continent of Africa towards the South. The Caspian Sea and Caucasus Mountains formed the northern border while the Greek mainland marked the western boundaries. Persia had consumed the former Neo-Babylonian Empire, Lydia, Cilicia, Egypt, the Media city-states, but now this large, wealthy, powerful cosmopolitan super-state that united Eurasian civilization was facing gradual decline. So it came to pass that Artaxerxes II had reigned for four decades and six years. He was buried in a tomb located in Persepolis, Iran.

Artaxerxes III
(358 B.C.E.—338 B.C.E.)

Artaxerxes III real name was Ochus, the same as his grandfather, who assumed the throne name of Darius II when he came to power. Remember, Darius II real name was "General Ochus" when he served as the satrap of Egypt. His grandson [**Artaxerxes III**] ascended to the throne in 358 and ruled the Achaemenid Empire for 20 years with his rulership ending in 338. Artaxeres III was the son of Artaxerxes II and queen-mother Stateira. He came to power in a bloody revolt. In the latter-days of his father's Artaxeres II reign, he plotted to seize the throne. Some suspect Artaxerses III conspired to avenge the death of his own mother Stateira. Artaxerxes III believed that his father Artaxerxes II was complicit with his grandmother Queen Parysatis in the murder of his mother Stateira. During this time Artaxerxes III also killed several of his own brother-princes. Afterwards,he sought to consolidate control over all the Persian satraps. He reversed the policies of his predecessors and demanded that all Greek fighters be expelled from the service of the empire. He is known as the last great military commander of the Achaemenids. Between the two years of 345 to 343, Artaxerxes invaded Phoenicia and reconquered Lower Egypt after a 13 year bloody war there. He defeated Nectanebo II driving him from Egypt then reestablished Persian domination over the land of Kemet. Historical sources differ over the cause of Artaxerxes's death. Some say he and his eldest sons were poisoned by his cupbearer Bagoas, who was also a palace eunuch and military general. Other sources, such as the cuneiform texts in the British Museum, theorize that he died from natural causes in 338 B.C.E.

Artaxerxes IV or Ares
(337 B.C.E.—335 B.C.E.)

Artaxeres, *pronounced* Ar-takh-sa-ca IV, was the youngest son of King Artaxerxes III. His real name was Ares. His short reign lasted for only two years from 337-335 B.C.E. He came to power after the eunuch Bagoas poisoned several members of the royal family. Again, other sources continue to reject that narrative. The cuneiform tablets in British Museum still suggest the emperor died from natural causes. Whatever the case, Ares accepted the throne name of his father [Artaxerxes III] and grandfather [Artaxerxes II], thus he became Artaxerxes IV.

The death of his father Artaxerxes III caused major unrest throughout the Achaemenid domain. Two of the empire's major provincial leaders revolted: Egypt again, and the other was Babylonia. To the far west, a major new military development took place in Asia Minor (modern Turkey). Phillip II, king of Macedonia, had forced the Greek city-states into one united front. The Macedon ruler then launched an offensive against Persian troops. His general, Parmenion, led the frontal assault crossing over to Hellespont in 336. As he advanced into Asia Minor, more Greek cities closed ranks with the emerging united Greek state.

King Ares and his courtiers were divided over foreign policy. Prince Artasala, a nephew of Artaxerxes IV and the satrap of Armenia, wanted to immediately counter the Macedonian offensive head-on. Several other influential noblemen supported his strategy. Ares did not have time to stabilize his royal court or the vast empire. Greek sources said Artaxerxes IV wanted to remove Bagoas. Bagoas, being the intelligence expert that he was, perceived that Ares wanted him removed. So in the summer of 336 Bagoas poisoned Ares, his children, and a host of other princes.

Ares had ambitions of restoring the Temples of Esagila and the Tower-Temple of Etemenanki in the royal residence of Babylonia. Although his reign was cut short, historians contend that his reign was important because it sowed the seeds for the ultimate downfall of imperial Persia.

After this, the cuneiform texts known as the Dynastic prophecy said Prince Artasala marched on Persepolis and seized the throne. Of course, Bagoas sided with Prince Artasala and welcomed his overwhelming military presence. Artasala then became king and assumed the throne name of Darius III Kodomannus.

Darius III Kodomannus
(335 B.C.E.—330 B.C.E.)

The title Darius III was the throne name chosen by Prince Artasala, the former satrap of Armenia, who assumed the mantle of power during the waning days of the empire. This nostalgic name represented the need for a great leader and a hope for the return to the glory days for the empire. Nonetheless, the Achaemenid dynasty and the Persian superstate was rapidly declining. One of his first acts was the removal of the eunuch Bagoas from the royal court. He personally gave Bagoas a taste of his own medicine and forced him to open his mouth and swallow poison. As King David once said in **Psalms 9: 17,** *"the wicked* [in this case Bagoas] *man is snared by his own devices."*

Darius III, an experienced military commander, temporarily united the empire once again, He was also successful in subduing the rebellion in Egypt once and for all. Darius III employed Grecian mercenary forces to halt opposing Grecian military advances in Asia Minor. On the Grecian mainland, King Phillip of Macedon was assassinated during October of 336. For the next two years, Memnon of Rhodes, the mercenary commander, fought to a draw with the Macedon general Parmenion. Phillip II was succeeded by his young son **Alexander III**, who eventually became known as **"The Great"**. Upon ascending to the throne, Alexander quickly joined General Parmenion in May of 334 and started a new advance that would eventually topple the Achaemenid empire. Greek forces crossed over into the Near East for the first time in world history. Unbelievably, a small, primitive Aryan kingdom with no more than 50,000 soldiers was able to overthrow an ancient empire that once encompassed almost 8 million square kilometers, 50 million citizens, and spanning three continents: Asia, Europe, and Africa. Persia was once the largest empire the world had seen. This gigantic ancient empire included the modern territories of what we call Iran, Turkey, Iraq, Kuwait, Syria, Jordan, Israel, Palestine, Lebanon, all significant population centers of ancient Egypt. Persia's contacts with the far west extended from Libya,to Thrace,Macedonia, Bulgaria, most of the Black Sea, the coastal regions consisting of Abkhzaia, Armenia, Georgia, Azerbaijan, and parts of North Caucasus. The long arms of Persia also stretched into parts of Central Asia, Afghanistan, India and western China. The Arabian Peninsula also came under Persia's sway.

Darius eventually fled to Ecbatana along with a personal stash of 8,000 talents of gold as the Achaemenid Persian empire crumbled around him. There Bessus, the satrap of Bactria, slew him, left his corpse in the middle of the road as a decoy as he fled into Central Asia,hoping to delay Alexander who was in hot pursuit. Alexander brought the corpse of Darius back to Persepolis for a royal-state funeral, but he continued his pursuit against Persian resistance.

Unfortunately, just as Darius III had succeeded in quelling the Egyptian insurrection,

Alexander and his battle-hardened troops were arriving on Persia's doorsteps. Darius had spent great manpower and treasure recapturing Egypt. His troops were not ready for another fierce war, especially against the wild Grecians. Alexander and his forces quickly decimated Persia's armies at Granicus in 334, followed by another triumph at Issus in 333, and last but not least at Gaugamela in 333. After this, Alexander set his sight on imperial cities of Susa and Persepolis. The Grecian garrisons entered renown Perseopolis in 330 B.C.E. where Alexander found over 200,000 talents of pure gold besides additional treasures the Macedons had already plundered in Phoenicia, Damascus, and Egypt. Afterwards the famous royal city was burned by Alexander and his mighty men. The majority of this newfound wealth was shipped back to the Macedonia to upgrade their inferior city-states. From Persepolis, he headed to Pasargadae where he visited the Tomb of Cyrus the Great. Alexander had long revered Cyrus as a deity, who was a brown-skinned man he had heard of as a young Aryan lad in Cyropedia. When Alexander arrived at the tomb, he was horrified to discover that looters had vandalized the memorial and removed all of its luxuries.

Bessus renamed himself Artaxerxes V and attempted to rally and unite the eastern part of the empire. This effort failed. Alexander found him, put him on trial in a Persian court then sentenced him to death in a cruel and barbaric execution.

The time zone for the Achaemenid Persians—**The Breast and Arms of Silver** was now a part of the annals of world history. Alexander had conquered vast swaths of territories and he needed an infrastructure to establish a stable alternative, which he did not possess. Still, a brand new prophetic time zone—**Its Belly and Thighs of Brass**—had emerged from the Aryan inhabitants of the isles of the Gentiles. Meanwhile, restlessness erupted throughout the former Persian empire. As the prophet **Daniel** had declared, *"YAH changes times and seasons, YAH removes kings [empire-kingdoms] and installs kings [empire-kingdoms],"* in **chapter 2: 21**.

In hindsight, one of the major reasons for the collapse of the Persian Empire was the heavy tax burden placed on the provinces. The massive tribute led to discontent and economic decline among the subject provinces. In many ways, the modern empire-kingdoms of the United States, Russia, China, and several other modern economies are repeating the same mistake of the ancient Persians. Today, these latter-day modern kingdoms, both **toes of iron and miry clay**, have placed high tax rates on their citizens and imposed other heavy burdens. This makes it more difficult for their citizens to purchase anything besides basic necessities. Citizens in the 21st century are required to pay sales taxes on all retail purchases, pay rent, buy food, gas, automobiles, all types of insurance, clothes, etc. It is a known fact these heavy burdens on the poor and lower middle-class causes stagnation, and decreases overall economic growth and prosperity.

As I said earlier concerning Africa, he who rules **the land of gold** is the head of the world. Persia's actions definitely proved that point during their two centuries of rulership. The Achaemenids always fought to maintain domination over **the land of gold—Kemet**. They had been the rulers **[Pharaohs]** during the 27th Dynasty in (525-404 B.C.E.), and again during the 31st Dynasty in 343-332 B.C.E.).

In the year 332 B.C.E., King Alexander of Greece defeated King Darius III and replaced him as the ruler of the ancient global order.

Ancient Athens, Greece

Olympia

The Brass Age—(Its Belly and Thighs of Brass)
Grecian Era—PART ONE "the belly"
"then yet a third kingdom [empire] of brass which will rule over the whole earth;"
Daniel 2: 32,39

"YAH changes times and seasons, HE removes kings(kingdoms) and install kings(kingdoms); HE gives the wise their wisdom And knowledge to those who know"   **Daniel 2: 21**

Greece is a southern European country that consisted of a mountainous mainland situated on the Aegean Sea. It also contains 2,500 miles of coastline with approximately 2,000 small nearby offshore islands. It was for this reason the region was known as **"the isles of the Gentiles,"** spoken of in **Genesis 10: 5** by the prophet Moses. The Grecians were dispersed from Marseilles in the west to western and central Asia in the east.

It reads on this wise: "The descendants of Japheth—[the Aryan, Indo-European (so-called white people): Gomer, Magog, Madai, **Javan [Greece]**, Tubal, Meshech, and Tiras. The descendants of Gomer: Ashkenaz, Riphath, and Togarmah. The descendants of **Javan [Greece]**: Elishah, and Tarshish, the Kittim and the Dodanim. These are isles of the Gentiles, by their lands, each with its language, and their clans."

When you talk about Greece, you have to talk about two different periods of time. In fact, ancient Greece has three histories: The first one is the 3000—1100 B.C.E. Minoan civilization which reached its peak on the island of Crete in 2000 B.C.E. and later expanded to the mainland. The next ancient Grecian civilization was the barbaric Mycenaean which came into existence in 1600 B.C.E. after overthrowing the Minoan dominion. The truth of the matter is the first ancient Grecian civilization was ruled by non-Indo-Europeans, meaning black people who were originally known as Egyptians, Phoenicians, Hittites, or Canaanites after sailing from the Near East. These black people created a sophisticated culture that included cities with palaces, seafaring with extended trade routes, and written documents [cuneiform]. The ruins from excavation have revealed that those palaces contained paved street and piped water. The second Greece was the invasion of the barbaric, warlike [white Aryan] Indo-European Mycenaeans who came from the northern mountains. These people learned all of their life skills from the early Minoans. The Mycenaeans were later overthrown by another wave of northern invaders who were known as the Dorians. After this, Greece plunged into a Dark Age for several centuries, not to rise again until the emergence of Greece's third history: classical Greece which began to evolve around 750 B.C.E., when the Aryans established independent city-states on the coastlines. From there, the classical Greeks traded with their black and brown neighbors and also traveled into Asia Minor, Egypt, and the Near East to learn from the ancients.

Another fact that should be stated is that the classical Greeks were the first white (Indo-European) kingdom to ever rule over the earth. Before them, all ancient empires, including the Egyptians, Ethiopians, Syrians, Philistines, Israelites, Assyrians, Babylonians, Persians, Phoenicians, and Canaanites were populated and ruled by black and brown-skinned people—who were non Indo-Europeans. In early Greece there was never one centralized and unified state. Instead, classical Greece consisted of scores of independent city-states scattered across the mainland and small islands. These Aryan tribes were divided by various mountain ranges and the sea.

For the sake of our prophetic discussion we will start our Grecian focus on the period of classical Greece during 5th Century B.C.E.. This is when King Darius I, the Kings of Kings, ruler of Persia decided to invade the Grecian mainland. That intervention, which was repelled by the Athenian rulers, sparked a series of Greco-Persian wars for the next two centuries which eventually propelled the small European city-state into a world empire.

As Daniel had revealed to Nebuchadnezzar centuries earlier, this third empire represented as **Brass** was a time zone when the idol-worshipping pale-skinned Greeks would rise to become the rulers of the entire earth. This image with a **Belly and Thighs of Brass** actually came into existence with the rise and fall of Phillip II, his son Alexander the Great, and the ascension of the Hellenistic culture throughout Europe, Asia, and Africa for the next three-hundred years. It should also be noted that classical Greece culture, which went on to influence the Roman Empire, also recycled itself and gave birth to modern-day life as we know it today. That culture includes the arts, great temples, architecture, mythology and religion, life-like sculptures, democracy, and drama. Even today, Greece is credited as being the birthplace of Western civilization because it was the first country on the continent of Europe to establish a civilized society. It is also said that in order to understand the world around you in the 21st century, you must look back to the Greeks. This was done through interchanges with the surrounding African and Asian world. They borrowed the alphabet, navigational skills, and literary improvements from the black Canaanites known as the Phoenicians. The Greeks used their newfound knowledge of the alphabets to write poetry, plays, history, and philosophy. They learned to calculate and understand astronomy from the ancient Babylonian starbooks. They learned math, science, and architectural improvements from the Persians and Egyptians.

One aspect of classical Greek culture that was purely homegrown was their Hellenistic festivals that included revelry, athletic games, open sexual orgies, and plenty of joyous merrymaking. Greeks began to worship their fair-skinned women as goddesses. In their legends they were described as having skin "like unto the first fall of snow." Helena,

Aphrodite, Hera were all seen as lovely female divine being represented as white marble statutes. The female priestess were living representatives of the deities at the festivals. Men would pay tithes for sexual favors in bath houses during the occasions. Many of Grecian mythologies includes adult-children sex, homosexuality, lesbianism, and sex with animals. When you notice the majority of the Greek deities, whether men, women, or children, they were always naked with their bodies and genitals exposed. This was an indication of their open sensualities and sexuality. To be completely honest, the classical Greeks and Hellenes were one of the most perverse group of people to ever possess global power thus far. In terms of the observing the moral and sexual Laws of the MOST HIGH YAH, the Greeks were major offenders who continuously transgressed those standards. Let's take a brief look at **Leviticus, chapter 18: 1-30**, to allow me to prove my point: It reads on this wise:

"**YAH spoke to Moses saying,** *Speak to the Israelite people and say to them, I YAH am your ELOHIM, You shall not copy the* [sexual] *practices of the land of Egypt where you dwelt, or of the land of Canaan to which I am taking you; nor shall you follow their laws. My rules, by the pursuit of which man shall live: I am YAH. None of you shall come near* [sexually] *anyone of his own flesh to uncover nakedness* [no incest] *: I am YAH. Your father's nakedness, that is the nakedness of your mother, you shall not uncover; she is your mother* [no mother-son sexual relationship or father-daughter sexual relationship]—*you shall not uncover her nakedness. Do not uncover the nakedness of your father's wife* [stepmother-step-son sexual relationship or step-father-step-daughter sexual relationship; **no pedophilia**]; *it is the nakedness of your father. The nakedness of your sister—your father's daughter or your mother's; whether born in the household or outside—do not uncover their nakedness* [no brother-sister or step-brother-step sister sexual involvement; **no incest**];

The nakedness of your son's daughter [granddaughter; **no pedophiles**], *or of your daughter's daughter*—[granddaughter; no pedophiles] *do not uncover their nakedness; for their nakedness is yours. The nakedness of your father's wife daughter* [step-sister; no incest], *who has born into your father's household—she is your sister; do not uncover her nakedness. Do not uncover* [sexually] *the nakedness of your father's sister; she is your father's flesh. Do not uncover the nakedness of your mother's sister; for she is your mother's flesh. Do not uncover the nakedness of your father's brother*[uncle]; *do not approach his wife* [sexually]; *she is your* [aunt]. *Do not uncover* [sexually] *the nakedness of your daughter-in-law; she is your son's wife; you shall not uncover her nakedness. Do not uncover the nakedness of your* [Hebrew] *brother's wife; it is the nakedness of your* [Hebrew] *brother* [no type of sexual relationship-adultery]. *Do not uncover the nakedness of a woman and her daughter* [no sex with mother and her daughter]; *nor shall you marry her son's daughter*[step-granddaughter] *or her daughter's daughter*[step-granddaughter] *and uncover her nakedness: they are kindred* [**no sexual contact with close family members**]; *it is* **depravity.**

Do not marry a woman as a rival to her sister [two maternal sisters or close women friends] *and uncover her nakedness in the other's lifetime. Do not come near a woman* [sexually] *during her period of uncleanliness* [monthly cycle] *to uncover her nakedness. Do not have carnal* [sexual] *relations with your neighbor's wife and defile* [make yourself spiritually off-balance] *with her* [**adultery**]. *Do not allow any of your offspring to be offered up to Molech, and do not profane the name of your ELOHIM: I am YAH. Do not lie* [sexually cohabitation] *with a male* [**no same-sex intimacy**] *as one lies* [sexually cohabitation] *with a woman;* **it is an abhorrence** [**no homosexuality or lesbianism allowed**]. *Do not have carnal* [sexual] *relations with any beast* [**no sex with animals**] *and defile yourself thereby; and let no woman lend herself to a beast to mate with it;* [In Greek mythology the Greek goddess Helen had sex with Zeus who came into her in the form of a swan/bird. That is one example of how the Grecians copied the practices of Egypt and the Canaanites. **It is perversion**. *Do not defile yourselves in any of those ways, for it is by such that the nations that I am casting out before you defiled* [**corrupt sexual practices**] *themselves. Thus the land became defiled, and I* [**YAH**] *called it to account for its iniquity, and the land spewed out its inhabitants. But you must keep MY laws and MY rules, and you must no do any of those abhorrent things, neither* *the citizen* [Israelites] *nor the strangers* [foreign nations] *who resides among you; for all those abhorrent things were done by the people who were in the land before you, and the land became defiled. So let not the land spew you out for defiling it, as it spewed out the nation that came before you. All who do any of those abhorrent things—such persons shall be cut off from their people; You shall keep MY charge not to engage in any of the abhorrent practices that were carried on before you, and you shall not defile yourselves through them: I YAH am your ELOHIM."*

When we look at Greek history, religion, and mythology it reveals that they engaged in all of the above forbidden sexual and moral practices which the God (**ELOHIM**) of Israel **[YAH]** commanded HIS people not to participate in. Israelites were commanded to place a higher value on PRINCIPLES instead of unrestrained PASSIONS. Israelites were a spiritual people whose moral standards placed them on a higher moral plane than their ungodly neighbors who were now their captors. Israelites were instructed to control and rule over their spirits and passions, and not the other way around. On the other hand, one common factor between the pagans such as the Greeks, Persians, Babylonians, Canaanites, and Egyptians and animals were that they all shared similar sexual habits. Animals such as dogs, cats, lions, monkeys, etc. all engage in acts of incest, close sexual contact with family members, and other perverse sexual instincts. Ironically when you study the history of these pagan human beings you discover they shared similar sexual appetites with the bestial world. Those strange sexual practices are still prevalent among non-Israelite nations even today, especially in the Western world. One example of this type of decadent anti-YAH sexuality in our modern world is the Western European and American endorsement and legalization of homosexuality. These nations, like the Greeks before them, have no respect for the God of Israel's moral and sexual standards. That is why we refer to them as the **"people of the image"** or the **"people of idol kingdoms."** All of those empires in Daniel's vision, from **the head of gold down to the ten toes of iron and miry clay**, are made up of **uncircumcised people** who do not know YAH, nor would they ever choose to walk in HIS ways.

The Classical Grecian rulers Draco (621 B.C.E.), Solon (594-546 B.C.E.), Psistratus (605-527), Hippias (527-510 B.C.E.), Hipparchus (555-514 B.C.E.), Themistocles (525-462 B.C.E.), Cimon (449), Cleisthenes (506 B.C.E.), Pericles (495-429 B.C.E.), Cleon (422 B.C.E.), Alcibiades (450-404 B.C.E.), Agesilaus II (444-360 B.C.E.), Aeis (Name of 4 Spartan kings), Phillip II (359-336 B.C.E.), Alexander the Great (356-323 B.C.E.): After the death of Alexander, the Grecian empire split into 4 separate kingdoms ruled by four generals: Lysimachus (323-281 B.C.E.), Ptolmey I Soter (323-285 B.C.E.), Antipater (323-319 B.C.E.), Seleucus I Nicator (323-281 B.C.E.).

Draco
(621 B.C.E.—594 B.C.E.)

Draco, the tyrant of Athens, ruled from 621 B.C.E. as an Athenian lawyer who became the chief magistrate among the Council of 6. The Council of 6 consisted of six magistrates known as the smdetai who were chosen to record the laws. Draco prevailed among these men to become the sole judicial voice. He went on to enact measures known as Draconian rules which were known for its harsh penalties for both minor and major offenses. His decrees eventually caused major dissent among the Athenians. Critics of Draco once said, that *"his laws were not written in ink, but rather in blood."* Upon his death, many of his decrees were overturned by his successors, including Solon. During Draco's reign, Greece was still a very primitive collection of city-states composed of competing tribes.

Solon
(594 B.C.E.—546 B.C.E.)

Solon was the son of Execestides, of the family of the Codrids and Neleids. Like all of his predecessors, Solon trusted in graven images and attributed his birth to the idol named Poseidon. Although he was a politician, Solon was well-known for his poetry. He traveled throughout many parts of Greece and Asia to promote the interest of Athens. He was a major supporter of Athens drive to claim the island of Salamis. His poems actually motivated the citizens to rally around a military offensive to help the Athenians who lived on the island.

When Solon came to power there was violence and major discontent among the Athenians. Some of the city's oligarchy wanted relief from Draco's measures while other powerbrokers benefited as his allies. It was during this time Solon, who was seen as neutral and a breath of fresh air, became one of the magistrates on the Council of 6. Nevertheless, he still played a part in a coup known as the *"Conspiracy of Cylon"* which started after 12 years of oppressive Draconianism. He eventually positioned himself to enact a new humane code of laws which overturned Draco's edicts for Athenians. For example, under the old Draco's measures, a Greek could face forced labor as a slave in order to pay off his or her debts. Solon also ended the death penalty for nearly all offenses. It should also be noted that Athens was still considered a small, poor, primitive city-state in comparison to the other great kingdoms of Egypt, Babylon, Persia, Phoenicia, Samaria, Judah, and other Near East urban centers.

Peisistratus
605—527 B.C.E.

Peisistratus, [*pronounced* Pi-sis-tra-tus] was the son of Hippocrates, the ruler of the ancient royal city of Athens from 561 to 527 B.C.E. He was a distant relative of Solon from northern Attica who did not come from noble ranks, nor did he inherit wealth, power, or social status. In fact, he came to power as a populist and a champion of lower-class Athenians. He became well known as a fighter who captured the Port of Nisaea in nearby Megara. At the time of his ascension, Athens was divided among three classes of people: The Pedieis, Paralioi, and the Hyperakrioi. Peisistratus organized the Hyperakrioi, who were the poor hill dwellers. Known as a cunning warrior, it was believed that Peisistratus intentionally injured himself to galvanize the public into allowing him to increase his power and personal security. His new paramilitary force gave him the power to seize the Acropolis. After that triumph, Peisistratus became the paramount leader—the tyrant—of Athens.

Meanwhile, the only source of income for the Hyperakrioi was trading honey and sheep's wool. This group of vagabonds became the most powerful group among the three. Once empowered, he confiscated the lands of the aristocracy, cut taxes on the lower-class, restricted the privileges for the wealthy, and transferred many of their assets to the Hyperakrioi. Peisistratus was also known for redistribution of power and benefits to the masses instead of enriching himself. Some of his most important accomplishments were the establishment of the Panathenaic Festival, which included poetry recitations that showcased a version of Homeric epics, and the growth in theaters, arts, and the proliferation of Greek sculptures. He was accredited for building the first aqueduct in Athens which provided a large and reliable water supply for the large population. He also replaced private water wells for aristocrats with public fountain houses for the masses.

Although Peisistratus was popular among the citizenry, the Areopagus Council of northern Attica did not like his high-handed reforms. They plotted his ouster twice. The first ouster came in 555 B.C.E.. That exile lasted for 3 to 6 years. While Peisistratus languished in exile, dissension between the aforementioned three groups, the Pedies, Paralioi, and Hyperkrioi, became turbulent. As fate would have it, Peisistratus was able to escape from exile and return to Athens riding in a golden chariot. This came to pass after Peisistratus made an agreement with Megacles, who was a leading opposition figure, to marry his daughter. However, he lied. When he returned to the capital he was accompanied with a tall woman named Phye whom he passed off as the personification of the Greek goddess Athena. This betrayal of Megacles forced him to exit Athens once again. This was his second exile.

In Greek mythology, the female idol named Athena was a sculptured "fair and stately woman" believed to possess a masculine mind like her father's who loved to fight. This separated this sacred post from other Grecian deities. In Grecian fairy tales, it was believed she was an anti-marriage figurine that desired other women—dykism or lesbianism. So in Peisistratus superstitious mind he could not risk his life and marry Megacles daughter without being cursed by the goddess.

After this, Peisistratus created a new alliance with the powerbrokers of Athens and Attica which allowed him the opportunity to finally accumulate great personal wealth. He also reassembled his personal army and marched to the city of Marathon to suppress it. He re-entered Athens in 546 for his third and final reign as a tyrant of Athens. Peisistratus died in 527 and was succeeded by his two sons—Hippias and Hipparchus.

Hippias
(527 B.C.E.—510 B.C.E.)

Hippias *pronounced* Hip-pi-as succeeded his father Peisistratus. In the early days of reign, he maintained the same policies of his father. However, his tranquility was disturbed when his brother was murdered by two men whose names were Harmodius [*pronounced* Har-mo-di-us] and Aristogeiton [*pronounced* Ari-sto-gei-ton]. After the slaying of his brother, Hippias became increasing paranoid. He began to reverse many of the liberal policies of his father Peisistratus, and in fact, he became extremely oppressive. This reversal caused his inner circle and the citizens of Athens to turn against him and mount a revolt. It was the wealthy families who instigated the plot to remove Hippias. Cleisthenes, who was appointed as the chief instigator, bribed a demonist-priest who sacrificed at Delphi shrine to join in a confederacy against Hippias. Cleisthenes *pronounced* Cleis-the-nes promised to renovate the Delphi shrine and reform Athens into a democracy in exchange for his support. Both sides shook hands on the deal and the plot was set in motion. Later when Hippias saw himself losing his grip on power, he sought a military deal with the Far East superpower Persia. He managed to form this new alliance through the marriage of his daughter to the son of the tyrant of the city-state of Lampsakes whose name was Hippeklos. Hippeklos was able to arrange the meeting between Darius I King of Persia and Hippias.

Once the ruling families of Athens caught wind of Hippias proposed alliance with their arch-enemy Persia, the conspiracy against Hippias moved into high gear. In 510 B.C.E. Cleomenes I of Sparta, formed an alliance with certain Athenians, invaded Athens, and trapped Hippias inside the sacred grounds of the Acropolis. The invading forces captured members of Hippias family, namely his children. That year he was forced to flee Athens if he wanted the safe return of his children.

What happened next seemed to come from the pages of Greek mythology. The Spartans later turned against the Athenian ruling class because Sparta did not like the idea of a democratic government. Sparta viewed democracy as a threat to their ideology of tyranny. Spartan officials made secret contacts with the exiled leader Hippias, but Hippias had already escaped and made his way to the Persian capital of Susa. Persia gave him refuge and threatened to attack Athens if the aristocracy didn't immediately restore Hippias to the throne. Athens did not bulge despite Persia's fierce growl. Inspite of Persian support, it was recorded that Hippias still desired the collapse of Persia because of their domination of his homeland. Greeks were known to continuously fight each other, but, when it came to outside threats from the kingdom of Persia, the ancient Grecians, in most cases, united against their common foes. *(That has been the case since then until this very day.)* So, in the year of 510 B.C.E. the Peisistratus dynasty was officially over.

Hipparchus
(555 B.C.E.—514 B.C.E.)

Hipparchus *pronounced* Hip-par-chus was also the son Peisistratus. His eldest brother was named

Hippias. He was the statesman with a wise nature who governed by laws before Hipparchus murder. Now Hippias appointed his son as an archon and charged him adorning the city with figurines, erecting and dedicating an altar of twelve gods in the chief marketplace of Athens. Hippias also built a temple to the idol Apollo Pythius. In fact, when the works were complete Hippias son, whose name was the same as his grandfather, Peisistratus, was chosen to serve as the master of ceremonies.

On the other hand, his brother and co-regent Hipparchus was the wild one. He loved partying, music, poetry, drama, wine, all types of amusements, and lovemaking. It was noted that he summoned the famous poets Anacreon and Simonides to Athens for regular performances.

And it came to pass that Hipparchus's heart was hot with lust and he deeply desired a homosexual relationship with this man named Harmodius. Harmodius was known as a handsome man in the flower of his youth who was renown for his great beauty. The only problem was Harmodius was under the power of his lover named Aristogeiton, who was man of middle-class nobility. Harmodius did not want to become a part of love triangle. However, Hipparchus carnal lust for Harmodius grew day by day. He repeatedly attempted to initiate an intimate affair with him. Harmodius, being faithful to Aristogeiton, spurned his bribes and sexual advances. As this episode continued, Aristogeiton feared Hipparchus and began to mastermind a plot to slay him.

Meanwhile,Hipparchus feelings began to chance. Now, he could not restrain his anger against Harmodius for rejecting him, the co-regent of Athens. When the time of the Panathenic Festival came, Hipparchus became petty and used his influence to prevent Harmodius sister from being a basket carrier in the processions. In fact, he uttered a public insult against Harmodius calling him an effeminate man—*a flaming faggot*—during the festivities. Harmodius became enraged. After this, he and Aristogeiton moved the plot into high gear, paying accomplices to serve as spies and lookouts.

When the following Panathenaic Festivals in Acropolis came in the year of 514 B.C.E., the pair joined the procession route to keep track of Hippias and Hipparchus. Hippias stood at the end of the procession route while Hipparchus stood at the beginning spot. All the plotters stood by. One of the co-conspirators began to speak to Hippias to possibly deflect his attention. The others became paranoid, thinking a double-cross was in the works. Harmodius and Aristogeiton immediately broke through the procession and slew Hipparchus as he was arranging the procession by the Leocoreum. In return, Harmodius was immediately slain by the royal spearmen. Aristogeiton was captured then tortured until death.

Greece historians report that Aristogeiton survived lengthy torture sessions. In his last grasp of breath, he promised to provide Hippias with the names of co-conspirators if the remaining tyrant would shake his right hand to confirm the agreement. Hippias extend his hand to confirm the deathbed agreement. After tricking him, Aristogeiton laughed in his face and taunted him for shaking the hand of his brother's murderer. Hippias instantly smote him to death. Hippias, who was now the sole tyrant, became harsh and extremely bitter after this. He executed several Athenians, sentenced others to exile on abandoned islands, and ruled in deep suspicion of everyone around him until the Peisistratus dynasty came to an end in 510 B.C.E. .

Themistocles
524—462 B.C.E.

Themistocles, *pronounced* The-mis-to-cles whose name means *"Glory of the Law"*, was the son of Neocles, who was a poor man who lived outside the walls of Athens. He was raised up from the dust and dunghill after his birth in 524. Themistocles was known as a new breed of non-aristocratic politicians who rose to power in the early years of democracy. That new form of government provided each citizen of Athens with same amount of power, opportunities for public office, and equal treatment under the law. It could be said, *'Power belonged to the People'*. Each Athenian had the power of one vote to elect their representatives. In return, elected officials had to answer to the voters. This Greco rule-of-law was passed down to the Roman empire, Western Europe, and even to the United States of America. Democracy was one of the founding principles among the American Founding fathers. This proves that the influence of classic Grecce still impacts us everyday in the 21st century. This is why Athens is attributed as the birthplace of Western democracy, classical arts, and Gentile civilization. It has also been stated that America's Founding Fathers admired the ancient famous Greek general Themistocles. In fact, it was written that Thomas Jefferson compared John Adams to Themistocles, the Athenian statesman.

Themistocles was a populist. The common Grecians loved him and he was elected as an archon [magistrate] in 493. It was during this same time that Darius, the king of Persia, launched repeated attacks against Grecian interest in Asia Minor, and moved to invade the Grecian mainland. Themistocles convinced city officials that a major increase in naval warship production was needed. The Greeks had learned those maritime skills from the black Phoenicians and Egyptians who had sailed the Mediterranean and Aegean Seas for millenniums. Athens underwent a major shipbuilding campaign to build a fleet of 200 new ships to counter Persia's maritime advantage. When Persia invaded the mainland for the first time Themistocles, who was very young man, fought and won the victory at the Battle of Marathon. Again, he was also one the victorious generals who defeated the Persians at the Battle of Salamis by luring their fleet into the straits. This Greek victory came during Persia's second excursion under Xerxes I.

Themistocles battlefield fortunes had the negative effect of boosting his pride to new heights. Without the consent of the Athens magistrates or the Athenian people, he erected an elaborate temple for the goddess Artemis who was renown for her supposed love with other women goddesses. The Athenians rejected the female molten image Artemis as the chief deity of the Acropolis. Most Athenian men favored the statue named after the male figure Apollo who was considered the brother of Artemis. Both were considered the offspring of Zeus, the father of all deities within the pagan Grecian pantheon. To make matters worse, Themistocles erected the great structure near his home as if he was the high priest. Themistocles had already begun to boast of his military prowess and his role in those victories, especially his great exploits against the Persians. This new proud look caused the people of Athens to disfavor him. The Parthenon was the official shrine for the Athenians. This high place was dedicated to the pantheon of all Grecian deities. The gods of Olympus, Zeus, Apollo, Athena, and others were already located inside the sanctuary of the Delphi Oracle. This famed acropolis could not be replaced by Themistocles arrogancy.

While Themistocles grip on power was loosening, the kingdoms of Sparta and Athens sought temporary peaceful co-existence by signing a pact known as the Congress of Greece. This new agreement created an impartial body that would settle disputes between the chief city-states. Meanwhile inside Athens, Themistocles re-fortified the royal city as if he was in a state of war. That new move aroused hostility in Sparta, and both sides turned against the famed general. Sparta accused their chief general Pausanias of plotting to remove his own leader. Themistocles name was mentioned as a co-conspirator with the Spartan general Pausanias. Athens was already alienated by their leader's attitude and actions. So, in the year 473 or 472 the archons agreed to hand Themistocles over to the independent Congress of Greece tribunal. Themistocles fled into exile to Argos. The Spartans pursued him hoping to destroy him for his supposed participation with Pausanias. Someone had lied on the Spartan officer because he was later cleared of all charges. Nevertheless, Sparta still wanted Themistocles head on a platter. The Athenian general then fled to Argos and sought refuge with Alexander I of Macedon.

Once it was discovered that Themistocles was still on the Greek mainland all city-states who were signators of the Congress of Greece were obligated to arrest Themistocles so he could be summoned before the seat of judgement. Themistocles fled Greece in a ship bound for Asia Minor. Still fearing one of Sparta's allies could still detain him although he was hundreds of miles from the mainland, Themistocles volunteered to enter the service and protection of Persia as a paid mercenary under the monarch Artaxerxes I. Overjoyed to have a man of Themistocles caliber to defect to the side of the Achaemenids, he quickly appointed him to the governorship of Magnesia. Themistocles lived there for the rest of his life until he died of natural causes in 459.

Cimon
(510 B.C.E.—450 B.C.E.)

Cimon, *pronounced* Ci-mon, was the son of Mitiades. He was an Athenian statesman and strategos [general] who became the chief rival of his fellow Athenian Themistocles. He formed an alliance with Sparta. He was born into the ranks of nobility. His mother's name was Hegesipyle, the daughter of King Olorus, the ruler of Thrace. He married Isodice, who was the granddaughter of Megacles, a prominent member of the Athens-based Alcmaeonidae family. With Cimon's cooperation, Sparta actively conspired to remove Themistocles in favor of him. Although he was an Athenian, Cimon preferred Sparta's aristocracy rather than the democratic experimentation taking place in his own city-state. He, however, still fought shoulder-by-shoulder with Themistocles to turn back the Persian invasion of the mainland at the Battle of Salamis. At this time, many of the Grecian maritime cities around the Aegean Sea were happy to see the Persians defeated so they hastily switched their allegiance to Athens. This confederation became known as the Delian League. Because of his outstanding bravery against the forces of Xerxes I, Persia was decimated in the Battle of Salamis. Cimon was eventually promoted to the position of commander of the Delian League which was founded two years later in 478. This combination of Greek city-states based on the island of Delos, and led by Athens, united to counter the Persian onslaught. Under his leadership, Cimon created a powerful Grecian maritime fleet capable of challenging Persia on the high seas. After that, Cimon was appointed magistrate for nearly twenty years, from 480 to 461. The framework of Delian League called for Athens to supply commanders, access tributes to alliance states, and finance the war effort. The league achieved a major victory in 467-466 when Grecian forces drove out the Persian garrisons from Asia Minor and cleared their forces from the East Mediterranean Sea. This was one of Cimon's greatest military victories. The Persia's fleet and army were devastated in the battle on the Eurymedon River. After this, Cimon and the other leaders decided to move their new spoils from the Persia treasury back to Athens for security purposes. The spoils from the war were used to beautify and renovate the temples and thank the gods for their victory.

In 462, Cimon led an unsuccessful expedition to support Sparta against its lower-class majority known as the helots. Athens nobility did not support Cimon's policy and turned against him. Nevertheless, one positive aspect from Cimon's new approach was the temporary city-state unity. It actually was a precursor of the eventual rise of the Macedonian empire that would later unite all city-states during the next century. But in 461, Pericles accused Cimon of secretly working as an agent for Sparta and Macedonia. Cimon then sought allies with other neighboring city-states who favored aristocratic rulership. Nevertheless, his actions led to serious charges, his ouster, and a sentence of ten years in exile. Before he could complete his prison term, both of his arch-enemies Athens and Sparta, recalled him in 451 B.C.E. They both needed his counsel on brokering a five-year peace agreement. After returning home, he was slain in a fierce naval battle against Persia in 449. Meanwhile, Sparta did not like playing second fiddle to Athens, so the two city-states continued to struggle over mainland dominance.

Cleisthenes
(506 B.C.E.)

Cleisthenes, *pronounced* Cleis-the-nes, was born in approximately 570 B.C.E.. He was named after his maternal grandfather, Cleisthenes, the tyrant of the city of Sicyon. Cleisthenes was the son of Megacles and Agariste. He was a member of the influential Alcmaeonid family who were the city rulers. After growing up, Cleisthenes became one of the conspirators against the tyrant Hippias. After Hippias downfall, he and a man named Isagoras, who was a former ally in the treachery against Hippias, became rivals to fill the power vacuum in Athens. Isagoras and his supporter prevailed by persuading Cleomenes I, king of Sparta to assist in expelling Cleisthenes. Isagoras plot succeeded and he became the chief authority in Athens. He called for a mass expulsion of hundreds of Athenians whom he said were cursed by the gods. Isagora then dissolved the Boule, which was the council of citizens appointed to operate the daily affairs of the city-state. The citizen's council resisted Isagoras high-handed tactics and a mass revolt against him broke out. Isagoras and his supporters were forced to flee to the sacred shrines in Acropolis to save their lives. The mob pursued them and laid a 2-day siege against the disposed leader, but somehow, he was able to escape on the third day. Afterwards, the citizens of Athens summoned Cleisthenes back to the royal city and crowned him the new head of state. Realizing that the people were responsible for his resurrection to power, Cleisthenes immediately initiated reforms, sharing power with all segments of the population. As the redeemed Athenian statesman he served as the archon [magistrate] from 525 to 524 where he continued to advocate sharing power through democratic principles. This is why he is regarded as the father of Western democracy. Under his rule, the Greek constitution was reformed and the rights of commoners were equalized with the Athenian noble families and their clans.

The legacy of Cleisthenes is still remembered today in the United States. A sculptured head bust of him stands on the grounds of the Ohio Statehouse in Columbus.

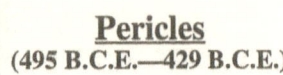
Pericles
(495 B.C.E.—429 B.C.E.)

Pericles ,*pronounced* Per-i-cles, the son of Xanthippus, grew to become an Athenian general and statesman. He was related to the influential Alcmaeonids who became largely responsible for the full development of Athenian democracy and the Athenian empire. He ascended to power sometimes after 461 and quickly implemented more democratic reforms than his predecessor Cleisthenes.

In foreign policy Pericles asserted Athenian control over Delian League and used the league's combined resources to rebuild the Acropolis which had been ransacked by the Persians. The Acropolis was located in Athens and considered one of the most impressive monuments of ancient Greek culture. Inside the Acropolis was the Pantheon which was a shrine dedicated to goddess Athena and all the other gods of the people.

His influential mistress Aspasia bore him a son outside of wedlock. However, his two sons by his wife died at a young age. In 447-446 Athens lost control of the city of Megara. This defeat gave their rival Sparta access to the enclave of Attica. Eventually Athens and Sparta signed a Thirty-Year peace agreement the following year in 446-445. During this time Pericles built the famed Long Wall which extended from Athens to the port of Piraeus. This wall protected the empire from foreign invaders. Fourteen year later in 431, another war with Artaxerxes I king of Persia broke out again. During this three decade war, Pericles relied on the Athenian naval fleet to continuously restock the city with essential supplies as the war raged. Athens fought hard and won. During this time Attica was once again brought under their sphere of its influence. As the war raged, the Grecian republic of Boeotia, which had revolted from Athens in 447, sided with Persia against the Athenians at the Battle of Deluim in 424.

Still, Pericles strategy saved the empire from the Persian invasion. However, the countryside in its rear was left exposed to Spartan and Boeotian League meddling and pillaging. In the latter part of his reign, a plague broke in Athens which killed twenty-five percent of the city's residents. The city's nobility blamed Pericles for the crisis, charging him with a fine and exiling him from the royal city. Several years later he was allowed to return and re-elected as a statesman. His reign was then cut short when he too became a victim of the plague still raging in the city. The city officials of Athens sponsored a great funeral ceremony and procession for Pericles. People from throughout Athens and surrounding areas came out overwhelmingly to pay their last respects to the father of Athenian democracy and **the Golden [Brass] Age of Athens.**

Cleon
(429 B.C.E.)

Cleon was an Athenian politician who was a first from among the merchant class. He emerged as the successor after the death of his arch enemy Pericles. Cleon was known as a hardliner who advocated Athens taking the offensive in the war against Persia during the Peloponnesian conflict. In the Athens conflict with Mytilene, he proposed that all its men be put to death, and their women and children enslaved for their roles in the rebellion against Athens. His proposal passed the citizen assembly, but the legislation was overturned the following day.

Cleon reached his pinnacle of fame when he captured the Spartan island of Sphacteria, only to be slain shortly thereafter in another conflict while fighting the Spartans while trying to retake parts of Thrace.

Alcibiades
(450 B.C.E.—404 B.C.E.)

Alcibiades, *pronounced* Al-ci-ba-a-des, was a descendant of Eurysaces, the son of Ajax. His mother was of the Alcmaeonid family whose name was Dinomache, the daughter of Megacles. He was born in 450 B.C.E. to a father who was an experienced and famed charioteer who served in the national war against Persia. His father was regarded as a mighty man of valor who fought in the sea battle at Artemisium. As the Thirty Year War raged on, he was eventually slain in the battle of Coronea. His two comrades, Pericles and his brother Ariphon, the sons of Xanthippus, adopted the orphan boy Alcibiades. Alcibiades was placed in boarding school under Socrates, the famed father of Western philosophical thought. Young Alcibiades was known as a beautiful little boy whose physique and natural vigor blossomed with age, even from his youth, into his teens, to manhood. This made young Alcibiades well-known and vulnerable to the fetishes of the men of Athens whose number one sexual passion and appetite was for adolescent boys. Even Ariphon wanted Alcibiades to be his child lover, but his brother Pericles convinced him not to pursue the lad. At that time pedophilia was a common and accepted way of life. Once he became a grown man, Alcibiades was reported to became a whorish homosexual with countless lovers.

Alcibiades conduct became the center of focus during the 399 B.C.E. trial against Socrates. Socrates was accused of corrupting young boys, like as Alcibiades, who had been under his supervision, causing them to question their loyalty to the Athenian government. Regardless of the soul-searching in Athens and the execution of Socrates, the old era of the classic Athenian empire was completed and the new era of Sparta hegemony was emerging.

AgisI, II, III, IV (The Name of 4 Spartan Kings)
(427 B.C.E.—359 B.C.E.)

According to Greek legend, Agis I was the first king of Sparta. He was the son of Eurydthenes and considered the first monarch of the dynasty that flourished in the 11th century B.C.E.. Again, according to Greek mythology, Agis I was the son of one of the twin dynasties who founded Sparta. His reign lasted only 1 year and he was succeeded by his son Echestratus. The 4th century Greek historian Ephorus wrote Agis I captured the city of Helos in Lacone, reducing the city to serfdom. Since then most of the kings of Spartan dynasty were named Agis, in his honor, as his successor. The order in which the four kings named Agis appear in Greek history are not in a consecutive sequence. Although all of their names—Agis I, Agis II, Agis III, and Agis IV—are the same, their actual lives were centuries apart.

Agis II
(427 B.C.E.—400 B.C.E.)

Agis II was the eldest son of Archidamus II by his first wife. He succeeded his father on the Spartan throne. He came to power in 427 B.C.E. as one of the commanders of operation for the Spartan regular army during most of the Peloponnesian War against Athens. He reigned for 28 years and a few months. In 418 while the Peace of Niclas was in effect, Agis II broke the agreement by invading the territory of Athens's ally, Argos, with the intention of invading Attica. After defeating the city, he made a truce and withdrew after cutting off the Argos army from its city. The Spartan aristocracy became angry with Agis because of his peace agreement with the Argos generals. Some of the officials wanted his house destroyed along with a fine of 100,000 drachmas. In the end they agreed to appoint a supervisory war council of 10 Spartans to determine strategy for the city-state. After this a series of earthquakes prevented any further advances. The following year Agis finally led his army into the city-state of Tegea, and continued on to the city of Mantineia. Agis developed a strategy to flood the lands of Mantinea. His plan worked. The army of Mantinea were drawn into a great battle where they were defeated. As the battle continued, their ally in Athens was also brought down to the ground. Sparta was totally victorious. This particular conflict known as the Battle of Mantinea has been regarded as one of the most important battles between the warring Grecian city-states.

In 413, another round of conflict began against Athens and Attica while Alcibiades was the ruler. Agis II and his powerful general Lysander led a force that once again occupied parts of Athens, causing severe hardship inside the city. In 404, it was General Lysander who was accredited with winning Sparta's final victory against Athens. Agis took no part in the peace settlement with Athens. Shortly afterwards in 401, war broke put again. This time with the city-state of Elis. Agis II forced the city-state to surrender and sue for peace. After this, the gravity of the Peloponnesian War eventually changed towards Asia. General Lysander became more powerful after the destruction of Athens. Within Sparta, however, paranoia and a conspiracy against Agis developed. His co-regent Pausanias was accused of treason, but he was later acquitted during a trial.

Later that year Agis II fell sick after returning from a thanksgiving sacrifice in the pagan shrine known as Delphi. The shrine housed all the image-gods of Greece, including Zeus, Apollo, Gaea, Pythos, and several others. He was at the city of Heraea in the province of

Arcadia when the mysterious ailment struck. A few days later he died as his entourage reached Sparta. He was buried in Sparta with a funeral that included unprecedented pomp, pageantry, and ceremonies.

In death, Agis II was survived by his son named Leotychides who was supposed to succeed him. However, there were questions about his birthright. What happened was Alcibiades, who was a playboy, once lived in Sparta while exiled from Athens. It was believed that Alciades slept with Agis's wife Timaea and fathered Leotychides. Once Agis discovered the treachery he sent his bodyguard Astyochus to slay Alciades. It was believed Queen Timaea was the one who tipped off Alciades, thus saving his adulterous life. The warning gave him the opportunity to flee the city before Agis II could have his head placed on a silver platter.

Socrates, the Philosopher, a Dirty Old Man

While in boarding school even Socrates became awe struck by Alciades physical beauty and spent personal time with him. It was said, Socrates believed Alcibiades possessed intellectual promise as well as physical beauty. As the head of a philosophy school Socrates had multiple relationships with several of his students and could not give Alcibiades his sole commitment. Both would later serve together in the Peloponnesian War, saving each other's lives on the battlefield.

(By today's standards Socrates would be regarded as a child molester and a dirty old man—think about it. An older man operating an all-boys school and having sexual relations with the students would be considered child molestation in the 21st century. This still remains a common practice among several European, Middle Eastern, Asian, and African countries. Even so-called black people in America have been found guilty of this abhorrent conduct. Peophilia remains to be a sexual and spiritual crime, even a sin, according to the law of YAH given to HIS servant Moses in Leviticus, chapter eighteen, as I pointed out earlier.)

By 420 he had become a commanding general who was known as brilliant, but an unscrupulous politician. In 415 he was on a foreign expedition in Sicily when he received orders to return to Athens. Once home he was placed on trial and charged with sacrilege for mutilating the great images of Hermes. However, he fled to Sparta for refuge. While there he assisted his once arch-rival Sparta against his own city-state Athens. The Spartans, nevertheless, still did not trust Alcibiades. From Sparta he fled into Asia Minor into the safe haven of Darius II, king of Persia.

For a while he switched sides and assisted Persia against his homeland, but an Athenian fleet eventually rescued him. He then switched sides again, directing Athens in new victories from 411 to 408. These new victories made him a national hero but his enemies would never allow him to live down his treachery. He was forced to flee again. This time he fled to Thrace. Hoping to still find favor back in Athens, he warned Athens of the danger building up against them at the Battle of Aegospotami. He eventually fled Thrace for a sanctuary in Phrygia. Left alone as a refugee, Sparta attempted to track him down and murder him for his previous treason against their city-state.

In 405-404 in the Battle of Aegospotami, Sparta won a naval victory over Athens in the final battle of the Peloponnesian War. The Spartans, led by General Lysander, surprised the Athens naval force at the anchor off the coast of Aegospotami in Thrace, destroyed their fleet, and cutting off their food supplies. The Athens naval fleet escaped with only 20 of its 180 ships. The Spartans then put over 4,000 Athenians to death. After this the Spartans marched on Athens, encircled the royal city, and forced the Athenians to surrender. Although Alcibiades had fled Athens, the Spartans tracked him down and conspired to have him murdered. In 403 Sparta allowed Athens to rebuild and once again establish self-rule.

 Socrates

Agesilaus II King of Sparta
(444 B.C.E.—360 B.C.E.)

Agesilaus II, *pronounced* A-ge-si-la-us, was born into the Euryponid family in 444 B.C.E. He was the son of king Archidamus II and his second wife Eupoieia. He was the brother of Cynisca, the first woman in ancient Greece to win an Olympic victory. Ironically, he was the younger half-brother of his predecessor Agis II. After the death of Agis II he assumed the mantle of leadership. Agesilaus came to power unexpectedly in his mid-40s with the assistance of his comrade General Lysander. The general was his manipulative confidant throughout most of his reign, and in fact, Agesilaus had been his homosexual child lover since he was a 12-year-old. As a child Lysander too had also been molested while growing up in poverty. The Spartan constitution sanctioned those types of same sex erotic relationships which were believed to be controlled by the idol Eros, the deity of sexual pleasure and perverseness. It was also believed that the Spartan constitution was written by the idol Lycurgus who issued a decree legalizing men [erastes]- boys [eromenos] sex. Therefore this carnal practice was common among Greeks. Although their male-male affair continued after Agesilaus began his rulership, it did not prevent Agesilaus from maintaining firm control over Spartan politics. Eventually the two fell out with each other.

Born in Cyrenaica which is now known as Libya, he was very small in statue, lame in one leg, and uncomely from birth, but he had a giant mind. He was regarded as a great leader of guerilla warfare who came to power during the suppression of the conspiracy by Cinacon in 398. After that quick victory, he crossed over into Asia Minor with 2,000 freed servants, 6,000 allies which included 30 other Spartan leaders who fought with him to liberate the Greek cities from Persia's grip. During this expedition he captured immense amounts of gold and silver as his forces trampled Phrygia, Lydia, Sardes, and other smaller cities on the Black Sea.

In the spring of 396, Agesilaus wanted to celebrate his good fortune by hosting a sacrificial ceremony at Aulis, which was in Boetia. The sacrifice was an offering to the idol-god Agamemnon requesting safe passage across the Aegean Sea. The site was well chosen because in Greek legend it was the place where the Spartan King Agamemnon had once sacrificed before winning the Battle of Troy. This time reality changed things. The Boetian coalition leaders from Thebes disrespected Agesilaus by interrupting the ceremony. Agesilaus never forgave the Thebians for this public insult.

In Greek mythology the idol-god Agamemnon was believed to be the son of the idol name Atreus. The idol was superstitiously believed to be the brother of a statue named Menelaus. The graven image was considered to be the king of Mycenae and the commander of Greek forces that attacked Troy. Agamemnon was worshipped as the male sculpture alongside a female figure named Clytemnestra, who was regarded as a goddess. It was believed that these two idols gave birth to three children gods named Oresles, a boy, and three girl idols named Iphigeneia, Electra, and Chrysothemis.

In Hebrew culture this Grecian belief system and pagan worshipping of man-made statues and graven images was forbidden and regarded as spiritual darkness and DIVINE error. The prophet **Isaiah** spoke of this in **chapter 44** verses **9** through **20**: It reads:

"The makers of idols all work to no purpose; And the things they treasure can do no good, as they themselves can testify: They neither look nor think, and so they shall be shamed; They are craftsmen, they are merely human. Let them all assemble and stand up! They are cowed, and they shall be shamed. The craftsmen in iron, with his tools work it over charcoal and fashions it by hammering, working with the strength of his arm. Should he go hungry, his strength ebb; Should he drink no water he would grow faint. The craftsman in wood measures with a line and marks out a shape with a stylus; he forms it with scraping tools, marking it out with a compass he gives it a human form, the beauty of a man to dwell in a shrine. For his use he cuts down cedars, he chooses plane trees and oaks. He sets aside trees of the forest or plant firs and the rain [from YAH] makes them grow. All

this serves man for fuel; he takes some to warm himself and he builds a fire and bakes bread. He also makes a god of it and worships it. Fashions an idol and bows down to it! Part of it he burns in a fire: On that part he roasts meat he eats the roast and is sated; He also warms himself and cries, "Ah, I am warm I can feel the heat!" Of the rest he makes a god—his own craving! He bows down to it, worships it; He prays to it and cries, "Save me, for you are my god!" They have not wit or judgement: Their eyes are besmeared; and they see not; Their minds and they cannot think. They do not give thought, they lack the wit and judgement to say: Part of it I burned in the fire; I also baked bread on the coals, I roasted meat and ate it— Should I make the rest an abhorrence? Should I bow to a block of wood?" He pursues ashes! A deluded mind has led him astray, and he cannot save himself. He never says to himself, the thing in my hand is a fraud!"

As you can see YAH revealed to the prophet Isaiah that the nations of people like the Egyptians, Babylonians, Persians, Assyrians, Canaanites, Greeks and others, were, and continue to be, idol-worshipper who are spiritually filthy, mentally deluded, and physically distracted by a fatal attraction to man-made objects, doctrines, and unholy practices. This is why YAH commanded the nation of Israel at Mount Sinai in the book of **Exodus chapter 20 verses 4 and 5:** *"You shall not make for yourself a sculptured image, or any likeness of what is in heaven above, or on the earth below, or in the waters under the earth. You shall not bow down to them or serve them."*

"Their idols are silver and gold, the work of men's hands. They have mouths but cannot speak, eyes, but cannot see, they have ears but cannot hear, noses, but cannot smell; they have hands but cannot touch, feet, but cannot walk; they can make no sound in their throats. Those who fashion them, all who trust in them, shall become like them [**spiritually dead**],"the ancient Hebrew psalmist wrote in **Psalms 115: 4-8.**

Therefore it is safe to say that the modern world today is still in a state of spiritual error just like the nations of the ancient world whom I mentioned earlier. We must keep in mind the spiritual errors of these various nations of people as we continue to walk through the annals of time according to the revelation that YAH showed to the prophet Daniel.

Now, lets return our focus back to the defiled life of Agesilaus. As king of Sparta, he presided over the decline and eventual fall of the city-state empire in the year 359 B.C.E. In the late 4th century, Sparta reigned as the preeminent city-state on the Greece mainland. During that era, Agesilaus was the commander of the Spartan army from 404 to 371.

After returning home from his Persian expedition, he moved offensively against the Boeotian League which comprised the city-states of Thebes, Orchomenus, Argos, and Corinth, thus provoking a twelve-year conflict from 395 to 387B.C.E. which became known as the Corinthian War. Sparta reigned supreme until the outbreak of that war. On one side you had the confederation of Athens, Argos, Thebes, and Corinth. On the opposing side, stood the city-state empire of Sparta. A series of battles ended in a stalemate. Sparta's dominion, however, continued for another 16 years until the city-state finally suffered a defeat at Leuctra in 371. This caused Sparta's wealth and influence to begin to wane. During the chaos Thebes was also weakened because it had also exhausted its manpower and treasure in its decade-long conflict with Sparta. In 362 Thebes and Sparta fought their final fight at the Battle of Mantinea. Thebes was able to thwart Agesilaus aggression, but their leader General Epaminondas was slain in conflict. Sparta lost territory in central Greece during that time. Those combined losses marked the decline of Sparta's hegemony. Two years later in 360 Agesilaus died at the age of 84 while returning from a mercenary mission in Egypt.

Phillip II King of Macedon
(359 B.C.E.—336 B.C.E.)

Phillip II was born in Pella, Macedon in 382 as the son of a man named Amyntas III and Eurydice I his mother. He was a descendant of the Argead dynasty, a people who traced their origins back to the island of Argos and the mythological god Hercules, who according to Greek religion was the son of Zeus. During his childhood, his city-state Macedon engaged in war against the city-state of Thebes. In midst of the conflict, young Phillip was taken captive by King Epaminondas of Thebes who treated him with respect by sending him to military and diplomatic school while in his custody. Nevertheless the royalty of Thebes, like those in other Grecian city-states, allowed man-boy [erastes-eromenos] sexual relationships. It was during this three year stay Phillip became the child lover [eromenos] of the commander named Pelopidas [erastes]. The erastes was the adult pursuer while the child was termed the eromenos.

While in Thebes his two older brothers, Perdiccas III and Alexander II, were slain. Perdiccas lost his life in a war against the city-state of Illyria. During this power vacuum Phillip returned home. The officials in Macedon appointed Phillip as the co-regent with his nephew Amyntas IV, who happened to be the young son of his slain brother Perdiccas III. Phillip, however, muscled his way into power and brought much needed experience and military skills to the Macedon table. By 359 B.C.E. Phillip seized the throne and came to power at the age of 23. He initially promoted peace among various Grecian city-states using this time for a military buildup. Up until this point, Macedon had always been regarded as the barbaric, primitive, backwards, lower-caste city-state when compared to other localities such as Athens or Sparta. Phillip changed that. He transformed the Macedon army into a great fighting machine. In fact, Macedon was under attack on several fronts when he came to power: the eastern portion of Macedon had been invaded by Thrace and Paion. Meanwhile, the city-state Athens sent a naval fleet against Macedon under the command of Argeus, who was a Macedon turncoat.

Phillip, a brilliant military strategist, disarmed Thebes and Paion by promising them tribute. This gave him time, resources, and opportunity to concentrate on a strategy against Athens. In one of his first confrontations with Athens, Phillip crushed 3,000 Athenian mercenaries. Being innovative, Phillip introduced new helmets and gear, a tactical war strategy consisting of a eight-man deep formation of heavily armed infantrymen standing shoulder to shoulder. He also developed a corps of engineers who constructed towers and catapults as a part of his advanced siege weaponry strategy. (Phillip borrowed these advanced military tactics from the ancient black Mesopotamians and Egyptians who had practiced those maneuvers millenniums earlier. These ancient techniques of the Afro-Asiatic world had now begun to reach Europe. Thanks to the Persians, Egyptians, Phoenicans, and other black nations who exported their ideas and know-how to the continent that one day would become known as Europe.)

In 358/357 B.C.E. Phillip warred against Bardyllis, the Illyrian king of Dardania although he had married the ruler's great-granddaughter. That union did not stop his declaration of war against the city-state. Historians recorded the conflict as a ferocious battle where 7,000 Illyrian soldiers were slain. After winning that major war Phillip established himself as the major leader of the Grecian mainland. Several other city-states joined into a Macedon confederation. This included Neoptolemus I, king of the city-state Epirus where Phillip married the princess Olympius, who eventually became the mother of Alexander the Great. By 356 Phillip military rampage became known as the Sacred War.

After those earlier victories, Phillip now possessed important lands, including the Athenian colony of Amphipolis where there was a forest with tall trees for shipbuilding and mineral-rich Mount Paragon. Phillip made a strategic deal with famed Athens, who had long controlled that valuable and strategic territory in exchange of the gold mines inside Mount Paragon. In exchange Phillip would receive the port-city of Pydna. Athens later declared war against Macedon after Phillip reneged on his promise and repossessed the valuable real estate.

Phillip then formed an alliance with the Chalcidian League of Olynthus. Afterwards, he ransacked the city of Polidaea and returned it to the Chalcidian League. In 356, the Macedon warrior-king conquered the gold-rich city of Crenides and renamed it Phillippi in honor of himself. He placed a large military battalion in the city to control gold production. This new wealth provided him with more cashflow to further his military conquests. Phillip had spent plenty of private time with princess Olympius who was now a queen of Macedon. She gave birth to Alexander in 356. Meanwhile Phillip's good fortune continued that year. He received reports that his racehorse was the victor in the Olympic Games and his army was continuing to crush their adversaries. The following year in 355/354, Phillip moved against Methone, the last Athenian ally on the Gulf of Therma. Phillip conquered the city, but, lost one of his eyes in the process. Athens intervened in the Methone-Macedon war by sending two naval fleets. That help was too little too late. The Macedon forces kept marching, subduing the cities of Abdere and Maronea along the Thracian coastline. At this point Phillip's army was on a roll, moving to consolidate the entire mainland. He even trampled Thessaly in the summer of 353. Thessaly proved to be a difficult nut to crack. It took several battles to secure a victory. This victory didn't come until the following year in 352. Phillip came with an army of 20,000 infantry and 3,000 horsemen. This conflict became known as the Battle of Crocus, a bloody scene. More than 5,000 were slain on the Thessaly side. 3,000 of them became prisoners of war and drowned.

After this victory Phillip became a renown leader. Several cities surrendered without war. This included Pherae and Pagasae. Only the two principal cities of Athens and Sparta stood in the way of bringing central Greece under his dominion. The next war came in 349 when Macedon attacked the city of Olynthus. Its ruler had switched sides and formed an alliance with Athens against Phillip. Phillip finally secured that victory the following year. Afterwards, he burned the city to the ground. That was the fate of all the other Grecian cities on the Chalcidian Peninsula who opposed his rule.

In 347 Phillip was marching again. This time the Macedon monarch warred against the city-state Hibrus. In 346 he used his powerful influence to end a war between Thebes and Phocia. After this, the hierarchy in Athens proposed a peace treaty with Macedon. The peace treaty was signed and ratified in Thessaly. With Athens now under his control, Phillip turned his attention towards Sparta. Phillip sent Sparta a message:"If I win this war you will be slaves forever. I will destroy your farms, slay your people, and raze your city." Sparta replied: "IF." For some unexplained reason Phillip chose not to attack Sparta. His forces withdrew. By 345, the Macedon war machine was grinding again. This time he laid seige to the city of Ardiaioi. Although he secured a hard fought victory, he was injured again. This time in his lower right leg. This did not stop him from moving northwards against Scythia, conquering the city of Eurnolpia and renaming it Philippopolis [*Phi-lip-pop-o-lis*] in honor of himself. Phillip began to view himself as the reincarnation of the sun-god Apollo. This was the second time a city was established where a cult-statue was commissioned to glorify the works of Phillip's hands.

Like a leopard on the prowl, the Macedon predator laid seige to Perinthus in 340. The following year in 339 he attacked the city of Byzantium. These two cities, however, resisted his conquest. This did not resolve Phillip's bloody appetite for fresh prey.

By 338 war broke out again. Phillip fought against the combined forces of Thebes and Athens in the Battle of Chaeronea. This victory propelled Phillip to the position of head of all Greece, except Sparta. He compelled the majority of the remaining neutral city-states to join him in the League of Corinth. Grecia was now one united kingdom for the first time in its existence as an Aryan nation. Grecia was now ready to challenge the authority of the Persian empire in Asia Minor. However, there was one major problem that stood between Phillip and challenging Persia: at the capital-city of Aegae there was infighting among his royal officials.

It was autumn of 336 in the month of October. All the Macedonian royalty had gathered in the capital for the marriage celebration of Alexander I, the ruler of Epirus, to Phillip's daughter Cleoparta. Now Cleoparta was the daughter of Phillip from his fourth wife Olympias. She was also the sister of Alexander III, who would later become known as *"The Great"*.

According to Greek historical sources such as the 16th book of Diodorus and the Aristotle report, Phillip's heart was merry and full of joy. He entered the townsquare to mix and mingle among the crowd of government officials, townspeople, and friends who were in attendance. Like a scene from the murder of Lee Harvey Oswald by Jack Ruby, the bodyguard Pausanias, who was one of the king's top seven security officials, stepped forward and stabbed Phillip II. The celebration had become a murder scene. Outside the gates of Aegae, Pausanias had co-conspirators with horses stationed nearby waiting for him to flee the murder scene. Pausanias wasn't so fortunate. He never reached the city's gates. Three of the king's bodyguards were also nearby. They immediately chased him. As Pausanias fled, he tripped up on a vine. He was immediately slain.

There were two accounts for the cause for Phillip's death. One account given is by the historian Cleitarchus who said that Phillip and Pausanias had been homosexual lovers. But Phillip had turned his attention to a younger man whose name so happened to be Pausanias as well. This infuriated the older Pausanias, so he began to verbally abuse the king's younger male lover. The young Pausanias couldn't endure the taunts from the older man so he committed suicide. However, the young homosexual was well connected and he had a government official friend named General Attalus who became angry at what the older gentleman had done. Attalus plotted by arranging to have dinner with the elder Pausanias and got him funky drunk then sodomized him. After sobering up, Pausanias sought the audience of King Phillip demanding that formal rape charges be brought against Attalus. Attalus, however, was very influential. He was like family to the king. He had arranged the marriage of his young niece Cleopatra Eurydice to Phillip. Politically speaking, the king needed ruthless Attalus expertise. He was planning to send Attalus on a mission in preparation for an impending Persian confrontation. Therefore Phillip decided against any type of formal reprimand of Attalus. Instead he hoped to appease the anger of Pausanias by promoting him into his inner security circle. This was a fatal mistake because it only gave Pausanias closer access to the king, and in fact, he began to blame the king for what had happened to him. While Attalus was on the foreign expedition in Asia Minor, Pausanias set in motion and carried out his bloody plan.

The second possible reason for the assassination of King Phillip II was the fact that Phillip had recently fell deeply in love with this younger beautiful woman named Cleoparta Eurydice. This new romance angered both Alexander and his mother Olympias who wanted her son to be king. To make matters worse, at the wedding banquet, which was Phillip's seventh marriage, his army general Attalus raised his cup of wine and invoked the name of the gods of Macedon to make the child from this new union the eventual heir to the throne. Phillip was so drunk he didn't realize or fully pay attention to the toast. However, both Alexander and his mother Olympias were furious over the gesture. A big argument broke out in midst of ceremony. Phillip punished both of them for their public disrespect, temporarily exiling his wife Olympias back to her native city Epirus while Alexander fled to Illyria. This is why some historians contend that, maybe, the mother and son may have had a hand in the plot with Pausanias against their own loved one. Ironically, on the same night of Phillip's death, Olympias and Alexander returned from exile. It has been reported by the historian Justin that Olympias placed a crown on the corpse of Pausanias and erected a burial memorial where she offered annual sacrifices in his honor. Olympias also arranged for the execution of the rival queen Cleoparta Eurydice and son Caranus. Her son Alexander immediately seized the throne of Macedon.

 ## Alexander III "The Great" King of Macedon
(356 B.C.E.—323 B.C.E.)

Alexander III [the Greek *meaning* of his name was ["**protector of men.**"] was born with a silver spoon in his mouth on July 20 in 356 B.C.E. in the capital city Pella to the royal parents of King Phillip II of Macedon and his fourth wife Olympias of Epirus. He was a member of the Aegean dynasty. According to ancient Greek history, the biographer Plutarch reported the following concerning the birth of Alexander: On the eve of the consummation of her marriage to Phillip, his mother Olympias dreamed that her womb had been struck by a thunderbolt that caused a flame that spread far and wide before dying out. Plutarch also reported that a short period afterwards, Phillip also dreamed a dream, and in his vision, the king saw himself placing a seal engraved with a lion's image on Olympias's womb. To the Greek oraculars, these dreams meant Alexander was born as a divine being, the son of the god Zeus. In Greek theology Zeus was viewed as the principal deity and the revered image [sacred post] among all Grecians.

As a young lad, he was raised like all Macedonian nobility. He was cared for by a nurse named Lanika who was the sister of the man who became the famous general Cleitus the Black. Growing up, he was taught by one of his mother's relatives Leonidus who was a strict disciplinarian. By the age of 13, he had been inducted into a boarding school under the instructions of Aristotle. Alexander's father, King Phillip, had razed the city of Stageira during his conquest of Greece. Stageria was the hometown of the Grecian wise man Aristotle. Phillip struck a deal with the famed philosopher promising to totally rebuild the city, repopulate it, and grant freedom to their citizens in slavery in exchange for teaching his son Alexander. Of course, Aristotle agreed. The classroom was within the chambers of the Temple of Nymphs at Meza. There he learned to read, write, play the lyre, ride and train horses, wrestle and fight, and hunt. Other boarding school classmates were future generals Ptolemy and Cassander. It was during this stage of his life that Alexander began to display courage and wit. His next step as a 16-year-old teenager was cadet training under General Lysimachus.

Alexander's lifelong friend named Hephaestion also attended boarding school with him. It has been reported that Alexander and Hephastion lived double lives as homosexual lovers before their marriage to women. Historians also point out that it was possible for two young men of roughly the same age to be sexually involved without their relationship being frowned upon. In Macedonia and throughout Greece it was a common practice for adolescent Royal Pages who were groomed in boarding schools to have intimate relationships with each other as well as with the king, princes, and his mighty men. Friendships and sexual affairs were common among the men, women, and children of this nation. In the Alexander Romance tales it was written: *"one day when Alexander was 15 years old sailing with Hephaestion his friend, he easily reached Pisa and went off to stroll with Hephaestion."*

By the age of 16, Alexander was being groomed for the throne of Macedonia. The short, stocky fair-skinned crown-prince served as the regent on the throne while his father Phillip was away on military expeditions. In 340 while Phillip was away laying seige to Perinthus the Thracians revolted, hoping to recover land from Macedonia it had loss in earlier confrontations. Alexander hastily summoned his standing army and drove the invaders from their territory. After defeating them, he secured the territory and moved displaced Greeks into the new city he founded named Alexandropolis. Once Phillip returned, he commanded Alexander to launch another offensive against Thrace and subdue it once and for all. After this, battle-hardened Alexander joined his father in the war against Perinthus. During this seige, Phillip almost lost his life, but Alexander saved him. After that, Phillip and Alexander also successfully fought wars against Illyria, Thermopylae, Elatea, Amphissa, Chaeronea, and Corinth..

For the next two years, crown prince Alexander and King Phillip II were riding side-by-side. In the Battle of Chaeronea, Phillip assembled a massive force of 30,000 against the united front of Athens, Achaea, and Thebes whose forces numbered over 35,000. Phillip, who had suffered a serious injury in previous battles, had to assign 18-year-old Alexander to the position of assistant general alongside other veteran generals. Alexander and the veteran commanders were outnumbered, yet, they defeated their foes using superior tactics and formations. The August 2, 338 victory propelled Phillip to the status of "chief commander of all Greece". Macedonian garrisons were placed throughout Greece to maintain control. Phillip used his new influence to call for a Greek unity gathering in the city of Corinth which was known as the League of Corinth. Alexander was next to his father when he was crowned Hegemon 'Supreme Commander' of the league. Phillip, the king of Greece, then announced his grand vision to attack Persia in Asia Minor and free the Grecian colonies from their dominion. Alexander was present at that Hellenic gathering and clearly understood all of his father's ambitions to free the isles of the Gentiles from centuries of brown-skinned Shemitic Persian subjugation. Philip, however, was assassinated in less than two years after that historic Corinthian meeting. Crown Prince Alexander would have to be the Macedonian leader to carry out the Aryan crusade against the Persians in Asia.

When the news of Phillip's sudden death reached foreign capitals many of them revolted, including Thebes, Athens, Thessaly, and the city-state of Thrace. Alexander had already quickly seized control as the new king and quickly extinguished all of those external threats. The army of Thessaly surrendered to Macedonia again after Alexander routed them at the passageway that crossed between Mount Olympus and Mount Ossa. Alexander accepted their surrender and added their cavalry to his mighty army. From there Alexander continued down south heading towards the Peloponnese Peninsula, stopping in Thermopylae where he was recognized as the leader of the Grecian city-states. Moving swiftly, Alexander and his army continued to the city-state Corinth, the very same city-state where his father King Phillip II had been crowned "Hegemon"—Supreme Leader only two years earlier. This time it was young King Alexander of Macedonia who was assuming the title of the *"Hegemon"* and appointed the commander of the war against Persia. Before launching an offensive against the Achaemenian Persian empire, Alexander launched several surprise frontal assaults against all northern opposition, starting with Thrace, Illyria, and Taulanti. After this, Alexander received reports of southern revolts in Thebes and Athens. Alexander demolished Thebes by burning it to the ground. Athens surrendered and accepted Alexander as leader of all Greece. With the Grecian mainland now secure, Alexander, the Aryan, finalized his plans to set out for conquest of the ancient black world of Africa and Asia.

Alexander then appointed one of his father's companions, General Antipater, as the regent homeland commander responsible for enforcing Macedonia's rule while he was absent attacking the forces of Darius III in Asia Minor. This was a smart strategic move by Alexander because while he was away in the East in 331 B.C.E., Agis III, king of Sparta, thought it was a good time to rebel against Macedon rulership.

Now Agis III came to power in 338 as the 21st Euryponid ruler and the son of the Spartan king Archidamus III. His scheme to revolt proved to be a fatal mistake, both for himself and the kingdom of Sparta as well. In the north, Macedonian General Antipater defeated Thrace and moved his 40,000 troops to Megalopolis to meet the Spartan challenge. Agis 20,000 infantry men and 2,000 cavalrymen proved to be no match for experienced Antipater. Sparta was crushed and King Agis III was seriously wounded in the bloody battle. Spartan forces were surrounded. Agis wounds prevented him from moving fast enough to escape the approaching enemy troops. Agis ordered his men to leave him behind. He then rose to his knees, slew several Macedonians before being fatally struck with a javelin. This skirmish gave the men of Agis time to escape. In the end, over 5,000 died on the Spartan side while Macedonia saw 3,500 of its troops slain.

Meanwhile in the east, King Alexander and his mighty force crossed the Hellenspont numbering 48,000 soldiers, 6,000 cavalrymen, a fleet of 120 ships with a naval crew of nearly 40,000. Greek historian Diodorus wrote that after Alexander landed in Asia Minor he illustrated his intentions of conquering the entire continent by thrusting his spear in the ground and proclaiming Asia as his gift from the gods of Greece. By 334, the Macedonian forces attacked the Persians at Granicus in a ferocious fight known as the Battle of Garanicus. Alexander was victorious in his initial confrontation. This gave him the additional confidence needed to keep marching towards Persepolis. After this, the Persian satrap in Sardis raised a white flag and surrendered without bloodshed. Several other cities followed suit. Alexander then warred at Halicarnassus in Caria where he launched his first large-scale offensive in Asia Minor against lackey Grecian mercenaries and Persian troops. Captain Memnon of Rhodes and his overseer Persian satrap Orontobates were forced to hastily flee by sea in order to escape death. Alexander, afterwards, handpicked the next vassal leaders of Caria then kept marching southwards. The city-states of Lycia, Pamphylia, Termessos, and Gordium all fell like dominoes. It was in the city of Gordium where Alexander solved the mystery of untieing the gordian knot, which according to legend, meant he would eventually become the king of all Asia. Alexander did not untie the complex knot. Instead he took his sword, chopped the knot into pieces, and proclaimed that it did not matter how the knot was untied.

By spring of 333 the leader of **the kingdom of the waist and thigh of brass** had crossed the entire Asia Minor [modern Turkey] passing over the Taurus mountains off the coast of the Mediterranean Sea. He was victorious at the Battle of Issus, capturing seaports to cutoff the Persian fleets. After this, Alexander fell sick and was forced to halt his advance into the ancient lands **[kingdoms] of gold and silver.** After recovery he moved into Syria and conquered it. From there he moved along the coast of the Levant and besieged the ancient black kingdom of Tyre, the golden Phoenician treasure-city. *(For millenniums these searfaring black Phoenican traders, navies, and armies that once ruled the people and waters of the Mediterranean and the Atlantic, establishing colonies in Carthage, Italy, Asia Minor, northern and western Africa, and the Americas.)*

King Alexander of Greece, an Aryan, faced the ancient sophisticated technology of the heavily fortified city built on a hill. It took three assaults and 7 months to finally subdue the black city-empire, thus shifting the balance of world power from Shemitc-Hamitic [black] into a world ruled by the descendants of Japheth [Javan] for the first time in human history. Before this victory, white people [the inferior metal of brass] had never ruled the ancient world of the kingdoms of gold and silver. The ancient and modern world would never be, and has never been, the same. Alexander was severely wounded in his shoulder during this prolonged seige. He finally prevailed, rounded up, and ordered the execution of all men, both old and young. The women and children were sold into slavery. After this, Alexander continued south, bypassing Jerusalem and advancing into **Egypt, the ancient land of gold**. *(After more than 4,000 years of indigenous black Kemitic-Shemitic rule, the land of the Pharaohs was now occupied by non-Afro-Asiatic people for the first time in human existence. Remember, Egypt was once the leading pillar of ancient civilization.)* By 332 B.C. E. the new Macedonian ruler had invaded Egypt where he was received with open arms as one who had liberated Egypt from Persian tyranny. In an elaborate ceremony the high priests of Kemet crowned Alexander as the son of god Ammon-Ra near a sacred shrine located at the Siwa Oasis. The young 24-year-old Gentile ruler was now regarded as a Euro-Pharaoh, the personification of Zeus-Ammon-Ra, a god-king, according to the manner of ancient Egypt whose customs dated back several thousands of years. The city of Alexandria was renamed in his honor where he studied in the ancient Kemetic royal libraries, exporting this newfound knowledge back to the city-states of Greece. Alexandria became a major influence in the development of Hellenism throughout the ancient Afro-Asiatic world.

One year later Alexander left Egypt in 331, marching eastward towards the second pillar of the ancient black world, into the land of the Sumerians, Babylonians, Assyrians, and eventually the Persians. *(Again, I cannot over emphasize the historic fact that these victories changed the 4,000-year orbit of the ancient world, eventually shifting human power into a new direction towards the Gentile people of Greece, Rome, and ultimately Europe and America.)* Alexander also defeated Darius III at the Battle of Gaugamela, thus capturing the birthplace of idolatry—Babylon. Darius III fled the battlefield into Ecbatana.

Alexander was now the ruler of known world, controlling both the kingdom of the head of gold **[Babylon]** and the ancient land of gold **[Egypt]**. At this point, the entire Macedonian war machine was at the doorsteps of the Achaemenid Persian throne. Alexander moved against the Persian capital Susa and looted the kingdom's treasury. From there he ordered his troops to march against the royal city of Persepolis via the Persian Royal Road. Upon entering the royal capital, his troops, unaccustomed to such a high standard of living, immediately raided the second Persian treasury in Persepolis, remaining there for five months feasting on the spoils of war. These conquests provided Alexander with vast sums of gold, silver, precious stones, clothes, ceramic tiles, dishes, and other valuables.

At the end of those five months, the city of Persepolis was totally burned to the ground. The fire started in the eastern palace of the late Persian monarch Xerxes I and spread across the entire royal residence. Thus, **the kingdom of the breast of silver** was now totally consumed as Daniel had prophesied. Some sources contend the fire was set deliberately as payback for the burning of the Acropolis in Athens by Xerxes I during the Second Persian War. Others say the fire was a fatal accident that occurred after a drunken stupor by Grecian soldiers. It was recorded that Alexander regretted the burning of the beautiful royal city. After returning to the site of the ruins, he came upon the fallen remains of the broken idol that was once erected in honor King Xerxes I. Alexander stopped to hold a conversation with the statue as if he was speaking to a live person. He reportedly told the statue: *"Shall I pass by and leave you lying there because of the expeditions you led against Greece, or shall I set you up again because of your magnanimity and your virtues in other respects?"* That conversation revealed Alexander's psyche during that time. He realized that he could not utterly destroy the ingenious Persian civilization because Greece needed their reservoir of architectural, intellectual, legal, and technological greatness and grandeur to advance his own cause. Instead, Alexander revised his empire based on joint Persian and Macedonian culture. It is a known fact, he was deeply impressed with Achaemenid way of life and heavily borrowed from Persia's dress code and royal protocol. This new Euro-Afro-Asiatic blend gave birth to the Hellenistic culture that extended from the northern borders of Thrace, down into Egypt in the south, over towards the Indus Valley in the far east.

Alexander continued to pursue the head of King Darius III whose empire had rapidly crumbled around him. Darius, however, fled for his life into the province of Media and continued into Parthia where he was finally stabbed to death by one of his own. The traitor's name was Bessus, a former Persian satrap who had proclaimed himself Artaxerxes V, hoping to rebuild the ruins of the Achaemenid empire. Bessus threw Darius corpse in the middle of the road then fled into Central Asia. The Achaemenid Persian empire had officially fallen from the pinnacle of world power into an ash heap. Meanwhile, Alexander commanded a pomp state funeral for the deceased ruler and continued to pursue Bessus, chasing him throughout Central Asia while extending the reach of his empire, and renaming cities in his honor, at the same time. His incursions led him into countries known today as India, the mountainous regions of Afghanistan, Tajikistan, Uzbekistan, and Scythia [southern Russia]. Eventually in 329 a former Persian satrap of the province of Sogdiana named Spitamenes arrested Bessus and turned him over to the Greek forces where he was tortured to death. Coincidentally, Spitamenes was later slain by Alexander after he too attempted to stage a revolt against Grecian dominion in former Persian territories deep inside Central Asia.

Seven years of constant fighting took its toll on the Macedonian army. Several plots against the life of Alexander began to surface. One of his officers named Philotas was executed for not informing Alexander of a plot to take his life. Philotas was the son of General Parmenion, who guarded the Persian treasury in Ecbatana. Alexander assassinated both the father and son. In Uzbekistan, Alexander and his general Cleitus the Black became embroiled in a drunken fight. (**In the book of Proverbs, chapter 20:1,** King Solomon once said: *"Wine is a scoffer, strong drink a roisterer; he who is muddled by them will not grow wise. The terror of a king is like the roar of a lion."*) Cleitus accused Alexander of forsaking his native Grecian culture and mismanaging the Asian campaign. The back and forth verbal exchanges, along with plenty of liquor, ended with the bludgeoned death of the veteran general who had earlier saved Alexander's life at the Battle of Granicus. Another royal court plot occurred during the Central Asia expedition when a royal page and historian, Callisthenes of Olynthus, attempted to halt Alexander's conversion to the Persian way of life. That conspiracy was also squashed. Needless to say, Alexander was headstrong and continued his merger of less-developed Aryan norms with superior Persian dress and customs.

By 327, the Macedon army had fought their way to the slopes of India where he commanded the former Persian satraps in Gandhara, a region known today as Pakistan, to submit to his new authority. Some the rulers beyond the Indus Valley obeyed his decree while others rejected the dictates of the new foreign invader. Alexander and his Indian allies built a bridge to cross over the Hydaspes River to engage in battles against King Porus, ruler of Punjab, and his allied Indian tribes in the Kunar valley, the Guraeus valley, along with the tribes of the Swat and Buner valleys. During these wars with the tribes in the Kunar valley, Alexander was seriously wounded in his shoulder. Again, he was seriously wounded in the ankle during the battle of Fort Massaga. He still continued his war effort and eventually overcame the city, slaying the entire population and burning the city to the ground. After these hard fought victories the Macedon generals began to realize the limits of their human power and did not want to continue the push eastwards into areas known today as Bangladesh. On the opposite side of the banks of the Ganges River, the kings of the region had assembled a force of 80,000 horsemen, 200,000 footmen, 8,000 chariots and 6,000 war elephants to await Alexander's attempt to cross over. Alexander wanted to push further, but his fighting machine was exhausted. Soldiers openly complained that "they longed to see their parents, their wives, children, and homeland." The King of Greece and Asia finally agreed to halt the advance into the east, reversing back through a new treacherous drought-stricken terrain to return back to Persia. Along the way he lost many of his troops due to fatigue and heat exhaustion.

Back in Persia in 324, it should be noted that it was during this time Alexander actually had his first known relationship with the opposite sex. Until then his only lover had been his boyhood and lifelong friend named Hephaestion, who was his bodyguard and second-in-command of the mighty Macedonian army. He was also the Chiliarch, the second-in-command of his newly installed Persian court. Once the Greeks moved into the Oriental world they discovered a society where the rulers were deeply polygamous. In order to solidify relations with his Persian subjects, Alexander dethroned a rebellion satrap in Bactria and married a princess named Roxana who was the daughter of a prominent and wealthy man named Oxyartes. In an elaborate Persian state ceremony, he also married the daughter of Darius III, Stateira II, and Parysatis II, the daughter of Artaxerxes III. Again, this was done to strengthen his ties to the Persian ruling class and its inner circles. His true lover was his closest friend and confidant Hephaestion. In fact, it has been said that Alexander was controlled by the thighs of his companion Hephaestion. We also cannot forget that both of them were taught by the philosopher Aristotle, who once described their friendship as "one soul in two bodies." In the Torah, Moses wrote in **Genesis 2: 24**: *"A man shall leave his father and mother and cleave unto his wife and they shall become one flesh."* In the Grecian world, however, those two souls, Alexander and Hephaestion, were of the same gender. It should be noted that a decade earlier at the beginning of the invasion of Asia Minor, Alexander and Hephaestion stopped at the city of Troy where they each laid a wreath at the tombs of two well-known homosexuals, Achilles and Patroclus. It has been recorded that Alexander laid his wreath on the gravesite of Achilles while Hephaestion placed his flowers on the tomb of Patroclus. Afterwards, they both undressed and ran naked in a race honoring their deceased heroes.

Nevertheless while back in the Persian capital of Susa, Hephaestion, like Alexander, also married into the royal family by uniting with a Persian princess named Drypetis who was another one of the daughters of Darius III. Many of the chief Macedonian officers followed the lead of the king and his bodyguard and arranged marriages with Persian noblewomen as well. After that, Hephaestion and several army units departed Susa in late 324 headed towards Ecbatana to confiscate the treasure of Persia. By the year's end he arrived in Ecbatana. Upon arrival, Hephaestion contacted a deadly fever. While still sick, he consumed a large breakfast of a boiled bird and a cooler of wine. After this large breakfast meal, his condition became worse and he died in a matter of days. When news of Hephaestion's death reached Alexander in Babylon, he immediately broke down in tears and headed towards Ecbatana. His open display of grief was so extraordinary that it was recognized throughout the kingdom. He called for a national period of mourning and ordered all the royal horses tails and manes be clipped short. All music-playing was banned. When Alexander arrived in Ecbatana he immediately embraced the corpse of his deceased lover. According to historic sources, he laid on Hephaestion's cold body all day and night in tears until his bodyguards forcibly removed him off the corpse. Alexander ordered the execution of Hephaestion's doctor, Glaucias, for negligence. For two days Alexander ate no food, didn't bathe, and laid on his bed crying. He also shaved his head and placed the hair in his companion's hand. Alexander's public display of grief was so intense that it even moved the battle-hardened Macedonian soldiers to tears as well. Alexander also dispatched envoys to Siwa, Egypt to meet the high priests of the god Amon to seek permission to molten the legacy of Hephaestion into a cult deity. The Egyptian priests told Alexander no, and instead, chose to regard Hephaestion as a 'divine hero.'

Hephaestion remains were cremated and his ashes became a part of a pomp funeral held in the great city Babylon. Alexander drove the hearse carriage a portion of the way from Ecbatana back to the city of the Hanging Gardens. Even the sacred flames inside the Temple of Bel-Marduk was put out when the funeral began. Normally, the Babylonian sacred flames were extinquished only for the Great King. Alexander, however, gave the honor to his friend and spared no cost, spending 10,000 talents of gold, in preparation of the ceremonies and the immaculate tomb for his companion. Babylon became the scene of grand festivities and funeral games conducted with thousands of participants. Finally, Hephaestion was buried in the city of ancient Babylon, the kingdom of **the Head of Gold**.

Many historians have reported that Alexander's countenance was not the same after the death of his friend. It came to pass in June of 323 Alexander succumbed to illness while living in the palace of Nebuchadnezzar there in Babylon at the age of 32. It has been reported that Alexander developed a fever in late May and for two weeks his health gradually deteriorated. Alexander had been involved in heavy drinking throughout the month of May. One of the last parties he hosted was the one for Admiral Nearchus, the head of his naval fleet, and Medius, of Larissa. After those rounds of heavy partying he became weak, sick unto the point the he could no longer talk, and eventually he died. Some historians have theorized that he could have been poisoned, while some say, the poisoning was his own fault due to his heavy drinking. Regardless of whichever theory is true, King Alexander the Great, the bloody conqueror of Greece, Asia Minor, Tyre, Syria, Egypt, and Persia, life had come to an end on June 10/11, 323 B.C.E.. All of that was done to fulfill the words of the prophet Daniel who said in **chapter 2: 20-21**: *"Let the name of ELOHIM be blessed forever and ever. For wisdom and power is HIS. HE* **[YAH]** *changes times and seasons,* **[YAH]** *removes kings* **[in this case Alexander]** *and setteth up kings* **[Again, in this case Alexander]**.*" So it had come to pass that it was YAH, the true Eternal KING of heaven and earth who had actually controlled Alexander's destiny, and, it was YAH who ultimately caused the Macedonian prince to give up the spirit of life and to sleep with his ancestors like all mortal men before him and after him, even unto this day.

Alexander's corpse was placed in a gold casket. The pallbearers placed the casket inside a large two-wheeled golden tomb filled with honey then locked the vault. The Macedonian hierachy wanted their native son's remains to return to their Grecian homeland. The large royal procession started from the royal residence in Babylon, the city Alexander had loved above all other royal capitals. As the entourage headed towards Macedon, the armies of General Ptolemy, one of Alexander's top four generals who ruled Egypt, overtook and seized the golden portable shrine and redirected the procession towards the city of Memphis where a lavish ceremony was conducted. The shrine remained there all the days of Ptolemy. His son and successor, Ptolemy II Philadelphus, eventually moved the tomb to Alexandria, Egypt where it remained throughout the times of the ancient world. It has been recorded that many Roman leaders visited the tomb after they conquered the divided Grecian empire.

In the following generations Roman General Pompey, Emperor Julius Ceasar, Emperor Augustus Ceasar, and Emperor Caligula all visited the gravesite of this Aryan conqueror to pay respects to his legacy. It should be always remembered that the Alexandrian Greeks were the first whites to ever rule ancient Afro-Asiatic civilization. This is why the Romans of antiquity and the Europeans of today still revere them until this very day. This is the reason why a majority of past and present white historians, for their most part, constantly attempt to sanitize the legacy of these people, whom they consider their founding fathers, while hiding the fact that black people of the ancient Afro-Asiatic world maintained a superior standard of living and academics thousands of years prior to the arrival of the Greeks, Romans, and Europeans into this region of the world.

With the sudden death of Alexander, the generals of the massive Macedon army realized that no successor had been chosen. Roxanna of Bactria was still pregnant with Alexander's child, so there was no living heir to the throne. Although Alexander had been seriously ill, no one thought the young 32-year-old king would actually die because he was revered as a god. Nevertheless while lying on his deathbed, his bodyguard Perdiccas received his signet ring, thus nominating him as the possible successor. Perdiccas chose not to immediately assume the throne. Instead Perdiccas chose to wait for the unborn child of Roxanna to be born to see if it would be a male-heir. Perdiccas viewed the other heir Phillip as feeble-minded and did not favour him. The other generals agreed with the plan of Perdiccas to wait for the child to be born, and, two months later in August 323, Alexander IV was born. Eventually, both sides agreed to a joint rulership by Alexander IV and Phillip. At this same time, Perdiccas proposed a partition of the united empire into four satrapies which unexpectedly provided each general with the opportunity to turn their province into an independent kingdom.

Another obstacle to a united Greece was the emnity between Perdiccas(of Babylon) and Ptolemy (of Egypt). The forces of Ptolemy had earlier hijacked the funeral procession for Alexander the Great and diverted the tomb into Egypt. Tensions between these two were not a good sign, and it was an indicator of the impending dissolution of the united Greek empire. Perdiccas eventually attacked Egypt, but his campaign failed. Those disagreements and rivalries between various leaders of the Macedonian army caused major cracks to appear in the massive kingdom that stretched from Thrace to India. General Lysimachus ruled over the provinces of Thrace while General Antipater maintained dominion over the kingdom of Macedon. In Egypt, General Ptolemy became the Euro-Pharaoh over Egypt as Seleucus reigned over Syria and Mesopotamia.

The Brass Age—(Its Belly and Thighs of Brass) *Continues*
Four divided Grecian Empires—PART TWO "the thighs"
"then yet a third kingdom [empire] of brass which will rule over the whole earth;"
Daniel 2: 32,39

"YAH changes times and seasons, HE removes kings(kingdoms) and install kings(kingdoms); HE gives the wise their wisdom And knowledge to those who know"   **Daniel 2: 21**

And it came to pass after the death of King Alexander in 323 B.C.E., General Perdiccas attempted to hold the kingdom together with a strategy of a joint kingship between Alexander IV, the son of Alexander the Great, and Phillip Arrhideaus, Alexander's half-brother. That plan also included the partitioning of the vast Grecian empire into four major provinces ruled by four governors. The governors were chief generals of the Macedonian army. General Lysimachus reigned over the province of Thrace while General Antipater continued his dominion over the homeland in Macedonia. General Seleucus possessed the province of Syria and Mesopotamia while his counterpart General Ptolemy became a Euro-Pharaoh who governed the kingdom of Egypt. This plan did not work for long. In 321 General Perdiccas was assassinated by his own soldiers after their military defeat in Egypt. While in Egypt Antipater was officially crowned regent at the meeting known as the Treaty of Triparadisus. The generals—Ptolemy, Antigonus, and Antipater—had joined forces to wage war against Perdiccas when they received a report that he had already been slain by his own troops. As part of a postwar settlement, Queen Roxana and the two Macedonia heirs-Alexander IV and Phillip-were brought back to Macedon. There in Macedonia, Alexander and Phillip became the victims in the crosswinds of murderous plots in Pella. The old Partition Plan once initiated by General Perdiccas along with the agreement of joint leadership was cast to the ground. In the process of time, each general-governor transformed their territories into four separate Grecian kingdoms, thus creating four Hellenistic dynasties that ruled over the ancient Afro-Asiatic lands.

Antipater, the regent of Macedonia, became the father of the Antipatrid Dynasty which lasted from (323-279 B.C.E.) before it was replaced by the Antigonid Dynasty which stood from (306-179 B.C.E.). Both dynasties ruled Macedon. During this same period of time Lysimachus became progenitor of the Thrace Dynasty (315-281 B.C.E.) while Seleucus I Nicator founded the Seleucid Dynasty which endured from (320-62 B.C.E.). In Egypt, Ptolemy I Soter began the first Ayan dynasty to rule over the land of the Pharaohs (323-30 B.C.E.). The time zone of world rulership for these **kingdoms of thigh of brass** continued under four separate dynasties. In antiquity the impact of their world influence became known as Hellenism, which was, as I said earlier, actually a blend of Greek and Oriental culture. This new Hellenistic period lasted from 323 unto the rise of Rome in146 B.C.E. Hellenism resulted in numerous Greeks leaving their homeland to establish Greco-colonies throughout the ancient world, mainly in Egypt, Israel. Lebanon,Syria,Arabia,Persia, Pakistan, and Afghanistan. Some of the great cities from those culture included Alexandria in Egypt, Antioch in Syria, Ctesiphon in modern Iraq, Seleucia in modern Syria, and Ai Khanoum in modern Afghanistan, along with several others. At least 20 cities had been Hellenized and named after King Alexander the Conquerer throughout the ancient world.

In a *New York Times, September 24, 2015*, newspaper article the headlines read **AFGHAN PRESIDENT VOWS TO CRACK DOWN ON SEXUAL ABUSE OF BOYS** by Matthew Rosenburg. He reported on sexual examples of continued Hellenistic influence over 2,300 years later. The focus of the article was the ongoing controversy in Afghanistan today where many high-ranking government officials have been accused of molesting young boys. The practice, which is known as bacha bazi, meaning boy-play, is still prevalent throughout Afghanistan, which was once territory under Alexander's control. In response to the global outcry, Afghanistan President Ashraf Ghani reminded critics that, *"Our Greek and Turkish heritage have generated periods of long practices [of* bacha bazi]. *Those require a large cultural social dialogue that require purpose and energy."* Rosenburg wrote: "Alexander the Great conquered much of Afghanistan starting around 330 B.C., bringing with him ancient Greek cultural practices that died out in their homeland millenniums ago. And though the sexual abuse of boys was a feature of life in the Ottoman Empire, it faded in the 19th century and is no longer accepted in Turkey. In Afghanistan, though, the rape of boys persists." So as we can see, the lingering effects of Hellenism are still rippling across the face of the earth well into the 21st century.

Now, let's turn our attention back to the divided Grecian empires.

The Antipatrid Dynasty (Macedonia)
(323 B.C.E.—294 B.C.E.)
First Division of the Alexandrian Empire

Antipater (323—319 B.C.E.), Polyperchon (319-318 B.C.E.), Cassander (318—297 B.C.E., however, he did not proclaim himself king until 302), Phillip IV (297B.C.E.), Alexander V(297—294 B.C.E.), Antipater II (296—294 B.C.E.), Antipater Etesias (279 B.C.E.).

Antipater of Macedonia
(323 B.C.E.—319 B.C.E.)

General Antipater was born in 397 B.C.E. and he grew to become a mighty man of valor. Eventually he became a trusted companion of King Phillip II during the early part of his career. One of his first assignments came in 346 when Phillip sent him as the envoy to represent Macedon at a religious unity meeting known as the Amphictyonic League in Delphi. Delphi was the central high place where all Greeks gathered to sacrifice to the sun-god Apollo. Four years later in 342 B.C.E., when Phillip was absent conquering various city-states across the mainland,

Antipater was appointed as the regent to govern Macedon. After another Macedon victory at the Battle of Chaeronea in 338, Phillip became recognized as the preeminent leader of all Greece and he dispatched Antipater as ambassador to Athens to sign a new peace treaty. On a personal level, Antipater was regarded as a faithful servant and confidant by King Phillip II. However, it has been suggested that he may have committed adultery with Alexander's mother Olympias, who was the king's wife. Some historians have stated that he could be, in fact, the true father of Alexander. When Phillip was assassinated in the autumn of 336, Antipater hastily moved to support Alexander's quest to become the new successor in Pella.

Once Alexander was crowned as the king of Macedon he continued his father's offensive against all rebellious city-states that did not bow to their dominion. King Alexander appointed Antipater to a second term as regent of Macedon while he was away in Asia, Egypt, and the Far East for 11 years. During this time the relationship between Olympias and Antipater became frosty as they both vied for the ear of the king. The bickering caused Alexander to order Antipater to bring fresh battalions of soldiers into Asia for backup. His lieutenant Craterus was appointed to the position of temporary regent. Ironically, shortly after Antipater departed, Alexander died in Babylon before Alexander could complete a transfer of power to Craterus. As uncertainty and instability began to surface, Alexander's assistant General Perdiccas became the temporary head of the kingdom. Hoping to stabilize the situation, General Perdiccas kept Antipater as the chief commander and regent of the homeland. His duty was to safeguard the lives of the heirs, Alexander IV and his disabled stepbrother Phillip III. He put down rebellions in Athens, Aetolia, Thessaly, and defeated Sparta at Megalopolis. Afterwards, Antipater strengthened the hands of the oligarchs and dictators across the mainland.

Polyperchon of Macedonia
(319 B.C.E.—318 B.C.E.)

Antipater's death was the result of natural causes. He was 78, sickly, and upon his deathbed, he appointed a trusted experienced friend named General Polyperchon. Born in 394 B.C.E., Polyperchon grew to become a loyal, conservative, and well respected warrior among the Macedonian troops. He was a capable soldier alongside Phillip in campaigns throughout Greece, and afterwards with Alexander in campaigns throughout Asia. After returning back to Babylon upon completion of the India incursion, Alexander sent Polyperchon back to Macedon. Shortly after his arrival back in Europe, Antipater, died in 319 and General Polyperchon was appointed regent of Macedonia and guardian of the two figurehead kings—Phillip III Arridaeus and Alexander IV. Antipater's son Cassander was appointed "the chiliarch", the second-in-command. Polyperchon was chosen to prevent any perception that Antipater intended to seize the throne of Alexander the Great. By 330 B.C.E. and due to conflicts with Antipater, former Queenmother Olympias chose to leave the royal city Pella to return home to live with royal family members in Epirus. Once power shifted in Pella, she quickly formed another alliance with Polypechon who had previously invited her to move back to the capital. She accepted. Being the vindictive and manipulative woman she was, she soon became a powerful force once again. Olympias had Phillip III Arridaeus, who was mentally unfit, and with no real power, along with his wife Queen Eurydice imprisoned. Her grandson Alexander IV, who was still a young lad, and his mother Roxanna, were placed under her care. The next move was a purge of Antipater's relatives. She ordered the execution of hundreds of members of the Macedonian ruling class and high officials. Prior to Antipater's death, Olymipas had already openly accused Antipater and his family members of being suspects in possible poisoning of her son Alexander the Great in Babylon.

In 322, three years before his death, Antipater had also joined in a confederation with Ptolemy, Antigonus, and Seleucus I to war against General Perdiccas, who was the regent in Babylon. General Perdiccas had attacked Ptolemy in Egypt and there were rumors circulating that he intended to seize control of the entire Grecian empire. This chain of events sparked The

First Diadochi War which lasted from 322 to 320.

It should be noted again that before Antipater died, Cassander totally disagreed with his decision not to make him ruler. So, he immediately formed an alliance to overthrow Polyperchon. Cassander eventually slew Queen Olympias, and Alexander IV, Queen Roxanna, Heracles, and opposed the glorification of the legacy of Alexander the Great. Polyperchon, who was 91, moved back to the Peloponnese Peninsula where he faded into the shadows. There he was regarded as a wise elder and he eventually passed in 303.

Two major actions taken by Polyperchon, which helped shape the course of history as we know it were, number one, his recognition of Cassander as king of Macedonia, and number two, his surrender of Heracles, the final heir of Alexander the Great and the Persian princess Stateira, over to Cassander who executed them. These actions represented Polyperchon's acceptance of the fact that defending the seed of Alexander the Great was a hopeless cause. The loyal veteran finally realized that the Argead Dynasty was now a relic of the past.

Cassander of Macedonia
(318 B.C.E.—297 B.C.E.)

Cassander was born in 355 B.C.E. as the son of the great general named Antipater. Cassander became co-regent and crown prince with his father in the homeland of Macedonia. Although he was an accomplished warrior, he never accompanied the Macedonian army on their foreign expeditions. Instead, he served as his father's representative in Macedonia and Greece. Cassander was a very covetous and power-hungry soul who hoped his father would promote him as successor to the throne of Macedon.

As a lad, Cassander attended the same boarding school in Lyceum as Alexander III, who later became known as "The Great." Both were taught by the famed philosopher Aristotle. Cassander rode side by side with his father Antipater as a young man. When the chaos surrounding the death of Alexander the Great began, Cassander and his father Antipater continued to rule Macedonia. Antipater eventually succumbed to old age. While lying upon his deathbed he choose Polyperchon, an elder-general, as his successor. Cassander became furious and sought military support from Ptolemy I Soter of Egypt, and Antigonus I of Asia Minor to confront Polyperchon. Polyperchon, an experienced commander, reacted quickly and found an ally in another warrior named Eumenes who was also a past enemy of Antigonus. Eumenes seized royal treasuries in territories under his command. The new treasure gave them the ability to purchase weapons and manpower. This infighting ignited the outbreak of the Second Diadochi War which started in 319 and concluded in 315.

In the spring of 318 Eumenes moved to the western flank to Phoenicia (a Black city-state) to purchase ships to build a navy for Polyperchon. He also intended to halt the advance of Ptolemy out of Egypt. By the autumn of 318 Polyperchon's hopes of building a strong naval force was shattered. His navy was defeated by the fleet of Antigonus in the Straits of Bosporus. At this point Polyperchon lost control of the Aegan Sea. Meanwhile in Greece, Polyperchon had weakened Cassander's influence by issuing a decree granting autonomy to all Greek towns where Macedonian garrisoned were presently stationed. This amnesty turned these cities into his allies on the homefront.

As this Second Diaodchi conflict raged, Cassander was the outsider. Polyperchon ruled the royal house in Macedonia, and he had invited, Alexander the Great's mother, Queen Olympias, back to Pella. Olympias had taken a self-imposed exile back to Epirus [modern Albania] with her cousin King Aeacides. In Pella, the elderly Polyperchon appointed a young Phillip III Arridaeus [*pronounced* Ar-ri-dae-us] to be the mere figurehead king. Meanwhile, Polyperchon, the true powerbroker, granted the custody of Alexander's widow, Queen Roxanna, and her son, Alexander IV, over to Queen Olympias. Not to be defeated, by the spring of 317, Cassander and his allies fought their way back into Greece and Macedonia. Polyperchon, Olympias, Roxanna, and Alexander IV along with others fled the capital. When Cassander re-entered Pella with his superior force, the young figurehead King Phillip III Arridaeus and his wife Queen Eurydice went out to greet Cassander as the liberator.

Cassander was now the the protector of the young figurehead Phillip III.

In the process of time, rebellions broke out in Greece which forced Cassander to leave Macedon again to campaign on the Peloponnese Peninsula. While Cassander was away, Olympias, Polyperchon, and their allied forces launched an offensive against Macedonia. The Macedonian army that was supposed to protect king Phillip III Arridaeus and his wife deserted the battlefield, refusing to war against the elderly general Polyperchon and the mother of Alexander the Great. Once the old general and former queen-mother reached the Pella, the bloodbath started. Phillip III Arridaeus was executed. His wife forced to kill herself, and the hierarchy decapitated. Once Cassander received the report of the uprising back in Pella, he hastily reversed course and returned to the capital with an overwhelming force.

Cassander maneuvered a surprise offensive that forced Polypercon, Olympias, and their allies to flee the capital a second time. Cassander pursued them and besieged them at Pydna and forced the city to surrender after a two-year seige. One of the terms of the surrender agreement was a promise not to kill Olympias and Polyperchon. Cassander agreed, but, after the deal was ratified there was a public outcry for vengeance against Olympias by the family members of those who had been slain during her earlier purge. She was forced to stand trial and sentenced to death. Some historians report she was stoned to death by their family members. Other historians state she was stabbed to death. Either way, in 310 B.C.E., Queen Olympias, the 58-year-old mother of Alexander the Great was now dead. Her corpse was left unburied like the remains of Queen Jezebel in the ancient Hebrew scriptures [**See 2 Kings 9:33-37**]. Let's compare the life of the Macedonian queen to the life of the ancient queen of Samaria. Both women lived very similar lives. Both grew up as powerful princesses from foreign lands that married powerful kings. Both oulived their powerful husbands and wanted their offsprings to inherit the throne. Both met their doom when new rulers came to power. In the case of Olympias, her birth name was Myrtle. King Phillip renamed her Olympias in honor of his racehorse that won the Olympic Games one year after they met in 356. She was a red haired 18-year-old fiery-tempered Aryan beauty when Phillip met her for the first time during religious ceremonies on the island of Samothrace, which is in the Aegan Sea between Macedonia and Troy. She was a sorceress and a devotee of the snake worshipping cult of Dionysos. A cult that included gluttonous wine drinking, orgies, and revelry. She was also well versed in the rites of magic and the handling of those serpents for cultic ceremonies. In fact, she was both famous and feared for her skills in controlling dangerous snakes during religious celebrations. Known to engage in extramarital affairs, there were rumors circulating that General Antipater could have been Alexander's true father. According to the historian Plutarch, one night King Phillip came to her bedchamber and discovered her having sex with a snake. After that his days of surprise visits to her bedroom were over. (For the record, King Phillip wasn't too much better. He was involved in several homosexual extramarital affairs throughout his reign, including one with his wife's brother, King Alexander of Epirus. A homosexual love triangle was one of the major reasons he was assassinated.) When Alexander the Great prepared to cross the strategic Hellenspot into Asia Minor, Olympias, acting as a spiritual-military adviser, came out to empower him, pulled him aside, and told him to be courageous because he was not a mortal man, the son of Phillip, instead he was a divine being, son of the god Zeus. That was the last time the mother and son would ever see each other again. Alexander died in Babylon.

Now back to General Cassander. Cassander had become alarmed at Antigonus increasing power and land grabs in both Asia and Greece. He then formed a new alliance which included Ptolemy, Seleucus, and Lysimachus to war against Antigonus who now controlled all Asia between the Aegan Sea to the Hindu Kush in the far east. This conflict was the beginning of the Third Diadochi War which began in 314 and raged until 311 B.C.E.

By 311, the generals—Cassander, Antigonus, and Ptolemy—agreed to end the war. They all recognized the young lad Alexander IV as the successor to the royal Macedonian throne once he reached the age of 18. However, years later a complete turnaround occurred. In 309 Cassander ordered his officer named Glaucias to secretly eliminate the 14-year crown prince Alexander IV and his mother. This treacherous act occurred four years before the heir was set to assume the throne. With no heir remaining, Alexander IV death represented the final nail in the coffin for the Macedonian royal house.

Cassander went on to marry a woman named Thessalonica, who happened to be one of the sisters of Alexander the Great. Cassander founded the royal city of Thessalonica in honor of her. **(It should be remembered that there is a epistle in the New Testament named after this city called the Book of Thessalonians. Those letters were written to new Greek converts of the emerging religion of Christo-Judaism which eventually became known as Christianity. These writings are not ancient Hebrew Torah or Prophets. They should not be regarded as holy scriptures for the ancient Afro-Asiatic Hebrew people.)**

In 302 he finally proclaimed himself king of Macedonia. During this time there were still continuous wars between Cassander and Antigonus, but, as fate would have it, Antigonus was slain in the Battle of Ipsus the following year in 301. In 297 the Cassander became sick and died from swollen tumors and other internal disorders. By 294 B.C.E. the Antipater Dynasty was gradually being replaced by Demetrius I Poliorceles, the son and heir of General Antigonus, who became founder of the Antigonid Dynasty over the kingdom of Macedonia. Although Cassander's sons Phillip IV, Alexander V, and Antipater II succeeded him, his desire for a long-lasting dynasty came to an abrupt end shortly after his death. The combined length of rulership for all three of his sons equaled a mere three years.

Phillip IV of Macedonia
(297 B.C.E.)

Phillip IV of Macedonia was the eldest son of Cassander, but the least known. He ascended to the royal throne after his father died from dropsy, a terrible disease that caused Cassander's body to become infested and covered with parasitic worms while he was still alive.

Not too much more is known about Phillip IV because his reign was so short. In less than one year Phillip IV was dead from a disease that caused him to rapidly lose weight and waste away.

Alexander V (Macedonia)
(297 B.C.E.—294 B.C.E.)

Alexander V was the third and youngest son of Cassander and Thessalonica of Macedon. He was co-regent with his brother Antipater II from 297 to 294. His brother Antipater II murdered their own mother Thessalonica and upsurged his brother's position as the king of Macedonia. Alexander V turned to Pyrrhus and Demetrius I Poliorcetes for help to recover his kingship. Once their alliance was confirmed, Antipater was oustered by Alexander. In exchange for Pyrrhus support, Alexander repaid them when he ceded the sea coast of Macedonia, along with the provinces of Ambracia, Asarnania, and Amphilochia. Shortly after those squabbles, the two blood brothers Alexander V and Antipater II settled their dispute and brokered a peace agreement among themselves. Arriving later after the brothers had made peace, Demetrius became the third party who was left out of their agreement. The brothers had finalized everything. Acting with subtility, Alexander still welcomed Demetrius. However in his heart, he intended to kill him to alleviate him as a future threat. His plan was to murder Demetrius at a banquet. However, Demetrius, who a keen observer, suspected something was not right. So the next day Demetrius left early, but Alexander escorted him as far as Thessaly. Once they came to the city of Larissa, the double-hearted pair stopped to eat. The two heads of state ordered their guards to leave. Alexander and Demetrius were left alone. Demetrius drew his sword and murdered Alexander, along with the other guests at the banquet table. Alexander's death represented the final nail in the coffin for the Antipatrid Dynasty. All of Cassander's three sons, Phillip IV, Alexander V, and Antipater II, were all gone in a matter of three years.

Antipater II (Macedonia)
(296—294 B.C.E.)

Antipater II was the second and middle son of Cassander and Thessalonica. After the death of his father, he became co-regent with his brother Alexander V. One thing for sure, Antipater II was a very jealous hearted man. Although his brother shared the throne with him, he was not content. When he suspected his mother of favoring his younger brother, he murdered her. He also rolled a stone and oustered his brother Alexander V. His brother Alexander V then requested outside help from Demetrius I and Pyrrhus to help him execute vengeance upon Antipater, but the helper became the hurtful one. Demetrius helped ouster Antipater II, forcing him to flee to Thrace, but he later turned around and murdered Alexander V. The Antipatrid Dynasty was now finished. Afterwards, the army of Macedon chose Demetrius I to become the first ruler from the Antigonid Dynasty to rule the kingdom of Macedonia.

Antipater Etesias
(279 B.C.E.)

Anipater Etesias was the nephew of General Antipater of Macedonia. His father, Phillip, was the brother of Cassander. His mother's name was not recorded in the annals of Macedonia's history. After the removal of Ptolemy Keraunos, he emerged as the last ruler of the Antipatrid Dynasty. His reign blew away as fast as it came into existence. It lasted only one month and 15 days—a mere 45 days. After him, the Antigonid Dynasty ascended to power over Macedonia for the next two centuries.

The Antigonid Dynasty (Macedonia)
(306 B.C.E.—179 B.C.E.)

Antigonus I Monophthalmus "One-eyed" (306—301 B.C.E.), Demetrius Poliorcetes (294—283 B.C.E.), Antigonus II Gonatas (276—239 B.C.E.), Demetrius the Fair (250 B.C.E.), Demetrius II Aetolicus (239—229 B.C.E.), Antigonus III Doson (229—221 B.C.E.), Phillip V (221—179B.C.E.), Perseus (179—168 B.C.E.).

Antigonus I Monophthalmus "One-eyed" was born in 382 B.C.E. as the son of a Macedonian nobleman. Like most of his contemporaries, he started as a soldier in the army of Phillip II and Alexander the Great. Under Alexander the Great, he became the governor of Greater Phrygia in 333. There he was responsible for defending the lines of communications and supplies for the extended Grecian empire as Alexander launched his offensive against the Persian empire. Following Alexander's victorious campaign at the Battle of Ipsus, Memnon, the mercenary commander of Rhodes, was paid to order a counter-attack into Asia Minor to cut-off Macedonian distribution routes. Antigonus, however, mounted a counter-strike and defeated the Persian adversaries in three different battles. After the sudden death of Alexander, Perdiccas the regent of Babylon, awarded the provinces of Pamphylia and Lycia to Antigonus. He eventually became the sole commander of Western Asia Minor. Shortly thereafter during the outbreak of the First Diadochi War, Antigonus and Perdiccas became enemies after Antigonus refused to assist his fellow comrade, General Eumenes, in his campaign to stabilize the neighboring province. The nearby provinces of Paphlagonia and Cappadocia had been given to General Eumenes. Perdiccas did not like the actions of Antigonus, so he mounted a campaign against his fellow comrade. Antigonus and his son Demetrius I fled to Greece to escape the massive offensive against them. From Greece, they joined Antipater, Ptolemy, and Craterus in a coalition against Perdiccas. This coalition also moved against General Eumenes, who allied himself with Perdiccas. Eumenes lost these battles and he was forced to flee to a fortress in the city of Nora in the province of Cappadocia. From there, he continued his opposition to Antigonus. Nevertheless, before Perdiccas could overcome these rebellions throughout the empire, he was murdered in 321.

Two years later, General Antipater, the regent of Macedonia, died in 319. Polyperchon was chosen to succeed Antipater instead of his son Cassander. In Asia Minor, Antigonus finally defeated General Eumenes by capturing his ruling Silvershield elite regiment and other portions of his army. The defeated officers of Eumenes handed him over in exchange for their release. Antigonus placed Eumenes on trial and executed him. These victories made Antigonus the strongest among the diadochis and gave him control of all the territories of the former Alexandrian empire, stretching from the borders of Syria in the east to Asia Minor towards the west. After that, he entered Baylon and Susa and raided their treasuries. General Seleucus, who served as the governor in Babylon after the death of Perdiccas, fled into Egypt for refuge with Ptolemy. By 315, Seleucus readily joined with the campaign of Ptolemy, Lysimachus and Cassander against Antigonus.

The following year in 314, Antigonus invaded the province of Phoenicia and besieged Tyre. However, by the year 312, his son Demetrius I was defeated by Ptolemy at the Battle of Gaia. This setback provided Seleucus with the opportunity to return to Babylonia. This time Seleucus built his own powerbase. This rift started the Babylonian wars between the two former generals of Alexander's once united army. During these conflicts Seleucus defeated both Demetrius and Antigonus and secured Babylon as his share of the empire. In the west, Demetrius continued his campaigns throughout the region. In 306 he conquered Cyprus. Following this victory, his father Antigonus declared himself King. After this move, the other regents, Cassander, Ptolemy, Lysimachus, and Seleucus, followed suit and declared themselves "Kings" over the territories they controlled.

After this, Antigonus assembled a large army and a massive naval fleet and appointed Demetrius I as the head of this mighty force. By 301, all these adversaries confronted each other at the Battle of Ipsus. The war was very intense. Antigonus met great resistance. Lysimachus outflanked General One-eyed forcing his son Demetrius to turn his attention and manpower towards the west. This gap in the frontlines left Antigonus vulnerable. General Seleucus maneuvered his hundreds of warrior elephants to split through the middle of their ranks, cutting off much needed help for Antigonus. Both Antigonus and Demetrius were defeated in this battle. At the age of 81, Antigonus was mortally wounded by a javelin's spear. Demetrius was forced to flee to Ephesus for his safety.

Demetrius I Poliorcetes
(294 B.C.E.—283 B.C.E.)

Demetrius I was born among the families of Macedonian nobility in the year of 337, which was exactly one year before Phillip II was assassinated. His father Antigonus named him in honor of the Greek goddess Demeter who was superstitiously believed to be a child of the idols Zeus and Rhea. The craved female statue of Demeter was regarded as a sacred post [goddess] which controlled the growth of cereal crops, such as wheat oats, rye, and barley, whom Greeks prayed to and worshipped as a protector against famine and starvation. The life of Demetrius I was very similar to that of his predecessor Alexander the Great in the sense that he and his father served closely together for several years just like the father-son team of Alexander and Phillip. He became known as Poliorcetes *"The Besieger"* because of his conquests under the directions of his father. Demetrius went on to establish control over central Greece. This advance caused a major rift between him and Cassander in Macedon and in the Aegean Sea. By 307 Demetrius conquered Athens and used the city for his powerbase. Athens was a place where he was worshipped as a *"Savior God"* because of his new policy of amnesty for the cities once under the tyranny of Antipater, Polyperchon, and Cassander.

While in Athens Demetrius launched a massive shipbuilding program to increase the size of his fleet. This buildup was intended to thwart the advances of Cassander from the west, Ptolemy from the south, and the forces of Seleucus to the east. Nevertheless, the showdown between Demetrius and Cassander was averted when Antigonus called him back to Asia Minor for backup support. Demetrius backup assistance was unsuccessful. They lost the battle at Ipsus and his father Antigonus was slain in the raging battle.

Following that setback, Demetrius was forced to retreat to the Grecian mainland. During this time, he consolidated his control in Greece. Meanwhile in Macedonia, his arch-enemy Cassander died of dropsy in 297 leaving the throne of Macedon to his dysfunctional and squabbling siblings. Case in point: Cassander's son Antipater II murdered his own mother Thessalonica because he believed she favored his brother Alexander V over him. To avenge the blood of his mother and get rid of his bloody brother, Alexander V requested support from Demetrius, who proved to be a false and double-hearted witness. In fact, the HELPER became the HURTFUL ONE. The reason I say this is because after Demetrius helped Alexander V reclaim the throne by overthrowing his brother Antipater II, he turned around a murdered Alexander V a few days later. After this, the army of Macedon and Greece named Demetrius the new king. Thus the House of Antigonus ascended to the throne over the kingdom of Macedonia replacing the House of Antipater.

After these devilish deeds, Demetrius initiated a massive renovation program throughout Greece. He reestablished strong garrisons at historic Corinth and improved the mountaintop temple-complex overlooking the city known as the *"Acrokornth"*. He also did the same for Chalcis and the city of Demetrias, which he built in his own honor and glory. To maintain control he also established a network of garrisons across the mainland.

In Macedonia, Demetrius was regarded as a stranger because of his upbringing in Oriental Asia. However, the benefits of Demetrius background was his further importation of Afro-Aisatic live skills into Greece and the throughout the Balkans. In 288, Demetrius faced an invasion from Pyrrhus of Epirus and Lysimachus of Thrace. The Macedonian army deserted Demetrius on the battlefield. Demetrius fled byway of the sea. Three years later he was captured by the forces of Seleucus, the regent of Babylon and eastern Asia. Seleucus placed Demetrius under house arrest in Cilicia where he remained until he died in 283 B.C.E..

Antigonus II Gonatas
(276-239 B.C.E.)

Antigonus II was born in 319 in the city of Gonnoi in the province of Thessaly. He was son of Demetrius I, the son of Antigonus I, and Phila, who was the daughter of Antipater. Following the Macedonian tradition, Antigonus was groomed to become a part of the country's fighting machine from a young age. Early on, he received the title *"Gonatas,"* deriving from the iron plate protecting the knee. By the age of 18 he was serving as a general for his father. In 288 B.C.E. Antigonus fought besides Demetrius when Seleucus, Ptolemy, Lysimachus, and Prryhus formed an alliance against them. Lysimachus attacked from the east while Prryhus invaded from the west. His father fled byway of the sea after the Macedonian army deserted him. Antigonus was left in charge. In absence of father, Antigonus meticiously gained control of Greece. After years of moving to various port cities, Demetrius was captured and died while under house arrest in Cilicia in 283. The body of Demetrius was returned to Antigonus II Gonatas via the sea in an elaborate display. Antigonus put his entire fleet, which he dedicated to the sun-god Apollo, to sea to receive the remains of his father near Cycladies. Antigonus then conducted a great ceremony in Corinth before interning his father's corpse in the city of Demetria. *(Remember. Demetria was the city built by Demetrius I in honor of himself in the province of Thessaly)*.

The following year in 282 war broke out between Seleucus and Lysimachus. Lysimachus was slain during this conflict. Hoping to expand his territory, Seleucus sought to claim the kingdoms of Thrace and Macedonia. However, Ptolemy Keraunos, the son of Ptolemy I, moved his forces into the region and murdered Seleucus, seized the throne of Macedon for himself. Continuous conflicts between Macedonia and surrounding city-states, such as Epirus and Thrace, persisted for several more years.

By that time, Antigonus had rebuilt his army and navy, and decided to move against Ptolemy to recapture his father's [Demetrius] throne and drive the Ptolemies from the Aegean Sea. Nevertheless, Antigonus lost the battles against Ptolemy Keraunos. Although it seemed Ptolemy's position was secure, his success was short-lived. In the winter of 279, Brennus, the leader of the barbaric hordes of Gauls, descended upon the Balkan Peninsula from the northern forest [Western Europe]. They crushed Ptolemy's army and slew him in the ensuing battle. With the uncivilized and uncultured Gauls now ruling the kingdom, Macedonia fell into complete anarchy, reducing it back into the stone ages. From there, the Gauls also moved into parts of Greece. However, by the year 278 Antigonus had mustered his army in defense of Greece against the European invaders. His strategy consisted of forming an alliance with a large mercenary force from Aetolia to check the advance of the Gauls. He was victorious in defeating them at Thermopylae and Delphi. After that victory, Antigonus sailed to Hellespont and ambushed to eastern flank of the Gauls and completely destroyed them at the Battle of Lysimachia, the following year in 277. After those events the fame of Antigonus II Gonatas spread and he proclaimed himself the "king of Macedonia". During this same time, Antigonus married his niece Phila who gave birth to their son who became known as Demetrius II Aetolicus.

And it came to pass after a thirty-seven year reign, and at the age of 80, Antigonus gave up the ghost and went to sleep with his fathers. His son Demetrius II Aetolicus ruled in his stead.

In retrospect, before we move forward to the legacy of the next ruler of Macedonia, there are several important things that we should note about Antigonus II Gonatas. One important fact is Antigonus increased the use of oriental culture in this newly emerging region of southeastern Europe. Secondly, it should be noted that he did not gain power as a great warrior. Instead he was a strategist who worked patiently to restore the military of his father and grandfather. In times of peace he prepared for war. He expanded the size of his naval force in the Aegean Sea with hundreds of large advanced ships. These new vessels gave him the strength to withstand the aggression by the Ptolemies. In addition, the Macedonian army strategy consisted of a cavalry brigade and phalanx formations with soldiers equipped with new **brass** helmets, shields, spears, and sarissas. He also instituted the heavy usage of mercenaries to assist his forces in all of his major battles.

Demetrius II Aetolicus
(239 B.C.E.—229 B.C.E.)

Demetrius II Aetolicus was born in the year 275. He was the son of Antigonus II Gonatas and Phila. Like his predecessors, he was trained in the art of warfare at a young age. While his father Antigonus II sat on the throne, he began to serve in the military. Historical records indicate his father promoted him into a powerful position as co-regent by the time he was 15. One of his first major victories was his triumph over Alexander II, the king of Epirus, in the battle at Dardia. This 260 B.C.E. victory saved Macedonia from utter ruin. Demetrius military skills enabled him to recover major portions of territories lost by his grandfather Demetrius I and father Antigonus II Gonatas. He also extended the borders of the Macedonian kingdom to Euboea, Magnesia, and Thessaly.

When Demetrius II came to power as the sole ruler in the winter of 239, he faced a coalition of enemies known as the Achaean League and the Aetolian League. These adversaries united against him, however, Demetrius defeated them and captured the city-state of Boetia. The kingdom of Macedonia actually experienced a revival under the leadership of Demetrius II.

In his personal life, he married a woman named Chryseis who bore him a son named Phillip V. Nevertheless towards the end of his ten-year reign, the barbarians known as the Dardanians descended from the wastelands of the north into the Balkans. The war against those fierce vandals ended in disaster for Demetrius. He was slain in the battle. Demetrius died leaving his son Phillip V, who was just a 9-year old child, as the next possible successor.

Antigonus III Doson
(229 B.C.E.—221 B.C.E.)

Born in 263 B.C.E., Antigonus III Doson came to power because his 9-year-old second cousin Phillip V was unable to assume the throne. Both, the generals in the Macedonian army and the aristocracy decided that Phillip's age was a liability to the interest of the kingdom. In their eyes the challenges and threats to the kingdom were too great to wait for Phillip to grow up. Instead, by consensus they chose another family member, a cousin, Antigonus III Doson, who happened to be an experienced soldier in the military.

Now Antigonus III Doson was the great-grandson of the dynasty's founder Antigonus I Monophthalmus. As I stated earlier, Antigonus I begat Demetrius I Poliorcetes, who begat two sons, Antigonus II Aetolicus and **Demetrius the Fair**. Now, **Demetrius the Fair and his wife Olympias begat Antigonus III Doson. His father Demetrius the Fair died in 250 B.C.E.** after leaving the royal house in Macedonia to live with his new bride the princess Berenice II in Cyrene. In a strange turn of events, after his arrival, Demetrius ended up falling in love with his bride's mother, Apama II, instead of becoming one flesh with his new fiancee. The expectant bride became extremely jealous, and felt bereaved, so she arranged a murderous plot and slew him.

Meanwhile back in Macedonia, the 13-year-old ophran Antigonus III Doson was raised by his uncle, King Antigonus II. Following the Antigonid Dynasty tradition, he attended military school and rose up through the ranks to become a general. Once he was chosen as regent, he worked wisely to secure the borders of the Macedonian empire. He also formed new alliances with the neighboring city-states of Epirus and the Achaean League, hoping to re-establish the kingdom's hegemony over the Grecian mainland through diplomacy. Two of his important military victories were his defeat of the barbaric Dardanian invaders and the suppression of the rebellion of Thessaly. These events stabilized his rule and he was then crowned "King of Macedonia". There were no rivals to Antigonus III Doson's claim to the throne, yet historians said he still viewed himself as the caretaker for his young cousin Phillip V.

In 228 B.C.E. he fought against Cleomenes, King of Sparta, at the Battle of Sellasia for control of the Peloponese Peninsula. The Macedonian phalanx outnumbered and overwhelmed the Spartans reducing their army and city-state to rubble. Cleomenes fled into Egypt with the Ptolemies for refuge. While Antigonus was in the south, the Illyrians invaded Macedonia from the north. Antigonus quickly returned back to Macedonia to repel the attackers. But during this 221 B.C.E. episode he won the battle, but loss his life in the battle by rupturing a blood vessel and bled to death.

During his lifetime he married Chryseis, the former queen and widow of Demetrius III Aetolicus, and mother of Phillip V. He also worshipped and participated in the Nemean Games held in the city of Nemea. These games were held in honor of the idol-god Zeus. Greeks also believed the athletic games were founded by the graven image Heracles.

Phillip V
(221 B.C.E.—179 B.C.E.)

Phillip V was born in Pella, Macedonia in 238 B.C.E. as the son of Antigonus II Gonatas and Phila, who was the daughter of General Antipater, the first regent and founder of the Antipatrid Dynasty over ancient Macedonia. When Phillip was born, unfortunately, his father had less than a decade to live. As I stated earlier, he was only nine years old when his father died from his war injuries. His older cousin Antigonus III Doson was selected to rule until

Phillip came of age. For eight years Phillip sat at the feet of his older cousin Antigonus and the council of advisors that trained the young lad for his eventual rulership. In 204 B.C.E., Phillip V turned 17. His opportunity to become king came when Antigonus III Doson died. In Greek society, he was known for his good-looks and a great charming personality which earned him the nicknamed *"the beloved of all Greece"*. However, on the battlefield he was regarded as a fearless warrior in the spirit of Alexander the Great. In the bedroom, he also possessed the perverse spirit of Alexander the Great as well.

In the beginning of his reign, one of first challenges came from a group of northern lower-class invaders known as the Dardanians. After reversing their advances, he went on to convene a conference known as Hellenic League of Greek states. This convention made him a regional leader throughout the mainland. The city-states of Aetolia, Elis, and Sparta opposed the unity gathering. Phillip then declared war on them. His attempt to extend Macedonia to its former glory sparked a three-year war which started in 220 and lasted until 217 B.C.E. Phillip's action forced his enemies to request help from the emerging Roman kingdom. Rome's intervention eventually led to the downfall of the entire four divisions of the former Hellenistic dynasties.

By 217 Phillip and Rome were open enemies. Yet, Rome had unfinished business to its south which prevent the Italians from swiftly moving into the region to assist any of their allies. Rome was involved in a lengthy war with King Hannibal, the ruler of Carthage, who had launched an offensive to invade the great city located on seven mountains. Meanwhile, Phillip invaded Illyria, which was a client state of Rome situated on the western bank of the Balkan Peninsula. He then challenged Roman influence on the eastern shore of the Adriatic Sea. These campaigns brought Phillip V into direct conflict with Rome, sparking the ten-year First Macedonian War.

To make matters worse, two years later in 215, Phillip made peace with Rome's arch enemy King Hannibal of Carthage, who had earlier plundered the Italians. He also expanded Macedon's maritime influence throughout the Aegean Sea. These high-handed moves by Phillip angered the Romans and war became inevitable. During the next decade Rome began to interfere in the political affairs on the Grecian mainland. In fact, in 207 Rome joined the Aeotian League uniting with Greek city-states that opposed Phillip. Nevertheless, Phillip defeated these city-states before Rome could come to their rescue. Phillip and his troops burned down the temples and public buildings in city of Thermum, which was the political and religious capital of the Aetolian League, then burned up to 2,000 graven image-gods and hauled away large quantities of gold, silver, and precious gems,15,000 brass shields and suits-of-arms. These shields were armors taken from the enemies of the Aetolians during their previous victories. This included the shields of the Gauls who had invaded in the third century. Phillip forced an independent peace treaty upon the city of Aeotila and worked a favorable peace agreement with Rome, halting their advance. This 206 B.C.E. agreement was known as the Peace of Phoenice. Instead of keeping the peace, Phillip started a war with the kingdom of Rhodes then joined King Antiochus III, ruler of Syria, and plundered the great treasures of Egypt held by the boy king Ptolemy V.

In the west, the Romans had finally overcome the Carthagians in the year 200. This allowed Rome to turn its attention eastward. During this same period Phillip faced a setback in his offensive against the kingdoms of Rhodes and Pergamum. By 201 the two-kingdom alliance had united to defeat the Macedonian forces in a sea battle near the coastal city of Chios. By now Rome's patience with Phillip had run out. The Roman legions moved into Macedonia, beginning The Second Macedonian War. By 199/198 Rome attacked both Macedonia and Thessaly. This attack, led by Roman general Titus Quinctius Flamininus, greatly weakened Macedonia's grip across Greece. This war also proved the superiority of the Roman legions over the famous Greek phalanx formations. This engagement took place in the city of Cynoscephaeae in the kingdom of Thessaly. Rome demanded Phillip sign a peace agreement to confine his armies to the borders of Macedonia. He was ordered to pay a 1,000 talents indemnity, leave his naval fleets, and hostages in Rome: included among the hostages was Phillip V's younger son Demetrius. These arrangements forced Phillip to make an alliance with Rome. He then joined in with their campaigns against their enemies on the Greek mainland and peninsula. During this time his son Perseus was the commanding general.

After years of good conduct, Rome rewarded Macedonia and returned all of their assets by 190. After this, Phillip spent most of his time restructuring his kingdom. He reorganized the treasury, transplanted various ethnic groups to different lands, and reopened the gold and silver mines to increase his wealth. During this time Phillip also introduced a new national currency and several local currencies throughout his realm. These reinforcements made Phillip's neighboring states very nervous. When the annual conference in Rome convened, the neighboring states accused Phillip of sedition against imperial Rome. At this point, Phillip was certain that Rome would invade his country once again. And they did. The Roman generals Scipio Africanus, Publius Cornelius, and Lucius Cornelius Scipio Asiaticus and their legions moved through Macedonia and Thrace.

Nevertheless from 184 to 181 B.C.E., Phillip launched a pre-emptive campaign throughout the western Balkan. Meanwhile, Rome had supplanted Phillip by secretly grooming his young son Demetrius to be their pro-Roman successor in Macedonia. However, Phillip wanted his older son Perseus to be heir on the throne. This led to a quarrel between his two sons. The next year an evil spirit of jealously and paranoia gripped Phillip moving him to slay his own son Demetrius, charging him with treason. This treacherous decision affected Phillip's fate. One year after taking his son's life, it came to pass that Phillip died in Amphipolis during 179 B.C.E. at the age of 59 while involved in a conflict between two barbarian tribes, the Dardanians and the Bastarnaes. Phillip had been a very popular ruler, however his long-term strategy for Macedonian expansionism never materialized. Rather, in the closing days of his reign, the Roman Republic expanded eastwards into the territories of the late Alexander the Great. His son Perseus ruled in his stead.

Perseus
(179 B.C.E.—168 B.C.E.)

Perseus was the oldest son of King Phillip V and his concubine named Polycreatia from the island of Argos. Born in 221 B.C.E., his father and mother named him after the Greek mythological idol called Perseus. In Grecian idolatry (legend) the god Perseus was considered the son of an imaginary sexual relationship between the idol Zeus and the female image called Danae. As the story goes, Zeus turned himself into a shower of liquid gold then poured himself through a small hole while Danae was imprisoned. This god of liquid gold laid on floor in love with Danae. Zeus then transformed himself and had sex with Danae and conceived Perseus. That was the origin and meaning of the name Perseus.

At the age of 42, Perseus ascended to the Macedonian throne, and in fact, he was actually the last of kings from the Antigonid Dynasty. A dynasty that had ruled the territory since the breakup of the united Grecian empire after the death of Alexander the Great in the year 323. Perseus path to the throne came after he staged a plot to turn his father against his younger brother. He convinced his father, Phillip V, that his young brother Demetrius had become a Roman traitor during his earlier exile in great city of Rome. As a result of this instigation, and, Phillip's own hatred for the new Roman overlords, Demetrius was charged with treason and executed.

Once Perseus gained power in 179 B.C.E. he made two strategic moves. The first one was his decision to renew his father's treaty with the Roman Republic. The second move was his plan to reconquer the entire Grecian mainland and restore Macedonian dominance throughout the region. Perseus exerted Macedonian influence over two Roman allies, Thrace and Illyria, and made special efforts to seduce the Greek city-states to support a native son instead of Roman outsiders. He even supported popular uprisings in the city-state kingdoms of Thessaly and Aetolia against Big Brother Rome. In the eyes of Rome, his next unpopular move was the suppression of the city of Golopia. After this victory, Perseus and his mighty men rode into the revered pagan sanctuary of Delphi. Greeks across the mainland were disturbed. Delphi was respected as the holy of holies in the Greco-Roman Hellenistic world. By 172, Eumenes

II, the ruler of city-state of Pergamum, turned against Perseus and dispatched envoys to Rome to enter a plea against his actions, accusing him of interference in his neighbor's affairs. Rome, in return, dispatched their ambassadors to Macedonia for talks and clarifications. Perseus refused to receive the diplomats. Those policies alarmed Rome and eventually led to direct confrontation known as the Third Macedonian War. The conflict lasted for three years,171-168, and ended with his capture. For three years Perseus held off the Roman advance until his army finally lost the western flank and the region of Illyria.

Perseus defeat came on the day of June 22,168 when he and the Roman General Lucius Aemilius Paullus faced-off on the battlefield near the city of Pydna in southern Macedonia. The Roman legions overpowered the Macedonian phalanx, sending the Grecian forces into retreat. Perseus was forced to surrender, stripped, and taken as a prisoner-of-war to Alba Facens, Italy where he died in the stockade. In restrospect, Perseus defeat came because he failed to see the handwriting on the wall. Little did he know,the days of [**the kingdoms of brass**] were rapidly disappearing and the prophetic [**kingdom of iron**] was emerging.

After Rome's complete conquest over Macedonia, Amphipolis grew into its first capital among four Roman mini-republics established on former Macedonian territory. In fact, Amphipolis became the chief city-state created by the Romans which they craved out of the kingdom of the Antigonids. A large naval base was located there along with several large luxurious temples dedicated to the image-gods of Greeks. In the days of Alexander the Great, several great Macedonian admirals came from there. That included Admiral Nearchus, Admiral Androsthenes, and Admiral Laomedon. Another reason which made this area a jewel of nature was the fact that the city was situated near the crossroads of Macedonian royal roads close to the Pargaon hills where there were large gold mines. Rome conquered this area and made it a part of their extensive Roman royal roads.

The Ptolemy Dynasty of (Egypt)
(323—30 B.C.E.) 2nd Division of Alexandrian Empire
The Beginning of The White Man Takeover of Africa

Ptolemy I Soter(323—285 B.C.E.), Ptolemy II Philadelphus (285—246 B.C.E.), Ptolemy III Euergetes (246—221 B.C.E.), Ptolemy IV Philopator (221—205 B.C.E.), Ptolemy V Epiphanes (204—181 B.C.E.), Ptolemy VI Philometor (181—145 B.C.E.), (169—164 B.C.E.)[**1st reign**] Ptolemy VIII Physcon [**2nd reign**](144—131 B.C.E [**3rd reign**]) 126 —116 B.C.E.), Ptolemy IX Soter II (116—110 [**1st reign**], 109—107[**2nd reign**], 88—81 B.C.E.[**3rd reign**]), Ptolemy X Alexander (110—109 B.C.E.[**1st reign**]107—88 B.C.E.[**2nd reign**]), Ptolemy XI Alexander II (80 B.C.E.), Ptolemy XII Auletes (80—51 B.C.E.), Cleoptra (51— 30 B.C.E.), Ptolemy XIII Theos Philopator (51—47 B.C.E.), Ptolemy XIV Theos Philopator II (47—44 B.C.E.), Ptolemy XV Caesarion (44—30 B.C.E.).

Ptolemy I[the First] Soter
(323 B.C.E.—285 B.C.E.)

Ptolemy I [the First] Soter was born in the year 367 B.C.E. as the son of a Macedonian nobleman named Lagus, of the city of Eordaea, and his wife named Arsinoe. His birth name was Ptolemy Lagus. Like most Macedonian youths during his era he underwent military training at a young age, serving as an infantryman with Alexander the Great's father, King Phillip II and working his way up through the ranks. When Alexander began his Persian campaign in the year 334, Ptolemy had been promoted to a general. By the time, the Greeks had conquered Asia Minor and the Near East, Ptolemy had become one of the Diadochi ["the followers"] who were regarded as the king's trusted generals. Eventually he was promoted to Alexander's inner circle as one of his chief seven bodyguards. Alexander trusted Ptolemy because he was a senior officer who supported his Hellenistic policy of mixing primitive Grecian culture with advanced Egyptian, Babylonian, and Persian customs.

After Alexander invaded Egypt he appointed a man named Clemones, a wealthy corrupt Greek banker, to control the export of Egypt's lucrative grain trade. There were many complaints about his unfair practices. Alexander, who was now regent in Babylon, replaced Clemones with his trusty general Ptolemy. King Alexander the Great established a Council of State to oversee the affairs of the province of Egypt and to maintain control. This arrangement worked well as long as Alexander lived. However, after Alexander's death, General Perdiccas, who became the second-in-command after the death of Hephaestion, did not share the same admirable feelings towards Ptolemy. Immediately after Alexander died on June 11, 323, Perdiccas became the regent in Babylon, which had become the new capital for the vast Grecian empire. Peridiccas summoned all the main officers of the Macedonian army to discuss the future of their new position as rulers of the Oriential World.

After back and forth jockeying, Ptolemy was officially promoted and assigned to the governorship over wealthy Egypt. This historic appointment shifted the orbit of the ancient world. For the first time in Egypt's 4,000 year history, a white[**Aryan**] man was sitting on the throne of Pharaoh as the ruling god-king of the land of Kemet. Ptolemy then proclaimed himself to be "The Soter" [The Savior] and established a succession of Euro-Pharaohs who became known as the 31st Dynasty that ruled the kingdom in Africa for nearly 300 years. Ptolemy also changed his name to the Egyptian name of Meryamum Setepenre which meant *"beloved of Amun, chosen of Re"*. He courted the native black population by acknowledging their historic greatness and married a daughter of Nectanebo II. He sent his Macedonian wife named Artacama back to the isles of the Gentiles. Ptolemy modeled his monarchy after the traditions of the ancient Pharaohs and in year 305/304 B.C.E. He demanded that his courtiers and populace address him with the title *"Pharaoh"*. He then proclaimed himself a god-king and shifted the center of Greek culture towards Egypt. Again, this blending and consolidation of Egyptian and Greek gods, temples and cultures along with a new geo-political reality gave birth to what we know today as the Hellenistic way of life. The truth of the matter was: Ptolemy never forsook his Euro-roots totally. This was shown when he also claimed that he was a descendant of the pure Greek deity Heracles who was regarded as the founder of the ancient Argeads [white people].

In Greek mythology the word Heracles meant *"Hera's glory"*. In reality Heracles was just another graven image which Greeks believed was the son of Zeus, who was also just another idol. Heracles was revered as the greatest hero among their pantheon of deities. In their psyche Heracles exemplified manhood and the champion of the Olympian order. They believed marbled statues possessed strength, courage, and sexual prowess. In terms of sexuality, Heracles was regarded as one who was sexually active with men, boys, and women. According to legend, one day Heracles was walking through the wilderness and he was jumped on by the Dryopians. Heracles overcame them and he killed their king Theidamus. The other assailants gave up and offered him Prince Hylas. Heracles took the young boy and made in his armourbearer and his child lover. Years later, Hylas joined the crew of Argo as an argonaut to journey to Mysia. Once Hylas arrived he was kipnapped by an island full of women known as nymphs. Heracles was heartbroken and searched for Hylas for a longtime. However, Hylas had fallen in love with the nymphs and never returned back to the arms of Heracles. In legend, Heracles was also known to possess several other male lovers that included Nestor, Iolaus, Elacatas, Nireus, Abderus, and Iphitus. Ptolemy, like all of Alexander's inner circle, practiced sodomy.

(Now back to reality! Man!, those Greeks were so perverse and delusional.)

In Egypt, Ptolemy founded the new cult of Serapis which joined both Macedonians and Egyptians together as one. He also studied heavily and gained deep insight at the Library of Alexandria which was filled with books and scholarship of ancient Egypt and the ancient world. This extensive research led Ptolemy to commission the translation of the Hebrew bible into the Greek language.

Meanwhile in Babylon, a feud broke out between General Perdiccas and General Seleucus. Seleucus fled to Egypt for refuge. In pursuit, General Perdiccas marched against Egypt with an army of 5,000 cavalrymen and an infantry of 20,000. Both armies confronted each other near Memphis, Egypt and Perdiccas lost the battle. After the loss, the officers in Perdiccas army mounted a mutiny and murdered him. General Seleucus then returned to Babylon.

During a moment of reflection on the deep divisions throughout the once united empire, Ptolemy was once quoted as saying these following words: "Within hours [after the death of Alexander] we were fighting like Jackal for his corpse. The wars of the world had begun. Forty years off and on, they [The Diadochi Wars] endured until we divided his empire in four parts. I think Alexander would have been disappointed in us." In fact, there were bitter and continuous wars between the Ptolemies and the Antigonids, Seleucids, and Thracians throughout this era. These conflicts were known as The Four Diadochi Wars.

In the year 283/282, Ptolemy I Soter died at the age of 84 and was buried in Alexandria in the royal necropolis. After his burial the Egyptian populace built a statue in his honor and elevated him to the status of a god[public hero].

Ptolemy II Philadelphus
(285 B.C.E.—246 B.C.E.)

Ptolemy II Philadelphus was born in the year 309/308 in Alexandria, Egypt as the son of Ptolemy I Soter and Berenice I[the First]. He grew and ascended to the throne to become the second king of the Ptolemy dynasty ruling over the land of Kemet. His reign lasted for thirty-nine years. After military training and school, he became co-regent with his father Ptolemy I Soter for his final three years of life during the years 285 to 282. After assuming power, he purged all his potential rivals, including close family members such as brothers, his first wife, and others. Ptolemy II first marriage was with Arsinoe I, the widow of King Lysimachus of Thrace. After the of death of King Lysimachus in the year 282/281, Ptolemy II then married his widow Arsinoe who happened to be his own maternal-sister. She then became known as Arsinoe II. He was also known to engage in homosexual acts like sleeping with his cupbearer Cleino, another one named Didyme the harp player, and Mnesis and Pothine, his flute players.

In Alexandria, Ptolemy royal court was filled with magnificent splendor and the highest standard of living for that era. His royal park was filled with exotic animals from far off lands. During the imperial festivals the processions were led by 24 chariots drawn by elephants, a procession of lions, leopards, panthers, camels, antelopes, wild asses, ostriches, a bear, giraffes, and rhinoceros. The parade also included a seven-feet tall golden statue led by four elephants.

However, Ptolemy II Philadelphus reign was marred with continuous wars against the Seleucids in Asia and the Near East, and the Antigonids in Asia Minor, and against the rulers of territories surrounding the Mediterranean and the Aegan Sea. In the year 258 Ptolemy lost a battle against Antigonus II Gonatas, king of Macedonia, at Kos, Greece. Ptolemy lost a major part of his fleet during the two-year conflict known as the First Syrian War which extended from 258 to 256. Nevertheless, the setback did not stop Ptolemy's meddling in Macedonia affairs and his command of the Aegan Sea. During the Third Syrian War in the year 250 B.C.E., Ptolemy defeated Antiochus II, the ruler of the Seleucids. **(This conflict was spoken of in the book of Daniel, chapter 11: 7-9.)** The powerful naval fleet of Ptolemy consisting of 112 ships inflicted heavy damage upon the Seleucids near the seaboard of Asia Minor. After his victory over Antiochus, both sides agreed to a peace treaty. In return, Antiochus married Ptolemy's daughter Berenice to seal the alliance.

Ptolemy was never able to provide the support needed by his allies in Athens and Sparta to overthrow the yoke of Macedonia. Instead, he also pursued diplomacy and marriage to maintain his sphere of influence on the Grecian mainland. Those alliances served as a buffer zone to protect Egypt from foreign invasions, which in turn, gave Ptolemy time to deal with several other challenges.

Ptolemy II Philadelphus was regarded as an educated, prudent, and enlightened leader known for his promotion of economic development and extensive renovations throughout his realm. He beautified the city of Alexandria by expanding the Museum and Library and increased the grandeur of the Egyptian royal court. He also made Alexandria the center for poetry and scholarship. These inclusive policies of culture exchange allowed the wisdom of ancient black Kemet to be taken back to white Greece and Macedonia. These exchanges served as the most important stimulus in the evolution of the Grecian people, and eventually all Europe.

Ptolemy III Euergetes "Benefactor"
(246 B.C.E.—221 B.C.E.)

Ptolemy III Euergetes, *pronounced* Eu-er-ge-tes which means [Benefactor], was born in Kos, Greece as the son of Ptolemy II Philadelphus and Arsinoe I. (Remember, Arsinoe I was the daughter of Lysimachus, the king of Thrace.) Ptolemy III Euergetes had been groomed to be the third Macedonian king of the Ptolemaic dynasty from his youth. His reign lasted for twenty-five years. One of the first things he did when he came to power in 246 B.C.E. was the construction of new statues to honor his mother and father as gods[**public heroes**]. He married Berenice of Cyrene. They bore six children: 1) Arsinoe III, born in 246/245, who grew up to marry her own blood brother Ptolemy IV. 2) Ptolemy IV, the second oldest child was born in 244, the third, Lysimachus, born in 243, the fourth, Alexander, who was born the following year in 242, the fifth, Magas, born in 241, and sixth, Berenice, who died as an infant child before the age of one.

Ptolemy III continued the policies of his predecessors, beautifying the royal city of Alexandria, expanding the royal library, conducting scientific research, and embracing Egyptian religious concepts. He is remembered for donating to the cults of the sacred cow Apis and Mnevis Bull. He also remodeled the Karnak temple. By 238 B.C.E. Ptolemy became the first known white ruler to issue a royal decree inscribed in both Egyptian hieroglyphics and the Greek language on massive stone blocks. The inscriptive stone stela became known as the Canopus Stone with priestly orders, poetry, and a written memorial to his daughter. The following year Ptolemy III Euergetes built the Serapeum which was the temple of Horus in the city of Edfu. Prior to this, the ancient Persians, Indians, Babylonians, and others had already used those ancient stone-block billboards centuries earlier.

On the international scene, the conflict between the Ptolemies and the Seleucids flared up again when Ptolemy III Euergetes's older sister Berenice Phemophorus, along with her baby, were murdered in Babylon. His rage was kindled. He invaded Syria, occupied Antioch, and besieged Babylon. As part of a peace agreement, Ptolemy received new territories on the northern coast of Syria. Meanwhile, in Greece, Ptolemy's foreign policy was centered on support for any of the enemies of kingdom of Macedonia.

Ptolemy IV Philopator
(221 B.C.E.—205 B.C.E.)

Ptolemy IV Philopator was born in the year 244/243 as the son of Euro-Pharaoh Ptolemy III Euergetes and his Euro-wife Berenice II. He was the king's firstborn son among their six siblings. He was surnamed Philopater, which meant, *"the man who loves his father."* His hereditary background fashioned him into a spoiled child who enjoyed a life of nobility, wealth, ease, and pleasure. He grew up in the king's court and became addicted to the "good life", wine, sexual orgies, and constant pleasures as a teenager. By the time he assumed the throne in 221 B.C.E. as the fourth Ptolemaic Pharaoh at the age of 23, he had already been corrupted by that extravagant lifestyle.

The hallmarks of his rulership were partying, daily-heavy drinking, multiple sexual partners, both men and women, the love of arts, poetry, drama, and hedonism. Those pursuits occupied the majority of his time during his 16-year reign. That is why the Greek historian Polybius reported that he remained under the influence of his favorites throughout his reign. Ptolemy was known to be indifferent about the low moral standards of his inner-circle as long as they carried out his day-to-day bidding. Namely, a man named Sosibius and the brother-sister tag team, Agathocles and Agathoclea. Both Agathocles and Agathoclea were his lovers. He fathered a child by Agathoclea, who was supposed to be the heir to the throne, but the child died at childbirth.

Sosibius, his other sexual partner, eased his burden of day-to-day governing, by becoming his number one chief minister. Sosibius was an experienced Alexandrian Greek known as a shrewd, capable, and cunning scoundrel who actually was the real power behind the throne. Sosibius became a member of the royal court around 235/234 during the reign of Ptolemy III. When Ptolemy IV came to the throne in 221, Sosibius became his chief advisers and held one of the highest post in the kingdom, serving as the Chief Priest of the Order of Alexander.

When Ptolemy IV came to power, Sosibius advised him to murder his mother, brother, and uncle. The queen-mother was poisoned. His brother, Magas, was scalded to death while bathing. His uncle was sentenced to death. In the end, Sosibius had all potential threats to Ptolemy IV removed.

Following the tradition of his father Ptolemy IV, he adopted the Egyptian name of Iwaennet-Erwy-Menkhwy-Setepptah-Userkare which meant *"heir of the two beneficent gods, Chosen of Ptah, Powerful is the Soul of Re, Living Image of Amun."* thus becoming a living god-king according to the Pharaonic tradition which dated back thousands of years. He married his own sister, Arisnoe, in order to maintain "royal blood". Together, they produced an heir to the throne. The brother-sister pair were regarded as the Benefactors, Father-Mother-loving, Saviour- state gods in the spirit of the Alexandrian cult. Meanwhile, Ptolemy and his court officials held continuous Feasts of Flagons involving drunkenness, orgies, and other base indignities. During the feasts honoring the image-god Dionysos, Ptolemy IV was honored as Dionysis by the multitudes who attended the celebration. He had a tattoo of an ivy-leaf printed on his body. The worshippers were called Gallus, meaning those devoted to the Great mother. Ptolemy and other men would dress in women's garb while masturbating and performing other freakish sexual acts during the parties.

Ptolemy IV Philopator was an ardent idolater. He composed a play and erected the Homereion, a pagan shrine honoring Homer. He also built the Great golden Horus for the Temple of Horus in the city of Edfu. He also constructed the Temple of Der-el-Medineh along with the Temple of Isis at Philae Tanis, the Khonsu Temple at Karnak, the Temple of Montu at Medannede, and the Ptolemaic Temple at Hathor. Ptolemy, a white man, built those monuments in hopes of persuading the native black Egyptian population into believing that he was just as good as a native black Pharaoh. Again, the Ptolemies were really foreigners with no real historic roots in Africa. This Ptolemy kingdom was really a private estate for the benefit of the Greek-Egyptians. In fact, the black Egyptians became restless during his reign. In terms of foreign policy, Ptolemy IV maintained a strong naval presence in the Mediterranean and Aegan Sea. But Ptolemy IV did not have not great interest in foreign affairs. It was noted that several of his allies, the rulers of Crete, the inhabitants of Cyclades, and others began to seek support from other regional powers because they believed Ptolemy did not have the will or desire to act with force. He lost territory that his predecessors had held for 20 years, principally parts of Syria. That is why many historians contend that the decline of the Ptolemaic dynasty over Egypt came during the reign of Ptolemy IV. In 220 B.C.E. Ptolemy married his own sister Arsinoe III. This incestuous brother-sister marriage produced the successor, Ptolemy V Epiphanes.

Nevertheless in the spring of 217 B.C.E. Ptolemy IV policy of isolationism had to change. Antiochus III, the king of the Seleucids, swarmed across Phoenica capturing Coele-Syria, portions of Israel, and he finally met Ptolemy's army at Raphia. This conflict became known as the Battle of Raphia. It took place on the edge of the Negev desert. Coincidentally, the Ptolemy-Seleucid battle between these two white Aryan kings was in the same location where the armies of the black kings of Assyria and Egypt engaged each other 500 years earlier.

Ptolemy army contained 70,000 foot soldiers, many of them native Egyptians, 5,000 horsemen, and 73 African elephants. Antiochus III had approximately 60,000 footmen that included several battalions of Asiatic mercenaries along with an equal amount of horsemen and 102 Indian elephants. Both sides engaged. In the heat of the battle, Antiochus III forces were routed in the Negev. His armies, consisting of white, black, brown, red, and yellow infantrymen, were outflanked and disbanded. King Antiochus was forced to flee back into Syria for his life. Ptolemy IV replaced him as the new lord over the land of Israel. After victory, Ptolemy restored his image-gods throughout Israel that previous rulers, the Persians and Seleucids, had destroyed. It should also be noted that Ptolemy IV was considered an enemy of the ancient black Israelites spoken of in the **Apocryphal** in **3 Maccabees**.

After the Raphia victory, the royal court commemorated the occasion with annual raucous celebrations. On the 20th of each month there was already a festival of revelry in honor of Ptolemy I and Berenice I. Ancient records reveal Ptolemy's royal palace was swarmed with alcoholics, writers, poets, whores, buffoons, philosophers, and other types of perverts.

If we looked for a modern example of what type of ruler Ptolemy was, we could look at former Russian President Boris Yeltsin as a great example. He was known as incompetent and a heavy drinker who allowed the Russian Federation to become weak during his reign in the1990s. Again, some historians contend that the decline of the Ptolemic dynasty over Egypt started during his 16-year reign. The reason being, the black generals, Harmacis and Amkmachis, from Upper Egypt launched a 20-year insurrection against the white Egyptian Greeks immediately after the Battle of Raphia, hoping to overthrow their foreign rule. This 20-year partition weakened the regime.

The most noted accomplishment for Ptolemy IV Philopater was his construction of a 420 ft. giant ship known as the *"Tessarakonteres,"* which means *"forty"*. This ship was a huge galley which was the largest human-powered vessel ever built. The ship could carry up to 2,850 mariners. However, in the end, Ptolemy's misconduct as the fourth Greco-god-king over Egypt brought the kingdom to a new low. The kingdom never recovered. In his final days, he and his sister-wife, retreated from the public eye. By the age of 50, his gluttonous drinking and other fetishes caused his health to deteriorate. Meanwhile, Queen Arsinoe withdrew into solitude too. Ptolemy died sometimes in the year 205, but no one knows for sure how and when he died. His courtiers kept his death a secret for a while. Finally on November 28, 203 B.C.E., his son Ptolemy V Epiphanes succeeded him on the throne in Alexandria, Egypt.

Ptolemy V Epiphanes
(204 B.C.E.—181 B.C.E.)

Born in Alexandria, Egypt in 210 B.C.E., Ptolemy V Epiphanes, [*pronounced* E-pi-ph-a-nes, meaning *"God Manifest"*] was the fifth Euro-Ptolemic ruler, who inherited the throne as a little child at the tender age of 5. His father, Ptolemy IV Philopator, had lived an extravagant lifestyle of wine, women, men, and song. In the year 205, he died near, or shortly thereafter, his 50th birthday, and left the kingship to his infant son. Although the child's mother, Queen Arsinoe III was still alive, her influence in the palace, and over the small boy's life, was next to none. In fact, she lived separately in another chamber of the palace and knew very little about the day-to-day affairs of the Ptolemaic kingdom. According to the historian Polybius, Queen Arsinoe III didn't even know her husband was dead for an entire year. Meanwhile, the two court favourites of the deceased Ptolemy IV Philopator, Sosibius and Agathocles, kept his death a secret while they plotted to murder her. They feared she would become the next powerful regent over her son and remove them from power. The mischievous two succeeded with their bloody plot. After they slew Queen Arsinoe III, the court ministers finally announced the deaths of the brother-sister, king-queen pair. By the year 204, the Sosibius-Agathocles clique had become the powerbrokers for the boy-king. Those chain of events caused deep unrest in the royal metropolis of Alexandria. Second only to Rome, the kingdom was now paralyzed. Overseas, the kings of Macedonia and Seleucid divided the possessions of the Ptolemies among themselves. Egypt was too weak to do anything.

By the year 202, the news of the king's and queen's death and the palace coup by Sosibius finally reached the frontline eastern outpost in Upper Egypt where one of the commanders of the army named General Tlepolemus was stationed. Tlepolemus[*pronounced* T-le-po-le-mus] and his garrison immediately broke rank and headed toward the capital.

Meanwhile, Sosibius and his clique set up a wooden platform in the public court of the palace. There they announced the death of the father and mother and introduced the boy-king to the audience. The crowd became a rowdy lynch mob with chaos spreading throughout the city. When Tlepolemus reached Alexandria he stormed the palace and took the boy to the nearby stadium in midst of the townsquare. His guardian Agathocles, the new chief minister, begged for his life once the heavily armed troops entered the palace. For some reason Sosibius was gone. Some say he had died in the year 203 while others contend he retired. Whatever the case, this confusion in Egypt caused weakness.

In Alexandria, the little king was taken to the center of the stadium and set on a throne. A royal diadem was placed on his seven-year-old head. A will was read aloud. Afterwards, one of the officers asked the lad if he wanted his parent's murderers to be put to death. The child, who was too young to know the difference between good and evil, nodded. Some historians believe the courtiers influenced the child, or made up a lie to dispose of the old regime. Regardless, the crowd interpreted his nod as a yes, and immediately there were demands for the heads of all the conspirators. Shouts of *"Its the king's will,"* could be heard ringing throughout the streets. Chief minister Agathocles, his sister, Agathoclea, and their mother, Oenanthe were dragged out the palace and carried through the streets. Their bodies were stripped naked and literally torn into pieces. Another member of the clique, General Philammon, who was also the governor of Libya [Cyrenaica], was beaten to death after returning home from duty in midst of the confusion. His son was strangled to death.

At the age of 12, the royal courtiers prepared a splendorous ceremony to officially anoint the young Ptolemy V Epiphanes as the king of Egypt. This made him the fifth Greek ruler to occupy the ancient black land of Kemet. The native Egyptian priests from the old capital of Memphis officiated the coronation ceremony. The extravagance of the ceremony made it fit for an ancient black Pharaoh. During these same festivities 12-year-old Ptolemy was crowned an Aryan god-king and received the surname *"Theos Epiphanes,"* which meant *"God Manifest."*

After Ptolemy grew into an energetic young man, he developed a selfish and harsh-temper. His cruelty and arrogance increased with his age until the point he was regarded as domineering. He loved to hunt and participated in open-air sports and other athletic activities. Ptolemy V Epiphanes violently put down a large scale Upper and Lower Egyptian rebellions by slaughtering their leaders and ruling the indigenous population with **brass** knuckles.

Eventually, the erratic young king found General Tlepolemus to be incompetent and replaced him with another official named Aristomenes. He later disposed of Aristomenes by forcing him to drink a cup of poisonous hemlock. He then selected Polycrates as his new chief of staff.

In the process of time, internal infighting caused external weakness. Eventually the empire of Ptolemy could not hold its grip on their overseas strongholds. Phillip V of Macedonia and Antiochus III of Seleucia divided the spoils of Asia and the Aegan Sea. In 198 B.C.E., Antiochus III captured the lands of Coele-Syria and Judaea. Five years later in the year 193/192, the Seleucid king gave his daughter Cleopatra I to young Ptolemy for marriage to conclude that treaty. The marriage produced the heir to the throne, Ptolemy VI Philometor.

When Cleopatra died, war broke out again. These two Gentile powers continued to fight each other for several decades, going back and forth in numerous wars with both sides exchanging control of the holyland for different periods of time. In the 11th chapter of Daniel, the Ptolemy dynasty is known as "the king of the south" while the Seleucid dynasty is termed "the king of the north". Eventually, the Roman empire subdued both sides and gained control of the entire region.

In hindsight, one of the most important parts of his legacy came when he became a young man. It was during this time that he commissioned the erection of a giant black basalt stone known as The Rosetta Stone. Although the Ptolemies used their native Greek language to administer state power, the giant billboard was written in three languages, classical Greek, ancient Kemetic hieroglyphics, and the Egyptian dialect. The monument also proclaimed the greatness of the Ptolemies, the power of the Egyptian priests, and other political commentaries.

In May of 181 B.C.E., Ptolemy V Epiphanes died suddenly leaving behind his wife Queen Cleopatra I of Syria as the regent for their son Ptolemy VI Philometor. He also had 2 more sons and 1 daughter.

Ptolemy VI Philometor
(180—145 B.C.E.)

Ptolemy VI Philometor was born in Alexandria, Egypt in 186 B.C.E. as the proud son of Ptolemy V Epiphanes and Queen Cleopatra I of Syria. Walking in the footsteps of his father, the baby boy Ptolemy VI assumed the mantle of power at the tender age of 6. Before the lad would know good from evil, his mother Queen Cleopatra served as his regent. Like most normal boys between the ages of 6 to 10 in his formative years, he was regarded as a *"momma's boy"*. He deeply loved the queen-mother and that affection earned him the surname *"Philometor"* which meant *"he who loves his mother"*.

In the year 176, however, his mother died while Ptolemy VI was a mere 10-year-old. The following year in 175, the royal court arranged a marriage between Ptolemy and his sister named Cleopatra II. It should be noted that it was customary for many Egyptian kings to marry their maternal sisters. The Ptolemaic Greeks adopted many of those same customs from the ancient inhabitants. In the following years, the incestuous union between this brother-sister couple produced 4 children: 1) Ptolemy Eupator, 2) Ptolemy VII Neos, 3) Cleopatra Thea, and, 4) Cleopatra III.

Meanwhile by year 170, arch-enemy Antiochus IV, the ruler of the Seleucid kingdom was on the rampage and took advantage of Egypt's inexperienced and weakened leadership. Antiochus IV passed the first blow in the Sixth Syrian War with the invasion of the land of Israel and two incursion into Egypt. In fact, he added Egypt to his territorial possessions and was crowned king of Egypt in 168. The Rome Senate intervened and demanded that he withdraw or face their legions. Antiochus withdrew. All of this strife occurred while Ptolemy was a teenager, no older than 17.

By the year 169, the kingdom's leadership had been reduced to a family triumvirate that consisted of the king, his queen-sister Cleopatra II, and his younger brother Ptolemy VIII Physcon. That arrangement lasted until 164 when Physcon rose up against Philometor and forced him to exit the throne. The Alexandrian Greeks did not agree with the coup d'etat of Physcon, and in the following year, Ptolemy VI Philometor was restored to power. After this, Philometor's countenance changed. An evil spirit came upon him and he ruled with brute force, cruelty, and suppressed all type of rebellions. Eventually, his brass knuckle policies did bring internal stability to the kingdom.

By 152, Philometor began to groom his son, Ptolemy Eupator, to be his successor, but, as fate would have it, his son died the same year. With Egypt stabilized, Philometor was able to turn his attention to foreign policy. In 150 B.C.E., he recognized a prince named Alexander Balas as the king of the Seleucid throne. To seal the deal, he gave his daughter Cleopatra Thea to the Syrian prince as a part of peace treaty. An elaborate ceremony was held in the city of Ptolemais Akko in the land of Israel. However, five years later in 145, while Prince Alexander Balas was away campaigning in Asia Minor, Ptolemy VI Philometor crossed him out. He took his daughter from Prince Alexander Balas and gave her to his rival Demetrius II. Then he invaded the land of Israel and Syria where he was crowned *"king of Asia"*. He then declared war on the Israelites who were led by Jonathan Maccabee. Afterwards in the east, the Egyptian forces continued their march into Syria where they also captured the capital city of Seleucia. When Alexander and his mighty army returned from Cilica, they were crushed by Ptolemy VI. Alexander I Balas fled to Arabia, but he was captured and slain.

For the first time since the days of Alexander the Great, Egypt and Syria were united under one authority.

However, shortly after those great triumphs, Ptolemy VI Philometor died from injuries he sustained after falling off his horse in Syria during the year of 145 B.C.E.. He was succeeded by his younger brother Ptolemy VIII Physcon.

Ptolemy VIII Physcon
(169—164 B.C.E.) 1st reign
(144—131 B.C.E.) 2nd reign
(126—116 B.C.E.) 3rd reign

Ptolemy VIII Physcon was born in Alexandria, Egypt during the year of 182 B.C.E. as the son of Ptolemy V Epiphanes and Queen Arsinoe III. Being one of the royal seed, he was always one of the potential heirs to the royal throne. In terms of his status among his siblings, he ranked as the youngest brother. The earliest historical records indicate that he was a man who loved to eat food. When he came to power, his surname became *"Physkon"*, meaning "sausage, pot belly, obese, or blubber. In other words, he was a very fat man. Although he was an Aryan, his weight reminds you of Eglon, the ancient black Moabite king spoken of in **Judges 3:17** which reads : "Eglon was a very fat man." Continuing, **verse 22** reads: "the fat closed over the blade so that he could not pull the dagger out of his belly; and the filth came out."

Physcon career began in 170/69 B.C.E. at the age of 12 when he was selected as an alternative king by the people of Alexandria to replace his brother Ptolemy VI. Now this is what happened. Antiochus IV, the king of Syria, invaded the land of Israel and moved south into Egypt. The Seleucid conqueror occupied every city in Egypt except Alexandria. Meanwhile, Antiochus IV declared himself king over Egypt, but used Philometor in the city of Thebes as a puppet king. Syria's actions caused alarm bells to go off in Rome and the Senate issued an edict to Antiochus IV demanding his withdrawal or face the **iron hand** of the Roman legions. In the year 168, Antiochus IV complied and returned to Antioch.

As I said earlier, during this time the rulers of Alexandria chose Ptolemy VIII Physcon as their leader. After the withdrawal, Ptolemy VI Philometor, their sister Cleopatra II, and Physcon agreed to co-rule as a triumvirate. There were rivalries, infighting, and deep divisions among the Ptolemies during that period. Philometor traveled to Rome to seek support for more power for his branch of power. Rome agreed and in May 163 B.C.E. Physcon was given the kingdom of Cyrenaica (Libya) as his base of power. Philometor and Cleopatra strengthened their rule throughout Egypt and control of the island Cyprus. This new Roman arrangement did not halt the power struggle between the two brothers.

Shortly afterwards, Physcon traveled to Rome to appear before the Senate requesting support his claim for the island of Cyprus. Of course, Philometor opposed his brother's claim. In 161 B.C.E., Physcon launched an invasion, but it failed. The infighting did not end. In the year 156/55, Philometor attempted to assassinate his brother Physcon. Physcon went to Rome a second time requesting additional support in his effort to reclaim the strategic island. The second invasion also failed, but this time Physcon was captured and taken prisoner. In a strange twist, Philometor spared Physcon's life and gave him his daughter, which was actually his young niece, Cleopatra Thea, in marriage. Both of them were sent back to Cyrenaica.

In the year 145 B.C.E., the older brother Philometor died from injuries sustained after falling off his horse at the Battle of Oinoparas in Syria. Immediately after that his wife Cleopatra II chose their son Ptolemy VII to sit on the throne. Physcon returned to Alexandria and proposed marriage to his older sister Cleopatra and co-rulership with her son. Cleopatra II accepted the deal and her brother's hand in marriage. A great wedding feast was planned. During the festivities Physcon had the young lad, who was actually his nephew, assassinated and became the sole heir to the throne. He then conducted a mass purge against all his opponents in the capital city. He expelled all the upper-class noblemen, including the philosophers, professors of geometry, musicians, painters, schoolteachers, and physicians. Many of those Macedonians returned to their mainland while others traveled to the barbaric parts of the northern forest to help civilize their less developed kinsmen.

By the year 144 B.C.E., Physcon proclaimed himself Ptolemy VIII Euergetes II, the new Pharaoh over Egypt. For the next twelve years, from 144 to 132 B.C.E., Physcon and Cleopatra II continued the arrangement until the latter-part of his second reign. This is what happened. Physcon, while still married to Cleopatra II, married his step-daughter whose name was Cleopatra III. Remember, Cleopatra III was the daughter of the brother-sister union of Ptolemy VI Philopator and Cleopatra II. This would make Cleopatra III the niece. *(She was his older brother's and sister's daughter)*. Now she had become the new wife of her uncle Ptolemy VIII Physcon.

Once Cleopatra discovered the secretive sexual union she became enraged and plotted against Physcon. The populace in Alexandria also turned against Physcon. Riots broke out, the royal palace was set aflame, and it was burned to the ground. Physcon, his wife, young Cleopatra III, and their children escaped and set sail to the island of Cyprus. Now that Cleopatra II was the sole regent, she appointed their 12-year-old son Ptolemy Memphitis as the new king. The agents of Physcon got a hold of Memphitis and cut the young lad into pieces. His remains were sent back to Cleopatra II.*(Think about it. This was his own son that he cut into pieces. Remember, Physcon had already murdered his nephew.)*

This rift caused a civil war within the Ptolemy-ruled Egypt. The city of Alexandria supported Cleopatra II while the majority of the country joined ranks behind Physcon. Fearing that she would be captured and slain, Cleopatra formed an alliance with the archenemy Seleucid ruler Demetrius II Nicator. The foreign invasion did not succeed. The Seleucid forces were not able to penetrate the fortified portions of the country. By the year 127 B.C.E., Cleopatra feared for her life and fled to Syria. After three years in exile, Cleopatra was allowed to return to Alexandria in 124. The Roman Republic intervened and by the year 118 a formal truce and amnesty was secured. Physcon was allowed to return to Egypt, but two years later in the year 116, the spirit of life departed from him. He died at the age of 66.

Ptolemy IX Soter II (known as) "Lathyros"
(116 —110 B.C.E.) 1st reign
(109—107 B.C.E.) 2nd reign
(88—81 B.C.E.) 3rd reign

Ptolemy IX Soter II was born in the city of Alexandria during the year 141 B.C.E. as the eldest son of Ptolemy VIII Physcon and Cleopatra III. He was also surnamed Ptolemy IX Lathy-ros, which meant *"grass pea"*. As a child and young man, he witnessed murder, adultery, stealing, false testimonies, and covetousness on a regular basis. Like a bunch of eggs in a nest, each waiting for their chance to burst out, Ptolemy IX waited in the wings until his mother brought him forth. Ptolemy IX came to power on this wise: His mother Cleopatra III wanted her younger son Ptolemy X to inherit the throne, but the people of Alexandria wanted the elder brother Ptolemy IX to be king. Cleopatra gave in to the wishes of the people and chose Ptolemy IX as the new Pharaoh. So at the age of 25 he began his **first reign** as a co-regent with his queen-mother in 116 B.C.E. Following the tradition of his father and uncle, the next year, he married his maternal sister Cleopatra IV, but his mother demanded that he write her a bill of divorcement due to her arrogancy. Instead she arranged another marriage for him with the younger, more tender-hearted sister named Cleopatra Selene. His mother then dispatched Ptolemy X to the island of Cyprus to serve as governor. In October of 110 B.C.E., the 31-year-old Ptolemy IX and his mother had a major dispute. Cleopatra never favored Ptolemy IX. She even accused him of plotting to murder her and banished him from Egypt to the governorship in Cyprus. She then summoned her other son Ptolemy X Alexander back from Cyprus to Alexandria where he served as the new Pharaoh.

In early 109 B.C.E., however, Ptolemy IX was allowed to return home to begin his short **second reign**, but by March of 108 he was forced back into exile again. He fled back to the island of Cyprus for a second time. While he was there, he strengthened himself. When his military buildup was completed, his forces invaded northern Syria and intervened in the

Seleucid civil-war. Meanwhile, his mother Cleopatra III and Ptolemy X also intervened in the regional battle on the opposite side.

While Ptolemy IX was in Cyprus again, his mother brought brother Ptolemy X back to Egypt to become the new Euro-Pharaoh. Six years later in 101 B.C.E. something went wrong and Ptolemy X Alexander turned against his own mother and murdered her. For the next thirteen years, Ptolemy, along with his niece-wife Berenice III, continued to reign as the sole heirs. Nevertheless, his rule was known as one of the most unpopular Ptolemaic kingships within the 31st Dynasty. During the latter-part of his reign there was a popular uprising against him. In the year 88 B.C.E. he was slain during sea battle.

After this, Ptolemy IX Soter II, also known as Lathyros, returned home to Egypt from Cyprus for a **third reign** on the throne.

Ptolemy X Alexander
(110—109 B.C.E.) 1st reign
(107—88 B.C.E.) 2nd reign

Ptolemy X Alexander was born as the youngest son of Ptolemy VIII Physcon and Cleopatra III among their five children. The lineup included Ptolemy IX, Ptolemy X, Cleopatra IV, Cleopatra Selene I, and Cleopatra Tryphaena. Ptolemy X was the youngest son, but his mother loved him more than his older brother. When their father Ptolemy VIII Physcon died, queen-mother Cleopatra II wanted the younger brother to sit on the throne but the people of Alexandria voted for Ptolemy IX. Cleopatra bowed to their wishes and Ptolemy IX became the ruler for one year. Within a year, the queen manipulated the ouster of Ptolemy IX and installed the younger brother for a one-year reign. This was his **first reign**.

By the end of the year, the tide turned against young Ptolemy X and his brother deposed him. He became the governor of Cyprus. But two years later, Ptolemy X was able to return to the throne again. His domineering mother remained his co-regent during this time, but in the year 101 he had his mother murdered. His wife and co-regent, Berenice III, who was actually his niece, ruled the land of Kemet together for the next thirteen years. Ptolemy X Alexander was slain in midst of a naval battle in the year 88. Upon hearing the news, Ptolemy IX returned back to Egypt and reclaimed the kingship. Seven years later, Ptolemy IX died in the year 81 B.C.E. and Berenice III took over for six months and ruled as the queen. By 85 B.C.E. Berenice III was forced to marry Ptolemy XI Alexander II. Nineteen days later he turned against her and murdered her. That cold-blooded act provoked a mass uprising. Ptolemy XI was captured and hung to death.

Ptolemy XI Alexander II
(80 B.C.E.)

Ptolemy XI Alexander II was born in Alexandria, Egypt as the son of Ptolemy X Alexander I. When his uncle died in 81 B.C.E., he did not have a son to inherit his position. So hia sister Berenice III seized the throne and won the favor of the people. She ruled for six months as the sole regent until Rome intervened. The Roman general and statesman Lucius Sulla wanted his puppet in charge of Egypt so he dispatched the son of Ptolemy X back to Egypt along with the will of the deceased monarch. The will requested that Rome chose the next ruler on the throne. Rome then commanded the young Ptolemy XI to married his step-mother Berenice III. The queen-mother followed the royal decree and married Ptolemy XI. In a strange turn of events, only three weeks after their marriage, 19 days to be exact, Ptolemy XI Alexander II murdered his new co-regent and bride. The people of Alexandria became enraged after they learned of her death because, as I mentioned earlier, she was greatly beloved. The citizens of Alexandria formed a lynch mob, tracked down and captured Ptolemy XI then hung him, ending his one-month reign. Following his death, his cousin Ptolemy XII Auletes came to power and reigned in his stead.

Ptolemy XII Auletes
(80—58 B.C.E.) 1st reign
(55—51 B.C.E,) 2nd reign

Ptolemy XII Auletes was born in 117 B.C.E. as the son of Ptolemy IX Lathyros and Cleopatra IV. Upon assuming the throne, at the age of 37, in 80 B.C.E. after the death of his uncle who did not have any male heirs to the throne, a search for any descendants of the Ptolemy lineage was conducted abroad. A son of Ptolemy IX by one of his Greek concubines was found living in the north-central Asia Minor city of Sinope. The boy was living in exile there in the court of King Mithridates of Pontus. Ptolemy XII was chosen to be the successor upon the Ptolemaic throne. He was given the name Ptolemy Neo Dionysos Theos Philopator Theos Philadelphos as his throne name, but his surname was actually Ptolemy XII Auletes. The meaning of the byword *"Auletes"* was—*the flutist or pipe player,"* which referred to his love of playing the pipes. During his reign, he was known to host musical concerts, parties, and competition in the palace. The king was also famous for his self-indulgence, drunkenness, and love of men, women, and children. Ptolemy XII Auletes was also known by the surname *"Nothos"* which meant *"bastard,"* referring to the fact the he was an outsider, a non-Alexandrian. His sister named Cleopatra Tryphaena became his wife along with her daughter Cleopatra VI Tryphaena.

Ptolemy XII had two periods of rulership. His **first reign** lasted 22 years, from 80 to 58 B.C.E. During this time he closely aligned Egypt with Rome by maintaining a close relationship with the Roman General Pompey. He sent him thousands of gold and silver coins. Ptolemy made an official visit to great city located upon seven mountains to sign a formal treaty with Julius Ceasar and Pompey. The agreement cost Ptolemy six thousand talents. Egypt then received protection from Rome against the Seleucids and Ptolemy XII's name was then placed on The Friends of Rome list.

Meanwhile in Egypt, he beautified the temples dedicated to the Greco-Egypt gods. He constructed the famed monumental gateway for the Edfu Temple which he decorated with pictures of him conquering his adversaries. Although Ptolemy had found peace with Rome, it was a different story on the homefront, and in 58 B.C.E., the people rebelled against his rule after he refused to denounce the Roman conquest of the island of Cyprus. The Ptolemaic kingdom had ruled Cyprus for several years. The revenues lost from this client-state greatly affected a people who were already murmuring about paying heavy taxes and bribes to Rome. Violence broke out in the capital, forcing Ptolemy XII, Cleopatra VII, and other cabinet officials to flee back to Rome for a three-year exile. In his absence, his two other daughters, Berenice IV and Cleopatra Tryphaena became co-regents and assumed the throne. However in the year 57, Cleopatra Tryphaena died. Some historians report that Berenice poisoned her. Berenice, who was strong-willed, covetous, and greedy, wanted all the power for herself. So she eliminated her sister.

She still faced other threats to her desire for exclusive rule. The Ptolemaic tradition was that the queen represented the female goddess, and it was required for her to have a co-regent king to represent the male god. So the people pressured Berenice to choose a husband-king. She eventually married a Seleucid prince, but she had him strangled to death. Again, she was alone. Her next marriage involved a relationship with a man who was disqualified from the beginning. He had already been appointed to a pagan priesthood by Rome to deal with religious matters. This incompleteness caused discontent in Alexandria and weakened her grip on power. It also caused her to fear an uprising against her rule. The truth of the matter was this: Berenice was only in her 20s, and she had bitten off more than she could chew. She was too young and inexperienced to hold the vast Ptolemaic kingdom together.

By the year 55 B.C.E. the Roman Senate backed a resolution for her father, Ptolemy XII, to return to power and reclaim his throne in Alexandria, thus beginning his **second reign** which lasted four years, from 55 to 51 B.C.E.,

And it came to pass that Ptolemy XII Auletes begat both Ptolemy XIII and Ptolemy XIV. In the year of 51 B.C.E. the spirit of life departed and he died at the age of 66. Afterwards, his son Ptolemy XIII became his successor.

Ptolemy XIII Theos Philopator
(51—47 B.C.E.)

Ptolemy XIII was born in 63/62 B.C.E. as the son of Ptolemy XII Auletes. He was one of the last members of the Ptolemaic dynasty to rule the land of Kemet. He was awarded the title: *"Theos Philopator—God Manifest, Father-Loving God, the First."* He succeeded his father in the spring of the year 51. He was a mere 11-year-old when he was promoted to the position of senior ruler by Pothinus, an eunuch, who served as the chief palace regent. Pothinus did not like the older sister of Ptolemy XIII who happened to be Cleopatra VII, an experienced, manipulative, whorish, strong-willed woman. Nevertheless, like most of the incestuous Ptolemies before him, Ptolemy XIII married his sister and they formed a co-rulership. Remember now, Cleopatra VII had already been married to her father, Ptolemy XII Auletes, as well. She had also established her own power base. Nevertheless, the people—the court clique of Pothinus, a native Egyptian general named Aichillas, and Theodotus, rallied around the young lad. This alliance caused a sibling rivalry. The envious court clique despised the fact that Cleopatra's image was represented on the minted coins of the kingdom. She was depicted as the goddess Aphrodite along with the infant-god Eros and her seal was placed on all official documents. Cleopatra was considered a beautiful woman who possessed a masculine energy, yet she was known to be a seductive woman who fired up men's blood.

During spring of the year 48, Ptolemy XIII and Pothinus plotted to dispose of Cleopatra VII hoping to completely seize the throne solely for the 15-year-old monarch. This expulsion sparked a civil war. Cleopatra fled Alexandria to save her life. At Thebaid, Cleopatra regrouped by raising an Arab army and moved to besiege the northern frontier city of Pelusium. In mid-Dec. of the year 48, the two factions fought in Alexandria. Alexandria was seriously damaged. Several of the great monuments and buildings, including the famous Library of Alexandria, were demolished. By now, another sibling of the Ptolemy dynasty, princess Arsinoe IV, the sister of both Ptolemy XIII and Cleopatra joined hands with her brother [Ptolemy XIII] and started claiming the throne as the new queen co-ruler. This further complicated a confusing situation. The Ptolemy dynasty was at its lowest point. It was beginning to crumble into a province of Rome. The Ptolemy dynasty had once ruled over several overseas city-states. All of those territories, Cyprus, Coele-Syria, and Cyrenacia, had been lost.

In midst of the two armies of Ptolemy and Cleopatra warring on the Nile, Roman politics inserted itself into the Ptolemaic fray. An internal conflict between the Roman generals Pompey and Julius Ceasar had turned into open warfare. Pompey had lost the battle of Pharsalus in Thessaly and fled into Egypt seeking refuge.

The palace clique, spearheaded by Pothinus and Achillas, advised the 15-year-old Ptolemy XIII to lure Pompey into an ambush under the pretense of asylum. On Sept. 29, 48 B.C.E., the Roman general was murdered and beheaded. Once Julius Ceasar learned that Pompey had fled into Egypt, he pursued him into the land of Kemet. When Ceasar arrived in Egypt, he was greeted with a state banquet. Ceasar demanded that both sides submit to the power of Rome, end the internal conflict, and meet for public reconciliation talks. Fearing she could be assassinated before she arrived, she secretly traveled to Alexandria via a boat rolled up in a large carpet. To the amazement of Ceasar, her soldiers unrolled the carpet in front of him and she popped out.

Hoping to earn the favor of Ceasar during talks at a royal toast, Ptolemy and his court clique presented the skull of his rival Pompey on a silver platter. Ceasar was not pleased. Instead, he reacted with anger and disgust. Ceasar ordered his generals to locate the body of Pompey and honor him with a Roman state funeral. This situation played into the hands of Cleopatra. She became Ceasar's mistress and lover. Now, the power of Rome backed her which allowed her to return to the throne as the sole ruler. According to the Ptolemaic tradition, she chose her younger brother Ptolemy XIV to serve as her figurehead co-regent. Ceasar ordered Cleopatra to execute Pothinus for his role in the murder of General Pompey. General Achillas was also slain.

Ptolemy XIII was not pleased with Ceasar's open preference of Cleopatra so he rekindled the flames of hostilities once again. Ceasar called in backup and additional reinforcements from his garrisons in Asia Minor to crush the enemies of his mistress. Roman forces out maneuvered his forces in a conflict known as the Battle of Nile of 47 B.C.E. Ptolemy was forced to flee the battlefield. He dived into the Nile hoping to escape, but he drowned while crossing on January 13th. His co-conspirator Arsinoe IV fled into Asia Minor to the city of Ephesus.

The wily Cleopatra had turned the power of Rome into her own personal instrument. She gave birth to the child of Julius Ceasar on June 23, 47 B.C.E. His name was Ceasrion in honor of his father. The native black priesthood at Hermonttars celebrated the birth of child with great festivities. Julius Ceasar was crowned as the personification of the Egyptian god Ra and the child, Ceasrion, was declared the Son of Ra. When Ceasar returned to Rome in the year 46, Cleopatra and young Ptolemy XIV left with him. Ceasar openly acknowledged the child. In Rome, the head of state dedicated a golden statue of Cleopatra in a new temple at Venus Genetrix. This was the same divinity which the entire Julian House claimed as their source of origins.

Nevertheless, the comforts of a queen in exile came to a screeching halt in March of 44 B.C.E. when officer Brutus and his fellows put a dagger into Julius Ceasar ending his life. This occurrence threatened Cleopatra's position so she and young Ptolemy fled back into Egypt. Ptolemy XIV died shortly after their return home, leading some to believe, Cleopatra poisoned him to make sure that her son Ceasrion would become the sole heir to the throne. Meanwhile in Egypt, Cleopatra viewed herself as the reincarnation of the Egyptian goddess Isis. At the Temple of Denderah, a colossal figure was also built in honor of her as the Egyptian goddess Hathor. These high places stood as a testament of her legacy which had begun at the age of 17 or 18 with the marriage of her father. Speaking of marriage, Cleopatra also married the Roman general Mark Anthony for two years from 32 to 30 B.C.E.. She was born in the great city of Alexandria in the year 69 and died on August 12th in 30 B.C.E. at the age of thirty-nine. She killed herself by allowing a poisonous snake bite her. Her lover Mark Anthony had already committed suicide after losing the Battle of Actium to Octavius's forces. Octavius later became known as Augustus Ceasar. Ptolemaic Egypt was now the territory of the growing **kingdom of iron**—the Roman empire.

Ptolemy XIV Theos Philopator II

(47—44 B.C.E.)

Ptolemy XIV was born in the royal city of Alexandria during the year 60/59 B.C.E. as the youngest son of Ptolemy XII Auletes. He was awarded the title: *"Theos Philopator"—God Manifest, the Father-Loving God, the Second."* As the younger brother, he was always used as a pawn by his older siblings. When his older brother Ptolemy XIII drowned after his defeat at the Battle of the Nile, he was proclaimed co-regent by his older sister Cleopatra VII. At the age of 11, his sister Cleopatra married him following the Ptolemaic tradition. Too young to make any important decisions, he was a mere figurehead who wielded no true power. In 46 B.C.E.,he traveled to Rome with his older sister until the assassination of Julius Ceasar forced both of them to flee. After the pair returned to Egypt, the young Ptolemy mysteriously died. Many historians contend she poisoned her younger brother to make way for her own son Ceasarion as the sole heir to the throne. By the age of 16, Ptolemy XIV was dead.

Ptolemy XV (Ceasar) Ceasarion
(44—30 B.C.E.)

Ptolemy XV Ceasarion was born on June 23, 47 B.C.E. in the royal city of Alexandria. He was the product of a love escapade between Queen Cleopatra VII and the Roman dictator Gaius Julius Ceasar. His birth name was Ceasarion. He was proclaimed co-ruler on Sept. 2, 44 B.C.E. along with his mother. He was three-years-old when his uncle Ptolemy XIV was poisoned. The young lad then became the male personification of the Egyptian deity Ra while his mother served as the female deity Isis. Besides that, the toddler was just like any other normal baby: unaware of good or evil. His mother Cleopatra was the true power on the throne of Egypt. Nevertheless, the long and turbulent reign of Cleopatra came to its end at the battle of Actium in the summer of 30 B.C.E. On one side you had the forces of Cleopatra, who was the ex-lover of Julius Ceasar, joined with her new lover, General Mark Anthony, pitched in a heated battle against the Roman forces of General Octavius. The queen of Egypt and her ally lost the battle. Shortly afterwards, Mark Anthony committed suicide instead of facing enemy soldiers. On August 12, 30 B.C.E., Cleopatra followed suit by picking up an asp and allowing it to bite her breasts. Young Ceasarion was left alone. After crushing his remaining Ptolemaic foes, General Octavius ordered the execution of 14-year-old Ptolemy XV Ceasarion on August 23th. His death came three days before his 15th birthday which would have been on Sept. 2.

By the time of his death, the kingdom of Egypt had been reduced to a puppet province of the rising Roman empire. The Ptolemy Dynasty, which began in 305 B.C.E., was now covered up in the annals of world history. *Sit in the dust, the great Ptolemaics had fallen, fallen, there was no more throne!*

I have mentioned on numerous occasions in this book that the death of Alexander the Great brought about the rapid division of his once united Grecian empire which the young emperor had fought so hard to establish. At the time of his death, the global empire extended from Thrace in the far west to the far eastern frontier in India. We must remember what Ptolemy I Soter once said: " *"Within hours [after the death of Alexander] we were fighting like Jackal for his corpse. The wars of the world had begun. Forty years off and on, they* [**The Diadochi Wars**] *endured until we divided his empire in four parts. I think Alexander would have been disappointed in us."* Nevertheless, all of these human affairs were being ochestrated by the DIVINE HAND and PLAN of YAH. We must never forget that it is **"YHWH** who setteth up kings (kingdoms) and overturn kings (kingdoms). What most people of the earth fail to realize is that it is **YAH, the Most High**, who ruleth among the entire kingdoms of men, and giveth power into the hands of whomsoever HE chooses. **YAH KHAI!!** YAH is the Ruler of Reality, HE is the ONE who is truly in charge of human affairs. Although these rulers, and even the rulers of the earth today, do not acknowledge **YAH, ELOHIM of the heavens and earth** who made an everlasting covenant with the ancient seed of Abraham, Isaac, and Yaacov, HE is the True Source of their power.

It is YAH who is creating each new day and each new night during these people's lifetimes. Each new spring, summer, autumn, and winter season and every new year on a perpetual cycle is the work of YAH'S Hands—**THE STONE CUT OUT WITHOUT HANDS**. It is YHWH who continues to rule among nations of the earth even today and forevermore. Not the graven images (world religions) that they serve. Because these nations do not understand DIVINE Reality, we will refer to them as **"the children of the image—rulers of the idol-worshipping kingdoms."** These rulers do not have the proper DIVINE respect for the true Creator-YAH, and this truth is reflected in the human conduct of these men and women. This is the true reason why we are walking down the historical timeline of the rulers and kingdoms. The biographies of these men and women prove that they are spiritually uncircumcised idol-worshipping people. They do not realize it, but each and everyone of them are fulfilling the prophecies of the **"great image of gold, silver, brass, iron, and miry clay"** spoken of in the dream which YAH placed in the mind (heart) of Nebuchadnezzar in **Daniel, chapter 2**.

Now back to the subject at hand: Remember, the **children of brass** are the four divisions of the Grecian empire. Let's concentrate on the Seleucid dynasty which became another one of those four prophesied parts of the divided Grecian empire. It evolved into another major center of Hellenistic culture, rivaling the Ptolemies in Egypt, with a heavy influx of Aryan Greek populations that migrated into this once Afro-Asiatic domain, changing its once black face into an European countenance: As it is until this day.

The Seleucid Empire & Dynasty
(312—63 B.C.E.)
Third Division of The Alexandrian Empire

Seleucus I Nicator (312—281 B.C.E.), Antiochus I Soter (281—261 B.C.E.), Antiochus II Theos (261—246 B.C.E.), Seleucus II Callinicus (246—225 B.C.E.), Seleucus III Ceraunus Soter (225—223 B.C.E.), Antiochus III Great (223—187 B.C.E.), Seleucus IV Philopator (187—175 B.C.E.), Antiochus IV Epiphanes (175—163 B.C.E.), Antiochus V Eupator (163—161 B.C.E.), Demetrius I Soter (161—150 B.C.E.), Alexander I Balas (161—150 B.C.E.), Demetrius II Nicator (1st reign 145 B.C.E., 2nd reign 138 B.C.E.), Antiochus VI Dionysus/Epiphanes (145—140 B.C.E.), Diodotus Tryphon (140—138 B.C.E.), Antiochus VII Sidestes/Euergetes (138—129 B.C.E.), Demetrius II Nicator (1st reign 129 B.C.E., 2nd reign 126 B.C.E.), Alexander II Zabinas 129—123 B.C.E.), Cleopatra Thea (126—121 B.C.E.), Antiochus VIII Grypus (125—96 B.C.E.), Antiochus IX Cyzicenus (114—96 B.C.E.), Seleucus VI Epiphanes Nicator (96—95 B.C.E.), Antiochus X Eusebes Philopator (95—92 B.C.E.), Demetrius III Eucaerus/Philopator (95—81 B.C.E.), Antiochus XI Epiphanes (95—92 B.C.E.), Phillip I Philadelphus (95—84/83 B.C.E.), Antiochus XII Dionysus (87—84 B.C.E.), Tigranes I of Armenia (83—69 B.C.E.), Seleucus VII Kybiosaktes/Philometor (83—69 B.C.E.), Antiochus XIII Asiaticus (69—64 B.C.E.), Phillip II Philoroniaeus (65—63 B.C.E.).

Seleucus I Nicator (Soter "The Saviour")
(312 B.C.E.—281 B.C.E.)

Seleucus I Nicator was the son of a Macedonian nobleman named Antiochus and his wife named Laodice. He was born in the city of Europos in northern Macedonia. Most historians place his year of birth somewhere between 358 to 354 B.C.E. He served as a teenage page for the king during his youth like most male offsprings of the ruling class clans. After rising through the ranks, he became a military commander and became one of the trusted "Companions" of Alexander's inner circle. In fact, he and Alexander were close to the same age. By 327 he had risen to become commander of the elite infantry corp. known as the "Shieldbearers." When Alexander the Great crossed the Hydaspes River into India, generals Seleucus, Ptolemy I, Lysimachus, and Perdiccas, his special assistant, accompanied him and cooperated with each other.

After the sudden death of Alexander in June of 323 in the great city Babylon, Seleucus was chosen as the second-in-command [Chiliarch] of the Royal cavalry as the special assistant to Perdiccas. Perdiccas had become the caretaker successor of Alexander at the Partition of Babylon. The next year, the Diadochi Wars broke out among the generals. Perdiccas and Ptolemy became enemies after Ptolemy hijacked the funeral procession of Alexander which was destined for his hometown of Pella, Macedonia. Ptolemy rerouted the corpse to Alexandria, Egypt. Perdiccas was extremely angry, he followed the corpse, then plotted a coup against Ptolemy in Egypt. Perdiccas lost that battle. His soldiers double-crossed him, including Seleucus who joined the mutiny. Perdiccas was assassinated in the city of Pelusium.

A year later in 321 B.C.E. at the Partition of Triparadisus, Seleucus was officially appointed as the satrap [governor] of Babylon. This established General Seleucus as the founding father of the dynasty that lasted for nearly two hundred fifty years. This leadership became known as the Seleucid empire, covering most of the territory in Near and Far Eastern frontiers.

In 317, there was a brief alliance between the generals Seleucus and Antigonus. Both of them warred against a general named Eumenes, governor of the province of Cardia. In 316, Seleucus executed Eumenes and claimed the territory of Cardia for himself. Antigonus wanted to divide the spoils and demanded an accounting of the province's income. Seleucus refused. To make matters worse, during the following summer of 315, a Chaldean astrologer delivered an oracle to Antigonus predicting that Seleucus would seek to murder him and become the new master of Asia. Immediately after hearing the deadly prophecy, Antigonus, the commander-in-chief of a larger army, ordered his cavalry to saddle up and bring head of Seleucus back to him on a platter. This forced Seleucus along with 50 of his chief horsemen to flee back into Egypt to save his life.

While in Egypt from 315—312 B.C.E., Ptolemy I Soter assisted him in rebuilding an armed force. He eventually fought his way back into power, recapturing the city of Babylon, and reclaiming the throne as governor of the East. This occurred on October 7, 312 B.C.E., Meanwhile Antigonus was occupied in Asia Minor and could not prevent Seleucus claim to the throne. Still, Antigonus and his son Demetrius I continued to launch raids on Babylonia for the next two years, 311 to 310, but they were unsuccessful.

From 312, Seleucus advanced the Aryan invasion of the Near and Far East, ruthlessly expanding his portion of the Alexandrian empire with the strong army which he had assembled. On continuous military campaigns, he acquired parts of Anatolia, the Levant, Mesopotamia, Armenia, Cappodocia, Persia, Bactrica, Arabia, Kuwait, Tapouria, Sogdia, Hyrcania, Afghanistan, Pakistan, Turkmenistan, and Arachiesia. Among all the generals, the boundaries of his empire became the most extensive in Asia.

The Seleucid dynasty developed a distinctive Oriential-style which interwined Macedonian culture with the various indigenous beliefs, philosophies to form a melting-pot Hellenistic culture. By 305, he declared himself "the King of Syria and Lord of Asia."

From 305—303 B.C.E., Seleucus continued fighting wars as far away as India. Afterwards, King Chandraguta Mauaya of India and Seleucus made peace. Seleucus relinquished his territorial claim on the Indus Valley in exchange for 500 war elephants. Strife and tensions near Asia Minor caused Seleucus to dispatch his new squadron of 500 fighting animals to his western frontier to engage in battle against Antigonus I in the Battle of Ipsus in the year 301. Seleucus I Nicator maneuvered his warrior elephants into position to split the ranks of Antigonus. Both flanks, controlled by Antigonus and his son Demetrius were defeated in the battle. In the heat of battle Antigonus was slain by a javelin sharpshooter. Demetrius fled to Ephesus.

Antiochus I Soter
(281—261 B.C.E.)

Antiochus I Soter was born somewhere between the territories of Mesopotamia or Persia during the year 324 B.C.E. as the son of General Seleucus I Nicator and Princess Apama, the daughter of Prince Spitamenes, the Persian satrap of the province of Sogdiana [present-day Tajikstan and Uzebkistan]. Even after the majority of the Greek warriors abandoned their foreign wives in groves after the death of Alexander the Great, Seleucus maintained his commitment and marriage to the Persian noblewoman. It was for this reason, Antiochus was considered biracial or a half-breed—half Sogdian [Persian] and half Macedon. It was believed that for this reason the three other pure-blooded Macedonian dynasties, the Ptolemiacs, the Macedonians, and the Thracians, did not readily offer one of their daughters to him at a young age. Antiochus did not get married until the age 30 in 294 B.C.E. after his father discovered he was heartbroken and slowly going down from loneliness and lovesickness. His father

Seleucus then gave away Stratonice, who was his own second wife, to his son Antiochus. Thus Antiochus I Soter married his step-mother, Stratonice. Once married, the royal union of Antiochus and Stratonice produced 5 children: Seleucus, Laodice, Apama II, Stratonice of Macedon, and Antiochus II Theos, who eventually became his successor.

Antiochus came to power in the year 292 as co-regent and the satrap of Bactria. For eleven years, he served as crown prince and co-regent under his father Seleucus. His responsibilities included the management of all provinces east of the Euphrates River. After the death of his father in September of 281 B.C.E., Antiochus assumed the throne as the absolute ruler.

Once in power, his main priorities became the consolidation of the kingdom by building several new cities to serve as buffer zones against foreign invaders. Those cities, scattered from Anatolia to Persia, consisted of Greek villages dominated by Greco-Macedonian rulers. He also expanded the trade routes and contacts in the Far East while exploring the Caspian Sea region.

In terms of his religious life, Antiochus created a cult that turned his father into a divine being, known as the Son, and the personification of the sun-god Apollo. Antiochus ordained his own priests who made monthly sacrifices into the memory of his father, who in their corrupt minds, thought he had resurrected with golden wings and flew into the pearly gates of heaven to dwell with the deity Apollo. For a while he stayed in the city of Babylon where he reconstructed the main temple dedicated to the deities Nabu (god of wisdom) and Nanaia (goddess of wisdom and writing). The Babylonian graven image Nanaia was the forerunner of the Greco-idol known as Artemis. He rebuilt the temple of Esagila where he bowed down before Marduk, the same golden statue that King Nebuchadnezzar once revered. The Seleucid king also restored the splendor of the Temple of Etemenanki. Throughout his empire, he had silver coins minted in his honor with an image of himself on front and a naked image of the sun-god Apollo on the opposite side. The white Seleucids also used the Babylonian calendar, adopted their religious concepts, and pagan festivals. On March 27, 268, he attended spring Akitu (New Year) Festivities in the royal city where he laid the foundation for the Ezida temple in honor of the god Nebo. The truth of the matter is, the brown Persians and black Egyptians were the idolatrous role models for the pale-skinned Greco-Macedonians. They had great respect for the native gods of these indigenous populations. Eventually, Antiochus founded the city of Seleucia in honor of his father. He then moved the Babylonian population into his new great city located near the banks of the Tigris River.

Throughout the reign of Antiochus there was constant conflicts between his kingdom and the southern kingdom of the Ptolemies. The region of Coele-Syria remained an open wound causing a series of wars. The Ptolemies occupied the territory, but the Seleucids claimed the same area as part of their empire.

In the year of 279 B.C.E., an horde of 20,000 barbaic Gauls migrated from the northern forest, which today is known as Europe, ransacking the kingdom of Macedonia and several other Grecian coastal cities. They almost ruined the rule of Antigonus II Gonatas.

The following year they crossed the Aegan Sea and broke into Asia Minor. The enemies of Antiochus recruited the Gauls for mercenaries against the Seleucids in the far western outskirts of their empire. Meanwhile, Antiochus was distracted with a raging Syrian conflict between his kingdom and the Ptolemy regime. By 275, Antiochus had settled the Syrian situation and was able to move against the Gauls in Asia Minor. Using Indian war elephants, Antiochus trampled the Gauls and saved the Grecian city-states from the Gaul's destructive path. This crucial victory earned him the title of "Soter"[Saviour] among the more civilized Macedonians and Greeks.

These events forced the two adversaries, Antigonus II Gonatas and Antiochus I Soter, to sign a peace treaty of non-interference in each other's territories. Meanwhile during this same period of time inside the kingdom, Antiochus was forced to murder his own oldest son, Seleucus, who had been named in honor of his grandfather Seleucus I Nicator. By 267, the younger Seleucus was disposed, charged with treason and executed. Ironically, his grandfather Seleucus I had been murdered fourteen years earlier by the Ptolemy Keraunos in September of 281 after he had murdered the Thracian king Lysimachus. The elder Seleucus had left Asia to live out his remaining years in his native land Macedonia. But when he had crossed into the territory of Thrace he was ambushed.

By 262, Antiochus I Soter was entangled in another conflict with the powerful city-state of Pergamum. Eventually, his army prevailed. He then moved to subdue the nearby city-state of Sardis. This time the reproach was returned upon his own head and he was defeated. This defeat was actually an omen for the Seleucid king because one year later, he died fighting the Galatians on June 1st or 2nd in the year 261 B.C.E.. He was succeeded by his youngest namesake son, Antiochus, who became known as Antiochus II Theos.

Antiochus II Theos
(261—246 B.C.E.)

Antiochus II was the younger son of Antiochus I Soter and Stratonice the First. He was born in the year 286 B.C.E. in the royal city of Antioch, Syria. As the youngest sibling, he played second fiddle behind his older brother Seleucus until he became the age of 18. In the year 268, his older brother, who had been the crown prince, conspired against his father Antiochus I Soter. His father executed his older brother and appointed Antiochus II as the new crown prince over the eastern provinces. For seven years he served as the co-regent gaining the experience needed to serve as the heir to the throne. In the early summer of the year 261, his father Antiochus the First was slain in a battle against the Galatians on June 2. This tragedy placed the scepter into the hands of 25-year-old Antiochus II.

One year after assuming the throne, the conflict between his kingdom and Ptolemaic Egypt, which was known as the Second Syria War, broke out again. This time the war raged along the expansive western coast of Asia Minor. Several years later at the end of the wars, the two combatants signed a peace treaty in the year 253. To seal the peace agreement, Ptolemy, the ruler over Egypt, arranged for his daughter Berenice to marry the young ruler of Syria. Prior to that, Antiochus was already married to his first cousin Laodice I, a noblewoman. She bore him 5 children, 2 boys: Seleucus II Callinicus, Antiochus Hierax, and 3 girls: Apama, Stratonice of Cappodica, Loadice II. Afterwards in the year 251, his second wife Berenice, the daughter of King Ptolemy II Philadelphus, gave birth to her only child, a boy who bore the name of his grandfather and father—Antiochus.

Antiochus II reigned for fifteen years in the capital city of Antioch. In the year 259 he liberated the famous city-state Miletus which was located in western Asia Minor, from the grip of a tyrant named Timarchus. The oppressed inhabitants were so thankful for their liberation that they named him *"Theos"* meaning "God". His new royal title became Antiochus II Theos. His new subjects viewed him as a white god [divine being] in the flesh worthy to be worshipped and praised. That type of pagan thinking was prevalent throughout ancient Hellenistic culture, and its influence was later transferred into Greco-Roman Christianity where popes are still considered infallible Holy Fathers *"Theos"*, the representatives of God [divine beings] in the flesh.

Although the governance of Antiochus II Theos, a warrior-king, was firm and secure, his palace situation was insecure and unstable. After his royal marriage to princess Berenice, it appeared that Queen Laodice was not very enthused or cooperative. In fact, the intense ill-will and confusion between the two Grecian women led to the divorce and exile of Queen Laodice back to the city of Ephesus. As long as her father lived, Berenice and Antiochus marriage represented peace between Egypt and Syria, but when King Ptolemy II Philadelphus died on January 28, 246 B.C.E. everything began to change for the worse. Their six-year-old marriage unraveled during the same period of time. Violent arguments between the pair led the king to put her down. Berenice resided in Antiochus, the royal capital, while the king traveled back to Ephesus to seek reconciliation with his first wife Queen Laodice. As the old saying goes, "there's a thin line between love and hate," so Queen Laodice pretended to lovingly welcome Antiochus back into her arms. However, through subtility, she poisoned the Seleucid monarch by early July of the year 246. It had been only six months since Ptolemy

II Philadelphus of Egypt had died.

After killing her former husband with a deadly brew, she ordered the murder of princess-queen Berenice and her five-year-old baby boy. Their deaths renewed tensions between Egypt and Syria sparking the Third Syrian War between the Seleucids and the Ptolemies. At the age of 40, Antiochus II Theos fifteen-year-old rule came to a complete end. And it came to pass that his eldest son Seleucus II Callinicus succeeded him as the new king on the throne in Antioch, Syria.

Seleucus II Callinicus
(246—225 B.C.E.)

Seleucus II Callinicus was born in the year 265 as the eldest son the Antiochus II Theos and Laodice I in Antioch, Syria. His surname was Callinius *which meant* "beautiful victor or gloriously triumphant." At the age of 19, the young crown prince was thrushed to power and inherited the throne after his mother Laodice poisoned his father. Remember, his father King Antiochus II Theos took a second wife, the Ptolemaic princess Berenice, angering his mother, the first wife. After leaving the royal palace to reside in the city of Ephesus, Laodice waited patiently for six years for an opportunity to kill her husband. By the 246, major brawls between his father and Berenice caused him to leave her. Afterwards, he traveled to Ephesus, attempting to repair his first marriage with Seleucus II mother. Like a black widow spider, she pretended to be happy to see him again, but she lured him in and poisoned his royal cup. She then chose their oldest son Seleucus II as the new successor over the Seleucid Empire.

Eventually he married his first cousin who had the same name as his mother: Laodice. She became known as Laodice II. They became the royal parents of five children, 2 daughters and 3 sons: The firstborn Antiochis was a girl. The second child was a boy named Alexander. He later changed his name to Seleucus III Keraunos. For some reason, the third child's name was not recorded in the annals of history. Antiochus III was the fourth child and the youngest son. For some reason their fifth child, a daughter, name was not mentioned.

The outbreak of war between Egypt and Seleucus occurred as soon as Seleucus assumed the mantle of power. This war involved a personal feud between the Ptolemaic family and the family of the Seleucus II. Now this was the case: Berenice was the sister of the new king in Egypt named Ptolemy III Euergetes. Her brother became enraged after he received the report that Queen Laodice had killed his sister Berenice and her baby boy Antiochus. That dynastic confusion sparked The Third Syrian War. Ptolemy III Euergetes swept through the land of Israel and invaded Syria with a massive force. Seleucus III was too inexperienced and unprepared for this major war at the mere age of 20. The Egyptian armies marched into the heartland of Syria capturing the cities of Seleucia, Antioch, and other cities near the Tigris River. He personally occupied the ancient city of Babylon well into the year of 245. The provinces in the east easily fell into the hands of Ptolemaic forces. Meanwhile, Ptolemy also launched a massive naval assault on Syrian satellite city-states along the coast of Asia Minor. The Seleucids suffered great setbacks during the Third Syrian War, but young Seleucus was still able to hold on to his territorial possessions in the interior landscape of Asia Minor.

Nevertheless, Ptolemy III Euergetes did not remain in conquered territories of Syria or Mesopotamia. He quickly withdrew his troops back to the luxuries and comforts of Alexandria, Egypt. Seleucus II Callinius then mounted military operations to recover his former possessions in northern Syria and western Mesopotamia. In Asia Minor, another scenario developed. Seleucus younger brother, Antiochus Hierax, a co-ruler in Sardis, turned against him and became his rival in the west. The civil war came to a climax in 235 B.C.E. in a conflict known as the Battle of Ancyra, which is located near modern Ankara, Turkey. There the armies of both brothers faced off. The army of Seleucus was crushed causing him to withdraw back to the east. Antiochus Hierax became the new ruler over portions of the western flank of empire beyond the Taurus mountains. He soon lost his control to Attalus the ruler of the powerful city-state of Pergamon. By the year 227, and after a final defeat, he was forced to flee into the kingdom of Thrace as a fugitive-of-law where he remained until death. Meanwhile back in the east, Seleucus II Callinius resided in Babylon where his military fortunes were no better. He lost portions of the eastern flank of the empire to the king of Persia.

It came to pass in the twenty-first year of his reign in the year 225, Seleucus II Callinius accidentally fell off his royal horse. At the age of 40, he died from his injuries. His older son Seleucus III Keraunos, who was an 18-year-old, succeeded him on the throne.

Seleucus III Keraunos
(225—222 B.C.E.)

Seleucus III Keraunos was born in the year 243 with the maternal name of Alexander. He was the older son of Seleucus II Calinicus and Laodice II. He came to power in December of the year 225 at the age of 18 after the accidental death of his father. In honor of his father, he changed his name from Alexander to the throne name of Seleucus III Keraunos. His surname "Ke-rau-nos" *meant* "Thunderbolt" which reflected his desire to recover the territorial possessions lost by both his father and uncle in Asia Minor. Most of his brief three-year reign consisted of battles with Attalus I Soter of the powerful city-state of Pergamon. He earned the title of "Soter" meaning "Savior" after winning a series of battle against the powerful adversary in Pergamon. However, he had a checkered military success pattern because he suffered several losses as well. His inner circle began to conspire against him during late spring and early summer of the year 222 while campaigning in Asia Minor. Seleucus was eventually assassinated through poisoning. It was those members of his army and inner court who carried out the conspiracy. Seleucus III was a mere 20 at the time of his death. His younger brother Antiochus III reigned in his stead.

Antiochus III Megas "the Great"
(222—187 B.C.E.)

Antiochus III was born in the year 242 B.C.E. as the youngest son of Seleucus II Calinius and Laodice II in Susa, Persia. In the year 222 he came to power at the age of 18 on the heels of his brother's assassination in western Asia Minor by his own army officers. When that happened, Antiochus was back east in Babylon serving as the crown prince. After ascending to the throne, he married his first cousin Laodice III. Together they had 8 children, four sons and four daughters: 1) Antiochus, a son who died in the year 193, 2) Seleucus IV Philopator, the oldest son, 3) Ardys, a son, 4) unnamed daughter, 5) Laodice IV, daughter who became Queen of Seleucia, 6) Cleopatra I of Syria, daughter who became a Queen of Egypt, 7) Antiochis, daughter who became a Queen of Cappadocia, 8) Antiochus IV Epiphanes, the youngest son.

When young Antiochus III came to the throne, the empire had been severely weakened by repeated losses to the Ptolemies in Syria and in several Asia Minor city-states. To restore confidence in the throne he established the cult worship of the king and queen as god-goddess of the empire. One of next moves he made was reducing the size of the provinces in order to govern them more efficiently. Throughout his reign, he also gave his daughters as wives to rulers of surrounding countries in hopes of improving relations.

External and internal pressures forced Antiochus to become a warrior-king like unto his father Seleucus Callinicus. Threats ranging from Ceole-Syria, to Parthia, and Asia Minor pressured the young leader into making quick decisions. He had to rely on his experienced chief minister named Hermeias. Hermeias recommended that the king attack the Ptolemiac possessions in Syria first. Next, he dispatched generals to Parthia to end the rebellions by the leaders, Molon and Alexander. Meanwhile in the far west another officer named Achaeus, who happened to be the cousin of Antiochus III, seceded then annexed territories in Asia Minor and declared himself king. None of Hermeias decisions proved to be correct. After listening to counsel from another advisor, notably a prince named Zeuxis, Antiochus decided he was not strong enough to confront Ptolemy III Euergetes, so instead during the year 221, he personally led the attack against the Parthian leaders Molon and Alexander where he won an important victory for his new leadership. Several of the other smaller cities surrounding Media also surrendered to Antiochus during this same time. The following year in 220, the young king arranged for the assassination of Hermeias.

By the year 219-218, the Fourth Syrian War had broke out. This new war between the Hellenistic rulers Antiochus III and Ptolemy IV Philopator lasted for three years, ending in the year 216. During the initial campaigns Antiochus was successful in recovering the royal city Seleucia, the port of Antioch, Coele-Syria, which is modern Lebanon, Tyre, and the land of Israel. By the year 217 Antiochus victories brought him to the doorsteps of Egypt, near the city of Raphia in southern Israel. There they faced off on the edge of the Negev Desert with their massive armies. Ptolemy's army numbered 75,000—70,000 foot soldiers, many of them native Egyptians, and 5,000 horsemen along with 73 African elephants. The army of Antiochus consisted of 60,000 foot soldiers, thousands of horsemen, several battalions of Asiatic mercanaries, and 102 Indian elephants. The battle was set in array in the holyland. In the midst of heated battle, Antiochus forces were outflanked and routed by the closed ranks of the Egyptian military, forcing Antiochus to retreat in haste. Ptolemy IV Philopator commanded his army to move northward and reoccupy the territories Antiochus had previously captured. Ptolemy became the new lord over the land of Israel. Antiochus still maintained his control over the city of Seleucia. Both sides accepted the new arrangements and a truce was enacted.

Antiochus quickly turned his attention to the rebellion in Asia Minor. By the year 216, he had formed an alliance with Attalus I, the powerful ruler of the city-state Pergamon, and months later, they launched an attack against his cousin Achaeus, the self-proclaimed king in his capital city of Sardis. After intense fighting, Antiochus finally captured the fortified stronghold after a three-year siege. Achaeus was captured and brutally tortured to death. Afterwards, he moved to secure control over several other northern and eastern city-states on the western outskirts of the Seleucid Empire. By the year 212, peaceful conditions on the mainland of Asia Minor gave Antiochus the opportunity to return eastward for a seven-year military campaign that reached the doorsteps of India. During the same year, he gave his sister's hand to King Xerxes of Armenia. He also conquered the Parthian provinces near the Caspian Sea. His next move included the conquest of the territories of Hyrcania, Bactria, where he allowed King Euthydemus [Eu-thy-de-mus] to remain in power under his supervision, along with the province of Gandara. Moving with the speed of a leopard, the armies of Antiochus crossed the mountainous Hindu Kush into the Kabul Valley [modern Afghanistan] and extended an olive branch to the king of India by the year 206. There Antiochus III met with King Sophagasenos [*pronounced* So-fa-ga-se-nos] in his capital Prakrit. The king of India gave the Aryan monarch food, water, wine, a total of 150 Indian war elephants, jewels, and treasures. After refreshment, the Seleucids departed back to Persia and eventually Syria.

Antiochus and his troops arrived back in the capital city Seleucia, which was located on the banks of the Tigris River, by late 205 or early 204. With the eastern portion of the empire secure, he then attacked the rival kingdoms located near the Arabian and Persian Gulf. Following in the footsteps of his predecessor Alexander the Great, his new title became Antiochus III **"Megas"**,**which** *is Greek for* **"The Great"**, the [Ayran] ruler of the East. As fate would have it, King Ptolemy IV Philopator became sick and passed away. His infant son Ptolemy V inherited the throne at the age of 5.

Sensing political and military weakness in Alexandria, Egypt, Antiochus the Great formed an alliance with Phillip V of Macedonia to divide the overseas possessions of the Ptolemies in Asia Minor and Syria-Israel among themselves. Egypt was too troubled with internal conflict to respond to this new Seleucid-Macedonia aggression. Under the agreement, Phillip received the territories along the Aegan Sea and the Cyrene [modern Libya] while Antiochus gained control of Lycia, Cilicia, Syria, Cyprus and Egypt itself. Antiochus then moved against the Ptolemiac possessions in Ceole-Syria and Phoenica [modern Lebanon]. Those new military moves by Antiochus sparked the Fifth Syrian War, beginning in 202 until Rome demanded he end his attacks against Egypt. Egypt was a vital trade partner with the emerging Roman Republic. The imperial city needed Egypt for its abundant food supplies. By the year 199,Antiochus controlled the land of Israel, but, under threats from Rome, he was forced to end all plans to invade the kingdom of Egypt. Ptolemiac Egypt never regained control over the land of Israel and Judaea again. At the end of that war, Antiochus gave his daugther Cleopatra of Syria to the young Ptolemy V Epiphanes to secure his advantage over the weakened Ptolemiac kingdom.

Not to be intimidated by Rome elsewhere, Antiochus the Great turned his attention and military power against the city-states of Cilicia and Lycia which were located on the western portion of Asia Minor [modern Turkey]. In 196, his fighting machine then moved northward into the kingdom of Thrace[modern Bulgaria] and conquered it, reclaiming territory that Seleucus I Nicator annexed in the year 281. Meanwhile, Phillip V, an ally of Antiochus III the Great, also ran into trouble with Rome after he attacked its allies, the kingdoms of Rhodes and Pergamon. By the year 200-196, Phillip's actions had provoked the Second Macedonian War with Rome, causing his own political downfall. Antiochus did not risk a war with Rome nor did he intervene to assist Phillip. Instead, he left Phillip to fend for himself.

Antiochus invasion of Thrace angered Rome and caused animosity between the two Gentile powers. Rome immediately dispatched their ambassadors to Antiochus demanding that he withdraw from Europe and give up his claims on the independent city-states in Asia Minor. Another point of contention between Rome and Seleucia was the fact the Antiochus offered asylum to the black general Hannibal of Carthage after his lost to Rome during the Second Punic Wars. After fleeing frum North Africa, Hannibal became a chief advisor to Antiochus in Syria.

In order for Antiochus to comply with Rome's demands he had to dissolve the western portion of the Seleucid Empire, a request he refused during talks with the Roman diplomats. With Hannibal on his side, Antiochus proposed an alliance with Phillip V of Macedonia in his new conflict with Rome. This time, Phillip refused Antiochus offer. In fact, Phillip had fallen under the sway of the **iron** rule of Rome and joined a Roman-led confederation with the city-states of Rhodes, Pergamon, and the Achean League. In the autumn of 192, Antiochus directly challenged Rome by invading central Greece with a company of 10,500 soldiers. The mainland Grecians did not welcome him with open arms. The following year a Roman legion numbering more than 20,000 mighty men pounced Antiochus forces in the city of Thermopylae while other battalions cut off all support from Thrace and elsewhere. Antiochus was forced to retreat and flee for his life. After escaping, he attempted to sail back across the Aegan Sea to the city of Ephesus on mainland Asia Minor, but the joint naval forces of Rome, Rhodes, and Perganom met him at sea and wiped out the fleets of both Antiochus and Hannibal. Following their victory at sea, Rome invaded Asia Minor for a final showdown against Antiochus. After negotiations which demanded that Antiochus relinquish all territorial claims in Europe and Asia Minor failed, the battle was set in array—70,000 Seleucid troops against 30,000 Romans and their allies—in the city of Magnesia ad Sipylum [*pronounced* Mag-ne-sia—ad—Si-pi-lem, located near the modern city of Manisa,Turkey]. The army of the Seleucids were routed and driven out of Asia Minor altogether. To solidify their victory Rome met with Antiochus and forced him to sign an agreement known as the Treaty of Apamea. The peace treaty called for the ruler of Seleucia to renounce all land claims in territories that were once the western portion of the expansive Seleucid Empire. This included all kingdoms in Thrace, Greece, and Asia Minor. The treaty also called for Antiochus to surrender his son Antiochus IV as a hostage, his fleet of Indian war elephants, naval vessels, and pay Rome 15,000 talents of gold over a 12-year period. The Seleucid kingdom now consisted of only Syria, Mesopotamia, and the western part of Persia. In the year 189, his son Seleucus IV Philopator was chosen as heir and co-regent.

By the year 187, Antiochus had returned back to Babylon angry and weakened. He needed at least 1,250 talents of gold each month to pay his indemnity to Rome. He began to rob and pillage many houses of worship to collect the needed treasure for the kingdom's expenses.

So it came to pass in the thirty-six year of his reign on July 3rd in the year 187, Antiochus the Great was attempting to pillage another temple. This time it was the temple of Bel near Susa, Persia being invaded, but at the age of 54 it was him who lost his life in a fierce battle to gain entry. During his lifetime, Antiochus served all the image-gods of the various Greek religions. His son Seleucus IV Philopator reigned in his stead.

Seleucus IV Philopator
(187—175 B.C.E.)

Seleucus IV Philopator was born in the year 220 B.C.E. as the second son of the royal seed of Antiochus III the Great and his wife Laodice III who also happened to be his first-cousin. He grew up and became his father's successor. At the age of 33, he became the seventh king of the Seleucid dynasty. Like most Greeks of that era, he married his own maternal sister Laodice IV who bore him three children: two sons, Antiochus IV Epiphanes, Demetrius I Soter, and one daughter: Laodice V. It should be noticed that King Seleucus came to power during one of the lowest points in the kingdom's existence. Betwwen the years 190-189, his father lost a decisive war against the Roman Republic. The kingdom's territorial possessions in Europe and Asia Minor were gone, and the empire owed Rome 15,000 coins of gold for the next decade. These constraints forced the king and his army to cancel all plans for overseas expeditions. Instead the Seleucid battalions remained in their barracks during his reign.

Seleucus only hope for restoring the former glory of the empire had to come through diplomatic means. In the ninth year of his reign, he arranged the marriage of his daughter Laodice V to the Macedonian king Perseus hoping to re-establish influence in that region. To ensure good behavior, the Roman Senate demanded that King Seleucus send his own son Demetrius to the imperial city in exchange for his youngest brother Antiochus IV. In Rome, Demetrius was held under home arrest while Antiochus IV was allowed to return back to Syria.

In the capital cities of Antioch and Seleucia the stress from the Roman indemnity caused hardships and financial difficulties for the kingship. The soldiers were disgruntled. King Seleucus dispatched his chief minister Heliodorus [pronounced He-li-o-do-rus] to collect revenues from the temple in Jerusalem to assist in paying off his national debt. However, an evil covetous and confusing spirit arose between Heliodorus and Seleucus after his return from Jerusalem. On September 3, 175 the chief minister Heliodorus rose up and slew King Seleucus then seized his throne. King Seleucus did not have an heir in the royal city. His only grown son Demetrius was under house arrest in Rome. Therefore, king's younger brother Antiochus IV Epiphanes plotted to retake the kingdom from the hands of Heliodrus. Eventually he regained control for the royal family. He then made a royal proclamation naming himself, and a baby brother who was also named Antiochus, as the new regents upon the throne. A few years later Antiochus IV murdered his infant co-regent and became the sole heir.

And it came to pass that Seleucus IV Philopator reigned for twelve years in the city of Seleucia. He served all the image-gods of the Greek pantheon during his reign according to the custom of all the Hellenistic rulers before him. He died at the age of 45.

Antiochus IV Epiphanes
(175—164 BCE.)

Antiochus IV Epiphanes [Epi-pha-nes which meant *"God Manifest"*] was born in the year 215 with the birth name of Mi-thri-da-tes. He was the son of Antiochus III the Great and

Laodice III. He became the 8th Seleucid Hellenisitc king at the age of 40 during the year of 175 after returning from Rome in exchange for his nephew Demetrius. I previously documented that Antiochus was a lad when he became a hostage and a pawn at the Treaty of Apamea. One of the terms in the agreement was for the 26-year-old Antiochus to be taken back to Rome as a surety to guarantee that his father Antiochus III the Great would abide by the terms of the 188 B.C.E. ceasefire pact.

While being held hostage in Rome from the years 188 to 175, the young Seleucid prince began to admire the Roman model of government and society. When Antiochus III died in battle, his older brother Seleucus IV Philopator became the successor. Rome demanded the king new to bring his own son Demetrius to Rome as a replacement for Antiochus IV. Antiochus was allowed to return home. Meanwhile in the royal city Seleucia [Babylon], a palace coup took place when Heliodorus conspired against King Seleucus, assassinated him, and reigned in his stead. Antiochus then contacted his friends in the powerful city-state of Pergamon and won their support to replace the usurper Heliodorus. Antiochus convinced King Eumenes II of Pergamon, who was a powerful trade partner with close ties with many wealthy and powerful noble ones in the Seleucid Empire, to join his plot. Through flatteries and manipulation, Antiochus oustered Heliodorus and replaced him as the rightful heir and new king on the throne. He proclaimed himself a co-regent with another one of his younger brothers who was also named Antiochus. But, in the year of 170, King Antiochus IV ordered his officer Andronicus to murder the young lad, his baby brother, Antiochus.

After that, his sister Laodice, who was now a widow from her marriage to his older brother Seleucus IV Philopator, then became his new wife. The pair became the royal parents of Antiochus V Eupator, Laodice VI, Alexander Balas, Antiochus, and possibly another daughter also named Laodice who became the wife of Mithridates III the king of Pontus. For the record, Alexander Balas was not the maternal son of Antiochus and Laodice. He was actually a poor Grecian lad from the western Asia Minor city of Smyrna whom he adopted to become his eromenos [child lover] throughout his reign. Those types of man-boy [erastes-eromenos] sexual relationships were common practice among all four of the Greek Hellenisitc empires.

In terms of his religious conviction, Antiochus was a patron servant of the Greek gods. Before he assumed the throne, he had already donated to Greek religious organizations to beautify the temple of Zeus and the amphitheater in Athens. His love for Zeus led him to believe that he was a personal manifestation of Zeus (God) in the flesh. He also expanded the cult of king and queen worship. His subjects bowed before his feet and kissed his ring. This is how he earned the title *"Epiphanes"* because he was worshiped as *God Manifest* during his reign. He was a lover of expensive and flamboyant apparel who enjoyed showing off his wealth and power. Antiochus IV Epiphanes undertook an expansive renovation campaign and added a Greek colony to the city of Babylon, built an aqueduct, a council hall, a marketplace, and a temple to the god Jupiter Capitolinus. He also built additional Greek cities to rule over the Oriental [Afro-Asiatic black] world. He developed a supremacist attitude wherein he viewed Greco-Roman Hellenisitc culture as superior to the customs of the Oriental populations in Mesopotamia, western Persia, Syria, and Israel. He then introduced a **brass** knuckle policy of imposing Hellenistic values upon native populations in a reign of terror that rivaled the persecution that Shadrach, Meshach, and Abednego faced when they were thrown into the fiery furnace during the reign of Nebuchadnezzar II centuries earlier.

During the first five years of his reign, Antiochus was forced to pay the remaining balance on the indemnity Rome imposed on the kingdom at the end of the Rome-Syrian war in 190-189. He completed the last payment of the debt in the year 170. Now he needed the new treasure to replace the enormous amounts given to Rome. So his mind was very covetous at that time. His army was strong and capable. During the annual military review parade near Antioch, an army of 46,000 foot soldiers, many of them Macedonian mercenaries equipped with the latest Roman weapons, along with 8,500 horsemen and 306 armored elephants were presented to the world.

Meanwhile in Alexandria, the elders of Egypt, who were caretakers of young Ptolemy VI, demanded that the Seleucid Empire return territory in Ceole-Syria taken in an earlier conflict.

Antiochus took their demand as a veiled threat and launched a preemptive invasion into both Israel and Egypt. Once in Egypt, Antiochus captured Ptolemy VI, but did not overthrow his throne. This was done to escape a renewed conflict with the **iron** fist of the Roman Republic. The people of Egypt then chose Ptolemy VII Euergetes as a rival to his brother. After Antiochus withdrew, the two brothers agreed upon joint rulership instead of a civil war.

But in the year 168, Antiochus IV launched a two-pronged attack, invading Egypt for a second time and sending his naval fleet to capture Cyprus.

On the road to Alexandria, Antiochus IV Epiphanes and his mighty army were stopped dead in their tracks by one Roman ambassador named Gaius Popillius Laenas, who drew a circle in the sand around Antiochus, and told the Seleucid ruler to retreat from both Egypt and Cyprus : "Before you cross this circle, I want you to give me a reply for the Roman Senate." The message was clear. If he wanted another war with Rome just step outside the circle. Antiochus decided to withdraw, then he and the Roman diplomat shook hands to seal the deal.

Enraged and resentful of the fact that he was forced to stand down in Egypt, Antiochus marched towards Jerusalem with blood in his eyes after learning that his handpicked governor Menelaus, a Hellenized Jew had been overthrown and replaced by a black Israelite, a Zadokite, while he was at war against the Ptolemies in northeast Africa. The following verses describe the scene of what happened according the **Book of Maccabees: The Massacre of Black Israelites.**

"When these happenings were reported to the king, he thought that Judaea was in revolt. Raging like a wild animal, he set out from Egypt and took Jerusalem by storm. He ordered his soldiers to cut down without mercy those whom they met and slay those who took refuge in their houses. There was a massacre of young and old, a killing of women and children, a slaughter of virgins and infants. In the space of three days, eighty thousand were lost, forty thousand meeting a violent death, and the same number being sold into slavery."

2 Maccabees 5:11-14

The truth of what happened in Jerusalem during this era has been hid from the world since the Greco-Roman Hellenistic white-supremacists have controlled the records of world history. The European Jewish converts and the Euro-Christian religious scholars have conspired against the Oriental Yehudees [Afro-Asiatic Hebrews] and cut off their existence from their annals of documented world history. According to 21st century popular opinion, there has never been a time when all twelve tribes of Israel [Yehudees] were Oriental, meaning Afro-Asiatic or black. The majority of the world was shocked during 1980s and 1990s when they learned that black Yehudees had lived in Ethiopia for thousands of years.

Now, this is what really happened in Jerusalem in 167 B.C.E.. **There was a civil war in Jerusalem between Black Israelites [Oriental Yehudees] and Hellenized Jewish converts.**

Centuries-old War Between Black Israelites and Judaic Converts

For several decades, even centuries, strangers who were not the descendants of Abraham, Isaac, and Jacob [**Afro-Asiatic Hebrews known as Oriental Jews**] entered the land of Israel and adopted the spiritual customs of the ancient Israelite people. This 722/721 B.C.E. occurrence is documented in **2 Kings 17:27-29:** "The king of Assyria gave an order, "Send one of the [ancient Levitical] priest who you have deported [into slavery]; let him come and dwell there, and let him teach them the manners of the God of the land. So one of the priests whom they had exiled from Samaria came and dwelt in Beth-el, and taught them how to worship YHWH. Howbeit every nation [of converts] continued to make its own god [man-made Judaic customs] and set them up in the houses [synagogues] of the high places which the Samaritans [Judaic converts] had made, every nation [of converts] in their cities where they dwelt. "

From that time onward, every superpower that ruled the land of Israel repopulated the holyland with his own religious converts who were not the original Afro-Asiatic Hebrew people. The king of Assyria was the first one to pursue this policy. You can read about it in **2 Kings 17; 24**:

"And the king of Assyria brought men from Babylon, and from Cuthah, and from Ava, and from Hamath, and from Sepharvaim, and placed them in the cities of Samaria instead of the children of Israel: and they possessed Samaria, and dwelt in their cities."

Continuing in **Nehemiah 4: 7-8:**
"But it came to pass, that when Sanballat and Tobiah, and **the Arabians,** and the Ammonites, and the Ashdodites **[Judaic converts]** heard that the walls of Jerusalem were made up, and that the breaches began to be stopped, then they were very wroth, and conspired, all of them together to come and to fight against Jerusalem [the **original Afro-Asiatic Hebrews**], and to hinder it."

Again **Nehemiah 6:10-14:**
"Afterward I came unto the house of Shemaiah the son of Delaiah the son of Mehetabeel, who was shut up: and he said, Let us meet together in the house of God**[ELOHIM]** within the temple; and let us shut the doors of the temple: for they will come to slay you; yea, in the night will they come to slay you. And I [Nehemiah] said should such a man as I flee? and who is there, that being as I am, would go into the temple to save his life? I will not go in. And I[Nehemiah] perceived that God**[ELOHIM]** had not sent him; but that he pronounced this prophecy against me: for Tobiah and Sanballat **[Judaic converts]** had hired him. Therefore was he hired, that I should be afraid, and do so; and sin, and that they might have matter for an evil report, that they might reproach me. My YAH, think upon Tobiah and Sanballat according to these their works; and on the prophetess Noadiah, and the rest of the prophets, that would have put me in fear."

Furthermore in **Ezra 4:1-10:**
"Now when the adversaries **[Judaic converts spoken of in 2 Kings 17:24]** of Yehudah and Benyamin heard that the children of the captivity **[descendants of the ancient Afro-Asiatic Hebrews known as Oriental Jews]** builded the temple unto YAH ELOHIM of Israel; Then they came to Zerubabel and to the chief of the fathers; and said unto them, "Let us build with you: for we **[Judaic converts]** seek your God **[YAH]** as you do; and we do sacrifice unto him since the days of **Esarhaddon king of Assyria**, which brought us up here. But Zerubabel and Yeshua **[the original Afro-Asiatic Hebrews]** and the rest of chief of the fathers of Israel said unto them, "You have nothing to do with us to build the house unto our ELOHIM; but we ourselves together will build unto YAH ELOHIM of Israel as **Cyrus the king of Persia** hath commanded us; Then the people **[Judaic converts]** of the land weakened the hands of the people of Yehudah [Shemitic Hebrews], and troubled them in building, And hired counsellors against them to frustrate their purpose, **all the days of Cyrus the king of Persia, even until the reign of Darius the king of Persia**. And in **the reign of Ahasuerus,** in the beginning of his reign, wrote they him an accusation against the inhabitants of Yehudah and Jerusalem, And in the days of Artaxerxes wrote Bishlam, Mithredath, Tabeel, and the rest of their companions, unto Artaxerxes king of Persia; and the writing of the letter was written in the Syrian tongue, and interpreted in the Syrian tongue. Rehum the chancellor, and Shimshai the scribe, and rest of their companions; the Dinaites; the Apharsathchites, the Tarpelites, the Apharsites, the Achevites, **the Babylonians [people of gold],** the Susanchites, Dehavites, and **the Elamites [Persians-people of silver]**, And the rest of the nations whom the great and noble Asnapper brought over [to occupy the territories of ancient Israel], and set in the cities of Samaria, and the rest that are on this side of the river, and at such a time."

Continuing in **Ezra 7:1-6:**
"Now after these things in **the reign of Artaxerxes king of Persia,** Ezra the son of Seraiah, the son of Azariah, the son of Hilkiah, the son of Shallum, **the son of Zadok,** the son of Ahitub, the son of Amariah, the son of Azariah, the son of Meraioth, the son of Zerahiah, the son of Uzzi, the son of Bukki, the son of Abishua, the son of Phinehas, the son of Eleazar, the son of Aaron the chief priest: This Ezra went up from Babylon: and he was a ready scribe in the law of Moses, which **YHWH ELOHIM of Israel** had given: and the king granted him all his request, according to the hand of YAH his ELOHIM upon him." These were the descendants of the ancient Afro-Asiatic Hebrews who had returned from the Babylonian and Persian captivities.

Like most of the aforementioned kings, Antiochus IV favored the foreign Judaic converts over the black Israelite returnees who struggled to remain faithful to the commandments of YAH. And it came to pass that before he invaded Egypt, he stopped in Jerusalem in midst of two feuding factions striving for control of Jerusalem. This was a civil conflict between Israelites and Hellenistic Judaic convert Jews. On one side you had a black Israelite named Jason, the last of the Zadokite lineage which dated back to King David. He opposed a man named Menelaus, a non-practicing Judaic convert whose faction had introduced many Hellenisitc customs into the holy city. Antiochus sided with Menelaus the Hellenized Jew and appointed him governor. During the era of Antiochus IV, [**Greek Judaic converts-people of brass**] had moved into the land of Israel and spread throughout the Greco-Roman world. Many Greco-Jewish synagogues were established throughout Syria, Asia Minor and Greece. Those non-practicing converts also represented a powerful anti-Torah force in Jerusalem as well as abroad. The Greco-Judaic converts did not undergo circumcision nor practice many of the laws of Moses in the diaspora where they dwelt. These Judaic converts became thorns and snares to the Afro-Asiatic Hebrews.

As we can see, this process of non-Israelite foreigners [**the Judaic converts**] moving into the land of Israel had begun over two millenniums earlier after the twelve tribes of the ancient Hebrew people were sold into slavery beginning in 721 B.C.E.(Israel) and 586 B.C.E.(Judah), proceeding up to the Trans-Atlantic Slave Trade(Judah). Beginning with the kingdoms of gold and continuing down to the kingdoms of iron and miry clay, various strangers have been transplanted into the land with the support of the ruling powers: Example: the kings of Assyria, the kings of Babylon, the kings of Persia, the kings of Greece, the kings of the four Hellenistic Grecians empires, the kings of Rome, the Ottoman kings, and continuing on down to the 1948 C.E. decision by President Harry Truman to support the creation of the modern state of Israel which is today ruled by [**Judaic converts**], who are not the descendants of the ancient Afro-Asiatic Hebrew people.

Antiochus IV returns to Jerusalem

As I mentioned earlier, Antiochus was enraged and resentful after being forced to withdraw from the land of gold, Egypt. So he marched back northward to Jerusalem with covetousness and blood in his eyes, especially after he learned that his handpicked governor had been deposed while he was at war in Egypt.

This is what happened.

While the Seieucid king was in Egypt a rumor spread throughout Jerusalem that Antiochus had been slain in battle. The Israelites rejoiced, thinking their adversary was dead. Their leader Jason, a lukewarm (Hasidic) Hebrew had been demoted by Antiochus. He then led a mob of 1,000 into Jerusalem and overthrew the Hellenized Judaic convert Menelaus, murdered many of his followers, and expelled the Seleucid troops. When King Antiochus returned to the city of David, he saw this coup by the black Israelites as a sign of blatant disrespect for his royal authority.

He immediately slew the ringleader Jason and routed all of his supporters. His army demolished the Holy of Holies, shutdown all Hebrew temple services, and plundered the treasure. The golden menorah candlesticks, golden altar, Torah scrolls, sacred vessels, and all other spiritual artifacts were looted. Antiochus then re-dedicated the Temple of YAH to his patron graven image Zeus which he erected in midst of the holy city. He sacrificed pig offerings on the inner court altar while demanding that Israelites bow before his graven image or face death. After slaughtering and torturing thousands of Israelites, Antiochus demanded that Israelites no longer circumcise their eight-day-old boys. He also forced them to indulge in all types of depraved acts. Anyone caught reading the Torah was immediately killed. Sabbath observation was abolished. In reality, Jerusalem became a Hellenistic stronghold where the gymnasium replaced the Temple as the gathering place. In order to maintain firm control they also built a military base known as Akra inside the holy city. The priests were ordered to practice sports, wrestle naked, and publicly profess allegiance to Greek religious beliefs. The prophet Daniel described those wicked acts as **"the abomination that maketh desolate,"** which meant the idolatry and sinful acts of the heathens that caused YAH to withhold HIS blessings from HIS land and people. These tensions provoked the War between the black Israelite Maccabees and the Gentile Seleucids. Large segments of the Afro-Asiatic Hebrews fled into Africa during this time and settled into the Elephatine community.

War Between The Maccabees and the pagan Seleucids

In the year of 165 B.C.E., the Syro-Greek officials continued to rule Jerusalem with heavy-handed fury. The Israelites and the Judaic converts were humiliated and brought low into subjection under their hands. Two years later in the year 167, Matthaniah Hasmon, an obscure priest from the city of Modein, a hilly region overlooking the city of Lydda, became angry after he witnessed a Seleucid officer in command of the Temple of Jerusalem forcing a fellow Israelite to commit a sinful act. He rose up and slew both of them. He, along with his family, and several others fled to the caves in the Judean desert and initiated a three-year guerilla war against the Seleucids. For the next three years, Judah the Maccabee, the son of Matthaniah, led a series of raids against their garrisons. By December of 164 B.C.E., the Maccabees liberated the temple from Greco-pagan influences. The remembrance and celebration of this victory became known as Hanukkah. The First and the Second Books of the Maccabees are historical accounts of the struggles faced by the Judaic converts and the remnant of Israelites who had returned to Jerusalem after Cyrus the Great, king of Persia had released them from Babylonian Bondage in 536 B.C.E.. Since then, however, the populations of foreigners and Greco-Judaic converts which had moved into the land of Israel had grown to outnumber the ancient Afro-Asiatic Hebrews (Oriental population). During this time, the people of the Dead Sea of Idumea [Edomites], Samaria, Moab, and Transjordan [Arabs] became Judaic converts under the newly emerging religion of Judaism. At various times, these converts became opponents of the Afro-Asiatic Hebrew returnees. These historical episodes are recorded in the Books of Ezra and Nehemiah.

Now back to the reign of **Antiochus IV Epiphanes**. By the year 167, troubles out of the east forced the Seleucid ruler to turn his attention away from the provinces of Samaria and Judah. Mithridates I, the king of Parthia [Persia] invaded the city of Herat disrupting the direct trade route between the Greek world into India. The raid threatened major commerce between the East and West regions. Antiochus assembled his mighty army and launched a military campaign against the king of Parthia by the spring of 164. Before departing for Persia, Antiochus left general Lysias in charge of the kingdom and co-regent for his nine-year-old son Antiochus V Eupator. Facing a gold and silver currency shortage, Antiochus hoped to gain needed money from looting temples along the way. He convinced King Artaxias of Armenia to surrender and recognize his rulership in the east. Nevertheless, this expedition into Elam would be his last. Near the end of the year 164 B.C.E. Antiochus IV Epiphanes died.

There are so many different accounts on how and why he died. Some historians report he succumbed to an illness because the gods were punishing him for attempting to loot the Temple of the god Nanaia in western Persia. The historic Scrolls of Antiochus recorded this sequence of events: "When Antiochus heard that his army had been defeated in Judaea, he boarded a ship and fled to the coastal cities. Wherever he went, the people rebelled and called him "The Fugitive," so he drowned in the sea."

The Second Book of Maccabees provides this testimony for his death:"The all-seeing Lord(**YAH**),the God (**ELOHIM**), struck him with an incurable and unseen blow. As soon as he ceased speaking he was seized with a pain in his bowels for which there was no relief and with sharp internal tortures—and that very justly, for he had tortured the bowels of others with many and strange inflictions. Yet he did not in any way stop his insolence, but was even more filled with arrogance, breathing fire in his rage against the Jews[black Yehudees], and giving orders to hasten the journey. And so it came about that he fell out of his chariot as it was rushing along, and the fall was so hard as to torture every limb of his body." Regardless, of which way he died, King Antiochus IV Epiphanes reign came to an end in the year of 164.

And it came to pass that the Seleucid king reigned for 11 years in royal capital of Babylon[Seleucia]. He served all the gods of the Greek religions, claiming to be the personal manifestation of the idol Zeus. During his reign, the coins were minted with his graven image on one side and the sun-god Apollo on the reverse side. Known to have an erratic behavior with an evil temper, his associates referred to him as Antiochus IV Epimanes, meaning "the Maniac." On his good days, however, he was known as man of the people, appearing at the public baths, and maintaining close contacts with municipal officials.

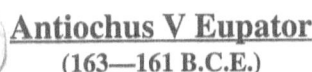

Antiochus V Eupator
(163—161 B.C.E.)

Antiochus V was born in the year of 172 B.C.E. in the western capital of Antioch as the oldest son of Antiochus IV and his sister-wife Laodice. When his father began his last military campaign in Persia during the year 165, he appointed young 9-year-old Antioch V as the crown prince and commanded General Lysias to serve as his co-regent securing the kingdom in his absence. Another General named Phillip, the usual caretaker of crown prince, accompanied King Antiochus IV Epiphanes on the Persian campaign. In his absence, General Lysias ordered the boy-king to attack Jerusalem. General Lysias launched a massive attack against the black Yehudees and Judaic converts to squash their rebellion. The Seleucids defeated the Israelites and their allies in the Battle of Beth-Zechariah. The brother of Judah Maccabee whose name was Eleazar Avram was slain during the conflict. The war was going well for General Lysias when he received a report that the king was dead and General Phillip and company were returning to the royal city. Fearing for his life and preparing for a possible war, Lysias instructed the boy-king to extend an olive branch to the inhabitants of Jerusalem. The Israelites and their allies accepted the plan. Before their departure, the Seleucids tore down the major walls around Jerusalem to ensure that the Israelites would not rebel again.

When General Lysias and his mighty ones arrived in the royal city Antioch, General Phillip and his forces were in complete control. A civil war between these two generals broke out. General Lysias, Antiochus V, and their loyalists recaptured the capital. Antiochus V assumed the throne with General Lysias serving as his chief advisor. In the midst of this turbulence, the Roman Senate decided against releasing the true heir, 22-year-old hostage Demetrius I Soter, the son of Seleucus IV Philopator. Rome felt that it was more safe dealing with a young lad and his co-regent instead of an unpredictable adult in his 20s. Therefore the Romans appointed the lad as king with the veteran-general serving as his confidant.

In recognition of his father, General Lysias bestowed the title "Eupator" which meant *"of a good father"* upon the young lad. Meanwhile the veteran-general took advantage of the young king's lack of experience and immaturity. Right under his nose, General Lysias started a military buildup which violated the terms of the twenty-seven year old Treaty of Apamea. The Romans sent an ambassador to Syria to verify the status of the agreement. They discovered that the Seleucids had more war elephants and ships in their arsenal than the treaty authorized. The Roman Senate approved a military operation to sink their warships and disable their war elephants, thus crippling their ability to threaten Roman interest. General Lysias did not challenge the Roman assault, but the population became incensed at their blatant disrespect for their sovereignty. In response, the Roman consul general Gnaeus Octavius was assassinated by a mob in 162 B.C.E. in the city of Laodecia. The Roman Senate issued a decree holding 11-year-old King Antiochus V Eupator responsible for the death of the their diplomat. After that, several Roman senators arranged for the escape of Demetrius back to Antioch. In Syria, Demetrius was welcomed as a hero and as the true heir of the throne. In the summer of the year 161, eleven-year-old Antiochus V Eupator and elder General Lysias were overthrown and executed.

It came to pass that Antiochus V Eupator had reigned as a ceremonial figurehead over the Seleucid Empire for three years. The young lad died without leaving any offsprings behind. He had not reached puberty.

Demetrius I Soter **(161—150 B.C.E.)**

Born in the year of 185 B.C.E. as the son of King Seleucus IV Philopator and Queen Laodice IV, Demetrius life began in the midst of political turmoil. When his grandfather Antiochus III the Great died in battle, his father Seleucus IV became the successor. With a new ruler on the throne, Rome wanted the son of Seleucus to become the new internee instead of the son of the deceased Antiochus III. So as a young child Demetrius was sent to Rome in exchange for his first-cousin Antiochus IV as the new hostage to ensure that his father King Seleucus IV Philopator would not violate the terms of the Treaty of Apamea. When King Seleucus IV was murdered, Antiochus IV Epiphanes rose up against the murderer named Heliodorus and succeeded him as the new king. After the reign of Antiochus IV Epiphanes, his 9-year-old son Antiochus V Eupator and his elderly co-regent General Lysias succeeded him on the throne. During this time in the year of 163, Demetrius petitioned the Roman Senate for release so he could return to royal capital of Antioch, but his request was denied. But two years later, the Roman government discovered that the rulers of the Seleucid Empire were violating the two-decades old treaty. Rome launched a pre-emptive attack against Antiochus V Eupator and General Lysias and disabled their warships and war elephants. The citizens of the Seleucid Empire became outraged at Rome's aggression and killed their ambassador Gnaeus Octavius. The Roman Senate passed an edict which held the rulers of the Seleucid Empire responsible. Certain members of the Roman Senate and their Greek allies initiated a plan to allow Demetrius to escape so that he could become the new ruler and a proxy for Rome.

Prince Demetrius arrived back in Antioch somewhere between late October of 162 and September 161. Once home, the hearts of the people turned towards him and he received a hero's welcome after two-decades of Roman captivity. After this, 11-year-old King Antiochus V Eupator and his mentor General Lysias were immediately captured and executed. Next, Demetrius was forced to fight another usurper, General Timarchus who had attacked the eastern capital of Babylon and proclaimed himself "the king". After killing Timarchus in 160 B.C.E., the Babylonians declared Demetrius **"the Soter"** *which meant* **"the Savior."** He also overthrew King Ariarathes of the city-state of Cappadocia. After these events, the Romans finally recognized him as the legitimate ruler of the Seleucid Empire. The elders of Antioch also agreed. Demetrius was declared "King Demetrius I Soter." He married two women: one named Apama and the other woman was his sister Laodice V. Through those marriages, he became the father of Demetrius II Nicator, Antiochus VII Sidestes, and Antigonus.

One of the first foreign policy flashpoints for the throne of Demetrius was the protracted war between his kingdom and the people in Israel [**the Maccabees and Judaic converts**]. Demetrius assigned General Bacchides to lead **the brass** knuckle war against the inhabitants of Jerusalem and crushed the uprising in Judah. Judas Maccabee was slain in midst of the battle. His brother Jonathan became the new leader of the rebellion. The conflict continued off and on for the next eight years.

Meanwhile in the east, the brother of the deceased Timarchus who was named Heracleides joined in a conspiracy against King Demetrius. Heracleides became the ally of the adopted son of Antiochus IV Epiphanes named Alexander Balas. Heracleides petitioned the Roman Senate on behalf of Prince Alexander. Heracleides eventually convinced the Latin officials that Alexander was the rightful heir of King Antiochus IV Epiphanes who should have succeeded Antiochus V Eupator—not his nephew Demetrius. Alexander also gained support from princess Laodice VI, the kings of Pergamon, Cappadocia, and Ptolemy VI Philometor of Egypt. In the summer of the year of 152, Prince Alexander I Balas proclaimed himself king with the political backing of Rome and its allies. He then assembled a small navy with mercenaries which landed and occupied the city of Ptolemais [in northern Egypt] and established a rival Seleucid headquarters. Alexander proclaimed peace to the Maccabees by recognizing Jonathan as the governor [Tishri] of the territory of Judaea. The Israelites and the Judaic converts became the allies of Alexander I Balas. Once King Demetrius learned about Alexander's mutinous actions, he hastily wrote a letter with the king's seal upon it that proclaimed more liberties to all the inhabitants of the Judaean province. The inhabitants of Judaea did not trust King Demetrius because of his long years of war against people of the covenant. The Israelites and Judaic converts rejected the offer and joined forces with Alexander I Balas. The history of these events can be found in **I Maccabees 10:25-45**. This Seleucid civil war actually provided the province of Judaea with a period of tranquility. Alexander I Balas and his army moved against King Demetrius I Soter and engaged in battle near Antioch. King Demetrius I Soter was defeated and killed.

And it came to pass that King Demetrius I Soter had ascended to the throne at the age of 24. He reigned for eleven years and served all the gods of the Greco-Roman religions. It appears that his long stay in Rome alienated him from the Seleucid people. He died at the age of 35 and Prince Alexander I Balas reigned in his stead.

Alexander Balas
(150—146 B.C.E.)

Alexander I Balas was a Greek native from the city-state of Smyrna in Asia Minor. His surname Balas [Ba-las] denoted the Semitic title which glorified the Babylonian god Bel. The ancient Babylonians superstitiously believed that the graven image (god) controlled the atmosphere (air-the holy ghost giving life). Bel was the (son/sun-god of order and destiny). It was a member of a trinity which included Anu(father) and Ea(mother). The Babylonians (**the head[kingdom] of gold**) believed the graven image brought forth severe storms and gentle spring winds. They also worshipped and praised the idol for their agricultural blessings. As we can see, the name Balas lets us know that the Grecian people(**the thigh[kingdom] of brass**) in Smyrna were still connected to that same religious ideology thousands of years later.

Now back to **King Alexander I Balas.** The year of his birth is unknown because he was not born in the royal palace at Antioch or Seleucia. This led many observers and researchers to believe that he was a bastard child, not his actual maternal son. The birth dates for the other children of Antiochus IV Epiphanes are readily available. Therefore it is highly probable that Alexander I Balas was an adopted son who was used as a child lover in a palace in an **erastes-eromenos [man-boy]** sexual relationship. Those types of relationships were common within the Hellenistic world.

Once he grew into a young man, Alexander came to the throne after being discovered by a disgruntled man named Heracleides[Hera-clei-des] who was the brother of the late Timarchus, a rebel who had lost his life fighting against King Demetrius. To avenge Ti-mar-chus blood, he supported Alexander I Balas in a coup against Demetrius. By 152 the conspiracy had gained support from the Roman Senate, their Greek allies, and the rulers of Egypt. In the summer of 150, a great battle between King Demetrius I Soter and Prince Alexander I Balas took place near the capital of Antioch. One of King Demetrius officers named Diodotus [Di-o-do-tus] conspired against the king and allowed Alexander's forces to capture the capital. Demetrius was slain during the raging battle. After Alexander was crowned the new king, he began to exalt himself as King Alexander *Epi-pha-nes,* which *meant "the manifestation of God."* on earth. He married Cleopatra Thea, the daughter of Ptolemy VI Philometor, princess of Egypt, and by the year of 147, they became the parents of Antiochus VI Dionysus.

During his short four year reign King Alexander ruled the palace in the manner of his Ptolemaic supporters. The sculptured potraits created during his reign featured Ptolemaic characteristics. Inside the palace he isolated himself and spent most of his time feasting and drinking, enjoying musical banquets, erastes-eromenos sexual orgies, along with acts of bestiality. As the old saying goes, *"the fruit doesn't fall too far from the tree."* Once in power, the adult King Alexander displayed the same type of behavior he had witnessed as the bastard child under his adopted father King Antiochus IV during his reign.

In the final year of his reign in 146 B.C.E. a revolt broke out in the western tributary city of Cilicia in Asia Minor. Cilician pirates took advantage of the weakened Seleucid navy which had been restricted by Rome. In the eastern portion of the kingdom, the native Parthian population **[Oriental-brown-skinned people]** rose up against the Seleucid Empire. Another challenge came when the father-in-law of Alexander, Ptolemy VI Philometor of Egypt, made an hundred-eighty-degree turn and supported the usurper Prince Demetrius II Nicator in the civil war. King Ptolemy and Demetrius captured the capital, but the king of Egypt was slain in battle. After that, Ptolemy's daughter, Cleopatra Thea, divorced Alexander and remarried Demetrius II. By August of the year 145 Antioch was completely surrounded. King Alexander I Balas attempted to escape the city, but he was captured and beheaded, along with his wife and eldest son, by the Nabatean Arabs who served as allies for Egypt and mercenaries for the rebel forces of Demetrius.

As the civil war raged, the chief minister Diodotus was able to remove Alexander's 2-year-old son, Antiochus VI Dionysus, from the danger of war. Then Diodotus proclaimed the infant child as king and another round of a civil war started. This time it was chief minister Diodotus and crown prince Antiochus VI Dionysus against the forces of Demetrius II Nicator.

So it came to pass that King Alexander I Balas died in the civil war against Demetrius II Nicator in August of 145 B.C.E.. He had reigned four years in the royal city of Antioch. During his brief reign he served all the gods of the Greek religion and walked in the abominable ways of his Greek ancestors who knew not **YAH**. His second-cousin Demetrius II Nicator reigned in his stead.

Demetrius II Nicator
(145—139 B.C.E. 1st reign)
(129—126 B.C.E. 2nd reign)

Demetrius II Nicator was the twelfth Hellenistic ruler over the Seleucid Empire. He was the son of King De-me-tri-us I Soter and Queen Laodice V. He was born in the year of 160 B.C.E. during the waning years of his father's reign. At the age of 10, his father experienced a mutinous civil-war against the armies of another Seleucid prince named Alexander I Balas, who "claimed" to be the son of late King Antiochus IV Epiphanes. With the support of Ptolemaic Egypt, the forces of Alexander I Balas surrounded the Antioch palace and eventually captured the entire capital city in the year of 150. As the battle raged, his father

King Demetrius I Soter, his mother, and older brother were slain. With the outcome of the war uncertain, young crown prince Demetrius II had been sent to the city of Cnidus, on the southwest coast of Asia Minor for safety. At that time, the Ptolemaic dynasty in Egypt ruled that territory near the island-state of Crete.

During this time, Ptolemy VI greatly interfered in Seleucid affairs. In the year 147, Demetrius II, at the age of 14, returned to Syria. During his four-year exile, the elder leadership which supported young Demetrius convinced Ptolemy to join their effort to return the teenage monarch to the throne.

The king of Egypt, Cretan mercenaries, and Seleucid supporters joined in a confederation to lay seige to Antioch to remove King Alexander I Balas. Ironically, Alexander had been the son-in-law of King Ptolemy VI Philometor. In the latest episode, Ptolemy commanded his daughter to divorce Alexander. Because of reports of Alexander's debased wild parties, neglect of kingdom affairs, his bad relations with his daughter Cleopatra Thea, the king of Egypt turned against Alexander and remarried his daughter to 14-year-old Demetrius II. Together they begat three children: Seleucus V, an unnamed daughter who married Phraates II, the son of Mithradates, king of Parthia, and Antiochus VIII Grypus.

King Ptolemy of Egypt and his allies eventually prevailed in conquering Antioch. The leaders of Antioch submitted to the rule of Ptolemy VI and offered him the Seleucid throne. The king of Egypt refused the offer in fear of offending the Roman Republic, realizing that such a move would be a provocation to the kingdom of Rome[**the kingdom of iron—pelvic and legs of iron**]. Rome would never allow the existence of a unified Ptolemiac-Seleucid Empire[**kingdom of brass—waist and thighs of brass**]. So in the summer of 145, Ptolemy VI appointed Demetrius II to sit upon the throne as the new Seleucid king. But in the autumn of that same year, Demetrius attacked his own Egyptian benefactors.

King Alexander I Balas was eventually captured by the Nabatean Arabs who cut his head off. The Egyptian victory, however, came with a heavy price. Egypt accomplished its goal of removing Alexander, but suffered the lost of their own revered king Ptolemy VI Philometor in the process. Howbeit in the year of 146, the young 14-year-old king Demetrius II did become the sole ruler for the next seven years. He was not very popular with the Seleucid people nor did they feel an intimate connection with him. They desired an older more capable leader. To make matters worse for young Demetrius, the Cretean mercenaries who had assisted in his victory over Alexander became disgruntled and turned against their allies in Antioch. They began pillaging the royal city. A terrible fight broke out. Many historians described it as a massacre, between the people of Antioch and the Creteans.

By the year 144, the engulfing chaos caused King Demetrius II to flee towards the eastern portion of the empire to Seleucia. When internal order in the royal city was finally restored by the year 142, a major shift had occurred. The leadership inside the Seleucid Empire had transfered into the hands of the chief minister and general Diodotus. Remember, this is the same Diodotus who was the general who turned against Demetrius I Soter and allowed the late Alexander I Balas to dethrone him. Remember, he also served as a cabinet official for Alexander during his brief four-year reign. At the end of Alexander's reign when Egypt and Demetrius II beseiged Antioch again, he fled the city with Alexander's two-year-old son Antiochus VI Dionysus. Now, five years later, he was back in Antioch at the helm of power again. He proclaimed the toddler as the new king of the Seleucid Empire to legitimize his scheme to rule. Meanwhile the disorder inside the kingdom caused the enemies of the Seleucids to rise up against them. King Mithradates I of Parthia reclaimed the territory of Media and Elam. He then launched an attack on the eastern capital of Seleucia [Babylonia] and conquered it. In October of the year 141, the king of Parthia attacked the city of Uruk and went on to conquer others parts of Mesopotamia. By the year of 139, Demetrius was forced to respond to the Parthian uprisings in the east. Demetrius won the initial round of this conflict which forced the Parthians to retreat to the Iranian mountains. But, the mountains proved to be a trap door for King Demetrius II and his army. They were defeated in the Persian high places, and during this combat Demetrius was captured and taken as a prisoner-of-war.

Meanwhile back in western capital of Antioch, Diodotus claimed the throne in the name of the 2-year-old Antiochus VI Dionysus. The large army which he had gathered temporarily gave him the support he needed to maintain a co-regent grip on power. The young 2-year-old lad Antiochus VI Dionysus crawled beside him as heir to the throne. For unexplained reasons, the young lad underwent surgery in the year 142 and died. Many historians suspect Diodotus killed him to claim the throne for himself. Diodotus maintained his control until the year of 139/138 when he was overthrown by Antiochus VII Sidestes.

Now let's switch back to the eastern side of the crumbling Seleucid Empire once again. By the late summer of 138, Demetrius II lost the war against Mithradates the king of Parthia. He was captured, and bound in captivity for nearly nine years. Nevertheless, the king of Parthia treated him well during his days in bondage. He even gave him a wife whose name was Rhodogune [[Rho-do-gune],a Parthian princess. The deposed monarch Demetrius still did not enjoy the niceties of incarceration. He continuously plotted to escape from the city of Hyrcania [Hyr-ca-nia] where he was held hostage. Hyrcania was an ancient Persian region, located near the southern and southwest coast of the Caspian Sea, which later became a Macedonian province under the Hellenistic invasions. Demetrius desire was to escape the province and return back to the royal city of Antioch to reclaim his throne. In one escape plot, a spy-friend of Demetrius named Kallimander secretly traveled from Antioch to Hyrcania to free him, but they were discovered. The king did not punish the pair for their attempted escape, but instead issued a pardon and a banquet. The second escape plot also failed when Mithradates uncovered his plans. This time the king of Parthia gave the humiliated leader a pair of golden dice, which symbolized a child's pacifier.

2nd reign
(129—126 B.C.E.)

And it came to pass that the Parthian king Phraates II, *pronounced* [fra-a-tes], the son of Mithradates released Demetrius II from captivity to return home to Antioch. King Phraates hoped that Demetrius and his brother Antiochus VII Sidestes, who was the new king in Antioch, would fight each other in a new protracted civil war. A war between the two brothers would alleviate an immediate threat to Parthia. That strategy did not work. The armies of Demetrius and Antiochus bypassed each other without confrontation. This is what happened. The army of Antiochus was defeated by the advancing Parthian troops and the winter season. Meanwhile, Demetrius II bypassed that entire war and returned to the capital to reclaim his throne and his queen-wife Cleopatra Thea. When Demetrius finally arrived back to the kingdom in the year of 129, its former glory was greatly diminished. It consisted of only Syria and Cilicia. Continuing a downward spiral, the Antioch population did not receive the resurrected kingship of Demetrius with much enthusiasm. Their reservations about Demetrius II included memories of his cruelty and lavish self-indulgence.

Another crisis that surfaced during Demetrius brief three-year reign from 129—126 B.C.E. was the political crisis in Egypt that spilled over into the affairs of the Seleucid kingdom. Egypt was wrecked with a civil-war between Ptolemaic siblings, Cleopatra II, a sister, and Ptolemy VIII, a brother. During this time the Egyptian queen Cleopatra was exiled in Syria where she spent her time building an army to challenge her brother back home in Egypt. Demetrius II supported Cleopatra in her scheme to replace her brother Ptolemy VIII by joining the attack near the city of Pelusium in northern Egypt. Demetrius also lost that battle in the year of 128. Once Ptolemy VIII gained knowledge of the Demetrius-Cleopatra conspiracy, he reacted by supporting a Seleucid rival named Alexander II Zabinas to challenge them. In the spring of 126, both arch-enemies met in a battle near Damascus. The army of King Demetrius II was defeated. He was forced to flee towards the city of Ptolemais. His wife, Queen Cleopatra Thea, forsook him, closed the gates as she left the city, and prevented his escape with her. He was then forced to board a ship, but was slain near Tyre.

And it came to pass that Demetrius II reigned over the Seleucid Empire twice. His first reign lasted seven years from 146—139 B.C.E. His second reign lasted from 129 to 126 B.C.E.

He came to power at the age of 14 and died at the age of 35. Demetrius II and Cleopatra Thea had two children: Seleucus V Philometor and Antiochus VIII Grypus.

Antiochus VI Dionysus
(144—142 B.C.E.)

Antiochus VI was born in the year 148 B.C.E. as the royal son of King Alexander I Balas and Cleopatra Thea. His birth came during the final two years of his father's reign. In fact, he was a 2-year-old when the armies of Demetrius II and his Egyptian allies beseiged the capital of Antioch. Once his father's defeat became apparent, his general named Diodotus grabbed the young lad Antiochus VI and fled the danger. After 14-year-old Demetrius II was given the mantle of power in 146 B.C.E., he was faced with an serious upheaval only two years later. The chaos forced the king to flee the royal city. His power-hungry general Diodotus Tryphon seized the throne as the co-regent for the heir Antiochus VI, the son of deceased King Alexander I Balas. Diodotus used the child as a pawn to legitimize his coup. For unexplained reasons, the child Seleucid monarch died in the year of 142/141. Some historians say Antiochus VI died in surgery while others contend he was murdered by his elderly co-regent Diodotus who wanted to claim absolute power for himself.

So it came to pass that Antioch VI Dionysus never actually reigned on the throne. He was a mere tool of Diodotus for two years, from 144 to 142 B.C.E. The ancient coins minted in his honor showed him on one side and the Greek gods Castor and Polydeuces on the reverse side. In Greek mythology, Castor and Polydeuces were two men who rode on horseback together. According to their legends, the male pair were inseparable in life and death.

He died under questionable circumstances at the age of 6. General Diodotus Tryphon became his successor.

Diodotus Tryphon
(142—138 B.C.E.)

General Diodotus was a chief minister and general for the Hellenistic Seleucid kingdom from 142—138 B.C.E. He was not a descendant or relative of the Seleucus I Nicator. Known as the most successful usurper in the history of the empire, Diodotus was born in the city of Casiana, a small town that consisted of the principalities of Apamea in Asia Minor. His year of birth is unknown because he was not a member of dynastic siblings. It appears that he was a hard-working individual who made personal and political connections to propel himself into a sphere of influence. As a young man Diodotus became a soldier in the Seleucid army. He advanced to the position of lieutenant general under the command of Alexander I Balas. Lieutenant General Diodotus became the commander of the forces in the royal capital of Antioch. When Alexander I Balas rose up against Demetrius I Soter, Diodotus became his chief minister in charge of the Antiochian palace. For four years he was a powerful prince in the royal court. But in the year 145, King Alexander I Balas was overthrown by Demetrius II. As the troops of Demetrius II and his allies surrounded the capital, Diodotus hid Alexander's son, Antiochus VI Dionysus, and defected to side of Demetrius II.

Demetrius assumed the throne in 145 B.C.E., but shortly thereafter chaos broke between the Cretean mercenaries and the Macedonian mercenaries which caused a major crisis inside the capital city. There was pillaging, bloodshed, and instability throughout Antioch that prompted King Demetrius II to flee for his safety. From the eastern capital of Seleucia, Demetrius was able to hold his sway over the single coastal city of Cilica, along with other coastal Phoenician and Syrian cities. In the process of time, war broke out on the eastern front once again. Demetrius was defeated and captured in this war against the kingdom of Parthia. Meanwhile General Diodotus, who had assembled a fighting force in Chalcis, a seaport on the eastern shore of Greece, used the situation to declare himself the new regent along with 2-year-old Antiochus VI Dionysus. The young lad was the heir of the late King Alexander I

123

Balas. During this time the realm of Diodotus only included the capital Antioch, Greater Syria, and the Grecian cities of Apamea and Chalcis. King Diodotus initially feigned himself to be a friend of the Judaea by offering an olive branch of peaceful relations to the **Greco-Judaic converts** in hopes of gaining their support. The Seleucid rulers had persecuted the inhabitants of the province of Samaria and Judaea throughout their existence. They were considered the enemy of the **Greco-Judaic converts and the lost sheep of the house of Israel**. In a reversal of policy, Diodotus solicited their support to maintain his control. The Jewish converts proved to be effective in battles against the forces of Demetrius. Nevertheless, King Diodotus Tryphon began to fear the increasing power and independence of his Judaic allies then turned against them. Diodotus lured the Judaic leader Jonathan Apphus near the banks of the Nile River to the city of Ptolemais. There Diodotus abducted him and held him for a bounty. After that didn't work, Diodotus murdered him and launched an offensive into the holyland to reduce the power of the Judaic conclave. The Seleucid kingdom was greatly divided. There were military flareups between pro-Demetrius forces and pro-Diodotus forces throughout Ceole-Syria.

In the year of 142/141, a mysterious event occurred. The young lad Antiochus VI Dionysus, who was only 6, underwent medical surgery and died. Some thought Diodotus had a hand in the matter, and may have murdered the child to become the sole heir on the Seleucid throne. Shortly after the child's death, the army elected Diodotus as king and bestowed the title *"Basileus"—"king"* upon him. He became known as King Diodotus Tryphon. He strengthened his close ties with the Seleucid military and Greco-Macedonian mercenaries. Graven images of Greco-Macedonian military helmets were inscripted on the reverse side of coins during his brief reign.

By the year of 139/138, Antiochus VII Sidestes, the brother of Demetrius II, left his hometown of Rhodes and traveled back to Antioch. While King Demetrius II was bound in captivity in Parthia, his wife Cleopatra Thea, married her brother-in-law Antiochus VII Sidestes. Many of the aristocrats of the capital city began to defect towards Antiochus VII Sidestes. The war between the two Seleucid factions quickly spread throughout Antioch. The army of King Diodotus was driven from the capital to the coastal fortress-city of Dora on the Ceole-Syrian coast. There King Diodotus was surrounded, so he fled by ship towards the Asia Minor city of Apamea, near his hometown. The army of Antiochus VII Sidetes continued to hotly pursue him. In the midst of the action, King Diodotus Tryphon died. Some historians report King Diodotus was put to death while other accounts contend he committed suicide.

And it came to pass that King Diodotus Tryphon died in the year 138 B.C.E. after reigning for four years in the city of Antioch. He walked in all of the corrupt ways of the kings of the Seleucid Empire who reigned before him. He served all the gods [graven images] of the Greek religion. Antiochus VII Sidestes succeeded him and reigned in his stead.

Antiochus VII Sidestes
(138—129 B.C.E.)

Antiochus VII Sidestes was born in the year of 159 B.C.E. as the middle son of the Seleucid King Demetrius I Soter and Queen Laodice V. He was a mere 8 or 9 year-old when his father's regime fell in 150 B.C.E. to an usurper named Alexander I Balas. *(His surname Sidestes reflected on the fact that he also lived in the city of Side, which was a famous city in southwest Asia Minor known for one of the best colossal arched theaters for the era.)* For safety, his father sent him to the island city-state of Rhodes where he remained until the collapse of his brother's first rulership in 141. His brother Demetrius was forced to flee to the eastern capital of Seleucia where he was later captured and held as a prisoner-of-war for nearly nine years before escaping in the year of 129.

At the age of 18, Antiochus returned to the royal capital of Antioch. Diodotus had seized the throne for himself while pretending to be the co-regent for Antiochus VI Dionysus, the 2-year-old son of King Alexander I Balas. Those events moved Antiochus VII Sidestes to leave the tranquility and comforts of his home in exile to enter the fray for rulership for the

Seleucid throne. His goal was to reclaim the throne for the true descendants of Seleucus I Nicator. When Antiochus VII Sidestes arrived, he married his sister-in-law, the wife of his older brother: whorish Queen Cleopatra Thea who had already been the bride of Alexander I Balas and Demetrius II. Her new union with Antiochus VII Sidestes brought forth one child: Antiochus IX Cyzicenus.

By August of the year 138, 21-year-old Antiochus had received a hero's welcome back in Antioch. Several influential groups joined ranks with him as he attacked King Diodotus Tryphon. Diodotus was driven from the palace to the coastal fortress of Dora where he was forced to escape by ship to Asia Minor. When he reached the city of Apamea he committed suicide while facing hot pursuit.

After these events, the energetic Antiochus VII Sidestes reigned on the Seleucid throne in control of the Ceole-Syria region. This led him into direct conflict with the inhabitants of the Judaean province. This included the **Greco-Judaic converts (whites)** and **the descendants of Judah, Benyamin, and Levi [lost sheep of the House of Israel](blacks)** who had returned to the region after the end of the Babylonian captivity in 536 B.C.E. In 137, Seleucid General Cendebeus attacked the **Judaic convert-ruled** Hasmonaean kingdom, but the integrated fighting force of Judaean warriors repelled the attack and turned the shame back on their heads. But years later, somewhere between the beginning of 134 and late 132, Antiochus assassinated the leader of the Hasmonaeans, Simon, the High Priest, when he invaded the land of Judaea for a second time. He built a seigemound around Jerusalem to bring the city of David to its knees. The new Hasmonean leader John Hyrcanus waved a white flag to the army of the Seleucids then raided the sepulchre of King David and removed 3,000 talents for ransom to halt the assault. Antiochus VII Sidestes accepted the Judaic offer and showed a renewed respect for the leadership and the inhabitants of Judaea. This benevolence earned him the title of "Euergetes" *which meant* "the Benefactor." After this, the Judaic inhabitants made peace with the Seleucids and joined their military as mercenaries in future wars for the next two decades.

After securing peace in Syria-Israel, Antiochus then turned his attention to the challenges he faced in the far east, mainly the Parthians. They had won their independence under Mithridates I "the Great" and his predecessors. Antiochus was victorious in the first and second confrontation with Mithridates. In fact, the elderly Mithridates was slain by Antiochus VII Sidestes during these early battles. Initially, the Seleucids prevailed and were able to recover Media and Babylonia. Now, it was 130 B.C.E. and Phraates, the son of Mithridetes, was seeking to reconquer their past territorial claims over Elam, Media, Babylonia, and all adjoining areas. In the midst of his warfare, Phraates made a calculated decision to release King Demetrius II from the confines of captivity in Hyrcania, hoping Demetrius II and Antiochus VII Sidestes would lock horns in a renewed Seleucid civil war that would alleviate a threat for him. That plan did not work. The two never crossed paths.

Instead, the 130-129 B.C.E. winter season caught both armies, the Seleucids and Parthians, off guard and forced them to disengage until the terrible weather passed over. Meanwhile, Demetrius II reached Antioch again while Antiochus VII Sidestes and his army retired to their winter quarters where they spent their time hunting, feasting, and heavy drinking. During this same time, several Media-Persian cities mounted, what appeared to be, a coordinated insurrection to cast out their Seleucid overlords. In the early summer of the year 129, Antiochus and his Royal Guards moved to support a garrison which had been isolated by the Parthian army, but he was ambushed and slain in a barren valley by King Phraates and his large force of Parthian warriors. The Parthians went on to reassert their dominion over the territories of Media, Babylonia, and large swarths of Mesopotamia that reached all the way to the Euphrates River. The land mass of the Seleucid Empire had decreased down to mainland Syria and the city-state of Cilica.

So it came to pass that Antiochus VII Sidestes reigned on the throne in Antioch for nine years from 138 to 129. He walked in all the ways of his Hellenistic predecessors. He came to power at the age of 21 and died at the age of 30. He married his brother's wife: Queen Cleopatra Thea. They had one child: Antiochus IX Cyzicenus.

Once Demetrius II reached the royal capital of Antioch in the same year of 129, he reigned for another three years until 126. Ironically, one brother perished on the battlefield while the other survived at the same time.

Demetrius II Nicator
(Historical account of Demetrius 2nd reign is being repeated again)
(129—126 B.C.E.)

(So Demetrius II actually came back into power a second time in the year of 129 after the death of his brother Antiochus VII Sidestes. Therefore I am reporting on Demetrius 2nd reign that lasted from 129 until 126 B.C.E. one more time because of the historical sequence inwhich those events occurred after the death of Antiochus VII Sidestes.)

And it came to pass that Parthian king Phraates II,*pronounced* [fra-a-tes], who was the successor and son of Mithradates released Demetrius II from captivity. He anticipated Demetrius and his brother Antiochus VII Sidestes would fight each other in a new protracted civil war and alleviate an immediate threat to his kingdom. The eastward campaign of Antiochus' Seleucid army was initially successful, but ultimately Demetrius and Antiochus never confronted each other because Antiochus army was defeated by the advancing Parthian troops and the winter season. Meanwhile, Demetrius II was able to return to the capital to reclaim his throne and his queen-wife Cleopatra Thea. When Demetrius finally arrived back to the kingdom in the year of 129, its former glory was greatly diminished. It consisted of only Syria and Cilicia. Continuing a downward spiral, the Antioch population did not receive the resurrected kingship of Demetrius with much enthusiasm. Their reservations about Demetrius II included memories of his cruelty and lavish self-indulgence.

Another crisis that surfaced during Demetrius brief three-year reign from 129—126 B.C.E. was the political crisis in Egypt that spilled over into the affairs of the Seleucid kingdom. Egypt was wrecked with a civil-war between Ptolemaic siblings, Cleopatra II, a sister, and Ptolemy VIII, a brother. During this time the Egyptian queen Cleopatra was exiled in Syria where she spent her time building an army to challenge her brother back home in Egypt. Demetrius II supported Cleopatra in her scheme to replace her brother Ptolemy VIII by joining the attack near the city of Pelusium in northern Egypt. Demetrius also lost that battle in the year of 128. Once Ptolemy VIII gained knowledge of Demetrius-Cleopatra conspiracy, he reacted by supporting a Seleucid rival named Alexander II Zabinas to challenge Demetrius. The two arch enemies met in a battle near Damascus in the spring of 126. The army of King Demetrius II was defeated. He was forced to flee towards the city of Ptolemais. His wife, Queen Cleopatra Thea, forsook him, closed the gates as she left the city, and prevented his escape with her. He was then forced to board a ship, but was slain near Tyre.

And it came to pass that Demetrius II reigned over the Seleucid Empire twice. His first reign lasted seven years from 146—139 B.C.E.. His second reign lasted from 129 to 126 B.C.E. He came to power at the age of 14 and died at the age of 35. Demetrius II and Cleopatra Thea had two children: Seleucus V Philometor and Antiochus VIII Grypus.

Alexander II Zabinas
(129—123 B.C.E.)

The exact year and place of birth for the Seleucid ruler Alexander II Zabinas [*pronounced* Za-bi-nas] is unknown for several reasons. The first explanation was he was not "royalty", a relative or family member of the dynasty of Seleucus I Nicator. Therefore, there were no royal court records for historians to examine for such details. The second reason for the lack of information is because Alexander came from a poor Greco-Egyptian background where records were not kept. The surname Zabinas meant *"the purchased slave,"* which suggest he could have been purchased by an Egyptian merchant-spy named Protarchus or by King Ptolemy for his personal satisfaction [**eromenos—boy sexual partner**]. This background indicate that he could have been an agent of Egypt to influence events in Antioch. His low self-esteem and poverty-stricken background made him very unique. He was the only Seleucid ruler to not glorify himself with the usage of a royal throne surname such as Epiphanes, Philometor, Euergetes, Soter, Eupator, Philopator, Nicator, etc.. To coverup his peasant origins, he claimed to be an adoptive son of Antiochus VII Sidestes.

Alexander Zabinas came to power while the Seleucid kingdom was suffering a defeat from the Parthians and the lost of all eastern territorial claims on Media, Elam, and Mesopotamia. In the west, Egypt and Syria were locked in another war. The internal turmoil in Alexandria, Egypt had expanded to the doorsteps of Antioch. In Egypt, Ptolemy VIII and Cleopatra II, a brother and sister, fought each other in a civil war during the year 132. By the year 128, Cleopatra II sought refuge in Syria where she rebuilt an army with the tactical support of King Demetrius II during his second reign. Once Ptolemy realized that Demetrius II had joined a confederacy against him, he sought a proxy to counter the Syrian underhanded move. King Ptolemy VIII Physcon found in Alexander Zabinas exactly what he needed: Someone to do his bidding: Attack Demetrius. For two years, from the year 128 to 126, Alexander Zabinas plotted and raised an army with Egyptian assistance.

The centuries-old Syrian [Seleucid]-Egyptian [Ptolemy] war exploded once again. The battle was set in array near Damascus. The armies of Demetrius II and Alexander Zabinas waged intense war against each other. Zabinas forced Demetrius to retreat and flee towards Tyre, near the Mediterranean Sea. He was slain in the year 126 and Alexander Zabinas reigned in his stead. For the next three years from 126 to 123 B.C.E., Alexander Zabinas ruled as king on the throne in Antioch. During his brief 5-year reign, Alexander hired **the Judaic converts** as mercenaries to conquer mainland Syria, but they did not accomplish that goal.

As duplicity would have it, the king of Egypt [Ptolemy VIII Physcon] acted double-heartedly and turned against Alexander to became an ally of Demetrius son and widow: Antiochus VIII Grypus and his mother Queen Cleopatra Thea.

In the closing days of the reign of King Alexander Zabinas, he robbed and plundered several local temples. According to one account, he once joked about destroying a graven image known as Nike by melting it down. The Seleucid people worshipped the image-god Nike as their source of power for victory. The craftsmen had sculptured the pair of image-gods, Nike and Zeus, holding hands. The hierarchy of Antioch loved those religious symbols and became outraged when Alexander Zabinas blatantly disrespected the deities of the Greek pantheon. On the other hand, he was still a pagan who worshipped the Greek god Zeus like all of his predecessors. It was recorded that he once stood in front of the statue and proclaimed, *"Zeus has given me Victory"*. Nevertheless, in the end the hierarchy forced Alexander out of the royal city. As he fled, he ran into marauders who captured him, and delivered him into the hands of Antiochus VIII Grypus who executed him on site. This occurred in the year of 123.

So it came to pass that King Alexander Zabinas reigned for 5 years from 128 to 123 B.C.E. over a weakened Seleucid kingdom. After him, Queen Cleopatra Thea, Seleucus V Philometor, Antiochus VIII Grypus, and Antiochus IX Cyzicensus all reigned in his stead as successors.

<u>Cleopatra Thea</u>
(126—121 B.C.E.)

Cleopatra Thea was born as the princess daughter of Ptolemy VI Philometor and Cleopatra II in Alexandria, Egypt during the year of 164 B.C.E. Her last name "Thea" *meant* "goddess." She was later surnamed Eueteria *which meant* "good harvest or fruitful season." She grew up in Egypt and became a ruler of the Hellenisitc Seleucid Empire through marriage to several powerful men. As a teenage girl somewhere between the age of 13 to 15, her father Ptolemy

VI gave her to Prince Alexander I Balas, an opponent of reigning King Demetrius I Soter, in a lavish and regal ceremony in the city of Ptolemais Akko. This marriage produced a son named Antiochus VI Dionysus in the year 147.

Five years later the king of Egypt turned against Alexander I Balas and helped Demetrius II, the son of Demetrius I, return to Antioch. Queen Cleopatra then switched sides and married the usurper Demetrius II Nicator. After marrying the new king, Demetrius II Nicator, she then became the mother, and later the ruling co-regent with both her sons Seleucus V Philometor and Antiochus VIII Grypus.

When King Demetrius II Nicator fell from power in 141 due to internal turmoil, he fled to the eastern capital of Seleucia. He was captured by the king of Parthia in the city of Du'uzu near southeast Babylon in 138. He was taken to prison in Hyrcania and held captive for nine years. During this time another usurper named General Diodotus seized the throne. At that time Demetrius's younger brother, Antiochus VII Sidestes, rose up to reclaim the throne for the family. Again, Cleopatra remarried this new king too. From this third incestuous marriage she begat another child. It was a boy. The lad's name was Antiochus IX Cyzicenus.

In 126 B.C.E., Cleopatra's son Seleucus V Philometor rose up and became king on the throne in Antioch. By the end of the year, Cleopatra turned against him and murdered him. From 125 to 121 she was the sole regent on the throne ruling Syria. To legitimize her reign, she shared the throne with her son Antiochus VIII Grypus.

Once Antiochus VIII Grypus grew up, however, he became uncontrollable. His mother Cleopatra wanted to eliminate him in the same manner she had gotten rid of Seleucus V Philometor. So she plotted. One day as he returned from hunting, Cleopatra Thea met with kind words and a flagon of wine. In the mind of Grypus, her behavior was very unusual, so he was very suspicious. He forced her to drink from her own cup. The wine cup was poisonous and Cleopatra died instantly. This incident occurred in the year of 121 B.C.E.. After this, Grypus re-organized the Seleucid kingdom for the next 8 years. His reforms marked a period of stability and economic recovery from years of unpredictably. However, this period of calm did not last long. In the year 114, Cleopatra's other son, Antiochus IX Cyzicenus arrived in Antioch to challenge his brother's kingship. That move kindled a new Seleucid civil war.

So it came to pass that Cleopatra Thea was killed by the hands of her own son at the age of 45. In her lifetime, she had been the queen-wife for three Seleucid rulers: First, Alexander I Balas who reigned from 150—145 B.C.E., then Demetrius II Nicator who reigned twice. The first time from 145 to 139 and a second reign from 129 to 126 B.C.E.. Then she married the younger brother Antiochus VII Sidestes who reigned from 138 to 129. She gave birth to children from all three marriages. Therefore all her children were both brothers and sisters as well as first-cousins.

Seleucus V Philometor
(126—125 B.C.E.)

Seleucus V Philometor [*pronounced* Phi-lo-me-tor] was the eldest son of Demetrius II Nicator and Cleopatra Thea. Like his younger brother Antiochus VIII Grypus, they both were born sometime after the year of 145 and before the year 141. The exact year of birth for both of them is not documented because they were born during turbulent days within the palace halls of Antioch. Remember, Demetrius II came to power in his first reign in 145, but he was deposed by 141. Both sons were born during the timeframe when General Diodotus came to power and overthrew King Demetrius II, he could have been the one who removed their birthdates from the royal Seleucid scrolls, or for some reason, maybe his mother Queen Cleopatra could have decided to remove their birthdates for some selfish underhanded reason.

Seleucus was a young lad during the nine years his father was held in prison by the king of Parthia. It was either Seleucus V Philometor or his younger brother Antiochus VIII Grypus who was mentioned as the young child ruler who was hastily crowned as king by Cleopatra Thea after death of Antiochus VII Sidestes in the year of 129. Whichever brother it was, his throne name was Antiochus Epiphanes, and he was peacefully removed from power once Demetrius II returned to Antioch to begin his second reign in the same year of 129.

Three years later in 126, King Demetrius II Nicator was murdered by a plot instigated by his own wife Queen Cleopatra Thea. After that, she seized the throne for herself and shortly thereafter killed her oldest son Seleucus V. Historians have stated two possible motives for why Cleopatra Thea, queen of Syria, had her own posterity put to death. One reason: Seleucus attempted to assume the mantle of power without her consent. The second explanation was she feared the young boy might avenge the blood of his father after he grew up. So she eliminated him.

And it came to pass that Seleucus V whose surname became "Philometor", *which meant* "mother-loving or lover of his mother, or derogatorily, motherfucker ", was actually slain by his own mother. In Greek idolatry, the surname Philometor derived from the belief in the goddess Philomela which was regarded as the princess of Athens, according to their graven imaginations. According to the legend, Philomela was raped by her sister's husband Tereus.

Now back to reality. Seleucus V Philometor had come to power in the year 126 between the approximate age of 17 or 18. He was murdered within a year by 125 B.C.E.. He walked in all the ways of the Greek Hellenisitc rulers that preceded him.

After Queen Cleopatra Thea slew him, she chose her other son Antiochus VIII Grypus and together they became the new regent and co-regent.

Antiochus VIII Grypus
(125—96 B.C.E.)

Antiochus VIII Grypus was the son of King Demetrius II Nicator and Queen Cleopatra Thea. He was born somewhere between the years of 143 and 141 in the royal capital of Antioch. His surname "Grypus" *meant* "hook-nose", which referred to his uncomely appearance and unusually large nose. After he became a young teenager, his mother Queen Cleopatra Thea slew his older blood brother Seleucus V, then arranged for him to be anointed as king over the Seleucid Empire in 125/124 B.C.E.. Shortly after taking hold of the reins of power, Grypus defeated the usurper Alexander Zabinas during battle in 123. Covetously desiring the throne for herself, his mother Cleopatra prepared a royal cup of poisonous brew to slay him, but young Antiochus was suspicious sensing something was not right. So instead he forced her to take the first drink. She died immediately.

Eventually Antiochus VIII Grypus married a Ptolemaic princess of Egypt named Tryphaena. Together they bore five sons who became five future kings of the waning kingdom. The oldest was Seleucus VI Epiphanes, then Antiochus XI Epiphanes Philadelphus, Phillip I Philadelphus, Demetrius III Eucaserus, and the youngest, Antiochus XII Dionysus.

According to historians, Grypus was an accomplished poet and a toxicologist who wrote about, and prepared, poisonous herbs himself. He was also a very popular leader who loved to party and believed in giving lavish gifts and enjoying the good life. Luxurious banquets consisting of wine, food, music, drama, and orgies were a major part of his royal court. The attendants brought guests into the banquet hall on shoulder-held carriages. When the parties ended, Grypus would give those guests camel loads of expensive food to carry home. Years of these parties eventually drained the treasury and caused strains on Seleucid society.

(**In Proverbs 23:20**, King Solomon warned in the spirit of DIVINE Wisdom, *"do not be of those who guzzle wine, or glut yourself on meat; For guzzlers and gluttons will be improverished, and drowsing will clothe you in tatters."* That is what happened to Grypus because he did not possess that type of proverbial intelligence.)

In 116 B.C.E., a hot dispute broke out between the two half-brothers: Antiochus VIII Grypus and Antiochus IX Cyzicenus. Both men were joined together as sons of the same mother, Queen Cleopatra Thea. However, they had different fathers who also happened to be blood brothers. Antiochus VIII was the son of Demetrius II. Antiochus IX was the son of Antiochus VII Sidestes. Both Demetrius II and Antiochus VII Sidestes were maternal brothers, the sons of Demetrius I. (Cleopatra Thea had children by both of those maternal brothers.)

By 113, the war between the two half-brothers forced Antiochus VIII Grypus to depart the royal capital and flee to the city of Aspendus which is located in southwest Asia Minor. There he remained for three years until his return in the year of 111. His arrival sparked a confusing civil war that split the Seleucid kingdom down the middle. Grypus gained the greater part of Syria while Cyzicenus held onto the larger portion of Ceole-Syria. The scourge of that division was a benefit to two unrelated parties. The first, and most important, it gave the emerging Roman empire (**kingdom of iron**) an opportunity to move its mighty legions into the region unchallenged. Secondly, it benefited (**the Judaic converts—the leadership of John Hyrcanus**) and (**the remnant of the Afro-Asiatic Hebrew Israelites of the tribes of Judah, Benjamin, and Levi**) which had returned when Cyrus the king Persia released them over four centuries earlier. The integrated Judaic enclave broke away from the Seleucids and declared their independence.

Grypus remained in power until the year of 96 B.C.E. reigning over a divided Syria. It came to pass that in the year of 96 his chief minister Heracleon slew him in an assassination plot. So he died somewhere between the age of 46 to 49. He walked in the ways of all the customs of the Seleucid kings before him, serving the gods of the wood and stone (Greek religion). The coins minted during his rulership featured him on front and gave honor to the deity Sandan on its reverse side. The graven image Sandan was sculptured standing upon a horned lion inside a mobile casket carried upon the back of an eagle. His brother Cyzicenus remained in power for another year.

Antiochus IX Cyzicenus
(113—95 B.C.E.)

Antiochus IX Cyzicenus was the only child of Antiochus VII Sidestes and Cleopatra Thea. He was born around 136 B.C.E. in the royal city Antioch. He was born during a tumultuous period that forced his father and mother to send him to the city of Cyzicus near the straits that separated Asia Minor from Greece. It was there he grew up and became a young teenager and met Cleopatra IV, the princess of Egypt. She was a divorcee in her early 20s. In the year of 115, they were married in an elaborate ceremony where his bride Cleopatra gave him a mercenary army for his dowry. After that, Antiochus joined in a rebellion with his new wife against his half-brother Antiochus VIII Grypus for the Seleucid throne. He invaded the country and annexed the southern portion of Syria. By the year 113, Cyzicenus overtook the capital Antioch and became the sole ruler over Syria for the next two years. Meanwhile Grypus maintained his grip over the city-state of Cilicia.

The following year in 112, Grypus recaptured the capital. Afterwards, his wife Tryphaena ordered the brutal murder of her own sister Cleopatra IV. Now Tryphaena, the rival Syrian queen, hated her sister Cleopatra IV who was married to the usurper Antiochus IX Cyzicenus. Nevertheless, Grypus had petitioned his wife, requesting her not to kill her sister. He warned her against disrespecting the sanctuary of the sacred temple for fear of offending the gods. He reminded his wife that the god Zeus would never be so merciless towards a woman. Meanwhile, Cleopatra hid in the temple of Apollo prostrating before the sacred altar begging the gods for help. The gods did not respond to her prayer. Soldiers, under the command of Tryphaena, entered the temple and executed her on spot in front of the sculptured image. Before she died, she cursed her murderers who had disrespected the hallowed sanctuary of the god Daphne inside the temple of Apollo.

By the year 110, Cyzicenus defeated his rival-brother and reconquered Antioch once again. But this time Tryphaena, the wife of Grypus, was the one captured and taken prisoner. The tables had turned. This time, Cyzicenus ordered the execution of Tryphaena in revenge for his wife Cleopatra IV. That victory did not last very long. The following year in 109, his brother Antiochus VIII Grypus recaptured the capital once again. This back-and-forth fighting greatly weakened the Seleucid Empire. Grypus held onto the greater part of Syria while Cyzicenus possessed the larger portion of Ceole-Syria.

In 103, Grypus married his deceased wife's maternal sister Cleopatra V Selene. She too was the daughter of Greco-Egyptian king Ptolemy VIII Euergetes Physcon. Seven years later in 96 B.C.E. Grypus died, leaving behind his widow who married his rival-brother Antiochus IX Cyzicenus. After Grypus's death, his son Seleucus VI Epiphanes continued the struggle for the throne. The sons of Antiochus VIII Grypus, namely Demetrius III and Philip I, united against Cyzicenus and seized the city of Damascus. In early 95, Cyzicenus was defeated and slain during the ongoing battles. So it came to pass that Antiochus IX Cyzicenus died at the approximate age of 47 after reigning off and on over a period of twenty-nine years. He walked in all the customs of the Hellenistic Seleucid kings that preceded him. After his death the Syrian civil war continued, but his son Antiochus X Eusebes continued to uphold his claim for the Seleucid throne.

Seleucus VI Epiphanes
(96—95 B.C.E.)

Seleucus VI Epiphanes was the oldest son among the five sons of King Antiochus VIII Grypus and Queen Tryphaena. He was born somewhere between the years of 122/121 B.C.E. in the royal city of Antioch. He grew up as the crown prince during the days when the Hellenistic Seleucid empire was deeply divided between feuding incestuous families. For twenty-six years he served as a regent to his father. After the death of his father by the hands of his chief minister Heracleon, who slew him in an assassination plot, his mother Queen Tryphaena married his arch-enemy, her brother-in-law Antiochus Cyzicenus. Cyzicenus hoped the marriage would put an end to the destructive civil war. Seleucus VI seized the throne in the year of 96 to avenge the blood of his father, and in his honor, he continued the civil war maintaining control over the northern portion of Syria.

By early 95 B.C.E., Seleucus and Cyzicenus engaged in battle. Seleucus slew his uncle Cyzicenus in the conflict, but his son Antiochus X Eusebes Philopator took up his mantle and seized the southern portion of the kingdom and continued the devastating internal conflict against the other branch of the family. As the war raged, Seleucus was forced to flee the royal capital and seek refuge in the city of Mopsuestia [*pronounced* Mop-su-es-ti-a] in the kingdom of Cilicia. The city became his capital in exile where he assembled a large army and lived fast and hard. He set up a luxurious court and lived a extravagant lifestyle. (**YAH warned the Israelite people against putting their trust in a man instead of HIM as the king. Read about the warning in I Samuel 8:11-18.**)

The city was not able to afford the high taxation and other demands of his pompous lifestyle. It eventually caused silver coin shortages. To avert a total collapse of the city's economy he minted coins of a lower standard. The kingdom of Cilicia had already been menaced by marauding pirates. The city leaders began to grumble and revolt against the expensive burden of granting refuge to Seleucus. The leaders conspired against Seleucus and aligned themselves with his arch rival Antiochus X Eusebes. Antiochus encircled the city outside. The city's inhabitants rebelled within. The mutineers along with Antiochus X surrounded Seleucus inside the hippodrome. The hippodrome in ancient Greco-Roman culture was a large oval shaped arena where horse and chariot races were held. Circuses, games, aerobatic, and horseback riding were also performed inside the hippodromes.

The revolters burned the hippodrome down to the ground with the king and his men inside. So it came to pass that Seleucus VI Epiphanes was burned alive in the city of Mopsuestia during the summer of 94. He was around 27-years-old. During his life he walked in all the abhorrent ways of his predecessors who served all the gods of the Greek pantheon. While reigning in the royal capital for a few months, the coins minted in his honor featured an image of the Greek god Zeus holding the goddess of victory Nike in his outstretched right hand.

Afterwards, Antiochus X Eusebes temporarily reigned as the successor. However, the brothers of Seleucus—Demetrius III Eucaerus, Antiochus XI Epiphanes Philadelphus, and

Philip I Philadelphus—continued the war. Meanwhile, Antiochus XI Epiphanes Philadelphus succeeded Seleucus VI Epiphanes in the northern portion of Syria. Those dysfunctional family feuds continued while Rome [**the kingdom of pelvic and legs of iron**] crept into dominance.

 ## Antiochus X Eusebes
(95—92 B.C.E.)

Antiochus X Eusebes was born approximately between the years of 114-113 B.C.E. as the son of Antiochus Cyzicenus and Cleopatra IV. He was born into a Seleucid civil war that had been raging since Cleopatra Thea begat two sons by two brothers: Demetrius II and Antiochus VII Sidestes. Every since then the rivalry between those offsprings of the two families caused a partition of the land of Syria into two kingdoms: The North and South. Growing up, his father Antiochus IX Cyzicenus, the ruler of South, inherited a brutal civil war with his half-brother Antiochus VIII Grypus, the ruler of the North. As a young lad he greatly admired his father and when he came to power he adopted his divisive strategies. He also used his father' surname "Eusebes", which meant the *"pious one"*. He employed the title *"Philopator"* as his throne name which affectionately meant *"father-loving* or *"my father's lover."* Therefore his official throne name was Antiochus X Eusebes Philopator.

His father Antiochus IX Cyzicenus was slain by his cousin Seleucus VI. Therefore Antiochus X Eusebes rage was kindled against his first-cousin and he sought revenge for the blood of his beloved father. Seleucus VI was driven out of Antioch and sought refuge in the Asia Minor city of Mopsuestia. Antiochus was not content with his conquest of Antioch. With blood in his eyes, he moved north into Mopsuestia to seek the head of Seleucus. The people of the city conspired against Seleucus and formed an alliance with Antiochus X. Antiochus X beseiged him inside the city's hippodrome. He burned it to the ground with Seleucus and his chief officers perishing inside the flames.

Antiochus X Eusebes came to power at the approximate age of 19 in the summer of 95 B.C.E. in midst of constant conflicts between enemies within and outside the gates of the fractured Seleucid Empire. He married his father's second wife, his stepmother. Her name was Cleopatra Selene I. By then she was almost past her child bearing years. Their unholy union produced only two children: Seleucus VII Kyhisosaktes and Antiochus XIII Asiaticus.

In her lifetime, Cleopatra Selene had been passed around like a communion cup as the wife of Ptolemy IX Soter, Antiochus VIII Grypus, Antiochus IX Cyzicenus, and now Antiochus X Eusebes.

After Eusebes burned up Seleucus VI, his brother Antiochus XI temporarily replaced him in the north and attempted to regain control of the royal capital Antioch. Eusebes repelled the invasion and slew Antiochus XI in the process. The victory gave Eusebes control over parts of the north, but the brothers of the slain Antiochus XI, who also controlled swaths of territory themselves, continued the war against Eusebes. The brothers were named Demetrius III Eucaerus and Phillip I Philadelphus.

The internal strife within the Seleucid kingdom gave **the Greco-Judaic converts** in the province of Judaea-Israel, under the leadership of Alexander Janneus, the advantage needed to rebel and declare their independence from Antiochus X Eusebes. His attention was severely diverted because of his homeland quagmire. Eusebes faced adversaries on several fronts. The new leader in the northern portion of kingdom, Antiochus XI Epiphanes Philopator, took up arms against him. In the east, the kingdoms of Parthia and the Arabs joined in a confederation against Eusebes. Eusebes was eventually slain in battles with Mithridates Sinaces and Aziz the Arab in the year of 89/88.

It came to pass that Antiochus X Eusebes died in the year 89/88 at the approximate age of 25 after reigning for seven years. In his lifetime, Antiochus X Eusebes served all the graven images of the Greek pantheon, walking in the ways of his predecessors who knew not **YHWH**. The political chaos in Syria persisted after Eusebes death. The brothers Demetrius III and Phillip I turned on each other and then vied for the same throne.

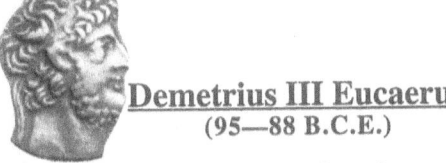

Demetrius III Eucaerus
(95—88 B.C.E.)

Demetrius III Eucaerus [*pronounced* U-cae-rus] was born somewhere between the years of 122 and 118 during the fragmented and turbulent days of the Seleucid Empire. He was the third of the 5 sons of King Antiochus VIII Grypus and Queen Tryphaena. After the death of his older brother Seleucus VI, Demetrius sought assistance from the king of Egypt, Ptolemy IX Soter Lathyros, who was then in exile. The king of Egypt agreed to help Demetrius and his brother Philip I Philadelphus in their quest to reclaim the throne from Eusebes. Their alliance proved to be successful. Demetrius was able to recover portions of the territory lost by his father Antiochus VIII Grypus. The two brothers, Demetrius and Philip moved into the southern portion of Syria. Demetrius set up his royal court in ancient Damascus while Philip ruled in the city of Beroea, which is now modern Aleppo.

(Historically and Prophetically speaking, this is the same area where the endtime battle often described as the Battle of Armageddon will take place. This is the same contested area where the ancient Neo-Babylonian armies of Nebuchadnezzar and the ancient Egyptian armies of Pharaoh-Necho engaged in Battle of Carchemish in 601/600 B.C.E., when the world was ruled by black kings[**head of gold**]. This is the same area where a modern war is raging between the Bashar al-Assad government and the majority Sunni Arab population in 2019. Today global superpowers, Russia, the U.S., Iran(Parthia-Persia), Turkey(Asia Minor), Saudia Arabia, Iraq,(Nabatean Arabs),Lebanon(Ceole-Syria), and **the modern Euro-Judaic convert State of Israel** are engaged in war as I write this book. From **the head of gold down to the ten toes of iron and miry clay,** this area has been, and continues to be a burdensome, and a trembling cup. You can read the book of **Joel 3:1-14, Ezekiel, chapters 38** and **39, Daniel 11:5-20, Daniel 11:40-45,** and **Zechariah 14: 1-2).**

Internal strife between **the Afro-Asiatic Hebrews** and **the Greco-Judaic converts** caused Demetrius III to intervene into the holyland. By the year of 93, the Seleucid king warred against the Greco-Judaic converts, led by Alexander Jannaeus, and defeated them, but turmoil and hostility among both local groups, **the Israelites** and **the converts,** forced him to withdraw.

Four years later in 89 B.C.E. the Parthians invaded the kingdom from the east. King Antiochus X Eusebes was slain in the battles. Once Demetrius III learned of Eusebes death, he called off his invasion of Israel and returned to Syria to capture the royal city Antioch. After that victory, his brother Philip became envious and a quarrel broke out between the two men who were once allies. Demetrius mounted his forces and moved northwards to encircle Aleppo. While Demetrius surrounded Aleppo, Philip send an envoy to Parthia requesting support. The Parthians came to his aid and Demetrius was eventually captured. Demetrius remained in captivity until his death in the year of 88/87.

And it came to pass that Demetrius III Eucaerus reigned for seven years and died in Parthian custody between the approximate age of 30 to 34. He walked in all the ways of the Seleucid kings who preceded him by serving all the idol-gods of Greek pantheon. The coins minted during the reign of Demetrius consisted of a potrait of him and a drawing of the god of fertility known as Atargatis seen holding flower and barley sheaves on her shoulders. His brother Philip I Philadelphus succeeded him as king.

Antiochus XI Epiphanes
((95—92 B.C.E.)

Antiochus XI Epiphanes was the second son of King Antiochus VIII Grypus and Queen Trypaena who was born somewhere between the years of 120 to 119. He was born during the days when the Seleucid Empire was deeply divided and partitioned into competing fiefdoms that ruled small swaths of territory. Antiochus XI came to power in the summer of 94 after his older brother Seleucus VI was burned alive inside the hippodrome by Eusebes. After Seleucus death, his brother Antiochus XI Epiphanes quickly seized the mantle of the northern branch of the kingdom. Shortly thereafter, Antiochus XI invaded the royal city Antioch and expelled Eusebes, but in less than one year, Eusebes recaptured the seat of power. By the end of the year the political tables had turned again. Eusebes's army gained control of Antioch for a second time. In less than two-years, the reign of Antiochus XI Epiphanes came to a premature end in the year 92 when he was slain during the conflict with Eusebes. Antiochus XI had attempted to regain the royal city once again, but his campaign was repelled. Antiochus XI Epiphanes was forced to retreat, but as he attempted to cross the Orontes River on horseback, he drowned in the river. The Orontes River flows 240 miles across Lebanon into Syria and Turkey before pouring into the Mediterranean Sea. Eusebes continued to take control of more territory deep inside the northern portion of the country.

So it came to pass that Antiochus XI Epiphanes ruled the northern branch of the Seleucid Empire for a mere 3 years. He died at the approximate age of 27. He too walked in all the detestable ways of the Seleucid rulers that preceded him, serving all the deities of the Greco-pantheon. His reign was so short that there were no coins minted in his honor during his brief reign. His brother Philip I Philadelphus reigned in his stead.

Philip I Philadelphus
(95—83 B.C.E.)

Philip I Philadelphus was also the third of 5 sons born to King Antiochus VIII Grypus and Queen Trypaena. His birth came somewhere between the year 118/117. He assumed the surname of Philadelphus which meant *"brother-loving"* or *"a man who loves his brother,"* which reflected his intimate passion for those of his own gender—*"brotherly love."* Philip I briefly ruled as a local Hellenistic duke in Antioch, but his blood brother Demetrius III maintained a separate sphere of power in another part of Syria. During his reign (95—83 B.C.E.), the once expansive and united Seleucid Empire was gone. Nevertheless, when he came to power in year of 95 a royal coronation was held in honor of him and his brothers, Demetrius III and Antiochus XI Epiphanes. That unity among the Seleucid siblings did not last long, and soon the three were up in arms against each other. During his reign the capital of Antioch exchanged hands back and forth among the competing kings. By the year of 92 he held sway in Antioch and withstood assaults from his brother Demetrius III. For the record, Philip I Philadelphus fathered only one son named Philip II Philoromaeus.

Four years later in 88 B.C.E., Demetrius moved north towards Aleppo and surrounded Philip. Philip dispatched a courier to the king of Parthia requesting support. The Parthians joined the war against Demetrius and eventually captured him. He remained there until he died. Philip seized the capital Antioch and was recognized as the king. His other rival-brother Antiochus XII Dionysus still ruled the south in the great city Damascus.

So it came to pass that King Philip I Philadelphus was slain in the year of 83 by the Nabatean Arabs. He died at the approximate age of 35 after reigning for seven years. And he walked in all of the ways of the Greco-Hellenistic Seleucid kings that preceded him. He served all the gods of the Greek religion. During his rule, the coins minted in his honor featured his potrait on front. On the reverse side the god Zeus is seen holding a scepter while the deity Nike is featured with wreath in hand.

The Seleucid Empire was rapidly crumbling on both sides: East and West. In the east, an Armenian king named Tigranes II the Great conquered Syria.

Antiochus XII Dionysus
(87—84 B.C.E.)

Antiochus XII Dionysus was the fifth and youngest son of King Antiochus VIII Grypus and Queen Cleopatra Selene I[Tryphaena]. He was probably born somewhere between the years of 120 to 118. During his childhood, his own family as well as the Seleucid kingdom was greatly divided. He and his blood brothers grew up and fought bitter wars against each other. He came to power in the year 87 when his brother Demetrius III departed Damascus in a military campaign against their other brother Philip I Philadelphus who resided in Beroea, which is modern Aleppo. Demetrius III almost defeated his brother in Aleppo, but Philip hastily dispatched an envoy to Parthia requesting support. Parthia agreed and sent troops. Demetrius was captured and taken prisoner by the Parthians. Demetrius never returned to Damascus again. Antiochus XII, his younger brother, seized the throne and assumed the mantle of local power and ruled four years in southern Syria near Damascus and surrounding areas. His brief rule included a confrontation with **the Greco-Judaic conclave** ruled by the Hasmonean leader King Jannaeus. This is what led to that confrontation. Antiochus XII was at war with Aretas king of the Nabatean Arabs and he sought passage through Judaea to face him at the Battle of Cana. (Cana was located in southern Jordan near the modern-day Uum Kais.) The two opposing armies faced-off in Cana. Antiochus won the first round of the conflict, but a brawl broke out between Arab soldiers. Antiochus XII Dionysus was caught in the midst of the confusion. He was killed by one of the Arab infantrymen.

So it came to pass the Antiochus XII, who had surnamed himself Dionysus which meant *"he was a servant of god Dionysus"*, died at the approximate age of 34. Like all the Seleucid Hellenistic rulers before him, he served the sculpture known as **Dionysus** which was believed to be *the god of wine, wild unrestrained revelry, and orgies*. He also surnamed himself **Epiphanes** which meant *"God Manifest"*, meaning believed himself to be *living god in flesh*. He also used the title **Philopator** as part of his official royal name. **Philopator** meant *"Father-loving,"* reflecting his affection for his father. Last, but not least, he also added the surname "Callinicus" to his royal title. The term **Callinicus** meant *"beautiful victor or gloriously triumphant."* Therefore his entire elongated royal surname was **Antiochus XII Dionysus Epiphanes Philopator Callinicus**. It also came to pass that Philip I Philadelphus succeeded Demetrius III after he was captured during the seige of Aleppo. Antiochus XII then seized the throne in Damascus and reigned for three years. He served all the gods of the Greek religion and walked in the ways of his predecessor who knew not **YAH**.

On the coins minted in his honor during his reign, his potrait of was featured on front. On the reverse side was a drawing of the cult statue **Hadad**, which was superstitiously believed to be the god[power] controlling storms, thunderings, and rainy seasons. The white Greeks adopted the same pagan belief system as the ancient black Arameans who had served the idol known as **Hadad** millenniums earlier. In fact, many of the ancient Aramean kings regarded themselves as the Sons[Ben] of the God [Hadad], Ben-Hadad. You can read about this in **I Kings 20:1-43** and **2 Kings 8:7-15** to confirm the point.

After the death of Antiochus XII in 84 B.C.E., the Nabatean Arabs went on to conquer Damascus. But King Tigranes I the Great eventually invaded the Seleucid territory the following year and ruled Syria for 14 years.

Tigranes II "Great" King of Armenia
(83—69 B.C.E.)

Tigranes II was the son of Tigranes I [*pronounced* Ti-gra-nes] born in the royal capital of Artashat[Ar-ta-shat] in the province of Ararat as a member of the Artaxiad Dynasty founded by Artaxias I. Born in approximately 140 B.C.E., while growing up he was captured somewhere between the years of 112—107 when his country and Mithridates II, king of Parthia, were at war. He remained there until he was almost a 40-year-old man.

In the year 95 B.C.E., his father Tigranes I died. He then petitioned the king of Parthia for the right to buy his freedom. In exchange, Tigranes II gave the king of Parthia 70 valleys in the province of Atropatene, which was territory within the land of Media. Atropatene was an ancient kingdom that was established and ruled by ethnic Iranian dynasties, beginning with Darius III of Persia, and later by Alexander the Great of Macedonia. Today this territory is known as modern Azerbijan and Iranian Kurdistan.

One of the first things Tigranes did was consolidate his kingdom. He established a centralist system that could maintain control over all the regions of the mountainous country.

Seven years later in the year 88 when Mithridates II "the Great" died, Tigranes II took advantage of the weakened state of affairs in Scythia, Mesopotamia, Syria, and Parthia. Eventually the First Mithridates War (89—85) gave way to peace between Parthia and Tigranes, king of Armenia. These two non-Seleucid/Roman powers agreed to divide the dominion of the eastern world. Tigranes of Armenia agreed to extend his control over the East while Mithridates IV warred against the kingdoms in Asia Minor, the Roman Republic **[kingdom of iron]**, and against other kingdoms elsewhere in what is now known as "southeastern Europe". According to the historical scrolls, Mithridates IV mounted an attack on Roman citizens and other Italians living in Asia Minor. Mithridates stroked the flames of discontent among the indigenous citizens, causing them to rise up against the Romans. 80,000 Roman citizens were slaughtered during the massacre known as the Asiatic Vespers. The Romans were incensed. The Senate chose Consul Luicius Cornelius Sulla to lead the military forces against Mithridates.

By the year 83, the strife between the Seleucid rulers continued as Tigranes crept into their affairs. One of the competing rulers decided to offer Tigranes the crown of Syria and titled him the protector of the Seleucid kingdom. Not only did Tigranes conquer Syria, he moved into Phoenicia and Cilicia. This officially ended the last remnants of the once mighty Seleucid Empire. Tigranes ruled from Asia Minor(**modern Turkey**) to Mesopotamia(**mordern Iraq**), stretching from **the Caspian Sea** to **the Mediterranean Sea.**

He married a woman named Cleopatra of Pontus. She happened to be the daughter of Mithridates VI, king of Pontus and Queen Laodice. Together they gave birth to three sons: Zariadres, Artavasdes II, and Tigranes, and two daughters that married the kings of Parthia and Media. It was during his reign that the kingdom of Armenia expanded its borders into the domain of the once mighty Seleucid Empire. Tigranes was the first non-Macedonian to conquer the territories once controlled by the Greek descendants of Seleucus I Nicator. This represented the downfall of Hellenistic dominion in Syria and Mesopotamia after three centuries of rulership.

For the record, Armenia is a country located in southwest Asia neighboring modern Turkey on its western border. The country of Iran (ancient Media) shares a southern border near the Black Sea. In the north, the Caucasus Mountains straddles the entire border. The Caspian Sea marked the eastern border.

So it came to pass that Tigranes II, who became known as "The Great" died at the approximate age of 85. His reign lasted for 40 years, from 95 to 55 B.C.E. in the royal capital of Artashat. He was buried in the city of Tigranocerta, in the modern city of Silvan, Turkey. He walked in the ways of all the heathen kings that preceded him serving the image-gods of the Armenian religion. A religion whose origins dated back to Indo-European and Urartian origins. Eventually, the Armenians incorporated the belief systems of Mesopotamia, Persia, and Greece into their form of worship. Known as nature worshippers, their principal deity was a statue known as Khaldi[Khal-di] or Uaidi[Uai-di], a god of storms. It was actually an Armenian version of Baal-worship. They also served the handcrafted sculptures regarded as Aramazad (Zeus), Anadatans, Anahit, the goddess of fertility and birth. The pagan Armenians, like the Greeks before them, also feared monsters and spirits known by the names of Mihr, Omanos, Tir, Tsovinar, Vahagon, and Spandaramet.

Moses instructed the Israelites in **Deuteronomy [Devarim] 18:10-11** of the Torah, *"Let no one be found among you who consigns his sons or daughter to the fire, or who is an augur, a soothsayer, a diviner, a sorcerer, one who inquries of the dead."* Those abhorrent practices were common practice among **the rulers and people of the kingdoms of gold, silver, brass, iron, and miry clay**, even unto this very day.

Seleucus VII Kyhiosaktes Philometor reigned as the arch-rival and opposition king during the same period of time as King Tigranes II of Armenia ruled in the years 83 to 69.

Seleucus VII Kyhiosaktes "Philometor"
(83—69 B.C.E.)

Seleucus VII Kyhiosaktes [*pronounced* Ky-hi-o-sak-tes] was born as one of the two sons of Antiochus X Eusebes and Cleopatra Selene. His birth came during the waning days of the crumbling Seleucid Empire. **(His brother's name was Antiochus XIII Asiaticus. He was one of the last kings of the Seleucid Hellenistic rulership).** Born in the approximate year of 95 B.C.E., the young boy-king Seleucus VII was thrust into power as a rival to the powerful Tigranes of Armenia who occupied Seleucid territory. At best, the Seleucid resistance controlled only a few cities. When he was a young lad, his mother Cleopatra Selene took him to Rome to petition the Senate for assistance and recognition of him as the legitimate king of Syria and Egypt. This occurred during the years of 75-73. Rome accepted him as heir to the throne in Antioch, but they rejected his bid to be crowned the king of Egypt. Although he spent most of his reign outside of Antioch, Syria, their goal was preservation of their bloodline and royal lineage. That's why, during his lifetime, his mother instructed him to marry the fair-skinned Ptolemaic queen Berenice IV of Egypt. Eventually his mother Queen Cleopatra Selene was captured by Tigranes and executed in the year of 69. After that, he most likely sought refuge in Alexandria, Egypt.

Eleven years later by the year of 58 B.C.E., 20-year-old Berenice IV had become the sole ruler in Alexandria because her father Ptolemy XII and his daughter-wife Cleopatra VII were exiled in Rome. Berenice advisors instructed her to find a male co-regent at home or from abroad. For Seleucus, the new marriage would promote him back into power. This time as king over Egypt.

But, Queen Berenice IV, who was nearly twenty years younger than Seleucus, loved luxuries and fashions. She loved men of the same stature who loved the same things. When Seleucus VII arrived in Alexandria somewhere between years of 71 to 69, Berenice was appalled at the older aristocrat's behavior. In her eyes, his mannerism was beneath her: "Horrible and foul, as if he had worked cutting tuna fish in the open market." Seleucus VII unpleasantness caused Berenice to plot his removal. In the year 58 B.C.E. Berenice had him strangled to death. This is how he earned his negative nickname "Kyhiosaktes" *which meant* "foul-smelling." Berenice IV continued her reign until 55 B.C.E. when her father returned from exile in Rome and cut her head off.

So it came to pass, Seleucus VII Kyhiosaktes Philadelphus died at the age of 37 after reigning for fourteen years. Most of his rule was spent hiding in Syria or exiled in [Rome and eventually Egypt] because the Seleucid kingdom was occupied by King Tigranes II of Armenia at the time. Seleucus VII was thrusted into the kingship at the approximate age of 12. He was 26 when he fled from Syria after the death of his mother in 69 B.C.E.. He lived 11 more years before being murdered in the year of 58 in Alexandria, Egypt. In his lifetime he walked in the abhorrent ways of the nations. He served the image-god Zeus and the pantheon of all other Greek gods according to the manner of all his predecessors who did not know **YAH ELOHIM Israel.** His brother Antiochus XIII Asiaticus reigned in his stead.

Antiochus XIII Asiaticus
(69—64 B.C.E.)

Antiochus XIII Asiaticus was the second son of Antiochus X Eusebes and Queen Cleopatra Selene. Born in the approximate year of 93/92 B.C.E., the young lad grew up when the Seleucid kingdom had been reduced to Antioch, Beroea (Aleppo), and surrounding areas. The threats came from the Romans in the West and the Armenians, Arabs, Arameans, and Parthians in the East. These continuous conflicts, along with internal chaos, reduced the empire to a mere faction of its former glory. When Tigranes II entered Antioch, Antiochus XIII was 9 or 10. He also accompanied his mother Cleopatra Selene and brother Seleucus VII to Rome.

By the year 69, Antiochus went to Rome to appeal for help in his war effort against the Armenians. The Roman Senate Consul agreed to help. General Lucius Lucullus was chosen to serve as the Supreme Commander in the eastern wars. The conflict became known as the Third Mithridatic War. Rome prevailed and defeated Tigranes II the Great in the Asian Minor city of Tigranocenta [Ti-gra-no-cen-ta]. Today Togranocenta near the modern city of Silvan,Turkey.

Once Antioch was liberated the same year, the populace chose Antiochus XIII as their new Seleucid king. General Lucius Lucullus agreed, and then appointed Antiochus XIII Asiaticus as the new caretaker and client ruler for the expanding Roman Empire.

However, shortly after that victory, General Lucullus was replaced by General Pompey as the Supreme Commander in the year of 68/67. Meanwhile internal fighting among the Seleucid siblings continued.

In 67/66 a large segment of the Antioch population along with a local ruler from Cilicia, supported another Seleucid cousin-brother named Phillip II Philoromaeus. He expelled Antiochus XIII from the city. The following year in 66/65 Antiochus XIII was restored back to the throne. This chaos disturbed the order of Rome and by the year of 65/64 Pompey deposed of Antiochus XIII by having him slain by a Syrian chieftain named Sampsicenamus [*pronounced Sam-psi-ce-na-mus*]. Pompey annexed the territory of the Seleucid Empire[Syria] as a part of the Roman Empire[**kingdom of the pelvis and legs of iron**].

So it came to pass that Antiochus came to power at the tender age of 14 and reigned for five years in Syria. Thus he died around the age of 19 or 20. Antiochus XIII walked in all the abhorrent ways of his Seleucid predecessors serving the idol Zeus and all the pantheon of Grecian graven images[religion]. After his death, Phillip II Philoromaeus seized the throne and briefly reigned in his stead. The infighting continued.

Phillip II Philoromaeus
(65—63 B.C.E.)

Phillip II Philoromaeus [*pronounced Phi-lo-ro-ma-e-us*] was born somewhere between the years of 99 to 95 as the son of King Antiochus VIII Grypus and Queen Tryphaena. He was between the ages of 12 to 14 when King Tigranes of Armenia conquered major parts of Seleucid territories. It appears his family supported the foreign rule of Tigranes, or at least, accepted his rulership. However, when Rome later removed the Armenians, the ruling class switched sides and welcomed the Roman legions as liberators.

It came to pass in the year of 65/64 that the Roman general Pompey dethroned the Seleucid ruler Antiochus XIII Asiaticus and chose Phillip II as the new client ruler in Antioch. To show his respect for his new overlord Phillip chose the surname "Philoromaeus" *meaning brother/lover of Rome*.

Two years later in 63 B.C.E. Rome declared Syria as one of its provinces. Phillip was replaced with a Roman official. Seven year later in the year 56, Phillip decided to marry the young 22-year-old Queen Berenice. However as I previously noted, Rome ruled Syria at that time, and their governor Aulus Gabinius did not approve of the new union. Instead, the Roman governor had Phillip killed. His death represented the final nail in the coffin for the Seleucid Empire. An empire that had spanned nearly three hundred years. The Seleucid rulers were once regarded as the most powerful and influential among the Hellenistic people. In the year of 63 they were reduced to a relic of the past.

So it came to pass that Phillip II had been chosen as king at the approximate age of 30 and reigned for only three years. He walked in all the abhorrent ways of the Seleucid kings that preceded him. He served the Greek deity Zeus and all the pantheon of Grecians deities.

As the prophet Daniel said in **chapter 2 verse 21:** *"YAH removeth kings [***Macedonian, Seleucid, Ptolemy, and Thrace empires-four divided kingdoms of brass***] and setteth up* *kings* [**Roman empire-kingdom of iron**]. We must not forget:YAH ruleth within the kingdoms of the children of men and gives it to whomsoever HE wills. This completes the rulership of the Seleucid Empire, and, at this point, YAH closed their historic Book of Life.

Thrace Dynasty (Thrace)
(305 —148 B.C.E.)
Fourth Division of the Alexandrian Empire

Lysimachus (305—281 B.C.E.),Ptolemy II Ceraunus (281—279 B.C.E.),CotysII (300—280 B.C.E.),Raizdos(280 B.C.E.),Odroes(280—273 B.C.E.),Adaeus co-ruler(280—273 B.C.E.),Skostodos(275—265 B.C.E.), Orsoaltios(265—260 B.C.E.), Kersivaulos (260 B/C/E/),Cotys III(260—250 B.C.E.),Teres III(250—240 B.C.E.),Riasscouporis I(240—215 B.C.E.),Seuthes(215—213 B.C.E.),Pleuractus(213—208 B.C.E.),Abrapolis(200—172 B.C.E.),Amadokos III(184—183 B.C.E.),Teres IV(183—172 B.C.E.),Teres V(172—148 B.C.E.) (148 B.C.E. Romans occupy Thrace and begin a large production of silver tetradrachums[coins]).

The region known as ancient Thrace was located in the area we call southeast Europe. Today, the modern countries of Bulgaria and northern Greece comprise that same ancient territory. In antiquity, the area of Thrace was inhabited by barbaric hordes that lived on hilltops and on mountains. Those primitive people lived similar to their Celtic, Gallic, and Slavic cousins who roamed the northern forest millenniums before Europe became the urban center it is today. At this time the people did not have an advanced system of government, buildings, roads, advanced writing, music, poetry, crafts, or industries. In the eyes of their Macedonian, Greek, and Asia Minor neighbors, they were considered barbarians. This is why the detailed history on this portion of the Divided Alexandrian Empire will be the shortest of them all. Their subculture had very little documentation after the death of Lysimachus. Remember, Lysimachus was a member of the inner circle among Alexander's chief generals who was given the territory of Thrace after his death. He advanced the province and attempted to incorporate it into the kingdoms of Macedonia and the Seleucids, but he was assassinated in 281 B.C.E.. After that, a power vacuum developed in the Balkans, and eventually by 279 B.C.E., an invasion by the Gauls, who were also barbarians, overwhelmed the province for a period of time. Their destructive campaign plundered Macedonia, Greece, and Illyria. Barbarism is the reason why there is no recorded history or cities being built in Thrace during these centuries. It remained a primitive place for several more years to come until the Romans came in 168 B.C.E..

Lysimachus
(305—281 B.C.E.)

Lysimachus [*pronounced* **Ly-si-ma-kus**] was born in Pella,Macedonia around the year of 360 B.C.E. with Greek roots that originated in Thessaly. He was the son of a nobleman named Agathocles [**A-ga-tho-cles**] who was a man of high rank in the royal court of King Phillip II in Pella. Historical sources report his father Agathocles was a lover and intimate friend of King Phillip, and one of his favourites. During this same time Agathocles was a married man and father of several sons, among them Lysimachus, who all were royal pages. In this environment it is highly probable that while young Lysimachus grew up and served as a royal page in the king's court, he was educated in the art of warfare and groomed in an erastes-eromenos [man-boy] relationship like all of his contemporaries.
During the early years of Phillip II's reign from 347—342 B.C.E., he conquered the province of Thrace, subduing the province into a vassal state of Macedon. Six years later in 336, the Thracians rebelled again during the reign of his son Alexander the Great. Thrace was the

region bordering the Danube River known today as northern Bulgaria and southern Romania. Once again, the more civilized kingdom of Macedon was forced to defeat the barbarian Getae hordes and King Syrxmus,who was leader of the Tribali hordes. Before Alexander departed for his Persian campaign, he appointed an officer named Zopyron as the governor of province of Thrace, but the Getae barbarians slew him in a fierce battle. During this time Lysimachus joined Alexander on his conquest of the Oriental world as one of his top bodyguards and commander of his fleet. He earned notoriety for his battlefield bravery and loyalty during the wars in India. (He was also known to have accompanied Alexander on lion hunts.) In his book *The Campaigns of Alexander* historian Arrian wrote the following words about Lysimachus during the Seige of Sangala: *"Throughout the seige Alexander lost a little under 100 men; the number of wounded, however, was disproportionately large, over 1,000 among them Lysimachus, of Alexander's personal guard, and other officers,290."*

By the year 324, Lysimachus was known as one of the Companions in the inner-circle known as the Diadochi. However, the following year Alexander the Great died, leaving his massive empire in a state of uncertainty without a capable heir. Peridiccas, the general who had been second-in-command besides Alexander, became the interim leader. He chose Lysimachus as the strategos [Governor] over his native territory and dispatched him back to Thrace to replace the deceased Zopyron.

Like most men of this Hellenistic period,Lysimachus had been raised to prefer his own gender and was not deeply interested in the opposite sex. Following suit of his contemporaries, he ultimately married for political, not intimate, reasons. First, he married Nicaea, the daughter of the Macedon regent Antipater to strengthen his powerbase. Together they had two children: Agathocles, his son, and Eurydice, his daughter. Ironically, he killed his own son at the instigation of his third wife Arsinoe II, the daughter of Ptolemy I Soter. His firstborn Agathocles grew up to become a respected and popular commander of the army. However, Lysimachus hearkened to the counsel of his other wife who trumped up treason charges against Agathocles provoking Lysimachus to also smite him to death. Along the way he married Amastris, a widowed Persian princess who was queen-mother of the Asia Minor city of Heraclea. His army needed somewhere to stay before the impending showdown with Antigonus I. She granted his request for lodging, but her own two sons from a previous marriage who were unhappy with that union, killed her. In return, Lysimachus slew the pair.

Back on the battlefield Lysimachus still faced difficulties fighting the fierce Thracian barbarians. During that era, various branches of the Thracians lived along the Danube River in mountains, caves, and the hinterland forests known as Europe today. These prehistoric Indo-European people covered their bodies with tattoos. They were described as being red and yellow-haired. There were no royal cities in their territories, instead they roamed uncultivated areas living nomadic and primitive lives.

By the year 306 all the chief generals of the divided Alexandrian Empire had declared themselves *"Basileus,"* meaning *"king"*. Lysimachus was among the four who assumed the sacred title, thus becoming the King of Thrace, which was the least and poorest province among the four, yet it was strategically important because it was located between Asia Minor and Europe. Lysimachus concentrated his efforts on creating a civilized powerbase in Thrace and attempted to avoid the War of Successions being waged by the other three generals. It could be said that initially the Persians and after them Greeks, like Lysimachus, Phillip II, and Alexander, were the ones who helped civilize the barbaric kinsmen. Lysimachus could not completely subdue the Thracians who were led by a king named Seuthes III. These conflicts were the beginning of a long series of wars between the two sides.

Stalemated in Europe, Lysimachus then turned his attention to Asia Minor, crossed over the Hellespont in 302, and overran the city-state Phrygia and reduced the entire region into serfdom. That added the title "King of Asia" to his resume.

By the year 301, Lysimachus massive army joined a confederation with the armies of Seleucus I Soter, Ptolemy I Soter, and Cassander to confront the threats posed by powerful Antigonus in the famous battle known as The Battle of Ispus. In order to crush the powerful army of Antigonus, which was a massive force that controlled territories extending from

Mesopotamia to Asia Minor, those three kings were forced to unite. Antigonus army consisted of 70,000 infantrymen, 10,000 cavalry, and 75 elephants while his three opponents mustered a fighting force of 64,000 infantrymen, 15,000 cavalry, 400 elephants, and 100 state-of-art chariots. The battle was set in array almost 50 miles northeast of the great city of Synnada, near the village of Ipsus in central Asia Minor. Just before the first arrow was shot, the army of Seleucus I Soter and his son Antiochus arrived on the battlefield after traveling from the far east to join the campaign against his arch-rival Antigonus. Demetruis, the son of Antigonus, and the commander of the cavalry, launched an attack against Antiochus and forced him to retreat from the battlefield. Meanwhile, in the heat of the battle, Antigonus commandeered the phalanx forces. Unintentionally, Demetruis hot pursuit of Antiochus left a large unprotected gap in his father's, Antigonus I "One-eyed" Monophtalmus, frontline. Demetrius tried to return back to the center of the battlefield, but he was blocked by Selecus I Soter's mechanized divisions of war elephants. In the heat of the battle, the infantry launched a hail of spears and darts. One of them hit Antigonus, killing him. A remaining part of his forces surrendered. The victors, Lysimachus, Seleucus I Soter, Ptolemy I Soter, and Cassander, divided the spoils. Lysimachus was given Asia Minor where he continued to expand. Ephesus became his new capital where he built the Belevi Mansoleum. He had already erected a city in his own honor named Lysimacheia.

It was the year 299 when Lysimachus married Arsinoe, the daughter of Ptolemy I Soter and later Berenice I, the daughter of the Macedonian regent Antipater. Again, those marriages were done for political reasons as I mentioned earlier.

Contention over who would rule Macedonia continued between Lysimachus and Demetrius I for several years, but in the year 294, Lysimachus temporarily relinquished control of Macedonia to Demetrius. Meanwhile, Lysimachus turned his attention back to troublesome Thrace, attempting to extend his power further north near the Danube River, but he and his son Agathocles were defeated and taken as prisoners of war. While Agathocles was detained, his father Lysimachus still fought against the nomads, but he too was captured. Dromichates, [*pronounced* **Dro-mi-ka-tes**] the fierce barbarian ruler over the Getae nomads whose prowness halted Lysimachus advances, held both of them as bargaining chips until the year 292 when he set them free. In exchange for their freedom, Lysimachus surrendered all claims on lands he had captured in Thracian territory.

Strife between Lysimachus and Macedonia flared-up again. In the year of 288/287, Lysimachus joined hands with Pyrrhus and invaded Macedonia toppling Demetrius I. The offensive forced Demetrius to flee the country into Asia Minor where he was captured by Seleucus I Nicator. By 286, the alliance had conquered all of Macedonia and Thessaly. Lysimachus initially agreed to allow Pyrrhus to wear the crown as king and ruler of Macedon for the first seven months. But, the following year he changed his mind in a very indecisive manner, expelled Pyrrhus then seized complete control for himself. Thus adding the title of "King of Macedon" to his lengthy political resume. Palace intrigue and infighting did not cease. His third wife Arsinoe convinced him that his eldest son Agathocles, who was the son of his first wife, was plotting against him. He executed Agathocles. His first wife Nicaea, the daughter of Antipater, and her relatives were extremely disturbed by his treachery. The widow of Agathocles named Lysandra, fled for safety in Babylon to Seleucus I Nicator. After those provocative events, Seleucus and Lysimachus became open enemies which culminated at the Battle of Corupedium.

It was February of 281 B.C.E. on the mainland of western Asia Minor when the armies of Seleucus and Lysimachus faced off at Corupedium. Lysimachus had crossed the Hellespont into Lydia to confront the Seleucid army. The Seleucid army overran the forces of Lysimachus. He was slain in the midst of the battle. Seleucus continued his pursuit westward into Thrace hoping to add the uncivilized terrain to the western borders of his empire. Days after the war was over, Lysimachus body was found in the open field. His faithful dog stood nearby protecting his corpse from the birds of prey. His remains were eventually given to his younger son Alexander who interned him at the royal city of Lysimacheia.

So it came to pass that Lysimachus died at the approximate age of 80. He had walked in all the abhorrent ways of the Grecian rulers who preceded him doing evil in the eyes of **YAH ELOHIM Israel**. He built a city adorned with a temple where he served all the graven images [**sacred post**] of gold, silver, brass, wood and stone according to Greco-religion. And it came to pass that Ptolemy II Ceraunus succeeded him and reigned in his stead.

<u>Ptolemy II Keraunos</u>
(281—279 B.C.E.)

Ptolemy II Keraunos [*pronounced* **Ke-rau-nos**] was born between the year 320/319 as the eldest son of the ruler of Egypt Ptolemy I Soter and his second wife Eurydice, who happened to be the daughter of Antipater, the regent of Macedonia. His father, Ptolemy I Soter took another wife, Berenice I, and begat another son, who was born around the year 309/308, who was also named Ptolemy. He became known as Ptolemy II Philadelphus. Although Keraunos was 10 years old older than Philadelphus, their father began to favor the younger son. A dispute between the king and his mother Eurydice led to the disfavor. During the final three years of his father's life [285-282 B.C.E.], he chose the younger Ptolemy II Philadelphus as the co-regent and heir to the throne. When Ptolemy I Soter died, Philadelphus assumed the throne and began a violent pre-emptive campaign to slay all potential rivals. He slew his brothers, his first wife, and other close relatives. In midst of the chaos, Keraunos fled from Alexandria to the royal court of Thrace where he received a warm reception from Lysimachus who reigned as king. It was a family affair between Egypt and Thrace. King Lysimachus was married to his half-sister Arsinoe, who was the queen. His maternal sister Lysandra was married to the son of King Lysimachus. His name was Agathocles, co-regent and crown prince. Nevertheless, infighting between the wives inside the palace of Lysimachus caused major problems. The rivalry did not cease. His wife Arsinoe convinced him that his eldest son Agathocles, from his first wife, was plotting against him. He hearkened to her counsel and executed his own firstborn son. Fearing for her safety as well, Lysandra fled to Seleucus I Soter in Babylon for refuge. Ptolemy II Keraunos followed suit and followed his sister into Babylon. King Seleucus, an opportunist, saw this new development as a chance to gain power over Thrace and Macedon and reunite the empire of Alexander the Great. The 84-year-old Seleucid leader took up arms against 77-year-old Lysimachus. The armies faced-off at the Battle of Corupedium where Lysimachus was slain. Seleucus was the victor and potentially the new ruler of Macedon and Thrace, but there was discord between Seleucus and Keraunos. Seleucus did not desire to share power with anyone else. *The Seleucus Chronicle* stated: "Certain military men rebelled against him and killed him. This ended his conquest of Thrace and Macedonia. He was stabbed to death by Ptolemy who then received the nickname Keraunos which meant *"thunderbolt"* because of his treacherous deed. He became known as to be man on the prowl looking for an unscrupulous adventure or prey. This backstabbing took place between August 26—Sept. 24, 281 B.C.E.. Keraunoss slew his former protectorate in order to seize power for himself. He then rushed to the city of Lysimacheia where he proclaimed himself king.

Keraunos had made close friends with the soldiers of the Seleucid army. He had also been an ally of Lysimachus. Soldiers from both kingdoms respected him as a skilful military officer and he was the grandson of Antipater, the great regent of Macedon. With Lysimachus and Seleucus dead, the soldiers of Macedon chose Ptolemy II Keraunos as the new king of Macedonia. Once he was anointed king of Macedonia he relinquished his longstanding claim to the Egyptian throne which was held by his half-brother Ptolemy II Philadelphus. Afterwards, Keraunos asked the widow of Lysimachus ,his half-sister, Arsinoe to marry him. Arsinoe consented, but she was not happy with her new relationship with Keraunos. While he was away on a campaign, she conspired against him with the assistance of her two sons. Keraunos sought to kill them. The younger son was slain, but the older son fled northwards towards the territory of the barbarian Dardanians. Meanwhile Arsinoe fled back into Egypt where she married her other brother Ptolemy II Philadelphus and became known as Arsinoe II.

Two years later in 279 B.C.E., the barbarian hordes from northern Bulgaria known as the Galatians swarmed into Macedonia and Greece. Ptolemy was no match for them. The Thracian tribes asked Keraunos to help them against the Galatians but he refused to help them. Keraunos was hoping the Galatians would weaken the Thracians and thereby assist Macedonia against the potential threat. But, the barbarian Galatians forced the Thracians to join them in an attack on Macedonia. The battle was set in array in the spring of 279. The savage barbarians, led by a leader named Bolgas, swarmed into the royal city Pella. The army of Ptolemy II Keraunos was defeated, he was captured, and his head cut-off. Those fierce warriors were known by the Greek term "Celtic" which meant barbarian. Their dwellings extended from what is known today as eastern France into southern Germany over to Romania and Bulgaria. In the 5th and 4th centuries B.C.E., those tribes expanded West into countries where they all spoke a common language which modern scholars refer to as "Celtic" and practiced a common culture known as "La-Tene." The offsprings of those primitive people are known today as Western Europeans, and in the 21st century that region has become one of the world's richest.

Ptolemy II Keraunos death caused more confusion among the Greek states. All the Grecian states once unified were in a constant state-of-war with each other. After his death, his brother Meleager seized the throne for two months until the officers of Macedonia forced him to resign. Eventually, Antigonus Gonatas rose up and defeated the Galatians in a battle near the city of Lysimachia in the province of Thrace during the year of 277 B.C.E. After that victory, Gonatas was recognized as the new king of Macedonia. His power extended from there into southern Greece.

It came to pass that Ptolemy II Keraunos died between the approximate age of 49 to 51. He reigned for two years walking in all the ways of the Greco-Hellenistic kings that preceded him, serving all the gods of the Greek pantheon. After his death and his brother Meleager, the kingdom of Thrace was overran by various barbarian tribes. And it came to pass that Cotys II, a barbarian of the Odrysian kingdom of Thrace became the new leader of the nomadic people. His succession began a lineage of independent mountain dwellers who remained free until the invasion of the Romans [kingdom of iron] in the year 148 B.C.E..

Cotys II (Odrysian)
(300—280 B.C.E.)

Cotys II was king of the barbarian Odrysian kingdom of Thrace who succeeded his father Seuthes III. He ruled over an underdeveloped system where there were no libraries or a king chamber filled with historical scrolls. There were no crafts or metalworking skills. Those skills were eventually obtained adopted later from the Persians and Greeks. When Darius, Phillip II, Alexander the Great, and Lysimachus invaded those areas, They turned the Thracian people into their vassals. Even then, it was centuries later before the Odrysians ceased to be a nomadic people roaming to and forth throughout the wasteland without a capital or royal city. This Odrysian kingdom consisted of the unification of nearly 50 barbaric tribes which established over 20 kingdoms over a four century period of time. Collectively, they became the strongest powerbases dwelling near the flatlands near the Hebrus River. Their hordes were known to consist of a powerful army with as many as 150,000 fighters.

Today that territory is known as southeastern Bulgaria, parts of Turkey, and northeastern portions of Greece. Over a period of time these early inhabitants became renown for their fierce fighting, horseriding skills and gluttonous winebibbing. In appearance and fashion, they resembled the Scythians. Eventually they learned to build roads and developed trade. By the year 320 B.C.E. they had developed a kingship with Seuthes III as the vicar. He even established the city Seuthopolis in his own honor, but the Celts destroyed it in 281.

So it came to pass in the year 280 that the reign of Cotys II came to an end. Raizdos became his successor ruling over the diverse tribes.

Raizdos (Odrysian)
(280 B.C.E.)

Raizdos was possibly the son of Cotys II. We are not certain because, as I said earlier, these primitive people did not have an established governmental order like Macedonia, Seleucid Syria, or Ptolemy Egypt. These people were mountain and cave dwellers without historians who recorded their daily activities on papyrus scrolls. Raizdos, sometimes called Roigos, rose to power as the new ruler of the pre-historic Indo-European Thracians. Their social status did not change until the Romanization of southeastern Europe in the second century before the common era. It was the war between Macedonia and the Roman Empire that had the side effect of bringing advanced civilization to Thrace. It came to pass that a man named Odroes succeeded him as the next leader of the Odrysians.

Odroes (Odrysian)
(280—273 B.C.E.)

Odroes became the new leader of the Odrysians after the reign of Raizdos. It is uncertain why his rulership lasted for only 1 year. There are no historical records or evidence to further elaborate on his life. It is presumed that lack of recorded history occurred because the primitive intellectual and social status of early Thracians. A barbarian ruler named Adaeus succeeded him as the next leader.

Adaeus Odrysian)
(280—273 B.C.E.)

Adaeus was the new leader of the mountain-dwellers. The physical geographical borders of ancient Thrace included the high ranges of the Balkan Mountains, the Rhodope Mountains, and the Bosporus. His reign is marred in obscurity because the Odrysians were a primitive people without written documents. There is no certain way to probe their daily activities. Another member of the hordes named Rostodos became the new leader.

Rostodos (Odrysian)
(275—265 B.C.E.)

Rostodos succeeded Adaeus as the next leader of the mountain-dwellers. There is no recorded history of his lineage, place of birth, or chronicles of daily Odrysian affairs during his reign. During these ancient times, this uncivilized Thracian landscape was already being referred to as "Europe," a designated title that would be eventually used to describe all the Aryan people living across the entire continent. So it came to pass that Rostodos ruled the rugged terrains of Thrace for ten years serving as the head of this primitive people. Another member of the hordes named Orsoaltios succeeded him on the throne.

Orsoaltios (Odrysian)
(265—260 B.C.E.)

Orsolaltios was the new ruler of the Odrysians, the roaming mountain-dwellers. As they moved around, they branched off into subgroups such as the Getaes, Tribal, Dardanians, or Dacians. Other splinter tribes that broke away from the principal group included the Sabokoi, Germanics, Celtics, Edones, Geto, Paionians, and the Agrianes. It came to pass that Orsolatios reign came to an end during the year of 260 B.C.E.. His successor was another mountain-dweller named Kersivalous.

Kersivalous (Odrysian)
(260 B.C.E.)

Kersivalous was the successor of Orsoaltios as the new leader of mountain-dwellers which lived the areas we refer today as southeastern Europe. Again, his exploits are not known because scribes or historians were not among their ranks. For whatever reason, Kersivalous rulership over the fierce nomadic warriors lasted for only one year. He was succeeded, possibly overthrown, by Cotys III in the approximate year of 260.

Cotys III (Odrysian)
(260—250 B.C.E.)

Cotys III assumed the mantle of power after succeeding Kersivalous as the ruler. Like all of the Odrysian kings before him, details about his rulership are obscure or nonexistent. One thing we do know is that he was named after two rulers, Cotys I and Cotys II, who had succeeded him. Cotys I ruled in 384 B.C.E. while Cotys II reigned two decades earlier in the year of 280. Besides that, we know that he was named after an ancient Thracian goddess who was worshipped in rites of homosexual orgies, human sacrifice, fire worship, gluttonous wine-drinking, and other frenzied activities. The festivals were held in the wild on the hills. The symbol for the goddess Cotys was a mere musical instrument.

There were no scribes or accomplished historians among the Odrysians during this time. So it came to pass that Tires III succeeded him as the next leader of the mountain-dwellers.

Tires III (Odrysian)
(250—240 B.C.E.)

Tires III succeeded the barbarian leader Cotys III as the next ruler over the Odrysian hordes. There are no historical documentation of his rulership. Like all the Odrysian leaders before him, he ruled over a nomadic people without skills to build royal capitals with palaces and stadiums made of precious stones. There was no king's throne, cabinet officials, craftsmen who built monuments, wheeled-charioteers, horsemen, scribes, philosophers, historians, skilled musicians, or a trained standing army. Those advancements did not occur until the Romanization of southeastern Europe. Tires III reigned for ten years until he was replaced by another nomadic ruler named Rascouporis.

Rascouporis I (Odrysian)
240—215 B.C.E.

Rascouporis I, sometimes spelled to Rhescuporis I, ascended to become the next strongman to hold the Odrysian hordes together. His twenty-five year rule indicates that he was a successful leader who was able to maintain control over wild mountain-dwellers. There is no recorded history of his rulership. What is known is that the Odrysians were a pagan people who worshipped a stone-idol named Zagreus which was a counterpart of the Greek deity Dionysus. Participants performed homosexual orgies, human sacrifice, gluttonous wine-drinking, and fire rituals. Seuthes succeeded Rascouporis as the next Odrysian ruler.

Seuthes (Odrysian)
215—213 B.C.E.

Seuthes became the next ruler over the Odrysian kingdom in Thrace during the year of 215 B.C.E.. He too was the ruler of the wild nomadic Thracians who lived in province of Thrace. There was no extensive written history on him as well. Like all the Odrysian rulers which I previously mentioned, Seuthes was the leader of a primitive people who did not advance to the level of Macedonian, Ptolemy, or Seleucid civilizations until hundreds of years later. It appeared that Seuthes was not a strong leader because he reigned for only two years, or maybe some type of misfortune befell him. So it came to pass that another nomadic leader named Plearatus emerged as the next ruler of the wild mountain-dwellers.

Plearatus (Odrysian)
213—208 B.C.E.

Plearatus emerged as the next ruler of the Odrysian people that lived in the province of Thrace. There were no cultural advancements for these nomads during his five year reign. For the record, it should be known that it was the Greeks who gave this region the name of Thrace and called the people by the name Thracians. In Greek mythology, Thrace was the name of an ancient female witch who was the daughter of a god named Oceanus and Parthenope. According to these legends, Thrace was the sister of the god Europa. Europa is the root word for both Europe and European. Eventually, the designated title was given to all the Aryan people who once roamed across the entire uncultivated continent. It was millenniums later before Europe became the home of the advanced civilization it is today. So it came to pass that Abrupolis eventually succeeded him.

Abrupolis (Odrysian)
200—172 B.C.E.

Abrupolis became the next leader to emerge after an eight-year gap in succession of Odrysian kings. We can not be sure why this occurred because, as I have repeated explained, there were no Thracian recorded history at this time. It appears that, maybe, internal strife or some type of uncertain situation caused this interruption. Whatever the cause, Abrupolis did not assume the mantle of leadership until the year of 200 B.C.E. During his 28-year reign, it appears that the strongman Abrupolis was challenged by another nomadic leader named Amadokos. During this time in the year 197, Rome assigned this nomadic wasteland to the kingdom of Pergamum

Amadokos III (Odrysian)
184 B.C.E.

It appears that Amadokos plotted a coup to topple the leadership of Abrupolis in the year of 184. Remember, the 28-year reign of Abrupolis lasted from 200 to 172 B.C.E. So in the year of 184 when Abrupolis was in the 16th year of his reign, it seems Amadokos challenged his authority that year. His revolt had to be unsuccessful because it lasted for only one year while Abrupolis hold on power continued for 12 more years until the year of 172. It came to pass that Amadokos claim to leadership did not continue. He was succeeded by Tires IV.

Tires IV (Odrysian)
183—172 B.C.E.

Tires IV became another leader who also claimed power during the same time when Abrupolis reigned as the true leader of the tribesmen. It appears Tires IV came to power one year after the revolt of Amadokos. Maybe Tires IV succeeded Amadokos as the next rebel leader against Abrupolis. There were no king's chambers with written historical scrolls that would provide us with a closer look into the daily affairs of these hordes. As I have repeatedly said earlier, the Odrysian tribesmen were split into several sub-tribes and became known by various other names such as the Pannonians, Breucis, Geto-Dacians, Napaes, Celtics, and the Germanics. The fact that 3 tribal leaders had the same dates for rulership tells us that there was a great division among the Odrysian mountain-dwellers. By now, the Romans began to expand their influence into this area with plans of modernization. This gradual and steady Romanization of Thrace lifted the province out of the dark ages.

So it came to pass that all these three, Abrupolis, Amadokos, and Tires IV, all vied for the mantle of authority during the years 184 to 172 B.C.E. until they were all succeeded by another barbarian leader named Tires V. During this time, the Odrysians were being weakened by internal strife and external pressure from the emerging **kingdom of pelvis and legs of iron—Rome**.

Tires V (Odrysians)
172—148 B.C.E.

Tires V emerged as the new leader of the Thracians in the year of 172 after years of infighting between power-hungry competitors Abrupolis, Amadokos, and Tires IV. It was said that he was the son of Cotys IV. By now, the Romans had defeated the Macedonians in the Battle of Pydna during the year of 168. That victory expanded the influence of Rome into southeastern Europe for the first time. After that victory, the fierce Roman legions gradually began to invade the province of Thrace over the next 20 years. Ironically, this invasion by Rome expanded their empire, but on the other hand, it brought a new level of modernization to the Odrysians inspite of their military defeat. Once Rome occupied the province and discovered large silver deposits, this area became a valuable center for the kingdom's coin production.

As we already know, Tires V ruled over a primitive people who were unable to record such events. So it came to pass that Tires V reigned for 24 years. His fate is unknown, but it seems possible that Tires V was killed during the uprising of another barbarian leader named Andriscus.

It should also be noted that during the reign of Tires V that the Third Macedonian War occurred. This conflict was between King Perseus of Macedonia and the Roman Republic. In the initial battles, Perseus enjoyed victory against the Roman legions, but Perseus was later forced to surrender following his defeat at the Battle of Pydna on June 22,168 B.C.E. That marked the beginning of Roman ruleship over Macedonia and Thrace. The wild Thracians continued their revolt against foreign powers, including Rome.

In the year of 149, Andriscus, the leader of the nomadic Thracians, invaded the kingdom of Macedonia and ransacked the Roman legions who were under the command of the Roman praetor Publius Juventis. The following year Andriscus popular uprising was crushed by the Roman legions during the Second Battle of Pydna. After that, Rome established a permanent residence in Greece. After those events, the Achaean League of Greek States rebelled against the Roman presence in the Grecian heartland, but Rome swiftly defeated their rebellion. The Roman legions then marched on the city-state of Corinth and burned the city to the ground. Rome then formally annexed Greece, including Macedonia and Thrace and assumed direct control throughout the region. This new Roman presence represented the formal destruction of the Odrysian kingdom. Nevertheless, there were two other barbarian hordes known as the Canites and the Odrissae which continued their nomadic independence.

The Iron Age—(Its Pelvis and Legs of Iron)
Roman Era—PART ONE "the pelvis"
"its legs were of iron—But the fourth kingdom will be strong as iron; just as iron crushes and shatters everything—and as iron that smashes—so will it crush and smash all these."
Daniel 2: 33, 40

"YAH changes times and seasons. HE removes kings (kingdoms) and install kings(kingdoms); HE gives the wise their wisdom and knowledge to those who know" **Daniel 2: 21**

The metal of **iron**, which is **the pelvis and the legs** of the image, is actually a metaphor for the Prophetic Time Zone when the Roman Empire would rise to dominate world affairs. The ascension of Rome solidified a historical and prophetic trend of Aryan people ruling the kingdoms of the earth. It started with the emergence of **the kingdom of brass**, the Macedonian Empire, and continued among the four Aryan empires that evolved from it, and proceeded down to the rule of Rome. The rise of Rome guaranteed that Europe and its inhabitants (white people) would become the new controllers of world affairs. The ancient people of Israel were destined to remain in captivity under the yoke of this strong global power.

The History of Rome

Ancient Rome started out as a primitive Aryan settlement situated on banks of the Tiber River at the top of the Palatine Hill. During this pre-civilization era the settlement was ruled by barbaric Latin tribes while the highly civilized black Phoenicians (Canaanites) who navigated the Mediterranean from Tyre, Sidon, and other Canaanite cities settled nearby. They became known as Etruscans, the builders of advanced colonies. Eventually, during the Bronze Age in 1500 B.C.E. the city was built on the central plateau in midst of the seven mountains that surrounded it. As I said earlier, the Latin natives did not civilize this city-settlement for another thousand years. The city of Rome did not have any grandeur, recorded history, or nobility in those days. The village did not become a recognized city until early 500 B.C.E..

The name of the city became Rome. The origins of the city's name derived from the mythological belief in two infant graven images. One idol was called Romulus and the second god was termed Remus. According to their legend, on April 21, 753 B.C.E., these baby twins were found and raised by a she-wolf. The two images, Romulus and Remus, were regarded as the offsprings of the gods Mars and Rhea Siliva. The twins went on to build their own city, but Romulus killed Remus in a quarrel over the location of the kingdom. Therefore, Romulus gave the city its name: ROME.

(Black) Phoenician discoverers create new kingdom Etruria on Italian peninsula

During these early years, Rome was dominated by the powerful Phoenicians who used the peninsula as a trading post. Those explorers manufactured its minerals and natural resources as part of their ancient global commerce. In the process of time, these black settlers became known as Etruscans. Their kinsmen who settled on the neighboring northern African coast of the Mediterranean Sea became known as the Carthaginians. Together, these black Hamitic seafaring conquerors ruled the entire Mediterranean region known today as southern Europe and northern Africa.

By 1000 B.C.E. the Phoenician **[Etruscan]** civilization in central Italy was flourishing in numerous seaport cities. These discoverers introduced the alphabet, built extensive road networks, architectural palaces, burial grounds, sculpturing, wall painting, pottery, clothing, religious beliefs, and other aspects of Oriental culture to the uncivilized way station. It would be centuries later before the native Latins created a similar civilization. *(So, for the record: the myth of Romulus and Remus is actually a black Etruscan fable. Thus, the name Rome itself actually derives from those black people. I bet your history professors have never taught you those hidden historical facts, have they?)* By the 5th century B.C.E. the native Greeks and the Latins began to rebel against the Etruscan dominance of the lands and seas. Many repeated wars were fought between these blacks and whites. Eventually, the Greeks expelled the Phoenicians, Etruscans, and Persians by the 3rd century B.C.E. while the Latins overthrew the Etruscans and Carthaginians in the 2nd century B.C.E. after successive Punic Wars.

After the earlier period of servitude, the Latins eventually rose to power between the 200-year period of 753 to 509 B.C.E. They adopted many of the practices of their ex-rulers, but step-by-step the Aryans established their own Roman monarchy and state. The name Rome was preserved by the new rulers of the city. The name was later adopted by the Roman Republic, and finally transferred to the entire empire. Around the year 509 B.C.E. and continuing up to the year 27 B.C.E., the small city-state began to evolve into a renown republic.

As the old saying goes, *"Rome was not built in one day,"* and for the next five hundred years (27 B.C.E. to 476 C.E.), the Latin **(kingdom of iron)** became one of the largest autocratic empires of the ancient world, replacing the four divisions **(kingdoms of brass)** of the Greco-Macedonian empire of Alexander the Great. At its zenith of power, the great city of Rome reigned over an estimated 90 million inhabitants of the earth covering over 5 million kilometers of the earth's landscape. The areas included all the territories surrounding the Mediterranean Sea, all the domains extending from the Atlantic Ocean to the Arabian Sea, and from those ranging from the mouth of the Rhine River [modern Germany] into northern Africa. As the Roman Empire expanded across Europe, it provided the blueprint of skills for construction of palaces, public facilities, monument building, roads, aqueducts, law, politics, society, engineering, religion, warfare, language, arts, literature, and technological know-how among the various **(ten toes of iron)** barbarian nomads that wandered the northern hinterlands. For those Aryan nomads, Rome represented law and order, professionalism, and a system of governance that served as a foundation for the future kingdoms of France and the United States over one millennium later.

Ancient Roman-Punic Wars
(White-Aryan) verus (Black-African) domination of the Mediterranean Sea

The word Punic originates from the word Phoenician. The Phoenicians were the biblical Canaanites who were the first inhabitants of the land of Canaan and Lebanon. Their greatest cities were Sidon and Tyre. They were the world's first mariners who navigated the Mediterranean Sea as early as 1000 B.C.E. establishing colonies in Greece, Italy, Carthage, and throughout northern Africa. Around the year 814 B.C.E., the Phoenicians founded colony of Carthage, which was located north of modern-day Tunis. It grew from a minor seaport into the most advanced, richest, and most powerful city in the Mediterranean region. They built a powerful navy which dominated the great waters for centuries. By the 3rd century B.C.E., when Rome began to emerge, Carthage barred Roman trade in the western Mediterranean Sea. At that time Rome was a little city with no navy. Carthage reigned supreme. If any Roman traders were caught in Carthaginian waters, their ships were taken and the sailors drowned. During this era, Rome's relations with Carthage were peaceful, but subservient. Rome was dominated by several treaties which gave Carthage the advantage.

First Punic War
264—241 B.C.E.

Carthage controlled the island of Sicily. A conflict broke out between sailors from Syracuse and the Latin inhabitants of Sicily. Carthage sided with the navy of Syracuse. The city of Rome supported their kinsmen of Sicily. This conflict became the nucleus of the **First Punic War** between Rome and Carthage. A war that lasted twenty-three years from 264 B.C.E. until 241. During this lengthy conflict the city of Rome defeated the Carthaginians and consolidated its control over the entire peninsula. Rome expelled Carthage from the island of Sicily, and several other islands where the black invaders had ruled for centuries. Over the course of this First Punic War, Rome also built a powerful navy and learned naval tactics from their enemies. At the outset of the war the Romans had no knowledge of shipbuilding. However when the war ended, Rome emerged as an aggressive naval power. Yet, due to its inexperience at sea warfare, Rome loss countless ships and crews in battles and powerful storms. Historians report Rome lost 50,000 soldiers and 700 ships during the two decade conflict, but the great city would never give up until they forced a withdrawal or a stalemate. This deadlocked maritime war was a victory for Rome. For the first time Carthage had to respect their Aryan foes as equals and the Republic of Rome maintained sovereignty over the waters near their own Italian borders.

Second Punic War
218—201 B.C.E.
Hannibal the Great
(219—201 B.C.E.)

For the next 23 years, from 241 until 218 B.C.E.,the Roman Republic continued to strengthen their navy and army in preparation for the next round of warfare against Carthage. During this same time Carthage had to expand its presence in the western Mediterranean Sea to make up for its losses after the First Punic War. Carthage established a base in Spain in the year of 237 under the leadership of Hamilcar Barca. Barca was the father of the famous Carthaginian general named Hannibal Barca who became known as **Hannibal the Great**. Before he died in 229 B.C.E. Barca made his young 10-year-old son Hannibal, *whose name meant "grace of Baal or Baal has been gracious,"* dip his hands in the warm blood of a sacrifice and made him vow that he would one day destroy Rome. Born in approximately 247, Hannibal was 16-years-old when his father Barca drowned in a battle to conquer Spain. His son-in-law named Hasdrubal succeeded him for the next eight years. During his reign Hasdrubal maintained a truce with the Roman presence near Spain. That truce was broken in the year of 219 when Hasdrubal was assassinated. Hannibal then declared war on Rome and destroyed the city of Saguntium. Saguntium was an Iberian city under the protection of Rome. After that initial attack the 26-year-old military strategist mounted an infantry of 90,000, 1,200 cavalrymen, along with countless elephants in a march from Spain across the Alp Mountains into Italy. Hannibal crossed the Alps with African elephants but became entangled in the snowy mountains. Hannibal's chemists designed a toxic brew that blasted the mountain cliffs into pebbles. His forces descended down the Roman side of the mountains and scored victories at Ticinus, Trebia, Lake Trasimene, and Cannae. Using superior cavalry tactics, Hannibal surrounded Roman armies twice his own size and inflicted massive casualties upon his foes. The only problem was that Hannibal could not bring his massive siege machines through the Alps which he needed to subdue the Roman fortifications. This led to a bogged down invasion that lasted for 15 years without a clear victory. By the year 203, Hannibal was forced to abandon his conquest of the Italian peninsula in order to defend against the new Roman naval offensive in North Africa. This military readjustment and retreat spelled the end of Carthage's empire in the western Mediterranean, leaving Rome as the sole ruler in Spain and Italy. Rome's aggression forced Hannibal to sue for peace. Carthage was forced to give up its naval fleet, ending their seapower superiority. The kingdom was also forced to pay a large sum of silver as indemnity to the Roman victors. The peace agreement allowed Carthage to retain only its territory in North Africa. Rome's army, navy, and political alliances in Sicily gave them the power needed to achieve victory and expel the Carthaginians for once and all.

for once and all.

The heavy indemnity on Carthage caused internal political tensions. In order to pay the peace settlement, Carthage had to rid itself of corruption. Some of the Carthaginian nobility did not like the new economic restraints forced upon them. Some accused Hannibal of mismanaging the war and the economy. So the ruling class plotted to surrender Hannibal in hopes of easing their financial burden along with better relations with Rome. In 201 B.C.E. Hannibal fled to Tyre to save his life. This effectively concluded the Second Punic War. Afterwards he escaped to the royal court of Antiochus in Ephesus and became his chief advisor in his war against Rome. With the ex-Carthaginian ruler on his side, Antiochus proposed a new strategic confederation with King Phillip V of Macedonia to halt Rome's expansion. Phillip refused. Neither did the new anti-Roman alliance work. Antiochus the Great was defeated by the Roman legions. When the peace treaty was signed between Antiochus and Rome at Magnesia in 190 B.C.E., Rome demanded that the Carthaginian ex-ruler be surrendered as part of the agreement. Hannibal was on the run again. This time he fled deeper into Asia Minor and hid among white Greeks, Turks, and Latin colonizers. He found refuge temporarily with King Prusias of Bithynia where he became his naval commander and defeated King Eumenes II of the city-state Pergamum. Regarded as a genius military strategist, Hannibal threw baskets of snakes into his enemy's ships. That terroristic warfare at sea was regarded as one the first recorded examples of biological warfare.

After the Bithynia-Pergamum war was over, Rome once again demanded at third party to hand over Hannibal the Great. The king of Bithynia betrayed the black leader to Rome. This time Hannibal fled into the fortress city of Libyssa and hid there. After hiding in the city for a while, Hannibal sent his envoy into the townsquare to survey all the possible secret exit routes. The messengers told Hannibal all exit points were guarded with hostile armed soldiers. Hannibal sensed his end was near. He did not want to be captured and desecrated. He wanted to die with his honor intact, so he mixed and drank a cup of deadly poison ending his own life. So it came to pass that Hannibal, the hater of Rome, died in city of Libyssa in the year of 183 B.C.E. at the age of 64. During his lifetime the Carthaginian king had been regarded as one of the greatest military strategist in ancient and modern history. He was deemed the *"father of strategy"*. Even his arch enemy Rome adopted elements of his battlefield tactics in their fighting strategies. Hannibal had been revered as a brutal commander who would slay a soldier for a mistake as simple as wrong directions. If a Carthaginian soldier detected, he would seize his wife and children, then burn them alive. He cruelly enforced loyalty among his troops and intimidated his enemies. However, in the end Hannibal's mission to the destroy Rome—**the kingdom of iron**—was a failure. The prophetic decree from **the Most High YHWH** was on Rome's side at that time.

The north African kingdom of Carthage was also known for continuing the old Canaanite ceremonial practice of child sacrifices to the gods. Unearthed historical records have shown that during the waning days of the Punic Wars, 500 innocent children of the nobility were sacrificed to Baal in a fiery baptism in hopes of gaining spiritual power against emerging Rome.

Third Punic War
(149—146 B.C.E.)
Aryan People (Whites) Takeover North Africa and western Mediterranean
(Continent known as Africa renamed after a Roman named General Scipio Africanus)

52 years had passed since the Battle of Zama and the collapse of the regime of Hannibal the Great. Yet certain members of the Roman Senate still viewed Carthage as a threat. These members included Cato the Elder and several of his hawkish allies. Those senate members lobbied their colleagues to join them in their campaign against Carthage. In their eyes, Carthage was a threat even in its weakened state. Their fears were confirmed in 149 B.C.E. when Carthage broke its treaty with Rome by declaring war against the neighboring state of Numidia. Rome immediately dispatched its army and navy to North Africa, sparking the Third Punic War.

The Third Punic War was different. Rome was the aggressor this time. In the year of 148 B.C.E. the Roman legions disembarked and besieged Carthage for two years. A young Roman general named Scipio Aemilianus Africanus was the commander of the war. By the spring of 146, Africanus mounted a new assault on the harbor side of the great city. His troops pushed inside the city, destroying house after house, and slaughtering every inhabitant that resisted. After a 7-day massacre, the royal city was obliterated. The remaining Carthaginians surrendered. At least 50,000 black Carthaginians were taken by ship to Rome to be sold as slaves. Great seafaring Carthage with its massive naval fleets had fallen from the pinnacle of power to become a vanquished city-state. In fact, Carthage was the last great black kingdom of antiquity. Its defeat represented the final nail in the coffin for the ancient great black Hamitic-Shemitic kingdoms like Egypt, Ethiopia, Nubia, Babylonia, Assyria, and Canaan. The Aryan Ptolemies, Seleucids, and Macedonians were ruling the ancient black world in the East and Aryan Rome ruled the Mediterranean regions in the West. In North Africa, Rome established a proconsul to incorporate the former Carthaginian territory into a Roman province. The province was renamed in honor of the Roman general **Scipio Africanus** who won the victory. The title Africanus was eventually extended to include territories of Numidia, which is modern Libya. Between the years of 30 B.C.E. and 180 C.E. the territories of Cyrenacia, Manmaria, and Mauretania became Roman provinces designated as parts of their empire. Eventually the entire continent became known as Africa in honor of the late Roman general. Since then the continent of **Havilah** where human civilization began has been renamed **Africa**.

Also in the same year of 146, the Roman army also launched an offensive against Phillip V of Macedonia. These series of battles became known as the Macedonian Wars. Rome crushed Phillip, and by the end of the year of 146, **the kingdom of the pelvis and legs of iron** ruled over a global empire that extended from off the Atlantic coast of Spain in the west towards the borders of Grecia and Asia Minor in the east.

The Roman Republic
(146—60 B.C.E.)

Rome reigned as the supreme power throughout the western Mediterranean after the destruction of Carthage. The spoils from foreign conquests and the tribute exacted from its subjects provided the stimulus for the great city, which was situated in the midst of seven mountains, to grow into an imperial city. The grandeur of the great city included magnificent public buildings, palaces, arched-bridges, temples dedicated to a pantheon of Roman gods, public bath houses, theaters, and stadiums.

The government consisted of two consuls and the Senate. The Senate was regarded as the people's assembly. It was comprised of two popular groups. The patricians and the plebeians. The patricians, who were known as the *Comitia Centuri*, were the wealthy aristocratic class. They usually held the highest positions in government. The plebeians, *Concilium Plebis*, were the poorer class who filled the rank-in-file as members of the Roman legions. The plebeians for the most part did not possess wealth or political authority. There was constant tensions between these two groups in the upper and lower houses of the Senate. Still, both groups were extremely popular. The people expressed their opinions through the institution and considered it as their voice. The members of the Senate served for life. Their responsibilities included proposing laws, overseeing foreign policy, finances, and maintaining civil order.

The two consuls served as joint executive leaders of the republic. The consuls presided over the Senate. One consul could veto the decision of the other. Their 1-year term was determined by the Senate. The consuls also commanded the armies. After serving in the office of consul, the former officeholder could be reappointed to serve as a proconsul. The proconsuls were the governors of the republic's foreign territories. Those positions enabled the officeholder the opportunity to enrich himself during the term. Other positions included the financial administrator known as the quaestor. Their responsibilities consisted of urban planning for roads, water, food supplies, and organizing annual games and festivals. The censor was charged with counting the people and property of the citizens.

Three centuries after disposing of the black Etruscan monarchy, a council of Aryan Latin assemblymen came together to write a constitution for the Roman Republic. That was done in the year of 450 B.C.E. The document became known as the Twelve Tables, a code of law enacted to assist the poor, define family life, and define property rights. The law granted protections against imprisonment for debt, and the right to appeal the decision of a magistrate. The legal code enshrined the political and personal rights for the poor. For example, a plebeian could marry a patrician and move up the ranks and become a consul. Nevertheless, the wealthy ruling class still represented the true powerbrokers in the republic. By the 3rd century B.C.E., the city of Rome controlled the entire Italian peninsula. The following century the Roman Republic expanded to most of areas we call Western Europe today, North Africa, and the Near East.

In the early 1st century Rome had grown into a great kingdom. Their constructional teams built the Ponte Altinate bridge which spanned a branch of the Brenta River in Padua, Italy. They also built the Pont Ambroix bridge in southern France. Rome also built gravel-paved roads that linked the royal city with the provinces of western Europe. There were countless temples built for their image-gods, and a theatre in Switzerland near the Rhine River. Western Europe basically became the ten provinces of the emerging Roman empire. There was a massive expansion of the Roman legion during this same period. The Roman Republic fought and won the Punic Wars, the Macedonian Wars, the Mithridatic Wars, the Seleucid, and Ptolemaic Wars during the first and second centuries.

However, as the Roman Republic continued its prosperous expansion, internally, there was increasing political turmoil. There was growing conflict between the patricians-[aristocrats] and the commoners-[plebeians]. By 133 B.C.E. the city of Rome's cosmopolitan population had grown more rapidly than jobs and business opportunities, causing economic stagnation, poverty, and homelessness. Roman victories on the battlefield also contributed to large number of slaves being imported into the royal city. These large slave populations caused numerous slave revolts. On top of that, there was also dissension within the military causing an upheaval known as the "Roman Revolution". When the revolution finally ended, the Roman Republic was gone and the seeds had been sown for the birth of the Roman Empire.

 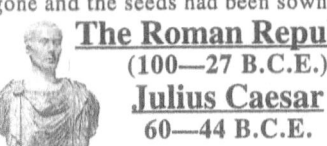 

The Roman Republic
(100—27 B.C.E.)
Julius Caesar
60—44 B.C.E.

It is believed Gaius Julius Caesar was born on July 13 in the year 100 B.C.E. as a child of the patrician class. At a young age he became involved with financial duties when he assumed the position of quaestor. Moving up the ladder, Caesar became a magistrate serving as an assistant to the consul before he eventually became a statesman. His political career started when he served as the consul of the Roman province of Spain during the year of 61/60 B.C.E. The Roman Republic was governed by three powerful military leaders. This included Ceasar, Pompey and Crassus. By the year 60 B.C.E. the threefold rulership was known as the First Triumvirate. Ceasar continued his military campaigns in Western Europe, killing hundreds of thousands. In the year 59, Ceasar became the proconsul of the Gaul province, known today as France. He also crushed dissension in Illyria the following year in 58. By the year of 55/54 Ceasar crossed the English Channel and invaded Britain. Continuing his military campaigns, he then crossed the Rhine River the next year in 53. By now, Pompey, the commander of the eastern forces and the Roman Senate, had become increasingly alarmed at Ceasar's growing power and popularity. The Roman Senate sent a decree to Caesar instructing him to cease his role as commander of the Roman legions. Ceasar then requested that he and Pompey resign their roles as commanders of the forces at the same time. The Senate refused Ceasar's demand. In the year of 49 the mutiny began. Ceasar mounted his soldiers, crossing the Rubicon River, which was located in the province of Gaul and Italy, sparking the Roman civil war. Ceasar defeated his opponents in Rome, forcing them, including Pompey to flee the royal city. Pompey fled to Egypt where he was murdered by Ptolemy XIII as Ceasar followed him in hot pursuit. Nevertheless, Julius Ceasar became the military backer, lover, and the father of a child by the Aryan queen Cleopatra. By the year of 46, all of Ceasar's enemies had been crushed and he had been exalted and crowned as the *"Dictator for Life."* Julius Caesar did not accept the title of *"king"* because he knew of his people's dislike for a monarchy.

Despite Caesar's reluctance to assume the crown as king, there was still simmering jealousy of his notoriety within the Senate and military. Two of the main conspirators against Caesar were Marcus Junius Brutus and Cassius Longinus Gaius. Both were generals and members of the Senate who had fought alongside Pompey in the civil war, however, after the conflict ended, Caesar pardoned them in hopes of creating an atmosphere of national reconciliation. Caesar even became more popular after his victories in the civil war. Meanwhile, an elaborate plot to restore the republic, with as many as 60 conspirators, was set in motion to assassinate the presiding ruler. Hatching their deadly scheme, they met in small groups to prevent detection. On March 15, 44 B.C.E. Caesar entered the Senate House and was stabbed to death where he fell at the foot of the statue of Pompey. After the murder of Caesar, the conspirators fled the royal city to Macedonia where they formed an army to defend themselves. In Rome, a Second Triumvirate, consisting of General Octavian, General Mark Anthony, and General Lepidus, seized the moment and assumed dictatorial power. The three leaders penalized the institution for its role in the mutiny. Senate's powers were greatly reduced.

The conspirators and the armies of the triumvirate met at the Battle of Philippi during the year of 42. General Octavian and his forces were routed by the army of Brutus and Cassius in the first battle. Nevertheless, in the second round, the forces of Octavian and Mark Anthony crushed their mercenary foes. Brutus committed suicide once he realized his cause was lost. Cassius also ordered one of his armourbearers to smite him to death. The conspiracy had been defeated. Mark Anthony was chosen to serve as commander of the eastern provinces. But, by the end of the year 33, the Roman Consul had ordered Anthony to end his role as proconsul in Egypt because he had divorced his wife, General Octavian's sister, and became the new lover of the whorish Cleopatra VII.

Another internal conflict erupted. This time between Octavian and Anthony. General Octavian had built a powerful military force in the western half of the empire. In the year 32 he dispatched General Lepidus. The following year in 31 he declared war on Egypt. Both sides met at the Battle of Actium in 31 B.C.E. where he defeated Mark Anthony. Cleopatra committed suicide by allowing a poisonous snake bite her breasts. General Octavian then became the undisputed commander of the western and eastern Roman legions. He reorganized the Roman government into an imperial principate where he controlled all major aspects of the empire as sole consul. In the year 27 B.C.E. he was awarded the title *"Augustus"*. Four years later in 23 B.C.E., he was granted imperial powers as the emperor. Thus Augustus Caesar became the first emperor of the newly evolved Roman Empire.

The Julio-Claudian Dynasty: **Part 1—The Pelvis and Legs of Iron**—Augustus (27 B.C.E.—14 C.E.), Tiberius (14 C.E.—37 C.E.), Caligula (37 C.E.—41 C.E.), Claudius (41 C.E.—54 C.E.), Nero (54 C.E.—68 C.E.), **Part 2**—Galba (68 C.E.—69 C.E.), Otho (69 C.E.), Vitellius (69 C.E.), Vespasian (69 C.E.—79 C.E.), Titus (79 C.E.—81 C.E.), Domitian (81 C.E.—96 C.E.), Nerva (96 C.E.—98 C.E.), Trajan (98 C.E.—117 C.E.).

Julio-Claudian Dynasty
The Roman Empire

Augustus Caesar
(27 B.C.E.—14 C.E.)

Augustus Caesar was born on September 23, 63 B.C.E. in Rome with the parental name of Gaius Octavius. His father's name was the same: Gaius Octavius. His mother's name was Atia. He was born into a well-known wealthy family that lived in the town of Velletri, located 25 miles south of the royal city. But, at the age of four his father died and his mother remarried another man who did not favor the young Gaius Octavius. The lad left his mother's home and was raised by his grandmother Julia, who happened to be the mother of Julius Caesar. Young Gaius loved his grandmother dearly. However, in the year of 52/51 she died while he was 12. After her death, his mother and stepfather, Luicius Marcius Philippus, brought him back into their home.

By the age of 16, Octavius was elected into the College of Pontiffs. The following year he was placed in charge of the Greek games held in the newly constructed temple built by his uncle Julius Caesar which honored the goddess Venus Genetix. By now, he was also eager to join the Roman legions but his mother Atia was very protective. He wanted to join Julius Caesar's campaign into Hispania, modern Spain, but he fell sick and was forced to remain behind. Once he recovered, he sailed towards the battlefront but the vessel shipwrecked. Octavius and his group were forced to cross enemy's territory to join Caesar. That courageous act greatly impressed his uncle, and from that day forward he was allowed to ride with Caesar in the commander's carriage. The Hispania campaign ended in a victory for Caesar. When he returned to Rome, he visited the temple of Venus where he met female gatekeepers known as the Vestal Virgins. There he deposited his will that named young Octavius as his beneficiary.

As I stated earlier, Julius Ceasar's enemies had been subdued by the year of 46 B.C.E. In the eyes of the people he was esteemed and crowned as their *"Dictator for Life"*. However, Julius Caesar did not accept the title of "king" because he knew of his people's dislike for a monarchy. Despite his modesty, there were still jealous foes in the Senate and military. Octavius was a mere 17-year-old. By March 15th of the year 44 when his uncle Julius Caesar was assassinated, Octavius had reached 19. He was studying and undergoing Roman legion training in Apollonia, Illyria. Once news of Caesar's death reached the troops in the east, Octavius rejected the advice of some senior officers to flee for safety in Macedonia. Instead he sailed towards Italy to see whether he had any fortune or position. He knew his uncle did not father any children, and he had been very close to him, even possibly involved in an eromenos-erastes sexual affair, so he made haste towards the royal city. Roman law made him a potential inheritor of a great fortune. For the record, an eromenos in ancient Roman culture was a male child lover. The erastes was the adult Roman male. Those same gender relationships were commonplace in the ancient Greco-Roman world. Roman consul and elder statesman Mark Anthony later criticized Octavius interference into Roman politics. He later scolded Octavius as being a puppet and sexual tool of Julius Caesar who should stand down.

Before arriving back in Rome, General Octavius landed at the city of Lupiae, located near military stronghold of Brundisium. Brundisium was a garrison city which served as a staging ground for Rome's wars against Parthia. General Octavius made another controversial decision when he used 700 million Roman coins stored at Brundisium to pay each soldier 500 denarii. He soon learned of the contents in his uncle's will which granted him two-thirds of Emperor Julius Caesar's estate. This is when he decided to become the political contender for one of the three consul seats. Meanwhile, General Octavius was receiving more warm receptions from Julius Caesar's former troops.

On May 6, 44 B.C.E. General Octavian entered Rome where tensions were high. There was a shaky truce between the Senate, the group responsible for Caesar's death, and the consul, the executive branch of Roman Republic power. Consul Mark Anthony had granted a general amnesty to the murderers of Julius Caesar. Regardless, the majority of the conspirators still fled to Macedonia. At the funeral of Caesar, Mark Anthony gave an arousing eulogy where he railed against the plotters. The speech caused a majority of Romans to turn against the perpetrators. Many fled Rome for safety in Macedonia. Mark Anthony and Octavian were both known as supporters of Caesar, however, behind closed doors they were rivals who vied for political advantage. Mark Anthony also refused to release the funds Julius Caesar left in his will for Octavian. Octavian then reached out to the great Senate orator Marcus Cicero to advance his personal position. Cicero was well respected. He had been one of the chief opponents of the dictatorship of Julius Caesar, however after the Roman Senate was granted amnesty by Anthony, he preferred this new alliance with the younger and more flexible Octavian over the elder statesman Mark Anthony. Cicero openly called for the restoration of the republican order and denounced Anthony as a threat to its revival. In a series of speeches known as the *Philippics*, Cicero advocated the abolishment of the office of dictator. Anthony's term as consul was complete by January of the year 43. Hostile public opinion and Octavian increasing power caused Anthony to seek the new position of proconsul of the Cisalpine Gaul province. The Senate granted him control, but Anthony faced one problem. There was an usurper named Decimus Junius Brutus who had been living there since his participation in conspiracy against Julius Caesar. Brutus refused to relinquish control to Anthony. Anthony attacked the city of Mutina. The Roman Senate demanded Anthony to cease the attack. Anthony ignored the directive from Rome. Rome declared war on Mark Anthony.

Meanwhile back in Rome, Cicero used his influence to induct Octavian into Senate membership on the same date of January 1, 43. Octavian was then promoted to the position of Commander of the Roman legions. Remember, Mark Anthony's term as consul had ended on January 1. The Senate appointed two other men to fill his consul vacancy. Their names were Hirtius and Pansa. These two men joined General Octavian into battle to bring order back to the Gaulic province. Both of those men were slain in the battles. Octavian became the sole commander of both of their armies, and added more military power behind his personal position. However, after the war concluded, the Roman Senate praised Decimus Junius Brutus for the victory instead of Octavian and then attempted to elect him as the Commander of Consul legions. Octavian saw this clever senatorial move as an attack to weaken the Office of Consul altogether. He countered by demanding that the Roman Senate rescind the decree that Mark Anthony was a public enemy. The Senate refused his request. Octavian marched on Rome unopposed with eight Roman legions. By summer, June of 44, Octavian had won over 3,000 more former Caesar's men into his fold. Those soldiers were stationed at Campania. During this time, Octavian increased his ranks with a private army to confront Mark Anthony.

That summer on August 19, Octavian was elected consul in Rome. In the Gaul province, Mark Anthony and another former Caesar general named Marcus Aemilius Lepidus signed an agreement of peace between their armies. By October, the three warriors laid down their weapons and met in the northern Italian city of Bologna. They all agreed to unite to work together in a new coalition known as the Second Triumvirate. Backed by their Roman legions, the triumvirate strengthened the Office of Consul, initiated a purge of the Roman Senate, seized the property, money, slew all their enemies, and anyone else connected to the death of Ceasar. Hundreds were caught up in the political purge. Even Cicero, the great thinker and manipulator in the Senate, had his head and hands cut off and placed in the center of the Roman Forum for public exhibition. In the end, all of their enemies in Rome were consumed.

With Rome stabilized, the triumviratè dispatched Anthony to the east to resume the campaign against the Parthians. Anthony experienced several setbacks on the battlefield. He requested 20,000 soldiers from Octavian and Lepidus, but Octavian dispatched only 2,000. Meanwhile, Anthony refused military support from Cleopatra, the queen of Egypt, to makeup for the shortage of manpower. Anthony, who had previously married the sister of Octavian, divorced her, sent her back to Rome, and became romantically involved with the Ptolemaic queen. Those moves angered Octavian and he began to rail against Anthony as being unpatriotic and favoring the Oriental world over Rome.

On January 1, 33 B.C.E. Octavian was re-elected to the Office of Consul for another term. Shortly afterwards, he burst into the Temple of Vestal Virgins to seize the personal will of his adversary Mark Anthony to determine his true intentions. He found out Anthony intended to grant all his territories under his command to his son Alexander Helios. His will also stated that he desired for his remains to be interned in Alexandria, Egypt with Queen Cleopatra VII, and not in Rome. By late 32 and early 31 B.C.E., Octavian and his allies in the Senate suspended General Anthony's authority as the consul in the east. Furthermore, he declared war against the queen of Ptolemaic Egypt. Octavian naval forces routed the fleets of Egypt and Anthony off the west coast of Greece, trapping them by land and sea. In a last ditch effort Anthony sought to break out of the blockade. Octavian's naval forces caught up with Anthony's ships in the Bay of Actium and nearly wiped them out completely. The backup forces of Cleopatra provided Anthony with the opportunity to retreat with a remnant of his ships. Nevertheless, the legions of Octavian relentlessly pursued them both into Egypt. Surrounded and outnumbered, Anthony fell on his own sword and Cleopatra committed suicide by allowing a venomous snake bite her breasts. Octavian then slew 14-year-old Caesarion, the son of Cleopatra and Julius Caesar. Octavian was propelled into a position to become sole consul. Octavian and his commander Agrippa entered Rome triumphantly and the Roman Senate elected them both to dual consulships. Throughout the region, Octavian cruelly destroyed all his enemies. By August 29 B.C.E., the successive battles in the civil war had come to a halt. Rome celebrated his triumph with a great celebration. He entered the royal city through the famed gateway. During ceremonies he closed the doors of Temple of Janus, which housed the two-faced statue-god which represented a new beginning, and marked a return to internal stability. According to Roman tradition, the temple doors were opened during times of bloodshed and closed during times of peace.

On January 16, 27 B.C.E. Octavian was given two new titles: One was *Augustus*, meaning *increase or the illustrious one*, and the other was *Princep*, meaning *the first head, the most powerful leader of Senate*. From this point, Octavian received his throne name of Augustus Caesar, "the Commander Caesar, son of the deified One." A crown with purple drapes were hung over his office door. He was given the golden shield normally encased in the halls of the Roman Senate. Augustus's financial power also greatly increased. He divided power among the consulship and the Senate, however, he still skillfully retained complete control over legion forces and the client states. By July 1, 23 B.C.E. the full powers of judicial authority along with a perpetual consulship was granted to him. In public he wore the imperial Roman insignia while clothed in a purple robe and the civic crown. On March 6, 12 B.C.E. co-consul and high priest Marcus Aemilius Lepidus died. Augustus assumed his position as the new Pontifex Maximus where he presided over the religious affairs of ancient Rome. Throughout Greece and Asia Minor several city-states built temples in honor of Rome where they deified Augustus as a god. In many city-states where Seleucid and Ptolemic kings were once esteemed as god-kings, divine beings, or sons of God, the worship of Augustus replaced those ruler cults. This new development created the merger of Roman and ancient Grecian culture, birthing what is now known as Greco-Roman culture. From the provinces of Western Europe to the Mediterranean world, the Rome standard [Pax Romana] was the new center of world power with Augustus being heralded as the sole master.

Internally, Augustus initiated reforms to bring internal stability, halt misgoverning, and reduced corruption. His improvements included the development of a network of royal Roman roads, a postal courier service, creation of a civil administration of career public servants who served for long periods of time. These new actions held the empire together, laying the foundation for a civil service force of police and fire-fighters which eventually became a standard among all Roman city-states in the western provinces. Augustus also reformed the Senate by dividing control between the two branches of power—consul and Senate. Militarily, Augustus built a unified military command for his professional military force of 300,000 soldiers who were exclusively loyal to the Roman state. The new structure prevented mutiny by individual imperial governors and their standing armies. The permanent army also served as a buffer on the frontier edges of the empire to prevent barbarian invasions in the western provinces. In the far east, the army was a deterrent to the Parthians and Armenians.

In the western provinces, the Roman legions organized magistrates and councils to attempt to civilize the masses of Germanic barbarians beyond the Danube River. The Romans also built urban cities in the netherlands where they colonized the hill people. Eventually, those hordes became Romanized over periods of time. Those once primitive Aryan nomads evolved to be the people now known as Western Europeans today.

For the next two decades Augustus Caesar reigned as the head of the Roman Empire.

In the year of 19 B.C.E. Rome had become a cesspool of wickedness with rampant sexual perverseness, adultery, incest, sodomy, and debauchery. Even Caesar Augustus, who was married three times and divorced twice, and widely known for his effeminacy, womanizing, and love of little girls and young boys, was prompted to command the Senate to pass legislation to rein in widespread adultery and open fornication. He also attempted to control excessive and extravagant spending in the royal capital.

By the year of 16/15 B.C.E. the Roman legions were conducting military expeditions into western areas now known as Switzerland, Austria, Germany in the west. Rome expanded the frontiers of the empire into the upper Danube River to subdue the Germanic barbarian hordes. On the eastern European frontier in areas now known as Croatia, Serbia, and Hungary, Augustus appointed his stepson Tiberius to serve as commander. His other stepson Drusus was leader of the western campaigns. He advanced both grown stepsons to the position of chief commander. Drusus died after being thrown from his horse. Tiberius left his post to be by his brother's side in his final days in 9 B.C.E.. Tiberius replaced him as the commander of the western forces. Caesar Augustus was now 69-years-old and aging. He held a great celebration for his adoptive stepson Lucius Caesar. Lucius Caesar was one of the sons of his deceased best friend Marcus Agrippa. It appeared the sons of his best friend Agrippa were favored over the sons of his wife Livia. To appease his other adoptive son Tiberius, Augustus made him the Tribune of the Roman Senate, a position which gave him great power. But this did not satisfy Tiberius, and in the year of 5 B.C.E., he retired from public office and left Rome for the island of Rhodes. However, a few years later both adoptive sons died. First, Gauias Caesar, who was only 24, died in 4 C.E., and his younger 20-year-old brother Luicus died in the city of Mars two years later in the year 2. After those developments, Tiberius was summoned to return from self-imposed retirement. During this same time his daughter named Julia was banished from her father's Augustus presence because of her widely known open sexual activities. She had many lovers while Tiberius was away in retirement. Augustus forced his adoptive son Tiberius to marry his daughter Julia, who happened to be Tiberius step-sister as well. Neither one of them wanted the marriage. Tiberius had already been married to one of Marcus Agrippa's daughters. Before Marcus Agrippa's death, Julia had already been his wife. Because of her promiscuity, Augustus once described his own daughter as "a disease to my flesh." To be totally honest, the pleasure in the palace of Augustus was no less infectious than the abhorrent behavior of his daughter Julia.

Outside his royal residence young men and women would dress up as spring goddesses. As the guests arrived at the royal gates, the young boys and girls, who were known as nymphs and coquettes, would openly prostitute themselves for a fee. There was unrestrained and excessive indulgence of all manner of sexual desires. There were small rooms in secluded nearby retreats known as "nooks".

Inside the imperial clifftop villa there were tables of the finest wines, foods, and pleasures served by nude handmaidens. There was no restraint to the type of sexual activities the guests would indulge in. Gross sensuality and lewdness was the hallmark of those types of gatherings throughout Italy and the Roman Empire.

So it came to pass that Caesar Augustus, who was born Gaius Octavius, died at the age of 75 on August 19, 14 C.E.. He had reigned for 41 years doing evil in **the eyes of YHWH, the CREATOR of the heavens, earth, seas, and all therein.** He walked in the ways of the heathens according to the abominable manner of Greco-Roman rulers that had preceded him. He served all the pantheon of the ancient Roman image-gods. It has been recorded that he died of natural causes, however, there have been unconfirmed rumors for ages that his wife Livia may have poisoned him. His adoptive son Tiberius succeeded him as emperor in the great city that sitteth upon seven hills.

Tiberius Caesar
(14—37 C.E.)

Tiberius Claudis Nero was born on November 16, 42 B.C.E. as the son of Tiberius Claudis Nero and Livia Drusilla. While he was a young lad his mother divorced his father in favor of an adulterous relationship with Octavian, who later became known as Emperor Augustus Caesar. That marriage is how Tiberius became the adoptive son with the new name of Tiberius Julius Caesar. At the tender age of 9 he delivered the eulogy for his biological father at the rosta in Rome. The Rosta was a large platform built during Republican and Imperial days of Roman rule. Speakers would stand on the podium to deliver public speeches before crowds in the royal city. At the age of 13 he was allowed to ride with Augustus in the triumphal chariot in celebration of the defeat of the Mark Anthony and Queen Cleopatra at Actium. As a young man he married Agrippina, who was the daughter of Marcus Vipsanius Agrippa, a great general and close friend of Augustus Caesar. In the year of 24 B.C.E. his adoptive father Agustus appointed him to the position of quaestor handling various financial affairs for the emperor. He was also granted the right to compete in the elections for the position of praetor and consul. Tiberius was only 18 or 19 years-old when he began to work inside the government. Eventually, he began military duty and by the year of 20 B.C.E. he was assigned to the Roman legions stationed in the East under the command of his father-in-law Marcus Agrippa. There he began to distinguish himself as a great soldier. The Parthians had previously defeated the Roman legions. After a year of negotiations, Tiberius led a massive army into Armenia to secure the eastern frontier of the Roman-Parthian border. During these years, he served in military expeditions to subdue hostile hordes in territories now known as Croatia, Serbia, and Hungary. Augustus also appointed two other stepsons, who were grown men, as the leaders of Germania campaigns. His other stepson Drusus was the chief commander of those western campaigns. However, Drusus died after being thrown from his horse. Augustus replaced Drusus with his brother Tiberius, who was emerging as one of great generals of the ancient empire. Tiberius also fought the barbarian hordes in the Alps and the Transalpine Gaul. Those people eventually became known as the French.

General Marcus Agrippa, the best friend of Augustus Caesar, died in 12 B.C.E. at the age of 51 in the city of Campania. Tiberius had already been elected as consul during the previous year. General Marcus Agrippa had been married to Augustus's daughter Julia. But after Agrippa's death, Augustus forced his adoptive son Tiberius to divorce Agrippina, the daughter of his deceased general, and remarry his daughter Julia. Remember, Tiberius had already been married to Agrippa's daughter Agrippina. Thus, Tiberius had married both the widow, Julia, and the daughter, Agrippina, of the same man during his lifetime. That also made Tiberius both the adoptive son and son-of-law of Augustus. It was a known fact that Julia was publicly promiscuous with many lovers. She had already made sexual advances towards Tiberius while she was still married to her former husband. In Rome, adultery and incest were standard practices. It had also been said that neither Tiberius nor Julia really wanted to marry. Augustus, using his absolute authority, forced the pair to unite in an union that was openly turbulent. Tiberius found himself married to a woman he hated, who publicly shamed him with night time affairs in the Roman Forum. Meanwhile, Tiberius was forbidden to see the woman he truly loved. One day, Tiberius ran into his former wife Agrippina in public. He followed her home crying and begging forgiveness. After Augustus Caesar learned of this encounter, he summoned Tiberius to the palace. Steps were taken so that the two would never run-in to each other or meet again. Tiberius was brokenhearted, longing for his former wife Agrippina. After that experience, Tiberius became dark and reclusive. There were also another problem for Tiberius. He became insecure and jealous of Agrippa's two sons which Augustus also adopted. He feared he would be swept aside in favor of one of them. It was for those reasons Tiberius left Rome for a self-imposed exile on the famous island of Rhodes. After living there for a while he longed to return, but Augustus denied him the right to return. However, two tragic incidents occurred during Tiberius absence. In the year of 2 C.E. Luicus

Agrippa, the 20-year-old younger adoptive son of Augustus Caesar died in the city of Mars. Two years later in 4 C.E. his 24-year-old adoptive brother Gaius Caesar Agrippa also died. After this Tiberius was allowed to return to Rome where he received tribunal powers. Meanwhile, Julia, the daughter of Augustus Caesar and the second wife of Tiberius, was banished from Rome by her own father because of her outlandish conduct.

By the year of 13 C.E. Tiberius power was elevated to status of co-princep which was equal to Emperor Augustus. Almost eight years later, he was assigned to the role of Tribune in the Roman Senate which greatly increased his personal power and influence. In early 14 C.E., crown prince Tiberius was recalled from a mission back to Rome. The Emperor Augustus was seriously ill in the last days of life. Tiberius spent the whole day with his ailing stepfather. On August 19, 14 C.E., at the age of 75, Augustus Caesar died. He was buried in a regal ceremony which had been pre-arranged. In death, he was deified as a god. During the funeral his will was read. Tiberius was declared the heir to the throne. One month later on September 18, the Senate convened to confirm Tiberius' position as the new Princep. Augustus accomplished his goal of peacefully handing authority to a successor. All the powers of Augustus were smoothly extended to him. Unaccustomed to public adulation, Tiberius initially refused to accept the civic crown and laurels as the emblems of his new authority. This refusal was an awkward beginning for many in the Senate. It actually dampen the tone between the two branches of power.

Initially, Tiberius started out as a passive leader who wanted the Senate to act independently of his authority. In the days of Augustus, who was an aggressive leader, the Senate served as the emperor's personal tool. Tiberius wanted to transfer civil responsibility to the Senate. Tiberius once complained, the Senate was an institution *"full of men fit to be slaves."* This criticism came amidst his struggle to motivate the Senate to abandon its self-imposed subservience to his office of Princep. Shortly after the beginning of his reign, Tiberius experienced a mutiny by the Roman legions stationed in Pannonea and Germania. The troops were angry because they had not received pay bonuses promised by Augustus before his death. In response, Tiberius dispatched a small elite force to quell the rebellion. His son Drusus Julius Caesar and another general named Germanicus led the emperor's forces. By 17 C.E. the rebellion was squashed. Rome celebrated the western frontier victories with full ceremonies. After those victories, General Germanicus was awarded complete control over the eastern parts of empire to secure those borders. One year later, General Germanicus mysteriously died from poisoning. Some suspected Emperor Tiberius of being jealous of Germanicus' rising popularity. They accused him of orchestrating the incident. Another memorable event that occurred in the year 17 C.E. was the great earthquake in the Asia Minor that destroyed the city-state of Smyrna. Tiberius completely restored the city to its former glory. As a sign of gratitude, the rulers of Smyrna built a marbled statue honoring Tiberius as a god. By 22 C.E. Tiberius became more withdrawn from day-to-day governance. He started to share tribunal authority with his son Drusus. Drusus also became commander of the annual campaigns into Campania, but he too died mysteriously in the following year. After his son's death, Emperor Tiberius elevated his Praetorian Prefect Luicus Aeluis Sejanus to co-regent status. Tiberius referred to him as *Socius Laborum* (**Partner of my Labours**). Sejanus became more and more visible, replacing the face of Tiberius as he withdrew from public appearances. This time he retired to the island of Capri. He appointed Sejanus as the chief of daily operations for the entire Roman state. Queen Mother Livia was the only pillar of power that challenged Sejanus political designs. Nevertheless, Sejanus moved to purge his opponents with public trials against senators and wealthy equestrians. Eventually he removed all people who were capable of opposing his power. At the same time, Sejanus increased his own treasury. It appears Sejanus attempted to gain total supreme authority for himself. He even restationed the loyal Praetorian guards in Rome as part of his scheme to consolidate his control. Tiberius had trusted Sejanus to be his personal agent to wield power for him, not replace him. Although Tiberius refused to re-enter Rome again, he still closely monitored public affairs. So, Sejanus overplayed his hand, and in the year 31 C.E. his plot was exposed. He was subpoenaed before a Senatorial meeting. The official letter (epistle) from Emperor

Tiberius was read aloud. It condemned Sejanus and called for his immediate execution. Sejanus was then placed on trial along with several of his friends and cohorts. The following week Sejanus was executed. After that, a politician named Naevius Satorius Marco replaced Sejanus as the chief operating officer. This time the recluse Roman emperor kept an even closer eye on the politics of Rome. When a financial crisis occurred in 33 C.E., he intervened to save the Roman economy. He also crushed rebellions in the provinces of Gaul, Africa and Thrace with an **iron fist**.

Meanwhile in the tranquility of the city of Capri, Tiberius, who was known to engage in homosexual relationships, presided over a sexually devious palace where sexual inmates, consisting of men, boys, and girls, were collected from throughout the empire. Those sexual mates were interned in a private sporting house used for the emperor's fetishes. They knew what was expected of them. At the same time, naked waitresses served the royal guests. There were also nearby groves that were filled with boys and girls who solicited money from palace visitors in exchange for sex. Inside the palace Tiberius had little boys known as "tiddlers" who teased him with oral sexual favors as he swam in the palace pool. Tiberius, who was known as the old goat, had a secret team of anal and oral sexual experts, who were paid by the government that gratified him with all types of deviant sexual escapades. These palace servants, known as the Spintriae, would regularly masturbate in front of him to excite him. Tiberius also had a team of unweaned babies that sucked his penis as if the infants were breastfeeding. On his bedroom wall, he laced the quarters with exotic pictures of the Grecian gods Atalanta and Meleagar performing oral sex. There he maintained an erotic library filled with manuals from Elephantis, Egypt depicting sexual positions and other pornographic paintings. It was also reported that Emperor Tiberius was known to rape male performers during religious ceremonies.

And it came to pass that Emperor Tiberius, who was born Tiberius Claudius Nero, died on March 16, 37 C.E. at the age of 78 in a villa in Misenum, Italy after reigning for twenty-two years. He was interned in the Mausoleum of Augustus in the great city of Rome. He had walked in all the manner of the Greco-Roman rulers that had preceded him doing evil in the eyes of **YHWH, the CREATOR of the heavens, earth, seas, and all therein**. He served all the traditional pantheon of ancient Roman image-gods. He was succeeded by his great nephew and adoptive grandson Caligula.

Caligula
(37—41 C.E.)

Caligula [Ca-ligu-la] was born with the birth name Gaius Julius Caesar Germanicus on August 31, 12 C.E. in Antium, Italy as the maternal son of General Germanicus Julius Caesar and Vipsania Agrippina, common referred to as Agrippina the Elder. His father had been a popular general who led successful campaigns against Gothic hordes. He later led military missions in the east where he died in Antioch, Syria in the year 19 C.E.. Some sources accused Emperor Tberius of contriving his death by sending one of his agents to Syria to poison him. In the eyes of Tiberius, Germanicus popularity made him a potential rival, and after all, he married his ex-wife Vipsania Agrippina. During this time, Caligula was a 2 or 3 year-old young lad who accompanied his father Germanicus on missions in the north near Germania. His father's comrades began to view him as their mascot. He wore a miniature soldier's outfit with boots and armor. He became known as *"caligula"* which meant *"little soldier's boot"*.

After the death of his father Germanicus, his mother Agrippina along with her six children returned to Rome. A bitter feud broke out between his mother Agrippina and Emperor Tiberius which sunk family relations to a new low. The king would not allow Agrippina to remarry, fearing her new husband would represent a new threat to him. By 29 C.E., his mother and brothers had been imprisoned where they eventually died. Caligula, the sole male survivor, became an orphan. He was sent to live with his great-grandmother Livia, who happened to be Tiberius mother. It came to pass that his great-grandmother Livia died and

Caligula was sent to live with Livia's daughter which was his aunt Antonia. Antonia was the sister of Emperor Tiberius.

During his childhood Caligula was afflicted with a falling disease, known today as epileptic seizures. As emperor, he was known to talk to the full moon because in ancient Rome, epilepsy was long thought to be associated with the moon.

The historian Suetonius also reported, that after the banishment of Caligula's mother and brothers, the young Caligula and his sisters became child inmates of Tiberius detained by Roman soldiers by the year of 31 C.E. It is reasonable to assume that Caligula and his sisters were sex toys for the depraved emperor. Tiberius was known for his sexual perversion, especially on the island of Capri. Caligula adapted well by being a good actor. He never displayed open animosity towards the emperor although he had cut off his father. It was said, *"never was there a better servant*[**Caligula**] *or a worst master*[**Tiberius**]*."*

In the year 33, Tiberius appointed Caligula to the honorary position of quaestor. He maintained that position until his ascension as emperor four years later in the year 37. Tiberius never considered Caligula as a possible heir because he was paranoid over the fact of what he had done to his family. However, one of Tiberius trusted officers named Naevius Sutorius Marco, who had exposed the mutinous plot of Sejanus, spoke well of Caligula in the ears of Tiberius. Tiberius had appointed Marco as the new chief of staff after he directed the purge against Sejanus and his allies. After his recommendation, the loyalty of Caligula was never questioned in the mind of Tiberius.

Nevertheless, at one point, it was said Caligula had in fact planned to avenge the blood of his family. He allegedly came into the bedroom with a dagger, but once in the bedroom, he threw the dagger down on the floor and fled. Some allege Tiberius knew of this episode, but never mentioned it to his confused male lover and adoptive grand nephew. In the year of 35, Caligula was named joint-heir to the throne by Emperor Tiberius along with his cousin Tiberius Gemeluis. Two years later, Tiberius became extremely ill. According to the Roman historian Tacitus, crown prince Caligula, under the supervision of Naevius Sutorius Marco, took power immediately in early March before actually confirming the death of Tiberius. Tiberius was very ill and persistently deteriorating. Tiberius was even heard summoning food. Fearing a backlash and embarrassment if Tiberius recovered, Marco ordered a huge pillow of clothes placed on his face and suffocated him. *(It's amazing how history repeats itself over and over again. This exact act occurred centuries earlier during the reign of King Benhadad II of Syria when crown prince Hazael smothered his leader to death).* **Read 2 Kings 8:15** which reads: "And it came to pass on the morrow, that he took a thick cloth, and dipped it in water, and spread it on his face, so that he[**Benhadad**] died: Hazael reigned in his stead.") Other historians have disagreed with this account and contend Emperor Tiberius died from natural causes. Either way, Tiberius died on March 16, 37 C.E. in Misenum, Italy at the age of 78. Caligula was immediately chosen as the successor. After promising Marco the post of consulship over Egypt as a reward for his role in the deadly act, Caligula had him arrested in the port city of Ostia as he embarked for the land of Kemet. His wife accompanied him on the journey, but she was released. Shortly thereafter, Marco committed suicide while in custody. To be completely honest, this was the second time that Caligula had double-crossed Marco. He had already had an adulterous affair with his wife back in 34 C.E., but Marco turned a blind eye and forgave him hoping to get closer to the pleasures of the ruling family. In his will, Marco left a large donation for the construction of an amphitheater for his hometown of Alba Fucens.

Nevertheless, twelve days later on March 28, Caligula accepted the powers of the Principate which were formally conferred upon him. The new 24-year-old leader entered Rome in the midst of celebrations and throngs of well-wishers. He was hailed as *"our baby and our star."* For three months there were public parties with nearly 200,000 animals sacrificed in the royal city. Caligula was the first Roman leader to enjoy support throughout the entire empire from the outset of his reign. He was very popular and beloved by almost everyone because he was the son of the famous general Germanicus.

The first six months of his reign were marked by his noble and moderate leadership, but after adjusting to his new role as emperor he veered towards a path of ruthlessness, sadism, extravagance, and sexual perversion. He worked to increase his powers to the point that he held unconstrained power that railed against all opposing powers. Absolute power corrupted Caligula more and more, leading him to conceive himself a living god. Nevertheless, Caligula was a sickly man who became ill after eight months of sitting on the throne. Remember, he had already been known to suffer from epileptic seizures since childhood. He couldn't even learn to swim as a child although swimming was a requirement in Roman imperial education. His physical disability prevented that. It is believed that this psychologically drove him to always prove his machoism. That, along with his personal insecurity, drove him insane. After recovering from the brief illness, Caligula started murdering those close to him and exiling others. The odd behavior caused feuds with the Roman Senate. That is why most historians from his era accused him of being mad, arrogant, always angry, and insulting.

Otherwise, his rule was known as an era of empire expansion. The Roman legions annexed the kingdom of Mauretania in northwest Africa as a province. The empire also expanded into Britain through military excursions. Internally, Caligula launched several massive interior construction projects, including the Great Obelisk which he brought from Egypt to Rome. This was one of his centerpiece projects which stood in the midst of a large chariot racing stadium in the center of the Imperial City. There, he also held expensive and lavish spectacles for the Roman public, including gladiator games as well. He also built a luxurious palace and massive aqueducts in Rome. He built several fancy yachts for his personal pleasure. He was known to love expensive clothes and he was very fond of expensive shoes. He even went so far as to build a miniature palace for his favorite horse and declared the horse stable as an office consulship with full powers.

Another major move Caligula made during his brief reign was his destruction of the Tiberius treason papers, declaring that era as a thing of the past. He even recalled those who had been sent into exile. He initiated a tax reform plan that helped those who had been overburdened by the imperial tax system. During his four-year reign, he also brought the remains of his mother and brothers back to Rome placing them in Tomb of Augustus in Rome. Although, Caligula was a sexual deviant in his own right, he still banished certain sexual perverts from the royal city. It has been reported that Caligula was sexually active from his early Roman childhood. He was said to have engaged in sexual intercourse with all three of his sisters and even his niece. His sister Drusilla was a young virgin when he took her virginity as a teenager. His grandmother caught him having sex with another sister named Antonia. Those sexual escapades continued well into the girl's adulthood, and didn't stop even after they were married. He was known to engage in homosexual affairs with several men, including actors and other noblemen as well. He spent his nights in unrestrained glutton orgies where he sometimes dressed as a woman. As I said earlier, Caligula, the one-man ruler, became a megalomaniac who viewed himself as a living deity. It was also said he would sit in temple to be worshipped as a god, receiving offerings and adulation. In Roman mythology, the bloody-mouthed god Jupiter was believed to have ripped open and eaten the fetus of his own child by his sister-god. Some historical accounts have accused Caligula of imitating this action of the image-god Jupiter in real life. He even ordered a bridge to be built that extended from his palace to the Temple of Jupiter.

Regardless, the actions of Caligula were separating him from the people. He isolated himself inside his fortress-palace. The Roman citizens began to hate their emperor, whispering against him while fearing his erratic behavior at the same time. In his paranoia he reimposed the treason trials and began a purge that put many people to death. Meanwhile he loved to watch the slow agonizing tortures and executions.

By now a conspiracy had been put in place. A gang from among the Praetorian Guard ranks along with certain senators who wanted to restore the Roman Republic, some of his own slaves, and others who bore grudges formulated a plot to assassinate Caligula. The bloody scheme was set in place on January 24, 41 C.E. and led by a certain chief palace guard named General Cassius Chaerea. That evening, Caligula attended the Palatine Games first and afterwards he went to the theater. Later that night, Caligula was caught alone and stabbed 30 times and bludgeoned to death. Some gossipers reported that the assassins savagely ate parts of his flesh. His wife and son were also slain and their remains were dumped in a shallow grave. The emperor was dead, but the plans of the plotters did not materialize. On the same exact date of the slaying of the king, the majority members of the Roman Senate and leadership of the Praetorian Guard hastily declared Caligula's uncle named Claudius as the new emperor. After that, the Senate approved an order to destroy all statues previously erected in honor of the fallen ruler, hoping to erase his legacy from the annals of Roman history.

So it came to pass that Emperor Caligula Caesar, who was born as Gaius Julius Caesar Germanicus, was bludgeoned to death at the age of 28 after reigning nearly fours years, 3-yrs. and 10 months to be exact, on the throne of Rome. He came to power on March 18, 37 C.E. and ceased on January 24, 41 C.E. Before his death, Caligula's corrupt mind and benighted lips once uttered these ungodly words: *"I have existed from the morning of the world and I shall exist until the last star falls from the night. Although I have taken the form of Gaius Caligula, I am all men, as I am no man, and therefore I am a God."* But Caligula died like all mortal men who had reigned before him. In **chapter 14 verses 12 through 15** ancient Hebrew prophet **Isaiah** spoke against the pagan mentality of rulers like the Roman emperors when he prophesied, "*How art you fallen from heaven, O Lucifer, son of the morning! how art you cut down to the ground, which did weaken the nations! For you have said in your heart* [**Caligula**], *I will ascend into heaven, I will exalt my throne above the stars of God*[YAH]; *I will sit also upon the mount of the congregation, in the sides of the north. I will ascend above the heights of the clouds; I will be like the Most High, yet you shall be brought down to hell, to the sides of the pit."*

Caligula had walked in all the abhorrent practices of the Greco-Roman rulers that preceded him serving all the graven-image gods of the Roman religion. He knew not YAH. And it came to pass that Claudius Caesar assumed the mantle of power in the Imperial City that ruled the entire world from the British Isles to Asia Minor, and the far east.

Claudius
(41—54 C.E.)

Emperor Claudius was born with the name of Tiberius Claudius Drusus on August 1, in the year of 10 B.C.E. as the son of his father Nero Claudius Drusus Germanicus and his mother Antonia Minor. He was the first Roman emperor born outside of mainland Italy. He was born in the province of Gaul (modern France) in the ancient city of Lugdunum (modern Lyons). His father Germainicus was a popular general who died from an illness in year of 9 B.C.E. while on a military campaign in Germania leaving behind two sons: Germanicus[Jr.] and Claudius. Beginning at a young age, his older brother Germanicus began to walk in the ways of his father, a renown and great soldier known for his valor. Claudius was different—the ugly duckling. He was a sickly cast away child known to foam at the mouth. He had a running nose and walked with a limp. He was known to be hard of hearing, probably because he was partially deaf in one ear. He was kept out of the sight of the Roman public as a youth because he was handicapped. He was only a 1-year-old when his father Germanicus died. His mother Antonia did not like him, publicly calling him a monster and stupid. In her eyes he was an embarrassment, completely opposite of his father and older brother. She eventually sent him away to be raised by his grandmother Livia, who was the sister of Julius Caesar. She thought he lacked will-power due to laziness. She too frowned upon him and hired a former mule-driver to teach him the necessary discipline for a member of the royal family. In the year 4 C.E., Uncle Tiberius adopted Claudius.

By his teenage years, he showed signs of discipline and the proper mindset. His family started to notice his scholarly capabilities. At the age 17, Claudius was studying under the famous philosophers Sulpicius Flavius and Athenodorus where he received praise as a talented student. He also became a student of Roman history, writing about the Civil War.

Claudius pursuit of academics, along with his lifelong sickness, kept him in the right place at the right time, away from the center of political drama, infighting, and even bloodshed. For most of his life, he was left alone in the background.

When Emperor Augustus died in 14 C.E., Claudius was then a twenty-three year-old. He was chosen to head the knights at the funeral procession. His uncle Emperor Tiberius, who was his father's brother, had assumed the mantle of Caesar. Claudius petitioned him for a position with the cursus honorum. The cursus honorum was the Roman Empire chain-of-command for obtaining political offices. Many aspiring public servants obtained their appointments to roles as military tribune, praetor, aedile, or quaestor through that system. Tiberius gave his nephew some token royal consular ornaments, but snubbed him, refusing to grant him an entry level job. Instead, Tiberius assigned his unfavored nephew to the position of the low level priesthood. After that, Claudius heavily indulged himself in drinking, gambling, and chasing women. Besides that he returned to his scholarly pursuits and gave up hopes of ever becoming a Roman statesman. By now, certain officials had begun to notice Claudius. They lobbied the Emperor requesting that Claudius be granted the right to debate in the General Assembly. Tiberius also turned that request down. When Claudius house burned down, the Senate agreed to rebuild his residence, but his uncle vetoed against that measure as well.

However, as fate would have it, 23 years later, near the fifth year of his reign the new Emperor Caligula, who happened to be his younger nephew, selected his older uncle Claudius to his first public position as co-consul in the year 37C.E. Claudius was now a 47-year-old middle-aged man. Although Caligula was younger, Claudius continued to face constant degradation from Caligula, his younger relative. For example, Claudius was known to dose-off during royal banquets. When he did fall asleep, Caligula would urge the guests to throw olives and dates at him for laughs. That type of treatment kept Claudius out the public eye where he still concentrated on his writing ability. He wrote volumes on Etruscan history, early Roman Republic history, and Roman and Carthage wars.

The four year reign of Caligula came to an end on the evening of January 24, 41 C.E. The conspirators inside the Praetorian Guard who desired to restore the Roman Republic joined forces with a group of senators. It was said that some of his own slaves, and others, who bore grudges also participated in the assassination plot. Afterwards, his wife and child were brutally murdered inside the imperial palace. During the palace coup, a frightened Claudius ran for his life and hid behind curtains on a balcony in the theater. The usurpers searched the theater and found Claudius, but instead of slaying him, they saluted him as Rome's newly chosen ruler. Many senators did not like what happened, but they were forced to accept the terms of the bloody coup and agree to amnesty for the plotters.

Upon assuming the throne at the age of 50, Claudius strengthened his position. He granted clemency to all those who participated in the assassination of Caligula. He also issued a new coin with the image of the goddess Pax Nemesis on one side. In Roman mythology, the idol Pax Nemesis represented subdued vengeance and mercy. To secure his position, Claudius strategically emphasized his connection to the Julio-Claudius lineage. He chose the title Caesar. He also used the title of Augustus in his throne name just as both of his predecessors Caligula and Tiberius had done. Therefore his complete throne name was Tiberius Claudius Augustus Caesar Germanicus. After that, he commissioned the building of a marbled statue of his grandmother Livia, who was one of the wives of the late emperor Augustus Caesar. He also publicly reminded the populace that his late brother Germanicus was a mighty warrior for the empire.

Unlike his predecessors, Claudius became a hands on chief justice who was imitately involved in daily legal cases of the Roman judicial system. However, Roman historians reported, Claudius was easily swayed and inconsistent in his rulings. He was not known for establishing one uniform code of law. For example, in the matter of the Temple of Aesculapius [*pronounced* Ae-scu-la-pi-us], there was a dispute over the treatment of slaves by their evilhearted rich slaveowners. Claudius sided with the slaves. This was the case: The Temple of Aesculapius was located on Tiber Island. Slaveowners used the location as a dumping ground to abandon their sick slaves instead of providing medical assistance, some of the masters killed their slaves. On the other hand, if the slaves recovered from their illness, the owners came back and re-enslaved the survivors. Claudius ruled against the slavemasters. He decreed that slavemasters should be charged with murder and the slaves who recovered should be automatically freed.

Internationally, Claudius was known to be directly involved in many final decisions abroad. He arbitrated grievances in far away provinces, such as the Letter to the Alexandrians. In the epistle, Claudius settled an argument between the Greeks and the Afro-Asiatic Israelites. During this time there was a great migration of black Yehudees(Jews) to Egypt due to the Romanization of the holy land. The Aryan Greeks wanted to halt this influx of new immigrants. Claudius upheld the rights of the Israelites to move into Egypt (Africa), but he also decreed that the Israelites could not move into the Euro-Ptolemaic capital of Alexandria en masse. That decision upheld a population balance between the two ethnicities. In fact, Claudius was regarded as a fair leader among the Euro-Judaic converts who controlled Jerusalem and Judaea as a province of the Roman Empire. Israelites also benefited from Claudius tolerance of Judaic culture as well. Mauretania, in northwest Africa, became a province during his reign. Lycia, in Asia Minor, was also annexed by Claudius. Thrace, in southeast Europe, came under Rome's the **iron rule**.

In Rome, Emperor Claudius, who was once regarded as a dimwitted object of scorn, proved to be a clever and capable leader. He avoided confrontations with the Roman Senate. He purchased the loyalty of the Praetorian Guards with an offering a 15,000 sesterces for each man. Those who once thought his disabilities would make him vulnerable or weak found out differently. It appeared his ailments may have improved after he assumed the mantle of power. He later told his confidants that he used to pretend to be a dumb weakling to protect himself.

Inspite of his appeasement towards the Senate, he still face opposition from some who viewed him as an illegitimate leader. He spent the majority of his 13-year reign dodging murder plots and bickering with the Roman Senate. In response, Claudius killed many senators for disrespect. In terms of foreign policy, he launched one of the most expansive 1st century military campaigns into the far away province of Britain. It was the first attempt by the Roman legions to conquer the territory. In 43 C.E., he assembled a force of 40,000 soldiers along with war elephants to cross the English Channel. Claudius also visited the frontline of Britain for 16 days. After returning to Rome, he received a hero's welcome. Now he was known as the strong leader *"who brought the barbarian people beyond the Ocean for the first time under Rome's sway."* By the year of 49 he married again. This time he became intimate with his niece named Agrippina the Younger who had already pregnant with a child named Nero from her previous marriage. Claudius had already married a woman named Messalina nine years earlier. After becoming the emperor, he murdered her because she was scheming to murder him.

During his reign, Claudius greatly improved the Imperial City. By the year of 52, he built two famous aqueducts known as Aqua Claudia and Porta Maggiore ("The Larger Gate") which guaranteed more abundant water supplies. Claudius also constructed many roads and canals across the empire. Throughout the time zone of **the kingdom of iron** Roman engineers constructed numerous aqueducts throughout Europe bringing water into cities and towns from distance sources. The water supplied public baths, latrines, sewers, foundations, and private households. Those aqueducts, which also supplied water for mining operations, cattle markets, milling, farming, and gardening, were made of stones, bricks, and concrete. Some were dug as tunnels while others were built on bridgework and carried through pipes made of lead, ceramic, or stones.

Emperor Claudius also improved sports and entertainment for the populace in the great city situated on seven hills. He sponsored and attended regular chariot races. He deeply loved gladiator competition. He stayed glued to his royal skybox seat for hours enjoying sadistic bloodshed. He cherished every moment of the competition, joining the audience to count aloud as gold pieces were paid to the victorious gladiators. For more pleasure, he once staged sea battle exercises consisting of 19,000 sailors in ships on Fucine Lake.

So it came to pass on October 3, 54 C.E. the 13-year reign of Emperor Claudius came to an end. His own niece-wife, Agrippina the Younger, poisoned him at the age of 63. Throughout his lifetime and during his thirteen-year reign **he did evil in the eyes of YHWH** serving all the graven images of the Greco-Roman pantheon. He knew not YAH instead he followed the abominations of the heathens. He was buried in the Mausoleum of Augustus in Rome, Italy. His adoptive son and nephew Nero succeeded him as the new Princep upon the throne of the Roman Empire.

Nero
(54 C.E.—68 C.E.)

Emperor Nero was born in Antium, Italy on December 15th in the year 37 C.E. with the birth name of Lucius Domitius[*pronounced* Do-mi-ti-us] Ahenobacbus[*pronounced* A-heno-ba-chus]. He was the biological son of Gnaeus Domitius and Agrippina the Younger. Now, Nero's father Gnaeus Domitius was the son of Marcus Agrippa, the trusted general of Augustus Caesar. Domitius's mother was Julia the Elder, the daughter of the late August Caesar. Domitius grew up and married a woman known as Agrippina the Younger who was the daughter of Germanicus, who was the brother of Emperor Claudius.

They became the parents of the future ruler who became the last Roman emperor connected to the Julio-Claudian dynasty.

In the beginning of his reign he assumed the throne name of Emperor Nero Claudius Caesar Augustus Germanicus. His father Domitius died in 40 C.E. when young Luicius [Nero] was only three years-old. So, his mother Agrippina raised him. She was very domineering and kept a tight rein over him. She remarried twice. Her second marriage came in the year 41 when she joined hands with a wealthy two-term consul named Gaius Sallustus Crispus Passienus. In her mid-30s and after a decree from the Roman Senate, she was allowed to marry her own uncle 59-year-old Emperor Claudius, who uncovered her nakedness. She became his fourth wife in the year 49. By then Nero was a 12-year-old. After the uncle-niece royal marriage, she persuaded Emperor Claudius into adopting her son. She also had the famous philosopher and historian Luicus Annaeus Seneca to return from exile to become Nero's private tutor. Emperor Claudius agreed to all her new moves. Claudius even recognized Nero as his new son and renamed him Nero Claudius Caesar Drusus Germanicus. He then publicly awarded Nero with the formal honor of heir. After that, Nero became very popular.

As a young lad, Nero had lived in poverty because his mother had been sentenced to exile on the island of Ponti. Her brother Emperor Caligula suspected her of treason. However, while his mother was in prison, Caligula was assassinated. Claudius released her once he came to power. The mother and son were reunited. Years later in the year 51, Nero began his political career at the age of 14. At age 16, he married his own step-sister Claudia Octavia, who was the daughter of Emperor Claudius.

It came to pass in the following year 54, Emperor Claudius was poisoned. Historians have implicated his new wife Agrippina as one of the co-conspirators. It's also been said that Agrippina became more powerful than 63-year-old frail Claudius himself. Agrippina still feared Claudius would choose his own biological child named Britiannicus instead of her son Nero. That fear motivated her to hatch a deadly plot. She also manipulated the Praetorian Guard, making sure her allies were in charge. Namely a man named Sextus Afranius Burrus, the Prefect, who would place Nero on the throne as the next emperor. Claudius had been murdered. Shortly afterwards, his son Britiannicus died after eating at a dinner party for the imperial family. He too was poisoned before reaching the age of manhood. So it came to pass that Nero came to power without incident on the date of October 13, 54 C.E. at the inexperienced age of only 17. For the next five years, his mother continued to serve as one of his chief counselors, continuing to smother him like a child although he was now the emperor. So, on March 23, 59 C.E. he turned against his mother and ordered her murder while she was in her villa in Balae, Italy.

It appeared the prediction of the Roman astrologers had come true. While Nero was growing up, his mother once sought counsel from diviners. The astrologers predicted that her son Nero would surely rise up and become the emperor, but they warned her, he would kill his mother. Her response: *"Let him kill me, provided he becomes emperor."* That is exactly what happened. After the death of his mother Agrippina, Nero began to exert more authority over kingdom affairs. Under his command, General Corbulo led the Roman legions in a successful campaign against the kingdom of Parthia. In Britain, General Paulinus also squashed a barbarian rebellion. Now in his mid-20s, Nero began to concentrate on trade, foreign relations, and improving society. He commissioned the building of theaters, chariot racing stadiums, and a host of other athletic games. In fact, Emperor Nero loved pleasure. The young ruler was known for his public participation as a theatrical playwright actor, poet, musician, and charioteer. Many of the old-fashioned Roman politicans and arisocrats saw Nero's action as a desecration of the royal standard.

Meanwhile, Nero spent lavishly on empire-wide programs for private individuals and the public. Those massive spending projects forced him to increase taxes on the upper and middle class. They became discontented. Even his courtiers devised several assassination attempts against the crown. Each time the plots were discovered and the culprits were put to death. By the year 62, this treachery caused Emperor Nero to reconvene treason trials against his political foes. Many of his political rivals were put to death. He even forced his former counselor and tutor, Luicus Annaeus Seneca, to commit suicide.

He killed his wife Octavia, accusing her of lesbianism and adulterous affairs. Nero castrated a younger male named Sporus, turned him into a female, and married him as a wife. He also joined hands with his male cupbearer named Pythagoras in unholy matrimony. As a Roman youth, Nero had been involved in same- sex eromenos[child]-erastes[adult] relationships. As an adult ruler, he openly practiced homosexuality, bestiality, and other forms of sexual perversions. One example of his perverseness was the relationship with the man named Sporus whom I just mentioned. In Nero's pschye, the man resembled his second wife, so he married the man, had him castrated and made into palace eunuch where he was used as his sexual partner until he murdered him.

Rome experienced a devastating tragedy on July 18/19, 64 C.E. when a devastating 7-day fire broke out in the Imperial City. The blaze started on the slopes of the Aventine Hill, which is one of the seven mountains of great city. The fire totally consumed the Circus Maximus, scores of mansions, royal residences, and several of the temples dedicated to the gods. The damage in Rome extended over towards the Palatine Hill. Three of the city's fourteen districts were totally consumed and 7 others suffered severe damage. Some thought Nero ordered the fire so he could rebuild Rome in his own image. Others maintained the fire was purely accidental. Regardless, Emperor Nero blamed the new Christian cult as the culprits behind the deadly fire. He then instituted a new policy of persecution of the worshippers of Jesus. Many were rounded up and fed to the dogs and lions. Others were crucified and tortured.

After that, Nero started a massive rebuilding program. He built a 100 to 300-acre palatial complex, beginning with the Golden House known as the Domus Aurea which included elegant landscaping. He also built a 100-ft. tall bronze statue known as the Colossus of Nero, glorifying himself as the sun god Sol. *(Remember, King Nebuchadnezzar of Babylon did that same thing in* **chapter 3** *of the book of* **Daniel**). Emperor Nero's main focus was on Rome where he spent extravagantly to restore the Imperial City to its former glory. His steady renovations eventually caused financial strains in the empire. Nero placed heavy tax burdens on his subjects in the provinces who were already experiencing hardships. Meanwhile, there were uprisings in the far away frontiers of the empire. In Britain, the barbarian queen Boudicca organized a rebellion against the Roman units stationed there. The rebellion was eventually quashed by the Roman legions. In the far east, Rome lost a war against the kingdom of Parthia and was forced to give up their plans to incorporate Armenia into their sphere of influence.

In 66 C.E., the emperor, who was a lover of Greek culture, made a foreign expedition to classical Greece to participate in the games and revelry. The competition was rigged in favor of Emperor Nero so he could win.

By 68 C.E. one of his generals named Vinfex, who was the governor of the province of Gaul, initiated a plot against Nero. He was joined by another general named Galba, who ruled the territory of Hispania, modern Spain. The conspiracy gained strength and many Roman military and civil officials joined ranks against the tyranny of the young ruler. Once the emperor learned of the plot he fled the capital on June 8th. Shortly afterwards, the Praetorian Guard, which was his own personal bodyguards, denounced his leadership. The next day on June 9 a majority of Roman Senators declared Nero an enemy of the state and tried him in absentia, sentencing him to death. Emperor Nero, who was really an effeminate man, feared that he would be slain. He fled with no one but his servant named Epaphroditus [Epa-fro-di-tus] at his side. Some historians had said that Nero was too big of a coward to even kill himself. They believed his servant helped him commit suicide. Nevertheless, Nero reportedly killed himself, putting a knife to his throat as he heard the sounds of the Praetorian Guard horsemen approaching his hideout. Ironically, Nero was still very popular in the eastern part of the empire at the time of his death. His consistent building of arenas and theaters throughout the empire was supported by the lower-class, slaves, and entertainment lovers. The popular legend surrounding Nero was that *"Nero didn't die, yet he would return again in a Second Coming."* It was even reported that several leaders in the east presented themselves as the reincarnation of Emperor Nero hoping to gain support from the populace.

So it came to pass that Emperor Nero fell upon his own sword in the year 68 C.E. at the age of 31 after he had reigned for fourteen years in the imperial city of Rome. He came to power at the childish age of 17 as the ruler of the mightiest empire on earth. He did evil in the eyes of **YAH ELOHIM of Israel** according to the doings of all his predecessors who served all the image gods of the Greco-Roman pantheon. During his 14-year reign he was very selfish and self-absorbed. He shed much innocent blood, slaying his step-brother, mother, wives, Roman subjects, and his male lovers. After his death Rome descended into a period of civil war with competing generals vying for the throne. This contentious period became known as The Year of Four Emperors: Galba(68-69 C.E.),Otho(69 C.E.),Vitellius(69 C.E.),Vespasian(69-79 C.E.).

The Year of Four Emperors
Galba(68-69 C.E.), Otho(69 C.E.), Vitellius(69 C.E.),Vespasian(69-79 C.E.)

Galba
(68 C.E.—79 C.E.)

Galba was born in the city of Terracina, Italy with the birth name of Servius Sulpicius Galba on December 24 in the year of 3 B.C.E. His father's name was Gauis Sulpicius Galba and his mother's name was Mummia Achaica. He was born into a wealthy aristocratic family with close ties to royal Julio-Claudian dynasty. He rose through the ranks as a capable member of the Roman Senate before becoming a consul in 33 C.E. during the reign of Tiberius. After serving as a consul for six years, Galba became the commanding governor of the Upper Germany legions in the year 39. He also was the proconsul of Africa for several years. Years later at the age of 62 he came out of retirement and was appointed to the governorship of Hispania Tarraconensis, which is now known as Nearer Spain. For eight years he amassed wealth and prestige while serving faithfully as the governor of the far western province. But informants told him that Nero planned to assassinate him. This made him paranoid and vengeful. By spring of 68 the once loyal statesman began to organize a rebellion against the dysfunctional Nero. While Nero concentrated on rebuilding, arts, and entertainment, his army's command and control was gradually deteriorating right around him.

By the summer of the year 68, the Roman Senate chose Galba as their new emperor after Nero's suicide. Galba and his troops entered Rome in October of that year. He chose the throne name Galba Servius Ceasar Augustus. He went on a killing spree executing many influential Romans, even those who had voted for him. Galba came to power when the empire's finances were in shambles. He attempted to correct the misappropriations of his predecessor Nero. But, another problem Galba faced was the low morale within the Praetorian Guard. Galba had promised the military a bonus in exchange for their support. They became extremely upset when the elderly general was unable to deliver on his promise. To make matters worse, Galba's close advisors were corrupt men who demanded compliance. Yet their actions were marred with briberies and other acts of selfishness.

By January 69 C.E. the Roman legions in Upper Germany rebelled against Galba. Meanwhile in Rome, the turning point for Galba's 7-month reign came when he attempted to appoint a successor. The men of war were already angry because Galba hadn't paid them their donation. So, on January 15 while Galba was walking in the middle of the streets of Rome, he was cut down by guardsmen on horseback. His inner circle and other close associates were also slain. Immediately after this bloody experience, the Roman senate proclaimed General Otho as the new emperor. Galba was the oldest man to ever serve as emperor. He was short, hunchback, and 70-years-old with a frail appearance when he came to power. He reigned only 7 months. His attempt to impose austerity measures upon the corrupt elite and his failure to pay the military their bonus doomed his brief rulership.

At the same time when Galba was slain and Otho chosen as the successor, another general named Julius Vindex, governor over the Gaulic province, also rose up to claim the title of emperor. Rome was in the midst of a leadership crisis.

Otho
(69 C.E.—69 C.E.)

Marcus Salvius Otho succeeded Emperor Galba as the next leader of the Roman Empire during the Year of The Four Emperors. He was born in Ferentium, Italy on April 23, 32 C.E. as the son of Lucuis Otho and Terentia Alba. He was of moderate height, bowlegged, and duck-footed. In his late teens and early 20s he was a favourite of Emperor Nero. His wife also had an adulterous relationship with Nero as well. Nero wanted his wife Poppaea Sabina for himself. He forced Otho to divorce her then sentenced him to 10-years of military service in Lustania, which is modern Portugal. Otho and Galba joined forces in the plot to seize the throne of Rome. Otho accompanied Galba when he entered Rome in October 68. Galba was the old man at the age of 70 and Otho was his young heir at the age of only 36. Otho's goal was to succeed the old general, but when he chose another successor instead of him, he revolted and hatched a plot to murder Galba. He purchased the services of 23 Praetorian Guards. On the same day of Galba's death, the Roman Senate elected Otho as the new Princep. The Roman populace liked Otho because he reminded them of their cherished flamboyant Nero. His throne name was Marcus Salvius Otho Caesar Augustus.

Otho was an effeminate man who wore a wig, shaved all his body and facial hairs. In memory of his lover, Otho restored the statues of Nero and recalled all the freedmen and household officers back to their jobs. Meanwhile, in far away places such as the northern forest of Germania Inferior, a war raged between two factions of the Roman Legions. Vitellius, the commander-in-chief of German forces, rebelled against Otho. The battle was set in array at Bedriacuim. The bloody conflict left 40,000 casualties on the battlefield, but after the war, both sides announced peace. Otho remained in rear with a large contingent of fresh troops which could have fought another round. But Otho did not want anymore blood to be spilled. After a good night sleep, Otho rose early on the morning of April 16, 69 C.E. and stabbed himself in the heart with a dagger which he kept under his pillow.

So it came to pass that the astrologer's prediction came true. The soothsayer told Otho that he would succeed Galba, who was childless and aged. However, what the familiar spirit didn't know or foresee was that Otho's reign would last only a mere 91-days [3 months]. After Otho committed suicide, Vitellius was proclaimed the new leader in Rome. Otho was dead at the age of 36 in the city of Brescello. He was the second emperor to briefly reign as Princep during the turbulent Year of The Four Emperors.

Vitellius
(69 B.C.E.)

Emperor Vitellius was born on September 24, 15 C.E. with birth name of Aulus Vitellius. He was the son of a man named Lucius Vitellius and Sextilla, who was the daughter of a wealthy man. It was reported that when Vetillius was born, his parents visited the astrologers to have his horoscope read. What they heard horrified them. It was predicted that Vitellius would grow to become an adversary to his own house. His father never forgot that prediction, and when Vitellius sought the consulship in the year 48 C.E. his father actually lobbied against his selection. As a young man he became close associates with the Tiberius clan and his successor Caligula. Vitellius and Caligula were both fond of chariot-racing, gambling, and dice games. This love of pleasure brought him into the inner circle.

Vitellius was married twice, but while growing up, he spent time of the island of Capri with Emperor Tiberius. As a husband, he was a scoundrel who had his own son killed to inherit the fortune the grandfather had left for the grandchild in his will. By 60 C.E. he was selected as pronconsul of Africa by Emperor Nero. Vitellius was tall, obese, with a huge belly. He was known for his overly friendly nature, but he was also regarded as lazy, self-indulgent, and a lover of food and drinks. Nevertheless, when General Galba seized the throne in the year of 68, he selected Vitellius as the new commander of the forces in Germania Inferior. Meanwhile in Rome the new emperor Galba faced a new uprising by his younger officer Otho. While Vitellius was stationed in Cologne, the forces in Germania Inferior and Germania Superior drafted him to be the new emperor. The forces in Gaul, Britannia, and Raetia joined ranks. When the large contingent reached Rome Otho had overthrown Galba. The armies of Otho and Vitellius were set in array against each other. In midst of battle, Otho committed suicide and Vertillius was proclaimed the new ruler in Rome.

During the brief reign of Vitellius, the city of Rome became undisciplined, the center of riots and massacres. His forces terrorized the Imperial City. For pleasure, he sponsored gladiator contests, chariot-racings, and unrestrained partying. Vitellius became known as a glutton who loved rare foods and hosted festive banquets four times a day.

As emperor, he chose the throne title Aulus Vitellius Germanicus Augustus. To secure his new position, he immediately reassigned his personal guards as the leaders of the notorious Praetorian Guard. In hindsight, this decision actually became a noose around his own neck because once the news of a rebellion in eastern provinces surfaced, these same guards would not allow him to surrender.

During Vitellius brief 8-month reign, he reportedly had his own mother starved to death after astrologers told him he would rule longer if she died first. Some said he gave his mother poison to kill her. Either way, Vetillius was self-absorbed. He then banned astrologers from the royal city in October of that same year after some spoke out against him. Certain astrologers responded by publishing their own epistle. In return, Vitellius went on a killing spree and executed all the astrologers in Rome.

Vitellius's claim to the throne was immediately challenged by the other Roman legions stationed elsewhere throughout the eastern provinces. By July 69, Vitellius learned of the mutiny among the eastern forces who did not acknowledge him. Instead, they chose their commander-in-chief Vespasian for their next emperor. Some of Vertillius close associates decided to defect. Even Vertillius decided to surrender and awaited Vespasian. However, his Praetorian Guard would not allow him to quit. They forced him to return to the palace.

When Vespasian forces reached home another war broke out. Vitellius forces were defeated at the Second Battle of Bedriacium in northern Italy. Vitellius went into hiding in a doorkeeper's lodge. He was found and dragged from the hideout and driven to the famed Gemonian Stairs where he was thrown down the flight of stairs. Afterwards, he was beheaded and his head was paraded throughout the Imperial City. His corpse was later thrown into the Tiber River. His brother and son were also slain during the purge. His wife's life was spared and she gave him a funeral. So it came to pass that Emperor Vitellius died on December 22, 69 C.E. at the age of 54 after reigning only eight months in Rome. He had walked in all of the ways of his predecessors who served image gods, practiced sodomy, and maintained an ungodly livelihood. When the dust from this latest round of chaos settled, Vitellius was the last of the three short-lived successors within the span of a year who strived to rule on the throne of Nero.

In the end Vitellius was succeeded by another Roman general named Vespasian on December 22, 69.

Vespasian
(69 C.E.—79 C.E.)

Emperor Vespasian was born on November 7, 9 C.E. in the city of Falacrinae, northeast of Rome. His birth name was Titus Flavius Vespasianus. His father was Titus Flavius Sabinus I and his mother was Vespasia Polla. He was born into a poor family that rose from dust and ashes to become capable functionaries for the Julio-Claudian rulers. After his father's military exploits on the battlefield, his father became the Prefect in the camp. This allowed the family to move up. This provided Vespasian the opportunity to start his career as a low-ranking quaestor in an outpost in Crete. After that, he began his military career in charge of street cleaning. He later served as a military tribune in Thrace, rising up the ranks under the reign of Caligula. In the year 43 he joined the Roman campaign to crush the barbaric tribes in southwest Britain. Vespasian devastated the primitive hill-people and reduced their settlements to rubble. It was during that time that Vespasian began to be known for his military prowess.

By 51 C.E. Vespasian was promoted to senatorial ranks where he served as a consul during the reign of Claudius. At the age of 54 he came out of retirement to become the governor of the province of Africa. Vespasian became known as an intelligent and witty man who possessed a commanding personality. In 66 C.E., Nero appointed Vespasian to lead the war against the province of Judaea. His troops quashed **the Euro-Judaic convert and Afro-Asiatic Hebrew rebellion** that raged across the holy land. The rebels had slain the previous governor of Egypt and threatened the governor of Syria. Meanwhile as Vespasian laid siege to Jerusalem to put down the rebellion, Nero committed suicide back in Rome. Thousands of Euro-Judaic converts and the lost sheep of the house of Israel were slain during this conflict. Vespasian captured the Euro-Judaic convert Josephus at the Siege of Yodfat. Josephus was a historical writer who mastered the Greek language and led one of the factions that resisted imperial Rome domination. However, after his capture Josephus became an ally of Vespasian and wrote favorably about him. By the summer of 68, Vespasian had captured some black Israelites from the Essene sect in Qumran and took them to the Dead Sea. Vespasian had heard that the salt waters would not allow a person to drown, but he doubted it. So he shackled the Israelites together, and threw them into the waters to see if they would perish. To Vespasian's amazement, the captive Afro-Asiatic Hebrews did not drown. They popped up to the surface after been bound and thrown overboard.

Shortly afterwards news of infighting between various commanders, Galba, Otho, and Vertillius, became known. The forces in Egypt and Syria elected their commander Vespasian as their choice for emperor. This occurred on July 1, 69 C.E. Five months later on December 20, 69, Vespasian defeated his rival Vitellius and the Roman Senate proclaimed him emperor. He chose the throne name Titus Flavius Caesar Vespasianus. Vespasian left the battlefield for the throne in Rome. He appointed his oldest son Titus to oversee the military campaign to crush the Judaean rebellion.

In Rome, Vespasain became a mild-mannered ruler known for his frank language. He reformed the financial system. He also initiated reforms to give the office of the Princep a permanent electoral college to prevent future infighting and coups. In the year of 70 C.E., he announced a new tax policy that affected Rome's grain supply which originated from Egypt.

The new policy caused a rebellion to break out in Egypt. His son Titus eventually crushed the rebellion in Egypt and destroyed Jerusalem and the towns throughout Judaea.

Meanwhile, Vespasian became a great renovator of the Imperial City. He built the Flavian Amphitheater which became known as the Roman Colosseum. He built the Temple of Peace, the Temple to Deified Claudius, and in the year 75, he finished the colossal statue of Apollo, the sun-god, which had been started by the late Emperor Nero.

Vespasian married twice. He was the father of three from his first marriage to a wealthy woman named Domitilla the Elder. She died in the year 69. His second wife was a woman named Caenis. There were no children from their relationship.

In the year 79 Vespasian became ill while in the city of Campania. His sickness caused him to return to Rome, but he soon left Rome to rest at his summer estate. There his illness worsened and he began to experience diarrhea. As his condition worsened, Vespasian felt death coming, and told his assistants, *"dear me, I'm becoming a god."* While sick, he still carried out his emperor duties from his bed. He also said, *"an emperor ought to die standing."* So he struggled to be sit upright and stand on his feet. But he died in the arms of the assistants who tried to help him to his feet. He was 69-years-old.

During his reign, Vespasian was an adversary of the lost sheep of the house of Israel, the Afro-Asiatic Hebrews, in both Judaea and in Egypt. In 70 C.E. when his son Titus destroyed Jerusalem, he also ordered that all the descendants of David, the original Hebrew people, be hunted down from province to province. Josephus had told Vespasian of the Messianic expectations among the black Israelites during that time. Emperor Vespasian viewed a Hebrew Messiah as a threat to Roman rulership. The lost sheep of Israel were forced to flee deep inside the interior of Africa to escape Roman forces. Centuries later, many of their descendants traveled the trade routes from eastern Sudan over to the west coast of Africa.

So it came to pass that Emperor Vespasian died on June 24 in the year 79 C.E. at the age of 69 after reigning ten years in the city of Rome. He did evil in the eyes of **YHWH** like all of his predecessors before him. He served all the image-gods of the Greco-Roman pantheon.

His eldest son Titus succeeded him as the next emperor. This made Vespasian the first emperor since the demise of the Julio-Claudian dynasty to have his heir to rule in his stead. Vespasian was the fourth and last emperor to rule in the year 69 during The Year of The Four Emperors. His dynasty continued for 27 years.

Flavian Dynasty
Titus (79 C.E.—81 C.E.)   Domitian (81 C.E.—96)

Emperor Titus was born with the birth name of Titus Flavius Vespasianus on December 30, 39 C.E. His father was his predecessor Emperor Vespasian. His mother was Empress Domitilla. He was the oldest among the three siblings. His sister, known as Domitilla the Younger, was born in the year 45 and named in honor of her mother. His younger son's name was Titus Flavius Domitianus who was born in 51. He was known as Domitian. Titus's ancestors came into power working under the Julio-Claudian dynasty, amassing wealth and marrying wealthy women. His father Vespasian started a political career serving as a quaestor, aedile, and praetor before moving up to membership in the Roman Senate. It was said that Titus was raised in the presence of the royal court as a childhood friend of Emperor Claudius son named Britannicus. It was even said that Titus and Britannicus had been playing the evening before Britannicus was poisoned during dinner.

At the age of 20, Titus was a military conscript in the Roman province of Germania. He later joined Roman forces when they returned to the British Isle to crush the revolt by the barbarian queen Boudica. After the Roman army suppressed the Celtic tribes, the invading army returned to Rome. Shortly afterwards, Titus first wife Arrecinus Tertulla died. Being a young man Titus did remarry into a family of nobility. However, once married, Titus found out the family was involved in a plot against Emperor Nero. Titus divorced the daughter of the family. Her name was Marcia Furnilla.

Titus continued to practice Roman law and he rose to the rank of quaestor until the turbulence in Judaea forced him back into military service. The ethnic violence broke out in the year 66 C.E. Titus was now 26-years-old. The Israelite and the Jewish convert hatred of the pagan Romanization of the holy land reached a boiling point. The Judaeans fought and won a battle against Cestius Gallus, the consul of Syria in the city of Beth-Horon. They later forced Roman legions stationed in Jerusalem to abandon their post. The Israelite and Jewish converts then sought to slay the Idumean Jewish king Herod Agrippa II. The king and his sister were forced to flee northwards to the Roman outpost in the city of Galilee where they surrendered to Roman authorities. Emperor Nero appointed General Vespasian as the commander to crush the Israelite and Judaic rebellion. His son Titus, who was the commander of another legion, joined him in the city of Ptolemais. Together their forces numbered 70,000 soldiers. From there, they moved across Galilee towards Jerusalem. The Roman-allied Jewish historian Josephus recorded the 4-year Roman conquest of the holy land in his book *The Wars of The Jews*.

When the Romans invaded the land of Israel the following year in 67, Josephus defected to the side of Rome and served Vespasian as his assistant and local commander in his conquest of the city Yodfat which was located in northern Israel. Josephus joined the month and a half-long siege where 40,000 were slain, a mixture of religious Jewish converts and Israelites. Within a year the Romans controlled northern Judaea along with the entire coastline of the land of Israel. The Roman legions then headed towards Jerusalem. But the news of Emperor Nero's death halted their planned offensive. Vespasian wanted to wait and see who would be the new Emperor before he completed his mission. He dispatched his son Titus back to Rome to greet the new leader. While traveling towards Rome, Titus received reports of infighting among the generals. Galba had been slain and replaced by Otho. He then received another report that General Vitellius and his forces stationed in Germania were heading towards Rome. Then news of Otho's suicide reached the young 30-year-old commander. Titus feared being caught up in the uncertainty, so he returned to safety with his father's forces in Judaea. Once the 60,000 troops learned of the ensuing political chaos, they chose their own commander Vespasian as the next Princep. This development took place on July 1, 69. By December 21, the Roman Senate confirmed Vespasian role as the new Emperor. Vespasian then placed Titus in charge of subduing the Judean uprising.

It was now 70 C.E. and the Siege of the once city of David, Jerusalem, was about to begin.

The Siege and Destruction of Jerusalem
70 C.E.

"And after threescore and two years shall Messiah **[the anointed remnant, not one person]** *shall be cut off* **[the destruction of the people and the city]**, *but not for himself* **[for the sins of their fathers]**: *and the people* **[The Romans]** *of the prince* **[Princep Vespasian and Titus]** *that shall come shall destroy the city* **[Jerusalem in 70 C.E.]** *and the sanctuary* **[Temple]**; *and the end thereof shall be with a flood, and unto the end of the war* **[between the children of YHWH and the children of the image—Satan]** *desolations* **[lost sheep of Israel cut off in spiritual graveyards]** *are determined."*

[Daniel 9:26]

The Crucifixion of Anointed[HaMashiach] People and City

According to the revelations of Daniel, the final prophesied conflict between the Roman Empire and the inhabitants of the land of Israel was now set in motion. The majority Jewish converts and Israelite minorities courageously faced a superior force. Initially, they had early successes in their initial skirmishes against the mighty Roman legions. But, these same Judaean nationalists also fought among themselves. Although all factions hated Rome, there was not a prepared strategy against the superior battle-hardened adversaries. It was more of an impulsive riot than a guerilla war. The rebel factions, known as the Judaean Free Government, had gained control of the city after the 66 C.E. riots. Meanwhile, Israelites fought among themselves while also fighting against the Idumean Jewish converts and the Romans.

Unfortunately, the siege of Jerusalem came only weeks before the Memorial of the Passover in 70 C.E. Jerusalem was filled with Israelites and Jewish converts who became trapped in the siege. Titus commanded his forces to surround the city of David. Three of his legions were stationed on the western side. The fourth legion arrayed themselves on the Mount of Olives on the eastern side. The Roman engineers then erected ramparts to demolish the walls of the city. Afterwards, the Roman strategists then built another ring around the city to starve the population. Food became scare. There was no water. Lawlessness ruled the streets of Jerusalem as the famine became more severe. Some Jerusalemites were forced to eat dung. It was very similar to the horror experienced by the Israelite kingdom of Samaria centuries later spoken of in **2 Kings 6:25-29:**

"And there was a great famine in Samaria: and, behold, they besieged it, until an ass's head was sold for fourscore pieces of silver, and fourth part of a cab of dove's dung for five pieces of silver. And as the king of Israel was passing by upon the wall, there cried a woman unto him, saying, Help, my lord, O king. And he **[King Yehoram]** *said, If YAH do not help you, how can I help you? out of barnfloor, or out of the winepress? And the king said unto her, what aileth you? And she answered, this woman said unto me, give your son that we may eat him to day, and we will eat my son tomorrow. So we boiled my son, and did eat him: and I said to her on the next day, give your son, that we may eat him: and she has hid her son."*

By July, the Roman mighty ones had scaled the Fortress of Antonia. The battle was still fierce. Several Roman soldiers were slain as well. Before Titus issued the deathblow of total annihilation, he sent Josephus as part of a mediation team to command them to surrender instead of being slaughtered. One of Judean defenders shot a member of the negotiation team with an arrow. Immediately after that, the Roman legions rekindled the flames of plunder. Roman soldiers crowded together around the gate entrances. Once the battering rams breached the gates, more Roman soldiers entered the city slaughtering every person in sight. There was no mercy. The old, young, feeble, hungry, and unarmed were murdered on sight. Then the walls of Jerusalem were set on fire. The people of the prince continued to enter the city ransacking everything in sight. One Roman soldier entered the Temple and threw a burning stick onto the Temple wall. The temple quickly caught fire with flames spreading throughout the structure and the entire city. Around the altar there were piles of corpses stacked high. Some of the bodies were slithered from top to bottom. The Holy of Holies turned into a river of blood from the piles of slain bodies. The remaining artifacts, such as the shewbread table, the menorah, the incense stands, were looted and taken back to Rome. Dead bodies littered the entire city of Jerusalem like dung on the ground. The overall death toll of Judaean combatants from all, the First and Third, Roman/Israelite-Jewish convert Wars totalled 350,000 from the year 66 to 70.

By August, the city and the sancutary were totally captured and destroyed. Roman legions continued to crush the remaining resistance. Most of the Israelites and Jewish converts fled through secret underground tunnels and sewers. Still, some continued to fight in the Upper City with no chances of victory. They were eventually subdued. On September 7, Herod's Palace was consumed. The next day, Sept. 8, Rome's conquest was completed. The true Messiah **[anointed]** the Prince **[holy people]**—**the anointed remnant**—the firstborn of YAH had been totally cut-off from the holy city and scattered among the nations into the spiritual desolations as spoken by Daniel and the other Hebrew prophets.

Romans continued to pursue the Judaeans throughout the land and the entire Mediterranean region. Israelites were forced to flee deep inside the interior of Africa to escape their Gentile pursuers. At least 30,000 Israelites and Jewish converts died in this final round of fighting. According to Josephus, over one million civilians died during this 6-month siege. 97,000 combatants were taken back to Rome as slaves to entertain their citizenry as gladiators. Others were forced to serve as laborers to build the famed Forum of Peace and the Colosseum. This was done while his father Vespasian was the reigning emperor.

Praise, glory, and honor was bestowed upon General Titus for his decisive victory over the turbulent Judaean province. In the holy city he was regarded as the champion of the Rome. Titus and his soldiers celebrated the victory upon returning to Rome. There was a procession of soldiers carrying the Menorah along with Table of Shewbread throughout the streets. Up until then, no Gentiles had ever seen those sacred items. The desecration of these holy objects were memorialized in the famed Arch of Titus which was erected in his honor in celebration of the Roman conquest.

> *"I will apply to Jerusalem the measuring line of Samaria and the weights of the House of Ahab; I will wipe Jerusalem clean as one wipes a dish and turns it upside down. And I will cast off the remnant of MY own people* **[The Messiah the Prince]** *and deliver them into the hands of their enemies [The* **Romans**]. *They shall be plunder and prey to all their enemies because they have done what is evil to ME and have been vexing ME from the day that their fathers came out of Egypt to this day."* **[2 Kings 21;13-15]**

Josephus Eyewitness Account of the Destruction of Jerusalem in the Year 70 C.E. by the Roman Army

"Now as soon as the army had no more people to slay or to plunder, because there remained none to be the objects of their fury, for they would not have spared any had there remained any other work to be done. Titus Caesar gave orders that they should now demolish the entire city and temple, but should leave as many of the towers standing as they were of the greatest eminence; that is Hippicus and Mariamme; and so much of the wall enclosed the city on the west side. This wall spared in order to afford a camp for such as were to lie in garrison (in the Upper City) as were the towers (3 forts) also spared in order to demonstrate to posterity what kind of city it was, and how well fortified, which the Roman valor had subdued; but for all the rest of the wall surrounding Jerusalem, it was so thoroughly laid even with the ground by those that dug it up to the foundation, that there was left nothing to make those that came there believe Jerusalem had ever existed or inhabited.

This was the end which Jerusalem came by the madness of those that were for innovations; a city otherwise of great magnificence, and of mighty fame among all mankind. And truly, the very view itself was a melancholy thing; for those places which were adorned with trees and pleasant gardens, were now become desolate country in every way, and its trees were all cut down. Nor could any foreigner that had formerly seen Judaea and the most beautiful suburbs of the city, and now saw it as a desert, but lament and mourn sadly at so great a change. For the war had laid all signs of beauty quite waste. Nor had anyone come [suddenly upon] it now, would he have known it again. But though he, a foreigner, were at the city itself, yet [he]would he have inquired for it."

In other words, if you had seen Jerusalem in the years before 70 C.E. and you then witnessed it after the Roman invasion, you wouldn't be able to believe your eyes. The city and people of Jerusalem were completely leveled to the ground and erased from the presence of the humanity. The city of Jerusalem was nothing but a great heap of stones and debris. Both—**the city and the people**— were totally cut-off, which now continues to be the case even today, nearly two thousand years later in the 21st century. **The Messiah the Prince—the anointed remnant**—continues to be cut off not for himself, but because of the sins of the fathers and the continued iniquities of the children generations after generations.

When you think about all the hard work and battles that King David fought to establish Jerusalem as the city of ELOHIM, and you see how his descendants did not continue in his righteous ways, but rather served other gods, you as an Israelite should feel a personal pain and sadness for what has happened to Jerusalem. We should join hands and share a personal obligation to unite to restore it to its former glory. Jerusalem, O Jerusalem the city where the Presence of YAH once dwelt, now laid in rubbles and ruins. The anointed people, prophets, Levite priests, and sons of David—**The true ancient Hebrew concept of the Messiah the Prince**— the Firstborn of YAH were cut off from the Presence of YAH for ages to come, even unto the end of heathen dominion. This is what the Angel Gabriel was informing **Daniel** of in **chapters 9 verses 25** and **26**. He was NOT predicting the coming of Jesus or Yeshua to die on the cross for the sins of Israel or the world. Those explanations of Daniel's vision are false, malicious, and misleading Gentile-based misinterpretations of the ancient Hebrew prophecies. As lawful Israelites, we MUST stay away from those erroneous, devilish thought patterns and reject all of those foreign-based ideologies. We must free our minds and return back to a YAH-Mind exclusively.

Now back to the subject at hand. After the war, Titus remained in the holyland where he entertained himself with elaborate Greco-Roman games. Eventually, he departed the land of Israel for Mesopotamia to meet with the king of Parthia where he received a crown. He also visited the city of Antioch where he spoke favorably with the Jewish converts in Syria. From there Titus traveled to Egypt where he stopped in the city of Memphis to worship the golden calf Apis in the Temple of Sacred Bull. During the ceremonies he received a royal diadem as a gift from the high priests. Although Titus received the honors of a king, he exalted the name of his father to make sure that his loyalty was unquestionable. When Titus finally arrived home back in Rome in 71, he was joined with his father and brother in a triumphal parade throughout the capital. The parade contained large amounts of gold and silver carried in wagons along the route. The leaders of the rebellion, including Simon Bar Giora and others, were executed in the Forum. The ceremonies finally concluded at the Temple of Jupiter, one of the chief image-gods of Rome.

Titus was awarded the title Caesar and awarded several consulships. Later on, he became Praetorian Prefect, the personal assistant of his father, and made Senate appearances on his behalf. He was known as a strong defender of his father who would execute suspected traitors without due process.

On June 23, 79 C.E. Emperor Vespasian died from an infection. At the age of 39, his son Titus succeeded him on the throne without contest. He adopted the throne name: Imperator Caesar Flavius Vespasianus Augustus, meaning *"the popular and perfect youth"*. He proved to be a competent Roman leader. One of his first actions as the new emperor was ending treason trials based on the testimony of secret informants. Since the days of Augustus, countless Romans had been put to death based on the words of corrupt and false witnesses. Titus also held the office of Pontifex Maximus in order to secure fairness for all sides. His reign was known for stability and free of major conspiracies. However, there were two exceptions: There was a Nero Impersonator named Terentius Maximus who portrayed himself as the Second Coming of Nero. He galvanized the masses in the eastern provinces where Nero was regarded as a folk hero. Once Titus caught wind of the conspiracy, he sought to capture the Nero impersonator. The usurper fled into Parthia to escape Roman territory. The other conspiracy came from his jealous-hearted younger brother Domitian. It appeared Domitian was envious of the good hand and honorable position of his older brother. Once Titus learned of his younger brother's evil eye he overlooked his ill will.

Another notable deed that Titus carried out during his reign was the completion of Colosseum, also known as the Flavian Amphitheater in the year 80. The colossal structure was an entertainment center hosting gladiatorial combats, horse and chariot races, plays, all types of sexual gratification, and a host of other pleasurable activities. The construction of the amphitheater started in 70 C.E., the same year the Temple in Jerusalem was destroyed. It had taken 10 years to complete the architectural wonder. Upon completion, Emperor Titus hosted inaugural competition and festivities that continued for 100 days. Titus extreme love for pleasure, games, and revelry rivaled Nero's. He built new bathhouses near the new Flavian Amphitheater. Men and their male companions could conveniently leave the games and enjoy their evenings in the bathhouses. This male only facility was known as the Baths of Titus. During his reign Titus built a temple, erected a statue of his father Vespasian, and deified him as a god as part of his revival of the imperial cults borrowed from Hellenistic cultures of Egypt, Syria, Mesopotamia, and Asia Minor. He also laid the foundation for a new temple in honor of himself and his father which later would be known as the Temple of Vespasian and Titus.

Two natural disasters occurred during the reign of Emperor Titus. The first act of **YHWH** was the eruption of the Mount Vesuvius volcano on August 24, 79 C.E. The eruption completely destroyed the cities and resorts of Pompeii and Herculaneum with lava, ash, stones, and killing thousands. All the communities around the Bay of Naples were consumed. Titus appointed two former consul-men to organize a relief effort. Titus opened the vaults of the imperial treasury to assist the victims affected by the calamity. It was if the CREATOR-YAH had visited DIVINE Retribution upon Emperor Titus for his destruction of Jerusalem nine years earlier.

The second strange occurrence came the following spring of the year 80. A major fire broke out in the royal capital. Several great buildings were consumed by the flames that rapidly spread across parts of the city destroying the Agrippa Pantheon, Temple of Jupiter, the Diribitorium, portions of Theater of Pompey, along with the Saepta Julia. To make matters worse, an unexplained plague broke out while the flames ravished a sector of the Imperial City.

One of the last recorded acts of Emperor Titus came in the latter-part of the year 80. That's when he dedicated the new Flavian Amphitheater to the gods of Rome during the opening games, races, and ceremonies. Shortly thereafter, he became ill while traveling in Italy. He was taken to a nearby farmhouse for rest and medical care. Ironically, it was the same farmhouse his father had died in two years earlier. As fate would have it, the spot became the final resting place for his son Titus too.

So it came to pass that Titus died from a fever at the age of 41 on September 13, 79 after reigning as Emperor for a mere two years. It has been recorded in certain Judaic writings that **YAH** plagued Titus by allowing an insect, even a gnat, fly into his nostrils, which in turn, developed into a brain tumor. He did evil in the eyes of **YHWH ELOHIM Israel** according to all that his predecessors had done by serving all the image-gods of the Greco-Roman pantheon. Titus was spoken of in the book of **Daniel** as *"the prince who would destroy the city of Jerusalem and the Sanctuary."* His actions fulfilled those Words of YAH. His younger brother Domitian succeeded him as the new emperor upon the throne of the Roman Empire.

Domitian
(81 C.E.—96 C.E.)

Domitian was born on October 24, 51 C.E. as the youngest son of Emperor Vespasian and wife Domitilla the Elder. His birth name was Titus Flavius Domitianus. When he was born in the year 51, his father Vespasian served as a consul under Emperor Claudius. Much of Domitian's childhood was spent in the shadows of his older brother and father. During his teenage years, both his mother, Domitilla the Elder, and his older sister, Domitilla the Younger died. His father and brother, both military men, were away on military campaigns while Domitian lived with his uncle Sabinus II. As a young child of the senatorial class, Domitian received a higher education. He studied literature and rhetoric where he developed great speaking skills. As a young man, he developed expert marksmanship skills with bow and arrows. As far as appearance was concerned, Domitian was considered tall and handsome according to Roman standards.

At the age 18, after the death of Nero and the civil war between the various Roman factions, Domitian found himself under house arrest by Emperor Vitellius. A war broke out between his father Vespasian's troops and Emperor Vitellius troops ending in defeat of Vitellius. The

Roman Senate then proclaimed Vespasian the new Emperor when he entered Rome in September of 70 C.E. His father elevated his older Titus to crown prince whereas Domitian held only ceremonial positions. He still remained in the shadows for a few more years.

Domitian eventually became the representative of the Flavian dynasty in the Roman Senate. He would make appearance as spokesman of the Emperor. He was granted the honorary title *Caesar* and appointed praetor with consul power.

Years later when his older brother Titus fell deadly ill. Domitian showed little sympathy for him while he laid on his deathbed. After the death of his brother, he was crowned emperor by the Praetorian Guard without any incidents on September 14, 81 C.E at the age of 29. His throne name became Imperator Caesar Domitianus Germanicus. He married a woman named Domitia Longina, the daughter of a general. Although when he was younger, his father Vespasian wanted him to marry Titus daughter, his niece named Julia. He refused to marry her, but he privately maintained an adulterous affair with her. His wife Domitia was no better. She carried out a secret affair with her brother-in-law Titus. Meanwhile, Domitian and Domitia had one child. The child died at the age of 3. In honor of his child and wife, he deified them both with a statue. The royal couple did not have anymore children, in fact, he later exiled her and replaced her with his niece. However in the year 84, he summoned her back to the royal court.

Domitian moved the center of influence and power away from the Senate towards the imperial court. He then marginalized their power. Domitian's ego led him to believe he ruled as a divine monarch who could dictate moral and cultural values. He became an authoritarian ruler who strived to strengthen the Roman economy. He governed the empire with a stern hands-on policy, executing countless offenders, and involving himself in all daily details. He demanded loyalty and kept corruption to an all-time low. Corruption among provincial governors fell to record lows because he rigidly collected taxes throughout the empire.

When Domitian came to power imperial Rome had been badly damaged by the Great Fire of 64, the Civil War of 69, and the tragic Great Fire of 80 C.E. During his reign he initiated a major reconstruction program to restore the Imperial City. With an earnings of $1.2 billion sesteriis, Domitian built the Villa of Domitian, the Palace of Domitian in Palatine Hill, the Stadium of Domitian, completed the Temple of Vespasian and Titus, the Arch of Titus, Colosseum, and nearly 50 other structures throughout the royal city. One-third of his billion-dollar budget went towards the world's largest standing army—the Roman legions. He also constructed a vast network of roads, forts, and watchtowers established along the Rhine River in Germania.

In terms of pleasure, Domitian was the typical Roman emperor who sponsored and loved sensual pleasures like adultery and other sorts of debauchery, chariot races, mock naval battles, female and dwarf gladiators. In terms of military campaigns, On the western edge of the empire, Domitian fought wars against the British tribesmen in the northern part of the island which eventually known as Scotland. On the eastern edges of the kingdom, he was also personally participated in warfare in Illyricum, which is modern Albania on the Balkan Peninsula.

It came to pass that as Domitian aged, he developed a protuding belly and walked with a limp. He also became bald and wore wigs to hide his baldness. Domitian's cruelty and disrespect for the Senate caused deep divisions in the capital. A deadly plot was set in motion by certain officials. On September 18, 96 C.E.,Domitian sat down on his throne that afternoon. Domitian had begun to come to the imperial court in the afternoon because an astrologers had warned him that he would die around midday. So,Domitian was always uneasy during lunchtime. However, on this day the emperor sat down on the throne in the late afternoon. He was approached by a certain courtier named Stephanus. Now Stepanus wore a large bandage to appear as if he was covering a injured part of his body. Hidden underneath was a sharp dagger. On this day, Stephanus removed the dagger from his bandage and hid it behind his back. He then delivered the official papers to Emperor Domitian as he normally did. Domitian began to look downward as he read the papers. Stephanus grabbed his dagger and bludgeoned the emperor in the groins, turning his royal purple into a pool of red blood. More courtiers gathered around Domitian. More stabbings followed. Even the attacker

Stepanus was slain in the ensuing confusion. This assassination did not only kill Domitian. It ended the 27-year reign of the Flavian dynasty. He was succeeded by another unrelated court official named Marcus Cocceius Nerva. The 15-year reign of Domitian represented stability after years of violent and brief rulership by his predecessors. His reign had been the longest since the twenty-two year reign of Tiberius which occurred in 14 C.E. to 37 C.E.

During his rule, Domitian viewed himself as the *"new Caesar"*, the enlightened one whom the gods of Rome ordained to guide the Roman Empire into a new era of human brilliance. He had started a personality cult deifying himself, his family, and others as divine beings. His image was seen on all religious, political, and military documents. Because he had lavishly funded the Roman Legions, he was once very popular with the army. But, his anti-Senate policies caused him to be viewed as a tyrant. On the other hand, his autocratic reign provided him with the space and time to develop cultural, economic, and political programs to propel the Roman Empire for another one hundred years into the 2nd Century common era [C.E.].

So it came to pass that Emperor Domitian died at the age of 44. He had done evil in eyes of **YHWH ELOHIM of Israel the CREATOR of the heavens, earth, and seas**. He served all the image-gods of the Greco-Roman pantheon according to the abhorrent traditions of his predecessors. He also built the Forum of Transitorium which housed the Temple of the image-goddess Minerva. As I said earlier, Marcus Cocceius Nerva, a man who had served as an imperial courtier, was chosen by the Roman Senate and reigned in his stead, beginning a dynasty which became known as The Nerva-Antonine Dynasty.

The Nerva-Antonine Dynasty (also known as Years of 5 Good Emperors)
Nerva (96 C.E.—98 C.E.) Trajan (98 C.E.—117 C.E.) Hadrian (117 C.E.—138 C.E.) Antoninus Pius(138 C.E.—161 C.E.) Marcus Aurelius (161 C.E.—180 C.E.) Commodus (177 C.E.—192 C.E.)

Marcus Cocceius Nerva was born in the village of Narni, one-mile north of Rome on November 8, 30 C.E. as the son of Marcus Cocceius Nerva and Sergia Plautilla. He grew up as a member of Roman nobility. He was a descendant of a prominent family that served in the imperial court for generations. His family's service dated back to his great-grandfather, grandfather, and father. When he was a child, his father served as the Suffect Consul while Emperor Caligula reigned of the throne. Nerva moved into the imperial circles as a young man possessing skills as a diplomatic strategist, serving as a personal advisor to Emperor Nero. In the year 65, his keen eyes successfully detected and unveiled the conspiracy to slay Emperor Nero. Nero greatly enriched and honored him in the royal court. Statues of his likeness were placed throughout the palace.

His imperial service continued until 71 C.E. when Emperor Vespasian elevated him to consulship. Vespasian and Nerva were members of the royal entourage when Nero visited Greece in the year of 66. After Vespasian, his son Domitian chose him for consulship in the year 90 C.E. During this time, the hatred for Domitian continued to grow until a conspiracy was hatched. In the year 98, conspirators approached the courtier Nerva with a plan for him to become the political successor of Domitian. This was right before the planned assassination. Emperor Domitian was slain in the Imperial Court on September 18th. Within hours, after the news of Domitian's death reached the public, the Senate hastily nominated Nerva as the new emperor. At the age of 65, failing health, and childless, Emperor Nerva assumed the mantle of power and sat down on the throne of Augustus. He who had once served the emperors was now the emperor himself. Nerva had been loyal to all the emperors before Domitian. But Nerva personally saw the extensive damage and anarchy caused by the year-long civil war in 69 after the fall of Nero. He know if he didn't step forward now the empire would experience a repeat of The Year of Four Emperors. He assumed the throne title of Imperator Marcus Cocceius Nerva Caesar Augustus. In his two-year reign, his image appeared on coins and statues of the emperor were erected in the royal city. He worshiped in the Forum Nerva to invoke the names of the gods for help.

Although Nerva was known as honorable and popular within the Senate, his prestige among the mighty ones inside the Praetorian Guard was totally opposite. They did not view him as a strong capable leader. In fact, mutinous pressure from the Roman Army played a role in Nerva adopting the young popular soldier Trajan as his son and heir.

So it came to pass that on January 1, 98 C.E. when Nerva was about to start his fourth term as a consul, he suffered a massive stroke while entertaining a private audience. A few days later he experienced a high fever. For the entire month of January, Nerva laid in agony at his Gardens of Sallust villa before expiring on January 27. Nerva died at the age of 67 without a family or child. He had spent his entire life in the inner court engaging in all types of sexual peverseness, including homosexuality, bestiality, and pedophilia.

Marcus Cocceius Nerva did evil in the eyes of **YHWH ELOHIM of Israel** like all his predecessors before him, serving the image-gods of the Greco-Roman pantheon. However, Nerva, like Emperor Domitian before him, had a special fetish for the idol Minvera which he favored above all the other idols. In the Roman religion Minerva, the sacred post, was believed to be the female goddess of handicrafts, the professions, arts, and war. Emperors Domitian and Nerva bowed down before this man-made object seeking divine protection. Trajan, his adoptive son who was widely known as a lover of young male flesh, became the next Emperor on the throne of Caesar.

Trajan
(98 C.E.—117 C.E.)

Trajan was born on September 18, 53 C.E. in the city of Italica. It was located near a city which is now called Seville, Spain . His birth name was Marcus Ulpius Trajanus. His father's name was the same, Marcus Ulpius Trajanus, and his mother's name, Marcia. The Roman Republic established colonies of the Hispania Peninsula as early as 206 B.C.E. Successive Roman rulers sent Roman legions there to build military colonies occupied by native Italians. It was normal for Roman settlers to intermingle with Iberian natives. The lineage of Trajan started with one of those mixed ethnic origins. He came from a poor background. Under these circumstances, he joined the Roman Army to eat. Through his valor, he rose to become a high-ranking Roman general. He rose to notoriety under Emperor Domitian assisting him in quashing a revolt by an usurper named Antonius Saturninus. Under Emperor Vespasian, Trajan was actively involved in combat during Rome's war in Syria. Eventually, Trajan became an officer in command of a Roman legion receiving large shares of the spoils from successful military campaigns. This is how he enriched himself.

Now General Trajan came to power on this wise. During the brief reign of Emperor Nerva, pressure from the Praetorian Guard reached a contentious point. Praetorian Prefect Casperius Aelianus demanded the killers of the late Emperor Domitian be executed. Nerva knew he needed support from the Roman Legions to prevent an assassination plot. So, during the summer of the year 97, Nerva named Trajan as his adoptive son and heir to the throne. This union between Nerva and Trajan most likely was sealed with intimacy between the two Roman male-loving officials.

In the year of 86, Trajan's cousin, Publius Aelius Afer, died leaving behind two young children as orphans: a boy and a girl named Hadrian and Paulina. Trajan and a male companion named Publius Aciluis Attianus became co-guardians of the children. Every since the days of Plato up until this era it was common for Greco-Roman men to engage in sexual relationships with each other and young teenage boys. Five years later in he year 91, Trajan was elevated to a consulship. Although Trajan was a publicly known wanton homosexual, he later participated in a bisexual marriage with a noblewoman named Pompeia Plotina who was from a Roman settlement in France.

One year after adopting Trajan, Emperor Nerva died on January 27, 98. With the help of the Senate and military, Trajan inherited the throne of Augustus on the same day. He assumed the throne name Imperator Caesar Neva Trajanus Divi Nervae Filius Augustus. The Senate named him *"optimus princeps"* meaning *"the best ruler"*. There were no rivals.

Under Trajan, Rome experienced its greatest military expansion since the recording of the Roman historical culture. In the far east by the year 106, Trajan had expanded the empire deep inside the Nabatean Arab territory, which is now parts of modern Jordan and northern Saudi Arabia. Further east, he warred against the Parthian Empire capturing the capital city Ctesiphon. He went on to annex Armenia and Mesopotamia. Large mineral deposits were discovered in the province of Dacia during Trajan's reign as well. Ancient Dacia is modern Romania in eastern Europe.

In late 117 C.E. Trajan, while was sailing back to Rome, became ill and died on August 8, 117 C.E. from a stroke just like his older predecessor Nerva. His ship was diverted to the city of Selinus, Cilica which is located in southern Turkey. Immediately after his death, Trajan was deified by the Senate and a graven image was erected in his honor. His remains were cremated, his ashes were placed in the foot of the Trajan's Column in Rome.

During his reign he added to the grandeur of the imperial city by constructing the Trajan Forum, the Trajan Market, and but not least, Trajan's Column. Inside the Imperial Palace, his promiscuity rivaled the sensualities of Tiberius and Nero's pleasure palaces. The royal pages in the Imperial Court satisfied his sexual taste buds.

So it came to pass that Trajan, who was known as the soldier-emperor, died at the age of 63 after reigning on the throne of Augustus for 18 years in Rome. He was the second emperor of the Nerva-Antonine Dynasty. He did evil in the eyes of **YHWH ELOHIM of Israel** and served all the image-gods of the Greco-Roman pantheon according to the abhorrent practices of those before him. He openly celebrated his love for same sex marriage and intimacy with men in violation, and contrary to **YHWH's DIVINE Principles** spoken of in **Leviticus 18:22** and **Leviticus 20:13**. Trajan's adoptive son and lover Hadrian became the new emperor over the vast Roman empire.

Hadrian
(117 C.E.—138 C.E.)

Hadrian was born with Latin name of Publius Aelius Hadrianus on January 24, 76 C.E. in a Roman settlement in Italica, which is located near Santiponce in modern Spain. His father's maternal name was Publius Aelius Hadrianus Afer and mother's name was Domitia Paulina. Hadrian's father was a senator and first cousin of Emperor Trajan. He died while Hadrian and his sister Paulina were the only children. For some reason, Trajan, the elder second-cousin, and his male friend adopted the pair. It is a widely known fact that during this era Roman men normally engaged in sex with male children. It appears that was the case for Trajan and Hadrian. It was also normal for Roman men to get married for procreation purposes only. According to that tradition, Hadrian married Trajan's grand niece named Vibia Sabina. Their marriage was known to be unhappy and their union did not produce any children. Again, Hadrian was known to prefer male lovers over his wife.

In the process of time, Hadrian became very close to Trajan's wife. She lobbied Trajan's friend and personal advisor Lucinius Sura to speak favorably to the emperor on behalf of Hadrian becoming the successor to the throne. During the year 117, while sailing back to Rome, Trajan became ill and eventually died from a stroke. Hadrain stepped forward, informing the Senate in a letter that Trajan wanted him to be the next emperor. Hadrain warned the Senate that the Roman State could not be without an emperor and asked the assembly to consider him as the best choice. On August 10, 117, Hadrian became emperor after gaining the support of the Praetorian Guard and the Senate. He chose the throne name Imperator Caesar Publius Aelius Traianus Hadrianus Augustus.

As soon as Emperor Hadrian came to power, four senators who opposed his ascension were put to death. This arbitrary move by the new emperor caused tensions between the two branches of power. The Senate held him accountable for the death of their colleagues. Hadrian, however, held on to power by rewarding the Roman Legions lavishly for their continued loyalty. Public ceremonies were organized throughout the Imperial City and Empire. His ascension was described as a *"divine election"* by all the gods. Hadrian immediately defied his predecessor Trajan as one of those gods.

Four years later in 121, Hadrian began construction of the Temple of Venus and Roma. It took 20 years to complete the structure which was not completed until the reign of Emperor Antoninus Pius in 141 C.E. The temple was the largest temple ever built in ancient Rome spanning 350 feet long and 150 feet wide, standing at a 52,500 square feet shrine. The huge pagan sanctuary housed a cult statue dedicated of the image-goddess Venus Felix and Roma Aeterna. It was located on the Velian Hill situated between the eastern edge of the Forum Romanui and the Colosseum. He also renovated the Pantheon of all the Roman deities. Hadrian was the total opposite of his predecessor Trajan. Trajan was a man of war while Hadrian was a man of flesh and sensualities. He loved ancient Greek culture and sought to remake the city of Athens into the cultural capital of the Roman Empire. He viewed the world through Pan-Hellenic visions and constructed opulent temples throughout the empire. He desired one Roman standard for the entire empire. He established an universal cult in honor of a homosexual boyfriend named Antinous who drowned in the Nile River at the age of 20. He even built a city in his honor near the scene of his death named Antinoplis. Back home in Italy, Hadrian built a temple honoring his lover and the seven planetary gods in the city of Tivoli, which was 16 miles northeast of Rome.

Hadrian also reversed the policies of Trajan in terms of expanding the empire. Hadrian did not launch any military offensives to gain territory in Armenia, Assyria, or Mesopotamia. In certain areas he did not enforce the gains of Trajan, and in other places, he withdrew. To his credit, he did encourage discipline, military preparedness, and the fortification of Roman defensive borders. One example was the 10-feet high, 80-mile long Hadrian Wall which was built to fortify the empire's northwestern border against the Picts barbarian invasions who roamed the north, which is now known as Scotland.

Hadrian's reign was known as a time of peace, but there was one stain of turbulence and bloodshed that continued to trouble the empire. That stain flared again when Hadrian outlawed circumcision provoking rebellions in the province of Judaea. This time it was a Judaean named Simon Bar Kokhba who lead a rebellion against the Roman Empire. *(This rebellion took place between the years of 132 to 135. Most of the ancient Afro-Asiatic Hebrews had already been driven from Jerusalem and Judaea in 70 C.E. when Titus decimated the city of David 62 years earlier. So it would be safe to assume that this rebellion was led and supported by Judaic converts and not the original descendants of the 12 tribes of Israel. The majority of the Israelites had fled deep into the interior of Africa to escape execution by emperors Vespasian, Titus, and Domitian.)* Again, the **iron** hand of Rome crushed that uprising as well.

In midst of the latter-part of his reign Hadrian began to experience chronic illness. So in the year 138, he eventually adopted Antoninus Pius as his possible successor, based upon one condition: He must choose both Marcus Aurelius and Lucius Verus as the next two in line as future successors. That same year Hadrian died on July 10, 138 C.E. at the age of 62 in the city of Balae, which was located near Rome close to the Gulf of Naples.

So it came to pass that Emperor Hadrian reigned for 20 years and 11 months doing evil in the eyes of **YHWH ELOHIM of Israel** according to all the abhorrent practices of all the pagan rulers who proceeded him. He was intimate with the same gender: mankind instead of womankind. He erected and bowed before graven images, and slew innocent souls without repose. Antoninus Pius succeeded him as the next Emperor of Rome.

Antoninus Pius
(138 C.E.—161 C.E.)

Antoninus Pius was born September 19, 86 C.E. in the city of Lanuvium, Italy which was located 20 miles from Rome. He shared the same birth name as his father, Titus Aurelius Fulvus Boinus Arrius Antoninus. His mother, Arria Fadilla, was the daughter of two-term consul named Arrius Antoninus. He was raised on a large estate in Lorium where his family members were large landholders. The neighborhood consisted of members of the Roman Senate who once served in southern Gaul.

As a young man he was raised by his grandfather due to the fact that his father died in the year 89. He inherited property and became wealthy. This allowed him to work his way through the ranks of government to become a quaestor, praetor, consul, and eventually a governor in Asia Minor. This aristocratic background, brilliant mind, gifted speaking ability, and scholarly persona propelled Antoninus into the service of Emperor Hadrian. On January 24,138, Hadrian adopted 51-year-old Antoninus as his son and heir. The official adoption took place on February 28, 138 C.E. with a dual ceremony for both Antoninus and Marcus Aurelius.

Now Antoninus married a woman named Annia Galeia Faustina, who became known as Faustina the Elder. They were parents of four children. Three of them died before Antoninus ascended to the throne in 138. He had one surviving daughter, Faustina the Younger. His wife, Roman Empress Faustina the Elder also died in late 140 or early 141 C.E. Now Antoninus came to power on this wise. Emperor Hadrian was suffering chronic illness, on the brink of suicide, when he realized he did not have any sons as an heir. Hadrian had spent his years pleasuring men and hadn't produced any offsprings. His first choice was a young man named Lucius Ceionius Commodus, but he died from tuberculosis while on an assignment in Pannonia. His next choice was a teenage boy named Marcus Ahrelius. Marcus was only 16. Hadrian knew he was too young to govern the vast empire. Therefore, he finally chose the honorable elder Antoninus, who was also known for his calm persona, based on one condition. Hadrian demanded that Antoninus adopt young Marcus Aurelius and his nephew Lucius Verus.

51-year-old Antoninus assumed the mantle of power on July 10,138. One of his first actions was the deification of the deceased Emperor Hadrian. After this, Antoninus was given the title *"Pius"* by the Roman Senate because of his loyalty to the memory of Emperor Hadrian. When his wife died two years later in 140/141 C.E., he erected a goddess statue in her honor. In ancient Rome, Empress Annia was considered a beautiful woman. In memory of her, he authorized the construction of a temple to be built in the Roman Forum where female priestess presided over all activities. Antoninus also minted coins with her potraits inscribed on front.

His throne name was Imperator Caesar Titus Aelius Antoninus Augustus Pius. He was considered one of the good emperors who did not oppress the Christians or any other subjects throughout the empire. He insisted that his government administrators be fair and impartial in their judgements. Trade and commerce flourished during his reign. The kingdom's treasury grew into a surplus while Antoninus held strict control over finances. At the same time, he was known to grant charity to the people and gracious donations to the military. Throughout the peaceful empire, the elder statesman helped many communities erect new monuments and restore older ones. Antoninus sponsored extravagant celebrations for the 900th anniversary of Rome. During his two decades reign, he completed many of his predecessor's renovation projects. He completed the Temple of the Deified Hadrian and the Temple of Faustina while he repaired the famous Colosseum.

In the northwest frontier, the Roman Legions still faced the barbarian onslaughts in Britain. To halt the invaders, Antoninus built another defensive wall known as the Antonine Wall. Roman forces abandoned the Hadrian Wall in favor of new security line.

So it came to pass that Emperor Antoninus Pius died on March 9,161 C.E. after reigning 23 years. He died at the age of 74 after eating a meal of Alpine cheese. He walked in all the abhorrent ways of his predecessors who served the image-gods of the Greco-Roman pantheon. He did evil in the eyes of **YHWH ELOHIM of Israel** like his predecessors Hadrian, Trajan, and Nerva who engaged in male sexual consummation. He sponsored an international homosexual festival known as the *Three Holy Days Involving The Divine Hadrian*. Still, his reign was remembered as the golden era of Rome, a time of peace. He was laid to rest in the Hadrian Mansoleum. As requested, Marcus Aurelius and Lucius Verus became co-emperors reigning in Antoninus stead as the late Emperor Hadrian had requested decades earlier.

Marcus Aurelius & Lucius Verus
(161 C.E.—180 C.E.)—(161 C.E.—169 C.E.)

Marcus Aurelius was born on April 26, 121 C.E. in the Imperial City of Rome. His birth name was identical to his maternal father's: Marcus Annius Verus. His mother's name was Domitia Lucilla, a wealthy woman who inherited a booming brickwork business and money. This allowed him to be raised in a princely environment as a young child. Dating back to the days of his great-grandfather who was a senator and a praetor, Marcus family had been connected the various emperors.

While he was growing up, his maternal father, Marcus Annius Verus III, died while serving as praetor during the year 124 C.E. while Marcus was only a three-year-old. His grandfather raised him as a child. During that era, it was a customary for women not to spend much time with their sons, especially among aristocrats.

Marcus Aurelius was educated in the halls of his family's aristocratic palace-villa on the Caelian Hill. By the time Marcus was an impressionable 11-year-old, he was involved in deep studies of Stoic philosophies, copying the dress and lifestyles of his adult tutors. One of his tutors was a man named Cornelius Fronto who was born in the Roman colony of Numidia and studied in Alexandria. Fronto was widely known for his carnal love for children and young men who lived in his study halls. According to the historical homosexual love letters between Aurelius and Fronto, the teacher and pupil, maintained a close and passionate relationship. It seem that the pair were emotionally inseparable. Marcus erected a personal statue of Fronto in his home and later commissioned the Roman Senate to erect another national shrine in his image when Fronto died in the year 176. During this time, he studied literature, language, poetry, music, painting, and philosophy. Although he spent most of his time with male tutors, he once told a Roman historian that his mother taught him about the need for religious commitment, how to avoid the ways of the rich, and living a simple life.

As a teenager it appears that Marcus's aristocratic background, in addition to his open sexuality as a boy toy, gained him access into the presence of the imperial entourage surrounding Emperor Hadrian. For eighteen years there were lavish parties and unrestrained sensualities. But in the year 136, Emperor Hadrian became chronically ill experiencing hemorrhages. He withdrew to his villa in the city of Tivoli for serenity. While lying on his sick bed, the ailing emperor realized he didn't have an heir. He hastily adopted another man named Lucius Ceionius Commodus and changed his name to Lucius Aelius Ceasar. The man was ailing, and during the public ceremony to anoint him as emperor, he died. Emperor Hadrian was forced to choose again. After his death, he chose the elderly Antoninus as the new ruler, but added an amendment to the deal. Emperor Antoninus had to choose Marcus Aurelius and his adoptive brother Lucius Catillus Severus as his successor.

So it came to pass that after the death of Emperor Antoninus Pius, Marcus Aurelius ascended to the throne on March 8,161 C.E. at the age of 39, one month before his fortieth birthday. According to Hadrian's wishes, his adoptive brother Lucius shared power and became his co-regent. Another interesting thing happened when Marcus Aurelius came to power. He gave his 11-year-old daughter, Annia Lucilla, hand in marriage to her uncle Lucius. In ancient Rome, uncle and niece marriages were common.

Aurelius was also formally elevated to the status of Pontifex Maximus, chief priest of the official Roman religion. His throne name was Imperator Caesar Marcus Aurelius Antoninus Augustus. Once he became the sole ruler eight years later, he changed his throne title to Emperor Marcus Aelius Aurelius Severus Caesar. He was considered the last of the so-called Five Good Emperors, starting with Nerva, Trajan, Hadrian, and Antoninus. Inside the empire, Marcus Aurelius placed the good of everyone in society over the desires and comforts of wealthy few. He passed laws to protect the treatment of slaves, reformed gladiator spectacles to promote a humane society. In fact, he was known as a follower of the Stoic philosophy. A belief system that dated back to the 3rd century Greek philosopher Zeno of Citium. The concentration of this school of thought centered on developing self-control and personal fortitude to overcome destructive temptations.

However, one group of Roman citizens that did not benefit from the good nature of Marcus Aurelius were the Christians. He persecuted the new Christian believers based on the premise that they were a threat to the Roman Empire. He also continued to hunt down and murder all Afro-Asiatic Hebrews in the decades-long campaign which started back in 70 C.E. under Vespasian and continued by all his successors.

Threats of war and barbarian invasions troubled Aurelius throughout his reign. In the north, he spent the majority of his reign fighting the Gothic and Germanic barbarians near the Danube River. He was not able to halt their migrations towards Italy, and in the year 167, the barbarian hordes invaded the Italian peninsula. In central Europe, Aurelius fought the hordes of Marcomanni, Quadi, and Samatian tribes. These were most likely Germanic barbarians who wandered into that area. Today this area is known as the Czech Republic, Slovakia, and Hungary.

In the Middle East, Imperial Rome locked horns with the kingdom of Parthia. Emperor Marcus Aurelius and co-regent Lucius Catillus Severus were the commanders-in-chief of the war effort. General Avidus Cassius led the Roman legions. Rome defeated the Parthian army and destroyed their capital of Ctesiphon in the year of 164. Four years later in 168, the two emperors returned to Rome from their military campaigns. Verus became sick with symptoms associated with food poisoning. Others associated his death with the outbreak of a widespread smallpox pandemic in Rome. Co-regent Lucius Verus died shortly thereafter in the year 169 leaving Aurelius as the sole emperor.

Now Emperor Aurelius married the late Emperor Antoninus Pius daughter Faustina. She was three months pregnant when Marcus came to power. While she was pregnant, she dreamed a dream. She saw herself giving birth to **two serpents**. One serpent was stronger than the other. It appears her dream was an omen because on August 31, the same exact date Emperor Caligula was born, she gave birth to **twin boys**. Their names were **Titus Aurelius Falvus Antoninus** and **Lucius Aurelius Commodus**.

In the days of Aurelius reign, Roman travelers expanded their reach to ancient China and other parts of southeast Asia. Towards the latter-part of his rule in 173 C.E. the emperor and empress traveled throughout the eastern provinces of **the iron kingdom**. This was the first time Aurelius traveled diplomatically outside of Rome. While he was co-regent under Emperor Antoninus Pius, he never left his side for twenty-three years. He visited Athens and declared himself the Protector of Philosophy and praised the gods of the Greco pantheon. His predecessor Hadrian had united Greece into a federation of city-states with Athens as the capital. Emperor Hadrian also renovated the shrines of Delphi and built the Temple of Zeus in the city of Olympia. Emperor Aurelius and his entourage toured all Grecian sacred sites.

Aurelius fell sick in the year 175. Rumors surfaced that he had died. Certain leaders of Roman legions rose up as competitors for the throne, but they were hastily repulsed after the people learned that Aurelius was still alive. For the next few years, Emperor Marcus Aurelius did not appear physically strong. The Roman historian Cassius Dio referred to him as a *"weakling"*. His 16-year-old son Commodus became his co-regent in the year 177. Three years later in the year of 180, Emperor Aurelius fell sick again and later died of natural causes on March 17. He had sought rest in a villa in the city of Vindobona, which is modern Vienna, Austria. His remains were returned to Rome where his ashes were interned in the Mausoleum of Hadrian. He was immediately deified as a god and a graven image was erected in his honor. Some historians said his death also represented the end of Pax Romana. The growing threat of constant barbarian invasions from the north and west marked the beginning of the end for the Roman Empire. Other interesting phenomenons that began to appear during this time were the increase in natural disasters. In the spring of 162, the waters of the Tiber River overflowed flooding the entire city of Rome, drowning livestock, causing pestilence, and famine. Afterwards, there was an earthquake in the city of Cyzicus.

So it came to pass that Emperor Marcus Aurelius had reigned for nineteen years in the city of Rome. He did evil in the eyes of **YHWH ELOHIM of Israel** according to all of the abhorrent practices of the Greco-Roman rulers that preceded him. He served all the pantheon of image-gods of the Gentiles. He came to power at the age of 39 and died at the age of 58.

His son Commodus succeeded him on the throne of Rome. *(A bronze statue of Emperor Marcus Aurelius riding a horse still remains in Rome today, thousands of years later).*

Commodus
(180 C.E.—192 C.E.)

Commodus was born August 31,161 C.E. in the city of Lanuvium, Italy as one of a pair of twin boys. They were the sons of Emperor Marcus Aurelius and Empress Faustina the Younger. *(As I said earlier, the empress was three months pregnant when her husband came to the throne.)* Commodus and his twin brother named Titus Aurelius Falvus were only two of a total of thirteen children, six boys and seven girls, to survive childbirth. His twin brother later died at the young age of four in the year 165.

Commodus complete birth name was Lucius Aurelius Commodus. He was *"born in the purple"* and grew up as a member of the royal household in Rome. Growing up, Emperor Aurelius made sure Commodus received extensive tutoring by many of Rome's best teachers and philosophers. However, the young lad Commodus showed signs of cruelty, excessiveness, and irrational behavior as an infant. To make matters worse, The Senate, in a jester of support to Emperor Aurelius, awarded the spoiled child the title *"Caesar"* on October 12,166 when Commodus was a mere 5-year-old. At the age of 11, he joined his father on the battlefield during the Marcomannic Wars in the year 172. He was given the victory title of *"Germanicus"* in the presence of the army at 12. When he returned to Rome, he entered the College of Pontiffs, beginning his public service. Four years later, he also joined his father when he visited Athens while touring the eastern provinces. During their pilgrimage the entourage visited the city of Eleusis where Commodus and his father Emperor Aurelius were initiated into the Eleusinian mysteries with ceremonies and religious rites that dated back to ancient Babylon and Egypt**(the head of gold)**. The principal festivities surrounding these famous Greco-celebrations evolved around the cult of Demter and Persephone. Participants used psychedelic drugs, magic, other forms of divination, transcendental meditation, yoga prayer, chanting, singing, dancing, and other sensual gratifications.

His father lobbied the Senate and, at the age of 16, Commodus became the youngest person in Roman history to ever serve as consul. He then used his power to cast his critics to lions. Any playmate who slighted him was put to death. The following year, his father promoted him to co-emperor, solidifying his role as his successor. On March 17,180, Emperor Marcus Aurelius died leaving his son Commodus as the heir to the throne. He chose the throne title Imperator Lucius Aelius Aurelius Commodus. He was finally inaugurated in the year 183. Early on, he was forced to crush several conspiracies and possible coups to maintain his grip on power. In many cases he simply slew people he didn't like whether they were friend, foe, man, woman, child, rich, poor, disabled, or a fellow gladiator. He once murdered an entire family because they were perceived as a threat simply because they were wealthy and well-respected.

Commodus reign was a time of external peace with the barbarians after a turbulent era during Emperor Aurelius rulership. Commodus used that time of stability to create a personality cult where he demanded to be worshipped as a living god. He commanded the builders to remove the face of Emperor Nero from the Colossus statue in Rome. He replaced it with his own likeness. Ruling by terror, Commodus pressured the Senate to bow before him as a god in flesh. He declared himself a personification of the Greek god Hercules. He draped himself in a cloak made of lion's skin. He commanded everyone to address him as *"Hercules, the son of Zeus."* Just like the mythological Hercules who was intimate with boys, each night Emperor Commodus demanded a young butt-naked boy be brought to him. He even changed the child's name to *"The Boy Who Loves Commodus."*

His administration of power was hands-off, totally opposite of his father. His subordinates were used to run the government on a daily basis. He sponsored lavish parties, expensive celebrations, and loved, and even, appeared naked to fight in the murderous gladiator games. Before beginning the competition, he would slay disabled people for pleasure to amuse the Roman crowds gathered at the arenas.

More conspiracies were uncovered and Emperor Commodus was forced to take control of day-to-day affairs. Commodus initiated more purges slaughtering scores of Roman senators while remaining popular among the Roman commoners and the Praetorian Guard because of his obsession with gladiator prowess. Meanwhile, Commodus became a brutal dictator ruling ruthlessly by royal decrees. He changed the name of the Imperial City from Rome to Commodiana in honor of himself. All the names of the months were changed to honor of him. August became Commodus. The month of September was renamed Hercules.

Although the Emperor possessed a harem of 300 concubines, the one woman he loved the most was his mistress named Marcia. She represented a hole in his amour. After years of seducing him as a trusted ally and lover, she subtilely began to work with others who wanted the madman emperor dead. This was the occasion. Commodus had planned to declare himself the sole supreme dictator of Rome. He also planned to slay all those in the Senate whom he hated. His mistress Marcia, who had supported him in all of his treacherous deeds, pleaded with him not to do it.

So it came to pass on New Year's Eve, December 31, 192 C.E., the plot was ready to be hatched. The adversaries were able to poison Emperor Commodus, but somehow he was able to vomit up the poison. He went to the bathroom. While he cleansed himself in the bathtub, the conspirators had a naked champion wrestler named Narcissus to come into his chamber and choked him to death as he bathed. He had reigned for 15 years in the Imperial City doing evil in the eyes of **YHWH ELOHIM of Israel** serving all the image-gods of the Greco-Roman pantheon. He ruled three years as co-regent with his father from 177 to 180. After his father died, he became sole emperor from 180 to 192 and reversed most of his policies. He walked in the abhorrent ways of the nations that did not know **YHWH** nor consider HIS ways. Emperor Commodus was guilty of shedding massive amounts innocent blood. He cruelly cursed the blind, casted stumblingblocks before the physically disabled and abused them for amusement. Immediately after his death, the Senate proclaimed a man named Publius Helvius Pertinax as the new emperor. Pertinax had served as the Prefect of Rome.

193 C.E.—The Year of The 5 Emperors

Pertinax (193C.E.) Didius Julianus (193 C.E.) Pescennius Niger (193 C.E.) Clodius Albinus (193 C.E.) Septimius Severus (193 C.E.—211 C.E.)

Pertinax
(193 C.E.)

Pertinax was born on August 1,126 C.E. in the city of Alba Pompeia with the birth name of Publius Helvius Pertinax. He was the son of Helvius Successus, who once was a slave but worked to gain his freedom. His mother's name was not recorded in the annals of Roman history for some reason. Maybe it was because of her low economic status. It is a fact that Pertinax came from a poor lower-class of people known as the plebeians. He worked his way through the ranks starting out as a teacher among his people before joining the Roman army. He was a good soldier whose performance on the battlefield elevated him into higher military and political circles. He was once chosen to serve as a provincial governor. Afterwards, he served as the City Prefect of Rome during the reign of his predecessor Commodus.

Pertinax came to power on New Year's Day, January 1, 193, under these circumstances. Two noblemen, Electus and Laetus, along with the emperor's mistress Marcia, arranged to have Commodus strangled to death. It appears Pertinax was the mastermind behind the assassination because as soon as the news of the emperor's death became known, Perinax was given the key to power and chosen as *"the new Caesar"*. His throne name became Imperator Caesar Publius Helvius Pertinax Augustus. He attempted to revive the Roman economy after years of mismanagement by Emperor Commodus. He had left the empire in financial straits, charging the state 1 million sesterces for each appearance in gladiator games. Pertinax attempted to rein in excessive spending. He informed the Praetorian Guard that he would not continue the policy of Commodus bestowing lavish gifts upon them. This angered the military and a plot was set in motion to remove Pertinax. So it came to pass on March 28, only three months after assuming the mantle of purple, Pertinax was murdered trying to stop the coup. After his death, the office of the Emperorship was placed on the auction block for the highest bidder. A wealthy man named Didius Julianus cast the highest bid and succeeded him on the throne. In the end, Pertinax's life resembled all of his Greco-Roman predecessors who worshipped the works of their own hands.

Didius Julianus
(193 C.E.)

Didius Julianus was born on January 30,133 C.E. in the city of Mediolanum, modern Milan. Some historians dispute that precise date and place, preferring to place his date of birth as February 2, in the year of 137. His birth name was Marcus Didius Severus Julianus. His father's name was Quintus Petronius Didius Severus, who was a member of one of the richest and prominent families in ancient Italy. His mother's name was Aemilia Clara, a black African woman from the former Phoenician colony Hadirumetum, which is now modern Sousse, Tunisia. Therefore it is safe to acknowledge that Didi Julianus was mulatto consisting of Roman and north African origins. Nevertheless, Julianus was raised as a pure blue-blooded Roman by the mother of the late Emperor Marcus Aurelius. At an early age he was placed in the Vigintivirate. The Vigintivirate, which means *"The 26 Men"* in the Latin. He attended a college consisting of 6 separate Boards where Roman youths were taught to administer justice, handle lawsuits, oversee road maintenance, join the police force and operate prisons.

At the age of 20, Julianus married a woman named Manlia Scantilla. Their union produced one child named Didia Clara. Julianus continued to rise through the ranks serving in the Roman government as a quaestor, aedile, a Praetor, consul, Governor of Bithynia, and eventually as a Proconsul of Africa.

Julianus came to power in Rome after the assassination of Emperor Pertinax who had been murdered on December 31, 192. After his death, the Praetorian Guard which had sunk low through drunkenness, rampant sex, and sensual pleasures, offered to sale the office of emperor to the highest bidder. His wife Manlia and daughter Didia overheard news of the impending auction. They immediately ran and told Julianus who was eating and drinking at a banquet. When Julianus arrived, the Praetorian Guard was auctioning off the throne. Eventually Didi Julianus ended up being the highest bidder by offering 25,000 sesterces to each soldier. The guards accepted Julianus generous offer and he was immediately declared Caesar. The Praetorian Guard then forced the Senate to accept their decision. It was now March 28, 193 C.E. and Julianus was now officially the new emperor of Rome. He chose the throne name: Imperator Marcus Didius Severus Julianus Augustus.

As I said earlier, Didi Julianus had a Gentile father and a north African mother. And although he had been courageous on the battlefield for several years, he was still a mulatto. The Roman population did not vote for him. *(Very similar to the treatment President Barack Obama received from Gentile America during his 8-year reign.)* Whenever and wherever he appeared in public, the crowds of native Romans would throw stones at him, shout insults, and salute him with groans and boos. The capital was in an uproar and near anarchy. News of public anger in Rome rapidly spread across the entire empire. Once the disturbing news reached the garrisons where Roman legions were stationed, three generals did not accept Julianus as emperor. Instead they fought each other for succession. **General Pescennius Niger in Syria, General Clodius Albinus in Britain,** and **General Septimus Severus**, another commander with thousands of armed men in the province of Pannonia. All of them sought the title of *"Augustus"*. General Septimus Severus and his troops were the closest to the capital of Rome in Pannonia. Today, Pannonia is modern southeastern Europe consisting of Hungary, eastern Austria, and former Yugoslavia.

Emperor Didius Julianus considered Severus the greatest threat to his survival. He declared war on Severus as they started their march towards Rome. His legions gathered more support along the way. When General Severus finally reached Rome, his force was too overwhelming for the undisciplined, corrupt Praetorian Guard in the Imperial City. They easily quashed all signs of rebellion forcing the Praetorian Guard to quickly surrender. The Senate hastily abandoned Julianus and proclaimed Severus the new leader. General Severus demanded that those responsible for his predecessor Pertinax death be prosecuted and sentenced to death. The Praetorian Guard apprehended the ringleaders and put them to death. General Severus then bestowed divine honors on the late Emperor Pertinax by erecting a graven image in his memory. Meanwhile the world crumbled around the current emperor Didi Julianus. The same people whom he paid to assume the mantle of power now sought his life. He was also sentenced to death. Unable to escape, Julianus was killed by a Roman soldier while he was still in the palace on June 1, 193. He had reigned for only 9 weeks in the turbulent city of Rome. His dying words were: *"But, what evil have I done? Whom have I killed?"* In the city of Rome it did not matter. Julianus had gotten swept up in the treacherous politics of the ancient **kingdom of iron**.

So it came to pass the Emperor Didi Julianus reigned from March 28 to June 1 in the year of 193. He had done evil in the eyes of **YHWH ELOHIM Israel** according to the traditions of the Greco-Roman rulers that had preceded him. He served all the image-gods of Rome. Emperor Didi Julianus died in Rome between the ages of 56 to 60. His corpse was given to his wife and daughter who buried him in the tomb of his great-grandfather in Via Labicana. General Septimus Severus reigned in his stead.

<u>Pescennius Niger</u>
(193 C.E.)

Pescennius Niger was born somewhere between the years of 135 to 140 C.E. and his birthplace was unknown or not recorded in the annals of the Roman chronicles. His birth name was Gaius Pescennius Niger [*pronounced* Gai-us Pes-cen-ni-us Ni-ger]. His father's name was Annius Fuscus and his mother's name was Lamprida. The word Niger means *"black"* or *"black neck"*, revealing that he was a black general. He grew to become the first member in his family to achieve any status. He was basically an unknown man in Rome until the 180s when Emperor Commodus chose him to serve as the Suffect Consul. A few years late in 191, Niger became an ambassador serving as the imperial envoy to Syria. Niger was still in Syria two years later when the news of the assassination of Pertinax reached the Levant. After that, there were more alarming reports that the throne of Rome was up for sale and the city was in an uproar because of the Roman populace rejection of the mulatto Didius Julianus. Turmoil was raging in Rome. Niger was a well-respected and popular man. Some of his friends suggested that he return to Rome to claim the throne as Caesar. Niger accepted their advice, and on April 9, 193, the battle-hardened Roman Legions of the east proclaimed Niger as their new emperor.

When Didius Julianus learned of the unfolding sedition, he dispatched an agent to Antioch to slay Niger. Meanwhile Niger sent an advance team of envoys to Rome to proclaim him emperor. At the same time, the black African general Septimus Severus mounted up his forces and headed towards Rome. When Severus reached the Imperial City in the early summer of 193, Emperor Didius Julianus had already been murdered.

A struggle broke out between the armies of Severus and Niger. Severus arrested the children of General Niger and held then as a bargaining chip. Meanwhile Niger attempted to consolidate power by sending ambassadors throughout Asia Minor, the Middle East, and Africa hoping to win over these city-states. Severus secured Rome and moved to confront Niger in Asia Minor. He dispatched his general Tiberius Claudius Candidus demanding that Niger surrender. Niger refused. Afterwards, a battle between the two armies started at Cyzicus in the autumn of the year 193. Niger's forces were defeated and his captain Aseillus Aemilianus was captured and slain. The forces of Severus then besieged the great city of Byzantium forcing the army of General Niger to retreat once again. Niger fled to another great city named Nicaea, but he was forced to retreat from there also. His forces remained behind in Byzantium to continue the fight against the forces of Severus.

Support for Niger began to erode in Asia Minor among the various wealthy city-states. Meanwhile the armies of Niger and Severus faced-off again at the Battle of Issus during the early summer of 184. The battle between the two armies was long and hard fought, but in the end the army of Severus overpowered the forces of Niger. He then attempted to flee back to Antioch and surrender to Parthia to save his life. However, by this time he was captured and beheaded. Severus had his scalp brought back to Byzantium to convince Niger's forces to surrender. They would not. The army of Severus eventually stormed the city, completely demolished it, and defeated the Roman legions defending Byzantium. The war was finally over two years later in the latter-part of 195. The head of Niger was taken back to Rome for public display. Severus also killed the children of Niger whom he had taken captured earlier. He also slew all of Niger's supporters in Rome, including his wife. All of Niger's property was taken away, blotting out his name from the midst of Rome.

So it came to pass that Emperor Niger reigned for only one month. He never actually set upon the throne in Rome. He perished in battle attempting to claim it. He came to power on April 9, 193, but he was beheaded four weeks later in May. He walked in all the abhorrent ways of the Greco-Romans serving all of their image-gods. He did not know **YAH ELOHIM of Israel** like all of his predecessors and successors. Pescennius Niger died somewhere between the ages of 53 to 59. In conclusion, the black African general Septimus Severus defeated his black rival Niger.

Clodius Albinus
(193 C.E.)

Decimus Clodius Septimus Albinus was born in the year 150 in the ancient Phoenician city of Hadrumetum, which is modern Sousse, Tunisia. In contrast to his other black African rivals Severus and Niger, Clodius Albinus was also an African man, but he possessed a light-skinned complexion that resembled an Italian skin tone. His father Ceionius gave him the surname *"Albinus,"* which meant *"albino* or *white"* because of his extraordinary pale appearance. His family became Romanized after the conquest of the territory. Albinus entered the Roman army at a young age. At the age of 23, he fought heroically for Emperor Marcus Aurelius when usurper Avidius Cassius rose up against the imperial throne. Without Albinus efforts, the outcome of the battle would have been different. Aurelius would have lost control of Asia Minor. Emperor Aurelius bestowed honors upon him, and advanced him in the army. Emperor Aurelius described Albinus as an African man who resembled one of his own countrymen.

Emperor Commodus promoted Albinus to the rank of commander of the Roman Legions in Belgium, and later in Britain. There he grew in stature in the eyes of his fighting men. When the news of Emperor Commodus outlandish conduct reached the frontiers of Britain, Albinus began to denounce him as a tyrant and called for more Senate control. Commodus was displeased with Albinus comments. He dispatched a man named Junius Severus to replace him. For whatever the reason, Albinus was never replaced, and his position outlasted Emperor Commodus and his successor Pertinax. The Senate was well-pleased with the strongman Albinus call for the restoration of their power. Many senators, who felt ignored after years of powerlessness, became his chief supporters.

After the murder of Emperor Pertinax and the chaos surrounding the ascension of Didius Julianus, Albinus proclaimed himself the next emperor with the support of Roman Legions in Britain, Hispania, and others provinces throughout Western Europe. When this conflict between the generals started, Albinus and General Septimus Severus were allies. They both had served together as co-consuls during the year 194. This time, however, these two former allies were on opposing sides. In the autumn of the year 196, Albinus left his stronghold in Britain and crossed the English Channel into Gaul with a force of 50,000-plus legions accompanying him. Albinus claimed Gaul as his territory. In the winter of 197, from February to be exact, the armies of Albinus and the armies of Severus arrayed themselves at the city of Lugdunum, which is modern-day Lyons, France. According to the Roman historian Dio Cassius, both armies contained 150,000 soldiers each. Some analysts dispute that amount and estimate that each army contained 50,000 soldiers. Regardless, it was a hard-fought bloody clash that left thousands dead. When the dust settled, Albinus troops had be overwhelmed and defeated. Albinus was slain. Some reported he committed suicide while others recorded him being captured and beheaded. All historians report General Septimus Severus took Albinus headless naked corpse, laid it in the road, then trampled over his remains with his horse. He sent the head to Rome to warn all of Albinus senatorial backers. He took Albinus wife and children and mercilessly executed them. Severus then sent another letter to Rome chastising the Senate for their role in the Albinus rebellion. Meanwhile in Lugdunum, all the supporters of Albinus were rounded up and executed. The entire city was demolished.

So it came to pass, Clodius Albinus died on February 19, 197 in the Battle of Lugdunum somewhere between the age 46 or 47. He never actually reigned upon the throne in the Imperial City. He walked in all the abhorrent ways of the Greco-Roman rulers that preceded him, serving all the image-gods of the Roman pantheon and did evil in the eyes of **YHWH ELOHIM of Israel**. General Septimus Severus finally became the first emperor since Commodus to remain in power more than a couple of months. Commodus had reigned for fifteen years from 177 to 192. Another interesting point that should be re-emphasized is that Severus was a black African. He was the father of **the Severan Dynasty, a dynasty of black African emperors of Rome** that extended for 42 years from the years 193 to 235.

THE BLACK AFRICAN EMPERORS OF ROME
The Severan Dynasty

Septimus Severus (193 C.E.—211 C.E.) Caracalla (198 C.E.—217 C.E.) Macrinus (217 C.E.—218 C.E.) Elagabalus (218 C.E.—222 C.E.) Severus Alexander (222 C.E.—235 C.E.)

Septimus Severus
(193 C.E.—211 C.E.)

Lucius Septimus Severus was born April 11,145 C.E. in the city of Leptis Magna, which was located in the Roman province of Africa. Today that area is known as modern Khos, Libya. His father's name was Publius Septimus Geta, a black Phoenician (Punic) of Hamitic ancestry who married Fulvia Pia, a woman of Italian blood. His family integrated into the flourishing Roman order and became a wealthy and distinguished clan. The blackness of Septimus Severus appearance was very pronounced. He spoke his native Punic language as well as Greek and Latin. As a young man he advanced in the Roman youth academy known as the cursus honorium during the reigns of Emperors Marcus Aurelius and Commodus. In 162, Severus journeyed north to Rome seeking to advance his public career. There he served as the overseer of road maintenance for the royal city. Aurelius had been emperor for only two years. Under the reign of Aurelius, he advanced into senatorial rank. As a black man Severus experienced overt racism and a glass ceiling which led him to return home to Libya where the atmosphere was more pleasant. Nevertheless, fate summoned him back to Rome by the year 169, and by December 5th, Severus had been officially enrolled into the Roman Senate. After the death of his father, he was forced to return home once again to assist his family. While there in Africa he received an order to be transferred to a new position as a quaestor to Sardinia. Years later in 173, an older relative named Gaius Septimus was appointed the proconsul of Africa. He then chose his younger cousin Septimus Severus to become a high ranking military officer. After completion of his term, Severus traveled back to Rome to work with the Senate once again. In Rome he became renown through his diligent legislative work.

Severus married twice. His first wife was named Pacca Marciana, a black woman of Phoenician ancestry. She died in the year 186 of natural causes. Once Severus became the

the age of 40 without a son or daughter. So he enquired of a familiar spirit, even an astrologer, who read his horoscope and foretold him he would meet the daughter of a king. In the process of time, Severus heard of a princess in Syria named Julia Bassianus, the daughter of the royal house of Samsigeramus [*pronounced* Sam-si-ge-ra-mus] and Sohaemus[*pronounced* So-hae-mus]. Her father was named Julius Bassianus, a high priest of a Syrian-Roman local cult of the sun-god Elagbaal. Severus eventually met the princess and proposed to her. She accepted his marriage proposal and they became happily married as husband and wife in the summer of 187. His wife proved to be a scholarly woman who studied philosophy. Septimus and Julia begat two sons, Lucius Septimus Bassianus known as Caracalla on April 4, 188, and Publius Septimus Geta on March 7,189.

One year before his assassination on New Year's Eve in the year 192, the Prefect of Rome named Quintus Aemilius Laetus advised Emperor Commodus to choose Septimus Severus to serve as the Governor of Pannonia Superior. Severus was dispatched to the eastern frontier of Europe. Months later, the successor of Commodus, Pertinax was murdered in a coup. In response to Perinax assassination, Severus was proclaimed emperor on April 14, 193 C.E. by his own legions and neighboring legions in the region. Meanwhile in Rome, the Praetorian Guard sold the throne of Augustus to the highest bidder who happened to be a wealthy man named Didus Julianus. The Roman citizenry rejected Julianus. Severus assembled his forces and marched towards Rome. Both the Senate and Severus rejected Julianus and sentenced him to death. There was no opposition to withstand Severus and his 50,000-plus Roman Legion.

Meanwhile the legions in Britain chose General Albinus while the legions in Syria rallied behind General Niger. Eventually Severus defeated Niger in the year 194 at the Battle of Issus and afterwards he subdued General Albinus at the Battle of Lugdunum in Gaul on February 19, 197. Following those decisive victories, Severus was declared the uncontested ruler of Rome. He chose the throne name of Imperator Caesar Lucius Septimus Severus Susebes Perinax Augustus.

The African emperor then consolidated his rule over the remaining western provinces. After that, another war with Parthians broke out. Severus won that war, destroying the capital Ctesiphon in the same year. While campaigning in the eastern provinces, he entered Byzantium and ordered that the tomb of his fellow black Carthaginian Hannibal be refurbished with marble stones. Five years later in 202, Severus campaigned in Africa and Mauretania. In the western provinces, he also traveled to Britain to strengthen the Hadrian Wall and restored Roman forces along the Antonine Wall. In 208, he invaded Caledonia, which is now modern Scotland, to halt barbarian invasions.

Known as a strong and capable leader, **the iron kingdom** of Roman Empire grew into a kingdom stretching 2 million square miles under Severus exploits. To support this great expansive empire, Severus raised taxes on the civilian population to finance the professional standing army. In Rome, Severus built the Arch of Septimus Severus and the Great Sephizodium in 203 C.E. The Sephizodium was an ancient temple monument dedicated to the seven planetary gods Saturn, Sun, Moon, Mars, Mercury, Jupiter, and Venus. It was said this standing monument was built to inspire the African population living in Rome. He also renovated his native city of Leptis Magna, beautifying the urban center with a Triumphal Arch and other grand structures. During his reign, Severus proclaimed his son Caracalla as co-emperor in 198 when he was born. He later proclaimed his son youngest son Geta in 209. Geta died in 2011. Severus ambitions were cut short in the year 210 when he fell sick while on military campaign. Severus died on February 4, 211 C.E. in the fort city of Eboracum, which was part of the Roman province of Britannia. Today it is the modern city of York and North Yorkshire, England.

So it came to pass that the African emperor Septimus Severus died at the age of 65 after reigning for 17 years in the city of Rome. He walked in all the abhorrent ways of the pale-skinned Greco-Roman rulers that preceded him who knew not **YAH** doing evil in the eyes of **YHWH ELOHIM of Israel**. He served all the image-gods of the Greco-Roman and Carthaginian pantheon. His sons Caracalla and Geta reigned in his stead as joint-emperors of the Imperial City.

Caracalla
(198 C.E.—209 C.E.)

Caracalla [*pronounced* Ca-ra-cal-la] was born with the name of Lucius Septimus Bassianus on April 4,188 C.E. in the city of Lugdunum in the Roman province of Gaul. His father, Septimus Severus and his mother, Julia Somna, both were both of ancient Phoenician (African) lineage. When he turned 7, his father renamed him Marcus Aurelius Antoninus as part of his strategy to gain favor with the House of Antoninus Pius and Marcus Aurelius. As a lad at the age of 10, he became a warrior accompanying his father Septimus Severus as his co-emperor until he reached the age of 21.

Publius Septimus Geta
(209 C.E.—211 C.E.)

Geta was born on March 7, 189 with the full name Publius Septimus Geta. His father was also Septimus Severus and his mother was named Julia Somna. As I pointed out earlier, both parents were both of ancient Phoenician (African) lineage. Like his father, he wore a long thick beard along with long hair. In the year of 209, the youngest son of Septimus Severus, and the younger brother of Caracalla turned 20. He also began to join his father and older brother as third co-regent. After the death of father Septimus Severus in 211, and in the same exact year, Caracalla arranged for the murder of his own younger brother Geta.

So it came to pass that Geta was assassinated on December 26, 211 during the Festival of Saturnalia in Rome, Italy. He was murdered by centurions of the Praetorian Guard as his mother watched. He died in her arms at the age of only 22. During the Feast of Saturnalia, the Roman graven image of agriculture was revered as a part of their harvest celebrations. Beginning on December 17 and continuing for 12 days, Saturnalia grew into one of the most popular Roman holidays. The worship of Saturn was also incorporated within Christmas and New Year celebrations in the western world. During Saturnalia, all businesses were closed, trees were decorated, gifts were exchanged, and slaves were granted token freedoms. The day of the week that we now refer to as Saturday, which is regarded as the day of weekly pleasure, was named in honor of that ancient Roman deity. Even in the 21st century C.E., people unknowingly continue to pay respect to that pagan idol during their participation in normal Saturday activities, and through their love for the annual twelve days of joy known as Christmas. **[Read Jeremiah 10:1-5]**. Co-Emperor Geta was slain during the conclusion of Saturnalia festivities.

Caracalla
(211 C.E.—217 C.E.)

The Roman Empire was rocked with internal instability during the reign of Caracalla as the sole emperor. As a black African emperor, he faced domestic hostilities from native Latins who resented his Hamitic ethnicity. That forced Caracalla to launch repeated massacres against rebellious citizens in Rome and elsewhere throughout the empire. At the same time, the external threat of Germanic barbarian invasions also increased.

In terms of matrimony, Caracalla was forced to marry Publia Fuliva Plautilla by his father. She was the daughter of Severus close friend named Gaius Fulvius Plautianus, who was also second-in-command. This was intended to be political marriage, but Caracalla was unhappy throughout the relationship. He loathed her and her father, threatening to kill them both. Once Caracalla became the sole emperor in 211 he did just that. He slew his wife, his father-in-law, and their entire family by strangling them to death.

Although his name was Lucius, he received the nickname Caracalla because he wore a fashionable hooded tunic. Inspite of the abundant bloodshed, Caracalla's reign was famous for a piece of legislation known as the Antonine Constitution, which was also known as the Edict of Caracalla. The new law granted Roman citizenship to nearly all free men throughout the Roman Empire.

In Rome, Caracalla built the Baths of Caracalla which were the largest man-made pools ever built in the Imperial City. The central room of the baths were larger than Saint Peter's Basilica. The baths could easily accommodate 2,000 Roman citizens.

Towards the end of his reign, Caracalla initiated a campaign against the Parthians, but he was unable to complete the mission. On April 8,217, he was assassinated by a disaffected soldier who served as his bodyguard. He was traveling from Edessa to continue the war.

Caracalla did not know **YAH** nor did he walk in HIS ways. Instead he walked in all the abhorrent ways of the pale-skinned Greco-Roman emperors which preceded him, serving all the image-gods of the Greco-Roman pantheon. He did that which was evil in the eyes of **YHWH ELOHIM Israel**. So it came to pass that Caracalla died at the age of 29 after serving as sole emperor for 6 years. He served thirteen years as co-emperor with his father Septimus Severus from 198 C.E. to 217 C.E. He served as co-regent with his brother Geta for two years before murdering him in the year 211. His successor was Macrinius, the Praetorian Prefect of Rome. Macrinius joined the conspiracy against the emperor to advance his own cause and to seize the throne.

Macrinius
(217 C.E.—218 C.E.)

Marcus Opellius Macrinius was born in the land of Mauretania. He was dark brown-skinned, and considered black of Berber descent. Born in the year of 165 in the Roman province of Mauretania Caesariensis which is today known as Cherchell, Algeria. Macrinius received a Roman education and developed into a skilled lawyer. He rose in prominence while serving under Emperor Septimus Severus. He eventually became a member of the equestrian class. When the son of Septimus Severus, Caracalla, became the emperor, Macrinius was chosen to serve as his Prefect of the Praetorian Guard.

It came to pass that Macrinicus went to consult a familiar spirit, even an astrologer one day. The astrologer prophesied that Macrinius would overthrow the Emperor Caracalla and succeed him. Macrinius feared for his life after hearing the forecast. He knew it was only a matter of time before the emperor would learn of the prediction. So he initiated a plot to murder Caracalla before he lost his own head.

In the spring of 217 Emperor Caracalla prepared a military campaign against Parthia. Macrinius was among his staff along with the other guards. On April 8th Caracalla stopped to visit the Temple of Luna near the battle site at Carrhae. Caracalla went to the temple with his personal bodyguard and Macrinius. Suddenly, the soldier named Justin Martialias, who had been recruited by Macrinius, stabbed Caracalla to death. In the aftermath, the assailant Justin Martialias could not escape, instead he was slain by one of the emperor's henchmen. For three days Rome did not have an emperor. Then on April 11, the Roman Legions declared Macrinius the emperor while he on the journey in the eastern provinces. Afterwards, the Senate also hastily confirmed Macrinius as the new Caesar. He chose the throne name of Imperator Marcus Opellius Severus Macrinius Augustus. Macrinius was a first for Rome in many aspects. He was the first emperor to ascend to the throne without serving, or, being connected to the Senate. He was the first emperor from the country of Mauretania and the third black emperor after Septimus Severus and Caracalla. As you can see, Macrinius added the name Severus to his throne title to pay respects to the late black emperor who was responsible for him becoming a well-respected Roman politician.

The Roman economy was in shambles during the reign of Caracalla. He had lavishly paid the Roman army. However, Macrinius attempted to reform the economy by devaluing the currency and cutting expensive military pay. He attempted to settle the wars with the kingdoms of Parthia, Armenia, and Dacia through diplomacy. Those political moves deeply angered the Roman Legions. Macrinius made all these decisions while he was still in Asia

Minor. He never returned to Rome to serve as the emperor. Instead, he reigned as the emperor while stationed in a royal palace in Antioch, Syria for his brief fourteen-month reign.

Emperor Macrinius married a woman named Nonia Celesa. He bestowed upon her the royal title of *"Augusta"*. They begat a son named Diadumenianus [*pronounced* Di-a-du-meni-anus] and together this father and son jointly reigned as emperor and co-emperor. Macrinius then bestowed upon his son Diadumenianus the title of Antoninius to honor the past Antonine dynasty.

After the murder of Caracalla, the war continued between Rome and Parthia with the situation turning sour for Macrinius as well. He was forced to flee the battlefield to return to Rome. He did not even get close to the Imperial City. He was captured in the city of Chaceldon and then taken to the city of Cappadocia, which is modern Bithynia, Turkey, where he was beheaded on June 8, 218 C.E. His son Diadumenianus, attempted to escape, but he was also captured as the battles raged. He was then executed. Once the news of his death reached Rome, the Senate declared both Emperor Macrinius and his son Diadumenianus enemies of the State. The Senate decreed that both of their names be struck from all records and all their standing images of deification be destroyed. Thus, the goal of the Latin Senate was to erase the presence of these two black emperors.

Meanwhile in Syria, a black woman named Julia Maesa, who was the aunt of the late Emperor Caracalla, took advantage of the power vacuum and uncertainty. She had already started to conspire against Macrinius with soldiers stationed there in Antioch. She had chosen her 14-year-old grandson named Elagabalus to be the replacement for Macrinius. On June 8, Elagabalus declared himself the next emperor of Rome with the backing of his aunt and the Third Roman Legion.

So it came to pass that Emperor Macrinius was slain at the age of 53 after reigning mere 14 months in the city of Antioch. He walked in all the abhorrent ways of the Greco-Roman emperors that had preceded him serving all their image-gods. He knew not YAH, instead he did evil in the eyes of **YHWH ELOHIM Israel.** Then Elagabalus, another **black emperor**, reigned in his stead on the throne of Augustus.

Elagabalus
(218 C.E.—222 C.E.)

Elagabalus [*pronounced* Ela-ga-ba-lus] was born with the birth name of Varius Avitus Bassianus in the year 203 in the city of Emesa. His father was Sextus Varius Marcellus and his mother was Julia Soaemias Bassiana. Both were of Punic (black) descent and both were of the equestrian rank. Thus, young Elagabalus was another member of **the black Severan dynasty—black emperors of Rome.** His family was relatives of Emperor Septimus Severus and served under his rule. While growing up Elagabalus served as a youth priest in the Cannanite-Syrian sun-god temple of Elagabal located in his mother's hometown Emesa, which is modern Homs, Syria.

During the reign of Caracalla, the relatives of Elagabalus migrated to the royal city of Antioch. However, when Mactinius came to power he dispersed the family back to their mansion in Emesa for safety precautions. That removal included Elagabalus, his grandmother, aunt, their daughters, and cousins. His aunt used the space and time to instigate a rebellion against Emperor Macrinius who resided in Antioch. Once Macrinius learned of the revolt, he dispatched his legions, led by commander Ulpius Julianus, to crush the uprising. Meanwhile, Elagabalus advisors bribed and assembled a large segment of the Roman army to support the young lad as the next king. The two armies met near Antioch. The mercenary troops of Elagabalus overpowered the loyalist army of Emperor Macrinius. The soldiers of Marcinius then joined forces with the troops of Elagabalus and turned against heir own commanders. Afterwards, the mutinous troops beheaded their own commander Ulpius Julianus and sent it back to the emperor. Once Macrinius saw his army had been defeated and his chief commander beheaded, he attempted to flee towards Rome. He disguised himself as a courier but he was intercepted at the city of Chalcedon. He was taken to the great city Cappadocia and executed.

At sunrise on May 16, 218 C.E., the commander of the Third Legion declared Elagabalus the new emperor of Rome. All of these events took place in Syria far away from the Imperial City. Nevertheless, Elagabalus still assumed the title *"Augustus"* without the approval of the Roman Senate. However, his advisors sent a Letter of Reconciliation to Rome informing them of the death of Macrinius and claiming that Elagabalus was the son of Caracalla. He also sought their approval for his new role as emperor. The senators responded by accepting both of his proposals: Elagabalus was the rightful heir. They also accepted Elagabalus claim to be the son of Caracalla. The Senate moved to build a standing image in honor of the late emperor Caracalla and his wife Julia Domna.

Elagabalus assumed the throne name Imperator Caesar Marcus Aurelius Antoninus Augustus. His aunt and grandmother were elevated to the honorary roles of *"Augustae"*. Now that Elagabalus had been declared emperor, the imperial entourage headed towards Rome. On the way back to Rome, Elagabalus displayed some disturbing behavior traits in the eyes of the Legions. For beginners, he continued to worship his native religion although he had been exalted to highest office in the empire. By autumn of 219 they finally reached their destination. Along the way, he had already killed an advisor who counseled him to live modestly with proper conduct.

Once in Rome, Elagabalus also performed rites as High Priest while worshipping his native religion, even going so far as removing the Latin face on Rome statue Jupiter and replacing it with the face of his Syrian-god named Elagabal. He also forced high-ranking members of the Roman government to participate in homosexual orgies and religious rites celebrating the Syrian deity. He viewed himself as the vicar of Baal and imposed Baal-worship on the entire empire. He also executed all of his opponents and promoted his lovers. Elagabalus was also widely known to be a homosexual who openly dressed as a transvestite. He even solicited men as prostitutes in local brothels. He also sold his sex while serving as emperor in the Imperial Palace. He even desired to undergo a sex change operation.

During his reign of gross pleasure, Elagabalus was known to give expensive gifts and favors to his same-sex lovers. Many of those lovers were his male couriers in the royal court. His outrageous behavior caused his two strongest allies, the Praetorian Guard and the Senate, to turn against him. In terms of moral decadence, Elagabalus was considered worst than the perverted Tiberius, Caligula, and Nero. His reputation also included long bouts of gross pleasure *(Emperor Elagabalus could be compared to Ru Paul in today's 21th century).*

In the halls of the Senate House Elagabalus commissioned the painting of the image-god Elagabal. The painting was hung over the statue **[graven image]** of the goddess known as Victoria. He blended the worship of the Syrian deity with the Roman sun-god Sol Invictus.

So it came to pass on March 11, 222 C.E. that the same people who had selected young Emperor Elagabalus conspired against him and slew him at the age of 18 in the city of Rome. He had reigned for only 4 years and did evil in the eyes of **YHWH ELOHIM** Israel. He erected and served all the image-gods of the Greco-Roman pantheon **[graven images]**, even wood and stone. He openly wore women garments, practiced sodomy, slew many, and reigned for nearly four years without the knowledge of **YAH**. After the assassination of Elagabalus, Severus Alexander, a close relative, rose to power and assumed the mantle of Augustus. His selection as Emperor represented the continuation of rulership for **the black Severan dynasty** over the Roman empire.

Black Emperors of Rome

Emperor Septimus Severus
(193—211 C.E.)

Emperor Caracalla
(211—217 C.E.)

Emperor Macrinius
(217—218 C.E.)

Black Emperors of the Roman Empire

Emperor Elagabalus
(218—222 C.E.)

Emperor Alexander Severus
(222—235 C.E.)

Alexander Severus
(222 B.C.E.—235 B.C.E.)

Alexander Severus was born in the year 207 C.E. in the city of Acra Caesarea in the region known as Syria-Phoenicia. His birth name was Marcus Julius Gessius Bassianus Alexianus. His father's name was Marcus Julius Gessius Marcianus and Julia Avita Mamaea was his mother's name. He was born into the black Roman nobility residing in the Mediterranean region. For centuries Syria-Phoenicia had been, and, it still was a majority black territory during that time. His family lived in the city of Emesa, modern Homs, Syria. They were close relatives of Elagabalus. In fact, Alexander Severus was his first cousin who was three years younger. He was a member of the royal entourage when Elagabalus traveled to Rome to assume the throne. Julia Maesa, the powerful kingmaker, was his grandmother. *(Remember, she was same woman who was responsible for the ascension of her other grandson Elagabalus to the throne.)* Alexander Severus was 15 when his eighteen-year-old cousin Emperor Elagabalus and aunt Julia Soaemias were murdered in Rome and their corpses were cast into the Tiber River. His diabolical grandmother was behind their murder. She had become disturbed at Elagabalus outrageous and decadent behavior. So, she turned to younger Alexander because she believed he was more level-headed with a better disposition. She cleverly advised her grandson Emperor Elagabalus to adopt Alexander Severus to ensure their dynasty. After that, she arranged the assassination of Elagabalus on March 11, 222 C.E. and the rise of her other grandson.

On March 13, the Roman Army backed her and declared 15-year-old Alexander Severus as the new emperor of Rome, bestowing the titles of Augustus and Pontifex Maximus upon him. He assumed the throne title: Imperator Caesar Marcus Aurelius Severus Alexander Augustus. Severus reign was marred by his heavy reliance upon his grandmother who dominated him until her death in 223. After her death, he relied upon his mother. This was seen as a character flaw that undermined his authority as a strong ruler. Otherwise, his 13-year reign was relatively peaceful in terms of foreign wars and upholding the status quo, however, the streets of Rome were plagued with lawlessness.

He attempted to halt the continued German barbarian invasions through diplomacy and bribery. In the eyes of the army this seen as another personal flaw. Last, but not least, the kingdom of Sassanid Persia threatened Rome's influence in the Middle East.

Under the advice of his mother and others, he restored the Baths of Nero. In terms of religious observance, he also allowed a Judaic-convert synagogue to be built in Rome. He wanted to build a temple to Jesus, but the priests of the traditional Roman gods opposed the idea. He also decreeed more rights for the men serving in the military.

In early 235, the Roman army and the Germans faced-off again on the battlefield. When Emperor Severus and his mother arrived at the battlefront there was a stalemate. His mother advised him to bribe the Germans into surrendering instead of confronting them with more violence. This angered many of the soldiers and some of them began to openly disrespect him. While he was meeting with his commanders in Moguntiacum, which is modern Mainz, Germany, the Roman Legion began a mutiny. Emperor Severus and his mother were slaughtered by the swords of their own men on March 19, 235 C.E. in the province of Germania.

So it came to pass, that Emperor Alexander Severus died at the age of 28 after reigning for thirteen years in the city of Rome. He did evil in the eyes of **YHWH ELOHIM Israel** like all of the Greco-Roman rulers that preceded him. He served all the image-gods of the Greco-Roman pantheon. After him, Maximinus Thrax reigned in his stead on the throne of Augustus. His death also represented the final nail in the coffin of rulership for the **black emperors of the Severan dynasty** over the Roman empire.

Maximinus Thrax
(235 C.E.—238 C.E.)

Maximinus Thrax was born in the year 173 in the former barbarian province of Thrace which is now known as southern Bulgaria. His birth name was Gaius Julius Verus Maximinus. He was born of low rank in territory that was not under Roman control, therefore his mother's and father's exact names and lineage were unknown. However, most sources report that his father was a Gothic nomad and his mother of Alanic origins.

After 42 years of successive black emperors, Maximinus represented a conservative backlash in favor of pale-skinned Aryan rulers upon the throne of Augustus. *(Very similar to the sentiments expressed by many white Americans after 8 years of black President Barack Obama in the White House.)* Maximinus Thrax also represented a return to mature elderly 62-year-old leadership. Both Elagabalus and Alexander Severus were minors—14 and 15 respectively—when they came to power as Emperors of Rome. Unlike the more cultured Romans, the ancient Thracians were known for their physical abnormalities. For example, Maximinus was a man of greater size than his fellow Romans. He was exceptionally tall with a frightening appearance, with some unconfirmed reports that his height reached 8 feet 6 inches, almost the size of biblical Goliath who was 9 feet and several inches with protuding eyebrows and a large nose and jaws. His thumb was said to be so large that is was wider that his wife's wrist. He wore her bracelet on his thumb. The historian Herodian said his appearance was a "colossal size, that there is no obvious comparison to be drawn with any of the best trained Greek athletes or elite warriors among the barbarians." Others said he resembled a barbarian bandit.

Maximinus started his career as a common soldier who rose to prominence through military service. He served in the army during the reigns of Emperor Septimus Severus, Caracalla, Elagabalus, and was promoted by Alexander Severus.

When Emperor Caracalla came to power he issued an edict granting citizenship to all freedmen, all nationalities, within the empire. The law assisted Maximinus in moving up the ranks within the Roman Legion. He was among the troops who became angry when Emperor Alexander Severus offered a bribe to the barbarians in Germania to avoid war. It was early 235 and the Roman army and Germans had been at war again. During a ceasefire Emperor Severus and his mother arrived at the battlefront. His mother advised him to bribe the Germans into surrendering instead of more violence. This angered the legion and some of them openly disrespected Emperor Severus. While he met with his commanders in Moguntiacum, which is modern Mainz, Germany, certain soldiers plotted to remove the young 28-year-old emperor. Emperor Severus and his mother were assassinated in the province of Germania on March 19. They also eliminated all of the emperor's senior advisors. The troops then proclaimed the stern Maximinus as the new leader. He then chose his son Maximus as his co-regent. The snubby Senate reluctantly accepted their choice of Maximinus because he was not viewed as a true Roman. They were displeased to have a peasant barbarian as the new emperor over the wealthy Roman Empire. The feelings were mutual. Maximinus was also a hater of the ruling class as well. In that tense environment, Maximinus was forced to foil several plots by groups of officers and their powerful senatorial henchmen.

Maximius was actually known as a barracks emperor instead of imperial royalty. His rule marked the beginning of the Crisis of the 3rd Century and the eventual fall of the Roman Empire. During these decades, the empire began to crumble between the years of 235 to 284.

The kingdom continued to experience barbaric invasions, a civil war, and an economic collapse. However during his reign, Maximinus fought and won continuous wars against the barbarians. But, these wars had to be financed, which in turn, required higher taxes. The tax collectors resorted to violent intimidation and illegal confiscations to meet the kingdom's expenses. This further alienated the ruling class from the commoners. To make matters worse, the soldiers paychecks were doubled in order to boost morale. This financial imbalance sowed the seeds for the future collapse of **the iron kingdom**.

Now, one of those plots against Maximinus came as early as 238 in the province of Africa when members of the Roman Legion murdered the governing officials and their bodyguards. The soldiers then proclaimed Marcus Antonius Gordianus Semiproanianus **[Gordian I]** and his son **[Gordian II]** as co-emperors. Back in Rome, once the news reached the Senate, they immediately switched their allegiance from Maximinus over to Gordian I and Gordian II and crowned them *"Augustus"*.

Meanwhile, the province of Numidia was located next door to the province of Africa. When Capelionus, the governor of Numidia, heard of the upheaval, he assembled a force to march against the royal city Carthage where Gordian I and II had been crowned only days earlier. Governor Capelionus was able to easily prevail against Carthage. The younger Gordian II was slain in the battle. The elder Gordian committed suicide and hung himself with his belt.

With both Gordian emperors dead in Africa, the Senate in Rome selected two men, **Pupienus** and **Balbinus** as the new emperors. Both of these men were from lower rank of society and the Roman citizenry did not favor them. Mob violence broke out in the Imperial City as the ceremonial procession passed by in the streets. Sticks and stones were thrown, street fighting broke out, and some in the crowd began to call for the selection of the grandson of Gordan I as the next emperor. The mob violence and discord caused Pupienus and Balbinus to reluctantly accept their demand that the eldest Gordian become the new Caesar.

At that time, Emperor Maximinus was far away from Rome fighting the prehistoric Germans inside their territories. Once he received the intelligence reports concerning the mutiny unfolding in Rome, he mounted up and started the march back home. However, when he reached the city of Aquileia the city leaders there closed the gates, denying him refuge. Maximinius then besieged the city to bring it into submission, but a famine and disease disrupted their assault. On May 10, 238, the soldiers in the camp revolted against Maximinus and murdered him, his son Maximus, along with all of his chief officials. They all were beheaded. Their heads were placed on poles and carried to Rome by the cavalry. During this chaos, Pupienus and Balbinus began to distrust each other, but meanwhile the Praetorian Guard turned against both of the co-emperors and slew them.

So it came to pass that Emperor Maximinus Thrax died at the age of 65 after reigning only three years upon the throne of Augustus. He did evil in the eyes of **YHWH ELOHIM Israel** like all of his Greco-Roman predecessors who shed innocent blood, served other gods, and walked in the abhorrent way of the nations that did not acknowledge the DIVINE Presence of the **CREATOR-YHWH,** the Maker of the heavens, earth, and seas. Instead he glorified standing images and all the image-gods of the Greco-Roman pantheon.

The Year Of The Six Emperors
(238 C.E.)

In the year 238 C.E. the Roman Empire experienced a turbulent civil war that saw 6 men being murdered in their quest and lust for the powerful throne of Augustus. These six emperors were **Maxim, Gordian I, Gordian II, Pupienus, Balbinus, and Gordian III**. In the end it was Gordian III who succeeded Maximinus Thrax was the next emperor.

Maxim
(238 C.E.)

Maxim was the son of Emperor Maximinus Thrax and his wife Empress Caexilla Paulina.

He was born somewhere between the years 217 to 220. His birth name was Gaius Julius Verus Maximus. After reigning one year, his father crowned him as the deputy emperor in the year 236. After that, he was given the throne name Gaius Julius Verus Maximus Caesar. He was a teenager when he was murdered along with his father on May 10, 238 after the mutiny that occurred during the siege of the city Aquilela. Disease and famine broke out among the troops and they turned against the father, son, and the royal advisors with swords and arrows.

Gordian I
(238 C.E.)

Gordian I was born in the year 159 in one of the eastern provinces of the Roman empire, possibly in the city of Phrygia in Asia Minor. His birth name was Marcus Antonius Gordianus Sempronianus. The name of his father was Senator Maecius Marullus and his mother's name Ulpia Gordiana. He came from a modest yet wealthy background and he married a woman named Fabia Orestilla. They were parents of two children: Gordianus II, a son, and Antonia Gordiana, a daughter.

Gordian I came from a family that rose to power as a member of the working-class. During the latter-part of the Roman Republic the family became members of the Senate. From that status, the family climbed the imperial hierarchy. During the beginning of his personal career when he was a young man, Gordian served as an aedile producing great shows and competitive games for the Roman public. His other responsibilities included maintenance of public buildings, law enforcement, and enforcing public order. This also allowed Gordian the opportunity to quietly move up the political ranks without any drama. He eventually became a senator during the latter-part of his life.

During the reign of Elagabalus, Gordian was chosen to become the commander of the Roman Legion in Syria. He also served as governor of Roman Britain in the year 216. In his 60s, and while Emperor Alexander Severus reigned, Gordian was appointed proconsul of governorship of the province of Africa while he resided in the royal city Carthage. Gordian's innocence and prudence preserved him. However, in the year 238, he was caught up in an African revolt against Emperor Maximinus Thrax.

Gordian II
(238 C.E.)

The mutiny occurred under these circumstances. While Gordian I was in retirement in the province of Africa, a riot broke out and the acting proconsul was murdered. The mob then turned to Gordian and demanded that he accept the call to become the Emperor of Rome. Gordian begged with tears in his eyes for them not to elect him as emperor of Rome. He protested that he was too old, but popular demand pressured him into accepting the title *"Augustus"* and *"Africanus"*. Eventually he accepted the Roman mantle of purple on March 22 with one stipulation. He insisted that his 46-year-old son, Gordian II, become his co-emperor. He chose the throne name:Imperator Caesar Marcus Aurelius Gordianus Semipronianus. Days afterwards, Gordian assembled a militia of uniformed soldiers and entered Carthage with overwhelming support. **[Gordian I] and his son [Gordian II]** assumed the roles of emperor and co-emperor at the same time. Immediately after the mutiny, Gordian I sent a delegation to Rome to meet the Senate, hoping to confirm his new status on the throne. The Senate received the Gordian delegation with favor and recognized him as the new emperor.

Meanwhile back in the province of Africa, another Roman governor named Cappellianus in the neighboring province of Numidia, assembled a large army to restore order for Emperor Maximinus. Both sides met for war in a conflict which eventually became known as the Battle of Carthage. **Gordian II** was the one who led the Carthaginian forces, but he was defeated and slain. After that, **Gordian I** committed suicide by hanging himself with a belt around his neck.

So it came to pass that both **Gordian I** and **Gordian II** reigned a mere 21 days away from Rome. Both of them died on April 12, 238 and both of them did evil in the DIVINE Presence of **YHWH ELOHIM Israel** who reigneth over "the kingdoms of the children of men". Gordian I died at the age of 79 while his son Gordian II, who was born in the year 192, died at the age of 46. Neither one of them ever reached Rome to sit upon the royal throne.

The city of Rome was filled with discontent and lawlessness. In this environment, some powerful senators and their allies in the Roman Legion rebelled against Emperor Maximinus Thrax. His chosen Praetorian Prefect was also slain. The Senate kingmakers then chose **Pupienus** and **Balbinus** as the next emperor and co-emperor.

Pupienus
(238 C.E.)

Pupienus Maximus was born somewhere between the years 165 to 170 C.E. His full birth name was Marcus Clodius Pupienus Maximus. The identities and names of his parents were uncertain. However, it is documented that he was the son of a blacksmith. He rose through the ranks because of his military valor. Beginning as a centurion before moving up to a military tribune, Pupienus became a professional officer within the Roman Army, the Praetorian Guard, and Proconsul. He grew in stature under the black Severan dynasty, serving several assignments as proconsul in different provinces. He also served as the Imperial legate of Germania. He won several victories against the barbaric German tribesmen. In the final years of the reign of Emperor Alexander Severus he was chosen to be consul of Rome for a second time. He was appointed Urban Prefect in the same year. He gained a reputation for being rigid, impartial, low down and cruel during his tenure. This made him unpopular with large segments of Rome's citizens.

When Gordian I and his son were proclaimed emperors in Africa, the Senate appointed a Committee of 20 to coordinate the plot to remove Emperor Maximinus Thrax from power. Pupienus was chosen to coordinate the plans to prepare Rome for the arrival of the Gordians. But three weeks later, news of the Gordians murder reach Rome. The senators met in closed session in the Temple of Jupiter Capitolinus. This time they chose two members to be installed as co-emperors. Pupienus and Balinus were chosen. On April 22, both received the official title of Pontifex Maximus which made them rulers of the state religion as well. At the age of 60, Pupienus had risen from dust and dunghill, the lowest and meanest origins, to become one of the heads of both the state and army along with Senator Balbinus.

Balbinus
(238 C.E.)

Balbinus was born as a member of the patrician class in the 178 C.E. There is not much known about his background. His parents names and identity were not known. His birth name was Decimus Caelian Calvinus Balbinus Pius. As a youth, he started his career as a Salil priest of the god Mars. During the reign of Emperor Caracalla, he served as a consul twice, once in the year 211 and again in 213. He was viewed as an intelligent judge who exercised fairness.

Balbinus was also known to be a great orator and poet who was well known throughout Rome. He was rich and well-connected and rose through the civilian ranks to become a senior senator. Although his reign lasted only three months, he was still greatly remembered for the building of a sacrophagus for himself and his wife. Sacrophagus were carved marble or limestone box-like caskets that were displayed above ground. Balbinus was in his early 70s when he became a part of the backstabbing plot to remove Emperor Maximinus Thrax. Balbinus was chosen to become co-emperor with the military man Pupienus.

Pupienus & Balbinus

Although Balbinus and Pupienus were chosen as the new emperors to replace the Gordians, there was an undercurrent of discontent with the senatorial decision. Behind closed doors, certain senators who favored the Gordians wanted to elect Gordian III, the grandson of Gordian I, as the sole heir to the throne. Meanwhile the plot against Emperor Maximinus Thrax thickened. Pupienus, the experienced warrior, drew up the plans and oversaw the campaign against Maximinus. He marched northwards to the city of Ravenna where he directed the war effort. Pupienus also hired German mercanaries to help him. However, Pupienus received news on the frontline that Maximinus had been assassinated by his own soldiers back in the city of Aquileia. Once the dust settled, Pupienus ordered his troops to return to their military bases in the outlying provinces. Pupienus returned to Rome along with his German bodyguard.

In Rome, his co-emperor Balbinus could not maintain public order. Lawlessness reigned supreme on the streets of the Imperial City. The unity between Pupienus and Balbinus became unglued. Each emperor moved into different sections of the imperial palace. The division between the two emperors played into the hands of the Praetorian Guard. They were already angry that the Senate had initially bypassed them for the selection of Pupienus and Balbinus in the first place. Pupienus, an experienced soldier suspected that the Praetorian Guard could be plotting against both of them. He attempted to warn Balbinus, but Balbinus feared that Pupienus had really hired the German bodyguard to eliminate him. So Balbinus refused to hire the German bodyguard for his protection. The two emperors argued back and forth. Suddenly, on July 29, 238, the assassins of the Praetorian Guard burst into their chamber, seized the pair, and dragged them back to the military barracks where both of them were tortured and brutally hacked to death in a bath house.

So it came to pass that Emperor Pupienus and Emperor Balbinus reigned together for a mere three months in the city of Rome. Both of them did evil in the eyes of **YHWH ELOHIM Israel** serving all the image-gods of the Greco-Roman pantheon and walking in all the abhorrent ways of the Greco-Roman rulers that preceded them. Pupienus died at the age of 60 while Balbinus perished at the age of 74. Gordian III became the successor upon the throne concluding the year when six men vied to become The Emperor of Rome and wear the title of *"Augustus"*.

Gordian III
(238 C.E.—244 C.E.)

Gordian III was born on January 20, 225 in the Imperial City of Rome. His father was an unnamed senator and his mother's name was Antonia Gordiana. His birth name was Marcus Antonius Gordianus Pius Augustus. He was the grandson of the well-respected consul of the African province Gordian I. He came to power at the age of 13, which made him the youngest sole legal emperor in the history of the **United Roman Empire (URE)**. Gordian III came to the throne because of the legacy and cherished memories of his grandfather and uncle. Both had been caught up in revolt against Emperor Maximinus Thrax. The Roman public remembered his grandfather and uncle as peace-loving intelligent statesmen.

This is what happened. Pupienus and Balbinus were not popular and respected among the citizens of Rome. The citizens of Rome were shocked to hear the news that the Gordians had been murdered. There were popular disturbances, military discontent, and a great fire that nearly consumed the Imperial City in the year 239. So, certain Roman legislators hatched a plot to anoint the 13-year-old Gordian as the next Augustus. The senators changed his name to the same as his grandfather. Afterwards, they voted to exalt young Gordian III to the rank of Caesar as the imperial heir of the throne.

Due to young Gordian's age, the government was ruled by the older, wealthy, aristocratic families who controlled the affairs of Rome through their cronies in Senate. In the year 241, Gordian, who was now 16, married a young woman named Furia Sabinia Tranquillina, who was his same age, and they became parents of one child named Furia. His wife was the daughter of the Prefect of Rome's Praetorian Guard named Timesitheus. Again, due to Gordian III age, Timesitheus was the true power behind the throne.

In the year 242/243, the Persians invaded Mesopotamia, a territory long claimed by Rome. In a declaration of war, the young emperor Gordian III opened the doors of the Temple which was dedicated to the image-god Janus. He also accompanied the Roman troops into the east where he defeated the Persians in the Battle of Resaena. The Mesopotamian campaign was a military success. Gordian III even made additional plans to launch an offensive inside enemy territory, but his Praetorian Prefect Timesitheus died under unexplained circumstances shortly after those battlefield victories. Back in Rome, two men, Gaius Julius Priscus and his brother named Marcus Julius Phillippus assumed the positions as the new Praetorian Prefects.

On February 11 in the year 244, another round of conflict started between the Romans and Persians. This time the battle site was near the city of Misiche in Mesopotamia. Gordian III was slain during this conflict. Misiche is near the modern city of Fullujah in central Iraq. *(Ironically this conflict took place in the same exact area where U.S. troops fought Sunni Arabs during the U.S.-Iraq war.)*

Some Roman sources dispute this version of events. They recorded that the Gordian III died far from Misiche. They placed him at Zaitha in northern Mesopotamia when he was slain in battle. Marcus Julius Phillippus, who was known as Phillip the Arab, arranged for the return of the body of Emperor Gordian III back to Rome where he honored him by deifying him with a statue in his likeness. Gordian III is still remembered today for being the youngest sole emperor of Rome. The misfortune with befell with grandfather, Gordian I, his uncle, Gordian II, and last but not least, befell Gordian III, who also died on the battlefield. For this reason Gordians have continued to hold a cherish place in the hearts of Romans, even until this day.

So it came to pass that Gordian III died at the age of 19 after reigning six years as the Emperor of Rome. He did evil in the eyes of **YHWH ELOHIM Israel** like all of his predecessors who served the image-gods of the Greco-Roman pantheon. He walked in the wicked imagination of his own thoughts doing whatever he conceived.

The Praetorian Prefect Phillip the Arab reigned in his stead as the next emperor of Rome.

Marcus Julius Phillippus
"Phillip the Arab" or "Phillip I"
(244 C.E.—249 C.E.)

Phillip I, also known as Phillip the Arab, birth name was Marcus Julius Phillippus. He was born in the year 204 in the city of Phillipopolis, a province in Arabia Petraea, which is modern Shahba, Syria, 56 miles southeast of Damascus. Phillip came from a very poor background and his parents identities or names were unknown. However, he had a brother who was well-connected whose name was Gaius Julius Priscus which served as a member of Gordian III security team. His brother advised the emperor to bring Phillip into the fold as a member of his Praetorian Guard. Gordian III consented. His brother's covetous goal was for both of them to control the teenage emperor and act as the true power behind the throne ruling the Roman world.

However, after mutinous soldiers slew Gordian III on the battlefront in Mesopotamia, and the death of Timesitheus, the Praetorian Prefect who happened to be the father-in-law of Gordian III, Phillip seized the purple robe of Augustus for him and his brother. Both of them fought beside Gordian in the military campaign against King Shapur I of Persia. With the command and control of the Roman legion divided, Phillip signed a peace treaty with Shapur, agreeing to withdraw the Roman army from disputed territory. This bold and shrewd move allowed Phillip the opportunity to remove his army from a dangerous situation and conflict.

In honor of Gordian III, Phillip deified him with a cenotaph in Mesopotamia. A cenotaph is an empty tomb or monument in honor of person whose body is elsewhere. After cremation, Phillip sent the ashes of the fallen ruler back to the Imperial City to be interned.

After that, Phillip made haste and returned back to Rome to seek approval from members of the Senate. Once he arrived home in the late summer of 244, he was confirmed as Augustus. He then commissioned the building of a standing image in memory of the 19-year-old emperor. He appointed his brother Priscus as the ruler of the Eastern provinces. Phillip made great efforts in maintaining good relations with the Senate.

During his reign, Emperor Phillip, in honor of himself, built his birthplace of Phillippopolis. He exalted statues of himself and his family throughout the city. He also built another city named Phillippopolis in the province of Thrace which served as his military headquarters while he fought against Germanic barbarians.

In the year 245 there was an uproar which forced Phillip to leave Rome due to rampant violence and lawlessness. Romans were in a depressed state due to death of the Gordian emperors, their lost to Persia on the battlefield, and Phillip's recent decision to end state benefits which many Romans depended upon for survival. By April 21, 248, the discontent had subsided and Rome returned to revelry as Phillip led them in the 1,000-year anniversary of Roman civilization. The jubilant celebrations, known as Ludi Saeculares included continued festivities, great gladiator games, circuses and theatrical plays, and other events in the Colosseums along with other gatherings and venues. Crowds saw processions of captured lions, leopards, hippos, giraffes, and rhinos as they toasted in drunken revelry. It was during this same time, Phillip nominated his son Marcus Phillippus, known as Phillip II, as his co-emperor and heir.

Although Phillip praised the old image-gods of the Greco-Roman pantheon, he was known to be a friend of the newly emerging Christian religion. He once attempted to attend Easter celebrations with the Christians in the city of Antioch, but the presiding bishop named Babylas made him stand with those who needed to repent first. Phillip also communicated in writing with a Christian theologian in Egypt named Origen.

Along the way, Phillip married a woman named Marcia Otacilia Severa, another daughter of Timesitheus, the deceased Praetorian Prefect. Together, they were the parents of three children, two sons and one daughter.

In late 248, problems in the eastern provinces appeared in two forms: rebellions and barbaric incursions. During this time, a certain Roman soldier named Tiberius Cloudius Pacatianus conspired against Phillip and declared himself emperor. This internal weakness and division gave the Germanic barbarians the opportunity to advance across the uncivilized frontier and move into the civilized Roman provinces of Pannonia and Moesia. During this same time the Goths plundered Moesia and Thrace, advancing across the Danube frontier. These low-level hordes also besieged the city of Marcianopolis. Meanwhile, another usurper in the Eastern provinces named Marcus Jolpianus rose up against Phillip's brother Priscus who was in charge of the Roman Legions stationed there. On top of that, two other adversaries, Marcus Silbannacus and Sponaianus, conspired against Emperor Phillip. It was successions of disrespect towards the reigning emperor, along with government cash shortages, which caused the discontent in midst of Rome's yearlong celebrations.

Phillip was overcome by those difficulties. In fact, he became very weary because of the continuous barbaric invasions and the backstabbings within the Roman Legion. So he offered to resign. However, he discovered there was still overwhelming support among the senators who refused to accept his resignation. Phillip was revived, so he accepted their endorsement and remained on the throne. He selected Senator Gaius Messius Quintus Decius to speak directly to the troops in the provinces. Decius diplomacy halted the revolt, but the legions in return proclaimed Decius as their own choice for emperor. Decius, disloyalty became apparent, and he accepted the nomination. He became their commander-in-chief and led the troops back to Rome.

Meanwhile, there were riots in Egypt which threatened the city of Rome's abundant wheat supply. This also caused more discontent within the Imperial City. In the summer of 249, Decius troops finally met the defenders of Emperor Phillip near the northeast Italian city of

Verona. The army of Decius easily won the series of battles. By September, Emperor Phillip had been slain during the ongoing battles. Others stated his own troops betrayed him and joined Decius. His 11-year-old son Phillip II was also slain. His brother Priscus fled and disappeared somewhere in exile.

So it came to pass that Emperor Phillip died at the age of 45 after reigning 5 years on the throne of Augustus. He did that which was evil in the eyes of **YHWH ELOHIM Israel** by serving all the image-gods of the Greco-Roman pantheon. He also served the new god Jesus Christ which was a newly emerging cult among the various gods throughout the Roman Empire. After him, Gaius Messius Quintus Decius reigned in his stead.

Trajan Decius
(249 C.E.—251 C.E.)

Decius was born in the year 201 in the city of Budalia, which is modern Martinci, Serbia. His full birth name was Gaius Messius Quintus Decius. Because of the low status of his father and mother at his birth, their names were not recorded in the annals of Roman history. Decius was the first in a long succession of Roman emperors who traced their origins back to the Danube provinces known as Illyricum. He worked his way up from the bottom to the top, beginning a career as an administrator before advancing into the senatorial ranks. At the age of 36, he became a Suffect consul. Afterwards, he served as the Governor of the Moesia, Germania Inferior, and Hispania Tarraconensis provinces. By the year 245, Decius had returned to the Senate. It was during this time in the year 248 or 249, Emperor Phillip called upon Decius to become the commander of the Roman forces stationed near the Danube River and quash the mutiny among the troops. However in a strange twist in events, once Decius arrived at the frontlines in the Moesia and Pannonia to speak to the troops in support of Phillip, they still rejected Phillip and chose Decius as their new choice for emperor.

After that, Decius and his troops marched towards Rome. Meanwhile Emperor Phillip and his forces moved northward towards the city of Verona where the two adversaries met. The troops of Decius easily overwhelmed the fighting men loyal to the emperor. Emperor Phillip was slain in September during the year 249. The Senate hastily confirmed Decius as the new emperor. They even bestowed upon him the title *"Trajan"* in memory of the beloved emperor, and clothed him in purple. His throne name was Imperator Caesar Gaius Messius Quintus Trajanus Decius Augustus. One of his first goals was restoring the Golden Age of Pax Romana, the military and economic strength of the Roman Empire. His second goal was restoring public allegiance to the traditional image-gods of Rome, thereby assuring the citizens of Rome that the empire was safe and sound. Several building projects were initiated throughout Rome, including the Baths of Decius and the repairing of the Colosseum which had been struck by lightning.

In January 250 during the annual sacrifice to the god Jupiter, Emperor Decius issued an imperial edict demanding all inhabitants of the empire appear before their local officials to sacrifice to the ancestral gods and burn incense before the standing image of an emperor, praying for his wellbeing. Those who refused to comply with this test of loyalty before a certain date were tortured and executed. Once a citizen bowed before the standing image, they would receive a certificate of compliance in their right hand. Various Christian bishops and their flocks did not comply with the edict. Even Pope Fabian was slain during the purge. Christians in Alexandria, Egypt, Carthage, and in the province of Africa were persecuted during this time. Because of his violence, the Christian Church viewed Decius as a "fierce tyrant". In the eyes of Decius, the Christians were a bunch of superstitious, socially disruptive dissenters.

Externally, the barbarian invasions by the Goths and others became more and more aggressive and organized, allowing them the opportunity to cross the Danube River to raid Thrace. During this time the barbarians sacked the Roman army and forced them into retreat. The primitive hills men returned to their territory with plenty of supplies, including some captives who happened to be members of the Senate.

After regrouping, Emperor Decius, his son Herennuis Etruscus, and the Roman legions returned with plans to overtake the barbarians and recover their Roman brethren. Decius met the Gothic barbarians at Abrittus, which is northeastern Bulgaria today. The battle took place on swampy grounds where the barbarians roamed. His son Herennius was struck by an arrow early in the battle and died. Decius continued to press the attack, saying his son's death was minor when compared to the Roman Empire. Decius encouraged his soldiers to fight harder. The Roman legions became entangled in the swamp and the barbarians devastated the Roman army. Many Roman soldiers lost their lives in that battle known as the Battle of Abrittus, including Emperor Decius. Some historians stated that he was betrayed by his successor Trebonianus Gallus who had made a secret deal with the Goths. Others have doubted that view. Regardless, he was dead in June of the year 251 at the age of 50 after reigning only two years in Rome. He did evil in the eyes of **YHWH ELOHIM Israel** and served all the image-gods of the Greco-Roman pantheon. He walked in all the abhorrent ways of the nations that did not know YAH.

During his lifetime, he married a woman named Herennia Etruscilla and begat two sons, one was named Herennius Etruscus and the other Hostillian. After his death, Trebonianus Gallus succeeded Decius on the throne of Augustus, but in Rome, Hostillian, the younger son of Decius, assumed the throne. When Gallus returned to Rome, he did not challenge Hostillian, instead he chose him to serve as his co-emperor.

There is one more notable occurrence that I should mention before we continue to move down the Prophetic Timeline. In the years between 251 to 266, there was a major epidemic known as the Antonine Plague that struck the city of Rome killing 5,000 each day. The Christians became the scapegoats for pandemic because of their anti-establishment views.

Hostillian
(251 C.E.)

Hostillian birth date or year was not recorded in the annals of ancient Roman history. However, he was the youngest son of his father Emperor Decius and mother Empress Herennia Etruscilla. His full birth name was Gaius Valens Hostillanus Messius Quintus.

His father Decius came to power in the year 249, and in May of 251, he elevated his older 24-year-old brother Herennius Etruscus to be co-emperor while choosing Hostillian to become Caesar.

After his father and brother were ambushed and slain by the Goths during the Battle of Abrittus, which is modern Razgrad, Bulgaria, during the summer of 251, Hostillian was elevated to the Imperial throne in Rome. On the battlefield, the soldiers chose Trebonianus Gallus, the governing commander of Moesia and Pannonia as their choice for the next emperor. Shortly afterwards, Gallus returned to Rome. He did not challenge Hostillian's role as Augustus. Instead, he elevated Hostillian to become his younger co-emperor, avoiding another disastrous civil-war. His throne title was Imperator Caesar Gaius Valens Hostillanus Messius Quintus Augustus. Four months later in November, Hostillian was dead. Some said he died from the plague ravishing the city while others contend the younger emperor was murdered by elder Trebonianus Gallus. After that, Gallus immediately chose his son Volusianus to be his new co-emperor the same year.

The Roman coins minted in honor of Hostillian during his brief 5-month reign bore an image of him on front, and on its reverse side, an image of the god Mars, Mercury standing, the goddess Roma seated holding the goddess Victoria. So it came to pass that Trebonianus Gallus succeeded him upon the throne of Augustus.

Gallus
(251 C.E.—253 C.E.)

Trebonianus Gallus was born in the year 206 in the country of Italy. It appears that he came from a similar background like unto the two emperors before him: Phillip the Arab and Trajan Decius. The reason I say that is because his father's and mother's names were unknown like his two predecessors. His full name was Gaius Vibius Volusianus Vibia Galla. Gallus rose through the ranks by holding several political and military posts. By the year 250, he had become a trusted servant of Emperor Decius who elevated him to Suffect Consul. He later became the Governor of the provinces of Moesia Superior. He married a woman named Afinia Germina Baebeana and became the father of two children.

In the summer of 251, Emperor Decius and his son co-emperor Herennius Etruscus were ambushed and slain in the battle against Cniva, the barbarian leader of the Gothic hordes. After that devastating loss, the Roman legions elected Gallus in the field. Gallus made a decision to make peace with the barbarians, allowing them to leave the Roman territory while keeping their captives and spoils. He also agreed to pay the primitive Goths a yearly subsidy to remain in the netherlands and halt their invasions.

Back in Rome, the Senate confirmed Gallus as the new emperor. He assumed the throne title of Imperator Caesar Gaius Vibius Afinius Trebonianus Gallus Augustus. Although Hostillian, the son of Decius, had already advanced to the throne before Gallus arrival, the two camps made peace and became joint emperors. However by November 251, Hostillian was dead. Gallus chose his own son Volusianus to be his new co-emperor.

During his two-year reign, Gallus added to the countless pantheon of emperor beatification by building a standing image in honor of Emperor Decius. He was an enemy of the Christian cult and he persecuted members of the faith in various provinces throughout the empire. He exiled Pope Cornelius in 253 and his successor Pope Luicius. Externally and internally, Gallus experienced a difficult reign. There were continuous barbarian invasions from the Goths and Scythian tribes. In 253, Scythian hordes penetrated the Roman defenses and reached the city of Ephesus where they burned the great temple of the god Artemis before they returned to their netherlands [**northern forest**] with plunder. In the far east, the Persians attacked Roman territory in Syria and Mesopotamia. Internally, there were a series of insurgencies in the eastern provinces. Mutinous soldiers chose Aemilianus as their new emperor. The news of the uprising reached Rome where Gallus began to prepare for a confrontation. He then recalled several of his legions to Rome for the impending battle. The troops in the province of Gaul were under General Publius Licinius Valerianus. Meanwhile, General Aemilianus continued his march towards Rome. He caught the army of Gallus at the city of Interamma, which is modern city of Terni in central Italy, and routed his forces before his support arrived from Gaul. Gallus and his son Volusianus lost those series of battles, and after this, it was reported that his own troops murdered him and his son in August of 253. General Aemilianus succeeded him as the next ruler of the ailing Roman Empire.

<u>Aemilianus</u>
"Another Black Emperor"
(253 C.E.—260 C.E.)

Aemilianus was born somewhere between the years 207—213 C.E. in the city of Girba in the province of Africa. Ancient Girba is modern Djerba, an island off the coast of Tunisia. He was a **Moor**. 12th century historian Joannes Zonaras described him as a Libyan(**Phoenician**) from eastern Libya near the western coast of Egypt. His full birth name was Marcus Aemilius Aemilianus. His parent's names were not known or recorded in the annals of Roman history. There is not too much known about his early life. Most likely he originated from the poor and needy class from throughout the empire. As a conscript he worked his way from the bottom to the top. Aemilianus, who was an African, also married a woman of African ancestry. Her name was Cornelia Supera and the two were married before Aemilianus left Africa. Now, he moved to the center of power during the reign of Emperor Decius. He was promoted to commander of the Roman army in Moesia where he was responsible for halting incursions by the Gothic barbarians from the uncivilized frontiers on the Balkan Peninsula. After the death of Decius and the ascension of Emperor Gallus, there was another outbreak of discontent among the fighting men. The soldiers were angry at Gallus because he had signed a peace treaty with the Goths and the Persians. During this time, Aemilianus launched an offensive against the Goths and defeated them. His victory inspired the demoralized legions and they decided to proclaim Aemilianus as their choice for emperor instead of Gallus. He chose throne name Imperator Caesar Marcus Aemilius Aemilianus Augustus.

Aemilianus moved back towards Italy in a blitz where his forces confronted the army of Emperor Gallus in central Italy in the city of Interamma. Gallus and the Senate passed an executive order declaring Aemilianus as an *"Enemy of the State"*. Nevertheless both sides engaged in battle and Gallus was defeated. Gallus and his son Volusianus fled the battlefield northward. His own guards, hoping to receive favors from the new emperor, stabbed Gallus and his son in their backs, assassinating them. Aemilianus then set his sight upon purging Rome. After an intense debate, the Senate agreed to officially award Aemilianus the title Pontifex Maximus, the priest of Roman state religion, not Consul. Regardless, the black emperor still declared his patriotism towards Rome, informing the Senate that he would fight for victory against the barbarians and the Persians in the far east.

Meanwhile, the larger army of reinforcements led by General Valerian finally arrived back to Italy. Fear of a civil war gripped the loins of the fighting men of Aemilianus as the larger contingency moved in. They then turned against their leader Aemilianus and slew him in the city of Spoletium near a bridge leading back to Rome. Although Aemilianus had fought courageously for the Roman Empire, he was viewed as an insignificant patriot. *(Keep in mind, Aemilianus was a black emperor ruling an Aryan Gentile empire, very similar to Barack Obama's eight-year reign upon the throne of George Washington in the United States. Obama was hated and also regarded as insignificant.)*

So it came to pass that Emperor Aemilianus died between the ages of 40 to 46 after reigning a mere three months over the Roman Empire in the year 253. He walked in all the abhorrent ways of the Greco-Roman emperors that preceded him doing evil in the eyes of **YHWH ELOHIM Israel**. Valerianus, a Caucasian, succeeded him on the throne of Augustus and restored traditional leadership inside the Imperial Palace.

Valerianus
(253 C.E.—260 C.E.)

Valerianus *[pronounced* Va-le-ri-an-us] was born somewhere between the years 193 to 200 C.E. into an aristocratic family with ties to the Roman Senate. However, for some reasons, his parent's names were not recorded in the annals of Roman history. Nevertheless, he was a nobleman from the traditional senatorial background. Unlike his predecessor Aemilianus, he was an Aryan of Latin lineage. He grew up at a time when the empire was in a state of instability, both internally and externally. It appears that during this time he began to enter public life and became a servant of the empire. He once served as a Consul. He was the leader among the senators who favored Gordian I to reign as emperor. He continued to serve in the Senate under Emperors Maximus, Balbinus, Gordian III, Phillip, and Decius.

Under Emperor Decius, he became a powerful official in Rome. In the year 253, when Decius left to war against the Goths, he was left in charge of civic affairs. Decius and his son Herennius Etruscus were slain by the Goths. Trebonianus Gallus replaced Decius. When Gallus had to deal with the rebellion by General Aemilianus, he recalled legions stationed in the province of Gaul which were led by Valerianus to support him in quashing the insurgency. However, Gallus was slain in a battle against Aemilianus before Valerianus arrived. Meanwhile, Valerianus troops proclaimed him their new emperor. His throne name was Imperator Caesar Publius Licinius Valerianus. He married a woman named Marinana and together they were the parents of two children.

Once the armies of Valerianus and Aemilianus confronted each other, the soldiers in Aemilianus army defected, killed him, then united behind Valerianus. The Roman Senate quickly acknowledged Valerianus as the new leader. He was one of their own—an Aryan. By October 22 in the year 253, he appointed his son Gallienus to serve as his co-emperor. In the meantime, Valerianus served as Consul from the year 254 to 257. The empire was in shambles. Barbarian incursions, along with low morale among the Roman Legions caused Roman affairs to go from bad to worse. In the east, the Persians invaded Syria, beseiged the royal city of Antioch, and eventually the city fell into their hands. The Persians, under King Shapur I, also occupied Armenia. These emergencies caused Valerianus and his son Gallienus to divide the responsibilities of empire into two spheres: West and East. The more experienced Valerianus chose to confront the Persian threat in east while Gallienus struggled to maintain stability in the west. In the year 259, Valerianus and his legions moved towards northern Mesopotamia to war against the Persians near the city of Edessa. *(Ancient Edessa is located in modern southeastern Turkey* **[Asia Minor]** *where northern Syria and Iraq intersect.)* Before the war started, a deadly plague broke out among the Roman soldiers killing enough of them to affect the outcome on the battlefield. When the war started the Romans were routed by the Persians, besieging them in the city of Edessa. Valerianus lifted the white flag to surrender and called for peace talks. King Shapur I deceitfully agreed to end the fighting. Nevertheless, when the meeting took place, the king of Persia seized the Roman emperor and detained him as a prisoner of war. This unprecedented loss caused shock waves of fear and instability to reverberate throughout the empire. Valerianus was the first Roman emperor to ever suffer that type of humiliation.

Before he fell from power, and while he fought against the Persians on the frontlines, Valerianus thoughts were not far from the domestic affairs in the city of Rome. He dispatched two anti-Christian epistles back to the Senate in the Imperial City. The first letter demanded that members of the Christian Church pledge allegiance to the pantheon of image-gods of Rome or face forced exile. The second epistle went a step further and ordered the execution of all Christian leaders. Even senators who professed Christianity were forced to bow before Roman statue-gods or lose their titles, property, and prestige. If they refused to receive and obey the order given by the emperor **[mark] [order] of the beast [king]**, they were put to death through execution. The persecution of Christians continued until his son Gallienus succeeded him. After his father capture in the year 260, he reversed his anti-Christian policies.

So it came to pass that Emperor Valerianus remained in the custody of King Shapur I of Persia for the remainder of his life. While there, according to reports, he was abused, used as foot stool by King Shapur to mount his horse. Eventually the Roman head of state was tortured to death while incarcerated in Persia for four years. He had reigned for six years, from 253 to 260, on the throne of Augustus Caesar. He died somewhere between the ages of 64 to 70. He had done evil in the eyes of **YHWH ELOHIM Israel** during his reign by serving all the image-gods of the Greco-Roman pantheon. During his reign he also shed much innocent blood, especially against the Roman Christians. In the end, Emperor Valerianus reaped what he had sown. As he had tortured many, so in the end of his days, he was flayed to death in the year 264 through torture. His son Gallienus, who had been his co-emperor throughout his reign, succeeded him as the next emperor of the crisis-ridden Roman Empire.

Gallienus
(253 C.E.—268 C.E.)

Gallienus was born in the year 218 C.E. in the central Italian city of Roman Eturia. He was the son of Emperor Valerianus and his mother Egnatia Marinana. His birth name was Publius Lucinius Egnatius Gallienus. As a young lad, he worked alongside his spiritual father Valerianus as mighty man of valor. He also served as Consul Ordinarius during the year 254. Once his father assumed the mantle of power, he placed the security of the Western provinces under his son's command. Valerianus defended the Eastern provinces.

When his father Valerianus became emperor on October 22, 253, one of his first decisions was to ask the Senate to confirm Gallienus as his co-emperor. At that time, Gallienus was approximately 35-years-old. As commander of Germania, Gallienus spent the major portion of his time fighting the primitive adversaries. He won several impressive military victories against those who straddled the Rhine and Danube Rivers. When his father was captured by the Persians besieging the city of Edessa, Gallienus was distracted by insurgencies and barbaric incursions into the Gaul and Hispania provinces, along with attempts to invade northern Italy. Confusion, infighting, unstable leadership, and repeated instances of barbaric invasions, along with diseases, almost caused the total collapse of the Roman Empire during the Third Century.

Gallienus chose the throne name of Imperator Caesar Publius Licinius Egnatius Gallienus Augustus. He married a woman named Cornelia Salonina which bore him three sons who became princes. But, two of them died before him. Valerian II died in 258. Saloninus was murdered in 260 by an army general. Marinanus, the third, was slain in 268 shortly after Gallienus was assassinated.

Before his death, Gallienus was forced to travel east to bring reinforcements to the frontline. During this period, several commanders inside **the kingdom of iron** began to openly defy Gallienus authority. Outside the kingdom, there were more massive invasions by barbarians overrunning civilized Rome. One of last battles that Gallienus fought was the Battle of Naissus, which was located near modern Serbia. In this round of conflict the Roman army crushed the Gothic barbarians, sending them into retreat. Meanwhile, a mutiny broke out in 268 when another commander claimed the throne for himself. This round of the insurgency took place near the city of Mediolanum, which is modern Milan, Italy. Gallienus and his army encircled the city, but he lost his life during the siege. Once the news of Gallienus death reached the capital of Rome, the Roman Senate voted to eliminate his entire family, including his wife, child, brothers, and sons.

So it came to pass that Emperor Gallienus died in the year 268 after reigning for fourteen years on the throne of Caesar Augustus. From the year 254 to 260, Gallienus was a joint emperor with his father Valerianus. From 260 to 268, he ruled as the sole emperor. He died at the approximate age of 50, after doing evil in the eyes of **YHWH ELOHIM Israel** according to all the abhorrent practices of the Greco-Roman leaders that preceded him. Claudius Gothicus succeeded him as the next emperor of Rome.

Claudius II Gothicus
(268 C.E.—270 C.E.)

Claudius Gothicus was born on May 20, 210 in the city of Sirmium, a province of Pannonia Inferior. Today this location is known as Sremska Mitrovica, Serbia. He was a descendant of the Illyrian people, the Indo-European barbarians who inhabited the western Balkans. It is apparent that his family became Romanized over a period of time. His birth name was Marcus Aurelius Valerius Claudius. He served in the Roman army all of his adult life, moving up the military ranks until Emperor Gallienus made him commander of his elite cavalry force. Although he was of babarian lineage, he spent his entire military career fighting against his own people who lived deep inside the interior of the mountainous areas known as southeastern Europe today. These bandit invaders would move from their uncivilized areas, which possessed no cities, roads, temples, homes, bath houses, cultural heritage, or literary records, into Roman territory hoping to plunder and murder them. Claudius, who was physically strong and known to be fierce, fought and won several battles against those enemies of the civilized Roman world. Claudius came to power after the death of Gallienus outside the city of Mediolanum when the troops proclaimed him the new emperor. Once the news of Gallienus death became widely known, the Roman Senate voted to execute all of his family members and supporters. Claudius attempted to spare their lives, but it was too late. The Senate's decree had already been carried out.

His throne title was Imperator Caesar Marcus Aurelius Valerius Claudius Augustus. He quickly moved to build a standing image in honor of his predecessor Emperor Gallienus and buried his remains in a family tomb in the Appian Way. With the empire in danger from repeated barbarian incursions, the Senate confirmed Claudius because they viewed him as the right man, a soldier emperor, who could defeat their primitive nomadic foes and restore order throughout the empire. Claudius military campaigns against the Goths were very successful. He conquered the territories along the Rhine and Danube Rivers. He took thousands of prisoners of war. He destroyed the Gothic cavalry, overthrew their fortified strongholds, and drove them deep inside the interiors of the uncivilized netherlands known today as Croatia, Bosnia, Slovenia, Montenegro, Serbia, and parts of northern Albania. Most of these victories were led by Gothicus cavalry commander Lucius Aurelianus who mercilessly massacred them. It was 100 years before the Goths were able to regroup from those defeats and pose a threat to empire again. Gothicus was also successful in his campaigns against the Alemammi barbarians at the Battle of Naissus. This is how he received the surname "Gothicus" *meaning* conqueror of the Goths.

Although Claudius was victorious in this campaigns against the Goths, internally the Roman empire was splintered with power bases in both the west, Britain, Gaul, Iberia, and the east, in Asia Minor and beyond. For decades, absolute power had slipped away from Imperial Rome. In the years 268 to 270, the grand vision of Claudius and the Senate was to reunite those lost territories back under Rome once again. Nevertheless, in late 269, Claudius II Gothicus traveled to the city of Sirmium to prepare for war against another barbarian tribe known as the Vandals who were raiding the province of Pannonia. But, at this time he fell sick and died from a disease referred to as *"The Plague of Cyprian"*. He died in January of the year 270.

So it came to pass that Emperor Claudius II Gothicus died at the age 59 after reigning for two years upon the throne of Augustus. He did evil in the eyes of **YHWH ELOHIM Israel** like unto all of his Greco-Roman predecessors. After his death, his brother Quintilius briefly seized the throne. The Roman Senate immediately voted for the deification of Claudius and commissioned a standing image in his honor known as "Divus Claudius Gothicus"

Quintilius
(270 C.E.)

Quintilius was born in the year 212 in the province of Pannonia in the Roman settlement-city Sirmium. Like his brother Claudius, he too was a descendant of the Illyrian people, the Indo-European barbarians which inhabited the western Balkans. His parent's names were not recorded in the annals of Roman History. His birth name was Marcus Aurelius Claudius Quintilius. Most likely, his ancestors were the ones which accepted Roman authority and were taught by their appointed Roman representatives. Like his brother, he also started his career as a low-ranking member of the Roman army. When his brother ascended to the throne in the year 268, Quintilius was chosen to serve as the Pocurator of Sardinia. When Claudius died, the soldiers immediately chose him as their choice for emperor. The Senate also approved their decision. According to Roman historical records, the Roman legions stationed in Germania were not included in the selection of Quintilius. They chose the military commander Aurelian as their emperor. This bloody showdown would mean another war between two large Roman armies. Instead of shedding the blood of others, Quintilius slit his own wrist, then opened his veins and bled himself to death. Some reports, however, contend his life came to an end through murder. Regardless, he died at the age of 58 in the city of Aquileia after reigning somewhere between a mere two weeks to six months. His opponent General Aurelian succeeded him as the next emperor upon the throne of Augustus.

Aurelian
(270 C.E.—275 C.E.)

Aurelian was born on September 9, 214, or in the following year 215, in the province of Pannonia in the Roman settlement-city of Sirmium. This was the same city where his two predecessors, Claudius II Gothicus and Quintilius, were born. His full birth name was Lucius Domitius Aurelianus. Born a poor man, his father, whose name was unknown, was a peasant farmer who received his name from his Roman landlord, who was a senator of the Surelius clan. It is also speculated that his mother, whose name was also unknown, came from a freedwoman background who once served as a priestess of the sun-god Sol Invictus in her village. Aurelian married a woman of his Illyrian lineage named Ulpia Severina.

He joined the Roman army at the age of 20, working his way up the ranks from the lowest ranks of society. He worked hard, building a solid record for bravery and military competence. Beginning his career serving as a foot soldier under Emperor Maximinus Thrax, Aurelian continued until he became cavalry commander under Claudius II Gothicus. He rode beside Emperor Gallienus when he traveled to central Italy to fight against the usurper General Auereolus. After the death of Gallienus, he supported the selection of Claudius II for emperor. He also participated in the Roman victory at the Battle of Naisscus when Claudius massacred the Goths in the year 268. Under Emperor Claudius II, he became the commander of his Dalmatian elite cavalry.

When Emperor Claudius died in 270 C.E., his brother Quintilius seized the purple robe and proclaimed himself the new emperor. The Senate initially approved his ascension on the throne. Aurelian, meanwhile, still viewed Quintilius as an usurper and declared war against him. Aurelian troops then declared him emperor. Both armies clashed and Aurelian's troops defeated the army of Quintilius. Quintilius then committed suicide and Aurelian succeeded him on the throne. He then chose the throne title Imperator Caesar Lucius Domitius Aurelianus Augustus. Continuing his military offensive against the enemies of the empire, Aurelian was able to halt the collapse of the Roman Empire and the Crisis of the Third Century. These victories earned him the title *"Restorer of the World"—Restitutor Orbis*. Amid these repetitive battles, he finally defeated the barbarian Alemanni, Goths, Vandals, Juthungi, Sarmatians, and Carpi tribes. Inside the empire, Aurelian was able to temporarily halt the splintering of the Roman Empire into two parts: Gallic [western] and Palmyrene [eastern **Roman empire in Syria**]. He overthrew several usurpers, including the autonomous leadership in Syria. As I mentioned earlier, he campaigned against the barbarians in the west and decisively ended their incursions into Roman territories. After those military triumphs, Aurelian was awarded the title *"Germanicus Maximus"*. He also gained notoriety as a great builder after he constructed a new system of walls around Rome to protect the Imperial City from the northern barbarians. The great walls became known as the Aurelian Walls. As emperor, he was devoted to the worship and reverence of the sun-god Sol Invictus. On the Roman coins minted in his honor, Aurelian was depicted as a personification of the sun-god. He was also the first emperor since Domitian to demand to be addressed as Dominus et deus—*"master and god"*. The title was written on all government documents.

By the year 275 the Roman emperor was on another military campaign against the Sassanid Persians, but he never reached the land of Persia. He was assassinated while waiting on a ship to cross over into Asia Minor. This is what happened. Aurerlian had been known to be a strict and heavyhanded ruler who did not tolerate corruption. One of his secretaries named Eros had told a lie to the emperor concerning a small matter. Fearing his first lie would be discovered, he devised more elaborate lies. He forged a letter in the emperor's name which was purportedly a hit list against several high-ranking officials. The fake secret indictment included names of several members of the Praetorian Guard. Alarmed and afraid of losing their lives, a conspiracy was set in motion to slay Emperor Aurelian. The soldier-emperor was assassinated in September of the 275. This bloody episode in Roman history occurred in the province of Thrace in the city of Caenophrurium. It is believed that his wife ruled for an interim period after his murder until the ascension of Tacitus as the next emperor.

So it came to pass that Emperor Aurelian died between the age of 60 to 61 after reigning five years on throne of Augustus. He did evil in the eyes of **YHWH ELOHIM** Israel according to all the Greco-Roman rulers that preceded him, walking in all the abhorrent practices of the nations that knew not YAH. When the dust settled, Tacitus became his successor.

Tacitus
(275 C.E.—276 C.E.)

Tacitus was born in the year 200 C.E. in Interamna, Italia. His mother's and father's name were not recorded in the annals of Roman history. His birth name was Marcus Claudius Tacitus. Not much is known about his childhood and early adult life. After become a grown man, Tacitus began to hold several positions as a civil officer. He advanced to become a Consul during the reign of Valerianus, and again during the rule of Aurelian.

After the 5-year reign of Aurelian, the Praetorian Guard decided to relinquish the process of selecting the emperor to the Senate. It was eight months before the Senate voted to elect 75-year-old Tacitus as the next emperor of Rome. The elder senator, who was no fool to the treachery of Roman politics, lobbied the Senate to see if his nomination was sincere or a part of some larger plot. Once he was convinced the nomination was sincere, Tacitus accepted the position as the Emperor of Rome. The Roman army also followed suit. He then chose the throne title of Imperator Caesar Marcus Claudius Tacitus Augustus, beginning his reign on September 25. He immediately requested that the Roman Senate support his building of a standing image in honor of Emperor Aurelianus. Another major move Tacitus made was the passing of law granting the Senate the authority to elect the Emperor, the Consul, the Provisional Governor, and control of the **iron kingdom's** treasury.

Tacitus was also confronted with the same external threats from the barbarians as all of his predecessors in the 3rd century. During his brief 8-month reign, he continued the wars initially fought by Aurelianus before his death, and new onslaughts carried out by the barbarian mercenaries that invaded Asia Minor. Those victories earned him the title *"Gothicus Maximus"*. On his way back to Rome. Tacitus received fresh reports of barbarian invasions in the Gaul province and northern Italy. The massive barbarian migrations across the ends of the Western Roman Empire were a continuous threat, as I mentioned earlier. It was during this time, some sources reported, Tacitus died in June of 276 after contacting a fever. Other sources stated Tacitus was assassinated. All of this suspense occurred in Asia Minor in the city of Tyana in the region of Cappadocia.

So it came to pass that Emperor Tacitus died in his camp at the age of 75 or 76 after reigning a mere eight months on the throne of Augustus. He walked in all the customs of the abhorrent nations that knew not **YHWH ELOHIM Israel**. His half-brother Florianus succeeded him as the next emperor in the Imperial City.

Florianus
(276 C.E.)

Florianus was born with the full name Marcus Annius Florianus. His birth date, parent's names, or place of birth were not recorded in the chronicles of Roman history. He was the maternal half-brother of Tacitus, who was largely unknown until Tacitus ascended to the throne. After the death of Tacitus in 276, Florianus declared himself emperor and received the co-signing from the Roman Senate. He chose the throne name Imperator Caesar Marcus Annius Florianus Augustus. Beginning his reign in July 276, Florianus faced an usurper named Probus. Probus had the backing of the eastern Roman legions in the Egyptian, Syrian, Palestinian, and Phoenician provinces. Both armies met in Asia Minor. Probus used the summer heatwave and a narrow pass through the Taurus Mountains, which was connected to the low plains of Cilica, to fight a longstanding war of skirmishes and attrition which lasted until September. So it came to pass that his war-weary soldiers turned against Florianus and assassinated him in September of 276. His reign lasted a mere 3 months and his opponent Probus was accepted as the new emperor in a matter of days.

Probus
(276 C.E.—282 C.E.)

Probus was born on August 19, 232 in the city of Sirmium, in the province of Pannonia. His birth name was Marcus Aurelius Probus. His father's name was Dalmatius, but some reason, his mother's name was not recorded. He too was a soldier-emperor whose historical roots dated back to Illyria among the ancient Thracians. Like his predecessors Maximus, Decius, Claudis II Gothicus, and Aurelian, he came from a very low estate, working his way from the bottom to the top. In the year 250 when he turned 18, he joined the Roman army. He became a decorated soldier known for his valor. During the reign of Valerianus [in 253-260 C.E.], Probus rose to the position of Military Tribune. He fought alongside generals Claudius and Aurelian participating in the military victories that ended barbarian incursions. He eventually became one of Aurelian's most valiant lieutenants. In the year 275, Emperor Tacitus chose him to serve as a powerful commander of the eastern Roman legions.

For the record, Probus initial support and powerbase extended to only a very small part of the total empire, mainly in the east. After his victory against the army of Florianus in Asia Minor, Probus sent a letter to the Roman Senate respectfully requesting their permission to become the new emperor. His control over the Egyptian grain supply increased his influence with the Senate. The Senate hastily approved his request. Probus became the new emperor of the Roman Empire. His throne name was Imperator Caesar Marcus Aurelianus Probus Augustus.

Probus continued his campaigns against the barbarian Goths tribes residing along the lower Danube River. Those victories earned him the title *"Gothicus Maximus"* and *"Germanicus Maximus"*—conqueror of the Goths and Germans. By the year 278, Probus was fighting wars in the province of Gaul against more invaders. According to historical reports, Probus massacred nearly 500,000 Germanic barbarians during these campaigns, even invading their barbaric homelands. The barbarian population known as the Lugil were completely wiped out. Hoping to halt the massive influx of nomads, Probus re-erected the ancient fortifications initially built by Emperor Hadrian between the Rhine and Danube rivers.

Probus then developed a new strategy of civilizing the conquered populations by settling them inside Roman territory and teaching them how to develop their own cities. Those provinces needed the barbarian population to replace the naturalized Roman citizens who had fled the frontiers due to wars, disease, army inscription, high taxes, and lack of support from the Imperial City. The settlements also served as frontline defenses against further invasions deeper inside Roman territories. Eventually these barbarian colonies grew into medieval European city-states before advancing into Western and Eastern European countries.

By the year 281, the soldier emperor had overcome at least three uprisings from within his own ranks. That was also the same year Probus returned to Rome in triumphal glory and celebrations. Probus wore a crown of laurel with a solid purple toga with gold-embroidered trimmings. The doors of Jupiter temple, situated on Capitoline Hill, were opened for sacrifices and thanksgivings to the image-god. The celebrations included a procession, feasting, and public games.

However, in September or October of 282, chaos broke out among Probus troops. The reasons for the mutiny differed. Some accounts said Probus was assassinated because they were disgruntled about their civilian assignments. Other accounts report his army overheard him complaining about the need for a standing army. Regardless of which account was true, Probus was murdered while preparing for another war against the Persians.

So it came to pass the Probus died as the age of 50 after reigning six years as the ruler of the ancient Roman Empire. He did evil in the eyes of **YHWH ELOHIM Israel**, the CREATOR of heavens, earth, and the seas, and all therein by serving all the image-gods of the Greco-Roman pantheon according to manner of all the nations that knew not YAH. A Roman general named Carus became his successor.

Carus
(282 C.E.—283 C.E.)

Carus was born in the year 222 in the city of Narbo in the Gaulic province of Gallia Narbonensis, which is modern southern France. His full birth name was Marcus Numerius

Carus. His father's and mother's names were not recorded in the annals of Roman history. During his days, there was a steep decline in literature, the arts, and historical records. Therefore, there is not much known about his early life. What is known is that he was educated in Rome and served in various government posts, both in the civilian and military departments. He eventually became a senator before being appointed Prefect of the Praetorian Guard under Emperor Probus in 282.

After the murder of Emperor Probus at Sirmium, Carus succeeded him as the commander-in-chief and emperor. He chose the throne name Imperator Caesar Marcus Aurelius Carus Augustus. He was 60 when he ascended to the throne, but he did not return to Rome to seek acceptance from the Senate. Instead, he arrogantly sent his proclamation by letter to the governing body. One of his first moves was to avenge the blood of his predecessor Probus. He also chose his two sons, Carinus and Numerian, as his co-emperors. Carinus was placed in charge of the western portion of the empire while Numerian joined him on his expedition against the Persians, moving through Thrace over into Asia Minor. From there, he advanced into Mesopotamia before pressing on to overthrow Seleucia and Ctesiphon before moving beyond the Tigris River. Carus victories avenged all the previous defeats suffered by the Romans, earning him the title *"Persicus Maximus"*. Unfortunately, Rome's hopes for further conquest was cut short by the death of Carus which occurred shortly after those victories.

There have been several conflicting narratives on how Carus died. Some sources, such as the Augustan history, stated his death was a natural one, and that he died from a sudden illness. Others believed he died from a wound received in war, or, he was assassinated by members of his Praetorian Guard. All sources agree that Carus died in the midst of a violent thunderstorm where the awe of the lightning terrorized the mighty fighting men. The Romans perceived his death and the storm as a sign from the gods. It was believed the gods of Rome did not want Rome to cross the Tigris. After Carus death Rome ceased its attempt to conquer Mesopotamia for a decade. Carus was succeeded by his sons Carinus and Numerian, creating a short-lived dynasty which lasted for only 2 years.

So it came to pass the Carus died at the age 61 beyond the Tigris River in Mesopotamia after reigning less than one year. He walked in all the ways of his Roman predecessors who knew not **YHWH ELOHIM Israel.** Instead, he served all the image-gods of the Greco-Roman pantheon.

Carinus and Numerian
(283-285 C.E.)—(283-284 C.E.)

Carinus date of birth was unknown, or erased from Roman inscriptions. His father was emperor Carus but his mother's name was not mentioned, or it was not known. His full birth name was Marcus Aurelius Carinus. There is very little known about his early life, however, it would be safe to presume that this part of his life was spent as a young soldier learning warfare with his father. From the year 282 to 283, he served as his father's co-emperor. When his father departed for his Persian campaign, he left Carinus, his oldest son, to handle the affairs of the western portion of the empire while he and his younger son Numerian marched towards Persia. During this time, in the year 284, Carinus later shared co-emperor status with his brother Numerian. Once he ascended to the seat of power, he chose the throne name Imperator Marcus Aurelius Carinus Augustus. He fought battles in the province of Gaul against the barbaric Quadi tribes. After subduing them, he left the Roman garrisons located on the Upper Rhine to return to Rome, leaving his commanders in charge.

Back in Rome, Carinus lived a reckless and promiscuous life. Although he was married to a woman named Magna Urbica, and the father of two children, he married nine other times and divorced each one of those women. During his one year reign he organized the annual celebrations of the Ludi Romani games to unparalleled extravagant levels. It was also reported that he bore a grudge against those who disrespected him before he became the emperor.

The news of Carus death, and afterwards the death of his younger brother Numerian, finally reached the Imperial City. After that, Carinus left Rome heading eastward to confront the troops and their new commander Diocletian. Along the way, Carinus had to quash an uprising by an usurper named Sabinus Julianus. Afterwards, he kept riding towards the province of Moesia. It was the summer of 285, in the month of July, the two armies met at the Marqus River. The battle was set in array. There are different accounts on how the conflict ended. One account said Carinus won the battle, but was slain by one of his disgruntled soldiers whose wife Carinus had committed adultery with in times past. The other account said Carinus lost the battle, his army deserted him, and then assassinated him. Either way, Carinus was dead in July of the year 285.

So it came to pass that Emperor Carinus died after reigning only two years, one year as a co-emperor with his father Carus and the second year with his brother Numerian. In the end Diocletian succeeded him as the next emperor of the ailing Roman Empire. Carinus did evil in the eyes of **YHWH ELOHIM Israel** according all the abominations of the nations that knew not YAH.

Numerian
(283 C.E.—284 C.E.)

Numerian's date of birth or year was unknown, or somehow erased from the annals of Roman inscriptions. His father was emperor Carus but his mother's name is not mentioned or it was not known. His full birth name was Marcus Aurelius Numerius. Like his brother Carinus, there is not much known about his early life. But, it would be safe to assume that the fruit did not fall to far from the tree, so if his father was a warrior, it is most likely he also spent the early part of life earning military experience as well. His father Carus was a general who was chosen to serve as Prefect of the Praetorian Guard under Emperor Probus.

After his father Carus became emperor, he chose Numerian as one of his co-emperors along with his older brother Carinus. Numerian joined his father Carus on his campaign against the Persians. His father died during a violent thunderstorm which his troops believed was an omen from the gods to retreat from Mesopotamia. His throne name was Imperator Caesar Marcus Aurelius Numerius Augustus. By March 284, the Roman forces had reached Emesa, which is modern Homs, Syria. At that time, his health was good. However, eight months later in November when they reached Asia Minor Numerian health took a turn for the worst. He was unable to endure the extreme heat wave, the rough terrain, and he suffered from inflammation of the eye, so he retreated in a closed carriage. He appointed the Prefect of the Praetorian Guard Arrius Aper to speak in his absence. Once the army crossed over into Thrace, some of the soldiers smelled an odor which reminded them of a dying corpse. They broke into the Imperial Tent, turned back the curtains, and found Numerian dead.

After this, the generals and the military tribunes called for a council of succession. They chose Diocletian, commander of the cavalry and the Imperial bodyguard, as the new emperor. Diolectian accepted their nomination, and afterwards he was awarded the purple vestments. He raised his sword to the light of the sun and swore an oath denying any responsibility for the death of Numerian. Diolectian accused Aper, the Prefect of the guards, of murdering the emperor. Aper was bound and dragged before the entire Roman army. As the soldiers looked, Diocletian took his sword and bludgeoned him in full view.

So it came to pass that Emperor Numerian died after reigning a mere 16 months. He never reached Rome to actually sit upon the throne. He died during those campaigns in the east. His age at the time is uncertain. We do know he died on November 20, 284 somewhere in the province of Thrace. He acted according to his father and his brother serving the image-gods of the Greco-Roman pantheon. He did evil eyes in the eyes of **YHWH ELOHIM Israel** according to the customs of the spiritually uncircumcised nations that knew not YAH. Numerian was known as a poet and great orator. Back in Rome, the Senate commissioned the building of a standing image in his honor.

Diocletian succeeded him and his brother Carinus as the next ruler of **the kingdom of iron**, the Roman Empire.

The Iron Age—(Its Legs of Iron)
Divided Western and Eastern Roman Empire—PART TWO "the legs"
"its legs were of iron—But the fourth kingdom will be strong as iron; just as iron crushes and shatters everything—and as iron that smashes—so will it crush and smash all these."
Daniel 2: 33, 40

"YAH changes times and seasons. HE removes kings (kingdoms) and install kings(kingdoms); HE gives the wise their wisdom and knowledge to those who know"   Daniel 2: 21

The History of Divided Roman Empire
[East] & [West] Roman Empires

In the late third century and early fourth century, the Roman Empire began to gradually transform and shift into two separate and distinct empires. One established in the Far West, which is now known as north-central and western Europe with its capital in the great city which sitteth upon the seven mountains. In the eastern capital Byzantium, Rome was no longer viewed as the unchallenged capital of the Greco-Roman world. During this new era Rome shared its once designated title of the capital of Roman Empire with Milan, Italy, Antioch, Syria, and finally the Imperial City of Constantinople. This division of **iron kingdom** was described as legs in the Revelation to Daniel. Just as all normal human beings have a right and left leg (2) legs, YAH foretold to Daniel that the Roman Empire would one day split into two parts, or two legs: West and East.

King Solomon once said in **Proverbs 21:1[Tanakh]**, *"Like channeled waters is the mind of the king in YHWH's Hand, HE directs it to whatever HE wishes."* So now, we will witness the mysterious Hand of YAH moving the uncircumcised minds of these Roman Emperors to fulfill HIS Word to create the Prophetic Time Zone within the Roman Empire known as the **two Legs of Iron**.

Diocletian
(284 C.E.—305 C.E.)
[East—West]

Diocletian was born on December 22 in the year of 244 in the city of Aspalathos, which is modern-day Split, Croatia. He was born into a family of low social status, rising through the ranks of the Roman legion in obscurity for his first 40 years. While growing up, the Roman Empire was on the brink of collapse because of civil wars and barbarian incursions. In the year 282 he was chosen to serve as commander of forces on the lower Danube River. The following year he was promoted to the office of Consul and commander of the elite cavalry for Emperor Carus. After the death of Carus and his son Numerian while campaigning against Persia, the soldiers chose him as their choice for emperor. However, the older son of Emperor Carus name Carinus still occupied the throne in Rome. Once Carinus received the report that his father and brother were dead and the troops had chosen a new emperor, he immediately left his post in the province of Gaul, arriving in Rome in January 284, before moving on to the east. The two adversaries met at the Margus River in the province of Moesia. The battle was set in array. Carinus mustered a larger army than Diolectian, and according to historical sources, his army initially prevailed, but in midst of the battle, Carinus soldiers turned against him and murdered him. It was said that many soldiers in Carinus army were angry with him because he had abused his power by having random affairs with their wives. They defected to Diocletian's side, thereby making him the victor of the Battle of Margus.

After the Battle of Margus in the summer of 285, Diocletian and his troops moved into northern Italy to pushback the barbaric invasions. This time it was the Quadi and Marcomanni invaders. Diocletian snubbed the Roman Senate, bypassing Rome for the city of Milan. He chose the throne name Imperator Caesar Gaius Aurelius Valerius Diocletianus Augustus. The one action Diocletian did take while near in Rome was replace the Prefect of Rome. He chose co-consul Lucius Caesonrus Bassus. Afterwards, the warrior-emperor marched back to the Balkans before winter. This time his battles were against the Sarmatian barbaric tribes. With unrest brewing in nearly all of the Roman provinces, ranging from the western province of Gaul to the eastern province of Syria, Diocletian adopted a fellow-soldier named Maximian to assist him in ruling the massive the empire as co-emperor.

During the winter of 290-291, Diocletian and Maximian met in Milan again. There was an elaborate ceremony and procession that displayed unity and confidence in their joint rulership. Maximian was responsible for defending the western frontiers while Diocletian fought to subdue all the adversaries in the eastern provinces. Maximian was having trouble securing the west against the Saxons, Franks, and other barbarian invaders, yet Diocletian still trusted him as his co-regent. In fact, Diocletian had returned from the east to support Maximian. During the imperial speeches at the anointing ceremonies in Milan, Italy Diocletian was praised as the representative of Jupiter, the sky-god, working on behalf of the statue on earth, elevating himself above the masses on earth. Both emperors shifted the public's attention away from military credibility towards divine trappings and religious authority. Those actions, along with successive military victories, halted the decline of the Roman Empire and returned normalcy throughout **the iron kingdom**. After Diocletian destroyed Ctesiphon, which was the capital of the Persian Empire in the year 299, he was credited with ending the Crisis of the Third Century. In the year 289 he received the title *"Sarmaticus Maximus"* because of his victorious wars against the barbaric Sarmatians. He then continued on into the eastern provinces where he strengthened the outlaying Roman cities and forced the Persians to relinquish their territorial claims on the land of Armenia. Bahram II, the king of Persia, was forced to sign a peace agreement with the Roman emperor. The King of Persia gave Diocletian all manner of precious gifts and opened a new chapter of non-aggression between the two longtime enemies. These acts caused Diocletian to be hailed as the founder of eternal peace.

As an administrator, he reformed the Roman tax system with one standardized rate. He restored government efficiency and stopped rampant corruption. He separated the civilian and military branches of power, ending the Praetorian Guard influence in the political process. He also reorganized the provinces into 12 dioceses with each being ruled by a vicar. Diocletian did not want to experience the same fate as his predecessors so in the spring of 293, he decided to form a new system of leadership known as a Tetrarchy—the rule of four emperors. The goal of this idea was to ensure an orderly succession of power. From his palace in the city of Nicomedia in Asia Minor, Diocletian, the Imperial Augusti, ruled the eastern provinces of the empire. His co-Augusti, Maximian reigned in Milan, Italy where he secured the borders of the western provinces, ranging from Britain to Gaul. Both of the Augustus then chose a co-Caesar to serve under them. Diocletian chose a man named **Galerius** who assisted in ruling the east. Maximian chose a man named Flavius Constantinus, the governor of Dalmatia, as his co-regent. Each emperor ruled a quarter of the empire with the responsibility of destroying all threats to Roman power. Diocletian established new administrative centers in Nicomedia, Mediolanum, Sirmium, and Tier. Those cites were closer to the empire's frontiers. As you can see, the true center of power was no longer in the city of Rome. Rome had been reduced to a ceremonial capital. In the mind of Diocletian, who snubbed the Imperial City, Rome was anywhere the emperor resided, meaning his capitals in Nicomedia and Milan were equal to Rome. In the new order, each emperor reigned as a sovereign Caesar with their own imperial courts, administrations, secretaries, and independent armies.

In terms of beliefs, Diocletian was a religious traditionalist who served the image-gods of the Roman trinity, the father Jupiter, the son Mars, and the holy ghost Quirinus. This placed him at odds with infant cult of Christianity which praised the new image-god Jesus. Both sides were critical of each other. In the year 299, the emperor resided in the city of Antioch, Syria, where he participated in a religious ceremony of sacrifice and divination, attempting to predict the future. The priests were unable to read the liver, the object used to foresee the future. *(This is the same type of divination King Nebuchadnezzar used in* **[Ezekiel 21:21]**, *and very similar to modern Ouija Boards).* The priests in the Imperial Court blamed the followers of Christianity for failure to receive an answer from the gods. All Christians were expelled from their government positions and military roles to pacify the wraths of the gods. **Co-emperor Galerius** called for the complete extermination of the Christianity from the empire. The two leaders then traveled to the city of Didyma to seek an oracle from the sun-god Apollo. The answer from the high priest of Apollo was that Christians were the enemies of the traditional gods, and they needed to be removed wherever they resided throughout the realms of the empire. Diocletian then razed all the churches, burned their scriptures, and confiscated all their tithes of precious treasures. In 302, he ordered his soldiers to cut out the tongues of Christians who had interrupted ceremonies and defied orders to bow before the traditional gods of Rome. On February 24, 303, Diocletian issued a decree that made it a crime for Christians to assemble. He continued his assaults against more places of worship, Christian scriptures, and believers. To make matters worse for Christians, a mysterious fire consumed parts of the Imperial Palace. The emperors superstitiously blamed the fire on Christians. Diocletian ordered more executions. Christians were stripped naked, flogged, scourged, and placed on crucifixes to die in agony. Salt and vinegar were poured in their open wounds. Others were boiled to death over open flames while others were beheaded. Ironically, a second fire broke out sixteen days later. Emperor Galerius was spooked and moved back to Rome. Diocletian followed him shortly thereafter.

(The oppression of the Christians had the opposite effects of its intentions. Instead of eradicating the new god, the persecution strengthened the resolve of the Christian faithful). The Diocletian Persecution lasted from 303 to 311. It was the worse official persecution of Christianity in the history of the Roman Empire.

In the month of November during the winter of 303, Diocletian entered Rome where he celebrated the 20th anniversary of his reign, the 10th year of the Tetrarchy, and his victory over Persia. Initially, he planned for both emperors to retire in Rome in an elaborate ceremony in the Temple of Jupiter. However, by December 20, 303, Diocletian, sensed disrespect to the Imperial throne of Caesar, so he hastily left Rome for Milan.

By November of the following year, which was the year 304, Diocletian appeared in public in his hometown of Aspalathos to dedicate the opening of a circus which was built right beside his palace. After the ceremonies, he collapsed and had to be carried away in a litter. He was taken to his palace where he remained for the entire winter of 304-305. He lost weight and looked bad. By summer of 305, he left for the city of Nicomedia to attempt to handle the kingdom's business. Weakened by lingering illness, Diocletian was forced to step down from the throne on May 1, 305, becoming the first leader in Roman history to peacefully retire. Ironically, Diocletian and the generals met on the same hill where he had been proclaimed emperor 21 years earlier, three miles outside of Nicomedia. In front of the statue-god Jupiter, the ailing emperor, who had once been a mighty man of valor, with tears in his eyes, told the officers he needed to rest. He then informed them of his intent to resign. He told the generals he needed to transfer the duty of Augusti to a more physically stronger person.

He lived out his final years in his palace on the Dalmatian coast off the coast of the Adriatic Sea. There, in solitude and serenity, he peacefully tended to his vegetable garden. His plans for an orderly succession did not materialize due to competing claims, interest, and selfishness on part of the potential heirs. In the end, the system of Tetrarchy collapsed. In the West, Emperor Maximian and his co-regent Caesar Constantius did not persecute the Christians. In 311, Galerius repealed the law against the Christian cult. Later in March of 311, Galerius left Rome to visit Diocletian on his sick bed. He planned to seize power for himself and his co-regent. He had already convinced the sickly Diocletian to comply to his wishes, but the others did not agree with the secret deal. Therefore, murder, chaotic envy, and jealousy broke out among the surviving tetrarchic emperors.

So it came to pass that Emperor Diocletian died at the age of 66 after reigning for 21 years. Diocletian retired in the year 305. His last six years were spent in retirement at his palace in the city of Aspalathos until he gave up the ghost. He did evil in the eyes of **YHWH ELOHIM Israel** according to all the abhorrent practices of the spiritually uncircumcised emperors that preceded him. He served all the image-gods of the Greco-Roman pantheon. During his lifetime, he married a woman named Prisca. They had one daughter named Valeria.

Diocletian lived in deep depression and illness for until he passed. Some say he killed himself, other contend he died from his grave illness. Either way, the fierce conquering emperor, a mighty hunter before YAH, was dead on December 3, 311.

King David once said, *"As for man[Diocletian], his days are as grass: as a flower of the field, so he flourishes. For the wind passeth over it, and it is gone; and the place therefore shall know it no more,"* in **Psalms 103:15-16**. Furthermore in **Psalms 37: 35-36**, he said: *"I have see the wicked in great power, and spreading himself like a green bay tree. Yet he passed away, and, lo, he was not; yea, I sought him, but he could not be found"*.

Once Diocletian was entombed, there were 7 men that vied to succeed him. There was Marcus Maximian, **Gaius Galerius[305-311], Flavius Severus[306-307], Gaius Lucinius[308-324], Marcus Maxicentus[306-312], Constantius Chlorus[305-306]**, and Flavius Constantine. After the dust settled from the civil war among the Tetrarchy, it was Constantine I who eventually ascended to the throne of Augustus.

Constantine I "The Great"
(312 C.E.—337 C.E.)
[West—East]

Constantine was born on February 27, 272 in the city of Naissus, Moesia Superior, which is present-day Nis, Serbia. His full birth name was Flavius Valerius Aurelius Constantinus. His father's name was Constantius Chlorus, a great general, and his mother's name was Helena, who was a woman of low status. He was born in the former barbarian territory of Illyria. His father worked through the Roman Legion ranks and became a junior Caesar, serving as the deputy emperor in the West under Emperor Maximian. By the age of 17, his father and mother were divorced. His mother Helena and her son Constantine were sent to the Imperial Court of Emperor Diocletian in Nicomedia where he grew up as a member of the ruling class, learning ancient Greek and Latin philosophies, the art of warfare and receiving extensive military training. Meanwhile, in the year 293, Constantine followed in the footsteps of his father as a man of war. He received orders to transfer to the east where he also rose through the ranks to become a military tribune in the imperial court of Emperors Diocletian and Galeriuis. He remained their for twelve years until his father arranged for him to come back to Britannia where he served under him as the junior emperor. His father died a year later in 306. The army at the Roman settlement at Eboracum, which is modern-day York, then proclaimed Constantine as the new Augustus. He received the purple robe and chose the throne name: Imperator Caesar Flavius Valerius Aurelius Constantinus Augustus.

His new role was not accepted by the entire Roman army and there were several contenders in the east. This included Maxentius, the son of Maximian, who fought against Constantine at the Battle of the Milvian Bridge. In that particular conflict Maxentius and his army were routed. Afterwards, they attempted to flee across the Tiber River, but Maxentius drowned. His body was later taken out of the river, his head cut off, and paraded through the streets of Rome. After that, Constantine continued to fight his way into power through several other wars against contenders such as Galerius, who was once-co-emperor under Diocletian. He also warred against contenders Valerius Severus and Lucinius. For twelve years, Constantine continued to battle his internal foes in a slugfest until he eliminated them. By September 19th, he emerged as the sole emperor of both the East and West during the year 324. After gaining complete control, Constantine began to enact administrative, financial, social, and military reforms to strengthen the Roman empire. He continued the reforms initiated by his predecessor Diocletian, separating the authority of the Senate and the Praetorian Guard. In terms of the military, he transformed the legion with mobile field units and garrison soldiers. In terms of economics, the emperor introduced a new gold coin known as the solidus. The gold coin became the standard for the Byzantine and European currencies until the Middle Ages. Externally, he successfully fought successive wars to halt the influx of the barbaric Frank,

Sarmartian, and the Goth tribes who attempted to invade, plunder, and occupy the territory of the western Roman provinces.

As I said earlier, Constantine was a member of Emperor Diocletian's imperial court in the city of Nicomedia during his teenage years. The emperor, who was a devout servant of the image-sun god Jupiter, also held elaborate ceremonies and great festivities in his new royal residence. Constantine and his mother Helena participated in those ancient Roman celebrations before their conversion to Christianity.

Constantine's conversion to Christianity came during October 312 during the Battle of Milvian. In the late evening before the battle, Constantine was commanded in a dream to draw an emblem of Cross on their shields. He followed the instructions in the dream and marked all the shields. The next day at noon on October 28, Constantine and his soldiers were marching and reportedly looked up and saw a vision of a Solar Halo with a Latin cross of light above the sun. On the cross he saw the Greek words Chi and Rho, which meant *"in this sign you will conquer."* All soldiers placed the symbols on their weapons. The battle between the two emperors was set in array. Constantine commanded an army of 100,000. His contender Maxentius had an army of 75,000. Both armies faced off at Milvian Bridge which was an important route over the Tiber River. Constantine decisively won the battle, killing Maxentius, and effectively ending the 4-man Tetrarchy of Diocletian.

Other historians place his mother's conversion somewhere between the time when Emperor Galerius issued the Edict of Toleration in 311, which ended the persecution of Christians, and 313 when Constantine and Lucinius agreed to **The Edict of Milan**.

The Edict of Milan

The imperial edict stated: *"Wherefore, for this our indulgence, they ought to pray to their god for our safety, for that of the republic, and for their own, that the commonwealth may continue uninjured on every side and that they may be able to live securely in their homes. The same shall be restored to the Christians without payment or any claim of recompense, and without any kind of fraud or deception. When you see that this has been granted to [Christians] by us, your worship will know that we have also conceded to other religions the right of open and free observance of their worship for the sake of the peace of our times, that each one may have the free opportunity to worship as he pleases; this regulation is made that we may not seem to detract from any dignity of any religion.*

All provincial rulers were commanded to enact the royal decree in haste with all the power entrusted unto them. The decree was meant to restore public order and the religious rights for all the various gods of Rome. During the reign of Diocletian, Christians were seen as disloyal critics of the Roman state, and unpatriotic towards the empire. Their new belief called for the overthrow of the temporal Roman empire, the ancient Roman state religion, and replacing it with the exclusive worship of the god Jesus. The edict was sponsored by both emperors, Constantine and Licinius. Both commanders, who traveled back from the Balkans, met in Milan, Italy during February 313 to finalize the agreement to change their policies towards the cult of Christianity. Thus, Constaintine became the first emperor of Rome to convert to the new religion. However, it should be noted that Constantine lived the majority of his life as a servant of the gods of the ancient Roman pantheon. Even after his conversion at the Battle of Milvian, Roman coins continued to be minted with the graven images of the sun-god Sol Invictus and other deities throughout his reign. He was depicted as a companion of the sun-god. In fact, after his conversion he still praised the sun-god Sol Invictus whose symbol was a Solar Halo. A solar halo is what Constantine claimed to have seen at the Battle of Milvian. The only difference was he saw a cross above the Solar Halo. When he commissioned the building of the Arch of Constantine, after his conversion, it did not contain any honors to the Christian god Jesus. Instead it was located to pay homage to the colossal standing graven image of Sol Invictus, which stood by the great Roman Colosseum. The emperor did not outlaw the sun-worshipping cult of Sol Invictus Mithras. Other cults flourished and continued throughout his reign until 326.

However, Constantine continued to fight under the protection of the Christian god for the duration of his rulership. He believed the Roman empire [**the kingdom of iron**] would be secure under the protection of the Christian god, which he viewed as the strongest among the pantheon of deities. Although Constantine continued to display pagan attributes, it should be noted that after his victory in the Battle of Milvian in 312, he did not honor the Roman national patron god Jupiter. He offered no sacrifices on the altar before the deity in Rome. He went directly to the palace bypassing the planned festivities. The other high officials who did not embrace Christianity readily stepped in to celebrate, offering sacrifices to the traditional pantheon of Roman image-gods. The list of gods included the man-god Jupiter and the female-goddess Juno, the man-god Neptune and the female-goddess Minerva, the male-image Mars and the female-image Venus, Apollo, the man-god, and Diana, the goddess, Vulcan, the male-idol and Vesta, the female goddess, and Mercury, the man-god, and Ceres, the female deity. For centuries, Romans had worshipped and honored these gods as a way of life. Constantine replaced the veneration of those deities with the worship of the man-god Jesus and the female-goddess Mother Mary.

Constantine began to play an influential role in the promotion of the Christian Church and the enforcement of the Edict of Milan. In the eyes of the Christian cult, he was their saviour that allowed the Christian religion to grow and flourish with government protection. The following year in 325 Constantine called for the first **Council of Nicaea**.

Council of Nicaea
"The Erection the graven doctrine/image of Jesus/Yeshua"

King Solomon once said in **Proverbs 15:26**, *"Evil thoughts* [**false doctrines and teachings**] *are an abomination to YAH; But pleasant words* [**Torah and Hebrew prophets**] *are pure.* He must have been prophesying about these pagan doctrinesmiths who gathered at the Council of Nicaea. Just like the ancient goldsmiths, silversmiths, and blacksmiths that preceded them, these mythmakers fashioned a religious doctrine according to the graven imaginations of their own froward hearts. Their followers were taught to bow before man-made words and ideas contrary to **"Thus saith YHWH"**. As Israelites, our minds must remain perfect with YHWH our ELOHIM and we must follow HIS holy decrees exclusively. We should not deviate. Instead, we should promote and embrace YAH's commandments forevermore. We must not allow ourselves to be caught up in these web of lies constructed by these Gentile men. We must be clear. The tenets of Council of Nicaea[**The New Testament**] were concieved by uncircumcised minds, and not with the DIVINE inspiration of YAH's Counsel.

"An ungodly man diggeth up evil; and in his lips there is a burning fire." **Proverbs 16:27**.

"An evil man seeketh only rebellion [**against YAH and HIS commandments**]*".* Proverbs **17:11.**

"A true witness [**Moses and the Hebrew prophets**] *deliverth souls: but a deceitful* [**Paul and New Testament writings**] *witness speakth lies".* **Proverbs 14:25**.

The purpose of the gathering of Gentile and African Christians was to produce a unified statement on Christian belief and doctrine. The final statement became known as the Nicene Creed or the Apostle's Creed. The creed stated the belief widely used by Christians in their liturgy, their profession of faith, and it outlined the important functions within the newly emerging Roman State Church, which eventually became known as the Roman Catholic Church.

The Council of Nicaea took place in the city of Nicaea, which was small town near the Bosporus Strait, located between the Mediterranean Sea and the Black Sea. Today, the city is known as Iznik, Turkey. The opening session began on a Thursday, May 20, 325. Approximately 250 to 300 people were in attendance, with only 5 coming from the churches in the western provinces. The meeting took place in a conference hall where a long table stood. All the Epistles of the Gospel were opened. It should be noted that no ancient Afro-Asiatic Hebrew people were in attendance and there were no major readings of the Torah according to the ancient Hebraic understanding. Instead, the ancient convocation was used to canonize what would later become known as the New Testament which they used to supplant the authority of the ancient Hebrew scriptures with their false interpretations. The churchmen replaced the reverence to **YHWH** with the worship of a man-god named Jesus/Yeshua. Another purpose of the meeting was to create one standard doctrine and mythology of Jesus/Yeshua. It should also be emphasized that no Levitical priest were present to refute these erroneous speculations concerning the ancient Hebrew prophecies. For example, the agreement of the new strange doctrine that defined the CREATOR as a Trinity, was, and continues to be, a Babylonian, Persian, Greco-Roman, Christian concept that believed there were three ways of being God. God, the Father, God, the son, and God, the Holy Spirit: 3 gods in one. YHWH never said anything about a Trinity to **Moses**. That concept would be considered "a strange god" or "false doctrine" in the ancient Hebrew scriptures. That point is confirmed in **Deuteronomy 6:4**, where YAH proclaimed: *"Hear O Israel YHWH is our ELOHIM is ONE"*. There was no mention of a pantheon of gods in Torah. The ancient pagans always worshiped man-gods, female-goddesses, and child-gods. It is clear Constantine and the those in attendance were influenced and adopted those pagan concepts and imported them into their newly emerging Church. Furthermore,in chapter **45:18** the prophet Isaiah stated: *"For thus saith* **YHWH** *that created the heavens: ELOHIM himself* [No Trinity] *that formed the earth and made it; HE hath established it* [Not Jesus/Yeshua] *HE created it not in vain, HE formed it to be inhabited: I am* **YHWH**: *AND THERE IS NONE ELSE!"*

*"Look to ME[***YHWH***], and be you saved, all the ends of the earth:*[**Israel and all Mankind**]; *I am ELOHIM and there is NONE ELSE* [**No Jesus**]. *I have sworn by* **MYSELF**; *the word is gone out of MY mouth in righteousness, and shall not return, that to ME[***YHWH***] every knee shall bow, every tongue shall swear. Surely, shall one say, in* **YHWH**[**Not Jesus**] *have I righteousness and strength: even to HIM* [**YHWH**] *shall men come; and all that are incensed against him shall be ashamed. In* **YHWH** [Not Jesus] *shall all the seed of Israel be justified, and shall glory.* [**Isaiah 45:22-25**].

All Israelites should read the **Book of Isaiah, chapters 40 through 45,** so that you are not deceived by the gospels of New testament, which is a mixture of distorted Hebraic and Gentile fabricated falsehoods. Israelites must rid ourselves of all NEW TESTAMENT concepts and deviations. Those lies have overspread the earth every since this Council of Nicaea.

Now let me go back to this first ecumenical **Gentile**, not Israelite, meeting known as the Council of Nicaea. The gathering was convened by Emperor Constantine and Bishop Hosius of Corduba. Constantine entered the hall wearing his imperial royal purple with jewel-encrusted, multicolored vestment. He was all alone with no bodyguards accompanying him. He spoke briefly, commanding the Christian bishops and elders to hammer out an agreement on the crucial matters causing dissension. Constantine told them, *"division in the church is worst than war."*

In the end, there were common agreements among most of the assemblymen concerning the new man-god Jesus Christ. Those agreements including the following:

Number one: Jesus was God in the flesh who should be worshipped. According to their new doctrine, Jesus was with God in the beginning of time, long before the 1st century. [These theologians had no **YHWH**-based scriptural proof for such a dramatic proclamation.] Another transgression committed by the participants at the Council of Nicaea was the total lack of Proper Divine Respect for the DIVINE **Name of YHWH**. [Israelites must never forget the everlasting DIVINE Instructions written in **Exodus 23:13, Deuteronomy 4:5-24, and Isaiah 54:5.**]

Number two: There was an agreement for the Church to abolish observance the ancient Hebrew Sabbath throughout the Roman Empire, and eventually, the entire world. They all agreed Easter should be observed on a Sunday annually, replacing the Hebrew Passover because the sacrifice of Jesus was in fact the true PASSOVER LAMB. Instead of recognizing the POWER that delivered ancient Israel out of Egypt, the focus was turned towards worshipping a man who served as an animal sacrifice. That too was a new and foreign concept, not based on the **Testimony of YHWH** given to the ancient children of Israel at Mount Sinai.

Number three: The ancient Levitical Priest were replaced. There was an agreement to ordain eunuchs as priest, creating a new rule that Christian priests should not be married men. Again this was a foreign concept not based on **Leviticus 21:13**, which clearly permits a Priest of ELOHIM to pro-create instead of being a part of the long church history of homosexual relations and child molestation. [These new Christian priests were not Levitical priest. Those Christian men were similar to the ones spoken of in **I Kings 12:31-33** where King Jeroboam ordained men similar to them during his reign.] It reads: *"And he [Jeroboam] made an house of high places, and made priests of the lowest of the people [eunuchs], which were not of the sons of Levi. And Jeroboam ordained a feast in the eighth month, on the fifteenth day of the month, like unto the feast that is in Judah, and he offered upon the altar. So did he in Bethel sacrificing unto the calves that he had made: and he placed in Bethel the priests of the high places which he had made. So he offered upon the altar which he had made in Bethel the fifteenth day of the eighth month, even in the month which he devised of his own heart, and ordained a feast unto the children of Israel: and he offered upon the altar, and burnt incense."* Pay close attention and you will notice that the Christian founding fathers did the same thing as Jeroboam. They devised these tenets of the Nicene Creed from the evil imaginations of their uncircumcised hearts. YHWH did not command them, nor did HE speak unto them. Nowhere in the Council of Nicaea do you read the words, *"Thus saith YAH"* spoken by anyone in attendance. None of them were ancient Afro-Asiatic Hebrews, nor were they Hebrew prophets. Therefore, it would have been a spiritual error for Hebrew Israelites to add, incorporate, or teach, those idolatrous concepts as part of their sacred way of life back in the first, second, and third centuries, and it is totally **WRONG** to do that today in the 21st century.

Words To The Wise

[We must not allow these man-made theories crafted by Gentile false prophets deceive us in 2019 and beyond. Israelites must be vigilant for the Torah and abandon the New Testament-Council of Nicaea thinking by returning to the total worship of the **CREATOR-YAH** alone. Always remember **Deuteronomy chapter 13** when reading and examining the New Testament. We cannot be deceived by the *false wonders* as YAH warned us of in **Deuteronomy 13th chapter**. Instead, we must compare these non-Levite apostles, bishops, preachers, and churchmen, beginning with Paul, to the *"dreamer of dream showing signs and wonders"* seeking to turn, you and I, and all Israel away from the worship of **YHWH** [Exodus 3:15, Exodus 6:1-2] towards the worship of Yeshua/Jesus.]

Back To The Council of Nicaea of 325 C.E.

Number four: There was a prohibition of kneeling to other gods besides Jesus on Sundays, and from Easter to Pentecost. The Christians also replaced the ancient YAH-focused Shavuot, feast of the first fruits, with the, speaking in tongues, Christian-Messianic concept of Pentecost.

Number five: There was an agreement among the Christian bishops for the need of baptism in the name of Jesus for personal salvation. Again, that too was another new and foreign concept according to ancient Hebrew culture.

Number six: There was also an agreement to canonize the letters[**Epistles**] of Paul into a book that would become known as the New Testament. The Christian founding fathers also agreed to promote the personal letters of Paul, which were written to the pagan Gentile Christians, into the new status of holy scriptures, even going so far as to comparing the Gentile-inspired gospels and epistles to the DIVINE Instructions of YAH found in the Hebrew scriptures. The long-term goal of these decisions were to replace the Hebrew scriptures. It was done by combining two diametrically opposite books, one glorifying the **CREATOR-YAH** and the other glorifying the man-god Jesus/Yeshua, into a single testimony—coining a new pagan phrase *"Old Testament and New Testament"*. That too was the work of error. The views of the Coptic Christians from Egypt and Ethiopia, which were opposite of the Latin Christians, were totally overlooked and ignored. In fact, the opinions expressed by the bishop from Egypt named Arius, who viewed Yeshua/Jesus as a human, were disregarded and he was labeled a heretic.

Number seven: In the end, the raucous convocation concluded with a unified Synod Epistle outlining the tenets for the universal Roman State Church which eventually splintered into the two branches of Christendom known as the Roman Catholic Church and the Greek Orthodox Church. It should be stated that both houses of Christianity were built upon the doctrine of Paul.

Who was Paul in the eyes of **YHWH ELOHIM Israel** and the Torah?

According to the New Testament, Paul was actually a Jew[Yehudee] from the tribe of Benjamin.

Right away, this is a major problem for the people of Israel in terms of him being a spokesman for YAH. Because first of all, as I mentioned earlier in **chapter 1** concerning **Deuteronomy/Devarim 18th chapter, verses 1 thru 15**, the prophets of Israel came from the tribe of Levi: men who were priests that were elevated to prophet status like Samuel, Isaiah Yeremiah, Isaiah, Eliyah, and others, all Levities. According to the New Testament writings, Paul/Saul was a Benjaminite. He was not a priest-prophet. YAH never ordained the Benjaminites to serve as HIS prophets, they were warriors. So Paul is disqualified in terms of being a true Levite prophet, and furthermore, he never called himself a prophet. YAH never mentioned speaking to an apostle in the Torah. HE [**YAH**] said, I will raise you up a prophet like Moses the Levite, not Saul the Benjaminite or Yeshua/Jesus of Judah. Both of those characters were not Levite Prophets of Israel.

Some observers doubt whether Paul was even a descendant of the ancient Hebrews based on the Acts 22: 25-29 which reads: "And as they bound him with thongs, Paul said under the centurion that stood by, is it lawful for you to scourge a man that is a Roman, and uncondemned? When the centurion heard, he went and told the chief captain, saying, Take heed what you doest; for this man is a Roman. Then the chief captain came, and said unto him, Tell me, art thou a Roman? He said, Yea. And the chief captain answered, with a great sum obtained I this freedom. And Paul said, But I was free born. Then straightway they departed from him which should have examined him: and the chief captain also was afraid, after he knew that he was a Roman, and because he had bound him."

As you can see, Paul openly declared himself to be Roman. This was during the 1st century C.E. when only native Aryan Romans were able to receive citizenship. How could Paul, an alleged black man, receive Roman citizenship when it was only offered to the Julio-Claudian dynasty, the wealthy, the Roman Senate, their government officials, and only people of social nobility and high rank in society. Blacks [Africans of Carthage, Mauritania, and elsewhere] did not receive Roman citizenship until the latter-part of the 2nd century and early third century. During the days of Paul, Roman citizenship was denied to black people. So either this entire New Testament writing was fabricated or Paul was actually an Euro-Judaic convert. The pale-skinned Euro-Judaic Herodians enjoyed close and cordial relations with the Roman Empire. In the first century, those Euro-Judaic converts were granted Roman citizenship, but during the time of Acts chapter 22 the Afro-Asiatic Hebrew people were denied Roman inclusion. Who was Paul? Was he Saul the Benjaminite, Paul the Roman, a Pharisee, a devout Jews who openly violated every tenet of Teaching of Moses, or was he a black man, or a Roman as he professed?

Paul was born in approximately 5 C.E. and he lived until the year 67. He died at the age of 62. It should be noted that the preachings of Paul did not occur until somewhere around the year 53 at least 20 years after the life of the alleged Yeshua/Jesus. Paul never met the man, yet he wholeheartedly worshipped and idolized the ground Jesus walked on.

Since when has **YHWH** ever commanded Israel to adore, praise, glorify, or bow before the name of another power beside HIM? The righteous answer would be NEVER. Never has YAH commanded HIS people to do such a thing. Therefore, we as Israel must be aware of all FABRICATORS such as the false prophet spoken of in **I Kings 13:11-18**. Please read it. Fabricators are pure liars, they devise their own testimonies from the imaginations of their own hearts. Then they turn around and lie in the Name of **YHWH**. Such as in the case I mentioned in **I Kings 13:18**. YAH did not command the Church bishops, Constantine, Paul, or Yeshua/Jesus, to speak the words coming from their mouths. You never read the proclamation *"Thus saith YAH"* or *"the word of YAH came unto me"*. I could certainly go on and on pointing out more discrepancies, distortions, and lies found in the New Testament, but by now, you should realize the point I'm making: Beware of devious Fabricators who deviate from the original **words of YAH** inscribed in the ancient Sacred Hebrew scriptures.

Now back to the final years of the reign of Constantine, the first Christian emperor of the Roman Empire. As we conclude, we must always remember that his decision to convene the first Council of Nicaea changed the course of human history in terms of spiritual understanding. Since that fourth century gathering at Nicaea, almost every human being on the face of the earth has been affected by the decisions that gave birth to the religion of Christianity in some shape, form, or fashion. Years later in 381, one year after Emperor Theodosius made Christianity the official religion of the Roman empire, a Second Council of Christian bishops took place in Constantinople.

A third Christian ecumenical gathering was convened in the city of Ephesus in the year 431. As I emphasized earlier, the ultimate goals of these convocations were to establish the canonization of the New Testament, create the myth of Jesus Christ, and to decree that the Christian Church was the heir to God's promise to mankind. The Church founding fathers were not Torah scholars. The Gospels of the New Testament were not based on historical accuracy or facts. The Gentile writers who wrote the book in the 2nd and 3rd centuries common era were not interested in historical facts, their main concern was teaching the faithful to believe in the so-called good news of the risen Christ and his Second Coming. Each author wrote differently, therefore, the gospels and epistles contain many contradictions. The Gospels of Jesus contain four diverse versions of the same subject matter with each differing in their versions of events. Each writer crafted their own story centered around the life and death of Jesus. None of the writers of the Gospel—Mark, Matthew, Luke, or John—personally knew or met the character they wrote about in the Gospels. Their compilations were written 200 to 400 years after the life of the so-called historical character. So, to be completely honest, most of their information was based on he-say, she-say, legends, and gossip [Gospels]. The author's writings were created to simply express the church attitude concerning Jesus, not historical facts. Therefore, we as Israelites cannot believe or base our proper course of action on what we read in the pages of those four legends.

In 326, Constantine's mother Helena, a devout converted Christian, made her pilgrimage to the holy land where she visited all the Christian sacred places throughout the land. She was a major influence upon her son, influencing him to undertake major building projects. He had already granted her the official title *"Augusta Imperatrix"* in the year 325 before she departed of her sacred visitation. Her position gave her unlimited access to the treasury of Rome. She influenced him to commission the building of The Church of The Holy Sepulchre on the alleged site of Jesus/Yeshua tomb. Eventually the church site became one of the most important sites in Christendom. The new Christian sanctuary buried the memory of the ancient Temple of **YHWH** built by King Solomon. From that day forward and continuing up through the Middle Ages even into 21st century, the Church of Rome has claimed the right to temporal power over Jerusalem based on this so-called church donation from Emperor Constantine. The emperor of Rome also commissioned the erection of the Church of the Nativity in the city of Bethlehem. He then ordered the construction of the Church of Eleona on Mount Olives.

In Rome, he commissioned the building of the Church of Saint Peter, which is known as Saint Peter's Basilica today. By May 11, 330, Constantine built a new imperial palace in the city of Byzantium, dedicating the city to himself. He eventually choose the great city as the new imperial capital for the Roman Empire, renaming it Constantinople,"the Second Rome", glorifying the works of his own hands.

In early 337, Constantine prepared for another offensive against the Persians, but he fell sick after reaching the city of Helenopolis. His doctors attempted to revive him but their treatments did not work. He was forced to abort his campaign, and instead, he headed back towards Constantinople. In route, his condition worsened causing him to seek a bed in the city of Nicomedia in the province of Bithyna. While Constantine laid on his sickbed, the imperial purple was taken off in exchange for a white robe. He was baptized by Bishop Eusebius of Berytus, modern Beirut, while lying on his deathbed. He gave up the ghost at the age of 65 in the Church of the Holy Apostle on May 22, 337 in the house of worship he had built during his lifetime. He was the father of 6 children and married twice. His first wife's name was Minervina. His second wife was named Fausta. After Constantine's death, Christian followers began to worship him as a god. He was venerated in the Syriac Orthodox Church, the Church of Antioch, the Eastern Orthodox Church, the Catholic Church, Oriential Orthodox Church, the Coptic Orthodox Church, and the Lutheran Church. This veneration of the first Christian emperor of Rome has continued non-stop since then.

So it came to pass that Emperor Constantine died after reigning 31 years on the throne of Augustus. During his lifetime he was a devout worshipper of the solar deity Sol Invictus. After 312, he became a converted worshipper of Christian sun/son-god and the cross of Jesus Christ. He did evil in eyes of **YHWH** and walked in all the abhorrent ways of the uncircumcised Greco-Roman rulers that preceded him, serving "other gods" and not acknowledging **YHWH ELOHIM Israel** or walking in HIS commandments. Instead, he commissioned the building of the graven sun-god, Son of God doctrine at the Council of Nicaea in 325, which led the nations away from the Mount Sinai message of YAH, as it is unto this day. After three centuries of persecution by the Roman state **[the kingdom of iron]**, Constantine was the first ruler to support the concept of a merger between the Christian Church and Roman State into one entity. Constantine also abandoned Diocletian's concept of a 4-man tetrarchy in favor of a imperial dynasty where his own son Constantine II reigned in his stead as the next emperor.

Constantine II
(337 C.E.—340 C.E.)
[West]

Constantine II was born in February 316 C.E. in the Roman settlement-city of Arelate in the province of Viennensis, which is modern southern France. He was the son of Emperor Constantine the Great and his second wife Empress Fausta. His full birth name was Flavius Claudius Constantius. At the age of 1 his father Constantine crowned him with the title "Caesar" of the western portion of the empire. At the age of 7 the young lad joined his father on his military campaigns against the Sarmatians. Three years later in the year 326, 10-year-old Constantine II became the commander of Gaul following the death of his half-brother Crispus. Crispus was the son of Constantine's first wife Minervina. By the year 332, the 16-year-old young crown prince, who was the oldest of Constantine the Great's three sons by Fausta, was made field commander in the campaign against the barbaric Goths.

Five years later on May 22, 337, Emperor Constantine the Great died after a thirty-one year reign. Constantine was a hard act to follow, so his three sons, Constantine II, Constantius II, and Constans, joined together in a triumvirate to divide power in order to preserve the Constantinian dynasty. The three brothers also shared power with their cousins Dalmalius and Hannibalianus. However, shortly after the agreement was made, the three sons of Constantine ordered the army to slaughter their relatives in a move to consolidate more power among themselves. On September 9, 337 the three met to formally divide the empire among themselves. More power led to covetousness and greed, and soon thereafter, the three sons of Constantine the Great were bickering among themselves, rupturing the unity built by their father in the Roman state and church.

Constantius II, the middle son, was given control over the Eastern Roman Empire. His throne name was Imperator Caesar Flavius Claudius Constantius Augustus. Constans, the youngest son, was chosen to serve as the Emperor of Italia(Italy) and Africa. Constans also gained more territories after the assassination of his two cousins Dalmatius and Hannibalianus. Constantine II, who was the firstborn, also felt he was entitled to more. He was given rule over the Western Roman Empire, including Gaul, Hispania, and Britannia. Those barbarian territories comprised the most primitive and undeveloped portions of the Roman World during that time. In hopes of keeping the peace between Christian brethren, the younger brother agreed to divide parts of Africa with his older brother Constantine II. However, another dispute broke out: who would gain control of Carthage and its outlying areas. By the year 340, tensions between the two emperors reached a boiling point. The infighting had provoked Constantine II and his forces to march from the western provinces towards Italy for a showdown. In advance, Emperor Constans dispatched his elite Illyrian Roman forces from Dacia. Constans and his forces followed from behind. Constantine II and his army were ambushed in the city of Aquileia, which is located in northern Italy. The 24-year-old died in the battle attempting to enter Italy.

So it came to pass that Constantine II reigned as Emperor for three years. His father Constantine the Great raised him as a Christian, a worshipper of image-god Jesus along with the cross of Christ. Like all of his predecessors before him, he walked in the imagination of his own heart. He did not serve **YHWH ELOHIM Israel** nor observe HIS commandments which HE instructed to HIS people Israel and all mankind. His youngest brother Constans reigned in his stead as the next Roman ruler along with his brother Constantinus II.

Constans I
(337 C.E.—350 C.E.)
[West]

Constans I was born in the year 323 in the imperial city of Constantinople, the city named in honor of his father. He was the youngest of the three sons of Constantine the Great. His mother was also Empress Fausta. He was educated in the royal court of his father where he was educated by the famed poet Aemilius Magnus Arborius. His full name was Flavius Julius Constans Augustus. Just like his older brothers before him, he was elevated to the status of Caesar in his youth with a great ceremony on December 25, 333 at the mere age of 10. When his father passed four years later, Constans was a 14-year-old teenager when he and his brother divided the Roman World between themselves. Constans started his career under the tutelage of his older brother Constantine II. Constans initially served as the Prefect of the Praetorian Guard of Italia and Africa. The Roman army proclaimed Constans as emperor, along with his two brothers, on September 9, 337, forming a Constantinian dynasty. Constans portion of the empire included Italy and the provinces of Africa. All three sons of Constantine joined in a conspiracy to eliminate their relatives Dalmatius and Hannibalianus because of their possible threat to their monopoly on power. The following year in 338, the three met in the city of Viminacium, modern Serbia, to discuss the boundaries for each of their portions of the empire. It appeared that Constans was the only one to benefit from the death of their cousins. He was the only one who received additional territories in Dacia and Thrace after their murders. His throne name was Imperator Caesar Flavius Julius Constans Augustus.

Back in Italy, and months after he received the purple robe, the barbaric Sarmatians attempted to penetrate the northern interior of the Roman empire. Constans was able repel the invasion and crush his enemies. After that, Constans was viewed as a national hero. Meanwhile envy and jealously began to creep in. His older brother Constantine II felt he had been disrespected at the earlier partition summit in Viminacium. After all, he was the oldest brother, yet he had received the worst landscape, the undeveloped western provinces. Constans attempted to appease him by handing over portions of the province of Africa, but that did not work. In a bid to overthrow Constans, his older brother, Constantine II, led his troops into Italy for war against his own younger brother. However, Constantine II was slain in an ambush by his brother's elite Illyrian bodyguards. Constans then inherited all the territories, Britannia, Hispania, and Gaul where his fallen brother continued to face more barbaric threats from the Franks and others. He was also successful in repelling their attacks.

For the next ten years, from 340 to 350, Constans shared power with his middle brother Constantius II. There were serious disagreements between the two brothers. Constantius was a strong believer in the Christian doctrine of Arianism, whereas, Constans adhered to the standards of the Council of Nicaea. Hoping to make peace with his older brother, Constans convened the Council of Sardica where he attempted to bridge the religious gap and mend political fences between the two Christian schools of thought. The ecumenical gathering ended in failure. By the year 346, these two sons of Constantine the Great were at the point of open warfare over their religious disagreements. They were able to resolve the conflict by agreeing to disagree: Each brother would support their own sect within their own territories while tolerating the other.

Although Constans claimed to be a Christian, he was known to indulge in sexual perversion. He was an open homosexual who was widely know to engage in relations with male barbaric captives whom he deemed to be handsome. In his royal court, he was dominated by his male lovers, preferring intimacy with his chosen bodyguards. Constans sexual submissiveness to his male subordinates in the imperial court caused the mighty men of the Roman legion to lose respect for him. Hypocritically, both Constans and Constintius II issued decrees that ruled same-marriages as "unnatural sex" and "a crime". The law did not outlaw homosexual activity, it simply outlawed formal marriages. It should be noted that homosexuality among men in ancient Rome **[the kingdom of iron]** was a large part of society, just like the men of ancient Athens. Male with male relations were the most common type, usually consisting of older men taking a young male lover. The older men were usually from the upper-class while their younger lovers were from the lower class, usually between the ages of 12 to 20. It was an unspoken rule that older males were the penetrator while the younger males were on the receiving end. This type of same-sex copulation was outlawed in ancient Hebrew culture. In ancient Rome, it was different. The Imperial City was a place where random same-sex male intercourse was common, especially at the bathhouses scattered throughout the royal city. It was said that a man looking for a homosexual affair would scratch his head with one finger. This was considered a signal to indicate he was sexually available.

In **Leviticus 18:22, YHWH**, the CREATOR of the heavens, earth, seas, and all therein, commanded Israelite men, *"You shall not lie* **[to be sexually intimate]** *with mankind* **[same gender]** *as with womankind* **[opposite gender]**: it is **ABOMINATION**. Furthermore, **YHWH** said in **Leviticus 20:13**, *"When a man also lie* **[to be sexually intimate]** *with mankind* **[same gender]**; *as he lie with a woman, both of them* **[penetrator and penetrated]** *have committed an abomination: they shall surely be put to death, their blood shall be upon them".* As you can now see, the acceptance of same-sex relationships was typical in Roman society whereas it was considered totally unacceptable in the kingdom of **YHWH**.

Now in the year 350, one of the generals of Constans named Magnentius rebelled against him by declaring himself emperor. General Magnentius was the commander of the troops stationed in the Gallic city of Augustdounim. He soon gained support from the other Roman forces throughout western provinces.

Meanwhile as usual, Constans was in the imperial court in the midst of his sensual pleasures when he received news of the rebellion. All the king's men forsook the emperor, forcing him to flee for his life. He fled Italy towards Hispania, but when he reached Pyrenees in southwestern Gaul, the supporters of General Magnentius spotted him. *(Today Pyrenees, Gaul is known as Elne, France.)* Constans attempted to flee inside a temple in the city, but he was captured and slain. Ironically when Constans was born, the astrologer told his father Constantine and mother Fausta that he would die in the arms of his grandmother. He died in a city of Vicus Helena which was named in honor of his grandmother Helena.

During his lifetime, Constans never married a woman. At one point in his life he was engaged to a woman named Olympias, the daughter of Ablabius, the Prefect of the Praetorian Guard, but he never married her. So he never did bear any offsprings during his lifetime. Instead, he spilled his seed on the ground like the sons of Judah, Onan and Er. (**See Genesis 38:7-10**). In the end, Constans was regarded as a man who ruled unjustly. His personal life of open homosexuality and other acts of depravity led to open hostility and disrespect. His assassination occurred somewhere between January and February of the year 350.

So it came to pass that Emperor Constans died at the age of 26 after reigning thirteen years on the throne of Augustus. He did evil in the eyes of **YHWH ELOHIM Israel** walking in the abhorrent practices of the nations that practiced sodomy and other unclean fetishes. He also served the image-god Jesus and the cross of Christ. He also tolerated the worship of other ancient gods according to Roman religion. In the east, his brother Constantius II continued to reign as Emperor of Rome until the year 361. In the west, General Magnentius reigned temporarily from the year 350 to 353.

Magnentius
(350 C.E.—353 C.E.)
[West]

Magnentius [*pronounced* Mag-nen-ti-us] was born in 303 in the city of Samarobriva, Gaul. His full birth name was Flavius Magnus Magnentius. His origins was from the the lower class. That explains why his father and mother names were not known. He advanced through the ranks to become a general of the Roman legions in the province of Gaul. He eventually became the commander of the Imperial Guard. When several army officers abandoned Emperor Constans because of his openly homosexual submissiveness with his royal bodyguards, the soldiers chose General Magnentius as their choice for Augustus in the west. This occurred on January 18, 350 C.E. Magnentius quickly received support from troops stationed in the provinces of Britannia, Hispania, and Gaul. He chose the throne name Imperator Caesar Flavius Magus Magnentius Augustus. However, Constantius, the older brother of Constans, did not accept his ascension. The adversaries fought battles for three years until General Magnentius was finally defeated in the Battles of Mursa Major and Mons Seleuci where the general lost 75 percent of his entire army. Once his army abandoned him, he knew he would be captured and tortured, so he committed suicide August 11, 353 in southern Gaul, leaving behind a wife named Justina without any children.
So it came to pass that the usurper Magnentius died at the age of 50 after reigning three years as emperor of the west. He did evil in eyes of **YHWH ELOHIM of Israel** by serving the image-god Jesus and by living in peaceful co-existence with the traditional image-gods of the Greco-Roman pantheon. Constantius II, the brother of the deceased Constans, rose up to take the kingdom back from Magnentius.

Constantius II
(337 C.E.—361 C.E.)
[East]

Constantius was born August 7, 317 in the city of Sirmium, in the province of Pannonia Inferior, which is modern Sremska Mitrovica, Serbia. He was the middle son among his two brethren. His father was Constantine the Great and his mother was also Fausta. His birth name was Flavius Julius Constantius. Like his two other brothers, he was raised up in the royal household. Constantinus II was crowned *"Caesar"* by his father at the age of 7 on November 13, 324. All three brothers possessed distinct personalities. Constantine II was thought to be the privileged one because he was the firstborn. Constans, the youngest of the three, was the spoiled one. Constantinus II was regarded as the fierce one. He was 19 in the year 336 when religious unrest between the Arian and Nicene Christians embroiled Armenia and several provinces throughout the empire. Although his father Constantine favored the tenets of the Council of Nicaea, his son Constantinus grew to prefer the Arian school of Christian thought. He, nor his brothers, were able to bridge the gap or solve the widespread religious differences that dominated fourth-century Christianity during their reigns. At this same time, tense relations between Rome and King Shapur II of Persia sparked a new war. His father Constantine I made initial preparations for the war, but he fell sick and could not go any further. Constantine then commanded his son Constantius II to continue the eastern campaign against Persia. The following year in 337, Constantine died on May 22, leaving the dynasty to his three sons and first cousins. Court intrigue, treachery, and greed among the brethren, and a bloody plot against their relatives was conceived.

It was said Constantius was the ringleader when he and his Christian brothers conspired to murder their own first cousins Dalmatius and Hannibalianus whom they viewed as challengers to their exclusive rights to the throne. Constantius sought to eliminate all threats. As fate would have it, there were two cousins that survived the Constantinian purge. They were Gallus and Julian.

After the killing of their relatives, the three sons of Constantine divided the empire among themselves. Constantinus was able to obtain the most wealthiest, historical, and prestigious provinces in the Roman World, mainly the eastern provinces. That included the new capital of the Roman empire Constantinople. His throne name was Imperator Caesar Flavius Julius Constantius Augustus.

After the death of his younger brother Constans in 350, Constantinus became the sole emperor, but he still faced one major challenge. General Magnentius, who was the murderer of his brother Constans, proclaimed himself emperor of the west. Constantinus did not accept Magnentius claim to the throne. Thus, a civil war started which lasted for three years until Magnentius was defeated at the battles of Mursa Major and Mons Seleuci. In the end, Magnentius committed suicide in face of defeat at the battle of Mons Seleuci. It was a costly and bloody experience for both sides. Constantius lost nearly half of his entire army while Magnentius lost seventy-five percent of all the men under his command. Thousands on both sides died in conflict.

When the dust from the internal conflict finally settled in 350, Constantius was the sole emperor, yet he immediately implemented the Diocletian Doctrine which meant dividing the empire into two spheres: West and East, then choosing a capable Caesar who could administer day-to-day governance, protect the emperor's interest, and protect the frontiers. In the following year, Constantius chose his only two surviving men relatives, Gallus and Julian, for his junior Caesars. At first, he selected Gallus in the year 351, but three years later in 354, Constantius turned against his cousin Gallus and executed him after reports of violence and corruption surfaced against him. That left Julian as the only surviving cousin. So, in the winter of 355 on November 6, Constantius promoted Julian to the position of Caesar. A few days later, Julian married Constantius sister named Helena, thus becoming the emperor's brother-in-law as well as his co-regent. His first assignment was to supervise kingdom affairs in Gaul.

Meanwhile from 351 to 357 in the western provinces, Constantius triumphed in defending the empire in successive wars against the barbaric Alamanni, Quadi, and Sarmatians, halting their incursions into fortified Roman cities. In 357, Constantius visited the Imperial City of Rome for his first and only time.

By the year 360, tensions between the two ancient superpowers—Rome and Sassanid Persia—flared up again when King Shapur of Persia demanded the return of occupied land. Constantius refused. Persia launched an attack against Roman cities in Mesopotamia. Constantius was forced to campaign in the east to answer this new crisis. Constantius needed re-enforcements to confront the massive Persian army, so he summoned support from Caesar Julian and his forces in Gaul. The Roman army in Gaul rebelled against the request of Constantius then proclaimed Julian as their choice for Augustus in the west. Once the news of Julian 's insurgency reached Constantius in the east, he could not immediately respond to his cousin's disrespect. His plate was full as he prepared to face-off with a resurgent Persian army. The only thing he could do was dispatch a messenger to Gaul in hopes of convincing Julian to remain loyal. Julian refused for an entire year, leaving Constantius no choice but to confront him on the battlefield. Meanwhile in the east, the armies of Persia and Rome were in the midst of a lull in between exhaustive and bloody battles. Both sides had loss manpower, property, and treasure. During this time, Constantius, mounted up, turned his attention towards his cousin's challenge in the west. As the troops moved from Mesopotamia into south-central Asia Minor, Constantius became gravely ill with a fever. He was unable to continue the journey. Fearing that death was near, Constantius requested Bishop Euzolus of Antioch to baptize him in the name of the Arian-Christian concept of Jesus. After that, he forgave his cousin Julian and relinquished temporal power to him. His fever continued unabated, and on November 3, 361, he died.

So it came to pass that Constantius II passed away at the age of 44 after reigning for a total of twenty-four years in the city of Constantinople. He shared power three years with older brother Constantine II from 337 to 340. He also reigned as co-emperor with his younger brother Constans for 13 years. Following those events, he reigned another 11 years as the sole emperor until he passed in the year 361. He did evil in eyes of **YHWH ELOHIM Israel**, the CREATOR of the heavens, earth, and the seas, and all therein. Instead he served the image-god Jesus and bowed before the standing image of the cross. He supported peaceful co-existence with those who served the traditional image-gods of Rome's state religion. He also walked in all the abhorrent manners of the nations that knew not YAH. He slew his own relatives in a quest to monopolize power. After him, Julian ruled in his stead as the next Augustus of Rome.

During the days of Constantius II, the Christian Church was divided between various interpretations of the new religion. One of the schools of thought was known as Arianism, of which, Constantius was a believer. His belief was the opposite of his father Constantine I, who supported the Nicene school of thought. Arianism was based on the belief that Jesus was the Son of God alone. The doctrine rejected the concept of the Trinity: God the Father, God, the Son, God, the Holy Ghost as agreed upon by the church fathers at the Council of Nicaea in 325. In fact, Arius, the Christian presbyter from Egypt and his followers were labeled offenders by the majority which supported the new Christian doctrine of Trinity.

The death of Constantius II represented the end of the Constantinian dynasty. He was the last of the three sons of Emperor Constantine the Great. As I said earlier, his cousin Julian reigned in his stead.

Julian
(361 C.E.—363 C.E.)
[West]

Julian was born in the year 330 C.E. in the imperial city of Constantinople. His father's name was Julianus Constantius and mother's name was Basilina. His full birth name was Flavius Claudius Julianus. His family was close relatives of Emperor Constantine the Great. While growing up, Julian underwent normal military training, studied classical Greek philosophy and religion, and became known as man of letters. He eventually became well-known as an author. At the age of 25, his first cousin Constantius II was the sole emperor of the expansive Roman empire. On November 6, 355 his cousin appointed him as his junior Caesar and commander over the western provinces. As commander of Gaul, he won several battles against the barbaric Alamanni and Frank tribes. One of his greatest victories came during the Battle of Argentoratum in the year 357 when he led an army of only 13,000 against a Germanic force that number nearly 50,000. *(Today, the modern city of Strasbourg, France is located where ancient Argentoratum once stood.).* By 360, Julian was promoted to senior Caesar in the West.

Meanwhile in the East, his cousin Emperor Constantius II faced a resurgent Persian army in both Syria and Mesopotamia. It was an intense and long-term struggle. He needed fresh support from his forces in the West. In a strange twist, his troops in Lutetiu, which is modern Paris, refused the emperor's request then, instead, proclaimed Julian as Augustus. Constantinus could not respond to this new rebellion. With his manpower stretched thin, Constantius had to concentrate on the war effort in the East. Julian used this time to gain more support from among other Roman forces stationed in Hispania and Britannia. Meanwhile in the east, the a lull in war between Rome and Persia occurred. There had been repeated exhaustive and bloody battles between the two armies. Both sides had experienced great losses. During this time, Constantius mounted up to confront his cousin Julian's challenge in the West. Constantius readied himself for another civil war.

As the troops moved from Mesopotamia into south-central Asia Minor, Constantius became gravely ill with a fever and was unable to continue the journey. Fearing death was near, Constantius made a request for Bishop Euzolus of Antioch to baptize him in the name of Jesus. After his confession, he forgave his cousin Julian and relinquished the power of the empire over to him. His fever continued unabated until he died on November 3, 361. After his death,

Julian assumed the mantle of power and became the next emperor of Rome. He assumed the throne name Imperator Caesar Flavius Claudius Julianus Augustus. Julian was seen as a continuation of the Constantinian dynasty, because after all, he was the first cousin of Constantius. Julian also inherited the war against Persia, which Constantius and his father Constantine fought for years. Julian was forced to move eastward to halt Persian advances against Roman interest in Syria and Mesopotamia.

By summer of 363 the flames of warfare between the Roman and Persian armies were rekindled. This time Emperor Julian, an experienced military commander, launched a pre-emptive strike which was initially successful. He then moved his troops outside the city of Ctesiphion where they enjoyed another victorious battle. But this time was different. The Persians created a trap door and flooded the area behind them. Emperor Julian was almost trapped, but he quickly withdrew up the Tigris River Valley. The conflict continued with another skirmish. This time Julian was fatally wounded, forcing him to leave his army trapped behind enemy lines in Persian territory. Emperor Julian eventually died from his injury. This forced the Roman legions to offer the return of confiscated Persian territory in exchange for safe passage.

So it came to pass that Julian died from his wound in the city of Maranga, Mesopotamia, near modern Baghdad, on June 26, 363 C.E. at the age of 32 after reigning a mere two years. He was an occultist who did evil in the eyes of **YHWH ELOHIM Israel** by promoting the traditional image-gods of the ancient Greco-Roman pantheon. Although Julian was raised as a member of the new Christian cult endorsed by the late Emperor Constantine the Great, he rejected the faith and reverted back to sun-worshipping which was prevalent during the reign of the late emperor Diocletian. His actions earned him the distinguished title of *"Julian the Apostate"*, the last non-Christian emperor. In Rome, Julian allowed the Christian Church and the devotees of ancient Roman religion to flourish side-by-side. However, during the latter-part of his reign, Julian shed much innocent blood, and rose up against the Christian Church with violence. During his lifetime, he was married a woman named Helena for five years, from 355 to 360. Their marriage did not produce any seed **[children]**. In the end, the Constantinian dynasty was completely gone, Julian gave up the spirit of life and his corpse was interned in the city of Tarsus. General Jovian succeeded him as the next emperor.

Jovian
(363 C.E.—364 C.E.)
[East]

Jovian was born in the year 331 in the city of Singidunum, which is modern Belgrade, Serbia. His full birth name was Flavius Jovianus. His father's name was Varronianus. For reasons unknown, his mother's name was not included in the annals of Roman history. While growing up as a young man, Jovian followed in the footsteps of his father Varronianus who had served as the head of the Praetorian Guard under Emperor Constantius II.

By the time Jovian had turned nearly 30-years-old, he accompanied Emperor Julian in the campaign against King Shapur II, the ruler of the Sassanid Persians. Emperor Julian was severely injured whereby he died from his mortal wound. Upon his death, the Roman army immediately turned to Jovian, who at this time was the commander of the Imperial bodyguards, and proclaimed him as their new choice for Augustus on June 27, 363. Jovian then chose the throne name: Imperator Caesar Flavius Jovianus Augustus. Still surrounded and outmanned, Jovian wisely retreated with the Persians still in pursuit. After escaping up the Tigris Valley, he attempted to construct a bridge to cross the river. Unable to perform the task, he was forced to sue for peace. The terms required him to give up Rome's claim to territory in Mesopotamia and Syria. All the territory that the late Emperor Diocletian had once conquered was relinquished.

After arriving back in the royal city of Antioch in Syria, Jovian became convinced that the Roman army suffered severe defeat because of Julian's apostasy with the traditional image-gods of the Greco-Roman state religion. Wherefore, Emperor Jovian issued an edict that re-established the new graven doctrine of Jesus Christ and the image of the Cross as the proper choice for the empire. This new decision by Emperor Jovian to officially re-impose the religious policies of the late Constantine the Great planted the seeds that gave birth to Roman Christianity and the rise of the Roman State Church, which eventually became known as the Roman Catholic Church.

Turning over the tables of toleration for other Roman religionists, Jovian then issued another decree which ordered book burning and total destruction of the Library of Antioch. By autumn of the year 363, Jovian decreed the death penalty and began to terrorize those who performed magic ceremonies and praised the ancient gods of Rome. By December 23, the royal decree extended to all citizens who privately and publicly praised any deity besides the new image-god Jesus Christ. Afterwards, he issued a church-state decree that made Bishop Athanasius the Pontifex Maximus of the Roman State Church. However, in terms of inter-church controversies, he urged toleration between the various branches of Christianity such as Arians, Nicenes, and others. His approach allowed the religion of Christianity to flourish in both the Eastern and Western Roman empires.

Jovian's popularity as emperor was another story. The Roman citizenry openly expressed their displeasure for the peace deal with Persia. Rome was forced to leave its cities on the eastern frontier defenseless at the mercy of King Shapur. Meanwhile, Jovian, needed time to refresh himself, so he hurried back to the Imperial City of Constantinople to fortify himself. Before he reached Constantinople, leaders from the western provinces informed Jovian that they would support him in any next conflict with Persia. However, when Emperor Jovian reached the city of Dadastana in Asia Minor, he was found dead on his bed in his tent on February 17, 364. According to history, he died from one of two causes: the first was a night of gluttonous wine and intoxicant mushrooms. The second reason was possibly death from carbon monoxide poisoning from his coal-burning stove. His remains were taken to the Imperial City of Constantinople where he was interned with his Christian emperor predecessors in the Church of the Holy Apostles. During his lifetime, he was married and later was survived by a woman named Charito. Together, they were the parents of two sons. One was named Varronianus, whom he appointed as consul in 364, and another one whose name was unknown.

So it came to pass, Emperor Jovian died at the age of 32 after reigning a mere 8 months. He walked in the ways of all his Roman predecessors who did evil in the eyes of **YHWH ELOHIM Israel** by not keeping in HIS commandments, laws, and judgements which YAH commanded to ancient Israel and to all nations. Instead, he knew not YAH, nor did he seek HIM. He served the false doctrine of Jesus Christ and bowed before the graven image of the Cross. After his death Valentinian I reigned in his stead as the next emperor of the divided **iron kingdom** of Rome.

Valentinian I "the Great"
(364 C.E.—375 C.E.)
[West]

Valentinian was born on July 3, 321 in the ancient city once known as Cibalae Pannonia Secunda, now known as modern Vinkovci, Croatia. This was the same year Constantine became the emperor of Rome. His father's name was Gratian the Elder. For some reason his mother's name was not recorded in the annals of Roman history. His full birth name was Flavius Valentinianus. As a young lad, he grew up on a family estate where he was educated in the art of painting and sculpturing. His father was a high-ranking military commander during the reign of Constantine the Great and during the days of his youngest son Contans I. Somewhere between the years of 328 to 332, his father was promoted to Count of the province of Africa. While serving on his post there, his father was accused of corruption and forced to resign.

Valentinian joined the army in the late 330s. While Valentinian served in the army, his father was recalled back to duty and asked to serve as the Count of Britannia. His duty was to protect Roman interest on the island. His father retired after completing his mission there, but years later when the usurper General Magnentius rose up against Emperor Constantius, his father sided with Magnentius. After Emperor Constantius II defeated Magnentius, he seized his father's property and left him destitute. Valentinian, however, was unaffected by his father's woes because he remained neutral during the three year civil war from **[350 to 353]** between Magnentius and Constantius II. When the civil war ended, Emperor Constantius II appointed his cousin Julian as one of the military commanders over troops in the province of Gaul. Julian then appointed Valentinian as one of his military tribunes whose job was to monitor the roads to prevent surprise attacks. During this time, stability in the Gallic province and Britannia was rapidly deteriorating. Barbarian raids by the Alamanni, Franks, and Saxons were becoming coordinated and sophisticated. These battles included hand-to-hand combat with their primitive opponents. And to make matters worse in Britannia, some of the Roman soldiers defected to the barbarian side and fought against Roman civilians because they had not received their salaries.

After the death of Emperor Julian, his fellow soldier General Jovian ascended to the throne as the next emperor. Julian dispatched a man named **Procopius [365—366]**, who was a notary, to announce him as the new Augustus. Procopius was the last descendant of Constantine the Great who still served in the Roman government. He rebelled against the eastern Emperor Valens, but he was defeated. He fled into the wilderness areas of the province of Phrygia where he remained until he was betrayed by his followers. He was executed on May 22, 366.

During Jovian's short eight-month reign, Valentinian was promoted to the position of tribune of the elite infantry regiment. As fate would have it, Jovian died eight months after receiving the purple robe. Jovian died while he and his troops were in route to Constantinople to regroup from their devastating loss to Persia. The army kept marching towards the capital, but stopped in the city of Nicaea to choose a new leader. The throne of emperor was offered to four different men. Two of choices declined the offer while two others were rejected by the civilian and military council. In the end, the assembly of officials turned to Valentinian, an experienced officer stationed nearby in the city of Ancyra.

On February 26, 364 Valentinian accepted his nomination as Augustus with a speech before the soldiers. Many of the soldiers did not trust Valentinian because they did not fully understand his intentions for the military. The situation was chaotic with some of the soldiers threatening to riot. Valentinian, who was very self-confident, was able to calm the crowd with a powerful speech. There was still opposition from officials in the eastern provinces. Valentinian realized the complexity of the situation, and one month later on March 28, he appointed an imperial co-regent to keep the kingdom united in the east.

Valentinian chose his brother **Valens [364—378]** to serve as the powerful emperor of the eastern Roman provinces, second only to Valentinian. He was born in the year 328 in the same city where his brother Valentinian was born, which was Cibalae in the province of Pannonia. In the East, Emperor Valens's royal court was in the city of Constantinople while Emperor Valentinian reigned in the royal city of Milan. In 378, Valens was slain after being struck in the face with a dart during the in the Battle of Adrianople. Other sources reported, he fled the battlefield, but was surrounded by enemy forces and slain.

Either way it came to pass that Valens died at the age of 50 after reigning fourteen years as emperor of the East. He did that which was evil in the eyes of **YHWH ELOHIM Israel** by serving the image-god of Jesus Christ and believing in the graven doctrine of Christianity. He also bowed before the graven image of the Cross. He knew not YAH nor did he observe HIS commandments, laws, judgements, and statutes.

Now back to Valentinian. He chose the throne title Imperator Caesar Flavius Valentinanus Augustus. He dismissed all of the court officials that had previously served under Emperor Julian. Nevertheless, during the reign of Valentinian, the barbarian incursions continued to intensify. The battles were relentless confrontations that were scattered across the western provinces. The Alamanni tribes were able to defeat the Roman army in several battles until Emperor Valentinian destroyed them in the Battle of Solicinius. There was the Great Conspiracy of 367-368 in Roman Britannia where the barbaric tribes of the

Picts,Scots,Saxons,Franks, along with some Roman deserters fought against Rome rulership. It wasn't until the spring of 368 when Roman forces crossed the body of water known today as the English Channel with relief support. A brilliant general named Theodosius the Elder served as commander of the fresh troops. Included among the new Roman troops was his son who would later be known as Emperor Theodosius. Meanwhile, the elder Theodosius was able to regain control and rescue Britannia from the grips of the ferocious tribesmen. He subdued both the southern portion of the island as well as the north, renaming it Valentia in honor of the emperor. After that, he later led troops on a mission to quell a rebellion in the province of Africa.

Throughout his reign in the city of Milan, Valentinian was known as a heavy-handed brute with a violent temper. Another interesting characteristic of Valentinian was the fact that he deeply despised the well-dressed and educated aristocratic class. On the other hand, he was very compassionate towards the lower-class, from which his father originated. He became the founder of several schools and provided medical assistance to the poor. Each of the Rome's fourteen districts had their own physician to provide care. He also outlawed baby killing which usually occurred when a child was born with a birth defect, unwanted pregnancies, or child sacrifice.

Nevertheless, Valentinian was known for his cruelty. He regularly executed his own courtiers for trivial matters. He reportedly kept two bears in a lion cage, which he transported everywhere he traveled, so he could carry out ravishing death sentences upon demand. Many people received capital punishment during his reign.

In his personal life, Emperor Valentinian was married to two women at the same time, making him a polygamist leader. One wife was named Marina Severa and the other one Justina. The women were very intimate with each other, they even bathed together and spent plenty of time alone. It was once said that Severa saw Justina naked in the bath and was awe struck by her bare nakedness. She told the emperor that Justina was so beautiful of a creature that she intimately desired her although she was a woman. Because of this relationship, Emperor Valentinian made it a law that a man could legally marry two wives. His first wife Marina Severa was the mother of his son Gratian. Justina became the mother of 4 children. Their son was named Valentinian II. Their three daughters were named Galla, Grata, and Justa.

Now it came to pass that Emperor Valentinian continued another military campaign into the city of Brigetio, which is modern Szony,Hungary,in the spring of 375. He arrived on November 17 and met a delegation of Quadi tribesmen hoping to establish peace. After meeting the Roman negotiators, the barbarian diplomats were granted an audience with the emperor. The Quadis told Valentinian that the building of Roman fortifications deep inside their homeland was the cause for war. The ambassadors also told Valentinian that some of the barbarian tribes would agree to a cease-fire and peace. They warned the emperor that they should not be held responsible for the actions of a few unruly tribesmen. Emperor Valentinian flew into a rage, screaming and verbally abusing the envoys. In the end his uncontrollable rage caused a blood vessel in his head to burst, causing a brain hemorrhage and instant death. This occurred on the same day he had arrived: November 17, 375.

Valentinian died at the age of 63 after serving as the sole emperor. One month before his death, he chose his brother as his co-emperor for the duration of his reign on the throne in Milan, Italy. For eleven years, he did evil in the eyes of **YHWH ELOHIM Israel** according to abhorrent practices of many of the Greco-Roman rulers that preceded him. He served the image-god Jesus Christ according to the graven doctrine of the Nicene Council. He also bowed before the graven image of the Cross. He did not walk in the commandments which YAH gave to Moses as the law for Israel and all mankind. His older son **Gratian [367— 383]** served as the senior Augustus over the western provinces until 383 C.E. He was born somewhere between April 18 and May 23 in the year 359. He was born in the city of Sirmium. His father was Emperor Valentinian I and his mother was Empress Marina Severa. Valentinian crowned him Caesar at the age 8. His full birth name was Flavius Gratianus Augustus. As a youth, he joined his father on military campaigns against the barbarians. After his father died in 375, Gratianus continued as emperor in the West, fighting Gothic tribesmen, for another eight years. In 383, he was assassinated by rebel soldiers in the city of Lyons, in the Gaulic province. So it came to pass that Gratianus died at the age of 24 after serving as a emperor for sixteen years. He served the image-doctrine of Jesus Christ and bowed before the image of the Cross. During his reign, he removed the statue of the Altar of Victory in the Roman Senate. Nevertheless, he still did evil in the eyes of **YHWH ELOHIM Israel** by not knowing HIS laws, commandments, judgements, and statutes nor realizing HIS ways. Before Gratianus died, he chose General Theodosius as his successor in the eastern provinces.

Now, upon the death of Valentinian I in November 375, his soldiers gathered together and declared his youngest son **Valentinian II[375—392]** as their choice for emperor in the West.

Valentinian II
(375 C.E.—392 C.E.)
[West]

Valentinian II was born in the year 371 as the son of Emperor Valentinian I and his second wife Justina. His full birth name was Flavius Valentinianus. When his father died on November 17, 375, he was only a 4-year-old lad living in the city of Brigetio in the province of Pannonia **[modern-day Szony, Hungary]**. Five days later on November 22, his father's soldiers chose the four-year-old Valentinian as the young child emperor without even considering his older 15-year-old brother Gratianus who was in Germany at the time, or his 37-year-old uncle Valens who was in east. The throne name Imperator Caesar Flavius Valentinanus Augustus was given to him. He reigned in the imperial court in the northern Italian city of Milan, which ranked as the third Rome, behind Constantinople and ancient Rome itself.

The child emperor Valentinian II was under his mother Justina's influence while growing up as a ruler. Unlike her deceased husband, Empress Justina was member of the Arian branch of Christianity while he had adhered to the tenets of the Nicene Council. In those days the evolving Roman state-church was governed by Ambrose I, a supporter of the Nicene Council. Their differences in religious theology led to open hostilities between the church and state. Those tensions came to a head during Easter of 385 when the bishop refused to allow the empress the right to use the Portian Basilica for the spring festival activities. The Roman Church had grown powerful enough to challenge the decrees of the 10-year-old emperor and his 45-year-old mother. Bishop Ambrose stood in the doorway to prevent the empress and her Gothic bodyguards from entering the sanctuary. The standoff caused riots throughout the city of Milan. Supporters of church rose up against the imperial court. The chances for a massive bloodbath were real. Had not Theodosius, the newly selected emperor of East, intervened, the city of Milan would have become the center of violence. Emperor Theodosius was forced to bring peace between the disputing parties. He then commanded Empress Justina to withdraw her imperial bodyguards which were surrounding the sanctuary. For the first time, Bishop Ambrose and the Roman church scored a victory against the Roman state which was ruled by the 14-year-old child emperor and his middle-aged mother. During this era, Roman unity in the western provinces was a relic of the past.

For example, two years earlier in late 383, a commander of the Roman armies in Britannia named **Magnus Maximus [384—388]** declared himself emperor of the West despite the fact Valentinian II had been chosen to succeed his father Valentiian I. Meanwhile Maximus gained the support from other commanders of troops who were stationed in Hispania and Gaul. Bishop Ambrose stepped in again. This time the powerful church statesman attempted to negotiate an agreement between the usurper Magnus Maximus and Valentinian II. After the death of Gratianus, Emperor Theodosius then chose Magnus Maximus to serve as the co-emperor of the West. In late 386 or early 387, Maximus crossed the Alp mountain range into northern Italy, seeking to oust Emperor Valentinian and his mother Empress Justina. The royal family fled to the city of Thessalonica where Emperor Theodosius reigned. Theodosius was forced to intervene again. He arranged for Magnus Maximus to marry Galla, the sister of

Valentinian. Maximus also agreed to restore the 18-year-old emperor upon his throne in the city of Milan. Nevertheless in the year 388, Emperor Theodosius made an one-hundred eighty degree turn and launched a military attack against Maximus and defeated him. So it came to pass that the usurper Magnus Maximus reigned for nearly 4 years doing evil in the eyes of **YHWH ELOHIM Israel** like unto all the Roman leaders that preceded him. Afterwards, Emperor Theodosius restored the young Valentinian II back upon his throne. But there was one major difference. In order to keep the peace, Theodosius, the powerbroker, decided to separate the imperial court of Valentinian II from Bishop Ambrose of Milan. The bishop remained in Milan while the imperial court was transferred to the city of Vienne in the province of Gaul. Meanwhile, Theodosius stayed in Milan for three years until 391.

Now Valentinian did not participate in the triumphal ceremonies celebrating Theodosius victory over Maximus. Theodosius used his influence to appoint key officials to rule the western provinces. He even had the coins minted to reveal his domination over the 18-year-old young emperor. During this time his mother Empress Justina died. Theodosius then appointed a Frank general named Arbogast to serve as a guardian over the teenage ruler. Unlike his father Valentinian I and his older brother Gratianus, Valentinian II was not a man of valor. While Theodosius militarily campaigned in the western provinces, Valentinian stayed behind in his palace in Vienne. This awkward relationship between the overseer and emperor caused tensions to flare-up.

Case in Point: By the 392, Valentinian II was a 21-year-old man who desired to lead the Roman army into battle against Gothic barbarian hordes which threatened northern Italy. Although Valentinian II was the emperor, General Argobast refused him the right to lead the armed forces while standing in front of them. Valentinian attempted to dismiss Argobast as commander of the army, but he refused to step down. Blatantly disrespecting him, Argobast then ripped up the written official order in his face. Argobast told Valentinian that he did not have the authority to remove him because he didn't appoint him in the first place. Valentinian then wrote to Emperor Theodosius, and even Bishop Ambrose in the city of Milan, complaining and begging for help. He told them Argobast had disrespected the imperial authority of the emperor.

Valentinian told Bishop Ambrose he was willing to convert to the beliefs of the Nicene Council in exchange for his support. He even invited him to Vienne to baptize him. However on May 15, 392 Valentinian II was found hanging in his palace in Vienne. Argobast told other officials his death was suicide while others contend Valentinian II was murdered by Argobast. Valentiniian's corpse was returned to the royal city of Milan for an elaborate funeral ceremony. Bishop Ambrose presided over his burial. His sisters Justa and Grata also publicly mourned his death. Valentinian was buried next to his brother Gratian in a stone box-like receptacle designed to encase a corpse and serve as a standing monument.

So it came to pass that Emperor Valentinian II died at the age of 21 after serving seventeen years upon the throne as Emperor of the western Roman empire. He did evil in the eyes of **YHWH ELOHIM Israel** by walking after other gods, even the doctrines of Arius and the Nicene Council. He bowed before the doctrine of the image-god Jesus Christ and the image of the cross according all the Roman emperors since Constantine the Great, except Julian the Apostate. Valentinian ruled 13 years in Milan **[375-388]** and 4 years **[388-392]** in the city of Vienne in the province of Gaul.

Now General Arbogast, the powerbroker, then chose a man named Eugenius as his choice for the next emperor. Argobast made this important decision without consulting with Emperor Theodosius. Theodosius accepted his choice. But the following year in January of 393, Emperor Theodosius selected his 8-year-old son Honorius as the new Augustus in the room of Valentinian II. This act sparked a division between General Argobast and Theodosius. The rift grew into another open civil war. In the end, Theodosius defeated both Eugenius and Argobast at the Battle of Frigidus River. So Theodosius reigned as the new emperor of both the eastern and western portions of the Roman empire.

Theodosius "the Great"
(379 C.E.—395 C.E.)
[East & West]

Theodosius was born on January 11, 347 in the city of Coca in the province of Hispania, modern Spain. His father's name was Theodosius the Elder and his mother's name Thermantia. He was born with birth name Flavius Theodosius. As a young lad, he began to learn the art of warfare by joining his father, who was a senior military officer, on campaigns. In the year 368, when he turned 20, his father was dispatched to Britannia to crush the Great Conspiracy against Emperor Valentinian I. He joined his father as he slaughtered the barbarians and Roman turncoats, and successfully quelled the rebellion and restored order to the province.

By 373, Theodosius was promoted to governor of Moseia were he warred against the barbaric Sarmatians, Quadi, and Alemannis. The following year in 374, he became the military commander while still facing continuous barbarian incursions. The neighboring province of Illyria was also invaded during that same time. Theodosius was able to halt those incursions, and he earned great notoriety for his courageous victories during his tenure. Coincidently, it was during this same time that his father Theodosius the Elder fell out of favor and executed. Theodosius fled to Hispania for refuge and safety. He retired from political and military service. While there, he lived as a provincial aristocrat on his family's estate.

Four years later in 378, Emperor Valens was slain in the Battle of Adrianople leaving the throne empty in the East. Gratian, who was temporarily the sole emperor without an heir, summoned Theodosius to take command of the Illyrian army in the East. Theodosius accepted the call back into public life. His elevation made him co-emperor of the eastern Roman empire. Less than three months after Theodosius became co-emperor, a church-state crisis erupted in the city of Milan. Bishop Ambrose stood in the doorway to prevent Empress Justina and her Gothic bodyguards from entering the sanctuary for Easter services. The standoff caused riots throughout the city of Milan. Supporters of church rose up against the imperial court. The chances for a massive bloodbath were real. Theodosius was forced to intervene to bring peace between the disputing parties. He then commanded Empress Justina to withdraw her imperial bodyguards which surrounded the sanctuary. For the first time, Bishop Ambrose and the Roman church scored a victory against the Roman state. During this era, Roman unity within the western provinces was nonexistent.

Another crisis in the western provinces occurred in late 386 or early 387 when Maximus crossed the Alp mountain range into northern Italy, seeking to oust Emperor Valentinian and his mother Empress Justina. The royal family fled to the city of Thessalonica where Emperor Theodosius reigned. Theodosius was forced to intervene in the affairs of the western provinces again. As part of the peace settlement, Theodosius arranged for Magnus Maximus to marry Galla, the sister of Valentinian. Maximus also agreed to restore the 18-year-old emperor upon his throne in the city of Milan. One year later in the year 388, Emperor Theodosius reversed course and launched a military attack against Maximus and defeated him in the Battle of Save on August 28. Afterwards, Emperor Theodosius restored the young Valentinian II back upon his throne. But there was one major difference. In order to keep the peace, Theodosius, the powerbroker, decided to separate the imperial court of Valentinian II from Bishop Ambrose of Milan. The bishop remained in Milan while the imperial court was transferred to the city of Vienne in the province of Gaul. Meanwhile, Theodosius stayed in Milan for three years until 391.

The Birth of The Roman Catholic Church

On February 27, 380, Theodosius joined Gratian and 5-year-old Valentinian II and issued a royal governmental decree declaring the Nicene belief in Trinity as the imperial religion of the Roman state. Theodosius declared the Roman state church as the only church entitled to call itself the Catholic (universal) Church. The tenets of the Nicene Creed were declared the universal standard for all Christians throughout the empire. Theodosius also issued a decree that made Nicene Christianity the official state religion of the Roman empire. Eventually the church became known as the Roman Catholic Church. Rome was able to recapture some of its glory when the great city situated on seven mountains was chosen as the capital of the new church.

In ancient Rome, the seven hills were the sanctuaries for praising the Roman image-gods Mars, Venus, Jupiter, Saturn, Sol Invictus, and others. Under the new Christian era, the seven mountains became sanctuaries for great church monuments of the Trinity, god the father, the son, and holy ghost. The Aventine Hill became the high place for the Basilica of Santa Sabina. The Caelian Hill became the altar for the Church of Santi Giovanni e Paola, the Church of Santo Stefano Rotondo, the Church of San Gregorio, and the Church of Santa Maria. The Esquiline Hill was the sanctuary of the image-goddess Minerva. It was replaced with the great chapel of the Church of Santa Maria. The Church of San Bonventura was erected on the Palatine Hill. The image-church known as the Church of Chiesa di Santa Susanna was reared up on the Quirinal Hill. The Basilica Papale di Santa Maria and the other great churches of Christianity were erected on the Viminal Hill. The great churches themselves became the new image-gods on the seven hill that people bowed before. Those 4th, 5th, and 6th century Christian worshippers attended church services to glorify the great cathedrals and uphold the tenets of the Nicene Council. The church began to regard itself as the true heir of the myth and ministry of the man-god Jesus. Rome was chosen as the new Jerusalem. The bishop of Rome became the Papal of the entire Church. **SUN**day was edified as the official **Day** of **Worship** worldwide. The seven sacraments: 1) baptism, 2) penance, 3) the Holy Communion, which was based of the statements *"this is my body and this is my blood"* believed to be made by Jesus, 4) matrimony, 5) ordination, 6) confirmation, and, 7) anointing of the sick. The church also adopted the royal colors of the Roman state, the purple, scarlet, and white togas(robes). The sculptured images of the Cross and pictures of the baby Jesus and mother Mary replaced the standing images of the former Roman deities.

By the 6th century the protection of Rome had been transferred into the hands of the Roman Catholic Church due to barbarian invasions and the collapse of the western Roman empire. By the 15th century, the bishop of Rome, who affectionately became known as the Pope, or Papacy, replacing the Roman Emperor.

The myth of Roman Catholic Church dates back to the year 64 when it is alleged St. Peter the Apostle became the first bishop of Rome. Since then, a succession of nearly 300 men have served as the bishop of Rome up until the writing of this book in 2019.

Back to the Reign of Theodosius

In the year of 381 during the month of May, Emperor Theodosius convened the Second Ecumenical Council in the imperial city of Constantinople. The goal of this second gathering, which took place 56 years after the first ecumenical convocation in 325 during the reign of Constantine I, was to close the religious gap between eastern and western versions of Christianity. In the end, the council established the concept of the Trinity as Christian orthodoxy. The bishops also established the rulership of the state church within the Roman Empire. They also agreed that Rome was the religious capital of Christianity, with Constantinople serving as the second holy city of the faith.

Another outcome from the second ecumenical gathering was Christian intolerance towards traditional Roman religion. Theodosius, a Christian hardliner, had only been emperor for two years before the gathering of the Christian bishops in Constantinople. After the council, he announced his intentions to enforce the earlier prohibition announced by Constantine the Great, which was never enforced. Theodosius then placed Christians in the judicial branches of government, outlawed polytheism, pagan holidays were turned into workdays, pagan associations such the Vestal Virgins were banned, along with others, and temples dedicated to traditional Greco-Roman standings images were demolished.

Theodosius the Sole Emperor

After Theodosius victory agasinst Maximus, Valentinian did not participate in the triumphal ceremonies in Rome. Theodosius, who was now the sole emperor of the empire, used his influence to appoint key officials to rule the western provinces. He even had the coins minted to reveal his domination over the 18-year-old young emperor. (During this time his mother Empress Justina died.) Theodosius then appointed a Frank general named Arbogast to serve as a guardian over the teenage ruler. Unlike his father Valentinian I and his older brother Gratian, Valentinian II was not a man of valor. While Theodosius militarily campaigned in the western provinces, Valentinian stayed behind in his palace in Vienne.

By the 392, Valentinian II was a 21-year-old man who desired to lead the Roman army into battle against Gothic barbarian hordes which threatened northern Italy. General Argobast refused him the right to lead the armed forces while standing in front of them. Valentinian attempted to dismiss Argobast as commander of the army, but Argobast refused to step down. Argobast ripped up the written official order in his face. Argobast told Valentinian that he did not have the authority to remove him. Valentinian then wrote to Emperor Theodosius, and even Bishop Ambrose in the city of Milan begging for help.

Valentinian told Bishop Ambrose he was willing to convert to the tenets of the Nicene Council in exchange for his support. He invited him to visit to baptize him. But on May 15, 392, Valentinian II was found hanging in his palace. Argobast ruled his death suicide while others believe Argobast murdered him. Valentiniian's corpse was returned to the royal city of Milan in an elaborate funeral. After those events, General Arbogast chose a man named Eugenius as his choice for the next emperor without consulting with Emperor Theodosius. Theodosius initially accepted his choice. But the following year in January of 393, he reversed course and chose his 8-year-old son Honorius as the new Augustus in the room of Valentinian II. This act caused a rift between General Argobast and Theodosius. The strain grew into open civil war. In the end, Theodosius defeated both Eugenius and Argobast at the Battle of the Frigidus River. This made Theodosius the last Roman emperor to reign over both the Eastern and Western Roman empire. He then chose the throne name Imperator Caesar Flavius Theodosius Augustus.

As emperor, Theodosius totally reversed the policies of his predecessors by allowing the Christian believers to destroy the sun-god Temple of Apollo in Delphi, Greece and the Temple of Serapeum in Alexandria, Egypt. In Rome, he dissolved the order of the revered Vestal Virgins. In the year 393, he also outlawed the pagan rituals of the Olympics. His policies forced the pagans to go undercover and allowed the Christians to become the new government officials. This new Roman church-state alliance propelled the new religion into a position of power that would affect the course of Roman, Middle Age, and modern Europe for thousands of years into the future, even until today. For those reasons, Theodosius was regarded as "The Great" in the Nicene Christian world.

During the latter-part of his reign, most of Emperor Theodosius attention was consumed with fending off barbarian invasions by Goths, Vandals, Taifals, and the Bastarnae. The provinces of Dacia **[modern Romania]** and eastern Pannonia Inferior **[modern Hungary, Austria, Croatia, Serbia, Slovenia, Bosnia]** were the localities for many of these bloody battles. In the end, the strength of the Roman army did not provide Theodosius with the ability to totally annihilate the populations of the barbarians. Therefore, he initiated a new policy of integrating the barbarians into the ranks of the armies, thus introducing classical Romanism to the far away primitive hinterlands now known as the countries of eastern and western Europe. One of Theodosius greatest diplomatic victories came when Athanric, the chief of the Visigoths, accepted his invitation to visit the imperial city Constantinople and agreed to assimilate his barbarian people into the empire. The beauty and majestic splendor of the famed city struck Athanric and his delegation with awe. They had never witnessed such advanced human development as the infrastructure inside Constantinople. They agreed to become one of the empire's autonomous allies. Shortly thereafter, Athanric died, but Theodosius arranged a royal state funeral on his behalf. That act of kindness endeared the

Visigoths to Theodosius. Northwest of Italy, the barbarian tribes of the Ostrogoths represented another threat. The Ostrogoths were led by a chief named Alathaeus who warred against the empire. Theodosius was able to defeat them in battle, but later signed a peace treaty which allowed the barbarians to be settle inside former Roman territories. Eventually the Franks, Scythians, the Goths, and all others were assimilated into the Roman way of life and the imperial armies.

Not all native Romans embraced the new Roman immigrants. One example of that rejection occurred in 390 C.E. in the city of Thessalonica when the city population rioted and rejected the presence of Gothic soldiers stationed in their midst. The Thessalonian people killed the commander of the troops. The blatant disrespect shown towards the emperor and his Gothic courtiers was unforgivable in the eyes of Theodosius. He ordered his troops to kill all the spectators in the circus arena. An eyewitness named **Theodoret** described the retaliation by the Christian emperor Theodosius in the following words:

"The anger of the Emperor rose to the highest pitch, and gratified his vindictive desire for vengeance by unheating the sword most unjustly and tyrannically against all, slaying the innocent and guilty alike. It is said 7,000 perished without any forms of law, and without even having judicial sentence passed upon them; but that, like ears of wheat in the time of harvest, they were alike cut down."

Although the Roman emperor Theodosius claimed to be a follower of peacemaker Jesus Christ, he was not a man who turned the other cheek. The fierceness of his wrath and the massive amount of bloodshed spilled in the aftermath of the riot caused Bishop Ambrose to intervene and suspend him from the Church. He demanded that Theodosius humble himself and seek forgiveness before he could re-enter the gates of the Christian Church. Theodosius compiled with the bishop's demands, and eventually months later, he was allowed to return to the fold as a member in good standing.

After the death of Valentinian II in 392, Theodosius continued his purge of non-Christian beliefs from Roman public life. He did not hearken unto any calls for toleration of other faiths. In fact, he repaid the pagans for all their intolerant acts of violence against Christians over the past three centuries. He tore down their sacred high places, burned their icons in the fire, and smashed their places of worship into rubbish. In the eyes of Theodosius, all non-Catholics were foolish madmen.

Although Frankish General Argobast chose a Roman named Eugenius as his choice for emperor after Valentinian's death, Theodosius chose his son Honorius as his co-emperor in the western provinces in January of 393. Theodosius and his new enemies, Argobast and Eugenius, warred against each other at the Battle of Frigidus. *(Both sides needed to recruit large armies composed of mainly barbarians to fill their ranks.)* Theodosius and his imperial army loss the first round of the conflict on September 5, 394. It was said that later that night Theodosius was visited by two heavenly riders dressed in all white. The heavenly riders told Theodosius to be courageous and not to give up. The next morning when the armies were set in array Theodosius was divinely assisted by hurricane-strength winds that blew against the armies of Argobast and Eugenius and destroyed their front lines. Theodosius army was able to storm the camp of Eugenius and Argobast. Argobast committed suicide. Eugenius was captured and executed. Theodosius was now sole emperor with his two sons as co-emperors. The following year on January 17, 395, Emperor Theodosius died a painful death after suffering from severe edema which caused his body to swell. Edema is caused when abnormal amounts of fluids accumulate in the intestines, or beneath the skin, or in body cavities causing swelling. This disorder causes severe pain throughout the body.

So it came to pass that Emperor Theodosius I died in the city of Mediolanum at the age of 48 after reigning 16 years as emperor of both the western and eastern halves of the Roman Empire. He did evil in the eyes of **YHWH ELOHIM Israel** according to all the Roman Christian emperors that preceded him. He served the graven image of the Cross and bowed before the graven doctrine of man-god Jesus Christ. He did not walk in the commandments which YAH commanded Israel and all nations at Mount Sinai.

During his lifetime he married two women. He married the first woman named Aelia Flaccilla in 385 which bore him 4 children: two boys and two girls. Arcadius and Honorius. Palcheria and Galla Placida. He married Galla, the daughter of Emperor Valentinian I in the year 394. They were the parents of one child: a daughter named Aelia Placida. She was the only child to later become an Empress. At his state funeral, Bishop Ambrose delivered the powerful eulogy praising Theodosius for his great works on behalf of the Church. On November 8, 395 he was finally interned in the imperial capital of the eastern Roman empire, Constantinople. After Theodosius death, his 10-year-old son Honorius reigned over the western portion of the empire while his 18-year-old brother Arcadius reigned over the East. Both young emperors were ruled by their adult guardians. Neither were capable of successfully ruling the vast provinces of the Roman Empire without a series of setbacks. One of most detrimental failures was the rapid deteriorating of the Roman army after their father's death.

Arcadius
(395 C.E.—408 C.E.)
[East]

Arcadius *[pronounced* Ar-ca-di-us] was born on January 1, 377 in the province of Hispania as the son of Emperor Theodosius and his wife Empress Aelia Flaccilla. His full birth name was Flavius Arcadius. As the old proverbs goes, "train up a child in the way which he shall go, and when he becomes older, he will not depart". That is exactly what his father Theodosius did. In the year 383, when Arcadius turned to be a 6-year-old lad, his father made him the new co-emperor in the East. Twelve years later when his father Theodosius died in the year 395 only two weeks after Arcadius had turned 18, he and his 10-year-old brother Honorius became successors of the vast eastern and western Roman empire. He chose the throne name Imperator Caesar Flavius Arcadius. However, Arcadius was the emperor in title only. His power-hungry ministers, which dominated his court politics, were known to rule over him, especially a man named Rufinus, the Praetorian Prefect. During the latter-part of his reign, another minister named Anthemius became his guardian. He too was member of the Prateorian Guard.

It was said, Arcadius was more interested in living as a Christian saint instead of being a political or military leader. This allowed his courtiers to do as they pleased. They saw him as a ruler who was extraodinarily weak and easily influenced. For instance, his ministers did not respect Gainas, the leader of the Gothic barbarians and his people, who had been integrated into Constantinople society. In fact, they became a part of the anti-barbarian reaction which mistreated them. These same ministers took matters into their own hands and raised a force to massacre multitudes of barbarians encamped in autonomous enclaves of the great city. The survivors fled to the neighboring province of Thrace. The imperial army tracked them down and slaughtered them while Gainas managed to escape to the Ostrogoths in Asia Minor.

During his 13-year reign Arcadius married a woman named Aelia Eudoxia, who was the daughter of a Romanized Frank general named Buto. During this era, the Franks, who had once been barbarians during the 1st, 2nd, 3rd, and early 4th centuries, were now integrated into Roman society. *(It should be noticed that it was Rome which created the foundation for the eventual rise of the kingdom of France in the years to come.)* The marriage between Arcadius and Aelia was arranged by his court ministers who chose her instead of another woman to control the emperor. It was said, Aelia dominated her new husband. They were parents of 5 children, one boy and four girls. His son was Theodosius II and his daughters were Pulcheria, Arcadia, Flaccilla, and Marina. After his marriage, his wife eventually became his sole advisor. In the year 399, the Ostrogoth barbarians, who had been previously integrated into Roman society in Asia Minor by Theodosius, rebelled against the rule of Arcadius. His wife then advised him to submit to the barbarians.

In July of 399, the 22-year-old emperor, who was a member of the Nicene branch of Christianity, issued a royal decree to tear down all remaining non-Christian temples in his realm. He began the construction of a new forum in his own honor known as the Column of Arcadius located on the seventh hill of the imperial city Constantinople. However, the column was completed years later by his son Theodosius II after his death.

So it came to pass that Arcadius died on May 1, 408 C.E. in Constantinople at the age of 31. He had reigned for 13 years and did that which was displeasing in the eyes of **YHWH ELOHIM of Israel** by serving other gods, even the doctrine of the man-god Jesus Christ and he bowed before the image of the Cross. He knew not YAH nor did he walk in HIS commandments, laws, statutes, or judgements.

In the eastern Roman empire his son **Theodosius II** reigned in his stead. Meanwhile in the West, Arcadius's brother **Honorius** continued to reign until the year 423.

Honorius
(395 C.E.—423 C.E.)
[West]

Honorius was born on September 9, 384 in the city of Constantinople. He was the son of Theodosius I and his wife Aelia Flaccilla. His full birth name was Flavius Honorius. His father, Theodosius promoted him to the imperial office of consulate at the age of 2 and later proclaimed him co-emperor at the tender age of 9 on January 23, 393. When his father Theodosius died, Honorius was only 10. Yet, he was promoted to the office of Augustus over the western Roman Empire. His throne name was Imperator Caesar Flavius Honorius Augustus. As a child emperor, he was controlled by a Romanized Vandal named Flavius Stilicho who determined his every move. After three years on the throne, he married Stilicho's daughter Maria in the year 398. Maria died in 407 and Honorius married her younger sister Thermantia the following year. During his reign, Western Europe was overran by constant invading Visigothic and Ostrogothic barbarians, and on top of that, there were several usurpers who sought to overthrow him.

In 401-402, the continued barbarian incursions forced the young emperor to move his imperial court from Milan to Ravenna, in northeastern Italy. For the next seven decades, Ravenna remained the capital of the western Roman Empire until its collapse in 476. Before its collapse, the city was arrayed with beautifully sculptured and magnificent monuments which served as enticement to the underprivileged Goths. To make matters worse, the imperial legions were overstretched and severely weakened, unable to defend the massive frontiers that extended from Britain to Italy. By 409, Emperor Honorius was forced to tell Roman citizens in Britain that Rome could no longer guarantee their security. In the year 405-406, other barbarian hordes consisting of Vandals, Alani, and Suebi crossed the frozen Rhine River to invade the Gaulic province. They also continued their incursions over into Hispania. Meanwhile, Honorius stayed in Ravenna while his loyal generals fought off all his challengers. His age and lack of military experience made him one of the weakest rulers in the history of the Roman Empire.

In 408, General Stilicho was able to avert another invasion, led by Alaric the ruler of the Visigoths, by forcing the Roman Senate to bribe the insurgents with 4,000 pounds of gold in exchange for their withdrawal from Italy. The barbarians accepted the deal. In the interim, Honorius brother Arcadius died that year. Stilicho convinced Honorius that he should go to the funeral instead of his own personal appearance. Honorius hearkened to the voice of Stilicho and allowed him to journey to Constantinople for Arcadius funeral. While Stilicho was absent, another advisor named Olympus stirred up Honorius spirit against his once trusted Praetorian Prefect. Olympius gained personal influence and convinced the 24-year-old emperor that Stilicho was a doublehearted servant plotting against him with the barbarians. When Stilicho returned to Ravenna, Honorius arrested him and executed him. He then slew all friends and family members of Stilicho. He also tortured several key officials and confiscated all of their possessions. Honorius continued his rampage by massacring the families of Stilicho federated barbarian troops. Many of the barbarian soldiers escaped and defected over to the barbarian chieftain Alaric. After the bloodletting, Honorius divorced his wife Thermantia and returned her to her mother. After that personal disaster, there was a palace revolution in his imperial court between those hostile to peace with Alaric and those who favored assimilation of the Goths.

The following year in 409, Alaric returned to Ravenna to claim more gold and to receive land. Before his execution, Stilicho had already agreed to the treaty. Honorius refused to comply with the terms of the treaty his once trusted general had okayed. Alaric departed Ravenna in rage and ordered his troops to march on Rome. After a short siege which caused a food shortages and a famine, Rome hastily agreed to pay Alaric a bribe to quit the siege. The Visigoths departed again. During the interim, Honorius requested assistance from his nephew Theodosius II, the new emperor of eastern provinces. By 410, Theodosius II had dispatched 6,000 legions to assist Honorius with the future battles against the barbarians. To their dismay, the forces of Alaric ambushed the eastern Roman legions en masse in route to Italy with only a few escaping. Emperor Honorius then declared Alaric to be an eternal enemy of the Roman Empire. After the declaration, Alaric marched against Rome for a second time. This time he destroyed the city. It was the first time in 800 years that Rome been invaded and sacked. Honorius miscalculation led to the destruction of Imperial City by the Goths. It should be noted that Honorius reign laid the foundation for Western Europe to transfer from Roman to Teuton dominion. In hindsight, it could be said that Honorius did nothing noteworthy to halt the infestation of barbarian enemies overturning their centuries of rulership. The **[iron kingdom]** of Rome was now permanently divided into two [East-West] parts **[legs-left/right]**. In terms of religion, Honorius adhered to the Nicene branch of Christianity, bowing before the doctrine of Jesus Christ and the image of the Cross.

By 411 another crisis arose when a usurper named **Constantine III[409-411 C.E.]**, commander of Roman armies in Britain, declared himself emperor of the West. His rebellion started in the year 407 in Britain. Once the mutiny started, he moved his capital to Gaul to confront any barbarians crossing the Rhine. Constantine III prevailed in the initial confrontations against Honorius. In the 409, both sides agreed to lay down their swords and Constantine III was proclaimed co-emperor to serve with Honorius. Constantine still faced multiple raids by the Saxons and others in Britain. He also faced low morale, desertions, and setbacks in Gaul where he was stationed. During his brief two-year reign, Constantine III appointed his son **Constans II[409—411]** as his co-emperor. Two years later, both Constantine III and his son Constans II relinquished their claim as co-emperors in the western provinces in 411. After Constantine III stepped down, he was apprehended by Praetorian Prefect and put to death. His son was also slain.

For the next several years the imperial army of Emperor Honorius fought back courageously against Visigothic barbarian incursions, and by the year 416, they had recovered the great city. There were men, women, boys, and girls celebrating the liberation of great city from the Visigoths in the streets of Rome. **Priscus Attalus [409 and in 414]** was the senator who had been previously handpicked twice: once in the year 409 and a second time in 414 by the barbarians as emperor. Priscus Attalus was forced to rejoice with his fellow Romans. He was later exiled to the Aeolian Islands as punishment for his treasonous support for the barbarians.

In the year 421, Honorius then recognized his Praetorian Prefect **Constantius III[421]** as his new co-emperor. He chose the throne name Imperator Caesar Flavius Constnatius. Prior to assuming his role as co-emperor, he had already married the sister of Honorius, Galla Placida. However, when Honorius notified his nephew Emperor Theodosius II in Constantinople, he refused to accept his new nominee. Constantius III became enraged and prepared his Roman legions for war against the East. But, before Constantius III could set forth for battle, he died in Ravenna on September 2, 421 after serving as co-emperor for only 7 months. His death represented the permanent division of the **two legs of iron [East-West**

Roman Empire].
During the years 420 to 422, another usurper named Maximus, a general in Hispania, threatened the throne. In the final days of his reign, the western provinces were in disarray. Britain, Hispania, and major parts of Gaul were under barbarian control. Although Honorius had been married twice, he fell deeply in love with his own half-sister in the final years as Augustus. She did not feel the same way about him. So Galla, the widow of Constantius III fled to Constantinople to escape his presence along with her little ones. Honorius also issued a royal decree which outlawed men wearing trousers in Rome and he also banned gladiator fights.

So it came to pass that Emperor Honorius reigned for 30 years before he died in Ravenna, Italy at the age 38 from edema, the same disease which had afflicted his father Theodosius. He died on August 15, 423 from the ailment that caused severe pain and swelling throughout his body. Although he died a natural death, a multitude of usurpers attempted to take his life and crown during his reign as Augustus. He did that which was displeasing in the eyes of **YHWH ELOHIM Israel** by serving other gods, even the doctrine of the Nicene Council, serving the man-god Jesus Christ. He also bowed before the graven image of the Cross. He knew not YAH nor did he walk in HIS commandments, laws, statutes, and judgements which HE commanded Israel and all nations. He was buried in Old Saint Peter's Basilica in Rome. Honorius did not have any sons to inherit the throne. So, his nephew Theodosius II was chosen to serve as emperor of the East while **Valentinian III** served as the emperor in the West.

Valentinian III
(423 C.E.—455 C.E.)
[West]

Valentinian III was born on July 2, 419 in the royal city of Ravenna. He was the son of Constantius III and Aelia Galla Placidia. His full birth name was Flavius Placicius Valentinanus. He was born into a very prominent family. His mother Galla was the princess daughter of the late Emperor Theodosius I. His father Constantius served as the Praetorian Prefect of the Imperial army, and later as co-emperor of the Western Roman Empire under Emperor Honorius, although his reign lasted for only seven months before he died.

In the year 421 when Valentinian III was a mere 2-year-old infant, his uncle Emperor Honorius granted the lad the title "Nobilissims [*pronounced* No-bi-lis-si-mus] which meant *"most noble"*. After his father's death, his uncle Emperor Honorius attempted to have an extramarital with his mother Galla, who happened to be the emperor's own sister. She spurned her brother's Honorius advances, and instead fled with the family to the eastern capital of Constantinople.

Meanwhile on November 20, 423 an usurper in Rome named Joannes, who was a senior civil servant, rose up after the death of Honorius. Joannes had been chosen by a man named Castinus, the new leader Praetorian Guard under Honorius after the death of Constantius III. For two years, from 423 to 425, Joannes proclaimed himself the new emperor of the West. He totally ignored Theodosius II, the emperor in the East. In the interim, Joannes strengthened himself with a large army and sought help from the Huns because he expected an attack from the eastern Roman army. He also moved his capital from Rome to Ravenna to defend against the expected assault.

Meanwhile in Constantinople, Emperor Theodosius II remained silent after the death of his uncle Honorius. During this time Galla, his elder aunt, lobbied him on behalf of her son Valentinian III. Emperor Theodosius finally consented two years and 2 months after Honorius death, and, on October 23th in the year 425, he proclaimed the 4-year-old Valentinian III as his co-emperor and Augustus of the West. This proclamation of Valentinian as emperor was a declaration of war to Emperor Joannes. Both armies met near the city of Aquileia. It was a hard fought campaign between two large armies and navies. The capital of the West, Ravenna, fell before the assault by the army of Theodosius. In the end, the soldiers of Joannes betrayed him by delivering him into the hands of his rivals. Joannes was bound and brought to the city of Aquileia for judgement. His hand was cut off. He was paraded on a donkey in the Hippodrome stadium. He was insulted, spit upon, and finally he was dismounted from the donkey and beheaded. This happened between the months June and July in 425.

The young lad was given the throne title Imperator Caesar Flavius Placidius Valentinianus Augustus. His mother Empress Galla became known as the regent who manipulated her son. After all, he was only a 6-year-old boy on the throne in Rome. For the next twelve years his mother was his guardian and chief advisor until he reached his 18th birthday in 437. She chose an experienced military officer named Felix as the commander of the imperial army. During this time Felix was able to negotiate a peace treaty with the Huns. The Huns had arrived too late to assist the usurper Joannes, who had already been put to death years earlier. Felix bribed the Huns to withdraw. Meanwhile, the western Roman army faced repeated barbarian invasions along the northern frontiers during 427 and 428. Some the battles ended in victories, however, those temporary victories against the Visigoths, Franks, and others along the Rhine River were not enough to reverse the gradual dismemberment of the Roman empire around Valentinian III. The Visigoths still occupied parts of the province of Gaul. In Hispania, the barbarian Vandals controlled parts of the landscape there. These pockets of resistance made it difficult for Roman commerce and taxation to flow smoothly as it had done for centuries. Those attacks also further weakened the economy of the Roman Empire. The Vandals also became rulers of the western part of North Africa during the reign of Valentinian III. This is how that happened: The barbarians, who had become pawns of the mutinous Roman general Bonifacius, turned against Bonifacius and crushed his army after Bonifacius invited them, then decided to reconcile with Emperor Valentinian III in the interest of unity. In the year 431, the Vandals overran the Roman garrisons, forcing Bonifacius to flee back to Italy. The Vandals then ruled the Roman province of Africa.

After General Bonifacius returned to the imperial court in Ravenna, Empress Galla, mother of Valentinian decided to replace him with another powerful general named Aetius. Nevertheless, Aetius declared war against the emperor, empress, and Bonifacius. A confusing civil war broke with Bonifacius finally defeating Aetius after a bloody conflict. Although Bonifacius won, he died from his deadly wounds. Aetius escaped to the barbarian lands of the Huns where he hired them to help him return to power. By 435, Valentinian was forced to negotiate in order to stabilize the dissolution of the western empire. In the interest of peace and stability, Aetius was allowed to return to his office. The Huns were given the new land in the Roman provinces of Pannonia and Savia. The Vandals were allowed to keep all conquered territories in exchange for tribute to the emperor in Ravenna. The western Roman empire, however, still continued its gradual decline as internal strife and external barbarian incursion constantly plagued the **[iron kingdom]**.

In the year 437 when Valentinian III turned 18, he became the sole emperor and married a woman named Licinia Eudoxia, who was the daughter of Emperor Theodosius II, the ruler of the Eastern Roman Empire. The royal marriage took place in the imperial city of Constantinople. He begat two girls by her: Eudocia and Placidia. Before his mother Empress Galla retired, she had been married several times, beginning with her union to Ataulf, king of the Visigoths, and continuing with her last marriage to the Praetorian Prefect named Constantius III.

Atilla the Hun
(434 C.E.—453 C.E.)

Throughout the decade of 440 to 450, the barbarian tribe of the Huns began invading the western provinces of the Roman empire located on the Danube River. Fearing an onslaught, Valentinian III offered the leader of the Huns the honorary title of "Magister Militum" meaning commander of armies of the western empire. In exchange, Attila, who was the chieftain of the Huns, agreed to withdraw his hordes from the western portions of the empire. Attila, a man who loved war, then turned his attention to menacing the eastern portions of the Roman empire. Born in 406, Attila grew to become the ruler of the barbarian people known as the Huns. These people migrated from parts of central Asia to inhabit territories known today as Central and Eastern Europe. Atilla's hordes consisted of Ostrogoths, Alans, and Huns.

By the year 449, the emperor's sister Honoria betrayed him after he attempted to force her into an incestuous marriage. She secretly dispatched a messenger to meet Attilla to offer him half of the western empire in exchange for saving her from the unwanted marriage. Attila readily agreed, and in the following year 450, he made an incursion into the province of Gaul after he made peace with the eastern emperor. Valentinian was deeply enraged and felt Attila had betrayed him. He soon discovered his sister Honoria had dispatched a messenger to seek military support from Attila. Valentinian arrested the messenger, tortured him to find out all of the details of the plot, then cut his head cut off. Valentinian wanted to do the same to his sister but his mother Empress Galla begged him to spare her life. General Aetius, the Praetorian Prefect, summoned a Roman army and gathered German barbarian mercenaries to confront the army of Attila. Aetius and his allies defeated the Huns, forcing them to retreat. In the following year 452, Atilla regrouped and invaded Italy again. This time Attila destroyed the cities of Vicentia, Aquileia, and Verona. The army of Aetius was not strong enough to confront the Huns. In response, Valentinian moved his imperial court back to Rome for safety reasons. In Rome, Valentinian asked Pope Leo I and the Roman Senate to intervene of behalf of the Roman state. Meanwhile, the troops of Atilla experienced a sudden outbreak of a pestilence which caused a famine. During this same time, Atilla learned that new eastern Roman Emperor Marican had attacked the Hun homeland along the Danube River. Those events forced Atilla to withdraw from Italy. Two years in later in 453, Atilla died in the province of Pannonia.

After the death of Atilla, the Hun invasions, and a temporary lull in other barbarian incursions, Valentinian turned his attention to his longtime Praetorian Prefect Aetius whom he now viewed as an adversary. The emperor then plotted to have him slain. A high-ranking senator named Petronius Maximus also had a score settlement with Aetius. He spoke evil words about Aetius in the ears of the Valentinian. Although Aetius and Valentinian were actually in-laws through marriage because the emperor's youngest daughter was married to the son of Aetius, it did not stop him from shedding his blood. This is what happened: It was September 21, 454 and Aetius came into the imperial court to read an official report before the emperor as he sat upon his throne. Before Aetius could complete reading his report, the emperor suddenly accused his trusted aide of being a depraved drunkard without morals. Furthermore, Valentinian accused Aetius of being the cause for all the kingdom's problems, and last but not least, he charged Aetius with plotting to usurp him. Valentinian suddenly rose up from his throne, drew his sword, and struck him in the head, instantly killing him on the spot. That was the only military action he ever saw during his entire 30-year reign. In his mind, Valentinian III thought he had slain someone who wanted to control him, but in reality he had slain his right hand man, his most trusted protector. In less than seven months after he slew Aetius, he too became the victim of an assassination plot. This is how it happened: Emperor Valentinian III rode his horse into the Campus Martius in Rome. He then dismantled his horse to practice archery with his bow and arrow. While his head was turned away, the two conspirators, Optelas and Thraustelas, attacked. Optelas delivered the deathblow on the side of his head just as he had done to Aetius only months earlier. In fact, the two murderers were bodyguard friends of Aetius who had been influenced by Senator Petronius Maximus. So in the end Emperor Valentinian III had reaped what he had sown. It was also recorded in the annals of Roman history that as the emperor Valentinian III laid on the ground, swarms of bees appeared, covered him, and sucked up the pool of blood.

At the time of Valentinian's death, the Roman Empire was only a reflection of its former glory. The **[iron kingdom]** was in shambles. North Africa had been taken from the empire. The barbarians had overrun western Spain and the majority of the province of Gaul. *"Rome was falling"*.

So it came to pass that Emperor Valentinian III died on March 16, 455 at the age of 35 after reigning for thirty-years in the royal cities of Ravenna and Rome. He did evil in the eyes of **YHWH ELOHIM Israel** by practicing astrology, sorcery, magic, and divination in violation of Teachings found in **Deuteronomy 18:9-14**. He was also a Christian who bowed before the graven doctrine of the Nicene Creed by believing in the man-god Jesus and he bowed before the image of the Cross. He did not know YAH nor did not he walk in HIS laws, commandments, judgements, and statutes. He lacked the stability to keep the empire together. He was known to be self-indulgent and a spoiled pleasure-seeker.

In terms of his religious standing, Valentinian III was devoted to contributing to the building of two great monuments: The Church of Saint Lawrence in Rome and the Church of Saint Lawrence in Ravenna. It should also be noted that Emperor Vatentinian III issued a decree on June 6, 455 which recognized the bishop of Rome as the Papacy. Rome was declared the religious capital of the Church and all Christianity. The tenets of the Nicene Creed were reiterated as the law of the Church. And most importantly, the emperor of Rome agreed to support the Church in enforcing Church law, thus redefining Roman state-church relations where the bishop was now equal to the emperor.

On the very next day after the assassination of Emperor Valentinian III, Petronius Maximus, paid a large donation to be proclaimed the successor and new emperor by the remaining Roman army stationed in Rome. Maximus, however, had bitten off more than he could chew. He was not prepared to takeover and stabilize the empire as he had thought. After 11 weeks, one week shy of three months, Emperor Petronius Maximus was stoned to death by a Roman mob.

Petronius Maximus
(455 C.E.)
[West]

Petronius Maximus was born in the year 396 C.E. with the birth name Flavius Anicius Petronius Maximus. His father's name was Anicius Probinus and his mother's name was not recorded in the annals of Roman history. Maximus came from humble beginnings although he grew to become a prominent aristocrat and wealthy senator. He started his career as a praetor before advancing to the position of "tribunus et notarius". He eventually became a member of the imperial bureaucracy as a *"comes"*. Afterwards, he became the executive authority and municipal administrator of Rome. He also served as the Praetorian Prefect, as a Consul, and Praetorian Prefecture of Italy. He was known to have built a Forum on the Caelian Hill in Rome and he was responsible for the restoration of the Old Saint Peter's Baslica.

During the reign of Emperor Valentinian III, Maximus had become a powerful politician and master manipulator. Both men were once friends and gambling companions. Valentinian and Maximus placed a bet on a game. Maximus lost the bet, and he did not have the money to pay his wager. So Maximus gave the emperor his ring as a surety. Valentinian, who was known to be lustful and self-indulgent, used the ring to bring Maximus wife to dinner behind his back. Now, Maximus wife was known as a beautiful woman, and when she arrived at the state dinner she and the emperor were all alone. She initially spurned the sexual advances of the emperor, but after long conversations, he was able to seduce her to the point where he could rape her. She left the palace in rage thinking her husband had betrayed her and agreed to the encounter. Maximus was enraged and swore to get revenge, but he had to first get rid of his bodyguard Praetorian Prefect Aetius.

Maximus set in motion a deadly plot. He first contacted a courtier named Heraclius who worked in the imperial court. Together, they convinced Emperor Valentinian III that Aetius was plotting to kill him. The emperor hearkened to their voices. So when Aetius came into the imperial court to read an official report, the emperor suddenly accused his trusted aide of being a depraved drunkard without morals. Valentinian then accused Aetius of being the cause for all the kingdom's problems, and last but not least, he charged Aetius with plotting to assassinate him. While Heraclius stood near, Valentinian suddenly rose up from his throne, drew his sword, and struck him in the head, instantly killing him. With Aetius out of the way,

Maximus was one step closer to his goal of revenge. However, being the clever politician he was, Maximus asked the emperor for the old position of Praetorian Prefect which the deceased Aetius held. But, Valentinian refused, based on prior counsel of his courtier Heraclius who had secretly told him not to do so. Maximus became angry again and decided it was now time to eliminate the emperor. He chose two Scythian bodyguards, Optelas and Thraustelas, who had once served under General Aetius. He convinced the pair that the emperor was responsible for Aetius death, and to sweeten the deal, he offered a reward.

On March 16, 455, Emperor Valentinian III rode his horse onto the Campus Martius in Rome. He then dismantled his horse to practice archery with bow and arrow. While his head was turned away, the two conspirators, Optelas and Thraustelas, attacked. Optelas delivered the deathblow to his temple. The pair then took the emperor's royal diadem and royal purple robe and brought it to Maximus. The next day, on March 17, Maximus secured the throne by distributing money to officers in the imperial palace. There were several potential rivals and successors to the throne, but his bribes helped him prevail. He chose the throne name Imperator Caesar Flavius Anicius Petronius Maximus Augustus.

In another act of revenge, Maximus forced the widow of Valentinian, Licinia Eudoxia, to marry him. Maximus also changed the marriage plans of Licinia's daughter named Eudocia. She had been engaged to Huneric, the son of the Vandal king Geiseric, but Maximus heavyhandedly canceled those plans. Instead, he gave Eudocia to his son. This breakup greatly angered the king of the Vandals. Geiseric then dispatched a fleet of ships towards Rome. Once Maximus learned the king of the Vandals had set sail towards Rome for war, he send his Praetorian Prefect named Avitius on a mission to gain support and troops from the Visigoths. But once the news of the impending Vandals invasion became known, and military support had notarrived fast enough , chaos broke out when the inhabitants in the city of Rome panicked . In midst of disorder, Maximus was somehow separated from his bodyguards. He was slain as he attempted to exit the city. He was stoned, his body stranded upon, and his corpse thrown in the Tiber River. Meanwhile, the Vandals sacked Rome and vandalized every property in sight. All of this occurred on May 31, 455.

It came to pass that Petronius Maximus reigned for only two and one-half months as the emperor of the Western Roman Empire in the city of Rome. He forcibly married Licinia Eudoxia, the widow of Valentinian III. He was father of one daughter, Palladius. Avitus reigned in his stead as the next emperor of the West.

Avitus
(455 C.E.—456 C.E.)
[West]

Avitus was born somewhere between the years 380 and 395 in the province of Gaul [**modern France**] in the Roman settlement city of Clemont-Ferrand. His father's name was Flavius Julius Agricola and his mother's name was not mentioned for some reason. It is a known fact that Avitus was a descendant of Romanized barbarians whose ancestors were elevated through their contacts with classical Roman civilization. During his days the Romanized barbarians were an intricate part of the western Roman empire's political and military leadership. For centuries the Romans had been unable to halt the incursions of Franks, Visigoths, Ostrogoths, Vandals, Alemanni, Goths, Avars, Bulgars, Angles, Saxons, Lombards, Frisii, Jutes, Huns, and others into Roman territories in the West. So by the early third centuries, various Romans started the process of integrating those barbarians into Roman culture. The lineage of Avitus originated from that background.

His full birth name was Marcus Maecilius Flavius Eparchius Avitus. He grew up in the province of Gaul where he eventually became a high-ranking officer in military administration and a Gaul-Roman aristocrat. He also became a fellow associate of the powerful senator Petronius Maximus. When Maximus became emperor, Avitus was recalled from retirement and chosen as his Magister Militum. When Avitus received his new position, there were many voices in the Roman hierarchy that were calling for the reduction of the empire down to the size of the land of Italy alone. Avitus, a powerful voice, opposed the downsizing of the Roman empire.

Although he lived on the Roman side of the border, Avitus was able to maintain good relations with the Visigoths. During the brief reign of his predecessor Emperor Petronius Maximus, the king of the Vandals had set sail towards Rome for war, the emperor sent an embassy, which included Avitius, on a mission to the city of Toulouse to gain support and troops from Theodoric II, king of the Visigoths, to withstand the assault by the Huns. Avitus did not return to Italy with additional support in time to stop the Vandal invasion. News of sack of Rome and the death of Emperor Petronius Maximus reached the court of Theodoric. Theodoric II then proclaimed Avitus the new emperor. The barbarian chiefs throughout the province followed suit. One month later, the Roman Senate agreed and conferred upon him title "Augustus". Avitus, however, remained in the province of Gaul for three more months to strengthen his hold on power. Gaul was the center of Avitus support.

Avitus came to power as the next Augustus on July 8th or 9th, in the year of 455. He finally returned to Italy, passing through the cities of Noricum and Ravenna, before reaching Rome on September 21 with an army that included large numbers of Gallic and Gothic troops. Included among those ranks were generals Remistus, Majorian, and Ricimer. General Remistus was assigned to the city of Ravenna. The other two generals remained with Avitus in Rome. His choice of throne title was Imperator Caesar Marcus Maecilius Flavius Eparchius Avitus Augustus.

By January 1, 456 Avitus gained control of the Consul in Rome reigning over what was left of the western empire. He appointed several Gallic-Romans, former barbarians who had been incorporated into Roman federated lands, into many key offices and public administration jobs. This new face of Roman government caused resentment among classic Romans. Furthermore, Rome was still suffering from the ruins, food shortages, and devastation wrought by Vandals who had recently sacked the city. The financial situation in Rome was so dire that Avitus was forced to meltdown bronze from the many statues to pay the wages of his officials and army. During this same time, the Visigothic barbarians invaded the province of Hispania with no resistance from the Roman Empire.

In Constantinople, the capital of Eastern Roman Empire, Emperor Marcian did not recognize the ascension of Avitus. This opposition solidified the division of the **[iron kingdom]** into two halves **[legs]**—East and West **[Roman Empire]**.

Back in Rome, the two firebrand generals Majorian and Ricimer rebelled against Emperor Avitus. He was forced to flee the imperial city in early autumn. By September 17, General Ricimer had the Roman Senate to despose of Avitus by murder. Avitus fought back by mounting up an army. Both sides met to battle at Piacenza. Avitus entered the city to attack, but Ricimer forces massacred the army of Avitus, forcing him to flee once again by October 18. Avitus was eventually captured and forced to resign. Ricimer showed him mercy and spared his life under one condition: He was forced to retire from government and serve as the Bishop of Piacenza.

So it came to pass that Avitus later died in late 456 or early 457 after General Majorian starved him to death between the approximate ages of 70 to 76 after he had reigned for one year in the city of Rome. He was buried in the city of Brioude next to the Tomb of Saint Julian. He did evil in the eyes of **YHWH ELOHIM Israel** serving the graven doctrine of Jesus Christ and bowing before graven image of the Cross according to the tenets of the Nicene Creed. Then Majorian succeeded him as the next emperor of the rapidly declining Western Roman Empire. Meanwhile in the eastern portion of the Roman Empire, **Emperor Theodosius II** reigned from 408 to 450 and **Emperor Marcian** ruled for seven years from 450 to 457.

Now, let's turn our attention to the Eastern Roman Empire for a few decades.

Theodosius II
(408 C.E.—450 C.E.)
[East]

Theodosius was born into the royal family on April 10, 401 in the city of Constantinople as the son of Emperor Arcadius and Empress Aelia Eudoxia. His full birth name was Flavius Theodosius Junior. He was proclaimed co-emperor by his father in January 402 even before he was an one-year-old infant. That made him the youngest male in Roman history to hold the title. Six years in later in 408, his father Emperor Arcadius died on May 1, leaving his only offspring, 7-year-old Theodosius, a child, as the sole Emperor of the expansive eastern division of the Roman empire. The young lad was given the name Theodosius II in honor of his grandfather Emperor Theodosius I who had reigned decades earlier.

For the majority of first decade as a ruler, the young lad was under a guardian. He was placed under King Yazdegerd I of Persia who treated him like his own son. The king of Persia sent a personal tutor to Constantinople to raise him. He also warned all usurpers that any attempt to overthrow the lad would be viewed as an attack on Persia. Meanwhile, the day-to-day governance of the kingdom was placed in the hands of Praetorian Prefect Anthemius. Under his supervision the great walls known as the Theodosian Walls of Constantinople were constructed. By the year 414 his older sister named Pulcheria rose up and proclaimed herself Augusta [Empress] to supervise her little brother. By the year 416, Theodosius had become a 15-year-old. He was mature enough to assume the mantle of power for himself, but his sister still remained as one of his chief advisors. He chose the throne title Imperator Caesar Flavius Theodosius Junior Augustus. He went on to marry a woman of Greek origin named Aelia Eudocia. The marriage did not last long because his sister Pulcheria did not like his wife. In the process of time the couple eventually separated. His wife moved on to a monastery in Jerusalem. After Aelia departed, his sister returned as the most important woman in his life. His sister had an inside courtier named Chrysaphius [*pronounced* Chry-sa-fi-us] who had sowed discord and worked on her behalf inside the imperial court.

By the age of 20, Theodosius had come under the heavy influence of New Age of Christian Theology. In fact, during his reign there was confusion and several versions of this new age paganism known as Christianity. Of course, you had the Nicene theology and Arianism, but you also had others such as Nestorianism and Eutychaianism. Those ideologies ranged from those who viewed Mary as the mother of God and Jesus as the birth of God, to others who saw Christ as pre-existence before the 1st century. The fact of matter was, none of those **idol ideas [ideologies]** were based of the Words of Torah or the Counsel of the ancient Afro-Asiatic Hebrew prophets. All of their interpretations were erroneous and every decision decreed was in violation of Words YAH spoken at Mount Sinai. The true people of Israel and all mankind must remember what King Solomon once said in **Proverbs 15: 26:** *"Evil thoughts*[**doctrines**] *are an abomination to YHWH"*. So with that being said, all humanity should know how YHWH truly views all of these various Christian ideologies or, better yet, these **idol ideas** crafted by the uncircumcised minds of those non-Israelite [goyim/**foreign Gentile**] men. This new age 1st, 2nd, 3rd, 4th, and 5th century Gentile doctrine represented a new falsehood which is now known as doctrinal idolatry. Doctrinal Idolatry is wrong ideas, which were crafted like great statues, that actually represent graven doctrines or anti-YAH thoughts.

Between the years of 421/422, Theodosius II turned against Persia, the country which once was his guardian. His sister Pulcheria influenced him to war against the Persians because they were persecuting Christians. The conflict ended in a stalemate. The Romans had to hastily return to Constantinople to defend the imperial city against the invasion of the Hun barbarians.

Months later, his uncle Emperor Honorius died leaving the western Roman empire in disarray. An usurper named Joannes then proclaimed himself the next emperor of the West.

(His aunt Galla Placidia, her son Valentinian III, and the other children had already fled before Emperor Honorius death because he had attempted to have a sexual affair with his own widowed sister, but she rejected him, and fled to Constantinople for safety.) By the year 424, Theodosius launched an offensive against the West and crushed the insurgency. The following year on October 23, 425, the young Vatlentinian III was crowned Augustus over the western Roman Empire. His mother Galla became his chief advisor.

On March 26, 429 Emperor Theodosius convened the Senate in Constantinople to announce his plans to form a committee to codify all the Roman laws dating back from 313 B.C. until completion. The effort took nine years to complete. The task ended with a collection of 16 books containing more than 2,500 decrees issued between the years of Constantine the Great in 313 to 437. The codes, known as the Codex Theodosiusanus, covered the political, economical, cultural, and socioeconomic issues affecting the Roman empire in the 4th and 5th centuries. Prior to codifying the laws of Rome, Theodosius founded the University of Constantinople where Greek, Latin, law, philosophy, medicine, arithmetic, geometry, astronomy, music, and rhetoric were taught. The large university was comprised of 31 chairs—15 were Latin and the other 16 were Greek. The institution actually represented the foundation for higher education in the Middle Age Europe and beyond.

Externally, the eastern division of the Roman Empire was plagued with the same problems of the western portion of **[the iron kingdom]**. Both divisions of the empire were threatened by continuous barbarian raids consisting of Huns and Vandals. In the decade of 420 to 430, the kingdom was forced to pay the invaders 300 pounds of gold to bribe them to cease attacking, but when Attila rose to power in the decade of the 440s to 450, the indemnity increased to 700 pounds of pure gold. Meanwhile, Sassanid Persia continued to drain manpower and treasure on the far eastern edges of the Mesopotamian and Syrian frontiers.

In the summer of 450, on July 28th to be exact, Emperor Theodosius II died from injuries he sustained in a riding accident. This left a power vacuum in Constantinople because Theodosius did not have a son to inherit his position. He had only one child, a daughter named Licinia Eudoxia. His elder sister Pulcheria returned to the court and seized the throne before her former ally Chrysaphius could become a kingmaker. She then became the kingmaker by marrying a general named Marcian and anointing him as the next emperor of the Eastern Roman Empire **[East]**.

So it came to pass that Emperor Theodosius II died at the age of 49 after serving forty-two years in the city of Constantinople. He did evil in the eyes of **YHWH ELOHIM Israel** like all of the Greco-Roman Christian emperors before him by serving the graven doctrine of Jesus Christ and bowing before the image of the Cross. He did not know YAH nor did he walk in HIS laws, commandments, judgements, or statutes none of the days of his life. General Marcian reigned in his stead.

<u>Marcian</u>
(450 C.E.—457 C.E.)
[East]

Marcian was born of low rank in the year 392. His place of birth was Thrace or Illyria, but his parental lineage was not recorded in the annals of Roman history. His full birth name was Flavius Marcianus. He was a descendant of the once barbaric Alanic tribe. Most likely his parents and grandparents were part of the Roman federations that grafted barbarians into Roman culture. As a youngster, he grew up working as a domestic servant under the a wealthy man named Ardabur whom he served for 15 years. Marcian also served his son named Aspar for a while. Marcian eventually joined the Roman army where he fought against the Vandals at Carthage. He was captured by the Vandals until they released him.

In the summer of the year 450, Emperor Theodosius II died from a riding accident. He had no sons, so it left a temporary power vacuum. This was the first succession crisis in the East in six decades. For a complete month various factions conspired to seize the vacancy on the throne. Aspar conspired to have Marcian, his former loyal servant, made emperor. Aspar consulted with Pulcheria, the older sister who was once Empress for Theodosius when he was a boy, and they agreed that Marcian was the best candidate for the throne. To seal the deal, Pulcheria agreed to marry Marcian. Marcian was now married to a former Empress, thus strengthening his connection to the Theodosian dynasty and his claim to be ruler. Pulcheria was now 52, and well beyond child-bearing age. This union was purely a showcase. She never had sex with him. During their marriage, she kept her commitment to virginity which she vowed at the age of 14.

Marcian was formally selected as Emperor of the Eastern Roman Empire on August 25, 450. His wife Pulcheria personally placed the crown on his head during his coronation. He then assumed the throne title: Imperator Caesar Flavius Marcianus Augustus. He chose a man named Flavius Zeno as his Praetorian Prefect in Constantinople. Once the kingdom was firmly established in his hands, he began to reverse many of the policies of his predecessor Theodosius II. He revoked all the peace terms with Atilla the Hun. In the year 452 while Atilla was ravishing northern Italy. Emperor Marcian launched a military campaign into the Hun flatlands and across the Danube River, defeating them and disrupting their territories. Meanwhile, Atilla and his army were away besieging northern Italy when a plague and famine broke out consuming his troops and the population. These actions forced Atilla to negotiate with Marcian and halt his incursions. One year later in 453, Atilla died and the Hunnic empire began to split apart. Many of the tribes chose to join the Roman federation in exchange for military service and other benefits.

In terms of religion, Marcian convened a religious gathering known as the Council of Chalcedon where he reversed many of the longstanding decisions already agreed upon at the earlier Second Council of Epheseus. Marican decreed Jesus had two natures: One divine and one human, in other words, Jesus was God and a man at the same time. In his uncircumcised mind, the CREATOR was born in a woman's womb, raised as an infant, grew into a child, matured into a teenager, and then aged into an adult. Those **idol ideas [ideologies]** were totally opposite of ancient Hebraic realization. Moses wrote: *"ELOHIM(God) is not a man"* in **Numbers 23:19**. A Hebrew scribe also wrote in **I Samuel 15:29** that, *"the Strength of Israel will not lie or repent: for HE is not a man, that he should repent"*. Furthermore in **Hosea 11:9** the prophet also proclaimed these words about the CREATOR, *"for I[YHWH] am ELOHIM(God), and not man: the HOLY ONE in the midst of you."* As we should be able to see, all of these decisions, such as the Jesus myth, baptism, the resurrection myth, and the Second Coming belief, which were edified by these various Christian convocations are the works, and doctrines, of errors **[idol doctrines]**.

So it came to pass that Emperor Marcian died on January 27,457 at the age of 65 after reigning seven years in the city of Constantinople. He did evil in the eyes of **YHWH ELOHIM Israel** by serving the graven doctrine of Jesus Christ and by bowing before the image of the Cross. He knew not YAH, nor did he walk in HIS commandments, laws, judgements, and statutes. He built a standing image in honor of his wife Pulcheria when she died. The dedication of the graven images in honor of Christian saints were known as the beatification process. Those new age statues replaced the ancient Roman idols of old. When he died the treasury of the Eastern Roman Empire stood at a surplus of 7 million solidus. Marcian had only one daughter named Marcea Euphemia from his previous marriage. She eventually married a man named **Arithemius** who became Emperor of the Western Roman Empire in the years 467 to 472.

After his death, **Leo I** was chosen to reign in his stead. In the West, the throne was now in the hands of general **Majorian**. As you can see, the infighting and division between the **two iron legs of Roman Empire** was permanent with each side not recognizing each other's respective leader.

Majorian
(457 C.E.—461 C.E.)
[West]

Majorian was born in the year 420. His full birth name was Flavius Julius Valerius Majorianus. It appears his background was of barbarian origins like his contemporaries Avitus, Aelius, Ricimer, and others who had rose to prominence through being incorporated into Roman federations. His parents were not recorded in the annals of Roman history. It is known that his grandfather, whose name was exactly the same as his, reached the position of commander-in-chief under Emperor Theodosius I. Following in grandfather's footsteps as a young man, Majorian became a part of the military aristocracy which comprised large numbers of barbarians, mainly tribespeople of the Gepids, Ostrogoths, Rugil, Burgundians, Huns, Bastarnae, Suebi, Scythians, and Alans. Majorian started his military career under the tutelage of the powerful general Aetius. But during the reign of Valentinian III, there was jealousy between Aetius and Marjorian. For example, Aetius wife stirred up contention between the two when she accused Marjorian of seeking to undermine his position. For that reason, Aetius put an end to Marjorian's career and sent him into retirement. Another problem came when Emperor Valentinian III, the father of two daughters and no sons, backed the marriage of his daughter Placida to Marjorian. Aetius annulled those arrangements. However, in a strange twist of fate, Marjorian was called back into public life in the year 454 by Emperor Valentinian III after he murdered Aetius. Valentinian feared the troops of Aetius would seek revenge and revolt, so he called Majorian back to power to put down any potential uprisings. Regardless of his precautions, the following year in 455, two Scythian staff officers murdered Valentinian III as he dismounted his horse. When the dust settled, a senator named Petronius Maximus outmaneuvered and bribed key officials to ascend to the throne to rule over what was left of the Western Roman Empire. Maximus then chose Majorian as his commander-in-chief of the imperial forces. Months later, Maximus was slain when the Vandals sacked Rome later that year. Afterwards, Avitus became the successor of Maximus, but he lost the support of the aristocracy after the pain felt from his economic reforms. In fact, Marjorian joined the revolt to depose of Avitus.

Avitus was dead. The throne was empty without an heir. With the **West** unable to appoint an emperor, it was left up to the **East** to choose a successor. Eastern Roman Emperor Marcian could not nominate anyone because he died on January 27, 457. His successor Emperor Leo refused to appoint a western emperor. Instead, he appointed two men to serve as "magister miltuim"—commanders of the army. He chose General Majorian and General Ricimer. After that, a band of 900 barbarians of Alemanni origins invaded Italy, the heart of the Western Roman Empire. They plundered everything in site before they were intercepted deep inside the territory near Lake Maggiore. General Majorian and his army ambushed the hordes and decisively crushed them. The people of Italy celebrated the triumph as a personal victory for General Majorian. He was greatly exalted through his valor. The Roman army then proclaimed him emperor. This occurred on April 1, 457. Majorian begrudgingly accepted, but the **East** still did not recognize his selection for another eight months until December 28 when his coronation finally took place. He chose the throne title Imperator Caesar Flavius Julius Valerius Majorianus Augustus.

After receiving the crown, Leo I and Majorian jointly assumed the consulate office. But in actuality the Eastern Roman Empire did not formally recognize Majorian in state affairs. Even the people in the western provinces still consulted with Leo I for issues such as tax reductions and other life necessities. But on the battlefield, it was Emperor Majorian, a man of action, who temporarily halted the crumbling of West. He defeated the attack by the Vandals in 458. In fact, he was the last western emperor to fight for the integrity of the longstanding Roman borders. When he came to power, the empire was only a shell of its former self. Hispania and Africa were lost to the Vandals. Major parts of the province of Gaul were in the hands of the Visigoths. Britannia was lost to the barbarians. Only Italy remained, and it too was under assault of barbarians.

For the next three years, Majorian campaigned to bring stability to the kingdom. In the year 458, he launched his offensive to bring Gaul under his rule again. He defeated Theodoric II. king of the Visigoths, at the Battle of Arelate. He also forced the barbarian Goths to abandon their strongholds in Septmania and Hispania, forcing them to return under Roman federate status. He attacked the Burgundians and defeated them. In 460, Majorian left the province of Gaul to restore order in Hispania. He was forced to hire barbarian mercenaries from the federate territories to strengthen his army. They came from the Alans, Suebi, Scythians, Ostrogoths, Bastarnae, Huns, and others. He won victories in Hispania and returned the vanquished to federate status. After those victories in Hispania, Majorian disbanded his mercenary force and headed back towards Italy. While Majorian was away on campaigns, a spirit of envy came upon General Ricimer. He began a plot to covet the purple robe and royal diadem. Ricimer had come under the influence of the Roman aristocracy which opposed Majorian's policies. Majorian had decreed reforms to improve government efficiency and taxation. Many wealthy Romans did not appreciate the increase in taxes demanded under his new reform efforts. Majorian had ignored the aristocrats pleas for relief. So they backed Ricimer bloody scheme to murder the emperor.

Marjorian and his imperial troops finally reached the city of Tortona, located in northwest Italy, on August 3. General Ricimer, accompanied with a military detachment, went out to meet him. When they met, Majorian was arrested and deposed on the spot. He was then stripped out of his royal attire and his royal diadem taken. He was severely beaten and tortured. After 5 days of torment, Emperor Marjorian was beheaded near the Iria River on August 7, 461.

So it came to pass that Majorian was slain at the age of 46 after reigning for four years on the throne of Augustus. He did evil in the eyes of **YHWH ELOHIM Israel** by not walking in HIS commandments, laws, judgements, and statutes. Instead, Majorian walked in the ways of all the Greco-Roman emperors that preceded him. After his murder, the throne was unoccupied for three months until General Ricimer, the kingmaker, finally appointed another man named **Libius Severus** to reign. **Severus** was a Roman senator before Ricimer drafted him to serve as his handpicked emperor over what was left of the western division of the empire. In Constantinople, Emperor Leo I did not recognize none the chaotic disorder in the West.

Libius Severus
(461 C.E.—465 C.E.)
[West]

Libius Severus was born in the year 420 in the city of Pyxous [**also known as Lucania**] which was located in the southern part of Italy. His father and mother names were not recorded in the annals of Roman history. His full birth name was Flavius Libius Severus Serpentius. Little is known about his past before his rise to prominence as a member of the Roman Senate from the city of Luciana. He had reached the age of 35 when the Vandals sacked Rome in the year 455. During the siege, Gaiseric, the king of Vandals, captured the wife and the two daughters of the former Emperor Valentinian III. The king of the Vandals wanted his son Huneric to marry Eudocia, the daughter of Valentinian to ensure a future role for his lineage in the Roman hierarchy. During this same time, the king of the Vandals also interfered in the affairs of the imperial Roman court in Ravenna. He attempted to handpick a man named **Olybrius** to serve as the successor to Majorian, but Ricimer rejected that idea. Instead, he searched and found a fainthearted and inexperienced emperor that he could easily control named Libius Severus.

The Vandals attempted to pressure Rome into submission by launching raids on the Italian countryside. The Vandals wanted Olybrius on the throne because he was already married to the other daughter of Valentinian named Placidia. Olybrius ascension to the throne would create family ties between Vandal king Gaiseric and the emperor of **West**. Ricimer ignored the Vandals and installed Libius Severus. The Italian aristocracy was well pleased with Ricimer's actions. So three months after the murder of Majorian, Severus was finally elected Emperor by the Roman Senate on November 19, 461. Like his predecessors, Severus held court in Ravenna. There was also another problem, Emperor Leo I did not recognize Severus. Normally, the eastern emperor had the duty to accept his western colleague in order to ensure peaceful relations between the two Romes, because technically speaking, the empire was still one entity. Regardless, he chose the throne title Imperator Flavius Libius Severus Serpentius Augustus. He did not have any real power like the earlier emperors of the Julian-Claudian dynasty. He was a figurehead who was unable to resolve any of the outstanding challenges facing the empire. It was General Ricimer, the commander-in-chief, who ruled as the real power behind the throne. As I said previously, Severus was powerless to overcome problems on several fronts. For example, one of his problems was the fact that Emperor Leo I, ruler of Eastern Roman Empire, did not recognize him as an heir on the throne. Another problem was the reality that several generals who had served under Majorian did not accept Severus as their legitimate emperor. They viewed him as an usurper. In terms of foreign affairs, the province of Illyricum, which once served as a Roman stronghold for the **West**, was now taken over by the **East**. The glory of Rome had rapidly declined. The temporary relief provided by Majorian no longer existed. Britain was permanently lost. There was now no chance to recover Africa with the Roman sword. Hispania had been overrun by the Visigoths, Vandals, and others. Gaul was almost autonomous, except for the federate lands. Meanwhile, the imperial Roman army in Italy was forced to fight for its life against successive barbarian incursions. Italy was all that remained of the once extensive Roman Empire.

General Ricimer controlled Severus throughout his 3 year 9 month reign, advising him on very important decision. Severus relationship with the Eastern Roman Empire was very contentious at best. So it came to pass the Libius Severus, who was 45, died of natural causes on August 15, 465. Severus did not have any heirs to the throne, sons nor daughters. Unlike his magister militim Ricimer, Severus was known as a pious Christian. Nevertheless, he did evil in the **eyes of YHWH ELOHIM Israel** by not observing HIS commandments, laws, judgements, or statutes. Instead he served the graven doctrine of Jesus Christ and bowed before the image of the Cross. So another General named **Anthemius** succeeded him and reigned on the collapsing throne of Augustus.

Anthemius
(467 C.E.—472 C.E.)
[West]

Anthemius [*pronounced* An-the-mi-us] was born in the year 420 in the royal city of Constantinople, the capital of the Eastern division of the **[iron kingdom]**. His father's name was Procopius and his mother's name was Lucina. His full birth name was Procopius Anthemius. He was born into a family of rank and nobility which maintained close ties with the various emperors over the decades. Growing up, he was groomed for leadership. He studied in Alexandria, Egypt where he learned philosophy, literary skills, government, and history. His loyalty and valor exalted him, and eventually his service caught the eye of Emperor Marcian. He became his son-in-law when he married his daughter named Princess Marcia Euphemia, and through their union, he begat six children.

After Anthemius marriage to Emperor Marcian's daughter, he began to wax stronger and stronger. He was elevated to position of *"Comes"*, which was the title for companion of the emperor, member of the inner circle. His first assignment was to build stronger defense lines and to bring order to the kingdom's frontiers along the Danube River. By 454, he returned to Constaninople where Marican promoted him to the position of Praetorian Prefect. The following year he was promoted to "Magister Militum", the commander-in-chief of the Roman army in the East. In the year 455, Marcian appointed Anthemius to serve as "Consulate" alongside Emperor Valentinian III. Anthemius close ties to the Emperor of East led many to believe that Marican wanted to install him as the Western Emperor after the removal of Emperor Avitus in hopes of reuniting the splintered empire. But, Emperor Marican died in January of 457 before he could fulfill his plans. For a while both empires, both **East** and **West,** were without reigning emperors. In the West, the power was in the hands of two generals named Rcimer and Majorian. In the East, the barbarian general named Alan Aspar exerted true power behind the scene. Aspar did not want to appoint an independent-minded or influential emperor such as Anthemius who would act independently. So he reached down and chose a low-ranking military officer named Leo to serve as the heir to the eastern throne. Anthemius continued as a loyal magister militum under Emperor Leo I, defending the empire against barbarian invasions. He defeated the Ostrogoths when they invaded Illyricum. In the winter of 466/467, Anthemius defeated Hormiedac the ruler of Huns after his hordes crossed across the frozen Danube River barefooted. They pillaged Dacia along the way picking up needed loot.

Meanwhile in the western capitals Ravenna and Rome, there were a succession of emperors that reigned for short periods of time. Emperor Libius Severus was one of them. After reigning a mere 3 years and nine months, Severus died in 465 leaving the West without an emperor once again. At this time, there were many pressing challenges facing the western Roman kingdom with various outside powers covetously seeking ways to have a say-so on who would next occupy the throne. One foreign power that attempted to sway the selection was Gaiseric, the king of Vandals. He wanted to install a man named **Olybrius** who was married to one of daughters of Valentinian III. The reason being, the Vandal king planned for his son to marry the remaining daughter of Valentinian III. This would make the new emperor a direct relative and in-law of Gaiseric. Gaiseric attempted to influence the election by attacking Sicily and Italian countryside, destroying everything in their paths. Gaiseric then invaded the Peloponnese Peninsula and other parts of Greece. Those attacks forced Emperor Leo I to take action against the Vandals.

On March 25, 467, Emperor Leo I met with General Ricimer. Ricimer consented to the idea that Anthemius would become the next designated Caesar of the Western empire. Anthemius, along with a strong army was dispatched to Italy to assume the mantle of power. The army was led by general named Marcellinus. On April 12, Anthemis was proclaimed Emperor while in route to Rome. His ascension to the throne was also celebrated in Constantinople. His throne title was Imperator Caesar Procopius Anthemius Augustus. He also exalted himself with the title *"Our Lord, Anthemius,* Pious, Fortunate, Augustus". In the beginning, the presence of Anthemius represented good diplomatic relations between the East and West Roman Empire. Both courts coordinated in choosing who would occupy the Consulate position. Once Anthemius arrived in the West, his goal was to solve the challenges facing the western kingdom. The Visigoths were launching raids under the new king Euric. The Vandals still held onto Rome's possessions in North Africa. In late 467, Anthemius formed an army to attempt to regain dominion over lost territory. He then organized the campaign with General Marcellinus serving as commander-in-chief. But, in this first mission the Roman fleet met turbulent winds and stormy weather at high seas which forced the Roman forces to return to their bases, aborting the mission. It was that act of **YAH** that prevented Anthemius from accomplishing his goal.

The prophet **Jeremiah** said in **chapter10:13,***"HE***(YHWH)** *makes vapors rise from the ends of the earth, HE makes lightning for the rain. And brings forth wind from HIS treasures."* After that mission, Anthemius planned a second mission against the Vandals in Carthage. Both emperors participated in the expedition, sending a fleet of 1,000 ships to filled with the armies of both the Eastern and Western Roman Empire. The cost of mission was financed by both sides, with the **East** paying the majority, but with treasury of the **West** being left totally depleted. To make matters worse, the fleet was defeated in the conflict known as the Battle of Cape Bon, off the coast of modern Tunisia. After the loss, General Marcellinus was slain at the hands of his own people.

In the year 468, Anthenmius served as the sole Consulate. The following year, the two consuls included the son of Anthemius named Marcian and the son-in-law of Emperor Leo I named **Flavius Zeno**. Zeno eventually became the successor of Leo in the East.

The coins minted in Rome during the reign of Anthemius portrayed two emperors. Their images represented the unity between Leo I and Anthemius. Even the coins featuring his wife included a portrait of Empress Marcia Euphemia, the wife of Anthemius, and the wife of General Ricimer, Alypia. Ricimer was the powerful magister militum and the most influential official in the Western Empire. In the process of time, Ricimer and Anthemius began to bump heads. Both men possessed strong personalities and long resumes of success. We must also remember that Anthemius had been exalted to power through the influence of the imperial court in Constantinople. So beneath the surface, he was seen as an outsider while some Romans accused him of being a pagan. The tense situation grew into open hostilities because of the Romanus Trial. In the year 470, Romanus, a patrician, friend of Ricimer, and influential Italian senator, was accused of treachery and conspiring against the throne. He was placed on trial, sentenced to death, then executed. The supporters of Anthemius and Ricimer began to battle in the streets. The church was called upon to end the rioting and chaos. But in early 472, the hostilities broke out again. This time Anthemius faked sickness and fled to Saint Peter's Basilica to escape Ricimer's supporters. *(The St. Peter's Basilica in Rome had been built by Constantine a century earlier.)*

As tensions grew worse, Emperor Leo I sent Olybrius to mediate between Anthemius and Ricimer. But, in a doublehearted move, Leo attempted to send a secret letter to Anthemius urging him to murder Olybrius once he arrived. But Ricimer, an experienced and crafty general, stationed a guard at the city of Ostia. The guard was tipped off and suspected foul play then intercepted the letter. He showed the letter to Ricimer, who in turn revealed the plot to Olybrius. Both men turned against Emperor Leo then proclaimed Olybrius the new emperor. The announcement sparked open warfare between the two camps. On one side, Anthemius, the Roman aristocracy, the people of Rome and on the other side Ricimer, the powerful general, with his barbarian army units consisting of 6,000. Ricimer blockaded Anthemius in Rome. For five months they fought until Ricimer breached the walls and took control of the port where food supplies entered. Ricimer then attempted to starve the supporters of Anthemius into submission. In a last ditch effort, Anthemius attempted to find help from abroad, but his supporters were defeated in their battles against Ricimer. Anthemius then attempted to mount an effort to break the siege, but his large army was slaughtered. Once again, Anthemius attempted to flee into Saint Peter's Basilica or Santa Maria for safety, but this time he was caught by the leader of Gothic barbarians, who was an ally of Ricimer and beheaded. These events occurred on, or near, July 11, 472, in the imperial city of Rome.

So it came to pass that Emperor Anthemius died at the age of 52 after reigning five years in the city of Rome as Augustus of the Western Roman Empire. He did evil in the eyes of **YHWH ELOHIM Israel** like all his Greco-Roman Christian predecessors by serving the graven Nicene doctrine of Jesus and bowing before the graven image of the Cross. He knew not YAH nor walked in his commandments, judgements, and statutes. Olybrius reigned after him as the next emperor of what was left of the crumbling Western Roman Empire.

Olybrius
(472 C.E.)
[West]

Olybrius [*pronounced* O-ly-bri-us] was born in the year 431 in the city of Rome. His full birth name was Anicius Olybrius. There is uncertainty as to who was his true father. Some sources recorded Anicius Hermogenianus Olybrius as his father while others contend it was Flavius Anicius Probus or Petronius Maximus. His mother's name was Anicius Juliana. He was born into an ancient powerful family of Italian descent. He grew to become a Roman senator and member of the aristocracy.

It is said that he fled Rome for the eastern capital of Constantinople when the Vandal King Geiseric invaded Italy and plundered Rome, the capital of the West in the year 455. He eventually married a woman named Placidia, the youngest daughter of the late Emperor Valentinian III. This marriage made him a member of the nobility. During the years 465 to 467 when the Western throne was empty after the death of Libius Severus, the king of Vandal attempted to pressure General Ricimer into placing Olybrius on the throne. The reason being, Geiseric, the king of the Vandals, wanted his son to marry the sister of Placidia, the eldest daughter of the late Emperor Valentinian III. Geiseric felt this marriage would give him leverage over the western empire and elevate his family status from a barbarian to Roman nobility. General Ricimer, the Magister Militum, rejected the pressure from the king of Vandals and, after a year, instead chose Libius Severus.

As tensions in Rome grew worse in the spring of 472, Emperor Leo I sent Olybrius to mediate between Anthemius and Ricimer. But, in a double-hearted move, Emperor Leo, who suspected Olybrius of favoring the Vandals, sent another secret letter by another envoy that trailed Olybrius. The letter urged Anthemius to murder Olybrius upon his arrival. Ricimer, an experienced and crafty general, had stationed a guard at the city of Ostia, southwest of Rome. The guard searched the envoy and found the letter. He revealed the plot to Olybrius. He then turned against Anthemius and convinced Olybrius to accept the purple robe as the new emperor. He consented and chose the throne title Imperator Caesar Anicius Olybrius.

Olybrius reign was short and turbulent. The Western Empire continued to face challenges and outslaught from the barbarian Vandals, Visigoths, Ostrogoths, and Burgundians. In fact, his reign lasted only 7 months before he died of the disease known as dropsy. He did not reign long enough to leave any lasting footprints in the sands of Roman history. His most notable action was the gold coins he had minted with the image of the Cross and the words *"SALVS MVNDI"*, meaning *"WELFARE OF THE WORLD"*. Although, he did not live to fulfill it, the slogan revealed Olybrius's hope and vision for the Roman Empire and Christianity.

His powerful Magister Militum, Ricimer, died August 18, 472 after serving several emperors as their right-hand man. Because of his barbarian background, he never attempted to occupy the throne of Augustus himself, but he was always the power behind the throne. His nephew Gundobad assumed his role as the Magister Militum of the West.

So it came to pass that Olybrius died four months after Ricimer at the age 41 after reigning a mere seven months on the throne of Augustus in Rome. He did evil in the eyes of **YHWH ELOHIM Israel** according to all the works of the Greco-Roman Christian emperors that preceded him. He was known as a pious Christian, but he knew not YAH nor did he walk in HIS commandments, judgements, and statutes. He served the graven doctrine of Jesus Christ and bowed before the image of the Cross. Afterwards, **Glycerius**, the commander of the palace guard, succeeded him on the throne as the next emperor of the disarrayed Western Roman Empire.

Glycerius
(473 C.E.—474 C.E.)
[West]

Glycerius date of birth was unknown. His full name was D.(Dominus N.(oster) Glycerius Augustus. His parents names were also unknown. He once served in the position known as *"comes domesticorum"* before he became commander of the palace guard during the brief reign of Olybrius. Although Olybrius died in November 472, it took four months before Glycerius was finally proclaimed Western Emperor on March 3, 473 by the Burgundian barbarian chieftain Gundobad, who was the successor of his powerful uncle general Ricimer.

His throne title was Imperator D. N. Caesar Flavius Glycerius Augustus. His rule was not recognized by Emperor Leo I of the Eastern Roman Empire. Glycerius ascended to power when the Western Roman Empire was in descent. The barbaric Visigoths continued their onslaught into Italy. Glycerius was able to force then to return to Gaul. He was able to temporarily hold off the invading Ostrogoths through a bribe. Meanwhile, Emperor Leo I nominated a man named Julius Nepos as his choice for Augustus on the western throne. He dispatched him to the West with a large army to invade Italy. Glycerius did not have any support to halt the invasion. Gundobad had departed Italy for his kingdom in the province of Gaul. Glycerius was all alone so he surrendered to Julius Nepos and his army. This occurred on June 24, 474. Glycerius was then appointed Bishop of Salona. A position he held onto until his death in the year 480. It was said that Bishop Glycerius could have played a role in the murder of Julius Nepos.

So it came to pass the Emperor Glycerius died after reigning one mere year. In the end, he became the personal bishop of Julius Nepos. His reign was so short that he was not able to really do anything. He was a Chalcedonian Christian who served the graven doctrine of Jesus Christ and bowed before the image of the Cross. He did evil in the eyes of **YHWH ELOHIM Israel** by not walking in HIS laws, commandments, judgements, and statutes. **Julius Nepos** succeeded him as the next Western Emperor of **[the iron kingdom]** which was rapidly descending into the abyss. Meanwhile in the capital of the Eastern Roman Empire, **Leo I** reigned in the imperial city of Constantinople.

Leo I
(457 C.E.—474 C.E.)
[East]

Leo I was born in the year 401 in a settlement on Dacia Aureliana near the province of Thrace during the reign of Emperor Arcadius. His father and mother names were not recorded during the time of his birth. This area was still a frontier outpost where Romans and barbarians intersected. For that reason, he was known as a Thracian. His full birth name was Leo Marcellus, but he became known as Leo the Thracian.

Leo was a low-ranking officer during the mid-450s. The eastern imperial court was deeply influenced by the barbarian general named Aspar the Alan who served as commander-in-chief of the army when Emperor Marcian died. Aspar was the power behind the purple and he wanted a puppet emperor that he could control. Flavius Valerius Leo was chosen by General Aspar to reign as the next Augustus of the Eastern Empire. On February 7, 457, Leo I was crowned emperor in a royal coronation officiated by the Patriarch of Constantinople. His throne title was Imperator Cacsar Flavius Valerius Leo Augustus.

After fourteen years on the throne, Leo grew more and more independent, and, in the process of time, he eventually made an alliance with another group known as the Isaurians, a fierce barbaric mountain people. They gave him the protection he need to get rid of Aspar. In 469, Aspar attempted to murder to Zeno, the leader of the Isaurians, but failed. In the year 471, Emperor Leo ordered the assassination of the powerful General Aspar. In the same year, Aspar's son named Ardabar was also caught up in a scheme to eliminate Emperor Leo. He too was assassinated by palace guards acting on the command of Zeno. In exchange for their support, Leo rewarded Zeno with his daughter's hand in marriage.

Emperor Leo I, a capable and long-term ruler, reigned for seventeen years as Emperor of the Eastern Roman Empire while the West experienced a rapid succession of emperors that included Majorian (457-461), Libius Severus(461-465), Anthemius(467-472), Olybrius(472), and Glycerius(472-474). During those two decades, Leo I was the first Roman emperor to legislate in the Greek language instead of Latin in the imperial court. He greatly influenced the West, and also participated in several attempts to assist the faltering **Western leg of the Roman Empire**. One of his greatest setbacks came in 468 when he attempted to assist

Anthemius in recovering Carthage from the Vandals. The Vandals defeated both armies which drained the treasury of the East and totally depleted the West. The war cost was 130,000 pounds of gold and 700 pounds of silver. The Roman fleet consisted of 1,113 ships carrying a total of 100,000 men. More than half of the fleet was lost in the Battle of Cape Bon.

In the East, the empire also faced the Ostrogoths who were ravaging the Balkan Peninsula and the coast of Greece. Those raids forced Emperor Leo to sign an expensive peace agreement with Gaiseric, king of Vandals. The Ostrogoths were led by Theodoric the Great who had been raised in the imperial court of Leo before turning against him. He understood the fundamentals of Roman government and military warfare. Leo also faced barbarian incursions from the Huns.

In Constantinople, Emperor Leo I abolished all non-Christian celebrations and activities in the imperial city on Sundays which was proclaimed the day of Jesus Christ. So it came to pass that Emperor Leo I died on January 18, 474 at the age of 73 after reigning seventeen years on the throne of Constantine in the imperial city of Constantinople. He died of dysentery, a disease which causes inflammatory infections in the intestines, especially the colon. It usually causes diarrhea and abdominal pain. In his lifetime he married a woman named Verina and they had three children. He did evil in the eyes of **YHWH ELOHIM Israel** according to all the Roman Christian emperors that preceded him by serving the graven doctrine of Jesus Christ and bowing before image of the Cross. He knew not YAH nor walked in HIS laws, commandments, judgements, and statutes. Leo II succeeded him as the next Emperor of The Eastern Roman Empire.

Leo II
(474 C.E.)
[East]

Leo II was born in the imperial city of Constatinople in the year 468 as the son of Zeno, the general of the Isaurians, and Ariadne, the daughter of Emperor Leo I. His birth name was Flavius Leo. At 5, his grandfather Emperor Leo I anointed him co-emperor on November 18, 473 at the Hippodrome. He was given the throne title Imperator Caesar Flavius Leo Augustus. Two months after his grandfather exalted him to the role of co-emperor, Leo I died in January of 474. The Ecumenical Patriarch of Constantinople crowned Leo II sole emperor of the Eastern Roman Empire on January 18 at the age of 6. One month later on February 9, the Roman Senate in Constantinople decreed that Zeno should be the official guardian for his son as his co-emperor. However, before the year of 474 was complete, the young child-emperor, who had just turned 7, died in Constantinople on November 10, leaving his father **Zeno** as the sole emperor.

So it came it pass, the Leo II died as a lad before he knew the difference between **good** and **evil**.

Zeno
(474 C.E.—475 C.E.) 1st reign
(476 C.E.—491 C.E.) 2nd reign
[East]

The earth shudders at three things;
At four which it can not bear:
A slave [Zeno] who becomes king **[Eastern Roman Emperor]**.
Proverbs 30:21-22

Zeno [*pronounced* Zi-nu] was born in a primitive city-settlement known as Rusumblada [*pronounced* Ru-sum-bla-da] in the year 425. The city was eventually renamed Zenopolis in his honor. He descended from a barbarian background as an offspring of the fierce Isaurian mountain-dwellers. Zeno's father's name was Kodisa and his mother's name was Lalliss. His full name was Tarasis Kodisa Rousombladiotes [*pronounced* Ta-ra-sis Ko-di-sa Rou-som-bla-dio-tes]. While he was a young man, his Isaurian tribe was bound under Roman federate authority. He joined the Roman legion to obtain favor inside the military, and eventually inside the imperial court. When Attila the Hun attacked Constantinople in 447 during the reign of Theodosius II,he fought courageously to prevent the invasion of the capital of the Eastern Roman Empire.

Zeno had competition in his quest to become a powerful influence in the imperial court. There was another former barbarian of the Alan tribe named General Aspar who was Magister Militum, commander-in-chief, and a powerful influence behind the throne at the imperial court in Constantinople. So it came to pass that these two Romanized barbarians, Aspar and Zeno, locked horns. Aspar then plotted against Zeno, but did not prevail. Aspar had a son named Ardabur[Ar-da-bur] that served as his assistant. In the year 464, Zeno uncovered a letter written by Ardabar in which he devised a plot to provoke a war with Sassanid Persia. He then promised in the letter to betray Emperor Leo I in support of the Persians. Ardabur was then dismissed from his position as second-in-command behind his father, reducing Aspar's power. Zeno was rewarded for his loyalty. He was chosen to serve as leader of the royal guard unit that protected the emperor. The dismissal of Ardabur caused tensions between Aspar and Leo I, and in following year 465, the general openly quarreled with his master. The dispute further weakened the hand of Aspar and strengthened the hand of Zeno, who became the chosen. As I said earlier, his birth name was Tarasis, but after his elevation he chose the Grecian name Zeno to make himself more acceptable to the aristocracy.

He also fought in military campaigns against the Goths, and by late 466, his valor earned him power and the hand of princess Ariadne, the daughter of Emperor Leo I in marriage. The following year in 467 their union brought forth a son who was named Leo in honor of his grandfather. The lad became known as Leo II. Two years later, Zeno was promoted to the office of Consulate before being chosen to serve as the Magister Militum in a military operation in Thrace. It was said that before Zeno departed on the military campaign, he and Leo consulted with a familiar spirit named Daniel the Stylite to see whether the mission would be successful or not. Daniel warned Zeno that certain forces who attempt to harm him. Leo then sent bodyguards to watch Zeno, but it came to pass that those soldiers were bribed by Aspar and his son Ardabur to kidnap him. Zeno perceived danger and fled to the city of Serdica. Afterwards he moved on to Antioch before paid agents could do him any harm. Zeno could not return to the imperial city because Aspar and Ardabur were still there. He had to wait outside for two years before he could re-enter the gates of Constantinople again.

While exiled in Antioch, Zeno faced religious dissension from among the various branches of Christianity, such as Monophysitism, Chalcedonian, and Orthodoxy. At times, the violence sparked by these opposing Christian mobs required the authority of the emperor to bring peace. Those development caused Zeno to bring early Christian leaders together where he helped them establish a document known as the *"instrument of union"* or *"Henotikin"*. The document was signed by all the Eastern Christian bishops in hopes to ending the divisions within the early Christian faith. The bishop of Rome did not attend the ecumenical convocation. Zeno was an Orthodox Christian, but he came into contact with member of the Monophysite faith. As I mentioned earlier, Monophysitism [*pronounced* Mo-no-phy-si-tism] was the Christian belief that the man Jesus Christ had one single divine nature as the eternal Son, and he was the Word of God. In other words, he was a human God in flesh, and not a man. *(Again, it should be noted that this new man-made doctrine was a perversion from the Words of* **YHWH** *found in the Torah. Therefore, the Israelite people should regard all these New Testament-based Christian edicts as pure falsehood.)*

Back in Constantinople, Emperor Leo I had General Aspar and his son Arbadur murdered in the year 471. Zeno and Emperor Leo's brother named Basiliscus approved of their elimination. Zeno then moved back to Constantinople where he became Magister Militum. In the autumn of 473, Leo I proclaimed his 6-year-old grandson Leo II as his co-emperor and

Caesar. *(Remember now, Leo II was the son of Zeno and Ariadane, the daughter of Emperor Leo I.)* Three months later, the elder Leo I died on January 18, 474, leaving his grandson as the Augustus of the Eastern Roman Empire. Now, Leo II was too young to assume any meaningful role in the daily governing of [**the Eastern iron leg**]. His mother Ariadne, the wife of Zeno, and Leo II grandmother Verina, the wife of the deceased Emperor Leo I, instructed the young lad emperor to chose his father Zeno as his co-emperor. He compiled, and on February 9, 474 he became the second-in-command over the Eastern Roman Empire. Months later, the young lad Leo II died, leaving his father Zeno as the sole emperor. His throne title was Imperator Caesar Flavius Zeno Augustus.

One of Zeno's first moves was the negotiation of a peace agreement with King Genseric, barbaric chieftain of the Vandals. A plan that halted their vandalistic incursions into civilized Roman territories, provided a prisoner exchange, and endorsed peaceful Christian relations between Orthodox Christians and other Gothic Christians. Zeno was a very capable ruler, but he experienced hatred by the Roman aristocracy because of his barbaric roots. He was seen as an outsider although he occupied the seat of power. Zeno realized his enemies surrounded him, so he strengthened his Praetorian Guard with Isaurian units for protection. This did not prevent his mother-in-law Verina from sponsoring a plot to remove her own son-in-law. The ex-Empress joined hand with her lover named Patricius and her brother who was named Basilscus to sow discord. The plot called for riots inside the capital. General Basiliscus also convinced the leader Theodoric Strabo to rebel against Zeno. This thickening mutiny caused Emperor Zeno to flee the royal city to save his life. There was a massacre of the Isaurian people which remained in the royal city. During this time, **Basiliscus[475-476]** ascended to the throne as Augustus over the East.

During his brief reign, Basiliscus turned against his co-conspirator Patricius and slew him. He murdered many Isaurian people, greatly increased taxes to fill depleted government coffers, and supported the monophysite branch of Christianity at the expense of Orthodox Christianity. He was also blamed for a great fire that ravished major sectors of the capital. Another strategic mistake he made was his failure to reward Theodoric Strabo for his support for the rebellion.

By the year 476, the people of Constantinople had turned against Basiliscus. When Zeno and his troops approached the capital to retake the throne, neither Theodoric Strabo, nor the generals of the eastern Roman army, stood up to fight against him. This time it was Basiliscus who was forced to flee the capital. He and his family ran into the sanctuary of the Church of Hagia Sophia for refuge. However, the church bishop, Patriarch Acacius, gave him up and delivered him over to the emperor after Zeno promised not to execute him and his family. Although Zeno did not immediately slay Basiliscus with a sword, he was sentenced to life in a fortress in the city of Cappadocia where he was placed inside a dry cistern and allowed to slowly die from thirst, starvation, and the weather.

2nd reign
(476 C.E.—491 C.E.)

"The Emergence of the Barbarian Kingdoms"
A slave [barbarians] who becomes king, **Proverbs 30:22**
[inheritors of the Roman Empire—Eastern & Western Europe].

When Zeno finally returned to power in Constantinople during the year 476, he faced more disrespectful domestic rebellions. *(It should also be noted that the Western Roman Empire collapsed in the same year[476].* In 479, an usurper named Marcian, the grandson of Emperor Marcian, raised his hand against the emperor. After him, General Illus lead a four-year rebellion, extending from 484 until 488. Meanwhile, Zeno was forced to pay bribes and award high positions to the Visigoths and Ostrogoths to prevent their continuous assaults against Constantinople. In the year 484, Zeno became the first emperor in Roman history to choose a non-Romanized barbarian, Theodoric the Great, to serve as the Magister Militum of the Eastern Empire. Nevertheless, two years later Theodoric the Great rose up against Zeno and attacked Constantinople, destroying its water supply. Again, Zeno negotiated another peace deal which relinquished the **western leg** to further barbarian invasions in exchange for withdrawal and non-aggression in the **eastern leg**. This agreement sold the birthright of the defenseless Western Roman Empire to the barbarian warriors by allowing them the right to establish their kingdom in the West without eastern military interference.

In the 480s, Zeno moved his army into the holy land where he met the Jewish converts known as the Samartians. The emperor met in the city of Sichem where he requested that the town convert to Christianity. They refused to convert to the doctrine of Jesus, Zeno then ordered for them to be executed. He slaughtered many Samartians during that time. He destroyed the local synagogue and rebuilt it as an Orthodox Christian Church. Most of this occurred in famed mountains known as Mount Gerizim.

Mount Gerizim is mentioned in the Torah[**Devarim/Deuteronomy 27:11-12**] as the high place where **the ancient Afro-Asiatic Hebrews tribes of Simeon, Levi, Judah, Issachar, Joseph, and Benyamin** stood before the monument where the Words of the Blessings of the Torah were written on a plastered stone. Ironically, one of the proclamation stated by the Levitical priest was *"Cursed be anyone who makes a sculptured or molten image, abhorred by YHWH, a craftsman's handiwork, and sets it up in secret. And all the people shall respond, Amen."* Undoubtably, that ancient Hebrew proclamation was violated by Emperor Zeno is the name of Christian religion. Zeno established a church in Mount Gerizim which contained many of the craftsman's handiwork, such edifices as sculptured images of the Cross, pictures of Jesus, Mother Mary, and statues of patron saints.

In 484, the Samaritans rebelled against Roman rule. They launched an attack on the city of Sichem, cut off the fingers of the Christian bishop named Terebinthus, and burned down five churches. Afterwards they chose a man named Justa as their king and moved the community to the city of Caesarea, which was heavily populated with Samaritans. The Samaritans had already destroyed the Church of Saint Sebastian, and killed many Christians. Another garrison of Roman troops initiated a campaign against Justa. This time Justa was defeated, beheaded, and his skull sent to Emperor Zeno. After that, Emperor Zeno traveled to Samaria to participate in the crushing of the Samaritan rebellion. The emperor reconstructed the Church of Saint Procopius in the city of Sichem, whose name had been changed to the Neapolis. Zeno banished all Samaritans from entering Mount Gerizim.

So it came to pass that Emperor Zeno died at the age of 66 on April 8, 491 after reigning seventeen years on the throne of Augustus over the Eastern Roman Empire. He died from the ailment of dysentery or epilepsy. During his lifetime Zeno did many things to stabilize the eastern empire. In his personal life, he honored his wife named Arcadia by erecting a statue of her likeness near the Baths of Arcadius. She bore him one son named Zenon. He did evil in the eyes of **YHWH ELOHIM Israel** all the days of his life. He did not know YAH, nor did he walk in HIS laws, commandments, judgements, and statutes. Instead he served the graven doctrine of Jesus as an Orthodox Christian. Like all the Roman Christian emperors that preceded him, he bowed before the image of the Cross and honored the name of *"another god"* named Jesus Christ. He participated in the crafting of The Great Deception known as The Immaculate Conception, which declared that the man Jesus as the only human being born without an earthly father. According to Zeno's belief, it was the holy spirit that was intimate with Mary to bring forth the child-god.

After Zeno's death, his wife Ariadne was instrumental in choosing **Anastasius I** as his successor. Meanwhile in the West, we must go back to the years of **474 to 476** during the reigns of **Julius Nepos** and **Romulus Augustus** to witness the destruction of the Western Roman Empire.

Julius Nepos
(474 C.E.—476 C.E.)
[West]

Julius Nepos was born in the year 430. His father was named Nepotianus while his mother name was not recorded in the annals of Roman historical records. However, it was known that she was the sister of General Marcellinus. His full birth name was Flavius Julius Nepos. He rose through the ranks in the Eastern Roman army until Emperor Leo I elevated him as his choice for Augustus of the Western Roman Empire. Emperor Leo I dispatched him to the West with a large army to invade Italy and replace Glycerius. Glycerius did not have any forces to withstand Nepos invasion. His only military ally, Gundobad, had left Italy for the province of Gaul. Glycerius had been abandoned. So Glycerius raised the white flag and surrendered to the army of Julius Nepos. This occurred on June 24, 474. Glycerius was then appointed Bishop of Salona. A role he served in until he died in 480.

Nepos then chose the throne title Imperator Caesar Flavius Julius Nepos Augustus. The following year in 475 Nepos faced the same fate as Glycerius. He was deposed by the Roman general named Orestes. Nepos made a fatal mistake by appointing Orestes, a powerful politician of Pannonian ancestry, to the position of Magster Militum. Orestes used his position to overthrow Nepos and take control of government in Ravenna. Emperor Julius Nepos did not have an army to fight, so he fled the capital for Dalmatia without a fight. Orestes had assembled an army consisting largely of Gothic barbarian mercenaries. The barbarian requested one-third of Italy in exchange for the help in overthrowing Nepos. Orestes denied their request. The mercenaries then turned against Orestes and warred against the crumbling Western Roman Empire. After that, the barbarians joined a Germanic barbarian chieftain named Odoacer and declared him king of the Roman Empire on August 23, 476.

So it came to pass that Emperor Julius Nepos continued to rule as the de jure ruler of the Roman Empire in the province of Dalmatia for another four years until 480. He was assassinated somewhere between late spring and early summer in the year 480. He had done evil in the eyes of **YHWH ELOHIM Israel** by serving the doctrine of Jesus Christ and bowing before the image of the Cross. He walked in the ways of all the Roman Christian Emperors that preceded him. He did not know YAH nor did he walk in the ways which YAH commanded Israel and all mankind. After him **Romulus Augustus** became the last emperor of the Western Roman Empire to reign in the stead of Emperor Augustus Caesar.

Romulus Augustus
(475 C.E.—476 C.E.)
[West]

"The Collapse of the Roman Empire in the West"

Romulus Augustus was born in the year 460. His father's name was Orestes [*pronounced O-res-tes*], however, like his predecessor Julius Nepos, his mother's name was not recorded in the annals of Roman history. His full birth name Flavius Romulus. His father, Orestes, was a Roman soldier and politician who had once served Attila the Hun as his secretary. After Attila's death, Orestes re-entered the Roman army in the West and rose through the ranks. During this time, the western empire was largely controlled by the East and ruled by Emperor Leo I. Emperor Leo I, known for his interference in the affairs of the West, nominated a man named Julius Nepos as his choice for new Augustus on the western throne. He dispatched Nepos to the West with a large army to invade Italy and overthrow the reigning emperor

Glycerius. Emperor Glycerius did not have any support to withstand Nepos invasion. His main ally and defender Gundobad had departed Italy for his kingdom in the province of Gaul. Glycerius was besieged, so he surrendered. Glycerius relinquished the throne and he was demoted to the position of Bishop of Salona. A position he held onto until his death in the year 480.

Meanwhile the new ruler, Emperor Julius Nepos, assumed the purple robe on June 24, 474. By 475, Nepos chose Orestes to be his Magester Militum-"commander-in-chief" of the army, hoping to secure his hold on power. Instead, Orestes, a backstabber, staged a coup and wrestled power from Nepos. Nepos did not put up a fight. He fled the capital-city of Ravenna to seek refuge in Dalmatia to save his life. From there, Nepos attempted to still rule as the Augustus, when in fact, all the dwindling power was left in Italy. In the year 480 Nepos was assassinated by one of his own.

"The Imperial City, great Rome has fallen, fallen"

On October 31, 475 back in the capital, Orestes chose his 15-year-old son, who was too young to make any decisions, to serve as the next emperor in the room of the deposed Nepos. He was given the throne title Imperator Caesar Flavius Romulus Augustus. However, he was known as Romulus Augustuslus, meaning *"little Augustus"*. Romulus reigned for 10 months, but trouble was building up. His father Orestes had used Germanic barbarian units to overthrow Nepos. The barbarian regiments, which were the largest components of his army, demanded one-third of Italian territory in exchange for their assistance in unseating Nepos. Orestes denied their request. The mercenaries then became dissatisfied and unruly. They revolted and chose Odoacer, leader of the Germanic units under Roman federate control. The Germanic units then proclaimed Odoacer king of Rome making him the first barbarian to ever rule the Roman Empire. Odoacer then defeated Orestes, captured him near the city of Placenza, and executed him August 28, 476 on site. Odoacer then destroyed every town and village in northern Italy. Afterwards, he advanced on Ravenna where he experienced a brief battle, before winning the conflict known as the Battle of Ravenna. He then entered Ravenna where he seized control. 16-year-old Romulus was captured, his life spared. This occurred on September 4, 476 C.E. After the conquest, Romulus was exiled to a castle in Campania where he eventually died. The Roman Empire in West had officially come to its end. Great Rome had fallen, the great world power situated on seven mountains, was no more. The lady of kingdoms had been seized. It was now ruled by *"the lowest of men"*. As fate would have it, Romulus Augustus ended the succession of Roman emperors over the Western Empire.

After the fall of Rome to Odoacer, the Roman Senate, acting on behalf of the conqueror, sent an official embassy to Constantinople requesting that Emperor Zeno, who was also of barbarian origins, to unite the two halves of the empire. The letter stated the following message: *"the West no longer required an emperor of its own. One monarch sufficed for the world.....the majesty of a sole monarch is sufficient to pervade and protect, at the same time, both East and West."* The Roman Senate also requested that Odoacer be appointed the Praetorian Prefect and administrator of Italy on behalf on Constantinople. Emperor Zeno wanted the deposed emperor Julius Nepos to be returned to power as his caretaker, but in the end he accepted the inevitable and appointed Odoacer as his appointed ruler in the West.

The order which the **[iron kingdom of Rome]** had established for 1,000 years since the beginning of Roman Republic was now the ash heap of world history. Even before the final blow by Odoacer, Rome had lost control over its provinces in Hispania, British Isles, parts of Gaul, Carthage, Illyria, and all other parts except mainland Italy. German generals like Odoacer and their units largely controlled the power behind the throne. Rome had fought the Germanic tribes for centuries, but by the 300s, the illegal immigrant barbarians had entered Roman territory in force. In the end, those non-stop waves of Germanic barbarian tribes sweeping into the Roman Empire in Europe were too numerous for one kingdom for withstand. There were at least **ten[10] barbarian tribes** that evolved into **ten[10] individual Romanized kingdoms** on the European continent. Among them were the Visigoths in the West, the Ostrogoths in the East, the Vandals, Angles, Saxons, Franks, Lombards, Picts, Scots, Scythians, and others. Those former tribesmen became more and more Romanized over the centuries in the post-Roman era. Eventually they replaced ancient Rome with their own versions of the Roman Empire. You had the Frank Holy Roman Empire, the Holy German Roman Empire, Spanish Holy Roman Empire, English Holy Roman Empire, and others. Although ancient Rome collapsed in 476, its culture continued to reverberate throughout Europe and elsewhere during the Middle Ages, in the Roman Catholic Church, the Age of Enlightenment, the Industrial Age, and in modern European and American societies.

When you study the reasons why ancient Rome collapsed, you will see that its demise came in gradual stages which included, most notably, continuous illegal immigration by barbarian invaders. But there were also several other reasons why Rome fell, including severe financial crises, several failed wars, government overspending, high and oppressive taxation on the people, a growing gap between the rich and poor, and rampant crime. In the year 410, the Visigoths, led by Alaric, reached Rome while it was unprotected. The hordes breached the walls, entered the city, looted, set on fire, and pillaged everything in sight throughout the city. The Visigoths plundered the city for 3 complete days, leaving it severely damaged. Rome never recovered.

Forty-five years later, Rome was besieged a second time in the year 455. This time it was the barbarian Vandals who scaled the walls, went on a rampage, and demolished the splendor of glorious Rome.

So, it came to pass that Romulus Augustus came to the throne at the age of 15 in the midst of these ruins and reigned for only 10 months before being deposed by the Germanic chieftain Odoacer at the age of 16. It is ironic that his name honored the two most important figures in Roman history, Romulus and Augustus. Romulus was regarded as the first legendary king of Rome, and founder of the city located upon seven mountains. Augustus was the title which honored the first emperor of the Roman Empire: Augustus Caesar.

(On a spiritual level, we should all realize that the heavy load of grievous iniquity in Roman society is what actually caused its downfall.) After the collapse of the Roman Empire in the West, the western provinces fell into turmoil. The chaotic disorder, known as the **Dark Ages**, lasted from the year 476 to the 10th century. It did not stop until the ascension of **Medieval Europe**. Prophetically speaking, we are now moving past the ancient Roman Empire down into the time zone of the long legs of the image known as the **[Legs of Iron]**. Think about it, the legs are the longest part of the human body, therefore **YHWH ELOHIM Israel** is informing us in this prophetic parable that the legs represent a long period of dominion inwhich Europe and the entire non-Israelite World would experience thousands of years of rulership from the 5th century well into 21th century. **[A long time—long legs]**. That explains why pale-skinned Roman European people **(iron)** have been able to rule over Africans, Asians, Arabs, and all indigenous nations **(miry clay)** of the earth for the past 2,000 years. This is a bitter pill to swallow, but this was ordained by YAH. Please read **Jeremiah 4:7, Jeremiah 5:6,** and **Jeremiah 5:15-17.** *"This captivity is Long"*, the prophet Jeremiah proclaimed to ancient Judah, **chapter 29:28**.

Dark Ages of Europe
(476 C.E.—1000 C.E.)

The Dark Ages was a period of time in Gentile history that occurred after the collapse of the ancient Roman Empire in the West. As I have repeatedly mentioned, Western Europe was once known as the "Northern Forest". The Northern Forest had no famous cities such as Amsterdam, Brussels, Madrid, Copenhagen, Munich, Warsaw, Moscow, Geneva, or Helsinki.

The area was covered with uncultivated mountainsides, hills, valleys, plains, plateaus, and other natural landscapes. The early Europeans, known as barbarians by the ancient Romans, had not learned the skills of brickmaking, writing, reading, domesticating animals such as horses, elephants, or law codes, clothes-making, sandalmaking, homebuilding, palace building, roadbuilding, or any of the skills that were a normal way of life for the Roman people. Unshaven, long beards, protuding body hairs everywhere, unbathed, unskilled in the use of utensils like the advanced Romans, the barbarians ate with their hands. The Romans had to educate, civilize them, and teach them humanistic norms that had been practiced in the ancient Afro-Asiatic World for thousands of years. Through countless wars over the centuries, the Romans and the barbarians of Western Europe came into contact with each other. There were periods of temporary peace when the Romans attempted to integrate the tribesmen into the army. The strategy of social integration was the only option for the Romans after they discovered the provinces of Western Europe contained millions of barbarians which outnumbered the Roman legions and the population. Therefore, the only sensible strategy was to seek peaceful relations through military alliances, which in return, created trade and cultural relationships. Thus, the foundation of European civilization was laid by the ancient Romans.

When the western empire fell in the **5th century [476 C.E.]**, the technological Romanization of the western provinces came to an end. For a long period of time, there was no federal Roman government to finance the development of the settlement cities. There was economic deterioration, political instability where various barbaric tribes warred continuously against each other. There was a lack of human progress. No records were kept verus a period when Roman scribes recorded everything and builders erected all types of structures. The barbarian tribes were not able to replace the Romans with those types of skills and human knowledge. This human knowledge and progress did not reoccur until the **10th century**, beginning with the Renaissance. Until then, Western Europe experienced a period of human darkness and backwardness that became known as the Dark Ages.

Prophetically speaking, **the Dark Ages** came during **The Time Zone of the Iron Legs of the Image.** These two legs represented the western and eastern civilizations that would evolve from ancient Roman civilization. Therefore, one leg should be regard as **the Western Leg** and the other **the Eastern Leg.** The Western Leg became known as the Western World and the other leg the Eastern World.

We are now moving down the legs of the Image which King Nebuchadnezzar had previously seen in his dream thousands of years earlier. We can now see and witness for ourselves that the **Words of YHWH** are true. It is apparent today that world events have unfolded within the kingdoms of men according to the explanation given by the ancient Afro-Asiatic Hebrew prophet Daniel.

The Iron Age—(Its *Long* Legs of Iron)
Divided Western and Eastern Roman Empire—PART THREE "the legs"
"its legs were of iron—But the fourth kingdom will be strong as iron; just as iron crushes and shatters everything—and as iron that smashes—so will it crush and smash all these."
Daniel 2: 33, 40

"YAH changes times and seasons. HE removes kings (kingdoms) and install kings(kingdoms); HE gives the wise their wisdom and knowledge to those who know"   Daniel 2: 21

The History of Divided Western World

Clovis I of the Franks (486—511 C.E.) Theodoric the Great of Ostrogoths (454—526 C.E.) Charlemagne the Great of the Franks (742—814 C.E.) Otto I Great of Germany (912—973 C.E.) Charles IV of Bohemia of France & Northern Spain (1294—1328 C.E.) Louis IV of Germany (1283—1347 C.E.) Charles V of France (1500—1558 C.E.) Henry VIII of England (1491—1547 C.E.) House of Bourbon (1327—1861 C.E.)

United Kingdom of Great Britain (1603—1900) (United States of America (1619—1900)

As we move down the legs of the image, we will start with **the Western Leg first**, the body part that experienced the Dark Ages. The Eastern Leg of the body continued for another thousand years as the Byzantine Empire. We will look at that leg afterwards. Now, we will follow the **HAND of YHWH** as it affects the children of image in the West. We will see the **Spirit of YAH** move the West through *the Dark Ages, Middle Ages, Age of Enlightenment, Industrial Age into the Modern Age of the 21st century*. The legs are long. We will begin with the most influential rulers who reigned during **The Time Zone of Iron Legs.**

[Western World]

Clovis I
(486 C.E.—511 C.E.)
[The Dark Ages]

Clovis was born in the year 466 in ancient northern Frank city settlement known today as the city of Tournai in the country of Belgium. He was the son of a barbarian chieftain named Childeric I. His mother Basina of Thuringa. As a child, he grew up as a paganist in an environment where his people were not accepted by the superior Romans.

His father Childeric fought against the Romans who had established their advanced enclaves in their midst. Clovis succeeded his father in the war against the Romans. During Clovis days, a Roman general named Syagrius was the military commander of the Roman enclave known as the kingdom of Soissons which continued after the collapse of Roman rulership in Ravenna and Rome.

Clovis turned against the Roman commanders and defeated them in battle. He then moved to conquer all the smaller Frank kingdoms throughout Gaul. He moved against the Alemanni tribes in the east. He warred against the Visigothic kingdoms of Aquitania in southern Gaul. In 496, he chose the city of Paris as his capital. By the year 508, he was then proclaimed *"king"* over what we refer to as France today. His name Clovis became the root word of Louis, a famous names used by a dynasty of 18 French kings. He also converted to the god of Catholicism on Christmas Day the same year. He had been deeply influenced by his wife Clotide. All of this was done so Clovis could imitate the manner of Roman emperors. After Clovis conversion, there was widespread conversion among the hordes of French people. That led to religious unification across areas known today as France, Belgium, and Germany. Those conversions greatly empowered the Roman Catholic Church, with the popes replacing the emperors of Rome as rulers, and serving as the preserver of the Roman way of life among the former barbarian kingdoms. The unity of the Crown and the Church continued for another three centuries until the reign of Charlemagne, and later with Holy Roman Empire under Otto the Great in the middle of the 10th century.

Clovis also advanced the once province of Gaul into a civilized state by becoming the fist Frank ruler to record written law. The laws were written by educated Gaulic-Romans who based their orders on Roman Law. Clovis also established the tradition of Frank and Catholicism as the rule of law for his **[new iron kingdom]**.

So it came to pass that Clovis I died on November 27, 511 at the age of 45 after reigning twenty-five years as the *"1st King of the Franks"*. He was buried in Paris, Francia in the church once known as the St. Genevieve Church. Today it has been renamed the Saint-Denis Basilica. After his death, the four barbarian sons of Clovis fought over the throne of their father. Those four sons were Clotaire I, Childebert I, Chlodomer, and Theuderic I. Their family rule became known as the Merovingian dynasty.

Before he died, Clovis formed an alliance with Theodoric the Great, king of the Ostrogoths, in hopes of creating an united western and eastern order. His sister Audofleda married Theodoric the Great. Regardless, the disorder of among the barbaric people continued while the lack of human progress was prevalent. The Western Roman Empire was still in the throes of the **Dark Ages** with only small enclaves of law and order.

Theodoric the Great, "King of the Ostrogoths"
(454 C.E.—526 C.E.)
[The Dark Ages]

Theodoric, of barbarian origin, was born on May 12, 454 on the banks of Lake Neusiedi near modern Austria in the Roman province of Pannonia. The area had been considered Roman federati territories for a long time. His father's name was Theodemir while his mother's name was Ereleuva [*pronounced* E-re-leu-va]. As a young 6-year-old boy he was caught up in a conflict between the Eastern Roman Empire and his people, the Ostrogoths. To ensure that the Ostrogoths would not invade Roman territories, Theodoric was held in Constantinople to guarantee their obedience. Although Theodoric came from a barbarian background, Emperor Leo I, who was a Thracian himself, took young Theodoric under his imperial wings. He lived with the emperor in the Great Palace of Constantinople where he received limited education. For that reason, Theodoric was known to maintain good relations with the Eastern Roman Empire during most of his reign. It should also be noted that Emperor Zeno manipulated Theodoric throughout his rulership.

At the age of 17, and three years before his father's death, Theodoric was allowed to return to his Ostrogothic people in Pannonia where he eventually succeeded his father as the leader. As the leader, he settled his people in lower Moesia. It is a known fact that Gothic hordes once roamed the countryside without an established city-state to call home. Theodoric focused on establishing his hordes into a stable people. However in the year 484, Theodoric came into conflict with another branch of the Ostrogothic tribes known as the Thracian Ostrogoths. Their leader was known as Theodoric Strabo. Theodoric I eventually overthrew Strabo's rule and united the Germanic tribes into one people.

In the year 488, Theodoric I was crowned *"King of the Ostrogoths"* by his people. The Eastern Roman Emperor Zeno crowned Theodoric with the title Patrician. Zeno then turned against his former ally King Odoacer, the conquerer of Rome, and appointed Theodoric to the position of Magister Militum—"commander of the soldiers". Zeno also awarded Theodoric with position of Roman Consul. All of that was done to appease Theodoric, who had turned against Zeno, and started to invade eastern Roman territories. Emperor Zeno bribes were intended to halt Theodoric assault on Constantinople. Instead, in the same year, Zeno ordered Theodoric to overthrow King Odoacer of Italy. In the eyes of Emperor Zeno, as long as the two barbarian chieftains fought each other, it alleviated a threat to him in Constantinople.

For the next four years, from 488 to 492, the armies of Odoacer and Theodoric fought repeated battles. The forces of Theodoric were able to capture most of the Italian peninsula by late summer of 490. The hostilities continued to rage until February 25, 493 when Bishop John of the Church of Ravenna mediated a peace agreement between the two barbaric contenders. Both sides agreed to end the bitterness of bloodshed. Odoacer had fled into the city of Ravenna for refuge. The city surrendered to Theodoric on March 5, 493. The agreement called for both leaders to meet March 15 to solidify the treaty. Theodoric rode into Ravenna pretending that bitterness of war had ended. Odoacer came to the formal dinner where Theodoric stabbed him to death. Theodoric then starved his wife to death, and dismantled all signs of Odoacer's rulership. After this, Theodoric became the new Ostrogothic King of Italy, settling his population of 200,000 to nearly 300,000 inside the Italian landscape. Afterwards, he went on to establish the city of Ravenna as the capital of his new kingdom where he ruled over the Romans and Goths. Through marriage alliances, Theodoric extended his control over other Germanic people known as the Burgundians and the Vandals. By the year 511, he had become the *"King of the Visigoths"* as well, extending his dominion from the Atlantic Ocean in the West to the Adriatic Sea in the East.

During the latter-part of his reign, Theodoric began to experience setbacks, such as the death of his son-in-law named Eutharic who was his heir. His orderly succession had been thrown into doubt. In the same year, he discovered that members of the Roman Senate were also plotting to eliminate him. The conspirators included a pair. One usurper was named Boethius, a philosopher and court official, and the other, his father-in-law Symmachus. Theodoric executed both of them. In the following year of 523, the Burgundians and the Vandals overthrew Theodoric's yoke.

Although Theodoric was known to be personally illiterate, meaning he could not read or write, he used a stamp to sign documents and worked hard to bring human norms to the Gothic people throughout Western Europe and parts of southeastern Europe. His reign was noted for bringing a semblance of law and order in the West not seen since the rule of Emperor Valentinian III. Theodoric was not a co-emperor with the Roman Catholic Church. Instead, he embraced another school of Christian thought known as Arianism. It was the belief embraced by Bishop Arius of Alexandria, Egypt who believed that God the Father gave birth to God the Son. Arius believed the Son did not always exist. Arius believed Jesus was begotten of God at some point. Arius contended Jesus was a creature distinct from the Father, and subordinate to him. The Arian doctrine was totally opposite of the belief crafted by the Nicene Council and Roman Catholic Church. Both churches, the Arian and Catholic, vied for religious authority among the emerging barbarian kingdoms. In fact, both churches sent missionaries to the uncivilized tribal territories across the Danube River to convert them and to establish peaceful relations in hopes of ending wars and incursions. It was during this era that the Germanic tribes began to settle, instead of roaming the countrysides, into the various western Roman provinces and establish their own kingdoms based on the ancient Roman model. The church missionaries served as the educators and torchbearers of ancient Roman culture among the Goths, Vandals, Burgundians, Franks, and others. Oftentimes, once the ruler converted to a certain branch of Christianity, he would force his countrymen to do the same, as in the case of Clovis I who forced the Franks to convert to Catholicism.

So it came to pass that Theodoric I, who had viewed himself as a Roman Emperor, and became known as "the Great", died at the age of 72 on August 30, 526 after reigning for thirty-three years. He was interned in the capital city of Ravenna, Italy in the Mausoleum of Theodoric. He was succeeded by his grandson Athalaric. He was married to Audofleda, the daughter of Clovis I, the King of the Franks. He was the father of four. Throughout his reign, his aim was to restore the glory of Rome. He maintained a Roman legal administration for day-to-day governance. He launched the largest building program to restore the glory of kingdom which had not been seen nor equaled for more than a century. He restored the aqueduct of Trajan and built a palace chapel known as The Church of Saint Apollinaire Nuovo which he dedicated to "Christ the Redeemer". He did evil in the **eyes of YHWH ELOHIM Israel** by not walking in HIS commandments, laws, statutes, and judgements. He did not know YAH. Instead, he served the doctrine of Jesus Christ according to Arian belief and bowed before the image of the Cross. In Nordic mythology, Theodoric continues to be revered as a god. There were standing images erected in his honor throughout the German lands. His reign was known for peace and prosperity among the emerging barbaric Germanic people who were slowly climbing out of **The Dark Ages**. Recorded history did not come to these tall, blond-haired Aryan people for another three hundred years later until the 9th century.

Charlemagne "Charles the Great"
(768 C.E.—814 C.E.)
[The Dark Ages/Early Middle Ages]

Charlemagne was born on April 2,742 in a settlement in the emerging country of Francia. His father was Pepin the Short and his mother was Bertrada of Laon. He was born during a time when his grandfather Charles Martel, known as *"the Hammer"*, ruled over the Franks. His father, Pepin the Short, succeeded his grandfather. Charlemagne came to power at the age of 26 when his father Pepin the Short died in 768. In the beginning, Charlemagne came to power on October 9, 768 alongside his brother Carloman I who served as his co-emperor. For unexplained reasons, Carloman died suddenly, only three years after coming to the throne in the year 771. That left Charlemagne as the sole emperor of the kingdom of the Franks.

Charlemagne, a heavily built and sturdy-looking man, moved to expand the Frankish state. By 774, he had expanded his territory and, in addition, he was titled *"King of the Lombards"*. He converted to the religion of Roman Catholicism and served as the protector of church interest. He removed the Lombards from power in northern Italy in the interest of the church.

The Roman Catholic Church, with Charlemagne serving as their enforcer, became responsible for lifting Western Europe from the secular and religious backwardness of the Dark Ages. His people became known as master horseback riders, skilled hunters, farmers, and established capital cities. For the first time in Frank history, courtyards, palaces with bedchambers, drinking cups, cauldrons, brass kettles, firewood, and other forms of human progress began to seen throughout the once uncivilized province of Gaul. The Frank people wore clothes and shoes, became swimmers, and, for the first time in their existence, they developed their own dialect. For centuries, the only language they had known was Latin, spoken by Romans, and Greek, spoken by the people of the Eastern Roman Empire. During this era, the Church was also responsible for bringing the educational Light of reading, and writing to the once primitive Frank people.

By the year 800, Charlemagne, under the guidance of the Roman Catholic Church, had fought and united much of western and central Europe, forcing the conquered Saxons and other tribes to convert to the Cross or face the Sword. In the same year Charlemage visited Pope Leo III at Saint Peter's Basilica in Rome for a royal coronation. This occurred on December 25, Christmas Day with Charlemagne wearing a Roman tunic, purple robe, and shoes. At this Saturnalia celebration, Pope Leo III crowned Charlemagne *"Emperor of the Romans"* and ruler of the Holy Roman Empire. For the next thirteen years, he united most of Western and Central Europe, for the first time since the collapse of the Western Roman Empire three centuries earlier, under one common Christian banner. For that reason, Charlemagne was regarded as the *"Father of Europe"*, and his rule ushered in the Middle Age.

Although Emperor Charlemagne was seen as a hero in the eyes of the people and leaders in the West, the Eastern Church, which became known as the Greek Orthodox Church, did not agree with the religious doctrine of Nicene Creed, or the authority of the bishop of Rome, or many other related church issues. The rift between the two churches **[the two gods (denominations) of the iron leg kingdoms]** continued for another two-hundred fifty years until it became a permanent split known as the East-West Schism of 1054. Even today in 2019, **the two diverse denominations (gods) of [iron legs], The Roman Catholic Church** in Rome **and the Greek Orthodox Church** in Constantinople, still suffer from a deadly wound of theological differences.

As I said earlier, Charlemagne's vigor spurred a resurgence of interest in ancient Rome. This Renaissance came through the Crown and the Church. It was a period in the kingdom of Francia, and other parts of western and central Europe, when former barbarians learned of cultural and intellectual activity. The Church, which possessed all the historical knowledge and limited documentation of ancient Rome, became the master of this evolutionary change known as Medieval Europe.

Black Moorish Conquest of Medieval Spain

Meanwhile, Christian Western Europe faced an external threat coming from neighboring Muslim Spain which was also known as Al-Andalus. Today this landscape consist of the countries of Spain and Portugal. The Caliph Al-Walid and his black Moorish army invaded Hispania in the year 711. Afterwards, the black Moors occupied the territory of Hispania, established great cities containing major educational centers, and brought cultural knowledge to a continent which was attempting to emerge from the Dark Ages. For the next 700 years, these dark-skinned Moorish rulers of Spain were known as the Umayyad dynasty, beginning with Caliph Al-Walid in 711 to 750, then Emirate of Cordoba, whose dynasty lasted from 750 to 929, continuing with the Caliphate of Cordoba from 929 to 1031, until the Aryan Queen and King Isabella and Ferdinand expelled them in 1492. Before their expulsion, there had been periods of time when the Moorish Islamic scholars [**miry clay kingdom**] shared their scientific insight, such as algebra, trigonometry, astronomy, surgery, pharmacology, and agronomy with their European contenders [**iron kingdom**].

Early Signs of a Latter-Day Conflict between Christians and Islamic World
[Iron Kingdom of Spain occupied by *Miry Clay Kingdom* of Moors *]*
(711 C.E.—1492 C.E.)

The Battle of Tours

In the 8th century, the Moors attempted to repeat the historic campaign of Hannibal by invading France. Their generals thought if they could advance across France, they would be able to capture Italy easily and move into central Europe. This era could be described as *The Age of the Caliphs*. A time when the dynasties of Sunni caliphs ruled over a vast Islamic Empire stretching from the Middle East to the Iberian Peninsula. Beginning in the late 7th and early 8th centuries, the Islamic armies had become the world's foremost military power pushing across Sassanid Persia to the east, and, North Africa and Spain to the west. This happened, for the most part, during a time when western and central Europe was still evolving from **The Dark Ages**. In the eastern Roman capital of Constantinople, the Islamic revolution also overran the Byzantine Empire and confiscated Syria, Armenia, and the holy land from their [**iron**] grip.

In the years 711 to 718, Tariq ibn Ziyad, general of the Moorish forces, led the military campaign to occupy Spain. He crossed the Strait of Gilbraltar and conquered the barbaric Visigothic kingdom of Hispania, then renamed the Iberian Peninsula *Al-Andalus*. For the next twenty years, the Umayyad [*pronounced* U-may-yad] dynasty tightened their grip on the native Iberians, forcing them into servitude. Once their control over Spain was secured, the black conquerors started to move eastward with military missions into the neighboring territory of the Franks. Using roads once built by the Romans, and moving through areas which were once provinces of the Roman empire, the Umayyads advanced easily into southwestern and central France. By the year 719, they had overran the southern Frank city of Septimania. The following year in 720, Narbonne was under their domain. By 725, the west-central region known as the Aquitaine, Burgundy, Bordeaux, and even Autun had been taken by the Islamic sword. The only resistance the Umayyads faced came from a leader named Odo who was the Duchy of Aquitaine. Odo had won one initial victory against the Moors with a surprise attack, but lost several other confrontations. Odo army had been destroyed by the Moor invaders. Odo warned Charles of the approaching Moors ravaging the southern and west-central countrysides. Odo appealed to Charles Martel for help. Charles, sensing an opportunity to extend his territory, told Odo he would help under one condition: only if he agreed to bring his enclave under his authority. Odo's back was against the wall, so he agreed.

Charles then prepared his army to confront the Moors. Strategically thinking, he avoided the main Roman roads, instead he used the hills, forest, and knowledge of the countryside to initiate a surprise attack.

By early October 732, Charles and his Frank army had reached the area near the city of Tours. He planned a surprise attack, amassing a defensive formation of soldiers side-by-side at the top of the hill in midst of the trees. The enemies were downhill. In order for the Moors to engage the Franks, their horsemen would be forced to separate in order to ride up the hills. Martel hoped his maneuvers would level the fighting field, knowing the Franks were less developed than their Moorish adversaries. Mounted cavalries had not been introduced into Western Europe or Central Europe since the decline of the Western Roman Empire nearly three centuries earlier. However, their determination and faith in their mission to liberate the lands of the Franks gave them the advantage over the Umayyads. Another advantage for the Frank troops was their also battle-hardened experience from their previous wars against other barbaric tribes in Europe.

The battle was set in array. The invaders had been caught out guard. A large force stood directly in the Umayyad's paths at the top of the hill. Martel had achieved his goal of choosing the place of engagement. Martel, assisted by Odo, the Duke of Aquitaine, led up to 20,000 soldiers. General Abdul Rahman Al-Ghafiqi, commander of the Arabs and Moorish Berbers, led up to 25,000 into the battle on October 10, 732..For the next few days, the two armies fought minor skirmishes testing each other's strength. The Umayyad fighters were uncertain of the size of the Frank army, therefore they did not instantly launch an offensive, so for a while, there was a standoff. After sizing up the opposition, Moorish general Abd-al Raham, trusting in his superior forces, commanded his cavalry forces to move uphill to attempt to destroy the formation of the Franks. The horsemen attacked, but the Frank infantrymen were able to withstand their frontal assaults. The Islamic army broke into the square where the Franks stood, but the warriors on feet were able to overpower the warriors who rode on horses. The following eyewitness report came from *The Chronicle of 754*, which described the historical battle:

"And in the stack of the battle the men of the North[Franks] seemed like a sea that cannot be moved. Finally, they stood, one close to another forming as if were a bulwark of ice; and with great blows of their swords they hewed down the Arabs. Drawn up in a band around their chief, the people of the Austrasians carried all before them. Their tireless hands drove their swords down to the breast of [their foe]."

At one point in the battle, the Umayyads did break into the Frank square and attempted to kill Charles Martel. His security guards were able to save him and force them to retreat. In the confusion of the battle, Charles dispatched scouts to disrupt their supply chain and bases behind their frontlines. They were commanded to attack and free the slaves being held as prisoners of war. A rumor surfaced among the Umayyad warriors that the Franks had breached their camp threatening their supplies. According to Muslim sources, some of the Umayyad fighters broke off the battle to secure their supplies in the city of Bordeaux. Once that occurred, other soldiers mistook their reversal as a full-fledged withdrawal, which it soon became. General Abd-al Rahmin attempting to stop the retreat, was separated from his security guards, and was struck in the chest and bludgeoned to death. After that, the Umayyad troops hastily withdrew altogether. The entire army fled from the Franks. The Franks ended the battle at sunset as darkness covered the skies. Charles Martel ordered his troops to reassemble in formation on top of the hill. There, they rested in formation all night, awaiting another round of battle the next morning. To the surprise of the Franks, the Moors did not renew the battle at daybreak as they had expected. Martlel's army did not come down from the positions of the hill.

After a waiting game, Martel finally commanded his scouts to spy upon the Umayyads. The reconnaissance soldiers discovered that the Moors had abandoned their camps, leaving their tents, supplies, and other spoils. The Moors had retreated by night, burning and looting as they withdrew. Nearly 12,000 Umayyad fighters had been slain. The Franks lost only 1,000 fighters. Their defeat marked the end of Islamic expansion **[miry clay kingdom]** in Europe. The Moorish loss signaled the end of the Umayyad enroachment on the former territory of the kingdom **[iron leg]** of the Western Roman Empire. Historically speaking, the western provinces had always been a part of the ancient Roman Empire, therefore the religion of Rome, which was Christianity, was viewed as the organic religion of the Germanic people of Europe. Martel's victory was a turning point in the preservation of Christianity throughout

Europe. Many scholars have stated that Europe would have become an Islamic continent if Martel had not stopped the northward advances of the Umayyads in the **West**. Christians viewed Martel's victory as a divine act that permanently expelled the Muslims. The triumph earned him the title *"Martel"* which meant *"The Hammer"*, the champion of Christianity. The victory established the dynasty of Charles Martel which became known as the Carolingian Dynasty. The victory also propelled the ex-barbarian province of Gaul into the first real imperial power in Western Europe after the collapse of the Roman Empire in 476.

So as you can see, Charlemagne success had already been paved by his grandfather Charles Martel, and his father Pepin the Short. His grandfather Martel died in 741, one year before Charlemagne was born in 742.

Reign of Charlemagne

Now back to Charlemagne. So it came to pass that Charlemage died in the city of Aachen, Germany at the age of 71 on January 28, 814 after reigning a total of forty-five years: Six years as King of the Franks. Twenty-six years as King of the Lombards and Franks, and thirteen years as Emperor of the Holy Roman Empire. He was buried in the Old Saint Peter's Basilica in Rome. It was said, Charlemagne had up to 10 wives although he was legally married to only 4 women. It was also said he fathered up to 18 children although only 5 children are recognized as his offsprings. Among his descendants were several members from various noble families and European dynasties, including the Habsburg.

In his medieval court, Charlemagne was known as a lover of roasted meats, a lover of music, book readings, especially Christian books and others about classical Rome. He was a private person who rarely entertained, except on special occasions with grand banquets. After him, all the succeeding Holy Roman emperors considered themselves to be the descendants of the Charlemagne Empire. The silver coins minted during his reign had the Latin inscription: *"Karolus Imperator Augustus"*, meaning *"Imperator Augustus Charlemagne"*. During his reign, he had been crowned *"Emperor of the Romans"* by Pope Leo III and Pope Hadrian. His son Louis the Pious became his successor as emperor of the Frank kingdom.

Otto I "the Great"
(936 C.E.—973 C.E.)
[The Middle Ages]

Otto I [**the First**] was born on November 23, 912 in the city of Wallhausen, East Francia. His father's name was Henry the Fowler, a skilled hunter of birds, and his mother's name was Matilda, who was his father's second wife and the daughter of a Saxon prince[**count**]. During his childhood, European human civilization had begun to spread rapidly across the population centers in central Europe.

In the same year Otto was born, his father became the duke of Saxony. By the time Otto became a 7-year-old, his father was the first non-Frank Germanic king of East Francia, which eventually became a part of western Germany. As a young man, Otto became a mighty man of valor, defeating the foes of his father. By the year 961, two years before his father's death, Otto overthrew King Berengar II of Italy, and became the King of Italy. In the year 936, his father, King Henry the Fowler, finally passed near his 60th birthday, leaving Otto, his oldest son, as his successor. His coronation took place at Aachen Cathedral in Germany on July 2. Otto was only 24 when he became the ruler of Central Europe. He traveled to Saint Peter's Basilica in Rome for his coronation on Feb. 2, 962. Pope John XII crowned Otto's kingdom as the successor of the ancient kingdom of Rome[**the kingdom of iron legs**]. With both Italy and Germany united under his leadership, Otto became the emperor of the Holy Roman Empire. That alliance between the church and state provided more power for the Roman Catholic Church, which had already dominated the Carolingian dynasty in the land of the

Franks.

Under Emperor Otto, the church became the authority in secular and religious matters. Their clerics, such as bishops and others, were appointed to government roles. Otto used the Catholic Church as his instrument to maintain authority over the people. With the blessings of all the popes, beginning with John XII in 962 and ending with Benedict VI in the year 973, Otto claimed a *"divine right"* to reign as emperor. He viewed himself as the guardian of the Christian faith. Throughout his reign, he continued the same policy of unification of the various German tribes which his father pursued. He forcibly converted the Slavic and Hunnic people with the edge of the Christian sword.

In August of 966, Otto heard of the disturbances in Italy. He then announced his plans to depart Germany, and introduced his plans to rule in absentia. By November, a rebellion in Italy led by a rebel militia, attacked the Church of Rome, deposed of Pope John XIII, and imprisoned him. Otto finally reached Rome later that month to crush the uprising. Otto entered the city without a struggle, apprehended the usurpers, hung them, and restored Pope John XIII back upon the throne of St. Peter. After those events, Otto changed his imperial residence to Rome. For the next six years Emperor Otto I reigned from the great city situated upon the seven great mountains. Nevertheless, during his prolonged absence from his native land, many Germans felt Otto had abandoned his German roots and neglected them, although his presence meant well-being and safety for the Papacy.

The following year in 967, the Pope crowned his son Otto II as co-emperor of the Holy Roman Empire.

A few years later during the latter-part of his reign in Rome, Otto sought good relations with the Eastern Roman Empire, although they did not view him as the heir of the Roman Empire. In fact, by April 972, Emperor Otto had arranged for his son, crown-prince Otto II, to marry the Byzantine princess Theophanu, who was the daughter of Emperor Nicephorus II.

However, in the process of time, the Crown and the Church began to experience conflicts. So in August of 972, Emperor Otto returned to Germany. At this time he was the most powerful man in Europe. After spending the winter back home, Otto visited Saxony where he celebrated Palm Sunday in the city of Magdeburg. For Easter, he visited the city of Quedlinburg where there was a great assembly. Otto also prepared for the upcoming days of prayer and fasting that were near. Seeking solitude for personal introspection, Otto then traveled to his palace in Memleben, the place where his father had died 37 years earlier. While there, Otto suddenly became seriously ill with a fever. In his final hours, he received his last sacraments. Shortly afterwards, Emperor Otto the Great died on May 7, 973.

So it came to pass that Emperor Otto I *"the Great"*, a bloody warrior who had slain many in battles, died at the age of 60 after reigning thirty-seven years as Emperor over Italy, Germany, and the Holy Roman Empire. Otto did evil in the eyes of **YHWH ELOHIM Israel** like all the Roman Christian emperors that preceded him. He did not seek YAH'S laws, commandments, judgements, and statutes. Instead, he served the graven doctrine of Jesus Christ and prostrated himself before the image of the Cross. He also erected several sculptured images in honor of Christian saints. During his reign, Otto also helped enrich the church by forcing all the citizens in Germany to pay tithes. The church did not have to comply with secular legal authority. Otto appointed clergymen to be representatives of the state. This arrangement led to massive amounts of abuse by church authorities and it eventually led to the Protestant Reformation centuries later.

His son Otto II, assumed power peacefully at the age of 17, and reigned in his father's stead as the next Emperor of the Holy Roman Empire.

Charles IV Bohemia "of Luxembourg"
(1346 C.E.—1378 C.E.)
[The Middle Ages]

Charles IV was born on May 14,1316 in Prague, Czech. His father's name was John of Bohemia who was a member of the House of Luxembourg. His mother's name was Elisabeth of Bohemia, a Czech of the House of Premyslid. When Charles was born, his parents gave him the name Wenceslanus [*pronounced* Wen-ces-la-nus] in honor of his grandfather. As a young lad, he was raised in the Frank imperial court of his uncle for seven years where he received a French education that included learning Latin, Czech, German, French, and Italian languages.

By 15, he became a man of war after gaining experience with his father while campaigning in Italy. By 1333, Charles was forced to assume more responsibilities as ruler because his father's gradual loss of eyesight. When his coronation came, he changed his throne name to Charles to honor his uncle Charles IV of France. Years later on August 26,1346, his father John of Bohemia, who had been blind for a decade, was slain. Many of his mighty men were also killed that day in midst of the Hundred Years War at the Battle of Crecy in northern France. Charles was also injured and forced to escape the battlefield. On September 2, one week after his father's death, Charles inherited the throne as the Count of Luxembourg and *King of Bohemia* during its Golden Age. A continent, once a uncultivated barbarian wasteland, was now home to several great evolving urban city-states.

After Charles victories in Italy, the prince-electors chose him instead of Louis IV as the *"King of the Romans"*. This occurred on July 11 during the summer of 1346. The formal coronation was officiated by Pope Clement VI that winter on November 26 in Bonn, Germany. When Louis IV suffered a stroke while bear hunting on October 11, 1347 one of Charles main adversaries was gone. Nine years later in the year 1355, Charles was elevated again. This time to the status of Emperor of the entire Holy Roman Empire. Two elaborate royal ceremonies were held in his honor. One in Milan where he received the Lombard crown in the St. Ambrose Basilica on January 6, and the second ceremony in Rome where he was crowned by a cardinal on April 5.

During his reign, Charles bowed before the Roman Catholic Church and became their representative. Charles also ceded vast territories in Italy and abroad to the Papacy. He promised the Church that he would overturn all of Louis IV prior decrees against the Church, and acted as the military enforcer of church authority. With the backing of various kings of the isles of the Gentiles, the Roman Catholic Church had become the most powerful institution in Western and Central Europe. On the other hand, the temporal leader Charles influence in places such as Germany was minimum, and none in Italy. Therefore Charles chose Prague, Czech as his seat of power. He rebuilt his capital-city in the image of Paris, the cultural capital of Europe at that time. He also built several abbey churches. Continuing the great works of his own hands, he commissioned the construction of a castle known as Charles Court. In 1348, he advanced Europe [**the Aryan world of the Legs of Iron**], to a new height when he founded the Charles University in Prague. This was the first university ever built in Central Europe. Keep in mind, the ancient [**Afro-Asiatic world of the Head of Gold**], which included the ancient kingdoms of Egypt and Babylonia, had already established colleges, universities, and libraries several thousands of years before the fourteen century common era. The Charles University served as an intellectual and cultural center for Central Europe, bring humanization to areas that had been covered in the Dark Ages for millenniums. The university became the training ground for lawyers and bureaucrats throughout Europe. Charles also built the Collegiate Abbey of Saint Apollinaris, the Monastery of Saint Mary of the Snows, and the fortress Montecarlo[*meaning* **mountain of Carlos**] during his reign.

The Western Schism [time zone of the iron legs]
"Can two [The Church and Crown] *walk together, except they be agreed?"*

During the reign of Emperor Charles IV, a deadly schism developed between the 14th century Roman Catholic Church and with the kingdom of France. This division became known as the Western Schism which resulted in the creation of the Avignon Papacy which was based in Avignon, France between the years 1309 to 1377, in the southeast portion of the country. The conflict started with a disagreement between Pope Boniface VIII and the Philip V, the king of France, who believed in the supremacy of the Crown. However, Pope Boniface declared the Papacy as the supreme authority [**god of the kingdoms of iron legs**], in all matters, both church and secular. Furthermore, Boniface proclaimed, the kings of Europe were subservient to the Pontiff of Rome. Philip V disagreed, and caused Pope Boniface death. After that, his successor, Benedict XI, died, forcing the church leaders to chose another successor. Philip intervened in church affairs and forced the undecided conclave to choose a French churchman named Clement V as the next head of the Roman Catholic Church. Clement then chose not to move to Rome. Instead, he established a papal residence there in Avignon, under the influence of the French crown. At that time, Avignon was a part of the kingdom of Arles, which belonged to the Holy Roman Empire. *(It should be noted that England and Germany were not pleased with the actions of Philip V king of France.)*

For the following sixty-seven years, the next 7 popes reigned in the city of Avignon, under French control, beginning with Clement V, then John XXII, Benedict XII, Clement VI, Innocent VI, Urban V, and Gregory XI, who eventually returned back to Rome in 1376. He arrived in Rome during the winter on January 17, 1377, ending what was referred to as the "Babylonian Captivity of the Church". A time of schism when there were two popes claiming to be the head of one church: One Pope was elected in Avignon and another one elected by the cardinals of Rome. The Roman Catholic Church referred to the popes in Avignon, France as the *"antipopes"*.

Meanwhile back in Prague, during the era of conflict between the church and French crown, Emperor Charles IV of Luxembourg, acting as a Church peacemaker, visited Pope Urban V in Avignon. After talks, he escorted Pope Urban V back to Rome for talks to heal the wound of division. During this time Charles also received another title and crown as the King of Burgundy. In the latter-part of his rule, Charles divided his great estate among his three sons and his nephews. In his lifetime, Charles had 4 wives and fathered 8 children.

So it came to pass that Emperor Charles IV of Luxembourg, a man of skills and courage, died on November 29, 1378 at the age of 62 from the painful inflammatory foot disease known as gout which most likely resulted from his royal lifestyle of heavy meat-eating, heavy beer drinking, and obesity. He reigned for 32 years as king of Bohemia, the Holy Roman Empire, and Burgundy. He was buried in Saint Vitus Cathedral in Prague, Czech. Charles IV served the graven doctrine of the Nicene Creed concerning Jesus Christ. He believed in Christianity according to tenets of the Roman Catholic Church. He did evil in the eyes of **YHWH ELOHIM Israel** according to all the abhorrent practices of all the European Christian emperors that preceded him who did not walk in YAH's laws, commandments, judgements, and statutes. In the 1848, the Czech government commissioned the building of a standing image in the likeness of Emperor Charles IV in the capital-city Prague.

One of the most important long-lasting decisions made by Charles was his decision to issue the Golden Bull of 1356. Written and mounted on a golden seal, it called for a continuous period of the next 400 years, from 1356 to 1756, for maintaining the constitutional structure of the Holy Roman Empire.

Ironically, centuries later, the young kingdom of the United States, emerged to inscribe many facets of the Roman constitutional structure in their Bill of Rights and the preamble of their Constitution. The new American Roman Republic was born in 1776, only twenty years after Charles IV decree expired.

In Prague, a prince named Sigismund reigned in his stead as the next emperor of the Holy Roman Empire.

The Black Death

Another important event that occurred during the reign of Emperor Charles IV of Luxembourg was the pandemic known as the Black Death, a deadly epidemic that extended from China, India, the Middle East, Eurasia, Asia Minor, and throughout Europe from 1347 to 1351, killing an estimated 200 million-plus inhabitants of the earth and making it one of the deadliest plagues in human existence. Nearly 100 million of those deaths occurred in Europe.

The plague, also known as the Black Plague, claimed between 30 to 60 percent of the total 14th century European population, causing religious, social, and monetary disruptions in the heavily populated cities. It is believed the plague originated from disease carrying rodents, their fleas, and lice. Many of these black rats lived in close proximity to these early Europeans. The rodents were known to be regular passengers on merchants ships traveling from the Mediterranean to Europe. They were known to run rampant in unsanitized populated urban cities. That is how the plague spread so rapidly throughout Europe. Poor hygiene also played a major role in the spread of the deadly pandemic. The lack of bathing and washing hands after constant contact with livestock and rodents helped transmit the plague. Those unsafe habits allowed the germs and bacteria to spread to humans. Smaller principalities, distant lands, and cleaner areas were able to escape the ravishing effects of the plague. Prague, Czech was one of those distant lands that escaped large scale devastation from the Black Plague.

Charles V, Holy Roman Emperor
(1519 C.E.—1556 C.E)
[The Age of Renaissance]

Charles V was born on February 24,1500 in the city of Ghent which belonged to the Habsburg dynasty in the Netherlands. His father, who was known as Philip the Handsome, from the city of Castile. His mother's name was Joanna. She too came from Castile. His father Philip was the heir to the throne behind Emperor Maximilian I, who was the grandfather of young Charles. His father Philip died in the year 1506 while Charles was a mere 6-year-old, leaving him, instead, as the future successor behind his grandfather Emperor Maximilian I. His grandfather placed Charles under the tutelage of his daughter Margaret, before she eventually became the Queen of the Netherlands. She was the overseer of both Charles and his brother Ferdinand. After the young Archduke of Bungundy Charles reached the age of 9, his grandfather transferred him to another tutor named William Croy. It was Croy who took Charles under his wings and helped to raise him to the role of Duke at a young age. Under him, Charles learned to speak French, Dutch, and Spanish. Charles once referred to the German language as the speech of his horse, meaning he spoke very little. Charles grew to depend upon the elder Croy to advance his position in the kingdom. Croy declared Charles a fifteen-year-old in order to orchestrate his appointment to the position of Grand Chamberlain. Another tutor that greatly influenced young Charles was a man named Adrian of Utrecht. Adrian later became Pope Adrian VI. Throughout his life, Charles praised the god of the Roman Catholic Church named Jesus. As a young boy growing up, he visited Paris several times. In fact, he fell in love with the famed city, which was the largest in Europe at the time, and the cultural capital of the emerging Renaissance Period. Charles once declared *"that Paris is not a city, but a world"*.

Five years prior to his father's death, his grandfather Emperor Maximilian had already experienced a serious injury from falling from his horse in the year 1501. His leg never fully recovered after the accident. He became so deeply depressed to the point that by the year 1514 Maximilian began to carry his coffin around everywhere he went. Emperor Maximilian I eventually died on January 20,1519. In his will, Maximilian instructed the morticians to cut off his hair, knock his teeth out, flog his body, then pour lime and ash over his entire body, and wrap his corpse in linen. Afterwards, he requested that his remains be placed on public display in the Castle Chapel in Wiener, Neustadt Austria to serve as a lesson on the vanity of earthly power, glory, and wealth. His tomb was surrounded by standing statues honoring the likeness of deceased Habsburg leaders.

Eight days before his grandfather died, Charles was chosen to succeed him on the throne as the Archduke of Austria. This occurred on January 12. At the age of 19, Charles had inherited the power of his grandfather, a mighty man of valor who had raised Europe to a new level through diplomacy, marriages, and wars. At the time of his grandfather's death, the Holy Roman Empire included territories ranging from Western Europe into Central Europe over toward Southern Europe, including Spain, Bohemia, Hungary, Poland, and Italy. The influence of his grandfather's actions lasted for centuries, greatly directing the course of events in European history. Charles was a member of the Habsburg dynasty which ruled Austria-Hungary until its collapse on November 3, 1918. For the record, the life of the Habsburg dynasty continued for exactly 399 years, 11 months, and 9 days after Emperor Maxililian died in 1519.

In the year 1516, three years before his grandfather died in 1519, Charles, at the age of 16, became king of the Spanish Empire. This is how that happened. In 1496, Maximilian I arranged for his son named Philip to marry a woman named Joanna who was the daughter of King Ferdinand II of Castile and Queen Isabella. Joanna became the Queen of Castile after the death of her mother Queen Isabella. Her father Ferdinand decided to step down from his kingship and chose to serve as the Governor and Administrator of Castile. This left the kingship to Philip and the queenship to Joanna. They became the parents of Charles. Ten years later Philip died in 1506 and left Joanna as a widow. For some reason, Ferdinand ordered the imprisonment of his own daughter. Then he ruled as regent until his death in 1516. Charles then became King of Spain while his mother remained in prison until her death. In the process of time, Charles was able to unite the Castile and Aragon kingdoms into one unified Spain. That earned him the title King Charles I of Spain.

On June 28, 1519, nineteen-year-old Charles was declared the *"King of Italy"*. He was also referred to as the *King of the Romans* and *Emperor of the Holy Roman Empire*. The following year Charles was officially crowned during a regal coronation ceremony in Germany on October 26, 1520. Ten years later, he traveled to Rome where he was crowned a second time on February 22, 1530. Two days later, he was proclaimed the new Emperor of the Holy Roman Empire. With the unification of the Holy Roman Empire with the Spanish Empire, Charles ruled over a Europe that resembled the first example of an united Europe since the collapse of the ancient Roman Empire.

Charles ruled over a Spain that developed into a powerful naval power. He oversaw the European expansion across the Atlantic Ocean into the Americas. Spanish conquistadores soon discovered silver in the New World, making it the chief source of wealth for his massive **[iron-legged kingdom]**. After discovery of massive amounts of silver and other natural resources in the New World, Charles okayed the conquest and destruction of the Aztec and Inca civilization. Spain conquered South and Central America. In the Far East, the Spanish armada also moved into Asia.

The Renaissance Period

After centuries of being known as the land of the barbarians, the entire continent of Europe finally emerged out of the Dark Ages and Middle Ages into the Renaissance Period. A time when Europe began to gain the human knowledge once known in the Afro-Asiatic World thousands of years earlier. 15th and 16th century Europeans surpassed the ancient black Phoenicians as the world's greatest navigators, sailing throughout the seven seas. European craftsmen designed armor with advanced metallurgical skills, their artists drew paintings with oil, scientific knowledge increased, scholarships in reading and writing moved to new heights. The invention of the printing press made literacy more prevalent among the European masses. For the record, the printing press was invented by Johannes Gutenburg of Mainz, Germany. He discovered a method of printing from moveable type. He started experimenting with the printing press in 1438. He had already worked in the crafts as a goldsmith and gem-cutter while living in Strasbourg, France and Mainz. He finally found a financial sponsor named Johann Fust twelve years later in 1450. Gutenburg's first printing was entitled the *"Forty-Two Line"* Bible which was completed in 1455. His invention consisted of a mold containing an alphabet that could be moved into different positions, stamping letters in various places on woodblock print. The new process eventually made large quantities of books available for commoners as well as aristocrats. It also became the basis for typesetting for the next 500 years. The system is still used today in the 21st century. The new printing press was actually created on the same design as those already used for winemaking and papermaking. During his reign, Charles commissioned a series of three monuments made with woodblock prints.

Another invention which came from the Renaissance Era was the introduction of stringed instrument known today as the guitar. It was brought into Spain in the early 16th century. Another new development which occurred was Charles development of the first modern professional army in Europe known as the *"Tercios"*. Throughout most of his reign, Charles' army which consisted mainly of German troops fought France over territory in Italy. His army also stopped the Ottoman invasion of Europe by defeating them at the Battle of Vienna in 1529.

The Protestant Reformation (Schism within Western Christianity)

Another important development that occurred during the Renaissance Period was the division of Christianity, the split between the Mother Church of Rome and the German Christians, which sparked religious wars with German princes. This religious rebellion, led by Martin Luther, against the authority of the Roman Catholic Church was defined as the Protestant Reformation. The advancement in human knowledge caused the European masses, especially in Germany, to question the dictatorship of the Papacy of Rome in all matters, both secular and religious.

By 1556, the mortality of Emperor Charles prevailed. Although Charles had been a powerful man like unto a robust native tree, he became exhaustive and resigned from his powerful position as ruler of the Holy Roman Empire. He vacated the turbulent throne to enter the tranquility of a monastery. However, in August of 1585, Charles became seriously ill with a sickness now known as malaria. So it came to pass that the sun did set upon the life of Charles V and he succumbed in the wee hours of the morning on September 21 at the age of 58. Initially, he was buried in the chapel of the Monastery of Yuste, but after the reading of his will, it requested the creation of a foundation to bury him besides his wife Queen Isabella of Portugal. His remains were returned to Spain where his son Philip II carried out his wishes and founded the Monastery of San Lorenzo de El Escorial. The monument was completed in 1574. Their bodies were transferred and re-interned beneath an altar erected in honor of the monastery itself. Inside the monastery stood a pantheon of standing images graven in the likeness of Charles, his wife Isabella, his daughter, and his sisters. In 1654, his great grandson Philip IV ignored the past will of his ancestor and moved their corpses. Many people accused him of disrespecting the legacy of his great grandfather.

In the end, Emperor Charles V died after reigning thirty-seven years as the ruler of the kingdom known as the Holy Roman Empire. During his reign, his imperial court was held in northern Italy and at other times in the city known as Brussels today. He did evil in the eyes of **YHWH ELOHIM Israel** by not observing HIS laws, commandments, judgements, and statutes. Instead, he bowed down before the graven doctrine of the Roman Catholic Church and served the graven image of Jesus. He also bowed before the image of the Cross according to the abhorrent practices of the European Christian emperors that had preceded him. He did not know YAH. His younger brother Ferdinand I, the Archduke of Austria, reigned in his stead as the next emperor of the Holy Roman Empire. His son Philip II was given the Spanish Empire, including Burgundy, known today as the Netherlands, and the lands of Italy. The two kingdoms remained close allies for centuries, even until the 18th century. It should also be remembered that Charles was a member of a powerful dynasty that stretched across Europe.

His sister Eleonor was Queen of France. His sister Isabella grew to become the Queen of Denmark. Another sister named Catherine was crowned Queen of Portugal while another one ascended to queenship in Hungary.

Although times had evolved for the better for Europeans in the 16th century and beyond, we should always be mindful of the historical facts that the royal Emperor Charles V, and his people, were descendant of the former Burgundian barbarians that the ancient Roman Legions once fought continuously twelve centuries earlier.

Henry VIII "King of England"
(1509 C.E.—1547 C.E.)
[The Renaissance Period]

Henry Tudor was born on June 28, 1491 in the Palace of Placentia, Greenwich, Kent. He was the third child of King Henry VII and Queen Elizabeth of York. He was baptized by Bishop Richard Fox of Exter. Before he knew good from evil, his father appointed him to the position of Constable of Dover Castle and Lord Warden of the Cinque Ports at the age of 2. The following year when he turned 3, he was given the title Lieutenant of Ireland. Although the young lad Henry held those titles, it was really his father Henry VII who acted as the true decisionmaker, holding all power himself and not sharing with other aristocratic families. Growing up, Prince Henry received a first-rate education from a personal tutor, learning to speak Latin, French, and limited amounts of the Italian language.

In the year 1502, his older brother Arthur married the princess of Spain, Catherine of Aragon. She was the daughter of King Ferdinand II of Aragon and Queen Isabella of Castile. In a strange turn of events, his brother Arthur died at the age of 15 only 5 months after his marriage to Catherine. Arthur's death forced his younger brother, 10-year-old Henry, to assume his position. Henry then ascended to the office of Duke of Cornwall. In February of 1503 he became the Prince of Wales and the Earl of Chester.

On June 23, 1503, a treaty was signed for a marriage between young Henry and the widow Catherine. Two days later, 12-year-old Henry and 17-year-old Catherine of Aragon were married in a royal ceremony. Three years afterwards, Emperor Maximilian I, the ruler of the Holy Roman Empire, invited Henry to his imperial court and crowned him a *Knight of the Golden Fleece*.

The English Reformation in England and The New World

His father Henry VII died on April 21, 1509, leaving the throne of England to his 17-year-old son. Two months later, Henry was inaugurated in a royal coronation on June 24, 1509. In his beginning, Henry started out as a youthful, attractive man. He became a talented and educated speaker, as well as a capable ruler known to be very accomplished due to the fact he started out handling assignments early in life. On the other hand, he was regarded as a self-indulgent, heavy spending, proud king who loved heavy eating and drinking while insisting he possessed *"the divine right of kings"* to govern. He also married six times to six different royal women during his reign. Most of those relationships ended with annulments or executions. At the age of 36 and after eighteen years as king, Henry desired to divorce from his first wife Catherine of Aragon, but Pope Clement VII refused to annul the marriage. At the time, he desired another princess named Anne Boleyn. *(However, in the process of time, he had her beheaded by his French swordsman.)* She was arrested and charged with adultery and incest. But, King Henry VIII was no better.

He was known to be intimate with his wife's Anne's own sister Mary as well. It is uncertain how true the following statement really is. It could be gossip, or it could be a deep dark secret. It was also said King Henry VIII was intimate his wife's mother Elizabeth Howard. A English nobleman named Sir George Throckmorton once told the king, *"it is thought you have meddled both with the mother and daughter"*. Of course, King Henry VIII denied the accusation by saying, *"never with the mother"*.

For the record, the Hebrew scriptures clearly speaks against those types of incestuous relationships in **Leviticus 18:17-18:** *"You shall not uncover the nakedness of a woman and her daughter, neither shall you take her son's daughter, or her daughter's daughter, to uncover her nakedness; for they are her near kinswomen: it is wickedness. Neither shall you take a wife to her sister, to vex her, to uncover her nakedness, beside the other in her life time".* King Henry VIII was accused of touching both of those forbidden fruits in his lifetime.

Now back to Catherine. Remember, Queen Catherine was the sister-in-law of Emperor Charles V of the Holy Roman Empire. Charles did not want his wife's sister to be put to shame, so he lobbied Pope Clement VII to deny the request of King Henry VIII. The Pope, under pressure from Charles, agreed that Henry and Catherine should remain united according to the dictates of the Roman Catholic Church. Henry, who was born, baptized, and raised as a Roman Catholic, totally disagreed with the stance of Pope Clement. Henry separated the Church of England from the regulations of the Papacy in Rome by asserting his sovereign supremacy over the Church of England. After all, the Church was located on English territory. He closed their monasteries and dissolved all of their convents. Christians in England no longer were obligated to adhere to the instructions of the Bishop of Rome.(*In history, this rift between Rome and King Henry VIII has been described as The English Reformation.*) Pope Clement, in return, severed ties with the Church of England by excommunicating the English monarch. This religious divorce gave birth to the Anglican Church, a separate Christian order independent of the influences of the Papacy. The Anglican Church reformed the old Catholic order with their own liturgies. The Archbishop of Canterbury was viewed as the new Protestant Pope.

In the process of time, the Church of England gave birth to the Episcopalian Church in the new English colonies across the Atlantic Ocean. When the American Revolution occurred over two centuries later, the American Anglicans separated their ties from the Church of England. This occurred in 1789. The American Anglicans renamed themselves the Protestant Episcopalian Church. The church, which was an offspring of the Church of England, which was an offspring of the Church of Rome, also accepted the tenets of the historic Nicene Council and the Apostle's Creed. In America, a new land where religious individualism and freedom flourished, several new denominations grew out of the Episcopalian Church. In the new land called America, European men and women created new graven doctrines and churches based on the imaginations of their own personal interpretations of the Bible.

(It should be noted that the Spanish and Portuguese European kingdoms **[legs and toes of iron]** *had already initiated the trans-Atlantic Slave Trade. It was in its beginning stages.)*

During the reign of Henry VIII, the Spanish kingdom built a mighty naval force that was unrivaled among their European competitors. France came in second place while England lagged behind. Henry commissioned massive shipbuilding plans. He invested heavily in the English Royal Navy, increased its size, dispatching more than 50 additional ships to sea.

Domestically, Henry had a checkered record. On one hand he was viewed as dictator who expanded royal power who accused many of treason and heresy without a fair trial, while on the other hand, some people continued to look at Henry as a good king who oversaw unity between the province of Wales and England. He fought wars with Francis I of France, and Charles V of the Holy Roman Empire. In those wars, he attempted to enforce England's sovereignty over territory claimed by France. These wars on the European continent were unsuccessful.

Another accomplishment for King Henry VIII was his elevation to King of Ireland in 1542 with the passing of the Crown of Ireland Act. That made him the first ruler, and, the only English Protestant dynasty to ever rule over Catholic Ireland, except for the small period of time in 1691 when the Irish Catholic Jacobites raised the white flag at the Battle of Limerick in surrender to the Protestants.

I mentioned earlier that Henry was considered a handsome young man in his younger days, but late in his life Henry doubled his weight and his waistline expanded to 54 inches. He was unable to walk, and had to be transported around in a mechanical invention, which was the forerunner of the modern wheelchair. His skin broke out with painful, pus-filled boils covering all parts of his body. He was also afflicted with the foot disease of gout. Henry gained most of weight after he experienced a jousting accident in late 1536 when he suffered a leg injury. The accident aggravated a previous injury, causing it to flare-up again. His personal doctors were not able to find a way to treat his infirmity. His wound festered for the rest of his life, becoming open sores. His level of physical activity became next to none. While physically restrained, Henry's confinement cause him to begin experiencing miserable mood swings with temperamental outbursts. Some historians suspect Henry had experienced traumatic brain injury from his accidents. Obese and covered with boils, Henry's physical ailments eventually shortened his days, and on January 28, 1541, King Henry VIII died. It was believed he died from a skin disease known as scurvy. It was preventable disease that could have been reversed by eating large quantities of fresh vegetables and fruits. Henry was a lover of meats and strong drink: *wine, women, and songs.*

So it came to pass that King Henry VIII, of Tudor, died in the Palace of Whitehall in London at the age of 55 after reigning thirty-eight years in the city of London. He did evil in the eyes of **YHWH ELOHIM Israel** according to abhorrent practices of all the Greco-Roman and European Christian emperors that had preceded him. He served the graven doctrine of Jesus Christ and bowed before the image of the Cross. He knew not YAH, nor did he walk in HIS ways, laws, commandments, and statutes that were commanded to Israel and all nations at Mount Sinai. His son **Edward VI** reigned in his stead as the next king of England. The succession of English kings and queens have continued, even unto this very day. In the end, the corpse of King Henry VIII was buried in Saint George's Chapel in the Windsor Castle in Berkshire.

The House of Bourbon
(1589 C.E.—1792 C.E.) 1st reign
(1814 C.E.—1848 C.E.) 2nd reign
France

(1700 C.E.—1868 C.E.) 1st reign
(1870 C.E.—1873 C.E,) 2nd reign
Spain
[The Age of Enlightenment]

"YAH changes times and seasons, HE removes kings(dynasties) and install kings(dynasties); HE gives the wise their wisdom And knowledge to those who know," **Daniel 2:21.**

The birth of the House of Bourbon dynasty date back to a man named Hugh Capet, who founded a Frank royal family known as the Capetians. His dynasty grew to become known as the House of France. He was born in Paris in the year 939. He ascended to become the King of the Franks in the 987 until his death in 996. He was the successor of Louis V, who was the last king of the lineage of Clovis the Great.

Hugh Capet was the son of a Frank duke named Hugh the Great. His mother was Hedwige Liudolfing, a duchess consort. He inherited vast estates in the regions of Paris and Orleans. That allowed him to become one the most powerful rulers in France. A position that threatened King Lothair, a descendant of the Carolingian dynasty. By 985, Hugh Capet had supplanted Lothair as the power behind the throne. Two years later in 987, he was formally elected king of Franks. Upon ascending to the throne, Capet immediately crowned his son as his co-emperor and eventual successor. His direct descendants continued the Capetian dynasty from 987 to 1328, creating a royal house whose offsprings ruled France, Italy, Luxembourg, and the region of Navarre, and Spain. The family extended their power through marriages into other royal houses in different European countries. Eventually, the House of

Bourbon increased their influence all across the continent.

In the year 1272, the French branch of Capetian dynasty became known as the House of Bourbon. This is how that happened. During this time, a descendant of the royal line named Robert Capet, who was the Count of Clemont and the sixth son of King Louis IX of France, married a heiress of the lordship of Bourbon. Their sons and daughters continued for the next 300 years, extending their power, by serving as a cadet branch in roles such as noblemen and noblewomen under several Capetian and Valois kings. **The kings of the House of Bourbons—Louis IX, Louis XI, Louis XII, Louis XIII, Louis XIV, Louis XV, and Louis XVI—** continued until the year 1792 when their monarchy, the royal family, Catholic officials, and other noblemen were rounded up, imprisoned, and massacred during the French Revolution. The following profiles are brief biographies of the kings of the House of Bourbon which I just named.

King Louis IX
(1226 C.E.—1270 C.E.)

King Louis IX was born into the House of Bourbon on April 25,1214. His father was King Louis VIII of France[**Christian iron kingdom**]. His mother Blanche of Castile. He inherited the throne at the age of 12. Louis led the 7th Crusade during 1248 to 1250 to regain control of the once city of David(Jerusalem) and Damascus. His troops were badly defeated by the Egyptians [**Islamic miry kingdom**]. On his return he organized the royal administrative system and minted one standardized coinage. He built the magnificent Saint-Chapelle to house religious images and relics. Upon his deathbed in 1270, he was declared a saint and a graven image was built in his honor. In the year 1297, he was canonized and placed among the pantheons of men and women that were revered by the Roman Catholic Church. In his legacy, he was revered as a just and pious man, becoming an idol known as Saint Louis. In the new land known as America, one the great cities was named in his honor, even Saint Louis, which is located in the state of Missouri.

King Louis XI
(1461 C.E.—1483 C.E.)

King Louis XI was born into the House of Bourbon on July 3,1423. His father was Charles VII, king of France. His mother was Marie Anjou. He ascended to the throne at the age 28. He was very popular among the masses of his Frank subjects. He plotted against his father Charles VII , and was forced to flee to the city of Dauphine where he ruled unchallenged until 1456. That year his father, King Charles, approached the city of Dauphine with a mighty army. Instead of fighting, Louis XI fled into the territory of Burgundy [the Netherlands]. He did not return to France until his father died in 1461. Then he became the king in his father's stead. During his reign, he sought to strengthen France.

King Louis XII
(1498 C.E.—1515 C.E.)

King Louis XII was born on June 27,1462. His father was Charles, Duke of Orleans and his mother was Marie of Cleves. He ascended to the throne at the age of 39. Although he was a Roman Catholic, Louis XII annulled his first marriage in order to marry another woman named Anne of Brittany, the widow of King Charles VIII of France. He was very popular with the Frank people. He was called *"The Father of the People"*. He died on New Year's Day, January 1, 1515 at the age of 52.

King Louis XIII
(1610 C.E.—1643 C.E.)

Louis XIII was born into the House of Bourbon on September 27, 1601. His father was King

Henry IV of France and his mother Marie de' Medici. He ascended to the throne at the tender age of 10. Therefore, his mother was his regent and the true power behind the throne. The mother-son relationship worked well until he was married. After that, he and his mother became estranged. His coming of age made him hate his mother's interference in almost every aspect of his life, both public and private. King Louis exiled her. However, the Roman Catholic Church brokered a peace agreement between the queen-mother and King Louis. After those events, the pair, queen-mother and son-king, reunited to ensure that France grew into the leading European power. King Louis XIII and Queen-mother Marie also consolidated their power against the rival Habsburg dynasty in Spain and Austria. Those two powerful dynasties fought the Three Years War. King Louis XIII declared war on Spain.

King Louis XIV
(1643 C.E.—1715 C.E.)

King Louis XIV was born into the House of Bourbon on September 5,1638. His father was King Louis XIII of France and Queen Anne of Austria. He succeeded his father Louis XIII to become a boy-king at the age of 4. He grew up during one of France's most brilliant period, *The Renaissance*. Once he became an adult, he became a believer in *the divine rights of kings* to rule, establishing a dictatorship in his own name. He viewed himself as God's representative, the vicar, on earth. He spent lavishly on the visual arts, literature, academic paintings, sculptures, decorative arts of Neoclassicism, architecture, extravagant palaces, such as Versailles. He became known as the glorious *"Sun King"* who reigned 72 years and became the longest reigning monarch in European history. He was a classic symbol of an aristocratic monarch for that time zone. He died in the Palace of Versailles on September 1,1715 at the age of 76.

King Louis XIV black illegitimate daughter
"black people living in early Renaissance Europe for various reasons"

King Louis XIV was an exotic king that enjoyed the best for his royal court. The kingdom of France conducted trade, cultural exchanges, and interaction with North Africa during the last part of the17th and early 18th centuries. Louis established a trading company known as Senegal Company for business in north and West Africa. Louis loved exotic animals for his royal park and Africa was full of them. But Africa was also full of something else that King Louis XIV and his other aristocratic men loved also, and that was African women. During the Renaissance, French men considered African women as beautiful, hot, and exotic. The women were brought into the homes and palaces of French nobility and used as house servants and sexual inmates. Louis had these type of house servants in his royal court at Versailles.
Another reason why King Louis XIV is known to have a black daughter is because of his marriage to the black Moorish Spanish princess Marie Therese of Spain.
It has been recorded that the black Benedictine nun Louise Marie Therese, known as the *"Black Nun of Moret"*, was actually the illegitimate daughter of King Louis XIV from his relationship with Queen Marie Therese. The famous portrait known as the *"Black Nun of Moret"* is a picture of the grown-up daughter of Queen Marie Therese. So, yes it is truth. King Louis XIV, and other nobility in Paris and throughout the former province of Gaul had babies by black women.
It should be noted that French nobility also included men like the younger brother of King Louis XIV named Philippe I. He was the duke of Orleans, who was an open homosexual. He dressed and conducted himself in a freely effeminate manner in public. Yet, he was a father of children at the same time. The two brothers—the king of France and duke of Orleans—were very, very close. Religiously, both were adherents of the doctrine of the Roman Catholic Church.

King Louis XV
(1715 C.E.—1774 C.E.)

King Louis XV was born into the House of Bourbon on February 15,1710. His father was Louis, the Duke of Burgundy and his mother was Marie Adelaide of Savoy. He ascended to the throne in 1715 at the mere age of 5. He reigned for 59 years, making him the second-longest ruling king in Europe's history. During his reign, he returned conquered territories his predecessors had won or claimed. He returned the territory of the Netherlands which was claimed by Austria. In the New World, he relinquished New France in North America, ceding France's overseas possessions to Spain and Great Britain after losing the Seven Years War. He was hated by his Frank subjects. He died on May 10,1774 in the Palace of Versailles.

King Louis XVI
(1774 C.E.—1792 C.E.)

King Louis XVI was born into the House of Bourbon on August 23,1754. His father was Louis, the Dauphin of France, and his mother was Maria Josepha, of Saxony. He ascended to the throne at the age of 37 in the year 1774. During his eighteen-year rulership, he resisted popular demands for democratic rule instead of his dictatorial monarchy. The royal family was forcibly transferred from Versailles palace to Tuileries Palace in Paris. He attempted to escape the capital in 1792, but he was captured and returned to Paris. After that, his wife Maria dominated him and persuaded him to abandon the Constitution of 1791 which he had previously sworn to uphold. In 1792, the Tuileries Palace was overrun by a large mob and militias that overthrew the monarchy and proclaimed the first French Republic. He was imprisoned and condemned to death. He was sentenced to the guillotine and beheaded in 1793. He faced death in dignity, showing no fear during the trial. That earned him great respect in the eyes of observers. He was slain on January 21,1793 at the age of 38 in Paris, France. The House of Bourbon had *fallen, fallen* to the dust.

Twenty-two years later in 1814, the House of Bourbon was briefly restored to the French throne. However, after the collapse of the First French Empire, their hold on power was restored until they were deposed again in the July Revolution of 1830. After their ouster, the royal house formed another cadet branch known as the House of Orleans, which ruled for another 18 years until their final demise in the year 1848.

So it came to pass that the dynasty of the House of Bourbon died after reigning for two eras. The first era extended from 1589 to 1792, even two-hundred and three years. Their second era lasted 34 years from 1814 to 1848. In the end the House of Bourbon dynasty had done evil in the eyes of **YHWH ELOHIM Israel** according to the abhorrent practices of the European Christian emperors that preceded them. None of the Frank kings of the House of Bourbon dynasty knew YAH, the Creator of the heavens, earth, seas, and all therein. None of them walked him in YAH's laws, commandments, judgements, statutes, and ordinances. They all served the graven doctrine of Jesus Christ crafted by the Nicene Council and espoused by Roman Catholic Church. Each of them bowed before the golden image of the Cross.

The House of Bourbon
(1700 C.E.—1868 C.E.)
(1870 C.E.—1873 C.E,)
Spain

Philip V King of Spain
(1700 C.E.—1724 C.E.) 1st reign
(1724 C.E.—1746 C.E.) 2nd reign
[The Age of Enlightenment]

The rulers of the Frankish House of Bourbon dominated neighboring Spain from the 1700s to the 19th century. Through wars, diplomacy, and marriages, this domination occurred. For example in the year 1700, the Spanish throne was empty. King Charles II died. He had named Philip V as heir in his will. Philip V, who was a mighty prince and a member of the French House of Bourbon, ascended to the throne as King of Spain on November 1, 1700. He was born on December 19. He was 17 when the mantle of power fell his way. The new unity of Spain and France under the House of Bourbon dynasty sparked fears of a strong force that could dominate all of Europe. His election triggered the 14-Year War of Succession in Europe. The conflict did not end until the signing of the Treaty of Utrecht which outlawed the unification of Frank and Spanish kingship. So it came to pass that Philip V stepped down after he had reigned over Spain for 24 years in favor of his son Louis. However, his son died after contacting smallpox. Philip was forced to return to the throne on September 6,1724 where he remained until his death on July 9,1746 after reigning another 22 years as King of Spain a second time. In the end Philip V of Spain was buried in The Royal Palace of La Granja San Ildefonso.

King Ferdinand VI
(1746 C.E.—1759 C.E.)

King Ferdinand VI was born into the Spanish branch of the House of Bourbon on September 23, 1713 in Madrid, Spain. His father was Philip V King of Spain and his mother was Queen Maria Luisa of Savoy. His father Philip was a passive man who fell deeply in love with his mother Maria. In fact, Philip did exactly what King Lemuel's mother advised men not to do in the book of **Proverbs in chapter 31 verse 3**: *"Give not your strength unto women, nor your ways to that which destroy kings"*. This is how that happened. According to history, Maria was known to be a beautiful and intelligent woman. He slept in her bed chamber at nights instead of the king's chamber, depending exclusively upon her for sexual gratification. His dependency became publicly known, even to the point that his grandfather Louis XIV warned him not to allow his queen-wife Maria to dominate him.

His mother Maria died from the effects of tuberculosis on February 14, 1714 while young Ferdinand was still a 5-month old lad. After his mother's death, Elizabeth Farnese married his father King Philip V and became Fredinand's caretaker. She did not attempt to nurture young Ferdinand. Instead, she became an active sex partner, an uncaring mistress and stepmother who only cared about her own children from a previous marriage, and her new position as the Queen of Spain. This caused him to live his childhood in loneliness. He became withdrawn, shy, and insecure in his own abilities. He grew up, and at the age of 16 he married the young bride Infanta Barbara of Portugal whom he espoused in 1729. She was the 18-year-old daughter of King John V of Portugal and Queen Maria Anna of Austria.

Seventeen years later, he ascended to the throne at the age of 33 on July 9, 1746. Domestically, one of his major acts after becoming king was the elimination of his overbearing stepmother Queen Elizabeth Farnese and her entourage. In terms of foreign policy, Ferdinand found Spain embroiled in a War of Succession against the Habsburg dynasty, Austria, and the various other major powers of central Europe. As the established ruler of Spain, he pursued a policy of non-involvement in the Seven Years War between France and Britain which broke out in the year 1756.

As fate would have it, Queen Barbara, his devoted royal highness who suffered from obesity and asthma, died on August 27,1758 as a childless woman at the age of 46. Her death broke the spirit of tenderhearted King Ferdinand VI. He stopped handling his kingly duties, he stopped shaving and bathing, he did not dress in his regal apparel, and he walked around in a nightgown all day. After her demise, he never ventured out of the royal park. He died also a year later the following August 10, 1759. His younger half-brother known as **Charles III** succeeded him as the next King of Spain from the House of Bourbon. His mother was

Elizabeth Farnese, the second wife of Ferdinand VI. Remember, she was Ferdinand's hateful stepmother.

Charles III King of Spain
(1759 C.E.—1788 C.E.)

Charles was born into the House of Bourbon dynasty on January 20,1716 as the son of King Philip V and his second wife Queen Elizabeth Farnese. He came to power as the King of Spain because his older half-brother Ferdinand VI died on August 10,1759 without choosing a successor. Charles's childhood was quite opposite of his older step-brother Ferdinand whose mother died while he was only a 5-month-old infant, leaving him as a stepchild. Whereas Charles mother, Queen Elizabeth Farnese, cared and nurtured him throughout his childhood.

Charles was 15 when he became the Duke of Parma and Piacenza on December 29, 1731. Three years later in 1734, he was awarded the title Charles VII, King of Naples, and Charles V, the King of Sicily, ruler of Italy. By 1738, Charles, a twenty-two year-old, desired Princess Maria Amalea of Saxony as his new wife. Princess Maria was an educated woman with aristocratic manners. She and Charles begat 13 children during their marriage. 5 of them died before reaching adulthood. The royal couple, Charles and Maria, remained in the royal city of Naples for nineteen years, from 1734 to 1753. While there in Naples, Charles grew to appreciate the doctrine of "enlightened absolutism" which called for increased individual rights at the expense of the monarchy and the Church. When Ferdinand died six years later, Charles ascended to the Spanish throne on August 10,1759 at the ripe age of 42. Once in power, Charles sought to enacted many reforms in the Spanish kingdom. He promoted science and university research, not Catholic dogma. He also increased trade and commerce, and modernized agriculture. In terms of foreign policy, Charles steered Spain away from conflicts and expensive military campaigns.

During his reign as King of Spain, Charles was charged with protecting Spain's interest in the West Indies. He also saw the birth of the United States of America in 1776 while he reigned in Madrid. So it came to pass that Charles III died at the age of 71 on December 14, 1788 after reigning 29-years as the King of Spain as a scion of the House of Bourbon. He was a Roman Catholic Christian who served the graven doctrine of Jesus Christ throughout his reign.

Charles IV
(1788 C.E.—1808 C.E.)

Charles IV was born into the House of Bourbon on November 11, 1748 in the Royal Palace of Portici in the kingdom of Naples in Italy. He was the son of King Charles III of Spain and Queen Maria Amalia of Saxony. Charles, the second son, gained his father's favor because his older brother's learning disabilities and epilesy. Charles, on the other hand, was active and loved sports, and grew to become a mighty hunter known as El Cazador *"The Hunter"*. During this time young Charles never showed any real interest in political affairs, preferring a simple life of friendship and pleasant mannerism.

It came to pass that his father Charles III died at the age of 71 on December 14, 1788 after reigning 29-years as the King of Spain. His father's death propelled his son Charles to into the fray of politics, and on the same exact date, he was chosen to succeed his father on the throne at the age of 40. His throne title was Charles the Fourth[IV]. Charles had never served as a duke, lord, lieutenant, co-regent, or any other official role in the Spanish monarchy. In fact, Charles IV was the total opposite of his father Charles III who had actively participated in reforming the Spanish kingdom. His father also actively promoted science, university research, and increased trade, commerce, and improved agricultural production. Instead, Charles IV allowed his 23-year-old wife to Queen Maria Luisa, and his prime minister, to handle kingdom affairs.

When he came to power, Charles IV did not possess any personal visions for the kingdom.

His goal was to maintain the policies of his father and retain his father's officials. So he retained his father's prime minister named the Count of Floridablanca. *(Notice the name:Florida-blanca. One of the states in the kingdom of the United States was named Florida. The Spanish Empire once controlled the territory of Florida and gave the land its name.)* Again, Charles IV did not care about details. His only demand was that he appeared as an absolute powerful monarch in public while others were the true power behind the throne. In the process of time, his father's prime minister Floridablanca was deposed and finally replaced by a man named Manuel de Godoy. Now Godoy took advantage of King Charles absence. He became powerful, and it was said he and the Queen of Spain maintained a secret adulterous love affair. Meanwhile, Godoy, a true backstabber, was the most trusted courtier and close friend of King Charles IV in his royal court.

In 1792, Louis XIV, King of France and fellow cadet of the House of Bourbon, was deposed and beheaded. King Charles protested the actions of the populist mobs and militias. In return, the new rulers of Republican France declared war on Spain. France, one of the most powerful armies in Europe, caused Spain and Portugal to unite in a defense pact to counter the French threat. After three years of conflict, Spain and France stood at a stalemate, but France held a slight edge. Spain was forced to make amends with France, then formed an alliance with France to war against the kingdom of Great Britain. The instability in foreign policies, economic troubles from conflicts, the sexual affair between the Queen and Prime Minister, and King Charles personal ineptitude caused discontent, riots, and massive revolts. The general discontent of 1808 caused King Charles IV own son, crown-prince Ferdinand, to rise up in a plot to overthrow his father. Riots and popular revolts continued in Spain. The violence reached the winter palace Aranjuez forcing King Charles IV to vacate the royal throne. The people then declared his usurper son Ferdinand as their new ruler. His son then assumed the throne title Ferdinand VII King of Spain. However, there were 100,000 Frank soldiers stationed on Spanish soil. King Charles appealed to General Napoleon Bonaparte to help him recover the throne. Instead, Napoleon summoned both, the father and son, before his presence in the city of Bayonne. Napoleon did not take sides in the Spanish family dispute. Instead he forced both of them to relinquish their claims on the throne and declared the end of the House of Bourbon in Spain. France already had deposed of the House of Bourbon in 1792. Napoleon chose his own brother Joseph Bonaparte as the new ruler over Spain. He assumed the throne title King Joseph I of Spain.

Napoleon Bonaparte
(1804 C.E.—1814 C.E.)
France

Napoleon Bonaparte was born on August 15, 1769 in the settlement of Ajaccio on the French island of Corsica. His father was Carlo Bonaparte and his mother's name was Letizia Ramolino. As a young lad, Napoleon spoke his native tongue of Corsica. He was not fluent in the French language, and in fact, he experienced difficulties speaking French. For this reason, the children meddled his accent, and because he was of a short stature, the children also bullied him. Those early life experiences caused him be insecure and to develop an inferiority complex, which would later cause him to become a brutal man and warrior.

His family was poor, and they were of Italian origin, so he joined the military as a young 16-year-old where he served as a low-ranking artillery officer in the French military. Napoleon had turned 20 when the French Revolution erupted in 1789. The army, mobs of people, and the Enlightenment Age leaders of the protest movement all joined ranks against the House of Bourbon scion King Louis XIV. This upheaval gave Napoleon the opportunity to rise through the ranks quickly. He seized the opportunities which the revolution had provided. When the revolution subsided in 1793, Napoleon, who was only 24, had risen to the rank of general in command of the French army. In the following years, he campaigned against the Egyptians, Austrians, the Italians, the Spanish, and the Haitians in the New World. (It *should be noted that Emperor Napoleon and his French army lost the war against the lost sheep of the house of Israel known as Haitian people.)* His military success propelled him into power as a war hero, and by May 18, 1804, he had already orchestrated a coup and proclaimed Emperor of France. He was later crowned with a royal coronation on December 2,1804 in the famed Notre Dame Cathedral in Paris.

By 1805 a confederation of European countries gathered against Napoleon. He defeated both Austria and Russia at the Battle of Austerlitz in one of his greatest military victories. On March 17, 1805 he became the King of Italy. The next year he defeated Prussia at the Battles of Jena and Auerstedt. By 1807, Russia had regrouped and warred against Napoleon again at the Battle of Friedland. He defeated Russia again, and forced the Czar of Russia to sign Treaty of Tilsit, ending the coalition of nations against France. However, one of his setbacks came when he lost the Battle of Trafalgar against Britain. The lost against Britian did not break Napoleon's grip on Europe. He dominated both Europe and global affairs for more than a decade as he led France in a continuous series of wars which became known as the Napleonic Wars. He later led an army of 450,000 men into Russia into enforce the Treaty of Tilsit which both countries had signed nearly a decade earlier. He suffered great losses in that campaign against Russia and he was forced to retreat from Moscow in shame. As he retreated, he was met by a coalition at the Battle of Leipzig which inflicted more wounds on a weakened army. Even the royal city Paris itself was attacked and taken. Napoleon was forced to flee and vacate the throne in the year 1814. He was exiled to the solitude of the island Elba where he remained for one year. At that time, the House of Bourbon scion King Louis XVIII was temporarily restored to the throne. The following year in 1815, Napoleon managed to return from exile and recover his throne for one hundred days, from March 20, 1815 to June 22,1815, before he was severely defeated again at the Battle of Waterloo. This time Napoleon was captured by the British army then sentenced to life in exile inside the Longwood House on the island of Saint Helena which was located in midst of the Atlantic Ocean between Europe and Africa. He lived there in exile under harsh conditions: cold weather, damp floors, poor rations, and loneliness. During this time his health began to deteriorate. By the month of February in 1821, Napoleon's health was rapidly deteriorating. He contacted the Roman Catholic Church to make amends with his conscious. After confession on May 5, 1821, Napoleon, one of the greatest generals in European history, died from stomach cancer. He was buried on the island of Saint Helena in the area known as the Valley of The Willows where he remained until December 15,1840 when his remains were returned to France. Napoleon was then enshrined in a stone above ground casket and placed in the Les Invalides royal palace in Paris. His legacy includes transforming military organization and training. His tactics are studied in military schools worldwide. He was known to introduce several reforms such as civil administration to French government as well.

Another abominable aspect of Napoleon, **in the eyes of YHWH,** was his support of homosexuality. In 1791,Napoleon passed a series of laws known as the Napoleonic Codes which legalized same-sex marriages and men co-habitation with men. After ancient Greece and Rome, France became the first European nation to openly legalize consensual sexual relations between adults of the same sex. So it came to pass that Napoleon did evil in the **eyes of YHWH ELOHIM Israel** by not following HIS laws, commandments, judgements, and statutes. **King Louis XVIII (1814—1830),** of the House of Bourbon returned to power a second time after the final ouster of Napoleon. **The House of Bourbon** remained in power until 1830 when a popular uprising removed them from power for the final time.

Now Back to King Charles IV of Spain.

King Charles, his wife Queen Maria, and Prime Minister Godoy were taken back to France as captives. They were held in the city of Marseille for three years. Eventually, the puppet government installed by Napaleon collapsed and Ferdinand VII made his way back to his throne in Spain. Both Charles and Queen Maria were also released. The ex-king and queen then traveled throughout Europe until they ultimately chose the Palazzo Barberini in the great city situated on seven mountains—Rome. That was his final place of retirement in 1812. For the next seven years, Charles lived a life of simplicity. His wife, and mother of all 14 of his children, died on January 2,1819. Shortly afterwards, Charles, the scion of **The House of Bourbon**, also died only eighteen days afterwards on January 20. Only six of their children survived to become adults. His corpse was returned to Spain where he was interned at a monastery called the Royal Site of San Lorenzo El Escoria, which was located 28 miles northwest of Madrid. During his lifetime, he served the graven doctrine of Jesus Christ crafted in the Nicene Creed and espoused by the Roman Catholic Church throughout all his life. He bowed before the Image of the Cross, and he knew not **YHWH**.

The Age of Enlightenment in Europe & New World

The Age of Enlightenment was a European **[Gentile]** intellectual movement of the 18th century. For the first time in the history of the isles of the Gentiles, the area known as Western and Central Europe today, was inhabited by men and women who had achieved a high level of human intelligence. Remember, these are the same areas where the Roman Empire once fought continuous wars against their barbarian ancestors who once roamed the uncultivated North Forest [consisting of the countries of France, Germany, Luxembourg, Belgium, the Netherlands [Northern land], and Switzerland]. For the first time in history, superior human intelligence had reached this part of the world. The Europeans, for the first time in their existence, established records of human progress. Europe became the place where ideas, reason, art, philosophy, medicine, law, economics, and politics flourished. The Enlightenment thinkers celebrated the greatness of their thoughts and independent personal liberty. They praised their ability to learn from science and investigate nature with unfettered minds, uninfluenced by the Roman Catholic Church.

For centuries, after the ascension from the Dark Ages and progressing through the Middle Ages and Renaissance, the kings, dukes, and other rulers ruled their kingdoms with an **[iron]** authoritative hand. The monarchs ruled by divine right, believing they were the enlightened one who knew what was best for the masses. The monarchs maintained a policy known as "Enlightened Absolutism", meaning the kings and their officials knew what was best. Beginning in the 1600s, popular resentment against both the church and monarch increased. The intellectuals and philosophers dominated these movements. An English man named John Locke (1632-1704), a physician and philosopher, was one those leaders during that era. He opposed the divine rights of kings and became known as the "Father of Liberalism". He published a document known as the *"Natural Rights (Life and Freedom)"* where he stated the government was bound to protect the people's rights, and on occasion that if it failed, the citizens maintained the right to replace it with a new order. *(Newton's Law of the Universe was also published in 1687).*

In France, those ideas inspired the 1789 French Revolution and led to the ouster and beheading of King Louis XIV in 1792. The Enlightenment Age occurred between 1715 and continued to 1789 in that country. French intellectuals addressed large crowds and demanded reforms such as "a government of the people", religious tolerance, and celebrated the power of the ongoing scientific revolution. The leaders of the movement wanted to apply this discovery of new knowledge of analytical thought to total society, changing the face of governance into our modern era.

The Age of Enlightenment actually undermined the authority of monarchs and the Roman Catholic Church, and Protestant churches, across Europe, and especially in the New World across the Atlantic Ocean. The free thinkers in the 13 colonies on the North American mainland were participants in the progressive movement of that era. Benjamin Franklin, one of the Founding Fathers of the American Republic, visited Europe several times where he participated in scientific and political debates. Thomas Jefferson, another Founding Father of America, particpated in the Age of Enlightenment movement. Many of the ideas found in the American Declaration of Independence were based on European ideas of social liberalism where individual rights surpassed government authority. James Madison, another Founding Father of America, also supported those ideas, such as personal liberty, separation of church and state, and incorporated them in the writing of the U.S. Constitution in 1787. In fact, all the founders of the United States of America were supporters of the Age of Enlighenment where shrines of scientific academies were erected. Masonic Lodges and fraternal orders flourished. Groves of literary salons, coffee shops, printed books and pamphlets were built on every high hill and in every valley. Men of this era were fascinated with their rediscovery of ancient pre-Christian Greek and Roman history. Unlike the early church fathers who were critics of the pre-Christian Greco-Romans, these New Age intellectuals embraced paganism along with their liberal Christian thoughts and church attendance. Pagan holidays such as Halloween [**worship of dead, ghosts and necromancy**], Christmas [**worship of the sun-god Saturn**], Easter[**worship of the queen of heaven Ishtar**], New Year celebrations [**reverence of the Roman New Year and two-headed god Janus**], Valentine [**worship of god Cupid**], were embraced by these Neo-Classic 18th century philosophers and intellectuals who were also known as respected Christians.

The Erection of The Statue of Liberty, a Symbol(Idol) of The Age of Enlightenment

On October 28,1886, U.S. President Grover Cleveland dedicated the Statue of Liberty, the sculptured image of Gentile Freedom, with a pomp ceremony that included New York's first ever ticker-taped parade. The structure had been crafted by the French sculptor named Frederic Auguste Bartholdi who first came to the U.S. in 1871. He had initially attempted to pitch the idea of a colossal woman statue with an upraised hand to the ruler of Egypt. He proposed building the statue on the mouth of Suez Canal. However, the Egyptian leader declined the offer.

The French sculptor then sailed to America where he again pitched the idea. This time in New York, he told potential donors that his inspiration for the statue came from a dinner party in Paris with the French scholar and American supporter Edouard Rene' Lefebvre de Laboulaye. Bartholdi told Americans that Laboulaye had favored the idea of erecting a monument in honor of America's freedom. Bartholdi began fundraising entertainment venues and started soliciting donations from private donors from both France and America. This is how the Statue of Liberty was financed. The standing image, which stood 151-ft. tall, was greatly influenced by the ancient [**female Roman goddess Liberas**]. Bartholdi convinced Americans that the standing image would serve as a symbol for the Liberalism movement, and to reaffirm the ideas rooted in the Age of Enlightenment.

This New Age Idolatry, which consisted of graven ideologies, came during the **Time Zone of the Legs of Iron.** It was a concept where European men and women [**iron people**] began to view themselves as the greatest and wisest of all humanity. Their expansion of old sciences eventually led to new inventions. Their World of Ideas included an appreciation of the arts, architecture, music, and ways to improve their usage. This new human progress was a new phenomenon for people in this part of the earth, but it should be noted that several civilizations during the **Time Zone of the Head of Gold** and **Chest and Arms of Brass** had already experience this level of human progress several thousands of years earlier. It is true, the European people did improve human existence through their graven ideas of science. They began to worship science as if it was the absolute sum of perfect understanding. The DIVINE Presence of **YHWH** was not recognized by those 18th century academic pagan great thinkers, nor did their European successors, even until this day. They did evil in **the eyes of YHWH.** They did not consider HIS laws, commandments, judgements, and statutes. Instead, they trusted in the works of their own hands and pursued a world of ideas without the reverence and acknowledgment of **YHWH** as the ultimate Source of all wisdom, knowledge, and understanding.

The Kingdom of Great Britain
(1707 C.E—1900 C.E.)
[Industrial Revolution]

The kingdom of Great Britain was officially born on May 1,1707 with the ratification of the Acts of Union. The new 1801 law united the four countries of England, Wales, Scotland, and eventually Northern Ireland. That is why Great Britain was referred to as the United Kingdom [UK]. Great Britain is a large island *"isles of the Gentiles"* [Indo-European or Aryan people, commonly referred to as white people—biblical Gentiles. **See Genesis 10:5**]. Britain is located in the North Atlantic Ocean, off the northwest coast of the continent of Europe. Britain is the ninth largest island on the face of the earth.

Once the land of the Picts, Scots, Britons, Angles, and later the Saxon barbarians, the people evolved to build one of the greatest and most powerful kingdom among the families of the European Gentile nations. The Age of Enlightenment also touched the island of Great Britain, which was formerly dominated by the kingdom of England. In 1603 King James VI, a Scot, inherited the throne of England when his wife Queen Elizabeth I died. This personal union of the kingdoms was known as the Union of the Crowns.

(It should also be mentioned that in the late 1600s, John Locke, a leading English philosopher, became a strong voice for the rights of commoners during this same era.)

In the late 1600s, King Charles II did not have a heir to the throne. His brother James was unpopular because he still believed in the Christian doctrine of the Roman Catholic Church. Charles II, who was childless, raised his two nieces, Anne and Mary, as Anglican Christians. When King Charles II died his brother James did succeed him as the new King of England. King James reigned for three years before being overthrown in the 1688 Glorious Revolution. Princess Mary and her husband William III of Orange seized power and succeeded King James on the throne. Princess Anne was not a part of their inner circle. King William and Queen Mary did not have any children. Queen Mary died in the year of 1694, leaving William to reign as the sole ruler for eight more years until he died in 1702. This left the outsider Princess Anne as the successor and new Queen of Great Britain.

Queen Anne of Great Britain
(1707 C.E.—1714 C.E.)

Queen Anne, of the House of Stuart, was born in Saint James's Palace in Westminister, England on February 6, 1665. She came to power on March 8,1702 as ruler of England, Scotland, and Ireland. She was crowned with a royal coronation on April 23,1702. She was the ruler of England when the Acts of Union was signed which unified England, Wales, Scotland, and Northern Ireland into the United Kingdom of Great Britain. She reigned for 12 years while experiencing health problems. She and her husband Prince George of Denmark too were childless after experiencing up to 17 miscarriages. After reaching the age of 30, she became obese. By 1701, the kingdom of England passed a law known as the Act of Settlement which excluded Roman Catholics from sitting upon the throne of great kingdom. Queen Anne died on August 1,1714 and she was buried in Westminister Abbey. Her successor was her cousin named George I of the royal house of Hanover. *(For the record, the name George derives from the Greek name Georgios meaning tiller of the soil , or farmer, and famous bearer. In English Christian mythology, the patron Saint George fought with a fire-breathing dragon which symbolized the Devil. In ancient Greek mythology, the imaginary character Gorge was a female who had an incestuous affair with her own father and bore an idol named Tydeus.)*

George I King of Great Britain
(1714 C.E.—1727 C.E.)

George Louis, of the House of Hanover, was born in Brunswick-Luneburg, in the Holy Roman Empire on May 28, 1660. He was the son of Ernest Augustus, an Elector of Hanover. His mother was Sophia of the Palatinate, the granddaughter of King James I of England. As a young man, he fought valiantly against the French in the war of the Spanish Succession. From 1708 until 1714, he was a prince-elector in the House of Hanover. When his cousin Queen Anne died, George was the closest Protestant relative available. King George I soon became the first ruler of Britain from the Hanover dynasty. Queen Anne had many relatives who were potential heirs to the throne, but all them professed Catholicism. A 1701 law known as the *Act of Settlement* outlawed Catholics from occupying the British throne.

George I ascended to the throne of the United Kingdom of Great Britain on August 1,1714 immediately after the death of his second-cousin Queen Anne. His royal coronation came two months later on October 20.

Prior to his rise to power in London at the age of 54, George had already served as a Duchy and held a position as one of the prince-electors in the Hanover Electoral College in the Holy Roman Empire. During his reign, George strengthened Britain's economic standing through the policy of mercantilism. Mercantilism was the overseas policy of the British, and other European countries during this era, where government and merchants worked together to enrich their individual kingdoms. Under this policy, the throne and the merchants were partners in crime, increasing their wealth through human trafficking, overseas possessions, and any other methods to multiply gold and silver in Great Britain's treasury. King George I collected the taxes and duties while the merchants increased their profits. King George also continued the buildup of the Royal Navy, projecting British power in North America, the West Indies, and developing the beginning stages of the British presence in India. During his reign, many Britons left the country in favor of becoming citizens in the new 13 colonies in North America.

Throughout his reign, George was unpopular due to his German background, mannerism, and his choice of a German mistress instead of a British princess. So it came to pass that George died in the year 1727 somewhere between June 11 to June 22. He suffered a stroke while visiting Prince Bishop Ernest of Brunswick-Luneburg in his native city Hanover on August 1. He was later buried in the Leineschloss Palace in the city of Hanover, becoming the last British ruler to be interned outside of the United kingdom of Great Britain. In 1974 the palace was converted into the University of Osnabruck. He served the graven doctrine of Protestant Christianity and bowed before the Image of Cross all the days of his life. His son George II reigned in his stead as the new King of Great Britain.

George II King of Great Britain
(1727 C.E.—1760 C.E.)

George Augustus, who became known as George II, was born with a silver spoon in his mouth into the royal House of Hanover somewhere between October 30th and November 9th, 1683. His mother Sophia Dorothea of Celle gave birth to him inside the Herrenhausen Palace in the city of Hanover. His father was King George I of Great Britain. Therefore, he received a royal upbringing while growing up in northern Germany. Like his father before him, George II was also a prince-elector in the Hanover House as a young man while his father George I reigned in London. His father had inherited the throne of Great Britain after the death of both his wife Sophia and Queen Anne, who was his second-cousin and a Protestant. His father George I reigned for thirteen years until his death on June 11, 1727.

After the death of his father that summer, his son George II ascended to the throne as the next king of the United Kingdom of Great Britain. Two weeks later, he received the crown in a royal coronation. George II was the new king, but the British Parliament was very powerful. Their opposition limited George's ability to rule by direct control. The agents of the Roman Catholic Church, who were known as Jacobites, attempted to overthrow King George II, but failed. King George traveled back to Hanover each summer to meet with the other electors.

Those electors had direct control over the affairs of various kingdoms. By 1743, Great Britain became embroiled in the War of the Austrian Succession where he courageously led the army at the Battle of Dettingen. After that conflict the British Parliament forced the king's prime minister named John Carteret to resign. A man named William Pitt was chosen to replace Carteret as the new Prime Minister of Great Britain. He too was later forced to resign.

In 1756, the outbreak of the Seven Years War began, causing the major European kingdoms **[the emerging ten iron toes]** of Britain, France, Spain, Portugal, Austria, Russia, Saxony, Sweden, Prussia, and the Electorate of Brunswick-Lineburg to war against each other. It was a worldwide conflict fought on several fronts, including India, Europe, and North America. France and Britain clashed over ownership of the 13 North American colonies.

In the thirty-third year of his reign in October of 1760, King George II suffered blindness in one of his eyes along with the loss of normal hearing. On the morning of October 25, the king rose as he normally did. He drank his cup of hot chocolate and went to the stool in the king's chamber. A few minutes later, his courtier heard a loud crash in the room. He entered and found King George II unconscious on the floor. He lifted the king up and dragged him to his bed. He immediately summoned his daughter Princess Amelia, but when she arrived at his bedside, he had already died. It was only days before his 77th birthday. His cause of death was a heart rupture. King George II was the last Britain monarch to be born outside of Great Britain.

During his lifetime, King George II married a woman named Caroline of Ansbach. Together they bore eight children: 1) Frederick, Prince of Wales. 2) Princess Anne of Orange. 3) Princess Amelia. 4) Princess Caroline. 5) Prince George William. 6) The Duke of Cumberland William. 7) Mary, the Landgravine of Hesse-Kassel. 8) Queen Louisa of Denmark and Norway.

The grandson of King George II, whose throne title was George III, succeeded him upon the throne of Great Britain.

George III King of Great Britain
(1760 C.E.—1820 C.E.)

George William Frederick became known as George III. He was born into the House of Hanover on June 4,1738. As the grandson of a king, he was born in the Norfolk House in Saint James Square in London. He was the son of Frederick, the Prince of Wales. His mother was Princess Augusta of Saxe-Goyhu. He grew to become the third monarch of the House of Hanover to rule upon the British throne. He spoke English as his first language, unlike his two predecessors—George I and George II—who spoke the German language better.

He ascended to power at the age of 22 in midst of the Seven Years War when Great Britain defeated the kingdom of France and propelled Great Britain into the most powerful European nation in the Americas, Africa, and India. However, when King George III came to the throne on October 25,1760, there was still confusion among his advisors. His chief minister John Bute forced William Pitt's resignation. Yet, Pitt's ouster still did not solve the problem. Even Bute resigned later in 1763. That is the type of internal dissent King George faced within his own ranks, the Tory Party. He attempted to reach out to the opposition, the Whig Party, but those overtures were rejected as well. Inspite of all those difficulties George was able to survive the turbulence, and in 1770, he chose another Prime Minister named Lord North to handle the kingdom's affairs. Prime Minister Lord North inherited difficulties. The kingdom was in financial distress after the costly Seven Years War [1756—1763] which had greatly depleted the nation's treasury.

"And the toes were part of iron"
The birth of The United States of America
(1775 C.E.—1781 C.E.)

"YAH changes times and seasons, HE removes kings (**King George III King of Britain**)

and install kings **(President George Washington of the United States of America)**; *HE gives the wise their wisdom And knowledge to those who know,"* **Daniel 2:21.**

After 1763, the [**iron**] kingdom of Great Britain needed new sources of revenues. The king's cabinet proposed, and the British Parliament embraced, the idea of taxation of the colonies for defense and protection against France. King George III also supported the proposal. After all, in the eyes of the crown and parliament, the 13 North American colonies were prosperous and living tax-free. Across the Atlantic Ocean, the viewpoint was totally opposite. The idea of Great Britain taxing the colonies without American members in the British Parliament was an abomination to the leaders in the colonies. The disagreement sparked a revolt which grew into the American Revolution. In 1773, American colonists refused to allow British tea ships to dock in the Boston Harbor. The colonists boarded the ships and threw the tea overboard. Two years later, the war started when British troops and a local militia confronted each other at Lexington and Concord, Massachusetts on April 19, 1775. The Americans trapped the British army in Boston and apprehended the loyalists who supported the Crown. In 1776, the Americans declared the independence of the United States of America [**the little iron toe**]. General George Washington led the small U.S. Army. The new nation received assistance from Britain's arch-enemy France, the Dutch Republic, and Spain. The war, known as the American War of Independence, lasted for seven years until the American revolutionaries forced the British to surrender in October 1781. Tens of thousands died on both sides. Parliament blamed King George III and Prime Minister Lord North for losing the war against the Americans. Prime Minister North was forced to resign. This time, a man named William Pitt the Younger was selected for the position. King George lost control of Parliament and wasn't able to pursue the war. The war ended with both sides meeting to sign a peace agreement known as the Treaty of Paris. Britain [**the elder iron toe kingdom**] relinquished all claims to the North American mainland. [The **new iron toe kingdom**]

(Now back to King George III.)

Soon afterwards, there was an insurrection in Northern Ireland, which was the home of a Roman Catholic majority. Pitt had the nerves to propose political emancipation for the Roman Catholics as a solution to end the disturbance. King George III wholeheartedly rejected the proposal and forced Pitt the Younger to resign as a result. In the end, there was a union of the two countries Great Britain and Ireland on January 1, 1801. King George III was now King of Great Britain and King of Ireland.

On October 12, 1814, King George III was crowned King of Hanover although he was then insane and had never personally visited there. He had already inherited the title *"Duke"* and *"prince-elector"* of Brunswick Luneburg [city of Hanover] of the Holy Roman Empire decades earlier since 1760.

In the following decade between [**1810—1820**] King George III mental illness reoccurred. As a younger man, he had already experienced bouts of mental instability for short periods of time. However, these new bouts of bipolar disorder caused the British Parliament to pass a new law which declared his son **George IV** as co-regent. George III health continued to deteriorate. He became totally blind in one eye, deaf in one ear, and developed dementia. He didn't even realize he had been declared King of Hanover back in 1814. The following year in 1815, the army of Great Britain was able to crush Napoleonic France at the Battle of Waterloo without King George guidance.

During his lifetime, King George III married a woman named Charlotte of Mecklenburg Strelitz, a princess. Together they were parents of 15 children of the royal seed. She passed away in the year 1818. During the next two years, George's dementia worsened. He also became virtually blind with cataracts while experiencing pain in his joints. He became incapable of knowing and understanding anything. In his last days, he even lost the ability to stand or walk. King George III finally succumbed at 8:38 p.m. on January 29, 1820 at the age of 81. He died in the Windsor Berkshire Palace in the royal city London. He was buried in Saint George Chapel in Windsor Castle. Although King George III bowed before the Image of the Cross and adhered to the graven doctrine of Protestant Christianity, his imperial court was marred with scandals of adultery, secret love affairs, and other sexual perversions. His son George IV reigned in his stead.

George IV King of Great Britain
(1820 C.E.—1830 C.E.)

George Augustus Frederick, who became known as George IV, was born into the royal family known as the Hanover House on August 12, 1762. He was the firstborn of his father King George III and his mother Charlotte of Mecklenburg Strelitz. His birthplace was Saint James's Palace in the royal city of London. Growing up as the son of the king of Great Britain, young George IV was raised in a regal and imperial environment. He was a very intelligent young lad who learned to speak French, German, Italian, as well as mastering his native English language. As the son of the king, the prince inherited the titles Prince of Wales, the Duke of Cornwall, and the Earl of Chester on the day he was born. As an one-month-old, he was inducted into the Anglican Church when he was baptized by the Archbishop of Canterbury Thomas Secker on September 18, 1762.

When young George turned 18, his father King George III empowered him with his own bureaucracy and budget. The young teenage prince used his wealth, prestige, and popularity to host extravagant parties with plenty of wine, women, and songs. The young prince of Saint James's Palace was totally opposite of his father who was a quiet introverted man who shunned the wild lifestyle. These two opposite, yet distinct, personalities led to father-son clashes. Young George even plotted behind his father's back and married a Catholic woman inspite of the established law known as the Act of Settlement which forbade such sexual unions. When King George III discovered what his son had done, he immediately sought to annul their secret marriage.

Another area of continuous strife between the king and crown-prince of the kingdom of Great Britain was his loose spending habits. Although George IV was a wealthy crown-prince, he faced indebtedness several times due to his lavish lifestyle. He dressed in the best fashions of his era. He loved all sorts new leisures, styles, and tastes. He commissioned the architect John Nash to build the Royal Pavilion in Brighton. He also remodeled the famed Buckingham Palace in London. He also commissioned Sir Jeffrey Wyattville to remodel Windsor Castle. His charm and love of aristocratic culture earned him the nickname *"the first Gentlemen* **[Gentile man]** *of England,"* but his open disagreements with his father and mother, and his bad marriage was a stain on his personal image in the eyes of conservative aristocrats. He was a disappointment to his father King George III.

By 1811,the mental issues and awkward behavior of the elder King George III caused the British Parliament to declare him insane. His son George IV was chosen as the regent in his stead. While his father was incapacitated, George handled the day-to-day duties of the kingdom [**one of the kingdoms of iron toes**]. Technically speaking, George IV was in charge of the army when Great Britain faced France at the Battle of Waterloo in 1815, but George did not provide true leadership in times of crisis, nor did he act as a model for his people, before or after his father's death. Eventually his father passed on January 29,1820. George ascended to the throne at the age of 58 on the exact same date his father died. He chose the throne name George IV. His royal coronation was held the following summer on July 19,1821.

King George IV reigned for 10 years. Throughout his reign, he was under the influence of his *"favourites"* and ignored the will of the people. For that reason, the British taxpayers were angry with him, and also because of his wasteful government spending.

King George IV gained a tremendous amount of weight in his 40s to 50s. His heavy drinking and big meals had begun to take its toll on his health. He was afflicted with gout, coronary artery disease, dropsy, and bipolar issues. He began to spend entire days in bed and suffered breathing problems. He too suffered partial blindness due to cataracts. By the spring of the year 1830, King George was confined to his bedroom in blindness and pain. By June, the king was unable to lie down at night, so he was forced to sleep upright in a chair. On June 26, King George IV woke up around 3 a.m. to pass bowel movement. His bowels were mixed with blood. According to some reports, he clutched his stomach then muttered,"this is death". He died at 3:15. The cause of his death was determined to be from gastrointestinal bleeding and the rupture of a blood vessel. A large tumor the size of an orange was found attached to his bladder.

He was buried two weeks later on July 15th in Saint George's Chapel at the Windsor Castle. He served the graven doctrine of Protestant Christianity according to the tenets of the Nicene Creed and the dictates of King Henry VIII. He bowed before the Image of the Cross according to all the European Christian monarchs that preceded him. He did evil in **the eyes of YHWH ELOHIM Israel.** He did not keep HIS laws, commandments, judgements, and statutes according as HE commanded Israel and all mankind at Mt. Sinai. During his lifetime he was married to a woman named Caroline Of Brunswick. He separated from the princess in 1796, years before he ascended to the throne. They only had one child, Princess Charlotte of Wales.

So it came to pass that his uncle **William IV** reigned in the stead of his deceased nephew King George IV. **William IV** was the third son of his grandfather King George III. After William another ruler named Ernest Augustus succeeded him. After him George V succeeded him.

The lifespan of the kingdom of Great Britain has continued from the **Time Zone of the Legs of Iron** in the *Dark Ages, Middle Ages, Renaissance,* and *Age of Enlightenment* down into the **Time Zone of Toes of Iron** during the *Industrial Revolution,* and continued until the **Time Zone of The Toes of Iron and Miry Clay** during the reign of the United Nations in this *Modern Age* during 2019. The longevity of Great Britain has continued from the **[upper part of the iron leg—occupied by the ancient Roman Empire in the Third and Fourth centuries Common Era]** down to the **Twenty-first century C.E.** where it is one of the latter-day permanent members **[latter-day iron toes]** of the modern-day United Nations Security Council and G-20. The G-20 and the United Nations Security Council are the global governing bodies which represent the **[ten toes of iron mixed with miry clay]** according to the Revelations of **YHWH** spoken to Daniel.

The kingdom of the United States of America
(1607 C.E.—1900 C.E.)

"A small [Gentile] *toe hold in the New World"*

The birth of the great **[iron toe]** kingdom known as the United States was conceived in the womb of the 13 North American colonies which were connected to the 17th century umbilical cord of the Crown of England. The first breath taken was the English settlement known as James's Fort which came into existence on the banks of the James River on May 4, 1607. The venture was owned and operated by the Virginia Company of London. Except for the brief abandonment in the year 1610, Jamestown served as the capital of the English presence in North America for the following four decades, beginning in 1616 and continuing on to 1699. The settlement was named in honor of **King James VI**, who ruled Scotland from 1567 until his death in 1625. He also ruled the kingdoms of England and Ireland as **King James I** from 1603 until 1625. When the European settlers arrived, the black, brown, and ruddy indigenous native Americans were already established with their own civilizations across the North American mainland. Those indigenous tribal kingdoms had been there for thousands of years prior to Columbus arrival.

For the record, North America had been visited by the kingdoms **[iron toes]** of Spain and France centuries before England. England was the last among the three **[iron toes]**.

1492 Christopher Columbus Discovery of The Americas

It was the kingdom of Catholic Spain which backed Christopher Columbus, the Spanish navigator and explorer, on his first historical European voyage to the New World. Columbus began his career as a young seaman in the Portuguese marine, and by the time he reached the age of 40, he found favor in the eyes of both King Ferdinand II and Queen Isabella I who financed the mission to reach Asia by sailing westward over the open seas. Columbus set sail on his first voyage in August 1492 with three ships—the Santa Maria, the Nina, and the Pinta. He sighted land known today as the Bahamas on October 12, 1492. He then sailed towards the north coast of Hispaniola, then returned to Spain the following year in 1493. Columbus returned to Madrid to report his findings before the king and queen who issued a decree to conquer the lands in the New World. This time Columbus was viceroy of the West Indies for the second voyage which lasted from 1493 to 1496. This armada consisted of 17 ships which docked at modern Dominican Republic and founded La Isabella. During the second expedition, the Spanish conquerors began to spread and promote Catholic evangelization.

On the third Columbus voyage, which lasted from 1498 to 1500, the Spanish navigator reached South America and the Orinoco River delta after crossing the Atlantic. During this visit, reports of his poor administration and harsh treatment of his crew tarnished Columbus's reputation. He was replaced as viceroy and returned to Catholic Spain in chains. Once in Spain, Columbus recovered his position and was later commissioned to return to the New World a fourth time. This time he arrived off the coast of Honduras and Panama. Columbus, however, never recovered from his tarnished image. Columbus died a few years later in 1506.

Instead of Columbus, who was the first European navigator to set foot in the New World, receiving the honors of the new lands being named after him, the glory passed over to another Spanish navigator and explorer named Vespucci Amerigo. Born in Florence, Italy, Amerigo became the chief navigator for the Seville, Spain-based Commercial House of the West Indies. In the year 1491, one year before Columbus set sail, he worked for him outfitting the ships. He rose to the position of manager and accompanied Columbus on several voyages across the Atlantic. By 1499, he was captain of the Spanish expeditions to the New World which discovered the mouth of Amazon River. He later led a Portuguese expedition during 1501-1502.

After the death of Columbus in 1501, Vespucci Amerigo began preparing navigation charts to the newly discovered lands from data that was supplied by the ship captains. This is how the New World received his name *"The Americas—North America, Central America, and South America"*. The accounts of these voyages were first published in the 1507 report which defined the lands in the New World as the *Americas* in honor of the European Gentile navigator who had visited those lands. His career ended in fame and notoriety whereas Columbus career ended in disgrace. Born in Genoa, Italy, to a Spanish couple residing there, Columbus died at the age of 54 in Valladolid, Spain.

Tans-Atlantic Slave Holocaust in the North America

On **August 19,1619**, a mere twelve years after the establishment of the Jamestown, Virginia settlement, a Dutch warship carrying 17 African Hebrew men and 3 African Hebrew women captives arrived in the mouth of the Chesapeake Bay. These were the first Israelites in the British North American colonies. Those captives were part of a cargo of 300 who were kidnapped from Angola by Portuguese slave traders that was headed to Vera Cruz in New Spain, now known as Mexico. The Portuguese ship was attacked by Dutch and English ships and their human cargo stolen. The 20 African Hebrews brought into Jamestown were among the ones taken during the shipjacking. When the Dutch arrived in Chesapeake Bay, the provisions on the ship were exhausted. So the captain traded the 20 captives to local officials in exchange for food supplies. The Israelite captives from Angola were then used as bondmen and bondwomen to the Jamestown planters and colonial officials. By 1649, the captive population had grown to 300 in Jamestown. By the 1660s, chattel slavery began to take root. Records reveal that the African Hebrew captives were sold in slavery for all their lives. In 1661 the House of Burgesses made it official and passed a law that stated *"black slaves would retain their status throughout life"*. The following year in 1662 the House of Burgesses passed another law which stated a child's status was based on the status of the mother. If the African mother was slave, all children born to her were automatically bondmen and bondwomen. Additional slave codes were enacted between 1660 and 1710 which further hardened the yoke of institutional slavery in all the North American colonies. The new laws granted the colonies the authority to demand free and forced labor from all people of African descent. Slaves did not have the right to testify against British Americans in court, own property, or travel freely without the expressed consent of their masters. Captives no longer had the right to congregate in groups, enter into a contract, marry, or bear any arms. To make matters worse, the 1699 House of Burgesses passed a new slave code which exempted all masters from any type of charges if they killed their slaves while administering punishment. This new law was a green light for human-rights abuse such as beatings, torture, coercion, beheadings, family separations, and sexual abuse. In the 1700s, the system of chattel slavery expanded to the newly emerging southern states whose economies were totally dependent upon chattel slavery. All enslaved African Hebrews brought into the United States, and those already residing in the United States, were reduced to the status of a domesticated animals such as horses, cattle, or dogs. Many African Hebrew slaves gave first-hand reports that their Gentile masters cared more about horses and dogs than them as *"niggers"*. Another important development that occurred during this era was the fact that baptism into Christianity no longer protected Africans from a life of forced labor.

The other development which happened was the fast growth of the tobacco system in Maryland and Virginia in the 1700s. Demand for tobacco was extremely great throughout liberal Europe where all middle-class and aristocratic gentlemen smoked tobacco pipes, consumed plenty of rice, sugar, and desired regal clothing made from cotton. That phenomenon led to the explosive growth in cotton, sugar, and rice plantations in the South during the mid-1700s which lasted until the end of the American Civil War in 1865. These new agricultural industries needed large amounts of human labor to function. The ranks of the white indentured servants were too few. The native Americans knew their surroundings to well to be enslaved by the European foreigners who had invaded their homeland, so their enslavement was impossible. The only other option to fill this demand for free human labor was the Trans-Atlantic Slave Trade.

The European slave traders used extreme cruelty to impose this new world order upon the African Hebrew people, and upon other indigenous people in Africa and in the Americas. The settlers in the 13 North American colonies continued to purchase human cargo from West Africa until it was finally outlawed in 1808. It should be noted, however, that the black market in domestic slave trafficking continued to thrive for six more decades inside America. Before international slave trafficking was outlawed, all of the African Hebrew captives that arrived in America were transported across the Atlantic Ocean then sold at various American slave markets in Charleston, South Carolina, Richmond, Virginia, Baltimore, Maryland, Memphis, Tenn., Jackson and Natchez, Mississippi, Philadelphia, Pennsylvania, and eleshwhere. After the 1808 decree, U.S. traffickers still continued the business of selling slaves down the river from the east coast of Virginia into deep South Louisiana, Texas, Georgia, Alabama, and Mississippi.

Below is an eyewitness account of one of those voyages across the Atlantic Ocean which was known as the Middle Passage. The ancestors of today's African Americans arrived into the land now known as The United States of America under the conditions described below:

An Eyewitness Account of the Middle Passage Experience:

From West Africa to the New World

By far the worst part of the slave's journey was the "Middle Passage" from the African coast to the West Indies or American mainland. This voyage generally lasted between 40 to 60 days. The overcrowded conditions were indescribable. Most 18th century slave ships had two decks with the in-between deck space reserved for slaves. In a Newport Slaver, the average height between decks was 3 feet 10 inches. Men, women, and children were each placed in separate compartments on the slave deck, the men bound together with iron ankle fetters. The slaves were made to lie with their backs on the deck, the men secured to chains or iron rods attached to the deck, squeezed so tightly together that the space allowed to each person was about sixteen inches wide and 5 1/2 feet long. In the Liverpool ships, towards the end of the century, the average height between decks was five feet two inches. This permitted even worse crowding, for a shelf extending six to nine feet from the side of the ship was placed midway between the 2 decks, and both the lower deck and the shelf were packed tightly with slaves.

On the small sloops and schooners that lacked in-between decks, the slaves were placed on a temporary platform of rough boards laid over barrels in the hold. There are recorded instances where the space between such a deck and the one above was less than two feet. Most of the ships used after the trade had been outlawed were of this type, and during this later period of great risks and greater profits, slaves were stowed closer than ever, forced to lie on their sides, back to back, spoon-fashion. Where the space between the decks was two feet or more, the slaves were placed sitting, or crowded into each other's laps. Conditions like these were described by eyewitnesses. [Alexander Falconbridge, an 18th century [European Jewish] ship surgeon wrote:

"In favorable weather they are fed upon deck, but in bad weather the food is given to them below. Numberless quarrels take place among them during meals, more especially when they are put upon short allowance, when that frequently happens, if the passage from the coast of Guinea to the West Indies islands, proves of unusual length...Exercise being deemed necessary for the preservation of their health. They are sometimes obliged to dance when the weather will permit their coming on deck. If they go about it reluctantly or do not move with agility, they are flogged. The poor wretches are frequently compelled to sing also.

The hardships and inconvenience air is among the most intolerable. For the purpose of admitting this needful refreshment most of the ships in the slave trade are provided between the decks with 5 or 6 air-ports on each side of the ship, but whenever the sea is rough, and the rain heavy, it becomes necessary to shut these, and other conveyance by which the air is admitted. The fresh air being excluded, the Negroes rooms grew intolerably hot. The confined air, rendered obnoxious by the effluvia exhaled from the bodies, and by being repeatedly breathed, soon produces fevers and fluxes, which generally carries off great numbers of them... the floor of the rooms were covered with blood and mucus which had proceeded from them in consequence of the flux, i.e., dysentery, that it resembled a slaughterhouse.

It is not in the power of human imagination to picture... a situation more dreadful or disgusting. Numbers of the slaves having fainted, they were carried upon deck, where several of them died.... The surgeon, upon going between decks in the morning to examine the situation of the slaves, frequently finds several dead among the men, sometimes a dead and living Negro fastened by their irons together. When this is the case, they are brought upon deck, and being laid on the grating, the living Negro is disengaged, and the dead one thrown overboard."

The mortality from the blood flux or dysentery, smallpox, and other diseases was often considerable. There are cases on record where whole shiploads, including the entire crew, were blind from ophthalmia, first contacted by slaves in their filthy and crowded conditions. Very sick Negroes were sometimes thrown overboard, as were the underwriters would not pay for slaves who died on the ship. Although one recent authority estimates that on the average, slave losses in route were about 16 percent, there were many cases where one-half to two-thirds of the cargo perished. When the slave trade was nearing its peak, the number taken from Africa amounted to 104,000; of these, merchants in England and her North American colonies accounted for well over half the total. It has also been calculated that between 1680 and 1786 Great Britain alone sent to her North American and West Indian colonies a total of 2,110,000. One widely accepted enumeration placed the number of slaves who reached the New World in the three and a half centuries of the slave trade at nearly 15 million, about 900,000 arriving in the sixteenth century, 2,750,000 in the 17th century, 7 million in the 18th, and 4 million in the 19th. On the other hand, a very recent study argues that not more than 9 or 10 million Africans could have reached the New World.

Contrary to popular impression and despite (the social disruption) it caused, the Trans-Atlantic trade did not generally lead to (breakdown) in West African social and political organization. In Angola, it is true, the Portuguese slave trade led to the (disintegration) of the extensive Mani-Congo kingdom. Because its ruler opposed the traffic, the Portuguese turned to his provincial officials, who supplied slaves in exchange for firearms that enabled them to challenge their king's authority. In West Africa, from the Gold Coast to the Niger Delta and Old Calabar, the overseas slave traffic encouraged the development of a substantial mercantile group whose fortunes were based on the slave trade.

Where Europeans found (strong) despotic (kingdoms), and (rulers) willing to supply their wants, the trade thrived from the start. Where these did not exist in West Africa, the slave traffic called them into being, or, as in the Niger Delta, stimulated the establishment of oligarchic and monarchical city-states. With the profits derived from the trade, and more particularly with the firearms obtained from Europeans in exchange for slaves, old rulers strengthened their power, and new autocratic kingdoms such as (Dahomey) and (Ashanti) arose. The role of firearms was crucial. Just as the Moroccans had quickly destroyed the Songhai empire in the 16th century because the latter lack of guns, so the strategically placed societies of the rain forest and southern Sudan were able to overpower their poorly armed neighbors.

It is difficult to ascertain with any degree of precision how profitable the slave trade was. Complete records are lacking; profits and losses fluctuated from one voyage to another, depending on the prices both in Africa and America and the numbers surviving the Trans-Atlantic crossing. Recent research suggests that profits may not have been as great as they were once believed, but the voyages with monetary returns ranging from one-third to one-half or more on the original investment were frequent.

For the record, all of these horrific experiences came to pass because ancient Israel disobeyed the commandments of their MIGHTY ONE: **YHWH ELOHIM Israel.** They had done evil in **eyes of YHWH** and did not walk in ways which HE commanded them at Mount Sinai. According to **Deuteronomy 28:64-68**, the prophet Moses predicted, *"YHWH shall scatter you among all people, from he one end of the earth even unto the other: and there you shall serve other gods* [**false religions of Christianity**], *which neither you nor your fathers have known, even wood* [**Rugged Cross**] *and stone* [**the religion of Islam**]. *Among these nations shall you find no ease* [**persecution and oppression**], *neither shall the sole of your foot have rest* [**chattel slavery**]; *but YHWH shall give you there a trembling heart, and failing of eyes* [**hopelessness**], *and sorrow of mind* [**mental depression**]: *And your life shall hang in doubt before you; and you shall fear day and night, and shalt have none assurance of your life* [**no legal protection in the land of captivity**]: *In morning you shall say, Would ELOHIM* [**allow this to happen if**] *it were even! and at even you shalt said, Would ELOHIM* [**allow this** to happen if] *it were morning! for the fear of thine heart wherewith you shall fear; and for the sight of thine eyes which you shall see. And YHWH shall bring you* **[under the yoke of the trans-Atlantic Slave Trade]** *into Egypt* **[America]** *again with ships* **[in the galleys of slave ships]**, *by the way whereof I spoke unto you. You shalt see it no more again: and there* **[in America]** *you shall be sold unto your enemies for bondmen and bondwomen, and no man shall redeem you."*

"And YHWH shall scatter **[African Hebrew diaspora]** *you among all nations, and you shall be left few in number* **[a minority]** *among the heathen* **[unrighteous kingdoms]**, *where YHWH shall lead you.* **Deuteronomy 4:27.**

"Make a chain: for the land **[black [Israelite] community]** *is full of bloody crimes, and the city is full of violence. Wherefore I* **[YHWH]** *will bring the worst of the heathen; and they possess their houses; I will also make the pomp of the strong to cease: and their holy places shall be defiled. Destruction cometh: and they shall seek peace, and there shall be none."* **Ezekiel 7: 23-25.**

"Then the king of Babylon slew the sons of Zedekiah in Riblah before his eyes: also the king of Babylon slew all the nobles of Yehudah. Moreover he put out Zedekiah's eyes, and bound him with chains, to carry him to Babylon." **Jeremiah 39:6-7.**

"Wherefore I poured MY fury upon them for the blood that they had shed upon the land, and for idols wherewith they had polluted it: And I **[YHWH]** *scattered them among the heathen, and they were dispersed through the countries: according to their way and according to their doings I judged them. And they entered unto the heathen, whither they went, they profaned MY holy name, when they said to them, These are the people of YAH, and are gone forth out of HIS land."* **Ezekiel 36:18-20.**

When you look back at the **openng page of Chapter 1** you will see where I made statements about the correlations between so-called African American history and ancient Afro-Asiatic Hebrew history. I will now like to reiterate those statements again because Israelite history has repeated itself here in the Americas. This is what I said earlier: "One of the greatest lessons to be learned from studying this book is that prophecy has dual aspects, meaning that prophecies apply both to the past, present, and future, and they would be repeated over and over again. What happened to Daniel in ancient times was destined to happen again in succeeding generations. <u>The offsprings of these Israelites would also be taken into captivity to foreign lands just like their ancestors Daniel, Hananiah, Mishael, and Azariah.</u> Another example of this book's duality is found in the fact that Daniel and his brethren were bound in chains, shackled, and carried into exile to the ancient kingdom of Babylonia. After the holy people's arrival in Babylon, Daniel was castrated, placed on an auction block, then sold as a palace slave where his name was changed to Belteshazzar. The Hebrew culture that Daniel and all Judah once embraced no longer existed. They were forced to eat the king's meat and drink his wine. Those developments occurred over and over again wherever Israel and Judah went into slavery, starting at the ancient **Head of Gold** and continuing down to the modern **Ten Toes of Iron and Miry Clay.**

Black people in America should be able to relate to these horrific experiences because this is exactly what happened to them in these modern times. In fact, when you study history, you will see that <u>black people's origins here in this country began under the same circumstances as Daniel and his people's in ancient Babylon</u>, thus unmistakably proving the link between the ancient people of Judah and the so-called black people here in America today. This duplication of historical events was not, and is not, a coincidence."

The 13 Colonies Grow into the United States of America

By the late-1750s, tensions between the European great powers, Britain and France flared into the first global war known as the Seven Years War. Multitudes of battles took place in Europe, West Africa, India, the Philippines, and North America, costing at least a million deaths worldwide. In North America both powers, Britain and France, locked horns over the lucrative fur trade and land in the Ohio River Valley in the emerging North American colonies. The North American theater of this worldwide conflict became known as the French and Indian War, raging from 1754 to 1763. On one side of the battlelines stood the mighty French armies with their Indian allies and on the other side were the British, along with their colonial American and Indian allies. For the first four years, the French seemed to control the momentum of the conflict, but in 1758 Great Britain counteracted with a vigorous response. In the end, Britain prevailed and forced the kingdom of France out of North America all together. Britain also gained the territory of Canada from France. London also received Florida from Spain. In the end, Spain lost all of its North American possessions, marking their complete exit from North America. Four decades later in the 1803 after two years of negotiations, the kingdom of the United States also gained all of the North American territories west of the Mississippi after acquiring the land from France for 68 million francs.

When the dust cleared, there was no more French nor Spanish presence in North America. For the first time since the founding of the Jamestown settlement in 1607, only North American colonists controlled the new land. The only foreign presence, at that time, was the kingdom of Great Britain, the colonial overseer and victor in the French and Indian War. The new reality allowed the young kingdom to expand westward. After the French and Indian War, massive European immigration began to transform once virgin native Indian lands into an extension of Europe. America was seen as the new promised land for Europeans who came in record numbers fleeing authoritative kings, queens, and other despots while searching for new economic opportunities.

After the French and Indian War, the fraternal bond between Britain and its 13 colonies began to rapidly weaken. The war had cost the kingdom of Britain millions in pounds. Its treasury was in deficit, and the leaders were looking for additional revenues to finance the empire. Looking across the Atlantic Ocean, members of the British Parliament saw the colonies as a lucrative tax base. After all, the Crown defended the colonies against the French and Spanish ambitions and protected them from Indian assaults. In their eyes, the colonies were a part of the Crown, and the empire needed to be compensated for those noble deeds. Without consulting the leaders in the 13 colonies, the British Parliament began to pass several measures which authorized them to tax and regulate the colonial economy. The following year, the British Parliament passed the Sugar Act, allowing the Crown to raise revenues. In 1765, the British Parliament passed the Stamp Act which gave them the legal authority to tax all printed material, such as playing cards, newspapers, and deeds. Those arbitrary moves by the British Parliament sowed the seeds of discontent among the American colonists. The uproar caused the lawmakers in London to rescind the law. However, Parliament was still determined to exercise greater dominion over America.

For nearly 150 years, the Americans had governed themselves without foreign interference in areas such as trade and taxation. The new attempts to tax the colonies without representation were seen as a form of slavery by those freedom-loving Gentile men. In 1774, years before he was elected president, George Washington once said *"the crisis [has] arrived when we must assert our rights, or submit to every imposition, that can be heaped upon us, till custom and use shall make us lame and abject, as the blacks we rule over with such arbitrary sway"*. (In other words, I'll be damned if we allow Great Britain to treat us [**White Americans**] the way we have treated these powerless Negroes [enslavement].) For the record, 8 of the first 12 freedom-hating, wealthy slaveholding U.S. Presidents reigned for a total period of 149 years. Chattel slavery in the U.S. lasted for 246 years.

Determined not to be treated like Negroes, a large segment of American colonists were fired up. In the minds of the colonial leaders, there was no need for British protection of their new homeland. The French and Spanish were gone. All the 13 colonies needed was for Great Britain, the third Gentile power which occupied the little kingdom, to leave them alone. But, Britain viewed the little horn of 13 colonies as a portion of their empirical possession.

By the 1770s, anti-British radicalism was increasing rapidly. The colony of Massachusetts emerged as the heartbeat for the American War of Independence.

The American War of Independence

March 5, 1770: Anti-British sentiments were high. The people of the 13 North American colonies were upset at Great Britain's continuing attempt to restrict their trade and regulate their commerce. In Boston, Massachusetts, a crowd a workers who had been affected by British policies gathered that evening. The dockworkers were armed with clubs and sticks, and among them was an African Hebrew man named Crispus Attucks, a former slave, who became the most vocal. These men were seen as low-class seaman in the eyes of the British regiment which stood nearby monitoring activities. The large crowd began to approach the British troops. Captain Thomas Preston and the nine soldiers were outnumbered. One eyewitness said, Attucks, who stood 6 feet 2 inches and stout, struck one of the soldiers with a long cordwood stick. With their backs against the wall, Preston commanded his soldiers to fire upon the crowd. Crispus Attucks, who was 47, was first in the crowd to be shot. Four men died in the confrontation. Their coffins were taken to the famed Faneuil Hall where they remained for three days on public display. Attucks, and the three others, were proclaimed *"martyrs"* in the struggle for American freedom. Their deaths were called a massacre which became known as the 1770 Boston Massacre. Ironically, one of the founding fathers, John Adams, a lawyer, successfully defended the British troops in court. His cousin, on the other hand, Samuel Adams, disagreed and proclaimed the four dead men as *Patriots*. This event was a watershed moment that began to radicalize the North Americans against Great Britain. Great Britain was viewed as the great oppressor.

May 1773: The British Parliament passed another arbitrary law affecting the 13 North American colonies. This time it was the Tea Act. This law gave the British East India Company exclusive rights of control for all tea sold in the colonies. The British East India Company was deeply indebted and in need of revenues to redeem itself from bankruptcy. The lucrative market in North America was seen as the solution to their problems. The Americans rejected the idea of taxation on their tea. Instead they purchased their cheaper unregulated tea from the Dutch. The British Parliament rescinded the first law and instead chose to sell their pre-taxed tea through American distributors. Americans understood they were still paying taxes for their favorite drink.

December 16, 1773: 500 American protestors, some dressed as native Indians, boarded British ships in the Boston harbor and destroyed all the tea onboard. The Sons of Liberty Samuel Adams, Paul Revere, William Molineux, and others led the rebellion. This act of defiance marked the beginning of open rebellion against British rule, which in turn, gave birth to the American War of Independence.

March 1774: British Parliament passed the Boston Port Act which closed the Boston Harbour until the colonies paid the full price for the damaged tea.

June 2, 1774: Great Britain demanded that the colonies provide vacant buildings to house British soldiers.

July 18, 1774: Fairfax County, Virginia adopted a resolution that rejected British sovereignty over the American colonies. This was the county where George Washington lived.

October 20, 1774: Delegates from 12 colonies formed the Continental Congress and agreed to support a resolution to boycott British goods.

February 9, 1775: Great Britain declared the colony of Massachusetts to be a rebel state.

March 23, 1775: The Virginia Convention gathered in Richmond, Virginia. Patrick Henry delivered an impassioned speech where he vehemently declared, *"Give me liberty or give me death!"*

April 18, 1775: British troops were on the offensive. Paul Revere, who was a member of the Sons of Liberty and a Massachusetts watchmen, rode on horseback to warn the neighboring communities that British troops were headed their way. The following day on April 19, British troops and the American resistance battled at Concord and Lexington. Hundreds of combatants on both sides were slain.

June 15, 1775: The Continental Congress appointed George Washington as commander-in-chief of the new Continental Army. Washington initially banned blacks **[African Hebrews]** from fighting in the U.S. Continental Army. It wasn't until December 30, 1775 that he changed his mind and allowed black Israelites to enlist to fight for the liberation of white America.

April 6, 1776: The new Continental Congress adopted a resolution declaring all American ports closed to Great Britain ships. Ships from other European nations were allowed to dock in American ports.

May 1776: King of France Louis XVI agreed to aid the Americans against Great Britain. The secret package included one million dollars in weapons and ammunition.

June 1776: A British fleet of 30 warships, 300 supply ships, and 40,000 British soldiers invaded New York.

July 4, 1776: The Second Continental Congress adopted a law known as the Declaration of Independence which had been drafted by Thomas Jefferson and approved by the entire Congress in full session.

December 26, 1776: George Washington launched a surprise attack against British troops after losing three battles. This attack on British troops led to capture of 1,000 prisoners, and marked a turning point for American rebels. The victory provided inspiration to an army which had suffered nothing but losses on battlefield.

January 3, 1777: Washington scored another victory against a small regiment of British troops at the Battle of Princeton.

June 1777: The French Army joined Americans as an ally against Great Britain. French officer Marquis de Lafayette volunteered to assist Continental Army on battlefield. By late July, he had been commissioned to serve as a major general.

June 14, 1777: The U.S. Continental Congress approved their first national flag consisting of 13 stars and 13 stripes.

October 17, 1777: The U.S. Continental Army defeated British General Burgoyne forces at the Battle of Saratoga. This was America's greatest victory to date in the ongoing two-year war.

February 6, 1778: The kingdom of France became the first European nation to recognize the United States as a sovereign nation. Both nations signed trade agreements and established a formal military alliance.

February 23, 1778: A military officer from the Prussian Army named Baron von Steuben came to Valley Forge to assist George Washington with training the rag-tag Continental Army.

July 10, 1778: France formally entered the American War of Independence against Great Britain after British ships attack a French ship.

December 1778: The British Army invaded Savannah, Georgia and created new theater in southern United States.

October 19, 1781: The U.S. Continental Army surrounded British forces led by Lord Cornwallis. Unable to receive supplies by land or sea, the British were forced to surrender at Yorktown. This was the last major battle of the American Revolution.

April 19, 1782: The European nation of Holland became the 2nd European nation to formally recognize the United States of America.

February 1783: Britain and the United States met in Paris to sign the agreement known as the Treaty of Paris, formally ending the war between the two Gentile kingdoms. The kingdoms of Spain, Denmark, Russia, and Sweden recognized the United States of America as a new Gentile power **[one of the iron toe kingdoms]**.

November 25, 1783: The last foreign British regiment left New York to return to London with their heads hung in defeat.

December 23, 1783: General George Washington entered Congress to voluntarily hand in his resignation as commander-in-chief.

June 21,1788: The United States Constitution, written mainly by Thomas Jefferson and James Madison, was officially ratified after New Hamshire became the ninth state to sign the document.

March 4,1789: The Continental Congress agreed to begin operating as a new government under the ratified Constitution.

April 30,1789: George Washington sworn-in as the first President of the newly created United States of America.

"YAH changes times and seasons, HE removes kings(**kingdoms of France, Spain, and Britain**) *and install kings*(**all the Presidents of the newly created United States of America**); *HE gives the wise their wisdom And knowledge to those who know."* **Daniel 2:21.**

President George Washington
(1789 C.E.—1797 C.E.)

George Washington was born February 22,1732 C.E. in the city-settlement of Popes Creek which was located in the colony of Virginia. His father was Augustine Washington and his mother Mary Ball Washington. At the age of 24, he fought valiantly in the French and Indian War. At 43, he was chosen to lead the Continental Army against Great Britain in the American War of Independence. After several losses, he turned the tide in his favor after a 1776 surprise attack on British forces. He soon gained support from France, Spain, and Prussia. He eventually led the Patriot Army to victory against Britain. The war ended in 1783 after the last Britain troops departed in November. Washington ascended to the throne of the Presidency on April 30, 1789. He reigned for 8 years. He died at the age 67 from a throat and tongue disease, along with low blood, on December 14, 1799.

So it came to pass that he did evil in the **eyes of YHWH ELOHIM Israel** by serving the graven doctrine of Jesus taught by the Nicene Creed and Protestant Christianity. He also bowed before the image of the Cross. Also, he was a great oppressor of the African Hebrew people, even the lost sheep of Israel. He enslaved them and highly favored the system of chattel slavery which reduced them to the status of a beast of the field. He was succeeded by John Adams.

John Adams
(1797 C.E.—1801 C.E.)

John Adams was born October 30, 1735 in the city of Braintree in the province of Massachusetts Bay which was part of British America at that time. He grew to become one of founding fathers of the newly created United States of America. He served as the first vice-president under George Washington before he ascended to the throne as the second President of the United States in 1797. He was an accomplished lawyer who at times defended the British in court prior to the American Revolution. He also reigned 8 years. He died July 4, 1826 in Quincy, Massachusetts. He did evil in the **eyes of YHWH ELOHIM Israel** by not keeping HIS laws, commandments, judgements, or statutes. Thomas Jefferson succeeded him as the next President of the United States.

Thomas Jefferson
(1801 C.E.—1809 C.E.)

Thomas Jefferson was born April 13, 1743 in the city of Shadwell in the Colony of Virginia which was a part of British America at that time. His parents lineage was obscure. He grew to become a powerful voice in the campaign against British tyranny. He was the principal author of the Declaration of Independence along with John Adams. He was a strong advocate for democracy. He spoke out against British imperialism and advocated forming a new nation. He reigned 8 years and did evil in the **eyes of YHWH ELOHIM** Israel by not following HIS laws, commandments, judgements, and statutes. He too was a slaveholder who was known to have intimate relationships with teenage African Hebrew slave girls, some as young as 14. After him, James Madison was elected to the presidency of the United States.

James Madison
(1809 C.E.—1817 C.E.)

James Madison was born March 16, 1751 in Port Conway in the colony of Virginia which was ruled by Great Britain at that time. He was the son of James Madison Sr. and Neily Conway Madison. Raised by wealthy plantation owning parents, he inherited thousands of acres, slaves, and became a duke of the city of Piedmont. While growing up, he was home-schooled, tutored, and later attended the College of New Jersey. Later in life, he became known as the *"Father of the Constitution"* after playing an important role in drafting the document. He drafted the Constitution and the Bill of Rights, known as the preamble. He served in several government roles of the new kingdom, including vice-presidency, Secretary of State, the U.S. House of Representatives, and the Congress of the Confederation from Virginia. So it came to pass that he died at the age of 85 on June 28, 1836 after reigning 8 years. He did evil in the **eyes of YHWH ELOHIM Israel** by serving the graven doctrine of Jesus Christ according to Protestant Christianity. He also bowed before the image of the Cross. He greatly enriched himself as slaveholding planter. He was also an exploiter and oppressor of the African Hebrew people.

James Monroe
(1817 C.E.—1825 C.E)

James Madison was born April 28, 1758 in the city of Monroe Hall in the colony of Virginia which was governed by Great Britain at that time. Born in Westmoreland County, Virginia, he grew to become a wealthy planter. His father was Spence Monroe and his mother was Elizabeth Jones. He was also one of the original Founding Fathers. He also inherited a plantation with chattel slaves before joining the fight for freedom against British oppression. He was wounded in the shoulder during the war. He studied law under Thomas Jefferson for three years from 1780 to 1783. He also served as one of the Virginian delegates in the convening of the Continental Congress.

So it came to pass that President Monroe died from heart failure at the age of 73 in New York City. He had served for 8 years as the chief executive of the new kingdom, the United States of America before his death. He also did evil in **the eyes of YHWH ELOHIM Israel** by oppressing HIS people the lost sheep of Israel. He also served *"other gods"*, even idols of wood and stone, known as Jesus Christ and the Christian Cross. John Quncicy Adams was his successor.

John Qunicy Adams
(1825 C.E.—1829 C.E.)

John Quncicy Adams was born July 11,1767 in the Braintree province of Massachusetts Bay in British America. His father was the second president John Adams. His mother was Abigail Smith. Young John spent most of his childhood in Europe while his father served as a statesman. He grew to become a lawyer and he later established a law firm in Boston. President Washington appointed him to serve as U.S. ambassador to the Netherlands in 1794. He also served as a diplomat under President James Madison where he helped to end the War of 1812. He also negotiated for the state of Florida to become a U.S. possession.

So it came to pass that President Adams died at the age of 80 in Washington, D.C. after reigning for four years. He did evil in **the eyes of YHWH ELOHIM** Israel by hardening his mind against Torah and his people, the lost sheep of Israel. Andrew Jackson became his successor,

President Andrew Jackson
(1829 C.E.—1837 C.E.)

President Martin Van Buren
(1837 C.E.—1841 C.E.)

President William Henry Harrison
(1841 C.E.)

President Tyler
(1841 C.E.—1845 C.E.)

President James K. Polk
(1845 C.E.—1849 C.E.)

President Zachary Taylor
(1849 C.E.—1850 C.E.)

President Millard Fillmore
(1850 C.E.—1853 C.E.)

President Franklin Pierce
(1853 C.E.—1857 C.E.)

President James Buchanan
(1857 C.E.—1861 C.E.)

Abraham Lincoln
(1861 C.E.—1865 C.E.)

Abraham Lincoln was born February 12,1809 C.E. on the Sinking Spring Farm, near Hodgenville, Kentucky. He was born in the westward lands of Kentucky within the expanding United States of America. He was the son of Thomas Lincoln and Nancy Hanks. His ancestors originated from Hingham, Norfolk in England before his great grandfather Samuel Lincoln migrated to Hingham, Massachusetts around 1638. As the tiny 13 colonies expanded, Samuel Lincoln's grandson and great grandsons began to move westward where land was abundant. Initially, his grandfather moved to Virginia before moving onward to Jefferson County, Kentucky. While there his grandfather was slain by Indians while Lincoln and his father Thomas witnessed the tragedy. The native Indians viewed "white men" as intruders. After this, Lincoln's father was left to fend for himself and the family. To make ends meet, his father worked as a farmer, a cabinetmaker, carpenter, and maintained a farm.

However, land disputes between wealthy landowners and Thomas Lincoln forced the family to leave the area. By the year 1815, another land dispute forced the Lincoln's to move again. Young Abraham was a 6-year-old when all of these legal problems occurred. The family was forced to move to Indiana this time. As the young lad grew, the family's legal and financial problems continued. These experiences motivated Abraham to become educated. He was self-taught and grew to become a very intelligent man. Abraham eventually moved to Illinois where he studied law and became a lawyer. He then entered the arena of politics where he became the leader of the Whig Party in Illinois. He was elected to the Illinois House of Representatives. He campaigned on modernization of the American economy and criticizing the Mexican-American War. He only served one term in Congress before he returned to Illinois to practice law once again.

At the age of 44 and in the year 1854, Lincoln re-entered politics by becoming the new leader of the new Republican Party. In Illinois, the Republicans held a statewide majority. Four years later in 1858, Lincoln campaigned to become the United States senator from Illinois. Lincoln's opponent was Democrat Stephen A. Douglass. During the heated and highly contested race, Lincoln, for the first time, publicly spoke out against the expansion of slavery into Western states. Lincoln did not want the slaveholding states to gain more power in Congress and statehouses in new territories. It was a pure power move, and, it had nothing to do with Lincoln's love for the **lost sheep of the House of Israel** who were then known by the fictitious byword *"American Negroes"* at that time.

Lincoln lost the 1858 race, but he gained nationwide notoriety. His newfound popularity propelled him to the position of 1860 Republican Party nominee. In the 1860 national election Lincoln did not receive any support from the slaveholding Southern states. In fact, Lincoln's victory provoked 7 Southern slaveholding to secede from the United States of America. The Southern nation was called the Confederate States of America. Those events happened before Lincoln moved into the White House. After the South issued a declaration of succession, they demanded Union troops leave Fort Sumter in Charleston, South Carolina. South Carolina was a member of the new Southern nation. The Union troops refused to leave Fort Sumter. The Confederate army attacked Fort Sumter on April 11,1861. The following day, Union army surrendered the base. That was the beginning of the American Civil War.

On August 6, 1861, Congress passed the First Confiscation Act which stated: *Any property that belonged to Confederates and used in the war effort could be seized by federal forces. Any slaves used by their masters to benefit the Confederacy—and only those slaves—would be freed from the service of their plantation owners.*

Union General John C. Fremont exceeded the limit of the new First Confiscation Act. He freed all slaves in Missouri. President Lincoln quickly rescinded the general's directive. Lincoln ordered General Fremont to only free slaves actively used to aid the Confederate war effort. Lincoln did not want Missouri, Kentucky, Delaware, or Maryland to join the succession from the Union. In fact, Union commanders showed more concern for the interest of the Confederate slave owners than the people afflicted during chattel bondage. In May 1861, Union General George B. McClellan reassured Virginia slave owners *"we will, with an* **[iron]** *hand, crush any attempt at insurrection on their part".*

YHWH's DIVINE Purpose of The American Civil War

For the record, neither side, the North nor the South, had any interest in improving the conditions of **the lost sheep of the House of Israel**, *Negroes*, during the Civil War. It was an act of **YHWH** to deliver HIS people from chattel slavery which caused the evil spirit of mistrust, warfare, and self-hatred to occur among the American Gentiles that caused the American Civil War. *"I form light, and create darkness: I make peace, and create evil: I* **YHWH** *do all these things,"* in **Isaiah 45:5**.

Again, it was YAH who used the American Civil War to end the separation of African Hebrew families, brutality, economic and sexual exploitation, and oppression of HIS people which they faced at hands of the American people. YAH wanted HIS people to learn how to read and write so that could study Torah and Hebrew Prophets then return back to their ancient Hebrew culture, and not accept the slave master's religion in the land of their enemies. Then YAH would remember HIS everlasting covenant with Abraham, Isaac, and Jacob, and return to become their SAVIOUR and REDEEMER once again. (**Read I Kings 8:44-53, Deuteronomy 4: 27-31, and Ezekiel 36:17-38 to name a few verses.**) Negroes have not obeyed the Voice of YHWH, even until this day.

Lincoln made it clear from the outset of the conflict that the purpose of the American Civil War was not to end slavery or destroy the institutions that their economies depended upon. Negro leaders were outraged at Lincoln. They said: *"To fight against slaveholders without fighting against slavery, is but a half-hearted business and paralyzes the hands engaged in it. Fire must not be met with water. War for the destruction of liberty must be met with war for the destruction of slavery".* Regardless, Lincoln did not bow before Negro criticism. He held fast to micro-managing the war. Instead of allowing the Northern generals to destroy the Southern economy through abolishing slavery, Lincoln kept respecting the Southern aristocracy until 1863.

Another example: On May 9,1862, Union General David Hunter ordered an end of slavery in South Carolina, Georgia, and Florida. Lincoln quickly rescinded that order and reprimanded General Hunter. Meanwhile, thousands of African Hebrew slaves along the South Carolina and Georgia coast threw off their shackles and welcomed Union forces. Plantation owners, for the first time in American history, were forced to flee deep into the interior of the South.

The **Spirit of YAH** stirred up Lincoln, and eventually, **YAH** caused him to issue the Emancipation of Proclamation in 1863. That symbolic announcement weakened the South's agricultural based economy because southern slaves stopped working. Lincoln realized that without chattel slaves there would be no labor force, which in turn, meant no money to execute the war against the North. With the naval blockade preventing fresh overseas supplies and the loss of the African Hebrew labor force, the Southern economy laid in ruins.

In the end, Lincoln also allowed those escaped slaves to join the war against their former slave masters. For the first time in American history, Negroes were allowed to kill their masters under the umbrella of the Union army. On January 31,1865 YAH also caused President Lincoln to pressure Congress into passing the 13th Amendment which formally outlawed chattel slavery for the African Hebrew people. On April 9,1865, Confederate General Robert E. Lee surrendered to the Union army General Ulysses Grant at Appomatox, officially ending the American Civil War.

On April 14, 1865, five days after the war ended, President Lincoln and his wife Mary Todd attended Ford's Theater in the nation's capital for an evening performance. The presidential couple relaxed in his upstairs booth. A man named John Wilkes Booth, a Southern war supporter, entered from behind Lincoln's booth and shot him in the head. He died the following day, April 15 across the street in the Petersen House. So it came to pass that President Abraham Lincoln died at the age of 56 after reigning four years upon the throne of George Washington. He did evil in eyes of **YHWH ELOHIM Israel** by not keeping HIS laws, commandments, judgements, and statutes. Before he left office, Lincoln summoned the Negro leaders to the White House where he attempted to rid the kingdom of the lost sheep of Israel. Lincoln told the leaders that he believed the only true long-term solution for the race problem and slavery was compensation for the emancipated slaves followed up with the establishment of African Hebrew colonization outside the United States. Under Lincoln's plan, slave owners would be paid for releasing them to Africa, the Caribbeans, or Latin America. Negro leaders were totally outraged and refused Lincoln's proposal. President Andrew Johnson became his successor.

President Andrew Johnson
(1865 C.E.—1869 C.E,)

President Rutherford B. Hayes
(1877 C.E.—1881 C.E.)

President James A. Garfield
(1881)
President Chester A. Arthur
(1881 C.E.—1885 C.E.)

President Grover Cleveland
(1885 C.E.—1899 C.E.)

President Benjamin Harrison
(1889 C.E.—1893 C.E.)

President Grover Cleveland
(1893 C.E.—1897 C.E.)

President William McKinley
(1897 C.E.—1901 C.E.)

President Theodore Roosevelt
(1901 C.E.—1909 C.E.)

Theodore Roosevelt was born October 27, 1858 in New York City, New York. He was the son of Theodore Roosevelt Sr. and Martha Stewart Bulloch. He was home-schooled as a youth. As a young man, he entered Harvard College. Over the years, and especially after writing of book, *The Naval War of 1812,* he became recognized as an accomplished author. He established himself as a mighty man of valor, known as the Rough Riders, during the Spanish-Mexican War. He was the 26th President of the United States of America. He also served as the 25th Vice-President of the United States of America. His resume' also included service as the 33rd Governor of New York. He was a powerful voice of American greatness at the turn of 20th century. He was responsible for leading the United States into modern-age.

So it came to pass that he died at the age of 60 in Oyster Bay, New York on January 9,1919. He had done evil in the **eyes of YHWH ELOHIM** Israel by not keeping HIS laws, commandments, statutes, and judgements.

The lifespan of the kingdom of United States is still continuing today from the **Time Zone of the Legs of Iron** when Jamestown, Virginia was founded in May 1607 during the *Age of Enlightenment* on down into the **Time Zone of Toes of Iron** during the *Industrial Revolution.* It has continued until today's **Time Zone of The Toes of Iron and Miry Clay** in this *Modern Age* of 2019 and beyond. The longevity of the United States of America has continued down into the **Twenty-first century C.E.** where it has become one of the latter-day permanent members **[latter-day iron toes]** of the United Nations Security Council. The United Nations Security Council is the global governing body which represent the **[ten toes of iron mixed with miry clay]** according to the Revelations of **YHWH** spoken to Daniel.

America is definitely one of those iron toes which King Nebuchadnezzar foresaw in his dream over 2,600 years ago.

We have now completed the prophetic **Western Iron Leg** which began with the division of the ancient Rome until **Global Iron Toes** of the modern United States of America. The year 1900 C.E. marked the beginning of the **Time Zone of Iron Toes,** but before we continued further, I must go back and travel down the **Eastern Iron Leg** first. Once we complete **the Eastern Iron Leg,** we will then proceed into the final Time Zone of the **toes of the image.**

The world has changed so much technologically speaking since the beginning of human existence with **The Head of Gold.** We have traveled for thousands of years down the prophetic timeline. Let's look at some of the Inventions that have changed the World as we know it since *the Renaissance, Age of Enlightenment, Industrial Age, and Modern Age.* Every nation under the sun is using these inventions, even until this very day. After this brief recognition of Inventions, I will start profiling the kingdoms of the **eastern iron leg.**

"As The World Turns from Ancient To Modern"
Inventions That Changed The World

Inventions During Renaissance

The Parachute: Invented by Leonardo de Vinci
Thermometer: Invented by Galileo
Barometer: Invented by Evangelista Torricelli
Thermoscope: Invented by Daniel Gabriel Fahrenheit
Italic typeface: Invented by Aldus Manutius and Francesco Griffo
Violin: Invented by Andrea Amati
Robotic Knight: Invented by Leonardo de Vinci
Anemometer: Invented by Leonardo de Vinci and later English scientist Robert Hooke
Condom: Invented by Gabriele Falloppio
Scuba Diving Gear: Invented by Leonardo de Vinci
Clocks: Invented by Christian Huygens
Eye glasses: Invented by Giordano da Pisa

Flush Toilets: Invented by Joseph Bramah, John Harington, (first invented Ismail al-Jazari)
Gun Powder: Gunpowder came to Europe via the Chinese and Arabs.
Microscope Lenses: Invented by Zacharias Janssen
Telescope Lenses: Invented by Hans Lippershey
Printing Press: Invented by Johannes Gutenberg
Submarines: Invented by Cornelis Drebbel
Matches: Invented by John Walker
Wallpaper: Invented by Christophe-Philippe Oberkampf
Telescope: Invented by Galileo Galilel

Inventions During Age of Enlightenment

1712: The Newcomen Steam Engine:
1733: The Flying Shuttle: Invented by John Kay.
1764: The Flying Shuttle: Invented by James Hargeaves.
1790: The Sewing Machine: Thomas Saint
1792: Modern Semaphore Telegraph: by Claude Chappe
1793: The Modern Cotton Gin: by Eli Whitney
1795: The Hydraulic Press: by Joseph Bramah
1796: The Lithography: by Alois Senefelder
Plywood: by Samuel Bentham

Inventions During The Industrial Revolution

1800: Electric Battery: Invented by Alessandro Volta
1806: The Coffee Pot: by Benjamin Thompson.
1807: Steamboat Service on the Hudson River: Invented by Robert Fulton.
1821: Difference Engine: Invented by Charles Babbage.
1829: Graham Cracker: Invented by Slyvester Graham.
1830: Rail service between Liverpool and London, England.
1836: The Telegraph: Invented by
1836: The Pistol Revolver: Invented by Samuel Colt
1840: Trans-Atlantic Steamship Service: by Samuel Cunard.
1843: Processed Rubber: by Charles Goodyear/ The Rotary Printing Press: by Richard Hoe
   Computer Program: Invented by Ada Lovelace/ Fax Machine: by Alexander Bain.
1846: Sewing Machine: Invented by Elais Howe.
1847: Candy Bar: Invented by Joseph Fry.
1852: Paper Bag: Invented by Francis Wolle/ Elevator: Invented by Elisha Graves Otis.
1853: Potato Chips: Invented by George Crum.
1856: Henry Bessemer develops the Bessemer Converter: Iron Ore processed into Steel.
1858: Brick Making Mahine: Invented by John Williamson Crary/Can Opener: by Ezra
   Warner
1859: First commercial oil well drilled in Pennsylvania.
1860: Vacuum Cleaner: Invented by Daniel Hess/ Yale Lock: Invented by Linus Yale.
1866: The Siemens Brothers improve steelmaking by developing the open hearth furnace.
   Dynamite: Invented by Alfred Nobel
1867: The Typewriter: Invented by Christopher Sholes/ Baby Formula: Invented by Henri
   Nestle
1869: The Motorcycle: Invented by Sylvester Roper/ Air Brakes: by George Westinghouse./
   Air Brake: Invented by George Westinghouse
1870: Chewing Gum: Invented by Thomas Adams
1872: Lubrication System: Invented by Elijah McCoy[**an African Hebrew**].
1873: Blue Jeans: Invented by Jacob Davis and Levi Strauss/Barbed Wire: by Joseph Glidden

1875: Steel Industry: Invented by Andrew Carneige
1876: The Telephone: Patent and Invention given to Alexander Graham Bell
1876: The Refrigerator: Invented by Carl Linde/Carpet Sweeper: Invented by Melville Bissell
1876: Internal Combustion Engine: Invented by Nicholaus Otto
1877: Toilet Paper: Invented by Seth Wheeler
1879: The Electric Light Bulb: Invented by Thomas Edison/ Ivory Soap: Invented by Harley Procter. Phonograph: Invented by Thomas Edison
1882: Christmas Lights Decoration: by Edward Johnson.
1884: Roll of Photographic Film: Invented by George Eastman
1888: Kodak Camera: Invented by George Eastman
1886: Coca-Cola Soft Drink: by Dr. John S. Pemberton./ Avon Cosmetics: by David H. McConnell/ A Transformer: Invented by William Stanley
1895: Wireless Telegraph: Invented by Guglielmo Marconi/ Schwin Bicycle: Invented by Ignaz Schwinn
1893: Modern Architecture: by Frank Lloyd Wright
1889: Electromagnetic Theory of Light: by Heinrich Hertz/Automobile: Invented by Karl Benz/ Matches: Invented by Joshua Pusey.
1890: Punched Card machine: Invented by Herman Hollerith
1891: Swiss Army knife: Invented by Carl Elsene/Traveler's Cheques: Invented by Marcellus F. Berry
1893: Cracker Jack Popcorn: Invented by F.W.Rueckheim.
1895: Wireless Telegraph: Invented by Guglielmo Marconi
1896: Peanut Agricultural Science: Invented by George Washington Carver [**An African Hebrew eunuch**[
1897: Aspirin Pills: Invented by Felix Hoffmann/Jell-O: Invented by Pearle B. Wait.

After taking a close look at all of the inventions listed above which the [**iron kingdoms— Europeans**] have injected into **legs** and **toes** of human civilization, you should now be able to understand how, and why, the world looks the way it does. Those inventions transformed the world. Today, we see all types and models of automobiles instead of different species of horses. We drive trucks instead of wagons and buggies. We marvel at tall skycrappers such as the Sears Towers, the Empire State Building, and others instead of one-room log cabins. We use telephones and tell time with our own personal clocks, ride bicycles, motorcycles, listen to phonographs, all because these inventions listed above. Even the snack foods, such as candy bars, ice cream, popsickles, Graham crackers, Coco-Colas, and potato chips were among the inventions that newly came into existence. Those new food items that were listed above have changed the course of the human diet in a manner never seen before.

The ability to move faster across the open seas with ships powered by stream engines instead of sails provided the opportunity to expand trade, culture, and ideas. These inventions brought a new type of freedom to mankind which they had never experienced before. This period in human history is definitely noted for its advancements in movement, discoveries, and new human intelligence. In other words,these new inventions have given the Uncircumcised Minded Man the ability to walk to and forth, up and down throughout the whole earth with **Iron Leg Power**.

The Spiritual Meaning Behind The Iron Legs Of Image

Legs represents the movement, the overspreading, of the wicked man's dominion throughout all the ends of the earth. His legs would lead him to conquer and discover new lands from one end of the earth unto the other. The kingdoms of [**iron**], which grew out of the ancient Roman Empire, would use their legs to travel and transport their man-made anti-YHWH way of life wherever their legs would take him and her. The **[legs of iron]**, through the power of YHWH, would be allowed to conquer Asia, Africa, the Middle East, and the Americas during the Time Zone allotted them.

The former Germanic barbarians, the Franks[France], the Visigoths, Ostrogoths[Germany], Angles, Saxons[England, Wales, Scotland, Great Britain, the United States of America], Bungundians[Luxembourg],Vandals,Huns[Austria-Hungary],Slavs,and others rose to prominence after the collapse of the Roman Empire, *the Dark Ages, the Middle Ages, the Age of Enlightenment, the Industrial Revolution,* and *the Modern Age*. These various European kingdoms **[sons of Japheth]** have colonized Asia, Africa, the Middle East, and the Americas. In fact, these sons and daughters of Japheth are fulfilling the ancient prophecy of Noah in Bereshith[**Genesis**] **9:27:**

Fulfillment of Noah's Prophecy

"May ELOHIM enlarge Japheth, and let him dwell in the tents of Shem". Noah clearly prophesied that the descendants of Japheth[**the Indo-European Gentiles**] would one day rise up to replace the descendants of Shem[**the ancient Afro-Asiatic Shemitic people**] as rulers of the earth. Beginning with the Portuguese, Dutch, and Spain conquests of foreign lands in the mid-15th century until today, those **[iron legs]** have been moving to and forth, and up and down throughout the entire earth. Today, the Japhethic conquest of the earth is known as European colonialism and imperialism.

At this time we have officially completed our journey down **The Time Zone of the Western Iron Leg**. Now, let's get ready to switch over and travel down the **Time Zone of the Eastern Iron Leg**.

The Iron Age—(Its *Long* Legs of Iron)
Divided Eastern Roman Empire and Eastern World—PART FOUR "the legs"
"its legs were of iron—But the fourth kingdom will be strong as iron; just as iron crushes and shatters everything—and as iron that smashes—so will it crush and smash all these."
Daniel 2: 33, 40

"YAH changes times and seasons. HE removes kings (kingdoms) and install kings(kingdoms); HE gives the wise their wisdom and knowledge to those who know" **Daniel 2: 21**

The History of the Divided Eastern World

The Byzantine Empire (491—1453 C.E.) The Islamic Era (613—700 C.E.) Islamic Expansionism (700—1400 C.E.) The Khazar Empire (650 C.E.—969 C.E.) The Ottoman Empire (1453—1914 C.E.) China (1294—1900 C.E.) India (1283—1900 C.E.) West African Kingdoms (1375—2019 C.E.) Brazil (1400—1900 C.E.) Russia (1613—1917 C.E.)

The Byzantine Empire
(491 C.E.—1453 C.E.)
[The Eastern World]

Sometimes according to **YHWH's** Prophetic Destiny individuals are born and singled out, and then again, there are other times when the Creator has caused empires to be born and singled out. All of those developments are the Hand of **THE STONE CUT OUT WITHOUT HANDS—YAH**.

The Byzantine Empire was created out of the territory in southwest and southern Europe, and West Asia when it initially began as the city of Byzantium. It sprouted from the ancient Greek colony founded on the European side of Bosporus. On May 11, 330 C.E. Emperor Constantine the Great conquered the city and established it as the seat of power for the Eastern Roman

Empire, and renamed it Constantinople.

Fifty years after the death of Emperor Constantine, Emperor Theodosius I chose the royal city as the capital of the eastern portion of the empire. In those days the massive empire stretched from Britain in the west to Mesopotamia in the east. Towards the latter-part of his reign, he appointed his two sons to manage both **legs** of the great **[iron kingdom]**. His son Arcadius was chosen to rule over the Eastern leg from the years 395 to 408 while his other son Honorius reigned over the Western leg from 395 to 423. The barbarian invasion of Rome in 476 marked the collapse of Western Roman Empire, but the eastern half continued and became renown as the Byzantine Empire with Constantinople as its imperial capital.

In the process of time, the Eastern Roman Empire differed from the West in several ways: it was more urban, advanced, commercial, and in the end, it became the heir of the Hellenistic era for more than a thousand years until Europe emerged from the Dark and Middle Ages. Meanwhile, in the Eastern Roman Empire known as **[Byzantine]**, the following emperors reigned upon the throne.

Anastassius I
(491 C.E.—518 C.E.)

Justin I
(518 C.E.—527 C.E.)

Justin I was born February 2,450 in the city of Bederiana, near Scupi. He grew to become the commander in the Imperial Guard. He was the uncle of Justinian I who succeeded him. He ascended to the throne at the age of 68 and reigned for nine years. In the year 525, Emperor Justin repealed an old law which prohibited members of the aristocracy to marry members of the lower class. The new law allowed his nephew Justinian to marry a woman of a lower rank named Theodora, a former actress. Emperor Justin died on August 1, 527 at the age of 77. He was the founder of the Justinian dynasty.

Justinian I "the Great"
(527 C.E.—565 C.E.)

Justinian was born May 11, 482 in the city of Tauesium in the province of Dardania, exactly 152 years after Constantine the Great founded the city, May 11, 330, on the same date. His birth name was Petrus Sabbatius. He was the son of a man named Sabbnatius and his mother's name was Viglantia. Over the years, he moved through the ranks of the army to eventually become the Prefect of the Imperial Guard under his uncle Justin I. By April 1, 527, his elderly uncle Justin health began to deteriorate, he turned to his 45-year-old nephew Justinian to serve as his co-emperor. Four months later, on August 1, Emperor Justin died and Justinian ascended to the throne as his successor, receiving his official throne title Imperator Flavius Petrus Sabbatius Justinianus Augustus during his coronation on the same date. His wife's name was Empress Theodora.

One of the main aims of Justinian was a desire to restore the glory of the ancient Roman Empire in the western portion of the once unified **[iron kingdom]**. He ordered his generals, Belisarius, Narses, and others, to conquer the lands the Ostrogoths ruled. That included the lands of Dalmatia, Sicily, Italy, and Rome. After 50 years of Ostrogoth rulership over Rome, Justinian reclaimed the "Imperial City" as the city of the Romans. In fact, he became known as the "Last Roman," meaning the last non-barbarian to rule until after the Dark Ages in the Middle Ages. His general Belisarius also defeated the Vandals in North Africa. General Liberius reclaimed the southern portion of the province of Hispania. Those victories gave the Eastern Roman Empire control over the western Mediterranean Sea for the first time in hundreds of years, reviving a partial restoration of Rome's former greatness. The kingdom's treasury also increased by over 1 million solidi [gold coins] per year.

Those victories, along with his magnificent building program which included the Church of Hagia Sophia in the year 537 and other icons, earned him the title "Justinian the Great". The gigantic cathedral with a massive dome was the world's largest building, and it was considered an engineering marvel during its time. Meanwhile in the West, the Franks, Saxons, Angles, and others were in the throes of the undeveloped Dark Ages.

Another great feat Justinian is known for is his uniform rewriting of Roman law which continues to be the basis of civil war in many modern states in the 21 century. His reign also marked the blossoming of Byzantine culture. He is also known for bringing Roman culture to the east of the Black Sea for the first time. There he conquered the primitive Tzani barbarian people.

During the year 535, the Middle East and Europe experienced a series of unusual weather events, beginning with unexplained toxic air to the sun not providing much heat, along with a famine. In the 542, a devastating Bubonic Plague spread throughout the empire causing thousands upon thousands of deaths, even causing Emperor Justinian to become ill. Nine years later in July 551, a strong earthquake, with an epicenter in the city of Beirut, Lebanon, rocked the region, triggering a tsunami and killing a combined 30,000 people. Tremors were felt from Antioch, Syria to Alexandria, Egypt.

So it came to pass that Emperor Justinian I the Great died on the night of November 14, 565 at the age of 83 after reigning thirty-eight years in the city of Constantinople. He did evil in eyes of **YHWH ELOHIM Israel** by not keeping HIS laws, commandments, judgements, and statutes. During his lifetime he served the graven doctrine of Chalcedonian Christianity and bowed before the image of the Cross like unto the all Roman Christian emperors that preceded him. Justinian did not have any sons to inherit his position. His nephew Justin II succeeded him as the next emperor ruling the Byzantine Empire. Although the empire continued, the empire began to weaken in the process of time.

Justin II
(565 C.E.—578 C.E.)

Tiberius II Constantine
(578 C.E.—582 C.E.)
Maurice Tiberius
(582 C.E.—602 C.E.)

Phocas
(602 C.E.—610 C.E.)

Heraclius
(610 C.E.—641 C.E.)

Heraclonas Constantine
(641 C.E.)

Heraclonas
(641 C.E.)

Constans II
(641 C.E.—668 C.E.)

Constantine IV
(668 C.E.—685 C.E.)

Justinian II Rhinotmetus
(685 C.E.—695 C.E.)

Leontius
(695 C.E.—698 C.E.)

Tiberius III
(698 C.E.—705 C.E.)

Justinian II Rhinotmetus
(705 C.E.—711 C.E.)

Philippicus
(711 C.E.—713 C.E.)

Anastasius II
(713 C.E.—715 C.E.)

Theodosius III
(715 C.E.—717 C.E.)

Leo III
(717 C.E.—741 C.E.)

Constantine V Copronymus
(741 C.E.—775 C.E.)

Leo IV
(775 C.E.—780 C.E.)

Constantine VI
(780 C.E.—797 C.E.)

Empress Irene
(797 C.E.—802 C.E.)

Nicephorus I
(802 C.E.—811 C.E.)

Stauracius
(811 C.E.)

Michael I Rhangabe
(811 C.E.—813 C.E.)

Leo V
(813 C.E.—820 C.E.)

Michael II Balbus
(820 C.E.—829 C.E.)

Theophilus
(829 C.E.—842 C.E.)

Michael III
(842 C.E.—867 C.E.)

Basil I
(867 C.E.—886 C.E.)

Leo VI
(886 C.E.—912 C.E.)

Alexander Constantine VII
(912 C.E.—913 C.E.)

Porphyrogenitus
(913 C.E.—959 C.E.)

Romanus I Lecapenus
(920 C.E.—944 C.E.)

Romanus II
(959 C.E.—963 C.E.)

Nicephorus II Phocas
(963 C.E.—969 C.E.)

John I Tzimisces
(969 C.E.—976 C.E.)

Basil II Bulgaroctonus
(976 C.E.—1025 C.E.)

Constantine VIII
((1025 C.E.—1028 C.E.)

Romanus III Argyrus
(1028 C.E.—1034 C.E.)

Michael IV
(1034 C.E.—1041 C.E.)

Michael V Calaphates
(1041 C.E.—1042 C.E.)

Empress Zoe
(1042 C.E.—1056 C.E.)

Constantine IX Monomachus
(1042 C.E.—1055 C.E.)

As you can see, the Eastern Roman Empire continued from the ancient times until the 11th century when the term Byzantine distinctively described the character of the medieval empire.

The East and the West no longer shared a common Roman heritage. A controversy over which Christian saints would be venerated as standing images caused a great rift between the Eastern Orthodox Church and the Western Roman Catholic Church. This split in body of Christianity became known as **the Great Schism of 1054**.

The Great East-West Christian Schism of 1054 C.E.

The Eastern and Western branches of Christianity had long been separated and estranged over doctrinal issues such as the Trinity, the beatification of Christian saints, the limitation of the authority of the bishop of Rome, whether to eat leavened or unleavened bread during Eucharist, and other jurisdictional disputes. The two religious capitals of Christianity, Rome and Constantinople, had drifted apart of the centuries. There were language differences where the Christians of Constantinople spoke Greek whereas the Christians of the West spoke Latin, Italian, French, and other Germanic dialects. Eventually, the Eastern branch **[leg]** became known as the Greek Orthodox Church while the Western leg was regarded as the Roman Catholic Church. Both graven doctrines upheld the unnatural policy of celibacy for their high priests. Those man-made principles are in direct violation of the laws of **YHWH** found in

Leviticus 21:7 which states: *"They* **[The Levities]***shall not take a wife that is a whore, or profane, neither shall take a woman put away from her husband: for he is holy unto his ELOHIM."* Furthermore **Leviticus 21: 13** explained, *"And he* **[the priest]** *shall take a wife in her virginity."* Therefore it safe to say that Christianity is a man-made religion and not true YAH-based Spirituality fond in the Hebrew scriptures.

The arguments between these two Christian branches reached a head in 1053 when the Roman Catholic Church demanded that the Greek Orthodox churches in southern Italy shutdown or change over to their doctrine. In response, the chief bishop of the Eastern Orthodox Church Michael I Cerularius, who was based in Constantinople, ordered all Catholic churches in the royal city to be shuttered. The next year in 1064, Pope Leo IX dispatched a papal representative to Constantinople for talks. The Church of Rome sent a message refusing to recognize Michael I Cerularius as the Ecumenical Patriarch of the Eastern Orthodox Church. Pope Leo IX also demanded that he be recognized as head all of Christian churches worldwide. The main mission of the papal delegation was to seek military support from Byzantine Emperor Constantine IX Monomachus in the church's war against a group of rulers known as the Normans who had invaded southern Italy. The pope also asked the bishop in Constantintnople to command his local bishop in southern Italy to stop attacking the Church of Rome's use of unleavened bread during Eucharist and other Latin practices. Cerularius refused the demand of the papal delegation. At that point the leader of papal delegation, Cardinal Humbert of Silva Candida immediately excommunicated chief bishop Michael I Cerularius. Cerularius then returned the favor and excommunicated Humbert and all the delegates with him. Back in Rome, Pope Leo IX died while **the Greek-Latin talks** were in progress in distant Constantinople. His death allowed the breach to expand. In the end, the two branches of Christianity split along the lines of doctrine, liturgy, politics, language, and geography. Those differences were never healed, and in the end each leg worshipped their own god. The god of the **Western iron leg** was the Roman Catholic Church and the god of the **Eastern leg iron** was the Greek Orthodox Church. The split continued for another 130 years until 1182 when there was a massacre of Latins. The West responded with an attack and destruction of the city of Thessalonica in 1185 in the east. Both branches continued to exist in the territories throughout the Roman Empire, Each church appointed its own representative for every position, conforming the Schism between the two branches of the graven doctrine of Jesus Christ as agreed upon during the Council of Nicaea centuries earlier. Both branches of Christian thoughts and beliefs bowed before the image of the Cross.

Theodora
(1055 C.E.—56 C.E.)

Michael VI Stratiolicus
(1056 C.E.—1057 C.E.)

Isaac I Comnenus
(1057 C.E.—1059 C.E.)

Constantine X Ducas
(1059 C.E.—1067 C.E.)

Romanus IV Diogenes
(1067 C.E.—1071 C.E.)

Michael VII Ducas
(1071 C.E.—1078 C.E.)

Nicephorus III Botaniates
(1078 C.E.—1081 C.E.)

Alexius I Comnenus
(1081 C.E.—1118 C.E.)

John II Comnenus
(1118 C.E.—1143 C.E.)

Byzantine Emperors

Manuel I Comnenus
(1143 C.E.—1180 C.E.)

Alexius II Comnenus
(1180 C.E.—1183 C.E.)

The 9 Christian Crusades

1. (1095 C.E.—1099 C.E.)

2. (1144 C.E.—1155 C.E.)

3. (1187 C.E.—1192 C.E.)

4. (1202 C.E.—1204 C.E.)
   (1212 C.E.)

5. (1217 C.E.—1221 C.E.)

6. (1228 C.E.—1229 C.E.)

7. (1248 C.E.—1254 C.E.)

8. (1270 C.E.)

9. (1271 C.E.—1272 C.E.)

The First Christian Crusade came during the era of Middle Age Europe, between the years 1095 to 1099, when Pope Urban II dispatched a military campaign to help the Byzantine Empire against the Seljuq Turks who had conquered most of territory in Asia Minor and captured the Holy Land. After receiving a request for help from Byzantine Emperor Alexius I Comnenus, the Pontiff convened the Council of Clermont in southern France during November 18-28, 1095, where he called for a military expedition to rescue Constantinople and recapture **Jerusalem** from the Islamic armies and establish the kingdom of God on earth. The Pope's army was mainly comprised of Frank nobles and their armies[**iron kingdoms**].

The battles of the First Crusade took place in Asia Minor, modern Turkey, and in the Levant, which is modern Syria, Israel, and Jordan. The Christian Crusaders were victorious, recapturing the famed city of Nicaea, and returning most of western Asia Minor back to Byzantine control. The Christian armies also recaptured Jerusalem and placed the Levant under Christian authority. There were major casualties on both sides. During the spring and summer of 1096, the Crusade armies massacred thousands of European Jewish converts as they head towards the battlefront.

The Second Christian Crusade came between the years 1144 to 1155 as Middle Age Europe continued to advance. Pope Eugene III issued an edict to save the Eastern Roman Empire from Islamic conquerors after the city of Edessa fell to the Islamic army of Zengi [**emerging miry clay kingdom**] in the 1146. In response, Holy Roman Emperor Conrad III of Germany [**iron leg & toe**], King Louis VII of France [another **iron leg & toe**], and other European noblemen [other **iron leg & toes**] answered his request by joining forces to launch a Christian war against Islam. The battles took place in Egypt, Asia Minor, the Levant, and the Iberian Peninsula. The German and French armies traveled different routes to the battlefront in Asia Minor. Both armies experienced several small confrontations along the way, and both armies faced defeat by the Seljug Turks. Both armies lost ninety percent of their soldiers before they reached **Jerusalem**. Both armies were defeated in the 1148 in the Battle of Damascus. In the end, the Second Crusade was a disaster for Catholic Europe and a great victory for the Islamic kingdoms. Both European kings accused each other of betrayal and collaboration with the enemy.

The Third Christian Crusade came thirty years after the 2nd Crusade ended. It occurred between the years 1187 to 1192. It was a continuation of the series of wars between Christians and Muslims. The Third Crusade was led by King Richard the Lionheart of England, Phillip II of France, and Holy Roman Emperor Frederick I. The war was an effort to reconquer the Holy Land after **Jerusalem** had been overrun and captured by the Islamic Sultan Saladin in 1187. The bloody battles took place in Asia Minor and Ceole-Syria. This series of warfare ended with a victory for both sides on September 2, 1192 when

324

the King of England and Sultan Saladin signed the Treaty of Jaffa which allowed Jerusalem to remain under Islamic control, but a provision in the pact allowed unarmed Christian access to the holy city. The king of England started his journey back to his homeland one month later on October 9, ending the third crusade.

The Fourth Crusade came in the year 1202 ten years after the 3rd Crusade ended. Pope Innocent III called for the military campaign to recapture **Jerusalem**, which was still under Muslim control. The goal was for Western forces to attack Jerusalem after ferrying over to Egypt first. Instead, what happened was mutinous. In April 1204, Western European Crusaders launched a backstabbing war against the capital of Eastern Roman Christianity when they destroyed parts of Constantinople, its palaces, churches, monuments, and everything else in their sight. That treacherous act perpetually solidified the Schism between the two branches of Christendom until this day. Major battles of the Fourth Crusade took place in the Balkans which had been invaded by Muslims. The Crusaders were led by the Fulk of Neuil and consisted of French knights who vowed loyalty to the Papacy. Numerous Eastern and Latin Christians were slain during the siege. After that debacle, the war against the Muslims temporarily ceased. Eight years later in the 1212 there was another effort known as the Children's Crusade because the leader was a 15-year-old French peasant boy named Stephen of Cloyes.

The Fifth Crusade came between the years 1217 to 1221 as Western Europe began to experience a Renaissance. The Pontiff of Rome Innocent III called for the war effort which was led by King Andrew II of Hungary, Duke Leopoid VI of Austria, and John Brienne. The series of battles were another Western European effort to recapture **Jerusalem** from the powerful Islamic state in Egypt [**miry clay kingdom**]. The people of Europe were itching for another Christian crusade, especially after the disastrous results of the previous campaigns. Pope Innocent III offered rewards for those who would sign-up. However, Pope Innocent III died before his plans could be enacted. He was succeeded by Pope Honorius. In 1217, the Crusaders from Germany and Holland joined ranks to retake Jerusalem. In 1218, the Crusaders attacked the Egyptian settlement-city of Damietta. It lasted for several months and included the lost of several thousand lives before they eventually captured the city. Once the Crusaders razed the city, they discovered a motherload of gold, silver, jewels, and other treasures. That victory inspired the Christians to launch an assault on Cairo. As the Christians marched towards Cairo, the Egyptian people fled in fear as the massive European army approached. The Crusaders pursued them until the floodwaters of the Nile trapped them. With little food supplies and nowhere to go, the Crusaders began to retreat. The Egyptians then launched an attack causing many Christian casualties. The Crusaders called for a ceasefire and agreed to return Damietta. Shortly afterwards, the Crusaders were captured and the Fifth Crusade came to an end.

The Sixth Crusade came seven years later in the year 1228 and it lasted for only one year. The Christian military campaign was led by the Holy Roman Emperor Frederick II. This too was another Christian attempt to regain control of **Jerusalem** as a result of the previous 5th Crusade failure. This campaign did not consist of much fighting. It was a victorious diplomatic campaign by Frederick. Through political maneuvering he regained partial control of Jerusalem along with others surrounding areas such as Nazareth, Sidon, Jaffa, and Bethlehem in the Holy Land for 15 years. The small conflicts which took place occurred in Cyprus.

The Seventh Christian Crusade came 20 years after the previous crusade in the midst of the blossoming Renaissance in Western Europe, between the years of 1248 to 1254. It was led by King Louis IX of France. The French troops were defeated by the Egyptian army which was led by Sultan Turanshah and his allies. King Louis IX was captured in midst of the conflict. The French paid a ransom of 800,000 gold coins for his safe return. The major battles took place in Al-Manourah, Egypt. The king of France almost loss of his entire army in this campaign.

The Eighth Crusade came sixteen years later in 1270. It too was led by King Louis IX of France. This time the king of France launched an attack against the city of Tunis, which is modern Tunisia on the northern coast of Africa. The crusade failed because King Louis IX died as soon as he reached the shores of Tunisia. A plague also festered among his army, causing massive deaths and diseases. The Eighth Crusade was called off and the invaders headed back to Europe.

The Ninth Crusade came one year later, beginning in 1271 and continuing until the following year in 1272. This was the last major Middle Age confrontation between European Christian armies and Muslim forces over control of **Jerusalem** and the Middle East. The military campaign was led by Prince Edward, who later became known as King Edward I of England. He was supported by the King Charles I of France. The yearlong battles took place throughout the Near East, resulting in minor Christian victories and ending with the Treaty of Caesarea. The Crusaders were able to lift the sieges of Tripoli and Lebanon where Islamic armies threatened to overtake Christian armies. The Islamic Mamluk fleet was destroyed, forcing the Mamluks to agree to a ten-year truce between the **Eastern leg** and **Western leg**.

Continued List of Byzantine Emperors & Empress

Andronicus I Comnenus
(1183 C.E.—1185 C.E.)

Isaac II Angelus
(1185 C.E.—1195 C.E.)

Alexius III Angelus
(1195 C.E.—1203 C.E.)

Isaac II Angelus & Alexius IV Angelus (restored)
(1203 C.E.—1204 C.E.)

Alexius V Ducas Murtzuphius
(1204 C.E.)

Latin Emperors
Baldwin I
(1204 C.E.—1206 C.E.)

Henry
(1206 C.E.—1216 C.E.)

Peter
(1217 C.E.)

Empress Yolande
(1217 C.E.—1219 C.E.)

Robert
(1221 C.E.—1228 C.E.)

Balswin II
(1228 C.E.—1261 C.E.)

John
(1231 C.E.—1237 C.E.)

Nicaean Emperors

Constantine XI
(1204 C.E.—1205 C.E.)

Theodore I Lascaris
(1205 C.E.—1222 C.E.)

John III Ducas Vatatzes
(1222 C.E.—1254 C.E.)

Theodore II Lascaris
(1254 C.E.—1258 C.E.)

John IV Lascaris
(1256 C.E.—1261 C.E.)

Greek Emperors -restored.
Michael VIII Palaeologus
1261 C.E.—1282 C.E.)

Andronious II Palaecologus
(1282 C.E.—1328

Andronicus III Palaeologus
(1328 C.E.—1341 C.E.)

John V Palaeologus
(1341 C.E.—1346 C.E.)

John VI Cantacuzenus
(1347 C.E.—1354 C.E.)

Andronicus IV Palaeologus
(1376 C.E.—1379 C.E.)

John V Palaeologus restored to power
(1379 C.E.—1390 C.E.)

John VII Palaeologus
(1390 C.E.)

John V Palaeologus restored to power
(1390 C.E.—1391 C.E.

Manuel II Palaeologus
(1391 C.E.—1425 C.E.)

John VIII Palaeologus
(1421 C.E.—1448 C.E.)

Constantine XI Palaeologus
(1449 C.E.—1453 C.E.)

The Fall of Constantinople—The Eastern Roman Empire

Constantine XI Palaeologus was born February 8,1405 in the city of Constantinople. He was the son of Emperor Manuel II Palaeologus and Empress Helena Dragas. He ascended to the Byzantine throne on January 6,1449 as the successor of John VIII Palaeologus. He reigned for 4 years in the royal city of Constantinople. His reign came to end in 1453 when the Ottoman Turks besieged the royal city. Emperor Constantine was hard pressed to defend the sprawling capital. He attempted to stockpile food by strengthening the ancient Theodosian Wall, hoping to withstand the Islamic onslaught.

With the economy in poor shape, Emperor Constantine did not have enough resources to mutter a large army to match the size of the Ottomans. Neither could they defend every

the torch of Roman civilization is gone. There is no more throne."
So it came to pass that the Byzantine Empire died after existing for 1,400 years. All of the rulers did evil in the **eyes of YHWH ELOHIM Israel** and did not keep HIS laws, commandments, judgements, and statutes according as HE commanded Israel and all mankind. **The Islamic Era** and **Expansionism** succeeded the **Byzantines.**

The Islamic Era & Islamic Expansionism
(613 C.E.—700 C.E.)
[Eastern World]

"YAH changes times and seasons. HE removes kings (kingdoms) and install kings(kingdoms); HE gives the wise their wisdom and knowledge to those who know" **Daniel 2: 21**

The Islamic Era was born in the womb of Arabia during the 7th century in the lifetime of an Arab man named **Muhummad ibn Abdullah** who founded the world's third monotheistic religion. **Muhummad** was born in the year 570 in the city of Mecca in the Hejaz region. His father's name was Abdullah ibn Abd al-Muttalib and mother's name was Aminah bint Wahib. His father, a member of the Makhzum clan, was a merchant man and clay worker. He grew up as the only child who became an orphan at the age of 6. Before his conversion, pre-Islamic Arabia was a mixture of *"other gods"* including Christianity, Judaism, Iranian religions, and various Arabian beliefs. Different gods and goddesses were worshipped each day at the local shrine known as the Ka'ba Stone in Mecca. During this time Mecca was considered a holy city before Muhummad's conversion to the new religion of Islam. Muhummad was a part of the Hanif sect, which practiced a blend of Christianity and Hebrewism. At 35, he also helped to rebuild the Ka'ba Stone in the year 605, eight years before the birth of Islam.

According to Islamic tradition, he received his first revelation of the Quran in the cave on February 9, 610 when he saw the angel Gabriel in a vision while he was on Mount Hira. He told followers he was grasped by the throat by a luminous being who commanded him to respect the words of God[Allah]. After that experience, Muhummad began to preach publicly at the age of 43 during the year 613 in his hometown of Mecca and neighboring Medina. Earlier on, he was ignored and many of his distractors viewed him as crazy. His messages included calls for the destruction of the other 365 gods worshipped in Mecca on a daily basis. In the mind of Muhummad, only one of those gods, Allah, was viewed as the patron deity of the new faith. He also urged the wealthy traders to give to the poor and less fortunate. He gained disciples, but at the same time, he acquired enemies who plotted to eliminate him, forcing him to flee the city Mecca and Medina. Many Arabs depended upon idol-worshipping for their livelihood, so Muhummad's message did not impress them, Muhummad was on the run. This flight became known as the "Hegira", *meaning* emigration, which marked the beginning of the Islamic era. He then invited his close family members to the new religion. Afterwards, he made a declaration at Mount Safa encouraging all Arabs to convert to Islam, a religion whose new tenets included belief in one Arab god Allah and walking in the footsteps of Muhummad, the messenger of Islamic tradition.

After escaping Mecca, he fled to the city of Yathrib, a prosperous city which welcomed him. There, he found a strong following who viewed him as prophet, religious, political, and judicial leader who could settle disputes. Yathrib was then renamed Madinat-at Nabi, *"the city of the Prophet"*. Muhummad responded to the economic hardships by organizing raids on merchant caravans. His greatest success came when he won a victory at the city of Bedr when he slew hundreds traveling from Mecca.

By January of 623, Muhummad established the Constitution of Medina which created the 1st Islamic State. Shortly afterwards, the followers of Islam expelled the Bani Qainuqa [**black**] Jews and Bani Nadir [**black**] Jews from the city of Medina because they rejected his claim judicial leader who could settle disputes. Yathrib was then renamed Madinat-at Nabi, *"the city of the Prophet"*. Muhummad responded to the economic hardships by organizing raids on merchant caravans. His greatest success came when he won a victory at the city of Bedr when he slew hundreds traveling from Mecca.

By January of 623, Muhummad established the Constitution of Medina which created the 1st Islamic State. Shortly afterwards, the followers of Islam expelled the Bani Qainuqa **[black]** Jews and Bani Nadir **[black]** Jews from the city of Medina because they rejected his claim to be a continuation of Abraham, Moses, and the Hebrew prophets. During the same year, Muhummad changed the direction of prayer from Jerusalem to Mecca. He also changed the Hebrew Sabbath to Friday. In 629, the Islamic army, under Muhummad's control, returned to Mecca to fight in the Battle Mu'ta. By 630, Muhummad conquered the city of Mecca. After those exploits, the entire Arabian Peninsula converted to the religion of Islam. His military might continued to grow stronger and stronger. With Mecca subdued, he ordered the wealthy to give to the poor. The new strength was seen as a confirmation of the power of his new religion. In their eyes, *"Allah had given Muhummad the power, and the other gods were worthless"*.

On March 6, 632, Muhummad made his farewell pilgrimage to Mecca. Later that year in the early summer on June 8, Muhummad died. He was the father of 3 sons and 4 daughters. All except his daughter Fatimah died before him. His daughter grew to become the wife of Ali-Ibn Abu Talib. All of descendants of Muhummad came through her. Muhummad was a descendants of Ishmael, son of Abraham and his Egyptian wife Hagar. The ancient Hebrew prophets referred to the Arabs as the Ishmaelites.

The Ishmaelites [Arabs], a blessed People, not the Covenant People

The origins of the Arab people is found in **Genesis[Bereshith] 16:11-12** which reads: *"And the angel of YAH said unto her, Behold you are with child and you shall bear a son, and shall call his name Ishmael because YAH has heard thy affliction. And he shall be a wild man, his hand will be against every man, and every man's hand against him: and he shall dwell in the presence of all his brethren"*. Continuing in **Genesis 17:20**, Moses wrote: *"As for Ishmael, I have heard thee. Behold, I have blessed him and shall made him fruitful and I will multiply him exceedingly; twelve tribes shall he beget, and I will make him a great nation* **[the Islamic Empire]**. However, **YHWH** also said in **Genesis 17:19**: *"Sarah your wife shall bear you a son, you shall name him Isaac, and I will maintain MY covenant with as an everlasting covenant for his seed in their generations"*. These verses prove that the ancient Afro-Asiatic Hebrews are the spiritually blessed covenant people.

As we all know, this great nation known as the Islamic empire has continued from the 7th century all the way down into today's 21st century during **[the endtime ten toes of iron mixed with miry clay]**.

So it came to pass that Muhummad's teachings and practices were opposite of the words which **YHWH ELOHIM Israel** spoke to Abraham, Isaac, Jacob, Moses, and all the ancient Hebrew prophets thousands of years earlier. He died at the age of 60 and he was buried in the Green Dome at al-Masjid an-Nabawi in the city of Medina after reigning nineteen years from 613 to 632. After his lifespan, his followers venerated him by studying his life and miracles, and his devotions and reflections throughout his ministry. His followers erected a doctrine in his image known as the Quran. Nevertheless, Muhummad, who was not a Levite priest, did not adhere to the DIVINE Principles already prescribed in the Torah for Israel and all mankind. He, nor any of his disciples, followed **YHWH's** laws, commandments, judgements, and statutes given at Mount Sinai. Instead, he altered Torah, and his followers devoted their attention to praising him as being the perfect example of an Islamic servant of Allah. He married a rich widow named Khadijah and together they produced six children. She died in the year 619, only six years after his ministry started. Altogether, he was married to 13 women. After his death, the new Arab-based Islamic Empire **[the emerging miry clay kingdom]** continued to expand throughout the four corners of the earth during the Time Zone of the **Eastern iron leg**.

Islamic Expansionism
(700 C.E.—1400 C.E.)

After the death of Muhummad in 632 C.E., the force of Islam exploded beyond the Arabian Peninsula under the Raishidun Caliphate during 632 C.E. to 661C.E., and the Umayyad Caliphate in 661 C.E.. The Islamic conquest of Persia came during the 7th century when the Sassanid rulers were overthrown. Islamic rulers also conquered Syria, Palestine (Israel), Armenia, Egypt, and Northern Africa. The rapid expansion of the Muslim Empire is what caused the Byzantine Empire to suffer setbacks and eventual defeat. The first Arab siege of the Byzantine capital Constantinople came in 674.

The momentum sparked by the successive Islamic victories caused a Spirit of Aggressiveness to come upon the Islamic warriors. With the Arabian Peninsula experiencing economic hardships, the warriors started plundering neighboring lands to lift the Islamic economy out of its downfall. The armies met little resistance, so their appetites for more treasures continued to grow, causing the empire to rapidly spread. As they plundered, the Islamic warriors would force the new vassals to submit to Islam. Caliph Abu Bakr then declared a holy war in support of the raids. This Islamic call to arms signaled the beginning of one of the greatest imperialism since the conquests of Cyrus the Great, Alexander the Great, and other famed conquerors.

Rashidun Caliphate
(632 C.E.—661 C.E.)

The Rashidun Caliphate grew to become the first of four major caliphate kingdoms that were established after the death of the prophet Muhummad in 632. Led by Caliph Abu Bakr, a close companion of the founder, the Muslim army invaded Bahrain, Oman, Yemen, and Hadramaut in 633. The following year, Caliph Bakr died on August 22, 634. Umar ibn Al-Khattab succeeded him as the second caliph. After him, Caliph Uthman reigned for 12 years until his assassination on June 17, 656. After him, the leader of the conspiracy Ali ibn Abi Talib reigned in his stead. He reigned a mere 5 years, from 656 until 661, because his bloody hands caused a major rift, which became known as Sunni and Shia branches, of this new religious tree of the knowledge of good and evil that had been founded by their predecessor Muhummad.

Sunni-Shia Islamic Schism

It should be noted that another major development that occurred after the year 632 was the great division of the Islamic Empire known as Sunni and Shia Schism. The Rashidun Caliphate represented the Sunni branch. This is what happened. There was political division among the followers of Muhummad after his death over who would be his successor. The majority of the Islamic community wanted the people to decide. The smaller group, namely his family members, felt his direct relative, the son-in-law, who had married to his daughter Fatimah should occupy the throne. His name was Ali ibn Abi Talib. Ali was a early convert to the new religion who helped him foil an assassination plot against the anointed Muhummad. He also fought besides Muhummad as he gained power. When the Arab religious-political leader died, some claimed Muhummad did not name a successor while others claimed Muhummad had named Ali. The controversy over Ali's claim to the throne led to the first battle of the Islamic civil war. At that time, the third Caliph named Uthman reigned as the leader of Islam until his assassination. The leaders of the conspiracy proclaimed Ali, the son-ln-law of the deceased Muhummad, as the new Caliph of Islam. A civil war erupted, splitting Islam into two distinct camps known as Sunnis, *the majority*, and the Shias, *the minority*, the family members of Muhummad. Ali's political and religious stance grew into a movement known as Shiite Islam. His followers demanded that each new caliph be a lineal descendant of Ali and Fatimah, the daughter of the founder. *(Even today in 2019, Shiites constitute only*

10 percent of the world's Muslim population while Sunnis make up 90 percent. However, Shiites are the majority in Iran and Iraq). The majority of the Muslims never accepted Ali was the rightful heir of the Prophet Muhummad.

The Birth of the Quran
[The Holy Book of the Muslims]

Almost 30 years after death of Muhummad in the year 651, there were quarrels and disputes over Muhummad's views on various issues. Caliph Uthman, in an attempt to end the divisions of opinions, ordered the formation of a Committee. Their job was to collect Muhummad's messages into one standard book to be called the **Koran [Quran]** in hopes of establishing clarity. The book drew from the memories, traditions, and oral history of Muhummad's conversations. Once the Koran was completed, many people across Arabia became angry because they held different interpretations. Five years later Caliph Uthman was slain.

In 660, the Koran is published for the first time. The book described the non-believers as evil, those who can expect war from Allah. But on the other hand, the Muslim book called for peace, love, and grace with non-Muslims who possessed peaceful intentions. It was recorded that Muhummad wanted Christians, Israelites, and Judaic converts to be a part of his realm. Non Muslims, however, paid taxes while the faithful were exempted. Through close observation, you will discover that the Koran borrowed heavily from the New Testament and the Hebraic teachings.

In the 661, Ali, the son-in-law of Muhummad, experienced an assassination attempt. He eventually died from his wounds. His death further aggravated the deadly Shia-Sunni Schism. Meanwhile in Damascus, Syria, the Sunni Muslims established a new Caliphate there. The Rashidun caliphate, led by Umar ibn Al-Khattab, also conquered the city of David **Jerusalem** during this same period. Muslims captured the entire holy land during this same time. In the year 683, the Caliph Abd al-Malik started building the Dome of the Rock in Jerusalem, transforming the **YHWH**-centered ancient Israelite spiritual capital into an Islamic sacred place, along with a Christian and Judaic presence already occupying the holy place.

In the year 680, another rebellion between the two branches of Islam broke out again. Opponents of the Umayyad Caliph rebelled against the Sunni authorities. This time, the son of Ali named Husayn bin Ali, led the uprising. He was hopelessly outnumbered by the Sunni army at the Battle of Karbala, which is located in modern-day southern Iraq. But Ali would not accept defeat. He and his companions fought until their last breathe. For that reason, Husayn bin Ali became a revered Shiite Muslim martyr who is honored annually among their followers. Millions of Shi'a Muslims beat themselves with chains and sticks causing blood to gush from their bodies in remembrance of the famous Shiite-Sunni battle.

By 683, several cracks appeared in the Islamic armor: the Shia-Sunni schism and a Sunni civil war. This time it was the Caliphate of Damascus Abd al-Malik verus the rival Caliphate in Mecca Abd allah-ibn az-Zabayr. Malik dispatched his trust general Al Hajjaj ibn Yusuf with a large army of 10,000 to retake the city. It took a 7-month siege along with continuous bombardment of Islamic holy city to bring it under General Hajjaj's control. There was intense fighting inside the city around the sacred Islamic object, the Kaaba Stone. The usurper Abd allah-ibn az-Zabayr, his youngest son, and his faithful followers were killed in the fighting during October 692.

As the new religion Islam reached 100 years-old and expanded to the Asia, Africa, and Europe, the number of non-Arab Muslims outnumbered Arabs of the Islamic faith. Although, some of the Arab leaders did not support the integration between Arab Muslims and non-Arab Muslim, the expansion of the new faith made it impossible to resist. The Islamic Empire created by the Arabs was swallowed up by their conquests of foreign lands. For example in the year 700, Umayyad Caliphate, led by Abd al-Malik, invaded East Africa and converted Somalia before moving westwards to North Africa and subduing the pagan Berbers and converting them to Islam. That pattern continued throughout West Africa and Europe as well, and by the end of the 8th century the global Muslim population totalled one percent of the entire world's population.

By the year 711, the Muslim empire had expanded into **the Far West** and crossed the Strait of Gilbraltar and started the conquest of Christian Spain and Lisbon, Portugal. The black Israelites living in Spain welcomed the dark-skinned Moors as liberators because the Visigoth king Egica had sentenced them to slavery, accusing them of aiding the Muslims. In **the Far East,** the religious Arab empire crossed the western borders of China. During May-September of 751, the Islamic Army in Central Asia fought and defeated the Chinese at the Battle of Atlakh. After that, the Muslims replaced the Chinese as the dominant influence along the Silk Road. Islam also reached the Caucasus Mountains, including Armenia, during this same era. The **powerful legs of Islam was walking to and fro, up and down, throughout all the ends of the earth**. During his three-year reign from 717 to 720, Caliph Umar ibn al-Aziz II granted tax exemptions to all the believers while taxing non-Muslims. Caliph Umar II accumulated great wealth from those looting campaigns.

Great Human Achievements of Islam

The Islamic Moorish occupation of Spain began in 711 when Caliph Tariq-ibn Ziyad crossed the Strait of Gilbraltar from northern Africa. The Moors brought advanced African civilization to primitive Europe. At that time, there were no lands in 8th century Europe in that compared to the African civilization which developed in Spain. The Moors ruled Spain for 800 years, and during this time, they introduced new scientific techniques such as an astrolabe to the continent. It was a device used to measure the position of the stars and planets. Under the Moors, Spain enjoyed scientific progress in areas of chemistry, mathematics, geography, philosophy, and physics with 17 universities in the cities of Almeria, Cordova, Granda, Andalos, Seville, and Toledo. There were only 2 universities throughout Europe during that time. In fact, education was universal in Spain during the Islamic millennium. The majority of the kings and queens of Europe could not read or write while in Spain it was totally opposite. The entire population of Europe was also illiterate. In the 10th and 11th centuries, Moorish Spain had 70 public libraries while they were non-existent in Europe. In the city of Cordova, there was the famous Cordova Public library which housed 600,000 manuscripts. The city also had 900 public baths were the poor could bathe and receive bread. It was also the site of The Great Mosque of Cordoba, which was considered one of the architectural wonders of the world. *(When the European Christian Spaniards overthrow the Muslims, the mosque was converted to a Catholic Church.)* The mosque had a low scarlet and gold roof supported by 1,000 columns of marbles and jasper. It was lit by thousands of brass and silver lamps which burned perfumed oil.

Another area of Islamic advancement in Moorish Spain was housing construction. Moorish rulers lived in palaces while the monarchs of Germany, France, and England dwelt in big barns without windows, no chimneys and only a hole in the roof. The Alhambra Palace, known as the red one, was one of Islamic Spain's architectural masterpieces. Alhambra was the seat of Muslim power from the 13th to the end of the 15th century. The streets were paved with raised sidewalks for pedestrians. During the night, 10 miles of street were well illuminated by lamps. Those developments took place hundreds of years before there were paved streets in Paris or street lamps in London.

In the year 750, Arab mathematicians began using a number system that originated in India which is more advanced than the Roman numeral system. The Moors eventually passed this system over to the Europeans who were emerging from the Dark Ages.

In 822, Moorish musician Ziryab "the Blackbird" came to Spain. He, and other Moorish musicians, introduced the lute, the guitar, and kithara into European culture. Moors changed the style of eating, breaking meals into separate portions, such as beginning with soup, then the main meal, and ending with dessert. In terms of communication, the Moors introduced paper to Europe and the Arabic numeral which eventually replaced the older Roman system. In terms of agriculture, the Moors introduced many new crops such as oranges, lemons, peaches, apricots, figs, sugar cane, dates, ginger, pomegranates, saffron, and rice. They were also the first to trade in cotton and silk.

It should also be noted that the Moors ruled and occupied neighboring Lisbon, named Lashbuna at that time, and the rest of the country until their expulsion in the 12th century. They were finally defeated by King Alfonso Henriques at the battle at the Castle of St. George.

However in the final analysis, it was the Moors who brought the compass, and other knowledge of China, India, and Arabia into Europe byway of Africa. Therefore, it can be safely said that the Moors, through warfare and cultural exchanges, played a major part in indirectly laying the foundation for the development of Europe during *The Middle Ages, Renaissance*, and *The Age of Enlightenment*.

Islamic Expansionism *continued*
(1000 C.E.—1100 C.E.)

The Golden Age of Islam continued during the 11th and 12th century. Islamic medical research, science, economic development, and cultural works flourished throughout their worldwide domain. In the 1054, Abdullah ben Yassim started his Muslim conquest of Ghana, and other parts of West Africa. Seven years later in 1061, another Islamic dynasty known as the Almoravids of northern Africa crossed the Gilbraltar and began their conquest of Spain. In the year 1063 Marrakesh conquered northern Africa and established Morocco.

In 1071, Alph Arsian, the leader of the Seljuk Turks, defeated the Roman Byzantine army and seized control of Asia Minor, known today as modern Turkey. At the close of century in 1098, Islam suffered a setback when the Christian Crusaders defeated them at the Battle of Antioch. The following year in 1099, the Frank Crusaders recaptured Jerusalem. Godfrey of Bouillon was selected to serve as the King of the city of **Jerusalem**. During this time, Islam **[miry clay kingdoms]** and Christian **[iron kingdoms]** vied for control in the holy land, Syria, and northern Africa.

Islamic Expansionism *continued*
(1100 C.E.—1200 C.E.)

The Golden Age of the Islamic Empire continued with the Almoravids Caliphate expanding across northern Africa for 26 years from 1121 to 1147 under the leadership of Ibn Tumar I who reigned from 1120 to 1130 and Abd al Mu'min who reigned from 1130 to 1163. Afterwards the Almoravids were replaced with Marinid suzerainty.

From 1100 to 1166, Muhummad al-Idrissi designed some of the world's most advancement world maps.

During the first half of the 1100s until 1400, the Islamic Empire of Mali, founded by the Mande-speaking people flourished in West Africa. The kingdom was known for its wealth and great rulers like Mansa Musa. It was renown for its famous cities such as Jenne and Timbuktu. Both were striving commercial centers serving as key spots along trade routes. Timbuktu also served as a religious and intellectual center for Muslim scholars.

During the 12th and 13 century, Islam also flourished on the eastern side of the continent of Africa—East Africa and the Indian Ocean. Cities in eastern and southern Africa served as key intersections of Indian Ocean trade. Swahili merchants in cities such as Kilwa and Mogadishu served as middlemen for goods traded from the African interior to the Arabian Peninsula, and vice versa, goods from the west coast of India that flow into the African interior. Gold mined in east Africa highlands provided large profits for Swahili merchants. They used the island of Madagascar, off the east coast, as a key trade spot in the booming Indian Ocean trade. The location served as a fusion place which allowed Islamic teachings to spread to numerous ethnic groups and cultures worldwide.

Islamic Conquest of Israel

In 1186, Prince Saladin, a Kurdish Muslim prince, defeated the Frank Crusaders and drove them out of **Jerusalem**. For the following 700 years, **Jerusalem** and the entire land of Israel remained under Egyptian and Ottoman Muslim control until 1917 when the British army forced the Ottomans out of the area.

The Sub-Saharan and Indian Ocean Slave Trade
(700 C.E.—1600 C.E.)

As the [**Eastern iron leg kingdoms**] continued to expand north, south, east, and west, the continent of Africa flourished through sub-Saharan trade. Merchants along the trade route traded in valuable items such as salt, gold, and eventually, the trade in human beings. Islamic rulers purchased slaves to serve as their bondmen and bondwomen throughout Europe, the Arabian Peninsula, the Middle East, and as far away as western India. Slavery evolved into a valuable and significant part of the Mediterranean and Indian Ocean economies. Scattered towards the **East**, millions of African captives were traded during this period. This sub-Saharan slavery occurred hundreds of years before the trans-Atlantic Slave Trade began in the Americas. Human trafficking in the **West** didn't start until the late 1400s.

Africans captured in the sub-Saharan Slave Trade were indoctrinated in Islamic teachings found in the Quran and forced to become Muslims or face death. Men slaves were assigned to various roles, such as the military, sailors, domestic servants, and plantation laborers while the African women served as concubines to rulers. Most of men were castrated for population control in their new strange lands. It was the brown-skinned Arabs and dark-skinned Berbers who were the masters and rulers of the black sub-Saharan slave trade. *(The only reason I mentioned the skin complexions of the Arabs and Berbers is to make the point it is not the color of a man's skin that makes him or her evil. It is because of the color of his or her mind: evil-minded. We see that pale-skinned Aryans, brown-skinned Arabs, dark-skinned Berbers, and black Africans all participated in the evil acts of sub-Saharan and Trans-Atlantic human trafficking.)* Human trafficking, transmitted by the religion of Islam, started in the 8th century and continued up to the 17th century. Slave ports included Algeria, Tunisia, Tripoitania, Morocco, Somalia, and the island of Madagascar. It should also be noted that **White Slavery** existed during this same era. White chattel slavery was the enslavement of pale-skinned Aryan Europeans by dark-skinned non-Europeans such as Berbers, Arabs, and Moors. The captive Europeans were taken to their master's homelands to serve in different capacities.

Islamic Expansionism *continued*
(1200 C.E.—1300 C.E.)

The Muslim Ayyubid and Khwarazmians sacked **Jerusalem**, defeated the Christian-backed kingdom of Jerusalem, in the year 1244.

Islamic expansionism met a reversal in Mesopotamia during the year 1258 when the Mongols besieged Baghdad for two weeks and overthrew Caliph Al-Musta'sim, executed him and several other officials, and replaced the Abbasid dynasty. The Mongol Army included 40,000 Mongols accompanied by Chinese, Armenian, and Kazakh soldiers. Many observers viewed the overthrow of the Sunni Caliphate as the end of the Golden Age of the Islamic Empire. However in the following two years, the Islamic Empire prevailed again. This is what occurred: The Mongols, who were feeling aggressive after their conquest of Baghdad, continued a western military campaign towards Syria, Israel, and Egypt. Those territories were controlled by the Mamluk Sultan of Egypt. The two armies met on September 3, 1260 at Ayn Jaiut, near Nazareth in northern Galilee. The Mongol army was totally destroyed, halting the Mongol's westward expansion. Baibars, the commander of the Egyptian army, ascended to throne of the Mamluk Sultan in 1261. He was the fourth Sultan who became known as Sultan Abu al-Futuh. The Mamluk dynasty continued from 1261 to 1517 when the Ottoman Turks overthrew the Egyptians.

In the year 1291, the Mamluks defeated the Crusaders for the final time and maintained control of the holyland.

Islamic Expansionism *continued*
(1300 C.E.—1400 C.E.)

By now, Islamic expansionism had lasted for nearly 700 years. However, politically speaking, the religious empire was divided. Although neighboring populations practiced the common religion of Islam, their local difference still caused conflicts. Muslim merchants centered in the heart of the Middle East worked to establish the region as the most important in the world, connecting Africa, Europe, and Asia. That is why the region became known as the *"Middle East"*. An intersection that provided commercial networks and a path for converting local populations and peasants to Islam.

Meanwhile in West Africa, the Mali Empire reached its zenith during the 25-year reign of Mansa Musa from 1312 to 1337. Musa was one of the world's wealthiest rulers. Musa became renown when he made the pilgrimage across the sub-Sahara trade route to the Islamic holy city of Mecca in Arabia. His entourage included 60,000 with a train of 100 elephants, and a huge amounts of gold. At this time **Jerusalem** was back in the hands of Muslim rulers where it remained until 1517 when the Ottomans conquered the holy land.

So it came to pass the Islamic Expansionism continued to reign for over the entire earth for nearly 1,400 years. The rulers of the Islamic Empire did not serve **YHWH ELOHIM Israel** nor walk in HIS laws, commandments, judgements, and statutes. Instead, each caliph walked in the imaginations of his own heart doing whatsoever was right in their own eyes according to all the nations that preceded them. **The Ottoman Empire** reigned in their stead.

Nevertheless, the Islamic Empire has continued even until this day. It is presently one of the latter-day United Nations non-European **[miry clay toes kingdoms]** of Saudi Arabia, Egypt, Libya, Tunisia, Algeria, Morocco, Sudan, Chad, Somalia, Yemen, Qatar, Oman, Bahrain, the United Arab Emirates, Syria, Lebanon, the Palestinians, the Kurds, Iran, Iraq, Jordan, I.S.I.S., and other Islamic warrior organizations that continuously oppose to the latter-day United Nations Christianized Europeans **[iron toes kingdom]** because *"iron and clay do not cleave one to another"*.

Before we look at the Ottoman Empire, we must note the acts of the Khazarian Empire first, an **[iron kingdom]** of European Jewish converts located in eastern Europe.

Khazar Empire
(650 C.E.—969 C.E.)
[The European Jewish-convert Kingdom]

The Khazar Empire was born in the 7th century C.E. along the north shore of the Black Sea near modern-day southern Russia, in the area known today as Azerbaijan. The Khazars were a non-Shemitic Turkic people mixed with the European bloodline. In the process of time, the Khazars expanded westwards and pushed the Bulgars south across the Danube River where they founded the country we call Bulgaria today. The European captives taken during warfare were sold to Arabs and Byzantines. The Aryan captives who were known as Slavs, meaning slaves. They became known as victims of **white slavery**.

During the 7th century in the year 650, the kingdom of Khazaria was strategically located as a crossroads between the Middle East, Eastern Europe, and southwest Asia while serving as a buffer state between the Byzantine Empire to the **West** and the Arab Islamic Empire on the **Eastern** border. Before then in the 6th century, between the years 550 to 630, it was once a part of the western Turkic empire. Even then, its unique location allowed all types of religious doctrines to pass through the borders, causing Khazaria to become home to the religions of Tengrism, Buddhism, Christianity, Islam, and various other native beliefs.

In the year 740, during the 8th century, a historic occurrence happened when King Bulan invited representatives from the three major religions to visit his capital. He summoned representatives from each religion to come to his imperial court to explain the tenets of their religion. In the end, with the urging of his wife Serakl, he was convinced to adopt Rabbinical Judaism. The ruling elite of Khazaria followed him and accepted Judaism as well. It is believed that after Bulan's conversion he chose the Hebrew name *"Sabriel"* which was a Turkic variation of the Hebrew word *"Gavriel"*. That is why some scholars refer to him as *"Bulan Sabriel"*. For the record, the word **Bulan** meant *"elk"* or *"Moose"*. In the Turkic language **Bulan** meant *"the one who finds"*.

On the other hand, other Khazar scholars contend Bulan and Sabriel were two different individuals. Either way you look at it, it is a historic fact written in the *Schechter Letter* that these non-Shemitic people converted to Judaism. In the same letter an unnamed Khazar official wrote to a Euro-Judaic dignitary named Hasadai ibn Shaprut who lived in Constantinople. The letter also referred to some Jews from Persia and Armenia who migrated to Khazaria to flee persecution. There these Jews mingled with the nomadic Khazars and were totally assimilated into a Turkic people. The *Schechter Letter* has been housed in Cambridge University since 1898. The fragmented text also revealed that the Khazars saw themselves as new leaders of worldwide Judaism.

There are other books that confirm the fact that most of today's Ashkenazi Jews are descended from the Khazarian Jewish diaspora which migrated westward after Rus barbarians in the 10th century pushed them into Poland, Germany, France, and England. From there, the European Jewry dispersed across East, Central and Western Europe. The names of the two other books are *The Jews of Khazaria* **by Kevin Brooks** and *The History of the Jewish Khazars* **by D.M. Dunlop**. When king Bulan accepted Judaism, he did so in order to maintain his kingdom's independence in face of the dominant Byzantines to his West and the Sassanid Persians and Arabs in the east.

The Lineage of Jewish Khazarian Rulers
King Bulan

Bulan's father and mother names remain unknown. His date of birth was not recorded in Khazarian history. In fact during the 8th century, the Khazars were very primitive without recorded scholarship. King Bulan converted to Rabbinical Judaism in the 8th century in the year 740 C.E.

King Obadiah
(9th Century)

He was one of the sons of King Bulan.

King Zachariah
(9th Century)

King Mannasseh
(9th Century)

King Benjamin
(9th Century)

King Aaron
(10th Century)

King Joseph
(10th Century)
King Joseph of Khazaria also traced his lineage back to King Bulan.

King David
(10th Century)

King Georgios
(969 C.E.)

So it came to pass that the **Khazarian Empire** was dispersed across Eastern and Western Europe after three centuries because of the invasion of the **Rus people** who succeeded them as the rulers of the crossroads of the Middle East, Eastern Europe, and southwest Asia. Each Khazrian ruler did evil in **the eyes of YHWH ELOHIM Israel** by not walking in HIS laws, commandments, judgements, and statutes. Instead, they served graven doctrines created from the imaginations of their uncircumcised minds. In the 8th century, their king Bulan, the ruling elite, and large segments of the Euro-Turkic population converted to the religion of **Rabbinical Judaism.** It should be noted that *convert Judaism* is not the same as the everlasting Levitical covenant that **YHWH** made with the ancient Afro-Asiatic Hebrew people from Africa(Egypt). [**Please read 2 Kings 17:24-41. It clearly documents the beginning of the religion of convert Judaism**]. Centuries later, the descendants of these same Khazarian people migrated to the holy land to establish the State of Israel in the year 1948 C.E.

And it came to pass after these days, even centuries later, that **the Spirit of YHWH** gave birth to the **Ottoman Empire**. Therefore, the Ottoman Empire will now become our focus as we continue to walk down the prophetic [**East iron legs of the image**]. We as conscious Israelites must always keep in mind that the **DIVINE Presence of YAH** is creating each new evening and each new morning, each new year, each new decade, each new century, and each new millennium, even until this very day.

The Ottoman Empire
(1453 C.E.—1914 C.E.)

"YAH changes times and seasons. HE removes kings (Byzantine Empire) and install kings (Ottoman Empire); HE gives the wise their wisdom and knowledge to those who know"
Daniel 2: 21

The birth of the **Ottoman Empire** came into existence in the year 1299 in northwest Asia Minor in the town called Sogut. The founding father was a Turkish tribal leader named Osman I.

Osman I was born with the birth name Osman Ghazi. He grew to become the leader of the pale, olive-skinned, and yellowish Indo-Turkic people in 1299 C.E. He founded what became known as the Ottoman dynasty over the land mass known as Asia Minor. Today this area is known as the country of Turkey.

The city of Athens was the royal capital of classical Greece. The revered pagan shrine known as the Acropolis stood in its midst. Inside stood a pantheon of graven images known as Zeus, Athena, Nike, Apollo, Artemis, Aphrodite, Atalanta, and several other statues dedicated to polytheistic Greek religion.

This map highlights western Asia Minor, known today as Turkey, and southeast Europe, which is now the country of Greece. Ancient Greek civilization strived in this region until the rise of Alexander the Great. During and after his reign, primitive Greek culture became more advance after Greek conquest of Asia and Africa. Their new culture became known as Hellenism.

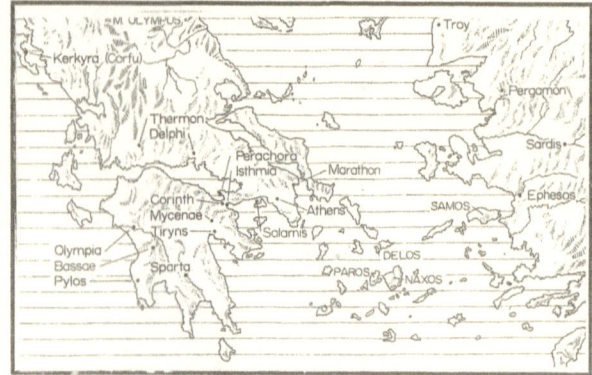

The Greeks were the first Indo-European civilization on the face of the earth. Before then, all prior Near East civilizations were Afro-Asiatic.

Black Biblical History:

Top Left: A paintinting of ancient Egyptians and Shemitic tribespeople. Both the Egyptians and the Shemities are non-Europreans known today as black people. [See Genesis 10:6].

Top Right: A sculptured drawing of King Darius I of ancient Persia on the Behistun relief. The Persians were the biblical Elamites who were also non-Europeans. [See Genesis 10:22].

Above: A monument depicting the black people who built the world's first city-states located on the Euphrates River. [See Genesis 10:10].

Map Below: The empire of Alexander the Great extended from Greece in the West to India in the Far East. This was the first Caucasian Gentile kingdom to become a world power. Before then, the Afro-Asiatic kingdoms of Egypt, Babylon, Israel, Persia, Ethiopia, Assyria, Canaanites, Phoenicians, and others were black kingdoms. [Genesis 10:4-5].

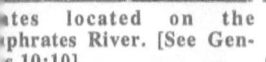

King Philip II of Macedon, the father of Alexander the Great, united the Grecian mainland and laid the foundation for the rise of the first Aryan [Indo-European] empire.

339

In the wall relief above King Hammurabi of Babylon is seen standing before the Babylonian sun-god Shamash who is seen sitting on his throne. The Babylonians and Egyptians were the first inhabitants of the earth who worshipped the Sun. The Persians, Greeks, Romans, Byzantines, Ottomans, Mongols, Arabs, Japanese, Chinese, and Christian Europeans have continued this sun and moon-veneration through their modern religions(gods). In the religion of Christianity, the modern Church has renamed one of the days of the week in honor of the sun, which is known as Sunday. The Day to venerate the Sun/Son.

Osman I, a Muslim prince, was the son of man named Ertugrul [*pronounced* Er-tug-rul], the leader of Turkic Kayi tribe. In generations earlier, the Kayi tribe originated from Central Asia, however, when the Mongols started their westward expansion, they forced the Kayi tribe into Asia Minor. His father Ertugrul was the leader of the Kayi tribe while his mother's name was unknown. His son Osman I ascended to tribal chief after the death of his father in 1280. From the northwest, Osman started his conquest of Bithynia and expanded across the entire mainland, overthrowing the Seljug dynasty in the year 1300. Forty-five years later in 1345, Ottoman troops swept into southeastern Europe and conquered the Balkan Peninsula.

On July 20, 1402 the Ottoman Empire experienced a major temporary setback when Timur, the chieftain of Mongolian-Tumurid Empire invaded Asia Minor. Timur and his army of 100,000-plus horsemen swiftly swept across Asia Minor, destroying every village and city in his path. Meanwhile, **Sultan Bayezid I**, the ruler of the Ottoman Empire, was away on a foreign expedition besieging the city-states of southeastern Europe on the Balkans Peninsula. Once Bayezid received news that the Mongols had invaded their homeland, he hastily called off the European conquest, withdrew, and returned to confront Timur's advancement. Pressing his fighting men to return back across the Bosporus Strait into Asia Minor, his troops did not have the opportunity to eat or refresh themselves after their extensive campaign in the Balkans. In fact, they were extremely weary. Nevertheless, both sides met at the Cubak plain near the city of Ankara. To make matters worse, the Ottomans were outnumbered nearly 2 to 1 with 140,000 Mongols and allies against only 85,000 Turks. The Mongols outflanked the Ottoman and surprised them from the rear. The Battle of Ankara was an extremely bloody battle with both sides losing 40,000-plus men. In the end there were still 100,000 Mongols standing and a mere 45,000 Ottomans remaining. When the battle ended, dead bodies laid everywhere, and the Ottomans had lost. **Sultan Bayezid I** and his sons were captured and slain. However, this was only a temporary setback for the Ottomans. Three years after this gigantic victory, Timur, the chieftain of the Mongol Empire, died in 1405, allowing the Ottomans the opportunity to fully recover from that defeat. *(Meanwhile, the Byzantine Christians were observing this war between these two Muslim superpowers.)*

In the process of time fifty-one years later, the Ottomans were fully recovered and on the march once again. This time their leader **Sultan Mehmed II** led the Islamic army against the capital of Eastern Christianity and destroyed Constantinople. This defeat occurred on May 29, 1453, signaling the collapse of the Eastern Roman Empire and the birth of the Ottoman capital, and the renaming of the city to **Istanbul**. By the end of the 15th century, the Ottomans inherited the Byzantine and Arab empires in the Middle East, North Africa, and parts of eastern and southern Europe. This was the beginning of the high point of Ottoman power beginning in the 14th century until the 20th century. Below is the chronology of the rulers of this vast Muslim empire.

Chronology of Ottoman Rulers

Osman I "the Warrior"
(1299 C.E.—1323 C.E.)

Osman I defeated the Byzantine army in the year 1301-1302. This victory brought him to notoriety.

Orhan "the Warrior"
(1323 C.E.—1362 C.E.)

Murad I "The Most Exalted Sultan"
(1362 C.E.—June 15, 1389 C.E.)

Bayezid I
(June 15, 1389 C.E.—July 20, 1402 C.E.)

Isa Celebi "co-Sultan of Anatolia"
(1405 C.E.—1406 C.E.)
Isa Celebi "Sultan of the Western Anatolian Territory"
(1405 C.E.—1406 C.E.)

Emir Suleyman Celebi "The First Sultan of Rumelia"
(July 20, 1402 C.E.—February 17, 1411 C.E.)

Musa Celebi "The Second Sultan of Rumelia"
(February 18, 1411 C.E.—July 5, 1413 C.E.)

Mehmed Celebi "The Sultan of Anatolia"
a) Sultan of the Eastern Anatolian Territory
(1403 C.E.—1406 C.E.)
b) Sultan of Anatolia
(1406 C.E.—July 5, 1413 C.E.)

Murad II
(June 25, 1413 C.E.—May 26, 1421 C.E.)

Abdicated the throne in favor of his 12-year-old son Mehmed II in 1444. Murad II later reclaimed the throne to handle the Christian Crusade. Mehmed regained the throne after he died in 1451.

Mehmed II "The Conqueror"
(1444 C.E.—1446 C.E.)

Mehmed was born in the year 1432. At the age of 12, Mehmed ascended to the throne of the Ottoman Empire. However, he was replaced once more by his father two years later.

(February 3, 1451 C.E.—May 3, 1481 C.E.)

Mehmed was now a 19-year-old and soon thereafter began to strategize his conquest of Constantinople. In 1453 C.E. he captured the royal city and restored the glory of the city in the image of the Ottomans after casting down the Byzantine crown to the ground. The city was became the largest city in Europe with the grandeur of an imperial city. During the next two decades, Mehmed II conquered the Balkan Peninsula while strengthening civil and criminal laws in the empire. In his reign, Mehmed established a library with Greek and Latin writings. He also built 8 colleges for the Ottoman empire while there were not 8 universities throughout all Western Europe.

Beyezid II "The Saint"
(May 19, 1481 C.E.—April 25, 1512 C.E.)

Selim
(April 25, 1512 C.E.—September 21, 1520 C.E.)

Suleiman I "The Magnificent"
(September 30, 1520 C.E.—September 6-7, 1566 C.E.)

During his reign the Ottomans controlled Persia, Arabia, Hungary, and the Balkan Peninsula, and he invaded Austria. By the end of the 16th century, the Ottoman defeated the Mamluks of Egypt and Syria and crushed their navies. The Ottomans, short afterwards, seized control of the Mediterranean Sea, namely the Barbary Coast. During this era, the rulers of the Ottoman Empire assumed the title of *"Caliph"*, which also indicated that the rulers were also considered the spiritual of Islam as well.

<u>Selim II</u>
(September 29, 1566 C.E.—December 21, 1574 C.E.)

<u>Murad III</u>
(December 22, 1574 C.E.—January 16, 1595 C.E.)

<u>Mehmed III "The Just"</u>
(January 27, 1583 C.E. —December 21, 1603 C.E.)

<u>Ahmed I</u>
(December 21, 1603 C.E.—November 22, 1617 C.E.)

<u>Mustafa</u>
(November 22, 1617 C.E.—February 26, 1618 C.E.)

<u>Osman II</u>
(February 26, 1618 C.E.—May 19, 1622 C.E.)

<u>Mustafa I</u>
(May 20, 1623 C.E.—September 10, 1623 C.E.)

<u>Murad IV</u>
(September 10, 1623 C.E.—February 8-9, 1640 C.E.)

<u>Ibrahim</u>
(February 9, 1640 C.E.—August 8, 1648 C.E.)

<u>Mehmed IV "The Hunter"</u>
(August 8, 1648 C.E.—November 8, 1687 C.E.)

<u>Suleiman "The Warrior"</u>
(November 8, 1687 C.E.—June 22, 1691 C.E.)

In 1683, the Ottomans besieged Vienna, Austria in Europe. The Ottomans were eventually defeated and forced to withdraw. The Ottomans were forced to relinquish the lands of Hungary 16 years later in 1699. Although the Ottomans were a Muslim kingdom, Suleiman was forced to deal with continuous reports of corruption and decadence which ultimately undermined his policies and foreign expeditions. In fact, the Ottomans attempted to conquer Vienna, Austria during two separate periods, once in 1683 as I just mentioned, and once before in 1529. Both attempts ultimately failed.

Ahmed II
(June 22, 1691 C.E.—February 6, 1695 C.E.)

Mustafa II
(February 6, 1695 C.E.—August 1703 C.E.)

Ahmed III
(August 22, 1703 C.E.—October 1-2, 1730 C.E.)

Mahmud I
(October 2, 1730 C.E.—December 13, 1754 C.E.)

Osman III
(December 13, 1754 C.E.—October 29-30, 1757 C.E.)

Mustafa III
(October 30, 1757 C.E.—January 21, 1774 C.E.)

Abdul Hamid I
(January 21, 1774 C.E.—April 6-7, 1789 C.E.)

Selim III
(April 7, 1789 C.E.—May 29, 1807 C.E.)

Mustafa IV
(May 29, 1807 C.E.—July 28, 1808 C.E.)

Mahmud II
(July 28, 1808 C.E.—July 1, 1839 C.E.)

Abdulmejid I
(July 1, 1839 C.E.—June 25, 1861 C.E.)

Abdulaziz
(June 25, 1861 C.E.—May 30, 1876 C.E.)

Murad V
(May 30, 1876 C.E.—August 31, 1876 C.E.)

Abdul Hamid II
(August 31, 1876 C.E.—April 27, 1909 C.E.)

Mehmed V "The True Path Follower"
(April 17, 1909 C.E.—July 3, 1918 C.E.)

The Ottoman Empire loss its remaining European territories during the 1912-1913 Balkans Wars, forcing out the Muslim Empire from Eastern Europe. The Ottomans supported Germany during World War I. The treaties signed after the war dissolved all Ottoman claims of European soil.

Mehmed VI
(July 4, 1918 C.E.—November 1, 1922 C.E.)

Abdulmejid II
(November 18, 1922 C.E.—March 3, 1924 C.E.

The Republic of Turkey was founded in 1923 by Musatafa Kemal Ataturk, a Turkish army officer who became a reformist politician, who abolished the autocratic monarchy. The capital was switched eastward from **Constantinople (Istanbul)** to the city of Ankara on the mainland a few days later on October 13, 1923.

In the end **the Ottoman Empire**, which had been ruled by a dynasty of Muslim sultans, was expelled from power in Asia Minor in 1924 C.E. and replaced by the **Grand National Assembly of Turkey**. The new democratic leaders completely abolished the Caliphate monarchy. Afterwards, Turkey became a constitutional monarchy. **Constantinople**, once a Christian capital, was officially renamed **Istanbul**, and turned into a Muslim royal city in 1930.

At its zenith, the Turkish Empire, which once was one of the most powerful empires, controlled major parts of southeast Europe, Western Asia, the Middle East, and North Africa for a period extending 625 years, beginning in 1300 until its demise on March 3, 1924. So it came to pass that the Ottoman Empire did evil in the **eyes of YHWH ELOHIM Israel** by not keeping HIS laws, commandments, judgements, and statutes according as HE commanded the ancient Afro-Asiatic Hebrew people at Mount Sinai after HE had delivered them out of hand of Pharaoh the king of Egypt.

The other important **[Eastern iron leg]** empires that reigned concurrently with the Byzantines, Arabs, and Ottoman Empires were the Far Eastern kingdoms of *China, the Mongols, Japan,* and *India*. As we continue to move down the **Prophetic Time Zone of the two Legs of Iron,** we will now focus of these great empires which were a part of **YHWH** Revelation to Daniel which he explained to Nebuchadnezzar to benefit and Guide us today.

The Far Eastern Kingdoms & Dynasty
(1400 C.E.—1900 C.E.)
[Far Eastern World]

The Chinese Empire(1368 C.E.—1912 C.E.) The Kingdoms of Japan(1392 C.E—1912 C.E.) Mongolian Empire(1206 C.E.—1636 C.E.) Empires of India(1206 C.E.—1857 C.E.)

"YAH changes times and seasons. HE removes kings (The Ming Dynasty) and install kings(The Qing Dynasty); HE gives the wise their wisdom and knowledge to those who know"
Daniel 2: 21.

The Ming Dynasty(1368 C.E.—1644 C.E.) The Qing Dynasty(1644 C.E.—1911 C.E.)

The birth of successive Chinese dynasties came forth out of the vast mainland territory located in southeast Asia off the coast of the South China Sea. Over the past centuries, the mainland has been the homeland of several Empires that ruled in one form or another. China was, and continues to be, a land with civilizations and dynasties dating back to the second millennium B.C.E. During that time, the Shang dynasty ruled over China from 1600 B.C.E. until the year 1000 B.C.E. The ancient people were very intelligent, creating a writing system and developing calendars during this same period of time. Even today in China, there remains an ancient relic of the past confirming their existence known as the Shang Tomb of Fu Hao.

Beginning in the year 1046 B.C.E., the Zhou dynasty, founded by King Wu, emerged from the Yellow River Valley to overthrow the Shang dynasty. The conflict continued for another 790 years until its Eastern Empire collapsed in the year 256, making the eastern dynasty the longest lasting in Chinese history. In contrast, the Western Empire fell years earlier in the year 771. During this same era, there was new growth in chariot warfare and everything else. In fact, 256 B.C.E. This period was known as **the Golden Age of China**, a time of peace and stability.

From 750 B.C.E. to 600 B.C.E., the Chinese were already printing books such as *Books of Poetry* compiled from earlier contemporary poems. By the year 500 B.C.E., the Chinese had developed and mastered iron technology. During this era, the ideology of Chinese philosopher Confucius flourished. His words and opinions became revered as a religion known as **Confucianism**. Born in 551 B.C.E. as Kongfuzi, he grew to be a teacher, philosopher, and political theorist. He came up poor living in the state of Lu. As a young man, he earned income by working in horse stables and eventually became a bookkeeper. He self-educated himself and became well-rounded in the skills as a charioteer, archery, calligraphy, arithmetic, music, and rituals. By the age of 30, his mastery of history and poetry earned him a role as a teacher for the Chinese aristocracy. His goal was to revive and improve Chinese institutions. He eventually became a visionary who addressed issues such as family life, education, community life, the state, and the kingdom as a whole. He also served in government roles and advanced to the post of Minister of Justice in Lu. However, his views were not popular, and in the end he resigned and went into a 12-year self-imposed retirement. It was during this time that his views became popular among young Chinese student. So at the age of 67, he returned to his hometown Lu and served again as an instructor in writing. His life and thoughts were recorded in a book known as the *Lunyu* or the *Analects of Confucius* and, as I said earlier, the Chinese people began to trust in his man-made ideas and he grew into a deity. He died in 479 B.C.E. in Lu. (*The prophet* **Jeremiah** *warned ancient Judah about following the paths men such as Confucius in* **chapter 17:5.**)

Now let's return back to the subject of King Wu. The Zhou dynasty initiated a feudal system that worked as long as King Wu kept the peace. However, when the founder died a few years later in 1043, a civil war broke out. Those events took place when the European people, on the other side of the world, **[Western iron leg kingdoms]** were still slowly emerging from *The Dark Ages*. Meanwhile in China, philosophers there were creating a new religion known as the **Tianism**. This new Chinese theology evolved around the worship of heaven.

Below are the names of the various Chinese dynasties that ruled the mainland for next 800 years.

Various Chinese Dynasties
Han Dynasty
(206 B.C.E.—220 C.E.)

The Han people dominated central China, stretching from the Shaanxi province to Wuhan. The Han dynasty seized power in 206 B.C.E. with Lui Bang becoming the first emperor. During their reign, the Hans ended the ban on Confucianism. They also appointed Doug Zhougshu, a Confucian as the state scholar. The theory of yin/yang cosmology then became the patron school of thought. In the spirit of religious tolerance, the Han Dynasty also introduced the religion of Buddhism into the kingdom as well. Their leaders led an aggressive effort to expand the field of arts while at the same time seeking to expand their territories. The dynasty crumbled, collapsed, and became a part of the annals of history in 220 C.E. after reigning 426 years.

China Divided into Separate Feudal Dynasties
Han Dynasty
(220 C.E.—581 C.E.)

By 350 C.E. the religion of **Buddhism**, which had reached China three centuries earlier, became the most powerful religious force in China. Buddhist cave temples, along with paintings, and sculptures adorned the mountains, valleys, hills, and plains enshrined inside numerous houses of worship nationwide. This religion and philosophy had been founded in northeast India in the 5th century B.C.E.. The religion was based on the Teachings of Siddhartha Gautama who was known as *"the Buddha"* or *"The Enlightened One"*. His teachings were accepted as the gospels. His views were transmitted verbally by his devoted followers to millions of others. Buddha built high places, called monasteries, to uphold his religious order. Some of his ideas came from the religion of **Hinduism**, namely the concept of *karma*. His teachings were known as the *Four Noble Truths*.

Meanwhile, this was also a time for great Chinese calligraphers who were renown for their advanced artistic skills.

Sui Dynasty
(589 C.E.—617 C.E.)

Tang Dynasty
(618 C.E.—907 C.E.)

During this era of the Tang Dynasty, Buddhist temples and images continued to proliferate the kingdom. Buddhism, which originated in India, also blanketed Sri Lanka, China, Korea, and Japan. Today in the 21st century, Buddhism has grown into one of the world's major religions with 400 million followers worldwide. In the era of the Tang dynasty, Chinese calligraphers continued to advance their internationally known artistic skills.

Five Dynasties Period
(907 C.E.—960 C.E.)

1. Song Dynasty
(960 C.E.—1279 C.E.)

2. Northern Dynasty
(960 C.E.—1127 C.E.)

3. Southern Dynasty
(1127 C.E.—1279 C.E.)

4. Yuan Dynasty
(1279 C.E.—1368 C.E.)

Great Paintings continued to flourish during the 1300s-1400s.

The Imperial Ming Dynasty
1368 C.E.—1644 C.E.

Expensive hardwood floors and furniture became commonplace. Most ordinary homes in China had elegant gardens.

Taizu "Hongwu Emperor"
(1368 C.E.—1398 C.E.)

The founder of the Ming dynasty, Zhu Yuanzhang, led a military rout against the remnant of the army of the Yuan dynasty and re-established Chinese rule. The capital Nanjing was transferred to Bejing where it became the new imperial city.

Born in the city of Haozhou on October 21,1328 as one of seven children, Zhu came from a poor peasant family. His father's name was Zhu Shizhen and his mother's name Lady Chen. He ascended to the throne as the first ruler of the Ming dynasty on January 23,1368 and became known as the Hongwu Emperor. He reigned for 30 years until his death in 1398.

Huidi "Jianwen Emperor"
(1399 C.E.—1402 C.E.)

Chengzu "Yougle Emperor"
(1403 C.E.—1424 C.E.)

Renzong "Hongxi Emperor"
(1425 C.E.)

Yuanzong "Yuande Emperor"
(1426 C.E.—1435 C.E.)

Yingzon "Zhenglong Emperor"
(1436 C.E.—1449 C.E.)

Daizong "Jingtai Emperor"
(1450 C.E.—1456 C.E.)

Yingzong "Dienshun Emperor"
(1457 C.E.—1464 C.E.)

Xianzong "Chenghua Emperor"
(1465 C.E.—1487 C.E.)

The years between 1480 to 1487 consisted of an era that produced massive state expansion through warfare. The constant wars were financed through heavy taxes on the Chinese citizens.

Wuzong "Zhengde Emperor"
(1506 C.E.—1521 C.E.)

Western Iron Leg kingdom of Gentiles Reach Far East: The first European traders, the Portuguese, arrived in the South China Sea in 1514 after receiving the report from explorer **Marco Polo,** who journeyed from Europe to Asia from 1271 to 1295. Two centuries later by 1557, the Portuguese had gained control of the autonomous region of Macao near Hong Kong. It remained in Portuguese hands until 1999 C.E.

Shizong "Jiajing Emperor"
(1522 C.E.—1566 C.E.)

Muzong "Longqing Emperor"
(1567 C.E.—1572 C.E.)

Shenzong "Wanli Emperor"
(1573 C.E.—1620 C.E.)

Guangzong "Taichang Emperor"
(1620 C.E.)

Hsizong "Dianqi Emperor"
(1621 C.E.—1627 C.E.)

Ssuzong "Chongzheng Emperor"
(1628 C.E.—1644 C.E.)

The Imperial Qing Dynasty
(1644 C.E.—1911 C.E.)

In the mid-1600s, an adversary rose up against the Ming Dynasty. His name was Nurhaci, a poor peasant rebel and member of the Aisin Gioro clan from the Manchuri region of the country. He was born April 8, 1559 in the city of Hetu Ala. He started his military career as a soldier working for a general of the Ming dynasty. In the year 1616, Nurhaci started his revolution against the Ming leader Ssuzong. He was successful in his goal to unite the various Manchu tribes. Afterwards he was able to launch attacks against Ming soldiers, and eventually conquering the entire northeastern parts of China. However, Nurchai died on September 30, 1626 before he was able to complete his mission of removing the Ming emperor. His ten-year effort, known as the Xinhai Revolution, did in the long run lay the foundation for the eventual removal of the Ming dynasty and the rise of the Qing dynasty.

His son Hong Taiji succeeded him as the leader of the Xinhai Revolution, consolidating the gains of his father, and serving as the founder and first emperor of the Qing Dynasty. Hong Taiji was born November 28, 1592. He was 33 when he ascended to the throne on October 20, 1626. He reigned for 17 years until his death on September 21, 1643 at the age of 50.

Shizu "Shunzhi Emperor"
(1644 C.E.—1661 C.E.)
Birth Name: Fulin

In the year 1645, the armies of the Qing Dynasty overthrew the remaining armies of the Ming Dynasty. In May of that year, Shizu oversaw the slaughter of as many as 800,000 in a bloody massacre. He was also the first Emperor of the Qing Dynasty to reign in Peking, presently known as Bejing today.

Shengzu "Kangxi Emperor"
(1662 C.E.—1722 C.E.)
Birth Name: Xuanye

Shengzu was the longest reigning Emperor of the Qing Dynasty. He ascended to the throne on February 5, 1661 and reigned until his death on December 20, 1722. And it came to pass that he reigned for a total of 61 years.

Shizong "Yungzheng Emperor"
(1723 C.E.—1735 C.E.)
Birth Name: Yinzhen

Gaozong "Qianlong Emperor"
(1736 C.E.—1795 C.E.)
Birth Name: Hongli

Renzong "Jiaqing Emperor"
(1796 C.E.—1820 C.E.)
Birth Name: Yongyan

Xuanzong "Daoguang Emperor"
(1821 C.E.—1850 C.E.)
Birth Name: Minning

Wenzong "Xianfeng Emperor"
(1851 C.E.—1861 C.E.)
Birth Name: Yizhu

Muzong "Dongzhi Emperor"
(1826 C.E.—1874 C.E.)
Birth Name: Zaichun

Tezong "Guangxu Emperor"
(1875 C.E.—1908 C.E.)
Birth Name: Zaitian

Puyi "Xuantong Emperor"
(1908 C.E.—1912 C.E.)
Birth Name: Puyi

Emperor Puyi was the last emperor of the Qing Dynasty which reigned from 1644 until its collapse in 1912. So it came to pass that the dynasty known as the Great Qing reigned for a total of 268 years over a multi-cultural Empire. None of these Chinese emperors knew **YHWH ELOHIM Israel** nor observed HIS laws, commandments, judgements, and statutes according as commanded at Mount Sinai. Each of them walked in the imaginations of their own minds and served graven doctrines and graven images on every lofty mountain, on hills, and under any luxuriant tree where they served the gods of Confucianism, Buddhism, Taoism, Tianism, Islam, Christianity, Shamanism, and other traditional Chinese religions. In the end, the successor to the Qing Dynasty was the Republic of China which came to power in 1912 unto 1949.

In 1949, **Chairman Mao Tse-tung, leader of the Chinese Communist Party,** led a successful socialist revolution and established the People's Republic of China which has reigned for 70 years and has remained in power until today in 2019. In these last days of the 21st century, China has become **one of the latter-day toes of miry clay** which is in opposition to, and, *does not cleave* unto **[the iron of the Western-capitalist kingdoms]**.

Great Chinese Inventions which eventually arrived in the West

Paper Making 105 C.E.
Moveable Type Printing/Printing Press 960 C.E.—1279 C.E.
Gunpowder 1000 C.E.
The Compass 1100 C.E.
Alcohol 2000 B.C.E.—1600 C.E.
Mechanical Clock 725 C.E.
Tea Production 2,737 B.C.E.
Silk 6,000 years ago
Umbrella 1,500 years ago
Acupuncture 2,300 years ago
Iron Smelting 1050 B.C.E.—256 B.C.E.
Porcelain 581 C.E.—618 C.E.
Earthquake Detector 132 C.E.
Rocket 228 C.E.
Bronze 1700 B.C.E.
The Kite 3,000 years ago
The Seed Drill 3,500 years ago

Row Crop Farming 6th Century B.C.
The Toothbrush 1498 C.E.
Paper Money 9th Century C.E.

In conclusion, **The Chinese Empires** were responsible for numerous of other inventions, both small and great, which advanced and changed the course of human civilization worldwide. In fact, they were first in many more categories than I mentioned. Even today, **The West** continues to be indebted to **The Far East** for many reasons, all which advanced the course of human history in both Europe and the Americas.

The Kingdoms of Japan
(1392 C.E.—1912 C.E.)

Muromachi Period (1392 C.E.—1573 C.E.) Momoyama Period (1573 C.E.—1615 C.E.) Edo Period (1611 C.E.—1867 C.E.) Meiji Period (1868 C.E.—1912 C.E.)

"YAH changes times and seasons. HE removes kings (The Muromachi Period) and install kings(The Momoyama Period, The Edo Period, and Meiji Period); HE gives the wise their wisdom and knowledge to those who know" **Daniel 2: 21.**

Japan is populated by one single Asian ethnic group. It is an island country situated off the east coast of Asia in the West Pacific Ocean. It consist of four main islands—Hokkaido, Honshu, Shikoku, and Kyushu. The islands are separated from China by the East China Sea. The Sea of Japan separates the island kingdom from North and South Korea, and Russia. Since the 17th century, Tokoyo has been the imperial capital. Four-fifths of Japan's surface is covered with mountains and hills. The sceneries provide the perfect setting for Shinto Buddhist temples to be built everywhere.

Japan is an ancient country with a history that began in 660 B.C.E.. The first unified Japanese state was established during the 4th and 5th centuries by the Yamato Court. Buddhism arrived in that same era byway of Korea. It is a well known fact that the Japanese borrowed heavily from Chinese culture for several centuries. But, by the 9th century C.E. Japan began to sever their links with mainland China. The prominent Fujiwara family held imperial power through the 11th century. In 1192, Minamoto Yoritomovo established Japan's first Shogunate. The Shogunate was a powerful government administration that served the interest of the Emperor. The head of the Shoginate was known as the *shogun*. In the Japanese language Shogun meant *"Commander-in-Chief of the Expeditionary Forces Against The Barbarians"*. From the 12th thru 19th century, the office of shogun grew into a de facto military dictatorship controlling every aspect of Japanese life, from foreign policies to domestic policies. The servants who carried out the duties for the shogun were called *bakufu*. Below is a list of the Emperors of Japan dating back to the 14th century and continuing to the 20th century.

Muromachi Period
(1392 C.E.—1573 C.E.)

Emperors of Japan

Go-Komatsu
(1382 C.E.—1412 C.E.)

Go-Komatsu was the 100th Emperor of Japan according to the traditional Japanese order of succession. During this period, **The Ashikaga Shogunate** ruled the feudal military government. The shogunate faced continuous warfare between powerful families. The Ashikaga Shogunate lasted from 1336 C.E. to 1573 C.E.) which was 237 years.

<u>Shoko</u>
(1412 C.E.—1428 C.E.)

<u>Go-Hanazono</u>
(1428 C.E.—1464 C.E.)

<u>Go-Tsuchimikado</u>
(1464 C.E.—1500 C.E.)

<u>Go-Kashiwabara</u>
(1500 C.E.—1526 C.E.)

<u>Go-Nara</u>
(1526 C.E.—1557 C.E.)

<u>Oogimachi</u>
(1557 C.E.—1586 C.E.)

Emperor Oogimachi, whose birth name was Oda Nobunaga, was able to bring peace among the rival powerful families and renew the process of unifying Japan. **The Ashikaga Shogunate** assisted the Emperor in restoring law and order.

Momoyama Period
(1573 C.E.—1615 C.E.)

The Azuchi Shogunate came into power in 1573 during the reign of Emperor Oogimachi. The powerful military administration replaced the Ashikaga Shogunate, however in the end, the military wing of the emperorship didn't last but a mere 27 years, from 1573 to 1600. It was replaced by the **Tokugawa Shogunate** in the year 1600 during the days of Emperor Go-Yozel.

<u>Oogimachi</u>
(1557 C.E.—1586 C.E.)

<u>Go-Yozel</u>
(1586 C.E.—1611 C.E.)

The Tokugawa Shogunate came to power in the year 1600 during the 25-year reign of Japanese **Emperor Go-Yozel**. This was a time when the feudal military government was strong. In fact, many historians believed Emperor Go-Yozel was Japan's greatest ruler. The powerful shogun reigned in Edo. In 1603, the powerful Tokugawa Ieyasu chose the city Edo as the new capital. Edo is present-day Tokoyo and it continues to serve as the kingdom's capital today, five centuries later. In 1605, Tokugawa Ieyasu resigned and gave his position to his son Tokugawa Hidelada, although he remained the power behind the throne.

<u>Go-Mizuo</u>
(1611 C.E.—1629 C.E.)

Edo Period
(1611 C.E.—1867 C.E.)

In terms of literature, Japan experienced a renaissance which featured great stage performances and stage presentations. There were comic compositions and an increase in writing humorous novels. Live actors and puppet shows were very popular. Samurai wrestling also emerged as a beloved sport. Buddhist temples and shrines with statues of Buddha adorned the mountainous countryside. The Japanese, along with the Chinese, were among the world's first people to use moveable woodblock printing. In this era, the Japanese mastered the use of multicolored woodblock print.

<u>Go-Mizuo</u>
(1611 C.E.—1629 C.E.)

<u>Meisho</u>
(1629 C.E.—1643 C.E.)

<u>Go-Komyo</u>
(1643 C.E.—1645 C.E.)

<u>Go-Sai</u>
(1654 C.E.—1663 C.E.)

<u>Reigen</u>
(1663 C.E.—1687 C.E.)

<u>Higashiyama</u>
(1687 C.E.—1709 C.E.)

<u>Nakamikado</u>
(1709 C.E.—1735 C.E.)

<u>Sakuramachi</u>
(1735 C.E.—1747 C.E.)

<u>Momozono</u>
(1747 C.E.—1762 C.E.)

<u>Go-Sakuramachi</u>
(1752 C.E.—1770 C.E.)

<u>Go-Momozono</u>
(1770 C.E.—1779 C.E.)

<u>Kokaku</u>
(1779 C.E.—1817 C.E.)

<u>Ninko</u>
(1817 C.E.—1846 C.E.)

<u>Komei</u>
(1848 C.E.—1867 C.E.)

<u>Meiji</u>
(1868 C.E.—1912 C.E.)

In 1867, Yoshinobu, the last shugunate of the Tokugawa lineage, stepped down and relinquished his position as the military chief and second-in-command to Emperor Meiji. All temporal power was now consolidated in the Emperor's hands.

Emperor Meiji, a visionary, adopted a constitution and started a program of modernization and **Westernization** of the **Far East kingdom**. Waxing stronger and stronger, Japan grew into an imperial power and in 1894 went to war with China. In 1904, Japan initiated a war against Russia. By the 1910, the island kingdom had annexed Korea, and two decades later in 1931, Machuria was a part of its colonial possessions in southeast Asia.

Sparking World War II, the imperial Japanese power attacked the United States in the Philippines and Hawaii during December 1941. In 1945, the emerging superpower United States dropped atomic bombs on Hiroshima and Nagasaki, killing hundreds of thousands. Imperial Japan surrendered immediately to the United States and other Allied Powers. After the war, the U.S., led by General Douglas MacArthur, occupied Japan and ordered the kingdom to adopt a Western-styled democratic government. After the U.S. departed, Japan underwent a monumental rebuilding program, and by the 1980s, it was one of the world's largest economic powers, rivaling the United States, Canada, and Western Europe.

In the latter-days, Japan has become one of the **10 principal miry clay kingdoms** spoken of in Nebuchadnezzar's dream. Although, Japan **[miry clay]** was conquered by the United States **[iron kingdom]**. Both countries still continue to disagree on several major issues, such as trade, finance, the stationing of U.S. military installations in the country, fishing rights, and North-South Korean relations. We must remember: **[iron]** and **[clay]** *"do not cleave one to another"* as Daniel foretold.

So it came to pass that all the Emperors of the kingdom of Japan knew not **YHWH ELOHIM Israel** nor walked in HIS laws, commandments, judgements, and statutes according to the standard **YAH** commanded Israel and all nations at Mount Sinai.

The Mongolian Empire
(1206 C.E.—1636 C.E.)

The Mongolia state was straddled across the central portion of north-central Asia south of Siberian Russia and north of eastern China. It was, and continues to be, a mountainous country where the heights of the Khentil Mountains peak at 9,200 feet and covers a range of 4,600 square miles of elevated landscape in the northeast portion of the country. For centuries, Mongolians were known as the steppe dwellers, whose habitations were built in mountain clefts.

During the 3rd century B.C.E., Mongolia became a part of the Xiongnu empire in China. From the 4th thru the 10th centuries C.E., the Turks rule Mongolia. At other times, Mongolia faced invasions from Siberian Rus tribesmen and infighting among the various Mongol tribal federations. However, Mongolia's fortune began to changed in the midst of the 12th century when a **Mongolian chieftain named Yesugel** and **his wife Hoeiun** became parents of a young lad named **Temujin** in the year 1162. Temujin was born in a dusty settlement known as Delun Boldog near the 8,000-feet tall Burkhan Khaldum mountains. At the age of 9, his father arranged a marriage between his young son and a neighboring Mongolian princess of the Khongirad clan. Her name was Borte. His father traveled through the land of a people known as the Tartars to arrive in the land of the Khongirads. After his arrival, he decided to allow Temujin to remain with his bride's family so he could learn their customs. On the way back home, his father traveled back through he land of the Turkic-Tartar people. This time, his father Yesugel was poisoned by someone. Once young Temujin learned what happened, he rushed to see his father, but he was dead before he arrived.

After those events, the elders of the clan abandoned the mother of Temujin. They were left alone, so his mother took the family back to the mountains to live. There, 11-year-old Temujin grew into a young warrior, killing his own younger brother for hoarding food during a famine, and becoming the companion of another warrior named Jamukha. The two young warriors made a blood oath to work together to plunder and liberate their territories.

Years later, Temujin decided to return to the land of the Khongirads to reunite with his wife Borte. His father-in-law granted him his request. But shortly after he redeemed his 1st wife, another Mongolian clan named the Merkits kidnapped her. Temujin barely escaped.

Several months later, Temujin requested support from another tribal leader named Toghrui who agreed to assist him. The three leaders, Temujin, his blood brother Jamukha, and his new ally Toghrui, assembled 20,000 soldiers to do battle with the Merkits. They defeated the Merkits and recovered Temujin's wife Borte. It was joyous occasion, but the egos of the three began to collide. Many feared Jamykha would seize power for himself. So, the Mongolians gathered at the sacred mountain Burkhan Khaldun and chose Temujin as their leader and received the throne name **Genghis Khan**.

"YAH changes times and seasons. HE removes (The Chinese, Turks, Siberians, and other foreign powers) kings and install (The Mongolian Empire) kings; HE gives the wise their wisdom and knowledge to those who know"

Daniel 2: 21.

Genghis Khan
(1206 C.E.—1227 C.E.)

1201: Born with the name Temujin, the 39-year-old leader was initially opposed by his blood brother Jamukha and Toghrui. Temujin prevailed.

1202: Temujin destroyed the Tartars and revenged the death of his father. In this same year, he defeated his once close friend Jamukha after several battles. Eventually, his generals betrayed him and delivered him into the hands of Temujin who slew him by breaking his spine in the autumn of 1204.

1203: Temujin created a new elite Imperial military guard known as the *Kheshig*. The following year, he began his military campaigns.

1205: Khan united the various Mongol tribes and began his conquest of central Asia. The Mongol Army conquered northwestern China.

1206: Temujin received his throne name **Genghis Khan** which meant *"Oceanic Ruler of the Mongol Empire"*. He was anointed by Kokochu, the chief shaman of the Mongols. His coronation was held at the Kurultal on the sacred mountain Burkhan Khaldun. The Mongolian people worshipped the mountain and the sun as gods. They bowed before and prayed to the spirit of the Burkhan Khaldun mountains daily.

Ogedei Khan
(1229 C.E.—1241 C.E.)

Khan's son Ogedie reigned in the Emperor's stead. Ogedei also conquered the Jin(Chin) dynasty in China.

Guyuk Khan
(1246 C.E.—1248 C.E.)

Mongke Khan
(1251 C.E.—1259 C.E.)

Kubai Khan
(1260 C.E.—1294 C.E.)

Kubai Khan established the Mongolian Dynasty (Yuan) in China in the year 1279. After the 14th century, the Ming Dynasty of China was able to restrict Mongolian incursions. The Chinese confined the Mongols to their homeland in the steppes.

Temur Khan
(1294 C.E.—1307 C.E.)

Kulug Khan
1307 C.E.—1311 C.E.)

Ayurbarwada Guyantu Khan
(1311 C.E.—1320 C.E.)

Gegeen Khan
(1320 C.E.—1323 C.E.)

Yesun Temur
(1323 C.E.—1328 C.E.)

Ragibagh Khan
(1328 C.E.)

Jayaatu Khan Tugh Temur
(1328 C.E.—1329 C.E.)
(1329 C.E.—1332 C.E.)

Rinchinbai Khan
(1332 C.E.)

Toghon Temur
(1333 C.E.—1370 C.E.)

Biligtu Khan
(1370 C.E.—1378 C.E.)

Togus Temur
(1378 C.E.—1388 C.E.)

Jorightu Khan
(1388 C.E.—1392 C.E.)

Engke Khan
(1392 C.E.—1393 C.E.)

Elbeg Khan
1393 C.E.—1399 C.E.)

Gun Temur Khan
(1399 C.E.—1402 C.E.)

Orug Temur Khan(Gulichi)
(1402 C.E.—1408 C.E.)

Oljei Temur Khan
(1408 C.E.—1412 C.E.)

Delbeg Khan
(1412 C.E.—1415 C.E.)

Oyiradai
(1415 C.E.—1425 C.E.)

Adai Khan
(1425 C.E.—1438 C.E.)

Taisun Khan
(1433 C.E.—1453 C.E.)

Agbarjin
(1454 C.E.)

Esen Tayasi
(1454 C.E.—1455 C.E.)

Markorgis Khan
(1455 C.E.—1465 C.E.)

Molon Khan
(1465 C.E.—1466 C.E.)

Mandulun Khan
(1475 C.E.—1478 C.E.)

Dayan Khan
(1479 C.E.—1517 C.E.)

Bars Bolud Jinong
(1525 C.E.—1531 C.E.)

Bodi Alagh Khan
(1519 C.E.—1547 C.E.)

Darayisung Godeng Khan
(1547 C.E.—1557 C.E.)

Tumen Zasagt Khan
(1558 C.E.—1592 C.E.)

Buyan Sechen Khan
(1592 C.E.—1604 C.E.)

Ligden Khan
(1603 C.E.—1634 C.E.)

During his 30-year reign, Ligdan Khan united the Mongol tribes in defense of Manchu, but after his death in 1634, his efforts failed and **the Mongolian Empire became a part of the Chinese Qing Dynasty.**

Ejen Khan
(1634 C.E.—1636 C.E.)

In the end, the Mongolian Empire collapsed and was swallowed up by the Chinese Emperor Hong Taiji, founder of the Qing Dynasty, and incorporated into the kingdoms of the **Chinese Empire** in the year 1644.

So it came to pass that the Mongolian Empire died after reigning 430 years. All of their rulers, beginning with the cruel Genghis Khan in 1206 C.E. and ending with Ejen Khan in 1636 C.E., did evil in the eyes of **YHWH ELOHIM Israel.** They did not walk in YAH's laws, commandments, judgements, and statutes written in the Torah for ancient Israel and all nations of the earth. Instead, all of them walked in the imaginations of their own minds doing whatever was good in their own eyes.

The Expansion of the Mongolian Empire
In the Spirit of Nimrod—Genghis Khan and Khan Dynasty—*"mighty hunters before YHWH"*

1207: The Mongols conquered Western Xia and parts of Tibet in a three-year campaign which lasted until 1210. Genghis Khan overthrew the Uyghur Turk dynasty that ruled northern China from 1115 C.E. to 1234 C.E..

1215: Khan captured the imperial city Zhongdu in the Battle of Zhongdu expanding the Mongol conquest of China.

1218: Mongol ambassadors visited Shah Muhummad II of Khwarezmain, which was northern Persia near the Caspian Sea, but they were slain. Their deaths enraged Khan provoking him to think about westward expansion for the first time. The following year the Mongolian cavalrymen, known as the Golden Horde, crossed the Jaxartes River into Central Asia destroying every kingdom that did not submit to the rule of Genghis Khan. Those territories includes areas known today as Kyrgyzstan, Uzbekistan, Tajilistan, Kazakhstan. Between 1219 to 1221, the Mongols reached the kingdom of Khwarezmia and launched a four-pronged attack against the city to repay them for what they had previously done to the Mongol envoys two years earlier. Khan commanded his elite forces to capture Shah Muhummad II, but he fled to an island somewhere in the Casipan Sea. Meanwhile back east, Mongol armies, with blood in their eyes, had penetrated deep inside southern China.

1223: Mongolian horsemen and their Rus allies had penetrated areas known as Ukraine in eastern Europe today. The Mongols defeated the Aryan warriors known as East Slavic tribesmen in the Battle of the Kalka River. At this time, the Mongolian Empire extended from the Pacific Ocean in the **East** to the Caspian Sea in the **West**. In only two decades the **Mongol kingdom** had grown into a 10 million mile Empire which equaled the size of the continent of Africa.

1227: Genghis Khan, a ruthless, unmerciful, bloody man who grew into one of the most successful military leaders in human history, died on August 18 at the age of 65. He slew millions during his 21-year reign. He was buried on the Burkhan Khaldun Mountain in a secret location. All of the pallbearers were slain after the funeral in order to keep his burial site a secret.

1229: On September 13, Ogedei ascended to the throne as the new Great Khan. Two years later in 1231, Ogedei, following in the footsteps of his father, ordered the conquest of Korea.

1232: Ogedei ordered the Siege of Kaifeng to war against the Jurchen Dynasty, which had refused to submit to Mongol rule for two decades. Ogedei dispatched two armies, one led by him and the other by his brother Tolui. It was a fierce battle with the Chinese soldiers counter-attacking with fire lances and bombs of gunpowder, killing countless Mongolian soldiers. The Mongols also used rocket launchers to inflict damage on Kaifeng. As the siege continued, a famine and sickness started to plague the city. As the battle raged on, the Chinese proposed a peace treaty, but a Mongol diplomat was slain and the talks were ended. The Chinese Emperor Aizong fled for his life, leaving for refuge elsewhere in the city of Caizhou. General Cui Li, sieged the throne in Kaifeng, executed all the officers and townspeople loyal to the former emperor, and promptly surrendered to the Mongolians. Although the Chinese lost the battle, they introduced missile-rocket technology to the world. The Jurchens were the first to use such skills during this time in human history. But, for the record, the ancient **Afro-Asiatic World** had already used such technology thousands of years earlier before this prophetic Time Zone. [**Read II Chronicles 26:11-15** for confirmation. You will see the **ancient Afro-Asiatic Hebrew king of Judah Uzziah** had used those weapons.]

Afterwards, the Mongols chased after Emperor Aizong in Caizhou. The Caizhou quickly fell before the Mongol onslaught. Emperor Aizong committed suicide.

1236: The Mongols, under the command of General Chormaqan, continued their westward expansion with the more conquest of eastern Europe, subduing both Georgia, Poland, Hungary, Croatia, and Armenia. During the same year on the other side of the world, the Mongol generals in the East initiated a new campaign against the Song Dynasty in eastern China.

1241: Mongols invaded Bulgaria.

1257: Mongols invaded Vietnam.

1258: Mongols invaded Mesopotamia and laid siege to Baghdad and overthrew the Abbasid Caliphate. Mongol cavalrymen in eastern Europe expand their conquest by invading Lithuania.

1259: Mongols invaded Syria.

1260: A civil-war broke out among the offspring of Genghis Khan. Kubai Khan and Ariq Boke were at odds, ending the era of an united Mongolian Empire. In 1271, Kubai Khan

eventually established the Yuan Dynasty. Two years later, he issued paper money throughout his realm. The paper money was known as *chao*.
1279: The Mongolian Dynasty reigned over all China. Trade flourished along the Silk Road.
1281: Mongols invaded the island kingdom of Japan for a second time.
1315: Mongols converted to Islam.
1368: The native Chinese Ming Dynasty overthrew the yoke of the Mongolian Yuan Dynasty. Mongol leader Toghon Temur was forced to flee northward to Shangdu.
In the end, the vast empire of the Mongols, which once extended from eastern Europe to eastern China, was confined to its own borders on the steppe lands of Mongolia. The Golden Horde was conquered by the Musovites. The Ming Dynasty incursions ended their unity and by the 15th and 16th century, only a loose federation of tribes existed.
King David once said, *"Man, his days are like those of grass; he blooms like a flower of the field; a wind passes by and it is no more, its own place no longer knows it,"* in **Psalms 103: 15-16**.
Another very important point that should be made about the Mongolian Empire was its impact upon the cosmopolitan nature of the human population. The empire, through conquest and interactions, consisted of a mixture of people with diverse physical features, and bloodlines, ranging from Chinese, Turks, Rus, Arabs, Persians, Europeans, to Africans that were brought under one common fold. Genghis Khan was known to take beautiful wives from all the kingdoms he conquered, and some even said, that one in every 200 people alive during his lifetime had Mongolian blood running through their veins. Biblically speaking, Khan's kingdom included all the sons of Noah: Japhethic sons and daughters who were Aryan pale-skinned, to Shemitic yellow-skinned, olive-skinned, brown-skinned people, along with Hamitic reddish-brown and black-skinned people living under one common Mongolian standard extending from the Far East, Central Asia, Middle East, Africa, into parts of Europe.

The Kingdoms of India
(1206 C.E.—1857 C.E.)

The Delhi Sultanate (1206 C.E.—1526 C.E.) Mughal Empire (1526 C.E.—1857 C.E.) Bengal Sultanate (1352 C.E.—1576 C.E.) Vijayanagara Empire (1336 C.E.—1646 C.E.) Maratha Empire(1674 C.E.—1818 C.E.)

"YAH changes times and seasons. HE removes kings and install kings; HE gives the wise their wisdom and knowledge to those who know" **Daniel 2:21.**

India is an ancient great, fertile, and vast South Asian country with a rich history which dates back to 7,000 B.C.E. when early dark brown-skinned and black **Afro-Asiatic** men and women built an urban civilization that thrived in the Indus Valley. **[Read Genesis/Bereshith 11:2]**. By 2,600 B.C.E., urban civilization thrived in the Indus Valley. The expansive 1.2 million square mile subcontinent is situated by the waters of the Bay of Bengal on its eastern border. The Bay of Bengal flows into the Indian Ocean. The Arabian Sea covers the western border and the Indian Ocean also surrounds the southern borders. The Himalayas Mountains covers India's northern border. China is located on the opposite side of the mountain range. The Indo-Gangetic Plain is another major geographical area, along with the Deccan Plateau in the southern portion of the vast land.
(Today, the countries of Pakistan and Afghanistan are neighboring countries. During early, middle, and late Medieval India, the territories known as Pakistan and Afghanistan today were a part of India. The same is true for Burma and Bangladesh.)
In the 6th century B.C.E., the religions of Buddhism and Jainism thrived. Eventually, the land became the home of Hinduism, Sikhism, Christianity, and Islam. The people of India were just as diverse as their multitude of gods. There were a varying mixture of ethnicities, Aryans, Africans, and Asians, who settled in the ancient land before the recording of human history. India also developed into an abundant breadbasket for rice, wheat, sugarcane, coconuts, spices, teas, coffee, and in the modern era, a source of tobacco, rubber, and cotton.

The kingdoms of India included the classic Maurya Empire, the Satvahana dynasty, the Middle kingdoms of the Gupta Empire in the 5th century C.E. ,and eventually the Muslims. The Muslims invaded India in 1,000 C.E. and, by the 13th century, they had established **the Islamic-based Delhi Sultanate.** For the historical record, the economy of India was the world's largest from the 1st century C.E. to 1,000 C.E., comprising 1/3 to 1/4 of all the wealth in the entire world, surpassing the Roman Empire and Middle Age Europe.

The Delhi Sultanate
(1206 C.E.—1526 C.E.)

The Delhi Sultanate was an Islamic sultanate based for the most part in Delhi. The empire stretched over large swaths of the northern Indian sub-continent for nearly three centuries. During that time, there were five separate dynasties that ruled the Delhi Sultanate, beginning with **1) Mamluk dynasty, 2) the Khalji dynasty, 3) the Toghlaq dynasty, 4) the Sayyid dynasty,** and ending with **5) the Lodi dynasty** in the 16th century C.E..

The Delhi Sultanate was born on June 25, 1206 when a Turkic slave general named Qutb ud-Din Albak of Central Asia, under the command of the Sunni-Islamic Mamluk Empire, led an invasion into the Gangetic heartland of northern India to establish control over the new areas.

1) The Mamluk Dynasty
(1206 C.E.—1290 C.E.)

Qutb ud-Din Albak
(1206 C.E.—1210 C.E.)

Born in 1150 in Turkestan, Qutb ud-Din Albak, a fair-skinned Indo-Turk, was raised as a slave in Persia, and grew into a military commander under a Mamluk general named Muhummad Ghor. He led the conquest of northern India with Albak serving as his assistant. After securing a victory, Ghor, founder of the Ghurid dynasty, returned to Persia where he was later murdered. He had already appointed his slave Qutb ud-Din Albak as the ruler in his absence. That is why the *Delhi Sultanate* is also referred to as the Ghurid *dynasty* or the *Slave dynasty*. For 14 years, from 1192 to 1206, Albak had served as Ghor's administrator. During this time, Albak and other generals conquered more territories. He chose the great city Lahore as the first capital for his Islamic Caliphate of India. He also repaired the great mosque, The Quwwat ul-Islam Mosque, in Delhi and attempted to erase all traces of Hinduism in the process. He died from injuries suffered after he fell off his horse while playing polo in the year 1210 at the age of 60. The official language for the sultanate was Persian.

Aram Shah
(1210 C.E.—1211 C.E.)

In the year 1210, the son of Qutb ud-Din Albak, who was named Aram Shah, ascended to the throne. During his reign, the capital of the Delhi Sultanate was moved to the city of Badayun.

Shams ud-Din Ittatmish
(1211 C.E.—1236 C.E.)

Ittutmish was the third fair-skinned Turkic ruler of the Mamluk dynasty. He too had been a slave. He was once a slave to Qutb ud-Din Albak. After marriage to Albak's daughter, he became the son-in-law and the lieutenant of the founder of the Delhi Sultanate. He was serving as the Governor of Baduan when he rose up against his brother-in-law Aram Shah, the biological son of Qutb ud-Din Albak, and deposed of him after his 1-yr. reign. In 1214, Ittutmish changed the capital of the Delhi Sultanate to royal city Delhi was first time. Delhi remained the capital of the empire for the following 113 years until 1327.

Rukn ud-Din Firuz
(April 30, 1236 C.E.—November 20, 1236 C.E.)

The son of Ittatmish reign for only 6 months and 21 days before his ouster.

Ruzia Sultana
(October 10, 1236 C.E.—October 14, 1240 C.E.)

Ruzia Sultana was the only woman to rule upon the throne over the Delhi Sultanate. Ruzia was a brown-skinned woman of the Egyptian based-Mamluk dynasty. She was born in 1205 in the heart of India. Her confidant **Jmal ud-Din Yaqut**, was an African slave who rose through the ranks to become an important recognized official in her inner court. It is believed that Yaqut was her secret lover. Many of the fair-skinned Turkic Muslims resented Yaqut's influence, along with the fact that a woman reigned as the monarch.

Muiz ud-Din Bahram
(1240 C.E.—1242 C.E.)

On May 15, 1242, Muiz ud-Din Bahram was murdered by officers in his own Islamic army.

Ala ud-Din Masad
(1242 C.E.—1246 C.E.)

Nasir ud-Din Mahmud
(1246 C.E.—1266 C.E.)

Ghiyas ud-Din Balban
(1266 C.E.—1286 C.E.)

Muiz ud-Din Qaiqabad
(1287 C.E.—February 1, 1290 C.E.)

Shams ud-Din Kaumars
(February 1, 1290 C.E.—June 13, 1290 C.E.)

On June 13, 1290, Shams ud-Din Kaumars, his father Muiz ud-din Qalqabad, and others were murdered by a man of Khalji lineage named Jalal ud-Din Firuz Khalji. Afterwards, he seized the throne of the Delhi Sultanate and established the new Khalji Dynasty in northern India.

2) The Khalji Dynasty
(1206 C.E.—1290 C.E.)

Jala ud-Din Firuz Khalji
(June 13, 1290 C.E.—July 19, 1296 C.E.)

Alauddin Khalji
(July 19, 1296 C.E.—January 1316 C.E.)

Shihabuddin Omar
(January 5, 1316 C.E.—April 1316 C.E.)

Qutb-ud-Din Murbarak
(1316 C.E.)

Khusrau Khan
(1320 C.E.)

Khusrau Khan, whose throne name was Sultan Nasiruddin Khusrau Shah, served as the last ruler of the Khalji dynasty which had begun in the year 1206 after the overthrow of the Qutb ud-Din Albak dynasty. Khusrau Khan's reign was noted for lastiing less than one year. Ghiyath al-Din Tughluq succeeded him and established a new dynasty known as the Tughluqs.

3) The Tughluq Dynasty
(1321 C.E.—1413 C.E.)

Ghiyath al-Din Tughluq
(September 8, 1321 C.E.—February 1325 C.E.)

Ghiyath al-Din Tughluq rose up and ascended to the throne as the founder of the Tughluq dynasty over the Delhi Sultanate on September 8, 1321.

Muhummad bin Tughluq
(1325 C.E.—March 20, 1351 C.E.)

The city of Daulalabad served as the capital for the Islamic Empire for seven years from 1327 unto 1334 before Muhummad bin Tughluq switched the capital back to Delhi. After 1337, Delhi remained as the royal capital of the Sultanate for the next 172 years, from 1334 to 1506.

Firoz Shah Tughlaq
(1351 C.E.—September 20, 1388)

Ghiyas ud-Din Tughlaq II
(September 20, 1388 C.E.—March 14, 1389 C.E.)

Abu Bakr Shah
(1389 C.E.—1390 C.E.)

Muhammad Shah ibn Firuz Shah Tughlaq
(length of rulership uncertain)

Mahumd Tughlaq
(length of rulership uncertain)

Nusrat Shah
(1413 C.E.)

Nusrat Shah was the last ruler of fair-skinned Turkic-Indian Tughluq lineage. During his reign the Tughluq dynasty was deeply divided. He ruled from the royal palace in the city of Firozabad. He ruled over several great cities while his rival Sultan Mahmud ruled over the Sayyid dynasty in the cities of Siri and Old Delhi. A covetous usurper named Khizi Khan succeeded him as the ruler of the Delhi Sultanate in northern India. During his reign, Timur, the ruler of the Mongols, invaded northern India and overthrew the Tughluqs.

4) The Sayyid Dynasty
(1414 C.E.—11451 C.E.)
Khizr Khan
(1414 C.E.—1421 C.E.)

Khizr Khan, whose throne name was Sayyid Khizr Khan ibn Malik Sulaiman, ascended to the throne on May 28, 1414. During his 7-year, he did not challenge the Mongolian rulership of Tamerlane. He did not even mint coins in his image during his reign. He died on May 20, 1421 and his son Murbarak succeeded him as the second ruler from the Sayyid dynasty.

Mubarak Shah
(1421 C.E.—1434 C.E.)

The Sayyids continued to be vassals to the Mongolian Empire.

Muhummad Shah
(1434 C.E.—1445 C.E.)

Ala ud-Din Shah
(1445 C.E.—1451 C.E.)

He assumed the throne name Alam Shah when he assumed power. He became known as a leader who was unable to command the respect of his subordinates. By 1448, he was forced to relinquish power in Delhi and retire to the city of Budaun. For three year a power vacuum existed until a rebel leader named Bahlol Lodi finally succeeded in overtaking Delhi after failing in two previous attempts. Lodi was declared the new ruler of the Delhi Sultanate in 1451.

5) The Lodi Dynasty
(1451 C.E.—1526 C.E.)
Bahlul Khan Lodi
(April 19, 1451 C.E.—July 12, 1489 C.E.)

Sikandar Lodi
(July 17, 1489 C.E.—November 1517 C.E.)

During the reign of Sikandar Lodi the capital city was changed from Delhi to Agra. Agra remained the capital city for 20 years, from 1506 until the demise of the Lodi dynasty in 1526.

Ibrahim Lodi
(1517 C.E.—April 26, 1526

Ibrahim Lodi was the last ruler of the Lodi dynasty and the Delhi Sultanate. He was slain during the Battle of Panipat in 1526 when the armies of Muhammad Babur attacked Agra and her other strongholds. After that, **The Delhi Sultanate** was abolished, disappeared, and replaced by Zahir ud-Din Muhummad Babur, the founder and first Emperor of the Mughal Dynasty. In the end, the Delhi Sultanate reigned for 320 years. Throughout **their Prophetic Time Zone** the Delhi Sultanate did not acknowledge **YHWH ELOHIM Israel** nor did they walk in HIS laws, commandments, judgements, and statutes according as HE commanded ancient Israel and all nations of the earth.

The Mughal Dynasty
(1526 C.E.—1857 C.E.)

Zahir ud-din Muhammad Babur
(April 26, 1526 C.E.—December 26, 1530 C.E.)

Zahir ud-din Muhummad Babur was born February 14, 1483 in Andijan in the Fergana Valley in an area now known as Uzbekistan. He was a man of Turkic-Mongol roots with a light yellowish-brown complexion. A fierce warrior, Babur conquered dark-skinned northern India and created a leadership known as the Mughal Dynasty. He was a fierce warrior which led the Mongol armies into the Indian subcontinent and overthrew the weakened Delhi Sultanate and the Lodi dynasty then established the Mughal Empire in northern India. The Mughal Empire was ruled by yellowish-brown, pale, and olive-skinned Mongolian men from areas in Central Asia. They became known as the Timurid dynasty, which began in the 15th century and continued up to the mid-19th century. They conquered dark-skinned northern India and created a leadership known as the Mughal Dynasty.

Nasir uddin Muhammad Humayun
(December 26, 1530 C.E.—May 17, 1540 C.E.)
(February 22, 1555 C.E.—January 27, 1556 C.E.)

Humayun ruled at a time when the Mughal Empire was at its peak. Except for the southern portion of the vast land, Humayun almost ruled the entire **Afro-Asiatic** Indian subcontinent in the area known as Hindustan. Those areas now include countries known as Pakistan and Afghanistan.

Muhammad Akbar "Akbar the Great"
(1556 C.E.—October 15, 1542 C.E.)

Akbar was born on October 15, 1542 in an area known as Pakistan today. He became the third Mughal Emperor at the age of 13 when his father Humayun died. By the time he reached the age of 34, he had defeated all of his enemies and increased the size of the Mughal Empire to twice the size it was when he assumed power. Like his predecessor, Akbar was not able to conquer the southern portion of the subcontinent. On a personal level Akbar was a multitalented individual who possessed a multitude of skills that ranging from being a warrior, to an armourer, animal trainer, inventor, technologist, carpentry, and an accomplished artist. He fell sick with a dysentery attack on October 3, 1605. Twelve days later, he died at the age of 63. He was buried in a mausoleum in Sikandra, Agra.

Nuruddin Muhammad Jahangir
(1605 C.E.—1627 C.E.)

Shah Jahan
(1628 C.E.—1658 C.E.)

Shah Jahan reigned for 31 years during the time known as the **Golden Age of Mughal** arts and architecture. During his reign, he erected splendorous monuments throughout the kingdom. He built the famous dome-shaped pure white marble stone **Taj Mahal** mausoleum built on the Yamuna River in the city of Agra during 1632 to 1648. The Taj Mahal, which was made of semi-precious stones, was a tomb in memory of Jahan's beloved wife Mumtaz Mahal who died in 1631. He initiated the project the following year in 1632. It took 22 years, even until 1654, to finish the massive architectural undertaking. The beautiful monument is flanked with two identical redstone buildings, one serving as a Mosque and the other one housing with two minarets. In front of the building is a square-shaped garden arrayed with beautiful flowers. Inside the large garden are several smaller ones. In 2019, nearly 350 years later, many historians contend the men whose architectural hands built the Taj Mahal constructed one of the world's most beautiful buildings. The artifacts, literature, and great monuments reveal a period of great wealth in India and a rich culture with beautiful clothing and aristocratic lifestyles.

It was said, Shah Jahan wanted to build another great Taj Mahal made of glistering black precious stones. But, his son Aurangzeb put him in prison where he remained until his death in 1666.

Aurangzeb
(1658 C.E.—1707 C.E.)

Born on November 4, 1618, Aurangzeb ascended to the throne at the age of 40 in the year 1658 and reigned for forty-nine years. Throughout his reign, there was constant warfare which allowed him the opportunity to expand his territorial holdings. He was an ambitious, well-educated Muslim ruler. In 1681, Aurangzeb launched an offensive against southern and western India. He led an army of 500,000 troops, expanding the Mughal Empire as he advanced. The Maratha people later rebelled against their imperial invasion. After his reign, there were a succession of weak and insignificant leaders that ruled over the Mughal dynasty. Aurangzeb was the last major leader until Shah Zafar II arose one-hundred thirty years later in 1837.

Shah Zafar II
(1837 C.E.—1857 C.E.)

Muhammad Bahadur Shah Zafar, a light-brown complexion man, was born October 24, 1775 in Delhi, India. He came to the throne at the age 62 on September 28, 1837 after his father Akbar II died. During his reign, the Mughal Empire had become a rump state, only a fraction of what it use to be. He fought against the British in the Indian Rebellion of 1857. His army lost the battle, he was captured, convicted of conspiracy, and sent into exile in the city of Ragoon, modern Burma. He remained there until his death on November 3, 1862 at the age of 87. After him, the Mughal dynasty officially collapsed and the Indo-European British Raj Empire succeeded them from 1858 until 1947.

The Bengal Sultanate
(1352 C.E.—1576 C.E.)

The Bengal Sultanate of India was born in the year 1352 out of the womb of the Muslim conquest of the Indian subcontinent. It grew into the first unified Bengali kingdom on the mainland. Today this area is the modern kingdom of Bangladesh.

Shamsuddin Ilyas Shah, a medium-brown skinned man of Afghan origin, was the founder of the Bengal Sultanate. The kingdom straddled that pathway from Persia and India into China, therefore it grew into **a melting pot of ethnicities** from throughout the Muslim world, from Africa, Central Asia, Asia Minor, and China in the Far East.

The Afro-Asiatic Presence of India

The Bengali Sultanate kingdom consisted of pale-skinned Aryans, brown-skinned Arabs, olive and yellow-skinned Turks, black Africans, native Afro-Aisatic Indians, olive-skinned Mongols, and others. Bengali society was inclusive for all these people, and although it was a Muslim society, it allowed Hinduism, Buddhism, and Christianity to flourish. It also became another center of the intermingling of bloodlines and ethnicities.

We also should be mindful of the historical facts that the subcontinent of India was the home of several African kingdoms and communities at various times, mainly ones such as **the Indian African Siddi community** in the southwest region in the city of Karnataka who were brought to India during **the sub-Saharan Slave Trade**. The Muslim rulers of the 12th century brought them to India for their bondmen and bondwomen. Those Africans became an intricate part of Indian society and moved up the ranks and became military leaders and some even became rulers. Others simply found soulmates and assimilated into the local surrounding Indian communities. Meanwhile, there were millions of other **black Afro-Asiatic of India** that had lived throughout the vast country since the days of Indus Valley civilizations.

Bengal Sultanate Emperors
(1352 C.E.—1578 C.E.)

Shamsuddin Ilyas Shah
(1352 C.E.—1358 C.E.)

Sikandar Shah
(1358 C.E.—1390 C.E.)

Ghiyasuddin Azam Shah
(1390 C.E.—1411 C.E.)

Saifuddin Hamza Shah
(1410 C.E.—1412 C.E.)

Although the Bengal Sultanate continued until 1578 C.E., a Muslim-Hindu civil-war broke out, pitting neighbor against neighbor. Saifuddin Hamza Shah ascended to the throne in 1410, but the civil war started in the second year of his reign in 1412. His slave named Shihabuddin hatched a plot and slew him.

Shihabuddin Bayazid Shah
(1413 C.E.—1414 C.E.)

He maintained good relations with China. He once sent a Chinese emperor a letter written on a gold leaf and he also gave the emperor a giraffe as a gift.

Alauddin Firuz Shah
(1414 C.E.—1415 C.E.)

The last Muslim successor of the Bengal Sultanate. The throne was seized by the brown-skinned Hindu leader Raja Ganesha who established himself as the new ruler.

Raja Ganesha
(1415 C.E.—1435 C.E.)

Ras Ganesha, a man with a dark complexion, established his own Hindu dynasty to rule the Bengal Sultanate.

Jalaluddin Muhammad Shah
(1415 C.E.—1416 C.E.)
(1418 C.E.—1433 C.E.)

The Hindu-Muslim civil war continued with both sides going back and forth temporarily gaining control only to lose it once again.

Shamsuddin Ahmad Shah
(1433 C.E.—1436 C.E.)

Nasiruddin Mahmud Shah
(1435 C.E.—1459 C.E.)

Rukunuddin Barbak Shah
(1459 C.E.—1474 C.E.)

Shamsuddin Yusuf Shah
(1474 C.E.—1481 C.E.)

Sikandar Shah II
(1481 C.E.)

Sikander was chosen to serve as the next emperor, but only days after receiving the mantle of power, he was removed for a lack of mental balance.

Fatah Shah
(1481 C.E.—1487 C.E.)

The Habshi Dynasty "A Black Dynasty of India"
(1487 C.E.—1494 C.E.)

Shahzada Barbak
(1487 C.E.)

Shahzada Barbak, a black man, founded the Habshi Dynasty, which consisted of former Abyssinians-*Ethiopians*-who had become important members of the Bengal Sultanate.

Jalaluddin Fateh Shah
(1487 C.E.)

Jalaluddin Fateh Shah resented the rising power of the former Abyssinians known as the Habshi. He attempted to enact policies to weaken their influence in the royal court. Shahzada Barak, commander-in-chief of the palace guards, conspired, then murdered Jalaluddin. Afterwards, the black Habshi dynasty briefly rose to power.

Saifuddin Firuz
(1487 C.E.—1489 C.E.)

Saifuddin Firuz, a black man ascended to the throne as the second ruler of the Habshi Dynasty. He once served as a army commander for previous Bengali dynasties.

Mahmud Shah II
(1489 C.E.—1490 C.E.)

Mahmud Shah II was an infant child when the mantle of power passed his way. Of course, he was too young to know good from evil, so Habash Khan served as his regent. Both, Mahmud and Habsh, were murdered by a rival usurper named Shamsuddin Muzaffar Shah.

Shamsuddin Muzaffar Shah
(1490 C.E.—1494 C.E.)

Shamsuddin Muzaffar Shah's reign was cut short when he was murdered by Habash Khan, the adult regent for the boy-king Mahnud Shah.

Shahi Dynasty
(1494 C.E.—1538 C.E.)

Alauddin Husain Shah
(1494 C.E.—1519 C.E.)

The infighting within the Habshi Dynasty provided the usurper Alauddin Husain Shah with the opportunity to rise up against Habash Khan and his child co-regent Mahmud Shah. He slew them both, then swept away the black Habshi dynasty and installed his Shahi Dynasty.

Nasiruddin Nasrat Shah
(1519 C.E.—1533 C.E.)

Alauddin Firuz Shah II
(1533 C.E.)

Ghiyasuddin Mahmud Shah
(1533 C.E.—1538 C.E)

During the reign of Ghiyasuddin Mahmud Shah, the kingdom of the last Bengal Sultan was conquered by the Sher Shah Suri, a light olive-skinned man who founded of **the Suri Empire**. The Suri Empire also succeeded **the Mughal Empire** in northern India as well.

Vijayanagara Empire "The Black Empire of India"
(1336 C.E.—1646 C.E.)

The Vijayanagar [*pronounced* **Vi-ja-ya-na-ga-ra**] Empire was born in the heart of black southern India during the 14th to the 17th century. It was an indigenous Afro-Asiatic empire also referred to as the Karnata Empire or the Kingdom of Bisnegar. The historical roots of the people that comprised the Vijayanagara Empire were the Kannada people. The Kannadas were the offsprings and a branch of the ancient Dravidian ethnic group that occupied and ruled southern India for thousands of years before the migration of Indo-Aryans, i.e., white people, into the southern Indian subcontinent. These black people were the descendants of the people from the great Indus Valley civilizations which dated back to 2,600 B.C.E..

Now, the Kannadas were closely related to another branch of nearby Afro-Asiatic people known as the Hoysalas. The Hoysalas had built an empire centuries before in the same region. The Hoysala Empire lasted from 1026 C.E. to 1313 C.E. The area today is a part of the Karnataka State in southwestern India. The ancient Hoysalas were famous for their development of sculpture and arts, architectural wonders, and religion. These black people built numerous great temples to the names of their gods. They built colossal graven images dedicated to their deities. One of their kings, King Vira Someshwara, who reigned from 1235 to 1263, built a great temple known as the Lakshminarayana Temple in the city of Hosaholalu. Today, it is a small town in the state of Karnataka in modern India.

The Vijayanagara Empire was founded in 1336 by black men named Harihara I and Bukka Raya I, his brother. Together, they established the Sangama Dynasty.

Sangama Dynasty
(1336 C.E.—1485 C.E.)

Harihara I(1336 C.E.—1356 C.E.)

Bukka Raya I(1356 C.E.—1377 C.E.)

Harihara Raya II(1377 C.E.—1404 C.E.

Virupaksha Raya(1404 C.E.—1405 C.E.)

Bukka Raya II(1405 C.E.—1406 C.E.)

Deva Raya I(1406 C.E.—1422 C.E.)

Ramachandra Raya(1422 C.E.)

Vira Vijaya Bukka Raya(1422 C.E.—1424 C.E.)

Deva Raya II(1424 C.E.—1446 C.E.)

Mallikarjuna Raya(1446 C.E.—1465 C.E.)

Virupaksha Raya II(1465 C.E.—1485 C.E.)

Prauha Raya(1485 C.E.)

Saluva Dynasty
(1485 C.E.—1505 C.E.)

Saluva Naeasimha Deva Raya(1485 C.E.—1491 C.E.)

Thimma Bhupala(1491 C.E.)

Narasimha Raya II(1491 C.E.—1505 C.E.)

Tuluva Dynasty
(1491C.E.—1570 C.E.)

Tuluva Narasa Nayaka(1491 C.E.—1503 C.E.)

Tuluva Narasa Nayaka(1491 C.E.—1503 C.E.)

Vira Narasimha Raya(1503 C.E.—1509 C.E.)

Krishna Deva Raya(1509 C.E.—1529 C.E.)

Achyuta Deva Raya(1529 C.E.—1542 C.E.)

Venkata I(1542 C.E.)

Sadasiva Raya(1542 C.E.—1570 C.E.)

Aravidu Dynasty
(1542 C.E.—1565 C.E.)

Aliya Rama Raya(1542 C.E.—1565 C.E.)

Emperor Rama Raya died fighting in the Battle of Talikota in 1565. His death served as an omen for the Vijayanagara Empire that their days were numbered.

Tirumala Deva Raya(1565 C.E.—1572 C.E.)

Sriranga I(1572 C.E.—1586 C.E.)

Venkata II(1586 C.E.—1614 C.E.)

Sriranga II(1614 C.E.)

Rama Deva Raya(1617 C.E.—1632 C.E.)

Venkata III(1632 C.E.—1642 C.E.)

Sriranga III(1642 C.E.—1646 C.E.)

Eventually, the Aravidu dynasty, and the entire empire itself, fell before the combined forces of the neighboring Muslim kingdoms of Mysore, Nayakas of Keladi and others that joined together against the once mighty empire.

So it came to pass that the Aravidu [*pronounced* A-ra-vi-du] Dynasty was the last dynasty to reign over **the Afro-Asiatic Vijayanagara Empire** in southern India. The empire, like its ancient Afro-Asiatic predecessors, did evil in **the eyes of YHWH ELOHIM Israel** and did not walk in the ways YAH which HE had commanded the ancient children of Israel and all nations. Instead, the Vijayanagara people, like their forebearers who built the 57-ft. high statue of Bahubali, served graven images. The 57-ft. image was dedicated to the god Jain. It continues to stand in southern India, and it is now regarded as one of world's largest statues still standing nearly 500 years later. In the city of Vikthala, they worshipped the sun, and in the city of Hampi, they built a shrine known as the Garuda Shrine in reverence of **the sun-god**. The religious monument was a sculptured stone fashioned into a temple chariot. They also served the god of **Hinduism**.

As I emphasized earlier, ancient, and even modern India today, is a majority Afro-Asiatic South Asian country. However, over the millenniums there have been repetitive pale-skinned Indo-Aryan, yellowish and olive-skinned Indo-Turkic invasions, and brownish Persian and Arab invasions that created a kaleidoscopes of diversity in hair texture and skin complexions.
For the record, another **Afro-Asiatic kingdom** of India was the **Janjira State**.

The Janjira State
(1489 C.—1948 C.E.)

The Janjira State was a princely state located in the Kathlawar Peninsula on the Gujarat coast. The rulers were descendants of the Siddis. The Siddi people were the offsprings of the Bantu people of East Africa who had journeyed to the region. Over the centuries, some immigrated there as merchants, crewmen on ships, mercenaries for Muslim invaders, and last but not least, multitudes came as bondmen and bondwomen during sub-Saharan slave trafficking. In 1489, it was said that an Ethiopian, in service of a Muslim sultanate, took over the island of Janjira and established the Afro-Asiatic dynasty. Their rulers were titled *nawab*, meaning *prince*. This dynasty over the black state of India continued on the coast of Koukan off southwest India, even during the era of the British Raj. At that time, from 1858 C.E. to 1948 C.E., it was known as the Prince State of British India in union with Jafrabad. In the end, Janjira came under the dominion of the rulership in Bombay.
So it came to pass that the kingdom of Janjira continued for 459 years, even from 1489 C.E. to 1948 C.E., before it was absorbed into the kingdom of India as one of its states when the central government of India won its independence from Britain in the year 1948.

Maratha Empire
(1674 C.E.—1818 C.E.)

The expansive Maratha [*pronounced* Ma-ra-tha] Empire was born in the heart of India during 1674. It grew to dominate the majority of the entire subcontinent of India from the mid-17th century to the early 19th century. This empire of India was ruled by a mulatto, light yellowish-brown and medium-brown people that believed in Indian self-rule. They rebelled against he **[iron]** foreign rule of the of the Mughal Empire and craved out their own indigenous kingdom.

Maratha Emperors
Shivaji (1674 C.E.—April 3, 1680 C.E.)

In 1627, Shivaji was born into an aristocratic family. Shavaji, an indigenous man of India, resented foreign domination of his people. They faced the Indo-Turk Mughals to the north and the black Muslim kingdoms to the south, namely the Bijapur Sultanate and their neighboring allies. This foreign pressure led Shivaji and his followers to call for "self-rule". He led the resistance to free his people from outsiders. Shivaji chose the city of Raigad as the capital of new kingdom.
The Maratha Empire started out as a tiny entity, consisting of only 4 percent on the Indian subcontinent. At the time of Shivaji's death six years later, the kingdom was rapidly expanding. During his reign, Shivaji built over 300 forts, a cavalry of 40,000 horsemen along with 50,000 infantrymen, and a strong naval presence on India's west coast. In the process of time, the Maratha Empire replaced the Mughal Empire and grew into a prominent kingdom across the mainland.

Sambhaji (January 16, 1681 C.E.—March 11, 1689 C.E.)
Sambhaji followed in his father's footsteps and continued the expansion of the empire. He also fought wars against the Portugese as they attempted to penetrate the Afro-Asiatic

subcontinent. In 1681, Mughal leader Aurangzeb attacked the kingdoms to its south. That included the Maratha kingdom, the Bijapur kingdom, the Vijayanagara kingdom, and all others in its path. Aurangzeb assembled a fighting force of 500,000 men for the campaign. Sambhaji led the resistance against the Mughal invaders. Throughout the 8-yr. conflict, Sambhaji never lost a battle or a fort to Aurangzeb, but on February 1, 1689, He was ambushed, captured, and executed. The Mughals charged him with torturing their people, raping their women, wholesale killing, and plundering their lands.

Rajaram I (March 11, 1689 C.E.—March 3, 1700 C.E.)
After his brother's murder, Rajaram ascended to the throne.

Shivaji II (1700 C.E.—1704 C.E.)
(1710 C.E.—1714 C.E.) Kolhapur State-a rival throne
Arguments over who would occupy the seat of power caused a rivalry among the Marathas.

Shahu I (January 12, 1708 C.E.—December 15, 1749 C.E.)
When Mughal Emperor Aurangzeb died in 1707, his successor released Shahu I, the grandson of the dynasty's founder, from their custody. After a brief power struggle, Shahu assumed the mantle of power and appointed a man named Balaji Vishwanath as his assistant. Vishwanath and his sons became powerful prime ministers serving ShahuI. They were instrumental in expanding the Maratha empire in all directions across the subcontinent: north, south, east, and west. During this era, the Maratha kingdom was the strongest military power inside in the lands of India.

Rajaram II (December 15, 1749 C.E.—December 11, 1777 C.E.)

Shahu II (December 11, 1777 C.E.—May 3, 1808 C.E.)

Pratap Singh Bhosie(May 3, 1808 C.E.—September 5, 1839 C.E.)
Pratap Singh Bhosie was a figurehead leader over the remains of the Maratha Empire. His power had slipped into the hands of his prime ministers. Eventually, the imperial British forces removed him from power in the year 1839. Once he was deposed, the Indo-European British ended the succession of Maratha rulers in their former territories. Their kingdom was annexed as part of British India. The British Empire continued to officially rule India from the days of their Raj Empire [**Western iron leg kingdom**] in 1858 until their expulsion in 1948.

So it came to pass that **the kingdom of India** evolved into one of the latter-day [**miry clay kingdoms**] described as one of the 10 toes mixed [**integrated**] with iron [**British colonialism**] and miry clay [**exploited and underdeveloped by European imperialism**] spoken of by the prophet Daniel.

Mahatma Gandhi, the Indian activist and leader of the 1940s independence movement, was a descendant of the Maratha people. It is ironic that, in the end, Britain ended up returning political power back to the same people nearly 100 years later.

West African Kingdoms
1464 C.E.—2019 C.E.

The Empire of Songhai (1375 C.E.—1591 C.E.) The Kingdom of Dahomey (1600 C.E.—1904 C.E.) African Hebrews in America (1619 C.E.—2019 and beyond) Berlin Conference/The West Africa Conference(1884-1885 C.E.)

"YAH changes times and seasons. HE removes kings(The Mali Empire) and install kings(The Songhai Empire); HE gives the wise their wisdom and knowledge to those who know"
                                                                                    Daniel 2:21.

The Empire of Songhai
(1375 C.E.—1591 C.E.)

The birth of the Songhai Empire came in the year 1375 when Sunni Ali severed ties with the Mali Empire and established a dynasty over one of the largest kingdoms in Kemetic history. Located in the heart of West Africa and known as the Songhai Empire, the kingdom flourished with the great city of Gao serving as the capital along with two other great cities: Timbuktu and Djenne. The kingdom was centered in the area of the great bend on the Niger River in today's central Mali. At the height of its glory, the kingdom extended all the way to the Atlantic coast passing through areas now known as Niger and Nigeria.

The Songhai people prospered in this great kingdom by establishing trade caravans that traveled all the away from the [West] across the heart of Africa to the [East]. The Songhai people also cultivated cereals during the rainy seasons in June through November. They were great fishermen, raised cattle, and worked as farmers. The class structure of society consisted of the nobility, the commoners, the artisans, griots, and slave laborers. Eventually, it became an ancient Muslim power in West Africa until it was toppled by invading Moroccan Arab armies in the 16th century. Below in a list of the Songhai rulers, known as *Dia*, meaning *king*, who reigned over the Sonni dynasty.

Sonni Dynasty
(1464 C.E.—1493 C.E.)

Sunni Ali (1464 C.E.—1492 C.E.)

Dia Sunni Ali built a large infantry and a massive cavalry which he used to capture Timbuktu in 1468 and Djenne in 1475. He expelled the scholars from the University of Timbuktu whom he deemed unpatriotic, namely those from the brown-skinned Berber-based northern African tribes known as the Tuareg. Ali's prowess expanded the kingdom to heights that surpassed his predecessors of the Ghana Empire, which reigned from 400 C.E. to 1076 C.E., and its successor, the Mali Empire which lasted for 258 years from the 1210 to 1468.

King [Dia] Sunni Ali drowned to death in 1492 while crossing the Niger River. Some sources accused his sister's son Askia Toure Muhummad of murdering his uncle to succeed him on the throne. Reason being: Askia believed Ali's son Baru, who was his first-cousin and heir to the throne, was not a faithful Muslim.

Sonni Baru (1492 C.E.—1493 C.E.)

Sonni Baru ascended to the throne immediately after his father's death on November 6, 1492. He was attacked by his first-cousin Askia Toure Muhummad, who conspired with other generals, the following year on February 18, 1493. Sonni Baru fled into exile to save his life.

Askia Dynasty
(1493 C.E.—1592 C.E.)

Askia Toure Muhummad "The Great" (1493 C.E.—1529 C.E.)

Born in 1443, Askia was 50 when he overthrew his first-cousin. He reigned for 35 years in the royal city of Gao. His rule was noted for the continued expansion of the Songhai Empire which grew into the largest in the history of the entire continent. He extended the kingdom's borders into the Sahara northward. Westward, the empire reached deep inside the borders of ancient Mali. Eastward, the Songhai Empire encompassed the great routes through the Hausaland, which is modern northern Nigeria. He created a strong central government to control trade routes, replaced local chiefs, and appointed his family members as the local rulers throughout his realm. All localities were ordered to pay tribute to the kingdom, which in turn, greatly enriched the throne in Gao. Although Askia was a Muslim, he used a system of governance based of African tradition which improved life and brought stability during his reign. In fact, his reign was noted for his unparalleled use of a bureaucracy and one standard to advance the West African empire. At the age of 85, Askia had become elderly, senile, and blind. His reign was cut short through the treachery of his own son Askia Musia who slew him in 1529.

During his lifetime he made a pilgrimage to Mecca to walk around the famed Kaaba Stone seven times and bow before the god of Islam Allah. Unlike his father, he extended an olive branch to the Arabs in Morocco and those in Egypt. He allowed their Islamic scholars to come and teach in the University of Sankore Mosque at Timbuktu. The studies included Islamic law and theology, medicine, science, and mathematics.

So it came to pass that Askia Toure Muhummad, known as the Great, did not know **YHWH ELOHIM Israel** nor did he walk in the ways which **YAH** commanded the ancient Afro-Asiatic Hebrew people when he delivered them out of northern Africa and brought into the land of Canaan. During the days of Moses, Canaan was a province of Africa.

Askia Musa (1529 C.E.—1531 C.E.)

This man Askia Musa was a bloody man who slew his own father. However, his reign did not last long. He only reigned for two years before being assassinated by Askia Benkan in a small village on April 24, 1531. Musa attempted to slay all of his rivals, but as fate would have it, he could not do so. So it came to pass, just as he had shed the innocent blood of his father, so too, was his blood spilled on the ground. His own brothers conspired against him.

Meanwhile, his influence was gradually weakening as many local chiefs secretly practiced their native religions and remained loyal to their own chiefs. Islam's influence remained strong in the urban centers, but in the outlying areas which made up the vast majority of the Songhai Empire, people still practiced their own indigenous faiths.

Askia Benkan (1531 C.E.—1537 C.E.)

Askia Benkan seized the throne as the new **Dia [king]** inspite of all the ongoing chaos between the potential heirs. He enlarged and refurbished the royal court extravagantly. He dressed all of his courtiers in splendorous apparel and added musical instruments and entertainment into his royal service. Benkan's officials turned against him and deposed of him.

Askia Isma'il (1537 C.E.—1539 C.E.)

Askia Isma'il came to power through a cut-throat conspiracy against his predecessor Askia Benkan. One of the first things he did upon his ascension to the throne was release his father from prison on Kangaba Island. After a brief war against his rivals, he died in December 1539 C.E. after only two years upon the throne in Gao.

Askia Ishaq I (1539 C.E.—1549 C.E.)

Askia Ishaq I came to the throne as a ruthless ruler. He was very paranoid, and executed anyone who threatened his position. During his 10-year reign, he moved his troops to occupy the capital city of the once Mali Empire, even Kangaba.

To understand the size of the Songhai Empire, I will describe the range of its borders in modern terms. The entire Songhai kingdom included territories of the modern African countries of Chad, Niger, Mali, Guinea, Burkina Faso, and parts of Ghana, Togo, Benin, and Nigeria. The latter-part of his rulership was filled with tensions between the black Africans and brown Arabs. The Moroccan Sultan Muhummad al-Arak demanded that Askia Ishaq I relinquished the salt mines in the territory of Taghaza, north of the empire. In response, Ishaq I ordered a company of 2,000 cavalrymen to raid a market city in the Dara Valley located in southern Morocco as a show of strength. He ordered his warriors not to kill anyone. This show of force only aggravated tensions between the brown-skinned Ishmaelites and the black

Africans. In the end, Askia Ishaq I died in the town of Kuklya and he was buried there.

Askia Daoud (1549 C.E.—1583 C.E.)

The Songhai Empire reached the peak of its glory during the reign of Askia Daoud between 1549 to 1582. Nevertheless, the reality of life was changing in West Africa. The Portugese had established trading centers along the Gulf of Guinea in the last 15th century. Those moves raised concerned for the Arabs in Morocco, fearing their loss of trade in salt, gold, slaves, and other African riches. The presence of the Portuguese marauders threatened their conquest of the region and provoked them to make a first move. It should be noted that the rulers of the Songhai Empire had cooperated with these same North African Arabs during the sub-Saharan Slave trade. Many of those slaves ended up as far east as India. Now those Arabs were turning their guns on the African rulers of the Songhai Empire.

Askia Ishaq II (1588 C.E.—1591 C.E.)

Dia [king] Askia Ishaq II was overthrown by the brown-skinned Berber-led Saadi dynasty which ruled the North African kingdom of Morocco from 1549 to 1659. This is what happened: In 1591, the king of Morocco sent an army of 4,000, consisting of Arabs and Spanish mercenaries, armed with the new technology of rifles and cannons into Western Sahara to lay siege to the royal city of Gao. Many of the soldiers died in route to the battlefront, however, those remaining carried firearms. The Songhai soldiers, armed only with bows and lances,could not withstand the barrage of bullets and cannon balls. The Moroccan Arabs and mercenaries totally destroyed the Songhai army. In the final analysis, the empire crumbled under the weight of the foreign invaders who trampled Gao, and scattered the once renown African Empire towards the four winds of heaven.

So it came to pass that the Songhai Empire lasted for 128 years from 1464 C.E. to 1591 C.E. when it ceased to be. None of its rulers served **YHWH ELOHIM Israel** nor walked in the ways of the ancient Afro-Asiatic children of Israel. Each ruler walked after the other gods. **The Kingdom of Dahomey** succeeded them as the next great power of West Africa.

The Kingdom of Dahomey
(1600 C.E.—1904 C.E.)

"YAH changes times and seasons. HE removes kings(Dahomey Kingdom) and install kings(The French Colonial Empire); HE gives the wise their wisdom and knowledge to those who know"

Daniel 2:21.

The kingdom of Dahomey came to life in the early 1600s when a man named Do-Aklin led the Fon people to the Abomey Plateau. Located inland off the Gulf of Guinea in the area now known as the country of Benin, the first name of kingdom was the same as the plateau on which they built their settlement: The Aja settlement grew into the kingdom of Abomey. In the 1700s, the kingdom of Abomey expanded into a regional power, through warfare, to include the city-states of Allada, Whydah, and Ouidah on the Atlantic coast. *(For the record, the kingdom of Ouidah[**Yehudah**], which was conquered and sold as slaves to Europeans by the Dahomeians, was one of the 42 Hebrew kingdoms of Africa.)* Eventually, the Abomey kingdom became recognized as the kingdom of Dahomey. In the process of time well-known powerful tribes like the **Yoruba** and **Fulani** people became minorities within their far-reaching empire.

The West African kingdom continued to flourish into the early 19th century until the French finally conquered the territory and enslaved them. In the end, the kingdom of Dahomey itself became a victim of French colonization of West Africa. By the 17th century, the French had already built forts throughout the area to begin their conquest. Many of Dahomeians ended up as French captives while others were mortgaged off in the Trans-Atlantic Slave Trade. Below is a list of the sovereign African kings of Dahomey before the French arrived.

The Rulers of the Kingdom of Dahomey
(1600 C.E.—1894 C.E.)

Do-Aklin (1600 C.E.—1620 C.E.)

Dakodono (1620 C.E.—1645 C.E.)
In the year 1620, Dakodono started his conquest of the entire Abomey Plateau, bringing all the inhabitants under his dominion.

Houegbadja (1645 C.E.—1685 C.E.)
Dahomey society included a royalty, commoners, and those taken as slaves. The West African kingdom was structured with a centralized bureaucracy which carried out the king's instructions. The expansionist kingdom was organized with a strong army built to capture territory and take their captives for the Trans-Atlantic Slave Trade. Women horse riders were among their mighty warriors.

Akaba (1685 C.E.—1716 C.E.)
From 1604 to 1690, the kingdom of Dahomey worked as a vassal under the Portuguese during the thriving Trans-Atlantic Slave Trade.

Agaja (1718 C.E.—1740 C.E.)
During the period of 1724 to 1727, King Agaja conquered the kingdoms of Allada, Whydah, and Ouidah. At this time, Dahomey rulers were actively participating in the Trans-Atlantic Slave trade.

Tegbessou (1740 C.E.—1774 C.E.)
The kings of the Dahomey were known as the *"Ahoshu"* meaning *"King"*.

Kpengla (1774 C.E.—1789 C.E.)

Agonglo (1789 C.E.—1797 C.E.)

Adandozan (1797 C.E.—1818 C.E.)

Ghezo (1818 C.E.—1858 C.E.)
During the reign of Ghezo, also spelled Gezu, the slave trade with the Europeans reached its high point within the kingdom of Dahomey. The kingdom became one of the chief suppliers of the human cash crop. He defeated the Oyo Empire and brought all its territories under Dahomey control.

Glele (1858 C.E.—1890 C.E.)

Behanzin (January 1890 C.E.—1894 C.E.)
King Behanzin changed his name to Kondo. At this time, the sovereignty of Dahomey was encroached upon by the growing French presence. Their forts were sprouting up throughout the area. He was the last king. He was defeated by the French and, in the end, the kingdom was annexed by their colonial empire.

Agoli-agbo (1904 C.E.)
So it came to pass that the kingdom of Dahomey, which was born in 1600 C.E., was removed from power by the superior weapons of the French colonial forces in 1904 C.E.. For 304 years, the black kingdom had reigned over West Africa. It had once thrived upon the human trafficking of their fellow Africans, many whom were African Hebrew people, but in the final analysis, the Dahomey Empire reaped what it had sown. The pale-skinned Aryan French colonized their empire, enslaved, and exploited them.

The rulers of Dahomey served the religion of Vodun and had done evil in the DIVINE Presence of **YHWH ELOHIM Israel** by disobeying HIS laws, commandments, judgements, and statutes written in the Torah. Instead, each of them had walked in the imaginations of their own self-will without regard for DIVINE Instructions.

In the late 19th century, Dahomey began exporting palm oil which did not earn anything close to the profits they once earned through Trans-Atlantic slave trafficking. So in the end, the land of **[gold]** was reduced to a **[miry clay]** kingdom in economic decline.

African Hebrews Taken Into Slavery in North America
(1619 C.E.—2019 C.E. and beyond)

"YAH changes times and seasons. HE removes kings(African Hebrew kingdoms of West Africa) and install kings(The United States of America); HE gives the wise their wisdom and knowledge to those who know"

Daniel 2:21.

The House of Bondage
"YHWH will bring you into Egypt again in ships"
(1619 C.E.—2019 C.E.)

(August 19, 1619C.E.—August 19, 1719 C.E.)
100-Years

On **August 19, 1619**, the first 20 African Hebrew captives arrived on a Dutch ship into Hampton and Jamestown, Virginia from the west coast of Africa. The captives, originally bound on a Portuguese ship, were taken from the port of Luanda in Angola. The Dutch raided the Portuguese ship at sea and kidnapped the 20 captives on board and sailed towards the English settlements in Chesapeake Bay. *(The Portuguese had colonized Angola since 1571.)*

For the next 100 years, from 1619 to 1719, slave ships continued to arrive into American colonial ports bringing hundreds of African Hebrews per ship for the next century. Among those African captives were the lost sheep of the house of Israel. Those ports included Boston, Baltimore, Charleston, New Orleans, Natchez, Richmond, Virginia, Philadelphia, Jackson, Mississippi, Memphis, and other slave auctioning places throughout the growing 13 North American colonies. The men and women arrived with yokes of iron on their necks, bound in chains, and fetters of iron upon their ankles. When they unloaded from the galleys, the Hebrews were naked, bare feet, cramped, seasick, and met with lashes of whips, evil faces, and immediately separated by gender in holding pens. This was a strange land and oppressive environment for these captives. For the next one hundred years families continued to be separated and sold of auction blocks where no man could redeem them. There was no might or earthly power in their hands. In fact, their faces pined in sadness and agony as their offsprings were ruthlessly sold away never to be seen again. To make matters worse, their American masters spoke a strange language which these captives could not comprehend.

During the 1700s, the thirteen colonies prospered through tobacco planting, sugar cane, and eventually a profitable cotton planting industry. All of their great European Gentile wealth was created upon the backs of the enslaved African Hebrews. A free labor system with human rights abuses were the rule of American law. It was unlawful for these captives to read, write, and think as a human being. The once tribal identification as Ashanti, Songhai, Ebos, Ouidah, Whydah, Yoruba, Fulani, Hausa, Mandinka were stripped, and they were reduced to the status of names like niggers, colored, Negroes, black, African Americans, dogs, whores, bitches, and other negative bywords and proverbial insults.

At this time I would like for you to recall what I said in chapter one. In chapter I said, and

I quote:
"One of the greatest lessons to be learned from studying this book is that prophecy has dual aspects, meaning that prophecies apply both to past, present, and future, and they would be repeated over and over again. What happened to Daniel in ancient times was destined to happen again in succeeding generations. The offsprings of these Israelites would also be taken into captivity to foreign lands just like their ancestors Daniel, Hannaniah, Mishael, and Azariah.

Another example of this book's duality is found in the fact that Daniel and his brethren were bound in chains, shackled, and carried into exile to the ancient kingdom of Babylonia. After the holy people's arrival in Babylon, Daniel was castrated, placed on an auction block, then sold as a palace slave where his name was changed to Belteshazzar. The Hebrew culture that Daniel and all Judah once embraced no longer existed. They were forced to eat the king's meat and drink his wine. Those developments occurred over and over again wherever Israel and Judah went into slavery, starting at the head of gold and continuing on down to the ten toes of iron and miry clay."

Please go back and read the first page of chapter one. Meditate on it. You will see for yourself how it happened again in our lifetimes. Our ancestors were carried across the Atlantic Ocean into the so-called New World to be bondmen and bondwomen for the **[iron]** kingdom of the United States, and other kingdoms throughout the Caribbean, Central America, Brazil, and other countries in South Americas.

All of these negative realities I mentioned were the results of ancient Israel's abandonment of the laws, commandments, judgements and statues written in Torah and spoken by HIS servant Moses for Israel and all mankind. So it had come to pass that the children of Israel had sinned against **YHWH their ELOHIM** and served the gods of Islam, Vodun, and other traditional gods when they resided in West Africa. Even unto this day, they do the same. After their forced arrival in the United States, the descendants of the lost sheep of Israel, even the Hebrew people, have converted to Jesus, the god of Christianity, although it was against the law for them to read or write. How could they truly understand what was being taught them? They couldn't read the Torah to identify the lies the Christian missionaries were force feeding them. So, they just trusted and believed in those who introduced them to the graven doctrine of the Nicene Creed and the idolatrous New Testament. This is the truth about the **Black Church in America** until this very day. **Black America**, the lost sheep of Israel, which embrace the religion of their Gentile captors, Christianity, will not serve **YAH**, nor will they hearken to those who come in **the Name of YHWH** to educate them to their spiritual heritage.

One bright spot in early American history that should not be overlooked is that the territory of Florida, which was under the dominion of Spain, an adversary of England, allowed escaped Israelite slaves to flee southward from the oppressive British colonies. This was the First Underground Railroad during the year 1693, hundreds of years before Harriet Tubman.

Significant Events In Captivity

1612: Tobacco was cultivated and emerged as the number one cash crop.
1624: First documented African Hebrew child born at Jamestown, Virginia.
1640-1670: Chattel slavery began to emerge in Virginia.
1693: Spanish Florida open door for escaped slaves fleeing British colonial slavery.
1700: Rice became the major crop in South Carolina. Additional slaves needed.

<u>(August 19, 1719 C.E.—1819 C.E.)</u>
200-Years

The Destruction of the African Hebrew People

In this era, the kingdom of England, even Great Britain, dominated and wrested control of the slave trade from the Portuguese who had been involved since the 15th century. During this time, chattel slavery was reaching a high point with ships crisscrossing the Atlantic nonstop for another 100 years before it was abolished by Great Britain in 1807 C.E. and the following year by the newly formed United States of America in 1808.

During the mid-1700s, a war broke out between the colonies and Great Britain in the year 1774. By 1776 C.E., the 13 North Americans broke away from Great Britain's domination and declared their independence. After a three-year war Britain surrendered and the 13 colonies became a sovereign kingdom known as the United States of America. The founders of the American dynasty agreed by consensus to establish a constitutional monarchy for pale-skinned Aryan Anglo-Saxon Gentiles who embraced Protestant Christianity only.

For Israelite captives, their beginning in America was totally different, and not an episode glorifying freedom. Here is a testimony of one captive that made it to the New World to talk about it. His name was Olaudah [*pronounced* **O-lau-dah**, which is a derivative of the Hebrew word **Ye-hu-dah**] Equiano.

The following words are the testimony of **Olaudah Equiano:**

"the white slave traders with their "horrible looks, red faces, and long hair," appeared to be savages who acted with "brutal cruelty" that went beyond anything previously experienced."

Many of these African Hebrew captives feared that Europeans were cannibals who would take them to their country for food. Deliberate European brutalization of these captives was a part of an attempt to destroy African self-respect and self-identity. After being held in slave dungeons on the West Coast of Africa for weeks, and sometimes months, they were finally boarded below deck, chained down, and shipped abroad.

For the next century, the descendants of the uneducated African Hebrew captives were converted to the religion of their slave masters in massive groves. Leaders of the enslaved Africans such as Richard Allen, Absalom Jones, Jupiter Hammon, of Long Island, New York, Daniel Coker, John Chavis, Lemuel Haynes, Prince Hall, and countless others became prophets of the graven image of the blue-eyed, blond hair, white Jesus. Those men built houses of worship for their graven New Testament writings, and all the idolatrous tenets of 4th century Gentile church leaders. The Black Church was taught to hate ancient Israel, the Torah, and the prophets. The captives were taught by Christian missionaries that European Jews were God's chosen people spoken of in the Old Testament. We must remember: During 1719 to 1819 it was still an automatic death sentence if a slave was found reading or writing. The same Christian missionaries taught the slave population that they were Gentile people with no hope for salvation unless they accepted white Jesus as their lord and saviour. All of those events transpired in order to fulfill **Deuteronomy 4:27-28:** *"And YAH shall scatter you among the nations* **[the United States]**, *and you shall be left few in number* **[a minority]** *among the heathen, whither YAH shall lead you. And there you shall serve gods, the work of* **[Gentile]** *men's hands, wood and stone, which neither see, nor hear, nor eat, nor smell."*

It should be remembered that in 18th and 19th century the enormous profits earned from human trafficking during the trans-Atlantic Slave Trade, along with huge profits from tobacco, rice, indigo, and sugar cane, were instrumental in funding the Industrial Revolution in both America and England. Many early U.S. political leaders waxed filthy rich through the abhorrent practice of chattel slavery. For the record, eight of the first 12 presidents of the United States were thriving slaveholders.

Significant Events In Captivity

1770: Crispus Attucks, born a slave, escaped to the abolitionist city of Boston where he was slain during the Boston Massacre.

1773: Phillis Wheatley, an African Hebrew woman, shocked Gentiles in United State when she publishes a book of poetry.

1776: The United States of America declared its independence from Britain 169 years after the establishment of the Jamestown Colony in Virginia in 1607.

1781-1783: 20,000 African Hebrews that sided with Great Britain departed the U.S. with the British army. During the same year 1781, the Gentile rulers of America ratified the Articles

of Confederation. Six years later in 1787, they held a Constitutional Convention.
1789: Virginia planter and slaveowner George Washington became the 1st President of the United States. Chattel slavery accepted by founding American Republic fathers.
1795: Benjamin Banneker, an intelligent Israelite, who was a renown astronomer and mathematician, published his almanac entitled the *Pennsylvania, Delaware, Maryland, and Virginia Almanac*. In 1790, he was appointed to the commission to survey the site for capital city Washington, D.C. He wrote a letter to Thomas Jefferson denouncing his belief that blacks were inferior. He also criticized Jefferson's published article which stated African Hebrews were intellectually inferior. He also wrote several articles denouncing slavery.
1800: Virginia planter and slaveholder Thomas Jefferson was elected 3rd President of the United States. Brutal chattel slavery was strictly enforced although Jefferson wrote a Constitution declaring all men were created equal. In 1803, President Jefferson, ruler of America, purchased 828,000 square miles from Emperor Napoleon, ruler of France, expanding the newborn kingdom all the way to the Pacific Ocean.
1808: Virginia planter and slaveholder James Madison was elected 4th President of the United States. Brutal chattel slavery continued to be strictly enforced although Madison was also one of the signatories of the U.S. Constitution declaring all men equal—except his slaves.
1820: Daniel Coker became leader of a movement of African Hebrews to return to Liberia.

(August 19, 1819C.E.—August 19, 1919 C.E.)
300-Years
A Holocaust

In this era, the kingdom of the United States continued to rapidly expand southward and westward, prospering through the introduction of cotton as a new cash-crop into their booming agrarian economy. At the same time, chattel slavery also continued to expand southward and westward to include Georgia, Arkansas, Mississippi, Alabama, Florida, Louisiana, and Texas as well.

In the beginning of the 19th century, the young United States experienced its first major financial crisis on January 2,1819 known as the *Panic of 1819*. Meanwhile in the same year on February 15, the U.S. House of Representative passed the Tallmadge Amendment which barred the entry of slavery in new Missouri territory. There were presently 21 states in the American union at the time of the 1819 amendment—10 anti-slavery states and 11 pro-slavery states. This conflict between those who favored slavery and those who opposed the institution of chattel slavery was a precursor to the civil war that would break out four decades later. The harsh treatment inflicted upon the lost sheep of Israel intensified year after year in the 19th century, and it did not stop in the 20th century.

Significant Events In Captivity
1822: The Denmark Vesey conspiracy was discovered. The Freedom fighter was slain.
1831: Nat Turner rebellion against chattel slavery ended with Freedom fighters slain.
1830: The United States underwent a transportation revolution. The increased building of roads, canals, and railroads connected the growing kingdom. The growing transportation network cut time, shipping cost, and encouraged big business with the idea of monopolies.
1845: The Narrative of the Life of Frederick Douglass, *An American Slave* was published. In this autobiography he details the treatment that African Hebrew people were receiving during his lifetime, nearly 225 years after the arrival of the first captives in Jamestown, Virginia back in 1619. The following words are quotes from his own mouth proving our ancestors were experiencing a **Holocaust** on the North American mainland:

"It would astonish one, unaccustomed to a slaveholding life, to see with what wonderful ease a slaveholder can find things of which to make occasion to whip a slave. A mere look, word, or motion—a mistake, accident, or want of power—

are all matters for which a slave may be whipped at any time. Does a slave look dissatisfied? It is said, he has a devil in him, and it must be whipped out. Does he speak loudly when spoken to by his masters? Then he is getting high-minded and should be taken down a button-hole lower. Does he forget to pull off his hat at the approach of a white person? Then he is wanting in reverence, and should be whipped for it. Does he ever venture to vindicate his conduct, when censured for it? Then he is guilty of impudence—one of the greatest crimes of which a slave can be guilty. Does he ever venture to suggest a different mode of doing things from that pointed out by his masters? He is indeed presumptuous, and getting above himself: and nothing less than a flogging will do for him. Does he, while plowing, break a plough—or, while hoeing, break a hoe? It is owing to his carelessness, and for it a slave must always be whipped." To make matters worse, enslaved African Hebrews were forbidden to read and write in their new strange land. They could not maintain a normal family life because either one of them, father, mother, son, or daughter, could have been sold at any moment. There was no protection for them under the U.S. Constitution. The brutality on Southern plantations was unimaginable, and worse than the treatment that European Jewish people ever experienced in Nazi extermination camps or Auschwitz concentration camps during World War II. American Hebrew slaves were tortured with 900 lashes until the fabrics from torn shirts were engraved inside the flesh of their bleeding backs. Bloodhounds were dispatched to chase runaway slaves, and when they caught them, they bit them to death. Rape of African Hebrew women was commonplace. All human dignity was denied and no civil liberties or rights were granted to the American Negro, who had also been stripped of all of their heredity and ancestral identities. The American slaves who lived during the century of 1819 to 1919 had long forgotten the greatness of the ancient Ashanti kingdoms of Ghana, Mali, Songhai, Whydah, Ebo, Hausa, Mandinka, and Ouidah kingdoms on the West Coast of Africa. In America, these men and women were regarded as chattel property such as a horse, dog, cattle, or pig. In regards to the U.S. Constitution, for census purposes, they were counted as three-fifths of a human being. And in reality, they were treated worse than the beasts of the field.

1857: Dred Scott Decision stated: The American Negroes were not entitled to protection under U.S. Constitution. Chattel slavery was an ongoing experience for the African Hebrew people as the domestic slave trade thrived with captives being sold down the river into Georgia, Mississippi and Louisiana.

1849-1860: As the Holocaust continued, African Hebrew Freedom fighter Harriet Tubman courageously led nearly a 100 lost sheep captives to safety in the Underground Railroad.

1858: Arkansas ordered all free Negroes to leave state or face re-enslavement.

1860: The African Hebrew slave population in the United States is estimated to be 3,953,760.

1860: Abraham Lincoln elected as 16th President of the United States.

1860-1861: The 11 slaveholding states secede from the United State of America. Shortly afterwards, the American Civil War began. **YHWH** fights for lost sheep of Israel.

1863: The **Spirit of YHWH** stirred up President Lincoln and YAH caused him to issue the Emancipation of Proclamation decreeing an end to chattel slavery. YAH saw the oppression of the lost sheep of Israel under the hands of the Gentile plantation owners, so he raised up President Abraham Lincoln to carry out HIS Will. Lost sheep of Israel receive compassion from YAH.

1864: Former African Hebrew slaves in the Union Army were massacred at Fort Pillow, Tennessee. General Nathan B. Forrest, a sworn adversary of the lost sheep of Israel, ordered the killing of hundreds of Negroes after they surrendered.

1865: The North is victorious in American Civil War. The Thirteenth Amendment is passed and chattel slavery is abolished after 246 years.

1866: The domestic terror group, the Klu Klux Klan organized to declare war on the lost sheep of Israel. Countless Negro men and women were slain by the powerful militia. In the same year, there was a massacre of hundred of former slaves in Memphis known as the 1866 Memphis Massacre.

1868: The 14th Amendment passed. The African Hebrew people were supposedly granted the rights of citizenship. However, the former slaves did not have any land, 40-acres or a mule, did not have advanced education, nor were they paid living wages: only crumbs from their former master's tables. Regardless of their new hardships, these former captives were overjoyed, and preferred captivity under the North instead of chattel slavery under the brutal South.

1890s-1920s: The former African Hebrew griots, who transformed into American musicians, created a new musical art form known as blues and jazz. Blues music was actually a storytelling experience of the hardships and pain of slavery disguised in subliminal messages about personal relationships, very similar to hymns that were sung in the cottonfields. Jazz music was an expression of the joy and pain felt by the former captives living in northern urban cities. Jazz musicians told stories through their instruments very similar to their vocal blues brethren in the South. Although the Gentile American general public was extremely racist, they loved both art forms and paid to hear and see the performances of these African folklore blues and jazz musicians.

1892: African Hebrew newspaper publisher and Freedom fighter Ida B. Wells spoke out against the lynching of her three friends in Memphis, Tennessee in 1892. They operated a successful grocery store across the street from a white store owner who resented their success. Forced by Gentile Memphians to flee to Chicago, she continued her anti-lynching crusade there. Born in 1862 C.E. in Holly Springs, Mississippi as a slave, she grew to be owner of the *Memphis Free Speech* newspaper. She died in 1931 at the age of 69 after championing the cause of free speech for the lost sheep of the House of Israel. *(In fact, she was one of my journalistic and freedom fighting mentors. She was a very courageous sister.)*

1896: *Plessy v. Ferguson* court ruling clearly stated Negroes and Gentiles should be kept "separate but equal", upholding racial segregation as a lawful practice.

1896: The **Spirit of YHWH** rose upon a former African Hebrew slave named **William Saunders Crowdy** revealing to him that the Negroes in America were the descendants of the biblical children of Israel. **The Great Awakening of lost sheep of Israel** in America began. Known as Prophet Crowdy, the 49-year-old Hebrew spokesman started his ministry in Lawrence, Kansas before moving to the East Coast. He established congregations in Philadelphia, Washington, D.C., New York City, Suffolk, Virginia, and several other cities. He proclaimed the name of the God of Abraham, the God of Isaac, and the God of Jacob to the former slave population. Renown **Israelite author Elder Moses Farrar** is a member of the 123-year-old congregation whose headquarter is in Suffolk, Virginia.

1905: The Chicago Defender newspaper begin publication.

1908: Springfield, Missouri Massacre of African Hebrew people. Hundreds of African Hebrews fled the city for Oklahoma City turning a majority black Missouri city into nearly a totally white Gentile enclave.

1909: The NAACP, the civil-rights organization known as the *National Association of Colored People,* was established to fight against lynching and segregation.

1914: World War I started in Europe. The bloody war lasted until 1918, ending with 10 million dead, 21 million wounded, and another 8 million missing or imprisoned. America and Britain were victorious against the Central Powers of Germany, Austria-Hungary, and Ottoman Empire.

1914: President Woodrow Wilson, a strong supporter of segregation, is elected as the 28th President of the United States.

1914: Marcus Garvey established UNIA, the *Universal Negro Improvement Association,* in Harlem, New York. **Rabbi Arnold Josiah Ford** was appointed choirmaster of UNIA. He chose James Weldon Johnson's *Lift Every Voice and Sing* as the national anthem of UNIA. It eventually became the national anthem of all Black America.

1915: Booker T. Washington died. Washington, a southerner with no memory of Africa, was the most influential Negro leader at the turn of century because of his promotion of submissiveness to Gentile supremacy. Washington believed Negroes should remain in labor force and avoid the pursuit of education which was promoted by W.E.B. DuBois.

1917: East St. Louis Massacre of African Hebrew people.

1917: Houston Massacre of African Hebrew people.

1919: Chicago Massacre of African Hebrew people.

1919: Eliane, Arkansas Massacre of nearly 1,000 lost sheep of Israel in southeast Arkansas city. The Oct.1-3 killing spree was supported by the U.S. Army stationed in Arkansas. Machine guns were used to kill unarmed black sharecroppers.

1919: Rabbi Wentworth A. Matthew established the **Commandment Keepers Ethiopian Hebrew Congregation** in Harlem, New, York. Matthew was a supporter of the Garvey-based UNIA and defended black people's cultural connection to ancient Hebrewism. Matthew established a Rabbinical Board to trained a generation of black men in rabbinical studies. Some of the prominent men that emerged from his institution were **Rabbi Yehoshua Yahonatan, Rabbi White, of Newark, New Jersey, Rabbi James Poinsett, Rabbi Levy Ben Levy, Rabbi Green,** and hundreds of others who are dispersed in various cities across the United States. Second and third generation leaders included **Cohen Levy Ben Levy, Rabbi Yeshurun, Cohen Michael Ben Levy, Moreh Mishael Ben Levi, Moreh Eleazar Ben Yehudah, Doraishiel Baynasher, and Rabbi Shlomo Ben Levy.** Other Israelite spokesmen that emerged during the turn of century were **Prophet Cherry,** of Chattanooga, Tennessee, **Chief William Christian, Rabbi David ben Itzoch, Grover Cleveland Redding, Elder Warren Roberson, Rabbi Israel ben Newman, and Leonard Percival Howell.**

1919: Marcus Garvey established the Black Star Ship Line to return lost sheep of Israel to Liberia. European powers opposed Garvey's plan of repatriation because of their colonial interest. In the end, like Frederick Douglass said seventy years earlier in 1845, *"They took him down a button-hole or two,"* with a federal indictment and incarceration. In other words, slavery persisted well into the modern era. In the eyes of FBI Director J. Edgar Hoover Garvey did not have the freedom to organize a *"Back to Africa"* movement. So, a government-sponsored modern-day public *whipping*, called a counter-intelligence plan, was created to flog Garvey and everyone associated with his movement.

<u>**(August 19, 1919C.E.—August 19, 2019 C.E.)**</u>
400-Years
A Holocaust *Continues*

The 300th year of captivity came to an end, but the Holocaust against the descendants of those brought to America in the hulls of ships as bondmen and bondwomen continued unabated. However in the Gentile world, the progress of the *Industrial Revolution* and the *Modern Age* propelled America and Europe to heights not seen among the family of nations since the beginning of **Head of Gold** down to **10 Toes of Iron and Miry Clay**.

In this era, major U.S. and European cities began to be modernized with architectural wonders such as skyscrapers and other high-rise buildings with elevators and escalators, paved roads where motorized cars replaced horses and buggies, telephones, typewriters, motion pictures, airplanes, the washing machine, radios, the refrigerator, instant cameras, jukeboxes, televisions, electric razors, the light bulb, and electricity were a part of everyday life. The strangers within our midst waxed greater and greater while the majority of the lost sheep of Israel lingered further and further behind in the ghettoes of America. Nor did technological progress necessarily mean progress in the human spirit concerning racism and overt hatred. The *Dark Age* oppression, such as daily lynchings and burnings at stake, of the African Hebrew people persisted without the protection of the U.S. Constitution well into the 20th century.

Another phenomenon in this era was the beginning of the prophetic **Time Zone of Toes of**

Iron which occurred in the early 1900s. For America, time zone started with the winds of conflict that caused their involvement in World War I and World War II. The United States was victorious in both wars. It was during this era that this great kingdom, which had started out as 13 little colonies, expanded into 50 states, and continued to grow into a global empire known in this 21st century as a **[Western]** economic, military, political, and cultural superpower. Prophetically speaking America became, *Great Babylon,* or sometimes it is referred to as *the daughter of Babylon,* the most wealthiest and most technologically advanced kingdom in modern times.

Significant Events In Captivity

1920: Unable to participate in or attend mainstream Gentile baseball games, the Negro Baseball League was founded by Andrew "Babe" Foster. Negroes, dressed in their best clothes, attend the baseball games after church services each Sunday during spring-summer baseball season.

1921: On May 31, a black man was accused of raping a white woman. Angry mobs of white Gentile men converged on black section of town known as Black Wall Street and began to destroy kill innocent men, women, and child and vandalize their neighborhood, leaving a booming enclave in rubble. Hundreds of lost sheep of Israel were slain in the mayhem.

1923: The entire city of Rosewood, Florida was razed to the ground and the lost sheep of Israel massacred.

1925: A. Phillip Randolph organized the black Brotherhood of Sleeping Car Porters labor union to assist African Hebrew train employees.

1926: Carter Woodson organized the celebration of Negro History Week to commemorate the achievements of the lost sheep of Israel within human society. For 300 years, Woodson realized that American society and education system had told black people they never contributed anything to advance humanity. Woodson hoped his celebration would promote black self-respect and counter those negative types of Gentile stereotypes. Eventually, the entire month of February became known as Black History Month.

1931: The Scottsboro Boys were arrested and charged with raping two white women mill workers on March 25, 1931. The women were allegedly raped in a Southern Railroad freight car. The 9 African Hebrew boys were sentenced to death before their sentence was overturned by the U.S. Supreme Court.

1934: Elijah Muhummad, an African Hebrew who practiced Islam, became the leader of the Nation of Islam. In 1954, Malcolm X became Minister of Harlem Temple No.7 and assisted Elijah Muhummad in advancing the organization into one of the most prominent black grassroots organization in American history.

1938: President Franklin D.Roosevelt appointed a cabinet of black leaders to assist his administration in improving conditions for African Hebrew people.

1938: African Hebrew boxer Joe Louis defeated German heavyweight Max Schmeling.

1939: World War II began with the Axis Powers fighting against the Allied Powers. The Axis Powers were Germany, Italy, and Japan while the Allied Powers included France, Britain, the United States, and the Soviet Union. The United States entered the war in 1941. There were at least 35 to 60 million casualties, including people killed, injured, missing, or imprisoned. It also includes the 6 million European Jewish converts slain.

1945: President Franklin D. Roosevelt died. President Harry Truman became the 33rd President of the United States. He ordered the bombing of two Japanese cities, Hiroshima and Nagasaki, with atomic bombs killing hundreds of thousands which ended World War II. With Europe in shambles and Japan devastated, the United States emerged as a global superpower at the end of the war. The new global order, known as the United Nations, was also created during this same year.

1948: UN mediator Ralph Bunche, an African Hebrew, helped establish the borders for the State of Israel. Jewish State of Israel recognized by the United States on May 14, 1948.

1954: Brown v. Board of Education reversed centuries-old policy of segregation. For the first time in American history, African Hebrew people would be able to move with protected civil liberties.

1955: Birmingham, Alabama bus boycott became the linchpin for the Civil Rights Movement. The bus strike led to more protests against discrimination, racism, and overt hatred.

1955: African Hebrew spokesmen gathered in Washington Park in Chicago, Illinois each Sunday [Yom Rishon] to teach black people in America that they were the descendants of the ancient Afro-Asiatic Hebrews. The spokesmen that emerged from those gathering included **Elder Lucius Casey Sr., his son Lucius Casey Jr. "Aaron", Rabbi Robert Devine, Rabbi James Hodges, Cohen Richard Nolan, Moreh Eliyahu Buie.** Other Chicago leaders from that era were **Rabbi Green, Rabbi Yaccov Johnson, Ben Yacov, Aliazar Ben Yehudah, and numerous others.** These Chicago men were responsible for spreading the grassroots Israelite message throughout the deep South, the Midwest, and out West. Beneath the surface of the well-publicized Civil Rights movement, the currents of the Israelite Spiritual Rights movement were flowing with silent strength, awakening multitudes of unknown men and women in most American urban centers. The cities of New York, Newark, Philadelphia, and Chicago were the historical foundation for the Israelite movement in the United States. Today in the United States, you can find conscious Israelite people and places of worship in small, medium, and large urban centers from coast to coast.

1965: African Hebrew leader Malcolm X, who converted to the religion of Islam, was assassinated in the Audubon Ballroom in Harlem New York. After serving as Elijah Muhummad's assistant for 11 years, he broke away after being suspended over comments he made after the assassination of President John F. Kennedy in 1963. Many observers, such as the late Dick Gregory, said the rift between the members Nation of Islam provided the green light for outside forces to assassinate him and blame it on the Nation of Islam. The late **Dr. Alufiel Ben Yehudah**, of New Jersey, assisted Malcolm in publishing the first issue of the Muhummad Speaks newspaper. **Dr. Yehudah** owned a printing company.

1967: The Israelite congregation, Abeta Hebrew Israelite Culture Center, of Chicago, Illinois made Exodus from United States to Liberia where they remained for two and one-half years before journeying to the land of Israel on December 19, 1969. Members of this historic movement included **Danyel Knight, Ben Yaacov, Elder Eliyahu Buie, Moshe Buie, Ben Ammi Israel, Gavriel Katan, Isaiah Winters and family, Mekhael Ben Yehudah and family, Gavriel HaGadol, Rockamem, Elkanah Israel, Yaacov Johnson, and numerous other unnamed women and men nationwide.** After entry into Israel, other men and women became attracted to the bold redemptive move. The new members, which included **Dr. Sheleak Ben Yehudah, Prince Asiel Ben Israel, Prince Rahm Ben Yehudah, and Ameeshida Ben Israel,** declared the Dimona-based community as the Kingdom of God[YAH] on earth. Soon thereafter, Ben Ammi Ben Israel was recognized as the Messiah until his death in December 2014.

1968: Dr. Martin Luther King, an African Hebrew leader of the Christian-based Civil-Rights movement, was assassinated in Memphis, Tennessee on the balcony of the Lorraine Hotel at 6:00 p.m. on April 4, 1968. King, a charismatic speaker, had galvanized and led a 13-year effort to integrate the lost sheep of Israel into American society. Dr. King sponsored non-violent marches, boycotts, and other forms of peaceful demonstrations to tear down the barrier between the descendants of former slaves and the offsprings of their masters. His death was caused by those who opposed the end of segregation and tolerance towards black people. However, if segregationists thought King's death would bring an end towards integration of American society, they were totally wrong. In fact, his death served as a catalyst for more social changes than our ancestors thought were possible here in this land.

1978: Minister Louis Farrakhan became leader of the Nation of Islam after years of turbulence following the death of the founder Elijah Muhummad. Farrakhan visited the Israelite community in Dimona in 1977. At the time, Farrakhan met and received a security team from the Dimona-based community until he rebuilt the Fruit of Islam. **Prince Asiel Ben Israel** was instrumental in that effort.

1979: Yehoshaphat Israel and his wife **Leah Baht Israel** attend Israelite Bible Class in Memphis, Tennessee where Aaron Casey, son of Lucius Casey Sr, was the Hebrew Teacher. Yehoshaphat Israel and his wife begat 8 children: **Israel, Samaria, Sarai, Judaea, Ophrah, Joshua, Aijalon, and Ariel.**

1980: Moses Israel, who later changed his name to **Yahweh Ben Yahweh**, established the Nation of Yahweh in Miami, Florida. Yahweh, a charismatic speaker and strong organizer, established temples throughout the United States and gained a large following. Dressed in all white from head to shoes, the members of Yahweh were seen in their hotels, restaurants, and other businesses. Viewed as the Messiah by his followers, Yahweh gained a reputation of ruling with an iron fist. In the early 1990s, he and his top leadership were indicted under the federal RICO law for racketeering. He remained incarcerated from 1991 until his release in 2005. He died two years later in 2007. Even in death, he is still revered and his teachings studied.

1990: Cohen Richard Nolan, spiritual leader of the Universal Kingdom-House of Israel in Harvey, Illinois and his wife **Mattanah Baht Levy,** and **family** established the **Israelite World Federation(IWF).** The goal of organization was to bring Israelite congregations together nationwide in order to establish a national agenda for the Israelite community. The IWF hosted a national convention in 1990 and 1992 in Chicago-Harvey, Illinois. In 1992, several future Israelite leaders attended, including **Aliazar Ben Yehudah, Cohen Nathanyah HaLevy, now living in Ghana, Moreh Elisha Yisrael, who later founded the national Sacred Laws Conferences, Rabbi Capers Funnye, presently the Chief Rabbi of Israelite Board of Rabbis, Ambassador Michael Israel, of Tacoma, Washington, Yehoshaphat Israel,** publisher of the *Jerusalem Chronicle Newspaper* **and chairman of the Yisraelite Spiritual Action Committee(Yis-SAC).** Yehoshaphat Israel also received the 1992 IWF Community Achievement Award during the banquet ceremonies.

1990: Yehoshaphat Israel established the *Jerusalem Chronicle Newspaper* as part of a graphic arts class project at Tennessee Technology Center. The project required students to design a front page of a newspaper. Israel decided to add 7 additional pages to complete 1st edition of *JCN* in March 1990. Since 1990, the *JCN* has been a voice for the Israelite community. His wife Leah served as assistant editor while the children served as his newspaper staff.

1997: Rabbi James Hodges, Prince Danyel Ben Yosef, Hadassah Baht Israel, Habakkuk Ben Levi, Obadiah Israel, Zephaniah Israel, and other Chicago Israelites created a nationwide organization known as Yisraelite organizations of Unity(YOU). After two years of planning, the first national convention was held at Inner City Studies in Chicago. Hundreds of participants from all parts of the U.S., Africa, and Israel attended. Supported by **Rabbi Capers Funnye,** many of strategy meetings were held at Beth Shalom Ethiopian Hebrew Congregation on South Houston.

2000: Yehoshaphat Israel and Eliyahu Ben Israel, of Vicksburg, Miss., visited the land of Israel during New World Passover observances in May 2000 as the special guests of **the Kingdom of YAH(KOY)** based in Dimona, Israel. During their 2-week journey, both men visited the city of David, even Jerusalem. While in Jerusalem, Yehoshaphat Israel offered a special prayer to **YHWH,** based on Daniel 9th chapter, for the redemption of the lost sheep of Israel.

2008: Barack Obama, a man of Kenyan father and European mother, was elected as the 44th President of the United States of America. It was the first time in American history an openly non-European president occupied the White House to sit upon the throne of George Washington. Obama reigned for eight years, even from 2008 to 2016. During his reign, the kingdom was deeply divided with anti-African Hebrew sentiments and open expressions of hatred resurfacing in ways not seen since the 1950s. The lost sheep of Israel revered Obama, but many Gentiles did not respect him as their President. Their deep frustrations led to the election of Donald trump as the 45th President of the United States of America. On a personal note, President Barack Obama married a woman named Michelle, who was the second-cousin of **Rabbi Capers Funnye.** Funnye's mother, whose maiden name was Verdelle Robinson, was the sister of Fraiser Robinson Jr. Fraiser was the grandfather of Michelle.

2010: Israelite Community host a National Day of Remembrance on September 18. Prayer vigils were held in various cities nationwide. The main event was scheduled for Jamestown, Virginia. Some Israelites disagreed with the fact that the planned event was held on the same date as the sacred appointment of Yom Kippurim (Day of Atonement). The main gathering, held in Blackjack, Missouri, was spearheaded by **Hudurah Baht Yisrael**. Participants included **Yehoshua Ben Israel, Tamar Israel, Alimah Ben Israel, Katriel Ben Israel, Avraham Ben Israel and scores of others**.

2012: The **Yisraelite Spiritual Action Committee(Yis-SAC)** was started on December 18, 2011 with a teleconference meeting organized by Yehoshaphat Israel. The initial name of the group was Yis-PAC, Yisraelite Political Action Committee, but after dialogue between participants, it was agreed that the core of Black America's problems were spiritual, not political. The name was changed to Yis-SAC, Yisraelite Spiritual Action Committe. Members included **Yehoshua Ben Israel, of Cincinnati, Ohio, Jeremiah Ben Israel, of Columbus, Ohio, Yahmaan Yashaahla, of Norfolk, Virginia, Yachanan Daveed Yisrael, of Senatobia, Mississippi, Chanak Ben Abisawa, of Memphis, Tennessee, Yachanan EL, of Memphis, Tennessee, NehemYAH Israel, of Halls, Tennessee, and Yeshoshaphat Israel, of Memphis, Tennessee**. During Passover 2012, Yis-SAC member Yahmaan Yashaahla visited Memphis to fellowship with the local community. During his visit to the city, Chanak Abisawa led him on a tour of the Civil Rights Museum. Inside it featured a wall with a timeline which started at 1619 until 1968. When Yahmaan saw the mural, it said, *"the assassination of Dr. King was not the assassination of one man, it was the destruction of a people"*. During the next bi-weekly Yis-SAC conference, the members discussed the topic. From that discussion, Yeshoshaphat Israel asked Yahmaan if we could come to Jamestown to pray to YAH on behalf of our people. The destruction of the people was viewed as a **Holocaust**. Thus, the decision was made to journey to Norfolk, Virginia for the **1st Israelite Holocaust Remembrance & Observance Day**, (Friday) **August 17, 2012**. The Shabbat services were entitled **Reconciliation Shabbat, a spiritual move to reconcile Israelites with YAH on August 18**. On Yom Rishon (Sunday) **August 19, 2012**, Yis-SAC went up to Jamestown, VA. for the first Day of Return. The **Spirit of YHWH** led the group to an unknown green historical marker acknowledging 1619 as the year of arrival for African Hebrew people. No one is the group knew anything about the historic marker until that day. The group could not believe they mysteriously stumbled upon the marker. Yis-SAC members called it the *Miracle at Jamestown*. Since then, the site has become well known within the Israelite community. It has been proclaimed to be the center of the August 19, 2019 Day of Return prayer vigil acknowledging the completion of 400-years of slavery in America.

2013: Yis-SAC sponsored the 2nd Israelite Holocaust Remembrance and Observance weekend in Norfolk and Jamestown, Virginia.

2014: Yis-SAC sponsored the 3rd Israelite Holocaust Remembrance and Observance weekend in Norfolk and Jamestown, Virginia.

2015: Yis-SAC moved the annual Holocaust observance to the deep South in Memphis, Tennessee. The 4th Israelite Holocaust Remembrance and Observance weekend held at the University of Memphis. Yis-SAC founding member Yahmaan Yashaahla, author of the Yis-SAC Israelite Constitution, died.

2016: Yis-SAC sponsored the 5th Israelite Holocaust Remembrance and Observance weekend at University of Memphis for second time. **Elder Yachanan Daweed Yisrael, Chanak Ben Abisawa, Yehoshaphat Israel,** and the *JCN* Foundation, consisting of active participants **Leah Baht Israel, Judaea Naomi Israel, Managing editor Ophrah Sherah Israel, Joshua Zamael Israel. Aijalon Keliah Israel, and Ariel Nathan Israel,** continue the Yis-SAC agenda.

2017: Yis-SAC sponsored the 6th Israelite Holocaust Remembrance and Observance weekend in Memphis, Tennessee for third time.

2018: Yis-SAC sponsored the 7th Israelite Holocaust Remembrance and Observance for the fourth time.

2019: The President of the kingdom of Ghana Nana Akufo Addo declared the year 2019 as the Year of Return for the descendants of African Hebrew people who were carried away to the North American colonies as bondmen and bondwomen, fulfilling the prophecies of **Genesis 15:13-14**. After the 400th-year captivity, West African kingdoms begin to Welcome the lost sheep of Israel back home to rebuild and restore themselves. *(HaleluYAH, Todah YHWH!!)*.

2019: The Israelite community will gather at Jamestown, Virginia on August 19, 2019 at the historic marker on the banks of the James River. Yis-SAC formed an alliance with the movement known as **Shoob Petach HalelYAH,** *meaning* **Door of Return to YAH.**

2019: On June 19th, the **Yisraelite Spiritual Action Committee(Yis-SAC)** host national press conference to address the spiritual significance of 2019 for Black America.

The DIVINE Plan of Redemption
(Genesis/Bereshith 15:13-14)

"And HE said to Abram, "Know well that your offspring shall be strangers in a land not theirs, and then **1) shall be enslaved and oppressed four hundred years,** but **2) I will execute judgement on the nation** they shall serve, and **3) in the end they shall go free with great wealth.**"

2019 C.E. and beyond

Within the Israelite community there must be a new *"latter-day"* Realization of the DIVINE process of YAH: Phase **1):** Completion of the 400-year captivity. Phase **2):** After 2019, we will be one step closer to our Redemption. However, once the 400 years are completed: YHWH will begin to execute spectacular and extraordinary judgements on this nation whom the African Hebrew people have served since 1619. These DIVINE Judgements will occur repeatedly, taking place over a number of years until this great kingdom can no longer hold the lost sheep in captivity. We must be patient and sing praises to YAH during this process as YAH goes before us like a cloudy pillar by day and a pillar of fire by night. Phase **3):** After years of DIVINE chastisement, "in the end, the lost sheep will go free with great wealth."

Israelites must realize that 2019 is a part of a DIVINE process, not some kind of end of the world Christian-like cultic prediction. We, the African Hebrew people, merely realize we have completed Phase 1. Now, YAH has spiritually issued the Emancipation of Proclamation from heaven and opened the Door of Return in Ghana on earth beneath, and after the Battle of Armageddon, we will return to Zion, even Jerusalem, with everlasting joy. We are YAH's witnesses, therefore we must acknowledge the outstretched **ARM** and mighty **HAND** of **YHWH,** who alone is **THE STONE CUT OUT WITHOUT HANDS,** our Eternal Saviour and Redeemer. **YHWH** will visit us, like Harriet Tubman in the night, and break us free from the bondage of 21st century America with great wealth.

Now that YAH is about to free us from these 400-years of chattel slavery, we must raise our thinking to new levels and begin to once again practice living with the Blessed Mindset spoken of in **Deuteronomy 28:1-13.** We must begin to develop proper nationalistic leadership, with a strong YAH-based educational and economic base, and most of all, Israel must develop their YAH-based own health care system in our new homeland. In the final analysis, only YAH knows the actual date and time of the Redemption for whole family of Yisrael and Yehudah, even the twelve tribes of Israel. *(Therefore, O YAH our eyes are fixed on YOU to see what YOU will do.)*

1884 Berlin Conference or 'West Africa Conference"
(1884 C.E.—1885 C.E.)

A Germanic-Portuguese-European Plan to Conquer, Divide, and Exploit Africa and peacefully share the spoils of war among themselves **[the 10 iron toes]** comprising the wealthy modernized European nations (1884 C.E.—Present)

"YAH changes times and seasons. HE removes kings (sovereign African kingdoms) and install kings(The European colonial powers); HE gives the wise their wisdom and knowledge to those who know" **Daniel 2:21.**

A Plan of Destructive Colonization

During the late 19th century and early 20th century, the prosperous European powers **[the 10 iron toe kingdoms]** sought to control the abundant resources of the undeveloped continent of Africa—**the land of gold.** The Indo-European and Indo-Turkic Ottoman plan consisted of colonizing the entire continent by establishing new European-imposed borders that would allow each European country the ability to exploit the mineral resources. This latter-day European influence over the land of gold would prophetically qualify the **10 Gentile powers** as the endtime **Head of Gold**. (Remember, what I said earlier, *"he who controls the land of gold controls the world"*. That is why all global empires, spanning from ancient Babylon to the modern Berlin Conference, have sought to rule the Garden of Eden. *(All of them have been the Serpent in Midst of the Garden.)*. German Chancellor Otto von Bismarck, the ruler of united Germany, convened the meeting in Berlin, Germany on November 15, 1884 and continued until February 26, 1885. The 14 European kingdoms in attendance at the Berlin Conference were **Belgium, Denmark, France, Germany, Great Britain, Italy, the Netherlands, Portugal, Spain, and the United States.** Those countries are the maternal offsprings of the ancient Roman Empire. Collectively, they are the prophesied **[10 toes of iron]**. The four other kingdoms in attendance were neutral Sweden-Norway along with Austria-Hungary, Russia, and Ottoman Turkey **[3 miry clay kingdoms]**.

The goal of the conference was to regulate European colonization, which was already underway, and to control trade on the continent in order to prevent conflicts among themselves. During this era, Germany was a great kingdom which emerged as an imperial power. However, it was the Portuguese who called for the meeting to combat the growing misunderstandings among the competing colonial powers on the continent. The decisions made in Berlin did not respect the sovereignty of the kingdoms of Africa, nor were decisions made in the interest of the indigenous people. The kingdoms of Africa waxed poorer and poorer, becoming a continent mired in colonial servitude and poverty. Prophetically, Africa became a bruised underdeveloped Third World **[miry clay kingdoms]** living under the **[iron]** yoke of the European imperialistic taskmasters. The independent glory of ancient kingdoms such as Kemet, Ghana, Mali, Songhai, Dahomey, and Zimbabwe were broken into pieces.

According to the European decrees coming from Berlin, all 11.7 billion square miles of the African continent, the second-largest in the world, belonged to them. Those changes of borders made life worse for the tribal people on the ground. All of a sudden, numerous African tribes found themselves separated by political boundaries that did not respect their ancestral landmarks. African borders, which had not changed for generations, now were established in the interest of the far away 10 iron toe isles of the Gentile kingdoms that trampled the **land of gold** under their feet. It should be noted that there were no African chiefs or leaders invited to Berlin for the 3-month conference.

The Berlin Conference gave birth to the policy of apartheid throughout Africa where Europeans separated themselves in modernized enclaves while they established businesses to take advantage of the natural resources to export the riches back to Europe and America. Africans were used as their domestic servants and tour guides to assist them in exploring very corner of the continent. At other times, their colonial policies included terror. For example, after the Berlin Conference, Germany annexed Namibia and changed the country's name to Southwest Africa. During that time, imperial Germany massacred thousands of Herero and Nama tribespeople during their late 19th and early 20th century occupation of Namibia. Others were starved to death and placed in concentration camps while the Germans controlled the diamond mines. Tons of raw diamonds have been excavated from the soil of

Namibia and exported back to Europe and America for processing into jewelry and other important manufactured products. Namibia also had some the world's most fertile agricultural farmland. German farmers harvested plenty as the indigenous Namibians waxed poor and hungry, becoming worthless miry clay.

The ideology of the Berlin Conference also strengthened the rise of Afrikaners in South Africa. The Afrikaners were the offsprings of the Dutch—from *Holland*—and the Huguenots from *Britain* and *France* who had already settled in the area since the year 1652. They arrived in the area as farmers known as the Boers. The Boers viewed themselves as the superior European children of God dwelling in the midst of a black pagan heathenistic wilderness. The Boers established self-sufficient communities where they developed their own Eurocentric culture and language. The European settlers, i.e., invaders, enforced a policy of brutality against the majority black population, creating a supremacist theology and separatist policy which eventually became known as apartheid. Economic exploitation of the country's natural resources was their number one goal. From 1899 to 1902, the Boers fought a war against the British who contested their executive claims over all the riches in South Africa.

In the process of time, European explorers found that South Africa contained the world's largest gold reserves. As the Modern Age continued, they mined coal, diamonds, copper, titanium, platium, oil, and countless other precious minerals. In 1900, Louis Botha was chosen as the first prime minister of apartheid South Africa.

As I said earlier, the 1884-1885 C.E. Berlin Conference assisted Europe in robbing Africa of its natural resources and served as a catalyst to advance the Industrialized World into the 21st century. Minerals such as copper, cobalt, industrial diamonds, titanium were used to build aircrafts, spacecrafts, missiles, and to produce atomic energy. The continent of Africa became essential to the growth and development of advanced European societies.

In the Congo, the [iron] kingdom of Belgium was given the mineral-rich kingdom located in the heart of the continent as their booty. The Belgians named the land the Congo Free State. The Belgians mined diamonds, gold, cobalt, rubber, coffee, palm oil, tea, cocoa, cotton, and limitless other mineral wealth. As their country Belgium grew into small powerful world power, the indigenous African people of Congo, including their chiefs and rulers, waxed low into one of the poorest countries of the face of the earth. Congo became one the poor [miry clay] kingdoms among the family of nations.

The Berlin Conference granted the kingdom of France the right to annex the area known as French West Africa. It occurred in 1895 when the territory consisting of the countries of Benin, Ivory Coast, Burkina Faso, Guinea, Mali, Mauretania, Senegal, and Niger came under their [iron] heels. The French exported palm oil from Benin. In the Ivory Coast, they took advantage of that country's world's largest cocoa supply. The French also exported coffee, bananas, rubber, timber, diamonds, and cotton back to their European cities. In Niger, the French developed an agricultural base and mined precious metals. In Mali, the French mined iron ore, bauxite, gold, nickel, and copper. Their farmers created a breadbasket of crops that included millet, sorghum, corn, rice, and peanuts. And, the French used the indigenous Africans of Mali to pick their cotton as well. In Senegal, the French exported peanuts, and also mined iron ore. The riches from French West Africa caused France to become one of Europe's most industrialized world powers. France also ruled the North African country of Algeria.

In Nigeria, Great Britain exploited their abundant oil supply and found fertile lands that produced enough crops to export agricultural products back to London. The British conducted the same policy in Ghana where they mined gold, diamonds, and harvested cocoa. The United States developed the rubber supply of Liberia for export back across the Atlantic. In Botswana, Europeans found diamonds and a bountiful supply of livestock for ivory, animal skins, and food. The same was true for Zimbabwe, Mozambique, and all the other black African countries of the sub-Sahara. As you can see, the Berlin Conference fulfilled the prophecies concerning the [10 iron toes] who were extensions of the ancient Roman Empire.

With the force of **iron,** all of the pale-skinned Aryan leaders at the roundtable in Berlin, Germany decided to treat Africa and its people with harshness and domination. As a result, the **land of gold** became worthless as dirt or **miry clay** to the indigenous Africans. All of Africa's valuable lands and its natural mineral resources were colonized, owned, and exported back to Europe and America. Since the agreements at the 1884-1885 **Berlin Conference,** limitless types of raw materials have been shipped back to the great cities of the Gentiles, producing items such as cars, planes, trains, telephone lines, wire, rubber tires, jewelry, chocolates, and countless other finished products.

The kingdom of Brazil
1501 C.E.—1914 C.E.)
"Iron People ruling a Miry Clay Kingdom"

"YAH changes times and seasons. HE removes kings (The indigenous Indian populations) and install kings(The Portuguese-Brazilians) HE gives the wise their wisdom and knowledge to those who know" **Daniel 2:21.**

    The country of Brazil is located on the northeastern tip of the continent of South America, south of Venezuela and Guyana with Colombia and Ecuador to its west. The Atlantic Ocean covers the entire eastern coastline.
    The Brazilian landscape is comprised of 3.2 million square miles, making it the second-largest country in New World behind the United States in North America. The land of Brazil is divided into two sections which include the Amazon River Basin and the Brazilian Plateau. In 1494 C.E., the two kingdoms of the Iberian Peninsula, Spain and Portugal, signed an agreement known as the Treaty of Tordesillas. It gave the land now known as Brazil to Portugal **[iron kingdom]**. However, since prehistoric times, indigenous people had already inhabited the vast array of lands that eventually became the kingdom of Brazil. The Tupinamba, Guarani, and Ge Indians were among the multitude of 7 million indigenous people **[miry clay]** who lived in those territories long before **Pedro Alvares Cabral** and his fleet **[iron]** arrived on their way to India on April 22, 1500. By navigational mistake, Pedro Alvares Cabral landed on Bahian shores in Porto Seguro, between Salvador and Rio Janeiro.
    Regardless of his error, Pedro Alvares Cabral laid claim to the vast sub-continent in the name of King Manuel I of Portugal **[iron toe kingdom]** after his arrival. Once there, the Portuguese settlers began to notice the limitless supply of redwood trees known as brazilwood trees. The Portuguese called them pau-basil. The Portuguese established a lucrative trade in exporting the trees, using them to make red dye. Eventually, the colony and settlements began to be called by the name Brazil, in honor of the brazilwood trees. It was Portuguese prosperity, and Dutch covetous eyes, that prompted the Dutch to invade Brazil in 1630. However, the Portuguese did not allow the Dutch to rob them. Instead, the Portuguese claimed total ownership of Brazil in 1654.
    By the late 17th century, the Brazilian population started to grow with an influx of Portuguese settlers along with their African slaves who were brought there to clear the fertile forest lands for plantations. The African Hebrew slaves included the Bantu people and West African population, consisting of Yoruba, Ewe, Fonti, and Ashanti tribes. By the end of the 17th century, the Portuguese settlers had discovered emeralds, diamonds, and gold in the city of Minas Gerais. During this time, the European settlers began moving farther inland while the Indians welcomed them. Both the Portuguese and Indians initially worked together harvesting brazilwood trees.
    In 1808, a war raged between France and Portugal. In midst of conflict, Napoleon invaded Portugal and forced King John VI to seek refuge across the Atlantic Ocean and change his seat of power to Brazil temporarily, from 1815 to 1821. After the war ended, the king of Portugal sailed back to Lisbon. Once King John returned to Portugal, Pedro I proclaimed Brazil's independence the following year in 1822.

Brazilian Rulers:
(1822 C.E.—1909 C.E.)

Dom Pedro I "the Liberator" (December 1, 1822 C.E.—April 7, 1831 C.E.)

Dom Pedro I was born on October 12, 1748. He was the founder and the first ruler of independent Brazil. He was the son of Joao VI of Portugal and Carlotta Joaquina of Spain. He reigned for 9 years before he died on September 24, 1834 at the age of 84. He was also recognized as King Pedro(Peter) IV of Portugal.

Dom Pedro II (April 7, 1831 C.E.—November 15, 1889 C.E.)

Pedro II, was the son of Pedro I, and he was deposed from power on November 15, 1889. At that time, the Brazilian monarchy was abolished in favor of a constitutional republic which was identified as the First Brazilian Republic. A man named Deodoro da Fonseca was elected as President. He led the coup to take over the government of Brazil from Emperor Dom Pedro II. However, one very important matter that the imperial king Pedro II did address during his brief reign was the issue of *Slavery*. On May 13, 1888, he issued a decree to abolish chattel slavery in Brazil, making it the last country in the Western Hemisphere to abolish slavery. The following year Pedro II was overthrown.

Presidents of First Brazilian Republic
(1891 C.E.—1909 C.E.)

Floriano Peixoto (November 23, 1891 C.E.—November 14, 1894 C.E.)

Peixoto rose to power at age of 51 after advancing through the ranks as a Brazilian soldier, and he eventually became a politician. Known as the **Iron** Marshal, Peixoto fought in the bloody 1864-1870 Paraguayan War. The Brazilian army joined in an alliance with Argentina and Uruguay to war against Paraguay. It was the worst war in South American history with hundreds of thousands lives lost. Paraguay lost over 300,000 people in the war. There were only 28,000 Paraguayan men left among a population of 221,000 when the six-year conflict ended. The kingdom of Brazil and its allies were victorious. As a result, Brazil expanded its southern borders to the present size. Peixoto was a 25-year-old when the war broke out.

Prudente de Morals (November 15, 1894 C.E.—November 14, 1898 C.E.)

Morais was the first ruler of Brazil to be elected by the popular voting of Brazilian people. His ascension to power was based on 1891 Brazilian Constitution. He ordered the Brazilian army to crush the settler revolt in the 1898 War of Canudos. The powerful Brazilian army overran the village and killed nearly all 30,000 inhabitants. It was regarded as the worst civil-war incident to occur in Brazilian history.

Manuel Ferraz de Campos Sales (November 14, 1898 C.E.—November 14, 1902 C.E.)

Francisco de Paula Rodrigues Alves (November 15, 1902 C.E.—November 14, 1906 C.E.)

Afonso Pena ((November 15, 1906 C.E.—June 14, 1909 C.E.)

Alfonso Pena, a legal scholar, an attorney, and once a member of the Supreme Court, ascended to the position of President of Brazil at the age of 59. He was the first leader to die in office. Pena passed on June 14, 1909 C.E. at the age of 61 after reigning a mere two years.

Appointment of Military Officer-President
(1910 C.E.—1914 C.E.)

Hermes Rodrigues de Fonseca (November 15, 1910 C.E.—November 14, 1914 C.E.)

Fonseca, a military leader, was appointed President by his predecessor Alfonso Pena. His ascension to power represented an end to republic rule and the beginning of a military dictatorship. During the 20th century, the population of Brazil increased greatly as more Portuguese and other Europeans immigrated to the vast country. There was also a growth in manufacturing during this time. Nevertheless, there were frequent military coups, like the selection of Fonseca, and suspension of civil liberties. During this time, the outbreak of World War I occurred in Europe.

Brazil, the Number 1 destination during in the Trans-Atlantic Slave Trade

Between 1501 to 1866, over 5 million Africans arrived in Latin America. Only 400,000 of those captives were taken to the United States. The remaining ones were destined for Latin America. In Latin America, the ports in Brazil were the number one points of sale. The slave trade in Brazil was very similar to what also occurred in the United States—the only difference was Brazil's slave system was much larger. When slave trafficking in Brazil finally ended on May 13, 1888, millions of African captives, many whom were the descendants of the lost sheep of Israel, had been taken into that South American country as bondmen and bondwomen to serve under the Portuguese-Brazilians. *(Even today there are more African Hebrew people living in Brazil than in the United States. In Brazil, the black population stands at 55 million while in America there are only 40 million African Hebrew people.)*

Slavery officially began full force in Brazil as early as 1530 when the Portuguese started building a sugar plantation system that was entirely dependent on African slave labor. The African kingdom of Dahomey supplied the Portuguese with a steady flow of captured men, women, and children to clear land, plant and harvest sugar cane, and operate their alcohol distilleries. For over 300 years, the Portuguese Gentile rulers **[iron people]** of the kingdom of Brazil continued to enforce the institution of chattel slavery, *with an iron hand*, against the descendants of the enslaved Africans and the indigenous Indians **[miry clay people]**.

The population of Brazil is now 47 percent European Portuguese-Brazilian and 53 percent indigenous Indians and Africans. Just think about it. At one point in history, Brazil was once upon a time 100 percent indigenous and zero percent European-Portuguese, but after more than 400 years of Portuguese conquest, the total indigenous population of Brazil fell to less than 35 percent of the overall population while the number of white Brazilians, who lived by the edge of the genocidal sword, climbed up to nearly fifty percent.

The Destruction of Great "Miry Clay" Latin American Empires

Brazil is located in the heart of South America, and for that reason, it is considered an intricate part of Latin America. It was the historical site of various indigenous empires established centuries before the arrival of Europeans. Latin America is comprised of 22 countries that cover Central and South America. They include Peru, Venezuela, Chile, Guatemala, Ecuador, Cuba, Bolivia, Haiti, Dominican Republic, Honduras, Paraguay, Uruguay, Mexico, El Salvador, Nicaragua, Costa Rica, Panama, Puerto Rico, Guadeloupe, Martinique, French Guyana, Argentina, and, of course, Brazil. All of those black, brown, and red-skinned countries shared an indigenous cultural and economic connection prior to the arrival of the Spanish conquistadors, and later the French and Portuguese warriors. The Aztec, Inca, Olmec, and Mayan civilizations, along with many others reigned prior to the discovery of the area by Amerigo Vespucci and Columbus. When the Europeans arrived, their primary goals were to enslave those indigenous Indian populations, exterminate others, and find new treasure for themselves and the Crown. The ill-treatment of those indigenous people also caused the spread of diseases, which in the end, helped to diminish their great empires. In the eyes of the European conquerors, Latin America was viewed as a mere annexation of Europe, and not their beloved homeland. That was that reason, Brazil, and other Latin American countries, were mistreated and remained a part of the developing countries of the earth. The truth of the matter was that the [iron] European people, in reality, were a minority in the midst of an indigenous [miry clay] majority in Latin America.

Latter-day Brazil: A Miry Clay Kingdom

Brazil, nor any other country in Latin America, is not considered a member of the wealthy developed countries of the earth. Although, Brazil is the largest economy in South and Central America, it, along with their other Latin American brethren, are still considered developing Third World nations because of their small industrialized base, low gross domestic product(GDP) per capita, low living standards, high infant mortality rates, and several other factors such as education and crime. The plunder of its resources has caused deforestation in Brazil and other Latin American countries. Air and water pollution have become serious problems. There are environmental damages resulting from heavy mining activities. The illegal drug trade, illegal wildlife trading and illegal poaching are other serious problems in Brazil and Latin America as well.

So it came to pass that the early rulers of the kingdom of Brazil knew not YAH nor did they walk in HIS ways. Instead, each one of them did evil in the eyes of **YHWH ELOHIM Israel**, by shedding the innocent blood of the indigenous Indians and the enslaved African Hebrews, and served the graven doctrine of Jesus Christ according to the idolatrous teachings of the Roman Catholic Church according to the dictates of the Council of Nicea in the 4th century C.E..

During these last-days of **the kingdoms of iron mixed with miry clay toes**, Brazil has become a member of a trade group representing developing countries known as BRICS in 2019. BRICS includes the developing nations of Brazil, Russia, India, China, and South Africa—**all miry clay kingdoms.**

The kingdoms of Ideas -idol ideologies
1884 C.E.—1917 C.E.)
"Ideas That Oppose Western European/Roman Supremacy"

"YAH changes times and seasons. HE removes kings (Western ideologies) and install kings (Anti-Western ideologies) HE gives the wise their wisdom and knowledge to those who know"
Daniel 2:21.

Friedrich Engels(1842 C.E.—1895 C.E.) Karl Marx(1842 C.E.—1883 C.E.) The Russian Revolution of 1917 (1917 C.E.) Vladimir I. Lenin(1922 C.E.—1924 C.E.) (Joseph Stalin (1924 C.E.—1928 C.E.)

Friedrich Engels
(1842 C.E.—1895 C.E.)

Friedrich Engels was born November 28, 1820 in Barmen, Germany in the kingdom of Prussia. He was the son of Friedrich Engels Sr. and Elisabeth "Elise" Franziska Mauritia von Haar. His father Friedrich Sr. was a wealthy German cotton textile manufacturer. Both of his parents were devoted Pietist Protestant Christians.

Growing up, it appeared young Friedrich was the opposite of his father. Instead of being diligent, he drifted off, and dropped out of high school while he was only 17. The following year in 1838, his father sent him to intern as an office clerk in the city of Bremen, hoping this would persuade him to follow in his footsteps as an accomplished businessman. It did not. While in Bremen, started to read the philosophy of a well-known teacher named George Wilheim Friedrich Hegel. His teachings were popular among the German masses at that time. Engels became more rebellious while living there. He also joined anti-business demonstrations which strained his relationship with his parents even further. During this time, he also developed atheistic opinions concerning religion as well.

Engels started a writing career when he published his first poem in 1838. His early writings also included the *Letters From Wuppertal*, which was an eyewitness investigative report highlighting the ill side effects of rapid modernization. By 1840, he was working at the family business by day and indulging in radical activities in the night. Afterwards, he began writing newspaper articles criticizing the negative effects of German industrialization. A year later in 1841, he joined the Prussian Army where he was stationed in Berlin. There he served as a member of the Household Artillery. While he was in Berlin, he attended university debates and joined a left-wing intellectual group known as the Young Hegelians. His association with the group prompted him to start writing again. This time he published articles that exposed the poor living conditions experienced by factory workers. Ironically, the magazine editor was Karl Marx. Engels and Marx finally met in Cologne, Germany in the year 1842.

In October of the same year, Engels eventually moved to Manchester, England to assist the family business there. He also continued to write in various European periodicals. In 1844, he wrote an in-depth essay entitled *Outlines of a Critique of Political Economy* in a publication where Karl Marx had become the co-editor. Marx was highly impressed with this new writing, and afterwards, the two men became long-term friends and intellectual contemporaries.

The following year in 1845, Engels wrote a book entitled *The Condition of the Working Class in England*. Written in German, the book contained an analysis of alienation of the working class in 19th century England. He exposed the unsanitary streets in the midst of crowded urban slums that were used as housing for workers. Engels criticized the unsafe factories, the degrading of blue collar workers, the negative impact that factory employment posed on English family life, such as long hours, the abuse of workers, and the disruption which jobs caused in poor people's lives. Engels' book was regarded as *"the best invective ever written . . . against industrial society and its conditions."* After the great impact of the this book, Engels and Marx's relationship evolved to even a higher new level. However, Engels was forced to leave England, go in hiding, and join Marx in Brussels where the pair joined hands to lay the foundation for an international revolutionary movement that would eventually grow to challenge Western capitalism [**iron ideology**] with [**Anti-western ideas— miry clay ideology**] worldwide.

In the following years, Engels and Marx worked together closely on several radical-thinking projects. In 1845, they authored the book *The Holy Family*, and in 1846, they wrote *The German Ideology*.

Two years later in 1848, Friedrich Engels Jr. and Karl Marx wrote their greatest work, a book entitled the *Communist Manifesto* which would one day spark changes worldwide, causing violent uprisings against Western capitalism. The pair spoke before various worker's groups, radical political parties, and secret socialist societies and eventually formed the **International Communist League—miry clay ideology**]. Although the *Communist Manifesto* was popular, the book did not help the pair find many communist converts in Brussels, so in 1849, both of them traveled through Switzerland to return to England. Engels returned to his father's textile business in Manchester while Marx went to London and resumed his penmanship. Engels used profits from the business to support Marx and his own leftist activities. In fact, Engels became the mouthpiece for Marx's movement. In 1859, Marx wrote a complicated book entitled *Das Kapital*, which was a critique of 19th century capitalism. Few understood his writing on dialectical materialism, but it was Engels who studied his writings and explained the concepts to working-class audiences. It was also Engels who popularized the doctrine of Karl Marx and defended him as a leading political thinker. When Marx died in 1883, it forced Engels to become the international ambassador for Marxism. Using his old quotes and unfinished manuscripts, Engels published *Volume 2* of *Das Kapital* in 1885, and nine years later in 1894, he completed *Volume 3*. For the remainder of his life, Engels continued to emphasize classism as the root of all evil. He steadfastly held the position that the working class in Europe [miry clay people] needed to revolt against the ruling class [iron people], and their political lackeys which held the poor European masses in servitude. So it came to pass that Friedrich Engels Jr. died on August 5,1895 at the age of 74. His corpse was cremated and his ashes were scattered off the coast of England on Beachy Head.

During his lifetime his consort was a woman named Lizze Burns. Engels, was not a ruler himself, however, the ideas that he and Karl Marx crafted were made into a graven doctrine known as socialism and communism, influencing world leaders such as Joseph Stalin, Vladimir Lenin, Leon Trotsky, of **Russia**. Russia is presently a communist [miry clay] superpower. Chairman Mao Zedong, the great ruler of [miry clay] Communist **China**, was also influenced by the *Communist Manifesto* ideas of Friedrich Engels and his companion Karl Marx.

Friedrich Engels did not know **YHWH ELOHIM Israel,** nor did he acknowledge HIS DIVINE Presence which eternally filled the entire heavens and earth, and seas during his lifetime. Instead, he walked in the imagination of his own ideas. Even today, many students of socialism and communism in all nations around the earth continue to trust in his **kingdom of ideas**, or a variation of his thoughts, for their political guidance.

Karl Marx
(1842 C.E.—1883 C.E.)

Karl Marx was born May 5, 1818 in Trier, Germany as the son of Heinrich Marx and Henriette Pressburg. Born into a Jewish family with long lineage of rabbis, his grandfather was a Dutch rabbi. During the time of his father, the German Rhineland had turned into an anti-Jewish stronghold, forcing his father to convert to Christianity for safety and prosperity. His father also received a secular education and grew to become a wealthy lawyer that owned vineyards. Therefore, young Karl Marx grew up in a prosperous middle-class household. Although he was European Jewish, Karl was baptized into the Lutheran Church in August 1824 at the age of 6.

At the age of 17, Karl Marx left home to attend the University of Bonn in 1835. Even then, Marx had a love for philosophy, but his father Heinrich insisted that he study law. He spent less than a year in the military because he was discharged for a medical condition known as a "weak chest". He returned to college again after a brief time in the military. Marx joined a radical college political group known as the Poet's Club. On the positive side of the coin, he started his career in writing, but on the negative side, he began attending wild college parties and became a member of the drinking society. His father forced him to transfer to the University of Berlin to continue his studies where he could regain focus.

While at the University of Berlin, Marx became fascinated with debates, political lectures, and philosophy. It was during this time that he was introduced to the writings and the ideas of the late G.W.F. Hegel, a widely known European socialist philosopher. In Berlin, he joined the Doctor's Club, a group known as the Young Hegelians, where he discussed Hegelian ideas. Marx became involved with the group and became a radical thinker.

In 1842, Marx moved again. This time to the city of Cologne where he became a journalist working for a radical newspaper. His journalistic skills attracted more than just readers. It attracted the watchful eyes of Prussian government censors as well. His newspaper was forced to submit their publication to government inspectors before printing a new issue. By October 1843, Marx was on the move once again. He left Germany for Paris. In Paris he became employed as a co-editor of a new radical leftist newspaper dedicated to uniting French and German revolutionaries. On August 28, 1844, Karl Marx met Friedrich Engels, who was also a German socialist. Engels showed Marx his recent writing, *The Conditions of the Working*

Class In England, which called for the working class workers to unite into one global order [**miry clay kingdoms**] to become agents of historical change for the final revolution to remove the ruling class of [**the iron kingdoms**]. Remember, *"whereas you sawest the feet and toes, part of potter's clay* [**opponents of the iron**] *and part of iron* [**opponents of the miry clay**]; *the kingdom shall be divided,"* and, as we all know the kingdom of ideas espoused by Engels and Marx divided Europe right down the middle between capitalism [**iron**] and socialism —communism [**potter's or miry clay**].

By April 1845, Marx was forced to move again. This time his revolutionary kingdom of ideas had become *non-persona grata* in both Germany and France[**iron kingdoms**]. While in Brussels, Belgium, he worked on his *11 Thesis on Feuerbach* and studied the inner workings of capitalism and the political economy. Engels moved there with him. There the pair met other exiled members of the underground group known as the *League of Just*. Two months later in July, Marx and Engels departed Brussels for England. Engels told Marx about an underground socialist movement called the Charlists which he had supported for the past two years in 1842 to 1844 while he lived in the United Kingdom. Engels returned to his family's business in Manchester while Marx studied and wrote pamphlets in London.

In 1848, he and Engels wrote the *Communist Manifesto* for the leftist group in London. That same year, he organized the first Rhineland Democratic Congress in Germany and opposed the king of Prussia when he called for the dissolution of the Prussian Assembly.

In the end, Marx stayed in exile in London from 1849 for the remainder of his life. For years his family lived in poverty and two of his children died. During those lean years Engels supported him. Marx helped himself by working part-time as a European correspondent for the New York Tribune newspaper from 1851 to 1862. He also wrote Volume 1 of a pamphlet entitled *Das Kapital*. Marx was also a leading figure in the First International from 1862 to 1872.

Karl Marx deified into the god of Marxism
"the power of the miry clay people"

Karl Marx died on March 14,1883 at the age of 64 in the city of London. Since his death, he has been regarded as one of the chief architects of modern political science and one of the most influential figures in human history. The reason being, Marx's thoughts and ideas were developed into a graven doctrine made in his own likeness known as Marxism. Marxism is the ideas and socio-economic theories developed by Karl Marx and Friedrich Engels in the mid-19th century. The tenets of Marxism is that all people are entitled to the fruits of their own labor, but people were prevented from doing so because of a capitalistic economic system. Marx said, in capitalism there were two classes of people: the non-owning workers [**miry clay—proletariat**] and the non-working owners [**iron—ruling class**]. Marx referred to this situation as an "alienation" of reality, creating the *haves* and *have nots*.

Marx prophesied that alienation and class division would one day come to an end once the workers were allowed to repossess the fruits of their labor. His theories were regarded as the gospel of truth among leftist radicals worldwide. He proclaimed class struggle as the driving force behind human history. Marx envisioned, and called for, a working class revolution [**miry clay**] that would unseat the ruling classes of the industrialized world [**iron**].

However, the 1848 *Communist Manifesto* biblical pamphlet did not spark the instability of social revolutions across Europe which Marx and Engels had hoped would materialize. However, students of socialism began to analyze the Marxist theory and adapt it based on their own variations, such as Russian leader Vladimir Lenin, who developed Leninism based on Marxism, and Chairman Mao Zedong, who crafted Maoism on the pedestal of Marxism.

Prophetical Analysis of Marxist Theory
[Iron] Ruling Class——Class Antagonism——Working Class [**Potter's Clay/Miry Clay**]

The [**iron**] represents strength, power, riches, and wealth of the business owners and lenders. Those are the non-working owners of all the machinery that control production and distribution of resources. Included in their ranks were private individuals, their families, their industrialized companies, and their powerful governments and militaries which dominated the **[miry clay]** impoverished working-class, the poor, the needy, non-owning borrowers in 19th century Europe. To overcome the gap between *the haves* and *have nots,* Marx proposed a classless communist society where only community ownership of all property was allowed. All the benefits from production and distribution were to be shared by all citizens according to the need of each. According to Marx's vision, the leadership of government would be in the hands of the proletariat, and not an aristocracy or a ruling family. In the eyes of Marx there would be a gradual end to state authority and ruling class **[iron kingdoms]**.

In the 20th century, the Marxist **kingdom of ideas** spread like a devastating *miry clay* plague into *Eastern Europe, Russia, China, Yugoslavia, North Korea, Vietnam, Cuba, Ethiopia, Angola, Mozambique*, and *elsewhere*, opposing and toppling *iron* Western-backed capitalist governments around the globe. Since the death of Marx and Engels, their *Communist Manifesto* has been used by revolutionary grassroots movements as a guiding philosophical light. Since then, it has become a historical fact that the **miry clay doctrine of Marxism** has given birth to **miry clay kingdoms in Asia, Africa, and Latin America.**

Karl Marx was buried in London on March 17, 1883. During his lifetime at the age of 25, he married a Dutch Jewish woman named Jenny von Westphalen on June 19, 1843. They were the parents of 5 children.

So it came to pass, that Karl Marx did not acknowledge **YHWH ELOHIM Israel, nor** did he walk in YAH's ways to do good and right in HIS sight according to the deeds of the ancient Afro-Asiatic children of Israel who observed HIS laws, commandments, judgements, and statutes. Instead, Marx devised thoughts and ideas according to the imaginations of his own mind. After him, **Vladimir Lenin** became the successor to his **kingdom of ideas** during the early 20th century **Russian Revolution of 1917.**

The Russian Revolution of 1917
(1917 C.E.)
"Kingdom of miry clay ideas became a miry clay kingdom"

"YAH changes times and seasons. HE removes kings (Czars of Russia) and install kings (Bolsheviks) HE gives the wise their wisdom and knowledge to those who know"
Daniel 2:21.

The seeds of the *Communist Manifesto*, which called for the working-class to rise up and violently overthrow the exploitative ruling classes, pollinated in 20th century Russia. In 1917, the imperial Romanov Dynasty continued to reign over the great kingdom of Russia. The word *Romanov*, which means *Romans*, had been a dynasty that had ruled over the land for 300 years, even since 1613. In the year 1917, the people of Russia were very discontented. As Marx had said, there were two classes: the imperial Romanov family which had been extremely corrupt and **iron-handed** and the dejected, impoverished Russian majority who were also angry about Russia's losses during World War I as well. To matters even worse, the majority of Russians were deeply mired in poverty—**miry clay**— without any opportunities to share the wealth of Russia with the royal Romanovs. Below is the lineage of the Romanov rulers of Russia: The rulers of Russia were referred to as *Czars*, meaning *Ceasars*.

<u>Romanov Dynasty over Russia</u>
(1613 C.E.—1917 C.E.)

Michael III(1613 C.E.—1645 C.E.)
Alexis (1645 C,E,—1676 C.E.)

Fyodor III (1676 C.E.—1682 C.E.)
Peter I (1682 C.E.—1725 C.E.)
Ivan V-co-regent (1682 C.E.—1696 C.E.)
Catherine I (1725 C.E.—1727 C.E.)
Peter II (1727 C.E.—1730 C.E.)
Anna (1730 C.E.—1740 C.E.)
Ivan VI (1740 C.E.—1741 C.E.)
Elizabeth (1741 C.E.—1761 C.E.)
Peter III (1761 C.E.—1762 C.E.)
Catherine II (1762 C.E.—1796 C.E.)
Paul (1796 C.E.—1801 C.E.)
Alexander I (1801 C.E.—1825 C.E.)
Nicholas I (1825 C.E.—1855 C.E.)
Alexander II (1855 C.E.—1881 C.E.)

Czar Alexander II lost the Crimean War during 1853 to 1856. European powers fought over domination of southeast Europe. Great Britain, France, Turkey, and Sardinia armies fought to defeat Russia. Russia lost the peninsula of Crimea situated in southwest Ukraine, extending out into the Black Sea.

Alexander III (1881 C.E.—1894 C.E.)
Nicholas II (1894 C.E.—1917 C.E.)

The Russian Revolution of 1905 came after years of food shortages and other imperially imposed hardships. Thousands of Russian people staged a massive peaceful demonstration in Petrograd. Nicholas arrogantly ordered Russian troops to crush the protest, killing over 200, injuring nearly a thousand, and arresting 7,000. After that, massive general strikes took place across the Russian Empire. Czar Nicholas was able to suppress the revolt, but the Bloody Sunday Massacre was seen as the beginning of the downfall of the Romanov dynasty and the ascension of the Bolshevik Soviets.

The Russian Revolution of 1917 began on February 23,1917 when there was massive protest in the nation's capital Petrograd, present-day St. Petersburg. Russian people were angry over long bread lines and the Russian monarchy's food rationing program. There were armed clashes with police and the army. The armed conflict, along with demonstrations lasted more than a week. Some soldiers in the Russian army started to join forces with the demonstrators. The violence and chaos caused the crown of Czar Nicholas II to be cast to the ground. There was no more throne or a Romanov dynasty any longer. Soon afterwards, more and more rank and file Russian soldiers began to desert their posts, leaving a power vacuum. The city of Petrograd became a center of anarchy where nearly 1,500 were slain in raging conflicts. All of this happened in February 1917. In the midst of the disorder, Prince Georgy Lvov attempted to establish a Russian Provisional Government which was forced to share power **[iron mixed with miry clay]** with the people's council of Petrograd who became known as the Soviets, *meaning* assembly, or council, of the people. In August of 1917, General Lavr Kornilov, the military leader for the Provisional government, attempted a coup to seize power for himself. His attempt failed.

Eight months later, the second phase of the revolution known as the **October Revolution** started on October 24,1917 when the provisional army launched another offensive against the Bolsheviks in Petrograd. In response, the Bolshevik revolutionaries seized control of government buildings from the Provisional government. Two weeks later on November 8, the Bolsheviks seized control of the former Winter Palace of the Czars in Petrograd and immediately called for national elections. On a local level, workers across Russia continued to organize into councils known as soviets. On a national level, the Congress of Soviet was established to serve as the governing body. Bolsheviks and other leftist groups then assumed government roles within the Russian new state. The royal family was placed under house arrest.

After the votes were counted, the Bolsheviks did not win as many seats in the 715-member Russian assembly as they had expected. They only gained 175 seats in the legislative body while the majority of the votes were received by the Socialist Revolutionary Party who won 370 votes. Once the Bolsheviks realized they did not have the votes, they sought to delay the transition of power to the new representatives while they consolidated their dictatorial hold on power. The Bolshevik power grab caused tensions with other revolutionary parties. The ill-will from these misunderstandings caused an outbreak of a five-year Russian Civil War which lasted from 1917 to 1922

Meanwhile, the Bolsheviks did not allow General Lavr Kornilov the right to grant exile to the imperial family to flee to safety in England. The Bolsheviks demanded that all members of the royal family remain in the city of Yekaterinburg under house arrest and face a people's tribunal. On July 17, 1918, Czar Nicholas II and his entire family were executed in a cellar, ending their 300-year reign as the Romanov dynasty. The Russian Revolution was led by Bolsheviks Leon Trotsky and Vladimir Lenin. Lenin then organized the armed forces known as the Red Guard to protect their power. The Red Guard served under the appointed Military Revolutionary Committee as their enforcers.

On December 30, 1922 C.E., the land of Russia officially became known as **the Union of Soviet Socialist Republic(U.S.S.R.).** It was historically the world's first proclaimed socialist state, making Russia the vanguard in adopting the ideas of Karl Marx and Friedrich Engels as part of their national patriotic cause. **Vladimir Lenin** was chosen to serve as the chairman of the Council of People's Commission of the Soviet Union.

Vladimir Lenin
(December 30, 1922 C.E.—January 21, 1924 C.E.

Vladimir Lenin was born on April 22,1870 in the city of Simbirsk in the Czarist Russian Empire. His actual birth name was Vladimir Ilich Ulyanov. He was the son of Ilya Nikolayevich Ulanov and his mother Maria Alexandrovna Blank. Lenin was raised in a middle-class family. However, he was deeply affected by the death of his older brother who was slain by Czarist security forces over accusations that he was involved in a plot to murder Czar Alexander III. At the age of 19, he began to study law where he was introduced to the teachings of Karl Marx. While still studying law, Lenin was baptized in Marxist theology, and by 1895, his activities caught the attention of the czar's security forces. He was arrested, charged with subversion, and sentenced to exile in Siberia. In the loneliness of exile, he found his wife Nadezhda Krupskaya. After the year 1900, the couple moved to the Western World, residing in London. In London, he was chosen as leader of the Russian Social-Democratic Worker's Party, known as the Bolsheviks. Just like his predecessors Marx and Engels, Lenin was a journalist. He actually published several revolutionary newspapers.

Once Lenin became the chairman of the Bolsheviks, he developed his own theories of the inner working of socialism. Lenin saw a need for the Russian Social-Democratic Worker's Party to serve as the vanguard of the people. He also envisioned a centralized body of socialists organized and led by a core of professional revolutionaries. His ideas became known as **Leninism.**

In 1905 when the outbreak of the Russian Revolution occurred, Lenin decided to return to the frontline in Russia and directed the guerilla campaign against the Romanovs. After the Romanovs quelled the rebellion, Lenin decided to return to Siberia and direct his campaign from his hideout. Twelve years later, the Russian masses staged massive demonstrations against government policies. Lenin returned to Petrograd to direct the revolution. During the chaos, a fellow socialist named Trostsky was chosen to serve as the visible leader while Lenin led from hiding. Lenin orchestrated the seizure of the Provisional government buildings, thus seizing control of the Russian government.

Afterwards, Lenin changed the foreign policy of Czarist Russia by signing the Treaty of Brest-Litovsk with Germany. Lenin withdrew the Russian army from World War I. In fact, Lenin wanted to turn World War I into an uprising of the European working classes against the ruling classes across Europe.

From late 1917 until 1922, the Russian Revolution turned into a Russian Civil War with various leftist factions fighting against the Bolsheviks. In the end, Lenin and the Bolsheviks prevailed to form a dictatorship of the proletariat spanning from eastern Europe and to Siberia. Tens of thousands of opponents were eliminated nationwide. Thousands more were placed in concentration camps and starved to death.

During those years the Russian economy experienced an economic crisis as it transitioned from capitalism to socialism, forcing Lenin to initiate a New Russian Economic Policy. However, ill-health began to take its toll on Valadimir Lenin from 1922 onward. He died on January 24, 1924 after suffering a stroke at the age of 53. After a royal funeral, his corpse was entombed in a building called the Lenin Mausoleum located in the new capital of the U.S.S.R. which was Moscow. His comrade **Joseph Stalin** became his successor.

In the process of time, Lenin became a member of the pantheon of socialist philosophers who were revered by followers worldwide. His doctrine was erected upon a pedestal besides the doctrine of Marx, thus becoming known as Marxism-Leninism.

So it came to pass that Vladimir Lenin did not acknowledge the DIVINE Presence of **YHWH ELOHIM Israel** nor did he take heed to any of the DIVINE Instructions found written in the Torah.

Joseph Stalin
(1924 C.E.—1928 C.E.)
"Gog, the chief prince of the land of Magog"
Miry clay kingdom: Enemy of the iron kingdoms in the West

Joseph Stalin was born December 18,1878 in the hilly city of Gori located in the province of eastern Georgia, which was a part of the Czarist Russian Empire. His actual birth name was Iosif Vissarionovich Dzhugashvili. His father's name was Besarion Jughashvili, a cobbler by trade, and his mother's name was Ekaterine Geladze. He was born into a peasant family that was mired in poverty. Growing up, he studied in the seminary, but by the time reached the age of 21,he was expelled because of his political activities. The seminary officials were anti-Marxists and pro-Russian Orthodox Christians. However, on the streets the Marxist message was very popular among grassroots individuals like Stalin. In 1903, by the time he had reached 25, Stalin joined the Bolshevik Russian Social-Democratic Worker's Party. Eventually, like Karl Marx before him, he abandoned religion altogether, and became the editor of the anti-church Russian Communist Party newspaper Pravda. In reality, he adopted the throne name Stalin, which meant *"steel"*, to reflect his internal commitment to the Russian revolutionary struggle. *(Remember, he was born with last name Dzhugashvili)*. Stalin grew to become the communist party's enforcer and gangster who raised funds through robberies, kidnappings for ransoms, and protection schemes. He was arrested several times by the Romanov police, and, he was sentenced to exile just as many times.

In October 1917,the Bolsheviks seized control of the headquarters of the Provisional government and hastily created a one-party monopoly on power under the banner of Marxist communism. 38-year-old Stalin, who by now had become a disciple of Lenin, was invited to join the Bolshevik Central Committee known as the Politburo. As fate would have it, by 1924, Lenin's health deteriorated to the point that he experienced a massive stroke which claimed his life in January of 1924. Joseph Stalin then out-muscled his rivals, Trotsky, Zinovyev, Kamenev, Bukharin, and Kykov, to assume leadership over one of the largest sovereign land masses on the face of the earth. For the record, Russia's western border extended into eastern Europe. The eastern borders extended deep into North Asia. The 6.5 million square mile perimeter stretched from Moscow to Siberia. The land and its environment was very diverse, including the mountainous ranges of the Ural Mountains to the cold forest lands of Siberia. The country's highest peaks included the Kamchatkra mountains. The great rivers of Volga and Northern Dvina flowed through the Russian plain. The Ob, Lena, Amur, and Yenisey rivers poured into the Siberian plains. In the southern part of the massive kingdom there were natural habitats of forests, fertile farmlands, and mountainous steppes. In ancient times, the land mass was roamed by the barbaric Sythicans, Goths, Huns, Avars, Kievan Rus, and other nomadic tribespeople.

The Birth of the graven doctrine of Stalinism
Stalinism joins Marxism and Leninism as gods of communism

In the 20th century, the same land mass was now ruled by the Union of Soviet Socialist Republic under the leadership of Joseph Stalin. Stalin had a vision of a new authoritarian dictatorship in the newly crowned Soviet Union. In 1924, he put forth the theme of *"Socialism In One Country"*. According to this concept, the Soviet Union strived to create the conditions to further socialism while simultaneously building an industrialized economy. His rival Trotsky envisioned a concept termed *"Permanent Revolution"* where Russia accepted assistance from other centers of the global revolution. By 1925, Trotsky and others were totally gone. Stalin had stripped his rivals of their personal power and positions. He removed them and appointed only those faithful to his vision. Stalin initiated a nationwide campaign very similar to a great church revival including red Soviet banners, flags, and other forms of pageantry. Stalin implemented a religious revival-type atmosphere meant to secure loyalty and adulation of the communist state. Large pictures of Politburo leaders were displayed in parades and military processions.

Stalin's goal from that period forward was to secure his hold on power and transform the once-capitalist Czarist Russian economy into a socialist beacon of light. This period was known as the *"Great Change"* or *"The Five Years Plan"*. Stalin restructured the Soviet Union into an independent major industrialized power capable of competing with the West in all sectors. He passed decrees to build the kingdom of Russia into a modern military power with machinery **[miry clay kingdom]** capable enough to stand up to hostile capitalist power such as Germany, France, Great Britain, and eventually the United States **[iron kingdoms]**.

At the end of the Stalinist revolution, the entire capitalist structure of imperial Russia was eliminated. All segments of the economy were turned into socialist sectors. Stalin's revolution did not fare well in the agricultural sectors. Poor peasant farmers who once earned small incomes from planting were stripped of those ways of doing business. The farmers were forced into state-sponsored collective farms where they were told what to plant, and how much to plant. There were wholesale rebellions in the Ukraine and the Caucasus regions. Farmers burned their crops and slaughtered their animals in defiance of Stalin's new regulations. Stalin ordered the Soviet Army to enforce his new policies. According to most reports, 5 to 6 million people died during that period of time. Millions others were interned in labor camps in rigid Siberia and the Russian Arctic where many of them perished.

On the other hand, Stalin was successful in consolidating his hold on power. His reign lasted for 29 years. He was also successful in transforming the Russian military into one of the world strongest military powers. The socialist-communist revolutions in Russia set in motion the transformation of that country into one of the prophesied **[10 miry clay] kingdoms in the feet and toes of the image** spoken of in the latter-days. The **kingdom of Ideas** constructed by Friedrich Engels and Karl Marx now stood as deities in the halls of power in Moscow. The Marxist theology was the mantra in a literal kingdom of men who believed in the founder's ideas. Those ideas represented a head-on collision with the ruling families, industrial tycoons, and governments of the **[10 iron toes]**.

O House of Israel and all mankind, we have now entered the **Prophetic Time Zone of the Feet and Toes of the Image.** In the 21st century, **YHWH** is now fulfilling this portion of the dream HE gave to King Nebuchadnezzar 2,600 years ago.

Black Biblical History

660 B.C.E. wall relief depicting a delegation of four ancient Afro-Asiatic Hebrews visiting Assyria. The portrait clearly reveal the Afrocentric physical features of the ancient Israelites. The wooly hair with locks, the broad noses, and lips are non-European. In the 20th and 21st century, the Caucasian Jewish religious converts have claimed the heritage of the ancient Shemitic tribes of Israel. The relief is further proof that today's European Jewish converts in the 1948 State of Israel are not the same as the historic biblical Israelites on the wall relief above.

The wall relief above is a portrait of the historic Canaanites in Egypt. The African features of the Canaanites in the picture above is obvious, proving the biblical Canaanites were a black people.

President Donald Trump, leader of the Iron Kingdom United States of America confer with President Xi Jinping, the ruler of the Miry Clay kingdom of China. Trade wars and military-poliical confrontation prove that these two spheres of power do not cleave one to another.

Miry Clay kingdom Russia has threaten to war against Iron U.S.

The Iron and Potter's Clay Age—
(And whereas you saw the feet part of potter's clay and part of iron)

I. (Iron Toes kingdoms and Miry Clay Toes kingdoms)
II. Iron Mixed with Miry Clay
III. Brief Historical Profile on the 10 Partly Iron Toes Kingdom
IV. Brief Historical Profile on the 10 Partly Miry Clay Toes Kingdom
V. The Creation of the United Nations
VI. G-20

"And whereas you saw the feet part of potter's clay and part of iron, the kingdom shall be partly strong and partly broken. And whereas you saw iron mixed with miry clay, they shall mingle themselves with the seed of men, but they shall not cleave one to another, even as iron is not mixed with clay. . . ."
Daniel 2:40-43

"YAH changes times and seasons, HE removes kings (kingdoms) and install kings (kingdoms), HE gives the wise their wisdom and knowledge to those who know."
Daniel 2:21

I. (Iron Toes Kingdom and Miry Clay Toes Kingdom)

In the dawn of the late 19th Century C.E. and continuing into both the 20th and 21st century, the prophetic clock finally reached the feet of the image which King Nebuchadnezzar had seen in his dream over two thousand years earlier. As we already know, each section of the body of the image, **gold, silver, brass, iron,** and **potter's clay**, represented a shift in global power from one people(kingdom) to another. This new, yet, final time zone represented the era which the prophet Daniel described as *"the latter-days"*. During this shift of power in the latter-days, YAH revealed to Daniel that the world would be divided among two distinct groups: Iron and Miry Clay. These two diverse powerful spheres would be known as **The Age of Iron and Miry Clay(Potter's Clay) or ten toes.**

As we traced the birth, the development, the rise, and the fall of the kingdoms, beginning with Babylonia, Persia, Greece, and Rome, we all have learned that Roman civilization is depicted by the metal of **Iron** which is one of the strongest and abundant metals on earth. It was the Europeans who became the inheritors of the extensive Roman domain and grew to become one of strongest people on the face of the earth. The use of iron, which the Europeans learned to process into steel for usage as tools and weapons, became one main elements used to advance world civilization. Beginning in the late 19th century, world civilization was centered in Europe. For the first time in history since the existence of human civilizations,

Europe was now the seat of world power. The Europeans, who are prophetically the **Iron People**, through their discoveries, inventions, and advancements in technologies, transformed the entire earth into one connected global community. During the era of the 1800s to 1900s, the discovery of the light bulb, electricity, the telegraph, telephones, bicycles, automobiles, trains, airplanes, the modern printing press, radio, television, typewriters, cameras, and the increased use of iron machines to perform tasks once performed by humans changed day-to-day life for all inhabitants of the earth while propelling the sons and daughters of Japheth, the isles of the Gentiles, into worldwide leadership. European civilization advanced with the federation of these powerful European/Roman toes which prophetically represent "The Ten Iron Kingdoms". Geographically, their territories extend all the way from Australia to Canada, and covering both continents, Europe and North America.

The Iron People, i.e. the Europeans, also transformed warfare with the use of gunpowder for firearms. The use of aviation, scientific discovery of atomic energy, and others weapons of destruction changed the world negatively, bruising every country on earth with weapons that caused massive deaths. The strength of the Europeans allowed them to be cruel, merciless, and powerful enough to demand global control. The Iron Kingdoms became oppressive, selfish, and the most dominant culture among the children of men. They amassed the world's wealth among themselves, the ten toes, with an economic system known as capitalism.

The ten principal latter-days Iron Kingdoms that have inherited this power in since the collapse of the Roman Empire have been France, Germany, Britain, Italy, Belgium, the Netherlands, Spain, Portugal, Luxembourg, and eventually the United States. For several centuries, these Aryan people have promoted their technological advancements as methods to gain wealth, rank, prestige, and power over indigenous people worldwide, dividing the world into the "civilized" and poorer "uncivilized" zones. Like their predecessors the ancient Romans, the global strategy of the Iron Kingdoms was to integrate the family of nations under their Pax European control and culture. Beginning in the first century B.C.E. until late 1800s C.E., the Iron Kingdoms have endured and expanded from one side of the earth unto the other, covering all 7 continents.

However in the latter-days of these kingdoms of men, and in accordance with Daniel's prophecy, European/Roman domination over the earth would begin to face violent uprisings from colonized indigenous nations in Europe and worldwide. During these last-days, the ancient lands, which once comprised ancient civilizations, will rise up to oppose the brutal **iron tyranny** of European colonialism which has crushed their national pride into poverty-stricken miry clay, even into dust. For centuries, the iron kingdoms used their strength to dominate the human affairs of others, extracting their natural resources for the benefit of their own iron kingdoms. These global policies caused great divisions and inequities between the descendants of the iron kingdoms (Europeans) and the descendants of the miry clay kingdoms (**Modern Third World**). Centuries of injustices and frictions between the rich iron nations and the poor miry clay nations have continue to cause tensions and turmoil, wars, diseases, famines, and poverty, fulfilling the prophecy of *"whereas you saw the feet part of potter's clay and part of iron, the kingdom shall be divided"*. The feet of the image represented the latter-days, or the last heathenistic era before **The Age of YAH—The STONE Cut Out Without Hands**. So, in the latter-days, Daniel foresaw an endtime global order ruled by a **group of toes [nations]** which were divided into two uncircumcised mindsets: **Iron and Potter's Clay, and also referred to as Miry Clay**.

The endtime Miry Clay kingdoms are presently known as the modern Third World countries. They are the nations with major populations, however, the minority iron kingdoms are the ones which control the lion's share of the world's wealth through their strong **ironclast** economic system. Europeans/Romans make up only 6 percent of the world population, yet they control over 60 percent of the world's wealth. This gap between wealth distribution and population growth has caused wars between indigenous Miry clay kingdoms and invading Iron kingdoms. They have fought over natural resources such as oil, opium, precious metals, minerals, water, farmland, and other valuables. Oftentimes, the Iron Kingdoms have laid claims to natural resources in far away places thousands of miles away from their own territory in Europe. In the Hebrew scriptures, Europe is known as "the isles of the Gentiles". **[Read Genesis 10:5]** They have used their strength to command advantage in economic, political, military, and social relationships throughout the global kingdom. However, since 1945, the indigenous miry clay people have rebelled against the iron people and crafted their own leadership and developed their own ideologies. During these divisive wars the **Miry Clay kingdoms** broke away from the **Iron kingdoms** and chose their own economic, political, and religious doctrines.

Therefore YAH revealed to Daniel that power within the global kingdom would be divided among several groups of nations like toes on the image's feet. These partly iron and partly clay broken toes representing an international civilization divided between the 10 wealthy Industrialized European nations verus the 10 most powerful Third World countries.

The 10 principal latter-day Third World nations that represent the prophetic **Miry Clay Kingdoms** are Russia, China, Brazil, India, Indonesia, Saudi Arabia, Iran, North Korea, South Africa, and Mexico. Together these 20 countries comprise the G-20, the 10 partly iron and 10 partly miry clay toes of the image. Collectively, these 20 nations are the controllers of the world economy, the possessors of the world's most powerful militaries, the world's wealthiest trading partners whose net worth is more than the other 175 nations combined. Founded in 1999, many nations that are members of G-20 were already members of the G-7, the seven richest nations, G-5, the five largest Third World economies, OPEC, the Arab League, the European Union(EU), permanent members of the UN, and permanent members of the United Nations Security Council—**groups of toes**.

All of these groups of nations, both **Iron** and **Potter's Clay**, are equally guilty of practicing the falsehood of Paganism which is the concept that every human being can do as he or she desires regardless of the standard ordained by the CREATOR of heavens, earth, and seas in the Torah. For example, all nations, rich and poor, continue to be guilty of violating the standard written in **Deuteronomy 16:21-22** which spiritually outlawed the custom of monument building:

"You shall not set up a sacred post besides the altar of YAH your ELOHIM or erect a stone pillar such YHWH your ELOHIM hates."

All nations have made a spiritual decision to commission sculptured images of their own leaders and all manner of people. Worldwide, you have monuments and statues of men and women such as Jesus, Taj Mahal, Buddha, Confucius, Virgin Mary, Venus, Athena, Diana, golden calves, sacred astrological symbols, and countless other religious symbols and man-made edifices. So as you can see, Paganism is the custom of promoting or believing in man-made ideologies and objects. An erroneous custom that had been practiced by all the kingdoms of gold, silver, brass, iron, and clay for thousands of years before this modern era. In the latter-days, the same wicked customs are still practiced by the **Iron Kingdoms** and the **Miry Clay Kingdoms**. The main contention between the two is: which graven image deserves praise and honor. For example in the Iron Kingdom of the United States, a monument is built to praise George Washington, but overseas in the Miry Clay kingdom of China the monument is built in honor their Communist Party founder Chairman Mao. In Rome, the cathedral is built in honor of the god of iron Jesus, whereas in Mecca a monument is built in honor of the god of miry clay Allah. The same is true in Russia where Karl Marx is regarded as a great man, but overseas in America, Thomas Jefferson is revered as the greatest thinker. Again, these are two competing spheres of image-worship:Iron worship verus Miry Clay worship: Christianity verus Islam, Buddhism verus Christianity, Communism verus Capitalism, and western lifestyle verus eastern, Mediterranean, or African lifestyles.

Keep in mind, both of these spheres of power walk in the imagination of their own uncircumcised hearts, following their own belief systems, doing according to all their unrighteous predecessors. Both kingdoms—**iron and clay**— allow their citizens to call upon the names of other gods besides **YAH ELOHIM**. These uncircumcised nations worship stone pillars, sacred posts, and objects, and various handcrafted images. In *the latter-days* these pagan worshippers, blinded through their spiritual ignorance, have turned their minds away from YAH to serve other doctrines and beliefs. None of them recognize the **DIVINE Presence of YAH ELOHIM, the CREATOR of the heavens, earth, and seas** whose Spirit is in the midst of all mankind. Paganism has closed the spiritual eyes of **the children of iron** and **the children of miry clay**, leaving them unable to see **the Presence of YAH** standing before them. Each group of toes **[kingdoms]** have built their own way of life, own political systems, and selfish national interest without a YAH-Mind. Both divisions are the **Children of The Image** who have built idolatrous altars which their own hands have wrought.

II. (Iron Mixed with Miry Clay)
Europe and The Non-Western World

The latter-day **Iron kingdoms** are the descendants of the ancient iron Roman civilization which started at the pelvis and legs of the image. These are the offsprings of the Germania, British Isles, Gaulic, and Hispania hordes who assumed control of the Roman provinces when the ancient Roman Empire collapsed in 476 C.E. These primitive Romanized hordes eventually evolved into Western European civilization, consisting of the people of Germany, France, Britain, Belgium, the Netherlands, Spain, Portugal, Italy, and eventually Canada, the United States, and others. These European countries are the ones who are continuing to carry the legacy of the Roman empire within their judicial, architectural, political, cultural, social, and economic ways of life. The belief systems of the ancient Roman empire, both paganism and Christianity, is deeply ingrained in their societies. The strength of iron within these kingdoms have provided them with the nucleus to rise into industrialized superpower status.

Another interesting observation you can witness for yourself is the appearance of ancient Roman leaders in sculpturing. Compare them to photos of modern European leaders. You will notice the striking resemblance for yourself, proving without a shadow of doubt that these are the same people. This will prove that **the long iron legs** of Roman influence has continued for thousands of years from the days of ancient Rome, the Roman Catholic Church, Medieval Europe, the Enlightenment Era, down through the modern eras of World War I, World War II, and continuing until this very day in 2019-2020 and beyond.

The latter-day **Miry clay kingdoms** were, and continue to be, the offsprings of the kingdoms that have opposed the domination of the iron kingdoms since the beginning of the ancient Roman Empire. For example, the kingdoms of the Parthians, the Armenians, the Egyptians, the ancient Syrians, the kingdoms of Mesopotamia, the Carthaginians, and even the Huns or Turks. Those rulers and their people have opposed Roman domination since the early days of the Roman Republic. Those kingdoms have molten their own self-images which do not include the likeness of Rome. Instead, they fought Roman influence for centuries to maintain their own sovereignty, and to serve their own traditions, myths, and to bow before their own sacred posts which they had chosen, and not those imposed upon them by the **iron-hands** of the Roman legions.

Today, the miry clay kingdoms are the ones with non-European beliefs and customs, such as the Arabs, the Chinese, Iranians, Russians, North Koreans, Somalis, the Sudanese, Brazilians, Mexicans, and others with the earthly power to oppose foreign domination. Another interesting discovery you will find through observation is that miry clay people come in all human skintones. You have pale-skinned Russians, Yellow-skinned Chinese, brown-skinned Arabs, dark-brown and black Africans, and reddish-brown skinned Latin Americans. So, it is correct to say that **miry clay** is a "State of Mind" within all nationalities of the human family. It represents a separate **bloc of power** which is opposite of the **iron.** Yet, both blocs of power live on the same planet and share the world's resources. They are mixed, or *integrated*, in one world, but they *"do not cleave one to another"* for various reasons which we've already discussed earlier. You will also notice that the **[miry clay]** kingdoms were always an undercurrent living concurrently during the long reign of [**the iron legs**]. They were always there and strong enough to go to battle against the Roman-Europeans. And, even if they lost a war against Rome/Western Europe, they would rebuild and fight at another date and time, never relinquishing their way of life to the [**iron**] Roman Empire.

Even today in 2019, world power is mixed, or *shared*, by the hands of the iron and miry clay in the United Nations and other global organizations such as the G-20, which is comprised of 10 iron nations and 10 miry clay nations.

However, before I go any further, let's look at a brief historical profile on each of the **10 latter-day toes of partly iron,** and afterwards we will briefly look at the **10 latter-day toes of partly clay** as we prepare for our redemption to usher in **the Age of YHWH—The STONE CUT OUT WITHOUT HANDS.**

III. Brief Historical Profile on the 10 Partly Iron Toe Kingdoms

"YAH changes times and seasons, HE removes kings (kingdoms) and install kings (kingdoms), HE gives the wise their wisdom and knowledge to those who know."

Daniel 2:21

1) Germany

By 1862, a Germanic leader named Otto Von Bismark came to power in Prussia, and over the next decade he reunited the German empire. The territory of Prussia included northern Germany and western Poland. The empire collapsed after its loss in World War I. Germany was stripped of its territorial possessions and all of its overseas colonies. After the loss of World War I, the Weimar Republic was established. This German dynasty lasted from 1919 to 1933. Troubled with economic problems, especially the Great Depression, and political instability, the German people voted Aloph Hitler and his Nazi Party into power establishing the Third Reich. Hilter reigned for twelve years, from 1933 to 1945, and he envisioned the re-creation of the Holy Roman Empire ruled by Germany. His invasion of neighboring Poland is what plunged the continent into the Second World War.

Chancellor Adolph Hitler
(1933 C.E.—1945 C.E.)

Born on April 20,1889 in the city of Braunau am Inn, Austria as the son of Alois Hitler and Klara Polzi. He moved to Germany in 1913, and a year later at the age of 25, he joined the army of the German Empire. Although Germany lost the war, young Hilter became a renown soldier. The kingdom of Germany was severely weakened after its defeat in the First World War. These hardships moved Hilter to become involved in German politics, and by 1921 he was appointed leader of the National Socialist German Worker's Party. Jailed in 1923 for his involvement in an attempted military coup, Hitler wrote the famed Mein Kampf, his strategy for takeover. After his release, he became very popular by denouncing Germany's acceptance of the terms to end Word War I and promoting pan-German nationalism while condemning European Jewish economic control of both capitalism and communism.

By 1933 the National Socialist German Worker's Party had become the most dominant political party and on January 30th, Hitler was crowned the new Chancellor. Hitler then initiated a purge, overthrowing all traces of the Weimar Republic and installing a one-party Nazi state. All European Jewish converts were regarded as enemies of the state. Hitler considered them as foreign agents whose sole purpose was to keep Germany weak through economic subjugation. In Hitler's eyes, Paris, France, London, England, and New York City were viewed as the behind-in-scene puppeteers controlling German politics. He later established concentration camps to single them out for persecution. This twelve years of suffering became known as the European Jewish Holocaust, resulting in a death toll of nearly six million. Nevertheless, these moves to reclaim German sovereignty made him very popular among the German masses. He then strengthened the German military with a massive rearmament program. On September 1,1939, Hitler ordered his forces to invade Poland. In response France and Britain declared on war on Germany. For two years Hitler's troops moved across Europe and also claimed territories in North Africa. In the year of 1941 C.E., Hitler expanded the war by declaring war on the United States. By 1945, the Allied **iron kingdoms of the United States, Britain, and France** along with additional support from the **miry clay kingdom of the Soviet Union** defeated Hitler and removed him from power.

So it came to pass that on April 30,1945 that 56-year-old Adolph Hitler, and his newlywed Eva Braun, committed suicide as the Allied Forces from the west and the Soviet Union from the east invaded Germany. Hitler reigned twelve years serving the image gods of Christianity, even Jesus Christ, and he did evil in the eyes of **YAH ELOHIM of Israel** like all of his Germanic predecessors and his successors, even until this day. During his reign, Hitler shedded massive amounts of innocent blood.

Latter-day Germany

After the defeat of Germany at the end of World War II, Germany was divided among the Allied Powers, represented by Britain, France, and the United States, and Russia. A disagreement between the Allied Powers and Russia led to the division of Germany into two spheres of power with the Berlin Wall serving as the border between the two:**Iron** and **Miry Clay**. Communist East Germany and Capitalist West Germany. Western Germany became a strong prosperous parliamentary democracy while Eastern Germany became a one-party state ruled by Communist leaders under Soviet Union control. Russia went on to create an eastern European defense federation known as the Warsaw Pact. The Allied Powers established a counter force known as NATO—North Atlantic Treaty Organization.

In 1989 the east German people overthrew the communist government in a peaceful revolution. The next year the two Germanys reunited into one. In the following years, the united Germany has moved towards political and economic integration as part of the European Union. Today **iron** Germany is one of the wealthiest countries in the world. In 2018-2019, a German woman named Angela Merkel served as the Chancellor of the united strong and wealthy north-central European kingdom.

2) France

So, in the process of times those Frankish kingdoms continued down the **long iron legs** through the time zones into 20th and 21st century France.

During the year of 1940 C.E. in the beginning of World War II, France was invaded and occupied by Nazi Germany. The Germans then rounded up European Jewish converts and many were slain. After years of Nazi occupation, the Allied Powers of the United States and Britain joined forces to reclaim France. In the summer of 1944 C.E. France was liberated and Charles deGaulle established a multi-party democracy known as the Fourth Republic. In 1958 de Gaulle re-established another government known as the Fifth French Republic.

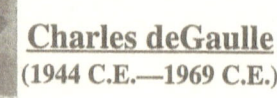

Charles deGaulle
(1944 C.E.—1969 C.E.)

Charles Andre Joseph Marie deGaulle born on November 22,1890 C.E. as the son of Henri deGaulle and Jeanne-nee Maillot in the city of Lille, France, a northern French city near the border of Belgium. Raised in a traditional family as an observant Catholic by an intellectual father who taught at a Jesuit College, deGaulle grew into a knowledgeable young man who loved his country. He joined the army in 1913 at the age of 23 before the outbreak of World War I. Once France became involved in the war, deGaulle served as a mighty man of valor where he became a distinguished soldier. During the war, he was wounded and taken prisoner where he spent almost three years in a German prisoner-of-war camp. DeGaulle attempted to escape several times and was moved to solitary confinement in a high-security facility where he remained until the war ended on December 1, 1918 C.E. Afterwards, deGaulle was allowed to return home to France and continued to serve in the military. By 1925 he was promoted to the staff of The Supreme War Council. By the time World War II began, deGaulle was the brigadier general and undersecretary of state for defense. Initially, he led the French Resistance against the Nazis. But after French forces were defeated by the Germans he fled to England.

While in England, he started the Free France Movement and established a government-in-exile. After the liberation of Paris, deGaulle returned home to lead the Provisional Government of the French Republic from 1944 to 1946. The following year, he stepped down to support the *"Rally for the French People"* movement. From August 20, 1944 to January 20, 1946 he served as Prime Minister. He also served as co-Prince of Andorra while serving as prime minister. In the year of 1953 C.E. deGaulle retired for the first time. At the time, he was the most dominant leader in French politics during the postwar era.

Five years later in May of 1958, the National Assembly summoned deGaulle out of retirement to be re-appointed as prime minister for the second time. This time he served from June 1 until January 8, 1959. DeGaulle then became the President of France and Co-Prince of Andorra from January 8, 1959 until late 1968 when he was forced to step down because of widespread protests by students and workers. He also served simultaneously as Minister of Defense and Minister of Algerian Affairs at the same time. He wrote a new French constitution and established the Fifth French Republic while in office. DeGaulle made his country the fourth nuclear power by launching an independent nuclear-weapons development program. He withdrew France from the American-led NATO defense alliance, instead preferring to an independent power while he strengthened ties with Germany and pursued peace with the Soviet Union and other Eastern European countries.

The French [**iron kingdom**] involvement in the war in Algeria [**a miry clay kingdom**] caused major problems for the deGaulle government inside France. Eventually he was forced to withdraw and grant Algeria its independence. He later withdrew France from 12 former African colonies and declared them independent states. France withdrew from Vietnam [**another miry clay nation**] as well.

So it came to pass that President Charles deGaulle died on November 9, 1970 C.E. at the age of 79 in the city of Colombey-les-Deux-Eglises, France. For 26 years he served in various leadership roles to guide the kingdom back to stability and prosperity after the devastation of World War II. He served the image-god Jesus of the Roman Catholic Church and all the other gods of the Greco-Roman pantheon like all of his predecessors. After his death, several streets and standing monuments [**statues or graven images**] were built in his likeness and dedicated to his honor and legacy throughout France.

Latter-day France

At the end of World War II, France became one the 5 permanent members of the newly formed United Nations Security Council, the global organization created to establish one global order [**iron mixed with miry clay**]. France became the central figure in the reconciliation of Europe which led to the creation of the European Common Market, the forerunner of the European Union. Today, France is one of the wealthiest and powerful nuclear [**iron**] kingdoms among the 193 nations of the earth. In 1981, the French voters elected a socialist, Francois Mitterand, as the country's president. During the 1990s France joined with Germany to solidify European political and economic integration. In the 2017 French national elections, Emmanuel Macron became the new President of France.

3. Britain

From the early modern period of the 19th and 20th century, Britain grew into a global power with technological, political and diplomatic influence among the kingdom of men. Britain is world renown and enjoys the elite status as the one of leading kingdom on the face of the earth.

Prime Minister Winston Churchill
(1940 C.E.—1945 C.E.)

Winston Leonard Churchill was born on November 30, 1874 C.E. in the city of Oxfordshire, England as the son of Lord Randolph Churchill and Jennie Jerome. He was born during the era when his country was the world's number one power and the sun never set on the British Empire. He was a descendant of the Dukes of Malborough, and his family was a member of the aristocracy. Born with a silver spoon in his mouth he lived among the elite as a lad. He was known to be a spoiled brat that misbehaved during his boarding school days where he later complained of being beaten by his overseers. He later became an intelligent student with a great interest in history. While growing up, his father served as the Viceroy to Ireland and later served in British parliament. His grandfather had served in parliament as well. His parents separated during his teenage years. His mother, the daughter of a wealthy American family, was known to be whorish with many admiring lovers. Churchill only saw his father on rare occasions. He grew up estranged from both of them.

As a maturing young man Churchill believed in the greatest of Britain and Gentile supremacy worldwide. He joined the British Army and fought in wars against India, the Anglo-Sudanese War, and the Second Boer War. Churchill combined his literary skills, which he learned in aristocratic schools and his experiences in war to write about those military campaigns. He became famous from his writings and won a Nobel Prize for Literature. His fame propelled him into public life.

He was first elected to parliament as a member of the Conservative Party in 1900 at the age of 26. He later switched to the Labor Party in 1904 C.E. Four years later in 1908 he became the President of Board of Trade. He also served as Home Secretary from 1910 to 1911. Before the outbreak of World War I, he served as the Chancellor of the Duchy of Lancester in 1915. He also served as the First Lord of Admirality during this same time. When the First World War stated, Churchill was chosen as the Minister of Munitions under Prime Minister David Lloyd George. Britain and France, along with U.S. troops in 1917, united to defeat Germany to end the First World War. The war was costly with 10 million dead, 21 million injured, and another 8 million missing or imprisoned, however, Britain continued as the preeminent European power for another 20 years until the outbreak of World War II. During that time, Churchill was a member of the Liberal Party, but that changed during events leading up to the Second World War. Germany, under Hitler, initiated a strong rearmament program to restore their fortunes. Churchill took the lead calling for a strong British military in face of the Nazi threat. In 1940, Churchill replaced Prime Minister Neville Chamberlin, who was seen as an appeaser of Germany. Britain, under Churchill, joined France against Germany to crush their aggression. Churchill oversaw Britain's victory to become a victorious wartime national hero.

In the eyes of the British people, Churchill was seen as one of the most important figures of the 20th century who defended their liberal democracy against fascism. Many of Churchill critics described him as a vengeful butcher based on his decision to bomb Dresden, Germany during the closing days of the Second World War. Beginning in early 1945 C.E., the U.S. and

Britain agreed to send 722 British Royal Air Force bombers along with 527 United States Air Force bombers, and 784 North American P-51 Mustangs on around-the-clock air raids, dropping 3,900 tons of highly explosive and incendiary devices on the German city. The bombs destroyed over 1,600 acres in the downtown area and other important infrastructure, killing nearly 25,000 Germans.

Ironically, Churchill was defeated in the 1945 national election. While out of power, Churchill became the war hawk leader of the opposition calling for a strong national defense in face of the emerging Cold War with the Soviet Union, the communist powerbroker which controlled the Eastern European side of the Iron Curtain. For one year, beginning in 1951 he temporarily served as Minister of Defense. He then called on the British defense establishment to develop an atomic bomb, joining the United States and Russia.

2nd reign of Winston Churchill
(1955 C.E.—1955 C.E.)

Churchill second term as Prime Minister began on October 26, 1951 C.E. after replacing the Labour Party leader named Clement Attle. During his second term the Third World countries (**Miry Clay kingdoms**) that were once a part of the British Commonwealth rebelled against the colonialist power (**Iron kingdom**). This included **Malaya, India, Kenya, Syria, and others**. Churchill became more aggressive as a British imperialist. He sought to ruthlessly suppress these anti-British campaigns, butchering countless numbers of his non-European enemies. **In Asia**, Britain was engaged in a guerilla war against the Malayan Liberation Army and the Malayan Communist Party. **In Africa**, British troops killed at least 20,000 Kenyans in a war against the Kenyan liberation army known as the Mau Mau. **In the Middle East**, Britain found itself at loggerheads with France over the fate of Syria. On May 19, 1945, French troops occupied Syria. The Syrian Arabs protested French occupation of the Levant. French troops fired on protestors causing heavy casualties. British troops were stationed next door in neighboring Jordan. Churchill spoke out against French actions. He later ordered British troops stationed in Jordan to use force if necessary to enter Syria and protect the Syrian nationalist protestors. By July 19, 1945 C.E. British troops enforced a cease-fire between the combatants. After these events, the French eventually withdrew from the Levant and Syria gained its full independence. Churchill also backed an Iranian coup in 1953 before resigning from the Prime Minister's office two years later in 1955. After resigning the position as the head of state, Churchill returned to the British Parliament where he worked for prison reform, worker's social security, and a host of liberal reforms for nine more years until stepping down in 1964.

So it came to pass that Winston Churchill died from a stroke while in his home the following year on January 24, 1965 C.E. at the age of 90 after serving as the ruler of Britain twice. He did that which was evil in the eyes of **YHWH ELOHIM Israel** like unto all his Greco-Roman-European predecessors before him. According to sources close to Churchill, he was a closet homosexual. In 1895 while he was accused of gross immorality with a fellow cadet at Sandhurst Military Academy. During his reign, sources stated Churchill had "a series of close platonic relationships with attractive young men". Nevertheless, he was married to a woman named Clementine Churchill, who was also known as Baroness Spencer-Churchill. They became the parents of 5 children: 1 son and 4 daughters. Churchill did not believe in the traditional Jesus Christ as a divine being. While stationed in India during his early military years, he developed an interest in eastern mysticism. He saw Jesus as only a prophet. He rejected the religion of Christianity which taught otherwise, and loathed the Roman Catholic Church as an institution of errors. Instead, he blended the mystic thoughts of India with pseudo-Christian thought, fashioning his own belief system. On January 30, 1965 C.E. Churchill received a British royal ceremonial state funeral before being laid to rest in the churchyard village of Bladon, near his birthplace in Oxfordshire. Even Queen Elizabeth II, who normally attended only burials of family members, came from of hallowed halls of Buckingham Palace to attend Churchill's funeral.

Latter-day Britain

Now, back to the focus on Britain. During 19th century civilization of Europe, the continent was free from the dangers of war, and the old French monarchy was gone. The sun never set on the British empire as Britain stood at the top of the mountain possessing financial and commercial supremacy along with maritime dominance. Britain's rulership continued well into the 20th century with the Victorian era. Not even World War I, which began in 1914 to 1918 C.E., was able to diminish Britain's status as the world's leading power. Led by Winston Churchill, Britain continued to grow until the outbreak of World War II in 1939 C.E. when **the iron kingdom** of Germany invaded Austria in 1938 and annexed Czechoslovakia the following year in 1939. In 1940, Germany defeated Poland and divided the country with **the miry clay kingdom** of the Soviet Union. Britain and France declared war on Germany. Germany responded by invading France and launching bombing campaign on London. It took the combined Allied Powers of **the iron kingdoms** of Britain, France, the United States, along with the **miry clay kingdoms** of China, and Russia to eventually crush the Axis Powers of Germany, Italy, and Japan in 1945. The expenses from the Second World War caused Britain's overseas possessions to become a burden, and shortly after the war, Britain granted independence to its commonwealth subjects in **Africa, Asia, the West Indies,** and **elsewhere.(Miry Clay kingdoms)**. After WWII, Britain also joined the United States in a strong anti-communist foreign policy. Britain became a principal participant in the formation of the North Alliance Treaty Organization(NATO), and later joined the Western European defense alliance under the European Union umbrella. In 1973 Britain joined the European Union but in 2018 the island kingdom exited the union.

On July 13, 2016 C.E., Queen Elizabeth II appointed a British female politician named Theresa May to the throne of Prime Minister replacing David Cameron. She served as the Home Secretary from 2010 to 2016. She is continuing to lead Conservative Party in 2019. There are intervals of five years between each British national election. Therefore the next elections for the House of Commons and Prime Minister are slated for May 5, 2022 C.E.

4) Belgium

Belgium is located in the northern portion of Western Europe strategically located in its center in a part of an area known as the Low Countries. It is only 12,000 square miles making it one of the smallest countries in the world. The royal-capital city is Brussels. Its population is Aryan Indo-Europeans who are known as the Flemings, who make up the 59 percent majority. The Walloons and Flanders are European minorities. Its ancient history date back to 57 B.C.E. when Julius Caesar conquered the Celtic barbarians. His successor Augustus Caesar made it a Roman province known as Gallia Belgica. After the collapse of the Western Roman Empire in 476 C.E. and the Dark Ages, the Franks conquered the area. Since then, its history has been interwined with its neighbors, such as the Netherlands, who were also known as the Dutch, Holland, Germany, France, and Luxembourg. For the most part, Belgium has been annexed and divided as a part of a neighboring kingdom's territory, mainly the Carolingian Empire, Germany, and the kingdom of Luxembourg. In the late 15th century, the territory came under the Habsburgs who ruled the Netherlands. At that time, Belgium grew into a center for European commerce. In 1801, the kingdom of France incorporated the area into the northern portion of their stronghold. Fourteen years later in 1815, Belgium broke away from France and reunited with Holland. In 1830, the people revolted against Dutch rulership and declared their own independence as the modern **[iron kingdom]** of Belgium.

The **[iron toe kingdom]** of Belgium advanced to participate in the Industrial Revolution of the late 19th and early 20th centuries. Unfortunately, the tiny European kingdom possessed no natural resources. So importing raw materials from abroad became key to Belgium's growth and development. So Belgium looked overseas to Africa where it colonized a number of mineral rich African lands, principally the Congo and Rwanda. Belgium grew into a major colonial power that waxed rich from its exploitation of the mineral riches found beneath the soil of Africa. From 1885, the year before the Berlin Conference of 1886, to 1960, Belgium ruled the Congo. From 1916 to 1962, Belgium reigned over Rwanda.

King Leopold II
(December 17, 1865 C.E.—December 17, 1909 C.E.)

King Leopold II was born with the birth name Leopold-Louis-Phillippe-Marie-Victor on April 9,1835 in Brussels, Belgium. He was the son and successor of King Leopold I and Queen Louise of Orleans. Young Leopold was raised in the royal palace. He ascended to the throne after the death of father Leopold I. Once he secured his hold on power, King Leopold II led the first European effort to develop the Congo River Basin. By 1865, King Leopold II formed the Free Congo State and declared himself the sovereign ruler. (**Think about this**): The territory of the Congo in the heart of Africa which King Leopold II ruled was 76 times larger than the territory of tiny Belgium in Europe. Yet, he was their master.

During the next decade, the king of Belgium formed private exploration associations to search for the natural riches in the Congo. He appointed Sir H. Stanley as his main agent to protect his interest. There were discoveries of gold, diamonds, cocoa, coffee, and rubber. Leopold shipped large cache of weapons to Congo to enforce his colonial rule. Congo became the scene of limitless human-rights abuses, ranging from mutilations, amputations, rapes, and other horrors that would make your ears tingle. King Leopold II, the ruler of Belgium, was a cruel colonial master. By 1905, the bloodletting against the Congolese people had reached such heights that the atrocities were reported in international news. During that time, Britain and its daughter, the United States, protested against Belgium's ongoing conduct in Congo. In the end, America and Britain pressured Leopold to relinquish his personal claim over the Congo. The territory was then placed under the auspices of the kingdom of Belgium in 1908.

So it came to pass that King Leopold II died on December 17, 1909 at the age of 74 after reigning 44 years in the royal city of Brussels. He did evil in **the eyes of YHWH ELOHIM Israel** and did not walk in HIS laws, commandments, judgements, and statutes. Leopold II committed many abominable acts in Belgian Congo according to all that the other European rulers did which preceded him. Instead, he served the graven doctrine of the Roman Catholic Church and bowed before the graven image of Jesus and the Cross.

Latter-day Belgium

The kingdom of Belgium is one of 6 founding countries of the European Union. Its capital Brussels is the royal city where the European Commission, the Council of the European Union, and the European Council are all located. Belgium is also a founding member of the **Eurozone, NATO, OCED, WTO**, and several other major global organizations, such as **the United Nations** and **G-20**. Today, **iron** Belgium is a developed country with an advanced high-income, which has propelled the tiny kingdom into superpower status. The country has a high-standard of living, peace, and a high-quality health-care system. Belgium is also considered one of the safest places on the earth to live. It is also regarded as one of the most peaceful countries in the world. Belgium is a constitutional monarchy with King Philippe as the Chief of State. The head of government is the Prime Minister. The federal parliament is comprised of two chambers: the Upper House for the senators and the Lower House for the lower middle-income citizens.

5) Italy

In the 15th through the 18th centuries, the kingdoms of Italy were ruled by neighboring France, the Holy Roman Empire, Spain, and Austria. When Napoleon's rule in Italy ended in 1815, the kingdom reverted back into a grouping of independent states. Italy was once the ancient homeland of the united Roman Empire. It is located in southern Europe consisting of a peninsula that is shaped like a boot extending out into the Mediterranean Sea. The city of Rome, which is situated in the center of seven great mountains, has served as its capital-city for millenniums. Italy is a fertile land known for its olive oil, wine, fruits, and tomatoes.

In the early 20th century, Italy entered World War I as an ally of the British Empire, France, and the Czarist Russian Empire. In the aftermath in 1919, Italy regained territories from Austria-Hungary in post-World War I peace treaties. The end of the war Italy started experiencing political and economic unrest. During this instability, the Italian leader Benito Mussolini rose to prominence. By the year 1922, Mussolini suppressed all of his opponents to become a strongman. In 1929, Italy signed the Lateran Treaty with the Roman Catholic Church which established Vatican City as a sovereign state government—even a global Latin Christian theocracy. In 1935, Mussolini ordered the invasion and occupation of Haile Selassie's Abyssinia, known now as Ethiopia. Years later in 1940, Mussolini declared war against Allied forces, joined forced with Nazi Germany to form an Axis of power, and launched an assault in Greece and northern Africa. Italy also occupied British Somaliland in East Africa during this same period of time.

Benito Mussolini
(October 31, 1922 C.E.—July 25, 1943 C.E.)

Benito Mussolini was born July 29,1883 in the kingdom of Italy in the city of Predappio with the birth name Benito Amilcare Andrea Mussolini. His father' name was Alessandro Mussolini and his mother was Rosa Maltoni. Growing up, he was known to be very intelligent, but unruly. As a 29-year-old young man, he became a socialist, a student of Karl Marx ideology, and served as the editor of their newspaper *Avanti!*. At the beginning of World War I, Mussolini opposed the war, but he reversed course and began to favor his country's participation. The socialist party oustered him. He started his own newspaper called Popolo d' Italia and joined the Italian army to support the cause. After the war, he returned to publishing his newspaper. The war changed his views. Mussolini began to see the need for a strong centralized government. In 1919, he formed his own political party which called for a close relationship between corporate industry, landowners, and government known as fascism. Fascism was the antithesis of communism. The centerpiece of the political doctrine was that government was supreme and should be protected, citizens are commanded to be obedient, and individual rights came secondary to state authority. Under fascist rule severe punishments were meted out for all dissenters.

Mussolini was a gifted orator who rallied the masses to his side. He organized the March on Rome in 1922 to prevent a general strike planned by the socialists. After the collapse of government in power, Mussolini, who was 39, was chosen to serve as Prime Minister of the new government. Shortly afterwards, Mussolini decreed that his party, the Fascist who were known as *Il Duce* meaning *"The Leader"*, should be the majority party and the ruler of the government. Mussolini used a strong security force to restore order to a turbulent society. He instituted social reforms and improved public works for the masses. Those actions were very popular among the majority of Italians. Mussolini envisioned the restoration of the Roman Empire. Hoping to make his vision a reality, he invaded Abyssinia in 1935.

By late 1938, Mussolini began to form a strategic relationship with Nazi Germany, led by Adolph Hitler. By 1940, Italy declared war on the Allied Powers. Italy invaded Greece and North Africa, experiencing setbacks on both battlefronts. The losses caused widespread condemnations of Mussolini's policies. When the Allied Powers invaded Sicily in 1943, the Italian hierarchy, known as the Fascist Grand Council, turned against Mussolini and ordered his resignation from office. He was arrested and imprisoned. Nazi German special forces were able to rescue him from prison. Mussolini was then installed as the puppet-ruler for Nazi rump state in the city of Salo in northern Italy. Allied Forces defeated German forces throughout Italy, liberating Rome in 1944. The remaining German defense lines rapidly collapsed before Allied forces, forcing Mussolini to attempt to escape to Austria, but he was spotted and captured by Italian peasants. Mussolini was placed on trial, condemned to death, and executed by a firing squad. His corpse was placed in his hometown Predappio at the San Cassiano cemetery.

So it came to pass that Benito Mussolini died at the age of 61, only four days shy of his 62nd birthday on July 25, 1945. He reigned for 20 years in the city of Rome. He did not know **YHWH ELOHIM Israel** nor did he acknowledge **YHWH ELOHIM Israel's DIVINE Presence** like predecessors who had eyes but could not see and ears that could not ears, and an uncircumcised mind that did not desire to understand, or overstand, as some say.

Latter-day Italy

After the liberation of Rome, the Italian people went to the election polls in 1946 and chose to form a republic and abolish the monarchy. Italy would be governed by a president, prime minister, and two legislative houses. In 1955, Italy joined **the United Nations**, becoming one of the members of the global organization. Two years later in 1957, Italy became one of the prophesied *"latter-days"* **[10 iron toes]** which descended from the ancient Roman Empire when it became one of the founding members of the pro-Western European Economic Community. Italy continues to be governed by a stable western democracy, however, the republic has faced internal turmoil between Italian socialists **[miry clay ideology]** and other democratic parties **[iron ideologies]**. For example, Italian communists parties, renamed themselves *Democratic Party of the Left*, and won elections in 1976 and 1978.

Today, Italy still is one of wealthiest industrialized countries in the world and it remains a staunch member of the industrialized European Union. However, the latter-day kingdom of Italy also remains to be the epicenter of a contentious co-existence between leftist **[miry clay]** and **[iron]** western political parties vying for control of Italian politics. The uncertainty makes it difficult for new governments to meet European Union budget guidelines or to pass legislation to fund national budgets for annual government expenditures.

So it came to pass that Sergio Mattarella ascended to the throne as the 12th President of the Italian Republic on February 3, 2015.

6) The Netherlands

The country of the Netherlands is located in northern section of Western Europe. The land that comprise the Netherlands are plains and a few high ridges. It is situated below sea level. Therefore, the Dutch people are forced to build a network of dykes to prevent flooding. Known as one of the Low Countries, along with Belgium and Luxembourg, the Netherlands has stood as the crossroads of many European conflicts dating back thousands of years. The area was once the home of Celtic and other Germanic hordes that roamed the *"nether'* or *"northern"* forest lands. In the times of the 3rd century, Roman commerce flourished in the same territory. When the Romans influence disappeared, the Germanic barbarians became resurgent and took the territory from the Romans in 406-407 C.E.. After the Roman era, the Merovingians of France moved in. In the 7th century C.E., the Carolingian Empire moved into the area, bring Roman Catholicism with them. In the 12th through 14th centuries, the area became a battlefield of Europe, as it withstood the spread of the Holy Roman Empire into their territory. In 1581, seven of the northern provinces declared their independence from

Catholic Spain. The Spanish kingdom was forced to recognize Dutch independence in 1646 following the Thirty Year War.

By the 17th century, the kingdom of the Netherlands reached its golden age, advancing with intellectual freedom, great painting masterpieces, shipbuilding, fishing, beer brewing, and a textile industry which lifted the low-lying area to new heights. During the same era, the Dutch East India secured African and Asian colonies thousands of miles away. The influx of capital from slaves, silk, diamonds, gold, and other resources advanced Amsterdam, into a banking center. By 1806, Napoleon led his French forces conquered the region and renamed the territory Holland.

John Calvin
(July 10, 1509 C.E.—May 27, 1564 C.E.)

John Calvin was born July 10, 1509 in the city of Noyon, France. Calvin grew to become a French Protestant theologian and major leader of the Reformation movement spreading across Europe. He studied religion at the University of Paris and he studied law at the University of Orleans. After college, he returned to Paris in 1531 where he became part of a movement that opposed Catholic doctrine and tyranny of individual's lives. Calvin believed salvation by grace rather that works. The Catholic-dominated government in France did not share the views of Calvin. He was forced to move to Basel, Switzerland. By 1536, Calvin gained a great reputation among fellow Protestant leaders, all whom opposed Rome. He moved to Geneva to help establish Protestantism there. The city elders expelled him two years later. In 1541, Calvin was allowed to return to Geneva once again. The town elders also decreed that the Church should follow the order of service prescribed by Calvin. His views on sexual mortality and the rejection of Catholic absolutism were also adopted by council decision.

By 1555, Calvin succeeded in establishing a theocracy in Geneva where he served as the chief pastor of the city. He also headed the Geneva Academy where he wrote sermons, biblical commentaries, and letters that formed the graven doctrine of Calvinism.

Calvinism In The Netherlands
16th century —19th Century

Calvinism became a major part of the anti-Catholic protest, known as Protestantism, that swept Europe, beginning in 16th century Germany with Martin Luther and continuing with Calvinism in France, Switzerland, and eventually the Netherlands. The theology of Calvinism was the views put forth forward by John Calvin. His followers further developed his ideas and laid the foundation of the Reformed and Presbyterian Churches in the Netherlands.

After Calvin's death, his follower, Theodore Beza, succeeded him as the next church pastor, furthering his doctrine. The Netherlands embraced the doctrine of Calvinism because of its spirit of independence from Catholic authority. The Netherlands had long frowned on Catholic imperialism. In fact, when the introduction of Calvinism came to the Netherlands, Dutch noblemen and commoners embraced the liberation theology. Dutch people who once viewed themselves as non-believers in the church, which served as God on earth. The people of Dutch considered themselves to be atheists. *(Even today in 2019, millions of people in the Netherlands profess that there is no higher power, making it a majority atheist country).*

The doctrine of Calvinism maintains that life is predestined. It purports that God extends grace and grants salvation for only the chosen or elect. Calvin believed the bible to be purely literal. In Calvin eyes, the Church hierarchy consisted of Christ at the head and all followers of Christ were equal, thus undermining and rejecting the Papal hierarchy where the Pope was seen as the vicar of Christ on earth.

As I said earlier, the doctrine of Calvinism arrived in the Netherlands in the 1540s, finding converts among noblemen, politicians, and grassroots people. Dutch statesmen adopted

Calvin's teachings, making his teachings a powerful force, although he never personally feet foot in the Netherlands during his lifetime. The Netherlands accepted the his teaching as a national honor. The Dutch people embraced him as one of their own.

William of Orange
(1533 C.E.—1584 C.E.)

Following the footsteps of Calvin, William of Orange, a Calvinist Dutchman fought against Catholic Spanish occupation of their kingdom. William united the northern provinces and became the governor in 1559. An ardent Calvinist, William strived to keep the Netherlands free from foreign domination. William inherited the principality of Orange from his cousin. His father was William the Count of Nassau-Dillenburg. Growing up, he had been educated in the Habsburg royal court in neighboring Brussels.

William also secretly, yet successfully, assisted in the negotiation of the Treaty of Cateau-Cambrisis. That earned him the throne name "William the Silent". His policies definitely separated the powers of the church from lordship over the Dutch state. In 1584, a Catholic fanatic, who was unhappy over William's social reforms which broke the yoke of the Catholic Church, murdered him.

Latter-day Netherlands

The Nazis sacked the Netherlands during the Second World War. When it ended in 1949, the Netherlands, which is one of the latter-day toes, joined the North Atlantic Treaty Organization(**NATO**). NATO is a military alliance that was formed to protect the [**10 iron toes**] of Western Europe from aggressive powers, mainly a possible Soviet assault from their bases in Eastern Europe [**miry clay kingdoms**].

Meanwhile in 1949, the Netherlands lost their overseas possession, consisting of the Netherland Indies, which is now known as the country of Indonesia.

In 1958, the kingdom of the Netherlands, joined the European Economic Community. Since then, the Netherlands has grown into a center of international law with the **United Nation's** International Court of Justice located in the Peace Palace in city of Hague. Today, the Netherlands is a wealthy developed industrialized kingdom that is a major banking, trade, and insurance center. The Netherlands is also a member of **the United Nations, the European Union, and the G-20.**

7) Luxembourg

The country of Luxembourg is located in the heart of Western Europe. The small kingdom contains a mere 1,000 miles perimeter and it is known as one of the Low Countries along with the Netherlands and Belgium. The terrain is a high plateau with river valleys. In 57 to 50 B.C.E., the Roman legions conquered the area. At that time, it was inhabited by the Belgic and Trevert tribes. Centuries later in 400 C.E., large hordes of Germanic tribes descended upon the region.

During the days of Charlmagne, Luxembourg became a part of his empire. It territory was ceded to the House of Burgundy in 1441. Like its two Benelux neighbors, Belgium and the Netherlands, Luxembourg was also the scene of many battles in Europe. By 1867, the European powers guaranteed the neutrality and independence of Luxembourg. In the latter-part of the 19th century, Luxembourg began to use its strategic crossroads for roads and railways. With the discovery of abundant iron-ore deposits, Luxembourg built a great steel industry. During World War II, Luxembourg was once again the battlefield of Europe as Nazi German troops occupied the centerpiece of Western Europe.

Influential Luxembourg Rulers
Henri of Luxembourg (October 3, 2000 C.E.—Present)
Grand Duke of Luxembourg
Jean of Luxembourg (November 12, 1964 C.E.—October 7, 2007 C.E.)
Grand Duke of Luxembourg
Jean Claude Juncker (January 20, 1995 C.E.—December 4, 2013 C.E.)
Prime Minister
Pierre Werner (July 16, 1979 C.E.—July 20, 1984 C.E.)
Prime Minister
Gaston Thorn (January 20, 1981 C.E.—January 6, 1985 C.E.)
President of the European Commission
Gaston Thorn (June 15, 1974 C.E.—July 16, 1979 C.E.)
Prime Minister of Luxembourg

Latter-day Luxembourg

Following the conclusion of the Second World War, the leaders of the kingdom of Luxembourg abandoned their policy of neutrality. Luxembourg joined NATO in 1949, allowing their country to become a stronghold for Western European-Roman warfare. Luxembourg, became one of the **[10 iron toes]** when the kingdom joined the European Economic Community in 1957. Luxembourg later joined the pan-European Union. From the late1950s until now, the Luxembourg economy continued to expand to the point to where it is now the kingdom with the world's second-largest per capita income behind number one Switzerland. In the 21st century, its capital city Luxembourg City has become the center of international trade, industry, banking, and finance. Luxembourg is ranked as one of world's richest financial centers. It is also the seat of the European Court of Justice along with several other European administrative offices of the European Union. Luxembourg is also a member of the **United Nations and the G-20**. The majority of its population is ethnic French and German.

8) Spain

The country of Spain is located in southwest Europe on the Iberian Peninsula, extending deep out into the Atlantic Ocean on its west coast. In the south is the Mediterranean Sea. The terrain of Spain is a large plateau surrounded by mountains with rivers running down into valleys. Today, it is one of largest countries in Europe whose capital city is Madrid. Off the coast of the Iberian Peninsula across the Mediterranean Sea, there are two archipelagoes that belong to Spain near the coastline of Africa. The enclaves are Ceuta and Melilla. Those enclaves make Spain the only European country to have a physical border directly next to an African country, which is Morocco. The Canary Islands and the Rock of Gibraltar are also located nearby.

Celtic nomads arrived there in 800 B.C.E. The Romans moved into the territories centuries later. The Romans built settlement-cities and remained there until they were eventually overthrown by the Visigoths. In the 8th century C.E., the Islamic Moors invaded Spain and ruled until the 15th century. After those years, the Spanish Christians rebelled against their occupation and gradually began to expel them.

In the 15th century, Spain was the first European kingdom to establish a presence across the Atlantic in the Americas. As we all already know, Spain was one of the first participants in the Trans-Atlantic Slave Trade along with their brethren, Portugal. Meanwhile, the Habsburg dynasty ruled Spain from 1516 until 1700. Phillip V, the first ruler of the House of Bourbon, succeeded them. Phillip's elevation to the throne sparked the Spanish War of Succession, a conflict in which Spain ended up losing the majority of their overseas American possessions. Spain ceded its remaining American territories of Cuba and Puerto Rico after their defeat in the Spanish-American War of 1898. In the Far East, Spain lost their overseas colonies of Philippines and Guam in the same conflict. All of Spain's former empire came under the United States dominion. In the year 1931, the people of Spain decided to form a Republic, but five years later in 1936, a civil war erupted shortly thereafter. The Iberian internal conflict raged for three years until Spanish strongman General Francisco Franco finally emerged as the next ruler of the kingdom of Spain.

General Francisco Franco
(October 1, 1936 C.E.—November 20, 1975 C.E.)

Francisco Franco was born December 4, 1892 in the city of Ferroi, Galicia, in the kingdom of Spain. His birth name was Francisco Paulino Hermenegildo Teodulo Franco Bahamonde. His father Nicolas Franco y Salgado Araujo was a naval officer. His mother Maia del Pilar Bahamonde y Pardo de Andrade was a devoted mother and faithful Roman Catholic. Young Franco was baptized 13 days after his birth on December 17, 1892. He grew up in a middle-class conservative household, and as a young man, he too joined the navy and rose through the ranks. He advanced as a career military officer. By the age of 43, he was regarded as a skillful leader and he was chosen to serve as the Army Chief of Staff in 1935. When the Spanish civil war broke out the following year, Franco joined the insurgents against the regime. He was proclaimed "El Caudilio" *meaning* "the Leader of Spain".

Franco and his nationalist forces won the 1936-1939 civil war which claimed 500,000 lives. As the new Head of State, Franco established himself as an authoritarian military dictator, outlawing all other political parties, turning the Republic into a one-party rulership. In Francoist Spain, the communists, anarchists, liberal democrats, Catalan, and Basque separatists were all repressed by his national police. His repression, which included forced labor camps and executions in concentration camps, claimed as many as another 400,000 lives during his reign.

When World War II exploded across Europe, Franco declared neutrality for the kingdom of Spain. However, he did provide military support for both Italy and Germany, allowing their ships and submarines to dock at Spanish ports. The war ended with the defeat of fascist Italy and Germany. Spain continued the rule of Franco, but he was somewhat isolated from the rest of Europe which embraced multi-party democratic governments.

In Madrid, Franco officially declared the kingdom of Spain to be a monarchy in 1947. The throne, however, remained vacant until 1969 when Franco, proclaimed himself regent for life and occupied the seat of power. In the eyes of Western Europe, Franco was a relic of the past, but he had one strong asset in his favor. The Cold War with Russia started and he was a staunch anti-communist. It was for this reason, the Spanish economy was able to experience a miraculous recovery. Spain, strategically located at the mouth of the Mediterranean Sea, was asked to join the military NATO alliance. Billions in investments flowed into the kingdom as the U.S. and other European powers built fortifications on the Iberian peninsula. In 1953, U.S. President Dwight Eisenhower visited Spain and signed a treaty known as the Pact of Madrid. During the remainder of his reign, Franco maintained his authoritarian rule. He was regarded as a Spanish nationalist who embraced Catholicism, mixing politics and religion. His religious conviction led him to embrace the clandestine Catholic Opus Dei while fiercely opposing freemasonry. Opus Dei agents, who were modern technocrats, were strong backers of his government. In 1969, he chose Prince Juan Carlos to be his successor.

So it came to pass that General Francisco Franco died on November 20, 1975 at age 82. He had reigned for 36 in the city of Madrid. Although he was a highly educated man, Franco did not know **YHWH ELOHIM Israel,** nor did he walk in HIS laws, commandments, judgements, and statutes which HE iterated to the children of Israel for the betterment of all mankind.

Instead, during his lifetime, he served the graven doctrine of the Roman Catholic Church and bowed before the graven image of Jesus Christ and the Cross. He also shed much innocent blood in his quest for earthly power. In the end, like all mortals before him, he fadeth away into dust and ashes while **YHWH**, the CREATOR of the complete heavens, the earth, the seas, and all therein continued to reign upon HIS Eternal throne observing leaders and empires rise and fall, as HE orchestrates it all—from the **Head of Gold** down to the **20th century Spanish Toe of Iron**.

Latter-day Spain

The kingdom of Spain joined the 12-member North Atlantic Treaty Organization (**NATO**) in the spring of 1949 on April 4. On December 14, 1955, Spain moved to become a member of the global **United Nations** order. In 1986, Spain finally joined the pan-European Economic Community. The European Community was created in 1957 with the Treaty of Rome. The original signatories were Belgium, France, Italy, Luxembourg, the Netherlands, and West Germany. Ireland and Denmark did not join until 1973 C.E., and as I said earlier, Spain didn't join the pan-European order until the late 1980s. Spain is now one of the **[iron toe]** member of the **European Union** and the latter-day **G-20**.

9) Portugal

The country of Portugal is located on the west coast of the Iberian Peninsula in southwest Europe directly facing the Atlantic Ocean. The land of Spain borders Portugal to the north and eastward. The Atlantic Ocean surrounds its western and southernmost borders. In fact, Portugal is the westernmost kingdom on mainland Europe. Portugal, which is an Aryan Gentile nation, has two isles that are part of their dominion. The isles that belong to the Portuguese Gentiles are Azores and Madeira in the Atlantic. At one point in antiquity, the territory now known as Portugal was named Lusitania. Eventually, the word Lusitania became modified into Lisbon, which became the name of the capital city.

In the 1st millennium B.C.E., Celtic hordes reached the Iberian peninsula. They were the barbarians the Romans referred to in their writings when their legions reached the area in 140 B.C.E. The Romans remained there until the Germanic Visigoths and Suebi tribes invaded the area in the 5th century C.E.. *(We should remember that the black Phoenicians, who were known as Carthaginians, also occupied the area in 2nd century B.C.E.)* The Muslim Moors invaded the area in the year 711 C.E. Four centuries later in 1179, the indigenous Aryan Portuguese people finally liberated the land and recovered the territories from Muslim hands. On May 23, 1179, the Roman Catholic Church immediately recognized them as the rightful heirs of those lands in Europe. Within the next century, the boundaries of modern Portugal were established in 1270 under the leadership of King Alfonso III.

In the 15th and 16th centuries, the kings of Portugal encouraged their navigators to explore Africa, India, Indonesia, China, the Middle East, and South America. It was during this prophetic time zone, **[the long iron legs of the image]** *when the children of men walked to and forth, up and down the earth,* that the Portuguese navigators sailed beyond the Cape of Good Hope in 1488. Three years later, the Portuguese discovered the sea route to India, beginning in 1491 and continuing to 1498. In the year 1500, the **Spirit of YHWH** allowed the Portuguese to discover Brazil. The Portuguese, who had become Europe's first great global maritime empire, dominated the spice trade during this era. At that time, Portugal was also a military, political, and economic power.

Portugal also established foreign colonies in East Africa, West Africa, India, Indonesia, and the enclave of Macao in China. *(And, as we all already know, the Portugal and Spain were the first participants in the Trans-Atlantic Slave Trade.)* Nevertheless as fate would have it, several major events took place which erased the entire presence of the global maritime empire. The first one was the great earthquake of 1755 which completely devastated the capital city Lisbon. The second event was the fact that Portugal lagged behind in the Industrial Revolution and the Seven Yeas War. Then, Napoleon invaded and occupied Portugal. Shortly thereafter, Brazil declared its independence in 1822, reducing the once mighty empire into only a fraction of what it used to be. In the year 1910, a revolution overthrew the monarchy and established the Portuguese Republic.

Portuguese Kings of their Maritime Empire
(1415 C.E.—1578 C.E,)

John I(April 6, 1385 C.E.—August 14, 1433 C.E.)

King John I reigned for 48 years, and he was the first Portuguese ruler to establish territories in Africa. He was also the first king to envision a Portuguese maritime empire. His son Henry the Navigator led the maritime expansion during Portugal's Age of Discovery. Prince Henry the Navigator was also appointed the Grand Master of the Military Order of Christ. He also initiated a massive shipbuilding program.

Edward King of Portugal (August 14, 1433 C.E.—September 9, 1438 C.E.)

Alfonso V (September 13, 1438 C.E.—August 28, 1481 C.E.)

King Alfonso V united the kingdom of Portugal with the southern Algarves region.

John II King of Portugal(August 28, 1481 C.E.—October 25, 1495 C..)

King John II renewed his country's exploration and exploitation of Africa. He also commissioned the Portuguese armada to sail towards the Orient.

Manuel I King of Portugal(October 25,1495 C.E.—December 13,1521 C.E.)

Portugal possessed the largest armada in the world during the reign of King Manuel I. The armada was used to import African Hebrew slaves into the New World as part of the Trans-Atlantic Slave Trade. The kingdom of Portugal was at the height of its maritime glory during Manuel's reign. The discovery of Brazil also came during his rulership.

John III King of Portugal (December 13,1521 C.E.—June 11,1557 C.E.)

King John III of Portugal made contacts with the Far East, reaching China and Japan. The country of Brazil was colonized during his reign, continuing the lucrative Trans-Atlantic Slave Trade.

Sebastian King of Portugal (June 11, 1557 C.E.—August 9,1578 C.E.)

During the reign of King Sebastian, the demise of the Portuguese maritime empire began. Other European powers had built large maritime forces to compete with Portugal in global trade, including the slave trade. The Dutch, French, and England were also great naval powers that reduced Portugal's once lion's share of all European overseas booty.

Latter-day Portugal

The kingdom of Portugal experienced a second democratic revolution in 1974. In 1999, Portugal relinquished the Macau province to China. Portugal had ruled the overseas colony since 1557, making Portugal one the longest reigning colonizers in world history.

Portugal solidified its position as 1 of the 10 [iron toe] kingdoms when it became one of the founding members of the North Atlantic Treaty Organization(**NATO**) in 1949. Portugal sovereign European states among the descendants of the 13 colonists and the influx of new European immigrants from around the world who flooded the shores of [**the new iron kingdom**] searching for wealth, freedom, and opportunities in the new Gentile Promised Land.

When World War I broke out in 1914, the United States joined the Allied Powers of Britain, France, Italy, and Russia. American troops became directly involved in the European war in 1917, and remained there until it ended in 1918. At the end of the war, the United States began to inherit the overseas possessions of Great Britain as their power waned. By 1924 C.E., all Indian lands [**miry clay kingdoms**] had been taken away and the indigenous tribes were now offered citizenship in the [**iron**] American kingdom.

In 1929, the U.S. stock market collapsed and within four years, over half of all U.S. banks in the kingdom had failed, causing a Great Depression. Thirty percent of the labor force was unemployed. The Great Depression caused much upheaval in the U.S. and in Western Europe. In America, it led to the election of Franklin D. Roosevelt as the 32nd President of the United States of America.

Latter-day Presidents of the United States of America
(1933 C.E.—Present)

President Franklin Delano Roosevelt(1933 C.E.—1945 C.E.)

Franklin Delano Roosevelt was born on January 30, 1882 in Hyde Park, New York. He was the son of a Dutch American named James Roosevelt and Sara Roosevelt. He attended Havard University where he received a bachelor's degree. He also attended Columbia University. He was attracted to politics by his cousin former President Theodore Roosevelt. From 1910 to 1913, he served in the New York State Senate. He was appointed U.S. assistant Secretary of the Navy during 1913 to 1920 during World War I. In 1920, he was nominated, but not chosen, to serve as the vice-president. The following year, he was stricken with polio which caused him to be wheelchair bound. Nevertheless, he still remained deeply involved in politics. He was governor of New York from 1929 to 1933. In the year 1932, he was chosen and nominated as the Democratic candidate for President. He easily defeated President Herbert Hoover and became the 32nd President of the United States.

In his first 100 days in office, he initiated The New Deal. A plan to revive the depressed U.S. economy. In 1936, Roosevelt was elected for a second term. During this term the threat of war became a reality with Germany's occupation of Austria in 1938 and their invasion of Czechoslovakia the following year in 1939. Germany invaded Poland in September 1939, sparking a conflict between Allied Powers and Axis Powers worldwide. In 1940, Roosevelt was elected to a third-term as President. The U.S. remained neutral in the raging Europe War. But, on December 7, 1941 C.E. when Japanese bombers destroyed the U.S. military base in Pearl Habour, Hawaii, the United States immediately entered the global conflict.

Roosevelt met with British Prime Minister Winston Churchill to draft an agreement known as the Atlantic Charter which formed a military alliance between the United States and Great Britain to war against the Axis Powers of Nazi Germany, fascist Italy, and Japan. In America, the president mobilized domestic industries to produce the military hardware needed to confront the kingdom's adversaries.

The United States emerged as the latter-day Head of Gold [Great Babylon]

In 1943, the president of the United States, Soviet Union leader Joseph Stalin, and Churchill— [**iron kingdoms, Britain and U.S. and miry clay kingdom, Russia**]—gathered in Tehran, Iran. Two years later in 1945, the three met again in Yalta, near Crimea Soviet Union. The meeting of these three great diverse kingdoms was a Prophetic Signal that the world was entering the new era of **The Age of Iron** [capitalist world] **mixed** [sharing world power] with **Miry Clay** [communist world], two separate spheres of world power: **toes partly iron and partly potter's clay**. It was during this Yalta meeting that same year that the international empire known as the United Nations was created by these three rulers. The goal of the global order was to secure peace and security among all nations of the earth: both poor and rich, capitalist and communist, developed and undeveloped **[iron and miry clay]**. The great city of New York was chosen as the world headquarters for the new global kingdom. Within the next two decades, all nations around the world joined the United Nations, setting the stage for the beginning of the end.

At the end of World War II, **the United States** replaced Britain and emerged as **the new undisputed leader of the iron Western World** while **Russia** assumed the mantle as the new **undisputed leader of the miry clay East**. Since then, the world order has been plagued with continuous tensions, disputes, and violent confrontations between the two UN Security Council members who have opposed each other on a majority of most important international events. They have not been able to cleave one to another. During this time, Roosevelt also commissioned the development of the atomic bomb.

President Franklin D. Roosevelt, whose health was steadily deteriorating, was re-elected for a fourth term in 1944, making him the longest-reigning constitutional monarch in U.S. history. Today, historians regard his presidency as the greatest in modern U.S. history. Roosevelt died on April 12, 1945 in Warm Springs, Georgia only three months into his fourth-term reign.

President Harry S. Truman (1945 C.E.—1953 C.E.)

Harry S. Truman was born May 8,1884 in Lamar, Missouri. He served as vice-president for President Franklin D. Roosevelt, and when he died in 1945, Truman assumed the mantle of power. He oversaw the conclusion of World War II and final stages of the creation of the United Nations. He ordered the dropping of two atomic bombs on Japan, one on Hiroshima and second on Nagasaki, killing tens of thousands and forcing Japan's surrender. Truman also approved the Marshal Plan which called for the reconstruction of Western Europe which had been devastated by World War II. The war had reduced Western Europe into mini-republics under the North American superpower (NATO). Another important part of Truman's legacy, was his approval of the creation of the European Jewish State of Israel in 1948.

President Dwight D. Eisenhower (1953 C.E.—1961 C.E.)

Dwight D. Eisenhower was born October 14, 1890 in Denison, Texas. There were unconfirmed reports that his mother Ida Stover, was a bi-racial woman. He rose to power as a five-star general in the U.S. Army during World War II. He was the supreme commander of the Allied Powers in Europe and he also supervised the invasion of North Africa. After the war, he was chosen to serve as the Supreme Commander of NATO forces. In an unprecedented move in 1951, he sent federal troops to Little rock, Arkansas to integrate the local school system. In terms of foreign policy, he established the **[iron]** Eisenhower Doctrine which provided military and economic assistance to all anti-communist governments around the world. During his reign, the Cold War heated up, as the **[miry clay]** Soviet Union and other communist governments provided arms and training to anti-western resistance fighters in Egypt and other Arab kingdoms. The goal of the Eisenhower Doctrine was to contain the global spread of communism. Alaska and Hawaii became the 49th and 50th states in the 1959.

President John Fitzgerald Kennedy (1961 C.E.—1963 C.E.)

John F. Kennedy was born on May 29, 1917 in Brookline, Massachusetts. His father was Joseph P. Kennedy Sr. and his mother was Rose Fitzgerald. He was the 35th President of the United States. When he came to power at the age of 43, international tensions between the **iron** West and **miry clay** communist East had reached a boiling point, especially with Russian plans to install long-range missiles on the nearby Communist island of Cuba, located 90 miles off the coast of the United States. He also started the U.S. war effort in to prevent the rise of communism in Vietnam. Kennedy, the second-youngest constitutional monarch to joined the **United Nations** on December 14, 1955 C.E. On January 1, 1986, Portugal joined the European integration process by joining the **European Union**. Portugal is also a member of the global **G-20** order.

Portugal is a developed industrialized kingdom with an advanced economy, providing one of the highest living standards in the world. It is regarded as the 4th most peaceful country on the face of the earth. Out of a total of 193 United Nation kingdoms, **[iron]** Portugal ranks as the 15th most stable place in the world to live and ranks as the 20th most prosperous kingdom on the face of the earth with some of world's best roads for doing business. Last but not least, Portugal is a Gentile kingdom known for its freedom of the press and moral freedoms, such the kingdom's open acceptance of lesbian, gay, bisexual, and transgender perversion.

10) United States of America
"the latter-day Babylon the Great"

The kingdom of United States is located on the continental mainland of North America. The kingdom is comprised of 48 continental states. The isle of Hawaii in the Pacific Ocean is also an additional state along with Alaska in the extreme northwest, adjacent to Russia. The kingdom is surrounded by waters on three sides. On the east coast in the Atlantic Ocean. On its west coast is the Pacific Ocean. In the south are the waters of the Gulf of Mexico. In the north are the inland Great Lakes and the extensive border with the **[iron kingdom]** of Canada.

Before the arrival of Europeans in the 15th century, the North American continent was inhabited by various indigenous dark-brown, reddish-brown, and olive-brown skinned tribes that had lived on the continent for thousands of years. The **[miry clay kingdoms]** of the Inuit, Yupik, Aluet tribes, Folsom tribe, Seminoles tribe, the Cherokee tribe, Chickasaw tribe, Blackfoot, Sioux, Navajo, and innumerable others shared the entire North American mainland. Their civilization was totally eradicated by the **[iron hands]** of Spain, the France, Great Britain, and ultimately by the hands of the European settlers in the newly emerging little 13 North American colonies. The first English colony was established in Jamestown, Virginia in 1607. Twelve years later in 1619, the 20 African Hebrew captives were brought into Chesapeake Bay, beginning chattel slavery for millions of **the lost sheep of the house of Israel** under the rising Gentile kingdom which would come to be known as the United States of America.

Britain and the colonists fought their first battles in 1775, and in 1776, the 13 colonies declared their independence from the dominant **[first iron kingdom]** of the Great British Empire. An eight-war of independence erupted, and in the end the colonists defeated Britain in 1783. In 1803, **[the second iron kingdom]** of France sold their portion of the United States to President Thomas Jefferson, doubling the size of America and extending it to the western Pacific Coast. Continuing to grow by leaps and bounds, the little horn of the United States withstood a second assault by Britain and emerged victorious three decades later in the War of 1812. Seven years later in 1819, the little United States acquired the territory of Florida from the **[third iron kingdom]** of Spain. From that time forward, the entire continental North American mainland has belonged to the small **[new iron horn]** named the United States. In 1830, the rulers moved westwards and passed laws legalizing the removal of indigenous Indians from all lands east of the Mississippi, and enforcing a system of interning natives to reservations. In 1848, when the discovery of gold occurred in the Far West, European settlements expanded rapidly at a record pace. By the end of the 19th century, North America had become a predominately Aryan Gentile kingdom where the indigenous populations had been crushed into minorities through warfare, diseases, and other upheavals wrought by the invasion of European setters known as Americans.

By the beginning of the 20th century, stage coaches, wagon trains, and locomotive trains traveled from the East Coast to the West Coast. The territories were now divided into ever reign in the White House, was assassinated on November 22, 1963. His death was very reminiscent of what happened to Emperor Julius Caesar in ancient Rome. *(Go back to the era of the ancient Roman Republic and read the historical profile of Julius Caesar and check out his assassination. Those closest to Caesar were responsible for his death).*

President Lyndon Baines Johnson(1963 C.E.—1969 C.E.)

Lyndon B. Johnson was born on August 27, 1908 in Stonewall, Texas. He ascended to the throne as the 36th President of the United States after the death of his predecessor President Kennedy. Johnson, a high school teacher who worked as a congressional assistant before becoming a member of the House of Representatives, passed legislation known as The Great Society during his reign which improved life for African Hebrew people in America, such as the Voting Rights Act of 1965, a ban on racial discrimination is public facilities, interstate commerce, housing, the workplace, and legalizing interracial marriage for the first time in American history since 1619. His policies did not calm the discontent among the masses of Black America at that time. There were riots in several major cities across the United States in the 1960s. The National Guard militiamen were called in to patrol urban neighborhoods until law and order was restored. Dr. Martin Luther King was assassinated during his presidency on April 4, 1968 at 6:01 p.m.

In terms of foreign policy, Johnson deepened the [**iron kingdom**] of the United States involvement with the Gulf of Tonkin resolution. Eventually, tens of thousands of American servicemen and women were dispatched to the Far East to confront the Vietcong communist rebels who were backed by China and Russia [**miry clay kingdoms**]. Due to turbulent rumbling throughout American society, Johnson decided not to run for a second term. Instead, he returned to his ranch in Texas for the remainder of his life. He died on January 22,1973 in Stonewall, Texas at the age of 64.

President Richard Millhous Nixon (1969 C.E.—1974 C.E.)

Richard M. Nixon was born on January 9,1913 in Yorba Linda, California. His father was Frank Nixon and his mother Hannah Milhous. He attended the University of Duke. He returned to California where he worked as an attorney for five years, from 1937 to 1942. He served in the U.S. Navy Reserve during world War II. After the war, he became involved in politics. He ran and won the U.S. House of Representative seat of California in the 1947 midterm congressional elections. He was elected to the Senate in 1951. The following year, President Dwight Eisenhower chose him as his vice-president. Nixon also served as his vice-president for a second term in 1956. In 1960 U.S. presidential race, Nixon narrowly lost to John F. Kennedy. After losing the 1962 California governor's race, Nixon retired from politics for six years. In the year 1968 C.E., Nixon returned to the national scene to run against Democratic nominee Hubert Humphrey in the presidential race. This time Nixon won. While in office, Nixon expanded U.S. involvement by ordering the covert bombing campaigns against North Vietnamese military infrastructure in neighboring Laos and Cambodia. The bombings sparked widespread condemnation by anti-war activists across America. In 1972, Nixon won re-election against Democratic nominee George McGovern.

During the beginning of his second term, he made a historic visit to Bejing to visit Communist Chinese leader Mao Zedong to open communications with the developing Far Eastern kingdom. The Chinese used the opportunity to enter the world trading system, and today, they are world's second-largest economy rivaling the United States. Nixon also signed a bilateral **SALT (Strategic Arms Limitation Talks)** with the Soviet Union. However, his success was circumvented when he became embroiled in a re-election scandal known as Watergate, forcing him to resign from office in August 1974. Nixon died April 22, 1994.

President Gerald Rudolph Ford (1974 C.E.—1977 C.E.)

Gerald R. Ford was born was born with the birth name Leslie Lynch King Jr. on July 14, 1913 in Omaha, Nebraska. Ford attended the University of Michigan and later studied law at Yale Law School. He later practiced law in Michigan before becoming a Michigan congressman. Nixon chose him as his 1972 vice-president. He ascended to the throne as the 38th President of the United States of America on August 9,1974 after the resignation of President Richard Nixon. One month later, he pardoned Nixon. The United States lost the war in Vietnam during his presidency. Ford lost his bid for his own four-year term when Democratic challenger Jimmy Carter rose to defeat him in the 1976 presidential race.

President Jimmy Carter (1977 C.E.—1981 C.E.)

Jimmy Carter Jr. was born October 1,1924 in Plains, Georgia. He was the son of James Earl Carter Sr. and Bessie Gordy. He attended the Georgia Institute of Technology and earned a B.S. at the United States Naval Academy. From 1963 to 1967, Carter served as a Georgia state senator before he became the Governor of Georgia from 1971 to 1975.

In 1976, he won the Democratic nomination and defeated the reigning president Gerald Ford. The nation's electorate was still angry at the Republicans about the Watergate scandal. During his reign, he brought Israeli Prime Minister Menahem Begin and Egyptian President Anwar Sadat to Camp David where he negotiated a peace agreement between two Middle East foes: Arab Egypt and Jewish Israel. He also signed an agreement to return the Panama Canal to a neutral zone status in the year 2000.

The year 1979 was another turbulent period for his presidency. The [miry clay] Soviet Union invaded Afghanistan. He faced a hostage crisis with the [miry clay] new Shiite Islamic fundamentalist government in Iran which had overthrown the Shah of Iran. Iranian protestors invaded the U.S. Embassy compound and held American personnel hostage for a year. He also established full diplomatic relations with [miry clay] Communist China.

He lost his 1980 bid for re-election to Republican nominee Ronald Reagan.

President Ronald Reagan (1981 C.E.—1989 C.E.)

Ronald Reagan was born February 6, 1911 in Tampico, Illinois. He was the son of Jack Reagan and Nelle Clyde. He attended Eureaka College and worked as a sport announcer. He left his home state for Hollywood in the year 1937 where he acted in over 50 films. He was elected twice as the President of the Screen Actors Guild. He later served as a spokesman for General Electric, the parent company of NBC, and hosted the company's television theater program. Over the years, he changed his political views from liberalism to Republican conservatism. He was elected governor of California in 1967 and served to 1974. In 1980, Reagan defeated the sitting president Jimmy Carter to become the 40th President of the United States of America. In 1984, he won re-election against Democratic challenger Walter Mondale.

During his two-term presidency, Reagan started America's biggest peacetime military buildup. Shortly after winning the 1984 presidential election, John Hinckley fired pistol shots, wounding him in an assassination attempt. His popularity waned after the American public discovered his administration's involvement in the Iran-contra Affair. Under his administration's supply-side economic policies, the U.S. became a debtor nation. His vice-president George H.W. Bush succeeded him as the 41st President of the United States. The Iran-Iraq war raged during his presidency.

President George Herbert Walker Bush (1989 C.E.—1993 C.E.)

George H.W. Bush was born June 12,1924 in Milton, Massachusetts. His father was Prescott Bush and Dorothy Walker. When Japan attacked the U.S. on December 7, 1941, the kingdom of America was in an uproar. Bush, who was 18 and entering college, chose to join the U.S. Navy where he trained in aviation. During the 2nd World War, he rose to the rank of as a lieutenant. After the war, he resumed higher education, this time at Yale University where he graduated in 1948.

Bush moved to West Texas and started his own oil company where he waxed rich and became a millionaire. He entered politics in 1966 C.E. when he won a seat in the U.S. House of Representatives. By 1971, Bush had been chosen by President Nixon to serve as U.S. ambassador to the United Nations. He became the chief liaison to China from 1974 to 1976.

In 1980, Bush ran for the office of U.S. president. He lost the race to Ronald Reagan, but Reagan chose him as his vice-president for both of his four-year terms, from 1981 to 1989.

In 1988, he won the presidential race against Democratic contender Michael Dukakis to become the 41st President of the United States of America. Once in office, Bush maintained the supply-line economic policies of his predecessor Reagan. He ordered the invasion of Panama which toppled General Manuel Noriega during his first year in office. The following year in 1990, Bush moved the United Nations to impose embargo sanctions on Iraq because of their invasion of Kuwait. The sanctions did not force Saddam Hussein into compliance, so he authorized a U.S.-led air campaign that served as an opening salvo in the first Persian Gulf war. Bush's war effort was successful. Kuwait was liberated. No fly-zones were imposed on airspace in the southern and northern portions of Iraq, and the stage was set for the ultimate removal of Saddam Hussein.

An economic recession affected U.S. voters in 1992, forcing President Bush to renege on his promise of "no new taxes", which in turn, provided Democratic challenger William Jefferson Clinton with the opportunity to replace Bush after he served only one term as president. So it came to pass that President George H.W. Bush returned to Texas where he retired for public office until he died on November 30, 2018 at the age of 94. Nevertheless, his dynasty continued through his two sons, Jeb Bush and George W. Bush.

President William Jefferson Clinton (1993 C.E.—2001 C.E.)

William Jefferson Clinton was born August 19, 1946 C.E. in Hope, Arkansas. He was the son of William Jefferson Blythe Jr. and Virginia Cassidy. He attended Georgetown University where he earned a Bachelor of Science degree. He later attended Oxford College and Yale Law School. He served as the Attorney General of Arkansas from 1977 to 1979. He ascended to the throne at the age of 46, becoming the third-youngest president in U.S. history, and presided over a period of economic expansion during his 8-years in office. He initiated at the North American Free Trade Agreement with Canada and Mexico. He reformed welfare, making it difficult for millions of poor people to continue to receive assistance, and started the push for a mandatory national health care program.

In the year 1996, Clinton won a second-term against Republican challenger Bob Dole. In the same year he committed U.S. troops to a peacekeeping force in Bosnia and Herzegovina to subdue the Serbian nationalists. Two years later in 1998, he became the second president to be impeached because of a sexual affair with a 22-year-old White House intern named Monica Lewinsky. He was acquitted at his Senate trial. Regardless of his moral infidelity, his two-terms continued to see monetary growth which caused budget surpluses year after year. This was the first time in 30 years that the economy performed in such optimal levels. Clinton retired and his vice-president Albert Gore lost the 2000 presidential race against Republican candidate George W. Bush, the son of former president George H.W. Bush.

George Walker Bush (2001 C.E.—2009 C.E.)

George W. Bush was born July 6, 1946 in New Haven, Connecticut. His father was George H.W. Bush and his mother Barbara Bush. He grew up in the Houston, Texas area where he attended high school. He attended Yale University and the Harvard Business School. While he was a young man, the United States became deeply involved in the Vietnam War. Bush joined the Texas Air National Guard and later in Alabama Air National Guard. Bush, who was in his mid-20s and dealing with alcohol abuse at this stage in his life, did not face the live fire on the battlefront in southeast Asia.

Following in his father's footsteps, he spent a decade in oil business with limited success. He earned enough money to become a partial owner of a professional baseball team, the Texas Rangers. Afterwards, he followed his father's path into politics when he ran for the governor's office in Texas. Bush Jr. won, and in 1994, he became the 46th Governor of Texas. His tough-on-crime, refusal to pardon death-row inmates, and western mannerism made him popular in the Lone Star State. Bush won a second term in 1998. In the 1999, he entered the 2000 presidential race and won the party's nomination. His lavish fundraising helped him raise more money than any other presidential candidate in American history. The Democratic nominee was Vice-President Al Gore. The November general election ended in a stalemate with Florida holding the key to determine which candidate would receive the majority votes in the Electoral College. In the end, the Florida Supreme Court and the United States Supreme Court were forced to make the final decision, awarding the popular vote to Bush and thereby giving him the 25 electoral votes needed to capture the White House. When the dust settled, George Walker Bush was the 43rd President of the United States of America.

Bush came to power in early 2001, and by September 11, 2001, the U.S. had been hit with the most deadliest terrorist strike since America came into existence. The twin towers of the World Trade Center were completely demolished and thousands died. *(On the other hand, some skeptics have accused the U.S. of orchestrating the entire incident to justify their War on Terror).* Either way, President Bush started the War on Terror in October 2001 when he ordered the invasion of Afghanistan, a land full of opium fields and precious stones. In March 2003, Bush ordered the invasion of Iraq in the name of destroying the country's hidden arsenal of weapons of mass destruction. The invasion toppled the government of President Saddam Hussein. American troops still remain in Iraq in 2019.

In 2004, Bush won re-election for a second-term. He defeated Democratic challenger Senator John Kerry of Massachusetts. One year later in August 2005, **YHWH** sent a mighty winds, *known as Hurricane Katrina*, against the coastal cities in the Gulf Coast, affecting Mississippi, Louisiana, and portions of Alabama. The winds caused billions in damage and killed hundreds. The city of New Orleans, which was majority black, was the hardest hit location. Entire sections of the city were destroyed when the levees burst in midst of the downpour. Bush was slow to react to the suffering of black people in the metropolis, and for that reason, he became very unpopular in their eyes. Another negative factor was the daily reports of the deaths of U.S. servicemen in Iraq.

In 2007, the United States housing market collapsed, sending the economy into a tailspin. The U.S. entered the longest post World War II recession since the Great Depression of 1929. The 2007-2008 downturn was referred to as the Great Recession. The severity of the slowdown forced Bush to pass emergency legislation to preserve the tottering U.S. financial structure. The deep recession occurred right in the middle of the 2008 presidential race, giving Democratic nominee Barack Obama the leverage he needed to make his bi-racial ethnicity a non-factor among white American voters.

President Barack Hussein Obama II(2009 C.E.—2017 C.E.)

Barack H. Obama was born August 4, 1961 in Honolulu, Hawaii as the son of Barack Obama Sr., a native of Kenya, and Ann Durham, an European American. After high school, Obama attended Occidental College in Los Angeles before he transferred to Columbia University in New York. His final educational stop was at Harvard University. After college, Obama moved to Chicago where he became an attorney and an influential community activist-organizer which propelled him into politics. In the 1997, he was elected as the Illinois state senator from District 13. He held the office until 2004 when won the U.S. Senate seat. Senator Obama held that office from 2005 to 2008. He then entered the 2008 presidential race.

In the 2008, the Democratic Party had two strong candidates: 46-year-old Senator Barack Obama and former First Lady Hillary Clinton. The party's nomination process was a slugfest between the two titans. At the end of the primary season, Obama made U.S. history when he became the first African American, not a descendant of the people whose ancestors were brought to Jamestown in 1619, chosen as the nominee for President of the United States. Regardless of whether Obama was African Hebrew or just Kenyan, in the eyes of Black America, Obama was the Messiah who came in the footsteps of Dr. Martin Luther King Jr. Black America hoped Obama's ascension to power represented an end of racism, inequality, and the beginning of a new post-racial era in their **House of Bondage**. All of those hopes proved to be a delusion. After the 2008 presidential race against Republican John McCain, racism re-erupted to new levels unseen since the waterhosing days of the 1950s. Police brutality re-emerged as a major concern for African Americans. Hardly, a week passed without incidents of an unarmed black person being shot by a police officer, or some other form of open racism, being shown on news or social media.

During his two-terms in office, white conservatives demonized Obama, denying his American citizenship, his constitutional right to serve as president, and his lack of political credentials needed to occupy the White House. White conservatives from both the Republican and Democratic side opposed Obama's liberal policies on immigration, gay rights, and his mandatory health care plan which, they claimed, he imposed upon the American people without congressional consent. Obama also made it clear to African Americans that he was President of all Americans, and not just African Americans. So in the end, the 400-year captivity continued for the lost sheep of the House of Israel, known as Black America. Moses words proved to be when he predicted, *"no man shall redeem you,"* in **Deuteronomy 28:68**. Obama, during his first year in office, also won the 2009 Nobel Peace Prize.

In 2012, President Obama, the 44th chief of state, defeated Republican contender Senator Mitt Romney and remained in the White house for another four-year term. Senator Joe Biden also continued to serve as his Vice-President. In the final analysis, the hallmarks of his presidency were the DREAM Act, assisting illegal immigrants, and his support of LGBT rights, advancing the cause of lesbians, gays, bi-sexuals, and transgender Americans. Again, in the end, Black America, for the large part, came up empty. The Messiah did not arrive.

In terms of foreign policy, Obama initially decreased the size of troops in Iraq and Afghanistan, but in the end he was forced to increase their ranks once again. External threats in places such as North Korea and Islamic terrorists continued to grow. Russia and China continued their conquest for dominance. One bright spot for Obama was the international agreement between Iran and the P5+1 nations, which included the U.S., Britain, France, Germany, Russia, and China, that required Iran to reduce its research and development of civilian or military nuclear technology. Obama also ordered the bombing of Libya which led to the removal of Colonel Moammar Gaddafi. Obama also stabilized the U.S. economy, which teetered on the brink of depression, when he came into office. At the end of his eight years, Vice-President Joe Biden decided not to compete in the 2016 presidential race. Instead, he bowed out allowing former First Lady Hillary Clinton to become the Democratic nominee once again. She lost again in 2016. This time Clinton won the popular vote, but lost the electoral vote, to Republican contender, billionaire Donald J. Trump.

So it came to pass that President Obama and his wife Michelle, along with their two daughters Malia and Sasha, retired to private life after his presidency.

President Donald John Trump (2017 C.E.—Present)

Donald J. Trump was born June 14, 1946 C.E. in Queens, New York City as the son of Fred Trump and Mary Anne MacLeod. He attended the Wharton School of Business where he earned a B.S. degree. He inherited a real estate business from his father and he was appointed as the regent. Through craftiness, he expanded the family business into an empire, owning skyscrapers, hotels, casinos, and golf courses worldwide. Today, Trump is known to be worth $3.1 billion, making him the wealthiest president in U.S. history.

Trump, a career businessman and dealmaker, had not gotten directly involved in politics until the Obama administration. He emerged as one of his most vocal political opponents, and many conservative voters began to view him as the answer to Barack Obama's liberalism. Campaigning to erase the legacy of Obama, Trump emerged number one among a crowded field of 16 Republican contenders. His flamboyant style and straight talk greatly impressed average white voters who despised Obama. This gave him the edge to receive the party's nomination. In the general elections, Clinton won the popular vote with 65,844,610 votes verus Trump's 62,979,879. However, Trump won in the states with the most electoral votes, which gave him 306 electoral votes verus Clinton's 264. Without prior political experience as a mayor, governor, congressman, or senator, Donald John Trump was now the 45th President of the United States. He chose Mike Pence, the former governor of Indiana, as his Vice-President.

Since taking office on January 20, 2017, President Trump has dealt with a multitude of issues. Domestically, his number one goal has been to dismantle Obama's national health care reform plan, and any other part of his legacy that can be removed by executive order. As far as foreign policy is concerned, Trump has been unpredictable. For example, when he came into office he ordered 59 Tomahawk missile strikes against a Syrian airbase suspected of harboring planes which dropped chemical gases on civilians. Two years later, he is demanding the withdrawal of U.S. troops from Syria. He also came into office threatening to destroy North Korea, but in the process of time, he met with President Kim-Jong-un and called him a decent guy and good negotiation partner. His relations with Russia and China have been very similar. On one hand, China is embraced as a good trading partner, but on the uther hand, he slapped tariffs on Chinese products for unfair trade practices. On one hand, he seeks good relations with President Vladimir Putin, but the U.S. plans to station medium-range nuclear missiles in eastern Europe. So, the verdict is still out on the Trump presidency thus far. The most troubling problem facing President Trump is the intense investigation of Trump personal and business affairs. Democrats and other opponents of Trump accused Russia of interfering and influencing the 2016 election. An investigation that started out as a Russia collusion investigation has turned into a probe to remove him from office, thus creating a still-born presidency.

Latter-day United States of America

The United States of America has been the headquarters for the **United Nations** since its beginning in 1945. It is the chief backer of the North American treaty Organization(**NATO**) since its conception in 1949. The United States is the most influential nation within the **World Trade Organization (WTO)** because, since the end of World War II, the U.S. market has grown into the most lucrative place to earn billions annually from car sales, electronic devices, smartphones, clothes, tennis shoes, jeans, jewelry, wines, music, foods, minerals, crude oil, cocoa, coffee beans, cocaine, opium, rubber, exotic animals, and countless other items in a nation where money-making activity never ceases. From the time of the rising of the sun in the morning until the switching on of electrical lights in night, the human motion of labor, inventions, pleasures, and personal pursuits of riches never ends. This latter-day **Head of Gold**, the United States of America, is actually one of latter-day **10 [iron toes]** of the Image spoken of in the book of Daniel. The United States of America, the Leader of Western World, the undisputed champion of the democratic free world, and the capitalist paradise, is the daughter of Babylon, the gate of the gods, the land known for its freedom of religion. *(All prophecies in the Hebrew scriptures concerning the latter-day Babylon the Great apply to the United States and its* **[iron toes]** *global allies*—**Isaiah 47, Jeremiah 50, Jeremiah 51***).*

IV. Brief Historical Profile on the 10 Partly Miry Clay Toe Kingdoms

"YAH changes times and seasons, HE removes kings (kingdoms) and install kings (kingdoms), HE gives the wise their wisdom and knowledge to those who know."

Daniel 2:21

1) Russia
"they shall not cleave one to another"

After World War II, the republic of Russia was a member of Union of Soviet Socialist Republic(**USSR**). The Soviet Union was the colossal communist government consisting of 15

430

socialist republics that ruled the great kingdom that stretched from Siberia to Ukraine.

In 1949, the Soviet Union exploded their first exploratory atomic bomb in their pursuit to match the military power of the **[iron]** United States. The following year in 1950, the Soviet Union and China signed a 30-year defense pact to oppose the West, forming a **[miry clay]** socialist security alliance. The outbreak of the Korean war came during the same year and lasted until 1953. The Far East conflict caused greater tensions to an already tense situation between the two opposing spheres of power. Communist leader Joseph Stalin died the same year on March 5. He was replaced by Georgi Malenkov as Prime Minister and Nikita Khruschchev, as first secretary of the Central Committee of the Communist Party. Soviet scientists were still hard at work. They tested and exploded a hydrogen bomb, continuing the Cold War arms race.

To counter the NATO threat, the Soviet Union established the Warsaw Pact, bringing the East European socialist nations of Bulgaria, Czechoslovakia, East Germany, Hungary, Poland, Romania, and Albania into a military alliance. The **[iron]** NATO and **[miry clay]** Warsaw Pact divided Europe right down the middle fulfilling the prophecy in Daniel 2:42 which states: "And *as the toes [kingdoms] of the feet [latter-days] were part of iron* **[capitalist Roman advanced kingdoms]** and part of clay **[socialist undeveloped anti-West]**, so the kingdom **[the global order]** shall be partly **[divided between]** *strong* **[rich and industrialized]**, *and partly broken* **[poor and undeveloped]**. Europe was definitely divided between two spheres of power represented by the Berlin Wall in Central Europe, even Germany. On the West side were the capitalist, free, democratic, industrialized Romanized nations and on the East side were the state-controlled, one-party, poor, undeveloped East European nation. Soviet troops helped crush an uprising in Hungary during 1956. Khrushchev also held a secret meeting where he made a speech denouncing the previous practices of Stalin. He condemned the graven personality cult of Stalin which he had created during his reign to mold the Soviet masses into the ideology in his own likeness. He condemned Stalin and labeled him a dictator.

Khrushchev was elevated to the position of Prime Minister and Communist Party Chief in 1958. He also maintained a hardline stance against the **[iron]** West and in 1960 the Soviet Union shot down a U-2 spy plane flying over their territory. In response, he attempted to position Soviet missiles in Communist Cuba, only 90 miles from the coast of U.S. territory, sparking threats of open warfare between the two nuclear powers. After the near miss, the U.S., Britain, and Russia signed a treaty banning atmospheric nuclear testing. The U.S. and Russia created a crisis hotline for emergencies such as the Cuban missile crisis.

In 1964, Leonid Brezhnev replaced Khruschev as the First Secretary of the Communist Party. In the fourth year of his reign, Brezhnev and his **[miry clay]** Warsaw allies invaded Czechoslovakia to stem the turn towards liberalization. He also created a policy known as the Brezhnev Doctrine which gave the Soviet Union the right to intervene directly or provide military assistance to communist countries under threat anywhere around the globe. In the mid-70s relations with the U.S. improved with President Nixon in the White House in Washington. Brezhnev died in 1982. KGB chief Yuri Andropov succeeded him as the new First Secretary of the Communist Party, but he died after only two years in office. Andropov was replaced by Konstantin Chernenko. Two years later, Chernenko died and was replaced by Mikhail Gorbachev as the next general secretary of the Communist Party.

The 1980s was the most turbulent era for the Soviet Union. Nationalists movements in Kazakhstan, the Baltic Republic, Armenia, and Azerbaijan rebelled against Soviet authority in Moscow. By 1989, there were revolutions that swept all communist Warsaw Pact countries in eastern Europe from power, including Poland, Hungary, East Germany, Bulgaria, Czechoslovakia, and Romania. On November 9, East Germans, in unprecedented numbers, gathered at the symbol of division, the Berlin Wall, where they held mass rallies and eventually tore down of the structure that stood as a reminder of the division between **the iron kingdoms** and **the miry clay kingdoms**. Another sign that the Soviet empire was collapsing was their forced evacuation from Afghanistan that same year after losing a decades-long war against the Islamic fundamentalists.

In 1990, the Communist Party voted to end one-party rule. The people of Russia moved to form their own republic known as the Russian Soviet Federative Socialist Republic. On December 25,1991, the Russian parliament voted to exit the USSR. **Boris Yeltsin** was elected as the new leader of the Russian Republic. The Russian government then moved to takeover all the offices once used by the USSR.

Vladimir Putin
(May 7,2000 C.E.—Present)

Vladimir Putin was born October 7,1952 in Leningrad, Russia. He was the son of Vladimir Spiridonovich Putin and Maria Ivanovna Putina. In his late teens, he entered college at Leningrad State University. He graduated at the age of 23 and entered the military as a KGB officer. He served in that capacity, moving up the ranks, until political turmoil pressured him to leave the behind-the-scene clandestine intelligence world to step forward to save the crumbling Soviet Union empire in 1991. He joined the Yeltsin administration as an assistant, and in the process of time, he maneuvered himself into second in command. When Yeltsin stepped down, Putin was chosen, on December 31, 1999, to step forward as the President of Russia.

Putin was the antithesis of Yeltsin. For example, Yeltsin was known to be a heavy drinker whereas Putin was focused, physically fit, and non-drinker. Yeltsin entertained Western cooperation whereas Putin came to power to check Western influence which had crept into the former Soviet Union after the collapse of the Berlin Wall and the Warsaw Pact. Putin saw those developments as a direct threat to Russia and its satellites from Siberia to Crimea.

One of his main goals was to re-nationalize the Russian economy first, and eventually the entire former Soviet Union. The Russian oil and banking oligarchies with close ties to the West were shutdown, taken over, and their owners criminalized, forcing them to flee to Britain and the United States. In 2018, Putin was accused of his sending agents to Britain to eliminate some of those former undercover agents who were in the process of opening Russian markets and selling large shares of the Russian economy to Western companies. Putin completely erased the pro-Western cozy legacy of Yeltsin. Those economic reforms sparked a revival of the Russian economy and gradually began to reverse the economic depression.

In 2014, Putin ordered the invasion of eastern Ukraine and the annexation of Crimea, prompting the West to impose international sanctions upon Russia. In 2015, Putin entered the Syrian civil-war to support his allies, Syrian President Bashar al-Assad, and Iran, to prevent the downfall of another anti-western Arab leader, such as Gaddafi and Saddam Hussein. The intervention also countered Western plans to self-impose a no-fly zone over Syria. During this same period of time, the U.S. and its NATO allies announced possible plans to station medium-range missiles with nuclear warheads in former Warsaw countries. In the eyes of Putin, the plans violated the spirit of understanding that has existed since the collapse of the Berlin Wall.

In late December 2018, Putin announced the development of a new hypersonic missile system that, he says, is invulnerable to U.S. defenses. Putin announced that the Avangard hypersonic missile system will enter service in 2019. Putin said these following words: *"Russia is the first in the world to receive a new type of strategic weapon and this will reliably ensure the security of our state and of our people for decades to come. This is a wonderful, excellent gift for the country for the New Year."* The Russian Tass agency said the missiles can fly 15,000 miles per hour, and as it reaches its target, the missile with a maneuverable gliding warhead, can adjust both altitude and direction to avoid defenses and fly low enough to avoid most interceptors. Many American analysts are skeptical of Putin's announcement, calling the announcement a fabrication.

Regardless of whether the new missile announcements are true of false, it clearly signals the mindset of Putin and Russia. The point is clear: Russia is prepared to engage the United States and NATO in Europe and, intercontinentally, against the United States. There are several ongoing crises that could spark a direct confrontation between the two nuclear powers: Ukraine, the stationing of missiles in eastern Europe, Syria, Iran, North Korea, or a joint-war alliance with China against the United States.

Latter-day Russia

Russia has supplied billions of dollars in advanced weaponry to Iran, the new regional superpower in the Middle East. Iran, a kingdom that straddles the Persian Gulf, has also mastered the technology of uranium enrichment, giving the radical Shiite Islamic kingdom the ability to use those deadly skills for peaceful or military purposes. Meanwhile, the Jewish State of Israel does not trust the radical Shiite regime which has repeatedly called for the Jewish State to be wiped off the face of the earth. Russia and Iran have joined ranks as members of the Caspian Sea alliance, an alliance that extends from Central Asia into the Middle East as well as their strategic confederation in Syria and other global matters.

Inside the kingdom of Iran, Russian technicians and other experts have assisted Iran in developing its own nuclear facilities and other infrastructure. Iran has consistently maintained that those skills are for peaceful purposes such as medical treatments and alternative energy. Iran has built multiple facilities in several cities scattered across the kingdom.

According to the prophet Ezekiel, Russia will play a major role in the downfall of the State of Israel and the United States. Russia, most definitely, will be one of the nations to participate in the Battle of Armageddon. Described as a Gentile people in **Genesis 10:2**, and from the remote parts of the land of the north, Gog, the chief prince of the land of Magog in Ezekiel 38th and 39th chapters, YHWH forecast that the kingdom of Russia will form a global alliance of **[miry clay kingdoms]** and invade the land of Israel and launch nuclear-tipped ICBM missiles against the United States of America in the latter-days. Ironically, Russia dispatched thousands of its soldiers to Syria in September 2015. According to the Words of YAH, Russia is destined to become a world power that only **YAH, the STONE CUT WITHOUT HANDS,** will be able topple.

2) China
"they shall not cleave one to another"

Four years after World War II ended, China's peasant-led Communist revolution swept the Chinese Nationalists out of power and thrust the People's Republic of China into power. The Communists then implemented major reforms that outlawed feudalism and expelled foreign powers from the Chinese mainland. The Communists, led by Mao Tse-tung, whose name was later changed to Mao Zedong, defeated the Nationalist Chinese, who were led by Chiang Kai-shek. The nationalist Chinese were driven from the Chinese mainland and exiled across the Taiwan Straits to the island of Taiwan. The following year in 1950, the Chinese troops intervened in the Korean War to assist the communist forces. A few years later, the **[iron kingdom]** of the United States intervened in China's internal conflict, siding with the nationalists. President Dwight Eisenhower lifted the U.S. naval blockade of Taiwan in support of Chiang Kai-shek. The nationalists then deployed thousands of troops to the Quemoy and Matsu islands in the Taiwan Straits. The Communists responded with a shelling campaign against both islands. After those events, Washington signed a mutual defense treaty with the nationalist Taiwan government. Mainland China continued its shelling until the spring of 1955 when the United States threatened them with a nuclear attack. The threat forced the mainland to agree to negotiations where they agreed to end the bombing. The Nationalists then agreed to withdraw from Dachen Island. Communist-Nationalists tensions flared up again in 1956 C.E., and again in 1996. Those misunderstandings persist until this day.

In 1959, China enforced its dominion over the province of Tibet. In response, the Tibetan people staged widespread uprisings. Chinese troops killed thousands of Tibetans. Their leader, Dalai Lama fled to neighboring India. The United States intervened again. This time to assist the Tibetan resistance and the U.S. continues to do so until this very day.

Inside China, the leader Mao implemented his own variation of the socialist doctrine of **Marxism-Leninism** on Chinese society. His policies became known as **Maoism,** which included a *Five-Year Plan* to improve peasant and farm life. His other plans included *The Great Leap Forward* and the 1965 *Cultural Revolution*. Those plans ended in widespread hunger and discontent, forcing Mao to later admit that his plans were a disaster. Nevertheless, the graven image of Mao and his *Red Book* graven doctrine of Maoism was adopted by socialist revolutionary groups such as the Khmer Rouge in Cambodia, the Vietcong in Vietnam, African and Latin American liberation armies, as well as black revolutionary organizations in the United States during the 1960s and 1970s.

In October 1964, China successfully tested its first atomic test for the development of an atomic bomb. The test came while Mao had ordered thousands of troops on their border with Vietnam, posing a possible threat to U.S. forces fighting the Vietcong.

In July 1971, Secretary of State Henry Kissinger made a secret trip to China where he met with Chairman Mao. The two opposing leaders struck a deal of peaceful coexistence between their **[iron]** and **[miry clay]** kingdoms. The People's Republic of China replaced Taiwan in 1971 as the representative for China at the global UN. Kissinger and President Nixon decided to give Communist China the permanent seat on the United Nations Security Council for strategic reasons. In February 1972, President Nixon visited Peking where the two leaders agreed to a thaw in their country's relations. Nixon agreed to open U.S. markets to certain Chinese products in exchange for China's cooperation against the Soviet Union. After all, the two Communist giants, the Chinese and the Soviets, had frosty relations. They had already experienced a border conflict three years earlier in 1969, and China had also expelled Soviet personnel a decade earlier.

On September 10, 1976 Mao Zedong, *The Father of The Chinese Revolution,* died at the age of 82. He was born December 26, 1893. He was succeeded by Hua Guofeng as Chairman of the Communist Party.

Hua Guofeng (October 7,1976 C.E.—June 28,1981 C.E.)
General Secretary Hu Yaobang (September 12,1982 C.E.—January 15,1987 C.E.)
Chairman Deng Xiaoping (September 13,1982 C.E.—November 2,1987 C.E.)
Premier Li Peng (March 25,1988 C.E.—March 17,1988 C.E.)
Zhao Ziyang (January 15,1987 C.E.—June 24,1989 C.E.)
President Jiang Zemin (June 24,1989 C.E.—November 15,2002 C.E.)
Hu Jintao (November 15,2002 C.E.—November 15,2012 C.E.)
Xi Jinping (November 15,2012 C.E.—Present)

Mao Zedong

Latter-day China

In 1989, Communist China launched a government crackdown on a massive student protest staged in Tiananmen Square in its capital-city Beijing. The West criticized the Chinese government for human-rights abuse and called for China to lose its bid to host the 2000 Olympic Games. Five years earlier in 1984, the **[iron]** kingdom of Britain agreed to return the colony of Hong Kong, a global financial center, back to Chinese rule. This move greatly enriched the Chinese government.

During this same era, there was also a gradual normalization of trade relations between the West and China, and by 2001, China gained entry into the **World Trade Organization (WTO).** China re-adjusted its **[miry clay]** socialist foundation in favor of state sponsored-capitalism to become a member of the **[iron]** Western-dominated global economy. Although, the Chinese sought close economic ties with the United States, it still maintained a hardline on national security. In 2001, a U.S. reconnaissance plane collided with Chinese jet fighters forcing the U.S. to make an emergency landing on Chinese territory. China reclaimed the South China Sea as their territorial possession and built a chain of island fortifications scattered across the sea.

Throughout the 2000s, China announced budget increases to strengthen their military readiness. Under their military modernization program, the Communist power established a space presence with manned and unmanned rockets and satellites, commissioned squadrons of aircraft carriers, added to their long-range nuclear missile arsenal, and assembled one of the world's largest armies. China also share a border with Afghanistan and trade ties with Iran, making it an integral part of the Middle East process as well.

In February 2011, the [miry clay] kingdom of China surpassed Japan to become the world's second largest economy with a net worth of $1.3 trillion. In September of 2008, China surpassed Japan as the largest holder of U.S. treasury bonds totalling $600 billion. However, growing interdependence has not been able to end continuous trade tension between the two spheres of power. China, which is one of the largest countries in the world that equals the size of entire Europe, has restricted foreign investments and maintained strict controls over its massive economy, making sure that its consumer market, which is one-fourth of the world population, is held under Communist control while earning massive trade surpluses from Western Europe and the United States. Some critics of China's unfair trade practices with the West has described Bejing's policies as economic warfare.

In recent years, [miry clay] China and Russia have mended fences and strengthened their communist ties once again. In 2015, the two communist superpowers conducted their first ever large-scale naval exercises in the Mediterranean Sea. In September 2018, China tested three hypersonic missiles simultaneously. The missiles, which are a direct threat to existence of the [iron] West, cannot be stopped by enemy counter measures. According to the Hebrew prophecies, China will join in the anti-Western confederation of chief prince Gog, ruler of the land of Magog—which is **Russia**. In the final analysis, the two Communist superpowers will join ranks to oppose the United States, the European Union, and the State of Israel **in the Battle of Armageddon**.

According to most global economic indicators, and regardless of whether there is war or peace in the future, China **[miry clay kingdom]** will overtake the United States **[iron kingdom]** as the number one economic power in the world by the year 2027. Chinese officials and people believe they deserve the new role as world leaders because, after all, they are the people who discovered the art of papermaking nearly 1,800 years ago. They also invented the moveable typeset 800 years ago. They were the first to use gunpowder, and most of all, China is the land with one of the world's oldest civilizations dating back nearly 4,000 years ago.

3) Brazil
"the kingdom shall be partly broken"

Besides Mexico, Brazil was the only other South American country to actively participate in World War II. Brazil was the only South American country to experience direct casualties in the conflict. On July 31, 1943, a Brazilian passenger ship and the freighter *Bage*, the largest commercial vessel in the South American Country's fleet, was purposely torpedoed and sunk off the coast of Brazil. The *Bage* was hit while 129 passengers were aboard along with 102 crew members. The ship was enroute from Berlin, Germany to Rio de Janeiro when a German U-boat attacked the unarmed ship. A total of 78 people perished, 41 passengers and 37 crew members.

By July 2, 1944, Brazil dispatched its first 5,000 soldiers to the battlefront in Europe aboard the USNS General Mann. By September, Brazilian pilots entered the European conflict by air along with Brazilian troops on the ground.

Inspite of the fact that Brazil supported the Allied Powers in World War II, the Brazilian Communist Party won nearly 10 percent of all votes in state elections to become the third party in the state of Sao Paulo in 1947, two years after the end of WWII. The same year, the

Brazilian Socialist Party was founded. Two years later in 1949, the general election was won by the Social Democratic Party, which became the largest party in both chambers of Deputies and the Senate. Growing unrest continued along with the proliferation of pro-communist terrorist attacks. The turmoil persisted throughout the 1960s.

Natural and man-made plagues in Brazil

In October of 1957, 26 swarms of Africanized bees were accidentally released from laboratories in Brazil, spreading across South America and reaching North America in 1985. The predator bees, which destroy other species of bees, are known as killer bees. The bees were man-made by scientists that cross-bred African honey bees with different kinds of bees from Italy and Spain hoping to increase honey production. The hybrid Africanized bees were the outcome of their experiments. The hyper-aggressive bees are known to chase people up to a quarter of a mile and they have killed up to a 1,000 people since their conception. They have also killed horses, cattle, and other animals.

On March 5, 1966, a massive theft of nuclear material was revealed. A year later on September 13, 1987 another radioactive contamination accident occurred in the city of Goiania. This is what occurred: Some ionized radiation equipment was taken from a closed hospital. Several people handled the material, causing 4 deaths. At least 100,000 people were affected while 249 of those being serious cases of infections. The International Atomic Energy Agency described the incident as "one of the world's worst radiological incidents".

"A den of dragons"

After the defeat of Nazi Germany in Europe, it has been proven that the Roman Catholic Church in Germany, Italy, and Spain assisted the vanquished Nazi soldiers in escaping capture. Many of those ex-Nazi soldiers were airlifted to South America with Brazil being one of their main destinations. One of those soldiers was Josef Mengele. Mengele was a physician renown for human experimentation on inmates at Auschwitz concentration camps. Mengele, who changed his name to Wolfgang Gerhard, suffered a stroke and drowned while swimming in a pool. His remains were found in 1985 in the city of Emba das Artes. Many more former Nazis are known to be in hiding in the South American countries of Bolivia, Argentina, Peru, Chile, Paraguay, and Uruguay.

South America is also home to other terror-related entities such as Iran and Hezbollah. Both anti-Jewish groups are known to operate in Brazil and elsewhere. Carrying the banner of former Nazis, Iran and Hezbollah are believed to have attacked the Association Mutual Israelita Argentina(AMIA) on July 18,1994, killing 85 people and injuring more than 300. Ibrahim Hussein Berro, a 21-year-old member of Hezbollah from southern Lebanon, was accused of the deadly crime. Argentine, Israeli, and American officials contend Hezbollah and its operative were responsible. Hezbollah has categorically denied the allegations as "false".

Pre-Meditated Murder

On June 1, 1980, a disgruntled pilot attempted to crash his plane into a hotel owned by his mother-in-law after he argued with his wife. He was angry at both the mother and daughter after he discovered she committed adultery. He attempted to fly the plane into the hotel, but failed to hit his target. He ended up hitting several objects and crashed his plane into an accounting office. He killed 6 and injured 4 others.

Political turmoil

Brazil had been ruled by a military government for 20 years, from 1964 until 1984 when suddenly one million Brazilians staged the largest protest in Brazilian history. Brazilians occupied the streets of Sao Paulo and demanded direct presidential elections, forcing the military government of Joao Figueiredo to resign.

Brazil, the home of One of the 7 Modern Wonders of The World

On July 7, 2006, the New 7 Wonders Foundation, which is based in Zurich, Switzerland declared the 98 ft.-tall Christ the Redeemer statue as one the new wonders in this modern world. Situated up high on top of the 2,300 feet Corcovado Mountain in the Tijuca Forest National Park in Rio de Janeiro, the soapstone image has become a symbol of Christianity across the world. The 98 ft.-tall sculptured image of Jesus is fixed on top of a 25 ft.-tall pedestal. It was designed with its arms stretched out, extending 92 ft. wide, symbolizing peace. The Christ the Redeemer molten image was crafted by French sculptor Paul Landowski and constructed by Brazilian designer Heltor da Silva Costa and his French counterpart Albert Caquot. Romanian sculptor Gheorghe Leonida crafted the head of the statue. The official dedication of soapstone image came on October 12, 1931 after nine years of hard work. The image can be seen for miles away as it stands 125 feet exalted high upon one of Brazil's tallest mountains.

The statue is visited, venerated, and bowed before by multitudes of people from all around the world speaking various languages. The statue has become a global attraction similar to an amusement park. The are escalators, walkways, and elevators which assist the people in gathering before the shrine. There are nearly 50 other replicas of the same Christ the Redeemer statues worldwide.

Lightning bolts have struck the 125 ft.-tall soapstone image on several occasions. During a violent February 10, 2008 thunderstorm caused major damage to the graven image's fingers, head, and eyebrows. Lightning also struck the image again on January 17, 2017 ripping off a finger on the statue's right hand.

Latter-day Brazil

Brazil is one of the epicenters of the discontent between [iron] and [miry clay] relations. By that I mean, you will find both iron and miry clay influences in Brazil. You have the instability, extreme poverty, crime, the assassinations and military coups such as those in the Third World. There are major accidents due to poor regulations, airplane crashes, and mass killings that reflect miry clay status. Then, you have a Brazil that has experienced an Economic Miracle for decades, growing with a gross domestic product increasing 10 percent annually. The government, in return, has invested in new highways, bridges, railroads, steel mills, factories, hydroelectrical power plants, petrochemical plants, and nuclear reactors. For the record, Brazil is a nation with great expertise in nuclear technology. All of those are traits of the iron kingdoms. That is why I say, Brazil is one of the epicenters of the partly iron and clay toes. But, on the other hand, Brazil practices state-capitalism which is the kind of capitalism Communist China practices. Under state-capitalism the government owns the profit-making ventures, not individuals or private entities.

Since 2009, Brazil has been a part of an international organization known as BRICS [**miry clay toe kingdoms**]. The BRICS nations consist of (B)razil, (R)ussia, (I)ndia, (C)hina, and (S)outh Africa. These nations represent the majority of the world's population. These are Aryan pale-skinned people, olive-skinned, brown-skinned, and black people in BRICS which make up three-fourths of the 7 billion people on earth. However, the economies of these governments are considered developing or emerging. Those economies are not regarded as advanced, industrialized, wealthy, or First World. This is why **YHWH** has deemed them "**miry clay**" and not "**iron**". The goal of BRICS is to strengthen the economies of the member nations in order to compete more efficiently against the Western powers. BRICS members are considering their own international currency.

In 1991, Brazil signed the Treaty of Asuincion and joined the South American Common Market(Mercosur) with Argentina, Uruguay, and Paraguay [**miry clay kingdoms**]. In the final analysis, the kingdom of Brazil, and other kingdoms like it, represent the toes of miry clay that are *partly broken* as spoken of by Daniel. In the last-days, the entire global order is destined to become *partly broken* like Brazil with instability, economic chaos, man-made and natural disasters, dens of dragons around the world, pre-meditated murders, and

international turmoil.
Last but not least, the South American country of Brazil is the site of the Great Whoredom that sitteth upon the minds of people worldwide, which is the belief in the Christ the Redeemer statue. That too is a metaphor for the spiritual blindness of all the inhabitants of the earth. **YHWH** has consistently warned Israel and all humanity not to make any graven images, yet Brazil and all **[the kingdoms of toes made of iron and miry clay]** have persistently done the opposite. Brazil is also a member of the global United Nations(**UN**) and the global World Trade Organization(**WTO**).

4) India
"the kingdom shall be divided"

At the close of World War II, the **[iron]** kingdom of Britain, due to economic hardships from war and the lost of manpower, was forced to relinquish its colonial control over the vast subcontinent of India which was located in southwest Asia. For three hundred years, beginning in the 18th and 19th centuries, the British Empire trampled the dark-skinned people of India with an oppressive iron hand, reducing one of the richest golden lands into one of the world's poorest **[miry clay]** localities.

India's independence came on August 15,1947 when the British Crown divided the huge 1.2 million square miles into two separate kingdoms. Unfortunately, the independence set the stage for religious and ethnic enmity, conflicts, and bloodshed for generations to come. The kingdom of India, which received the largest central tract of territory, became the independent secular Hindu nation whereas neighboring Pakistan, the territory once formally known as western India, became an Islamic Republic one day earlier on August 14, 1947.

The Birth of Religious and Ethnic Bloodshed

Months after two manner of kingdoms were separated from the bowels of one soil, India and Pakistan went to war for the first time, feuding over the Himalayan region of Kashmir. In September 1965, India and Pakistan fought a large-scale war over the Kashmir a second time. The **United Nations** was forced to intervene, demanding a cease-fire. Six years later, Hindu India and Muslim Pakistan fought a third large-scale war. This time the two adversaries clashed over East Pakistan, which was another Muslim-dominated area of India. The war ended when 90,000 Pakistani troops surrendered. India, however, agreed to cede the territory to the Muslim majority. Afterwards, the kingdom of Bangladesh was established on February 7,1971.

Surrounded by two Islamic kingdoms, Pakistan on the west and Bangladesh to the east, India conducted an underground nuclear test on May 18, 1974 for deterrence, and became a nuclear power shortly thereafter. Not to be outgunned, Pakistan conducted its first underground nuclear test and joined the ranks of the nuclear powers as well. Again, in May 1998, the rivalry continued when the two enemies sent messages of deterrence to each other by both sides conducting nuclear tests. The following year in 1999, India launched another offensive against Pakistani-backed infiltrators who had attacked the city of Kargail in Indian Kashmir. Tensions erupted in the same area a decade later when Pakistani separatists rose up against Indian rule.

The Hindu verus Muslim enmity has persisted nonstop since the day the agreement was signed between the three parties, Britain, India, and Pakistan. On December 6,1992, Hindu zealots tore down the renown 16th century Islamic mosque in the northern city of Ayodhya. The vandalism sparked nationwide riots between Hindus and Muslims, ending with 3,000 dead whom were mostly Muslims. Months later, Muslim guerillas planted a series of bombs across Bombay, the kingdom's commercial capital, and slew 257 people, mostly Hindus.

Inspite of the ongoing tug-of-war between Hindus and Muslims, the leaders of India have maintained the country's independence while the kingdom has grown into one of leading developing countries of the Third World.

The Prime Ministers of India

Prime Minister Jawaharla Nehru (August 15,1947 C.E.—May 27,1964 C.E.)
Nehru was chosen as the first nationalist leader of independent India after the Indian National Congress had successfully overturned British rule which had existed since 1885. Five months after he came to power, **Mahatma Gandhi,** the leader of the grassroots independence movement, was assassinated by a Hindu fundamentalist who opposed his decision to agree to the British plan to partition India into two countries: India and Pakistan. On January 30,1948, Gandhi was shot during a prayer meeting in New Delhi. Gandhi, who had become the symbolic nationalist leader after he returned from South Africa in February 1920, led the uprising which forced the British to leave. In the autumn of 1920, Gandhi started the non-cooperation movement. Indian masses refused to buy British goods and instead used local handicrafts. Indians picketed British liquor shops and returned to Indian values. One of his greatest acts of civil disobedience was his walk to the coast of India to harvest salt. The British taxed all salt production. Therefore, Indians could not harvest salt without British oversight and permission. The British would severely flog those found illegally harvesting salt.
Nehru died on May 27, 1964 at the age of 74 in New Delhi.

Prime Minister Guizarilal Nanda (January 11, 1966 C.E.—January 24,1966 C.E.)
Indira Gandhi (Jan. 24,1966 C.E.—Mar. 24,1977 C.E.) (Jan.24,1966 C.E.—Mar.24,1977 C.E.
Prime Minister Indira Gandhi was the daughter of the deceased President Jawaharla Nehru. During her first reign, she conducted a major purge and declared a state of emergency censoring the press and arresting 100,000 people. In January 1980, she came to power for a second term. However, she was assassinated by Sikh bodyguards. Hindus killed around 3,000 Sikhs in revenge rioting after her death.

Prime Minister Rajiv Gandhi (October 31,1984 C.E.—December 2,1989 C.E.)
Prime Minister Rajiv Gandhi was the son of Prime Minister Indira Gandhi.

Prime Minister V.P. Singh (December 2,1989 C.E.—November 10,1990 C.E.)
Prime Minister Rajiv is assassinated by a Tamil suicide bomber during an election campaign seeking a second term. The Congress Party won the general elections, ending decades of socialist control over the economy. The Congress Party then initiated new government reforms and launched new economic policies.

Prime Minister Chandra Shekhar (November 10,1990 C.E.—June 21,1991 C.E.)
Prime Minister P.V.Narasimha Rao (June 21,1991 C.E.—May 16,1996 C.E.)
Prime Minister Atal Bihari Vajpayee (March 19,1998 C.E.—May 22,2004 C.E.)
Unable to gain the majority, Prime Minister Atal Bihai Vajpayee, of the nationalist Bharatiya Janata Party (BJP), formed a coalition government. Vajpayee was the first prime minister who was not a member of the Indian National Congress Party.

Dr. Manmohan Singh (May 22,2004 C.E.—May 26,2014 C.E.)
Prime Minister Narendra Modt (May 26,2014 C.E.—Present)
Prime Minister Modi is a member of the Hindu nationalist Bharatiya Janata Party.

Latter-day India

In December 2001, ethnic and religious tensions exploded once again when gunmen attacked the Indian parliament. New Delhi blamed the assault on Pakistan-based extremists, and in response, New Delhi severed all transportation and diplomatic links with Islamabad . Another war was barely averted as both rivals made preparations.
In such an environment even accidents are viewed as acts of war. For example, In February/March 2002, there was a fire on a train that killed 59 Hindu activists while traveling in the western state of Gujarat. In a spirit of hateful revenge, Hindus across India went on a riotous rampage killing 2,500 Muslims.

India has the world's second-largest population, trailing only China. Unfortunately, large segments of that population live in poverty. To compound the dire situation, the land is filled with various religious groups such as Hindus, Muslims, Sikhs, Tamils, and others that hate each other to the core. The most dangerous crisis among the feuding parties is the Pakistan-India conflict. The reason being, both nations possess nuclear weapons which could kill millions on both sides, making the death and destruction experienced by Hiroshima and Nagasaki look like a minor skirmish. Both Pakistan and India have the ability to share their nuclear knowledge and create a proliferation crisis internationally. Pakistan is suspected of already sharing their skills with Saudi Arabia. Therefore, the kingdom of India, which is definitely one of the [miry clay toes], *represents* the human misery caused by religious and ethnic strife throughout the world.

Another negative aspect of India's prophetic existence is the fact that it also *represents* one of the world's worst industrial disasters. In December 1984, deadly gas leaks from a pesticide plant in the city of Bhopal claimed 6,500 lives. The plant was owned by Union Carbide Corp., a company from the [iron kingdom] of the United States. International companies from wealthy nations are known to build dangerous facilities in poorer nations where lax regulatory oversight exist. It allows them to earn greater profits while maintaining their unsafe businesses abroad, out of sight of the watchful eyes of the iron kingdoms. Meanwhile, thousands of poor people in Third World countries die each year from accidental oil spills, gas leaks, explosions from underground mining, and other preventable incidents.

In terms of morality, the **miry clay kingdom of India** joined the ranks of **the iron kingdoms of the West** in the spiritual Sodom and Gomorrah anti-YHWH international movement which legalizes homosexuality. On September 6, 2018 C.E., a panel of 5 Supreme Court Indian judges amended the kingdom's constitutional law making same-sex marriages legal, striking down centuries-old laws which once punished sodomites with a death sentence by street mob violence or a 10 year prison sentence.

5) Indonesia
"the kingdom shall be divided"

The [miry clay] kingdom of Indonesia is an archipelago nation located off the coast of Southeast Asia in the midst of the Indian Ocean and the Arafura Sea to its east. It is also north of Australia. The kingdom consist of 13,670 islands straddled over 3,200 square miles stretching from Sumatra in the West to New Guinea to the far East. The total boundaries of the sprawling kingdom equals 750,000 square miles. More than half of the chain of islands are uninhabited. The major islands are Java, where over half the total 200 million people of Indonesia reside. Other major islands are Bali, Lonbok, Sambawa, Timor, Borneo, Celbes, and the North Moluccas. The islands are to be rugged volcanic terrain with mountains and rain forests.

The capital city of Indonesia is Jakarta located on the island of Java. There are 300 various ethnic groups within Indonesia which speak 250 diverse languages. It is a Muslim majority kingdom where 80 percent of the population are members of the faith. Islam was brought to far away Indonesia in the 13th century when Indian traders introduced the religion to the islanders. The remaining 20 percent of the Indonesians are members of Hinduism and Buddhism.

After World War II, the people of Indonesia declared their independence from the Dutch[iron]. The Dutch had colonized the country from the late 1600s to 1942. During that time the kingdom was known as the Netherlands Indies. In 1949, the independent Indonesian Republic was established when the Dutch consented to the demands of the indigenous people and downgraded their relations to only nominal ties. The new government was comprised of a President who served as the head of state along with two legislative chambers.

Indonesian Presidents Since 1949

President Sukarno (August 18,1915 C.E.—March 12,1967 C.E.)
Born as Kusno Sosrodihardjo on June 6,1901, President Sukarno became the first president of the new republic. He implemented a plan known as the New Order administration which called for a strong centralized administration and a military dominated government. During his 31-year reign, he was able to maintain stability over a sprawling and diverse kingdom. Sukarno was known for his staunch anti-communist stance. His anti-communism gained him respect and diplomatic support from the West. In 1965, he aborted a coup, and as a result, he killed over 300,000 alleged communists and assumed dictorial power.
During his reign, he was able to personally amass between $15 to $35 billion. His policies consisted of a strong push towards industrialization which sparked economic growth for decades. Sukarno died at the age 69 on June 21,1970, leaving a legacy as one of the most corrupt leaders in modern history. U.S. intelligence agents also described his anti-communist slaughter as the worst mass murder of the 20th century.

President Suharto (March 27,1968 C.E.—May 21,1998 C.E.)
Suharto coveted all power to himself. His government incorporated East Timo into Indonesia during 1975-1976. Suharto was born June 8,1920 in the city of Kernusuk in the Yogyakarta Sultanate. During his reign, the kingdom was beset by political, economic, and environmental turmoil. Suharto was deposed in 1998. He died January 27,2008 at the age of 87.

President Bacharuddin Jusuf Habibie (May 21,1998 C.E.—October 20,1999 C.E.)

Prime Abdurrchmad Wahid (October 20,1999 C.E.—July 23,2001 C.E.)
President Wahid was the first leader elected by national elections. Habibie liberalized the press and allowed other political parties to compete in the political process.

President Megawati Sukarnoputri (July 23,2001 C.E.—October 20,2004 C.E.)
Sukarnoputri was the first woman to serve as the President of Indonesia.

Susilo Bambang Yudhoyono (October 20,2004 C.E.—October 20,2014 C.E.)
Pudhoyono defeated incumbent Sukarnoputri in national elections.

President Joko Widodo (October 20,2014 C.E.—Present)

Latter-day Indonesia

In the early 2000s, [miry clay] Indonesia relations with the [iron] West made a hundred and eighty-degree change for the worst. The Far East kingdom in the Indian Ocean, which was once a hospitable pro-western haven, turned into an unwelcome center for global Islamic terrorism. The beginning of that reality check came on October 12,2002 during the Bali bombing. Islamic warriors attacked Westerners in two nightclubs in the city of Kuta's tourist district. The terrorists were suicide bombers who wore bomb vests while others drove cars packed with bombs. The attacks killed 202 people and injured another 209. Indonesian investigators connected the bombing to two well-known Islamic groups, Al-Qaeda and Jemaah Islamiyah. The terrorists released a statement citing the attacks as direct responses to the U.S. *War on Terror* and Australia's role in the independence of Timor. Three years later in 2005, Jemaah Islamiyah struck again in the city of Kuta of the island of Bali. That attack came October 1, when the attackers launched a series of suicide bombings and car bombs at two sites on Jimbarau Beach Resort.

The Islamist group, Jemaah Islamiyah launched an attack in the capital-city of Jakarta in July 2009. Terrorists struck the JW Marriot Hotel and the Ritz-Carlton Hotel in the tourist section of Setiabudi in south Jakarta. All targets were hit by separate bombings in 5 minute sequences. 7 people died and 53 were injured. Two suicide bombers were among the casualties.

More bloodshed came on January 14th, two weeks after the New Year of 2016. ISIS attackers plotted to attack a shopping mall in central Jakarta. There was gunfire and multiple explosions at a downtown intersection. A bomb exploded at a nearby Burger King. Another blast occurred at the neighboring McDonalds. 8 people died in that incident, four of them were attackers. There were 24 non-life threatening injuries. ISIS was blamed for that attack as well.

In 2016, terror attacks, inspired by believers in Al-Qaeda, Jemaah Islamiyah, and ISIS ideologies, struck in far away places such as Berlin,Germany. ISIS-inspired terrorists rammed a truck into a crowd and killed 12 and injured another 56 in that incident. Islamic State of Iraq and Syria-inspired assailants drove cargo trucks into crowds in Nice, France a few weeks later, killing 86 and maiming 458 others.

Extremist assailants launched another truck ramming attack in Westminister, Britain on March 22, 2017,killing 6 and injuring 49. Among the fatalities were 4 pedestrians, 1 police officer, and one attacker. Two months later, several thousands of miles away back in the Far East, ISIS struck again in Jakarta, Indonesia on May 24th. Two explosions detonated at a bus terminal in Kampung Melayu, East Jakarta. Investigators uncovered evidence that the explosions were caused by devices found in the toilet and in another part of the terminal. Bombers killed 5 people. Three victims were policemen and the two others were the attackers. ISIS also claimed responsibility for that attack.

On June 3, 2017, ISIS-inspired terrorists rammed another vehicle into a crowd. A van was deliberately driven into people walking on a London Bridge before crashing on the south bank of the River Thames. 11 people died, eight victims and three attackers, in that assault. A total of 48 people were injured. 24 of those injuries were critical. The war between the **[iron]** West and the **[miry clay]** Islamic fighters reached peaceful Stockholm, Sweden in the same year when ISIS-inspired terrorists drove another truck into a crowd, claiming 5 more lives and seriously injuring another 14 innocent bystanders.

On May 13, 2018 Islamic attackers struck again. This time the battlefields were three Christian churches in the second-largest city of Surabaya where 28 were killed and 57 injured.

Prophetically speaking, Indonesia *represents* one of the **10 miry clay toes** of *the latter-days*. It is a member of the **United Nations** and **the G-20**. All of the Islamic inspired attacks worldwide, which are related to the ongoing Middle East conflict between Western influence and Islamic fundamentalists, can be traced to Indonesian-based group such as Al-Qaeda, Jemaah Islamiyah, and ISIS. Those Islamic hardliners oppose all Western European and American influence within their sphere of power. Those groups are committed to international bombing campaigns that include car bombings, truck-rammings, explosive vest wearing suicide bombers, chemical attackers, stabbing attacks, and even *allegedly* commandeering jetliners into the World Trade Center. Their worldwide battlefield include Brussels, Belgium, Paris, France, London, England, Copenhagen, Denmark, Madrid, Spain, New York City, San Bernardino, California, Damascus, Syria, Beirut, Lebanon, and Mali, West Africa. The global conflict between Islam and the West will certainly continue to raise its ugly head at any time in any place around the world.

Economically speaking, Indonesia has a gross national product of $1.01 trillion which is larger than the Philippines and Malaysia combined. Indonesia produces over 500,000 barrels of oil per day, making it a large oil exporter. The kingdom is also a major producer of rice along with large forests of timber and rubber. Indonesia, a large garment maker, is also known for its low labor cost. The kingdom is comprised of people with bronze, light-brown, and dark-brown complexions.

6) Saudi Arabia
"you saw iron mixed with clay, they shall mingle themselves with the seed of men: but they shall not cleave one to another, even as iron is not mixed with clay"

The **[miry clay]** kingdom of Saudi Arabia is located on a flat plateau in the region referred to as the Middle East. Biblically speaking, it is a part of the area known in the Hebrew scriptures as the Garden of Eden. Arabia is situated near the crossroads which extended from the continent of Africa where the Gihon and Pison Rivers flow. Northeast of Arabia, the Tigris and Euphrates flow through Syria and Iraq. Geographically, Saudi Arabia is located in Southwest Asia on the Arabian Peninsula. The desert kingdom's boundaries are the Red Sea on the west coast and the Persian Gulf on the east. The kingdom's 30 million population is totally Arab with foreign African and Asian migrant workers and other international wayfaring men and women.

Known as the birthplace of the founder of the religion of Islam, the cities of Medina and Mecca in Saudi Arabia are revered as holy shrines by 1 billion Muslims worldwide.

From 1915 to 1927 after World War I, the British gained control of the territory that comprise the kingdom of Saudi Arabia today. The British forces defeated the Ottomans and removed them from Arabia and the entire region. In midst of the war, the British formed secret ties and funneled weapons to the Arabs, encouraging them to rise up against the Ottomans. In the end, Britain accepted the sovereignty of the kingdoms of Hejaz and Najd in 1932. The two Arab kingdoms then unified as the Kingdom of Saudi Arabia.

1st Saud Dynasty
(1765 C.E.—1932 C.E.)

Muhammad ibn Saud (1726 C.E.—1765 C.E.)

In 1744, Muhammad ibn Saud joined forces with religious leader Muhammad Abd al-Wahhab, the founder of the strict Sunni branch of Islam known as Wahhabism. Saud was the chief of an Arab village that had never fallen under Ottoman control. The two men rose to power together and formed a sect of Islam known as Wahhabism.

Abdul-Aziz bin Muhammad bin Saud (1765 C.E.—1803 C.E.)

Abd-Aziz conquered most of territory on the Arabian Peninsula.

Saud bin Abdul-Aziz ibn Muhammad bin Saud (1803 C.E.—1814 C.E.)

Saud conquered Medina in 1804, and two years later, he re-established Saud rule in Mecca in 1806. The Al-Masjid al-Haram Mosque is located in Mecca. The Al-Masjid an-Nabawi Mosque stands in Medina.

Abdullah bin Saud (1814 C.E.—1818 C.E.)

During this time, the Ottomans ruled the entire Middle East. The Ottoman sultan ordered his Mamluk viceroy in Egypt to lead his mighty soldiers to Arabia and crush the Saudi move towards independence.

Turki bin Abdullah bin Muhammad (1819 C.E.—1820 C.E.) (1823 C.E.—1834 C.E.)

Turki, the grandson of the founder Muhammad ibn Saud, made the city of Riyadh his capital. He also established the 2nd Saudi state in 1824.

Faisal bin Turki (1834 C.E.—1838 C.E.) (1843 C.E.—1865 C.E.)
Saud bin Faisal bin Turki (1871 C.E.) (1873 C.E.—1875 C.E.)

After the death of Faisal, a civil war erupted within the House of Saud. Power did not return to the Sauds until 1902 when ibn Saud recaptured Riyadh and established the kingdom of Saudi Arabia. In 1932, Ibn Saud issued a royal decree announcing the modern Saudi kingdom. His sons have been the successors every since then.

Lawrence of Arabia (1915 C.E.—1918 C.E.)

So it came to pass that the British hatched a plot to undermine the Ottoman Turks who were fighting alongside their arch-enemy Germany. The man with the plan was Thomas Edward Lawrence. Born August 16, 1888, he became known as Lawrence of Arabia because of his proficiency in the Arabic language. He also studied history and military strategy at Oxford University. As a lieutenant in the British Army, he came up with a plan to *mingle himself with the seed of Arab men* in support of Arab rebellions against Ottoman Turks. His goal was to undermine Ottoman dominion by bogging down their forces through guerilla warfare. Dressed in Bedouin attire to masquerade as an Arab, his guerilla campaign was conducted behind Ottoman battlelines. By 1917, he conquered Aqaba. In another operation he was captured but managed to escape. He rejoined his Arab guerilla army and they attacked Damascus. At the end of World War I, he was dispatched to India. After retirement, he died on May 19,1935 at the age of 46 in a motorcycle accident only three months after being discharged from the British Army.

2nd Saud Dynasty
(1932 C.E.—Present)

ibn Saud (September 23,1932 C.E.—November 9,1953 C.E.)

Ibn Saud was the first king and founder of modern Saudi Arabia. He is also regarded as the first ruler of the Third Saudi State. He was a man with many wives and the father of 45 sons, and not including daughters. He strengthened his control over the kingdom by bringing every city under his command. Twenty years after the end of World War I, petroleum was discovered in Saudi Arabia on March 3,1938. Shortly afterwards, several more oil discoveries were found in the eastern province. Large-scale development of the oilfields began in 1941 under United States control. Since then, oil has provided Saudi Arabia with economic prosperity and global influence. Saudi Arabia has become the world's second largest producer of oil. Vast quantities of natural gas were discovered beneath the sands of Saudi Arabia as well. With the discovery of oil, Saudi Arabia became an intricate part of the international transportation industry, providing crude oil to be processed into fuel for cars, trucks, motorcycles, airplanes, boats, ships, and all types of vehicles that need petroleum.

Saud of Saudi Arabia (November 9,1953 C.E.—November 2,1964 C.E.)
Faisal of Saudi Arabia (November 2,1964 C.E.—March 25,1975 C.E.)

In 1972, Saudi Arabia gained a 20 percent stake in the oil company Aramco, gaining more control over their own natural resources for the first time. The nationalizing move decreased American control over Saudi oil. In 1973, King Faisal led Saudi Arabia when the kingdom joined the boycott against Western countries that supported Israel in the Yom Kippur War against Egypt and Syria. In 1975, King Faisal was assassinated by his nephew Prince Faisal bin Musaid. He was succeeded by his half-brother Khalid. Oil prices shot up 400 percent, earning billions for a people who were once poor.

Khalid of Saudi Arabia (March 25,1975 C.E.—June 13,1982 C.E.)

By 1976 C.E., Saudi Arabia had become the largest producer of oil in the world. King Khalid saw an economic boom and social development explosion that transformed the desert kingdom into a Middle East metropolis. He transformed the infrastructure and educational system. He also supported close ties with the United States and the West.

Fahd of Saudi Arabia (June 13,1982 C.E.—August 1,2005 C.E.)
Abdullah of Saudi Arabia(August 1,2005 C.E.—January 23,2015 C.E.)
Salman of Saudi Arabia(January 23,2015 C.E.—Present)
co-regent Muqrin bin Abdulaziz(2015 C.E.—Present)

Latter-day Saudi Arabia

Since the end of World War II the[**miry clay**] kingdom of Saudi Arabia has cleaved to the side of the Palestinians in their struggle against the Jewish State of Israel while at the same time embracing close relations with the United States. By the mid-1990s, a growing segment of the kingdom's citizen did not share their ruler's affinity with the U.S. and her Western allies. Many Saudis began to complain of the U.S. presence in their country, labeling it the American occupation of the Arabian Peninsula. Although the [**iron**] United States and the [**miry clay**] House of Saud had sought *"to cleave one to another"* for seven decades, a spirit of militancy was incubating inside the desert kingdom that would not allow the two spheres of power to *"mix together"*, even as secular westernism is totally opposite to conservative Islam.

By 1999, a new generation of Saudis, ranging in ages 19 to 40, but mainly in their 20s, left behind their wealthy families and the comforts of their royal palaces to join one of their brethren named Osama bin Laden in Afghanistan. Laden was a member of a wealthy Saudi family. Bin Laden established training camps in the mountains of Afghanistan where he plotted acts of international terrorism inside caves. The terrorist boot camps taught young men from Saudi Arabia, and other places such as, Yemen, Morocco, Syria, Chad, Mauritania, and elsewhere how to launch terror strikes anywhere in the world. During Obama's reign of terror, Saudi Arabia grew into a source of Islamic extremism with a recruitment infrastructure inside his homeland funded by sympathetic local Saudis.

On September 11 ,2001, the World Trade Center in New York City became the battlefield between radical Saudi Islam and the capitalist West. Two jetliners commandeered by Al-Qaeda recruits slammed into the twin skyscrapers killing several thousand people and totally destroying the building. Eleven of the 15 were accused of being Saudis. Many skeptics have expressed doubts about what happened that day. Some critics have labelled the building's devastation as an implosion and, not an explosion, used as a pretext to initiate *The War on Terror* against Afghanistan, Iraq, Libya, and Syria. Regardless, by early 2002, and after the U.S.-led invasion of Afghanistan and the fall of the Taliban, hundreds of Saudis returned to their homeland. This time, bin Ladin instructed the Al-Qaeda returnees to go on the offensive and launch attacks against the kingdom because of their pro-Western ties. Since then, Saudi authorities have arrested thousands of militants. At least 150 have been slain in shootouts and other attacks. Saudi Arabia has a strong internal police known for torture and human rights abuse.

Prophetically speaking, the kingdom of Saudi Arabia is located in the midst of the holy land. In these latter-days, the kingdom is the chief representative of all the energy-producing countries worldwide. It is bordered by the land of Jordan and Iraq to the north. The kingdom of Kuwait is to its northeast. Qatar, Bahrain, and the United Arab Emirates are located on the eastern border. Oman is southeast of Saudi Arabia and the kingdom of Yemen shares the southern border. Saudi fighters have been involved in conflicts in Kuwait, Yemen, Iraq, Syria, Bosnia, Chechnya, Afghanistan, and Lebanon. Radical elements within pro-western Saudi kingdom continue to clandestinely support international terror campaigns against the West and its pro-Western allies. This ongoing international terror campaign could strike any nation, any locality, or make any group of people possible victims within a moment's notice.

Last but not least, the kingdom of Saudi Arabia, which is **one of principal 10 miry clay toe nations**, is a regional power backed by one of the world's largest oil and natural gas reserves. From 2010 to 2014, Saudi Arabia held the title as the world's second largest weapons importer. It is the leader of Gulf Cooperation Council(**GCC**). The GCC is a group of majority Sunni-Arab kingdoms located on the eastern side of the Arabian Peninsula. It is one of the leading member states within the Arab League and the Organization of Islamic Countries. It is also one of founding members of the Organization of Petroleum Exporting Countries(**OPEC**). Saudi Arabia is also a member of the World Trading Organization(**WTO**), the United Nations(**UN**) and the **G-20**. The kingdom's net worth is $2.1 trillion. The **[miry clay]** kingdom, which *"has cleaved unto"* the **[iron]** United States and the State of Israel, is now involved in nuclear research with assistance from Pakistan and the West.

7) Iran
"the kingdom shall be divided"

The **[miry clay]** kingdom of **Iran** is located on the banks of the waters of the Persian Gulf in southwestern Asia. Formerly known as the ancient land of Persia, Reza Shah Pahlavi officially switched the country's name to Iran in the year 1935. Iran, a land once occupied by black Shemitic Elamite people, was the birthplace of another one of the world's first civilizations which date back 4,000 years. Today, Iran is comprised of a majority 61 percent Persian, along with Kurds, Arabs, Lur, Turkmen, Bakfityari, and Baluchi minorities. The size of the population totals 81 million, making it the 17th largest country in the world.

The Land of the North

North of Iran are the central Caucasus Mountains where the ancient Scythians resided. The Scythians became known as southern Russians and Medes. Iran ceded this historic territory to Russia after the Second Russian-Persian war in 1828. Today, the countries of **Russia**, Armenia, and Azerbaijan occupy that area which straddles the Caspian Sea to the east. The waters of the Persian Gulf and the Strait of Hormuz are Iran's borders to its west. The countries of Iraq and Turkey conjunct at Iran's western border. The countries of Afghanistan and Pakistan are located on the eastern border. Historically, the land of Iran has housed the Median Empire, Achaemenid Empire, the Parthian Empire, the Sassanid Empire, the Buyid Empire, the Safavid Empire, and since 1979, the current fundamentalist Shiite Islamic Republic.

Soviet Union, the land of North, join Britain to attack Iran

During World War II, the kingdom of Iran became one of the main theaters of the global conflict. The Allied Powers of Britain, the U.S., and the Soviet Union felt Reza Shah Pahlavi was too sympathetic to the German cause. So, on August 25,1941 the British and the Soviet Union united to launch a joint invasion of Iran. The purpose of the assault was to ensure that the supply of crude oil coming from the Iranian oilfields would not be cut-off or used by the Axis Powers. The invasion lasted nearly one month until September 17. In the end, the Allied Powers replaced the father Reza Shah Pahlavi with his young son Mohammad Reza Pahlavi.

Mohammad Reza Pahlavi ascended to the throne on September 16,1941. Born on October 26,1919 in Tehran, Persia, the Shah of Iran ruled as the kingdom's hereditary monarch.

In 1951, Mohammad Mossadegh came to power as the 35th Prime Minister of Iran. He was a progressive politician. He attempted to initiate major social reforms such as higher taxes on the wealthy, land reform, other measures to bring equality to Iranian society. The most far-ranging change he attempted during his brief two-year reign was the nationalizing of Iranian oilfields. It was the **[iron kingdom]** of Britain which had built the **[miry clay kingdom's]** oil industry, beginning in 1913 one year before the outbreak of First World War.

In order to keep control over Persia's natural resources, the British intelligence agency and the U.S. Central Intelligence Agency plotted a coup against Mosasadeq. The head of Iranian Armed forces General Fazlollah Zahedi assisted in the scheme and he was chosen as the handpicked successor as his reward. With Zahedi now serving as the 36th Prime Minister, the Shah of Iran Mohammad Reza Pahlavi returned from exile to reclaim his throne. After those events, the Shah commissioned the SAVAK secret police to monitor all opposition movements and to keep a firm grip on society. By 1963, the Shah announced a national plan known as *"The White Revolution"* which called for land reform, economic and social modernization. Those actions greatly improved the Iranian infrastructure. However, the Shah of Iran continued his harsh rule with **[a rod of iron]** inspite for his material improvements.

In the late 1970s, things began to turn for the worse for the Shah of Iran. By September 1978, the royal monarch's policies had alienated the Shiite clergy. His harsh authoritarian rule led to riots, mass demonstrations, and general strikes. The Shah retaliated by imposing martial law. By January 1979, law and order had deteriorated into chaos. The Shah and the royal family were forced to flee to the United States for refuge. The following month in February, Islamic cleric Ayatollah Ruhollah Khomeini returned from 14 years of exile in Iraq and France. Relations between the United States and Iran sunk to new lows in the following months. The new government in Tehran demanded the return of the Shah to face trial. The

United States granted asylum to the Shah, who was suffering from cancer. In retaliation, Islamic militants broke down the gates of the United States Embassy in Tehran and seized 52 American diplomats as hostages. The hostages were held as captives until President Ronald Reagan took office in January 1981, 444 days later.

The Supreme Leaders of Iran
(1979 C.E.—Present)

Grand Ayatollah Ruhollah Khomeini
(December 7,1979 C.E.—June 3,1989 C.E.)

Born September 24,1902 in the city of Khomeyn, Persia, the young lad named Ruhollah Musavi Khomeini experienced violence while he was infant when his father was slain before he reached the age of 1. As a young lad, he began studying the Koran and learning the Persian language. He married a woman named Khadijah Saqafi and together they were the parents of 5 children. By 1964, he had become an enemy of the Shah of Iran and was forced into exile in neighboring Iraq among his Shiite kinsmen before moving on to Paris, France. From exile, Khomeini would send underground recorded messages to Iranian supporters calling for the overthrow of the corrupt Shah. Khomeini envisioned a kingdom ruled by Islamic theocratic political jurists.

By late 1978, there was mass discontent in Iran. The Islamic clerics supported the protesters who were demanding a voice in government. Riots, general strikes, violence, mass demonstrations forced the imperial monarch, Shah Mohammed Reza Pahlavi, to abdicate the throne and flee for his life. Ayatollah Ruhollah Khomeini returned to Tehran, Iran in February 1979. Returning from exile at the age of 77, Khomeini was revered as a national father known as a charismatic leader. He became a man with a great name in the earth. By November 1979, the new government had been established. It was the Islamic Republic of Iran. Khomeini was crowned the Grand Ayatollah, the Supreme Leader. His position was regarded as the highest-ranking political and spiritual authority in the new nation. He was regarded as the founder of the Islamic Republic and the leader of the 1979 Revolution. His rise to power represented the end of 2,500 years of Persian monarchies. The new republic was governed by a Prime Minister elected by the Iranian people and a Parliament ruled by elected representatives. Under his spiritual guidance, Iran nationalized their oilfields and oil industry. He became anti-US. and West after rising to power, although he had lived in France during exile. He referred to the United States as the *"Great Satan"*. He was not fond of the Soviet Union neither. Khomeini referred to the Soviets as the *"Lesser Satan"*.

During his 10-year reign, Khomeini executed thousands of his of his opponents. He slew street criminals, war criminals, political prisoners, and others who spoke against the new Shiite theocracy. Internationally, Khomeini became the known as the leader of Shiite Islam. He attempted good relations with the Sunnis, but those attempts were marred by the 8-year Shiite Iran-Sunni Iraq Islamic War. Ayatollah Khomeini died in the city of Tehran on June 3,1989 at the age of 86. He was buried in a gold-domed tomb at the Mausoleum of Ruhollah Khomeini in Tehran. His successor was Ali Khamenei.

Grand Ayatollah Ali Khamenei
(June 4,1989 C.E.—Present)

Born in the year1939 in the city of Mashhad in the Khorasan province of Iran with the birth name Sayyid Ali Hosseini Khamenei, 49-year-old Khameini became the successor of Ayatollah Khomeini on June 4,1989. He had already served as the third President of Iran from 1981 to 1989. During those days, he aligned himself closely with Ayatollah Khomeini. He faced an assassination attempt in 1981 which left one of his arms paralyzed. During the reign of the Shah of Iran, he was arrested several times. Like his predecessor Khomeini, he was also forced into exile where he remained for three years.

Khamenei is regard as the militarist Supreme Leader because he was one of the military leaders during the 8-year Iran-Iraq War. Since becoming the 2nd Supreme Leader, he has maintained close ties with the powerful Revolutionary Guard, watching over his country's development of an advanced long-range missile production programme. In 2014, Iran announced the development of long-range missiles with multiple warheads known as Qiam missiles. These missiles were built in anticipation of a future war with the Jewish State of Israel and U.S. military bases in the region.

In 1989, Khameini was chosen by Khomeini in the closing days of his life. Khomeini then advised his crown princes, known as the Assembly of Experts, to confirm his choice. Khameini ascended to the throne on June 4, one day after the death of his predecessor. He currently serves as the Head of State of Iran and controls the armed forces as commander-in-chief. In 2003, he issued a religious decree condemning the use and storage of nuclear weapons.

Ayatollah Khameini married a woman named Khojaste Bagherzadah in 1964. They became the parents of 6 children. Khameini is currently the second-longest serving head of state in the entire Middle East.

Latter-day Iran

[Miry clay] Iran verus the [Iron] West

Since the ascension of the radical Islamic Republic of Iran in 1979, the **[miry clay]** kingdom of Iran has been on a collision course with the United States and the West. In 1995, President Clinton imposed oil and trade sanctions upon the Islamic Republic because of the regime's sponsorship of international terrorism and its quest for nuclear arms. Iran is hostile towards the Israeli-Palestinian peace process and has called for the destruction of the Jewish State.

In 2002, President George W. Bush, leader of the **[iron]** kingdom of the United States characterized the **[miry clay]** kingdoms of Iran, Iraq, and North Korea as the *"Axis of Evil"*. Bush accused all three regimes of proliferation of long-missile technology. During the same year, Russian technicians started construction of the Iranian nuclear reactor in the city of Bushehr. Russia ignored U.S. strong objections to the construction of the nuclear reactor. Shortly afterwards, Iran started its uranium enrichment program at the facility, but by November 2005, Iran agreed to end their uranium enrichment programme and permit inspectors from the UN to visit nuclear facilities. Months later, UN inspectors accused Iran of not allowing them to access to certain nuclear activities.

In late August and early September 2005, Iran announced it had resumed processing uranium at the Isfahan nuclear facility for peaceful purposes. Meanwhile, the International Atomic Energy Agency(**IAEA**) once again accused Iran of violating the nuclear non-Proliferation Treaty. The following year, the Iranians resumed uranium enrichment at the Natanz nuclear facility. Iran also failed to comply with an United Nations Security Council deadline to stop possessing nuclear fuel. **IAEA** said Iran failed to suspend their programme. In 2007, President Barack Obama imposed the toughest sanctions against Iran in 30 years. The UN Security Council joined him in September 2008 and unanimously passed a new resolution demanding Iran cease enriching uranium. No new sanctions were imposed.

Iran's relationship with West made another turn for the worse in September 2009 when the Islamic regime admitted it had built an uranium enrichment plant near Qom for peaceful purposes. Iran also test-fired a series of medium and long-range missiles capable to striking U.S. bases in the region and the State of Israel. In June 2010, the UN Security Council imposed another round of sanctions against Iran as it continued to defy the Western World, mainly the **[iron kingdoms]** of the United States, Britain, France, and Germany. The countries, Russia and China, **[miry clay kingdom]** have supported Iran throughout the tough negotiations with the global UN authority. Nevertheless, the powerful West enforced an arms embargo, tightened financial restrictions, and attempted to isolate Iran diplomatically. By 2011, the Bushehr nuclear power plant was connected to the national electrical grid and supplying energy for the kingdom. The IAEA reported Iran had doubled its production of uranium at the Fordo nuclear plant. Meanwhile, Iran refused the IAEA access to their Parchin military base.

In 2014, the IAEA reported that Iran had neutralized half of its highly enriched uranium stockpiles. That allowed the **P5+1** nations, *the U.S., Britain, France, Russia, China, and Germany* the opportunity to reach a deal on limiting Iran's nuclear production. In return, the P5+1 nations would agree to lift the international sanctions, release frozen assets, and grant Iran access to the world trading system.

In 2018, the newly elected U.S. President Donald J. Trump announced the U.S. withdrawal from the 2015 [P5+1] international nuclear deal with Iran. Iran in turn, announced it would resume and increase its uranium enrichment if the 2015 deal collapsed.

Prophetically speaking, the kingdom of Iran **[Persia]** will continue to strengthen its geopolitical, economic, and military cooperation with Russia, which is prophetic Gog, the chief prince of the land of Magog. Iran and Russia are already working closely together in Syria in support of President Bashar al-Assad. Along with Israel's nervousness over Iran's missile program, the conflict inside Syria has also brought Iran and the State of Israel into the possibility of direct confrontation in the near future. Most of all, Iran is mentioned as one of the nations allied with Russia in the latter-day alliance that will invade the land of Israel. [**See Ezekiel 38:5**]. That alliance, Russia, China, Iran, Syria, Hezbollah, and Shiite militias from Iraq, is exactly what we see unfolding in the Middle East right now. The confederation will play a major role in the upcoming **Battle of Armageddon**.

Shiite Iran verus Sunni Saudi Arabia

Another conflict raging in the Middle East today is the ongoing Islamic civil war between Shias and Sunnis. In September 2018, gunmen opened fire on a military parade in the city of Ahvaz in the Khuzesen province, which has a large Arab population. A Sunni-Arab nationalist group and ISIS claimed responsibility for that attack. 25 people were slain. A year earlier in June 2017, several people were killed in a coordinated attack on Parliament and the Shrine of Ayatollah Khomeini. The Islamic State of Iraq and Syria(**ISIS**) claimed responsibility for both of those attacks. Shias and Sunnis are also involved in conflicts in Yemen, Bahrain, Iraq, Syria, and Pakistan. Saudi Arabia is the major backer of Sunni politics and warfare while Iran does the same for Shia politics. This has placed them on opposing side in proxy wars in Yemen, Bahrain, Syria, and Iraq. Both kingdoms are rivals in a contest to become the leading regional superpower. Saudi Arabia is presently allied with the West and Israel in their quest for prominence whereas powerhouse Iran is wholly anti-Saudi Arabian, anti-Israeli, and anti-United States.

It should also be remembered that the kingdom of Iran shares a border with an important waterway known as the Strait of Hormuz which flows into the Persian Gulf. Several sqaudrons of United States aircraft carriers and other battleship armadas confront Iranian patrol forces on a daily basis in those important waters. Iran claims control of the strategic Strait of Hormuz where two-thirds of the world's crude oil supplies originate. A hot conflict is simmering among these antagonists as we speak.

For the record, Iran was one of the original signatories of the **United Nations** when it was established on October 24, 1945.

8) North Korea
"part of clay, partly broken"

The **[miry clay]** kingdom of North Korea, which is officially known as the Democratic People's Republic of Korea, is located on a portion of the Korean Peninsula in East Asia. North Korea share a western and northern border with Communist China. Its southern border is surrounded by the Yellow Sea. The Sea of Japan surrounds the eastern coastline.

Known as the hermit kingdom because of its isolation from the broader world, the kingdom is a mere 50,000 square mile landscape, consisting of mountain ranges and peaking highlands, with a population of 25 million Koreans. The capital-city is Pyongyang.

The history of the Korean Peninsula goes back to the 7th B.C.E., beginning with the civilization known as the First Kingdom. It was followed by the Three kingdoms, the North-South kingdoms, the Goryeo dynasty, Joseon dynasty, the Korean Empire, the Japanese-Korean Treaty, and on September 9,1948, the Democratic People's Republic of Korea was established.

After the defeat of Japan after World War II, the socialist Soviet Union moved in and occupied the [**miry clay**] northern portion of the peninsula while the territory of the south was possessed by the [**iron**] capitalist United States. In 1950, the ceasefire between the two spheres of power ended when the North launched an invasion seeking to unite the entire peninsula by force. The regional conflict turned into a global war when **UN** troops entered the conflict. In response, the Chinese sent troops to reinforce the North. The war ended three years later in 1953 with an armistice between the warring parties.

North Korean Supreme Leaders
(1948 C.E.—Present)

Kim II-sung (September 9.1948 C.E.—July 8,1994 C.E.)

Born on April 15,1912 as Kim Song-ju, he grew to become the founder of the Democratic People's Republic of Korea at the age of 36. Kim II-sung rulership was a classic definition of *Potter's clay* or *Miry clay*. Kim was the Potter and the North Korean people were the Clay. This meant the leadership of North Korea and its people were those who demanded to fashion their own system of rulership not based on the values of the powerful capitalist Western world. During his reign, Kim II-sung handcrafted a harsh regimented society based on his own Korean likeness. Compared to the industrialized [**iron**] kingdoms, the Miry clay kingdoms are poor, but they refuse to be dominated by the wealthy Iron kingdoms. This continuous struggle between the two diverse kingdoms is causing the global order to be *partly strong* and *partly broken* with neither side *mixing* or understanding one *another*.

Kim ordered the invasion of South Korea in 1950, hoping to unite the iron and potter's clay, however, it ended in 1953 as it began with two opposing spheres of power. The 1953 death toll stood at 1.3 million South Koreans,1 million Chinese, 500,000 North Koreans, 54,000 Americans, and many others from various countries serving in the **UN armed forces**, totalling nearly 3 million.

After the war, North Korea established a centralized state-controlled economy owned by Kim II-sung and his close associates. And since then, the kingdom hasn't expanded pass cooperative farms, steel and chemical production, and textiles.

In the 1980s, North Korea secretly began its nuclear and missile programs. After 20 years of hard work, his successor Kim Jong II oversaw the country's first test of a nuclear device in 2006.

Kim Jong II(October 8,1997 C.E.—December 17,2011 C.E.)

Born in the year 1942 in Vyatskoye, Russia, Kim Jong II followed in his father's footsteps by becoming Secretariat of the Worker's Party of Korea in his late 20s. By the age of 32 he was the leader of the Central Committee of the Worker's Party of Korea. During his reign, the Korean People's Army(KPA) grew into the fourth-largest standing army in the world with 1.2 million soldiers in uniform. China has the 3rd largest, the United States is in second place, and India has the world largest standing army.

On the slip side, Kim Jong II oversaw one of the worst famines in Korean history. As I already mentioned, North Korea's agriculture system was based on cooperative farms where rice, corn, barley, and vegetables are grown. When weather conditions prevented the harvest of those crops, the kingdom endured extreme food shortages where millions of Koreans died from starvation. Regardless of those hardships inside North Korea, Kim involved his country in anti-Western policies around the globe through state terrorism, weapons sales, and the sell of missile technology to [**miry clay**] Middle East countries such as Iran, Syria, Libya, and Pakistan. North Korea was also known for international counterfeiting of currencies, drug dealing, and money laundering. Throughout his 14-year reign, and despite human misery, Kim Jong II main concern was the strengthening of North Korean military capabilities. Today, the kingdom continues to be minerally rich with coal, iron ore, and magnesite, yet the gross domestic product for 2014 was still a mere $40 billion. In 2015, their gross domestic product dropped dramatically to $25 billion, making North Korea one of the poorest kingdoms [miry clay] among the family of nations. The average income is a meager $1,800 per person.

Still, Kim Jong II should be credited with initiating some economic reforms. He built the Kaesong Industrial Park in 2003, using the Chinese model of state-owned capitalism as an example. In the year 2000, Kim Jong II came out of isolation to attend a summit with his South Korean counterpart. The meeting, the first in 50 years, raised hopes of reconciliation between the two Koreas situated on one peninsula. On a personal note, Kim was the father of 5, and when he died on December 17, 2011, his son Kim Jong-un became his successor.

Kim Jong-un (December 17, 2011 C.E.—Present)

Born on January 8, 1983 in Pyonyang, North Korea, young Kim Jong-un followed in the footsteps of the founder of the dynasty, his grandfather, and his own father. He served as Chairman of the State Affairs Commission, Chairman of the Central Military Commission, Leader of the Presidium of the Politburo, and Supreme Commander of the Korean People's Army before his ascension to the throne as the new Supreme Leader.

Kim Jong-un came to power as the Great Successor one month before his 28th birthday. Before coming to the throne, he also earned two college degrees, one as a physicist and the other as a military officer.

For the first six years of his reign, Kim conducted numerous long-range missile tests, exploded underground nuclear devices, and repeatedly threatened to confront the United States if provoked. United States Donald Trump came to power as the new leader in Washington on January 20, 2017. Kim was in the midst of his missile testing when Trump began to demand an end of such activity. Kim responded with more provocative testing. The conflict became personal when the U.S. leader described Kim Jong-un as a *"Rocket Man"* before the diplomats gathered at the September 2017 UN General Assembly.

American military intelligence also believe North Korea has successfully reduced a nuclear device small enough to be outfitted on a warhead. North Korea's goal is to deploy intercontinental ballistic missiles capable of reaching American cities. However, the relationship between Trump and Kim Jong-un has changed for the better. On June 12, 2018 and again in early 2019, the two diverse leaders met for summits. The first meeting convened in Singapore while the second round of talks were held in Vietnam. The summits were the first direct talks between a reigning U.S. president and a North Korean leader. The major focus of the discussions were the ongoing North Korean nuclear and missile programs.

Prior to those talks, North Korean Supreme Leader Kim Jong-un and South Korean President Moon Jae-in had already met in April 2018 for the first time to discuss better relations.

Latter-day North Korea

The reason North Korea is one of the [10] principal [miry clay kingdoms] is not because of its economic, political, or social superiority. It is because of its military superiority and its potential to destroy the wealthy capitalist United States and her military installations in the regions, including her allies such as Japan and South Korea. North Korea has a 1.2 million man standing army, the fourth largest among all nations, yet its 2015 gross domestic product reached only $25 billion, five times less than the gross domestic product of the West African kingdom of Ghana.

Economically poor, North Korea has mastered the technology of launching intercontinental ballistic missiles, and along with that, it is now known to be a nuclear power. This technological combination makes North Korea a national threat on the level of governments like Russia, China, and even a greater threat than radical Iran. This is why poor [miry clay]

North Korea is regarded as one of greatest kingdoms of the earth during these latter-days of the toes of the feet made of **"partly iron and partly clay"**. Strategically, North Korea is allied with neighboring wealthy China which has been their economic lifeline during international sanctions and economic isolation. Those economic ties could easily turn into military cooperation during a protracted war in the South China Sea which China claims as its own. China has fortified the South China Sea with a chain of weaponized man-made islands to control movement in the waterway. Those developments have placed the United States and China on a dangerous course that could lead to a regional war involving North Korea as one of the Chinese allies. On the other hand, North Korea has the military strength to engage the United States on their own.

It is a known fact that North Korean technical experts were building a nuclear reactor for Syria before it was destroyed by the Israelis in a pre-emptive strike. North Korea has also provided missile expertise to Iran in exchange for economic assistance. Therefore, North Korea should be regarded as an enemy of the State of Israel that supplies all the destructive materials needed to assemble a dirty bomb or missile to strike the Jewish State. Wealthy guerilla groups such as Shiite Hezbollah, Sunni Al-Qaeda, or Sunni-ISIS, all have the resources available to purchase those weapons of mass destruction, and most of all, North Korea needs the hard currency.

Both North Korea and South Korea joined **the United Nations** in 1991.

9) South Africa
"part of clay, partly broken"

The [**miry clay**] kingdom of South Africa comprises 500,000 square miles and 42 million inhabitants. It is located at the farthest southernmost point on the continent of Africa. The country was built on a broad interior plateau surrounded by mountainous ranges with a narrow coastal plain leading out into the Indian Ocean. The annual weather is a subtropical climate. Three-fourths of the population is indigenous African, consisting of the Zulu, Xhosa, Sotho, and Tswana. Aryan Europeans make up only one-eighth of the total population. The remaining minorities are the mixed races and Indians. Within the territory of South Africa, the kingdom of Lesotho continues to flourish. Pretoria is the capital-city of the down South kingdom which is a Republic. The republic consist of two houses and a president that serves as a head of state and the government.

The country of South Africa came into existence when Dutch settlers invaded the area in 1652. In the process of time, the settlers became known as Boers, and later the Afrikaners. The Europeans viewed themselves as superior to the [**miry clay**] black Africans. After nearly 300 years of multiplying, the [**iron**] Europeans formally instituted the supremacist policy of apartheid, meaning separation of the two diverse people [**iron and clay**] while exploiting their natural resources. Under apartheid, the Afrikaners practiced white supremacy and cruelty against the black population. The Republic of South Africa then broke away from the British Commonwealth in 1961.

South Africa is a minerally rich land possessing the world's largest gold reserves. It is also one of the leading producers of coal, diamonds, platium, and the mineral vanadium. However, the wealth of this lush land was seized by the European settlers while the indigenous population was reduced to poverty-stricken Third World status.

Discontent and violence brought South Africa to the brink of a race war in the mid-1980s until the release of black South African nationalist leader Nelson Mandela in 1990. Sensing the kingdom was about to implode, white South African President F.W. deKlerk opened the jail cell for Mandela after he had spent 26 years in confinement. Hailed as a national hero and the leader of the black uprising against apartheid, Mandela was elected as the country's first ever black President of South Africa. Mandela saved the [**iron**] white Afrikaners from total eradication because [**miry clay**] black extremist groups where plotting to massacre all white Afrikaners as revenge for hundreds of years of cruelty against them. Mandela prevented their violent overthrow and the bloody destruction of the former apartheid rulers. He also prevented the socialist idea of nationalization of black South Africa's abundant natural resources held under foreign [iron] Boer, British, and American domination.

In the first free non-racial general elections where indigenous people were allowed to vote along with their Afrikaner counterparts, Mandela easily won the crown as the new President of the multiracial [iron mixed with clay] Republic of South Africa.

Post-Apartheid South African Presidents
(1994 C.E.—Present)

Nelson Mandela (May 10,1994 C.E.—June 16,1999 C.E.)
Mandela was the potter and black South Africa was the clay

Nelson Rolihlahla Mandela was the son of a Xhosa chief born in the [miry clay] village in Mvezo, South Africa on July 18,1918. At the age 23, Mandela qualified to enter the University of Witwaterstand University where he studied law. Identifying the unrighteousness in [iron] apartheid society, he joined the struggle against apartheid with the African National Congress(ANC) in 1944. Mandela was also involved in the South African Communist Party as well. After the 1960 Sharpeville Massacre, Mandela abandoned his nonviolent stance. The Sharpeville Massacre occurred on March 21, after thousands of demonstrators had protested all day. Some of them headed towards the police station in the township of Sharpevile. The unarmed protestors were met by white South African policemen firing a hail of bullets which killed 69 and injured 180. After those events, Mandela helped to start the Spear of the Nation, which was the military wing of the ANC. Mandela was arrested several times for those activities. In 1962, he was finally sentenced to life in prison without parole. His wife Winnie Madikizela kept his name alive among the South African masses. He retained nationwide support among the masses during his 27 years in prison on Robben Island.

On February 11,1990, **the Spirit of YHWH** moved upon white South African President F.W. deKlerk, who feared a racial civil war. Those fears forced him to release Mandela from the dungeon. Upon his release, he received a hero's welcome internationally. He was even invited to the international capital of the capitalist world, [iron] New York City, where he received a ticker tape parade with thousands of New Yorkers lining the streets to sée a glimpse of him as he passed by in a motorcade.

Back in South Africa, Mandela replaced Oliver Tambo as the president of the African National Congress the following year in 1991 until 1997. In 1993, Mandela and President deKlerk received international Nobel Peace Prize for their efforts to end the separatist ideology of apartheid. The new South Africa would be integrated into the new global order where iron and clay were mixed together. Both men worked on the transition of South Africa from the old to the new. In 1994, the first nonracial general election in South African history occurred. Mandela was unanimously elected as the first black president in the country's history.

Mandela reigned for 5 years until he stepped down in 1999. His political platform called for an end to institutional racism. During his reign, he established the Truth and Reconciliation Commission which investigated the human rights abuse that occurred during the days of apartheid.

On personal note, Mandela was married three times. His first wife was Evelyn Ntoko Mase, his second wife was Winnie Madikizela, and his third one was Grace Machel. He was the father of 6 children. When Mandela stepped down in 1999, he was the most universally respected ruler in post-colonial African history. He was called by his clan name Madiba, which meant "Father of the Nation". Mandela died on December 5,2013 at the age of 95. His remains were interned at the Honghton Estate in Johannesburg.

Thabo Mbeki(June 16,1999 C.E.—September 24,2008 C.E.)

Thabo Mbeki was born June 18,1942 in the Xhosa village of Mbewuleui in Cape Province in the Union of South Africa under the [iron] rule of apartheid. He was the son of Govan Mbeki and Epainette Mbeki. His father Govan was an activist who worked in the African National Congress and the South African Communist Party. That is why Thabo Mbeki was quoted as saying, *"I was born into the struggle"*. He also said there were pictures of Karl Marx and Mohandas Gandhi **[miry clay]** leaders on the wall in his home. He grew and eventually departed the townships of South Africa to attend and graduate from Sussex University in London. He also received military training in the Soviet Union as well. Mandela appointed him as his deputy president after the first multiracial general elections in 1994. Mbeki was chosen to control the new government's day-to-day operations.

In 1999, when 81-year-old President Nelson Mandela decided against seeking a second-term, Mbeki ascended to the throne as the new President of black-ruled South Africa. The South African economy grew under Mbeki's leadership. A new black middle-class emerged consisting of newly trained professionals. This new group grew as more opportunities opened up for those who had been marginalized for centuries. Mbeki initiated the Black Economic Empowerment which advanced more blacks into industries once reserved for whites only.

South Africa also became a member of a group of developing economies known as BRICS, consisting of (B)razil, (R)ussia, (I)ndia, (C)hina, and (S)outh Africa. The goal of the group was to build bridges and strengthen businesses, trade relations, and investments among themselves without Western interference. Mbeki, who believed in quiet diplomacy, also served as a peacemaker by covertly intervening in the Burundi crisis, the Congo crisis, and the Ivory Coast civil-war. He also witnessed the transition of the Organization of African Unity into today's African Union.

Mbeki, on the other hand, was very vocal in his non-aligned positions at the United Nations. He also called for reforms at the UN Security Council. He demanded an end to *"global apartheid"* where a small minority of rich **[iron]** nations ruled over a great number of impoverished **[miry clay]** nations. Mbeki viewed those inequalities as a source for global tensions and world conflicts. He once said these following words, *"a global human society based on poverty by many* **[miry clay]** *and prosperity for a few islands of wealth* **[iron]**, *surrounded by a sea of poverty is unsustainable* **[cannot cleave one to another]**.*"*

Although Mbeki enjoyed great success during his 8-year reign, there were several negative factors that troubled his near decade rulership. There was still a large pool of unemployed, unskilled slum dwellers that comprised a large segment of South African population. Under black rule, the black townships became extremely violent where lawlessness reigned.

Meanwhile, Mbeki and his Health Minister Manto Tshabalala Msimang faced a serious health crisis known as HIV/AIDS afflicting southern Africa. Both men suspected pharmaceutical industry mischief. Msimang attempted to overhaul the industry, but he faced heated criticism because of his stance in banning anti-retroviral drugs. Mbeki and Msimang accused their critics of racism and ignoring the connection between poverty and the AIDS epidemic. His critics said nearly 500,000 people died due to both men's policies.

Mbeki resigned during his second-term in 2009 after getting caught up in a scandal. The National Executive Committee of the ANC accused Mbeki of allowing his deputy Jacob Zuma to engage in corruption. A judge later dismissed the charges against Zuma, but Mbeki did not return to office. **Kgalema Motlanthe** became his successor.

President Kgalema Motlanthe (September 25, 2008 C.E.—May 9, 2008 C.E.)
President Jacob Zuma (May 19, 2009 C.E.—February 14, 2018 C.E.)
President Cyril Ramaphosa (February 15, 2018 C.E.—Present)

Latter-day South Africa

The reason the kingdom of South Africa is considered one of principal **[10] miry clay** kingdom is because of two reasons: 1) It is home of the world's largest gold deposits on the face of the earth, making South Africa, **the Head of Gold**, the wealthiest place on this planet.

Yet, the indigenous black South Africans are one of the world's most poverty-stricken [miry clay] people of this *latter-day* global order. 2) It is also the region where the HIV/AIDS epidemic originated under questionable circumstances. Some call it one of the worst man-made plagues to ravage the inhabitants of the earth. Prophetically speaking, South Africa symbolizes the deep-rooted corruption in Africa and the entire world economic system. A system that allows rich nations to dominate and exploit indigenous poor people worldwide by paying them slave wages, no benefits, while robbing their lands of all the gold, diamonds, platinum, cobalt, iron, coal, vanadium, nickel, and all other natural resources. The African governments are controlled by the rich foreign governments and their wealthy investors. Meanwhile, the miry clay people of South Africa, and throughout the entire continent of Africa, live daily lives lanquishing in despair.

The Worldwide Plague of HIV/AIDS ravage South Africa, all Africa, and Third World

Meanwhile, the plague of the HIV/AIDS virus has ravaged these same communities during this time. In fact, the global pandemic has severely afflicted South Africa where 8 million are infected with the man-made plague designed to control population growth. Further north, 3.2 million Nigerians are infected. Meanwhile, 20 percent of the Africans living in Swaziland, Lesotho, and Botswana are HIV/AIDS positive. Elsewhere in other African countries such as Namibia, Zimbabwe, Zambia, Mozambique, Malawi, Mozambique, Uganda, Kenya, Equatorial Guinea, and nearly every other country on the continent of Africa, people are infected. In India, 2.1 million people suffer from the disease. In Indonesia, there are 500,000 confirmed cases of the global scourge. There were also hundreds of thousands reported cases of the HIV/AIDS in Latin America causing loss of life, sickness, and other disruptions.

10) Mexico
"the kingdom shall be partly broken"

The [miry clay] kingdom of Mexico is located on the southernmost portion of the North American continent. The country shares a northern and eastern border with the United States of America. The kingdom is located on a high Mexican plateau surrounded by several mountain ranges. The entire boundaries of the kingdom cover 750,000 square miles. The west coast of the country is surrounded by the blue-green waters of the Pacific Ocean. The southern border is shared with the country of Guatemala. The country has two peninsula: the Bali California peninsula in the northwest and the Yucatan peninsula in the southeast part of the country. The population totals 95 million people with 60 percent Mestizo, 30 percent American Indian, and the remaining 10 percent being of European ancestry.

Mexico is a diverse country that comprise nearly 10 percent desert, well-known beaches for tourists, mountains, and jungles. Mexico is also a land of great history where several pre-European civilizations strived. Beginning with the Olmecs, the Toltecs, Mayans, and Aztecs [miry clay] kingdoms, and various indigenous kingdoms extending from Central America to the borders of what we call the western and southwest United States today. The Spanish began conquering the area in the year 1521. Mexico remained under Spain's [iron] authority until 1821 when they rebelled and declared their independence. In 1845, the [iron] United States and [miry clay] Mexico fought after the Americans invaded their territory, claimed, and annexed the lands now known as California, Texas, New Mexico, and Arizona

Today, Mexico remains a wealthy kingdom that is the world's 7th largest crude oil producer and exporter. The major crops grown are corn, beans, wheat, rice, coffee, and cotton. The minerals celestite and bismuth are very plentiful there. The capital-city of the kingdom is Mexico City.

The Post-World War II Mexico Leaders
(1940 C.E.—Present)
President Avita Camacho (1940 C.E.—1946 C.E.)

President Camacho, the 45th President of Mexico, joined ranks with the United States and declared war on the Axis Powers in 1942. The symbolic gesture represented Mexico's close ties with the United States. Mexico also joined the U.S.-backed United Nations in 1945 as one of the founding members.

President Miguel Aleman (1946 C.E.—1952 C.E.)

President Aleman, the 46th President of Mexico, joined the Organization of American States in 1948 C.E.

President Adolfo Ruiz Cortines (1952 C.E.—1958 C.E.)
President Lopez Mateos (1958 C.E.—1964 C.E.)
President Diaz Ordaz (1964 C.E.—1970 C.E.)
President Echeverria Alvarez (1970 C.E.—1976 C.E.)
President Jose Lopez Portillo (1976 .E.—1982 C.E.)
President Miguel de la Madrid (1982 C.E.—1988 C.E.)
President Carlos Salinas de Gortari (1988 C.E.—1994 C.E.)

President de Gortari ratified the North American Free Trade Agreement (NAFTA), linking the United States, Canada, and Mexico economies together in a free trade agreement allowing goods and services to flow across each other's borders without tariffs or surcharges.

President Ernesto Zedillo (1994 C.E.—2000 C.E.)
President Vicente Fox (2000 C.E.—2006 C.E.)
President Felipe Calderon (2006 C.E.—2012 C.E.)
President Enrique Pena Niet (2012 C.E.—2018 C.E.)
President Manuel Lopez Obrador (December 1,2018—Present)

Latter-day Mexico

After World War II, the kingdom of Mexico maintained close political and economics ties with the United States. In terms of war or peace, Mexico, like its northern counterpart Canada, was a safe haven. Mexico was a nonviolent neighbor, the opposite of adversarial nations like Cuba, Nicaragua, Grenada, Panama, or Venezuela.

International Drug Trafficking "Mexican Drug War"

All of that changed for the worst once Mexico became a transit point for tons of cocaine, marijuana, and opium destned for the United States. Since then, cocaine drug trafficking has involved people from all the countries of Central and South America. Beginning with Mexico, Cuba, Haiti, Jamaica, Colombia, and Peru, the Mexican border has become, strategically, the most important border to international drug trafficking originating from South and Central America. 93 percent of all cocaine coming from South America goes directly through Mexico. Mexico is directly connected to the United States by virtue of a long unsecured border spanning nearly 1,500 miles. Both Mexican and Central American drug cartels have invaded this territory, spreading crime, causing violence, and infesting the United States and Mexico with an unparalleled narcotic epidemic. Mexico is fighting to not be overran by Mexican and Colombian traffickers. Drug tunnels stretching from Mexico into California have also been discovered in recent years. An estimated 70 tons of cocaine a year come through Mexico alone earning the Mexican cartels between $20 to $30 billion,corrupting the Mexican law enforcement and judicial system, leaving broken families, drug addicts, hundreds of gang murders, violence, property theft, crime, jail sentences, loss of productivity, academic failures, and mayhem in Mexico and across U.S. urban centers. At least 55,000 people have been slain since 2006 when Mexico declared its *War on Drug*.

Illegal Immigrants "Modern-day babarians"
A U.S. National Security Threat across U.S. southern border

Thousands upon thousands of illegal immigrants have also been aware of the long unsecured U.S.-Mexican border which extends all the way from California to Texas. Countless illegal

Mexicans, and others, have used the unprotected northern Texas-Mexico border to simply walk over to the American side. This is why the new U.S. President Donald Trump has demanded that the U.S. build a wall to separate the United States from Mexico, hoping to halt the invasion of illegal immigrants and drugs flooding U.S. cities. The hordes of illegal immigrants walking, driving, boating, and hitchhiking towards the southern United States border via Mexico is undoubtedly reminiscent of the hundreds of thousands of primitive Gothic barbarians that invaded the Roman Empire, and eventually destroyed it in the 5th century. The Roman legions were unable to halt the flow of barbarians invading their frontiers and pillaging their settlement-cities. Illegal immigrants today are coming from all parts of [miry clay] Central America, such as Guatemala, Belize, Honduras, El Salvador, Nicaragua, Costa Rica, and Panama, before they crossover into Mexico. These homeless waves from Central America greatly outnumber the U.S. Border Patrol, making it unlikely the illegal hordes will be stopped until they reach their U.S. destinations to join their families already in the United States.

The flow of illegal immigrants coming into Mexico has provoked an international humanitarian crisis on the U.S. southwest border. Mexican authorities, under pressure from the U.S., have attempted to halt the flow by placing police guards at hundreds of border checkpoints on its southern border with Guatemala.

Prophetically speaking, Mexico *represents* Latin America, the entire Central American drug crisis, and the illegal immigrant invasion extending from its southern border to the northwest border of Colombia. The ongoing humanitarian crisis has deeply affected the security of [miry clay] Mexico first, and their pleasure-loving northern neighbor, the [iron] United States, secondly.

V. The Creation of the 1945 United Nations signaled the *"Beginning of the Last Days"*

"YAH changes times and seasons, HE removes kings (Nationalism) and install kings (Globalism), HE gives the wise their wisdom and knowledge to those who know."
Daniel 2:21

The United Nations, the Fulfillment of YHWH'S Prophecies

"And whereas you sawest [iron-rich nations] *mixed, meaning* [one integrated world order] with [miry clay-poor, undeveloped nations], they shall *mingle* [globalism] themselves with the seed of man: but they shall not cleave one to another; even as iron is not mixed with clay."
Daniel 2:43

The Birth of Globalism [Groups of Toes]

During the closing days of World War II, the leaders of the great powers, the [iron] kingdoms of United States and Britain and the [miry clay] kingdom of the Soviet Union met at the Yalta Conference in Iran to plan a new world order after the defeat of Germany and Japan. U. S. President Franklin D. Roosevelt, British Prime Minister Winston Churchill, and Soviet Premier Joseph Stalin met in February 1945 where they demanded the unconditional surrender of the Axis Powers, divided the spoils of war, and separated world power into four groups [toes]: 1) United States, 2) Britain 3)Soviet Union 4)France. The leaders scheduled another meeting in April 1945 in San Francisco, California to create a plan for an international organization to maintain global peace and security. The leaders expressed hopes of developing friendly relations among nations based on equality. The plan was to mingle with the seed of all mankind from every nation into one body [one group of toes mixed with [iron] rich, industrialized nations and poor, [miry clay] undeveloped nations] known as the United Nations. The agreements at Yalta did not work out, *"they did not cleave one to another"*, and the instability of the Cold War started shortly thereafter. The [iron] West accused Stalin[**miry clay**] of reneging on the Yalta agreements by not allowing free elections in Eastern Europe. Stalin accused the West of initiating an arms race and Western dominance in West Germany and Western Europe(**NATO**), threatening Eastern Europe and the Soviet Union.

By 1955, the Soviet Union responsed by creating the Warsaw Pact. This group of nations[**toes**] included the Soviet Union, Albania, Bulgaria, Czechoslovakia, East Germany, Poland, Hungary, and Romania. The goal of the bloc was to create an unified command and control for all their militaries in case of an attack from NATO. The nations of the Warsaw Pact were kingdoms that believed in the ideas of Joseph Engels and Karl Marx. They were one-party, state-controlled economies that were poorer than their Western European brethren. This group represented [**miry clay**].

Inspite of continued frictions, tensions, conflicts, and other rumblings of war, the United Nations remained strong. There was strength of [**iron**] in the global order with six principal world departments known as the Economic and Social Council, the UN General Assembly, the International Court of Justice, the UN general-secretary, who served as a global president for a 5-year term, the UN Security Council, which served as a global Parliament, and the UN Trusteeship Council. This Leviathan would involve itself in the affairs of all nations, including economic standards, cultural recognitions, regulation of international postal standards, civil aviation, and international communication standards. Eventually, the powerful world body would address the issues of nonproliferation of nuclear, chemical, and biological weapons of mass destruction.

In **1948**, the United Nations oversaw **the creation of the State of Israel** when Ralph Bunche, an African Hebrew, who served as the UN mediator for Palestine, met with European Jewish political authorities to bring the Jewish State into the international fold.

In 1949, the kingdom of the United Nations dispatched peacekeeping troops to the Kashmir region to keep the peace between India and Pakistan.

Iron and Miry Clay Conflicts during the Latter-days of United Nations

1950-1953: U.S., South Korea fought against North Korea, China, and Russia (Korean War)
1962: The United States against Soviet Union during Cuban Missile Crisis
1967: Six-Day Arab-Israeli War
1973: Arab-Israeli War
1960s-1970s: The United States against North Vietnam rebels (Vietnam War)
1982: Israeli-Lebanon War
1980-1988: Iran-Iraq War
1982: Britain-Argentina War
1991: Iraq invaded Kuwait starting the 1st Gulf War
2003: The United States invaded Iraq starting the 2nd Gulf War
2000s: Iran uranium enrichment and use of nuclear energy [**P5+1 nations against Iran**]

There are countless other conflicts I could mention where iron and clay did not cleave one to another, but by now, I'm sure you can see for yourself the two spheres of power [**iron and clay**] in world affairs during our lifetimes. These conflicts are proof that **the Spirit of YHWH liveth**, and the interpretation given by Daniel was wholly accurate.

New York City, the capital of the World

The wealthy, advanced, industrialized [**iron**] United States was chosen as the host country for the New World Order. New York City, the number one financial center of the world, was chosen as the capital-city for the global kingdom. Geneva, Switzerland was chosen as its European capital.

Rich and Poor countries join the United Nations

Once the United Nations was established on October 24, 1945, 49 diverse nations joined hands, ranging from extremely poor to wealthy industrialized. Various ethnicities, racial complexions, different political systems, and religious persuasions became as one. They all agreed to cleave one to another within this new global kingdom, which was an extension of the ancient Pax Romana Empire. These latter-day 49 nations, prophetically speaking, represented two distinct spheres of power:**iron and miry clay**. An imbalanced world divided between the powerful and wealthy verus the weak, poverty-stricken,underdeveloped, or developing nations. I will start with the miry clay nations first because they are in the majority. I realize that I have already emphasized these points earlier, but I will focus on those points one final time as we prepare to close out this era and enter the new **Prophetic Time Zone of the Age of YHWH**.

Again, the miry clay people **[kingdom/toes]** are the ones with large population growth. The desire of these miry people is to formulate their own human history where their own leadership is the potter and they agree to be the clay, and not to ruled by a colonial power with a rod of iron. These socialist, underdeveloped European and Third World countries demand to develop their own independent policies and views of the world. Historically speaking, the miry clay people are the descendants of some of earliest recorded civilizations, but in the process of time, they lost their glory. In the latter-days, they are now forced to fight and struggle for respect from the rich capitalist industrialized nations based in Western Europe and North America.

As I pointed out earlier, these inequities are the root causes of many of global crises, tensions, violence, and unresolved conflicts the **United Nations** must manage during these last days. The racial composition of the miry people range from anti-Western pale-skinned Europeans, to yellow and olive-skinned Orientals, to reddish-brown Asians and Latin Americans, to black Africans.

The following nations comprised the first **Miry Clay Nations** which participated in the October 24,1945 birth of the global kingdom known as the United Nations: Argentina, Belarus, Brazil, Chile, China, Dominican Republic, Egypt, El Salvador, Haiti, Iran, Lebanon, Iraq, Guatemala, Honduras, Uruguay, Ecuador, Venezuela, Bolivia, Panama, Ethiopia, apartheid South Africa, Mexico, India, Peru, Costa Rica, Liberia, Colombia, Yugoslavia, Ukraine, Poland, Soviet Union, Saudi Arabia, Syria, Turkey, Philippines, Paraguay, and Nicaragua.

Now, let's look at the influential dominant **Iron Nations**. The following nations were the first **Iron Nations** which participated in the birth of the **united toes** of *iron mixed with miry clay:* Denmark, France, Belgium, Norway the Netherlands, Canada, Greece, Australia, the United States of America, the United Kingdom, New Zeland, and Luxembourg. This exclusively Europeans-only **[group of toes]** are the ones who set the high standards for the world in terms of technology, inventions, and global dominance. Their values are based on the **ancient brass Greco-iron Roman model**.

Since the conception of the UN nearly 70 years ago, the United Nations has grown into a powerful transnational global kingdom consisting of all 193 nations on earth.

"you saw iron mixed with miry clay"

One of the main goals of the United Nations global kingdom has been to create strategic global cooperation between nations to maintain the order of the world system. Yet, the same nations at the UN consist of governments that demand to establish their own agenda, not necessarily in the image of the Greco-Roman model. However, in the latter-days, these two competing systems, **iron and miry clay**, will seek to peacefully *mix* and *co-exist* through diplomacy and global UN resolutions.

Over the past seven decades, the UN has intervened in numerous conflicts, sent support for those afflicted by natural disasters, and legally prosecuted various leaders for war crimes from around the world. This global cooperation and intervention has prevented more deaths in places like Rwanda, Congo, Liberia, Yugoslavia, Serbia, and in several other regional and global hotspots since 1945.

"they will mingle with the offspring of men"

During this era of global cooperation and multinational integration, the human family from all four corners of the earth assembled under one great Tower of Babel speaking one language: English. All of the sons of Noah, Shem, Khem, and Japheth, *cleaved one to another* in economic, political, cultural matrimony, as well as in marriage.

Today, in the era of the **feet** [latter-days] of **toes of iron and miry clay** the intimate integration of the family of nations is commonplace. It is common for men and women from any racial background to join hands in love, *cleave one to another*, in holy matrimony. Some examples of these prophesied relationships were the parents of Bob Marley, whose father was British and his mother a black Jamaican. President Barack Obama, the son of a Kenyan man from East Africa and his mother of European descent. That is another example of the mingling of the seed of men with the **[iron]** people. It is not unusual for a so-called black man to marry an European woman, a Korean, a Filipino woman, a Japanese, or an African woman. Nor is it unusual for a black woman to marry an European man, an Arab, an African, or Oriental man. White people (Europeans) will now openly marry other nationalities without a second thought. Look at the recent marriage of British Prince Harry and biracial Princess Meghan. A Cuban person will readily marry a Canadian person. A British man will go to Africa to find a bride. A native American will marry an European American. The late King Hussein of Jordan, a Hashemite Arab, was married to a French woman. Serena Williams, an African Hebrew woman, married an European man a few years ago. Recording artist and actress Janice Jackson was once married to a wealthy Arab prince of the United Arab Emirate. To make a long story short, interracial and diverse relationships are a direct result of the prophetic words of **YHWH** revealed to Daniel. This is why relationships that were once frowned upon in the older days are now accepted as commonplace. These human contacts, which started as transnational interactions, have caused men and woman to cross their ethnic borders in the name of human love.

"but they will not cleave one to another, just as iron does not mix with miry clay"

As I said earlier, the UN Security Council is the branch of the global kingdom whose primary responsibility is to maintain international peace and security. Its original permanent members were **[miry clay]** China, **[iron]** France, **[iron]** Britain, and **[miry clay]** Soviet Union (**3 iron + 2 miry clay = 5 nations**). There was also a system of another six rotating members elected by the other 44 nations of the original 1945 United Nations General Assembly. The UN General Assembly is the international Congress where diplomats from each nation on earth assembly under one roof to handle world affairs. Every two years since its beginning, the members of the UN General Assembly are called upon to elect 6 members for two-year terms. Those six members along with the 5 permanent members are the Arbitrators of international affairs. In 1965, the non-permanent UN Security Council membership expanded to 10 nations **[10 toes or iron mixed with miry clay]**. Under the new global order, member-states are bound by UN Security Council resolutions. The UN Security Council acts as the investigators of disputes. Afterwards, the council serves as the referee to resolve the conflict, prevent the war, or authorize economic sanctions, or military action against a guilty leader.

The major flaw in the UN global kingdom is the need for unanimous consent in order for the Security Council to implement any actions. Many times, the iron nations and the miry clay nations have found themselves on the opposites sides of resolving regional conflicts, making an uanimous decision nearly impossible. For example, the division among UN Security Council permanent members have prevented a decision concerning Iran. On the issue of Palestine, the UN Security Council has been split down the middle with the **[miry clay]** kingdoms of China and Russia favoring the Palestinians and the **[iron]** kingdoms of the United States, Britain, and France vetoing every resolution they deem anti-Semitic or anti-Israeli. The differences between these two spheres of world power have made the two-state solution between Palestinians and Jewish people nearly impossible. The same is true in New York City at the **United Nations** headquarters where it is extremely difficult for the **iron** and **miry clay** nations to *cleave together* to implement uanimous UN Security Council decisions. The United Nations General Assembly can pass resolutions based on a majority vote, but there is one glitch. The resolutions that the General Assembly issue are purely symbolic because they are non-bidding, meaning there are no real enforcements. Some critics have complained that non-enforcement of their resolutions reduces their governing body into a toothless tiger. It is for these reasons that the United Nations has not been able to live up to its full potential. The upper house, known as the Security Council, is a divided body, making unified decisions extremely difficult. The lower house, known as the General Assembly, lacks enforcement powers. Oftentimes the UN process has ended in protracted stalemates without any meaningful movement forward. The continuous failures of the United Nations has led to the creation of other global organizations [**groups of toes**] in order to establish international law and order. These global groups include the European Common Market, which grew into the European Union(**EU**), the World Trade organization(**WTO**), the **G-7**, the **G-8**, North American Free Trade Agreement (NAFTA), and finally, at the turn of the century, in 1999, a group of 10 wealthy and 10 developing nations joined hands to *cleave together as one* to create a new global order known as the **G-20**.

VI. The Birth of G-20 [Group of 10 Iron and 10 Miry Clay Toes]
(The Final Days of Serpent Dominion Has Arrived)

The G-20 is the new global kingdom which is the latest outgrowth of the post-World War II United Nations era. It has the same agenda as the United Nations, but it is reserved for only the 10 principal wealthy industrialized nations and 10 principal developing nations. This kingdom is the final stage of the prophecy which King Nebuchadnezzar saw in his dream. Remember, Daniel said he saw the toes of the image. Each individual toe was partly iron and partly clay. Keep in mind each individual whole toe is divided into two distinct groups. Therefore you have 10 partly iron toes and 10 partly clay toes that equals 20 nations or G-20. For thousands of years, Christian theologians have erroneously taught that these 10 toes only represented the Revived Roman Empire. But there was one major problem with that viewpoint. What about 10 partly miry clay toes. Each metal represented a people beginning with gold representing the Babylonian people, the silver representing the Persian people, the brass representing the Grecian people, and the iron representing the Roman people and their 10 offsprings. Now, what people do the miry clay represent? They are not part of the iron. These are partly miry clay kingdoms that share one toe which is also partly iron. Therefore, when this global kingdom came into power on September 26,1999 C.E., it was **a sign from YHWH** that HIS dreadful dream to King Nebuchadnezzar was certain and Daniel's interpretation was sure. Here we are today witnessing these two powerful groups of toes:10 partly iron and 10 partly miry clay, creating the G-20. This kingdom represents the final stages of the image [**the Serpent kingdoms**]. This global kingdom is the final world power spoken of in Nebuchadnezzar's dream.

The **10 partly iron toes** are the industrialized European Union, France, Germany, Italy, the United Kingdom, Belgium, the United States, Luxembourg, Spain, Portugal, and their junior allies in Australia, Japan, South Korea, Canada, and others worldwide. The **10 partly clay toes** are developing Brazil, China, India, Indonesia, Mexico, Saudi Arabia, South Africa, Russia, North Korea, Iran, and their secondary allies in Argentina, Turkey, and others elsewhere around the globe. Again, this group of whole 10 toes are divided into partly iron and partly clay, creating 20 fractured powers.10 half iron and 10 half clay united as one G-20. These 20 powerful nations combined govern the global economy and represent 90 percent of all the global wealth and trade. In other words, these 20 nations are far richer than the other 173 nations all put together. The G-20 also represents 80 percent of all world trade and their countries occupy one-half of all the earth's landscape. At the appointed time during the days of these kings known as the G-20, **YHWH, the ELOHIM of heaven, THE STONE CUT OUT WITHOUT HANDS** shall intervene in human global affairs because of their great overflowing wickedness.

O Israel, we have finally arrived at the **Age of YHWH.** HalleluYAH, **YHWH Khai!!**

For **YAH** of host(sabaot) has ready a DAY against all that is proud and arrogant. Against all that is lofty—so that it is brought low. Against all the cedars of Lebanon, tall and stately, and all the oaks of Bashan; Against all the high mountains and all the lofty hills,; Against every soaring tower and every mighty wall; Against all the ships of Tarshish and all the gallant barks. Then man's haughtiness shall be humbled and the pride of man brought low. None but YHWH shall be Exalted in that DAY.
Isaiah 2:12-18

Prepare to meet your ELOHIM, O Yisrael! Behold, HE who formed the mountains, And created the wind, And has told man what HIS wish is, Who turns blackness into daybreak, And treads upon the high places of the earth—HIS Name is YHWH,ELOHIM of host(sabaot) . Seek YHWH, who made Pleiades and Orion, who turns deep darkness into dawn, And darkens day into night. WHO summons the waters of the sea, and pour them out upon earth. HIS Name is YHWH.
Amos 4;12-13, Amos 5:7-8

The Age of YHWH (YAH)
—("I saw a STONE cut out without hands")—

"You sawest until that a stone was cut out without hands, which smote the image upon his feet that were of iron and clay, and brake them in pieces. Then was the iron, the clay, the brass, the silver, and the gold, broken to pieces together, and became like the chaff of the summer threshingfloors; and the wind carried them away, that no place was found for them: and the stone that smote the image became a great mountain, and filled the whole earth." Daniel 2: 34-35

2nd Coming of the Israelite era 'The Anointed People'

"And in the days of these kings shall the ELOHIM (G-d) of heaven set up a kingdom, which shall never be left to other people (people of gold, silver, brass, iron, miry clay), but it shall break in pieces and consume all these kingdoms, and it shall stand for ever." Daniel 2: 44

"YAH changes times and seasons, HE removes kings (kingdoms) and install kings(kingdoms), HE gives the wise their wisdom and knowledge to those who know."   Daniel 2:21

Developmental Stages of Return of the Age of YAH

a) YAH victorious through Natural Disasters and the Battle of Armageddon b) Universal Worship of the ELOHIM of Israel c) The Deliverance of 12 tribes of Israel d) Re-establishment of the Kingdom of YAH on earth with the throne of David, the Levitical priesthood, prophets of Israel, and Israel and Yehudah—the 12 tribes e) The Holiness of YAH rule the earth forever.

Since the Beginning of Existence, Time, and Creation, YAH has been here)

"In the beginning YHWH ELOHIM created the heavens and earth. *The earth was unformed with darkness over the surface of the great deep and a Wind (Spirit) moved over the waters. And ELOHIM said, Let there be Light: and there was Light. And ELOHIM saw the Light, that it was good, and ELOHIM divided the Light from the Darkness. And ELOHIM called the Light*

Day, and the Darkness HE called Night. And the evening and the morning were Day One." YHWH founded the Earth by Wisdom: HE established the Heavens by Understanding; By HIS Knowledge the depths burst apart, and the Skies distill Dew," King Solomon taught ancient Israel those spiritual facts in **Proverbs 3:19**. Those scriptures prove that **The Age of YAH** has always been here. From eternity to eternity YHWH is the SPIRITUAL ENERGY that governs life. It is YAH who spoke and brought all things into existence since the beginning of time. Therefore the CREATOR has created all reality that exist. Each day since the beginning of creation has been HIS (YAH's) Day because it is HIS DIVINE Wisdom that renews each day causing the sun to give Light by day and the moon and the stars to give Light by night. HE cause the winds to blow, the waters of the seas to flow, and provides air to breathe.—Each Day is the **Age of YAH**. The Torah opens in **Genesis** [Bereshith] **1:1** revealing the fact that YHWH spoke, meaning, HE created all the elements required to develop the universe. HIS Spirit [DIVINE Presence] moved over the surface guiding the development of our entire solar system into a living ecosystem. It was, is, and shall always be YAH'S Infinite Wisdom that set the distance from the earth to the sun. HE created mass and radius of all the planets. HE created the chemical reactions to produce molecules. Then HE went on to create and develop environments, set temperatures, atmospheres, and other geological phenomenons. YAH created vocal speech, the private thoughts of the individual mind and the wonders of the heart. (Blessed be the NAME of YHWH forevermore which is only worthy to be praised.)

Unfortunately, the former rulers of the kingdoms of gold, silver, brass, iron, and potter clay, did not recognize the existence of YHWH nor did they keep HIS commandments during their time zones of earthly dominion. They walked in the imaginations of their own minds and each empire believed in false doctrines and served gods graven by the hands of men, even wood and stone. *"It is I (YHWH), who made everything. Who alone stretched out the heavens and unaided spread out the earth; It was I (YHWH) who made the earth and created man upon it; MY own hands stretched out the heavens, and I marshaled all their host,"* the prophet Isaiah proclaimed in **chapters 44:24** and **45:12**. "

As we enter the time zone of the recognized reign of the **Age of YAH**, I would like to first and foremost publicly give all praise, glory, and honor to YAH ELOHIM of our ancient Hebrew ancestors, the ELOHIM of Abraham, Isaac, and Jacob our Eternal Saviour and Redeemer. HIS day of Judgement has finally arrived. A time when the CREATOR of the heavens, earth, and seas, will take control of the reins of earthly power for HIMSELF. Since the destruction of ancient Jerusalem and Yehudah, nearly three thousands years ago, YAH had been in Spiritual Exile from mankind which had been ruled by the Satanic kingdoms of gold, silver, brass, iron, and miry clay. Now, in the **Age of YAH**, HE becomes totally involved in the affairs of men once again. As the prophet Isaiah said: "the mountain of YAH'S house shall be established in the top of the mountains, and shall be exalted above the hills; and all nations shall flow unto it. Many people shall go and say, come you, and let us go up to the mountain of YAH, to the house of the ELOHIM of Jacob; and he will teach us of HIS ways, and the word of YAH from Jerusalem." **Isaiah 2:1-3**.

YAH also revealed to the prophet Daniel that HE was the STONE hewn without Hands. It has been, presently is, and shall always be YAH's DIVINE Presence that fills the entire heavens and the entire earth. HIS Eternal Spirit has not ever consisted of human hands which could have been nailed to a cross or handcuffed to a tree.

In the **Age of YAH** all humanity shall realize that YAH alone has measured the waters in the hollow of HIS hand, and measured the heaven with a span, comprehended the dust of the earth in a measure, and weighed the mountains in scales, and the hills in a measure. The world will understand that no one has directed the Spirit of YAH, or none was with HIM to be HIS counsellor. No one taught HIM. It will be common knowledge that YAH is the MASTER TEACHER. No one can rearrange HIS counsels of old. No one knows better than HIM or taught HIM in the paths of proper judgement. No one has more knowledge or DIVINE INSIGHT than YAH. None can show HIM a better way of understanding. **See Isaiah 40:12-15**. It is YAH who is Enthroned over the circle of the earth, and the inhabitants are as grasshoppers: YAH stretched out the heavens as a curtain, and spread them out as a tent to dwell in. **See Isaiah 40: 22,28**. In this **Age of YAH** all nations will understand that none can be likened or equal to the CREATOR. All praise, honor, and glory will be directed towards

YAH alone. In that day and at that time YAH will be openly regarded as the everlasting ELOHIM, the CREATOR of the ends of the earth, who fainteth not, neither weary. There is no searching of YAH's DIVINE understanding. In fact, the prophecies of Universal Recognition of YAH spoken of by Moses and Habakkuk will be fulfilled with the emergence of the **Age of YAH**.

"As truly as I live, all the earth shall be filled with the glory of YAH," **Numbers 14:21.**

"For the earth shall be filled with the knowledge of the glory of YAH , as the waters cover the sea." **Habakkuk 2:14.**

At that time, they shall call Jerusalem **"Throne of YAH"** and all nations shall assemble there, in **the name of YAH** at Jerusalem. YAH will create over **the whole shrine and meeting place of Mount Zion cloud by day and smoke with a glow of flaming fire by night**. Indeed, over all the glory shall hang a canopy, which shall serve as a pavilion for shade from heat by day and as a shelter for protection against drenching rain. The DIVINE Presence of YAH which appeared in the Temple which King Solomon built in Jerusalem in days of old will be restored once again. The prophet Ezekiel foresaw the visions of this restoration in **chapters 40 through 48** where he also saw the glory of the Presence of YAH which appeared at Mount Sinai return to holy city of Jerusalem. The Levitical priest will once again re-enter the Holy of Holies to bow before the DIVINE PRESENCE of YAH which will manifest itself as in the days of Mt. Sinai. As Moses said in **Deuteronomy (Devarim)4:5-20:** *"I have taught you statutes and judgements even as YAH my ELOHIM commanded me, that you should do so in the land where you go to possess it. Keep therefore and do them; for this your wisdom and your understanding in the sight of the nations, which shall hear all these statutes, and say, Surely this great nation is a wise and understanding people. For what nation is there so great, who has ELOHIM so near unto them, as YAH our ELOHIM is in all things that we call upon him for? Only take heed to yourself and keep your soul diligently, unless you forget the things which our eyes have seen, and unless they depart from your mind all the days of your life: but teach them your sons, and your son's sons: Especially the day that you stood before YAH thy ELOHIM in Horeb, when YAH said unto me, Gather me the people together, and I will make them hear MY words, that they may learn to revere ME all the days that they live upon the earth, and that they may teach their children. And you came near and stood under the mountain; and the mountain burned with fire unto the midst of heaven, with darkness, clouds, and thick darkness. And YAH spoke unto you out of the midst of the fire: ye heard the voice of the words, but saw no similitude; only ye heard a VOICE.* (Notice reader: Moses said ancient Israel did not see a similitude, meaning they did not see a figure of man(Jesus Christ/ Yeshua HaMashiach), the likeness of a female(Mary and other goddesses), the likeness of an animal, a winged fowl, anything that creeps on the ground, an image of a fish, the sun, moon, or stars. None of those physical entities appeared at Mt. Sinai. So it is safe to say that YAH is not, has not, nor never will HE be contained in the body of a man, woman, animal, insect, fish, or in the constellations. YAH has never appeared in the body of a man. YAH is the DIVINE PRESENCE that fills creation.) *And HE declared unto you HIS covenant, which HE commanded you to observe, Ten commandment; and HE inscribed them upon two tablets of* **STONE**. *And YAH commanded me at that time to teach you statutes and judgements, for you go to observe in the land that you are about to cross into and occupy.*

Therefore Israel and mankind should not be expecting YAH to return as a man, woman, animal, insect, fish, or a sun/son as God, moon, or stars (Age of Aquarius) etc. YAH will manifest HIMSELF on the THRONE in the TEMPLE as it is written in **Exodus/Shemot 24:16-17:** *"And the glory of YHWH abode upon Mount Sinai, and the cloud covered it six days; and the seventh day HE called Moses out of the midst of the cloud. And the sight of the glory of YHWH was like devouring fire on top of the mount in the eyes of the children of Israel."* That is the vision which ancient Israel saw 3,500 years ago when they departed ancient Egypt, and in the latter-days, this will be the vision that all mankind shall witness during the **Age of YAH**. There will be no man serving as YAH. YAH will represent HIMSELF (The Ancient of Days) with HIS cloudy pillar by day and a pillar of fire by night.

For the record, all other theories are not ancient Hebrew related. And honestly, we should cast those non-Torah theories away like a menstruous cloth: we should say unto them, *Get away from me!*. **See Isaiah 30:22.**

All nations will come up to Jerusalem to witness the DIVINE Presence of YAH and give praises to HIS Name in the manner of King David in **Psalms/Tehilim 29:1-11** where he said: "Ascribe to YAH, O mighty, ascribe unto YAH glory and strength. Ascribe to YAH the glory of HIS Name; bow down to YHWH, majestic in Holiness. The VOICE of YAH is over the waters; ELOHIM of glory thunders, YAH, over the mighty waters. The VOICE of YAH is Power; the VOICE of YAH is Majesty; the VOICE of YAH breaks cedars; YAH shatters the cedars of Lebanon (great powers of the earth). He makes Lebanon skip like a calf, Sirion, like a young wild ox. The VOICE of YAH kindles flames of fire; the VOICE of YAH shakes the wilderness; YAH shakes the wilderness of Kadesh. the VOICE of YAH causes hinds to calve, and strips the forest bare; while in HIS temple all say "Glory!"(YHWH alone). YAH sat Enthroned upon the flood; yea YAH is Enthroned forever. May YAH grant strength to HIS people; YAH will bless HIS people (Israel and Yehudah) with peace. The **Age of YAH** will fulfill this vision of Universal Recognition of YAH as ELOHIM of all the earth. All the cedars of Lebanon will bow before HIS glory and majesty.

The eternal reign of **The Age of YAH** will consist of a timeless period when the DIVINE Instructions of the MOST HIGH which HE had given to Moses will be become the DIVINE standard and rule of law internationally. When you read **Exodus/Shemot 31:18** you find that the Wisdom of YAH found in the two tablets of testimony, tables of **STONE**, written with the finger of ELOHIM **(Cut out without hands)** will settle disputes, wars, famines, diseases, and all problems ailing humanity.

The Stone Cut Out Without Hands

"The day that you stood before **YHWH thy ELOHIM (The STONE)** in Horeb, when YAH said unto me, Gather me the people together, and I will make them hear MY words **(Cut Out Without Hands)**,that they learn to fear ME all the days that they live upon the earth, and that they may teach their children.(You and I). You came near and stood under the mountain; and the mountain burned with fire unto the midst of heaven, with darkness, clouds, and thick darkness. YAH **(The God of heaven)** spoke unto you out the midst of the fire; you heard the **VOICE** of the words; but saw no similitude(no man with human hands); only you heard a **VOICE.(THE LIVING ONE—THE STONE).** HE declared unto you HIS covenant, which HE commanded you to perform, even Ten Commandments; and **HE(YAH)** wrote upon two tables of STONE. (without human hands). **Deuteronomy/Devarim 4:10-13/Daniel 2:34(KJV).**

"HE gave unto Moses, when HE had made an end of communing with him upon Mount Sinai, two tables of testimony, tables of **STONE**, written with the finger of ELOHIM. **Exodus/Shemot 31:18(KJV).**

"O that there were such a mind in them, that they would fear ME, and keep all MY commandments always; that it might be well with them, and with their children for ever! Go, say to them, "Return to your tents:" But you (Moses) remain here with ME., and I will give you all the commandments, and statutes, and judgements, you shall teach them, that they do them in the land which I gave them to possess. You shall observe to do as **YAH your ELOHIM** commanded you: you shall not turn aside to right hand or to the left." You shall walk in all the ways which **YAH your ELOHIM** commanded you, that you may live, and that it may be well with you, and that you prolong your days in the land which you shall possess." **Deuteronomy/Devarim 5:29-33(KJV).**

"Moses turned and went down from the mount, and the two tables of the testimony were in his hand: the tables were written on both their sides: on the one side and on the other were they written. **And the tables were the work of ELOHIM(God); and the writing was the writing of ELOHIM(God),** graven upon the tables.(Cut out without human hands) Exodus/

Shemot 32:15-16/Daniel 2:44(KJV).

"Know therefore that **YAH thy ELOHIM, HE is ELOHIM**(God), the faithful **ELOHIM**, which keeps covenant and mercy with them that love HIM and keep HIS commandments to a thousands generations." **Deuteronomy/Devarim 7:9(KJV).**

"Know therefore this day, and consider in your mind that **YAH is ELOHIM** in heaven above, and upon the earth beneath: there is _none else_. You shall keep therefore HIS statutes, and HIS commandments; which I command you this day that it may go well with you, and with your children after you, and you may prolong your days upon the earth, which **YAH thy ELOHIM** gives you _for ever_." **Deuteronomy/Devarim 4:39-40(KJV).**

"Behold, the heaven and the heaven of heavens is **YAH's thy ELOHIM**, the earth also, with all therein is.".........."For YAH your ELOHIM is ELOHIM of elohims, YAH, the great ELOHIM, a Mighty and Terrible, which regards not persons, nor take rewards." **Deuteronomy/Devarim 10:14,17(KJV).**

Jerusalem will be the city where all Celestial and Earthly decrees originate.

YHWH alone comes to sit on THRONE as KING of heaven and earth

A **THRONE** is a seat, to hold, support, firm; the chair on which a KING sits on formal and ceremonial occasions; A place of honor. The POWER or RANK of a KING; SOVEREIGNTY; Sovereign Ruler; The highest order in the hierarchy. **To ENTHRONE** means to place on a throne; make a king and accord the highest place for exaltation.

The complete HEAVEN is YAHAWAH'S Sacred Throne; A Seat where HIS DIVINE PRESENCE holds, supports, stands firm; A Spiritual Chair (Chamber) on which YAHAWAH rules both literally and figuratively. As the SOVEREIGN ONE, YAH is the Absolute Power and rank of the Universal KING; The Highest Cosmic Divine Power among all the Divine beings.

As servants of YAH we are commanded to enthrone and place (empower) YAH as KING of the Universe in our hearts, minds, and souls. YAH should be regarded as the MOST HIGH (The Highest) in the Celestial hierarchy. The heavens reflect the celestial wonders of the ONE (YHWH) who is Perfect in knowledge. It is YHWH who causes both spiritual rain and physical rain-clouds. See **Job 37: 15-18 and Job 37: 5,6,9, Isaiah 66:1, Amos 5:8, Psalms 11:4, Psalms 29: 10-11, Psalms 45: 6, Psalms 57: 5**

During The Age of YAH the mission of the Kingdom of Yisrael and Yehudah will be to Sanctify the name of YAHAWAH among the nations. As it is written: "I will be sanctified through you [Israel] in the sight of the nations."

HOW CAN THIS HAPPEN? This is done through SANCTIFICATION OF YAH: As servants of YAH, we should be exalting the name of YAH in the midst of our people and the nations. YAH, and YAH alone, should be our Sacred Shrine and Glory. This total exaltation of YAH in the earth will cause sanctification in the sight of the inhabitants of the earth.

"Hear O Israel: YHWH is our ELOHIM, YHWH is the ONE and ONLY. You shall love YAH your ELOHIM with all your heart, with all your soul, and with all your resources. And these matters that I command you today shall be upon your heart. You shall teach them thoroughly to your children and you shall speak of them while you sit

in your home, while you walk on the way, when you retire and when you arise." **Deut. 6: 4-7.** When we adhere to these DIVINE principles we display true sanctification. YAH is the KING on the THRONE is HEAVEN above and earth beneath, and in the waters beneath the earth.

SANCTIFICATION OF OURSELVES means to sanitize ourselves in the sight of the nations through wise behavior. This sanctification will be developed in stages. This national development will display wisdom, understanding, and knowledge.

These stages begin with pre-natal love and nurture, childbirth, 8-day male circumcision of boys, childcare, elementary, middle-school, and high school education, courtship, marriage, family, culture, and even how we handle our deceased.

[True Process of Sanctification Begins with the following]
1) Recognition of YAH as the SUPREME BEING and SUPREME INTELLECT **alone**; NONE OTHER **(Isaiah 43: 10-11; Isaiah 45: 18-23, Exodus 20:1-3)**
2) No falsehood such as Santa Claus, Easter Bunny, Tooth fairy, Christmas trees, Easter eggs, Cupid and St.Valentine's Day, all man-made religions and celebrations, etc.**(Exodus 20: 4-6)**
3) No disrespect or disregard of the name of YAH **(Exodus 20: 7)**
4) Observance of Hebrew Sabbath, observe YAH's Dietary laws **(Lev.11)**
5) Honor and Respect for the Elders and love for your neighbors.
6) No murder of any human being under any circumstances. Only self-defense.
7) No adultery, no carnal, sexual relations with your friend's girl, or partner's wife or girlfriend. All forms of homosexuality is spiritual crime (sin).
8) No stealing from any Israelites or any other nation of people.
9) No lying, con games, slick-ism, or bearing false witness.
10) No greed, lust, desire, strong feeling, or thirst for money, sex, material gain, or anything that causes you to do wrong, think wrong, and commit spiritual criminal acts against YAH's commandments, laws, judgements, and statutes.

Israelites must find honest, productive work, whether self-employed or a job, trades, or education to display honesty and righteousness in our day-to-day affairs. This Blessed Mindset will prepare the redeemed lost sheep of the House of Israel for their new role as the Priest of YAH and Servants of their ELOHIM(God). Yisrael shall enjoy the wealth of the nations and revel in their riches which YAH shall convert over to them. In this new age, YAH's righteousness shall be the hallmark of the Kingdom of Yisrael and Yehudah and all the nations of the earth. YAH will judge among the nations and Arbitrate for the many peoples. All nations will be commanded by YAH to beat their destructive warfare capabilities into peaceful technological skills that will save humanity while glorifying YAH. Nations will not take up swords against each other during the new era. YAH will cause them to never practice warfare again. All nations will espouse the Proverbial Wisdom found in **Proverbs 11:2** which states: "The righteousness of the blameless men(nations) will smooth the way. Also in the next verse, **verse 3**, it says:*"The righteousness of the upright nations will save them."* These nations will walk in the commandments of YAH. This obedience will create a new international harmony among all inhabitants of the earth. No harm will befall mankind. The past era of strife and conflict which the **kingdoms of gold, silver, brass, iron, and potter's clay** represented will be a relic of the past. The wicked rulers and unrighteous inhabitants of the earth will be bygone. All the great nations(cedars of Lebanon) that obey the VOICE of YAH will be deemed blameless. They will experience YAH's DIVINE Protection. Yisrael and Yehudah will be in the forefront as the world's leading YAH worshipping power. Yisrael will acknowledge and trust in YAH their ELOHIM who freed them from the land of the north and from all the other lands. HE has gathered them back to HIMSELF in Zion. This renewal of the covenant will be totally opposite of the former days when mankind worshipped other gods, the works of their own hands and followed pagan customs.

On a spiritual level, Yisrael earned their way back into YAH's LIFE. After millenniums of procuring evil upon themselves by turning their backs on YAH, Yisrael has regained HIS DIVINE Favor. The anointed(HaMashiach) remnant has passed the spiritual test by returning totally to YAH and forsaking the gods of gold, silver, brass, iron, and potter's clay. The anointed remnant will faithfully walk in the ways of YAH in the manner of their righteous ancestors during the reigns of King David, King Solomon, King Yehoshaphat, King Yotham, King Hezekiah, and King Yosiah. YAH has accomplished HIS Prophetic Utterances once proclaimed thousands of years ago by HIS servants the ancient Hebrew prophets. "Blessed be the Name of **YAH, ELOHIM of our Hebrew ancestors, Abraham, Isaac, and Yaacov our Eternal Saviour and Redeemer, the King of Israel**," will be the mantra of the 12 tribes of Israel. HIS Name is now exalted throughout the ends of the earth.

"For HE who made you has espoused you. HIS Name is **YHWH(YAH)** of host(**sabaot**). The **HOLY ONE of Israel** has redeemed you. HE is called **ELOHIM(POWERS)** of all the earth. **Isaiah 54:5.**

"**For I am YAH your ELOHIM, the HOLY ONE of Israel your SAVIOUR**. I gave Egypt as a ransom for you . . . Thus saith **YHWH your REDEEMER, the HOLY ONE of Israel,** for your sake I send to Babylon, I will bring down all their bars and the Chaldeans shall raise their voice in lamentation." **Isaiah 43:3,14.**

"Fear not, O worm Jacob(Yaacov), O men of Israel: I will help you declares **YAH. I am your REDEEMER, the HOLY ONE of Israel.**" **Isaiah 41:14.**

"I will make you(Yisrael-Yehudah) a threshing board. A new thresher, with many spikes; You shall thresh mountains to dust, and make hills like chaff. You shall winnow them and the wind shall carry them off. You shall winnow them and scatter them. But you shall rejoice in YAH and glory in the **HOLY ONE of Israel.**" **Isaiah 41:15-16.**

In this new DIVINE era, all Israel will acknowledge the fact that it was, is, and shall always be, YAH's DIVINE WISDOM that led them to this newfound freedom. It was the DIVINE plan of YAH that produced this new heaven on earth. The Israelite leadership will uphold the Sanctity of YHWH's Name and the importance of the commandments among the people.

"Know therefore that **YAH thy ELOHIM, HE is ELOHIM, the faithful ELOHIM,** which keepeth covenant and mercy with them that love HIM and keep **HIS commandments** to a thousand generations." **Deuteronomy 7:9.**

"And it shall come to pass, if you shall hearken diligently unto **MY commandments** which I command you this day, to love **YAH your ELOHIM**, and to serve HIM with all your heart and with all your soul." **Deuteronomy 11:13.**

"And shewing mercy unto thousands of generation of them that love ME and keep **MY commandments.**" **Deuteronomy 5:10.**

"Know therefore this day, and consider it in your mind that **YAH, HE is ELOHIM** in heaven above, and upon the earth beneath: there is none else. You shall keep therefore HIS statutes, and **HIS commandments**, which I command you this day, that it may go well with you, and with your children after you, and you mayest prolong your days upon the earth which **YAH thy ELOHIM** giveth you for ever." **Deuteronomy 4: 39-40.**

"And now, Israel what do **YAH thy ELOHIM** require of you, but to fear **YAH thy ELOHIM** to walk in all HIS ways, and love HIM, and to serve **YAH thy ELOHIM** with all thy heart and with all thy soul. To keep the **commandments** of YAH, and HIS statutes, which I command you this day for your good. Behold, the heaven and the heaven of heavens is **YAH's thy ELOHIM**, the earth also, with all therein is." **Deuteronomy 10:12-14.**

In that day and during those times, Yisrael and all mankind will possess the proper DIVINE respect for YAH spoken of in the Book of Deuteronomy. In fact, the people of Yisrael will serve as YAH's instrument to restore the YAH-Mind upon the face of the earth. The main component in achieving this YAH-Mind will be LOVE. A LOVE that could be described as deep and tender feelings of affection for DIVINE Instructions (**YAH's commandments**). All nations will feel this spiritual and emotional attachment towards YAH. This oneness of humanity will produce a feeling of brotherhood and goodwill towards each other. This LOVE of YAH thy ELOHIM will first activate the Redemption of lost sheep of Israel from captivity among the nations. Yisrael's unbreakable faith in YAH will actually be more powerful than any weapons of war. That strong passionate affection for YAH will be our national defense forevermore. The Presence of YAH will be confirmed through all these prophetic events as they actually unfold according to the testimonies of the ancient Hebrew prophets right before our eyes.

Nevertheless long ago, the visionary King David once foresaw this future day in **Psalms 102:16-17 [in the Tanakh] Psalms 102:16-17 [in the KJV]**, *"the nations will fear the Name of YAH, all kings of the earth, YOUR glory, For YAH has built Zion; HE has appeared in all HIS glory."*

Again in **Psalms 67:2-8[Tanakh/KJV]**, King David also envisioned the Universal Recognition of YAH when he said these words about YAH: *"may YOUR way be known on earth, YOUR deliverance among all nations. Peoples will praise YOU, O ELOHIM. Nations will exult and shout for joy, for YOU rule the peoples with equity, YOU guide the nations of the earth; all peoples will praise YOU, O ELOHIM; all peoples will praise YOU. May the earth yield its produce; may ELOHIM, our ELOHIM[YAH] bless us. MAY ELOHIM bless us, and be revered to the ends of the earth."*

However, as we know the **Age of YAH** will be ushered in through YAH's destructive outstretched ARM and mighty HAND of nature: HIS winters (extreme cold, snow, ice, blizzards, winterstorms), summers (extreme heatwaves, water and food shortages, famines, droughts), springtimes (drenching rains, floods, powerful winds), and autumns (mudslides, earthquakes, hurricanes, cyclones, tsunamis) will plague mankind every year until HIS Presence is known internationally. HIS DIVINE POWERS will be revealed before all mankind in order to first, get their attention and, secondly to humble their selfish and haughty spirits. YAH will act as one who circumcises an eight-day old Hebrew lad. It is a bloody and painful process for the young male child, but it brings him into compliance with YAH'S Will. This is what these bloody and painful judgements represent for all mankind in the latter-days.

These endtime judgements will also cut off the foreskin of wickedness that clouds the spiritual minds of **the kingdoms of gold, silver, brass, iron, and miry clay**. In the end, like the lashes of the slavemaster's whip that once afflicted the backs of the lost sheep of the house of Israel, these oppressive blows shall chastise mankind, and usher them into compliance with the rule of the **Age of YAH**.

a) YAH'S Judgement shall be upon the nations of the Earth
(As it was in the days of Ancient Egypt, so shall it be among all Nations in the Latter-days)

"and the magicians said to Pharaoh, This is the finger of ELOHIM! But, Pharaoh's heart stiffened and would not heed them, as YAH has spoken," **Exodus 8:15**

Number One. As I emphasized before, **The Age of YAH** will escalate with unprecedented NATURAL DISASTERS. These increased deadly natural disasters will serve as body blows to the global order, weakening it step by step until it crumbles under the weight of YAH'S outstretched ARM. As the latter-days come to a close, the outstretched ARM and mighty HAND of YAH will be revealed more and more. It will be very similar to the signs and wonders that YAH displayed in the land of Egypt thousands of years ago. Those **10 Plagues** in days of old destroyed the normal operation of the kingdom of Pharaoh. The lives of the Egyptian people were constantly upset by DIVINE upheaval. Each plague represented

DIVINE chastisement from YAH for two reasons. 1) YAH wanted the Egyptians to realize that their way of life was not the proper path to walk in. Their kingdom was absent of the reverence of YAH. Instead they built pyramids, obelisks, and glorified the works of their own hands. 2) The Kemetic Egyptians had brutally oppressed and practiced a war of genocide against the ancient Afro-Asiatic Hebrew people. YAH'S DIVINE Judgement broke the vice grip of power they held on the Hebrews. This is how YAH will break the vice grip of power that the **kingdoms of iron and miry clay(G-20)** hold upon the lost sheep of the House of Yisrael in this modern era.

40-years of continuous Global Plagues
Plague 1

There will be direct resemblances between the catastrophic plagues that once destroyed Egypt during the days of Moses and those that are covering the Earth in the 21st century to usher in **The Age of YAH**.

In **Exodus 7:17-18** it is written: Thus saith YAH ELOHIM of thy fathers, ELOHIM of Abraham, ELOHIM of Isaac, and ELOHIM of Jacob, I will smite the waters which are in the river, and they shall be turned to blood. And the fish that is in the river shall die, and the river shall stink, and the Egyptians shall loathe to drink of the water of the river.

Today: In **[2018]** waters off the coast of Florida turned red. The, occurrence, known as the red tide is caused by a species of algae known as Karenia brevis. The aglae turns the water into a muddy brown and red color. A series of other rivers, lakes, and other waterways have also turned blood-red. Of course, officials have always provided an explanation that downplayed all the incidents as man-made occurrences. On **[August 1, 2011]** in the state of Texas, the O.C. Fisher Reservoir which is located in San Angelo State Park turned blood red as a result of chromatlaceae bacteria, according to fishery officials. In **[2011]**, the Jiang River in northern China turned blood red. Chinese authorities contend the red color was caused by illegal dumping by workshops operating along the river. On **[Feb. 16, 2012]** the river that runs through Beirut, Lebanon mysteriously turned red.

Again, in the year 2012 there were additional reports of waters turning red. In southwest China, officials there blamed the mysterious red waters on pollution and sand. There was evidence of sewage dumping found during an ongoing investigation. In the city of Carargue in southern France, blood-red rivers appeared there. In **[Nov. 2012]** more red tides washed up on Bondo Beach in Australia.

During **[2013]** in the eastern European city of Myjava, Slovakia, a river turned red, however, officials reported they found a broken down slaughterhouse filtering system allowing animal blood to be dumped in the river as the cause for red waters. The following year on **[July 25, 2014]** rivers in the eastern Chinese province village of Xinmeizhou were baffled when their waters turned blood-red. Two years later the same phenomenon occurred in the salty waters of Lake Urima in Iran on **[Aug. 1, 2016]**. The deep green waters turned rich red. Iranian officials blamed algae and bacteria for the unusual occurrence. In Moscow, Russia: **[Sept.2016]**. "A river in the far north of Siberia turned bright red this week residents said, leading Russians to nickname the tributary the "blood river." The government ministry's investigation centered around a possible leak of industrial waste as the cause. However, the Russian government did not provide an official statement on what caused the discoloration.

On **[June 15, 2017]** the waters of a river running through Trelawny, Jamaica morphed into blood red as the villagers stared in amazement. In Indonesia: [August 7, 2017]. The Bah Bolon River in Indonesia suddenly turned red on Monday, Aug.7 in when the normally pristine river, a source of life-giving water for irrigation and drinking, turned bright blood-red. The river, normally teeming with life, became choked with dead fish." On **[August 22, 2017]** the water fountain in San Pedro, Costa Rica turned red without an explanation.

The waters throughout the earth are also being defiled by the pollution of countless oil spills dumping millions of gallons of oil into pristine waters killing sea life. Pesticides, industrial waste, waste treatment, and illegal dumping are some of the other ways drinking water and food supplies have been endangered as it was in the days of ancient Egypt. In the coming **Age of YAH** the waters of the earth will be more contaminated by man and DIVINE Retribution from YAH. As in the case of Flint, Michigan in 2016, the city's water supply became toxic and undrinkable due to human error.

In the **[Feb./March 1992]** *Jerusalem Chronicle Newspaper* it was reported: "**[On March 24, 1989]**, the oil tanker Exxon Valdez spilled 11 million gallons of oil into Alaska's Prince William Sound killing hundreds of thousands of fishes, destroying and disrupting lifestyles. The water was no longer fit for drinking, nor was it suitable for sea life. Two years later, **[March 18, 1991]**, 55,000 gallons of light oil spewed into Santa Monica Bay covering a five square mile area after a oil tanker pierced an underground pipeline. Lt. Reed Smith of the California Department of Fish and Game reported the spill could destroy the homes of sea lions and dolphins. Once again, the water was completely defiled.

Less than four months later, a burning tanker dumped almost three million gallons of oil into the Indian Ocean off the western coast. Australian officials reported that the spill was the worst in the country's history. Countless other toxic spills have also affected the earth's water supplies off the coast of Louisiana, Texas, New York, and New Jersey. Across the globe, off the western coast of Africa in Morocco, in the Middle East, and near India, toxic spills have affected the ocean's waters. In the Sea of Japan, hundreds of red tides resembling blood appeared off the coast of Osaka Bay leaving miles of polluted trails on the sea shores.

Not only have oil spills damaged the world's water supplies, but recreational boaters, fishermen, and oceangoing shippers have continuously dumped garbage killing millions of birds, mammals, and other marine creatures each year. Crack vials, needles, and syringes and other AIDS infected debris have washed up on the world's coastline constantly.

Meanwhile, the Great Lakes—Lake Superior, Lake Michigan, Lake Huron, Lake Ontario—are infested with zebra mussel. The small inedible shell fishes have clogged power plant pipes and destroyed plant life at the bottom of the lakes, endangering the food supply for native fishes. Margaret Dochoda, a biologist at the Great Lakes Fishing Commission, said "we estimate that it will cost $4 billion in the next ten years in the Great Lakes area alone." Zebra mussels colonies can grow quickly from 30,000 to 40,000 a square yard. Experts fear nothing can be done to prevent the dark brown shell-like creatures from spreading throughout the United States.

In **[1991-92]** it was predicted that man-made disasters such as oil, toxic spills, and zebra mussels would cause future water shortages. Ms. Postel, vice president of the Worldwatch Institute, also predicted "chronic water shortages to appear in northern China, western United States, and many Third World countries." She also cited rapid growth of the world's population, high demand from underground aquifers as more reasons for a decrease in water supplies. Water is the most essential resource for human existence. [**The loss of abundant water supplies would definitely resemble a biblical plague. It would spell major hardships for this modern human civilization just as it did in the days of old when the waters of the Nile River turned blood-red in ancient Egypt**].

Plague 2

Thus saith YAH, ELOHIM of thy fathers, ELOHIM of Abraham, Isaac, and Jacob, behold I will smite all your borders with frogs in **Exodus 8:1-15.**

Today: Since **[mid-2018]** a species of frogs known as the Cuban Tree Frogs have invaded the southern State of Florida. These frogs are known to be predators that prey upon native frogs killing them. They also secrete a poisonous mucus that causes temproary blindness with extreme eye-burning. Some humans have suffered asthmatic attacks. The frogs are also known to cause seizures and uncontrollable slobbing in pet dogs and cats. Swarms of the toads have invaded homes throughout parts of Florida causing plumbing and drainage problems. Swarms of toads have also invaded power boxes causing power outages.

On **[Dec. 22, 2014]** in Big Island, Hawaii the residents found themselves in a war with the coqui frogs. The frogs had overran large portions of Big Island preventing homeowners from sleeping at night. There were reports of more than 10,000 frogs per acre in hard-hit areas. Officials were worried that small quarter-sized frogs would eat the insects needed for pollination and destroy their plant sales. Originally from Puerto Rico, these same frogs invaded California during the summer of 2017. In 1935, scientists imported a species of cane toad frogs into Australia to fight a beetle infestation. The frogs were unable to eat the beetles because they lived in the upper stalks of plants. By **[June 2016]** the cane toads grew into an invading army spreading across northern Australia. The frogs are known to travel nearly 30 miles a day. There are now an estimated 1.5 billion of these toads in the Land Down Under. During **[Nov.2016]** the island of Madagascar was fighting a similar infestation of Asian frogs. As of late 2016, there were 4 million of those toads scattered over 100 kilometers. In the **[Feb./March 1992]** *Jerusalem Chronicle Newspaper* the following information appeared: In **[1991]** a plague of frogs overran Beddarides, France keeping residents up all night with a deafening concert from 9 pm at night until 6 am in the morning.

Plague 3

Thus saith YAH, ELOHIM of thy fathers, ELOHIM of Abraham, Isaac, and Jacob, smite the dust of the land, that it may become lice throughout the land of Egypt in **Exodus 8:16-18**.

Today: The dust**[soil]** of the earth has been smitten with spores of various kinds reproducing a number of small gnats, lices, fleas, and even anthrax deriving from animals who contact the plague. Anthrax is a disease caused by bacteria that spores retain. The virus originates from contaminated soil **[dust]** causing respiratory or cardiac complications. In **[2015]** scientists reported a plague of parasitic sea lice causing major damage to the supply of salmon fish worldwide. According to statistics, since 2015 the aquaculture sector loss $1 billion a year to the outbreak of tiny sea lice infesting and devouring salmon fish farms in the U.S., Canada, Scotland, Norway, and Chile. The small parasites attach themselves to the fish and eat on them, causing death or poisoning and making it unfit to consume. Farmers warn they are in a race against time to save their $15 billion industry.

"There are not enough tools right now to allow the farmer to really effectively deal with it," said Shawn Robinson, a scientist at the Canadian Dept. of Fisheries and Oceans. Since **[2004]**, the southern African nation of Namibia has experienced several rounds of anthrax caused by bacteria in the soil and eaten by animals. 300 hippos were killed by the dust disease during that year. Again in **[2010]** 82 more hippos and 9 buffaloes died from the plague. Seven years later in **[Oct. 2017]** more than 100 more dead hippo carcases, lying on their side, floated in the river with their legs sticking in the air.

In **[August 2017]** the Texas Animal Health Commission found that dust had contaminated 5 cows on a Crockett County farm.

The southeast Asian nations of Pakistan, India, and even China have also experienced a lice infestation in their poultry industries during **[2017]**. There were also confirmed reports of the plague in the countries of Egypt, South Africa, and throughout countries in Europe.

In **[2016]** Russia fought a mysterious anthrax outbreak caused by a global heat wave. In the remote corner of Siberia the frozen soil **[dust]** where reindeer carcases were once buried beneath the snow and ice now have become deadly spores. Without reversing the trend, northern Russia could face a pandemic in the coming decades.

"The soil in Yamal Peninsula is like a giant freezer," said Jean-Michel Claverice, of the National Center for Scientific Research in France. "Those are very, very, good conditions for bacteria to remain alive for a very long time." The infectious spores in the dust could spread the disease across reindeer grazing areas. Hoping to head off the outbreak, Russian authorities planned to kill 250,000 reindeers.

In **[2015]** in the Chinese Yunnan province, an outbreak of dust-spores causing anthrax in citizens erupted after the slaughter of cattle. The health scare caused itching, and blisters on their hands and arms. The plague started with cattle, horses, sheeps, and camels before infecting humans.

Meanwhile, scientists have reported an uptick in head lice worldwide. The new super head lice are immune to common medical treatment. In the U.S., California parents became concerned after an outbreak of head lice among children in the Santa Rosa County School District. The same disruption occurred when parents confronted the board of Thunder Bay Catholic District School.

In Salt Lake City, Utah the PTA **[Parent's Teachers Association]** asked the Hawaii State Dept. of Health & Education to reexamine its policy for dealing with head lice. Those affected by the head lice experience discomfort, distress, skin diseases, sores, or itching. There are 14 million American people affected annually by this pesty-itching hair problem, even in **[2015]**.

In the **[Feb./March 1992]** *Jerusalem Chronicle Newspaper* the following information appeared: "Beginning in 1984, a Bubonic plague carried by wild animals appeared to be spreading across several Western states infecting a record number of humans in the United States, William Rosser, state veterinarian for the West Texas region, reported. "This is the worst year on record, he continued. In medieval Europe this disease killed a third of Medieval Europe, it has spread steadily to at least 14 western states, including New Mexico, Arizona, Colorado, and Texas." He also said a record 40 human cases were reported in the U.S. last year.

Plague 4

Thus saith YAH, ELOHIM of thy fathers, ELOHIM of Abraham, Isaac, and Jacob, "I will make a distinction between MY people and your people. Tomorrow this sign shall come to pass.'" And YHWH did so. Heavy swarms of insects invaded Pharaoh's palace and into his servant's houses, and into all the land of Egypt: the land was corrupted by reason of the swarms of flies. **Exodus 8:23-24**.

Today: During **[Nov. 2004]** millions, possibly tens of millions, of locusts originating in parts of Senegal, Mauritania, and Mali on the western coast of Africa have swarmed into Egypt threatening important agriculture farmlands along the way. The multitude of these small insects created clouds of reddish-brown dust as they traveled eastward. UN Food and Agriculture Organization coordinator Christian Pantenius said the swarms were part of an infestation in West Africa caused by westward winds that blew them across the Sahara. The UN spokesman also said that the swarm seems to be heading towards the Red Sea where they breed during November and March. The good news was the swarms appeared not to be a threat to agriculture in the fertile Nile Valley.

One decade later in **[Nov.2014]** an extraordinary plague of fruit flies are surfaced in various sections of the United Kingdom during that winter season. The scientists blamed the swarms of flies on the unusually warm winter.

King David once said in **Psalms 74:16-17:** "The day is thine, the night also is thine: YOU [YAH] has prepared the light and the sun. YOU[YAH] has set all the borders of the earth: YOU[YAH] has made summer and winter." Therefore we, the Israelite observers today, realize that these modern-day plagues are temporary DIVINE signs from the everlasting ELOHIM-YAH right before our eyes.

In **[July 2014]** the British town of Avonmouth, Bristol was invaded by swarms of flies causing residents to eat and live in mosquito nets for refuge. The flies invaded despite attempts to kill them with electric traps and spraying. Authorities believe the infestation started when flies gathered on bales of damaged biofuel. The British Environmental Agency suspended the company's permit to store biofuel at the nearby Avonmouth Dock.

In **[2017]** the U.S. cities of San Francisco, Cincinnati each experienced an outbreak of swarms of various flies. At the same time**[July 2017]**, swarms of fish flies resembling a tornado covered the skies of Saskatchewan in western Canada. In the region of Manitoba, in central Canada, swarms of fish flies appear every year blanketing the areas with insects that smell like dead fish. Also in **[the summer of 2017]** authorities in the U.S. and the UK were forced to deal with swarms of mosquitoes spreading the Nile River virus. People bitten by the mosquitoes experience a fever, headaches, body aches, joint pain, vomiting, diarrhea, rashes, and even death in extreme cases. In the United States alone there were nearly 2,000 cases of people being affected by the disease-carrying insects.

In the **[Feb./March 1992]** *Jerusalem Chronicle Newspaper* reported this following information: "As early as **[1991]** Mexican fruit flies were discovered in southern San Diego County. Those Mexican fruit flies were similar to the Mediterranean fruit flies which injected eggs into soft fruit ruining the crop. The flies were a threat to California's billion dollar agricultural economy. In **[1990]** the Africanized killer bees were discovered in southern Texas. Government scientists discovered the first swarms of dreaded flies during that year. The Africanized killer bees were descendants of bees that escaped a breeding experimentation in Brazil in **[1957]**, according to government officials. The bees were known to kill livestocks, humans, and even domestic bees of a lesser species."

Nearly two decades later in rural parts of western Africa in **[2017]**, malaria is still a common parasitic disease which is contacted by bites from swarms of female anopheles mosquitoes. In other parts of Africa, such as the Democratic Republic of Congo, Equatorial Guinea, Eritea, and Ethiopia, there have been plagues of malaria-carrying mosquitoes. Swarms of various types of flies are afflicting all 193 nations of the earth worldwide during the 21st century, and with the increase of global warming, these infestations will certainly increase in frequency and severity.

Plague 5

Thus saith YAH, ELOHIM of the Hebrews, MINE HAND is upon thy cattle which is in the field, upon horses, upon the asses, upon the camels, upon the oxen, and upon the sheep: there shall be a very grievous murrain. **Exodus 9:1-7.**

Today: On **[Feb. 21, 2001]** officials in the United Kingdom declared an outbreak of foot-and-mouth disease throughout their country. Since then, the disease spread like a bush fire among farm animals—mainly sheep and cattle—reaching a total of 1,461 confirmed cases by **[April 20,2001]**. To halt a continuing pandemic the United Kingdom, along with the British military, killed more than 2 million animals. There was also one confirmed case across the English Channel in the Netherlands. The disease has also affected horses, donkeys(asses), sheeps, and cattle worldwide.

During the decade **[2004-2014]** there were several unexplained disease outbreaks among camels in the African nations of Mali, Niger, Ethiopia, Sudan, Somalia, and Saudi Arabia. At least 16 to 20 million camels in North Africa and the Middle East were mainly affected. Camels there are used for their meat, milk, wool, and skins. On **[March 30, 2012]** a new strain of the foot-and-mouth disease threatened modern Egypt and Sudan. The strain had never been seen before in those northeast African countries. Egyptian farmers lost 10,000 of their livestock to the plague.60,000 other animals were affected during the same outbreak. Another 6.3 million buffalos and cattle along with 7.5 million sheeps and goats were also at risk. The foot-and-mouth disease is an highly infectious viral disease that travels through the air. It targets animals with clovenfoot hooves. According to scientists, the plague lives in animal feces and urine for up to 3 days in the soil during summer. The virus can live up to 20 weeks in hay and straw. When left untreated, the disease causes animals to suffer pneumonia, arthritis, and tendinitis.

In **[2017]** the Ministry for Primary Industries **[MPI]** on the South Island of New Zealand detected a cattle disease known as *mycoplasma bovis* in 14 cows among their diary herd. About 150 others on the property showed signs of infection.

The foot-and-mouth disease became a pandemic since **[2009]** in the country of Nepal. A country of 28 million located between India and China. The disease has become a major concern because animals, especially among bulls which openly roam through the streets. The virus from these animals live in their manure for up to 2 days. It can spread to humans through clothes, contact, and breathing the air of infected animals. The European Commission has sent veterinarians to Nepal to gain field and clinical diagnosis experience and training in preparation for a possible global outbreak. More than 600 veterinarians from 50 countries have been through the programs. The disease does not kill, but it effects the animal's reproduction, drooling at the mouth, mouth lesions, and blistering feet. The virus can also get into the animal's blood, their milk, meat, saliva, nasal, and semen discharge.

Anthrax: Domestic and wild animals such as cattle, camels, oxens, and sheeps are infected when they breathe in or ingest spores in the contaminated soil, plants, or water. Anthrax is the most common in animals, but it can also be seen in people exposed to tissues from the diseased animals. People become infected with anthrax when the spores get into the body. The spores become active bacteria and spread inside the body. In **[2015]** traces of anthrax were found in the farming lands of Central and South America, sub-Sahara Africa, Central and Southwest Asia, Southern and Eastern Europe, and the Carribeans. Anthrax transmission occurs when people breathe, touch contaminated animal products like wool, bone, hair, or hides. The infection also occurs when the bacteria enters a cut or scratch in the skin.

In the **[Feb./March 1992]** *Jerusalem Chronicle Newspaper* the following article was reported: "Since **[1991]** U.S. government scientists have known of a virus similar to the AIDS virus which is common in U.S. cattle". The virus, known as BIV, bovine immunodeficiency, is spread through the blood of an animal's immune system. Evidence indicating that the virus could be transmitted to humans through the food chain had not been confirmed. However back in the early 1990s, officials did warn of the potential economic danger the virus represented for the $55 billion U.S. cattle and diary industry. In a war against pestilences, farmers have relied heavily on numerous drugs, some approved by the FDA(Food and Drug Administration) and others not, to halt the spread of diseases among U.S. livestock for the past 30 years.

Plague 6

Thus saith YAH, ELOHIM of the Hebrews, unto Moses and unto Aaron, Take to you handfuls of ashes of the furnace, and let Moses sprinkle it toward the heaven in the sight of Pharaoh. And it shall become small dust in all the land of Egypt, and shall be a boil braking forth with blains upon man, and upon beast. And the magicians (scientists) could not stand before Moses because of the boils; for the boil was upon the magicians, and upon all Egyptians. **Exodus 9:8-11**.*(This was a continuation of diseases originating from the soil to animals onto humans. Once transmitted, humans can infect each other through interaction)*

Today: A boil or furuncle is an infection of hair follicle caused by bacteria named staphylococcus aureus. Boils usually resolve by themselves but severe or recurring cases require medical attention, and oftentimes treatment. In the United Kingdom, a nation of 62 million, **[Between 1995 and 2010]** at least 164,461 individuals visited their doctors for boils and abscess. In **[2010]** alone, at least 280,000 Britons consulted primary care for boils and abscesses. Boils are usually found on the buttocks, abdomen, arms, hands, and posterior thigh.

In the small village of Setting, Alaska, which is located in the southwestern corner of the state, the Alaska Division of Public Health recorded at least 115 residents who were afflicted with at least one boil on their bodies. This comprised 25 percent of the villagers, including 2 who were hospitalized. This occurred between **[Jan. 1, 1995—Dec. 12, 1996]**.

Another form of boils is Staph infection. This infection is catagious and transmitted by contact with an infected sore, a wound, or a cut. The ailment causes a buildup of pus, redness in the skin, swelling, and pain in the affected area.

Toxic Shock Syndrome (TSS) is an illness caused by toxins secreted by staph. TSS causes fever, vomiting, diarrhea, and muscle aches. Eventually the plague causes low-blood pressure which has caused shock and death in several instances. This disease usually occur in menstruating women who use tampons.

In Lebanon **[2017]** an outbreak known as the "Aleppo boils" occurred among the northern Syrian population. The plague was spread by sand flies and transmitted to Arab inhabitants. Doctors in Lebanon have tried to control outbreak in midst of the Syrian civil war.

The following information was written in the **[Feb./March 1992]** *Jerusalem Chronicle Newspaper.* "In **[1991]** the World Health Organization announced that 10 million people could be infected by the AIDS virus by the year 2000. The AIDS virus causes an inflammatory swelling of flesh with sores that cover the entire body while contaminated blood causes a slow death that could take up to five years. In the 1990s, the epidemic threatened the health of all nations on earth. The National Commission on AIDS criticized the U.S. government, accusing President George H.W. Bush of failing to take the necessary steps to prevent the spread of the infection. At that time, researchers reported that one pint of contaminated blood could contain enough virus to infect 2 million people. Studies also revealed that although infected people appear well outwardly, the virus continues to reproduce infected cells inside the body. The virus can also be transmitted through blood plasma."

7th Plague

Thus saith YAH, ELOHIM of the Hebrews, I will cause it to rain a very grievous hail, such as hath not been seen in Egypt since the foundations thereof, even until now. Exodus 9:13-25.

Today: On [**October 9, 2017**] a massive thunderstorm struck parts of Johannesburg, Gauteng, East and West Rand, and Roodeport, South Africa with lightnings, hailstones, flooding, fires, and tornadoes causing one death and leaving scores of residents homeless. The Monday afternoon hailstorm left a trail of destruction that caused major power outages, ripped off roofs at a primary school, caused several fatal car accidents, and left thousands without their homes. The massive storm downed many trees with strong winds, prompted flash floods washed out roads, and overturned cars. The storm shutdown the Yaldwyn Power Plant Station, which is located near OK Tambo International Airport in Kempton Park, causing major outages.

A major hailstorm also hit parts of the country of Turkey during [**July 2017**].

On [**September 2, 2017**] severe weather rolled through central North Carolina uprooting scores of trees, damaging cars, buildings, homes, and properties. The large 70-mph wind gusts and golfball-sized hailstorm downed power lines causing major outages. In Holly Springs, North Carolina a lightning bolt struck a home setting it on fire. In the United States, a hailstorm devastated parts of the state of Wyoming on [**July 13, 2017**]. Two days later on [**July 15, 2017**] parts of Italy was struck with a hailstorm shattering glass, destroying properties, automobiles, and prompting tornado funnels. During [**June 2017**] in the far east, an American-owned AUS lotus tourism park located in midst of the Tanghe province of China was destroyed by a hailstorm causing huge losses for the uninsured business, costing $2.2 million A year before in [**June 2016**] 125-mph tornado winds along with heavy rains and a hailstorm struck the eastern province of Jiangsu, China killing nearly 100 people and injuring 800. It was the worst tornado to hit the region in 50 years. Roofs were blown off, walls collapsed, cars were submerged in canals, leaving broken windows everywhere, leaving $410 million in property damage. Hail is formed during thunderstorms when fast currents carry water droplets up in the sky where they freeze into hailstones. As more waters surround the droplets, these lumps of ice become heavy and fall onto the ground as hail. These hailstones can kill.

Kansas City was hit with a major hailstorm on [**February 28, 2017**]. Baseball-sized hail pummeled the city of Omaha, Nebraska was pounded twice with severe storms. The first one came on [**May 8, 2017**] and the second one came [**June 30, 2017**], causing $1.4 billion in damages. The May 8 storm also touched down in Denver, Colorado. Believe it or not, hailstorms surpassed wildfires as the state's costliest natural disaster, leaving a trail of $1.4 billion in damages. Weeks later, another hailstorm hit the suburbs of Minneapolis costing that city $1 billion in losses. The same storm extended from the state of Minnesota to Texas to Virginia to New York, leaving $2.5 billion in total losses. In Texas alone, severe weather made its way across the northern part of the state, hammering Collin and Dention counties with its goftball-sized hail, damaging homes, cars, and businesses that same year in [**2017**].

Hail is one of the most damaging weather phenomenons in the U.S. every year. From [**2010** to 2016] insurance industry sources reported $8 to $10 billion in property and agriculture losses. The costliest hailstorm in U.S. history came on [October 5, 2010] when Phoenix, Arizona was hit with a hailstorm causing $2.8 billion in damages. In the U.S., the worst states hit with hailstorms in the year [2014] were Kansas, Iowa, Pennsylvania, South Carolina, Nebraska, Missouri, Colorado, Illinois, and Texas.

Continuing during this same decade of [2010—2020], countless hailstorms struck many nations around the globe. On [July 12, 2011] beachgoers in Norosibirsk, Russia were caught off guard when a sudden storm with golfball-sized hail swept across the area. In [June 2014], several powerful thunderstorm systems moved across western Europe pelting the countries of France, Belgium, and northern Germany with damaging hail. Two weeks later on [July 8, 2014] another hailstorm struck Sofia, Bulgaria, costing 51 million euros. A year before on [July 27-28, 2013] a series of powerful hailstorms hit the cities of Pfortzheim, Baden-Wurttemburg, Wolfsburg, Hanover, Lower Saxony in Germany. The hailstorm caused large amounts damage, costing $3.6 billion. In the city of Keutlingen alone, 70 people were injured. Elsewhere in [2013] several villages in the state of Andhra Pradesh, India were severely damaged by hailstorms, killing 9, and leveling homes, crops, and livestock. The list of damaging hailstorms goes on and on throughout the seven continents of the earth affecting all 193 nations. *(I would never complete the remaining three plagues if I continued to document each and every hailstorm that has, and continues to, afflict the nations of the earth. So, I'll just name a few more incidents. However, YHWH will continue to pour out HIS Judgements upon the nations of the earth today as in the days of old.).*

On [May 18, 2000] the Chicago, Illinois area experienced the worst hailstorm in 30 years. The metropolis was struck with golfball-sized hail that caused $1/2 billion in damages. Roofs, cars, patios, furniture, skylights, and windows were destroyed by the storm.

Let's look back 40 years again. In the **Feb./March 1992 edition of the *Jerusalem Chronicle Newspaper*** these natural phenomenons occurred. In [July 1991] lightning struck the Alaskan interior igniting 270,000 acres of forestry. Dry weather and constant summer heat had baked the area one month earlier. A total of 152 wildfires burned throughout the state threatening the ozone layer with damage of carbon dioxide and dumping acid rain in surrounding states. Some of the Alaskan forest fires have tripled in size and conditions are ripe for more fires to reoccur in the near future. [In 2018-019], the conditions are now the same in California as well.

In [1988], the Yellowstone National Park was struck with a lightning storm that charred nearly a million acres of forestry. The giant fires extended from Wyoming, New Mexico, Montana, and reached as far south as Iowa. The state of California has experienced similar forest fires during [1989] and [1990]. Thunderstorms have triggered other massive natural disasters throughout the earth in recent years, such as mudslides, flooding, property damages, and deaths.

The following information was also reported in the [Feb./March 1992] *Jerusalem Chronicle Newspaper:* "On [April 30,1991], Bangleedash experienced a destructive cyclone which killed 250,000 men, women, and children, causing the prolonged horror of hunger, homelessness, and sickness. UN relief workers fear people in remote villages and offshore islands are quietly starving because no one knows of their plight.

Thunderstorms triggered an avalanche in Tione, Italy early last month [January 1992] burying scores and injuring an untold number of schoolchildren in the Italian city. Snow, mud, and stones covered portions of the city. [Meanwhile in America during the same time] floods devastated north-central Mississippi destroying tens of millions of dollars worth of farmlands, property, and livestock. The same occurred in the states of Oregon, Washington, and parts of northern California."

In [2019] and in the decades coming, these DIVINE ACTS of YAH shall continue to occur in frequencies, intensities, and ferocities that shall ultimately usher in the time zone when the **NAME of YHWH is KING** and **HIS POWER** is known, and seen, by all mankind, even HIS cloudy pillar in day and the pillar of fire in night, throughout the realms of all existence.

8th Plague

Thus saith YAH ELOHIM of the Hebrews, I will bring the locusts into thy coast: And they shall cover the face of the earth, that one cannot be able to see the earth: and they shall eat the residue of that which escaped, which remaineth unto you from the hail, and shall eat every tree which grows for you out of the field. **Exodus 10:1-6.**

Today: Swarms of locust consisting of millions covered several parts of southern Russia in 2017 beginning in East Kazahhstan. Reoccurring swarms of locust also covered the state of Dagestan during the same year. Four years prior to that plague, an infestation occurred in **June 2013** with swarms of locust covering 270,000 square miles in the same southern Russian state of Dagestan. The swarms of locusts created dark clouds that covered the sky blocking the sun, turning the brightness of day into darkness. Residents were forced to stop driving their vehicles and other activities. The situation created momentary chaos throughout the city. There were car wrecks, and loss of income. The infestation was of biblical proportions according to all observers. Meanwhile in the year of 2013, the island of Madagascar, which is located off the east coast of Africa, was afflicted with swarms of locust that ate up 50 percent of the rice and grain crops causing the worst plague of food shortages in 60 years. Millions of locust swarmed the island. A locust plague struck parts of war-torn Syria in **June of 2017**. The plague, which first appeared in 2016 in midst of the devastating civil war, grew consuming 60 percent of their wheat, barley, figs, and olives. In **September 2017** swarms of locust also hit the Caribbean island of Trinidad.

Several cities on the east coast of the United States were hit with cicadas infestations in the **spring of 2017**. These insects, known as the 17-year locust, typically re-appear every thirteen to seventeen years, damaging fruit trees, shrubs, a multitude of other type trees such as ash, beech, dogwood, pine, firs, willows, flowers, and vegetables before shedding their skeleton shells. The swarms of the noisy vibrating locust invaded northern Virginia, Illinois, Washington, D.C., Maryland, and Delaware. In Bowie, Maryland the cicadas took over trees throughout the city for two straight years in **2016** and **2017**. One year prior **in 2016**, massive swarms of cicadas numbering 1.5 million per acre were seen throughout the city.

From **March to May of 2013** swarms of desert locusts, which are the most dangerous species among a dozen different kinds, threatened 32 million square kilometers extending across 50 countries from West Africa to India. On **March 4, 2013** swarms of locusts crossed into Israel from neighboring Egypt raising fears that the biblical land of Israel would be struck before Passover season. Israel sent squadrons of planes into the skies to spray pesticide over agricultural fields to avert the dangers. Some scientists have blamed the increase frequency of locust infestations on climate change. In **2003-2004** swarms of locust invaded the west African country of Mali causing educational hardships that closed schools until the plague subsided. The plague also caused temporary unemployment for poor parents who depended upon agricultural work to feed their families.

. In the **[Feb./March 1992] edition** of the *Jerusalem Chronicle Newspaper* the following excerpts appeared in an article written by me titled, *Natural, and Man-made Disasters Resemble Biblical Plagues:* "The grasshoppers are so thick that the ground literally moves," said Michelle McLawthorn, spokeswoman of the Florida Department of Agriculture. Ms. McLawthorn was referring to the swarms of grasshoppers that had descended upon the counties of Pasco, Hernando, and Hillsborough in Florida, near the heart of the state's $1 billion-a-year citrus growing industry.

The swarming grasshoppers appear to be unstoppable. Farmers have used all available pesticides against the legions of grasshoppers, but the insects have developed immunity to the spraying. Scientists hope to end the biblical plague by bombarding the hatchings of grasshoppers with more toxic pesticides."

9th Plague

Thus saith YAH ELOHIM of the Hebrews, Stretch out thine hand towards heaven, there shall be darkness over the land of Egypt, even darkness which may be felt. **Exodus 10:21.**

Today: During the past 40 years there has been a minimal of 31 solar eclipses throughout various hemispheres of the world that caused the brightness of noonday to transcend into thick darkness during daytime. A solar eclipse occurs when the Moon passes between the Sun and the Earth. It causes the Moon to fully or partially block the sun causing darkness. Below are the respective dates when YAH, the CREATOR of the heavens and earth, has caused solar eclipses to appear before all mankind.

40-Year Record of Solar Eclipses

July 13,2018, Feb. 15,2018, Aug. 21,2017,March 9,2016,March 20,2015,Oct.25,2014,April 29,2014,Nov.3,2013,May 10,2013,Nov.3,2013,May 10,2013, Nov.13,2012, May 20,2012, Nov.25,2011, Jan.4,2011,July 11, 2010, Jan.15, 2010, July 22, 2009, Jan.26,2009, Aug.1,2008, Sept.11, 2007, March 29,2006, Oct.3, 2005, April 8,2005, Oct.14, 2004, April 19, 2004, April 19, 2004, Nov.23,2003. Dec.4,2002, June 21,2001,Aug. 11,1999, July 11, 1991, April 29, 1976.

Another major cause for daytime skies becoming abnormally darkened has been huge mushroom clouds of ash and debris blanketing and darkening skies. In the past 40 years thick carpets of debris from volcanoes have created deadly mixtures of fiery volcanic fragments with gases that have completed darkened daytime skies in many countries around the world.

On January 22 and 23, 2018, two powerful volcanoes in the Pacific basin known as the Ring of Fire erupted. The first mountain of fire to erupt was the Mayon volcano near Legazpi City, southeast of the capital of Manila, Philippines. The volcano spewed fountains of red-hot lava and massive ash plumes into the sky forcing 50,000 people to evacuate. The explosive eruption came at noonday and plunged several nearby villages into total darkness. Rivers of red--hot lava also flowed down the mountain slopes for two miles. When Mount Pinatubo erupted in 1991, plumes of ash darkened the skies in villages throughout surrounding area.

The next day of **Jan. 23** Mount Kusatsu-Shirane, which is located above a ski resort 120 miles northwest of Tokyo, burst into flames, spewing volcano rocks, red-hot lava, and a curtain of black smoke throughout the area. The sunlight was blocked out turning day into night. The same thing happened in Japan during **Sept. 2014** when Mount Ontake erupted.

During **April 2015** Mount Calbuco in southern Chile erupted sending columns of ash-smoke about 15 kilometers into the blue skies. A deadly flow of ash and hot air spewed covering the area and causing a daytime blackout of the sun..

In 2017, Mount Shiveluch in Russia exploded causing the same phenomenon of turning daytime skies into darkness. The same was true when the Villarrica volcano erupted in Chile. The eruptions of Mount Sinabung and Mount Agung in Indonesia also blanketed nearby areas with darkness. Also in **2017** the Turrialba volcano erupted in Costa Rica. Next door in Mexico, the Popocatopeti and Volcande Colima volcanoes exploded blanketing the skies with plumes of ash and blocking out sunlight. There were also volcanic explosions causing darkness when Mount Kilauea burst into flames in **2013**. Three years earlier in 2010, the Eyjafgallojkull [Ey-jaf-gal-loj-kull] volcano erupted on the island of Iceland. The massive clouds of ash smoke disrupted air-traffic in the skies above. On the earth beneath, the massive plumes of ash-smoke caused darkness.

There are at least 1,500 other known volcanoes scattered across the seven continents of earth. With each new eruption, the reality of daylight being turned into blinding darkness by plumes of ash-smoke is repeated over and over again.

In the **[Feb./March 1992] edition of the** *Jerusalem Chronicle Newspaper* the following story appeared: "**[In 1991]**, huge mushroom clouds of ash and debris exploded from Mt. Pinatubo in the Philippines in early June, blanketing a 25 mile area and darkening the skies, turning day into darkness. The thick carpet of debris came from the 4,795-foot volcano that had been inactive for over 6 centuries. The deadly mixture of the fiery volcanic fragments and gases completely darkened the U.S.Clark Air Force base below the volcano site. Over 50,000 people had to evacuate their homes, farms, and servicemen fled U.S military bases. "It rained Ash leaves light from Manila to this point, said R Del phe Wolcgnia eruption" on a

10th Plague

Thus saith YAH ELOHIM of the Hebrews, all the firstborn in the land of Egypt shall die, from the firstborn of Pharaoh that sitteth upon the throne, even unto the firstborn of maidervants that are behind the mill, and all the firstborn of beast. **Exodus 11:4-10.**

Today: In **early 2016** an infectious mosquito-borne epidemic known as the Zika Virus resurfaced in Latin America, Puerto Rico, and the southern United States causing brain damage, deformities, and abnormal heads in newborn babies. The mysterious plague rapidly spreaded among Brazilian women prompting health officials to tell women to avoid having children. Brazilian President Dilma Rouseff said there was no medical defense against the virus then called for a crusade to halt the spread of the disease. The Pan American Health Organization, which is a division of the World Health Organization, also advised all women of child-bearing age to avoid conception, thus cutting off all firstborns in the affected countries. Some health officials disagreed with the policy of avoiding pregnancies, instead they called for extreme caution in avoiding mosquito bites.

American health officials issued health alerts to citizens living in Puerto Rico, the U.S. Virgin Islands, the American Samoa, and the southern states of the Gulf Coast. 350 people in the U.S. were diagnosed with the infection, including 36 pregnant women. Most of the cases occurred on the Puerto Rico island of 3.5 million. American tourists, especially women travellers, who visited affected areas were the most affected. They were told to avoid pregnancy for 8-weeks after returning home. Men tourists were told not to impregnate a woman for 6 months if they had any signs of the virus. In **2013-2014** there was a Zika virus outbreak in French Polynesia. In the mid-1950s, the virus appeared in western Africa.

There are several other types of diseases plaguing babies when they first arrive in this world. For example, within European Jewish population there is a plague known as the Tay-Sachs Disease. The disease causes severe mental and developmental retardation when the child is 4 to 8 months old. The child usually dies between the ages of 5 to 8. Another childhood plague is the Niemain-Pick Disease(Type A). This mysterious ailment is a disorder that affects a newborn liver, spleen, lungs, and brain. Death usually occur before the child even reaches the age of 18-months. The list of firstborn plagues continues with another disease known as Trisomy 18 and 13. This disease is also a genetic disorder in new babies. This little known sickness causes different kinds of birth defects and mental retardation. Almost every organ in the newborn's system is damaged. Most of the babies afflicted with this ailment die at the age of 1. Cystic Fibrosis is another chronic illness that is fatal to newborns. The ailment prevents breathing in newborns. Graves Disease is another fatal disease occurring in newborns that causes thyroid problems. The disease then affects the baby's heartbeat, blood pressure, and results in heart failure. Oftentimes when the disease appears in the pregnant mother the outcome is a stillbirth child, a miscarriage, or pre-term birth. The genetic disorder that causes seizures, loss of vision, and a loss of motor skills in newborn's nervous system is called Batten Disease. All newborns with the disease usually die by their late teens or early 20s.

Health officials have also discovered another genetic disease that's called the Fragile X Syndrome. This sickness causes autism, seizures, and facial deformities. Doctors also cited the Gaucher Disease which is a rare disorder that causes a buildup of harmful substances in the body damaging the spleen, liver, bones, and marrow. As you can see there are numerous diseases affecting firstborns worldwide in the 21st century. The few childhood/firstborn diseases I mentioned serve only as a small example of the genetic, hemolyic diseases, neonatal infections, krabbe diseases, meningococcal diseases now plaguing newborns world-wide during **the time zone of the iron and miry clay kingdoms** in the latter-days.

In the [**Feb./March 1992**] issue of the *Jerusalem Chronicle Newspaper* the following article was reported; "A mysterious disease call crib death has puzzled doctors and health experts for nearly ten years. The death occurs while infants are asleep in the cribs. Most mothers have reported that their babies are in good health before death consumes their newborn. The disease has primarily plagued the white community, striking the rich as well as the poor.

The World Health Organization also reports that 7.6 million children worldwide are dying from diarrhea, respiratory infections, malaria, and other vaccine preventable diseases. The problem has become critical enough for UNICEF to request a "World Summit for Children" in September. The summit is to be held at UN headquarters in New York. "Developing countries spend a total of $145 billion a year on their military establishments," James Grant, executive director of UNICEF, the UN Children's Fund, reported. "7,000 a day die of dehydration caused by diarrhea, 6,000 die of pneumonia for a total of 7.6 million." Grant said more than 100 countries would attend the summit.

Eventually, these continuous disasters—both natural and man-made—will become so burdensome and expensive that YAH will alter and crush this present world's geopolitical, economic, and ecosystem, forcing them to "Let HIS People return back to the land of Canaan to serve HIM." Along with the 10 mentioned plagues all nations will also be afflicted with earthquakes, mudslides, wildfires, floods, tornadoes, hurricanes, tsunamis, volcanoes, earth-opening sinkholes, snowstorms, rainstorms, heatwaves, arctic cold fronts, droughts, famines, viruses, diseases, and other forms of unheard of DIVINE chastisements.

Last but not least, the final time zone of unrighteous heathenistic rulership will closeout with the downfall of **the kingdoms of iron and miry clay toes** during the era termed the **"latter-days"**. It will be a time of spiritual darkness, moral gloomiest, and physical warfare. This DIVINE chastisement is better known to most bible readers as the Battle of Armageddon. This conflict is caused by the uncircumcised thoughts, actions, and plots of the covetous world leaders. Their lust for oil wealth, continued terrorism, and each side's desire to conquer Jerusalem will actually bring this DIVINE, and man-made, disaster upon the nations of the earth. However, according to **YHWH's DIVINE strategy,** it will surely usher in **the Age of YAH** by assembling the world powers into the Middle East for **the Battle of Har Megiddo.**

The Battle of Armageddon

"For lo, I begin to bring evil on the city which bears MY Name, and should you expect to go unpunished? You shall not go unpunished: for I will call for a sword upon all the inhabitants of the earth, saith YAH of host[sabaot]. Therefore prophecy against them all these words, and say unto them, YAH shall roar from his holy habitation: HE shall mightily roar upon his habitation; he shall give a shout; as they that tread the grapes, against all the inhabitants of the earth. A noise shall come even to the ends of the earth; for YAH has a controversy with the nations, he will plead with all flesh; he will give them that are wicked to the sword, saith YHWH. Thus saith YAH of hosts; Behold, evil shall go forth from nation to nation, and a great whirlwind shall be raised up from the coasts of the earth. And the slain of YAH shall be at that day from one end of the earth; they shall not be lamented, neither gathered, nor buried; they shall be dung upon the ground. **[Jeremiah 25:29-33]**.

In the latter-days the Spirit of God Almighty(**El Shaddai—The STONE cut out without Hands—**) will cause the kings of the earth [**world powers**] to converge upon the region known as Ceole-Syria [modern Syria-Iraq] which is located in the eastern portion of the holy land. That area extends from the Golan Heights in Israel over to the Tigris and Euphrates River in ancient Mesopotamia. This location will be the site for global conflicts to control Jerusalem, the natural resources in the region, and to establish dominion and stability in the most turbulent landscape on earth. The Battle of Armageddon is actually an ongoing series of major wars that will ultimately lead to the destruction of **the kingdoms of iron and miry clay toes.**

At the end of these wars, the descendants of the ancient Afro-Asiatic Hebrews will be allowed to return from captivity among the nations to re-establish the kingdom of YHWH on earth Millions of people will die during these wars, countless others will be maimed, kings will be overthrown, and kingdoms will rise up against neighboring kingdoms. The inhabitants of this region will be consumed by famine, diseases, human oppression, and other forms of human misery.

In this part of the chapter we are closing out the Age of Human Idolatry and ushering in **The Age of YHWH**. Now, we will begin to look at the series of modern wars that are taking place in the land promised to the seed of Abraham, Isaac, and Jacob. For the record, there have been continuous wars in the land of Syria since the time zone of **the head of gold** down to today's time zone of **iron and miry clay toes**. It is these repetitive conflicts, that will increase in frequency and severity, that will surely spark the final wars known as the Battle of Armageddon. Man's evil lust for covetous oil wealth, their desire to exalt their idolatrous religions of wood and stone, and their disregard for human life will cause YAH to intervene for HIS Name's sake and for the sake of HIS people Israel. Until then, each war in the region will serve as the Countdown to Armageddon.

The 40-year Countdown To Armageddon

"In that day, a great tumult from YHWH shall fall upon them, and everyone shall snatch at the hand of another, and everyone shall raise his hand against everyone else's hand." **[Zechariah 14:13].**

1980s: On October 23, 1983 two truck bombs struck barracks where international peace-keeping forces were stationed in Lebanon, killing 241 U.S. soldiers who were a part of the peacekeepers. On December 21, 1988, a Pan Am passenger jet with 259 people on board exploded over Lockerbie, Scotland. Libyan agent Abdelbaset al-Megrahi was charged with the terrorist act of mass murder. The incident was directly connected with the ongoing Mideast conflict.

"In that day, a great tumult from YHWH shall fall upon them, and everyone shall snatch at the hand of another, and everyone shall raise his hand against everyone else's hand." **[Zechariah 14:13].**

1980-1990: Iran-Iraq War: The Iran-Iraq War started on September 22, 1980 when Iraq, led by President Saddam Hussein, a Sunni Muslim, attacked the new Shiite cleric led government of Ayatollah Ruhollah Khomeini in neighboring Iran. Hussein, sensing a weakness and instability in the new regime, took control of the oil-rich Khuzestan Province inside Iranian territory and the Shatt-al-Arab waterway which leads into the Persian Gulf. The Iraqi president feared the Shiite theocratic victory in Iran could cause unrest among its majority Shiite population. Sunni Muslims comprised only 30 percent of the population although they ruled Iraq for centuries. 60 percent of Iraqi citizens are Shiites.

Iraq was backed by Saudi Arabia, the Arab League, and the United States. The Iranians were supplied by China, Syria, North Korea, Libya, and Israel. The U.S. also funneled weapons to the Iranians as well. After early Iraqi gains from 1980 to 1982, the Iraqis lost the ground it had captured. Iraq announced itself ready to negotiate. Iran refused and the war continued nonstop for another six years. The large scale World War I type conflict, with 110,000 Iranian soldiers against 200,000 Iraqi fighters, raged until Iran agreed to a ceasefire in 1988. Nearly 1 million people died, half of them soldiers and the other half civilians. Hundreds of thousands were injured. Both sides claimed victory as the ceasefire continued until 1990.

After that, Iraqi President Saddam Hussein ordered an invasion of the small oil-rich Persian Gulf kingdom of Kuwait. During this war, Hussein finally agreed to a peace settlement between the two Middle East powerhouses. The war had been costly and destructive for both kingdoms. Both Iran and Iraq, **miry clay kingdoms**, have some of world's largest petroleum and natural gas supplies beneath their soil. This war eventually led to the downfall of Iraqi President Saddam Hussein and the ascension of the Shiite Islamic regime in Iran. After this war, Iran and the Soviet Union, which had changed into Russia, developed a close strategic partnership.

"In that day, a great tumult from YHWH shall fall upon them, and everyone shall snatch at the hand of another, and everyone shall raise his hand against everyone else's hand." [Zechariah 14:13].

1990-1991: Iraq-Kuwait War: This conflict began on August 2,1990 when Iraqi invaded and occupied the border kingdom of Kuwait. Iraqi President Saddam Hussein , the ruler of a **miry clay kingdom**, covetously annexed the oil-rich Arab kingdom as the 19th province of his country. Iraq accused Kuwait of stealing their underground oil reserves through slant drilling. Critics of Hussein said he had borrowed $14 billion to finance the earlier 1980-1990 Iran-Iraq War, and was in desperate need of cash. And on top of that, Kuwait was overproducing oil and keeping the international prices low. This angered Hussein, and Kuwait was a tiny kingdom with a small military. Iraqi forces easily overpowered the Kuwaitis during a 2-day campaign and installed a puppet leader. Most of the Kuwaiti ruling class, including the emir [king], Sheikh Jaber Al-Ahmad al-Sabah, fled to neighboring Saudi Arabia. For seven month President Saddam Hussein military looted Kuwait's vast wealth and tortured all resisters. The majority of the kings of the earth turned against Hussein and demanded that he withdraw from Kuwait immediately. Iraq refused their demand. The Gulf War crisis was placed on the table of the United Nation Security Council. The global government authorized a UN resolution authorizing the use of force to remove Iraq from Kuwait. The global war coalition was led by the **iron kingdoms** of the United States, along with France and Britain. This war became known as the 1991 Gulf War or the first Gulf war.

In the end, Hussein refused to give up his prey. So, in 1991 the UN authorized conflict, which was led by U.S generals, called Operation Desert Storm received a green light from the Security Council. On the battlefield, the global coalition of the willing easily overpowered the Iraqis. 400,000 U.S. soldiers were deployed to northern Saudi Arabia to participate in the war effort. In a matter of days, Hussein's forces had been routed and fled northwards back into Iraq. As they fled, the Iraqis torched 600 Kuwaiti oil wells. American fighter jet pilots killed hundreds of escaping soldiers. The final death toll from the brief war included 22,000 Iraqis, 4,200 Kuwaitis, 12,000 missing or captured Kuwaitis, and billions in damages.

When the dust settled from the military storm, the UN approved no-fly zone zones over the northern and southern portions of Iraq along with economic sanctions. In the north, Iraqi jets were denied the right to fly over northern Kurdish Iraq. In the south, the no-fly zones protected the majority Shiite population. President Saddam Hussein had been severely weakened by this war.

"In that day, a great tumult from YHWH shall fall upon them, and everyone shall snatch at the hand of another, and everyone shall raise his hand against everyone else's hand." [Zechariah 14:13].

September 11, 2001: Bombing of World Trade Center: Two passenger jet airliners commandeered by 19 alleged Saudi Arabian and Egyptian terrorist [citizens from **miry clay kingdoms**] slammed the planes into the twin towers of the 110-story World Trade Center in New York City. A third jetliner was flown into the Pentagon in Washington, D.C. The burning structure resembled a volcano spewing flames, dust clouds, and smoke, covering over 20 blocks and several miles of lower Manhattan. 2,996 people died, including the 19 suspected terrorists. Another 6,000 were injured. All 265 passengers perished in the tragedy. 125 people died in the Pentagon strike in the nation's capitol. Another jetliner crashed in Shanksville, Pennsylvania. Afterwards, another 2,753 died from cancer directly related to the toxic fallout.

The **iron kingdom** of America, the preeminent superpower and leader of the United Nations, NATO, the International Monetary Fund, the World Bank, and the most industrialized and wealthiest kingdom on earth, had suffered a crushing blow to its invincible pride. This Pearl Harbor-type strike against the U.S. greatly enraged President George W. Bush, the son of former President George H.W. Bush, moving him to become directly involved in the struggle over the holy land.

"In that day, a great tumult from YHWH shall fall upon them, and everyone shall snatch at the hand of another, and everyone shall raise his hand against everyone else's hand." **[Zechariah 14:13].**

October 7, 2001: U.S.-Afghanistan War: President George W. Bush began the War on Terror with the invasion of the **miry clay kingdom** of Afghanistan after the Taliban rulers refused to apprehend Osama Bin Laden and his Al-Qaeda army. The Sunni fundamentalist government known as the Taliban was known to harbor training camps for Al-Qaeda terrorist groups. Al-Qaeda was the same group that launched the attacks on the World Trade Center three weeks earlier. American forces moved into the Middle East and Central Asia in a great array, consisting of three Marine amphibious groups, four aircraft carriers, infantry troops, commandos, fighter jets, bombers, and intelligence forces. U.S. attack jets began around-the-clock pounding of Afghanistan destroying communication lines, government headquarters, energy depots, military installations, villages, mosques, and all moving targets. The American invasion has led to the longest war the U.S. has ever experienced. Nearly two decades later their military forces are still bogged down with guerilla wars against the re-emerging Taliban. By the year of 2016 C.E., 2,386 U.S. soldiers had died. Another 20,049 had been wounded in combat. 1,173 United States contractors have also died during the same period of time. The U.S. has spent $1.4 trillion to keep the military expedition moving forward. On the other side 149,000 Afghan and Pakistani soldiers and people combined have died has a direct result of war effort. Yet, in 2019 there is still no end in sight for this two decades-old mountainous slugfest.

"In that day, a great tumult from YHWH shall fall upon them, and everyone shall snatch at the hand of another, and everyone shall raise his hand against everyone else's hand." **[Zechariah 14:13].**

2003-2011: U.S.-Iraq War: Beginning on March 20, 2003 George W. Bush, the president of the United States, ordered airstrikes on the presidential palace of President Saddam Hussein, leader of Baath Socialist Party, beginning the overthrow of his regime. This was the first blow in another Mideast battle which became known as the 2nd Gulf War. According to U.S. intelligence reports, the Hussein government possessed a hidden arsenal of weapons of mass destruction. Secretary of State Colin Powell, his African American subordinate, went before the UN Assembly where he cited intelligence reports that certainly confirmed Hussein was assembling a biological, chemical, and nuclear arsenal. His reports were later found to be a total fabrication. However, his presentation convinced the international body that Hussein was a threat to world peace and he needed to be overthrown immediately. Without a final green light from the UN Security Council, the 21-day invasion dubbed "Operation Freedom, which included global forces from the United Kingdom, Australia, and Polish armies, roared into the capital city of Baghdad. (Russia was upset, yet too weak to respond.) Hussein and his inner circle fled the capital to save their lives as the 130,000 U.S. troops besieged their strongholds. By May 1,2003 the U.S. declared complete victory. In this first invasion phase,139 U.S. soldiers died, another 551 wounded, along with 33 British soldiers who also died.

In less than two months, the strongman of Baghdad known to be a brutal dictator, was erased from power. Hussein fled for his life, hiding in various places throughout the vast swaths of territory near his hometown of Tikrit in north-central Iraq. In the end, Hussein was found hiding on a rural farm. He was captured, a noose placed around his neck, and hung on Yom Shabbat [Saturday], December 30, 2006.

The suspected arsenal was never found nor unearthed after a seven-year search and destroy war mission. The conflict didn't end until December 18, 2011 when a new U.S. leader, President Barack Obama, withdrew the majority of U.S. troops, leaving behind only a skeleton crew of Special Forces. The U.S. installed-Shiite majority became the new leaders of Iraq, ending centuries-old Sunni dominion of Iraqi politics. This historic shift of religious power from the Sunnis to Shiites caused a Middle East earthquake with tremors felt in Iran, Saudi Arabia, Lebanon, and most of all in Syria. One unintended outcome was the emergence of the kingdom of Shiite-Iran as the new regional superpower, causing alarm bells to go off in Tel Aviv, Israel.

At the conclusion of the 2nd Gulf War, the United States had lost 4,424 soldiers, along with 31,952 wounded at a cost of $1.06 trillion. On the other side, 500,000 Iraqis perished during the seven years of the conquest. 132,000 of them were Iraqi soldiers and the other were 330,000 civilians who perished in the crossfires.

"In that day, a great tumult from YHWH shall fall upon them, and everyone shall snatch at the hand of another, and everyone shall raise his hand against everyone else's hand." **[Zechariah 14:13].**

February 14, 2005: Lebanese Bombing: A deadly explosion, 2,200 pounds of TNT, tore through the heart of Beirut shattering 15 years of calm, causing fears that Lebanon could erupt into another civil war or possibly become another front in the ongoing U.S.-Iraq conflict. Former Prime Minister Rafik Hariri, a close ally of the United States and Saudi Arabia and 19 others were slain. 100 others were wounded. Some Lebanese officials accused Syria, or one of its proxies, of being the culprits behind the attack. They called the bombing an assassination plot to murder Hariri. Hariri favored closer ties with Washington, and he was favored to return to power in the May 2005 national elections. Hariri opposed the presence of neighboring Syria and their ally Hezbollah. President George W. Bush **[iron kingdom]** called for a condemnation of Syria in the UN Security Council on the following day, Feb. 15. In response, the U.S. president threatened the Syrian regime **[miry clay kingdom]**. The Saudis began to support the underground opposition forces inside Syria, thus sowing the seeds for a future Syrian civil-war.

"In that day, a great tumult from YHWH shall fall upon them, and everyone shall snatch at the hand of another, and everyone shall raise his hand against everyone else's hand." **[Zechariah 14:13].**

March 2011: Syrian Civil-War: The Syrian civil war started out as daily demonstrations, a general strike, and calls for reforms by the Syrian populace. Syrian President Bashar al-Assad, who came to power in the year 2000, answered those outcries with a deadly military crackdown in cities across the desert kingdom. Over 80,000 were killed over the next twenty-four months. However, the Syrian government suppression did not extinguish the people's desire to replace the autocratic rule of the Assad family. A family which had ruled the country that straddles the Euphrates River for the past 40 years.

"Assad has ruled Syria for 11 years after succeeding his father Hafez al-Assad on his death. The Assad family belongs to the Alawite sect, an offshoot of Shiite Islam, in a majority Sunni country, and there are fears the uprising could break down into a full sectarian [Shiite-Sunni] conflict," Khaled Yacoub, a correspondent and reporter for Reuters, explained. By 2013, the internal conflict had drawn regional neighbors into the quagmire. Sunni-led Saudi Arabia, Qatar, and other Sunni-backed Arab league member-states aligned themselves with the majority Syrian population against Assad. The Assad regime found allies in Iran, Lebanese-backed Hezbollah, and other Shiite militias from Iraq, and Yemen. The United States **[iron kingdom]** soon joined the Saudi-led plan **[miry clay kingdom]** to topple Assad. Russia, meanwhile, closed ranks with Iran and Syria.

Neighboring Turkey **[miry clay kingdom]** soon became unnerved when the Syrian Kurds began to establish an autonomous homeland in northern Syria. Turkey was caught in the middle. On one hand, Turkey was a NATO ally and a supporter of the U.S., France, and Britain [**iron kingdoms**]. On the other hand, Turkey opposed the U.S. close alliance with the Kurdish minority in Syria. In the past, Kurds in Turkey fought armed struggles with Turkish authorities seeking to break away from the federal government in Ankara. The Turkish government feared the Kurds in their country might unite with those in Syria. Turkey has also publicly opposed the U.S. plan to join with the Syrian Kurds to topple Assad. It was this type of foreign interference that turned the Syrian civil war into a proxy battlefield for competing global powers. Turkey later deployed Patriot defensive missile batteries along their long border with Syria.

In late November of 2015, a Turkish warplane shot down a Russian SU-24 fighter plane prompting angry exchanges between the two powers. The Turkish military reported a Russian plane trespassing their airspace. One Russian crew member was killed in that incident. The two great powers mended their differences after that 2014 confrontation, and on Dec. 20, 2016, Russia, Turkey, and Iran met in Moscow to seek ways to bring an end to the raging Syrian civil-war. At the end of the conference, the three governments agreed to a tentative plan to end the fighting, but after the conference, the combatants on the ground continued to engage in military action. Weeks after the Moscow meeting, Turkey accused Syria of not abiding by the terms of the agreement. Russia and Iran were Syria's main backers in the international conflict.

On the ground inside Syria, Russian warplanes, Syrian troops, Iranian Republican Guards, and Hezbollah guerillas besieged the second largest city of Aleppo. Russian airstrikes were blamed for killing scores, wounding several others, and the destruction of hospitals and schools. Thousands fled the intense fighting for refuge in Lebanon while others sought refuge in Greece, Hungary, and Germany. By 2016 the balance of power shifted in favor of Assad, especially after September 2015 when thousands of Russian naval, air force, ground, and intelligence contingents became directly involved in the Syria civil-war. Until then, it appeared Assad could have faced the same fate as Iraqi President Saddam Hussein and Libyan President Moammar Gadaffi. Both were overthrown by foreign inspired uprisings.

Meanwhile, the United States still called for the removal of President Bashar al-Assad. The U.S. continued to finance anti-Assad forces who controlled large swaths of Syrian desert territory in the eastern portion of the country. Russia, Iran, and Turkey accused the United States and Israel of supporting the terrorist organization known as I.S.I.S.[Islamic State of Iraq and Syria]. I.S.I.S. was a continuation of the Sunni-based Al-Qaeda resistance movement. Many ex-soldiers of former Saddam Hussein joined the I.S.I.S. movement to resist America in Iraq. But in Syria, the U.S. and I.S.I.S. had a common agenda which was the removal of the Assad rulership. As the war continued, the United States eventually turned against I.S.I.S. in favor of more pro-western Syrian militias because scores of their radicalized Islamic fighters were implicated in several terrorist strikes in Britain, France, Germany, Denmark, and several other Western European countries.

By the year of 2018 C.E., the Syrian war had become an international crisis causing direct involvement of all nations in the entire Middle East and the world. The world body, the United Nations [**UN**], had become directly involved. On the battlefield and the diplomatic front, one side consisted of a multitude of armed Syrian opposition groups, including I.S.I.S.,the United States, Britain, France, Saudi Arabia, Jordan, Qatar, United Arab Emirate, Bahrain, Israel, various Palestinian groups, along with the Kurds of Syria and Iran. Their adversaries were the Syrian government, Russia, China, Iran, Egypt, Shiite rulers and militias of Iraq and Yemen, Lebanese-based Hezbollah. From afar, North Korea directly assisted Iran and Syria with the transfer of advanced missile technologies. As we approach the second decade of the 21st century, the UN Security Council resolutions will cause all nations to converge on the holy land to do battle in the name of world peace. Since the beginning of the Syrian civil war an estimated 414,000 people have died. The 2016 report by the UN High Commissioner for Refugees stated 4.8 million people have fled to the neighboring countries of Turkey, Lebanon, Jordan, Egypt, and Iraq. Another 6.6 million people became homeless and faced starvation. With no end in sight, one million other Syrians fled to Europe for comfort and safety.

As the Syrian war continues to rage unabated, two of the major prophetic opponents in this Countdown to Armageddon have emerged: The State of Israel and The Islamic Republic of Iran.

"In that day, a great tumult from YHWH shall fall upon them, and everyone shall snatch at the hand of another, and everyone shall raise his hand against everyone else's hand."
[Zechariah 14:13].

2005-2019:Israeli-Iran Cold War: The United States introduced the development of nuclear energy to Iran during the reign of the pro-Western Shah of Iran. In 1979, the Islamic revolution toppled the Shah and swept a radical Shiite cleric-led government into power. The new ruler Ayatollah Ruhollah Khomeini cut off ties with the United States, including their involvement in the country's new nuclear program. By 1984, China agreed to assist Iran in establishing a nuclear energy program by opening a nuclear research center in the central Iranian city of Isfahan. In early 1998 the U.S. became concerned that Iranian progress in their nuclear energy program could be a cover for the radical Islamic government to develop nuclear weapons. By 2003, the International Atomic Energy Agency visited Iran to survey the status of Iran's clandestine nuclear facilities. The head of the international agency also requested that Iran allow IAEA inspectors unfettered access to all their nuclear sites. Iran refused. The director, General Mohammed ElBaradei, issued a departing statement that said he found Iran's nuclear program to be for peaceful and civilian use. In June of 2003, the IAEA said Iran was in compliance with the international Non-Proliferation Treaty. However, the U.S. and Israel demanded stricter inspections after inspectors visited a nuclear plant in the city of Natanz and discovered traces of highly enriched uranium. In October of 2003, the European Union nations of Germany, France, and Britain visited the Iranian capital of Tehran. All parties agreed to peacefully settle the nuclear controversy. Iran agreed to temporarily suspend nuclear enrichment. In the following year during February 2004, A.Q. Khan, the chief scientist and brainchild for Pakistan's nuclear weapons development programme, publicly stated the he provided Iran and other developing nations with technological know-how and the equipment needed to enrich uranium. The leadership in the State of Israel became alarmed at Iran's rapid development of nuclear capabilities. Jewish leaders did not trust the Islamic Republic of Iran and suspected that the Persian kingdom could be secretly developing a nuclear bomb. In late 2005, Israeli Prime Minister Ariel Sharon planned a pre-emptive strike, but in 2006 he suffered a debilitating massive stroke. Israel continued to plot a pre-emptive strike, but another setback occurred when the liberal democratic President Barack Obama won the White House in 2008 and 2012. Obama opposed a strike against Iran and the Jewish State could not go to war without America's blessings. During this time Iran continued its buildup in preparation of war against the Jewish State, almost reaching military equality. In November, 2005 Iran launched a Sina-1 spy satellite that was capable of monitoring Israeli actions. This event marked the beginning of the Iranian space program. The Iranians also announced the purchase of $1 billion in ballistic missiles in Nov. 2005. Since then, the Iranians have learned how to develop their own long-range ballistic missiles.

In mid-Oct. 2005, the president of Iran said, "Israel should be wiped off the face of the map." Two months later in December of 2005, Iranian President Mahmoud Ahmadinejad reportedly said, "today they have created a myth in the name of the Holocaust and consider it to be above God, religion, and the prophets. If you committed this big crime, then why should the oppressed Palestinian nation pay the price?" Since then threats from both Israel and Iran have elevated Middle East tensions to dangerous new levels. Both nations possess large armies, navies, air forces, submarines, long-range missiles, cyberspace capabilities, nuclear, biological, chemical weapons, and a deep hatred for each other. The potential death toll from this future war will likely reach hundreds of thousands, and possibly millions. The State of Israel is believed to possess 75 to 400 nuclear warheads along with the strongest army, navy, and air force in the region.

The prophet **Zechariah** foresaw this disastrous latter-day Battle of Armageddon when he predicted in **chapter 14:12-13**: *"As for those peoples that warred against Jerusalem, YAH will* *smite them with this plague: Their flesh shall rot away while they stand on their feet;* [**nuclear, biological, and chemical warfare**]. *Their eyes shall rot away in their sockets; and their tongues shall rot away in their mouths. In that day, a great panic from YAH shall fall upon them, and everyone shall snatch at the hand of another, and everyone shall raise his hand against everyone's else hand* [**in regional conflicts involving all Middle East nations**]. One of the main reasons why everyone's hand will shed blood, and turn against each other, will be the ongoing Islamic civil war between Shiite and Sunni Muslims throughout the region.

2003-2019: Shiite-Sunni Islamic Civil Wars: The United States invasion of Iraq directly led to the heightening of Shiite and Sunni tensions. The overthrow of Sunni leader of Iraq Saddam Hussein and his replacement with a new transitional government led by Shiite leader Nouri al-Maliki was far reaching. The historic shift of Iraqi politics, in a country that lies in the heart of the Middle East, set in motion a chain reaction of events. 1) After the humiliating defeat of the Iraqi Army, the minority Sunni population strengthened themselves in the Anbar Province. They regrouped there, turning to the fundamentalist Wahabi faith for answers for their destruction. Their allies from abroad came to the Anbar Province to assist them in the war against the infidel United States and their Shiite lackeys. Volunteers came from Saudi Arabia, Jordan, Syria, and Afghanistan. Soon Iraq began to be plagued with a series of bombings . The destruction of the Askari Mosque in Samarra came in February of 2006, destroying the Golden Dome. Following that sectarian bombing, a cycle of retaliatory vengeance began. The next day 100 deaths were reported. In the following weeks, over a 1,000 people were slain in back-to-back revenge car bombings and suicide bombings. The Shiites responded by forming death squads and killing thousands of Sunnis. Iraq teetered on the brink of civil war. In 2007 President Bush dispatched 20,000 extra troops to Iraq to stabilize the country. The U.S.commanders dispatched troops to the Anbar Province to confront Sunni extremists. This caused the U.S. to become mired in a struggle for control of the Sunni heartland. The U.S. needed allies to overcome support from among the Arab population who saw them as foreign crusaders. The U.S. formed ties with the Arab chieftains and the clans who controlled the fighters. The U.S. supplied the Sunni groups with weapons to overcome Al-Qaeda of Iraq, the main anti-U.S. Sunni extremist group. The short term strategy worked with Al-Qaeda being expelled and the U.S. declaring victory. However, the Shiite-led government in Baghdad did not embrace the Sunnis who lived in the Anbar Province, the once a stronghold Saddam Hussein. Years later, the U.S. withdrew and the Sunnis felt abandoned, both by the U.S. and the central government in Baghdad. The sentiment of these displaced Sunnis gave birth to a new anti-Western Sunni extremist organization known as the Islamic State of Iraq [ISIS]. Many of their recruits were former Baath Party soldiers. Other recruits came from Sunni fundamentalist Saudi Arabia.

85 percent of all Muslims are Sunnis. They are the majority in Saudi Arabia, Egypt, Yemen, Pakistan, Indonesia, Turkey, Algeria, Morocco, and Tunisia. Shiites make up the majority population in only Iraq and Iran. They comprise large minorities in Yemen, Bahrain, Syria, Lebanon, and Azerbaijan.

Shiites in Iraq make up 63 percent of that country's population, and after gaining control in 2003, they fostered closer ties with neighboring Shiite Iran. The two countries which had fought a devastating decade-long war moved to a common Middle East kinship because of their shared faith. Meanwhile, the Sunnis in the Anbar Province, now under the umbrella of ISIS, moved to claim large swaths of western Iraq and eastern Syria. At one point ISIS controlled the northern Iraqi city of Mosul, with a population of 10 million people. They sold black market oil to finance their government, and placed the territory under Sharia law. By late 2016, however, the terrorist group had lost the majority of Mosul and held only 16 percent of their former territory. *(In ancient times the city of Nineveh was located in the same place as modern Mosul.)*

By the year of 2010 C.E., the two major Islamic powers of the Middle East were Saudi Arabia, which was a Sunni Arab populated kingdom ruled by the royal family. Modern Saudi Arabia dates back to the 1700s when Muhummad Ibn Saud founded the family dynasty. Saud formed an alliance with a religious leader named Abd al-Wahhab to start a religious order known as Wahhabism which became the state religion for the ultraconservative Arab rulers. Together they unified the Arabian tribes. Once petroleum reserves were discovered centuries later, the desert kingdom which today comprise 28 million people, became an economic superpower, possessing 16 percent of the world's proven oil reserves. Since then, the Saudis have used their wealth to finance Wahhabi centered mosques and religious schools throughout the earth. The other sphere of Islamic power is Iran, a Persian populated kingdom consisting of Shiite believers. Since 1979 Iran has been ruled by the Shiite fundamentalist clerics. Their first leader, Ayatollah Ruhollah Khomeini, led the revolution that deposed the pro-western Shah Muhammad Reza Pahlavi. Khomeini became the Supreme Leader choosing and directing all elected leaders. He openly denounced the Saudi royal family as pro-Western stooges of the United States, and not servants of Allah. The Saudis and Sunni Arabs fear the Islamic Republic of Iran ultimate goal is to build a Shiite Persian empire extending from Iran through Iraq, Syria, to Lebanon.

The religious split between the two is also aggravated by the economic competition over oil. The rivalry is based on who will reign over the Strait of Hormuz, a waterway which passes into the Persian Gulf where 20 percent of global energy originates. Six of world's largest oil-producing countries straddle the Persian Gulf. These Sunni Arab caliphates, known as the Gulf Cooperation Council [GCC], are Kuwait, Bahrain, Qatar, the United Arab Emirates, Saudi Arabia, and Oman. Per capita this is one of the richest areas on earth. One-third of all U.S. oil supplies come from this area. The U.S. has its 5th Fleet naval base in Bahrain to protect these valuable liquid gold supplies. Bahrain is one exception. It is ruled by a 30 percent Sunni minority over a Shiite majority.

For centuries Iran has claimed the Persian Gulf as theirs. The United States, and the Western World, consider the area to be international waters. Iranian and American forces have faced-off repeatedly for decades, making this area a potential flashpoint. In the event of a war, Shiite Iran has vowed to use its military power to shutdown commerce in the Persian Gulf.

In Syria, President Bashar al-Assad, a Shiite Muslim of the Alawite sect, rules the ancient holy heartland. The Shiites are only 13 percent of the Syrian population. The Shiites in Iraq and Iran have united with the Assad leadership. Iran is known to funnel weapons through Iraq into Syria over to the Shiite Hezbollah Army in Lebanon. Assad and his Shiite predecessors have a history of persecution and torture of the Sunni majority in Syria. Many of the ISIS fighters come from those Sunni ranks.

Another fault line in the Shiite-Sunni rivalry is Lebanon, a country divided between Christians, Sunnis, and Shiites. 49 percent of the Lebanese people are Christians, and 22 percent Sunnis. Shiites comprise the remaining 29 percent. From 1975 to 1990 Lebanon was mired in a costly civil war. During that time the Israelis invaded southern Lebanon twice. The Syrians also occupied the eastern part of the country. In 2006 Israel and the Shiite militia Hezbollah fought a protracted war. Hezbollah's ability to withstand an Israeli Defense Force assault helped the guerilla organization gain influence at the ballot box. They were seen as the defenders of Islam against Jewish occupiers. The Saudis, another major powerbroker in Lebanon, have opposed the Iranian-backed Hezbollah rise to power.

For the record, the Sunni-Shiite divide occurred in 632 C.E. when the prophet Muhummad died. Sunnis believed that the successor should have been elected. Those followers chose Muhummad's advisor Abu Bakr. On the other hand, the Shiites believed the next leader should have been his son-in-law Ali bin Abu Talib. The split established two schools of Islamic thought. The Shiites chose their own Imams whom they considered "holy men". Their leaders were viewed as true representatives, not the caliphates. Both sects shared a common belief in a god named Allah. Both believed in the Quran and considered Muhummad as a prophet. Both practiced the five pillars of faith: fasting, the hajj, pledge to the faith, prayer, and giving charity to the poor.

In the Arabic language, the word Sunni meant "one who follows the tradition of the prophet". Shia Ali was first to use the title Shiite which meant the "Party of All". The competition between these Arabs, Persians, and Kurds will serve as the catalyst which causes *"every man's hand to be against his neighbor"*—producung a series of regional conflicts.

In Egypt, an ancient kingdom situated on the Nile River, there is presently a 90 percent Sunni Arab population. However, there are two other prominent faiths: the Coptic Christians and the Shiite Muslims. In recent years, Coptic Christians and Shiites have been a persecuted minority facing bombings and other attacks. In 2011, the young population rose up against President Hosni Murbarak. The Muslim Brotherhood eventually became the voice for disenfranchised Egyptians. Muslim Brotherhood candidate Mohammed Morsi was elected president in 2012 national elections. However in 2013, the Egyptian military rose up and imprisoned Morsi. The following year the Egyptian army chief Abdul Fattah al Sisi won the 2014 national elections. The Muslim Brotherhood is a Sunni Muslim organization founded in Egypt during 1928 by Hassan al-Banna. Its initial purpose was to promote brotherhood, networking, charity, and spreading the faith. From Egypt, the organization expanded into Syria, Sudan, Jordan, Kuwait, Libya, and Iraq.

In the land of Jordan, the territory that once belonged to the ancient Israelite tribes of Reuben, Gad, and half of the tribe of Manneseh, there is another epicenter and potential powderkeg in the Countdown towards Armageddon. The kingdom is ruled by a 92 percent Sunni Arab and Palestinian majority. Nearly 60 percent of the Jordanian population is comprised of Palestinians. Jordan is now being affected by the civil war in neighboring Syria. Syrian refugees fleeing the conflict have been chased into Jordan by pro-Assad Shiites forces. Sunni Jordan has also allied with the United States. The Hashemite kingdom has declared peace with the State of Israel as well.

The country of Turkey, which was once known as the *"entering of Hamath"* or Asia Minor, is a Sunni majority Islamic kingdom. The leader, President Tayyip Erdogan, is a Sunni Muslim who was radicalized by the Syrian civil war and the Western support for Kurds in the war against Assad. In the eyes of Turkey, the Kurdish desire for an independent homeland, not ISIS, represented the greatest threat to their country. Kurds in Turkey, Syria, Iraq, and Iran have desired an autonomous region for themselves for ages. The U.S. support for the Syrian Kurds in the war against I.S.I.S. has created tensions between the U.S. and Turkey. It has also sparked another Turkish-Kurdish war. The new battle front was the unintended spillover of the Syrian civil war.

Last but not least, the State of Israel is the active volcano in Middle East politics. The state is composed of European Jewish converts from mainly Europe and North America who immigrated there, beginning in the late 1800s until the establishment of the Jewish State in 1948. The Palestinians, however, make up the majority population. The Palestinians are Sunni Muslims and Christians. Since its founding in 1948 the Jewish State [**supported by the iron kingdoms of the U.S., France, and Britain**] has expanded to include Judaea, Samaria, Jerusalem, and parts of Golan. The Sunni Palestinians are led by organizations named Hamas and the Palestinian Authority. Hamas has vowed to remove the Jewish State from the land of Palestine by violence. Although Hamas leaders are Sunni, they enjoy the full support of Shiite Iran [**supported by the miry clay kingdoms of Iran and the Arab world**]. Hamas has attacked Israel repeatedly with rockets, suicide bombings, stabbings, and successive intifadas. Israel has responded to Palestinian violence with continuous brutal crackdowns.

Jerusalem is also another point of contention between the two distinct people living in the ancient land of Canaan. The Palestinians claim East Jerusalem as the capital of their future state. In 2018 the State of Israel moved forward in totally conquering Jerusalem when the U.S. moved their embassy to the holy city. Since 1967, the Jewish State already controlled Jerusalem after their military victory over the Jordan. Successive Israeli governments have consistently expanded their territorial claims in and around Jerusalem, building settlement after settlement throughout the West Bank. The United Nations [**UN**] has called upon Israel to halt their settlement building. The UN has also called for both the Israelis and Palestinians to end their violence and agree to a two-state solution. The international decree demands both sides to lay their weapons down, live in peace, and divide the holy land.

"In that day, a great tumult from YHWH shall fall upon them, and everyone shall snatch at

the hand of another, and everyone shall raise his hand against everyone else's hand."
[Zechariah 14:13].

March 2015: Yemen Civil War: The outbreak of the Yemeni civil war came on March 22, 2015. A group of Shiite Arabs, known as the Houthis, from the northern part of Yemen near the Saudi Arabian border started the initial conflict as a low-level uprising beginning in 2004. The Houthis began to launch attacks against the Sunni-ruled central government and Sunni tribes. Their attacks soon expanded into neighboring provinces. The Houthis joined forces with supporters of the former president Ali Abdullah Saleh. Saleh opposed the new president Abdrabbuh Mansur Hadi. By 2014, the Houthis and their allied forces overthrew Hadi and gained control of the capital city Sana'a.

The Houthis and the central government were now involved in open warfare. Hadi fled to the southern stronghold city of Aden. The Houthis soon reached the center of power in Aden **[miry clay kingdom verus another miry clay kingdom—internal civil war]**. During this time the conflict became internationalized when a coalition of forces led by Sunni-Saudi Arabia launched military operations. The Saudis launched airstrikes hoping to restore President Hadi. The U.S. provided intelligence and logistical support for the Saudis in the widening war. The international community condemned the Saudis air campaign because they conducted widespread bombings of civilian neighborhoods. On the ground, the Sunni-backed terrorist groups, Al-Qaeda of the Arabian Peninsula and the Islamic State of Iraq and Syria, joined the fray. These Saudi-Al-Qaeda-ISIS joint operations helped them maintain control of nearly 40 percent of the country.

Since March 2015 to November 2017, nearly 10,000 people died, including over 5,000 civilians. Nearly 8 million people have been affected by a severe famine, and beginning in 2016, there was a cholera outbreak. With foreign involvement the death toll has continued to rise. The Houthis have been supported by pro-Saleh forces, Iran, Hezbollah, Qatar, and North Korea. Hadi has been backed by the Sunni-Yemeni population, Saudi Arabia, United Arab Emirates, Senegal, NATO, Sudan, Qatar, Britain, the United States, and France **[iron kingdoms verus miry clay kingdoms]**.

"In that day, a great tumult from YHWH shall fall upon them, and everyone shall snatch at the hand of another, and everyone shall raise his hand against everyone else's hand."
[Zechariah 14:13].

December 27, 2011: The Arab Spring: The internal **[miry clay verus miry clay]** grassroots uprisings that swept the Arab world in late 2011 became known as the Arab Spring, meaning a new generation of Islamic democratic rule in kingdoms that had been ruled by emirs, caliphates, military dictators, and other autocratic rulers for centuries. The first conflict in the internal revolts came on December 18, 2010 when an uprising, known as the Jasmine Revolution started as a resistance movement against a Tunisian government crackdown. The young generation of Tunisians demanded that the national government grant more reforms. The populace was angry at government corruption, poverty, a lack of meaningful jobs, and harsh treatment by the police. The rebellion grew into mass rallies, demonstrations, general strikes, and several Arabs burned themselves alive in fires. By January of 2011 the twenty-four year reign of President Zine El Abdine Ben Ali came to an abrupt end. Ali had come to power on November 7, 1987 and ruled the north African country with a **miry clay** fist for over two decades. After his ouster, the leaders and people held open and democratic elections to change the course of the Arab state. In the end, 338 people died and over 2,147 injured. The deposed monarch, Zine El Abdine Ben Ali fled to Saudi Arabia for asylum.

The discontent of the Arab Spring expanded to Egypt via the new Arab-owned global media outlet Al-Jazeera. The television station is owned by Qatar, a small wealthy natural gas rich caliphate located next door to larger Saudi Arabia. The station's support for free speech helped ignite the dissident movement, providing the fuel the needed for the strife to become contagious across the region.

By late January 2011, the internal strife that started in Tunisia reached the doorsteps of Egyptian President Hosni Murbarak. Inspired by the mass demonstrations in Tunisia, the young generation of Arab Egyptians took to the streets demanding an end to corruption, better jobs, and democratic reforms. For over two weeks there were violent battles between Egyptian police and protestors throughout Cairo and elsewhere. For days, demonstrators met in Tahrir Square in the downtown of the capital. Weeks later on February 11, President Murbarak was forced to resign. His 30-year reign had come to an end with 846 Egyptians dead and hundreds others injured. The military, under the banner of the Supreme Council of the Armed Forces, assumed the mantle of power. The entire country of Egypt burst into jubilant celebrations at the news of the removal of Murbarak. Again, the Qatari-owned Al Jazeera television network also supported the political Islamic dissidents of Egypt, angering Saudi Arabia and the United Arab Emirates. The wealthy autocratic monarchs of the Persian Gulf were disturbed about the uprisings taking place across the region, and they were especially upset at the Qataris. That was the beginning of a rift between the members of the wealthy Gulf cooperative Council.

By February 15, 2011 the upheaval and unrest that rocked Tunisia and Egypt swept into oil-rich Libya. The Libyans living in the eastern oil-rich city of Benghazi staged a protest against the autocratic government of President Moammar Gaddafi. Gaddafi responded to the mass demonstrations with warplanes dropping bombs on the dissidents. In 14 days, three hundred civilians were killed in aerial bombardments. As the daily death toll mounted, international rulers quickly brought the Libyan crisis before the UN Security Council for a vote to establish a no-fly zone over eastern Libya. 10 members voted in favor of the no-fly zone over Libya authorizing all necessary measures to protect civilians. Russia, China, and 3 others abstained, allowing the attack to take place. On March 31, NATO began air strikes that destroyed his air force. The no-fly zone gave the revolutionaries the opportunity to hold onto the eastern portion of the country, creating a division of two Libyas. The 42-year reign of President Gaddafi, who came to power as a colonel in 1969 after a bloodless coup that overthrew King Idris I, came to an end hastily. Before his death on October 20, 2011, Gaddafi had been the longest reigning Arab leader in the Middle East. But the Arab Spring swept him out of power.

After the death of Gaddafi, the once tranquil and peaceful oil-rich kingdom of 6 million people, which produced 1.6 million barrels per day, descended into chaotic political unrest. Over 300 warring militias took to the streets fighting for control of oil terminals, ports, the Tripoli airport, and major cities. The uprising completely halted all oil production and crippled the nationalized oil industry. Rival factions fought for control of those important facilities. The violence and conflict soon destroyed the economy and Libya soon became a failed state similar to Afghanistan, Iraq, Syria, and Yemen. During Gaddafi's reign Libyans received free health care and education.

With Gaddafi out of the picture, the UN Security Council recognized the dissidents from eastern Libya, along with other factions, as the new rulers under the banner of the National Transition Council (NTC). The warriors, turned politicians, promised to implement fair elections and a fair judicial system. All sides pledged to put away their weapons, establish a centralized security force, and promote peace. By July 2012, Libya held national elections with 2 million people going to the polls. After the elections, the NTC disbanded and was replaced with the General National Congress (GNC). The Libyan Supreme Court ruled that the General National Congress was unconstitutional after it attempted to cling to power after their two-year mandate had expired. Libya plunged further into political chaos with three major factions fighting for power and dividing territory. The violence reached the U.S. diplomatic post in oil-rich city of Benghazi by September of 2012 when a competing armed group stormed the compound. American ambassador J. Christopher Stevens and three others were slain during the intrusion. Remember, Benghazi was the city where the anti-Gaddafi uprising began. Many influential Libyans with close ties to international businessmen and investors lived there. Following that surprise attack, both the U.S. and Britain [iron kingdoms] removed their special mission staffs from the restless city.

By early 2014, rival factions warred in Tripoli. Meanwhile, Libyan fighters who once fought with I.S.I.S in Syria returned to North Africa and formed the Islamic State of Libya (I.S.I.L.). In May of that year with Gaddafi gone, a 1980s U.S. backed defector named General Khalifa Haftar joined the fray by returning to the country and forming the Libyan National Army. He launched a campaign known as Operation Dignity hoping to prevent the country from becoming a I.S.I.L terrorist state. He launched an offensive and seized control of key oil terminals and ports in the cities of Ras Lanuf, Al-Sidra, and Zuwaytania, and Brega. Afterward, the Libyan strongman fought armed groups in Benghazi and elsewhere throughout the east. He received political and military backing from Egypt, the United Arab Emirates, and France. Nevertheless, the country still remained deeply divided into two sections: East(Tripoli) and West(Benghazi). Two governments. Two competing National Oil Councils, and by 2017 Haftar made a 180-degree turn. He turned to Russia for support. The violence and human misery continued with Libya becoming a center for slave trafficking. Today, post-war Libya is ruled by the UN recognized National Transition Council. This council is comprised of the same armed Arab and Berber groups fighting each other on the streets. The death toll is estimated to be in the tens of thousands. An estimated 435,000 people have been displaced and another 2.5 million are in need of humanitarian assistance. The standard of living has fallen to the point where food supplies, clean water, and sanitation are nonexistent in some areas. Seven years later, oil production is only 700,000 barrels per day, nowhere near pre-war levels. Remember, Gaddafi was found hiding in a drainage pipe in downtown Tripoli on October 20, 2011. He was sodomized and executed on site by the leaders of the National Transition Council. The Western-backed international campaign to remove Gaddafi could be viewed as a *latter-day* Fourth Punic War where the descendants of the ancient Roman Empire(NATO) **[iron kingdoms]** destroyed the city of Carthage(Libya)**[miry clay kingdom]**.

By February 4, 2011 hundreds of Bahraini protestors gathered in front of the Egyptian Embassy in the nation's capital to join ranks with the Egyptian protestors in downtown Cairo. With the Al-Jazeera news network broadcasting the uprisings throughout the region, the Bahrainis were encouraged to start their own anti-government demonstrations. This was the first time Bahraini citizens had ever rose up against their caliphate. Ten days later on Feb. 14, the ranks of the protestors had grown to 6,000 throughout the oil-rich kingdom. Protestors demanded an end to corruption, political and economic reforms, and a release of political prisoners. Police responded with tear gas, rubber bullets, and rubber shotgun pellets. 1 person was slain by police during the various disturbances. The next day his funeral became a mass demonstration resulting in more clashes between mourners and police. Scores were injured and more deaths came in further clashes. Several dissident leaders were rounded up and held in custody. By Feb. 22, over 100,000 Shiite Bahrainis took part in a major defiance against the Sunni-ruled government. On March 14, Bahrain requested military assistance from member states of the Gulf Cooperation Council. Led by Saudi Arabia and United Arab Emirate armies, the soldiers entered the oil-rich kingdom and crushed the rebellion. After that crackdown, periodic demonstrations continued to surface for another two years with nearly a hundred protestors being slain. Over 3,000 people were injured and another 3,000 arrested. Since the infancy of the rebellion in 2011, Shiite Iran has supported the demonstrator's quest to unseat the minority Sunni leadership.

The Final Conflict

As I said earlier, it will be the continuous conflicts between the various great kingdoms of the earth that will eventually cause the final conflict known as the Battle of Armageddon. The enmity between the kings of the north, the kings of the south, the kings of the east, and the kings of the west will cause them to converge on the holy land where **YHWH** will judge them. For the record, I will provide the names of the countries that these kings represent today. The kings of the north is Russia and her allies in Europe. The kings of the south are the Arab, Iranian, and African countries. The kings of the east are China, North Korea, Japan, India, and other far eastern countries. And last but not least, the kings of the west is Western Europe, North America, and their allies.

Now, let's look at the current principal players in the ongoing Middle East where the prophesied endtime World War will take place. The king of the north, Russia, is presently involved in the Syrian civil war. The kings of the south, which are all the Arab kingdoms, Saudi Arabia, Egypt, Iraq, Syria, Yemen, Libya, Jordan, and Bahrain along with Persian Iran, are deeply involved in every conflict taking place in the region. These are *"the wild men whose hands are against every man"*. The kings of the east who are involved in the Middle East conflict are mainly China and North Korea. The kings of the west, which comprise Western Europe and the United States(NATO) are deeply involved in the ongoing holy land dispute. In fact, it was the kings of the west, the U.S., Britain, and France, which formally backed the creation of the State of Israel in May of 1948. It is this conflict between the occupants of the holy land, the European Jewish converts, the Islamic and Christian Palestinians, Shiite-Sunni Arabs, and their allies that will spark this commotion. For example, the Palestinians are backed by Iran, Russia, North Korea, and China. The European Jewish State of Israel is supported by the United States, Britain, France, and their NATO allies. The kings of south have opposed the creation of the State of Israel from its conception. They have fought several wars against the Jewish state, beginning in 1948, continuing in 1967, 1973, 1982, 2000, and 2012. Radical Arab states have called for the destruction of the State of Israel while moderate Arab rulers have demanded the division of the holy land into a Palestinian state alongside the State of Israel. This is known as the two-state solution. The Palestinians have claimed Jerusalem as the capital of their future state. At the same time, the State of Israel claims the city of Jerusalem as their historical and spiritual capital. The Jewish people also claim the Western Wall, which is the remaining wall from the second temple built by King Herod an Idumean in the 1st century common era, as their religious inheritance. The Palestinians and Arabs claim the Dome of the Rock Mosque as their religious inheritance in Jerusalem. The kings of the west, the home of the Roman Catholic Church and Western Christianity, also claim Jerusalem as part of their historical and religious inheritance. It will be this conflict between these parties that will ignite this endtime showdown.

The failure of the Mideast process will be one of the major causes for the Battle of Armageddon. The failure to find a peaceful solution between the Palestinian and Jewish inhabitants will spark the war. The Palestinians of the coastal towns of Gaza are known for terrorist strikes and shooting rockets into Israel killing civilians. In return, Israel has responded with devastating retaliatory strikes against the Palestinians. The Palestinians are angry with the Jewish inhabitants because they have seized their homes, lands, and established Jewish settlements throughout the West Bank. For the past forty years successive Jewish governments have built homes, highways, apartments, and completely transformed the areas into a Jewish stronghold.

To the north of Israel in southern Lebanon, the national security threat to Israel is very similar to the Gaza. The Shiite-Islamic Hezbollah militia is known to possess an estimated 50,000 rockets aimed at the State of Israel. In response, Israel has launched repeated retaliatory strikes into southern Lebanon to remove the missile threat. Hezbollah is allied with Syrian government of Bashar al-Assad. A strike against Hezbollah could inadvertently spread into a larger conflict with the Syrian regime. Syria is allied with Iran. Iran is known to possess long-range missiles that could devastate the Jewish state. Iran has vowed to destroy the Jewish state if they launched a pre-emptive strike against their suspected nuclear facilities. The State of Israel is also known to possess nuclear weapons. Russia, which is based in Syria, is also a nuclear power. The United States, the chief backer of the State of Israel, is a major nuclear power that opposes Russia's strategies in the region. Those threats and disagreements among world powers concerning the Middle East will pose dangers to the entire global order. Those controversies will cause the world leaders to seek advise from the United Nations Security Council. This international council, which represents *"all nations"*, will pass global decrees [UN Resolutions] that will gather all nations [UN peacekeeping forces] right into the midst of the Battle of Armageddon. It will be a combination of those ongoing conflicts that will lead to this final World War. This war will surely involve all the above mentioned "kings of the earth" and will result in the use of nuclear, atomic, chemical, and biological weapons. It will be YAH—**The Stone Cut Out Without Hands**—who will orchestrate all the events leading these ungodly kingdoms into the Valley of Decision where HE will pass Judgement against them. In that day and during that era of time, these following prophetic events will finally occur. The Countdown to Armageddon will be completed and the outbreak of the last major Middle East World War will begin with a HOLY Decree from YAH. **YHWH** will utter these words:

"In that day, a great tumult from YHWH shall fall upon them, and everyone shall snatch at the hand of another, and everyone shall raise his hand against everyone else's hand." **[Zechariah 14:13]**. As you can see, I have used that particular verse, Zechariah 14:13, over and over again throughout the 40-year Countdown To Armageddon. The reason I did that was because each Middle East conflict is a fulfillment of that prophetic vision, so I used it over and over again. Remember, I said earlier, the Battle of Armageddon is an ongoing process. Each of the aforementioned wars have occurred year after year, one after another, until ultimately, the nations are drawn into the last battle which the prophet Yoel foresaw.

[Joel 4:9 Tanakh or Joel 3:9 in King James Version KJV]

"Proclaim you this among the Gentiles **[powerful iron kingdoms]**; *Prepare war.* **[Major Middle East War]** *wake up the mighty men [militaries], let all the men of war draw near; let them come up: Beat your plowshare* **[farming, peaceful technology]** *into sword* **[destructive technology]**, *and your pruninghooks* **[technology to feed people]** *into spears* **[technology to kill people]**; *let the weak* **[miry clay kingdoms]** *say I am strong* **[build mighty armies to confront powerful iron nations]**: *Assemble yourselves* [into Ceole-Syria, modern-Syria-Iraq], *and come, all you heathen* **[UN]**, *and gather yourselves together round about: There cause YOUR mighty ones to come down, O YAH.*

Prophetically speaking, the children of Israel have finally completed their DIVINE Punishment of captivity which extended from **the time zone of the head of gold down to the time zone of the ten toes of iron and miry clay.** Now YAH has called the Holy Court back into session.

Blessed be the glory of the Name of YHWH from everlasting to everlasting, whose Mercies endure forever towards the seed of Abraham, Isaac, and Yaacov, the anointed people.

May all Yisrael and Yehudah rise to praise and honor the Mighty YAH. Court is once again in session. Every Israelite and all inhabitants of the earth must have the proper DIVINE respect for the Judge. Let us all humble ourselves and be silent in HIS DIVINE Presence. We will humbly present ourselves before our HEAVENLY FATHER with this petition/prayer by one of the sons of Israel, Brother Yehoshua Ben Israel of Cincinnati, Ohio: "We petition thee O YAH to hear our prayer and grant us the strength as we fast and pray for clarity in thy Holy Spirit. We petition thee O YAH for DIVINE Inspiration and DIVINE Protection. We petition thee O YAH for unity for the brotherhood and unity of the sisterhood, and unity for the nationhood. We petition thee O YAH for good health and a sound mind. We petition thee O YAH for financial blessings. We petition thee O YAH for the return home and the great assembly of YOUR people. O YAH, we the outcast people that the whole world hate, we beseech you O YAH with our whole heart, mind, and soul. All praises be to YAH. HallueYAH, HalleuYAH, HalleuYAH. Selah.

We, the servants of YAH—the Israelites, have learned our bitter lesson after thousands of years of slavery. We do not call upon the names of no powers besides YAH. We worship YAH alone. The prayers of our lips are dedicated to HIM wholeheartedly and without guile. We have cast away all strange gods and false doctrines like a menstrous cloth. We have nothing to do with idols. As Brother Yehoshua Ben Israel said, we seek YAH for all our needs and we dedicate ourselves to walking in HIS commandments as HE commanded us at Mt. Sinai. Israel's goal is to have clean hands and to be blameless as we enter HIS Heavenly Divine

Court of Justice. Let us all raise our right hand and recite this pledge: We pledge to comply and live by YOUR 10 DIVINE Principles known as the 10 commandments and all YOUR laws, judgements, statutes, and ordinances. We seek YOU with all our minds, hearts, and souls. We pray towards the land of Israel, the city of Jerusalem, and the ruins of the Temple once built by King Solomon. We invoke the Name of **YHWH** our Eternal Saviour and Redeemer and we ask YOU to pardon us and bring us back home. O YAH, we humbly and respectfully place this petition/prayer before your bench, even YOUR Holy Throne. Forgive us O FATHER, please have Mercy, please act on our behalf.

YAH's Heavenly Divine Court of Justice in the latter-days

"I call you to hear the word of YAH! I saw YHWH seated upon His throne, with all the host of heaven standing in attendance to the right and to the left of Him." **[I Kings 22: 19]**.

"As I looked on, Thrones were set in place, And the Ancient of Days (YHWH) took His seat, His garment was like white snow, and the hair of His head was like lamb's wool. His throne was tongues of flame, his wheels were blazing fire." **[Daniel 7: 9]**.

For YHWH is our JUDGE, YAH is our Lawgiver, YHWH is our **[Israel's]** *King. He will save us.* **[Isaiah 33:22]**.

It is now the 21st century and two millenniums have passed. YAH's Heavenly Court is once again back in session after 2,600 years of recess which started with the rise of **the head of gold,** the ancient Babylonian empire, and continued until the days of the **ten toes of iron and miry clay,** the United Nations, the G-20, NATO, and the European Union. One of the holy angels (the accuser) stepped forward to testify against **"the children of the image"**. The angel unsealed the secret indictment. With a strong voice, he began to read the long list of Spiritual Crimes that the heathen kings and their people had committed for centuries. The **Spiritual Indictment** read: O children of men, the people of gold, silver, brass, iron, and miry clay, you have done evil in the eyes of the CREATOR of the heavens, earth, and the seas. You have not walked in HIS ways or sought DIVINE Truth during the time zones of your rulership. This is the vision of YAH and we will tell you, the world governments, the interpretation of YAH's Pronouncements. You, O kingdoms of gold, silver, brass, iron, and iron and miry clay were the dominant superpowers among the kingdoms of men. YAH, ELOHIM who created the heavens gave you world power, economic strength, and triumphant military glory. Wheresoever the children of men dwelt, the beasts of the field and fowls of the heaven has dwelt, HE has given into your hands, and has made you the heads over all the world governments. Your kingdoms were the heads of world power. It was YAH, the Most High ELOHIM, who gave you wisdom and might. HE established your kingdoms and removed your foes. It is YAH who gave wisdom to your wise men and women, and revealed to them the abundance of all knowledge.

Yet, you O kingdoms of gold, silver, brass, iron, iron and miry clay, have not sought ME, the Living ELOHIM nor walked in MY righteousness. Instead, you have made graven images, erected sacred posts, and bowed before great monuments. You did not seek the DIVINE Presence of YAH, nor acknowledge HIS cloudy pillar by day and pillar of fire by night. You glorified lifeless craved statues. You chose to serve sculptured images, even man-made religions, such as Bel Marduk, Sin, Ishtar, Mithra, Zeus, Apollo, Jupiter, Venus, Saturn, Mars, Jesus, Mary, Allah, Buddha, Confuicus, rats, golden calves, and countless other false deities. I am YAH that made all things. I stretched forth the entire heavens alone. I spreadeth abroad the earth by MYSELF. Yet you, O idolatrous kingdoms, trusted in tokens from your liars. You sought divination and astrologers. A deceived mind turned you aside. Your eyes were shut to MY DIVINE Truth. You and your people were spiritual dullards who could not tell you were holding a lie in your right hand. You have praised the sun, moon, and stars, which I made, while you never acknowledged MY Presence standing before you. Instead you served the imaginations and ideologies which were graven into your uncircumcised minds. You, O idol worshippers took MY Name in vain and did not seek ME. Instead, you served the works of your own hands, even gods of wood, stone, gold, silver, brass, iron, and potter's clay. Therefore I will Judge you.

You did not acknowledge MY Holy Hebrew Shabbat. The citizens in your kingdoms had no respect for the elderly, murder was rampant, adultery was commonplace, stealing was a way of life, false witnesses were everywhere, and covetousness was an acceptable standard. Homosexuality and sexual deviations were the norm. Child sexual abuse occurred in every capital of **iron and miry clay** nations under the sun. Your wickedness is great, the press of perverseness is full, and vats of sins are overflown. And most of all, you have persecuted My people, the lost sheep of the house of Israel, from the head of gold down to the ten toes of iron and miry clay. Your inward thoughts were that your ungodly oppressive kingdoms would continue for ever. You have even named lands after your own names as if you created the earth.

After the Spirit of truth completed uttering the litany of spiritual offenses committed by the children of the image, YAH, the Self-Existing ONE who liveth forever and ever in truth, judgement, and righteousness, lifted up HIS hand holding the holy gavel, even the Scepter, and struck the bench then said: "**I hereby sentence you, O children of the image, to utter destruction in the Final Conflict of the Battle of Armageddon.**"

YAH's Heavenly Verdict against the Children of the Image

"Therefore wait you upon ME saith YAH, until the day that I rise up to the prey; for MY determination is to gather the nations; that I may assemble the kingdoms, to pour upon them MINE indignation, even all MY fierce anger: for all the earth shall be devoured with the fire of MY jealousy. **[Zephaniah 3:8].**

Some people may still wonder why the Creator would say such harsh things about the 7 billion people that make up humanity. The YAH-minded answer is found in **Isaiah 24: 5-6** which reads:*"For the earth is defiled under it inhabitants; Because they transgressed teachings, violated laws, broke the ancient covenant. That is why earth's dwellers have dwindled, And few men are left."*

So, as we see, the prophet Isaiah made it clear that all nations [**the kingdoms of gold, silver, brass, iron, and miry clay**], are bound to the Creator's moral laws. Yet during the reign of the children of the image, they were blinded by their trust and the belief in the anti-YAH way of life, consisting of man-made religions, military might, and economic power. However, the prophet Jeremiah, who was a black man, warned: "Thus said YAH: *"Let not the wise man glory in his wisdom; Let not the strong man glory in his strength; Let not the rich man glory in his riches, But only in this should one glory: In his earnest devotion to Me. For I YAH act with kindness, Justice, and equity in the world; For in these I delight declares YAH,"* **chapter 9: 22-23.**

Contrarily, the moral values within idolatrous kingdoms of gold, silver, brass, iron, and miry clay were not based on the sacred principles of kindness spoke by YAH. Their value systems were based on cruelty. There was no true justice among the nations. The rich [**iron kingdoms**] ruled the poor [**miry clay kingdoms**] with a rod of iron. Exploitation was the rule of law. There was no equity. The industrialized countries that made the rules, broke the rules, and wrote international laws which gave them advantages in trade. The iron kingdoms of the United States, France, and Britain, were the permanent members of the UN Security Council that worked against the miry clay kingdoms of Russia and China to control the global order. As I said earlier, the iron nations are the Euro-nations that dominate the International Monetary Fund, the World Bank, and all other international governing bodies in these latter-days.

Therefore YAH's Anger is presently kindled against the nations and shall He judge them according to the multitude of their iniquities. For their wickedness is great said the prophet Joel in **Chapter 3:13**, and *"This is YAH's day of retribution, The year of vindication for Zion's cause."*

THE VERDICT: **YAH's Pronouncements against all [Iron and Miry Clay] nations,** starting with HIS prophetic utterances against Jerusalem and continuing throughout the four corners of the earth. The DIVINE Judgement concerning Jerusalem is written in **Zechariah 12: 1-14**.

The pronouncement against America and Western Europe, the two modern-day offsprings of the ancient Roman Empire are found in [**Daniel 7: 7-8, 23-25**, **Jeremiah 51: 7-10, Isaiah 47: 1-15**]. The pronouncement against Russia is inscribed in [**Ezekiel 38:1-23**]. The Pronouncement concerning Iran (Persia) is also found in [**Ezekiel 38: 5**]. Continuing, YAH's pronouncement against the Arab world [the kings of the south], is found in **Daniel 11:40-45**], Those verses also include YAH's judgement against the far eastern Asian world. Their destiny is also foretold in [**Daniel 11: 44**] which predict that they will come to the region to participate in the final conflict.

Elsewhere, the prophecies concerning the continent of Africa are found in [**Isaiah 19: 1-21, Isaiah 20: 1-6**]. The prophecies in **Isaiah 34: 1-17, Isaiah 24: 17-23** are messages against all nations (**the United Nations**).

Ultimately, YAH's Judgements against all of these kingdoms will take place in the Valley of Yehoshaphat in the midst of the land of Israel. However, there will be many DIVINE judgements taking place, blow by blow, within the borders of many other countries at the same time. This DIVINE chastisement will be worldwide Judgements felt by all mankind.

The Final Battle of Armageddon kicks off

*"Let the heathen be wakened, and come up to the valley of Yehoshaphat: for there will I sit to Judge all the heathens round about. Put you in the sickle, for the harvest is ripe: come, get you down: for the press is full, the vats overflown: for their wickedness is great. Multitudes, multitudes in the valley of decision: for **the day of YHWH** is near in the valley of decision."* [**Joel 3:12-14 KJV/Joel 4:12-14 Tanakh**].

The Final Conflict of the Battle of Armageddon will involve millions of UN soldiers, and other warriors from individual countries worldwide. The State of Israel, Russians, Chinese, the United States, NATO, Turkey, the Arab League, Iran, various Arab militias such as Hamas, Hezbollah, Al-Qaeda, I.S.I.S., the Taliban, the Mahdi Army, North Korea, and countless others will drawn into the region for different reasons. Some of those nations will converge to protect their economic interest, others will gather to protect their idolatrous religious shrines in the holy land, and, most of all, many will converge to make war to achieve their covetous objectives. Regardless of what their evil thoughts may be or their personal motivations, it is YAH who is causing these nations to appear before HIM in the same manner as HE once caused the children of Israel to appear before HIM at Mount Sinai thousands of years ago.

*"For I know their works and their thoughts: it shall come, that I will gather all nations and tongues; and they shall come, and see my glory. And I will set a sign among them, and I will send those that escape of them unto the nations, to Tarshish, Pul, and Lud, that draw the bow, to Tubal, and Javan, to the isles afar, that have seen **MY** glory: and they shall declare **MY** glory among the Gentiles."* [**Isaiah 66:19-20**]. So as you can see, YAH reveals in this latter-day vision that HIS glory, even HIS cloudy pillar by day and HIS pillar of fire by night, will be openly revealed before the great Gentile powers of Western Europe and Russia to usher in **The Age of YAH**. [Read **Exodus 34:5-17** and **Exodus 24:15-18** to foresee how the Return of the Presence Of **YHWH** will appear in Zion and manifest Itself before all humanity].

"For, behold, YAH will come with fire; and with chariots like a whirlwind, to render HIS anger with fury, and HIS rebuke with flames of fire. For by fire and by HIS sword will YAH

plead with all flesh, and the slain of YAH shall be many." **[Isaiah 66: 15-16].** This fire which the prophet Isaiah referred to is: nuclear, biological, and chemical warfare. This reveals to us that **the Battle of Armageddon** will be a war where weapons of mass destructions are openly used by all sides. As the prophet said, *"the slain of YAH shall be many,"* even millions upon millions shall perish is the final round of this devastating war.

"And I **[YHWH]** *will overthrow* **(world capitals)** *the thrones of kingdoms* **(superpower nations)**, *and I will destroy the strength* **(their militaries)** *of the kingdoms of the heathen; and I will overthrow the chariots* **(fighter jets, long-range bombers, drones, aircraft carriers, frigates, tanks, jeeps, and all other support vehicles)**, *and those that ride in them; and the horses and their riders shall come down, every one by the sword of his brother* **[total chaos throughout the Mideast region]. [Haggai 2:22].**

It will be the glory of YAH returning to Judge the ends of the earth, especially the latter-day great world powers and their mighty armies. Notice, the prophet DID NOT mention any other Saviour besides **YHWH. YHWH Himself** is returning to overthrow the great capitals such as Bejing, Moscow, Paris, London, Madrid, Rome, New York, Washington, D.C., Capetown, New Delhi, and all other great cities. The New Testament is guilty of adding words and meanings to YAH's Sacred Counsel that HE never spoke. Therefore the New Testament, and all other so-called sacred books, are guilty of being False Witnesses that maliciously led the inhabitants of earth astray from the true meanings of the ancient Hebrew writings. YAH, the only CREATOR of heavens, earth, and the seas, will return to overthrow the strength of those lies and the great powers that support those false religions. It will be a bloody mess. Again, **The Age of YAH** will finally overthrow the corrupt 2,600-year dominion of the head of gold, the breast and arms of silver, the waist and thighs of brass, the pelvis and legs of iron, and toes of iron and potter's clay. YAH will accomplish HIS Will through the DIVINE chastisements of human warfare. The Spirit of YAH will provoke the multitudes of nations, ethnicities, and competing religious observers to raise their hands against each other in bloody warfare. The raging conflicts in Libya, Gaza, Lebanon, Syria, Iraq, Yemen, and ultimately, the war between Iran and Israel will fulfill the prophecies of Haggai, who was also an ancient Afro-Asiatic Hebrew spokesman.

"And it shall come to pass in that day, that I[**YHWH, not Christ, a Messiah, or a Lamb**] *will give unto Gog a place there of graves in Israel, the valley of the passengers on the east of the sea: and it shall stop the noses of the passengers; and there shall they bury Gog, and all his multitude: and they shall call it, The valley of Hamon-gog. And seven months shall the house of Israel be burying them, that they may cleanse the land. Yea, all the people of the land shall bury them: and it shall be to them a renown day where I shall be glorified saith YAH ELOHIM. And they shall separate out men for continual employment, passing through the land to bury with the passengers those that remain upon the face of the earth, to cleanse it; after the end of seven months shall they search. And the passengers that pass through the land when any see a man's bone, then shall he set up a sign by it, until the buriers have buried it in the valley of Hamon-gog.* **[Ezekiel 39:11-15].** As I said earlier, multitudes, even multitudes shall perish in this Battle against YAH.

"YAH also shall roar out of Zion, and utter HIS voice from Jerusalem: and the heavens and the earth shall shake **[great earthquake]**; *but YAH will be the hope of HIS people, and the Strength of the children of Israel. So shall you know that I* **[YHWH]** *your ELOHIM dwelling in Zion, MY holy mountain: then shall Jerusalem be Holy, and there shall no strangers* **[non-Israelites]** *pass through her any more.* **[See Joel 3:17 KJV or Tanakh 4:17].**

The Battle of Armageddon will spell victory for the children of Israel after serving as second-class citizens and perpetual slaves among the kingdoms of gold, silver, brass, iron, and miry clay for thousands of years. Jerusalem, which had been divided among three man-made religions, Judaism, Christianity, and Islam, will be purged from those three abominations that caused desolations. Jerusalem will return to righteous days of King David and King Solomon. Only the Presence of YAH, the cloudy pillar by day and the pillar of fire shall reign supreme in the newly reclaimed city of David. All the worshippers of those former religions will be eternally cast out of the holy sanctuary. No servants of strange gods shall be allowed to pass through the city of David any longer. **Jerusalem will be the Throne of YHWH forevermore.**

"Behold the eyes of YHWH ELOHIM are upon the sinful kingdoms, and I will destroy it from off the face of the earth; saving that I will not utterly destroy the house of Jacob, saith YAH. **[See Amos 9:8].**

This Holy Pronouncement by YAH confirms HIS true reason for gathering the nations into the region for Battle of Armageddon. The goal is to gather all nations, under the auspices of the United Nations, to the holy land for DIVINE Judgement. All 193 nations of the United Nations—both **iron and miry clay**—are sinful in the Presence of YAH. All those nations have allowed idolatrous man-made religions to flourish under the banner of religious choice. All of them are guilty of erecting great monuments of men, women, children, animals, insects, and creatures of the sea. All of the nations have citizens that engage in sun, moon, and astral research and worship. Out of all 193 nations with membership seats at the United Nations, none of them are wholly dedicated to the worship of **YHWH** nor have their rulers inclined their minds to accept YAH's Instructions. Therefore, they all take YAH's Name is vain. None of them totally observe the ancient Hebrew Sabbath by reframing from their personal pursuits and business practices. Instead in all of their respective capitals, altars are built for the glorification of Sunday worship and Friday worship. Along with that, racial hatred and tribalism continues to rage in many rich and poor nations. Elderly abuse is rampant in many nations worldwide, especially in the industrialized countries where old people are treated like a worthless commodity. Murder is a normal practice among the inhabitants of the earth. Adultery, broken families, child abuse, children sex trafficking, and homosexuality is accepted as normal practices in both the western and eastern world. The stealing of natural resources, malicious witnesses, and covetousness have been main reasons for a majority of today's regional conflicts. *(We won't even mention the other 603 laws inscribed in the Torah.)* All of those abhorrent practices have festered and grown among all **the children of the image: the kingdoms of gold, silver, brass, iron, and miry clay.** The prophet **Isaiah** spoke of them in chapter **5:20-21**: *"Ah, [you are] those who call evil good, and good evil: Who present darkness as light and light as darkness; Who present bitter as sweet and sweet as bitter. Ah, those who are wise in their opinion and clever in their wrong judgement"* The Holy One of Israel, the great KING, will eradicate all those improper mindsets and evil deeds during **The Age of YAH.**

"Come near, you nations **(United Nations)**,*to hear; and hearken, you people; let the earth hear, and all that is therein; the world, and all things that come forth of it. For the indignation of YAH is upon all nations, and HIS fury upon all their armies: HE hath utterly destroyed them, HE hath delivered them to the slaughter. Their slain also shall be cast out, and their stink shall come up out of their carcases, and the mountains shall be melted with their blood. And all the host of heavens shall be dissolved, and the heavens shall be rolled together as a scroll: and all their host shall fall down, as the leaf falleth off from the vine, and as a falling fig from a fig tree. For MY sword shall be bathed in heaven: behold, it shall come down upon* **Idumea**, *and upon the people of MY curse, to judgement. The sword of YHWH is filled with blood, it is made fat with fatness, and with blood of lambs and goats: for YAH hath a sacrifice in Bozrah, and a great slaughter in* **Idumea.**" **[See Isaiah 34:1].**

In the above mentioned prophetic utterances YAH revealed HIS true intentions, even HIS behind-the-scene Spiritual reasons, for orchestrating the Battle of Armageddon. On a base level, the children of the image perceive the war as a conflict about oil wealth, stamping out terrorism, and control of the holy land, but in the Mind of YAH this is about gathering the nations together for DIVINE Judgement. YAH is summoning the nations to judge them for their centuries of moral and spiritual corruption.

Although YAH denounces **"all nations"** in the vision,there is one nation that the CREATOR specifically pinpointed. That one nation mentioned was **"Idumea"**. This leads to the question, who is Idumea? Well, Idumea is the Greek translation of the Hebrew word "Edom". In the Hebrew scriptures, Esau was the father of the Edomite people. Moses described Esau as *"red all over like a hairy garment"*, in **Genesis [Bereshith 25:25]**. Esau was the first person whose skin color is explicitly mentioned. He appears to have suffered from a genetic disorder which caused a lack of melanin producing cells. That caused him to have a pale, reddish-white countenance. Both of his parents were dark-skinned, or what we refer to today as "black people". Esau eventually married black Canaanite women, established a family clan, and integrated in with the Horite people of Mount Seir. They were located south of the Dead Sea in Canaan. By the 13th century B.C.E.,the Edomite people became a dominant people in that area. The Edomites and the southern Israelites of the tribe of Judah were close neighbors. There were constant conflicts between the two nations.

When the kingdom of Judah fell in 586 B.C.E.,the Edomites joined forces with the Babylonians to fight against the people of Judah. Once the original inhabitants of the province of Judah was taken into captivity the Edomites moved northward into their abandoned territory. They remained there during the time zone of the Persians, Greeks, Ptolemies, Seleucids, and eventually the Romans. They began to practice the culture of the ancient people of Judah(Yehudah) and became known as "the Jews". They too became one of the converted nations spoken of in **2 Kings 17:27-29** which reads:

"Then the king of Assyria commanded, saying, Carry one of the priests who you brought from thence, and let them teach them the manner of the God of the land. Then one of the priests whom they had carried away from Samaria came and dwelt in Bethel, and taught them how they should fear YAH. Howbeit every nation [Edomites] made gods of their own, and put them in the high places [places of worship-synagogues] which the Samaritans had made, every nation in their cities wherein they dwelt **[strangers in the holy land practicing the culture of ancient Judah while adding pagan concepts of their own. This practice became known as Judaism]**.

When the anointed remnant returned,beginning in 536 B.C.E.—Zerubabel, Yeshua, Sheshbazzar and the 42,360 others—these squatters fought against the descendants of the original returnees. The conflict continued during the days of Ezra, Nehemiah, and Malachi.

During the reign of the Roman Empire, the Edomites, whose name had been changed to the **Idumeans,** became the rulers of Judaea under the auspices of Roman Gentile empire. One of most famous family of Edomites to emerge were the Herodian dynasty. Known as converted Jews, the family of Herod ruled from 37 B.C.E. until 44 C.E.. The family integrated in with the fair-skinned Aryan Romans. Around 37 B.C.E. Herod the Great began to reign. The Idumean king was appointed by **the kingdom of iron (Rome)** as the **"King of Judaea."** He was a pale-skinned Jewish convert who also supported General Mark Anthony during the days of the Roman civil-war. He later switched sides and became a supporter of Augustus Caesar. In return, Caesar increased his territorial claims over the holy land. The province of Judaea prospered under his reign. The Jewish kingdom expanded in trade. He built fortresses, aqueducts, theaters, and reconstructed the Second Temple in Jerusalem. Remains from the temple structure are still standing in Jerusalem today. It is presently known as "The Western Wall." When he died in the year of 4 B.C.E., his son Herod Antipas, the co-regent in Galilee, succeeded him on the throne. He reigned for 18 years in the former city of David. In the latter-days of his reign, the Emperor of Rome turned against him and banished the Jewish leader to province of Gaul **[modern France]**. As I said earlier, these close ties between the Idumean Jewish converts and the Roman empire allowed Judaism to spread throughout the realms of the massive empire. This is why there have been discovery of 2,000-year-old Jewish artifacts and archeological records of synagogues found throughout Asia Minor, parts of Europe, northern Africa, and the Middle East.

Another notable member of the Herodian dynasty was the grandson of Herod the Great. His name was Herod Agrippa. He came to power in the year of 41 C.E. and he too was known as the **"King of the Jews"**. Like his grandfather, he added to the Greco-Roman splendor of Jerusalem during his reign. He maintained close ties with Emperor Tiberius and Caligula. His reign came to an end in 44 B.C.E. The Jewish kingdom continued until the Roman armies destroyed Jerusalem in the year 70 C.E.

Nevertheless, the Jewish faith practiced by the Idumean descendants continued to flourish throughout Europe, Asia Minor, northern Africa, and elsewhere. The dream to return to Zion and rebuild the Jewish kingdom became the hallmark of the faith. During this time, the Arabs moved into the land of Canaan and became known as the Palestinians. During the absence of the Jewish people, the Arab Muslims flourished in the city of David and became the dominant population in the land for a thousand years. In the diaspora, the dream of a Jewish ingathering also flourished for the next thousand years. This dream became known as Zionism.

Another prominent people who became Jewish converts were the pale-skinned Khazars of eastern Europe. In the process of time Rabbinical Judaism from Constantinople [**Asia Minor/ modern Turkey**] eventually made its way into southern Russia. By 740 C.E. King Bulan and his ruling elite chose the religion of Judaism after listening to scholars from the three major world religions: Christianity, Islam, and Judaism. Khazaria was strategically located in southern Russia. It also served as a major trade route and religious corridor linking the East and West. The kingdom continued until it was destroyed by the Vikings in the 10th century C.E. Following their defeat, the Khazarian people were dispersed throughout eastern Europe into the countries of Russia, Hungary, Poland, and Germany. Their form of worship became known as Ashkenazi Judaism. By the Middle Ages, the Jewish converts had become major money traders, wealthy businessmen, and powerful politicians in several European countries. Many other Europeans also converted to the religion of Judaism becoming "religious Jews".

By 1948, the Zionist movement had received the backing of several European countries, mainly the United States, Britain, and France, and the State of Israel was created. The State of Israel became the heirs of the earlier Jewish kingdom of the Herod dynasty. Although, the historical Edomites or Idumeans were a Shemitic albino people and the Khazarians were a Euro-Turkish people, both were known as converted Jewish people that replaced the ancient Afro-Asiatic Hebrew people. Both of them historically hated and fought against the ancient people. Both claimed the title of **"the Jews"** which meant to imply they were the heirs of the seed of Abraham, Isaac, and Jacob. Both were a pale-skinned people. Both received the political backing of **the kingdom of iron**—the ancient Roman empire and its offspring the western European countries. Therefore in the latter-days **the Jewish-convert State of Israel** is the modern-day heirs of historical Jewish kingdom of Herod the Idumean. It is therefore the State of Israel which is pinpointed as prophetic "Idumea" in **Isaiah 34:1, Ezekiel 35:1-15, Ezekiel 36:1-5,** and **Obadiah 1:1-21.** They are the people who have sought to replace the original 12 tribes of Israel with their religion of Judaism. It is a certainty: The State of Israel will be one of the nations that will converge on Ceole-Syria for the Battle of Armageddon.

"Behold, the day of YHWH cometh, and your spoil shall be divided in the midst of you. For I will gather all nations (**United Nations**) *against Jerusalem to battle: and the city shall be taken, and the houses rifled, and the women ravished: and half of the city shall go forth into captivity, and the residue of the people shall be cut off from the city."* [**Zechariah 14:1-2**].

Based on this prophetic utterance all nations (**United Nations resolution condemning the State of Israel**) will join together in global criticism of Jewish kingdom. Supported by the UN Security Council, the enemies of Israel will make war against the possessors of the ancient city of David. In 1967, the Jewish State reclaimed the city of Jerusalem during the Six-Day War. Since then, the Jewish State of Israel has ruled and the Palestinian Arabs have fought against them. The United Nations has promoted the idea that Jerusalem is the city of three world religions: Judaism, Christianity, and Islam. The global order has also called for a two-state solution where both sides, Jews and Palestinians, share Jerusalem and the territory of Judah, and Samaria, known today as the West Bank. The State of Israel do not agree with the United Nations position. The Jewish State has claimed Jerusalem as their *"Eternal Capital."*

Bypassing the Palestinians, the Jewish government financed the construction of major cities, roads, and settlements throughout the West Bank, transforming a once Palestinian habitation into a Jewish stronghold. The State of Israel has also built one of the strongest militaries in modern history to defend their homeland. In the coming future, the State of Israel will crush the Palestinians on the battlefield. The only hope the victimized Palestinians will have is support from the international community at the UN. The Palestinian's goal is to bring international condemnation on the Jewish State and pressure them to surrender occupied territory. This will cause a global disagreement. The great **miry clay kingdoms** of Russia, China, and several powerful **iron European kingdoms**, Germany, Denmark, Canada, and Sweden are sympathetic to the Palestinian cause and they have called upon all nations to support the anti-Zionist cause. The other powerful **iron** nations, the United States, Britain, France, and other western European countries are strong supporters of the State of Israel. This disagreement among major powers will make *"Jerusalem a cup of trembling unto all people round about, when they shall be in the siege both against Judah and Jerusalem. And in that day will I make Jerusalem a burdensome stone for all people: all that burden themselves with it shall be cut in pieces* **[major war]**, *though all the people of the earth be gathered together against it. In that day saith YAH, I will smite every horse with astonishment, and his rider with madness; and I will open MINE eyes upon the house of Judah, and will smite every horse of the people with blindness."* **[Zechariah 12:2-4]**.

I know I said this earlier, but I'll say it again. The struggle between the competing groups of religious observers to control Jerusalem will actually serve as a catalyst for the latter-day Battle of Armageddon. In the final conflict, and in this last round of warfare, the United Nations will be forced to dispatch international peacekeepers, representing all nations, to the holy land to temporarily halt the indiscriminate bloodshed between warring Jewish, Iranian, Palestinian, and Arab parties. This endtime United Nations peacekeeping mission will only serve as YAH-inspired bait to get all nations involved.

b) Universal Worship of the ELOHIM of Israel begins with
The Destruction of the Idolatrous Nations usher in new era

"Then was the iron, the clay, the brass, the silver, and the gold, broken to pieces together, and became like the chaff of the summer threshingfloors; and the wind carried them away; that no place was found for them; and the STONE[YHWH] that smote the image became a great mountain and filled the whole earth." **[Daniel 2:35]**.

"The adversaries of YHWH shall be broken to pieces: out of heaven shall HE thunder upon them: YAH shall judge the ends of the earth; and HE shall give strength unto HIS king; and exalt the horn of HIS anointed (HIS people). **[The prayer of our beloved sister Hannah, a daughter of YAH, found in I Samuel 2: 10]**.

"YAH will be terrible unto them: for HE **[YHWH]** *will famish all the gods* **[man-made religions]** *of the earth; and men shall worship HIM***[YHWH]**. *every one from his place, even all the isles of the heathen."* **[Zephaniah 2:11]**.

It is the Presence of YAH[**The STONE Cut Out Without Hands**] who returns to restore righteousness upon the earth after 2,600 years of global pagan domination. The **time zone of the toes of iron and miry clay** has finally concluded. YAH's DIVINE Judgements of natural disasters and wars has consumed the great and powerful idol-worshipping nations. The falsehoods and moral corruption that ruled the minds of men, women, and children during **the era of the kingdoms of iron, clay, brass, silver, and gold** has been *swept away* by the wrath of YAH.

"The great day of YAH is near, it is near, and hastens greatly, even the Voice of the day of YAH: the mighty man shall cry there bitterly. That day is a day of wrath, a day of trouble and distress, a day of wasteness and desolation, a day of darkness and gloominess, a day of clouds and thick darkness. A day of the trumpet and alarm against the fenced cities and against the high towers. And I will bring distress upon men, that they shall walk like blind men, because they have sinned against YAH and their blood shall be poured out as dust, and their flesh as dung. Neither their silver nor their gold shall be able to deliver them in the day of YAH's wrath; but the whole land **[the earth]** *shall be devoured by the fire of HIS jealousy: for HE shall make even a speedy riddance of all them that dwell in the land* **[the earth]**. **[Zephaniah 1:14-18]**.

The Victory of YHWH

The Aftermath of the Final Conflict of the Battle of Armageddon: The glory of YAH has been universally recognized by all remaining inhabitants of the earth. **The Spirit of YHWH** has cleaned the earth of human misconduct. HIS DIVINE Presence, even HIS cloudy pillar by day and pillar of fire by night has been openly revealed to all mankind. **YHWH** has commanded HIS Angels *[the wind]* to destroy all evildoers throughout all ends of the earth. The Angels of YAH will go door-to-door worldwide until all spiritual criminals are *[swept away]*. Some will be pardoned to be reformed. Others will be executed on sight.

This DIVINE global offensive by YHWH will bring victorious universal recognition to HIS Name alone, ushering in **The Age of YAH [the** *STONE became a great mountain and filled the whole earth]*.

In that day and at that time the prophecies of Moses in the Torah and the pronouncement of Habakkuk shall be finally fulfilled. The glory of YAH will cover the earth like the waters that cover the seas. **[See Numbers 14:21 and Habakkuk 2: 14]**. *Wait a minute!* (We should all realize something here). The so-called Old Testament, as Gentiles call it, has not been fulfilled with the life and death of Jesus as the Christian theologians have falsely taught for thousands of years. Both of these prophecies by Moses and Habakkuk are not realized until the **latter-days in the Age of YAH.** So again, those Gentile religious authorities have blatantly taught falsehoods and poisoned the minds of people worldwide against the Hebrew Scriptures—which is the true name for the so-called Old Testament. **The Age of YAH** will finally clear up all New Testament lies and distortions such as "The Lamb, Christ is the son of David, the Rapture, the Second Coming, and all other idolatrous Epistle narratives.

"YHWH has made bare HIS holy arm in the eyes of all the nations; and all the ends of the earth shall see the salvation of our ELOHIM," **[not the return of Christ or Messiah]. [See Isaiah 52:10]**.

"For YHWH is our Judge, YHWH is our Lawgiver, YAH is our KING; HE will save us." **[Isaiah 33:22]**.

"Strengthen the weak hands, and confirm the feeble knees. Say to them that are of a fearful heart, Be strong, fear not: behold your ELOHIM will come with vengeance, even ELOHIM with a recompense; HE **[YHWH]** *will come and save you. Then the eyes of the blind shall be opened; and the ears of the deaf shall be unstopped. Then shall the lame man leap as an hart, and the tongue of the dumb sing: for in the wilderness shall waters break out, and streams in the desert."* **[Isaiah 35:3-6]**.

Immediately after the conclusion of the Battle of Armageddon, YAH will gather the lost sheep of the House of Israel from among the graveyards of nations, even the lands of their captivities. From all continents, the redeemed of YAH shall travel the Overground Railroad and the Freedom Highway to Zion. Thus saith YAH: *"I will set a sign* **[Universal Recognition]** *among them* **[all nations]**, *and I will send those that escaped of them* **[from the Battle of Armageddon]** *unto the nations, to Tarshish* **[Spain-NATO countries]**, *Pul, and Lud, that draw the bow* **[fight in war]**, *to Tubal* **[Russia]**, *and Javan* **[Greece-NATO countries]** *to the isles [of the Gentiles] afar off, that have not seen MY glory; and they shall declare MY glory among the Gentiles* **[Western and Eastern Europe]**. *And they shall bring all your brethren for an offering unto YHWH for an offering unto YAH out of all nations upon horses* **[in airplanes]**, *and in chariots* **[in all kinds of modern transportation]** , *and in litters* **[in ships]**, *and upon mules* **[in cargo trucks]**, *and upon swift beasts***[in fast-moving express trains]**, *to MY Holy mountain Jerusalem, saith YAH, as the children of Israel bring an offering in a clean vessel into the house of YAH. And I will also take of them for priests and for Levities, saith YHWH."*

Now that **the kingdoms of gold, silver, brass, iron, and miry clay** are vanquished, the twelve tribes will return home singing, "In YOUR temple, O Eternal, we meditate upon YOU and YOUR faithful care. These consecrated ones, the anointed sons and daughters of YAH will do as they have been commanded. They will meditate exclusively upon YAH their ETERNAL Saviour and Redeemer. The HaMashiach Remnant with praise YAH alone as the CREATOR of the heavens, earth, seas, and all that is therein is. The Israelite people will lead the global movement of praising YHWH. They will serve YAH their ELOHIM and act as a Light to the Nations teaching them how to praise, revere, and honor the Name of YAH.

The remnant will remember the DIVINE Instructions given by Moses and say: "Revere YAH our ELOHIM, walk in HIS ways only, love HIM with all our minds and souls. The twelve tribes will bring fame and notoriety to the Name of YAH worldwide. In China, Russia, India, Afghanistan, and elsewhere, men will know the difference between good and evil, and the difference between those who worship YAH and those who worship the works of their own fingers. The wise inhabitants of the earth will proclaim: YAH is the True Eternal, the everlasting Eternal, Supreme, Great, Majestic, Awesome in Power, and Glorious in wisdom, understanding, and knowledge. The nations will finally understand: *"The Gentiles shall come unto YAH from the ends of the earth, and shall say, Surely our fathers have inherited lies, vanity, and things wherein their is no profit. Shall a man* **[nation of people]** *make gods* **[religions]** *unto themselves, and they are no* **[true]** *gods*[**DIVINE Power**]. **[See Jeremiah 16: 19-20]**.

In **The Age of YAH** the redeemed Levitical priests will reinstitute the ancient Hebrew Shabbat. The days of praising other gods will be abolished. The only days of worship and praise allowed will be the Appointed Feast Days mentioned in the book of **Leviticus, chapter 23.** Beginning with the ancient Hebrew Shabbat, every seventh day from evening unto evening all inhabitants of the earth will be devoted to reflecting upon the majesty and glory of the CREATOR-YAH. **Yom Shabbat** will be honored in every nation under the sun. All nations will cease from their manual labors, their reaping and sowing, planting vineyards, cooking, sewing, constructing, slaughtering, washing, selling and buying, sports competition, and all other secular activities. **[See Isaiah 56:1-8, Isaiah 58:9-14]**.

"For as the new heavens and the new earth, which I will make shall remain before ME saith YHWH; so shall your seed and your name remain. And it shall come to pass, that from **one new moon** *to another, and from one* **Sabbath** *to another, shall all flesh come to worship before ME saith YHWH."* **[See Isaiah 66: 22-23]**.

HIS servants shall teach the nations how to observe the **New Memorial of The Passover** which commemorates the days when YAH brought forth the Israelites from the land of the north **[iron kingdoms]**, and from all other countries **[miry clay kingdoms]** where HE scattered them. **[See Jeremiah 16:15, Jeremiah 23:7-8]**. Israelites will instruct the nations in the proper course of observing **the Feast of the Firstfruits.** All mankind will undoubtedly understand the importance of honoring YAH first with their increases. Humanity will be honored to bring forth their offerings of bread, lambs, wine, and vegetables before the Presence of YAH—HIS cloudy pillar by day and the pillar of fire by night. There will be Universal Recognition of YHWH as the King of all the earth. All nations shall join together with the kingdom of Yisrael and Yehudah three sacred times each year observing **the Blowing of The Trumpets (Yom Zikron Teruah),** the Day of Atonement (**Yom Kippurim**), the Feast of Tabernacles (**Sukkot-Zechariah 14:16-21**). They will end the annual holy convocation with **Shmini Atzeret** shouting:*"YAH reigneth for eternity throughout all ages."*

Last but not least, all the inhabitants of the earth will follow Yisrael's lead in Loving YAH our ELOHIM will all their hearts and with all their souls, and with all their might. They will place the Sacred Name and Words of YHWH in their minds and will teach their children, speaking of them daily. All mankind [**nations**] will speak of the Words of YAH when they sit in their homes, when they travel throughout the earth, and when they return to their homes. Yisrael and Yehudah will teach the nations to **praise YHWH** when they rise in the morning and before they close their eyes to sleep at night. During **The Age of YAH**, the daily observance of the commandments spoken at Mt. Sinai will be the universally recognized standard for all humanity.

c) The Deliverance of the 12 tribes of Israel

"From beyond the rivers of Ethiopia [**from throughout the continent of Africa**] *MY suppliants, even the daughter of MY dispersed, shall bring MINE offering, "* said the prophet **Zephaniah in 3:8.**

"Thus saith YHWH[YAH] sabaot [host], In those days it shall come to pass that ten men shall take hold out of all languages of the nations, even shall take hold of the skirt of him that is Yehudah [**descendants of ancient Afro-Asiatic Hebrews of tribe of Yehudah**], *saying , we will go with you: for we heard that ELOHIM[God] is with you,"* said the prophet **Zechariah in 8:23.**

12 Prophecies of the Great Ingathering of the Latter-days

1) *"And it shall come to pass, when all these things are come upon you, the blessings and the curse, which I have set before you, and you shall call them to mind among all the nations, whither YAH thy ELOHIM has driven you, and shall return to YAH thy ELOHIM, and shall obey HIS Voice according to all that I*[**YAH**] *command you this day, you and your children, with all your heart, and with all your soul; That then YAH thy ELOHIM will return your captivity [slavery], and have compassion upon you, and will return and gather you from all the nations, where YAH thy ELOHIM has scattered you. If any of you be driven out unto the outmost parts under heaven, from there will YAH thy ELOHIM gather you, and from there will HE fetch you; And YAH thy ELOHIM will bring you into the land which thy fathers possessed, and you shall possess it; and HE will do you good, and multiply you above your fathers. And YAH thy ELOHIM will circumcise your heart* [**mind**], *and the heart* [**mind**] *of your seed to love YAH thy ELOHIM with all your heart*[**mind**], *and with all your soul* [**physical power**], *that you may live. And YAH will put all these curses upon thine enemies, and on them that hate you and persecuted you. And you shall return and obey the Voice of YAH, and do all HIS commandments which I*[**YAH**] *command you this day, and YAH thy ELOHIM will make you plenteous in every work of your hand, in the fruit of your body, and in the fruit of your cattle, and in the fruit of the land, for good; for YAH will again rejoice over you for good, as HE rejoiced over your fathers. If you shall hearken unto the Voice of YAH thy ELOHIM, to keep HIS commandments and HIS statutes which are written in this book of the law, and if you turn unto YAH thy ELOHIM will all your heart*[**mind**], *and with all your soul.*[**Deuteronomy 30:1-10**].

2) *"In those days, and in that time, saith YHWH, the children of Israel shall come, they and*

the children of Judah together, going and weeping; they shall go, and seek YAH their ELOHIM. They shall ask the way to Zion with their faces towards there, saying, come, and let us join ourselves to YAH in a perpetual covenant that shall not be forgotten. MY people hath been lost sheep:their shepherds have caused them to go astray, they have turned them away on the mountains; they have gone from mountain to hill, they have forgotten their restingplace." **[Jeremiah 50:4-6].**

3) "Thus saith YAH sabaot [of **host**]; the children of Israel and the children of Judah were oppressed together: and all that took them captives held them fast; they refused to let them go. Their Redeemer is strong; YHWH sabaot is HIS Name [not **Jesus Christ or Yeshua the Messiah**]: HE shall thoroughly plead their cause,; that HE may give rest to the land, and disquiet the inhabitants of Babylon. **[Jeremiah 50:33-34].**

4) "Surely the isles**[of the Gentiles]** shall wait for ME, and the ships of Tarshish first, to bring your sons from far, their silver and their gold with them, unto the Name of YHWH thy ELOHIM, and to the Holy One of Israel, because HE hath glorified you." **[Isaiah 60:9].**

5) "For HE**[YHWH]** saw that there was no man; and wondered that there was no intercessor; therefore HIS**[YHWH]** arm brought salvation unto HIM; and HIS righteousness, it sustained HIM. For HE**[YHWH]** put on righteousness as a breastplate, and an helmet of salvation upon HIS head; and HE put on the garments of vengeance for clothing, and was clad with zeal as a cloak. According to their deeds, according HE will repay, fury to HIS adversaries, recompense to HIS enemies; to the islands HE will repay recompense. So shall they fear**[revere]** the Name of YAH from the west, and HIS glory from the rising of the sun. When the enemy shall come in like a flood, **the Spirit of YHWH** shall lift up a standard against him. And the Redeemer **[YHWH-See Isaiah 54:5]** shall come to Zion, and unto them that turn from transgression in Jacob, saith YAH." **[See Isaiah 59:16-20].**

6) "For the nation and kingdom that will not serve you shall perish; yea those nations shall be utterly wasted. The glory of Lebanon shall come unto you, the fir tree, the pine tree, and the box together, to beautify the place MY sanctuary; and I**[YHWH]** will make the place of MY feet glorious. The sons also of them that afflicted you shall come bending unto you; and they that despised you shall bow themselves down at the soles of your feet; and they call you, 'The city of YHWH, The Zion of the Holy One of Israel. Whereas you have been forsaken and hated, so that no man went through you, I will make you an eternal excellency, a joy of many generations. You shall suck the milk of the Gentiles, and shall suck the breast of kings; and you shall know that I **[YHWH]** am your Saviour and your Redeemer, the Mighty One of Jacob.' For brass I will bring gold, and for iron silver, and for wood brass, and for stones iron: I will also make your officers Peace, and your exactors righteousness. Violence shall no more be heard in your land; wasting nor destruction within your borders; but you shall call your walls Salvation, and your gates Praise. The sun shall be no more your light by day; neither for brightness shall the moon give light unto you; but YAH shall be unto you an everlasting light, and thy ELOHIM your glory. The sun shall no more go down, neither shall the moon withdraw itself. For YAH shall be thine everlasting light, and the days of your mourning shall be ended. Your people also shall be all righteous: they shall inherit the land forever. The branch of MY planting, the work of MY hands, that I may be glorified. A little one shall be a thousand; and a small one a strong nation: I YAH will hasten it in HIS time." **[Isaiah 60:12-22].**

7) "But you shall be named the Priests of YAH; men shall call you the Ministers of our ELOHIM: you shall eat the riches of the Gentiles; and in their glory shall you boast yourselves. For your shame you shall have double; and for confusion they shall possess the double: everlasting joy shall be unto them. For I YAH love judgement, I hate robbery for a burnt offering: and I will direct their work in truth, and I will make an everlasting covenant

with them. And their seed shall be known among the Gentiles; and their offspring among the people: all that see them shall acknowledge them, that they are the seed which YAH has blessed. I will greatly rejoice in YAH, my soul shall be joyful in my ELOHIM [not the slave master's religion]. For HE has clothed me with robes of righteousness, as a bridegroom decketh himself with ornaments, and as a bride adorneth herself with her jewels. For as the earth bringeth forth her bud, and as the garden causeth the things that are sow in it to spring forth; so YAH ELOHIM will cause righteousness and praise to spring forth before all nations. **[Isaiah 61:6-11]**.

8) "*For I*[**YHWH**] *will restore health onto you, and I will heal you of your wounds, saith YAH; because they called you an Outcast, saying, this is Zion whom no man [nations] seeketh after. Thus saith YAH; Behold I will bring again the captivity of Jacob's tents, and have mercy on his dwellingplaces; and the city shall be built upon her own heap, and the palace shall remain after the manner thereof. And out of them shall proceed thanksgiving and the voice of them that make merry; and I will multiply them, and they shall not be few: I will also glorify them, and they shall not be small. Their children also shall be as aforetime, and their congregation shall be established before ME, and I will punish all that oppress them. And their nobles shall be of themselves* [**not a man returning on clouds as the 2nd Coming**], *and their governor shall proceed from the midst of them* [**again, not the return of Christ/Messiah**]: *and I will cause him to draw near, and he shall approach unto ME* [**not approach the Lamb or Christ**]: *for who is this that engaged his heart*[**mind**] *to approach unto ME? saith YAH. And you shall be MY*[**YHWH**] *people*[**YAH's People not worshippers of the Lamb**], *and I*[**YHWH alone**] *will be your ELOHIM*[**The Only POWERS**]. *Behold, the whirlwind of YAH goeth forth with fury, a continuing whirlwind: it shall fall with pain upon the head of the wicked. The fierce anger of YAH shall not return, until HE have done it, and until HE have performed the intents of HIS*[**YAH**] *heart*[**Mind**]: *in the latter days you shall consider it.*" **[Jeremiah 30:17-24]**.

9) "*At the same*[**in the latter-days**] *time saith YAH, will I be ELOHIM*[**YAH-Alone**] *of all the families*[**camps, congregations, communities, knessets, groups, tribes, etc.**] *of Yisrael, and they* [**all 12 tribes**] *shall be MY*[**YHWH**] *People. Thus saith YAH, the people which were left of the sword found grace in the wilderness, even Israel, when I went to cause him to rest. YAH has appeared of old unto me, saying, Yea, I have loved you with an everlasting love: therefore with lovingkindness have I drawn you. Again I will build you, and you shall be built, O virgin of Israel: you shall again be adorned with thy tabrets, and shalt go forth in dances of them that make merry. You shall yet plant vines upon the mountains of Samaria: the planters shall plant; and shall eat them as common things. For there shall be a day, that the watchmen upon the mount of Ephraim shall cry, Arise you, and let us go up to Zion unto YAH our ELOHIM*[**not visit the Lamb-Jesus or Yeshua, rather YAH our ELOHIM**]. *For thus saith YAH, Sing with gladness for Jacob*[**Black America**], *and shout among the chief of the nations: publish you, praise you and say, O YAH save YOUR people, remnant of Israel*[**not the Church, rather the faithful commandment-keeping people of 12 tribes of Israel**]. *Behold, I will bring them from the north country, and gather them from the coasts of the earth, and with them the blind and the lame; the woman with child and her that travaileth with child together: a great company* [**a great company, an untold number not 144,000. Also read Jeremiah 33:24-26.**] *shall return there. They shall come with weeping and with supplications will I lead them: I will cause them to walk by the rivers of waters in a straight way; wherein they shall not stumble: for I*[**YHWH**] *am a FATHER to Israel and Ephraim*[**the sons of Jacob, even the Israelite people**] *is MY Firstborn*[**not Jesus, Yeshua, Christ, the Messiah, or the Lamb**]. *Hear the word of YAH, O you nations, and declare it in the isles [of the Gentiles in Europe] afar off, and say, HE that scattered Israel will gather him, and keep him, as a Shepherd does for his flock. For YAH has redeemed Jacob*[**Black America**], *and ransomed him from the hand of him that was stronger than he. Therefore they shall come and sing in the height of Zion, and shall flow together to the goodness of YAH, for wheat, and for wine, and for oil, and for the young of the flock and of the herd: and their soul shall be as a watered garden: and they shall*

not sorrow any more at all. Then shall the virgin rejoice in the dance, both young men and old together: for I will turn their mourning into joy, and will comfort them, and make them rejoice from their sorrow. And I will satiate the soul of the priests with fatness, and MY people shall be satisfied with MY goodness, saith YAH.[**Jeremiah 31:1-14**].

10) *"Behold, I will gather them out of all countries where I have driven them in MINE anger, and in MY fury, and great wrath; and I will bring them unto this place [the land of Israel], and I will cause them to dwell safely. And they shall be MY*[**YHWH**] *People, and I*[**YHWH alone**] *will be their ELOHIM. And I will give them one heart*[**Mind**] *and one way, that they may fear ME*[**YHWH**] *for ever, for the good of them, and of their children after them: And I*[**YHWH alone**] *will make an everlasting covenant with them, that I*[**YHWH**] *will not turn away from them, to do them good: but I will put MY*[**YHWH**] *fear*[**reverence of YAH only**] *in their hearts*[**minds—The YAH Mind**]*, that they shall not depart from ME. Yea, I will rejoice over them to do them good, and I will plant them in this land assuredly with MY whole heart and with MY whole soul. For thus saith YAH: Like as I have brought all this great evil upon this people [The* **Curses of Deuteronomy 28:15-68**]*, so I bring upon them all the good that I promised them."* [**Jeremiah 32:37-42**].

11) *"Behold, the days come, saith YAH, that I will perform that good thing which I have promised unto the house of Yisrael and to the house of Yehudah. In those days, and at that time, will I cause the Branch of Righteousness to grow up unto David; and he shall execute judgement and righteousness in the land. In those days shall Yehudah be saved, and Jerusalem shall dwell safely: and this the name wherewith she shall be called, YAH our Righteousness.* [**Jeremiah 33:14-16**].

12) *"The remnant of Israel shall not do iniquity, nor speak lies; neither shall a deceitful tongue be found in their mouth: for they shall feed and lie down, and none shall make them afraid. Sing, O daughter of Zion: shout, O Israel; be glad and rejoice with all your heart[mind], O daughter of Jerusalem. YAH has taken away your judgements, HE has cast out your enemy: the King of Yisrael, even YAH* [**not Jesus Christ or Yeshua the Messiah**]*, is in the midst of you;*[**HIS majestic cloudy pillar by day and pillar of fire by night**]*; you shall not see evil any more. In that day it shall be said to Jerusalem, Fear you not; and to Zion, let not thine hands be slack. YAH thy ELOHIM in the midst of you is Mighty; HE will save, HE will rejoice over you with joy: HE will rest in HIS love, HE will joy over you with singing. I*[**YHWH**] *will gather them that are sorrowful for the solemn assembly, who are of you, to whom the reproach of it was a burden. Behold, at that time I will undo all that afflict you: and I will save her that halteth, and gather her that was driven out; and I will get them praise and fame in every land where they have been put to shame. At that time will I bring you again, even in the time that I gather you: for I will make you a name and a praise among all people of the earth, when I turn back your captivity* [**slavery**] *before your eyes, saith YAH."* [**Zephaniah 3:13-20**].

YAH'S Message To Black America

There are countless other scriptures that I could continue to pinpoint that expose the spiritual truths about the prophesied Redemption of the 12 tribes of Yisrael in the latter-days. If I attempted to write them all, I would never complete this book. There are so many of them. You can read more in: **Deuteronomy 4:29-31, Jeremiah 29:10-14, Ezekiel 20: 33-38, Ezekiel 36:22-38, Ezekiel 37:19-28, Zechariah 8:1-23, Zechariah 9:8-17, Amos 5:14-15, Hosea 13:4-5, Micah 7:15-20, Joel 2:23-32,** and **I Kings 8:46-61** to name a few.

The 12 Hebrew scriptures which I highlighted are totally clear. Without a shadow of a doubt, the various Hebrew prophets plainly cry out: **YAH our ELOHIM is the Saviour and Redeemer.** The covenant which YAH made with the 12 tribes is an everlasting agreement. YAH HIMSELF is the **"anointed CREATOR" "HaMashiach"** of HIS people. Those scriptures clearly expose us to the fact that YAH did not communicate any New Testament references of going up to heaven, Sunday-worship, the Second Coming of a middle man like a Christ, Messiah, or Lamb. Instead, YAH repeatedly command Yisrael to return to HIM with all their minds and souls. In the above mentioned scriptures which I emphasized, the prophets of Yisrael gave us high beam visions of the earthly seed of David being resurrected from the valley of dry bones to become the future earthly King of Israel, not a resurrected Christ descending from the sky. Please read the 12 Prophecies once more so it can soak in your brain and you really see this point for yourself. The visions of the Hebrew prophets, Moses, Isaiah, Jeremiah, Zepnaniah, Ezekiel, Amos, Zechariah, and all others, do not support the New Testament narratives that **the Laws of YHWH given to Moses** have been done away with, abolishment of the Hebrew dietary laws written in **Deuteronomy 14th chapter** and **Leviticus 11th chapter,** the 1st or 2nd Coming of Christ, the Lamb reigning on the throne of David, the Christian Church replacing ancient Israel as the covenant people, or any other pagan Greco-Roman self-conceived hypothesis. For the official Hebrew record, YAH did not speak any of those Words written in the pages of the Epistles. You never read the Sacred qualifying words of: "Thus *saith YAH ELOHIM,* or, *"The visions of YAH came unto me saying,* or, *"The Spirit of YAH came unto me saying thus and thus".* You never read those qualifying statements.

Another case in point, as I have already explained earlier in **Chapter 1,** is that the ancient Hebrew prophets were **like unto Moses** **of the tribe of Levi—Levitical priests**. Please re-read **Deuteronomy 18:15** from a Hebrew perspective, and not the Christian narrative. The men of the New Testament, especially the main figure, the man from Galilee, has two origins. One origin said he was from "the holy ghost" and the other origin said he was of the tribe of Judah. That too is a contradiction. Is he the seed of David or the seed of the holy ghost? If he is the seed of holy ghost, then, he is not the seed of David because his father is not one of descendants of David. On the other hand, if he is the son of David, he is not the only begotten son of God, all Israelites were considered YAH's Firstborn dating back to the days of Moses. Please re-read **Exodus 4:22**. The lost sheep of the House of Israel [**The American Negroes**] have been lied to since their arrival into this land of captivity. The slavemasters taught them their version of the bible, their interpretations of the scriptures, and most of all, taught them "the Old Testament has been done away with." This slave indoctrination has polluted the spiritual minds of the slave population for 400 years. However, in the latter-days the anointed remnant will cast off the yoke of those slave master's lies. They will withstand the slavemaster's religious whip that has scarred the spiritual minds of every generation since 1619. Like Frederick Douglass, the anointed remnant will take the religious whip out of the slavemaster's hand and stand up for YAH's Torah. As free-minded servants of YAH, they will cast away all foreign, slave-imposed or inspired religious teachings. They will refuse to be religious bondmen and bondwomen any longer. In return YAH will support their Redemptive Struggle and ransom them from the hand of their oppressors.

The anointed remnant will be the people who will finally make it to **"The Promise Land"** as Dr. Martin Luther King Jr. once predicted on April 3, 1968. YAH Power, the same power used by Moses, will be the salvation of the lost sheep of the House of Israel [**The American Negroes**]. On the other hand, their continued slavish belief in Christianity will prolong their days on the religious plantation. The majority of the lost sheep of Israel will not hear the Spiritual Decree of the YAH's Emancipation of Proclamation. They will continue to labor on spiritual, mental, political, economic, and social plantations long after the 400 years of captivity has been completed. Through ignorance, they will continue to pick cotton on various jobs many generations after YAH has decreed to open the Door of Return for those who desire to return to HIM and obey HIS Voice.

The lost sheep of Israel [**Black America**] must wholly return to YAH their ELOHIM and walk in HIS commandments as written in the Book of Moses. They must drop their belief and devotion to the slavemaster's inspired god named Jesus Christ. Once YAH awaken a brother or sister, he and she must not re-hatch the Christian narrative with a Hebrew twist. By this I mean, they turn white Jesus into black Yeshua. The philosophies of Yeshua is used to supplant the Teachings of the Torah. The lies of the apostles are accepted with the same respect given to the testimony of Hebrew prophecy. Brothers and Sisters that is pure ERROR and modern-day idolatry. The anointed remnant must drop the New Testament and the idolatrous worship of the man-god Yeshua falsely known as "The Messiah". YAH has never commanded or instructed HIS people Israel to believe in those false preachers and teachers who have spiritually led the American Negroes away from HIM who appeared at Mt. Sinai. We [**the lost sheep of Israel**] must believe and know only YAH, ELOHIM of our fathers, ELOHIM of Abraham, ELOHIM of Isaac, and ELOHIM of Yaacov as our only Eternal Saviour and Redeemer as written in **Exodus 3:15, Isaiah 43:3,11, Isaiah 45:15-18, 22, Isaiah 46:8-9, Isaiah 47:4, Isaiah 48:17-22, Isaiah 48:22-26, Isaiah 51:15, Isaiah 52:10-12, and Isaiah 54:5.** There are many other prophecies that support YAH as being the Saviour and Redeemer of the lost sheep of Israel, the American Negroes. In fact, the entire so-called Old Testament is actually buried American Negro history, dating back to once upon a time when we knew our Hebrew identity, but our ancestors still did not act righteously. This spiritual cold water may sadden millions of our sincere minded black brothers and sisters who have been misled into believing the Black Church is the WAY and the molten image named Jesus Christ is their lord and saviour. My Brothers and Sisters that message has been a message of 400-year-old brainwashing that was handed down to us by our foreparents who could not read or write. Therefore they did not make an intellectual decision when they accepted this Euro-Christian doctrine. But this bitter truth is intended to be like cold water poured upon you while you are asleep. It will wake you up to acceptance or anger you at the words of the prophets as in the days of old. Today, we must act wisely and the Negroes must let go of the religious doctrines of Pharaoh [**The Black Church**] and return to the 10 commandments [**Torah**] spoken by YAH at Mount Sinai. Then YAH will spiritually command Pharaoh to let MY Son—the Israelite People—go that he may return home to Freedom to serve ME. Once our people make the critical decision to amend their ways and return to YAH, Black America will once again become the true People of ancient Israel, the Servants of the Most High ELOHIM-whose name is poetically pronounced as **YAH**.

Once the anointed remnant return home their next step will be establishing a righteous government that represent the glorification of YAH exclusively and the exaltation of HIS commandments, laws, judgements, statutes, and ordinances which are written in the 12 Prophecies I just highlighted.

d) Re-establishment of the Kingdom of YAH on earth with the throne of David, the Levitical priesthood, prophets of Israel, and Israel and Yehudah—the 12 tribes

*"And I will clothe him [Hezekiah] with your robe, and strengthen him with your girdle; and I will commit your government into his hand; and he [Hezekiah, **a descendant of David**] shall be a father to the inhabitants of Jerusalem, and to the house of Judah. And the key of the house of David will I lay upon his shoulder; so he shall open, and none shall shut; and he shall shut and none shall open. [Isaiah **22:21-22 and Ezekiel 46:1-10**].*

The responsibility of self-governance will fall upon the shoulders of the anointed remnant after the destruction of the kingdoms of the image. The offsprings of Abraham, Isaac, and Yaacov will return from the lands of their enemies to rebuild the kingdom of YAH which had been destroyed thousands of years ago by King Nebuchadnezzar, **the head of gold**. The Blueprint of the Kingdom of YAH is revealed in **I Chronicles 28:1-9** where the scribe provided intricate details and wrote:

"David assembled all the prince of Israel, the prince of the tribes, and captains of the companies that ministered to the king by course, and the captains of thousands, and the captains of the hundreds, and the stewards over all the substance and the possession of the king and of his sons, with the officers and the mighty men, and with all their valiant men came

unto Jerusalem. [**National Unity**]. *Then David the king stood up upon his feet, and said, Hear my brethren, and my people: As for me, I had in my heart to build an house of rest for the ark of the covenant of YAH, and for the footstool of our ELOHIM, and had made ready for the building. But ELOHIM said unto me, you shall not build an house for MY Name, because you have been a man of war, and has shed blood. Howbeit YAH ELOHIM of Israel chose me before all the house of my father to be king over Israel for ever. For HE has chosen Yehudah to be the ruler [I* **Chronicles 28:1-9 is the fulfillment of Jacob's prophecy in Genesis 49:8-12. For 2,000 years, Christian theologians have falsely taught that this was a prophecy of Jesus the carpenter when in fact it was actually a prophecy of the coming of King David**]; *and of the house of Yehudah, the house of father; and among the sons of my father HE liked me* [**King David's Dynasty**] *to make me king over all Israel. And of all my sons, for YAH has given me many sons, HE has chosen Solomon my son to sit upon the throne of the kingdom of YAH over Yisrael. And HE said unto me, Solomon your son, he shall build MY house and MY courts [Isaiah* **43:7**]: *For I have chosen him to be* **MY son,** *and I [YHWH] will be* **his FATHER**. *Moreover,* ***I will establish his kingdom for ever****. If he be constant to do MY commandments and MY judgements, as at this day. Now therefore in the sight of all Israel the congregation of YAH, and in the audience of our ELOHIM, keep and* <u>seek for all the commandments of YAH our ELOHIM; that you may possess this good land, and leave it for an inheritance for your children after you forever</u>. *And you Solomon my son, know ELOHIM of your father, and serve HIM with a perfect heart*[**mind**] *and a willing mind: for YAH search all hearts [minds] and understand all the imaginations of the thoughts: if you seek HIM, HE will be found of you, but do not forsake HIM, HE will cast you off for ever."*

By this time this truth will be apparent to the anointed person who YAH has chosen to sit upon David's throne. This latter-day champion of the YAH Movement will be known for his spiritual victories against the children of the image. He will possess King David's courage and unselfish service in the liberation of YAH's people. Those positive attributes will earn him favor in the eyes of YAH.

"And I will clothe him [**the latter-day son of David**] *with your robe, and strengthen him with your girdle; and I will commit your government into his hand; and he* [**during The Age of YAH and the revived dynasty of David**] *shall be a father to the inhabitants of Jerusalem, and to the house of Judah. And the key of the house of David will I lay upon his shoulder; so he shall open, and none shall shut; and he shall shut and none shall open.* [**Isaiah 22:21-22**].

Although there will be many sons of David capable of occupying the position as "the son of David", it will be YAH who ultimately chooses this particular son of David above his other brethren. In that day and at that time the remnant will realize the importance of cooperation and national unity. No longer will be said, black people cannot organize or can't get along. These black people—the anointed remnant— will rally around righteous leadership and practice cooperative economics in their newly redeemed homeland. There will be no jealousy or envy among the righteous remnant. <u>This new style of leadership and DIVINE patriotism will be dedicated to exalting and glorifying of the Name of YHWH alone.</u> When you read **I Chronicles 28:1-9** you will see that this is exactly what ancient David did during his reign, and this is exactly what the descendant of David, who will raise up the tabernacle of David that is fallen, must do in the latter-days. *(This is the duality of prophecy I mentioned earlier in the opening pages of* ***Chapter 1.****)*

In the ancient kingdom of YAH the levitical priests always served as the spiritual spokesmen for YAH and the people, daily offering sacrifices and instructing the people on how to serve YAH. Judah, even David was the lawgiver with the scepter that did not depart from between his feet, and the sons of Aaron ministered before him. This is what will happen again in the new Kingdom of YAH. The prophet **Ezekiel** foretold this in **chapter 37:24-28**: *"And David MY servant shall be king over them: and they all shall have one shepherd; they shall also walk in MY judgements and observe MY statutes, and do them. And they shall dwell in the land that I* [**YAH**] *have given unto Jacob MY servant, wherein your fathers have dwelt;*

and they shall dwell therein, even they and their children for ever; and MY servant David shall be their prince for ever **[Re-establishing the Davidic Dynasty under YAH]**. *Moreover, I will make a covenant of peace with them; it shall be an everlasting covenant with them; and I [YHWH] will place them; and multiply them, and will set MY sanctuary*[**Shiloh spoken of Genesis 49:10**] *in the midst of them forevermore. MY* **[YAH]** *Tabernacle* [**not the Lamb or Christ**] *also shall be with them; yea, I [YHWH] will be their ELOHIM, and they shall be MY people. And the heathen shall know that I[YAH] do sanctify Yisrael, when MY sanctuary shall be in the midst of them forevermore."* In **the Age of YAH** this elected son of David, the anointed prince, will lead the people up to the gates of House of YHWH where YAH'S DIVINE Presence shall dwell [See **Ezekiel 46:1-24**]. *(Again, please notice that the Hebrew prophets never mention the name of J-E-S-U-S, Christ, the Lamb, of the 2nd Coming of a Messiah. Only the Name of YAH ELOHIM is mentioned. Therefore we, the conscious Israelites, must call all those Gentile-inspired beliefs a strange doctrine or a strange god).*

Not only did the prophet Ezekiel foresee the resurrection of the throne of David in the latter-days, he also foresaw the reestablishment of the Levitical priesthood in **chapters 40 through 48**. Through the Visions of YAH, he saw a new generation of prophets returning to the midst of Israel as in the days of Elijah [**See Malachi 4:4-6**]. In **The Age of YAH** these new Hebrew prophets will appear as spiritual directors for the anointed remnant. The 12 tribes will re-experience **Ezra 5:1-2**: *"Then the prophets Haggai the prophet, and Zechariah the son of Iddo, prophesied unto the Jews* [**remnant of black Yehudah, Benyamin, and Levi**] *that were in Judah and Jerusalem in the name of ELOHIM of Israel even unto them. Then rose up Zerubabel the son of Shealtiel* [**the son of David-See Haggai 2:23, Zechariah 4:6**] *, and Yeshua the son of Yozadak*[**Levities**]*, and began to build the house of ELOHIM which is at Jerusalem: and with them were prophets of ELOHIM [prophets] helping them."* So as you can see, these scriptures clearly illustrate that the main goal of the ancient remnant was to re-establish the Davidic kingdom upon their return from the Babylonian captivity in 536 B.C.E.. This will be the same goal during **The Age of YAH.** Once again, rebuilding the Davidic kingdom will be the main goal of the anointed remnant after their ingathering back to Jerusalem. The universal righteous order will be total reverence to YAH, the re-establishment of the throne of David, the revival of the Levitical priesthood, the re-establishment of Hebrew prophets, and the restoration of the twelve tribes of Israel back to Zion. This revived Kingdom of YAH will serve as the returned Messiah-Prince, YAH's Light to the Nations, in the midst of earth. The 12 tribes will bring humanity under the guidance of YHWH.

Total Reverence to YHWH, the CREATOR of the heavens, earth, and the seas
Throne of David
Levitical Priesthood
Hebrew Prophets
12 Tribes

e) The Holiness of YAH rule the earth forever.

"You [**12 tribes of Yisrael**] *are the children of YAH your ELOHIM: you shall not cut yourselves, nor make any baldness between your eyes for the dead. For you are an holy people unto YAH thy ELOHIM, and YHWH has chosen you to be a peculiar people unto HIMSELF, above all the nations that upon the earth.* [**Deuteronomy 14:1-2**]. In **The Age of YAH** every Israelite man, woman, and child shall understand the DIVINE concept of total reverence to YAH. The Teachings of YAH shall be written in their inward parts, and they shall publicly sing, "There is none like YOU, O YAH. YOU are great in Might. Who would not revere YOU, O YAH, King of the nations? For kingship befits YOU. For among all the wise men of the nations and in all their kingdoms it is known that there is none like unto YAH. YOU, O YAH are truly ELOHIM, a LIVING ELOHIM, the everlasting KING. YOU, O YHWH, made the earth with YOUR Might. YOU established the universe with YOUR wisdom and with understanding. YOU spread out heavens; YOU raised clouds from the end of the earth. YAH

makes lightning bolts for rain and continuously bring forth winds from HIS treasuries. Therefore we give honor and glory to YOU, O YAH our ELOHIM.

Wisdom belongs to YOU, O YHWH, so let not the wise men glory in their wisdom, let not the mighty ones glory in their might. Neither let the rich and wealthy glory in their riches. True success O YAH is earnest devotion to YOU. YOU act with kindness, justice, and equity throughout all realms. In these attributes you delight O HOLY ONE of ISRAEL. YOU, O YAH are the Throne of Glory exalted from of old. YOU, O YAH are our Sacred Shrine, the Hope of Israel. Therefore you have healed us and we are healed. YOU saved us and we have been saved. For YOU are our glory. Blessed is the one who trusts in YOU, O YAH. YOU alone are worthy of praise, glory, reverence, and honor. Blessed is the ones who trust in YOU alone. They will be as trees planted by the rivers of waters whose roots never fail. In YOU, O YHWH is everlasting life and continuous joy. Blessed be the glory of the HOLY ONE of Israel from everlasting to everlasting."

In those days and at that time, the minds of the Israelite people will be totally circumcised to YAH their ELOHIM. They will wholly understand the differences between truth and falsehood, light and darkness, and those who serve YAH and those who serve the "gods of others." The twelve tribes will make joyful noises praising YAH. The soulful vibrations from these redeemed psalmists will be felt internationally. All lands will join the global joyous chorus of praising YAH. The anointed remnant and all mankind shall go up to New Jerusalem to appear before the THRONE of YAH, even **the DIVINE Presence of YAH, even HIS cloudy pillar by day and HIS pillar of fire by night.** YAH will be continuously recognized as the **SOVEREIGN CREATOR** dwelling in the midst of HIS people Israel and all remaining inhabitants of the earth. In the true Kingdom of YAH the names of the twelve tribes of Israel shall be written on their gates as written in **Ezekiel 48:1-35.** Each tribe shall enter through their respective gate with gladness and thanksgiving to worship YAH, the Great King. All the inhabitants of the earth will bless **the Sacred Name of YHWH**. They will join the 12 tribes saying, "YAH is good, HIS mercies are everlasting and HIS truth spoken at Mi. Sinai endureth to all generations."

"*Thus saith YAH ELOHIM, Behold, I will lift up MINE hand to the Gentiles* [**Let MY people Go!**], *and set up MY standard to the people; and they shall bring your sons in their arms, and your daughters shall be carried upon their shoulders. And kings shall be your nursing fathers, and their queens your nursing mothers: they shall bow down to you with their face toward the earth; and lick up the dust of your feet; and you shall know that I am YHWH. For they shall not be ashamed that wait on ME.* [**Isaiah 49:22-23**]. In **The Age of YAH** the lawful captives, even the descendants of Daniel, Hananiah, Mishael, and Azariah—the anointed remnant—shall be finally taken away from the grips of **the kingdoms of gold, silver, brass, iron, and miry clay.** They will be finally taken away and delivered by **The STONE Cut Out Without Hands—YHWH.** All the powerful enemies of the Israelite people, even the oppressive superpowers, have been fed their own flesh and drunken with their own blood.

In this new eternal time zone known as **The Age of YAH:** "All flesh shall KNOW that I[YHWH] is the **SAVIOUR** and Israel's and mankind's **REDEEMER, the Mighty One of Jacob.** [**Isaiah 49:26**].

"*And he [YAH] said unto me, O Son of man, the place of MY THRONE, and the place of the soles of MY feet, where I will dwell in the midst of the children of Israel forever; and MY Holy Name shall the house of Israel no more defile, neither they, nor their kings, by their whoredom, nor by the carcases of their kings in their high places.*

In their setting of their threshold by MY thresholds, and their post by MY posts, and the wall between ME and them, they have even defiled MY HOLY Name by their abominations that they have committed: wherefore I have consumed them in MINE anger.

Now let them put away their whoredom, and the carcases of their kings, far from ME, and **I[YAH] will dwell in the midst of them for ever." [Ezekiel** 43:7-9]. The curse of the Spiritual Famine, which began at the head of gold continuing down to the 10 ten toes of

iron and miry clay, is completed. The Spiritual blessings of **The STONE Cut Out Without Hands** even **The Age of YAH** is here raining down wisdom, understanding, knowledge, freedom, prosperity, well-being, and everlasting life upon the seed of Abraham, Isaac, and Jacob .
Then the 12 tribes will sing in unison the old Negro spirituals, *"We Have Overcame"* and *"Free at Last, Free at Last, thank EL Shaddai we are free at last in Mount Zion at Jerusalem."*

The Perpetual Reign of YAH

"Then a cloud covered the tent of the congregation; and the glory of YAH filled the tabernacle. And Moses was not able to enter into the tent of the congregation, because the cloud abode thereon, and the glory of YAH filled the tabernacle. And when the cloud was taken up from over the tabernacle, the children of Israel went onward in all their journeys. But if the cloud were not taken up, then they journeyed not till the day that it was taken up. For the cloud of YHWH was upon the tabernacle by day, and fire was on it by night, in the sight of all the house of Israel, throughout all their journeys."
[Exodus 40:34-38]

The Holiness of YHWH shall reign forever and ever in truth, judgement, and righteousness . HIS Glory shall cover the earth like waters that cover the seas.
[Numbers 14:21]
[Habakkuk 2:14]

"The great God [YHWH] has made known to the king [Nebuchadnezzar] what shall come to pass hereafter: And the interpretation thereof sure"
[Daniel 2:49]

Chapter 3

The Great Whoredom "that ruleth the nations, languages, and tongues"

> "What profiteth the graven image that the maker thereof hath graven it; the molten image, and a teacher of lies, that the maker of his work trusteth therein, to make dumb idols? Woe unto him that saith to the wood, Awake; to the dumb stone, Arise, it shall teach! Behold, it is laid over with gold and silver, and there is no breath at all in the midst of it."
>
> **Habakkuk 2:18-19**

Global Falsehood

"These six behaviors YAH hates, yea seven are an abomination unto HIM; haughty eyes, a false tongue, hands spilling innocent blood, a mind plotting iniquitous thoughts, feet hastening to run to evil, a false witness sprouting lies, and one who stirs up strife among brothers."
[Proverbs 6:16-19]

King Nebuchadnezzar of Babylon from days of old, and the great leaders of the world today, are guilty of all those above mentioned abominable attributes. They are guilty of thoughts and actions which YAHAWAH considers anti-righteous. In fact, the Almighty continues to hate these mindsets and conduct even today. Throughout the Torah you will find that HE still considers their actions as abominable.

Through prudent observation you will discover that even in the 21st century the world rulers, pagan priests, officers, magicians, wizards, witches, and the global population are guilty of acting in those above mentioned ways. As conscious Israelites, the sons and daughters of the MOST HIGH-YHWH, we must be sure that we do not bring those types of aforementioned mindsets into the emerging Kingdom of YAH, the ELOHIM of heaven and earth, who alone is: [**The Stone Cut Out Without Hands**].

So in this chapter, my goal is to spell out and highlight all of those behaviors in relationship to the Torah. To be completely honest, that was the only reason I provided the biographies of the kings and people of **gold, silver, brass, iron, and iron and miry clay** in the last chapter. That is why I looked into their personal lives. Through reading chapter 2 you will see that all of **the kingdoms of gold, silver, brass, iron, and iron and miry clay** violated the 10 commandments on a daily basis: They built temples for man-made gods, they called upon the names of other gods, they disrespected the SANCTITY of the **YHWH**, they violated the Sabbath, they did not honor their fathers and mothers, they murdered, they stole, they committed adultery, they bore false witness against each other, and they acted very covetously in so many ways. This is why I refer to their dominion as the reign of "The Uncircumcised Mind" which is reflected through their anti-YAH behaviors.

Chapter 3 opens with King Nebuchadnezzar II undertaking a major monument-building project which took him several years to complete. The Babylonian ruler commissioned a mighty force of builders, carpenters, sculptors, metallurgists, hewers of wood and stone, goldsmiths, and blacksmiths to construct a temple with a courtyard large enough to house the 90 feet pure gold statue. This new sculptured graven image represented the introduction of a new world religion by a powerful emperor (**the head of the kingdom gold**). It is exactly the same act that **Emperor Constantine of Rome** committed eight centuries later in 321 C.E. when he was **the head of the kingdom of iron**. He announced that the religion of Christianity was the new state religion.

King Nebuchadnezzar represented all non-Israelite men claiming to be divinely inspired by God, with visions that are totally opposite and contrary to the Words of YAH spoken at Mt. Sinai. This is a scenario that would be repeated over and over again by various religious founders, from **the head of gold down to the ten toes of iron and miry clay**. A word to the wise: Do not trust in any of these world religions whose origins can be traced back to the prophetic time zones of the head of gold down to the ten toes. These world religions would include Babylonian mystery religions, Zoroastrianism, Judaism, Christianity, Islam, Buddhism, Hinduism, and any other new religions created during the past three millenniums.

Nebuchadnezzar, serving as the High Priest or Pontiff, of his new Mystery Babylonian order claimed a vision from God had instructed him to build this new edifice. The plans for the grand ceremonies included a national holiday where all the subjects throughout his global realm were commanded not to work on that day. It was very similar to the way it is for Christmas in these modern days.

On a spiritual level, Chapter 3 represented the Great Whoredom that the world would face for millenniums because of the fall and destruction of the people(kingdoms) of Israel and Judah. **The twelve tribes of Israel once represented the Presence of YHWH on earth.** This PRESENCE was reflected through their obedient to YAH'S Voice and walking in HIS commandments, judgements, laws, and statutes. Through Israel, the **PRESENCE of YHWH** walked in the midst of the earth. When the people of **the Kingdom of YHWH**, both Israel and Judah, strayed away "after other gods" instead of compliance to their True Power, the entire earth experienced a spiritual darkness that it would not recover from until the re-emergence of the Kingdom of YAH, ELOHIM of heaven and earth, who alone is: **[The Stone Cut Out Without Hands]**. That development would not occur until the latter-days. That process is described as a time, times, and the dividing of time—in other words, thousands of years later]. Until then, man-made religions (gods) along with their man-made doctrines would be the rule of law among the kingdoms of men. That explains why there are so many religions in the world today. These man-made belief systems bring the illusion of salvation to its worshippers. In reality, these lifeless icons and doctrines have no power, and, are not representatives of the Words of YHWH which HE commanded to the covenant people when they depart from ancient Egypt.

According to the spiritual and mental state of Nebuchanezzar II, his idol was the "Saviour" and personification of God on earth. This is why he wanted everyone to bow down before the Presence of his new religion (golden image). In Nebuchadnezzar's uncircumcised mind, his idol was the Creator of the heavens, the earth, and the seas. The Chaldean Pontifex Maximus believed his idol controlled man's destiny. His testimony was that his man-made god was the true path of Salvation and Redemption for all nations, kindreds, and languages. All non-worshippers were considered sinners.

Conscious Israelites of that era were fully aware that King Nebuchadnezzar's executive order was a violation of the 1st and 2nd commandments of YHWH which states:

> *"I* **[YHWH]** *am your* **[ELOHIM]** *who brought you out of the land of Egypt, the house of bondage: You shall have no other gods besides ME. You shall not make for yourself <u>a sculptured image</u>, or any likeness of what is in the heavens above, or on the earth below, or in the waters under the earth. <u>You shall not bow down to them or serve them.</u> For I* **[YHWH]** *your* **[ELOHIM]** *am an impassioned ELOHIM, visiting the guilt of the parents upon the children, upon the third and upon the fourth generations of those who reject ME, but showing kindness to the thousandth generation of those who love ME and keep MY commandments."* **[Exodus 20: 2-6]**

Nebuchadnezzar's thoughts, actions, and plans violated those DIVINE principles. First, he built a graven image to honor another power besides YAH. That was a violation of **Exodus 22: 19** which states:

> *"Whoever sacrifices to a god (belief-system) other than YAH alone shall be*

Secondly, he had <u>haughty eyes. Eyes that looked down upon and despised the 1st and 2nd commandments of YAH</u>. Secondly, he had a <u>false tongue</u> that <u>spoke against the DIVINE PRINCIPLES of YAH</u>. In the eyes of Nebuchadnezzar his graven image was greater than YAH. In his uncircumcised mind his golden deity commanded him to erect the monument in its honor. Again, the MIGHTY ONE of heaven, earth, and the seas did not command this ruler to commit these sins. The people who <u>refused to bow down to his god</u> were sentenced to be cast into a fiery furnace, therefore his <u>hands were guilty of spilling</u>

518

innocent blood.

The foolish leader attempted to murder Hananiah [Shadrach], Mishael [Meschech]. and Azariah [Abednego] in the fiery death chambers. His mind plotted iniquitous thoughts; thoughts that turned his spirit away from the commandments of ELOHIM. He was quick to run to evil, doing wrong, even after the truth had been shown to him. Remember now, Daniel had already recalled and interpreted the dream for him in the previous chapter. Yet, he quickly forgot the prophetic revelations.

> "He who turns a deaf hear to instructions, His prayer is an abomination,"
> **[Proverbs 28:9]**
> "Those who forsake instruction praise the wicked [Satan],"
> **[Proverbs 28:4]**

Instead, the king of Babylon declared a national holiday with a national parade featuring dancers, musical bands, and pageantry. That national holiday was not one of the Hebrew Holy Days commanded by YAH in **Leviticus 23: 1-44**, such as the Passover, the Shavuot, or High Holy Season [Yom Teruah, Yom Kippurim, Sukkot]. Therefore his feet hastened to run to evil. He was a false witness sprouting lies and stirred up strife among brethren. By this I mean, he plotted wars against surrounding kingdoms, dividing some into his allies and others into his foes. This policy of discord stirred up strife among the families of nations and allowed him to rule over them all.

As I said earlier, Nebuchadnezzar displayed all the seven above mentioned abominable traits. This is why the prophet **Isaiah** described him as "Lucifer, the son of morning", in chapter **14: 4-7**. He was Satan, the adversary of YAH in his days and times. Just as you have today, world leaders opposing the commandments of YAH and acting as the Satans [The Serpent] of this modern time zone we're living in now. Now let's read and discuss **Daniel, chapter 3** together. It reads on this wise:

> King Nebuchadnezzar made an image of gold, whose height was sixty cubits high [90 feet], and the width six cubits [9 feet]. He set it up in the plain of Dura in one of the provinces of Babylon. King Nebuchadnezzar then sent word to gather the satraps, prefects, governors, counselors, treasurers, judges, officers, and all the provincial officials to attend the dedication of the statue that King Nebuchadnezzar had set up. So the satraps, prefects, governors, counselors, treasurers, judges, officers, and all the provincial officials assembled for the dedication of the statue that King Nebuchadnezzar had set up, and stood before the statue that Nebuchadnezzar had set up. **[Daniel 3:1-3]**

After spending enormous amounts of the kingdom's treasury on this government project, the new monument was ready for dedication, world review, and salutation. All the noblemen and noblewomen, chief government officials, and their low-level workers were instructed to take the day off work. There was plenty of wine, music, women, men, along with children for sensual pleasures. Satraps and other officials from the provinces of Judah, Egypt, Syria, Zidon, Assyria, Persia, and Arabia were in attendance. Their hearts were merry and ready for a great celebration.

From a spiritual point of view, this religious gathering represented the **"era of the uncircumcised mind."** A time when men and women who were without the knowledge of Torah were in charge of world affairs. Instead of rulers like King David or King Solomon, you have corrupt minded Nebuchadnezzars, Cyruses, Alexanders, Ceasars, Czars, kings, queens, and presidents. These "strangers" represented rulers without the proper DIVINE respect for **EL Shaddai (God Almighty)—YAH**.

What makes this situation so bothersome is the fact that none of these human beings knew any better. They were all wicked men and women who were spiritually retarded—out of their righteous minds. Those participants were spiritual dullards with brains lacking true wisdom, understanding, and knowledge. Their minds were so dull they could not comprehend the least basic DIVINE principles such as the 1st and 2nd commandments even if it smacked them in the face. In their minds it was Christmas-time.

> "The herald proclaimed in a loud voice:[**"It's a national holiday**], "You are commanded, O peoples and nations of every language, when you hear the [**king's symphony**] sound of horn, pipe, harp, lyre, psaltery, bagpipe, and all other types of instruments, to fall down and worship the statue of gold that King Nebuchadnezzar has set up. Whoever will not fall down and worship shall at once be thrown into a burning fiery furnace."
> [Daniel 3:4-6]

The wondrous 90 feet tall glittering, shiny pure golden statue stood tall in midst of the royal courtyard. People gathered around like multitudes gathering during the lighting of the national Christmas Tree at the White House. The people, nations, and languages enjoyed the festivities like the multitudes who gather at Times Square in New York each January for New Year celebrations. There was one difference, however, everyone's participation was mandatory, like pledging allegiance to the flag or paying income taxes.

> "And so, as soon as all the peoples heard the sound of the horn, pipe, harp, lyre, psaltery, and all other types of instruments, all peoples and nations of every language fell down and worshipped the statue of gold that King Nebuchadnezzar had set up. Seizing the occasion, certain Chaldeans came forward to slander the Yehudees [Jews]. They spoke up and said to King Nebuchadnezzar, "O king, live forever! You, O king, gave an order that everyone who hears the horn, pipe, harp, lyre, psaltery, bagpipe, and all types of instruments must fall down and worship the golden statue, [**A Total Violation of Exodus 20: 1-3**], and whoever does not fall down and worship shall be thrown into a burning fiery furnace. There are certain **Yehudees [Black Hebrews of tribe of Judah]** whom you appointed to administer the province of Babylon, Shadrach, Meshach, and Abednego; those men were brought before the king.
> [Daniel 3:7-12]

What that historical development revealed was that the Israelite belief in ONE POWER, YAH, the DIVINE PRESENCE that filleth heavens and earth was totally opposite to the new world religion that was being introduced and forced upon the inhabitants of the earth by King Nebuchadnezzar.

Although the Israelite people were in Babylonian captivity, the righteous ones continued to observe Torah. The spiritual issue at hand was whether Shadrach, Meshach, and Abednego would cleave to the 1st and 2nd commandments or bow to public pressure and accept the new religion of their slave master. Similar to the situation our ancestors faced here in America when their masters forced them to serve their blond, blue-eyed statue and picture of Jesus Christ, which is the graven image of the

Europeans—modern-day Chaldeans or face death. Our ancestors were stripped, whipped, and beaten into submission of the religion of their slave masters. That is a well known fact, and it proves our connection to the ancient Afro-Asiatic Hebrew people, who received the same treatment. Our ancestors Hebrew names were changed to Belteshazar, Shadrach, Meshach, and Abednego. King Nebuchadnezzar did the same thing to our ancestors that American slave owners did to us thousands of years later. His aim was to intimidate the Israelite people into fearing him and bowing to his religion and forsaking YAH for fear of losing their lives. King Solomon once said:

> "The fear of man bringeth a snare: but whoso putteth his trust in YAH shall be safe." **[Proverbs 29:25]**

> King Solomon also stated: "An unjust man [**King Nebuchadnezzar**] is an abomination to the just [**Shadrach, Meshach, and Abednego**]; and he that is upright [**Shadrach, Meshach, and Abenego**] is hated [an abomination] by the wicked [**King Nebuchadnezzar**]. **[Proverbs 29:27]**

Those two proverbial life lessons explain why there has been, and continues to be, a constant conflict between the righteous servants of YAH and the idolatrous (people)kingdoms of the earth, beginning with the head of gold on down to the ten toes of iron and miry clay today. Throughout these various captivities, it has been difficult for the Hebrew Israelites to serve two masters: Obeying the Voice of YAH while serving Nebuchadnezzar (foreign leaders) at the same time. As we can see, oftentimes the slave masters of the earth have demanded conversion to their way of thinking and acting. The Israelite experience in this country has been exactly the same for nearly four centuries. Again, this is another example of the duality of prophecy which I spoke in the beginning of chapter one.

> "Then Nebuchadnezzar, in raging fury, ordered Shadrach, Meshach, and Abednego to be brought; so those men were brought before the king." **[Daniel 3: 13]**

Upon hearing the report that certain black men were not being patriotic, Nebuchadnezzar's merry heart turned into raging anger. In his mind, he controlled the Yehudees. They were his property to be used as he saw fit, and the last thing anyone of them would do is not obey his commands. The only protection these Israelites had was the DIVINE Presence of YAH. This heathen king intended to kill them.

> "Nebuchadnezzar spoke to them and said, "Is it true[you nigger boys], Shadrach, Meshach, and Abednego, that you do not serve my god [Jesus Christ] or worship the statue[man-made god and doctrine] that I [not YHWH] have set up? Now if you are ready to fall down[submit to] and worship the statue [slave master's religion] that I have made when you hear the sound of the horn, pipe, harp, lyre, psaltery, and bagpipe, and all other types of instruments, [well and good]; but if you will not worship, you shall at

once be thrown into a burning fiery furnace, and <u>what god [belief] is there than can save you from my power?"</u>
[Daniel 3: 14-15]

In other words, *"I know you [Yehudee] nigger boys are not disobeying your master, are you? My god is your lord and saviour, and if you don't confess his name and proclaim your belief in him, I will string you up, tar and feather you, torture you boys to death, and there ain't no God that can stop me. I am God to you boys. Do what I tell you now!"* Of course Nebuchadnezzar expected to see head scratching and grinning like the thousands of unmentioned Yehudees who did submit to his terror. Again he expected words like: *"No sir boss, we's ain't disobeying you. We love your instructions massa, we's believe everything you tell us. Sho' we believe in your gospel. We gon' worship the golden image boss."* Up until this point these Hebrew men had been model citizens. The last thing he expected to hear were words like these following defiant words:

""Shadrach, Meshach, and Abednego said in reply to the king, "O Nebuchadnezzar, we have no need to answer you in this matter, for if so it must be, our God [YAH], not the golden statue] whom we serve is able to save us from the burning fiery furnace, and HE will save us from your power, O king: But even if HE does not, be it known to you, O king, that we will not serve your god [religion] or worship the statue of gold that you have set up."
[Daniel 3: 16-18]

That was, *and continues to be*, a classic example of Israelites standing strong inspite of physical danger and displaying courage during very difficult times of spiritual persecution. Thousands of unmentioned Yehudees bowed before the golden statue and participated in the religious and cultural festivities of King Nebuchadnezzar. They forsook YAH their ELOHIM who had brought their ancestors out of the land of Egypt[Africa] and feared man (the king of Babylon) and submitted to his new man-made religion. On the other hand, you had these three ancient Hebrew men, Shadrach, Meshach, and Abednego, who possessed spirits similar to men that we know today like Nat Turner, Denmark Vesey, David Walker, William Saunders Crowdy, Rabbi Wentworth A. Matthew, Marcus Garvey, Arnold Josiah Ford, Elijah Muhummad, Malcolm X, Dr. Isaac Richmond, and many other known and unknown freedom fighters, who have stood against tyranny during this American captivity.

"Then was Nebuchadnezzar full of fury, and the form of his visage was changed against Shadrach, Meshach, and Abednego: therefore he spake, and commanded that they should heat the furnace seven times more than it was known to be heated. And he commanded the most mighty men that were in his army bound Shadrach, Meshach, and Abednego, and to cast them into the burning fiery furnace."
[Daniel 3: 19-20]

Like all past and present brutal slave masters and tyrants, Nebuchadnezzar did not tolerate disrespect from his slaves. He demanded that the Israelite people to convert to his new way of life, drink his wine, eat his meat, and serve his god (religion). The decision by the Hebrew men to cleave unto the commandments of YAH their ELOHIM and not to bow before the Chaldean graven image was viewed as a criminal act of defiance against royal authority. According to the psyche of this Babylonian monarch, his temporal decrees superseded YAH's DIVINE Decrees.

On a spiritual level, **Chapter 3** of the book of Daniel exposes the reader to a World Without YAH where the man-made gods of Idolatry replaces the worship of the Living God [YAH]. The Sacredness of Torah was replaced with the Profanity of false doctrines. Heathenism replaced the Righteousness of Hebrew culture. Sin became normal and the rule of Law.

The chapter also provides us with a classic example of reckless behavior by a world leader who cast the commandments of God [YAH] behind his back and acted lawlessly without moral consciousness. That lack of moral consciousness has been on high display by the majority of world leaders since then, beginning with the time zone of the head of gold on down to the time zone of the ten toes of iron and miry clay in which we live today. The mindset of heathen rulership has been *"May the king live forever"* although there was no respect for the DIVINE PRINCIPLES of YAH. The phrase *"May the king live forever"* means may the man-made humanistic leadership of the kings of the earth continue without end. Glory be to man and not to YAH, the ELOHIM of the heavens, earth, and seas. Today, that kingship is represented by the federal governments and central authorities of the nations of the earth that rule without YAH consciousness, which is HIS commandments, judgements, and statutes. Today, those powerful leaders, like King Nebuchadnezzar in days of old, are continuing to issue new laws that violate the commandments of the Almighty YAH and issue threats of penalties and incarceration for those who do not bow down and comply.

> "Then these men were bound in their coats, their hosen, and their hats, and their other garments, and were cast into the midst of the burning fiery furnace. Therefore because the king's commandment was urgent, and the furnace exceeding hot, the flame of the fire slew those men that took up Shadrach, Meshach, and Abednego. And these three men, Shadrach, Meshach, and Abednego fell down bound into the midst of the burning furnace.
> **[Daniel 3:21-23]**

Remember what King Solomon once said: One of six behaviors YAH hates was: "HANDS SPILLING INNOCENT BLOOD." That is exactly what Nebuchadnezzar intended to do. Murder Shadrach, Meshach, and Abednego and spill their innocent blood because of his haughty Satanic eyes. The famous golden image represented a spiritual error and fabrication of all world religions. However, the spiritually blind masses of the world population accepted this new world religious order. The fiery furnace represented the enslavement and the sword that Israel and all inhabitants of the earth would face if they did not accept the new religions. Throughout Europe, Asia Minor, Africa, and the Americas, people have been slain who did not accept the great images of Jesus, the crucifixes and crosses, the statute of Virgin Mary, and New Testament teachings. That persecution represented a fiery furnace. The same has been true for the history of Islam as well. The founders of the religion conquered Asia, the Middle East, southern Europe, and Africa, and all who did not submit to the Koran and bow before the Kaaba Stone were cast into a fiery furnace. In other words, once a hearalder cried aloud, and one did not obey, they became sheep for the slaughter. All of those new religions forced the conquered populations to submit or die by the edge of the sword.

The Fiery Furnace also symbolized the continuous persecution and hostile environments that the children of Israel would face traveling through the dark tunnels of captivities that would extend from the head of gold unto the ten toes of iron and miry clay in the latter-days. Since the fall of Samaria in 721 B.C.E. and the destruction of Jerusalem in 586 B.C.E., the children of Judah and Israel have experienced continuous persecutions in the pagan heathenistic kingdoms of Babylon, Persia, the Grecia, Rome, Africa, and even in the Americas.

In the fiery furnace of captivity in North America, the lost sheep of the House of Israel have faced 246 years of chattel slavery,beheadings,religious and cultural persecution, whippings, torture, hung in trees and on stakes, fed to bloodhounds, bitten by police dogs, slain by police, railroaded by justice system, mass incarceration, capital punishment, along with any other forms of torture to humble the captives into submission. It has been very difficult for the servants of the Most High YAH to serve HIM in this environment. Nevertheless, YAH commanded HIS servants to stand strong in the Torah and not bow down to "other gods". In antiquity, Shadrach, Meshach, and Abednego complied and obeyed YAH's Voice even when faced with intimidation and a death threat. Today, the descendants of Shadrach, Meshach, and Abednego, the lost sheep of Israel must do the same thing although we have been cast into a 400-year fiery furnace in this American land of slavery. *"Be strong and of good courage,"* King David told the twelve tribes in **Psalms 31:24**.(The children of Israel would have to follow those instructions throughout their various captivities.) In the United States there has been the 1811 Louisiana Massacre, the Rosewood Massacre, the Tulsa, Oklahoma Massacre, the East St. Louis Massacre, the Memphis Massacre, the Eliane, Arkansas Massacre, the Wilmington Massacre, the Clinton, Mississippi Massacre, the Chicago Massacre, the Cincinnati Massacre, the Atlanta Massacre, the Springfield, Illinois Massacre, the Washington, D.C. Massacre, the Savannah, Georgia Massacre, and countless other bloody and fiery episodes in this iron furnace.

"Then Nebuchadnezzar the king was astonied, and rose up in haste, and spake, and said unto his counsellors, Did not we cast three men bound into the midst of the fire? They answered and said unto the king, True, O king. He answered and said, Lo, I see four men loose, walking in the midst of the fire, and they have no hurt; and form of the fourth is like a DIVINE Being."
[Daniel 3: 24-25]

On a spiritual level, the children of Israel were being purified in the furnace of affliction. Daniel, Hananiah, Mishael, and Azariah experienced this spiritual purification in the land of Babylon. A land of spiritual poverty where those Hebrew men sanctified the NAME of YHWH openly with a wealth of knowledge and confidence in YAH's Holy laws, commandments, judgements, and statues in that YAH forsaken land. The spiritual strength displayed by those mighty soldiers of YAH brought about that purification. Daniel, Hananiah, Mishael. and Azariah should be considered our role models on how to survive captivity.

What lesson did YAH want us to learn from that miraculous experience? Answer: When you glorify YAH's NAME in the flames of captivity you purify yourself and the whole nation of

Israel. Once a man or woman becomes a representative of the nation, he or she, becomes a part of the anointed remnant with a YAH-mind. This new mind causes us to realize that this chastisement we have experienced has been an act of love by YAH. YAH, who is our Spiritual Father and Mother, has used this fiery furnace to create a higher spiritual awareness in HIS people. Today, the anointed remnant has a better understanding of right and wrong. The elect has retraced the children of Israel's personal and collective steps in order to renew the covenant with the Ancient of Days[YHWH]. In the final analysis, the ALMIGHTY is creating greater Hebrew men, women, and children out the fiery furnaces of captivity and oppression. Out of the adverse conditions, YAH is molding a people with a higher spiritual intellect who have been humbled from their afflictions for past misdeeds. The anointed remnant is duty-bound to walk uprightly before the Throne of YHWH, the Everlasting King of the Universe.

Thus, Shadrach, Meshach, and Abednego in days of old, and the anointed remnant today are fulfilling the prophecy spoken by the prophet **Isaiah** in **48:9-12:** *"For MY Name sake will I [YAH] defer MINE anger, and for MY praise will I refrain for thee, that I cut thee not off. Behold I have refined thee, not with silver; I have chosen thee in the furnace of affliction. For MINE own sake, even MINE own sake, will I do it; for how should MY Name be polluted? And I will not give MY glory to another. Hearken unto ME O Jacob and Israel, MY called; I am HE; I am the first, I also am the Last."*

Furthermore, this chapter revealed that it was, is, and shall always be YAH who had walked with HIS people throughout the fiery furnace of captivity, beginning in ancient Babylon and continuing up into the 21st century. When Shadrach, Meshach, and Abednego were thrown into the flaming furnace, they survived and became greater men unscathed by the forces of wickedness. As Moses said: "When we do what is good and right in the eyes of YAH ELOHIM Yisrael, the forces of evil will not overcome us. The commandments of YAH is our Protection. The same was true for Daniel when he was thrown into the lion's den. This proved that when Israel is loyal to YAH, HE will remain loyal to them, even in slavery, and will be their Protector.

Each man, woman, and child that comprise the anointed remnant should seek to become a new person with a higher consciousness and understanding. They should not allow the flames of slave mentality, which has burned down our people's sense of DIVINE Intellect, to consume their minds. They must walk with a YAH-mind in the midst of the hellholes and wicked vices of captivity. They must re-learn how to love YAH their ELOHIM with all their heart, soul, and might. Israel must re-embrace Torah and walk in YAH's commandments. Then Israel will once again be YAH's Son, even HIS firstborn (the Son of God) spoken of in **Exodus 4:22** and **Daniel 3: 25**. So metaphorically speaking, these captivities were meant to purify Israel into men and women who are like unto angels of God. See **II Samuel 14:17,20** and **Zechariah 12:8**. In other words,the DIVINE chastisement of Captivity (the fiery furnace) was not designed to totally eradicate the children of Israel(they walked loosed in midst of the flames). Instead, it was meant to be a rod of correction to refine them into acknowledging YAH, the ELOHIM of heaven, earth, and seas. Coming out of the flames of national destruction, Israel should realize that it was YAH alone who saved them from the Fiery Furnance in the same manner HE delivered their ancestors out of ancient Egypt with an

OUTSTRETCHED ARM and MIGHTY HAND in days of old. This is the same spiritual lesson that black people (the lost sheep of the House of Israel) in America must learn from their 400-year experience here in this country, which began in the year 1619. Israelites, from the 17th through the 21st century, must reject the golden statue of their slave masters (Jesus Christ) and praise only YAH, the God of their fathers, the God of Abraham, the God of Isaac, and the God of Jacob spoken of in **Exodus 3:15**.

> "Then Nebuchadnezzar came near to the mouth of the burning fiery furnace, and spake, and said, Shadrach, Meshach, and Abednego, ye servants of the Most High God, come forth, and come hither. Then Shadrach, Meshach, and Abednego, came forth of the midst of the fire. And the princes, governors, and captains, and the king's counsellors, being gathered together, saw these men, upon whose bodies the fire had no power, nor was an hair of their head singed, neither were their coats changed, nor the smell of fire had passed on them. Then Nebuchadnezzar spake, and said, Blessed be the God of Shadrach, Meshach, and Abednego, who hath sent his angel, and delivered his servants that trusted in him, and have changed the king's word, and yielded their bodies, that they might not serve nor worship any god, except their own God." **[Daniel 3:26-28]**

> The power of YAH the KING of heavens and earth made a believer out of King Nebuchadnezzar, the ruler of Babylon. After the miraculous appearance of the Angel of YAH, even Nebuchadnezzar had to recognize YAH's greatness and ability to deliver HIS people out of the hands of those stronger than them-

selves. As it is written in the Torah in **Exodus 23:20:** *"Behold, I send MINE Angel before you, to keep you in the way, and to bring you into the place which I have prepared."* King David also reaffirmed that point by saying, *"The angel of YAH encampeth round about them that fear HIM, and delivereth them,"* in **Psalms 35:7**. Behind enemy lines in the midst of Babylon, YAH sent that Angel to assist Shadrach, Meshach, and Abednego to deliver them from the power of the fiery furnace because HIS covenant endures forever. *"Have you not known? Have you not heard, that the everlasting ELOHIM, YAH, the Creator of the ends of the earth, faineth not, neither is weary? There is no searching HIS understanding. HE giveth power to the faint; and to them that have no might he increaseth strength. Even the youths shall faint and be weary, and the young men shall utterly fall: But they that wait upon YAH shall renew their strength: they shall mount up with wings as eagles; they shall run and not be weary; and they shall walk, and not faint,"* the **Prophet Isaiah** proclaimed in **40:28-31**.

Furthermore, the prophet **Isaiah** envisioned a day when kings like Nebuchadnezzar would bow down and acknowledge the DIVINE PRESENCE of YAH in **chapter 49:7**: *"Thus saith YAH, the Redeemer and the HOLY ONE, to him whom man despiseth, to him whom the nation abhorreth, to a servant of rulers, kings shall see and arise, princes also shall worship, because of YAH that is faithful, and the HOLY ONE of Israel, and HE shall choose you." "Look to ME and be saved, all the ends of the earth: for I am ELOHIM, and there is none else. I have sworn by MYSELF. The word is gone out of MY mouth in righteousness, and shall not return, that unto ME* **[YAH]** *every knee shall bow,* **[even Nebuchadnezzar bowed down]** *every tongue shall swear. Surely, shall one say, in YAH I have righteousness and strength:*

even to him shall men come; and all that are incensed against him shall be ashamed. In YAH shall all the seed of Israel [Shadrach, Meshach, and Abednego] be justified, and shall glory," said **Isaiah** in **45:22-25**. Make sure that you read the **Book of Esther, chapters 1 through 10** as well. It is another classic example and testimony of YAH's protection and salvation in the midst of the fiery furnace of captivity in ancient Persia.

The days are coming said YAH to the prophet **Jeremiah** in **chapter 3:15** that, *"At that time they shall call Jerusalem the throne of YAH; and all nations* **[from the head of gold down to the ten toes of iron and miry clay]** *shall be gathered unto it, to the Name of YAH to Jerusalem: neither shall they walk any more after the imagination of their evil hearts* **[worship of the golden images and all false world religions]**.

We should also listen to this YAH-inspired counsel coming from **Isaiah 51:12-13**: *"I[YAH] ,even I[YAH] am HE that comforteth you* **[not Jesus/Yeshua]**: *who are you, that you should be afraid of a man* **[Nebuchadnezzar]** *that shall die, and of the Son of man which shall be made as grass; And forget YAH thy Maker who stretched forth the heavens, and laid the foundations of the earth; and has feared continually everyday because of the fury of the oppressor, as if he was ready to destroy? And where is the fury of the oppressor?*

The answer is found in **Proverbs 21:1**: The fury of the oppressor is in the hand of YAH because *"the king's heart* **[mind]** *is the hand [under* **the control of]** *YAH, as rivers of water, he turneth it wheresoever HE will."*

So one of the main lessons that the children of Israel should learn from **Daniel chapter 3** is: Israelites must love YAH our ELOHIM with total reverence and not fear "other gods" which are represented by the rulers of the idol-kingdoms of the earth. Threats and intimidation should not cause the anointed remnant to become fearful and bow down to public pressure. Like Shadrach, Meshach, and Abednego of yesteryears, Israelites of the 21st century must always remember in the final analysis, YAH's WORDS will always prevail over the Satanic designs of uncircumcised world leaders whose dominion has extended from the head of gold down to the toes of iron and miry clay.

"Therefore I make a decree, that every people, nation, and language, which speak anything amiss against the God of Shadrach, Meshach, and Abednego, shall be cut in pieces, and their houses shall be cut in pieces, and their houses shall be made a dunghill: because there is no other God that can deliver after this sort. Then the king promoted Shadrach, Meshach, and Abednego, in the province of Babylon." [Daniel 3:29-30]

From a YAH-perspective, the unveiling of the 90-feet tall golden national monument represented an evil abomination. Its mere presence caused a great separation between God ALMIGHTY and the various people of the nations and languages that followed the dictates of King Nebuchadnezzar instead of the Creator's DIVINE PRINCIPLES. That spiritual gulf which causes a great disconnection between the ALMIGHTY and mankind is known as the Great Whoredom that ruleth over the earth. Due to spiritual illiteracy the majority of the inhabitants of the earth do not fully understand the first commandment spoken by EL SHADDAI [God ALMIGHTY] at Mount Sinai:

"And ELOHIM[God] spake all these Words, saying, I am YAH[the Lord] thy ELOHIM[God] which brought you out of the land of Egypt, out of the house of bondage. You shall have no other gods besides ME," **Exodus 20:1-3**. This DIVINE PRINCIPLE is the beginning of true

Spirituality. YAH alone created the heavens, the earth, and the seas, and all therein. HE only is worthy to be praised. HIS SPIRITUAL PRESENCE spans the entire heavens and the entire earth. The Torah instructs Israel that the eyes of YAH sees all things and HIS ears hears all things. Therefore a true Israelite worshipper should never bow down to or *"make any graven image, or any likeness of anything that is heaven above, or that is in the earth beneath, or that is in the waters under the earth."* **(See Exodus 20:4)**. Again, the Torah teaches that idolatry was a capital offense punishable by a death sentence. Read **Exodus 22:20** in the King James Version of the Bible and see for yourself. What King Nebuchadnezzar failed to realize was that he, himself, was a spiritual criminal who deserved death in the eyes of YAH for building the gigantic 90-foot tall graven image. His lawless conduct was in direct violation of the 1st and 2nd commandments of God ALMIGHTY(**EL SHADDAI**).

In the eyes of YAH, idolatry causes an altered and confused sense of reality. You can read about it in **Isaiah 44:9-20**. Idolatry is also spiritual filthiness which causes perverse thoughts, beliefs, and actions. The spiritual disease of idolatry causes mental delusions in those afflicted by it. Sufferers of ailment believe in pure fantasies and blatant falsehoods, and last but not least, they become physical distracted, which in turn, causes them "to forget about YAH." The symptoms from this Great Whoredom includes an atheist heathenistic mentality, self-conceitedness, disrespect for Torah, extreme lust for richness, sexual perversion, fame, and power. (**See Jeremiah 9:22-23**). All the nations, from the head of gold to the feet of iron and miry clay, are spiritually uncircumcised, meaning they maintain love affairs with religious monuments . Most often, the leadership of these uncircumcised kingdoms direct their constituents to violate the 1st and 2nd commandments of God by exalting their new religious edifice while debasing the Words of YAH and casting HIS laws behind their backs. (**See Jeremiah 9:25-26**). In the book of **Ezra 9:11**, the Levitical priest Ezra described Nebuchadnezzar's and other nation's foreign lifestyles as "unclean, the filthiness of the heathen people who have filled the earth with uncleanliness and abominations from one end to another".

Nebuchadnezzar, and all the idolatrous leaders and people of the image of gold, silver, brass, iron, and miry clay, are spiritually dead. They were, and continue to be, unable to behold and understand the glory of the true and LIVING ELOHIM-YAH. Those people are the *"children of the image"* that comprised all nations, tongues, and languages. All of the inhabitants of the earth praise human handiwork. Those idol-worshipping nations seek only advancement of man through their humanistic mindset. They have no regard for YAH's DIVINE INSTRUCTIONS. They create lies (myths) and (legends) in the name of their man-made belief systems.

> "Their idols are silver and gold, the handiwork of man. They have a mouth but cannot speak, they have eyes but cannot see, they have ears, but cannot hear, they have a nose, but cannot smell."
> **[Psalms 115:2-8]**

The Chaldean craftsmen who built the golden image for Nebuchadnezzar made sure they constructed hands for the golden statute, but, in reality, those handcrafted hands did not possess life to feel or handle a human or a DIVINE task. The craftsmen also made sure that the golden image stood on two handcrafted feet, but those feet did not have blood running through their veins, or the ability to walk. It was a lifeless object. Although, the builders made a mouth on the golden image, it did not possess a tongue to utter a sound through its handcrafted throat. People who believe in lifeless idols [**world religions**] are just as .

spiritually lifeless as the non-living graven image that they worship. *"They that trust in them [idols] are like unto them* **[spiritually dead]**," King David once wrote in **Psalms 115:8** and **Psalms 135:18**

> "The idols of the nations are silver and gold, human handiwork. They have mouths but they speak not, they have eyes, but they see not, they have ears, but they hear not, neither is there any breathe in their mouths. Like unto them shall their makers become [spiritually **dead**], so is everyone who trust in them." **[Psalms 135:15-18]**

Although the idol-worshipping kingdoms appear to be materially prosperous today, they are spiritually in poverty. They are blind, deaf, and dumb to that spiritual fact, and on top of that, those kingdoms of gold, silver, brass, iron, and miry clay are morally and spiritually bankrupt in terms of Obeying YAH's Voice and following HIS commandments. Therefore, the children of Israel must look these idol-worshippers straight in their faces and "not be afraid" of their insults and insinuations. Israelites must stand strong because King Solomon said in **Proverbs 25:26,** *"a righteous man falling down before the wicked one is as a ruined fountain and a polluted spring."* Shadrach, Meshach, and Abednego could not let the historical King Nebuchadnezzar rob them out of their spiritual manhood and dignity. Likewise, Israelites of this era must not allow these modern-day Nebuchadnezzars to rob them out of their spiritual dignity in this dispensation.

Instead of trusting in YAH, the idol-worshipping kingdoms create their own man-made holidays giving praise, glory, and honor to the sun[Sunday, Saturnalia, Jesus Christ, Christmas, etc.], moon [Monday, the moon-god of Arabia], and the stars. They continuously honor men, women, animals, rocks, mountains, and hills, naming them in honor of their false beliefs. None of their holidays give honor to the True and Living ELOHIM—**YHWH**. Blessed be HIS Name forever. All Israelites should Magnify **YHWH's** works, for HE is great, and only HE is worthy to be praised, and not Nebuchadnezzar's golden image or any other world religion.

A Prayer For Victory In Our Spiritual Struggle
Prayers of Yehoshaphat Israel

"Awaken, Awaken, O YAH, arouse YOUR Strength, that we may behold YOUR outstretched ARM and Mighty HAND. Awaken as in the days of old, as when you brought forth ancient Israel out of the land of Kemet, even Egypt.

YOU, O YAH, are the only ONE who comforts Israel and Yehudah. I must learn to trust in YOU and not be fearful of man, especially the unrighteous mortals. For they shall be as grass. In the Time of Judgement they shall wither away.

You, O YAH, stir up the great seas causing their waves to rage. YOUR Name is YAHAWAH, KING of the Heavenly host. O YAH, please place YOUR Words in my mouth and I humbly ask YOU to protect me and allow me to dwell in the shade of YOUR Hand and protection. Please cover me, O YAH, I humbly beseech

YOU. YOU implanted the heavens and set the foundations of the earth. Please issue a HOLY DECREE and say to Zion, you are MY people. I have not forgotten you. Thank you O YAH, thank you forevermore.

Awake, Awake, O YAH, arise for YOUR Name sake and for Jerusalem's and YOUR ancient people's sake. I have sinned, I deserved to drink from the cup of YOUR fury. We did not Obey YOUR Voice, nor heed YOUR Instructions or warnings. Therefore we have fallen and can not get up. There are none among us that have the answers. Only YOU, O YAH, have the answers. Our Power is gone. Among the children there are none to guide us. Therefore, we humbly request that YOU return to our midst O HEAVENLY FATHER and lead us as in days of old. Even a cloudy pillar by day and a pillar of fire by night. YOU are the LIGHT. Blessed be YOUR Name throughout the existence of time, even forevermore. **Selah.**

KING NEBUCHADNEZZAR II
the personification of the evil and wicked man
(spoken of in Psalms 140:1-14)

In conclusion, **Chapter 3** of Daniel revealed that King Nebuchadnezzar of Babylon was the living personification of <u>an evil and wicked man</u>. In **Psalms 140:1-14**, King David said that an evil man is one who is lawless. This means a person who is not restrained or guided by the Holy Authority of YAH. He or she would eagerly break the commandments of YAH without taking a second thought. This was the mindset of the king of Babylon and it has grown into the mindset of most of the inhabitants of the earth today. Just like the ancient Nebuchadnezzar who disregarded the 1st and 2nd commandment by erecting the golden image, people today are doing the same thing and eagerly violating the 1st and 2nd commandments by erecting the graven images in the their homes, houses of worship, and townsquares.

In **verse 2** and **3** of the Hebrew Tanakh it reads: wicked men *"minds are full of evil schemes, who plot war every day. They sharpen their tongues like serpents; spider's poison is on their lips."* In other words, their conversations and communications are totally anti-YAH. The <u>evil and wicked ones</u> proudly speaks against the laws, commandments, judgements, statutes, and ordinances of YAH. In fact, just like Nebuchadnezzar, their government policies do not consider YAH'S standard, which is the Torah. You can witness countless rulers of different nations devising evil schemes in their minds to murder, steal, commit adultery, bare false witness, and act covetously against their own citizens and other countries. That type of anti-YAH behavior and has been accepted as a normal code of conduct. Therefore it is safe say that the world today is under the influence of anti-YAH heads of state [serpents]. These Serpent kingdoms of gold, silver, brass, iron, and miry clay have waged a daily spiritual war against the code of ethics prescribed in the Torah. This is why the world is in a state of lawlessness today. These serpent leaders have cast the Torah behind their backs and chosen to walk in the imaginations of their own proud, brave, and bold evil hearts. (They believe their anti-Torah way of life is ordained by God [the **golden image/false belief system**].)

"*Arrogant men* [**Nebuchadnezzar and others**] *laid traps with ropes for me* [**built a fiery furnace, executed evil decrees, and carried out other forms of persecution against the righteous**]; *they spread out a net along the way, they set snares for me*" **verse 6** reads. Continuing three verses later in **verse 9** it reads: "*O YAH do not grant the desires of the wicked; do not let their plan succeed, else they be exalted.*"

Those verses clearly illustrate the fact that the contemporary evil and wicked ones of the earth, like Nebuchadnezzar in days of old, and all others, will conspire and seek to entrap the righteous even when they have done nothing wrong. The evil and wicked man will slander the innocent with his serpentine tongue that spew anti-YAH thoughts.

TIMEOUT: As you read this particular portion of the book, please put the book down for moment. Turn on your television. Switch your channel to the evening news, take a look at the multitudes of poor and upper-class political, religious, and economic leaders and people who're making the news. Examine their conduct. See if their behavior reflects the [**personality profile and behavior pattern**] spoken of in **Psalms 140**. If any of their behaviors fit the shoe size described by the Psalmist, then he or she is guilty of being an evil and wicked soul. Believe it or not, there are plenty of modern-day Nebuchadnezzars walking around in our midst today. They come in all shapes, forms, fashions, and income levels. Some are rich and some are poor, but they all share one common attribute. Their human desires and endeavors are anti-YAH to the very core. They trust and believe only in their own viewpoints and the works of their own hands, such as their own particular religions, man-made ideologies, money, technology, sciences, the arts, music, and vulgar materialism. Those man-made pursuits have become the 21st century version of worshipping the golden image. Thereby causing all the inhabitants of the earth to become a lawless Personification of this Evil and Wicked Man spoken of in **Psalms 140** who bow before these modern-day abominations of spiritual desolation. Its so amazing, even poor and lowly men and women of the inner-cities are possessed with this selfish, haughty, anti-YAH Nebuchadnezzar spirit. (A black person will spread a net to trap and harm another one faster than Nebuchadnezzar's men threw Shadrach, Meshach, and Abednego in the fiery furnace).

TIME IN: Our ancestor King David did not turn the other cheek in **verses 10-13** when he asked YAH ELOHIM of Israel: "*May the heads of those who beset me be covered with the mischief of their lips. May coals of fire drop down upon them, and they be cast into pits, never to rise again. Let slanderers have no place in the land; let the evil of the lawless man drive him into corrals.*" As we can see, the son of Jesse did not pray for those who hated him and sought to spitefully misuse him. Instead, in the spirit of self-preservation he invoked YAH's Name requesting that HE champion the cause of the righteous poor and needy Israelite people at all time.

Now since YAH has visited us with the Spirit of self-realization, we, the descendants of the ancient Afro-Asiatic Hebrew people, should wholly return back to YAH our ELOHIM with all our minds, souls, and resources. We should return to the laws, commandments, judgements, statutes, and ordinances of YAH and worship HIM alone. Then, we as a people, will make it back to the promised land and dwell in the Presence of YHWH according to HIS everlasting covenant. Blessed be the Name of YAH, the Creator of the heavens, earth, seas, and all therein. Thank you, O YAH our Heavenly Father, for YOUR DIVINE INSIGHT, the wisdom, the understanding, and the knowledge that YOUR Presence illuminates.

A Psalms of Praise Dedicated to YAH

YAH, ELOHIM of our fathers, ELOHIM of Abraham, ELOHIM of Isaac, and ELOHIM of Yaacov our ETERNAL SAVIOUR and REDEEMER. YOU, O YAH, are Great in Counsel, and Mighty in works. YOUR Eyes, O YAH, are open upon all the ways of the sons and daughters of men. YOU give to everyone according to the fruit of their doings.

YOU have set signs and wonders in earth even to this day, and in Israel, and among other men. YOU have made YOU a Great Name as it is until this day. YOU will once again bring YOUR people from among all the nations with great temptations, signs, wonders, and a Strong Hand and Outstretched Arm, and with Great Terror. YOU promised the land of Canaan to the seed of Abraham, Isaac, and Yaacov, even to all the seed of the twelve tribes of Israel. O YAH please have mercy upon us and allow us to return to the land which YOU described as a land that floweth with milk and honey.

Blessed be the Name of YAHAWAH, ELOHIM of our fathers, ELOHIM of Abraham, ELOHIM of Isaac, and ELOHIM of Yaacov our ETERNAL SAVIOUR and REDEEMER forevermore.

Selah.

YAH IS MY STRENGTH

Blessed be the Name of YAHAWAH, ELOHIM of our fathers, Abraham, Isaac, and Yaacov our ETERNAL SAVIOUR and REDEEMER. O YAH, the Strength of Israel, YOU will not lie, nor will YOU repent or turn back YOUR Holy Decrees. YOU are not a man that YOU would turn back.

YOU, O STRENGTH of ISRAEL, shall send YOUR fear before us and YOU shall confound the entire people among whom we shall come. Blessed be YOUR HOLY Name, O YAHAWAH our STRENGTH and POWER throughout all eternity. May YOU, O YAH, be the Arbiter and Judge between Israel and their adversaries. May YOU, O YAH, take note and uphold my cause and vindicate me against them.

Selah.

A Prayer Recognizing
"THE STONE CUT OUT WITHOUT HANDS"
By Yehoshaphat Israel

YHWH is from eternity to eternity; Since the beginning of time YHWH ELOHIM, the HOLY ONE of Israel has chosen Israel as HIS covenant people. HIS DIVINE PRESENCE formed the heavens, earth, and seas, and filled HIS Creation with wisdom, knowledge, and glory. HIS glory reach throughout the waters than cover the seabed.

THE ANCIENT of DAYS is the DIVINE Presence who existed before the Creation of day. YOU are YHWH, and besides are YOU there is none other. YOU are MOST HOLY, The HOLY ONE of Israel.

When YOU speak all Israel must be able to listen and heed YOUR Spiritual Voice. YOUR Voice is the same Voice who spoke and all the elements listened and obeyed then CREATION came into existence. YOU, O YAH, also spoke to Israel at Mount Sinai and commanded us to listen to YOUR commands. YOU said, *"I am YHWH thy ELOHIM that brought you out of the land of Egypt out the house of bondage"*. You commanded us: "O Israel shall have no other gods—powers, beliefs, or testaments—besides ME." YOU gave us DIVINE INTELLIGENCE and superior spiritual intellect. Therefore we will not heed no other Voice besides *"Thus saith YAH"* or *"the Word of YAH"* came unto me saying thus and thus. YOU, O YAH, have taught us that we verily, verily, need to walk in YOUR commandments, laws, statutes, and judgements and not listen to those who come in the their own name or in the name of another Power. YHWH is our Power from everlasting to everlasting. YOU, O YAH, have never been a man, woman, animal, insect, fish, sun, moon, or stars. YOU, O YAH, are the cloudy pillar by day and the pillar of fire by night. YOUR Spirit fills all creation, the heavens above, the earth beneath, and the waters that cover the seas. Besides YOU there is none other. Blessed be **the Name of YHWH ELOHIM of our fathers, Abraham, Isaac, and Yaacov forevermore.** May **YOUR DIVINE Presence** dwell in our midst forevermore. Please write YOUR DIVINE truths in our inwards parts so we can possess the Spirit that recognizing YOUR Spiritual Presence.

Teach us to proclaim YOUR NAME and **YOUR NAME alone**. Teach us to act justly, to know YOU, to believe and trust in YOU, and to understand and heed YOUR Presence. YOUR wisdom will teach us to be mindful of YOUR righteous ways at all times. Then, we will be YOUR Spiritual representatives on earth. We will boast ourselves in YOUR commandments. We will teach the nations to trust in YOU, O YHWH our Heavenly Father. For **YOU alone O YHWH are THE STONE CUT OUT WITHOUT HANDS**. When I look at the heavens above, the earth beneath, and the great waters, I see the Works of YOUR DIVINE SPIRITUAL HANDS, I realize YOU are not human hands that could be nailed to a cross, or hung on a tree, or one born of a woman with a birthdate, lifespan, and day of death. YOU, O ETERNAL ONE are the Spiritual Energy that governs the evenings and mornings of each day forevermore.

Selah.

References

Chapter 1

1. Tanakh, Holy Scriptures
2. Book of Daniel, chapter 1
3. Various verses taken from ancient Traditional Hebrew Text written in the book Genesis to Malachi
4. Notes from Aaron Casey Lectures of the House of Israel Hebrew Community of Memphis-1978-1994
5. Research and Notes of Yehoshaphat Israel from 1978-2012

Chapter 2

6. Tanakh, Holy Scriptures
7. Book of Daniel, chapter 2
8. Various verses taken from ancient Traditional Hebrew Text written in the book Genesis to Malachi
9. 2012 edition Merriam-Webster's Collegiate Encyclopedia

The Gold Age

10. The Neo-Babylonian Empire(612—539), History and Culture, Ancient World Civilization, pg.826
11. Babylon, History and Culture, page 251,252
12. Babylonians, History and Culture, page 256,257
13. Nebuchadnezzar II, Encylcopedia, Second Edition, Volume 15
14. Evil-Merodach, Encylcopedia, Second Edition, Volume 15
15. Neriglissar, Encylcopedia, Second Edition, Volume 15
16. Labashi-Marduk, Encylcopedia, Second Edition, Volume 15
17. Nabonidus, Encylcopedia, Second Edition, Volume 15
18. Belshazzar, Encylcopedia, Second Edition, Volume 15

The Silver Age

19. The History of Elam and Achaemenid Persia, History and Culture, Ancient World Civilization, pg.1014
20. The Rulers of Persia, from Cyrus II to Darius III, History and Culture,
21. Wikipedia.org, the Free Encyclopedia/The Personal Profile of all Rulers of Persia from Cyrus II to Darius III

The Brass Age

22. Tanakh, Holy Scriptures
23. Book of Daniel, chapter 2
24. Various verses taken from ancient Traditional Hebrew Text written in the book Genesis to Malachi
25. 2012 edition Merriam-Webster's Collegiate Encyclopedia
26. The Greekl Myths, Robin Waterfield, Perseus, pg. 91-97, 144
27. The Greek Myths, Robin Waterfield, Zeus, Apollo, Nike, pg. 10-102
28. Leviticus 18:1-30
29. Wikipedia.org, the Free Encyclopedia/The Personal Profile of all Rulers of Classical Greece from Draco to Alexander the Great, the Ptolemy Dynasty, the Seleucid Dynasty, the Macedonian Dynasty, the Thrace Dynasty, to Tires IV
30. www.history of Macedonia.org
31. The Armies of the Macedonian Successor States:The Antigonids. deadliestblogpage.wordpress.com
32. 2015 edition World Book Encyclopedia

Continued

The Iron Age
Tanakh, Holy Scriptures
33. Book of Daniel, chapter 2
34. Various verses taken from ancient Traditional Hebrew Text written in the book Genesis to Malachi
35. 2012 edition Merriam-Webster's Collegiate Encyclopedia
36. The History of Rome, Roman Republic, Roman Empire, History and Culture, Ancient World Civilization
37. The Rulers of Rome, from Augustus Caesar to Romulus Augustus, History and Culture,
38. Wikipedia.org, the Free Encyclopedia/The Personal Profile of all Rulers of Rome from Julius Caesar to Romulus Augustus

Western Iron Leg
39. Wikipedia.org, the Free Encyclopedia/The Personal Profile of Clovis of the Franks
    2012 edition Merriam-Webster's Collegiate Encyclopedia
40. Wikipedia.org, the Free Encyclopedia/The Personal Profile of Theodoric the Great of the Ostrogoths
41. Wikipedia.org, the Free Encyclopedia/The Personal Profile of Charlemagne the Great
42. Wikipedia.org, the Free Encyclopedia/The Personal Profile of Otto I Great—The Holy Roman Empire
43. Wikipedia.org, the Free Encyclopedia/The Personal Profile of Charles IV King of Bohemia
44. Wikipedia.org, the Free Encyclopedia/The Personal Profile of Louis IV
45. Wikipedia.org, the Free Encyclopedia/The Personal Profile of Charles V
46. Wikipedia.org, the Free Encyclopedia/The Personal Profile of Henry VIII
47. Wikipedia.org, the Free Encyclopedia/The Personal Profile of all the leaders of the House of Bourbon
48. Wikipedia.org, the Free Encyclopedia/The Personal Profile of the Presidents of the United States
49. Wikipedia.org, the Free Encyclopedia/The Personal Profile of Great Britain/United Kingdom

Eastern Iron Leg
50. Wikipedia.org, the Free Encyclopedia/The Personal Profile of all Rulers of the Byzantine Empire
51. Wikipedia.org, the Free Encyclopedia/The Personal Profile of all Rulers of the Ottoman Empire
52. Wikipedia.org, the Free Encyclopedia/The Personal Profile of all Rulers of the Islamic Revolution
53. Wikipedia.org, the Free Encyclopedia/The Personal Profile of all Rulers of Islamic Expansionism
54. Wikipedia.org, the Free Encyclopedia/The Personal Profile of all Rulers of Far East, China, Japan, Mongols, and ancient India/ 2012 edition Merriam-Webster's Collegiate Encyclopedia
55. Wikipedia.org, the Free Encyclopedia/The Personal Profile of Rulers of West African Kingdoms
56. Wikipedia.org, the Free Encyclopedia/The Personal Profile of Rulers of Brazil
57. Wikipedia.org, the Free Encyclopedia/The Personal Profile of Joseph Emgels, Karl Marx, Joseph Stalin/ 2012 edition Merriam-Webster's Collegiate Encyclopedia
58. Wikipedia.org, the Free Encyclopedia/The Personal Profile of all Rulers of the Soviet Union/Russia

The Feet and Toes of Partly Iron [1945 to Present]
59. Wikipedia.org, the Free Encyclopedia/Historical Profile of France
60. Wikipedia.org, the Free Encyclopedia/Historical Profile of Germany
61. Wikipedia.org, the Free Encyclopedia/Historical Profile of Britain
62. Wikipedia.org, the Free Encyclopedia/Historical Profile of Italy
63. Wikipedia.org, the Free Encyclopedia/Historical Profile of Belgium
64. Wikipedia.org, the Free Encyclopedia/Historical Profile of the Netherlands
65. Wikipedia.org, the Free Encyclopedia/Historical Profile of Spain
66. Wikipedia.org, the Free Encyclopedia/Historical Profile of Portugal
67. Wikipedia.org, the Free Encyclopedia/Historical Profile of Luxembourg
68. Wikipedia.org, the Free Encyclopedia/Historical Profile of the United States
    2012 edition Merriam-Webster's Collegiate Encyclopedia for all of mentioned nations.
Ziyon

Continued
Feet and Toes of Partly Miry[Potter's] Clay [1945 to Present]
69. Wikipedia.org, the Free Encyclopedia/Historical Profile of Brazil
    2012 edition Merriam-Webster's Collegiate Encyclopedia
70. Wikipedia.org, the Free Encyclopedia/Historical Profile of Russia
    2012 edition Merriam-Webster's Collegiate Encyclopedia
71. Wikipedia.org, the Free Encyclopedia/Historical Profile of India
    2012 edition Merriam-Webster's Collegiate Encyclopedia
72. Wikipedia.org, the Free Encyclopedia/Historical Profile of China
    2012 edition Merriam-Webster's Collegiate Encyclopedia
73. Wikipedia.org, the Free Encyclopedia/Historical Profile of South Africa
    2012 edition Merriam-Webster's Collegiate Encyclopedia
74. Wikipedia.org, the Free Encyclopedia/Historical Profile of Indonesia
    2012 edition Merriam-Webster's Collegiate Encyclopedia
75. Wikipedia.org, the Free Encyclopedia/Historical Profile of Saudi Arabia
    2012 edition Merriam-Webster's Collegiate Encyclopedia
76. Wikipedia.org, the Free Encyclopedia/Historical Profile of Iran
    2012 edition Merriam-Webster's Collegiate Encyclopedia
77. Wikipedia.org, the Free Encyclopedia/Historical Profile of North Korea
    2012 edition Merriam-Webster's Collegiate Encyclopedia
78. Wikipedia.org, the Free Encyclopedia/Historical Profile of Mexico
    2012 edition Merriam-Webster's Collegiate Encyclopedia
79. 2012 edition Merriam-Webster's Collegiate Encyclopedia/The United Nations
80. Wikipedia.org, the Free Encyclopedia/Historical Profile of the G-20

The Age of YHWH—THE STONE CUT OUT WITHOUT HANDS
81. Tanakh, Holy Scriptures
82. Book of Daniel, chapter 2
83. Various verses taken from ancient Traditional Hebrew Text written in the book Genesis to Malachi
84. 2012 edition Merriam-Webster's Collegiate Encyclopedia

Notes
1. January/February 1991 Jerusalem Chronicle Newspaper*(JCN)*
Article, Blacks Reject Bush's War Policy in Gulf, pages 1-2
February/March 1992 Jerusalem Chronicle Newspaper*(JCN)*
Article, Natural, Man-made Disasters Resemble Biblical Plagues, pages 8-9
2. November/January 2002 Jerusalem Chronicle Newspaper*(JCN)*
Article, Evil Begets Evil, 911 The U.S. Struck! pages 1,4,8
3. November/January 2002 Jerusalem Chronicle Newspaper*(JCN)*
Article, The Clash of Civilizations, page 5
4. April/August 2006 Jerusalem Chronicle Newspaper*(JCN)*
Article, Islamic World Explodes, page 1,9
5. September/October 2014 Jerusalem Chronicle Newspaper*(JCN)*
Article, U.S. Report says Tehran aims missiles at Dimona, pages 1,25,10
6. April/May 2016 Jerusalem Chronicle Newspaper*(JCN)*
Article, Showdown in the holylaand, Global Powers face-off in Syria, pages 1, 2,5,9,13,14
7. July/August 2017 Jerusalem Chronicle Newspaper*(JCN)*
Article, Trumps changes world11,13

Cheth

www.ingramcontent.com/pod-product-compliance
Lightning Source LLC
Chambersburg PA
CBHW020300010526
44108CB00037B/166